# Current Biography Yearbook 2015

H. W. Wilson

A Division of EBSCO Information Services

Ipswich, Massachusetts

**GREY HOUSE PUBLISHING**

SEVENTY-SIXTH ANNUAL CUMULATION—2015

International Standard Serial No. 0084-9499

International Standard Book No. 978-1-61925-707-8

Library of Congress Catalog Card No. 40-27432

*Current Biography Yearbook,* 2015, published by Grey House Publishing, Inc., Amenia, NY, under exclusive license from EBSCO Information Services, Inc.

# CONTENTS

# LIST OF BIOGRAPHICAL SKETCHES

## List of Biographical Sketches

## List of Biographical Sketches

## List of Biographical Sketches

# LIST OF OBITUARIES

## List of Obituaries

## List of Obituaries

# Current Biography Yearbook 2015

# Current Biography

## Hawa Abdi

**Born:** 1947
**Occupation:** Activist and physician

In November 2010, when Hawa Abdi and her two daughters were named the "women of the year" by Glamour magazine, Eliza Griswold, a freelance journalist for Glamour who had worked closely with the Somali obstetrician-gynecologist, called Abdi "equal parts Mother Teresa and Rambo." Abdi had founded a small clinic outside of Mogadishu in 1983, and that humble enterprise eventually mushroomed into an entire compound, providing housing, medical facilities, and a school to some ninety thousand people who had been displaced by Somalia's sectarian violence. While that mission earned her comparison to the late Mother Teresa, a nun who ministered to the poor and ill in India, it was Abdi's steadfast defiance of Somalia's various militias that led to her comparison with the tough action film hero Rambo. She has repeatedly refused to turn over Hawa Abdi Village, as the compound is known, to marauding militias, even after being kidnapped and held hostage.

Despite the adversity she continually faces, Abdi has remained stalwart in her mission to house, heal, and educate Somalia's most vulnerable citizens, and she has enlisted her two daughters to help keep the village running. "As I speak for millions of Somali women who have no voice," she wrote in her 2013 memoir, *Keeping Hope Alive: One Woman—90,000 Lives Changed*, "I also share their struggles in this complicated world we will forever insist on calling home."

### EARLY YEARS AND EDUCATION

Hawa Abdi Diblawe was born in 1947 in the Somali capital of Mogadishu. Her father, Abdi Diblawe, worked in the city's ports, and while the family was not wealthy, they owned a fenced-in, two-room home. As Abdi recalled in her memoir, "In those days, we had no running water; the well filled our jugs, and the entire Indian Ocean

Astrid Stawiarz/WireImage

was our bath and our Laundromat." Growing up, she spent a great deal of time with her maternal grandmother, whom she called Ayeyo, at the older woman's farm outside of the capital in the rural region of Lafole, enjoying the fresh milk and meat there.

When Abdi was twelve years old, her mother, Dahabo, died in the midst of a painful and complicated pregnancy. Abdi was at her side when she delivered a premature baby, no bigger than a woman's palm, and later when she died of related complications. After watching her mother suffer, Abdi, who was left to raise her three younger sisters, became determined to become a doctor. In 1963, one of her friends told her about a Russian cultural school that was giving scholarships to Somali students, where Abdi enrolled and became a serious and dedicated student. At the time, the Soviets maintained a strong presence in Somalia, and thanks to the recommendation of one of her Russian-born teachers, Abdi—an avid student who completed three years of academic work in one year—won a scholarship from the Soviet Women's Commission in Moscow to study medicine. In 1964, at the age of seventeen, she received her father's blessing and left Mogadishu for the Soviet Union. From Moscow, she transferred to Kiev for a yearlong preparatory course. Although many of her fellow African classmates began adopting a socialist ideology while studying in the Soviet Union, Abdi felt herself to be apolitical. "Of course I wanted our country to be built well, whether that was through democracy or socialism," she wrote in her memoir. "What I most wanted to take with me from the Soviet Union was the work ethic and the respect for science."

Abdi earned her medical degree in 1971 and returned to Somalia as one of the nation's first female obstetrician-gynecologists. She quickly found a post at a six-hundred-bed hospital in Mogadishu called Digfer, where she was placed on the pediatric rotation despite her experience and desire to work in the surgery department. After three months in the pediatric ward, Abdi was assigned to a rotation in the obstetrics and gynecology department. To further her education, she began attending the Somali National University in the evenings in 1972 and earned a law degree in 1979. She later taught as an assistant professor of medicine at the same university.

## A LIFE OF SERVICE

In 1983, Abdi relocated from Mogadishu to Lafole, where she opened a one-room medical clinic with twenty-three beds. Two months after its opening, the clinic was drawing about one hundred patients per day from the surrounding area. She later expanded the clinic to include a surgical ward.

Within a few years of the clinic's opening, civil war had broken out in Somalia, and in 1991 the country's president, Siad Barre, was overthrown in a coup. As clan-based guerilla groups battled for supremacy, Somalia descended into chaos. As injured people began arriving at the clinic from Mogadishu, Abdi and her employees began to perform emergency medical interventions as needed. Soon, word had spread that there was a safe haven not far from Mogadishu, and refugees from across Somalia began flocking to her. Although she had to sell many of her family's assets, including her late mother's gold, Abdi turned no one away. A few months after the coup, some four thousand people were living on Abdi's property. Her well, which was drilled with financing from the International Committee of the Red Cross in 1993, provided some of the only clean drinking water for miles around.

In 1993, due to her law background, she was called by the United Nations Operation in Somalia to help draft a new constitution for Somalia. In the early 2000s, she was asked to serve as a vice minister of labor and sports in the newly established Transitional National Government. She was later appointed as a vice minister of health and tasked with reopening the Banadir hospital in Mogadishu, although she was forced to resign from that post after receiving multiple death threats.

## EXPANDING HER EFFORTS

By 2012, as drought and famine caused widespread suffering and violent clashes continued, an estimated ninety thousand refugees had arrived at Hawa Abdi Village, which by then included a four-hundred-bed hospital, a school, and thousands of makeshift shelters. All who arrived were welcome to stay, Abdi has explained, provided they followed just a few simple rules. For example, she has forbidden wife-beating and established a rudimentary holding cell for men accused of striking their spouses. Even more important in a time of sectarian violence, she ruled that no one could speak of their clan kinships in the village. "We created a rule with no exceptions," she explained in her memoir. "In our place, we are all Somali. If you want to identify by your clan, you can't stay." The ban was meant to limit fighting between members of opposing clans in the village and to ensure that Abdi could not be accused of favoring any particular faction.

In addition to housing, health care, and schooling for the children, Abdi instituted a series of classes for the village's adults, aiming to teach them about various health and child care topics. "We couldn't survive without her," said Hamdi Nur Mire, one of the residents of Hawa Abdi Village, in an interview with Edmund Sanders for the *Los Angeles Times* (1 Aug. 2007). "She is doing what the government should be doing."

Abdi's other major goal is to make the village—and Somalis as a whole—as self-sufficient as possible, and to that end she has established a variety of fishing and agricultural projects. "The long-term solution in preventing another famine in Somalia is to promote self-reliance," she told Laila Ali for the *Guardian* (23 Aug. 2011). "Somalia has enough land and a big coast but, because there hasn't been an effective government for over twenty years, we need to educate people on how to use the land sustainably. Our policy is sustainment and development."

## MEETING ADVERSITY

The Hawa Abdi Village has proven to be a tempting target for militias, whose fundamentalist members often disapprove of a woman heading a major organization and are eager to commandeer Abdi's assets for their own use. In May 2010, more than five hundred armed members of the militant Party of Islam (also known as Hizbul Islam) entered the village and demanded that Abdi relinquish control of the hospital and refugee camp on her property. Holding her at gunpoint, the group, comprised mainly of teenage boys, ransacked the building, destroying X-ray machines, shredding records, killing two guards, and terrorizing the rest of the staff.

Abdi was held under house arrest for several days, during which time many frightened patients fled; some two dozen malnourished children died as their families hid in the bush. While confined to her room by gunmen, Abdi, who had attracted support from numerous foreign journalists, nongovernmental organizations, and Somalis living abroad, used her phone to summon help, and the militiamen quickly became the focus of international censure. Not only were they forced to withdraw, they issued a written apology to Abdi, who sternly chastised them for not doing anything of real value for their country.

In 2012, members of the al-Qaeda–backed militant group al-Shabab (the Youth), a group infamous for enforcing strict sharia law such as stoning adulterers and hacking off the hands of suspected thieves, made incursions into the village, falsely claiming that they had a deed to a portion of the land and bulldozing the shelters of refugees.

## AWARDS AND ACCOMPLISHMENTS

In addition to being named a "woman of the year" by *Glamour* magazine, Abdi has received numerous honors and awards, including the 2012 John Jay Medal for Justice, whose administrators cited her "strength of nonviolent resistance through decades of upheaval, facing down armed forces despite imprisonment and death threats." She is also the recipient of a Vital Voices' Global Leadership Award and a Women of Impact Award from the Women in the World Foundation in 2013.

In 2012, Abdi was nominated for the Nobel Peace Prize by the American Friends Service Committee, which asserted in its recommendation, "Dr. Abdi is a woman of extraordinary strength, courage, and tenacity, who has created a safe haven for

internal refugees from the protracted conflict in her country." (The honor ultimately went to the European Union rather than to an individual.)

## PERSONAL LIFE

Abdi married her first husband, Mohamed Hussein, at the age of twelve in an arranged marriage; their marriage ended in divorce. She married her second husband, Aden Mohamed, an engineer and former officer in the Somali Marines, in 1973. They separated in the early 2000s, and Aden died in 2011. Together, they had three children.

Abdi had one son, Ahmed, who died in a car accident in 2005. Her daughters, Deqo and Amina, are both physicians, and both now work with the Doctor Hawa Abdi Foundation. "[My mother] always expects us to do more," Deqo, who serves as the foundation's CEO, explained to the audience during a TED Talk in February 2010. She contrasted the hospital facility in the village to Western medical practices and said of her daily schedule, "It is not like beautiful offices here, twenty patients, you're tired. [In Somalia] you see three hundred patients, [perform] twenty surgeries, and [have] ninety thousand people to manage."

Abdi acknowledges that Deqo is correct about the incredible demands of the village, which now employs more than one hundred workers. As Abdi wrote in *Keeping Hope Alive*: "There is a Somali saying that when you finish hard work, life gives you more hard work."

## SUGGESTED READING

Abdi, Hawa. *Keeping Hope Alive: One Woman: 90,000 Lives Changed*. New York: Grand Central, 2013. Print.

Abdi, Hawa. Interview. "In Somalia, Mother and Daughter Are 'Keeping Hope Alive.'" *All Things Considered*. National Public Radio, 29 Mar. 2013. Radio.

Ali, Laila. "The Doctor Undaunted by Somalia's Insurgents." *Guardian*. Guardian News and Media, 23 Aug. 2011. Web. 22 Oct. 2014.

Griswold, Eliza. "Dr. Hawa Abdi and Her Daughters: The Saints of Somalia." *Glamour*. Condé Nast, Nov. 2010. Web. 22 Oct. 2014.

Ibrahim, Mohammed, and Jeffrey Gettleman. "Under Siege in War-Torn Somalia, a Doctor Holds Her Ground." *New York Times*. New York Times, 7 Jan. 2011. Web. 22 Oct. 2014.

Kristof, Nicholas D. "Heroic, Female and Muslim." *New York Times*. New York Times, 15 Dec. 2010. Web. 22 Oct. 2014.

Sanders, Edmund. "A Doctor Bound by Humanity." *Los Angeles Times.* Los Angeles Times, 1 Aug. 2007. Web. 22 Oct. 2014.

—Mari Rich

# Sheila Kay Adams
**Born:** March 18, 1953
**Occupation:** Storyteller and ballad singer

Sheila Kay Adams is a storyteller and ballad singer known for both her voice and her skill with a five-string guitar. As a member of the seventh generation of musicians and storytellers in her western North Carolina–based extended family, with roots in Appalachia and connections to several of the prominent musical families there—including the Chandlers, Nortons, Ramseys, Rays, Sheltons, and Wallins—she helps keep the region's traditional music alive. Her family was key in beginning that work, giving many songs to Cecil Sharp, a folklorist who traveled the area between 1916 and 1918.

Adams accompanies her own singing on banjo and guitar. In 1997 she won a Bascom Lamar Lunsford Award for the preservation of traditional music; the following year, she received the Brown-Hudson Folklore Award, given by the North Carolina Folklore Society. In the citation for the latter award, Daniel W. Patterson commented, "She has remarkable gifts—a lovely voice, great natural musicality, depth and feeling, and a memory that won't let any good song or story escape." Adams has also been awarded the 2013 National Heritage Fellowship, a National Endowment for the Arts grant that is the nation's highest honor in traditional and folk arts and carries a cash prize of $25,000. Her recordings of Civil War–era folk music have been used in the Steven Spielberg film *Lincoln* (2012) and the History Channel documentary *Lee & Grant* (2011).

## EARLY LIFE AND FAMILY

Adams's ancestors traveled to North America from England and Northern Ireland in the late 1600s and early 1700s. According to Adams, one of her maternal ancestors, Amos Norton—whom she described in an interview for the collection *Southern Appalachian Storytellers* (2011) as her "grandfather's four greats-back grandfather"— left England and settled first in Bermuda around 1690. Some of his children moved to James-

town, Virginia, then headed south to eastern Tennessee, where they received a land grant. They have been in Madison County since 1731.

Adams's parents, Ervin Adams and Neple Norton Adams, were both born in Madison County, North Carolina, near Walnut Mountain, in a community officially named Revere but almost always called Sodom or Sodom Laurel. According to legend, the area was dubbed "Sodom" during the Civil War by a Baptist preacher who said the sinning there was worse than in the biblical Sodom. The name was later changed to Revere, but the new name never caught on within the community itself.

Adams herself was born March 18, 1953, in a hospital in Greeneville, Tennessee, and also grew up in Sodom. A small, isolated, unincorporated mountain settlement, Sodom was not electrified until the end of the 1940s and had no telephone service until Adams was sixteen years old. She recalls her mother canning large quantities of homegrown food; she, her sister, and her father stayed up late stringing green beans as her mother put up three hundred quarts every summer. To keep his daughters amused during this task, Adams's father told stories.

Singing was as common as storytelling in Adams's family, particularly old ballads. They inherited the stories and songs of the border region between Scotland and England, including "love songs" (long ballads) and camp-meeting songs from religious tent revivals. Adams says she cannot remember a time in her life without music. Some of the songs were associated with particular tasks; she recalls that her great-aunt Dellie Chandler Norton, whom she called Granny, always sang "Young Emily" while milking the cows. Adams told Paul Stamler for *Sing Out!* magazine (Summer 2002), "Lots of times my cousins and I would use little sticks and cornshuck dolls, and we would reenact the ballads. Or we would get outside in the spring, when it first started warming up, and we would choose a ballad . . . and actually act it out, like it was a play." Of her more than seventy first cousins, approximately half became musicians.

Adams graduated from Mars Hill College in 1974 with a degree in education and began teaching history at public schools in North Carolina. She gave her first public performance in 1976 at Duke University, accompanying Norton and Norton's sister, Berzilla Wallin. She went on to record three albums—*Loving Forward, Loving Back* (1987), *A Spring in the Burton Cove* (1990), and the storytelling collection, *Don't Git*

*Above Your Raising* (1992)—before leaving her teaching career in 1993 to sing and tell stories professionally full time. By that time, she had been teaching for about seventeen years, and she feared that if she did not leave then, she would be caught in a thirty-year career.

## FAMILY, SONGS, AND STORIES

Cecil Sharp was a British collector of folk songs who also specialized in folk dances. He was in the United States several times between 1915 and 1918; during one such visit, he met Olive Dame Campbell of Asheville, North Carolina, who told him that many of the traditional Scottish and English folk songs were still being sung in Appalachia. Between 1916 and 1918, Sharp and Campbell made several trips through North Carolina together, gathering songs and stories; over the two-year period, Sharp collected more than sixteen hundred songs. While in Madison County, where Adams's extended family lived, he met the Wallin and Chandler families and heard them sing. He had arrived at just the right time; soon radio and electricity would change the region, and many singers would turn from the traditional music to newer country or bluegrass music.

Adams learned the old songs she sings by hearing them from family and neighbors, which gave them a greater value to her. "When you learned them the way that I did, you had to spend the time with them," she told Laurin Penland for NPR (4 Dec. 2011), referring to singers such as Inez Chandler, also a Sodom native. "There was no other way around it, and that meant more to me—and means more to me now—than the song itself. Anybody can learn a song, but to sit with Inez Chandler for three hours on her front porch . . . was an experience."

Family was also the source of her stories, and Adams says she retells them in her family's voices, using their dialect. She believes that mountain people have good memories for family stories because for many generations they were unable to read and write, so instead they had to repeat the tales and memorize them. Adams herself uses visualization to force her mind to recall events from childhood, relying on techniques such as remembering the color of a dress or shoes to bring an event or story to mind.

## FESTIVALS AND FILMS

Adams has performed in numerous settings, including the National Storytelling Festival in Jonesborough, Tennessee. The festival is hosted by the International Storytelling Center, also in Jonesborough, where Adams was a featured teller in residence for the 2014 Storytelling Live! program. She also performed at the Smithsonian Folklife Festival in 1976, as part of the US bicentennial celebrations, and again in 2003, when one of the featured programs was Appalachia: Heritage and Harmony.

Adams appeared in the feature films *The Last of the Mohicans* (1992) and *Songcatcher* (2000), the latter of which was based on the life of Olive Dame Campbell and also employed Adams as a singing coach and technical adviser. She was initially reluctant to be involved in *Songcatcher*, having had a less-than-optimum experience with her first film. "I had reservations," she said to Stamler. "I'm kind of by myself here; there's nobody left that's singing the old love songs the way that Granny, and her family, and all those wonderful people I learned from over there [used to] . . . I feel a certain amount of responsibility to that. I didn't want it to be stereotypical—you know, where all these mountain people lay around drunk on the porch, scratching fleas with the dogs."

However, the film's director, Maggie Greenwald, won Adams's trust. In an interview with Gaili Schoen for *FolkWorks* (Mar./Apr. 2002), Adams explained, "In my conversations with Maggie I knew that there was a real possibility . . . of being able to present the culture as it really was, as opposed to that miserable stereotype that you see so often about mountain people." Greenwald was also impressed by the strong female associations of the music; she told Stamler, "I realized that songs are very much a women's tradition—handed down from mother to daughters, from grandmothers to children around the house. It was really exciting to me to discover a form of music that was primarily created by women, passed down through the generations by women, and even discovered by women."

## BECOMING A WRITER

When Adams began writing down stories for her children, she never intended to publish them. In 1991, however, when she met the novelist Lee Smith, the man who introduced them mentioned that Adams wrote as well and suggested that she send Smith one of her stories. This led to the publication of Adams's first short-story collection, *Come Go Home with Me* (1995), for which Smith wrote the foreword. The book won the

1997 Clark Cox Historical Fiction Award from the North Carolina Society of Historians.

Writing does not come easily to Adams, who works in her home office. "Only if you are dying do you knock on my office door," she said to Clint Johnson for *Our State* magazine (Nov. 2006). "And if you are not dying, you soon will be. I am a real sporadic writer, and once I get into it, I get really mad if someone interrupts." Nevertheless, she produced a second work: *My Old True Love* (2004), a novel of the Civil War, based on family stories. The novel was a finalist for both the Southeastern Booksellers Association's and the Appalachian Writers Association's 2004 Book of the Year Award. A reviewer for *Kirkus Reviews* (1 Mar. 2004) praised the musicality of the language, writing that Adams's "text is permeated with . . . tragic vision and keening rhythms" and that "she has an equally faultless ear for the cadences of ordinary folks' speech."

## PERSONAL LIFE AND THE NEXT GENERATIONS

Adams still lives in Madison County, North Carolina, close to where she grew up in Sodom. She married Jim Taylor, a musician and instrument maker, in 1993. The two met while Taylor was recording an album of Civil War–themed music, for which Adams played clawhammer-style banjo, and they went on to become frequent collaborators. Taylor, Adams told Stamler, was "one of those disgusting people that can play several different instruments, but his main one would be the hammered dulcimer." He died in 2009.

Adams has three children from previous marriages, daughter Melanie Rice and sons Hart and Andrew Barnwell. Like Adams, Rice is a musician. While Adams learned folk songs and stories from family members; Rice has learned from hearing recordings. Several old tunes were preserved during the 1960s and 1970s, when musicians such as Joan Baez and Bob Dylan recorded reinterpretations of them. "It was different for me in that Mom heard it from a bunch of old people working in the garden, and I heard it from a bunch of folk revivalists from New York City sleeping on our front porch," Rice told Penland. "It's been a performance-geared situation. I've known Mom being on stage, and I've known big groups of people playing music. It was a big party. It wasn't as much as in the natural setting."

Adams has high hopes for a ninth generation of musicians; of Rice's son Ezra, her grandson, Adams told Penland (who is also the sister of Rice's husband, Nate Penland, and thus Ezra's aunt), "When he was a baby, we used to go all the way to the top of the mountain behind his house where he lives over in Sodom, and we would sing as we were going up the mountain." By age five, Ezra was already singing traditional ballads.

## SUGGESTED READING

Adams, Sheila Kay. Interview by Gaili Schoen. *FolkWorks* Mar./Apr. 2002: 3+. Print.

Adams, Sheila Kay. "Sheila Kay Adams." *Southern Appalachian Storytellers: Interviews with Sixteen Keepers of the Oral Tradition*. Ed. Saundra Gerrell Kelley. Jefferson: McFarland, 2011. 5–15. Print.

Patterson, Daniel W. "Sheila Kay Adams, Seventh-Generation Ballad Singer." *North Carolina Folklore Journal* 45.2 (1998): 115–16. Print.

Penland, Laurin. "From Knee-to-Knee to CD: The Evolution of Oral Tradition in Mountain Ballads." *NPR*. NPR, 4 Dec. 2011. Web. 2 July 2014.

Stamler, Paul J. "Just the Thought of Going Home: Sheila Kay Adams and the Singers of Madison County, N.C." *Sing Out!* Summer 2002: 60–72. Print.

## SELECTED WORKS

*Loving Forward, Loving Back*, 1987; *A Spring in the Burton Cove*, 1990; *My Dearest Dear*, 2000; *All the Other Fine Things*, 2004; *Live at the International Storytelling Festival*, 2007

—Judy Johnson, MLS

# Anat Admati

**Born:** ca. 1955
**Occupation:** Economist

Anat Admati is an award-winning economist. In 2013 she coauthored the book *The Bankers' New Clothes: What's Wrong with Banking and What to Do about It*, with Martin Hellwig. The book, which uses simple (but not simplistic) language, sheds light and insight on the instability of the banking system. The book questions why banks, unlike any other business, are allowed to operate by performing 95 percent of their business with borrowed money. Admati and Hellwig argue that banks are not special, but because they are treated as such, there is a greater likelihood of a financial collapse similar to the one experienced in 2008, which would significantly affect other businesses and individuals. "Her solution is to make banks behave more like other companies by forcing them to reduce sharply their reliance on borrowed money," wrote Binyamin Appelbaum for the *New York Times* (9 Aug. 2014). A year after the book's publication, *Time* magazine included Admati on its 2014 list of the hundred most influential people. Admati also appeared on *Foreign Policy* magazine's 2014 list of one hundred global thinkers.

## EARLY YEARS, EDUCATION, AND TEACHING

Anat Ruth Admati was born and raised in Israel and received her bachelor of science degree with distinction in mathematics and statistics from Hebrew University in Jerusalem in 1979. She then moved to the United States to attend Yale University in New Haven, Connecticut, where she received her master of arts and master of philosophy degrees in operations research and management science in 1981. Admati received her PhD with distinction in operations research and management science from Yale in 1983.

After graduation she moved to California, where she worked as an assistant professor of decision sciences at Stanford University's graduate school of business. In 1989 she spent a year as visiting professor of finance at Tel-Aviv University's Recanati School of Management. Seven years later Admati again took a year's leave of absence from Stanford to teach at Recanati. This time, she worked as a visiting professor in the economics department. Despite these two breaks, Admati has remained affiliated with Stanford University and its graduate school of business since she first began there in 1983. After promotions to associate professor of finance and economics in 1986 and then to full professor in 1992, she was named the Joseph McDonald Professor of Finance and Economics in 2000 and the George G. C. Parker Professor of Finance and Economics in 2009.

## THE PATH TO FINANCIAL ACTIVISM

In 2010 Admati became determined to understand how and why the 2007–8 financial crisis happened and what was wrong with the banking industry. As she researched the issue and spoke with various financial experts, she began to question several arguments she encountered. She was hesitant, however, to speak up, fearing her lack of banking expertise would make her less credible. She decided to enroll in a program called the OpEd Project, which trains underrepresented individuals—most notably women—to write opinion pieces in their areas of interest and expertise. Rather than finance, Admati, who at the time was a mother of two teenagers, looked to a problem that haunted her Palo Alto, California, community: increased numbers of teen suicide. She attended city council and school board meetings, enlisted the help of local citizens and the town's mayor, and helped to raise money for prevention and awareness of the issue. Her piece, "How the US Air Force Fought Suicide, and We Can, Too," was published in the *Palo Alto Weekly* (23 Apr. 2010). Her involvement with this issue was transformative because, as Michael Freedman of *Graduate School of Stanford Business* (28 Jan. 2013) explained, Admati realized that "any entrenched problem, whether local, national, or global, could be changed through the involvement of greater numbers of people."

After her opinion piece was published, she grew more confident and began to voice her concerns about the banking industry with colleagues and at a Federal Reserve Bank of New York conference. After the conference, one of the participants urged her to write up a detailed account of her presentation. Admati and several colleagues at Stanford spent the summer of 2010 writing a seventy-page paper that challenged current banking methods, specifically banking regulations. Despite being later appointed to the FDIC Systemic Resolution Advisory Committee, writing for and being published in national newspapers and financial news outlets, and being recognized by the international financial community, Admati felt that only through a book could she expand and elaborate on the issues and alter the conversations about the changes that were needed in the banking industry.

## THE BANKERS' NEW CLOTHES

In 2013 Admati and Martin Hellwig coauthored *The Bankers' New Clothes: What's Wrong with Banking and What to Do about It*. In it, the authors argue that poor financial regulations, coupled with ineffective enforcement of those regulations led to the 2008 financial crisis, and that despite a devastating and long-lasting economic downturn for the United States, there has been no significant financial reform since then. This, Admati and Hellwig explain, leaves everyone, with the exception of the banks, highly vulnerable to the consequences of another major collapse. The system, they state, is unstable and unsustainable, but it can be safer and more stable without significantly affecting society and economic growth. The authors explain that banks need to have more available capital and rely less on borrowed money to fund investments. Furthermore, regulations must be in place to ensure there are restrictions on the amount of money banking institutions are allowed to borrow. Banks disagree, however, and state that restricting their amount of debt in the form of borrowed money will only serve to hamper the country's economic growth because the number of loans to individuals and businesses will decline. Admati and Hellwig dismiss those arguments as misleading and false and claim that too many are too afraid to speak up. They explain in their article for *Bloomberg Business* (3 Feb. 2013) that "there is a pervasive myth that banks are different . . . from all other companies and industries in the economy. Anyone who questions this is at risk of being declared incompetent."

## REVIEWS AND RECOGNITIONS

The book received mostly positive reviews for its clear, simple arguments written in a style that is free of financial jargon. John Cochrane for the *Wall Street Journal* (1 Mar. 2013) commends the book for what the authors left out of it: he points out that in portraying the relationship between politicians, regulators, and banks, the authors could have engaged in "naming more names and quoting more nonsense, writing a gripping exposé dripping with their justified outrage. But . . . too much exposé would detract from the clarity of their ideas." Although Cochrane points out a potential problem with the book in that the authors did not offer a detailed regulatory plan, "this apparent omission, too, is a strength. A long, detailed regulatory proposal would simply distract us from the clear, central argument of . . . more capital and less debt, especially short-term debt, equals fewer crises, and common contrary arguments are nonsense." A reviewer for the *Economist* (13 Apr. 2013) praised Admati and Hellwig for having "done an admirable job in explaining how capital in the banking system works to absorb shocks, and how too little of it makes banks unstable." Martin Wolf for *Financial Times* (17 Mar. 2013) agreed with Admati and Hellwig, stating that they "demolish" such "popular fallacies" as it being safer to fund banks with debt than it is for banks to fund themselves with capital. Wolf concluded his review with a direct appeal to his readers:

"Read this book. You will then understand the economics. . . . you will also appreciate that we have failed to remove the causes of the [2008 financial] crisis. Further such crises will come."

*The Bankers' New Clothes* received numerous recognitions and awards in its first year of publication such as the 2013 PROSE Award in Business, Finance & Management from the Association of American Publishers, as well as several "best" awards from such notable publications as *Bloomberg Businessweek*, the *Wall Street Journal*, and *Financial Times*. The book was short-listed for both the 2013 German Business and Economics Book Award and the 2013 Spear's Book Award in Business. The following year *The Bankers' New Clothes* won a bronze medal in economics at the Axiom Business Book Awards.

## AWARDS, HONORS, AND PUBLICATIONS

Admati has received a number of prestigious and diverse honors, awards, and fellowships throughout her career. For instance, in 2014 she was named one of *Time* magazine's hundred most influential people and *Foreign Policy*'s hundred global thinkers, and in 2015 *Prospect* magazine named her one of their choices for the top fifty world thinkers. Admati was named a finalist for the 2014 Faculty Pioneer Award by the Aspen Institute for her work in bringing business together with government to solve problems and create solutions.

Also in 2014, Admati was awarded an honorary doctorate degree from the University of Zurich. She has been awarded several fellowships and grants, including the Alfred P. Sloan Research Fellowship (1987–89), the Batterymarch Fellowship (1987–88), a Q-Group grant (1989), a National Science Foundation grant (1993–95), and the Michelle Clayman Faculty Fellowship (2013–14).

Aside from her book, Admati has authored dozens of academic publications and research papers for such journals as *Econometrica*, *Journal of Business*, *Journal of Economic Theory*, *Journal of Finance*, *American Economic Review*, *Journal of Monetary Economics*, *UCLA Law Review*, and *Journal of Legal Studies*. She has also published articles for general audiences in mainstream media publications, such as the *Financial Times*, *Huffington Post*, *New York Times*, *Guardian*, *Washington Post*, and *Bloomberg*.

## SUGGESTED READING

Admati, Anat R. "We're All Still Hostages to Big Banks." *New York Times*. New York Times, 26 Aug. 2013. Web. 20 May 2015.

Admati, Anat R., and Martin Hellwig. "Emperors of Banking Have No Clothes." *Bloomberg*. Bloomberg, 3 Feb. 2013. Web. 23 May 2015.

Appelbaum, Binyamin. "When She Talks, Banks Shudder." *New York Times*. New York Times, 9 Aug. 2014. Web. 20 May 2015.

Cassidy, John. "Taking on the Banks: A Conversation with Anat Admati." *New Yorker*. Condé Nast, 5 May 2015. Web. 20 May 2015.

Cochrane, John H. "Running on Empty: Banks Should Raise More Capital, Carry Less Debt—and Never Need a Bailout Again." *Wall Street Journal*. Dow Jones, 1 Mar. 2013. Web. 20 May 2015.

Foroohar, Rana. "Anat Admati." *Time*. Time, 23 Apr. 2014. Web. 20 May 2015.

Freedman, Michael. "'What's Wrong with Banking and What to Do about It:' How, and Why, Stanford's Anat Admati Took on the Banking System." *GSB*. Stanford Graduate School of Business, 28 Jan. 2013. Web. 20 May 2015.

—Dmitry Kiper

# Noorjahan Akbar

**Born:** 1991
**Occupation:** Activist

Noorjahan Akbar is an Afghan human-rights activist and the cofounder of Young Women for Change, an organization that empowers young Afghan women to speak out against violence and harassment. "I'm an advocate, not a politician. I want to empower women to mobilize," Akbar told Stacy Brown for the Carlisle, Pennsylvania, *Sentinel* (18 Sept. 2012). "There are things essential and they include providing women the opportunities to tell their stories and providing them economic opportunities." In 2012 *Forbes* magazine named Akbar one of the most powerful women in the world, and in 2013 she was named one of the top ten college women by *Glamour* magazine for which she received an award of $20,000. Akbar is also a prolific blogger. She has written for the *New York Times*, *Al Jazeera*, the *UN Dispatch*, and *Safe World for Women International*. She also runs her own blog called *Daughters of Rabia: Free Women Writers*, also the title of a collection of women's writing that Akbar helped publish in 2013, named for the Persian poet Rabia Balkhi, who was killed by her brother around 900 CE for writing about and falling in love with a slave.

## EARLY LIFE AND EDUCATION

Akbar was born in Kabul, Afghanistan, in 1991. She was raised in both Afghanistan and Pakistan and attended school in the United States. Her parents, both teachers, were adamant that Akbar and her three sisters receive an education. Akbar's paternal grandmother, Bibi Jan, attended school until she was twelve, as was the custom for Afghan women. Akbar's grandfather was a mullah (a Muslim official educated in religious law) who encouraged his son, Akbar's father, to attend school despite social pressures, even for boys, to discontinue secular education. Akbar's father walked miles to middle school outside of his village and finished high school through a military program in Kabul. Akbar's mother attended the first girl's high school in Aqcha city, with aspirations of becoming a midwife. She was a part of the first generation of Afghan women to find employment outside of the home. Life for Afghan women improved through the 1970s and 1980s, only to decline with the rise of the mujahideen (Islamic guerrillas against the Soviets) in the late 1980s. In 1996 the Taliban came to Afghanistan, and Akbar's family fled to Peshawar, Pakistan, where her parents could teach and her sisters could go to school. "The Taliban closed all schooling for women," said Akbar, as reported by the Australian Broadcasting Corporation (11 Sept. 2011). "So in order for us to be able to go to school my parents they sold their house, their library, my mum's wedding ring and wedding gown, and basically sacrificed everything they had for us to be able to go to school." In Peshawar, Akbar learned to speak English and how to use a computer. When she was eleven years old, she created a homemade magazine for Afghan women and began working with Radio Azadi, or Radio Free Europe, writing for children's programs and translating.

## AFGANISTAN AND AMERICA

Akbar's family returned to Kabul in the winter of 2001, after the US–led invasion of Afghanistan and the subsequent collapse of the Taliban regime. "The city still smelled of bullets and bombs," Akbar wrote in an article for *Al Jazeera* (28 July 2011). Akbar's mother began teaching high school and resumed studying for a bachelor's degree to teach literature. Akbar, her sisters, and her father started a teaching center for Afghan women in the Qala-e-Fathullah neighborhood in Kabul, passing on the English and computer skills Akbar and her sisters had learned in Pakistan. When Akbar was a teenager, she won a scholarship to attend high school at George School, a Quaker boarding school in Newtown, Pennsylvania, for two years. She graduated in 2010 and, through the Afghan Girls Financial Assistance Fund, won a scholarship to Dickinson College in Carlisle, Pennsylvania, where she earned a bachelor's degree in sociology in 2014. Akbar went on to earn a master's degree in journalism and public affairs at American University in Washington, DC, in 2015. She planned to return to Afghanistan following her graduation.

## YOUNG WOMEN FOR CHANGE

In May 2011 Akbar and her friend, Anita Haidary, decided to organize a meeting of women in Kabul to discuss, as Akbar put in her op-ed for the New York Times (22 Nov. 2011), "sexual discrimination and gender inequality" in Afghanistan. They announced the meeting on Facebook, expecting about fifteen attendees. They were shocked when seventy-five women—and ten more via Skype—showed up. Thus, a group called Young Women for Change (YWC) was born. The formation was only the first step, however. The group was not allowed to meet at Kabul University, Akbar wrote, because the police "did not want women making problems for them." After an arduous process of registering as a nonprofit organization, YWC chose street harassment—an issue all of the women in YWC faced—as its first priority and first major campaign. "Every woman I know, whether she wears a burqa or simply dresses conservatively, has told me stories of being harassed in Afghanistan," Akbar wrote. The harassment—both verbal and physical—comes from men of all ages. Her mother "arrives home upset almost every day because of the disgusting comments she receives," Akbar wrote. Akbar herself was groped in front of the orphanage where she taught creative writing.

The YWC scheduled a march to protest public sexual harassment in Kabul on July 14, 2011. On the designated day, twenty-five women met in front of a restaurant. (The manager of the restaurant would not let them come inside.) They walked to Kabul University, where they were joined by twenty-five more marchers. On their way to the Afghan Independent Human Rights

Commission they were joined by an additional fifty-plus marchers. The success of the march, Akbar wrote, filled her with hope for a better future. "This was the moment I fell in love with Afghanistan."

## SAHAR GUL

In March 2012 the YWC opened a women-only Internet café, the first of its kind in Afghanistan, in Kabul. The café was named after Sahar Gul, a twelve-year-old who was sold into marriage with an older man and brutally tortured by her in-laws when she refused to become a prostitute. She was rescued after neighbors reported hearing screams coming from the family's cellar. While the details of Gul's case are particularly grisly, her tale is by no means unique. In 2012 the United Nations and the Afghanistan Independent Human Rights Commission reported that 56 percent of Afghan brides were under the age of sixteen. Violence against women was not officially made a crime until 2009—in a country in which 90 percent of women are subject to domestic violence—the same year that the Afghan parliament passed a bill making it illegal for a woman to refuse her husband sex. Despite international attention and domestic protest, women in Afghanistan are regularly subject to discrimination and abuse, but Akbar hopes to help change that.

### DAUGHTERS OF RABIA

Akbar left YWC in September 2012 to finish her degree. In 2013 she and activist Batul Muradi published a collection of women's writings called Dukhtarane Rabia (Daughters of Rabia), after the Persian poet Rabia Balkhi. They created a blog of the same name—Daughters of Rabia: Free Women Writers—publishing writing in Persian, Pashto, and Uzbek. Even though parts of the blog are available in English, Akbar began the project not as a means to reach an international audience but to "engage in conversations with my own people," she told Raluca Besliu for the blog Taking on the Giant (1 Mar. 2014). Like YWC before it, the Daughters of Rabia blog is intended as a safe place for Afghan women to share their experiences with other Afghan women in hopes of creating change. Besliu notes that literacy rates for women in Afghanistan remain abysmally low, but Akbar hopes both that increased access to education will improve those numbers and writing will prove to be a powerful tool for women, she told Besliu. Akbar is a regular contributor to the Daughters of Rabia.

In one essay, "Where Did I Learn about Freedom?" (16 June 2015), she writes about an American journalist who, in a profile of Akbar, suggested that her time in the United States made her an activist for women's rights because Western culture made her aware of her repression in Afghanistan. "The idea that freedom or liberation is a solely American or Western concept and therefore we must all have learnt about freedom in America, given [that] our own cultures are only oppressive, and [that] there are no notions of liberation at home is absurd," Akbar writes, noting the United States' own history of slavery and racial oppression. "Freedom is in my blood, and in the blood of millions of women and men who have never been to the USA, but know that as humans, they deserve the right to breathe fresh air and say their opinions without the fear of prosecution."

Akbar spoke to Joshi Herrmann of the London *Independent* (10 July 2015) about the rising number of Afghan women using social media. Her verdict: sites like Facebook are valuable forums for women but also leave them vulnerable to attacks. "Recently, there is a trend to publish photos of civil rights activists and defame them publicly on right-wing social media," she said. When she is not writing, Akbar travels the globe as a freelance public speaker.

## SUGGESTED READING

Agius, Connie, et al. "Long Road ahead for Afghan Women." *World Today*. Australian Broadcasting Corp., 11 Sept. 2011. Web. 7 Aug. 2015.

Akbar, Noorjahan. "Education Remains Only for Privileged Afghans." *Al Jazeera*. Al Jazeera Media Network, 28 July 2011. Web. 28 July 2015.

Akbar, Noorjahan. "Women Take a Stand in Kabul." *New York Times*. New York Times, 22 Nov. 2011. Web. 26 July 2015.

Besliu, Raluca. "Young Writer Changing Afghanistan for Women." *Taking on the Giant*. Taking on the Giant, 1 Mar. 2014. Web. 2 Aug. 2015.

Brown, Stacy. "Dickinson College Student Makes Forbes Powerful Women List." *Sentinel* [Carlisle, PA]. Sentinel, 18 Sept. 2012. Web. 26 July 2015.

Herrmann, Joshi. "How Social Media Is Empowering Young Afghan Women: The Facebook Effect." *Independent*. Independent. co.uk, 10 July 2015. Web. 2 Aug. 2015.

—Molly Hagan

# Folorunsho Alakija

**Born:** 1951
**Occupation:** Businessperson

The multitalented Folorunsho Alakija became the richest woman in her home country of Nigeria by 2012 and the twelfth wealthiest person in all of Africa by 2014 according to *Forbes* magazine. An oil tycoon, high-end fashion designer, author, and former banking administrator, Alakija has worn many hats and in so doing amassed a fortune that some estimate at $3.3 billion. While there is some debate about the exact size of Alakija's fortune, with some estimates placing it as high as $7 billion, most observers agree that with her oil company alone valued at a minimum of $3 billion, as well as a vast real estate portfolio and a $46 million private jet, she has surpassed Oprah Winfrey by at least hundreds of millions of dollars, making her the "richest black woman in the world," as Helen Pow called her in the London *Daily Mail* (8 Oct. 2013). "Wealth is beyond money and affluence," she once said, as quoted by Kemi Ashefon for *Punch*, a Nigerian magazine (7 Apr. 2013). "It can be classified as a large amount of something, ranging from experience to talent. . . . For instance, you could say someone has a wealth of interesting qualities. Many people have said the same to me because there are so many parts to who I am, who I have become, and who God has created me to be."

© AP Photo/AP/Corbis

## EARLY LIFE

Folorunsho Ogbara Alakija was born in 1951 in Ikorodu, a town in Lagos state, Nigeria. Her father, a man of great wealth who is sometimes referred to as Chief L. A. Ogbara, was a Yoruba leader. While Alakija's mother was his first wife, he went on to marry seven other women. Alakija is her mother's second surviving child and the eighth of her father's fifty-two children. Occasionally sources give conflicting accounts of her birth order. Although Alakija became a devout Christian in her forties, she has referred in interviews to having been Muslim in her youth.

"It was a happy childhood," Alakija recalled to Jessica Ellis in an interview for *African Voices* (16 Feb. 2012). "I enjoyed growing up. I learnt a lot with my guardian [Mrs. Coker], which was a totally different set-up to my mum's. She taught us etiquette, how to sit at a table, went through our homework with us." Alakija's mother worked as a textile dealer, and Alakija often helped out in her business when off from school.

Evincing some ambivalence about her upbringing, however, she had also told Ebun Sessou for the Nigerian newspaper *Vanguard* (9 Sept. 2011), "I know [my father] loved all his children and always wanted them around him. But, this was difficult to believe. I thought he hated me amongst his fifty-two children from eight different wives. Understandably, he was having problems managing domestic affairs."

## EDUCATION

When Alakija was seven years old, she traveled with her younger sister Doyin, the daughter of a favored wife, to northern Wales to attend primary school. "My parents' epoch-making decision became news in the dailies because sending children so young to study abroad was extremely expensive, and therefore rarely done at the time," she recalled to Sessou. "As soon as the news was out that they were sending not one, but two children to school in England at the same time, visitors started trooping into our house. Friends, family, and well-wishers came with goodwill messages and gifts." The girls excitedly shopped for clothes suitable for colder climes and African goods for relatives who had settled in the United Kingdom. Their arrival, amid a bustling port and tall buildings, was a shock; however, as she told Sessou, "I had never experienced life in another part of the world, and didn't know that things are different elsewhere." Alakija and her sister were reportedly the first two children of color at the now-defunct

Hafodunos Hall, and because their classmates were unable to correctly pronounce their names, they were known as Flo and Doyle. The two remained in Wales for four years before their parents, fearing that they might become overly assimilated and forget their Nigerian culture, summoned them home. "I regret that the school building, which is one of the most cherished buildings in Wales, has been sold," Alakija lamented to Ashefon. "I remember with nostalgia the etiquette lessons we got, [as well as the] elocution, horse riding, singing lessons, [and] stamp collection." She concluded, "I learnt a lot in those four years."

Alakija completed her secondary education at a Muslim high school in Nigeria, and while she has told interviewers that she would have liked to have attended law school, her father would not agree to send her, believing that the profession was unsuitable for a woman. Instead, she returned to the United Kingdom and completed secretarial training at Pitman Central College (now the London College of International Business Studies).

## BANKING CAREER

After graduation, Alakija took a series of administrative jobs at such institutions as Sijuwade Enterprises, a holding company that had been founded by the Nigerian monarch Alayeluwa Oba Okunade Sijuwade, and the First National Bank of Chicago, which had recently opened a branch in Lagos and later became known as Fin-Bank. As executive secretary to the managing director of the bank, she fought for better conditions for administrative staffers and was often called upon to make decisions about company logos and other such issues because of her discerning eye and sense of design.

She ultimately worked her way up to head of corporate affairs at what had by then become known as the International Merchant Bank (IMB), and she was later tapped to complete an intensive in-house banking course—the only staffer without a four-year university degree to do so. Still, she chafed at the restrictions placed upon her as a woman in the banking industry and became frustrated when men with fewer skills and less natural talent were promoted ahead of her. Determined to start her own business, she hit upon the idea of clothing design and traveled to London to attend fashion school.

## MAKING HER FORTUNE

In 1985 Alakija returned to Nigeria and rented an apartment in Lagos to use as headquarters for her fledgling fashion company, which she called Supreme Stitches (later renamed Rose of Sharon House of Fashion). She had made several high-profile contacts while working in the banking industry, and soon members of Nigeria's elite—including former first lady Maryam Babangida—were flocking to buy her colorful, eye-catching garments. Within a year Alakija had been named Nigerian designer of the year and had become the president of the Fashion Designers Association of Nigeria (FADAN). She remains a patron of the organization and is considered among the most influential figures in the history of the Nigerian fashion industry. Speaking of her success to Ellis, Alakija noted, "I've always believed that anything worth doing is worth doing well."

Most of her wealth, however, comes not from fashion but from oil. Noticing that many of her wealthy clients were applying for oil-prospecting licenses, Alakija did so as well in 1993. Thanks in some part to her friendship with Maryam Babangida, the government granted her oil rights to 617,000 acres located about 220 miles southeast of Lagos. While she knew little about the oil industry, she was savvy enough to hire Star Deep Water Petroleum, a subsidiary of the multinational Texaco, to advise her and conduct the exploration in exchange for a 40 percent stake.

When Deep Water discovered that the acreage was exceptionally rich in oil, the Nigerian government quickly took over 50 percent ownership of the enterprise. With Deep Water's support, Alakija engaged in a legal battle that spanned more than a dozen years. Finally, in 2012 the Nigerian Supreme Court ruled in her favor, deeming the government's move illegal. Oil production began in 2008. By 2014 she was listed in *Forbes* as the twelfth richest person in Africa, and she has since been acknowledged as the richest black woman in the world. Additionally, in 2015 she was included as number eighty-seven on the *Forbes* list of the most powerful women in the world.

Alakija remains in partnership with Chevron (which bought Texaco), and her company, Famfa Oil Limited, continues to own 60 percent of the plot, OML 127. Famfa is overseen by Alakija's husband and sons, while she serves as executive vice chair.

## OTHER WORK

Alakija holds traditional, conservative Christian views on marriage and gender roles. "Personally, I always make sure I seek the support and approval of my husband in whatever I plan to do, either for the day or for the future," she told Ashefon. "This is because I strongly believe he is the head of our home and God is in the center. As we honor and respect our husbands, God honors and uplifts the work of our hands." Alakija penned the nonfiction books *University of Marriage* (2011) and *The Cry of Widows and Orphans* (2013). She is also the author of an autobiography, *Growing with the Hand That Gives the Rose* (2011).

The plight of Nigerian widows—who can be forced to marry brothers of their late husbands or turn over their property to in-laws—is particularly important to Alakija; her philanthropy, the Rose of Sharon Foundation, is devoted to providing for them and their children. The nonprofit has led workshops, sponsored scholarships, and funded small-business loans to enable widows to support themselves and their families.

## PERSONAL LIFE

Alakija and her husband, Modupe, a lawyer by training, married on November 12, 1976. They have four sons. Nigerian recording artist and producer Rotimi Alakija, known professionally as DJ Xclusive, is her nephew, not her son, as some sources have claimed.

She is still known for her sense of style and is often photographed in the dramatic Nigerian headdresses known as *gele*. "Tying my *gele* comes to me naturally as it does not take me more than two minutes to do so," she told Ashefon.

## SUGGESTED READING

Alakija, Folorunsho. "Nigerian Billionaire Takes on Cause of 'Mistreated Widows.'" Interview by Jessica Ellis. *CNN African Voices*. Cable News Network, 16 Feb. 2012. Web. 20 June 2015.

Ashefon, Kemi. "I Have Passion for Fashion: Folorunsho Alakija." *Punch*. 7 Apr. 2013. Web. 20 June 2015.

Iyengar, Rishi. "Here's Who Just Unseated Oprah as the World's Richest Black Woman." *Time*. Time, 30 Dec. 2014. Web. 20 June 2015.

Nsehe, Mfonobong. "Nigeria's Richest Woman Folorunsho Alakija Reveals She Did Not Go to University." *Forbes*. Forbes.com, 1 Sept. 2014. Web. 20 June 2015.

Pow, Helen. "Move Over, Oprah." *Daily Mail* [London]. Associated Newspapers, 8 Oct. 2013. Web. 20 June 2015.

Sessou, Ebun. "My Life Is Full of Blissful Moments: Folorunsho Alakija." *Vanguard*. Vanguard Media Nigeria, 9 Sept. 2011. Web. 20 June 2015.

—Mari Rich

# Myles Allen
**Occupation:** Geoscientist

Climatologist Myles R. Allen teaches at Oxford University in England, where he is a professor of geosystem science in the School of Geography and the Environment. He is also the head of the Climate Dynamics Group in the university's Department of Physics. With the Climate Dynamics Group, Allen works to understand how humans and natural forces—"external drivers," as he called them in a column he wrote for the *Guardian* (11 July 2012)—affect the climate and influence climate forecasting. "Some of these drivers, like volcanoes, are things we can do nothing about," he wrote. "But others, like rising levels of greenhouse gases, we can. And quantifying how greenhouse gases contribute to extreme weather is a crucial step in pinning down the real cost of human influence on climate."

Most climatologists make predictions about what the world will look like a generation or two from now, given the rate at which greenhouse gases are warming the climate of the Earth. Allen, however, prefers to focus on the effects of climate change in present and recent weather events. He is known for creating a new method of statistical analysis called event attribution, which attempts to assess recent weather events and pin down exactly how much of their probability could be attributed to human-influenced climate change—a challenging task, to say the least. "These impacts are so complex that isolating them would be like taking the sugar out of a chocolate-chip cookie—nearly impossible, everything is so intertwined," Maggie Koerth-Baker wrote for the *New York Times* (27 Aug. 2013). "Event attribution tries to break through this ambiguity using brute force."

In 2010, Allen won the Appleton Medal and Prize, awarded to one scientist every two years, for his work in understanding and predicting the effects of climate change. He has served on the United Nations–sponsored Intergovernmental Panel on Climate Change (IPCC), an international committee of hundreds of scientists that has issued reports on climate change every five or six years since 1990. The IPCC won the Nobel Peace Prize in 2007. Allen served as the lead author of "Detection of Climate Change and Attribution of Causes," a chapter of the IPCC report *Climate Change 2001: The Scientific Basis*, and as review editor for the chapter "Global Climate Projections" in *Climate Change 2007: The Physical Science Basis*. In 2013, Allen coauthored an IPCC report that advised an unprecedented upper limit on greenhouse gases for the globe, and he has championed a technology called carbon capture and storage (sometimes called carbon capture and sequestration), or CCS, to address this limit. He occasionally writes a column about climate change for the *Guardian*.

## EDUCATION AND EARLY CAREER
Myles Allen graduated from St. John's College, Oxford, with degrees in physics and philosophy in 1987, and went to work for the Energy Unit of the United Nations Environment Programme (UNEP) in Kenya, where he became interested in climate change. He returned to Oxford, where he studied, according to his official biography, "atmosphere-ocean interactions and internally generated climate variability." He earned his PhD in atmospheric, oceanic, and planetary physics in 1992. Allen then took a job as a research fellow with the Space Science and Technology Department at the Rutherford Appleton Laboratory (RAL) in Oxfordshire. Allen also traveled to the Massachusetts Institute of Technology (MIT), where he worked alongside Professor Richard Lindzen as a National Oceanic and Atmospheric Administration (NOAA) Global Change Fellow. Lindzen, a meteorology professor, is notorious in the scientific community for his views on climate change. He believes that humankind is influencing the climate of the Earth but that influence is insignificant. Lindzen's research was championed by the George W. Bush administration in the early 2000s and was used to inform United States climate policy.

Allen collaborated with the Hadley Centre for Change Prediction and Research at the Meteorological Office, or Met Office, the United Kingdom's weather service, in the late 1990s. He later used Met Office data as the basis for his climate change prediction model in the early 2000s. Allen became a university lecturer at Oxford in 2001.

## CLIMATE PREDICTIONS MODEL

The concept of climate change is a complex one. Scientists have observed that greenhouse gases created by pollution and deforestation are warming the Earth's climate. Although the term *global warming* is commonly used when discussing climate change, this term is somewhat misleading, as such warming has a wide range of effects on the world's weather patterns, not limited to a change in temperature. Scientists such as Allen seek to determine the extent to which extreme weather events such as hurricanes, floods, and heat waves can be attributed to humankind's direct influence on the world's climate.

In October 1999, Allen published an article in the science journal *Nature* titled "Do-It-Yourself Climate Prediction." The article detailed the beginnings of his most significant contribution to climate science, a website called Climateprediction.net. Allen was inspired by one ongoing experiment in which scientists used computers to scan space continuously for radio signals that might be evidence in the search for extraterrestrial intelligence (SETI). The computers generated so much data that it was impossible for the scientists to comb through it all themselves. They decided to split the data into fragments and posted those manageable fragments on the Internet for people to scan using their home computers. They called the project SETI@home. Allen wondered what would happen if he applied a similar strategy to climate models. The answer to Allen's burning question of whether human-induced climate change has affected the likelihood of certain weather events would require thousands of computer simulations, so Allen began designing a climate model that would run on an ordinary home computer. If a significant number of people could participate in the study, just as a significant number of people had with SETI@home, then Allen might be able to get an accurate analysis.

The result of his efforts, climateprediction.net, officially launched in 2003. In his article for *Nature*, Allen argued that the website would be a direct and effective way of involving the public in the issue of climate change. "As long as politicians only propose targets that they think they can sell to a generally indifferent electorate, it seems unlikely that we will achieve the order-of-magnitude reductions in greenhouse-gas emission required to make a significant impact on the problem," he wrote. "As long as climate change research remains confined to large, centralized institutions, this indifference is likely to remain."

In February 2011, Allen and a handful of other scientists published a paper titled "Anthropogenic Greenhouse Gas Contribution to Flood Risk in England and Wales in 2000" in *Nature*. The study, which involved a displaced Atlantic jet stream that caused floods in England in 2000 (and again in 2003), relied on research garnered from the tens of thousands of volunteers running at-home simulations made possible by climateprediction.net. In the highly cited paper, Allen found that human-induced climate change increased the odds of the floods happening in 2000. "We found this out by using a detailed computer climate model from the UK Met Office to simulate autumn 2000 weather: first in a world as it was in autumn 2000, and then in a parallel autumn 2000 world that might have been had no greenhouse gasses been emitted in the twentieth century," Allen explained to Reuters.

Participation in the experiment was so encouraging that Allen and his team have begun looking at a number of different weather events through a climateprediction.net experiment called weather@home, which, like SETI@home, allows for a regular and effective coalition of analysts working via their personal computers. Allen's work on climateprediction.net earned him the prestigious Appleton Prize in 2010. The website was also featured in the BBC documentary *Meltdown: A Global Warming Journey* (2006), and Allen himself was featured in the 2013 documentary *Thin Ice*.

## RECENT IPCC FINDINGS AND "CARBON BUDGET"

In September 2013, the IPCC established a maximum limit on greenhouse gases for the world, above which humanity would face irreversible climate change. Allen and the other authors of the report endorsed a "carbon budget" for humanity, Justin Gillis wrote for the *New York Times* (27 Sept. 2013). This endorsement was particularly significant because it was so explicit. In the report, Allen calculated that more than half a trillion tons of carbon have been burned since the Industrial Revolution (a period of about 250 years) and estimated that humans would hit the trillion-ton mark—the IPCC's carbon budget—sometime around 2040 at the current rate of consumption. Allen notes that there are about three trillion tons of carbon still in the ground as fossil fuels.

Carbon dioxide, Allen explained in a video posted on the University of Oxford's Environmental Change Institute's website (23 Sept. 2013), "is not the most powerful greenhouse gas . . . but it matters because we emit an enormous amount of it." As humankind burns through its "budget" of carbon, through deforestation and the use of fossil fuels, that carbon is released into the atmosphere. Allen estimated that since the Industrial Revolution, humans have released over 500 billion tons of carbon into the atmosphere. Half of that amount—more than 250 billion tons—is still in the atmosphere and still affecting the climate. Allen noted that 1.5 trillion tons of carbon consumed correlates to warming the global climate about one degree. Humanity is on the path to warm the global climate by a total of two degrees, Allen warned, and he is working to prevent this measurement from being exceeded. There is no way to take the carbon out of the atmosphere, so scientists must determine how to prevent additional carbon from accumulating.

"The only way of stopping climate change is by stopping the flow of fossil carbon into the atmosphere," Allen said in the video. A technology called carbon capture and storage (CCS) might offer humans the chance to stop that flow by burying carbon emissions in the ground. CCS technology has existed since the 1930s and had been operating on a small scale since the 1970s. Allen and other scientists think that CCS is the best—and quickest—hope to slow the warming climate. "We can't rely on emission trading systems and carbon taxes to drive the development of carbon capture and storage," he said in the video. "Until carbon capture is made compulsory, made a condition of extracting fossil carbon out of the ground, we won't be building the technologies we need to avoid dangerous climate change."

**SUGGESTED READING**

Allen, Myles. "The Climate of the Climate Change Debate Is Changing." *Guardian*. Guardian News and Media, 11 July 2012. Web. 14 Apr. 2014.

Allen, Myles. "Do-It-Yourself Climate Prediction." *Nature*. Macmillan, 14 Oct. 1999. Web. 14 Apr. 2014.

Allen, Myles. "An Expert View on Carbon Capture and Storage." *Environmental Change Institute*. Oxford U, 23 Sept. 2013. Web. 14 Apr. 2014.

Gillis, Justin. "U.N. Panel Endorses Ceiling on Global Emissions." *New York Times*. New York Times, 27 Sept. 2013. Web. 14 Apr. 2014.

Koerth-Baker, Maggie. "Mutually Insured Destruction." *New York Times*. New York Times, 27 Aug. 2013. Web. 14 Apr. 2014.

Koerth-Baker, Maggie. "What Are the Odds? How Much Is Climate Change to Blame for Extreme Weather?" *Conservation Magazine*. University of Washington, 10 July 2014. Web. 17 July 2014.

—Molly Hagan

# Richard Alley

**Born:** August 18, 1957
**Occupation:** Geologist

Richard Alley is a Nobel Peace Prize–winning environmental scientist and an Evan Pugh Professor of Geosciences at Pennsylvania State University (Penn State). In 2000, he published an award-winning book called *The Two-Mile Time Machine: Ice Cores, Abrupt Climate Change, and Our Future*, and in 2011, he hosted a PBS miniseries about climate change called *Earth: The Operators' Manual*. He is best known as a glaciologist (someone who studies ice and glaciers)—the Alley Glacier in the Britannia Range of the West Antarctic Ice Sheet is named in his honor—and he is an expert on Earth's climate cycles. But as his students and fans can attest, Alley is also an excellent communicator. Andrew C. Revkin wrote for the *New York Times* (6 Feb. 2009) that Alley "has spent years trying out new ways to captivate students and the public with the science and significance of climate change."

Revkin described the eccentric professor as a cross between the neurotic filmmaker Woody Allen and the late popular scientist Carl Sagan. Alley is popular among students for his unusual style of teaching. He is famous for his "rock" (as in geology) videos, in which he rewrites the lyrics to popular songs to explain scientific concepts. Alone with his guitar, Alley has performed such hits as Johnny Cash's "I Walk the Line" (retitled "We Watch the Line") to describe the work of seismologists, "Rollin' to the Future" (to the tune of Creedence Clearwater Revival's "Proud Mary") about global warming, "Peaceful Easy Obduction" (to the tune of the Eagle's "Peace-

Richard Alley/Wikimedia

ful Easy Feeling") to describe plate tectonics, and a revision of Johnny Cash's "Ring of Fire" about volcanoes. The production of the videos is a family affair: his wife, Cindy, films them and his daughters sometime provide musical accompaniment. One of Alley's most popular courses, "Survey of National Parks," is taught online and offers "field trips" composed of Alley's own photo albums. The class has an enrollment of nearly one thousand students each semester.

**EARLY LIFE AND TEACHING CAREER**

Richard B. Alley was born on August 18, 1957, in Columbus, Ohio, and grew up in Worthington, Ohio. He has two siblings: an older brother and a younger sister. Both of his parents encouraged his scientific curiosity, and he recalls helping his mother in her garden from an early age. He spent a lot of time collecting rocks around an abandoned house near his own and later joined rock and mineral societies that took him on rock-climbing trips. As a senior at Worthington High School, Alley was chosen as a US Presidential Scholar, a long-running program that selects students based on academic achievement, artistic excellence, personal essays, and community service. Alley took his first airplane trip to Washington, DC, for the ceremony in 1976. He graduated the same year.

Alley attended the nearby Ohio State University, and after his freshman year, he was offered a choice of two different summer jobs. One in-

volved cleaning fossils with a toothbrush. The other involved working with a glaciologist. "I wasn't quite sure what the glaciologist did, but it sounded really interesting and I am still doing it to this day," Alley told Megan Caldwell of the State College *Centre Daily Times* (10 May 2014). During his sophomore year in 1978, Alley traveled to Antarctica for the first time to assist glaciologists in performing paleomagnetic sampling, a process by which scientists can decipher the direction of Earth's magnetic field at the time of a rock's formation. Alley was initially assigned menial tasks, but in later years his work on such excursions included studying cylindrical cores of ice, drilled from glaciers nearly two miles thick. Snow rarely melts on the ice caps of Antarctica and Greenland, and year after year, snowfall accumulates (trapping bubbles of air) and freezes. Ice cores are a sampling of layers of this snowfall, and they can tell scientists a lot about the history of Earth's climate based on their contents. For example, the level of sulfate present in a layer can tell scientists something about the level of volcanic activity that particular year, while the level of carbon dioxide provides information about temperature. Higher levels of carbon dioxide indicate a warmer climate and lower levels indicate a colder one.

Alley earned both his BS (1980) and MS (1983) degrees from the geology department at Ohio State University and completed his PhD at the University of Wisconsin–Madison in 1987, where the geophysicist Charles Bentley served as his mentor. After completing his postdoctoral work, Alley was hired by Penn State's Eric Barron, who was then the dean of the College of Earth and Mineral Sciences. Alley began working for Penn State in 1988 and became an assistant professor in 1989. He was an associate professor for many years before becoming an Evan Pugh Professor of Geosciences in 2000.

*THE TWO-MILE TIME MACHINE*

In 2000, Alley published a book called *The Two-Mile Time Machine: Ice Cores, Abrupt Climate Change, and Our Future*. According to a book review by J. A. Rial for the *American Scientist* (Mar.-Apr. 2001), Alley calls the book a "progress report" on abrupt climate changes, but Rial writes that *The Two-Mile Time Machine* is a more compelling and relevant read than that description suggests. The title refers to the experiences of Alley and his colleagues drilling ice cores in Greenland. The cores they removed, merely a few inches in diameter and a few feet long, totaling a length of more than two miles of compacted snowfall, give the scientists a view of Earth's climate over the last 110,000 years. "Alley's book focuses not on the long-term changes that may have caused the ice ages, but on more recent, newly discovered 'flickering' climate changes that the drilling through Greenland's ice cap revealed," Rial wrote. "He emphasizes that many of the important climate changes he and his colleagues have been able to read from the ice cores are sudden, abrupt, and enormous. The Earth's climate has at times changed drastically in just a few years from livable to glacially inhospitable or unbearably hot and sauna-like. If such changes were to occur today, we would face a climate catastrophe of proportions unprecedented in the history of humankind."

At the end of the book, Alley, using computer models, makes several predictions based on current, human-induced global warming. One scenario even included—perversely—the dawn of a new ice age. On the whole, Alley's research has shown that Earth's climate is extremely volatile; thus, the impact of human activity is something to be taken seriously, he warns. In his review, Rial put it a different way: "Some scientists warn that global climate is like a drunk: If left alone, a drunk will stay put, but a tap on the shoulder may cause him to panic, stagger, fall, and break his neck," he wrote. "With our notorious disregard for the environment, we humans could well become the tap on the drunk's shoulder." *The Two-Mile Time Machine* won the Phi Beta Kappa Book Award in Science in 2001.

### *EARTH: THE OPERATOR'S MANUAL*

In 2011, Alley hosted a three-hour PBS miniseries about abrupt climate change called *Earth: The Operator's Manual*. (He published a companion book with the same title the same year.) The series was funded by the National Science Foundation and written and directed by Geoff Haines-Stiles, the same man who produced Sagan's iconic *Cosmos* series for PBS in the 1980s. Filmed across the globe, *Earth: The Operator's Manual* aimed for an optimistic take on global warming. "The good news is that there are a lot of things that we can do," Alley told Terry Waghorn for *Forbes* (25 Jan. 2012). "They fall under three broad categories: mitigation"—slowing climate change—"adaptation, and the innovation that makes mitigation and adaptation easier."

Alley, who has described himself as a registered Republican, has met with politicians from both parties to discuss the effects of climate change and global warming, and in 2007, he accompanied a bi-partisan group of ten US senators from the US Senate Committee on Environment and Public Works on a trip to Greenland to study the impact of global warming.

### PERSONAL LIFE

Alley eschews the seated desk in his office in favor of a stationary bike. He suggested to Caldwell that he does his best thinking while in motion. Caldwell reports that Alley has five bikes—one in his office, three at various locations within his department, and one at home. In his spare time, he is an avid bird-watcher, gardener, and amateur soccer player. He met his wife, Cindy, a fellow geology major, as an undergraduate at Ohio State. The couple married in 1980. Cindy worked as a librarian while Alley earned his master's degree, and their first daughter, Janet, was born a few days after he defended his thesis. Alley and his wife live in College Township. Their daughter Janet is a schoolteacher in Seattle and their daughter Karen is a graduate student studying Antarctic glaciation at the University of Colorado.

In 2007, Alley was a coauthor on the United Nations' Fourth Assessment Report of the Intergovernmental Panel on Climate Change (IPCC). He and his colleagues share a Nobel Peace Prize with former vice president Al Gore for their work. Alley cares deeply about the future of Earth's climate and has worked not only to provide evidence of global warming but also to convey the gravity of that information to the lay public. "The warming influence of $CO_2$ on the planet is not something you 'believe in,'" Alley said in a keynote address at Albion College, as quoted by Jake Weber for the school's website (25 Apr. 2014). "It's physics."

### SUGGESTED READING

Caldwell, Megan. "Penn State Professor, Climate Scientist Continues to Rack Up Awards for Work." *Centre Daily Times* [State College]. Centre Daily Times, 10 May 2014. Web. 23 Oct. 2014.

Revkin, Andrew C. "Richard Alley's Orbital and Climate Dance." *New York Times*. New York Times, 6 Feb. 2009. Web. 23 Oct. 2014.

Rial, J. A. "Time Travel on Ice." *American Scientist*. Scientific Research Society, 1 Mar.–Apr. 2001. Web. 23 Oct. 2014.

Waghorn, Terry. "Richard Alley on Challenges, Choices, and Climate Change." *Forbes*. Forbes, 25 Jan. 2012. Web. 23 Oct. 2014.

Weber, Jake. "Expert Richard Alley Shares Facts, Optimism about Climate Change." *Albion College*. Albion College, 25 Apr. 2014. Web. 23 Oct. 2014.

—Molly Hagan

# Anthony Anderson

**Born:** August 15, 1970
**Occupation:** Actor

Anthony Anderson has racked up more than eighty credits to his name in both film and television, mostly as a supporting actor. He has also received considerable acclaim for his ability to slip between comedic and dramatic roles. He is perhaps best known for his supporting roles in films such as *Me, Myself & Irene* (2000), *Hustle & Flow* (2005), and *The Departed* (2006), as well as on television dramas such as *The Shield* and *Law & Order* and television comedies such as *All about the Andersons*. He is also a host on Food Network's *Eating America* series.

After a few false starts as a lead actor on television, he finally came into his own as the lead actor and executive producer on *Black-ish*, the breakout ABC comedy centered on an upper-middle-class African American family looking to maintain its ethnic identity. Inspired in part by Anderson's own experiences with his family, the show has garnered a large and diverse audience. For his work on *Black-ish*, Anderson was nominated for a 2015 Emmy Award in the category of outstanding lead actor in a comedy series. He believes his success is due in part to the creation of his personal brand. He told Carolyn M. Brown for *Black Enterprise* (1 Dec. 2012): "Part of building a brand is diversification and appealing to various people, creeds, religions, and so forth. . . . I want longevity, which means I must have the courage to turn left before anyone else does."

## EARLY LIFE AND EDUCATION

Anthony Anderson was born on August 15, 1970, in Los Angeles, California, where he was raised by his mother, Doris, a phone operator in Los Angeles County, and his stepfather, Sterling Bowman, who at one time owned several plus-sized women's clothing stores. Growing up, young Anthony wanted to have one of three professions: lawyer, pro football player for the Dallas Cowboys, or actor. Then he had something of an epiphany. Anderson told Britni Danielle for *Jet* (8 Oct. 2012): "I realized that if I became an actor, I could become all three of those things."

Much of Anderson's comedy has taken its inspiration from the crazy things he and his family did growing up—such as the time his stepfather put a padlock on the refrigerator. "Anthony and his friend were eating all the food," his mother, Doris, explained in *People* (17 Nov. 2003). "And [Sterling] put a pay phone in the living room. . . . You had to put a quarter in every three minutes." His mother once even attached him and his two brothers to a dog's leash to keep them from running off.

Anderson's path toward an acting career began in earnest when he was attending the Los Angeles County High School for the Performing Arts. There he won first place in the ACT-SO Awards from the National Association for the Advancement of Colored People by performing the famous monologue from *The Great White Hope*, a 1967 play written by Howard Sackler that gives a fictionalized account of boxing champion Jack Johnson's life and was adapted for the big screen in 1970. Winning the award helped Anderson earn a scholarship to Howard University in Washington, DC.

## CHARACTER ACTOR IN FILM AND ON TELEVISION

Anderson's first real show-business experience was when he tried stand-up comedy—and completely bombed. Despite this, Anderson found it to be a learning experience. "The stage taught me to be fearless," Miller told Danielle for *Jet*. "You must be willing to be vulnerable in order for your audience to go on that journey with you." After starring for a year as Teddy Broadis on the teen series *Hang Time* (1996–7), he had more success in small, supporting roles in film and television. One of his first high-profile roles was in the Eddie Murphy and Martin Lawrence comedy *Life* (1999) and in the Jim Carrey comedy *Me, Myself & Irene*, in which he played one of Carrey's sons. Other supporting film roles followed, including *Exit Wounds* (2001), *Barbershop* (2002), *Scary Movie 3* (2003), *Agent Cody Banks 2: Destination London* (2004), *Hustle & Flow* (2005), and *Scary Movie 4* (2006).

Anderson had even greater success on the small screen, where he was able to take leading roles in both situation comedies and dramas. He received critical acclaim—if not stellar ratings—for his work on the sitcom *All about the Andersons* (2003–4), about a struggling actor and single dad who moves back in with his parents. Although the show, which starred veteran actor John Amos as Anderson's father, was canceled after a single season, it garnered solid reviews. In *Variety* (9 Sept. 2003), Michael Speier wrote: "On paper, the WB's *All about the Andersons* is a routine sitcom with tried-and-true mechanisms, but there's something brewing here that feels more distinct. . . . [Anderson] displays a passion and a Ruben Studdard–like teddy bear allure while finally making a name for himself, as Bernie Mac did two seasons back, in a medium that serves his talents perfectly."

For his next major television role, Anderson branched into drama, taking on the role of a villain on *The Shield* from 2005 to 2007, a cop show that starred Michael Chiklis and featured veteran actor Glenn Close. Close was particularly impressed with Anderson's performance. "He's a really good actor," she was quoted as saying in *USA Today* (18 Apr. 2005). "My daughter knows him from all the funny movies, like *Me, Myself & Irene*. And I think comedy is harder than drama. So if he can do comedy, he should do well in drama."

For his next roles, Anderson appeared as a good cop in *The Departed* (2006), a crime drama directed by Martin Scorsese and starring Jack Nicholson and Leonardo DiCaprio, and in Michael Bay's 2007 big-budget adaptation of the TV cartoon series *Transformers*. In 2008, he returned to television to star as Detective Kevin

Bernard on the long-running drama *Law & Order*. He also starred on the short-lived comedy *Guys with Kids* from 2012 to 2013.

## BLACK-ISH

Anderson's greatest success to date has been his leading role in the television comedy, *Black-ish*, which first aired on ABC in 2014. In it, he portrays Andre "Dre" Johnson Sr., an advertising executive who worries that his family's affluence, suburban lifestyle, and association with upper-middle-class white families has made his children less "authentically" black, and he tries his best to incorporate his own less affluent and urban experiences into their lives to little effect. One of his sons is a nerd; his wife is biracial and ambivalent about racial issues; and their four children have no real memories of the United States before Barack Obama was president.

The show has earned praise from viewers for both for its comedy and for the performances of its lead characters, played by Anderson and Tracee Ellis Ross, who plays Dre's wife, Rainbow, a doctor who was raised by hippies and is less concerned about making sure their children have an "authentic" black experience. Critics have been impressed as well. In the *New Yorker* (9 Mar. 2015), Emily Nussbaum declared that in its first fifteen episodes, "the series has transformed from hokey formula into one of the goofiest, most reliably enjoyable comedies around. . . . In the best tradition of the mainstream sitcom, the show felt both new and familiar, giving the show's marriage emotional roots." In a review for NPR (24 Sept. 2014), Linda Holmes remarked: "While the racial politics of *Black-ish* are interesting and feel pretty fresh (especially for a broadcast show), what's even more unusual is Dre's mention of money. What makes the show interesting and the comedy more pointed, for me, is that there's a candor about the way that having money affects Dre and Rainbow's sense of who they are and how they're raising their kids that's very uncommon in a world where the obviously rolling-in-dough families on *Modern Family*, for instance, almost never discuss it." Anderson has also recently appeared in the miniseries *Anthony Eats America* (2013). His upcoming projects include the films *Hot Bot* and *Barbershop 3*.

## PERSONAL LIFE

Since 1995, Anthony Anderson has been married to his college sweetheart, Alvina, to whom he credits much of his success, as she helped to give him the stable home life he needed to make a creative impact in his profession. They live in Southern California and have two children, Kyra and Nathan. In an interview with *Black Enterprise*, Anderson told Brown: "I work in Hollywood, but we don't live in that world. I discipline my kids because they will not be an embarrassment to me. Of course, they have [luxuries] I didn't have, but whether they like it or not, it is paramount that they go to college. . . . I'm not their safety net. I will help them as best I can without enabling them." Anderson, who has type 2 diabetes, is also actively involved in campaigns promoting awareness, diagnosis, and treatment of the condition.

### SUGGESTED READING

Anderson, Anthony. Interview by Carolyn M. Brown. "Backtalk with Anthony Anderson." *Black Enterprise* Dec. 2012: 96. Print.

Danielle, Britni. "The Family Man." *Jet* 8 Oct. 2012: 26–27. Print.

Holmes, Lynda. "'Black-ish' and the Color of Money." *Monkey See*. NPR, 24 Sept. 2014. Web. 28 July 2015.

Nussbaum, Emily. "Home Cooking." *New Yorker*. Condé Nast, 9 Mar. 2015. Web. 3 Aug. 2015.

### SELECTED WORKS

*Life*, 1999; *Me, Myself & Irene*, 2000; *Scary Movie 3*, 2003; *All about the Andersons*, 2003–4; *Scary Movie 4*, 2006; *The Departed*, 2006; *The Shield*, 2005–7; *Law & Order*, 2008–10; *Guys with Kids*, 2012–13; *Black-ish*, 2014–

—Christopher Mari

# Jamie Anderson

**Born:** September 13, 1990
**Occupation:** Snowboarder

"Watching Jamie Anderson go down a hill on a snowboard is similar to listening to a well-performed Beethoven Concerto No. 5: it's smooth, flawless, and exquisite," Robert Piper wrote for the *Huffington Post* blog *Healthy Living* (28 Feb. 2014). Referring to a difficult move in which snowboarders make not one but two full rotations (720 degrees) while in midair, Piper wrote, "In the world of snowboarding, there

Quinn Rooney/Getty Images

are 720s, and then there are Jamie Anderson 720s."

Anderson specializes in slopestyle snowboarding, which involves performing tricks while descending a course filled with obstacles and challenging terrain features. In 2006 she won a bronze medal at the Winter X Games, held annually in Aspen, Colorado, supplanting Shaun White, one of snowboarding's most popular practitioners. At age fifteen, she was the youngest person ever to reach the X Games podium. The following year she became the youngest woman ever to win a gold medal at the popular extreme-sports showcase.

Anderson has racked up an impressive number of wins in the sport's other major competitions, the Winter Dew event and the World Snowboard Tour, as well. However, the pinnacle of her career to date occurred at the 2014 Olympic Winter Games, held in Sochi, Russia, where she won the inaugural gold medal in women's slopestyle competition. (Snowboarding became an Olympic sport in 1998, when the Winter Games were held in Nagano, Japan; the competition in Sochi marked the first time that slopestyle was included as an event.) The Olympics introduced Anderson to a wide audience, many of whom had never before seen snowboarding as a serious sport.

A relatively modern pursuit, snowboarding had its genesis in the mid-1960s, when engineer Sherman Poppen made a Christmas present for his two daughters by lashing two cheap skis together and adding a rope to make steering easier. He later patented the resulting forty-two-inch-by-seven-inch board, which he called the "Snurfer" (a portmanteau of "snow" and "surfer") and which sold more than one million units over the next fifteen years. In 1982, the ninth National Snow Surfing Championship—the first to be held outside of Poppen's hometown of Muskegon, Michigan—drew 125 contestants to a course outside Woodstock, Vermont, that featured a kitchen table as a starting gate and hay bales as crash pads.

The Olympics, of course, was a decidedly more high-profile affair. "The X Games is the biggest event in our sport," Anderson told Amy Donaldson for the *Deseret News* (9 Feb. 2014). "[But] the Olympics is the biggest event in all of sports, in the whole world, and there is such history to it." Still, Anderson, known for her laid-back persona and her fondness for meditation and yoga, explained, "At the end of the day, it's snowboarding. We all started it because of how much fun it brings. We're basically snowboarding on a playground up there."

## EARLY LIFE AND EDUCATION

Jamie Anderson was born on September 13, 1990, in the Lake Tahoe region of California. Her mother, Lauren, was a Vermont native who moved to California in her twenties and met Anderson's father, Joe, while working at a ski resort. Lauren ran a lawn-mowing business while her children were growing up; in 2013, she moved back to Vermont to become an alpaca farmer. Joe, who worked as a firefighter in Lake Tahoe after graduating from high school, eventually retired to a small, sled-accessible cabin at the foot of the mountains, where he could spend his time snowmobiling, fly-fishing, and hiking.

Anderson, her five sisters, and her two brothers were all home-schooled by Lauren. "I wanted them to be like children, playing outside, running and jumping and not sitting inside at a desk," Lauren told Vidya Rao for *Today* (11 Feb. 2014). "They got to be free, building their bodies, protecting their spirits and minds, and not being pushed or pressured." She continued, "There wasn't a big push for them to read and write and do arithmetic. I wanted them to learn how to get along and let life be the teacher. Character-building was more important than academics." Anderson's grandparents were less convinced; during family visits, they would ask the children to read out loud to them in order to make sure they knew how to read.

Lauren and Joe could not afford to buy their children much sporting equipment, but their oldest daughters, Joanie and Stacie, were given hand-me-down snowboards by a family friend. When Anderson was nine years old, she tried her sisters' snowboards for the first time. Within a year she was entering competitions at the local resort, Sierra-at-Tahoe, and beating children older than her. She helped out with Lauren's lawn business and sold golf balls she collected from a nearby course to earn money for snowboarding gear and entry fees, and she soon became good enough to attract sponsors.

## SNOWBOARDING CAREER

At first, Anderson competed in United States of America Snowboard Association (USASA) events, working her way up to national and junior world championships. When she was thirteen, she qualified for the 2004 Winter X Games in boardercross, a racing event. "I am still blown away when I look at a thirteen-year-old and realize how little I must have looked back then," she told Morty Ain in an interview for *ESPN* magazine's *Body Issue* (9 July 2014.) "But of course when you're thirteen you feel like you're an adult, you think you're twenty just kicking it. At least I did. . . . I was definitely a little firecracker."

When she was fifteen years old, Anderson signed her first sponsorship contract with clothing and sporting-goods company Billabong, which continues to be her main sponsor. Soon after, in January 2006, she took home a bronze medal in the Winter X Games' slopestyle event, becoming the youngest competitor ever to medal at the games. The following year, at the 2007 Winter X Games, Anderson successfully performed a 720 for the first time in competition and became the youngest woman ever to win a Winter X Games gold, again in the slopestyle event. (At the same games, Anderson's sister Joanie won the gold medal in the women's snowboard cross event.) She has stood on the podium in every Winter X Game since then—save for the 2009 games, when she did not participate due to a broken pelvis—becoming the most medaled female athlete ever in the Winter X Games slopestyle competition.

In another high-profile event, the World Snowboard Tour—formerly known as the Ticket to Ride (TTR) World Snowboard Tour—Anderson has won similar laurels, placing first in the

2007–8 and 2010–11 Overall World Tours and the 2011–12 and 2013–14 Slopestyle World Tours. She has also performed admirably in the Winter Dew Tour, which debuted in the winter of 2008–9, being crowned women's slopestyle champion for several years running. In addition, Anderson has twice been awarded ESPN's Excellence in Sports Performance Yearly (ESPY) Award for Best Female Action Sports Athlete, first in 2012 and then again in 2014.

In early 2013, the United States Ski and Snowboard Association (USSA), the US governing body for Olympic skiing and snowboarding, agreed to allow a Winter Dew Tour event in Breckenridge, Colorado, to serve as a qualifier for the 2014 Winter Olympics team. Few were surprised when it was announced that Anderson would be representing the United States in Sochi.

## SOCHI 2014

Vividly describing Anderson preparing for her final run at the Olympics—the one that would win her the gold medal—John Branch wrote for the *New York Times* (9 Feb. 2014), "Around her neck, under her jacket, she wore mantra beads . . . that Anderson said gave 'sacred energy.' There was 'power stone' and 'moonstone' of clear quartz. In her ears, she had the Nas song 'I Can' playing. . . . She took a deep breath and closed her eyes. She imagined her run, felt the landings, saw her family . . . cheering at the bottom, half a mile and forty-five seconds away. And then she went there."

Anderson's run included two seemingly effortless 720s and earned her the gold with a score of 95.25. While it was an outstanding performance, journalists seemed equally impressed with her calm demeanor throughout the event. "After she was through centering a group of stressed-out reporters on Internet deadlines, it wasn't clear whether she had just swept the slopestyle snowboarding events for the US or was set to open a restorative wellness center with a noon Ashtanga class," Mike Wise wrote for the *Washington Post* (9 Feb. 2014).

Others noted a sense of generosity and camaraderie among the women snowboarders that seemed unusual in elite competitive athletes. "As Anderson talked about the love between competitors, which was evident everywhere, including in the media maze where competitors shared smiles and tears and exchanged praise and love, [British snowboarder Jenny] Jones quipped, 'Can you tell she's a hippie from Tahoe?'" Don-

aldson wrote. "Anderson embraced the characterization, and the two then began a light-hearted exchange about the different ways they deal with stress." Anderson revealed that the night before, she had "burned some sage, had some candles going, did some yoga."

Not one to rest on her laurels, Anderson continued to shine in competition following the Olympics. Among her post-Sochi victories have been first-place finishes in the Dew Tour Mountain Championships in December 2014, the Burton US Open in March 2015, and the Audi Quattro Winter Games NZ in August 2015.

## PERSONAL LIFE

Anderson credits much of her good physical condition to her serious study of yoga. "My yoga has saved me through a lot of bad crashes," she told Ain. "Even flat landings that most people wouldn't land, I somehow have been able to land from all the work in yoga. When I'm snowboarding, I just feel stronger and more flexible and more able to trust my instincts—because there are times when you really do have to be mindful with the jumps you're hitting and the conditions that you're riding in."

She posed nude for *ESPN* magazine's 2014 Body Issue and told Ain that she was proud of every aspect of her body, including its ability to heal itself. "I ruptured my spleen like five years ago," she said. "Seeing the body heal itself and come back from injuries is something that just makes me value my body and health even more. I love everything about it."

Anderson is widely recognized for her devotion to the snowboarding community. She has spearheaded a sponsorship program, offering season passes and gear to Lake Tahoe middle school students with good grades and athletic ability who want to snowboard but cannot afford to do so. "Snowboarding is such an expensive sport," she told Natalie Langmann for *Huck* magazine (7 Mar. 2012). "I feel so lucky that I was given hand-me-downs from family friends, my sisters and everyone else, and that I eventually got to become this professional snowboarder. I also want to give back to the mountains that have supported me for a decade strong."

## SUGGESTED READING

Anderson, Jamie. "Jamie Anderson in Only a Smile." Interview by Morty Ain. *ESPN.com.* ESPN Internet Ventures, 9 July 2014. Web. 10 Sept. 2015.

Branch, John. "Jamie Anderson, Slopestyle's Star, Is on Top Again." *New York Times*. New York Times, 9 Feb. 2014. Web. 10 Sept. 2015.

Donaldson, Amy. "Sochi 2014: US Snowboarder Jamie Anderson Delivers under Historic Pressure to Win Slopestyle Olympic Gold." *Deseret News*. Deseret Digital Media, 9 Feb. 2014. Web. 10 Sept. 2015.

Langmann, Natalie. "Jamie Anderson: More than This." *Huck*. TCOLondon, 7 Mar. 2012. Web. 10 Sept. 2015.

Piper, Robert. "Olympic Gold Medalist Jamie Anderson: On Life, Snowboarding and Staying Calm." *HuffPost Healthy Living*. TheHuffingtonPost.com, 28 Feb. 2014. Web. 10 Sept. 2015.

Rao, Vidya. "Gold Medalist Jamie Anderson's Mom: I Didn't Push My Kids 'to Read and Write.'" *Today*. NBCUniversal Media, 11 Feb. 2014. Web. 10 Sept. 2015.

Wise, Mike. "Gold Medal, the Jamie Anderson Way: Meditation, Incense and Candles." *Washington Post*. Washington Post, 9 Feb. 2014. Web. 10 Sept. 2015.

—Mari Rich

Cindy Ord/Getty Images

# Gavin Andresen

**Born:** 1966

**Occupation:** Chief scientist of Bitcoin Foundation

Gavin Andresen is the chief developer of the open-source virtual currency system known as Bitcoin and a founder of the nonprofit Bitcoin Foundation. (Bitcoin, with a capital "B," is the name of the software system; bitcoins are the currency itself.) As the most prominent individual officially associated with the controversial currency, he has become quite influential as Bitcoin has grown in popularity. In many ways, bitcoins are a lot like US dollars—they have value and can be traded for goods and services—but there are also significant differences between bitcoins and other currencies. Dollars are "a so-called fiat currency," Noam Cohen wrote for the *New York Times* (3 July 2011), "valuable because the government says they are," and other traditional systems are specie currencies, linked to the value of precious metals. Bitcoins are neither, and so their value can fluctuate dramatically. Despite its volatility, the Bitcoin system provides potential advantages over traditional money such as privacy and confidentiality, ease of cross-border transactions, and protection from government confiscation. Andresen is the primary person responsible for maintaining and improving the Bitcoin software.

Although bitcoin is a functional currency with a growing following, it has generated significant interest as a social experiment. Andresen called the possibility of survival for such a stand-alone currency "an open question" in an interview with James Freeman for the *Wall Street Journal* (3 May 2013), noting that there was no model to follow. Bitcoin has been criticized as unnecessary, called an aid to criminals, and questioned due to the mystery surrounding its anonymous founder, a programmer known as Satoshi Nakamoto. Yet it has drawn support from those who question the philosophy of the established global banking system and its potential flaws. Andresen himself was attracted to Bitcoin out of interest in its disruptive potential and is committed to supporting the system to wherever users take it. "Can you get from where we are to the vision of billions of people all over the world using bitcoin just like they use any other currency?" he mused to Freeman. "That's the grand experiment."

## EDUCATION AND EARLY CAREER

Andresen was born Gavin Bell in Melbourne, Australia, and moved to the United States as a child. He graduated with a bachelor's degree in computer science from Princeton University in 1988. His professional career as a computer programmer began straight out of school when he took a job with Silicon Graphics Computer Systems, a technology company in Silicon Valley, California, where he worked for seven years. According to Andresen's autobiographical "Ask Me Anything" post on the social media site Reddit (21 Oct. 2014), he was involved in the development of the Internet 3-D graphics programs Open Inventor and VRML (Virtual Reality Modeling Language) before moving on to a number of other software start-up firms. Some of the other projects he worked on include a series of computer games that could be played by blind people, the computer science research archive search engine Rexa, and his own failed start-up company. He was also a coauthor of the book *The Annotated VRML 2.0 Reference Manual*, published in 1997.

Andresen discovered Bitcoin in 2010, a year after Nakamoto set the system in motion. Nakamoto, who was well known through blog posts and e-mail conversations among the programming community until he ceased all communication by early 2012, invented the currency as a response to the 2008 global financial crisis. "The root problem with conventional currency is all the trust that's required to make it work," Nakamoto wrote in one blog post on the P2P Foundation website, as quoted by Maria Bustillos in the *New Yorker* (1 Apr. 2013). Nakamoto devised a system in which a fixed amount of bitcoins could be released into circulation as computers "mine" the currency by solving complex mathematical problems. Every bitcoin generated includes a cryptographic identity to prevent copying and forgery and to bypass the need for a controlling authority such as a bank. By operating as a purely peer-to-peer system, bitcoins could theoretically remain independent from the online transaction costs extracted by intermediaries such as credit card companies as well as the influence and potential corruption of governments, banks, and other groups.

## EARLY BITCOIN INVOLVEMENT

Nakamoto's antiestablishment ideas appealed to Andresen, who told Bianca Bosker for the *Huffington Post* (16 Apr. 2013), "As I've gotten older, I've become mostly libertarian. I'm generally of the opinion that less government tends to be better just because I'm very suspicious of concentrated power. I realized that a lot of the evils in the world come from people who take

or are given too much power, and often the way they get there is through government." Andresen was so impressed with the concept for the independent virtual currency that he started a website called Bitcoin Faucet in May 2010 in order to promote the system. For fifty dollars, he bought ten thousand bitcoins and gave five coins to everyone who visited the site—for free. "It turns out that giving things away for free is a good way to become pretty popular," Andresen joked to Brett Tomlinson for the *Princeton Alumni Weekly* (13 Nov. 2013).

Andresen also began corresponding directly with Nakamoto, proposing changes and improvements to the Bitcoin code. As his contributions increased, so did his overall involvement with the Bitcoin phenomenon. Andresen told Bosker, "Over time [Nakamoto] trusted my judgment on the code I wrote. And eventually, he pulled a fast one on me because he asked me if it'd be okay if he put my email address on the Bitcoin homepage, and I said yes, not realizing that when he put my email address there, he'd take his away. I was the person everyone would email when they wanted to know about Bitcoin."

By December 2010, Andresen officially acknowledged that he was taking on a full-time leadership role to develop Bitcoin's core software with other volunteers, and in 2011 Nakamoto effectively ended his own involvement in the project. Although many observers attempting to solve the mystery of Nakamoto's identity have suggested Andresen's quick rise to prominence could mean the founder and his successor are one and the same, others note that their writing and coding styles are highly distinct. Andresen himself rejects such claims, stating "I am not Satoshi Nakamoto; I have never met him. . . . Nobody knows who he is, I think," as quoted by Tom Simonite in the *MIT Technology Review* (15 Aug. 2014).

## PUBLIC FACE OF BITCOIN

In his position as chief developer of Bitcoin's open-source software, Andresen began to take steps to secure the currency's stability and future. In addition to the technical aspects of maintaining and improving the code, he became involved in efforts to bolster the organizational framework necessary to allow Bitcoin to function and spread. As the project grew and gained wider attention in the media for its controversial revolutionary potential, challenges arose that required a unified presence to represent Bitcoin. In 2011 the bitcoin exchange Mt. Gox was hacked, causing a major crash in bitcoin prices and a significant setback in the currency's reputation. Some groups, such as the Internet rights advocacy organization the Electronic Frontier Foundation, have decided not to use bitcoins due to the uncharted legal issues involved. The same year Andresen presented a talk to the Central Intelligence Agency to explain how Bitcoin worked so the US government could evaluate its risks. "I expected it to have lots of speed bumps," Andresen said of Bitcoin's growth to Cohen, "But I didn't expect there to be so many speed bumps in a row."

In 2012 Andresen became the first developer to be paid for his work on the system, through the support of the Trucoin company. When that income stream ended, he helped to establish the Bitcoin Foundation, a nonprofit modeled after the Linux Foundation that supports the similarly open-source Linux software. The Bitcoin Foundation ensures that Andresen and a small number of other key developers can be paid to devote themselves to the Bitcoin program as it expands to greater levels of complexity and encounters new challenges. Andresen's salary is paid in bitcoins, calculated according to the dollar exchange rate for tax purposes, though he told Bosker "I've been diversifying out of bitcoins because it just doesn't make sense to have all your eggs in one basket." Andresen's title later changed from chief developer to chief scientist to reflect his expanded management duties.

## BITCOIN'S FUTURE

In early 2013, the Financial Crimes Enforcement Network (FinCEN), the federal agency within the US Department of the Treasury that enforces laws against money laundering, announced new regulations that stated, in part, certain bitcoin trading entities must register as Money Services Businesses (MSBs). While Andresen took issue with some aspects of the guidelines, he told Bustillos that he felt the announcement was a positive one. "In my opinion, the FinCEN guidance is fantastic news: it gives Bitcoin users and businesses clear rules on how they will or won't be regulated," he said. "It is great for ordinary users, because FinCEN said that using bitcoins to buy products or services is perfectly legal. And, long-term, it is great for businesses, because they now know how FinCEN will classify them and what regulations they must obey here in the United States."

Andresen outlined his vision of Bitcoin's future to Kim Hjelmgaard for *USA Today* (7 Nov.

2014), claiming that he wanted to focus his energy on eradicating Bitcoin's technical weaknesses and explaining that "I don't see myself as the king of Bitcoin. I don't want to be the king of Bitcoin." He addressed concerns about the increasing centralization of "mining," and regulatory clarity with characteristic calm. "Bitcoin as a globally distributed public ledger—that's the thing I'm most excited about going forward," he said. He also was careful to categorize Bitcoin as an ongoing experiment. "I use Bitcoin whenever I can, but can't pay my mortgage, buy a car—at least not at the car dealers where I live. I did ask and I would have if I could have," he told Hjelmgaard. "My day-to-day life is cash and credit cards like everyone else."

## PERSONAL LIFE

Andresen met his wife, Michele Cooke-Andresen, at Princeton. They moved to Amherst, Massachusetts, in 1998, where Cooke-Andresen is a tenured geology professor at the University of Massachusetts. The couple has two children. Andresen is an active Amherst Town Meeting member and enjoys riding his bicycle and unicycle.

## SUGGESTED READING

Andresen, Gavin. "I'm Gavin Andresen, Chief Scientist at the Bitcoin Foundation. Ask Me Anything!" *Reddit*. Reddit, 21 Oct. 2014. Web. 15 Dec. 2014.

Bosker, Bianca. "Gavin Andresen, Bitcoin Architect: Meet the Man Bringing You Bitcoin (And Getting Paid in It)." *Huffington Post*. TheHuffingtonPost.com, 16 Apr. 2013. Web. 15 Dec. 2014.

Bustillos, Maria. "The Bitcoin Boom." *New Yorker*. Condé Nast, 1 Apr. 2013. Web. 7 Dec. 2014.

Freeman, James. "Bitcoin vs. Ben Bernanke." *Wall Street Journal*. Dow Jones, 3 May 2013. Web. 7 Dec. 2014.

Hjelmgaard, Kim. "Gavin Andresen: I Don't Want to Be 'King of Bitcoin.'" *USA Today*. Gannett Satellite Information Network, 7 Nov. 2014. Web. 9 Dec. 2014.

Simonite, Tom. "The Man Who Really Built Bitcoin." *MIT Technology Review*. MIT Technology Review, 15 Aug. 2014. Web. 7 Dec. 2014.

Tomlinson, Brett. "Buying into Bitcoin." *Princeton Alumni Weekly*. Trustees of Princeton U, 13 Nov. 2013. Web. 7 Dec. 2014.

—Molly Hagan

# Mylswamy Annadurai

**Born:** July 2, 1958
**Occupation:** Aerospace engineer

Dr. Mylswamy Annadurai has been called the "moon man" by various publications. Annadurai was the project director of India's first mission to the moon in 2008, Chandrayaan 1, and he is now in charge of the Indian Space Research Organisation's (ISRO) first moon landing, Chandrayaan 2, scheduled for launch in 2017. Annadurai, who has been working with the ISRO since 1982, brought international attention to the organization after the Chandrayaan 1's Moon Impact Probe (MIP) found evidence of water molecules on the moon. He is now the project director of Mangalyaan 1, or India's Mars Orbiter Mission (MOM), which entered Mars's orbit on September 24, 2014, making the ISRO the world's fourth space agency to achieve the feat. India is the first Asian country to enter Mars's orbit and the first country to achieve the feat on its first attempt. The success of India's space missions has sparked the public's interest in space and rocket science. "Searching is part of the human condition," Annadurai told Kushalrani Gulab for the *Hindustan Times* (14 Dec. 2013). "Exploration, search, whether internal or external, that is what makes us human. The whole of science is driven by questions and the mother of all questions is:

Ram 121/ Wikimedia Commons

who are we? And for that answer, we have to see what's out there. If there once was life on Mars, why is there no life there now? If there is life only on Earth, why are we here?"

Annadurai was born in a rural village in the southern Indian state of Tamil Nadu and did not have electricity in his house until he was about twelve years old. He is invested in seeing young people who share his rural upbringing grow up to study science. He writes regular weekly columns for Tamil periodicals explaining rocket science using terms that are easy to understand, and he encourages Indian teachers to teach science in students' native tongues—for example, in Tamil as opposed to English—to encourage independent thinking. (Annadurai learned English during his first year of college.) "My father was a common man; today his son is leading an internationally reputed mission," Annadurai said in an interview for the *Hindu* (22 Nov. 2008). "It throws open immense opportunities for the common man and he is witnessing a slice of history unfolding right in front of his eyes. It is an uplifting moment for the whole community."

## EARLY LIFE AND EDUCATION

Annadurai was born one of five children in the rural village of Kothavadi (also spelled Kodhawady) near Coimbatore, Tamil Nadu, on July 2, 1958. His father, a retired headmaster, and his mother are extraordinarily proud of their son's accomplishments. His father named him after the former chief minister of Tamil Nadu, C. N. Annadurai, who was also a playwright. "I wanted him to get name and fame," his father said in an interview for the *Hindu* (24 Nov. 2008). Annadurai attended the Panchayat Union School in Kothavadi and later studied at the Municipal Boys High School in Pollachi, where, according to his former English and mathematics teacher C. K. Krishnan, he was a talented and inquisitive student. He used to walk ten kilometers (a little more than six miles) to school every day, and after classes, Annadurai and his classmates cultivated the land around the school. Annadurai was also an avid reader.

He completed his bachelor's degree in engineering at the Government College of Technology in Coimbatore in 1980, but he was also known to write poetry and song lyrics in his spare time. Some of his poems were published in the college's magazine. He then earned his master's degree in engineering from PSG College of Technology in Coimbatore in 1982. According to Peerzada Abrar for the *Economic Times* (25

Sept. 2014), Annadurai did not set foot outside of his district until after he had completed his master's degree.

## EARLY CAREER AT THE ISRO

Annadurai joined the ISRO at its headquarters in Bangalore in 1982, at the age of twenty-four. He began his career developing satellite technology for the ISRO, and in 1986, he delivered the first ever software satellite simulator, a training tool, for the organization. In 1988, he was promoted to spacecraft operations manager for the Indian remote-sensing satellites (IRS) mission 1A. He then served as operations manager for IRS 1B in 1989. Annadurai became the spacecraft operations manager of the Indian National Satellite System (INSAT) 2A and 2B missions in the early 1990s and later acted as the deputy project director of the INSAT 2C mission in 1994. He served as the mission director of various INSAT missions throughout the late 1990s and early 2000s. In 2003, as associate project director, he made significant contributions to the development of India's first educational satellite, EDUSAT, which was launched in September 2004. Annadurai's wife, Vasanthi, told Abrar that as a young scientist, Annadurai used to lie on their roof and stare at the moon for hours, but a serious discussion of an unmanned flight to the moon was first broached at a meeting of the Indian Academy of Sciences years later, in 1999, and at a meeting of the Astronautical Society of India in 2000.

By the early 2000s India's space race with China was just beginning to heat up. In 2003 Yang Liwei became the first Chinese citizen to orbit Earth. Developing countries such as India, Bruce Sterling argued in an article for *Wired* magazine (Dec. 2004), have a vested interest in devoting funds to their space programs. "With satellites, it's possible to see typhoons, floods, and dust storms coming and shout a warning to the victims-to-be," he wrote. "Monitor the weather and you can manage agricultural productivity so that massive populations don't starve." Of course, a thriving space program signifies prestige in its own right, and of late newer space programs, particularly ISRO, have been launching more cost-effective missions than their veteran colleagues in the United States and Russia.

## CHANDRAYAAN 1

In 2004 Annadurai was named the project director of India's first moon mission, Chandrayaan

1. (The word *chandrayaan* is Sanskrit for "moon craft.") Chandrayaan 1 was designed to carry instruments from ISRO, the US National Aeronautics and Space Administration (NASA), the European Space Agency (ESA), and Bulgaria. As Praveen Bose explained in an article for the New Delhi *Business Standard* (6 Oct. 2008), the instrumentation was selected to "accomplish systematic and simultaneous chemical, mineralogical, resource and topographic mapping of the entire lunar surface at high spatial and spectral resolutions." Annadurai told a reporter for India's *Z News* (19 Oct. 2008) that designing a spacecraft to accommodate these prebuilt payloads reminded him of his college days when he wrote lyrics to fit the tunes composed by his friends. But the instruments informed only one aspect of the design. In 2004, the ISRO decided that Chandrayaan 1 would be carried on the Polar Satellite Launch Vehicle (PSLV), which dictated how much weight the spacecraft could carry. The spacecraft's distance from Earth and the extreme climate of the moon were also contributing factors to the design. Given all the stipulations, it was fairly remarkable that the completed spacecraft was finished on time—and within budget. This last feat was particularly noteworthy, as the Chandrayaan 1 mission cost about one-fifth what other space agencies had spent on similar moon missions.

Chandrayaan 1 was successfully launched on October 22, 2008, and during its mission, it fulfilled its most important objective by finding evidence of water molecules on the moon. The discovery was an enormous coup for scientists everywhere. "When we say 'water on the moon,' we are not talking about lakes, oceans, or even puddles," Carle Pieters of Brown University said in a statement, as quoted by Helen Pidd for the *Guardian* (23 Sept. 2009). "Water on the moon means molecules of water and hydroxyl (hydrogen and oxygen) that interact with molecules of rock and dust specifically in the top millimeters of the moon's surface." The existence of those molecules, however, rekindled scientists' hopes of eventually building a manned base on the moon. Chandrayaan 1's successor, Chandrayaan 2, will use the maps drawn by Chandrayaan 1 to land on the moon following its proposed launch in 2017. A projected third mission could land Indian astronauts on the moon that could bring back samples from the moon to Earth.

## MISSION TO MARS

In 2010, two years after the success of Chandrayaan 1, ISRO began investigating the possibility of a similar orbital mission to Mars. The mission is officially called Mangalyaan (Sanskrit for "Mars craft"), but the scientists at ISRO prefer to call it the Mars Orbiter Mission (MOM). The MOM was the organization's first interplanetary mission and required a slew of new technologies, bringing a new set of challenges to the scientists at ISRO. The practical requirements alone were mind-boggling. Aside from weight concerns, the spacecraft had to have the capability to correct itself should anything go wrong with its trajectory. Launched in November 2013, MOM and ISRO have a communication lag (known as time drift) of about twelve and a half minutes each way. Even such rudimentary communication requires a network of powerful antennas planted across the globe. But ISRO's biggest challenge for India's first mission to Mars was scheduling. "The geometry of the sun, Earth, and Mars is such that a mission like this can only take place once in twenty-six months," Gulab wrote.

When financial approval for the project came through in August 2012, ISRO chair Dr. K. Radhakrishnan made a bold decision: the organization chose the first available window for launch in 2013 rather than wait until 2016. In no less than fifteen months, Annadurai and his team conceived, designed, created, tested, and launched MOM—all for a fraction of the cost of NASA's comparable Mars mission, the Mars Atmosphere and Volatile Evolution (MAVEN). Annadurai recalled to Gulab how he made a presentation about MOM more than a year before the launch and saw a MAVEN project director in the audience. "He thought I was joking. How could we possibly pull off such a mission with only one-tenth of the money NASA was spending, within one-fifth of the time frame. . . . Now both missions are on their way to Mars." The MAVEN mission cost NASA $671 million, while MOM cost ISRO $73 million.

India is truly innovative when it comes to cutting costs, Saritha Rai remarked in an article for the *New York Times* (17 Feb. 2014), but on the other hand, Indian aerospace engineers are often paid a fraction of what American engineers earn. The ISRO teams behind MOM scheduled their tasks by the hour, worked through weekends without overtime pay, and often slept at work to pull off the launch within the allotted time frame. "This is the Indian way of working," Annadurai remarked to Rai. India is the first country to successfully execute a Mars mission on its first attempt. MOM left Earth's sphere of influence (the area surrounding the planet over which it exerts a gravitational pull) on December 4, 2013, and officially entered Mars's orbit on September 24, 2014.

Annadurai received the Hari Om Ashram Prerit Vikram Sarabhai Research Award for systems analysis and space systems management in 2004 and the Team Excellence award for his contributions to ISRO in 2007. He has also received honorary doctorates of science from Pondicherry University, Anna University, and the University of Madras.

## PERSONAL LIFE

Each morning, Annadurai reads a few verses from the *Bhagavad Gita* and enjoys listening to old Tamil film songs and classical Carnatic concerts in his free time. Annadurai and his wife, Vasanthi Annadurai, have a son named Gokul Kannan. As of 2010, he was following in his father's footsteps, studying mechanical engineering at the Indian Institute of Technology in Kharagpur.

## SUGGESTED READING

Abrar, Peerzada. "ISRO's Mars Orbiter Mission: Mylswamy Annadurai & Other People Who Played a Key Role." *Economic Times*. Times Internet, 25 Sept. 2014. Web. 19 Nov. 2014.

Bose, Praveen. "The Man Who'll Give India the Moon." *Business Standard*. Business Standard, 6 Oct. 2008. Web. 19 Nov. 2014.

Gulab, Kushalrani. "Mangalyaan: Meet the Men behind India's Mars Mission." *Hindustan Times*. HT Media, 14 Dec. 2013. Web. 19 Nov. 2014.

K. J. "A Star Is Born." *Hindu*. Hindu, 24 Nov. 2008. Web. 19 Nov. 2014.

Pidd, Helen. "India's First Lunar Mission Finds Water on Moon." *Guardian*. Guardian News and Media, 23 Sept. 2009. Web. 19 Nov. 2014.

Rai, Saritha. "From India, Proof That a Trip to Mars Doesn't Have to Break the Bank." *New York Times*. New York Times, 17 Feb. 2014. Web. 19 Nov. 2014.

Sterling, Bruce. "The New Space Race: Why China and India Could Rule the Skies." *Wired*. Condé Nast, Dec. 2004. Web. 19 Nov. 2014.

—Molly Hagan

# Lloyd Austin

**Born:** August 8, 1953

**Occupation:** CENTCOM commander

In 2013 four-star US Army general Lloyd J. Austin III was named the commander of the United States Central Command, better known by its acronym CENTCOM, one of nine unified commands in the US military. CENTCOM's areas of responsibility are the twenty countries that make up the Middle East, Central Asia, and the Horn of Africa. It is also responsible for US–led anti-terrorism measures, including the air campaign against the terrorist group the Islamic State of Iraq and Syria (ISIS), which is also known as the Islamic State of Iraq and the Levant (ISIL). Austin previously gained considerable experience as a commander of large numbers of troops, having served for years in Afghanistan and Iraq, including as the last commander of US forces in Iraq in 2011.

Austin was appointed to lead CENTCOM by President Barack Obama in 2012, and after his Senate confirmation in March 2013, he became the twelfth overall commander and the first African American leader of the organization. In a long and distinguished military career spanning several decades and conflicts, Austin—invariably described as a soft-spoken leader who goes the extra mile for his soldiers—has been a trailblazing black commander. However, he does not

U.S. Central Command/Wikimedia Commons

want his race to be his defining characteristic. When asked about his groundbreaking status, he said, "I don't often reflect on it. I reflect most on trying to get the job done. . . . I am the first African American to take on a responsibility like that, but I think I'm prepared and I look forward to the challenge," as quoted by Ewen MacAskill in the *Guardian* (22 Mar. 2013).

## EARLY LIFE AND CAREER

The fifth of his parents' six children, Lloyd J. Austin III was born on August 8, 1953, in Mobile, Alabama, and raised in the small city of Thomasville, Georgia. There he played on his high school basketball and football teams, taking advantage of his imposing six-foot-four frame. After graduating from high school, he studied at the United States Military Academy at West Point, New York, where he earned a bachelor of science degree and was commissioned an infantry second lieutenant in 1975. He subsequently earned two master's degrees: one in education from Auburn University and one in business management from Webster University.

Upon graduating from West Point, Austin decided to make military service his career. He continued his military education at the Infantry Officer Advanced Course, United States Army Infantry School in Fort Benning, Georgia, at the United States Army Command and General Staff College in Fort Leavenworth, Kansas, and at the United States Army War College in Carlisle Barracks, Pennsylvania. As a young officer, he would serve in numerous staff and command assignments throughout his early career, including stations throughout the United States. Specific appointments included stints with the First Battalion, Seventh Infantry, Third Infantry Division, US Army Europe and Seventh Army; the Second Battalion, 508th Infantry, Eighty-Second Airborne Division at Fort Bragg, North Carolina; and the Second Battalion, Twenty-Second Infantry and First Brigade, Tenth Mountain Division (Light) at Fort Drum, New York.

In 1993 Austin became the commander of the Second Battalion of the 505th Parachute Infantry Regiment, Eighty-Second Airborne Division, based out of Fort Bragg. From 1997 to 1999 he was the commander of the Third Brigade, Eighty-Second Airborne Division. He then served for a time at the Pentagon as the chief of the Joint Staff's Joint Operations Division, J-3.

Austin's career was forever altered by the terrorist attacks of September 11, 2001. The attack sparked the NATO–led invasion of Afghanistan later that year in an attempt to destroy the al-Qaeda terrorist network, and then the 2003 US–led invasion of Iraq. Having proven himself an adept leader, Austin was primed to play an important role in these conflicts and climb his way further up the ranks of the US Army.

## COMMANDER IN IRAQ AND AFGANISTAN

The War on Terror would provide Austin with ample opportunities to use the skills he had honed as an army commander. In 2001 he took the position of assistant division commander (maneuver) with the Third Infantry Division (Mechanized), operating out of Fort Stewart, Georgia. In that position, he would—as the first African American general to maneuver an army division in combat—play a pivotal role in the invasion of Iraq in March 2003, as the Third Infantry served as part of the spearhead in the march on the Iraqi capital of Baghdad. Ann Scott Tyson wrote in the *Washington Post* (13 Jan. 2008) of Austin's strategic skills in that engagement: "When the 3rd Infantry met unexpected resistance . . . he was central to formulating a new plan that brought in other brigades to relieve his troops and maintain the momentum critical to the campaign's success." For his leadership in the invasion, he earned the Silver Star, which recognizes gallantry in combat.

From September 2003 to August 2005, Austin was the commanding general of the Tenth Mountain Division (Light), operating out of Fort Drum, and served as commander of the Combined Joint Task Force-180 in Afghanistan as part of Operation Enduring Freedom. "He's one of the best troop leaders we have," Major General Anthony Cucolo, who served with Austin in Afghanistan, told Tyson. "He goes everywhere he can. He will be standing on the walls at Shkin fire base [on the Pakistani border] to get a feel for what goes on there. He will fly to the deepest regions of Konar province to meet with village elders. . . . He'd never ask his soldiers to do anything he wouldn't do." Another of Austin's fellow commanders, Brigadier General Bill Weber, echoed those sentiments. "Lloyd's approach is, 'I'm a soldier like everyone else.' His style is flak vest, Kevlar, and a ton of ammunition," he told Tyson.

## RISING STAR

Austin served as chief of staff for CENTCOM from September 2005 to November 2006. He then commanded the XVIII Airborne Corps beginning in December 2006 and served as commander of the Multi-National Corps in Operation Iraqi Freedom from 2008 to 2009. This assignment made him the second most important officer in Iraq, charged with leading nearly 150,000 US and coalition troops. It was at this time the quiet general began to attract the notice of the media, in part because he was then one of only eight black officers in all branches of the US armed forces at or above the rank of lieutenant general or vice admiral. At the time of Austin's appointment as Multi-National Corps commander in 2008, fewer than 6 percent of over 900 total US officers were African American. "I certainly fully appreciate the fact that I am the first African-American to ever command a division in combat, the first African-American to ever command a corps in combat and there are a couple other firsts before that," Austin told Lennox Samuels for *Newsweek* (15 Sept. 2008). "Certainly when you have my job you consider yourself to be a role model for a number of elements in the community, not just African-Americans."

## LEADING CENTCOM

In August 2009 Austin was reassigned to the Pentagon, where he served as director of the Joint Staff for one year. The following September Austin was tapped by President Barack Obama to oversee the end of US military involvement in Iraq. Because there had been concern among a number of high-ranking military officials that Iraq might face increased conflict following a total US withdrawal, Austin advised keeping 24,000 troops in Iraq even after the end of official US involvement. Obama, however, declined that suggestion, and all US forces were withdrawn in December 2011.

From January 2012 to March 2013, Austin served as the US Army's first African American vice chief of staff. During that time Austin was nominated by Obama to take over the leadership of CENTCOM. The US Senate confirmed his nomination in March 2013, and he assumed command later that same month, marking another first for a black officer. Yet, despite becoming the country's top general in charge of the headline-grabbing Middle East, Austin was far from a household name. Ernesto Londoño, writing for the *New York Times* (9 Sept. 2014), explained that the general "shuns the limelight, largely avoids engaging in politics and seldom speaks to the press, often declining interviews," all of which have contributed to his lack of mainstream recognition.

Austin assumed command of CENTCOM at a critical juncture. The United States was engaged in talks with Iran about its nuclear program, US forces were looking to withdraw from Afghanistan, and the Middle East was facing a new crisis in the form of ISIS, a terrorist group that had begun in Iraq and took control of large swaths of territory in Iraq and Syria. Some political commentators, including Marc A. Thiessen for the *New York Times* (15 Sept. 2015), suggested that the rise of ISIS could have been prevented had Obama followed Austin's earlier advice and maintained a troop presence in Iraq. Londoño reported that, according to aides, Austin was "disappointed and worried when it became clear the US military would pull out entirely," though he did not publicly disagree with the president's decision. Regardless, Austin was anticipated to again weigh heavily in any renewed US military action in Iraq. As of 2015 CENTCOM oversaw hundreds of air strikes against ISIS, but controversy over committing ground forces continued.

**PERSONAL LIFE**

Austin married Charlene Denise Banner and has two stepsons. Throughout his career he earned numerous awards, including the Defense Distinguished Service Medal, the Legion of Merit, the Army Commendation Medal, and the Combat Action Badge. He is also an avid fisherman and is known to frequently joke about leaving the army to open a bait shop.

**SUGGESTED READING**

Londoño, Ernesto. "At the Helm of Military Mission in Iraq, an Invisible General." *Taking Note.* New York Times, 9 Sept. 2014. Web. 16 Mar. 2015.

MacAskill, Ewen. "General Lloyd Austin Picked for Top Job at US Central Command." *Guardian.* Guardian News and Media, 22 Mar. 2013. Web. 16 Mar. 2015.

Samuels, Lennox. "Lt. Gen. Austin the Quiet No. 2 in Iraq." *Newsweek.* Newsweek, 15 Sept. 2008. Web. 16 Mar. 2015.

Thiessen, Marc A. "Obama vs. the Generals." *Washington Post.* Washington Post, 15 Sept. 2014. Web. 16 Mar. 2015.

Tyson, Ann Scott. "Hands-On General Is Next No. 2 in Iraq." *Washington Post.* Washington Post, 13 Jan. 2008. Web. 16 Mar. 2015.

"U.S. Central Command Leadership." *CENTCOM.* US Central Command, n.d. Web. 16 Mar. 2015.

—Christopher Mari

# Brandee Barker

**Born:** 1970
**Occupation:** Public relations consultant

Brandee Barker was a public relations executive with the social networking website Facebook before launching her career as an independent image consultant in Silicon Valley. Barker has advised the founders of successful start-ups such as Uber, Airbnb, and Dropbox, and in 2013, she managed television interviews for Facebook COO Sheryl Sandberg in the lead-up to the publication of Sandberg's book *Lean In.* The book, and subsequent movement, encourages corporate working women to "lean in," or take charge of their own career. For example, Sandberg encourages women to be more assertive in asking for a raise. Her brand of bootstrap feminism has been taken to task because it foists institutional problems onto the individual—the fact that women are paid less than men, Sandberg reasons, is because women are not asking for raises. Still, Sandberg's ethos resonates with a number of women, including Barker, who wrote about her decision to have a child while working as an executive at Facebook on the *Lean In* website. Barker's personal investment in Sandberg's message might be why she famously lashed out at one of the book's detractors. The dust-up (which, appropriately, took place on Facebook) made headlines. "Brandee is a passionate advocate for people and causes she believes in," Sandberg told Sheila Marikar for the *New York Times* (10 Jan. 2014). "People want to work with her because of her great media relationships and the energy and commitment she brings to everything she does." In 2013, she cofounded a boutique consulting firm called Pramana Collective with Sean Garrett, formerly of Twitter, and Brian O'Shaughnessy, formerly of Skype. "While PR types don't usually get a lot of the attention, the joining of these three top Silicon Valley players is enough of a news event to warrant some mention," the well-known tech journalist Kara Swisher wrote for the *Wall Street Journal*'s tech news site, *All Things Digital* (14 Mar. 2013).

## EARLY LIFE AND EDUCATION

Barker was raised in Southern California. Her father owned a liquor store and her mother worked as a real estate broker. Her parents are divorced, and Barker is an only child. She attended Westlake High School in California and studied journalism at the University of Colorado at Boulder. After graduating with honors in 1993, she moved to San Francisco and took a public relations job with Stamps.com. The 1990s saw a proliferation of Internet companies, but by the end of the decade, the dot-com bubble had burst and few of those companies survived. (Stamps.com is still in business.) Following the bust, Barker sold all of her possessions and embarked on a solo trip around the world. "Climbing Mount Kilimanjaro in Africa was kind of my final thing," she told Marikar. "I summited it after five days and went home." In 2005, Barker was named vice president at the PR firm Zeno Group in San Francisco, where she represented brands like the clothing retailer Gap and the technology corporation Oracle. There she noticed that a coworker, who had recently graduated from Stanford, frequented a peculiar-looking website called Facebook.

Barker called Facebook and persuaded them to run a survey for the Gap. A few months after the survey was posted, Barker received a call. The social network had grown to seven million users—though it was still limited to certain schools and companies—and larger companies were clamoring to buy them out. In 2005, Viacom offered to pay $75 million for the site and a year later, Yahoo! offered to pay $1 billion. Facebook turned both offers down, but, as the executive who called Barker told her, they were desperately in need of a PR representative to head communications. Barker traveled to the Facebook headquarters in Palo Alto, and after a four-hour interview capped with a glass of chardonnay, the company offered her a job.

## FACEBOOK

Facebook, or Thefacebook, as it was first called, was founded by Mark Zuckerberg and several of his Harvard classmates in a dorm room in 2004. By 2007 Microsoft had valued the upstart start-up at over $15 billion. Barker joined the team as employee number 120 in 2006, just as the company was starting to get hot—though its status was not obvious from its set-up. "I started commuting three hours a day to work at a table with two other people in the middle of this big room," Barker recalled to Marikar, "And I still couldn't use it." (Facebook opened its registration—anyone with an e-mail address could join—in the fall of 2006.) As Barker wrote for Sandberg's *Lean In* website, she initially felt out of place in Facebook's predominantly male, youth-oriented culture. Start-ups are about sleeping on couches and living on Red Bull; Barker was thirty-six, married, and thinking about having a child, but she was worried about how pregnancy would affect her standing in the company. "I had counted myself out of work and motherhood before I faced any real decisions," she wrote. In the meantime, Barker assembled a communications team for Facebook that included Bill McGowan, the founder and CEO of Clarity Media Group. (In 2014 the journalist turned media guru wrote a book called *Pitch Perfect: How to Say It Right the First Time, Every Time*.) McGowan helped coach the founders on how to talk about Facebook to a variety of audiences. McGowan praised Barker's approach to the company. "For me, it's a matter of, 'How is the story unfolding?' Brandee focuses on, 'What are we trying to say?'" he told Marikar. "She has this ability to stay incredibly clear in her thinking and to also tailor her advice to what will be second nature to the client. She's never trying to make someone say, 'This is what I'm not.'"

Barker also played a more hands-on role with the young founders—Zuckerberg was only twenty when he started Facebook. In 2007 Zuckerberg was invited to the annual World Economic Forum in Davos, Switzerland, an international gathering of some of the world's most important people. He was famous for wearing only hoodie sweatshirts and jeans, though he may have been a trendsetter even in that regard. As consultant Tom Searcy later wrote, as quoted by Matthew Hutson for the *New Yorker* (17 Dec. 2013), "I have a number of super-successful Silicon Valley clients who dress in ripped denim, Vans shoes and T-shirts. It's a status symbol to dress like you're homeless to attend board meetings." Barker, however, was unimpressed. Before he flew to the gathering, she and another Facebook employee ran to the Nordstrom department store in Palo Alto to buy him a suit. She told Marikar she was "pretty sure that he did not wear it at Davos." He did, however, take the suitcase she bought him after she insisted that he leave his backpack at home. That same year, *PRWeek* named Barker as one of the top forty public relations professionals under forty.

## A GROWING COMPANY, STORMY SEAS

Barker's Facebook communications team gradually grew to include ten employees and a multimillion-dollar budget. During her tenure, she navigated some stormy seas for the company; every change to the site seemed to have users up in arms. In September 2006, the site introduced the news feed, the rolling ticker that tells users what all of their friends are posting. The blow-back was so quick and fierce, Samantha Murphy Kelly wrote for *Mashable* (12 Mar. 2013), that Zuckerberg felt compelled to write a blog post addressing the change titled "Calm down. Breathe. We hear you." Of the incident Barker later told Swisher for *All Things Digital* (8 Nov. 2010), "I had no idea when I took the job that it would be like that." Other crises included the spat (depicted in the 2010 movie *The Social Network*) over Facebook's founding—Swisher joked in her 2010 article that Barker obtained "a masters from Harvard University in Winklevii crisis management," referring to the Winklevoss twins' claim that Facebook was their idea—and frequent privacy issues. In 2009, for example, users complained when Facebook updated its terms of service in such a way that suggested Facebook owned users' content.

At the height of Facebook's rise in 2009, Barker learned that she was going to have a child and, as she wrote for the *Lean In* website, put aside her previous doubts to embrace both her pregnancy and her career. In 2010, after taking her maternity leave, she decided to leave the company and start her own private consulting firm. When Barker started her job with Facebook, the site employed less than 150 people and had 7 million users. By the time she left, the site counted more than 2,000 employees and more than 500 million users.

## INDEPENDENT CONSULTANCY

Barker began her career as an independent consultant in 2011. In 2013, while managing Sandberg's television interviews in the press tour surrounding her book *Lean In: Women, Work, and the Will to Lead* (2013), Barker sent a woman named Katherine Losse an angry private message via Facebook. Losse, Barker's former colleague at Facebook and author of the tell-all book *The Boy Kings: A Journey into the Heart of the Social Network* (2012), wrote a critical review of Sandberg's book for *Dissent Magazine* in 2013. Tweeting a link to the article, she wrote, "Shots fired." A few minutes later Barker sent her a message that read, "There's a special

place in hell for you." Losse immediately took a screen shot of the message—an uncharacteristically bad PR move on Barker's part, Tracie Egan Morrissey noted for the feminist website *Jezebel* (29 Mar. 2013)—and tweeted it out to her followers. It was a rare slip for controlled Barker, whom Swisher frequently referred to as Brandee "No Comment" Barker in jest, and journalists speculated that it stemmed from a more personal grudge, given Losse's condemnation of Facebook.

In 2013, Barker joined forces with two other former PR executives—Sean Garrett of Twitter and Brian O'Shaughnessy of Skype—to form the Pramana Collective, a boutique consulting firm for start-ups. (The word "pramana," Swisher wrote in her 2013 article, is defined as "the means by which one obtains accurate knowledge or true perception.") In July 2013, Barker worked with Drew Houston, the CEO of the file-sharing company Dropbox, to come up with the successful phrase "sync is the new save," Marikar reported. The firm continues to grow and recently hired PR executives from Facebook and StumbleUpon.

## PERSONAL LIFE

Barker met her husband, Neal Howard George, at a bar before flying to Peru during her backpacking trip. George is the head of sales at Tealium, a data distribution company. The couple have a young son named Logan, whom Barker (as she wrote for *Lean In*) calls "my other start-up."

## SUGGESTED READING

Barker, Brandee. "Brandee Barker—Communications Strategist." *Lean In*. Leanin.org, n.d. Web. 13 Feb. 2015.

Hutson, Matthew. "The Power of the Hoodie-Wearing C.E.O." *New Yorker*. Condé Nast, 17 Dec. 2013. Web. 13 Feb. 2015.

Kelly, Samantha Murphy. "The Evolution of the Facebook News Feed." *Mashable*. Mashable, 12 Mar. 2013. Web. 13 Feb. 2015.

Marikar, Sheila. "They Want Her on Their Side." *New York Times*. New York Times, 10 Jan. 2014. Web. 13 Feb. 2015.

Morrissey, Tracie Egan. "There's More to the Sandberg Publicist 'Cat Fight' Than Meets the Eye." *Jezebel*. Gawker, 29 Mar. 2013. Web. 13 Feb. 2015.

Swisher, Kara. "Exclusive: Brandee 'No Comment' Barker Finally Comments—Longtime PR Honcho Is Leaving Facebook." *All Things*

*Digital.* Dow Jones, 8 Nov. 2010. Web. 13 Feb. 2015.

Swisher, Kara. "The Pramana Collective: New Tech PR Firm Made Up of Old PR Hands." *All Things Digital.* Dow Jones, 14 Mar. 2013. Web. 13 Feb. 2015.

—Molly Hagan

# Danielle Bassett

**Born:** ca. 1981

**Occupation:** Physicist and neuroscientist

Danielle S. Bassett is a brain researcher at the University of Pennsylvania (Penn). In 2014 she was awarded a $625,000 "genius" grant through the MacArthur Foundation for her study of network science as it applies to the brain. At thirty-two, she was the youngest recipient in her class of twenty-one fellows. Bassett's official title is the Skirkanich Assistant Professor of Innovation in the department of bioengineering. She combines her love for mathematics and medicine with physics to understand how brain connectivity patterns change over time and how those connectivity patterns adapt to human behaviors. Bassett recently discovered that people with more flexible brains—people who can reconfigure their connectivity patterns easily—learn more quickly than people with less flexible brains. Understanding why that is could affect how people learn new skills or recover from brain injury or trauma in the future. Bassett's work has helped found a new subdiscipline, dynamic network neuroscience.

In addition to the MacArthur grant, Bassett was awarded a $50,000 Sloan Research Fellowship earlier in 2014. "She is tackling the problems that very few physicists want to get anywhere near," Lee Bassett, an assistant professor of engineering at Penn and Bassett's husband, told Tom Avril for the *Philadelphia Inquirer* (18 Sept. 2014). "She's interested in stuff like how we think and how we feel and how we interact. These are the problems that don't have easy or elegant solutions."

## EARLY LIFE AND EDUCATION

Danielle Perry Bassett was the second-oldest of eleven children and was raised in Lock Haven and Reading, Pennsylvania. She was homeschooled by her mother Holly Perry, who is an artist. Her father, John Perry, is an orthopedic

MacArthur Foundation/Wikimedia Commons

surgeon at Reading Hospital. Inspired by her father, Bassett enrolled in nursing school at the Reading Hospital School of Nursing, but after about a year and a half, she realized that she missed math and physics—subjects in which she had excelled in high school. She then switched her major and in January 2001 began studying physics at Penn State Berks, a campus of the Pennsylvania State University (Penn State), and began work on magnetic field lines project with Penn State professor and astrophysicist Dr. Ruth A. Daly. Bassett also studied world literature and poetry with Dr. Thomas Lynn, who recalled her enthusiasm for the subject, explaining to Andrew Wagman of the Reading Pennsylvania *Eagle* (20 Oct. 2014) that Bassett was "able to understand and respond deeply in many academic and creative disciplines." However, Bassett's passion for math and physics and the psychology of the brain remained. She reflected on this passion in her Meet the Fellows of 2014 video, which is produced through the MacArthur Foundation (17 Sept. 2014): "The brain is a very complicated system, so it requires extremely complicated methods to understand it. Math and physics give you the tools that enable you to understand those complexities in new ways that you would not be able to with traditional neuroscientific methods."

During her time at Penn State, Bassett received the Paul Axt Prize in the Schreyer Honors College, Most Achieving Undergraduate Woman of the Year, an Academic Achievement

Award from the Eberly College of Science, and the Academic Achievement Award in Physics. She graduated from Penn State's main campus in 2004 and became the first Penn State student to receive the Winston Churchill Scholarship, which is a fully funded year of study at Cambridge University in England. She also won a five-year National Institutes of Health Oxford-Cambridge University Graduate Partnerships Fellowship. Bassett earned her doctorate in theoretical physics at Cambridge in 2009, and she completed her postdoctoral work at the University of California, Santa Barbara, in 2011. She was a Sage Junior Research Fellow at the university from 2011–13, and she lectured about her work using information systems to understand neuroscience and human behavior at Yale University, Cornell University, and the University of Glasgow, Scotland. Before she joined the University of Pennsylvania faculty in 2013, she had already authored thirty-one publications.

## NETWORK SCIENCE

As a researcher at the University of Pennsylvania, Bassett and her team work in an interdisciplinary field known as network science. In this field, Basset studies, compares, and finds the interrelatedness of disparate phenomena, fundamentally unrelated occurrences such as cellular behavior and human behavior. Elizabeth Gudrais for *Harvard Magazine* explains Bassett's work and network science (1 May 2010), "It used to be that sociologists studied networks of people, while physicists and computer scientists studied different kinds of networks in their own fields." "But as social scientists sought to understand larger, more sophisticated networks, they looked to physics for methods suited to this complexity." Of course, Gudrais added, this exchange of systems "is a two-way street." Bassett is a physicist by training, but she works with bioengineers, medical professionals, and even artists in an effort to describe the complex inter-workings of the human brain. Most recently Bassett has been trying to understand the science of learning. "I'm fascinated by learning; I'm interested in how the brain's network configuration changes when our behavior changes . . . when we learn a new skill," Bassett told Ryan Briggs, a reporter for *The Pulse*, a program on Philadelphia's public radio station WHYY-FM (18 Sept. 2014). "What I'd like to be able to do is to understand how the brain evolves to enable that change and then how we could optimize that to enhance learning in an individual."

## THE SCIENCE OF LEARNING

To study how people learn, Bassett and her team use magnetic resonance imaging (MRI) technology to scan brain activity in order to determine how brain circuits work together while they perform and learn new yet simple skills. Briggs explained that by using MRIs, Bassett is able to watch different parts of a subject's brain "light up" when they are being used and as they communicate with other parts of the brain to perform and subsequently learn a new task. "We see connections moving in and out between different parts of the brain and rapid reconfiguration of networks," Bassett said. "Think of social networks, individual people, and how they're connected up. Those networks change drastically, they reconfigure very quickly." Bassett found that fast learners were able to make new connections and configure new networks with ease. She also discovered that fast learners have more flexible brains. She hopes to apply her findings to learning environments and to brain rehabilitation strategies in order to determine whether certain learning environments are more conducive to brain flexibility than others and if, in the case of neurological rehabilitation, certain parts of the brain can be stimulated to make the brain more flexible. In patients with schizophrenia, however, Bassett has found that the brain is almost too flexible—still, the information, Bassett told Gary Stix for *Scientific American* (30 Sept. 2014), will "give us a biological target to enhance rehabilitation."

## GRAPH THEORY AND COGNITIVE FUNCTIONING

A few of the concepts found in network science have proved helpful to Bassett, including graph theory, which is actually a branch of pure mathematics. Graph theory helps interpret the relationship among data using "nodes" and "edges"—often visually represented as a web in which the lines are edges and the places where the lines connect are nodes. Bassett likes to think of the brain as a network in which individual parts are nodes and the connections that form between and among those parts are edges. "The question in our group is how can we understand the configuration of those edges to better understand cognitive functioning," she told Stix. Bassett views the brain as multiple sets of graphs; this view is helping her to understand not only what the brain does when it is actively learning, but also what it does when it seems to be at rest, such as when a person is listening.

## MACARTHUR FELLOWSHIP

The MacArthur grant will help radically expand Bassett's research, she has said. Her work thus far has been straightforward, but areas she would like to explore—studying the brains of patients with diseases, for example—are considered less traditional and are therefore more difficult to fund. The grant will allow her to fund her own research as she sees fit. Still, optimization holds a particular appeal for Bassett, who wants to find out more about how the brain exists as a network and how people, knowingly or unknowingly, intervene to improve that network. The work is exciting and offers what could potentially be the base research of a new field called dynamic network neuroscience. Still, when Bassett received the phone call from the MacArthur Foundation in 2014, she was sure they were calling for a colleague. "Halfway through, I said, 'Are you absolutely sure you got the right person?'" Bassett recalled to Felicia R. Lee for the *New York Times* (17 Sept. 2014). "Then they read my bio to me."

## NETWORK VISUALIZATION PROGRAM

Bassett launched the Network Visualization Program at Penn in the summer of 2014. The program is a six-week internship in which undergraduate art students—in disciplines as dissimilar as computer graphics and fashion design—learn about network science. The artists attend a week of lectures with Penn researchers and faculty, and then they spend five weeks creating work based on what they learned. "Scientists aren't trained to look at data the way an artist is," Bassett told Madeleine Stone for the *Penn Current* magazine (28 Aug. 2014). "This program is enabling us to conceptualize our research in new ways."

The program, which was first launched during the summer of 2014, emphasizes the similarities between the scientific process and the artistic process. Bassett has explained that science is often difficult for students because it is hard to visually conceptualize. By encouraging interdisciplinary projects like the Network Visualization Program, Bassett hopes to make complex scientific concepts more accessible to all students. Some of the works created in the program are later used as educational tools in area schools. Bassett plans to use part of her MacArthur grant to help fund the Network Visualization Program.

## PERSONAL LIFE

Bassett is married to Lee Bassett, whom she met as a student at Penn State. He is an assistant professor of electrical and systems engineering at the University of Pennsylvania. The Bassets live in Wallingford, Pennsylvania, with their two young children.

## SUGGESTED READING

Avril, Tom. "Penn Researcher Danielle Bassett Wins a 'Genius Grant.'" *Philly.* Philadelphia Media Network, 18 Sept. 2014. Web. 10 Mar. 2015.

Briggs, Ryan. "MacArthur Fellow Danielle Bassett on Leveraging Brain Research to Enhance Learning." *Newsworks.* WHYY/Newsworks, 18 Sept. 2014. Web. 10 Mar. 2015.

Briggs, Ryan. "Danielle Bassett—Physicist." *MacArthur Foundation.* MacArthur Foundation, 17 Sept. 2014. Web. 10 Mar. 2015.

Gudrais, Elizabeth. "Networked: Exploring the Weblike Structures That Underlie Everything from Friendship to Cellular Behavior." *Harvard Magazine.* Harvard Magazine, 1 May 2010. Web. 10 Mar. 2015.

Stix, Gary. "MacArthur 'Genius' Winner: Math Might Help Crack Mysteries of Schizophrenia." *Scientific American.* Nature America, 30 Sept. 2014. Web. 16 Mar. 2015.

Stone, Madeleine. "Network Visualization Program Fuses Science and Art." *Penn Current.* University of Pennsylvania, 28 Aug. 2014. Web. 10 Mar. 2015.

—Molly Hagan

# Emily Bazelon

**Born:** 1971
**Occupation:** Journalist and academic

Emily Bazelon is a journalist and writer known for her coverage of such hot-button topics as abortion rights, rape, affirmative action, and bullying. A passionately left-leaning feminist, she frequently comes under fire for her views, drawing the ire of political conservatives and other opponents. "Controversy is like coffee: It gets the blood flowing and puts me on my toes," she told Dan Schawbel in an interview for the website *Personal Branding Blog* (30 Dec. 2009). "When it's about substantive debate, and real disagreement about interpretation of facts, then it's all to the good I think." Bazelon

Andrew Toth/Getty Images News

enjoyed a long career at the online publication *Slate*, where she cofounded "Double X," a section of the website dedicated to women's issues. After *Slate* Bazelon moved on to work as a staff writer at the *New York Times Magazine*. In 2015 Bazelon is known for her written work, as well as for serving as the Truman Capote Fellow for Creative Writing and Law at Yale University, her alma mater.

In 2013 Bazelon wrote the best-selling book *Sticks and Stones: Defeating the Culture of Bullying and Rediscovering the Power of Character and Empathy*. She had become immersed in the topic while reporting for *Slate* on the case of Phoebe Prince, a Massachusetts teen who committed suicide, in part due to bullying from a group of her classmates. Her *Slate* series won widespread praise for being a fair-minded look at a complex subject. Even critics bothered by Bazelon's examination of Prince's mental-health history and the severity of the punishment meted out to the teens involved, found it riveting and well researched. In a profile for the London *Guardian* (6 May 2013), Emma G. Keller described Bazelon as "a different voice in the current climate of judgmental snark." She added: "Bazelon is the woman who reads the entire book before forming an opinion. She doesn't want the shouting to drown out anyone's voice."

## EARLY YEARS

Emily Bazelon was born in 1971. Her father, Richard, is an attorney, and her mother, Eileen, is a psychiatrist. She has three younger sisters: Lara, Gillian, and Dana. Bazelon's family tree includes a pair of well-known figures: pioneering feminist Betty Friedan, a second cousin (Bazelon received a copy of Friedan's groundbreaking book *The Feminine Mystique* for her bat mitzvah), and her paternal grandfather David Bazelon, a well-regarded liberal judge on the US Court of Appeals. In the 1950s, at the height of Senator Joseph R. McCarthy's Communist witch hunt, Judge Bazelon upheld the rights of individuals to refuse to answer congressional questions that were not pertinent to the inquiry at hand. Later, in the 1970s, he ruled that President Richard M. Nixon must relinquish tape recordings sought by the Watergate grand jury, despite his claims of executive privilege. (When Emily Bazelon unearthed Phoebe Prince's mental-health issues while reporting on the suicide, observers pointed out that Judge Bazelon had been a staunch protector of rights for the mentally ill—including their right to privacy.)

Bazelon has written that she herself was bullied in middle school. "It was a transformative experience, and I don't use that term lightly," she recalled to Keller. "It just changed my whole view of myself. Ever since then I don't assume that people are going to like me. I'm always pleasantly surprised when it turns out OK."

## EDUCATION

Bazelon attended the Germantown Friends School, a private high school in a historic section of Philadelphia, Pennsylvania, where she worked on the school newspaper and graduated in 1989. She attended college at Yale University, where she became the managing editor of the *New Journal*, a student magazine that included personal essays, feature reporting, and more. At Yale, Bazelon took a nonfiction writing course, and during her senior year, she interned at a local alternative weekly, *The Advocate*. "My interest in long-form narrative journalism really comes directly from my undergraduate experience," she explained to Emily Rappaport for *Broad Recognition* (3 Nov. 2011), a feminist magazine published at Yale. "I was also one of the student coordinators of the Yale Women's Center when I was in college, and lots of people there thought a lot about issues surrounding feminism and sexuality and working women and all those things—

so they were both a personal and professional interest of mine, and they were intertwined."

Upon graduating from Yale in 1993, Bazelon accepted the Dorot Fellowship, which was established, as its website states, to "enliven the American Jewish landscape by seeding the community with a cadre of outstanding young lay leaders." Dorot Fellowships are awarded to people from a wide array of fields, who then live in Israel for one year. Bazelon worked as a freelance journalist during her time in the country. "The Oslo peace process was getting off the ground and that opened up avenues to all kinds of interesting stories," she recalled to Schawbel. "I think that ideally every journalist would have the experience of reporting from abroad. It's so good for honing one's skills as a cultural translator and for running with one's every curiosity."

She next moved to California and took an entry-level job as a reporter on a small newspaper. The pace of her new work was slow, however, and she soon hit upon the idea of returning to Yale to attend law school. Although she never really intended to become a practicing attorney, she realized that having a specific area of expertise could be a boon to her journalism career. Her studies at Yale helped her learn to ask questions and develop her investigative skills. Her law school experience also had a bearing on the specific topics she writes about. "Legal questions often frame my inquiry when I'm going into a subject, so I tend to choose things that are kind of at an intersection between law and issues of family or gender or kids," she explained to Rappaport.

Bazelon earned her juris doctor degree in 2000. She then began working as a clerk for Judge Kermit Lipez of the US Court of Appeals for the First Circuit.

## JOURNALISM CAREER

For a time, Bazelon combined her interest in law and journalism by serving as the senior editor of *Legal Affairs*, a general interest magazine whose features focused on how the law affected everyday life. It ceased publication in 2006. In addition to editing, she penned articles on such topics as the pollution generated by multinational oil companies, a judge's role in a democracy, and the courts in South Africa. She also found work freelancing for various publications, including *Slate*, an online magazine that was founded in 1996 and offers a blend of political analysis, business news, and cultural commentary. She

joined the staff on a full-time basis in 2005, writing her own pieces and editing others.

In 2007 Bazelon began contributing a section of the website called "Double X," aimed at *Slate*'s female readers. The section became so popular that within two years *Slate*'s managers agreed to spin it off into its own separate publication, which they dubbed *Double X*. Bazelon, along with fellow editors Hanna Rosin and Meghan O'Rourke, oversaw the website. "Our hope is that *Double X* will appeal to women who don't necessarily feel at home in the glossy mag world (me among them)," Bazelon wrote for the *Washington Post* (12 May 2009), when *Double X* launched. "Women's magazines surround their smart content with much straight-up, idealized coverage of beauty and fashion. That's an economic necessity for them. We're hoping that the web will free us from that. We're also hoping that men will join in and eavesdrop on our conversation, and feel more comfortable doing so than they would buying a glossy women's mag." Those hopes were not realized, however, and in the face of a dwindling readership, *Double X* was folded back into the main *Slate* website after a few months.

Another *Slate* project with which Bazelon became involved was more successful: *Political Gabfest*, a podcast that features Bazelon and fellow commentators John Dickerson and David Plotz discussing a wide variety of subjects. Episodes have touched upon the debate surrounding vaccines, campaign finance reform, and marriage equality. Among Bazelon's controversial and attention-grabbing pieces for the magazine have been a cover story on how women around the world are obtaining abortions in the wake of increasing restrictions and a profile of an Alabama judge trying to block same-sex marriage.

## BULLYING

In 2010 Bazelon started investigating a series on cyberbullying for *Slate*. Early that year, Phoebe Prince, a fifteen-year-old girl from South Hadley, Massachusetts, had committed suicide, and journalists were widely reporting that she had been driven to do so by a group of classmates. The six teens involved were facing serious criminal charges, and Northwestern District Attorney Elizabeth Scheibel was being particularly aggressive in seeking the most severe penalties possible.

Bazelon traveled to South Hadley to conduct an exhaustive set of interviews. On July 20, 2010, she wrote for *Slate*, "There is no question that some of the teenagers facing criminal charges treated Phoebe cruelly. But not all of them did. And it's hard to see how any of the kids going to trial this fall ever could have anticipated the consequences of their actions, for Phoebe or for themselves. Should we send teenagers to prison for being nasty to one another? Is it really fair to lay the burden of Phoebe's suicide on these kids?" Bazelon reported that Prince had had a long history of depression, suicide attempts, and self-mutilation, and she pointed out that Elizabeth Scheibel had a track record of overzealous prosecution—including threatening reporters who contradicted her actions.

Ultimately, five of the defendants were put on probation, while charges against the sixth were dropped at the request of the Prince family. The family later settled a suit against the Town and School Department of South Hadley for $225,000—a figure that was made public only after Bazelon, with the help of the American Civil Liberties Union, sued for its disclosure. For her work, Bazelon was a finalist for both the 2011 Michael Kelly Award, given by the Atlantic Media Company for journalism in "the fearless pursuit and expression of truth," and the 2011 Online Journalism Award from the Gannett Foundation for innovative investigative journalism.

The Prince case is just one of those examined in Bazelon's book, *Sticks and Stones: Defeating the Culture of Bullying and Rediscovering the Power of Character and Empathy*. In it, she also reports on two cases: Monique McClain, who became a target of a group of girls in Connecticut and was forced to switch schools, and Jacob Lasher, from upstate New York, who was tormented for being openly gay. Calling the book "intelligent [and] rigorous," Andrew Solomon wrote for the *New York Times* (28 Feb. 2013), "Bazelon includes chapters on anti-bullying measures with good track records. She reviews jurisprudence on bullying, and examines both the virtues and the pitfalls of treating it as a crime. . . . Bazelon is at her best as a storyteller, and the most interesting parts of the book are its human narratives."

## PERSONAL LIFE

Bazelon is married to Paul Sabin, who teaches environmental, political, legal, and economic history at Yale. They have two sons, Eli and Simon.

## SUGGESTED READING

Bazelon, Emily. "How to Stop Bullying." Interview by Gareth Cook. *Scientific American*. Scientific American, 26 Feb. 2013. Web. 6 Feb. 2015.

Bazelon, Emily. "Interview: *Slate's* Emily Bazelon on Feminist Media." Interview by Emily Rappaport. *Broad Recognition*. Broad-Recognition.com, 3 Nov. 2011. Web. 6 Feb. 2015.

Bazelon, Emily. "Personal Branding Interview: Emily Bazelon." Interview by Dan Schawbel. *Personal Branding Blog*. Personal Branding Blog, 30 Dec. 2009. Web. 6 Feb. 2015.

Bazelon, Emily. "What Really Happened to Phoebe Prince?" *Slate*. Slate Group, 20 July 2010. Web. 6 Feb. 2015.

Keller, Emma G. "Emily Bazelon's Fair-Minded Feminism: 'I don't think there's anything missing'" *Guardian*. Guardian News and Media, 6 May 2013. Web. 6 Feb. 2015.

—Mari Rich

# Yves Béhar

**Born:** May 9, 1967
**Occupation:** Designer

Swiss-born designer Yves Béhar is dedicated to creating products that are both pleasing to the eye and easy to use, but his overarching design philosophy is about much more than just beauty and functionality. For Béhar, design is also about storytelling; all objects, as he remarked in a February 2008 Technology, Entertainment, Design (TED) Talk, have the potential to tell stories. Even more important are the values associated with a well-designed product. "I think everybody agrees that as designers we bring value to business, value to the users also," he explained in his TED Talk, "but I think it's the values that we put into these projects that ultimately create the greater value. And the values we bring can be about environmental issues, about sustainability." Over the course of his career, Béhar has worked to design aesthetically pleasing, functional products that embody strong values, promoting causes such as truly personal communication, environmental sustainability, and accessible and affordable education.

An experienced professional with a strong background in industrial design, Béhar has created products in a wide range of industries. The

Lester Cohen/Getty Images for WIRED

founder of the design firm Fuseproject, he has collaborated with many well-known companies, from the furniture company Herman Miller to the shoe manufacturer Puma. He has also forged productive partnerships with nonprofit organizations, including One Laptop per Child and the See Better to Learn Better project. Above all, Béhar hopes to expand the boundaries of design with his work, taking physical design itself in new directions and challenging the traditional ideas of what a beautifully designed product can do. "Design is at the intersection of sustainability, social good, ergonomics, business, and beauty," he told Helen Chislett for the online publication *How to Spend It* (11 May 2010). "Everyone is going to have to rethink how things are done, but doing things differently is key to human evolution."

### EARLY LIFE AND CAREER

Yves Béhar was born in Lausanne, Switzerland, on May 9, 1967, the son of a German-born mother and a Turkish-born father. He and his two younger brothers grew up in Lausanne, a city bordering Switzerland's Lake Geneva. Béhar developed an interest in storytelling at an early age and noted in his TED Talk that he was particularly intrigued by the Turkish carpets in his family's home, which depicted battle scenes and other narratives. His exposure to such home decor instilled in him an awareness of the storytelling power of objects, which would prove

essential to his later career. In light of his love of stories, Béhar initially considered pursuing a career as a writer but by mid-adolescence had decided to focus on design.

After studying for a time in Europe, Béhar enrolled in the Art Center College of Design in Pasadena, California. As a student he was particularly inspired by the work of designers such as Charles and Ray Eames and Joe Colombo, whose work, as he explained to Peter High for *Forbes* (25 Aug. 2014), fell at the "intersection of design and culture change." Béhar earned his bachelor's degree in product design in 1991 and began his professional career in California's Silicon Valley, where a boom in computer technology was creating new, inventive areas of design. Despite the rampant innovation of the period, however, Béhar was ultimately dissatisfied with the type of design work Silicon Valley's tech companies had in mind, which was more focused on external appearance than on a harmonious melding of beauty and functionality. "They were really looking for us, the designers, to create the skins, to put some pretty stuff outside of the box," Béhar explained in his TED Talk. "I didn't want to be a stylist in this way."

### FUSEPROJECT

Seeking to explore the possibilities of design under his own direction, in 1999 Béhar founded Fuseproject, a design firm through which he has pursued many of his most famous projects. By 2015 the firm, which has offices in both San Francisco and New York City, employed numerous designers, strategists, and other design and branding professionals. As Béhar's own company, Fuseproject is shaped around his personal design philosophy and approach to creating products. "Good designers work like editors: reducing the features, creating a simple yet compelling experience, addressing users with emotional intelligence, making sure that every design element that is left, is to the service of the big idea," he told Aaron Britt for the *Journal*, the online magazine of the retail website Mr Porter (29 Apr. 2014). In addition to being designed at Fuseproject, prototypes are sometimes fabricated and often tested in house, allowing the firm's designers to interact with new products just as users would to gain a thorough understanding of consumers' needs. This process also allows Fuseproject to maintain a level of secrecy when designing products for high-profile brands.

In 2014 Béhar, who serves as Fuseproject's chief executive officer, sold a 75 percent interest in the company to BlueFocus Communication Group, a Chinese marketing conglomerate. This partial acquisition, he stressed in interviews, would not affect the firm's practices or guiding ethos. Rather, he hoped it would allow Fuseproject to expand the scope of its business and pursue new design opportunities in the global marketplace.

## FRUITFUL COLLABORATIONS

As head of Fuseproject, Béhar has participated in a number of high-profile design collaborations with prominent companies and brands. He has been affiliated with the technology company Jawbone since 2003 and has served as the company's chief creative officer since 2007. Jawbone, founded in 1999 as Aliph, initially created military communications technology but soon refocused on wearable consumer devices, most prominently headsets for use with cellular phones. The company later introduced a line of portable wireless speakers as well as fitness wristbands used to track data such as the number of steps taken by the wearer each day. In collaboration with Jawbone, Béhar designed a number of products in those lines, including the Jawbone ERA headset, the Jambox speaker, and the UP3 wristband.

Béhar has also received significant attention for his work with the furniture brand Herman Miller. This collaboration was an especially fitting one; two of the young Béhar's design inspirations, twentieth-century American designers Charles and Ray Eames, notably designed a number of iconic chairs for the brand that are now considered classics of midcentury modern design. Béhar's first project for Herman Miller was a small lamp known as the Leaf Personal Light, the first lamp produced by the company. The Leaf lamp, named for its twisted, leaf-like shape, used LED lighting and was thus significantly more energy efficient than similarly sized lamps featuring compact fluorescent lightbulbs. In recognition of both its efficiency and innovative design, the Leaf Personal Light won awards and praise from design and decorating publications as well as from several environmental organizations. Continuing collaborations between Herman Miller and Fuseproject resulted in the creation of the Ardea and Twist lamps, and in 2014, the furniture manufacturer debuted a line of office furniture designed by Fuseproject, including, most notably, the ergonomic SAYL office chair.

## ONE LAPTOP PER CHILD

In addition to consumer products, Béhar has worked to design products for nonprofit organizations. In 2006 he was named chief designer for One Laptop per Child (OLPC), a nonprofit organization that produces inexpensive laptop computers, which are then sold to the governments of developing nations and distributed to schoolchildren. Those laptops, which come preloaded with a variety of educational programs, are intended to be powerful educational tools that take into account not only the educational needs of the students but also the energy and connectivity limitations often faced in the developing world: the devices are energy efficient and can connect to each other even without Internet access.

Béhar was initially responsible for designing OLPC's XO laptop, a durable, lightweight machine with a colorful exterior that is visually appealing to children. This design strategy has remained consistent even as the laptops themselves have evolved, introducing features such as touchscreens and cameras, and the XO tablet has a similar physical appearance and functionality. As his previous work and commitment to design with strong values might suggest, Béhar takes OLPC's mission and his responsibility as the organization's chief designer very seriously. "These laptops are not a hand-me-down from the developed world to the developing one," he explained to Chislett. "They are not less efficient, less technically advanced, less of something in any way. There is just as much design in this laptop as in a very expensive one—arguably more."

## OTHER WORK

Although Béhar's collaborations with Jawbone, Herman Miller, and OLPC are among his best-known and longest lasting partnerships, he and Fuseproject as a whole have worked with numerous well-known companies, designing products in a wide range of areas. To do so, he follows what he described to High as "a methodology of designing from ideas," in which he and his team consider "a company's history or background or attributes, and then tak[e] that to a new place." He is often brought on board when companies hope to create products that introduce new functions or fulfill existing needs in new and innovative ways. Béhar has, for instance, designed several machines for the company SodaStream, which allows consumers to carbonate water and make soda in the comfort of their own homes. One of Béhar's projects was the SodaStream MIX, the first SodaStream unit designed for creating cocktails and featuring the ability to carbonate liquids other than water. Béhar was likewise responsible for the design of shoe manufacturer Puma's Clever Little Bag, an alternative to the traditional shoebox. Made of recyclable materials and featuring far less cardboard than a traditional shoebox, the bag reduced waste while still allowing for the safe transport and storage of shoes. In addition to those companies, Béhar and Fuseproject have collaborated with noteworthy brands such as Prada and GE.

Béhar has likewise worked with various companies and nonprofits seeking to make substantial changes within their respective fields. He was tapped to design the OUYA, a videogame console based on the Android operating system that was crowdfunded on Kickstarter, ultimately raising more than eight million dollars in funding. In addition to playing games, the console was designed with game development in mind, allowing both experienced developers and novices to design and test games for the OUYA with minimal technological or financial barriers.

Following his work with OLPC, Béhar partnered with Augen Optics to design a line of inexpensive glasses that are both durable and child-friendly in design. Those glasses were distributed to school-aged children in Mexico as part of the Ver Bien para Aprender Mejor (See Better to Learn Better) project, an attempt to improve the educational prospects of children with visual impairments. Béhar has also served on the board of directors for the San Francisco Museum of Modern Art and as chair of the California College of Art's industrial design program.

### PERSONAL LIFE

Béhar lives in Northern California's Bay Area with longtime partner Sabrina Buell, an art adviser and former gallery director. He has three children, whom he has cited as his greatest inspiration. "Having children makes you more sure of your choices and sure of your direction," Béhar told Alexandra Wolfe for the *Wall Street Journal* (27 June 2014). "They've made me a lot stronger and a lot softer."

### SUGGESTED READING

Béhar, Yves. "Designing Objects That Tell Stories." *TED.* TED Conferences, May 2008. Web. 8 July 2015.

Béhar, Yves. "Mr. Yves Béhar." Interview by Aaron Britt. *Journal.* Mr Porter, 29 Apr. 2014. Web. 8 July 2015.

Chislett, Helen. "It's Not All about Yves." *How to Spend It.* Financial Times, 11 May 2010. Web. 8 July 2015.

High, Peter. "Yves Béhar Is the Most Influential Industrial Designer in the World." *Forbes.* Forbes.com, 25 Aug. 2014. Web. 8 July 2015.

Wieners, Brad. "Yves Béhar: The Designer as Entrepreneur." *BloombergBusiness.* Bloomberg, 24 Jan. 2013. Web. 8 July 2015.

Wolfe, Alexandra. "Yves Béhar of Fuseproject on Tech Products and Design." *Wall Street Journal.* Dow Jones, 27 June 2014. Web. 8 July 2015.

—Joy Crelin

# Preet Bharara

**Born:** 1968
**Occupation:** US Attorney for the Southern District of New York

As the US attorney for the Southern District of New York (sometimes jokingly referred to as the "Sovereign District"), Preet Bharara wields a lot of influence. First and foremost, he goes after "bad guys": terrorists, drug traffickers, financial criminals, and cybercriminals. Since taking office in 2009, Bharara—nicknamed the "Sheriff of Wall Street"—has developed a reputation for being both tough and fair, employing both cutting-edge, sophisticated technologies to go after cybercrime and traditional, proven methods, such as court-approved wiretaps, to go after Wall Street criminals. Bharara has received a good deal of recognition for his efforts. He has been profiled in financial, mainstream, and literary publications, including the *New York Times, Fortune, Fast Company,* and the *New Yorker.* In 2012 a *Time* magazine cover featured a photograph of Bharara with the all-caps headline: "This Man Is Busting Wall St." Later that year, *Time* included him on its list of the world's one hundred most influential people. He had been mentioned as a possible replacement for US attorney general Eric Holder, but Loretta Lynch, US attorney for the Eastern District, was nominated instead.

### EARLY LIFE AND ROOTS OF PASSION

Preetinder Bharara was born in Ferozepur, India (in the state of Punjab), in 1968. When he was two years old, his mother and father left India for the United States, ultimately settling in Monmouth County, New Jersey. His father, a doctor, eventually saved enough money to send Preet, his oldest son, to the private Ranney School, in Tinton Falls, New Jersey. As a boy, Bharara was curious and loved to learn and to read; his parents were success-oriented, pushing him and his younger brother, Vinit, to work as hard as they could. (Vinit Bharara cofounded Diapers.com and sold its parent company to Amazon.com in 2011 for more than $500 million.) During his time at Ranney, Preet Bharara read a variety of books and was particularly impressed by the novel *To Kill a Mockingbird* (1960) and the play *Inherit the Wind* (1955). The latter, a fictionalized version of the 1925 Scopes "Monkey" Trial, was a court-trial story about teaching evolution in public school classrooms. When Bharara read the play, and other literary works about court trials, he decided he wanted to become a criminal lawyer.

During Bharara's time at Ranney, he served as the editor of the school newspaper, for which his history and literature teacher, Barbara Tomlinson, one of his favorites, was the adviser. His desire for accountability and fairness began at this time, too. Toward the end of his senior year, Bharara heard that Tomlinson was going to be fired for objecting to the school's plan to give teachers a raise but also to increase their hours. By this point, Bharara had been accepted to Harvard University, and Tomlinson asked him not to stir up trouble on her behalf, concerned that he might jeopardize his standing with Harvard. Bharara did not heed Tomlinson, instead organizing students to talk to the school's founder. Despite his efforts, however, Tomlinson lost her job.

After graduating from high school in 1986, Bharara attended Harvard, where he studied government and continued to follow social justice issues. During his sophomore year he served as a news anchor at the local student radio station. Although Bharara briefly considered a career in journalism, he ultimately settled upon law. He graduated from Harvard with a bachelor's degree in government in 1990.

## FROM LAW SCHOOL TO HARD KNOCKS

In 1990 Bharara began his studies at Columbia Law School. After graduating in 1993, he worked in private practice for Gibson, Dunn & Crutcher from 1993 to 1996 and for Swidler Berlin Shereff Friedman from 1996 to 2000. In 2000, he became an assistant US attorney for the

www.justice/gov/Wikimedia Commons

Southern District of New York, working on cases involving securities fraud, organized crime, and illegal drugs. According to an extensive profile by George Packer in the *New Yorker* (27 June 2011), Bharara "wasn't a star prosecutor, but his intelligence, wit, and skill at navigating the politics of a large and competitive institution caught the attention" of Democratic senator Charles Schumer of New York.

In February 2005, Bharara began work as chief counsel for Schumer, a top member of the Senate Judiciary Committee. The following year, Bharara was one of the leaders of the investigation in the firing of eight US attorneys under President George W. Bush. The controversial firings eventually led to the resignation of Attorney General Alberto Gonzales. During the investigation, wrote Packer, Bharara "stood out as a sharp, nonpartisan interrogator of witnesses who were to testify before the Judiciary Committee." Schumer was clearly impressed with his work, and he recommended him for the position of US Attorney to President Barack Obama in early 2009.

Bharara began serving as US Attorney of the Southern District of New York in August 2009. Even though he is based in New York, his job is to pursue crime on the federal level. He can charge someone with a federal crime—and therefore investigate them prior to doing so—if they have placed a telephone call, traded securities, or sent an e-mail or text message in one of several New York State counties, including those in New York City. His first big case began in October 2009 with the arrest of Raj Rajaratnam, the founder and manager of Galleon Group, a hedge fund worth $7 billion. Rajaratnam was charged with fourteen counts of securities fraud and conspiracy (insider trading). The investigation into his activities began a few years before Bharara took office: by early 2007, the Securities and Exchange Commission (SEC) had begun analyzing Galleon's electronic correspondences. The evidence against him was overwhelming. The SEC intercepted communications and seized electronic records that directly pointed to Rajaratnam getting illegal insider information about upcoming deals or investments worth billions of dollars and then using that information to buy stock before its price shot up.

During a press conference announcing Rajaratnam's arrest, Bharara said that the case represents the first time that (legal) wiretaps—fairly common in investigations of organized crime and drug cartels—were used to target insider trading. In 2011 Rajaratnam, who had been accused of making nearly $64 million from insider trading, was found guilty and sentenced to eleven years in prison; he was also fined nearly $93 million by the SEC. In numerous interviews Bharara both defended his use of court-authorized wiretaps and pointed out that his vigilance to prosecute such big cases is about holding perpetrators accountable and sending them to prison. Paying a fine—even one as large as that levied against Rajaratnam—is one thing, but being locked up is quite another. "When sophisticated business people begin to adopt the methods of common criminals, we have no choice but to treat them as such," Bharara told Packer.

## TRACKING DOWN CYBERCRIME

It did not take long for Bharara to develop a reputation as a tough prosecutor unafraid to go after financial crooks, terrorists, drug lords, and those engaging in illegal activities online. Bharara's Southern District office has successfully prosecuted a great variety of cases, including those of Faisal Shahzad, who attempted to detonate a bomb in the middle of New York's Times Square; Rajat Gupta, a Goldman Sachs board member who was allegedly involved in insider trading; and a growing number of criminals using the Internet for both financial dealings and illegal drug sales. "There are websites," Bharara told Max Chafkin for *Fast Company* (4 Mar. 2014), "whose business model is to use

the fact that they can't know everything that's going on as an excuse to look the other way. There are people who run companies whose websites are rife with tremendous amounts of illegal activity."

Bharara told Chafkin that he wants to be known not just as the "Sheriff of Wall Street" but also as the guy who "cleaned up the web." In particular, Bharara focused on the all-digital online payment network called Bitcoin, which allows anyone to "bank with near-complete anonymity." Bharara explained that there is nothing inherently wrong with Bitcoin, because there are legitimate reasons to want privacy in one's financial purchases, but online there are criminals who could steal one's money or sell illegal drugs. According to Chafkin, when Bharara began his job as a US attorney in 2009, his office had one prosecutor devoted to technology crimes. Bharara has increased that number to ten. Because of such resources and vigilance, his office has prosecuted high-profile cases such as those of Ross Ulbricht and Charlie Shrem. Ulbricht, a.k.a. "Dread Pirate Roberts," is the alleged founder of Silk Road, a site that dealt (with the purchasing power of Bitcoin) in illegal drugs, such as cocaine, heroin, methamphetamine, and various pills. In July 2013 undercover FBI agents arrested Ulbricht at a public library in San Francisco, California. Shrem, CEO of BitInstant and vice chairman of the Bitcoin Foundation, pleaded guilty and was convicted in 2014 of laundering more than $1 million via Silk Road.

## PERSONAL LIFE

Although there has been much speculation about what the future holds for Bharara—whether he will seek a high political office or move on to work for a private law firm—he has insisted that he is happy where he is and that he is doing the job he wants to be doing. Bharara and his wife have three children. He closely guards his private life, largely because of his position as a high-level prosecutor.

## SUGGESTED READING

Chafkin, Max. "The Most Dangerous Man in Bitcoin Isn't a Criminal." *Fast Company*. Mansueto Ventures, 4 Mar. 2014, Web. 12 Dec. 2014.

Cohan, William D. "Preet Bharara: The Enforcer of Wall Street." *Fortune*. Time, 2 Aug. 2011. Web. 12 Dec. 2014.

Horowitz, Jason. "When Preet Bharara Speaks, the Shady Get Nervous." *Washington Post*. Washington Post, 4 Apr. 2013. Web. 12 Dec. 2014.

Packer, George. "A Dirty Business." *New Yorker*. Condé Nast, 27 June 2011. Web. 12 Dec. 2014.

—Dmitry Kiper

# Arundhati Bhattacharya

**Born:** March 18, 1956

**Occupation:** Chair, State Bank of India

In 2013 Arundhati Bhattacharya became the youngest person—and the first woman—to be named the chair of the State Bank of India (SBI) in its more than two centuries of operation. She was also the first woman to ever lead a Fortune 500 company in India, and in 2014 *Forbes* magazine listed Bhattacharya number thirty-six on its list of the hundred most powerful women in the world. SBI is India's largest lender, with about 220,000 employees in 15,000 branches that control a fifth of India's banking assets.

Bhattacharya has won praise in India and abroad for her adept leadership and efforts to fix SBI's various problems. Most notably, bad loans, also known as nonperforming assets

Dibyangshu Sarkar/AFP/Getty Images

(NPAs), approved by her predecessors damaged the bank's reputation. Bhattacharya told a reporter for Mumbai's *Business Today* (10 Oct. 2013) that reducing the burden of NPAs was her "top priority" as chair. The Indian government, which owns 59 percent of SBI, hoped that the appointment of Bhattacharya would be a positive step in reforming the country's banking sector, including SBI's reputation for poor customer service and slow management.

In addition to loan management, Bhattacharya introduced a new, broader strategy for SBI focusing on new technologies, attracting new customers—as of 2014, the World Bank estimated that over half of Indian adults did not have a bank account—and improving internal corporate policies, with a focus on female employees. Although women in India's banking industry are more powerful than in any other country, controlling as much as 40 percent of all assets, true gender equality is still on the horizon. "The women are far outnumbered by the men," Bhattacharya told James Crabtree for the *Financial Times* (12 Dec. 2014), and the country's culture remains deeply patriarchal. Bhattacharya hoped to make it easier for women to get a leg up at SBI, noting that the challenge is less outright hostility and more the fact that women must break new ground to succeed in the banking world. She told Crabtree about her pioneering early career: "The difficulties that we had were more basic—whether there would be a separate women's toilet and things like that in some of the smaller branches, because they may never have seen a woman on staff."

## EDUCATION AND JOINING SBI

Arundhati Bhattacharya was born on March 18, 1956, and grew up with her two older sisters and older brother in the steel towns of Bokaro and Bhilai in east central India. Her father, P. K. Mukherjee, was an engineer at Bhilai Steel Plant. She excelled at St. Xavier's School in Bokaro; her maternal aunt Parbati Dutta told Divy Khare for the *Times of India* (9 Oct. 2013) that Bhattacharya was a "scholar student" who "always came first in class." Her teachers encouraged her to pursue a career in the arts, and Bhattacharya earned her BA in English literature from Kolkata's Lady Brabourne College and her MA in the same subject from Jadavpur University.

Bhattacharya dreamed of becoming a journalist and one day writing a book. After graduation, she decided, along with her college friends, to take the entrance examination for SBI positions on a whim in 1977. "It sort of just happened," she recalled to Anand Adhikari for India's *Business Today* (31 Aug. 2014), though she noted, "Those days, SBI was one of the best paymasters." Bhattacharya was the only one of her friends to take the job as a probationary officer, and she attended training school in Hyderabad to learn about banking under the Institute of Bankers. She officially joined the SBI as a direct recruit officer in September 1977.

Bhattacharya's first day of work coincided with the eve of the Hindu festival Durga Puja, during which the banks are closed, so her branch was flooded with customers taking out money before the holiday. "I was given the job of writing checks and entering their details," she recalled to Samyabrata Ray Goswami for the Kolkata *Telegraph* (9 Oct. 2013). "The branch was surrounded by hordes of people . . . soon they had to close the gates to manage the crowds and they started pushing in. I remember every bit of the day and my aching hands as I kept writing the checks in a daze, ensuring there were no mistakes. I remember the pressing crowds and their urgency to withdraw money before the bank closed for the festive season. It was a day of baptism by fire."

## CLIMBING THE LADDER AT SBI

Early in her career, Bhattacharya was tasked with overseeing some of SBI's numerous rural branches. Many of them did not even have electricity. Bhattacharya was horrified that the bank had to employ "punkwallahs," or servants to manually operate fans, and worked to modernize the facilities. "The first time I [saw this] I was so amazed that in the 1980s we still could have an abomination like this that, on the spot, I approved a diesel generator so that they could put in real fans," she said. It would be just the beginning of her efforts to bring SBI up to date, starting by setting a personal example.

A lack of electricity could be remedied with a single order, but one of the largest obstacles Bhattacharya faced was the SBI's patriarchal culture. Although she claims to have never faced acute discrimination from her male colleagues, the bank's managerial decisions consistently forced her to choose between her family and her job. Throughout her career, Bhattacharya served in branches across India, with frequent travel often interrupting her personal life. Yet through her dedication and patience from her family, she was able to succeed at every level and quickly

work her way up the ranks. In 1996 she was asked to run the SBI's New York City branch. She brought along her aunt to look after her young daughter. After encountering problems with her visa, Bhattacharya's aunt had to return to India, and Bhattacharya was forced to send her daughter back as well. She credits her aunt, sister, and mother for raising her daughter while she worked in New York for four years, gaining valuable leadership experience. The experience would inform her understanding of the unique challenges faced by women in the workforce.

## PAYING DIVIDENDS

In 2006 Bhattacharya was appointed general manager of the SBI branch in Lucknow, the capital of the Indian state of Uttar Pradesh. She was concerned that the move would hurt her family. "My worry was finding a proper school for my child," she told Adhikari (31 Aug. 2014). It was one move too many—she decided to quit. Her mentor, M. S. Verma, urged her to rethink her decision. He told her that she had come too far to give up. "You've worked long and hard," Bhattacharya recalled him saying to Mallika Kapur for *CNN* (4 Feb. 2015), "you are just about beginning to reap the awards, and you will not give up and you will try your best."

Bhattacharya went to Lucknow in 2006, and from then on she rose steadily within SBI with promotion after promotion. Her appointments provided experience in virtually every aspect of banking, including retail, corporate, and investment banking. In 2009 she was appointed chief general manager of new businesses. It was a turning point in her career. In her new position, she introduced a mobile banking platform, which proved enormously successful and generated substantial profits for the company. Bhattacharya was named deputy managing director of SBI in 2010, and in 2012 she was named managing director (MD) and chief executive officer (CEO) of SBI Capital Markets, one of the bank's subsidiaries.

Bhattacharya returned to SBI itself when she was named chief financial officer (CFO) and MD in August 2013. Less than two months later, she beat out several male colleagues to succeed Pratip Chaudhuri as chair for a term set to last three years. Her rise to the company's top position was historic but unsurprising to many because of her experience and length of service with SBI. According to Goswami, a personal intervention from then prime minister Manmohan

Singh, sealed Bhattacharya's appointment, signaling an overall effort to shift the management of SBI in a new direction.

## CHANGING THE CULTURE

After assuming her post in 2013, Bhattacharya sought to change the culture of the SBI both in terms of the way it does business and in its internal company policies. In 2014 Bhattacharya oversaw SBI's efforts to update its technology—and reach out to young, tech-savvy customers—through the opening of a number of digital branches. At a digital branch, customers could open accounts and be approved for loans with the click of a button. They could even talk to advisers via video link. "These branches are a first step in the journey of offering full digital services across the nation," Bhattacharya told Adhikari (17 Aug. 2014).

Meanwhile, SBI employees saw a major shift in policy regarding leave of absence. Under Bhattacharya's direction, the bank offered employees the opportunity to take up to three two-year sabbaticals during their career. The new policy was seen as a huge boon for female employees who felt pressured to quit their jobs to care for children or elderly relatives. "I still see a lot of recruitment of women. But I think we need to do more in order to get them to stay," Bhattacharya told Kapur. "There are still too few people staying put for them to have a good shot at the top jobs."

## PERSONAL LIFE

During her infrequent periods of down time, Bhattacharya enjoys traveling, trying new foods, and reading. She reads two or three books at a time, including books about her favorite topic, antiques. Her husband, Pritimoy Bhattacharya, is a former professor at the Indian Institute of Technology (IIT) at Kharagpur. They often maintain a long-distance relationship due to her continued busy travel schedule. They have a daughter, Sukrita.

## SUGGESTED READING

Adhikari, Anand. "Entering a Male Domain." *Business Today In.* Living Media India, 31 Aug. 2014. Web. 8 Apr. 2015.

Adhikari, Anand. "Fixing a Running Motor." *Business Today In.* Living Media India, 17 Aug. 2014. Web. 9 Apr. 2015.

Crabtree, James. "Women of 2014: Arundhati Bhattacharya, Head of State Bank of India." *Financial Times.* Financial Times, 12 Dec. 2014. Web. 8 Apr. 2015.

Goswami, Samyabrata Ray. "Steady Climb to the Top." *Telegraph* (Kolkata, India). Telegraph, 9 Oct. 2013. Web. 8 Apr. 2015.

Kapur, Mallika. "Arundhati Bhattacharya: India's Banking Titan Shakes Up 200 Years of Tradition." *CNN.* Cable News Network, 4 Feb. 2015. Web. 8 Apr. 2015.

Khare, Divy. "Bokaro Parties as Homegrown Arundhati Bhattacharya Becomes SBI Boss." *Times of India.* Bennett, Coleman, & Co., 9 Oct. 2013. Web. 8 Apr. 2015.

Mazumdar, Shreyanka. "How SBI Chief Arundhati Bhattacharya Banks on Breakthroughs." *Mid-Day.* Mid-Day Infomedia, 14 Dec. 2014. Web. 9 Apr. 2015.

—Molly Hagan

---

# Simone Biles

**Born:** March 14, 1997
**Occupation:** Gymnast

After only two years as a senior competitor, Simone Biles already held the distinction of being one of the most decorated female gymnasts in US history. She had an impressive 2013 senior debut, highlighted by all-around titles at the US nationals and the World Artistic Gymnastics Championships, where her three additional individual medals made her the first American woman to notch four medals at a World Championship since Nastia Liukin did so in 2005.

Biles proved that she was no fluke, taking home five medals (four gold and one silver) at the 2014 World Championships. With this, she joined Shannon Miller as one of two American female gymnasts to win back-to-back all-around titles. Biles is considered by many to be a gold medal favorite for the 2016 Olympics in Rio, including Liukin, who was Olympic all-around winner in 2008. "You can see that fire in her eyes," she told Nick Zaccardi for *NBC Sports* (9 Oct. 2013). "Her skills are just through the roof. It's not just her skills, but it's the way that she executes them."

## EARLY LIFE

Simone Arianne Biles was born in Columbus, Ohio, on March 14, 1997. At the age of three, Biles, whose single mother struggled with substance abuse issues, first entered the foster care

© Yang Zongyou/Xinhua Press/Corbis

*Illustrated* (8 Sept. 2014). "She was also what I call an 'air-sense savant.' She had an innate feel for what her body could do once it got off the ground."

Biles's confident poise and raw, acrobatic ability were on full display at the 2007 Texas Level 7–10 Statewide Qualifier, in Houston, where she competed at Level 8—the intermediate level for USA Gymnastics' (USAG) Junior Olympic Program. The program consists of ten levels of competition for young gymnasts of various ages. Gymnasts at Levels 6 and above choreograph their own routines but must also display certain skills on uneven bars, balance beam, vault, and floor. Biles finished first in the vault and had top-ten finishes in the uneven bars and the floor exercise. Her all-around score at the qualifier (a USAG–sanctioned meet) allowed her to advance to the Texas Level 8 State Championships, where she placed sixth in vault.

## DOMINATING LEVELS 9 AND 10

As a Level 9 gymnast, Biles had her best showing at the 2008 South Padre Extravaganza, where she earned the all-around title and finished first in vault and floor exercise, as well as second on balance beam. She followed that up with another first-place victory on floor and top-five finish in vault at the Region III Level 9–10 Championships. Her all-around runner-up status at regionals helped Biles advance to the final competition of the Level 9 season—the 2008 Western National Championships—and a fourth-place tie on vault.

In 2009 Biles, now at Level 10, remained dominant, amassing all-around titles at two meets: the Mary Lou Retton Invitational, where she was the floor exercise champion, vault runner-up, and third-place finisher in the uneven bars; and the Rose City Classic, where she reigned supreme on floor and vault, qualifying once again for the regional championships. There Biles replicated the previous year's performance, finishing first in floor and fourth in vault. Other highlights included the Alamo Classic, with top-five finishes in all four individual events and the all-around.

The 2010 season started off impressively for Biles, who added consecutive all-around titles from the Ricky Deci Invitational, Space City Classic, and Classic Rock Invitational. Her winning streak continued at the Jazz Invitational, where she finished first in almost every category, except for her runner-up finish on uneven bars. Biles more than held her own against many of

system. After spending time traveling between foster homes and her mother's place, Biles was finally taken in by her maternal grandparents, Ron and Nellie Biles, on Christmas Eve 2002. The Spring, Texas, couple formally adopted Biles, along with her younger sister, Adria. Biles's six other siblings had also spent time in the foster care system. While two of them were returned to their mother, another pair found a permanent home with Ron's sister; non-family members adopted the remaining duo.

Growing up, Biles was very energetic, according to her adoptive father, an Air Force veteran and former air traffic controller. Biles found the perfect outlet at age six, when she visited Bannon's Gymnastix with her daycare class. While copying some of the older gymnasts' moves, Biles attracted the attention of gym officials, who invited her to sign up for classes—an offer that Biles's parents gladly accepted. "My wife took it as a sign to save the furniture," Ron Biles told Melissa Murphy for the Associated Press's *Winter Games Sochi 2014* site (16 Oct. 2014).

## COMPETITIVE DEBUT

Shortly after observing Biles during a class and taking notice of her natural talent, head instructor Aimee Boorman appointed herself Biles's personal coach. By age seven, Biles was already performing back flips in the air and tumbling passes on the floor. "She was absolutely fearless," Boorman told Brian Cazeneuve for *Sports* the world's junior and senior elite female gymnasts at the Houston National Invitational, with wins on floor and vault, as well as third-place showings in balance beam and the all-around.

## JOINING THE RANKS OF THE ELITE

Also in 2010, Biles returned to the state championships, where she finally stood atop the podium after winning gold in vault and floor and gaining the all-around bronze. At the regional championships, Biles took home another first-place trophy on vault, as well as third place on floor. With fourth place in the individual all-around, she qualified for the 2010 Junior Olympic Nationals, in Dallas, Texas, where she had an impressive showing, winning the floor event while tying for third on vault. Biles attained Junior Pre-Elite status at the National Elite Qualifier.

Biles picked up right where she left off in 2011, claiming all-around titles at the Metroplex Challenge and the Gliders Elite Qualifier, the latter of which promoted her to Junior Elite. (At the Elite level, gymnasts can compete at international events, including the Olympics.) Biles's junior elite debut at the American Classic was an overwhelming success. In addition to winning gold in balance beam and vault, her bronze medal–winning performance in the all-around earned her a return trip to the CoverGirl Classic, this time as a junior elite. After achieving top-five finishes in floor exercise and vault, Biles made her first appearance at the Visa Championships, placing seventh in vault and tenth on beam. She was fourteenth overall in the all-around, narrowly missing a spot on the US National Team.

## JUNIOR NATIONALS

The following year, Biles further established herself as one of the best junior vaulters and tumblers. At the Alamo Classic, she successfully debuted one of the toughest vaults performed by women—an Amanar (a roundoff-back handspring with two-and-a-half twists and blind landing)—and received the highest score in floor. Her effort earned her gold medals in both events, along with two more for beam and the all-around and a silver in the uneven bars. Biles dominated both the vault and floor exercise at her next two meets: February's WOGA (World Olympics Gymnastics Academy) Classic, where she also won the bronze all-around, and March's Houston National Invite, where she claimed additional medals in the all-around (gold) and uneven bars (bronze).

A month later Biles reigned supreme over the junior women's competition at the American Classic. Not only did she win silver with her floor routine, she earned the highest score in vault. Her powerful Amanar helped propel her to another gold in the all-around. This performance qualified Biles for the Secret US Classic in May. With her superior jumping skills and a high-flying floor routine, Biles took first place in vault and all-around, along with runner-up in floor, despite struggles with the uneven bars and balance beam. In June she turned heads at the 2012 Visa Championships, a two-day event where she netted the junior vault title. She also finished with the all-around bronze and a spot on the junior national squad, giving her the opportunity to compete abroad.

## WORLD CHAMPIONSHIPS

In early March 2013 Biles made her international debut as a senior national team member at one of the season's first major competitions: the AT&T American Cup, a meet held in Worcester, Massachusetts, and sanctioned by the Fédération Internationale de Gymnastique (FIG). Stepping in alongside Katelyn Ohashi as a last-minute replacement for injured teammates Elizabeth Price and Kyla Ross, Biles showed early promise, taking the lead on a near-perfect vault and solid uneven bars routine—one of her traditionally weaker events. Despite a fall on beam and shaky floor performance, she placed second, behind Ohashi, in the all-around and won the vault and uneven bars titles.

Later that month Biles was equally instrumental in helping the senior national squad defeat Japan and Italy to capture team gold at the City of Jesolo Trophy. She nearly pulled off a clean sweep in the individual all-around competition, with first-place finishes in vault, beam, floor, and the all-around. Her stranglehold on first continued in the team finals, adding three more golds to her collection (in vault, beam, and floor). A week later Biles's second-place finish in the all-around helped get Team USA the gold at a friendly meet with Romania and Germany.

However, Biles's winning streak came to an end following an uncharacteristically shaky performance at July's Secret US Classic. After falling during her uneven bars routine, struggling to stay on the beam, and twisting her ankle during the floor exercise, she pulled out of the vault—and the competition, diagnosed with bone spurs in her foot. While preparing for the P&G Championships with physical therapy and acupuncture, Biles consulted with sports psychologist Robert B. Andrews. She also accepted a personal invitation to work out at the National Team Training Center in Huntsville, Texas, under the watchful eye of Marta Karolyi, US women's national team coordinator. "I reassured her about her potential, but also reminded her that the talent by itself doesn't make the results," Karolyi told Brandon Penny for the *Team USA* website (18 Aug. 2013).

By August Biles had returned to form at the P&G Championships, claiming gold in the all-around and silver on vault, uneven bars, vault, and floor. She subsequently accepted an invitation to attend qualifying camp at Huntsville, where she was selected to represent the United States at the 2013 World Championships in Antwerp, Belgium. She defeated teammates and Olympic gold medalists McKayla Maroney and Kyla Ross to become the seventh American woman to capture the all-around gold. Although she also notched the floor title in event finals, she finished second to Maroney on vault and third on beam, right behind silver medalist Ross.

## COMEBACK

After withdrawing from the American Cup and the Pacific Rim Championships due to a nagging shoulder injury, Biles, also recovering from off-season ankle surgery, made her 2014 debut at the Secret US Classic in July. She emphatically erased memories of the previous year's debacle with first-place finishes in the all-around, vault, beam, and floor. In August Biles successfully defended her P&G Championship all-around crown against runner-up Ross, who trailed her by more than four points, despite a fall during Biles's final routine. Her other golds (on vault and floor) and her balance beam silver earned her another selection to the Senior National Team—and a return to the World Championships, the scene of her greatest triumph.

In the world team finals, Biles guided her squad to a first-place finish while also claiming her second consecutive all-around and floor titles, along with another gold medal in beam and a silver in vault. During the all-around medal ceremony, Biles made headlines when she ran screaming from the podium after a bee attacked her ceremony bouquet.

Biles continued her success in 2015, sweeping the American Cup and helping the senior national team win gold at the City of Jesolo

Trophy, where she also took individual golds in vault, floor, and beam. Accolades include the Sportswoman of the Year Award (2014) from the Women's Sports Foundation and the ESPNW's Impact 25 (2014).

## PERSONAL LIFE

Biles, who is homeschooled, has been admitted to the University of California, Los Angeles, although she has decided to defer enrollment until after the 2016 Olympics. She will not be joining the college's gymnastics squad, however, having relinquished her amateur status to sign with the sports agency Octagon. Since February 2014 Biles has been training with Boorman at the World Champions Centre, a training facility founded and run by Biles's parents. Biles's sister Adria is also a competitive gymnast.

## SUGGESTED READING

Cazeneuve, Brian. "A Flying Start." *Sports Illustrated*. Time, 8 Sept. 2014. Web. 18 Aug. 2015.

Murphy, Melissa. "Biles Returns with 4 World Golds, No Bee Stings." *AP Winter Games Sochi 2014*. Associated Press, 16 Oct. 2014. Web. 18 Aug. 2015.

Penny, Brandon. "A New Champion: Simone Biles." *Team USA*. US Olympic Committee, 8 Aug. 2013. Web. 18 Aug. 2015.

Radnofsky, Louise. "Simone Biles Is Vaulting Gymnastics to New Heights." *Wall Street Journal*. Dow Jones, 17 Aug. 2015. 18 Aug. 2015.

Zaccardi, Nick. "USA Gymnastics' Future Bright with Rio 2016 on Horizon." *NBCSports.com*. NBC Sports, 9 Oct. 2013. Web. 18 Aug. 2015.

—Bertha Muteba

# Aloe Blacc

**Born:** January 7, 1979
**Occupation:** Singer

After years of recording music as an underground phenomenon as part of the hip-hop duo Emanon and then as a soul singer, Aloe Blacc became a mega-selling artist in 2013, in collaboration with producer Avicii on the international smash single "Wake Me Up." Blacc had a major-label debut with the 2014 release of *Lift Your Spirit*, which produced a number of hit singles, including the Billboard chart-topper "The Man," in February 2014. Although he appeared to many as an overnight sensation, it had taken Blacc about a decade to become an internationally renowned songwriter and recording artist, with his first hit—the hypnotic neo-soul single "I Need a Dollar"—coming only in 2010. "To my benefit, I started from ground up," Blacc remarked in an interview with Sarah Godfrey for the *Washington Post* (10 Mar. 2014). "Writing, recording, mixing, mastering, producing, doing all artwork, pressing, distributing, selling—everything from bottom to top. I found an indie to do that eventually, then a major, which has more resources and infrastructure, but there are no questions I can't answer about my own career. I can always be trusted to make the music that I know how to make."

## EARLY LIFE AND EDUCATION

Blacc was born Egbert Nathaniel Dawkins III on January 7, 1979, in Los Angeles, California, the son and only child of Panamanian immigrants. Blacc came to appreciate music, both through learning the trumpet and through his father. Blacc recalled to Guy Raz for NPR (29 Oct. 2010), "There was always music in the house. My dad had a stereo system, and he had this sign posted on the stereo system that said: If you value your life, do not touch my stereo." Blacc continued, "And he had a record collection, and of course, every Saturday morning, Sunday morning, the sounds that I can remember waking up to were—it's either some soul music, you know, from the states or salsa music from the Caribbean, calypso, soca, something that was just vibrant and energetic." It wasn't long before Blacc was devouring records by rap artists like Public Enemy and De La Soul, as well as those of pioneering soul musicians like Donny Hathaway and Marvin Gaye. By age nine, he had already begun writing rap lyrics. In 1995 Blacc and Exile (a.k.a. Aleksander Manfredi) started their DJ/MC duo Emanon—"no name" spelled backward. He put out his first hip-hop mix tape as a teenager in 1996.

Blacc's success as a straight-A high school student enabled him to attend the University of Southern California Dornsife on scholarship. While there, Blacc learned how to play guitar and piano as well. He graduated in 2001 with a bachelor of arts degree in communications and linguistic psychology. "It's kind of a nerdy interest," he said of his bachelor's degree to Dorian Lynskey for the *Guardian* (3 Apr. 2014). "It helps me to continue whetting my blade as a thinker. I don't play the new app of the week on my phone, I play with words. I put them together in little puzzles and see how they make me feel and then do this projection puzzle to the rest of the world and ask how they will make other people feel."

## HIS CAREER IN MUSIC—AND IN THE CORPORATE WORLD

After forming Emanon with Exile, Blacc took on the moniker Aloe because of his smooth style. The duo produced two major recordings, their first EP in 2002, *Anon and On*, and in 2005, the full-length album, *The Waiting Room*. Despite the success the duo were having as underground artists, Blacc found his heart really wasn't into becoming the next big thing. "Music was a hobby," he recalled of his early career to Lynskey. "There wasn't that urgency of feeling, like I needed to make it in the music industry. I'm glad I had a decade or more of doing it for fun so I know what it feels like and I don't do it for any other reason."

When not performing as a hip-hop artist, Blacc was having some success in the corporate world as a business consultant for the accounting firm Ernst & Young, where he worked to improve services for children's hospitals. Then, in 2005 he lost his job due to corporate downsizing.

## BREAKING OUT AS A SOLO ARTIST

Blacc knew he could find another job or return to school to earn his doctorate, but he felt an urge to continue to develop his musical career. One thing he knew for certain was that he did not want to return to hip-hop. In an interview with Raz he said, "I became disillusioned with hip-hop . . . a lot of the music . . . was just a string of lines that didn't connect." Blacc was also disillusioned with hip-hop's posturing and machismo. "What I wanted to do was write stories, you know? I want to be a storyteller. . . . And then, I wanted to become a better lyricist. So I started listening to Joni Mitchell and James Taylor and Nina Simone, and that's when I started singing, really."

In 2006 Blacc released his first solo record, *Shine Through*, on the distinguished indie label Stones Throw. *Shine Through* was a combination of retro-soul and Latin music and showed a distinct departure from his hip-hop past. It also highlighted his development as a singer of some ability. In the *New York Times* (19 Nov. 2010), Jon Caramanica called Blacc's first solo album "excellent" and described it as "a spiky collection of eclectic electronic soul."

Blacc's sophomore solo album, *Good Things* (2010), was also recorded for the Stones Throw label. Like his previous effort, the record impressed music critics who were captivated by Blacc's take on the growing soul revival in popular music. Otis Hart, reviewing the record for NPR (19 Sept. 2010), remarked, "Aloe Blacc's voice, while planted firmly in the mid-range, resonates with conviction, and the themes he explores—women and social injustice—revisit a time when love and politics didn't make such strange bedfellows." *Good Things*—a certified gold record in a number of countries—also received a huge boost from its hit single, "I Need a Dollar," which captured the recessionary spirit of the year. The single vaulted to the Top 10 on music charts around the world, including those in Great Britain and Germany, and was used as the theme song to the HBO show *How to Make It in America*. In interviews Blacc has described the success of "I Need a Dollar" as life changing, because it gave him the ability to pursue a full-time musical career. Other notable songs from *Good Things* include "Take Me Back," "Life So Hard," and "Green Lights."

Blacc's next major success came in 2013, when he cowrote and provided vocals for Swedish DJ Avicii's "Wake Me Up," which gave the Swedish producer a Top 5 hit on Billboard's Hot 100. In an interview with Patrick Doyle for *Rolling Stone* (28 Aug. 2013), Blacc discussed his feelings about the success of Avicii's worldwide hit single, which had reached number one in twenty-two countries: "As a songwriter, it is wonderful for the world to appreciate the lyrics you write. As a singer, it is even better for people to become a fan of your voice. I'm very happy that I have the chance to earn the respect of new fans with both my lyrics and my voice. A friend of mine told me he had to educate his coworker whom he overheard complementing Avicii's voice. He leaned over and said, 'That's not actually Avicii singing, that's Aloe Blacc.'"

## *LIFT YOUR SPIRIT*

In 2014 Blacc released *Lift Your Spirit* in the United States for Interscope. Originally released in October 2013, it was his third solo album and his first for a major record label. Blacc's own folksier and acoustic version of "Wake Me Up" appeared on the album, alongside another hit single, "The Man," which was inspired by Elton John's enormously popular "Your Song," which first hit the charts in 1970. Also on the album was the single "Here Today." With production from Pharrell and DJ Khalil, the album impressed music fans with its fresh and optimistic take on neo-soul, peaking at number four on Billboard charts.

Reviewers were similarly wowed by Blacc's most recent work. "Blacc [is] a welcome counterpoint to the prevailing style of modern soul men. All three top-selling R&B males—Justin Timberlake, Bruno Mars, and Pharrell—sing in light and lively voices, but Blacc goes deep. The other guys soar on sky high pitches, smooth tones and swooping phrases. That's fine, but where's the beef?" Jim Farber, in the *New York Daily News* (11 Mar. 2014), wrote. In a review of *Lift Your Spirit* for the *New York Times* (10 Mar. 2014), Jon Pareles declared that Blacc's voice "has the frayed-denim edge of Bill Withers, some of Stevie Wonder's twists and turns, and a little Sam Cooke grit. . . . Throughout the album, Mr. Blacc sings with the kind of earthy vitality that many studied neo-soul singers don't have the voice to match." In 2015 *Lift Your Spirit* was nominated for a Grammy Award for best R&B album.

## PERSONAL LIFE

Blacc is married to Australian rapper Maya Jupiter. They have a daughter, Mandela, born in September 2013.

## SUGGESTED READING

Blacc, Aloe. "Q&A: 'I Need a Dollar' Singer-Songwriter Aloe Blacc." Interview by Emma Cox. *Daily Mail*. Associated Newspapers, 28 June 2014. Web. 27 Apr. 2015.

Caramanica, Jon. "The Old-School Style, Unafraid to Be Imperfect." *New York Times*. New York Times, 19 Nov. 2010. Web. 16 Mar. 2015.

Farber, Jim. "Aloe Blacc, 'Lift Your Spirit'; Drive-By Truckers, 'English Oceans': Album Reviews." *New York Daily News*. NY Daily News, 11 Mar. 2014. Web. 16 Mar. 2015.

Godfrey, Sarah. "As Aloe Blacc Gets Noticed with 'Lift Your Spirit,' He Stays True to His Roots." *Washington Post*. Washington Post, 10 Mar. 2014. Web. 16 Mar. 2015.

Lynskey, Dorian. "Aloe Blacc: The Man of the Moment." *Guardian*. Guardian News, 3 Apr. 2014. Web. 16 Mar. 2015.

Pareles, Jon, Jon Caramanica, and Nate Chinen. "Albums from Aloe Blacc, Sara Evans and Ambrose Akinmusire." *New York Times*. New York Times, 10 Mar. 2014. Web. 16 Mar. 2015.

Raz, Guy. "The Evolution of Aloe Blacc." *NPR. org*. NPR, 29 Oct. 2010. Web. 16 Mar. 2015.

## SELECTED WORKS

*Shine Through*, 2006; *Good Things*, 2010; *Lift Your Spirit*, 2014

—Christopher Mari

---

# Malorie Blackman

**Born:** February 8, 1962
**Occupation:** Children's author

"One of Malorie Blackman's strengths as a writer for young adults is her directness and conviction," reviewer Linda Buckley-Archer wrote for the *Guardian* (5 June 2013). "She takes big themes and gets stuck in. With *Pig-Heart Boy* it was transplants and animal rights; with *Boys Don't Cry* it was teenage fathers; most famously, with the Carnegie-shortlisted *Noughts & Crosses* series, it was racism." Blackman, who was named the Waterstones Children's Laureate in 2013, is indisputably among the most popular, prolific, and critically acclaimed writers of books for children and young adults in the entire United Kingdom. She has been widely praised for introducing much-needed diversity and mul-

ticulturalism into her field. She explained for the website of Booktrust (1 Nov. 2008), the nonprofit organization that manages the Children's Laureate program, "My initial reason for writing was to write the books I'd missed as a child: mysteries and thrillers and adventure stories, which just happened to feature black children and had absolutely nothing overtly to do with race."

The news that she had been chosen as laureate for 2013 to 2015 (a role that calls for her to undertake various initiatives to encourage a love of reading in Britain's young people) was met with extensive approval. "Malorie Blackman is a superb choice as the new Children's Laureate," Martin Chilton wrote for the *Telegraph* (4 June 2013). "She's passionate, funny, and will not mince her words when it comes to promoting reading and tackling anyone trying to hold back literacy and the simple enjoyment of books." He concluded, "It's a bold and interesting appointment—one that clearly thrills her—and by the end of 2015, I'm certain there will be thousands and thousands more children reading because of Malorie Blackman. She's a Laureate for the 21st century."

## EARLY YEARS

Oneta Malorie Blackman was born on February 8, 1962, in Clapham, London. Her father, a carpenter, and her mother, a seamstress, had immigrated to England two years before her birth from their native Barbados, leaving their older son and daughter with relatives. Her older siblings eventually joined the rest of the family in England, and in addition to them, Blackman has younger twin brothers. The sudden shift from being the only child in her family to being the middle one of five was made even more difficult by the fact that her older siblings could not easily decipher her British accent, making communication with them problematic.

While Blackman was growing up, few black people were depicted in popular culture, aside from criminals on police shows or servants on historical dramas; Blackman recalled to Chilton how her entire family would run to the television when Nichelle Nichols, the black actor who played Lieutenant Uhura on *Star Trek* was on screen, so happy were they to see a black person portrayed in a positive light. (She now owns a replica of the uniform Nichols wore on the show.)

Blackman, who studied the piano and saxophone as a youngster, had always enjoyed writing poems and short stories, and after her parents divorced when she was thirteen, she turned increasingly to those literary pursuits. "I coped by making up fantasies for myself. I'd walk along inventing scenarios and dialogues," she wrote in her author's profile for Penguin Books. "I wrote out all the pain, all the feelings I couldn't share, in secret poems."

## EDUCATION

Blackman loved reading and, although her father preferred his children to consume only nonfiction in the hopes that it would further their academic and career opportunities, she was soon reading anything she could get her hands on. (Despite borrowing thousands of books from the library, Blackman searched in vain for one featuring a person of color on the cover.)

Her parents' divorce was not the only trauma Blackman suffered during her formative years. She has told journalists that she was regularly on the receiving end of racist taunts from other children, and as a teenager she was once attacked by a group of white men in a movie theater and sexually assaulted.

Blackman intended to study English and drama at Goldsmiths College, part of the University of London. But when she informed her careers advisor of her longstanding goal to become an English teacher, the counselor refused to write her a reference, telling Blackman that black people did not become teachers and that she should aim instead for a clerical job.

Resignedly taking that advice—despite the deep anger she felt at the counselor—Blackman enrolled at Huddersfield Polytechnic (now the University of Huddersfield) in West Yorkshire, where she majored in business studies. Even that circumscribed path was cut short, however, when Blackman, then eighteen years old, had an emergency appendectomy and was forced to withdraw from school. Blackman convalesced at her parents' house and ultimately recovered. She subsequently decided to study computer science at Thames Polytechnic (now the University of Greenwich) and worked as a computer programmer at a succession of companies, including Reuters.

## BECOMING A WRITER

Blackman found a measure of success as a programmer, but she did not lose her love of literature and writing. She spent hours each evening after work penning short stories, despite a decided shortage of black role models. "In all the thousands and thousands of books I read as a child and a teenager, I didn't read a single story that featured a black child like me, not one. I didn't read a single book written by a black author, until *The Color Purple*," she said in a feature on BBC Radio 3 (23 Jan. 2014). "It was never suggested and it certainly never occurred to me that maybe, just maybe, I could be an author, until *The Color Purple*. Reading Alice Walker's book in my early twenties blasted open a door which I thought was locked and barred to me; actually, it blasted open a door which I didn't appreciate even existed."

Blackman sent her drafts to a string of editors and agents, only to meet with repeated rejection. Accumulating more than eighty rejection letters during those first years, she finally succeeded in publishing her first book, a collection of horror and science-fiction tales titled *Not So Stupid!* in 1990. She followed that in quick succession with a wide variety of other books for children and young adults, including the enormously popular novel *Hacker* (1992), about a young tech whiz who breaks into a bank's computer system in order to prove her father innocent of stealing; *Whizziwig* (1995), the first in a series of books about a boy who befriends a small, pink alien (and the basis for a well-received children's television show on CITV); *Thief!* (1996), a time-travel adventure; and *Pig Heart Boy* (1997), about a thirteen-year-old boy dying of heart disease who undergoes an experimental surgery. (In 1999 the BBC adapted the latter novel into a BAFTA Award–winning television series.)

Blackman was insistent that her books feature black people on their covers, even though she was told repeatedly that they would sell better with white characters depicted. She was equally insistent about writing in a variety of genres. Publishers, as she told Amanda Craig for the London *Times* (31 Jan. 2004), generally expected her to "write about race and nothing else. But I like to confound expectations." She continued, "A couple of editors did say, 'We want something for our multi-cultural list', and I'd think, Well, you're not getting one from me."

## *NOUGHTS AND CROSSES*

Blackman was sometimes criticized harshly early in her career for not writing about racism, but, as she told Alison Flood for the *Guardian* (10 Nov. 2008), "Even having black characters on covers when I first started was a bit of a political statement." She began considering tackling that theme in the wake of a 1998 public inquiry into the murder of Stephen Lawrence. Lawrence, a black eighteen-year-old, had been the victim of a racially motivated attack in 1993, and the subsequent police investigation, as a public inquiry later determined, was tainted by impropriety and institutionalized racism on the part of officers. "I started thinking," Blackman told Booktrust, "what if I turned it on its head so that white people were the minority and the status quo was working for black people in society?" (She has also explained to interviewers that she drew upon a childhood trip to Barbados, where she had been fascinated by the fact that, unlike in England, all the news anchors and bank tellers were black.)

In 2001 Blackman published *Noughts & Crosses*, the first of her books to deal overtly with matters of race. The book's protagonists are teenage lovers Sephy, a Cross, as the members of the dark-skinned ruling class are known, and Callum, a Nought or member of a white underclass of former slaves. After a new law allows Callum to attend a formerly segregated high school, the two hope their relationship can be brought out into the open, but they quickly discover that integration poses its own set of problems. (Some editions of the book feature the title spelled *Naughts and Crosses*, and it has also been released under the title *Black & White*.)

When the book was made available in the United States, a reviewer for *Publishers Weekly* (20 June 2005) wrote that Blackman's plot is "an amalgam of 20th-century race relations. The setting resembles England, but the author mixes in issues similar to American history (such as a school integration scenario reminiscent of Little Rock in 1957). The naughts' protest organization (the Liberation Militia), however, more closely resembles the Irish Republican Army than members of the nonviolent U.S. Civil Rights movement." Popular audiences have also wondered at the book's transcendence of its place. "I've had a number of letters from Ireland where people are saying 'you're talking about the Protestant/Catholic situation, aren't you?'" Blackman told Flood. Perhaps in part because she only uses color language sparingly in the novel, others have also inquired as to whether the subject of conflict was the Catalonian separatist movement in Spain or the issue of Palestinian statehood in the Middle East. "Obviously people get what is relevant to their own life from it," she remarked to Flood. "It's really interesting to me, because I kind of thought it was obvious I was doing the black and white thing."

*Noughts & Crosses* was adapted for the stage by the Royal Shakespeare Company in the winter of 2007 and 2008, and Blackman has also written a series of sequels, including *Knife Edge* (2004), *Checkmate* (2005), and *Double Cross* (2008), which follow the lives of Callum, Sephy, and their daughter, Callie.

## OTHER BOOKS

Although Blackman was widely celebrated for the Noughts and Crosses young-adult series and its thought-provoking themes, she did not stop writing books on a wide array of topics for a variety of age groups. Her Betsey Biggalow series for beginning readers, for example, follows the adventures of a spunky young girl with big ideas, and the Girl Wonder series, meant for slightly more proficient readers, features a similarly engaging child, Maxine, and her twin brothers.

Blackman's other young-adult novels include *Dead Gorgeous* (2002), in which a teen meets a mysterious stranger with a tragic past; *Jon for Short* (2013), a chilling tale about a boy with recurring nightmares; and *Noble Conflict* (2013), a futuristic story set in a world that has been largely destroyed by war. She has also written poetry—*Cloud Busting* (2004), an uplifting tale of friendship that won a Nestlé Smarties Silver Book Prize—and she is the compiler of *Unheard Voices*, a 2007 anthology of short stories, extracts, and nonfiction pieces about slavery.

## CHILDREN'S LAUREATE AND OTHER HONORS

In 2008 Blackman was named an officer of the Order of the British Empire (OBE) for her services to children's literature. In 2013 she was named as the Waterstones Children's Laureate, a post awarded every two years to "an eminent writer or illustrator of children's books to celebrate outstanding achievement in their field." She is the eighth laureate to be named since the program was inaugurated in 1999, joining such luminaries as Quentin Blake, Anne Fine, Anthony Browne, and Julia Donaldson. As laureate, she has focused on getting parents and teachers to spend at least ten minutes a day reading to children and on encouraging teens to read by promoting a varied range of books, including graphic novels.

Blackman has accrued more than fifteen awards to her name. In 2014, Blackman landed the number-one spot on the 2014 Powerful Media Powerlist, an annual list of the most influential people of African and African Caribbean heritage in the United Kingdom. (Others near the top of the list included businessman Ken Olisa, Olympic gold medalist Mo Farah, and actor Idris Elba.)

## PERSONAL LIFE

Blackman and her husband, Neil, a white man of Scottish descent, met while they were working at a software company. They have been married since the 1980s and live in Kent. She credits him with encouraging her to write, even as rejection letters filled their mailbox.

After suffering two miscarriages, Blackman gave birth to a daughter, Elizabeth, in 1995. Lizzie, as she is nicknamed, is now an avid fan of rock music, and she plays both the drums and guitar. When asked about her greatest achievement by Rosanna Greenstreet for the *Guardian* (6 Sept. 2013), Blackman replied, "Having a daughter who is not afraid to stand up for what she believes."

## SUGGESTED READING

Blackman, Malorie. "Q&A: Malorie Blackman." Interview by Rosanna Greenstreet. *Guardian*. Guardian News and Media, 6 Sept. 2013. Web. 3 Sept. 2014.

Chilton, Martin. "Malorie Blackman Is a Great Choice to Inspire Children." *Telegraph*. Telegraph Media Group, 4 June 2013. Web. 3 Sept. 2014.

Craig, Amanda. "Malorie Blackman: The World in Photographic Negative." *Times* [London] 31 Jan. 2004. Print.

Flood, Alison. "Malorie Blackman: Developing Negatives." *Guardian*. Guardian News and Media, 10 Nov. 2008. Web. 3 Sept. 2014.

Johnstone, Anne. "As a Teenager, the World Seemed to Be One Big White Plot. Now, 50 Children's Books Later, It's a Different Story." *Herald Scotland*. Herald and Times Group, 31 July 2004. Web. 3 Sept. 2014.

Robinson, David. "Under the Skin of Racism." *Scotsman*. Johnson, 3 Feb. 2001. Web. 3 Sept. 2014.

## SELECTED WORKS

*Not So Stupid!: Incredible Short Stories*, 1990; *Hacker*, 1992; *Whizziwig*, 1995; *Thief!*, 1996; *Pig Heart Boy*, 1997; *Noughts & Crosses*, 2001; *Knife Edge*, 2004; *Checkmate*, 2005; *Double Cross*, 2008; *Boys Don't Cry*, 2010; *Noble Conflict*, 2013

—Mari Rich

# Charles M. Blow
**Born:** August 11, 1970
**Occupation:** Journalist

Charles M. Blow is a *New York Times* opinion columnist, a position he has held since 2008. In his previous nine-year stint at the *Times*, Blow rose through the paper's graphics department, first as a graphics editor and eventually as the department's director. Under his leadership, the department won awards for its coverage of the September 11 terrorist attacks and the war in Iraq. He eventually became the paper's design director for news before joining *National Geographic* magazine as its art director in 2006.

On his return to the *New York Times*, Blow became the national daily's first visual op-ed columnist. His op-ed column is published twice a week, on Mondays and Thursdays; his blog, *By the Numbers*, appears on the paper's website. Asked by Matthew Kassel for the *New York Observer* (24 Sept. 2014) how he saw his position at the respected national daily, Blow answered: "I love it, because the [op-ed] columnists are a sort of orchestra—everyone should be hitting a different note. Trying to figure out the thing that makes you stand out can take years to find. Eventually I decided that being the Southern guy, from the small town, from no means, was, in fact, the thing that made my voice different." In addition to his work for the *Times*, Blow has

© Beowulf Sheehan/Corbis

appeared as a television commentator on CNN and MSNBC, and as a guest on *Real Time with Bill Maher*, *Piers Morgan Tonight*, and *Anderson Cooper 360°*.

In 2014 Blow published his memoir, *Fire Shut Up in My Bones*, in which he reveals the sexual abuse and bullying he suffered while growing up in a poor, African American family in Louisiana, its impact on him in college and beyond, and his struggle with his identity as a bisexual man. Ranked a best seller according to the *New York Times*, Amazon, and Barnes & Noble, the book has received acclaim, with critics praising it as honest, riveting, and moving.

## EARLY YEARS

Charles M. Blow, the youngest of five sons in an African American family, was born on August 11, 1970, in the still largely segregated town of Gibsland, Louisiana. Blow's father, Spinner, was, as Blow wrote in his memoir, "a construction worker by trade, a pool shark by habit, and a serial philanderer by compulsion." As a young woman, Blow's mother, Billie, worked as a secretary at a chicken-processing plant.

After his birth, Blow lived in Arkansas with his maternal grandmother, who was called Big Mama, and her fourth husband, Jed, while Billie recuperated from a long series of illnesses. At three he moved back to Gibsland to the "House with No Steps," as he called the rundown structure. (For years, Billie was forced to carry children and groceries all the way to the back of the house to enter, because of the lack of front steps.) As Spinner became an ever more unreliable and itinerant presence in the life of Blow and his brothers—Nathan, William, Robert, and James—Billie returned to college. When Blow, a quiet and introspective child, was five, his mother found work as a home economics teacher at a nearby high school.

When she left Spinner for good, Billie and her sons moved into a home owned by Blow's maternal great-grandfather. While the family had been far from wealthy before, Blow had never felt truly deprived until this latest move. Blow and his brothers spent Saturdays at the local dump, scavenging. "Being a child with nothing, it didn't take much to satisfy me," Blow wrote in his memoir. "The smallest trinkets sparked the wonder of great treasure. . . . They were ideas made real in faraway places by unknown hands, things that somehow made their way into mine, things that, when touched, connected me to another world."

Blow craved his brothers' attention and counted the hours they spent huddled around their old television watching the popular dance show *Soul Train* as fond memories. Still, as they grew, the older boys became busy with their own pursuits. Blow, already introspective, became lonely during this time.

When Blow was seven, a teenage cousin visited the family and sexually molested him one night. Blow has vividly described the incident in both his book and newspaper columns. The damage to his psyche was further compounded when a trusted uncle who lived with the family attempted a similar act. Blow, by then slightly older, fled the room, and the incident was never discussed. At eight years old, having become the target of neighborhood bullies and wondering if he had done something to invite the abuse, he briefly contemplated suicide. While Blow—depressed and neglecting his school work—was at one point mistakenly put in a class for slow learners, he was in reality a bright and artistically skilled child who loved to read and draw.

## EDUCATION

Blow blossomed in high school, becoming a star athlete and class officer. He set his sights on entering politics one day and poured over etiquette books in order to refine his behavior. The valedictorian of his graduating class, he thought of attending Louisiana State University until a recruiter from Grambling State University, the historically black public university located right near his home, convinced him to enroll. There, Blow was elected president of his freshman class and joined a fraternity, rising to lead the Greek organization not long after pledging. Though he later became disgusted by the hazing rituals and hypermasculine posturing and dropped out of the fraternity, he still counts some of his fraternity brothers among his closest friends.

Blow has written often about one defining moment in college: when he received a phone call from the cousin who had molested him. His rage triggered by the casual tone in the man's voice, he grabbed a gun and sped off, intending to commit murder. "Then I thought about who I was now, and who I could be," Blow wrote in a column for the *New York Times* (19 Sept. 2014). "Seeing him in a pool of his own blood might finally liberate me from my past, but it would also destroy my future. I had to make a choice: drive forward on the broad road toward the unspeakable or take the narrow highway exit."

Blow chose to forgo revenge rather than waste his own future.

## EARLY CAREER AS A GRAPHIC JOURNALIST

Blow edited the student newspaper and majored in mass communications, and while still in school he won an internship at the *Shreveport Times*, where he created charts, graphs, and maps to illustrate articles. Once, when the police would not let him inside of a home where a family had died because of a faulty heater, he cajoled a neighbor with the same model house to let him sketch her floor plan. He then went to a hardware store and sketched a heater similar to the faulty one, and his illustrations were featured on the paper's front page the next day.

Later in his college years, he arrived without an appointment at a job fair at which the *New York Times* had sponsored a booth, and he waited all day until an interviewer finally agreed to see him. Although the *Times* had no graphic internship, the interviewer was so impressed with both Blow's portfolio and tenacity that the paper created one specifically for him.

After graduating from Grambling with honors in 1991, Blow took a post doing graphics work for the *Detroit News*. "An illustration is a visual editorial—it's just as nuanced," he explained to Julia Lurie for *Mother Jones* (23 Sept. 2014). "Everything that goes into it is a call you make: every color, every line weight, every angle."

## *NEW YORK TIMES* AND *NATIONAL GEOGRAPHIC*

Blow joined the graphic-design staff of the *New York Times* in 1994 and quickly rose to lead the department. At twenty-five, he was youngest department head the paper had ever had. In that role, he helped the *Times* garner an award from the Society for News Design for its information-graphics coverage of the September 11 terrorist attacks. It was the first time the prestigious prize had been given for graphics coverage.

In 2006 Blow quit the *New York Times* to become the art director of *National Geographic* magazine. During his long commute from New York to *National Geographic*'s offices in Washington, DC, he wrote the vignettes that would become his memoir. He returned to the *Times* two years later, however, to accept a coveted post as an op-ed columnist. "[It was] great to circle back to a first love, of language and writing," he recalled to Lurie. "But it has been the most excruciating and

public on-the-job training exercise I could imagine. . . . The Internet is ruthless. And people are very, very happy to let you know when they don't like something."

Blow's op-eds cover a wide range of topics under the categories of politics, public opinion, and social justice, and they often focus on high-profile and contentious news events involving structural racism and homophobia. Such events have included the murder of Trayvon Martin; the unrest and protests in Ferguson, Missouri, and Baltimore, Maryland, over excessive force used by police against African Americans; and in 2015 the efforts of conservative politicians to pass so-called religious freedom legislation that critics, including Blow, say would allow businesses to discriminate against gay and lesbian couples and other individuals.

Blow also writes about how such issues and others have touched his own family. His oldest son is an undergraduate at Yale, and on January 26, 2015, the columnist wrote about an incident in which a policeman, believing the young black man to be a burglary suspect, pointed a gun at him and forced him to spread out on the ground. "I am reminded of what I have always known, but what some would choose to deny: that there is no way to work your way out—earn your way out—of this sort of crisis," said Blow. "In these moments, what you've done matters less than how you look. There is no amount of respectability that can bend a gun's barrel."

## *FIRE SHUT UP IN MY BONES*

In 2009 Blow decided that he would publish the story of his own sexual abuse and bullying after hearing reports of two eleven-year-old boys who hanged themselves in separate incidents ten days apart. The boys had been the targets of bullies, and Blow figured that writing about his own experiences might help. As he said in a 2014 interview with Terry Gross for NPR's *Fresh Air*, "I know that pain. I know what that feels like. I know what it feels like to not think that you have another option. And I thought, this can't happen on my watch—that if there's something that I can do . . . then I have to do it."

Blow's memoir was published in 2014 to praise from reviewers such as Alice Walker, Henry Louis Gates, and Anderson Cooper, among many others. A *New York Times* Best Seller in several categories, *Fire Shut Up in My Bones* was named to several best books lists, including the *New York Times* Sunday Book Review's 100 Notable Books of 2014, *New York*

*Times* Sunday Book Review Editors' Choice, Publishers Weekly's Best Books of 2014, and the National Book Foundation's Pride Month Reading List for 2015. The book also won the 2015 Lambda Literary Award for bisexual non-fiction and the PEN Literary Awards Longlist 2015 open book award.

## PERSONAL LIFE

Blow married his college sweetheart, Greta, right after graduation. The couple had three children together, a son and a pair of twins (one boy and one girl). They are now divorced, and the children live with Blow in the New York City borough of Brooklyn.

## SUGGESTED READING

Blow, Charles M. "After Childhood Abuse, *Times* Columnist Says He Chose Life over Vengeance." Interview by Terry Gross. *Fresh Air*. NPR, 24 Sept. 2014. Web. 16 July 2015.

Blow, Charles M. "Up from Pain." *New York Times*. New York Times, 19 Sept. 2014. Web. 16 July 2015.

Blow, Charles M. "Library Visit, Then Held at Gunpoint." *New York Times*. New York Times, 26 Jan. 2015. Web. 16 July 2015.

Kassel, Matthew. "*New York Times* Opinion Columnist Charles Blow Celebrates Himself in New Memoir." *New York Observer*. Observer Media, 24 Sept. 2014. Web. 16 July 2015.

Lurie, Julia. "Charles Blow on Masculinity, Trayvon Martin, and Reliving Childhood Trauma." *Mother Jones*. Mother Jones and the Foundation for Natl. Progress, 23 Sept. 2014. Web. 16 July 2015.

—Mari Rich

# Matthew Bomer

**Born:** October 11, 1977
**Occupation:** Actor

In recent years, Matt Bomer has frequently been ranked as one of Hollywood's up-and-coming leading men, due in large part to his chiseled good looks, piercing blue eyes, and boyish charm. Best known for his portrayal of the smooth-talking con man Neal Caffrey for six seasons on USA's hit series *White Collar* (2009–14), he has since been celebrated for his star-making supporting performance as Felix Turner, an AIDS-afflicted writer, in *The Normal Heart*, a 2014 HBO film adaptation of

Vagueonthehow/Wikimedia Commons

Larry Kramer's famed play. His serious acting turn has drawn comparisons to those previously made by Tom Hanks and Matthew McConaughey, other actors once known for lighter performances who went on to award-winning dramatic roles.

More than anything else, Bomer wants to take on the kinds of roles that will challenge him as an actor and enable him to go beyond what he expects of himself. "I don't care about the size of the roles, or how they're marketed or billed or anything like that," he told Howie Kahn for *Details* (1 May 2014). "I would love to be a part of stories that tell us about where we've come from, where we are, where we're going—with great directors."

## EARLY LIFE AND CAREER

Matthew Staton Bomer was born on October 11, 1977, in Webster Groves, Missouri. He and his brother, Neill, and sister, Megan, were raised in Spring, Texas, a suburb of Houston, by their parents, Elizabeth Macy "Sissi" (née Staton) and John O'Neill Bomer IV. His father had once been an offensive lineman for the Dallas Cowboys and later worked as a shipping executive. The children were raised in a household with strong moral values: PG-13 movies were off-limits, and family members were required to attend church several times a week.

Bomer first became interested in acting as a fourteen-year-old, after reading Larry Kramer's play The Normal Heart (1985), about the devastating impact HIV and AIDS had on young gay men living in and around New York City in the early

1980s, a time when little was known about the disease. "It completely rocked my world," he told Kahn. "It's just such an amazing call to arms." He would later make his acting debut in the Alley Theatre, a respected venue in Houston.

After graduating from Klein High School outside of Houston in 1996, Bomer studied drama at Carnegie Mellon University in Pittsburgh, Pennsylvania, where he earned his bachelor of fine arts degree in 2000. This experience, which included "working on all the best plays," proved very rewarding for Bomer, as he told Leslie Hoffman for WHIRL magazine (1 Jan. 2010). "To me," he explained, "the great thing about college was that I got to work on things that I knew I was probably going to be cast for in the real world but I also got to stretch myself out."

Convinced that he would find his career onstage, Bomer moved to New York City, hoping to make a name for himself on Broadway. Although he did work onstage, his first success came through a small part on the television soap opera *All My Children* in 2001; he subsequently played a recurring character, the murderous Ben Reade, on another soap opera, *Guiding Light*, from 2002 to 2003. He left New York for the West Coast later that year, hoping to start a film career in Hollywood.

For a moment, it seemed he would hit the big time immediately—he was almost cast in the role of Superman for the big-budget film *Superman Returns* (2006), but he lost the part to Brandon Routh when the long-simmering project switched directors. His first notable part in Hollywood was in the 2003–4 season of the television drama *Tru Calling*. Following this role, he found work on television series such as *North Shore* (2004), *Traveler* (2007) and *Chuck* (2007–9) and in films such as *Flightplan* (2005), *The Texas Chainsaw Massacre: The Beginning* (2006), *Amy Coyne* (2006), and *In Time* (2011).

### WHITE COLLAR

In 2009, Bomer's breakout moment came when he was cast in the USA network series *White Collar*, which brought him back to New York City. Bomer played Neal Caffrey, a bond forger who, in exchange for avoiding a prison sentence, uses his underhanded artistic and financial expertise to help the Federal Bureau of Investigation (FBI) catch other white-collar criminals. Caffrey works under the direct supervision of FBI agent Peter Burke (Tim DeKay), the only person who ever managed to catch him. From the beginning, part of the series' draw was the way in which the duo played off of one another. In his interview with Hoffman, Bomer described his approach to his character as "one part Danny Ocean from *Ocean's Eleven*, one part Cary Grant's character from *To Catch a Thief*, one part *Catch Me if You Can*, and one part Ferris Bueller."

Bomer's performance proved incredibly popular with viewers across demographics—a particularly notable achievement at a time when fragmented audience viewership has been at an all-time high. "There are guys men gravitate to and guys women gravitate to. Rarely do we get both sides of the audience gravitating equally," Bonnie Hammer, the television executive who approved *White Collar* for USA, told Kahn. "With Matt you get both. Everybody sees him as the perfect leading man. That's rare."

Bomer worked for six years on the series, which became one of the most popular shows on cable television before completing its run at the end of 2014. Some of *White Collar*'s success was due to good timing: premiering shortly after the financial crisis that triggered the Great Recession (which officially began in late 2007), the series also debuted against the backdrop of the Bernie Madoff financial scandal, in which the once-respected investor was sent to prison after it was discovered that his wealth-management firm had been involved in a vast Ponzi scheme that resulted in the largest accounting fraud in US history. But much of the show's success was also due to the talents of its lead actor, a sentiment with which series creator Jeff Eastin agrees. "Neal is someone you could easily hate, but I think Matt Bomer brings so much boyish charm to him that you end up liking the guy despite that," Eastin said in an interview with Kathryn Shattuck for the *New York Times* (16 Oct. 2009).

Also a gifted singer, Bomer showcased his voice during a duet with the legendary Diahann Carroll in the second season of *White Collar*. Additionally, as a tribute to composer Jerry Herman, he performed "It Only Takes a Moment" from the musical Hello, Dolly! along with Broadway actress Kelli O'Hara at the 2010 Kennedy Center Honors. He followed this with another musical turn on the popular television series Glee in 2012—the same year in which he starred alongside Channing Tatum and Matthew McConaughey in Magic Mike, a comedy-drama by acclaimed director Steven Soderbergh. One year later, he even got a second shot at the Superman gig, this time as the voice of the superhero in the animated film *Superman: Unbound*.

### THE NORMAL HEART

Bomer's most celebrated performance to date came as part of the ensemble cast for HBO's adaptation of *The Normal Heart*. Directed by Ryan Murphy, the film describes the efforts made by writer Ned Weeks (Mark Ruffalo) and doctor Emma Brookner (Julia Roberts) to get help from various levels of government to fight the emerging HIV/AIDS crisis. Bomer plays Felix Turner, Weeks's lover and a *New York Times* lifestyle reporter who himself is killed by the disease.

To portray Turner's debilitating condition, Bomer, who had loved the play since high school and had actively lobbied for a role in the film adaptation, lost at least thirty-five pounds over a three-month period. The transformation, combined with the very serious turn he took for the role, mesmerized critics. Reviewing the TV movie for the *Atlantic* (23 May 2014), Sophie Gilbert wrote, "The power of Bomer's performance is in how believable he makes Felix's attraction to the older, prickly, pathologically awkward Ned."

In addition to the rave reviews Bomer received from critics, he also found himself a favorite during awards season. In 2014, he won a Critics' Choice Television Award and was nominated for a Primetime Emmy Award for best supporting actor in a movie or miniseries for his role in *The Normal Heart*.

## PERSONAL LIFE

In 2012, Bomer revealed his sexual orientation during his acceptance speech at the Steve Chase Humanitarian Awards ceremony by publicly thanking his husband, publicist Simon Halls, and their three young sons, Henry, Walker, and Kit. The longtime couple had married in 2011. Bomer has since admitted in interviews that he was surprised by the public's reaction to the fact that he is gay, since it was more or less an open secret in Hollywood. "I frankly did not think people would be that interested. I certainly didn't think it was going to be on the CNN ticker," Bomer told Shana Naomi Krochmal for *Out* magazine (6 May 2014).

While Bomer is glad that his sexual orientation is now public knowledge, he does not want to be defined by his sexuality. "What we really have to do is stop the adjective before the job title—whether it's 'black actor,' a 'gay actor' or anything actor," he told Marc Malkin for *E! Online* (25 June 2012). "Everybody thinks that equality comes from identifying people, and that's not where equality comes from. Equality comes from treating everybody the same regardless of who they are. I hope the media and the press catches on to that, because it's time to move out of 1992."

## SUGGESTED READING

Gilbert, Sophie. "*The Normal Heart*: One of TV's Best Portrayals of Gay Romance, Ever." *Atlantic*. Atlantic Monthly, 23 May 2014. Web. 24 Nov. 2014.

Hoffman, Leslie. "Business Man, Matt Bomer." *WHIRL*. WHIRL, 1 Jan. 2010. Web. 24 Nov. 2014.

Kahn, Howie. "Matt Bomer Is More Than Just a Pretty Face." *Details*. Condé Nast, 1 May 2014. Web. 24 Nov. 2014.

Krochmal, Shana Naomi. "The Bomer Method." *Out*. Here Media, 6 May 2014. Web. 24 Nov. 2014.

Malkin, Marc. "*Magic Mike*'s Matt Bomer Talks about Being Out as Gay: What Brought Him to Tears?" *E! Online*. E! Entertainment Television, 25 June 2012. Web. 24 Nov. 2014.

Maresca, Rachel. "Matt Bomer: I Didn't Think People Would Be That Interested When I Came Out." *Daily News*. NYDailyNews.com, 6 May 2014. Web. 24 Nov. 2014.

## SELECTED WORKS

*Guiding Light*, 2002–3; *Tru Calling*, 2003–4; *Flightplan*, 2005; *The Texas Chainsaw Massacre: The Beginning*, 2006; *Chuck*, 2007–9; *White Collar*, 2009–14; *Magic Mike*, 2012; *The Normal Heart*, 2014; *Space Station 76*, 2014

—Christopher Mari

# Raphael Bousso

**Born:** ca. 1971–72
**Occupation:** Physicist

Dr. Raphael Bousso is a theoretical physicist and professor at the University of California, Berkeley (UC Berkeley) who works in the field of cosmology, the study of the structure and origin of the universe. "It has been said that it's been a golden age for cosmology in the last fifteen years or so, and it's true. I was very lucky with timing," he said in an interview for *Edge* (22 Nov. 2011). Bousso has made key contributions to cosmological research, and he is known as one of the scientists who discovered the landscape of string theory. String theory is a strong contender in the ongoing quest for a unified field theory, also known as a theory of everything, which would unite quantum mechanics and gravity as described by Albert Einstein's theory of general relativity. According to general relativity, gravity is warps and curves in the fabric of space-time. These warps and curves are created by mass and energy. Earth is so massive that it perceptibly warps the space-time around it, pulling the moon into its orbit. Bousso's other research interests involve the confounding nature of black holes. General relativity predicted the existence of black holes—regions of infinite mass that warp and twist the surrounding space-time to a breaking point. The force of gravity within a black hole is so strong that it consumes matter, energy, and even light. General relativity also described what it would be like to travel through a black hole, but this description presented a peculiar problem. In the center of a black hole, gravity is infinite and time ceases to exist; in other words, the existing understanding of the physical universe falls apart.

In 2002, Bousso laid the groundwork for something called the holographic principle, which suggests that the universe functions like a hologram, storing three-dimensional information (or in the case of the universe, multidimensional information) in a two-dimensional space. Bousso is also interested in the firewall paradox of black holes, an extension of Stephen Hawking's information paradox. The firewall paradox involves the question of what might happen to people if they were swallowed by a black hole. Would they be stretched like pasta and then crushed into a speck of dust by infinite gravity, or would they be incinerated by the radiation of something within the black hole called a firewall? This quandary has some serious implications regarding Einstein's description of gravity, and Bousso said in a video interview for the World Science Festival in 2013 that the firewall paradox "keeps [him] up at night."

## EARLY LIFE AND EDUCATION

Bousso was born in Israel and attended Cambridge University in the United Kingdom, graduating with his PhD in 1998. While at Cambridge Bousso was a student of the physicist Stephen Hawking, with whom he studied the quantum properties of black holes and published several papers. Black holes present scientists with a peculiar set of problems because they are so unlike any other known object. They cannot be dismissed as singularities in themselves because there are so many of them and they appear to play a very important role in the universe. Most black holes are the remnants of dead stars. The Milky Way has a supermassive black hole at its center, and scientists have found overwhelming evidence that suggests nearly every other large galaxy in the universe does as well; they are still trying to determine why this is the case.

Black hole physics is an exciting, if frustrating, realm of cosmological research because the answer could hold the key to a better understanding of our universe. For now, general relativity provides a theoretical glimpse inside of a black hole. A black hole is invisible, but its edge is known as an event horizon. When scientists refer to a black hole's event horizon, they are talking about a point of no return—the point after which there is no escaping the pull of gravity into the center of a black hole. Hawking's controversial views on this subject would come into play later in Bousso's career when he studied the firewall paradox.

## HOLOGRAPHIC PRINCIPLE

Bousso went to Stanford University in California for his postdoctorate, working with theoretical physicists Andrei Linde and Leonard Susskind. (The latter debated with Hawking for years over the nature of black holes.) At Stanford, Bousso was interested in string theory as it is applied to cosmology. He also studied something called the holographic principle. Every object is made up of a very specific arrangement of particles—this is its information content. The holographic principle, Bousso said in his interview for *Edge*, "deals with the question of how much information you need to describe a regional of space-time at the most fundamental level, and surprisingly the answer is not infinity. Even more surprisingly, the answer doesn't grow with the volume of the region." He continued his research at Stanford and later explained to *Edge*, "One of the topics that I worked on was trying to understand whether this idea of the holographic principle is really correct, whether it can be formulated in such a way that it makes sense in all imaginable space-time regions, in cosmology, inside black holes, and not just in some harmless place where gravity is not important. That turned out to be true, and so that was very exciting."

Applied to one of the many quandaries of black hole physics, the holographic principle says that an object's information is not lost inside of a black hole; rather it is preserved in an image along the hole's event horizon. In other words, an object's information is encoded on the surface of a black hole, much like a hologram in which a three-dimensional image is encoded in a two-dimensional space. In March 2002, Bousso shared first prize in the Young Researchers Competition in Physics. His paper dealt with quantum gravity and the holographic principle. Bousso is credited with discovering the "covariant entropy bound," which expressed the relationship between the geometry of space and time and its information content. This relationship is the basis of the holographic principle.

Bousso went on to complete a postdoctorate at the Kavli Institute for Theoretical Physics at UC Santa Barbara and a 2002–3 fellowship at Harvard University. He joined the faculty at UC Berkeley in 2004.

## STRING THEORY AND DARK ENERGY

Bousso is a string theorist. There are various branches of the theory—those branches together are called M-theory—but at its most basic level, the theory describes a universe made up of tiny vibrating strings. Those strings vibrate at different frequencies, and each frequency produces a different particle. The theory also postulates that the universe is made up of ten dimensions, nine dimensions of space and one dimension of time, with some dimensions curled up inside of other dimensions. This is almost impossible to imagine visually, but Brian Greene, a leading string theorist and author, described it this way in a 2008 TED talk: imagine looking out of a window at a cable suspended on a pole that holds a traffic light. From the window, the cable looks two-dimensional. Now imagine an ant crawling along that cable. From the ant's perspective, the cable is three-dimensional. Likewise, Greene suggests that those "invisible" dimensions described by string theory require a perspective beyond our current scope to be seen.

Bousso thinks that string theory is the best explanation for the abundance of dark energy in the universe. "We don't really know what this stuff is," he told J. R. Minkel for *Scientific American* (7 Apr. 2003), referring to the mysterious form of matter that makes up almost 70 percent of the universe. There is evidence that dark energy is the force that is accelerating the expansion of the universe. The question, Bousso said, is "whether that dark energy is really what we call a cosmological constant, in which case its density is fixed and will never change. Or if it is something that acts for a while like a cosmological constant, accelerating the universe, but eventually gets diluted."

Bousso has been praised for his ability to think about the universe as a whole entity, a point of view that requires a theory such as string theory to sustain. "What does the universe look like on the largest scales?" he asked in his interview for *Edge.* "How special is the part of the universe that we see? Are there other possibilities?"

In 2011 Bousso appeared in two episodes of the documentary series *Nova.* In "The Fabric of the Universe: What Is Space?" (2 Nov. 2011), he and other scientists described experiments being carried out to help them determine what space is. In "The Fabric of the Cosmos: Universe or Multiverse" (23 Nov. 2011), he and other physicists were interviewed about the cutting-edge theory that the universe is one of an infinite set of universes known as the multiverse.

## THE FIREWALL PARADOX

In addition to his interest in string theory, Bousso is particularly intrigued by the firewall paradox, an extension of the black hole information paradox described by Hawking. If an object is crushed into nothingness when it reaches the infinitely dense core of a black hole, what happens to its information? In the 1970s, Hawking suggested that the energy of the object remains but the information is destroyed. This presented a problem—the information paradox—because quantum physics dictates that information can never be destroyed. In theory, this means that if one could collect all of the information from an object that has been destroyed, one could reconstruct it from scratch. But if Hawking was right and information could be lost, it had a profound impact on the real world. Most meaningfully, there would be no such thing as cause and effect; the past would have no bearing on the future, rendering predictability and memory moot.

Efforts to understand what happens to the information that falls inside of a black hole yielded a paradox: calculations showed that if information were to flow *out* of a black hole, the event horizon would actually be replaced by a ring of energetic particles known as a firewall. Science writer Dennis Overbye, writing for the *New York Times* (12 Aug. 2013), explained, "The existence of a firewall would mean that the [event] horizon, which according to general relativity is just empty space, is a special place, pulling the rug out from under Einstein's principle, his theory of gravity, and modern cosmology, which is based on general relativity." He added, "This presented the scientists with what Dr. Bousso calls the 'menu from hell.' If the firewall argument was right, one of three ideas that lie at the heart and soul of modern physics, had to be wrong."

In 2014, Hawking made another radical proposal. He said that black holes do not have event horizons at all, thus changing the very nature of black holes. "The absence of event horizons means that there are no black holes, in the sense of regimes from which light can't escape," Hawking wrote in his January 22 paper, titled "Information Preservation and Weather Forecasting for Black Holes," which he posted online. Instead, he argued, they contain "apparent horizons," which, as Charles Q. Choi explained for *National Geographic* (27 Jan. 2014), "only temporarily entrap matter and energy that can eventually reemerge as radiation. This outgoing radiation possesses all the original information about what fell into the black hole, although in radically different form. As the outgoing information is scrambled, Hawking writes, there's no practical way to reconstruct anything that fell in based on what comes out. The scrambling occurs because the apparent horizon is chaotic in nature, kind of like weather on Earth." Hawking's theory has yet to be peer-reviewed and is already drawing scrutiny from other physicists, including Bousso. For his part, Bousso told Adrianne Jeffries for the online magazine the *Verge* (25 Jan. 2014), "The idea that there are no points from which you cannot escape a black hole is in some ways an even more radical and problematic suggestion than the existence of firewalls."

### CONFERENCES

In January 2014, Bousso took part in a humorous reverse debate about the correct theory of quantum gravity with Carlo Rovelli at the Foundational Questions Institute conference, "The Physics of Information," in Puerto Rico. In the debate, the two physicists argued against the theories they support, with Bousso arguing against string theory and Rovelli attacking loop quantum gravity. Bousso is also a member of the international advisory committee for Strings 2014, a conference held at Princeton University and the Institute for Advanced Study, both in Princeton, New Jersey, in June of 2014.

### SUGGESTED READING

Bousso, Raphael. "Thinking about the Universe on the Larger Scales." *Edge*. Edge Foundation, 22 Nov. 2011. Web. 9 Feb. 2014.

Choi, Charles Q. "No Black Holes Exist, Says Stephen Hawking—At Least Not Like We Think." *National Geographic*. National Geographic Society, 27 Jan. 2014. Web. 9 Feb. 2014.

Jeffries, Adrianne. "Black Holes Should Be Redefined, Says Stephen Hawking in New Paper." *Verge*. Vox Media, 25 Jan. 2014. Web. 9 Feb. 2014.

Minkel, J. R. "Strung Out on the Universe." *Scientific American*. Scientific American, 7 Apr. 2003. Web. 9 Feb. 2014.

Overbye, Dennis. "A Black Hole Mystery Wrapped in a Firewall Paradox." *New York Times*. New York Times, 12 Aug. 2013. Web. 9 Feb. 2014.

—Molly Hagan

# John Boyega

**Born:** March 17, 1992
**Occupation:** Actor

"Acting careers don't come out fully formed," British actor John Boyega told Keith Watson for *Metro.co.uk* (20 Dec. 2013). In the case of Boyega's career, however, one might be excused for thinking that it had. The young actor first received international attention in 2011, following the premiere of the science-fiction film *Attack the Block*, in which he plays a character named Moses. The feature-length debut of British director Joe Cornish, the film follows a group of teenagers, led by Moses, from a low-income London neighborhood who are forced to protect themselves and their home from an alien invasion. Critics praised Boyega's performance, and over the next several years he found further work in films such as *Half of a Yellow Sun* (2013) and the television miniseries *24: Live Another Day* (2014).

It was a 2014 casting announcement, however, that transformed Boyega from an up-and-coming indie star into a well-known name among film buffs, science-fiction fans, and the general public alike. On April 29 of that year, the world learned that Boyega had been cast in *Star Wars: The Force Awakens*, the seventh episode in the iconic science-fiction series that began in 1977. Scheduled for release in December 2015, the film will follow a new generation of heroes and villains and also feature appearances by beloved classic characters such as Luke Skywalker and Han Solo. For Boyega, a Star Wars fan since childhood, the opportunity to join the franchise's rich universe was an incredibly exciting one. "I think the most surreal moment for me is when they walked out with a black box and open[ed] it up and handed me a lightsaber," he told Haleigh Foutch for *Collider* (16 Aug. 2015). "For me that was when I was like, 'Okay, I'm in a Star Wars movie and I have a lightsaber in my hand.'"

Gage Skidmore (CC BY 3.0)

## EARLY LIFE AND EDUCATION

John Boyega was born on March 17, 1992, in London, England, to Nigerian-born parents. His father, Samson, was a Pentecostal minister, while his mother, Abigail, worked with individuals with disabilities. Boyega and his two older sisters, Grace and Blessing, grew up in low-income housing in the district of Peckham, in southeastern London. Boyega has noted that although many journalists and individuals from other areas of London perceive his childhood neighborhood as a dangerous, violent area, that perception does not accurately reflect his experience. "A lot of people that look at you from the outside feel as if, 'Oh my gosh, how do you do it?'" he told Dave Itzkoff for the *New York Times* (22 July 2011) of the response to growing up in Peckham. "And it's like, 'How do *you* do it?'" In response to an April 2015 article in the *Telegraph* that focused on the gang activity that allegedly plagued the neighborhood when the actor was growing up, Boyega wrote on the social-networking site Twitter (24 Apr. 2015), "Inaccurate. Stereotypical. NOT my story."

As a child, Boyega developed an interest in acting that was encouraged by his parents, both of whom were film enthusiasts. His first experience with acting came in primary school, when he and his classmates were tasked with reenacting African folktales about the spider Anansi. "I went on all fours and I was playing this leopard, and I gave him character breakdown, and I was

doing the work and doing the research and creating a character," Boyega told *Interview* magazine (29 July 2011). "That is the greatest feeling ever. When you're young and you're like, 'Oh, this is quite cool, and I really, really want to do this.'" He soon began to take courses and appear in productions at Theatre Peckham, a performing arts program for children and young adults in south London.

Boyega went on to attend South Thames College and also studied at the Identity School of Acting, a part-time theater school for teens and adults. After graduating from secondary school, he enrolled in the University of Greenwich but ultimately left to focus on his acting career. Building upon his theatrical training, he initially found work on the stage, performing in productions at notable venues such as the National Theatre and the Tricycle Theatre.

## ATTACK THE BLOCK

In 2011 Boyega made his film debut in the science-fiction film *Attack the Block*. Although he was initially skeptical about the film, which he had learned about online, the script won him over, and he ultimately became one of nearly 1,500 young actors considered for its cast. Directed by Joe Cornish, the film is about a group of teenagers from a low-income London neighborhood who over the course of one night go from muggers to heroes as they defend their housing development from an alien invasion. Boyega plays Moses, the taciturn and resourceful leader of the group, and performed many of his own stunts in the film's action sequences.

To prepare for the role, Boyega consulted with individuals whose life experiences paralleled Moses's more closely than his own. "I've lived in south London all my life but I think there's a difference between living there and being part of some of what goes on there . . . things I'm not involved in," he explained to Rob Carnevale for *IndieLondon* (2011). "So, that enlightened me and opened my eyes so that I could understand him." The film was received well by many critics and gained a cult following among fans of science-fiction and horror films. A fan of comics, Boyega especially enjoyed having the opportunity to promote the film at Comic-Con International: San Diego, where he and the filmmakers held a screening and question-and-answer session.

After gaining notice for his role in *Attack the Block*, Boyega found further work in film and television, appearing in television programs such as *Law and Order: UK* and *24: Live Another Day*, the television films *My Murder* (2012) and *The Whale* (2013), and the historical film *Half of a Yellow Sun* (2013). He also appeared in the HBO pilot *Da Brick* (2011), directed by veteran filmmaker Spike Lee; however, the pilot was not picked up. Hoping to avoid being typecast, particularly after the success of *Attack the Block*, Boyega was determined to take on a diverse array of roles. "My biggest challenge is to not do urban movies for the rest of my life," he explained to Watson. By 2014, however, it seemed clear that Boyega would no longer have to worry about being typecast as "alpha hoodies," as he described the characters to Watson. Instead, his career trajectory took a sudden and exciting turn when he was cast in *Star Wars: The Force Awakens*.

## STAR WARS

For decades, fans of the Star Wars franchise speculated that filmmaker George Lucas, the creator of the series, would release both prequel and sequel films to the original Star Wars trilogy. Released between 1977 and 1983, the original three films were referred to as episodes four, five, and six in 1981, implying that the story had begun in medias res, and Lucas himself confirmed that he planned to continue the story through sequels one day. A trilogy of prequel films was released between 1999 and 2005, but sequel films seemed unlikely to materialize.

In late 2012, however, the Walt Disney Company acquired the production company Lucasfilm, which held the rights to the franchise, and announced its plans to produce a new trilogy of Star Wars films set after the original trilogy. The first such film, *Star Wars: The Force Awakens*, was scheduled for release in December 2015, and director J. J. Abrams was brought in to helm the project. In April 2014, the filmmakers announced that they had cast Boyega in one of the film's lead roles, alongside fellow British newcomer Daisy Ridley and American actor Oscar Isaac. The film would also feature appearances by Mark Hamill, Carrie Fisher, and Harrison Ford, among other actors from the original trilogy.

### THE FORCE AWAKENS

Boyega avoided telling his parents about his new role until the official announcement in an attempt to avoid jinxing it. Following the casting announcement, however, both the Boyega family and the world at large knew that the young actor had obtained a starring role in one of the most anticipated films of 2015, if not the decade. A fan of the Star Wars films since childhood, Boyega noted that his own excitement was dual in nature, posting on the photo-sharing social network Instagram (30 Nov. 2014), "Isn't it crazy that *Star Wars* is actually happening? I'm in the movie but as a Star Wars fan I am very excited!" While many Star Wars fans were supportive of Boyega's casting, a small minority responded negatively because of his race, particularly after the release of a teaser trailer in which Boyega's character appears wearing the franchise's iconic stormtrooper armor; some objected to the concept of a black stormtrooper, while others deemed Boyega's casting the result of political correctness run amok. Boyega, however, was not disheartened by such responses, instead commenting on Instagram (30 Nov. 2014), "To whom it may concern. . . . Get used to it."

Little is known about Boyega's character, Finn, and the role he plays in *The Force Awakens*, which is set three decades after 1983's *Return of the Jedi*. However, early promotional material provides some tantalizing hints: in trailers, Finn is seen wearing stormtrooper armor and at another point fleeing an explosion with Ridley's Rey, while a limited-edition poster for the film depicts the character armed with a lightsaber, the traditional weapon of the Jedi. Boyega himself has largely remained tight lipped regarding his role but has shared a select few details about Finn's story arc with Star Wars fans. "He's in incredible danger," he explained on a panel at the April 2015 Star Wars Celebration convention in Anaheim, California, "And the way in which he decides to react to this danger changes his life . . . and launches him into the Star Wars universe in a very unique way."

### SUGGESTED READING

"The Attack of John Boyega." *Interview*. Interview, 29 July 2011. Web. 31 Aug. 2015.

Boyega, John. "'Attack the Block'—John Boyega Interview." *IndieLondon*. IndieLondon. co.uk, 2011. Web. 31 Aug. 2015.

Boyega, John. "John Boyega: The Slave Movies That Are Coming Out Are Great but We Need to Be Doing Other Things as Well." Interview by Keith Watson. *Metro.co.uk*. Metro.co.uk, 20 Dec. 2013. Web. 31 Aug. 2015.

Breznican, Anthony. "'Star Wars: The Force Awakens': Forget the Clones . . . Meet John Boyega, the One-of-a-Kind Stormtrooper."

*Entertainment Weekly*. Entertainment Weekly, 26 Apr. 2015. Web. 31 Aug. 2015.

Foutch, Haleigh. "'Star Wars': Oscar Isaac and John Boyega Share Their Favorite On-Set Memories." *Collider*. Complex Media, 16 Aug. 2015. Web. 31 Aug. 2015.

Gonzalez, Robbie. "John Boyega Responds to 'Black Stormtrooper' Criticisms." *Io9*. Gawker Media, 30 Nov. 2014. Web. 31 Aug. 2015.

Itzkoff, Dave. "Keeping It Real with Aliens in the 'Hood." *New York Times*. New York Times, 22 July 2011. Web. 31 Aug. 2015.

## SELECTED WORKS

*Attack the Block*, 2011; *Junkhearts*, 2011; *My Murder*, 2012; *Half of a Yellow Sun*, 2013; *The Whale*, 2013; *Imperial Dreams*, 2014; *24: Live Another Day*, 2014; *Major Lazer*, 2015; *Star Wars: The Force Awakens*, 2015

—Joy Crelin

# Rosalind Brewer

**Born:** 1962

**Occupation:** President and CEO of Sam's Club

Rosalind Gates Brewer became the president and CEO of Sam's Club, a subsidiary of Walmart Stores, in February 2012. The first African American and the first woman to lead a division of a Wal-Mart, she had previously spent more than two decades of her career at the Kimberly-Clark Corporation.

## EARLY LIFE AND EDUCATION

Rosalind Gates Brewer was born Rosalind Gates in 1962, the same year that Wal-Mart founder Sam Walton opened the first Walmart store. She grew up in Detroit, Michigan, the youngest of five children of George and Sally Gates. Brewer enjoyed studying math and science, and with the encouragement of her parents, she initially planned to become a physician. However, she soon realized that a medical career was not for her due to her squeamishness.

Brewer and her siblings were the first generation of their family to attend college. Brewer attended Spelman College in Atlanta, Georgia, the country's oldest historically black college for women, where she was active in student government. She earned her bachelor of science degree in chemistry in 1984. Brewer later attended a program in advanced management at the Wharton School of the University of Pennsylvania and graduated from the Directors' Consortium, a professional program for corporate board members that features instruction from faculty at Stanford Law School and the University of Chicago Booth School of Business.

## KIMBERLY-CLARK CORPORATION

After graduating from Spelman, Brewer began her career as an organic chemist in the Kimberly-Clark Corporation's product development office near Atlanta. Founded in 1872 as Kimberly, Clark and Company, the company produces a wide variety of consumer products, specializing in personal-care products and managing such brands as Scott, Huggies, Kotex, Depend, and Kleenex, as well as creating products for the medical and professional sectors.

Although her work in research and development allowed her to make use of her degree in chemistry, Brewer found herself becoming more interested in the business side of the company's operations, and she soon transitioned to a new position. Over the course of her twenty-two years with the company, Brewer worked in a variety of positions in such areas as marketing and sales. As vice president of the company's nonwoven fabrics business, she succeeded in increasing her division's sales by more than 30 percent. In 2004, she became president of Kimberly-Clark's global nonwovens sector, in which capacity she was responsible for overseeing the manufacturing and development of various consumer products.

## WALMART STORES

Feeling that she had achieved as much professional growth as she could at the Kimberly-Clark Corporation, Brewer decided to make a major career transition. In 2006, she joined Walmart Stores as the regional vice president, overseeing operations in the state of Georgia, a role she held until being promoted to president of the company's southeast division. She was later appointed president of Wal-Mart East, overseeing more than fifteen hundred stores throughout the eastern United States and Puerto Rico.

In January 2012, Wal-Mart announced that Brian Cornell, the chief executive officer (CEO) and president of the company's Sam's Club chain of warehouse stores, was stepping down from his position. Brewer succeeded Cornell as Sam's Club president and CEO on February 1, 2012. She was the first woman and the first African American to serve as the CEO of a Wal-Mart company.

Sam's Club presented Brewer with a unique set of challenges. Unlike the company's main Walmart stores, Sam's Club stores are open only to members and primarily sell products in bulk to consumers and small businesses. As CEO, Brewer sought to increase sales and grow the company with the ultimate goal of doubling Sam's Club's revenue. To do so, she oversaw the opening of new stores throughout the United States and the introduction of new merchandise. She also worked to improve the company's e-commerce offerings and to foster a productive relationship between Sam's Club and American microbusinesses, which are small businesses with fewer than five employees, nearly half of which are owned and operated by women. In May 2014, Brewer announced that Sam's Club was awarding $2.5 million in grants to nonprofit organizations that provide educational and financial assistance to female entrepreneurs and small-business owners.

In addition to her work with Sam's Club, Brewer began serving as the chair of Spelman College's board of trustees in mid-2011. She also served on the board of directors of the technology company Lockheed Martin, the board of councilors of the Carter Center, and the board of trustees for Atlanta's Westminster Schools.

## IMPACT

In her role as president and CEO of Sam's Club, Brewer has been credited with fostering significant growth and encouraging innovation within the company. She has been honored as one of the most powerful women in business by *Forbes*, *Fortune*, *Working Mother*, and *Black Enterprise*, among other publications. In recognition of her work, Brewer was awarded the Legacy of Leadership Award at the Spelman College Women of Color Conference.

## PERSONAL LIFE

Brewer and her husband, John Brewer, have a son and a daughter. They moved to Arkansas, the home of Sam's Club's corporate headquarters, following her appointment as chief executive officer.

## SUGGESTED READING

Alderman, Mille. "From Chemist to CEO, Rosalind Brewer Knows a Thing or Two about Hard Work." *AY*. AY Magazine, Sept. 2012. Web. 23 July 2014.

Bahn, Chris. "Rosalind Brewer: Rising Star in Wal-Mart." *Arkansas Business*. Arkansas Business, 25 Feb. 2013. Web. 23 July 2014.

Brewer, Rosalind. "New Board Chair Rosalind Brewer, C'84, Shares Her Vision." Interview by Lorraine Robertson. *Inside Spelman*. Spelman Coll., 1 Sept. 2011. Web. 23 July 2014.

Brown, Carolyn M. "Rosalind Brewer Makes History as Sam's Club CEO." *Black Enterprise*. Black Enterprise, 23 Jan. 2012. Web. 25 June 2014.

"Rosalind Brewer, Named First Woman, African-American, CEO of Sam's Club." *Huffington Post*. The HuffingtonPost.com, 20 Jan. 2012. Web. 23 July 2014.

—Leland Spencer

# Dustin Brown

**Born:** November 4, 1984
**Occupation:** Professional hockey player

The Los Angeles Kings' captain and right winger Dustin Brown "is a clenched fist on the ice," Michael Farber wrote for *Sports Illustrated* (30 Apr. 2012). "He is not so much a star as a cornerstone, a straight-ahead player who can score off either wing, kill penalties, and hit harder than the news of a tax audit, all while showing remarkable durability given his abrasive style." A native of Ithaca, New York, Brown is particularly known for his ultra-physical style of play, which has consistently ranked him among the league leaders in hits since his debut with the Kings in the 2003–4 season as an eighteen-year-old. Rounding out his physicality is a superb offensive game that has helped transform the Kings from one of the worst teams in the National Hockey League (NHL) to an elite title contender. Brown, the youngest captain in Kings history, recorded five consecutive fifty-plus-point seasons from 2007–8 to 2011–12 and keyed improbable playoff runs by the Kings in 2012 and 2014 en route to the team's first two Stanley Cup titles. He is only the second American-born team captain to win the Stanley Cup.

Nicole/Wikimedia Commons

## A HOCKEY PRODIGY

Dustin James Brown was born on November 4, 1984, in Ithaca, a town in central New York. He is the youngest of the five children of Bryan and Sharan Brown. He has three sisters, Seanna, Staci, and Macaila, and a brother, Brandon. Growing up in hockey-obsessed Ithaca, Brown developed a passion for the sport early on. He learned how to skate at the age of three and, shortly thereafter, began playing competitive hockey in the Ithaca Youth Hockey Association. "I loved the game right away," Brown wrote in an article for the Kings' website (8 June 2011). "I couldn't wait to get on the ice whether it was a five o'clock practice in the morning or going to skate and shoot after school." Brown's parents fostered his early development as a hockey player, shuttling him to early-morning practices and games. As Brown got older he excelled in other sports as well before focusing on hockey.

By all accounts, Brown's hockey skills were apparent from the time he first stepped on the ice. Always the best player on his team growing up, he was initially made a defenseman because coaches wanted to give him the most amount of ice time. At the peewee league level (ages eleven and twelve), however, he began to play forward, which better complemented his speed and soft hands. It was during this time that Brown began honing the rugged, physical style of play he would become known for.

By the time Brown reached the bantam level (ages thirteen and fourteen), his shooting and puck-handling abilities were "light years ahead of the kids around him," as his bantam coach, Russ Johnson, noted to Tom Fleischman for the *Ithaca Journal* (31 Jan. 2014). "He could already stick handle and pass and shoot better than kids who were four or five years older than him." Brown's talent was such that he made Ithaca High School's varsity hockey squad as an eighth grader, but he played only two seasons before leaving school to pursue a professional hockey career. Brown first earned a spot on the Syracuse Stars travel team before joining the Guelph Storm, a major junior team in the Ontario Hockey League (OHL). After he was chosen in the OHL draft, Brown made the difficult decision to relinquish his eligibility to play for a college, reasoning that going directly to minor league hockey was a faster path to the NHL.

## EARLY NHL CAREER

Brown spent three seasons with the Storm, during which time he amassed ninety-seven goals and was named the OHL Scholastic Player of the Year for three consecutive years. Brown's performance in the OHL prompted the Kings to select him with the thirteenth overall pick in the first round of the 2003 NHL Entry Draft. By then he had established a reputation as "a grinder with a goal-scorer's touch," as Greg Wyshynski wrote for *Yahoo! Sports* (9 June 2014). Brown earned a spot on the Kings' roster after his first training camp and made his NHL debut that same season. Ankle injuries, however, limited him to only thirty-one games during his rookie year, in which he recorded one goal and four assists.

When the entire 2004–5 NHL season was canceled due to a labor dispute, Brown was assigned to the Kings' American Hockey League (AHL) affiliate, the Manchester Monarchs, in order to continue to develop his overall game. After tallying an impressive seventy-four points in seventy-nine AHL games, Brown returned to the Kings for the 2005–6 season. While his offensive play remained a work in progress, he emerged as one of the Kings' most physical players. "In my first [full] year, I wasn't looked upon as an offensive guy," Brown explained to Jim Stevens for *USA Hockey Magazine* (June 2008). "I needed to find a way to stay with the Kings, so playing physical helped fill the void."

## BECOMING A TOP PLAYER

Pairing up with the Kings' center Anze Kopitar during the 2006–7 season, Brown began to blossom offensively and scored seventeen goals and twenty-nine assists in eighty-one games. Meanwhile, he continued his aggressive play with 258 hits, more than twice the amount of any player on his team. Yet at the same time he faced significant challenges, reportedly including bullying by teammates.

Brown's struggles faded in the 2007–8 season as he "emerged as one of the top young players in the game," according to Stevens. He recorded career highs in goals (33), points (60), and hits (311), the latter of which led the NHL. His efforts were recognized as he was signed to a six-year contract extension. Though the Kings finished that year with the worst record in the NHL, there was optimism about the future. The team hired a new general manager, Dean Lombardi, and new head coach, Terry Murray, while committing to its talented young skaters. Brown became a symbol of the franchise's renewal when he was named the fifteenth team captain in Kings history. At twenty-three, he was the youngest captain ever on the team.

Brown rewarded the Kings' faith by putting up his second consecutive fifty-plus-point season in 2008–9, recording twenty-four goals and twenty-nine assists and earning his first career NHL All-Star selection. Despite missing the playoffs once again, the Kings showed significant improvement while playing with the youngest team in the NHL. Then, in the 2009–10 season, Brown helped the Kings secure their first playoff berth since the 2001–2 season.

## OLYMPICS AND THE STANLEY CUP

Brown made the US hockey team for the 2010 Winter Olympics in Vancouver, British Columbia, having previously played with the national team in world championship tournaments. The team performed well only to lose to Canada in the gold-medal game, earning the silver medal. Brown then returned to the Kings, who had high expectations for the 2011–12 season after first-round playoff defeats the previous two seasons.

The Kings got off to a rocky start, however, stumbling to a mediocre record and firing coach Terry Murray partway through the season. Murray's replacement, Darryl Sutter, planned to jumpstart the Kings' faltering offense with an aggressive brand of hockey that complemented Brown, who had been slumping along with the team and was the subject of trade rumors. Under Sutter's guidance, Brown helped lead the Kings to a remarkable second-half turnaround as he played in all eighty-two games for the third straight year, recorded fifty-plus points for the fifth consecutive season, and ranked second in the NHL in hits (239). "I knew I had to be better, and that went hand-in-hand with our team. . . . We put ourselves in a tough position entering the stretch, and guys responded," he explained to Pierre LeBrun for *ESPN* (4 June 2012). The team managed to secure the eighth seed in the Western Conference playoffs.

The Kings not only retained their momentum but enjoyed one of the most dominant postseason runs in history. After successively defeating the Vancouver Canucks, the St. Louis Blues, and the Phoenix Coyotes, the Kings faced the New Jersey Devils in the Stanley Cup Final. The Kings won the series in six games to earn the franchise's first Stanley Cup title and become the first eighth-seeded team ever to win hockey's top competition. Brown served as the catalyst for the team's success during the playoffs, in which he led all players in goals, assists, and points. He became only the second American to captain a team to the Stanley Cup.

## SECOND STANLEY CUP TITLE

The 2012–13 NHL season was shortened to forty-eight games due to another labor dispute, and Brown scored eighteen goals and eleven assists in forty-six games. The Kings advanced to the Western Conference finals for the second straight season but failed to defend their title, losing to the eventual Stanley Cup champion team, the Chicago Blackhawks, in five games.

In July 2013 Brown solidified his long-term future with the Kings after negotiating an eight-year contract extension with the team worth $47 million. Dogged by a nagging hamstring injury, his offensive output dropped considerably during the 2013–14 season, in which he played seventy-nine games but only scored fifteen goals and twelve assists. He also again played for the US Olympic team in Sochi, Russia, during the 2014 Winter Olympics and served as an alternate captain, though the team placed fourth and did not win a medal.

Brown's lackluster regular-season performance notwithstanding, the Kings earned their fifth consecutive playoff appearance in 2014. "Every player has gone through ups and downs," Brown told Lisa Dillman for the *Los Angeles Times* (21 Sept. 2014), "But it's about finding a way to get through it." The captain bounced back to play a pivotal role in the post-season, which saw the team put together another improbable championship run. The Kings won three dramatic game-seven playoff series before defeating the New York Rangers in the Stanley Cup Final to capture their second championship in three years.

Brown entered the 2014–15 season as the Kings' longest-tenured player. In contrast to the fiery motivational antics of many NHL captains, he has adopted a quiet, lead-by-example approach on and off the ice, earning him the respect and admiration of his teammates. "He's not the most talkative guy or loudest guy in the room," Kings defenseman Drew Doughty told Wyshynski. "He leads on the ice, always. He cares."

Brown married his high school sweetheart, Nicole Poole, in 2007, and the couple has three sons, Jake, Mason, and Cooper, and a daughter, Mackenzie. Brown is known for his family-oriented lifestyle and dedication to charitable work, and he was awarded the NHL Foundation Award in 2011 for his contributions to the community.

## SUGGESTED READING

Brown, Dustin. "My Story: Dustin Brown." *LAKings.com.* Los Angeles Kings Hockey Club, National Hockey League, 8 June 2011. Web. 24 Nov. 2014.

Dillman, Lisa. "Kings Captain Dustin Brown Is Better Than a Year Ago." *Los Angeles Times.* Los Angeles Times, 21 Sept. 2014. Web. 24 Nov. 2014.

Farber, Michael. "The Face of the Playoffs." *Sports Illustrated.* Time, 30 Apr. 2012. Web. 24 Nov. 2014.

LeBrun, Pierre. "Dustin Brown Turns It Around." *ESPN.* ESPN Internet Ventures, 4 June 2012. Web. 24 Nov. 2014.

Stevens, Jim. "Speak Softly, but Deliver a Big Hit." *USA Hockey Magazine.* USA Hockey Magazine, June 2008. Web. 24 Nov. 2014.

Wyshynski, Greg. "Dustin Brown Endures as One of the NHL's Most Criticized Captains." *Yahoo! Sports.* NBC Sports Network, 9 June 2014. Web. 24 Nov. 2014.

—Chris Cullen

# Carrie Brownstein
**Born:** September 27, 1974
**Occupation:** Musician, actor, and writer

Carrie Brownstein is best known as the co-founder of both the feminist punk-rock band Sleater-Kinney and the sketch-comedy show *Portlandia.* The show, which Brownstein co-writes and costars in along with former *Saturday Night Live* cast member Fred Armisen, premiered on the Independent Film Channel (IFC) in 2011 and quickly became a cult and critical favorite. Brownstein and Armisen met in 2003 at a *Saturday Night Live* after-party and have been close friends ever since.

At the time the two met, Brownstein was still in Sleater-Kinney, which she had formed along with bandmate Corin Tucker in 1994. After the band went on hiatus in the summer of 2006, Brownstein worked for six months at an advertising firm before leaving to pursue various writing projects, including a music blog for National Public Radio (NPR) and a handful of video-game reviews for the online magazine *Slate.* During this time, she and Armisen collaborated on a series of Portland-centric sketch-comedy videos that they posted online under the name Thunder-Ant. These videos were an early version of what eventually became *Portlandia,* which has earned Brownstein, along with Armisen and their fellow cowriters, three consecutive Emmy Award nominations for outstanding writing for a variety series (2012–14).

## AMERICAN PASTORAL

Carrie Rachel Brownstein was born on September 27, 1974, in Seattle, Washington. She and her younger sister, Stacey, grew up in the nearby suburban town of Redmond, now known as the headquarters of Microsoft but still fairly rural at the time. As a child, Brownstein played soccer and tennis and spent much of her free time riding her bicycle. She was fascinated by acting and drama, and she and her friends, and sometimes her sister, often performed pageants and plays for their parents.

When Brownstein was fourteen years old, her parents divorced, and she and her sister were primarily raised by their father, a corporate lawyer. Brownstein bought her first guitar around this time, a red Epiphone, with money she had earned from babysitting and working at a movie

theater. She began listening to bands such as the Jam, the Clash, and the Ramones and took a few lessons in basic guitar from a neighbor. She was an average student at Lake Washington High School, where she hung out with classmates who shared her interest in punk rock and its antiauthoritarian attitude.

For her senior year, Brownstein transferred to the Overlake School, an elite private school in Redmond. She "traded [her] Doc Marten boots for L. L. Bean duck shoes" and "went preppy," she recalled to Paul de Barros for the *Seattle Times* (3 Mar. 2012), joining the varsity tennis team and starring in the senior class play. Brownstein graduated in 1992 and was accepted to Portland's Lewis and Clark College, but because she could not afford the tuition, she attended Western Washington University in Bellingham instead. She dropped out before the end of her first term and moved to Seattle, which at the time was the epicenter of grunge rock, an alternative subgenre epitomized by such bands as Nirvana, Pearl Jam, and Soundgarden.

## ROCKIN' IN THE NORTHWEST

In Seattle, Brownstein worked a job delivering sandwiches and felt herself getting nowhere. "I was miserable," she told de Barros. "I had always assumed I would be in college by then." She eventually enrolled in the Evergreen State College in Olympia, the locus of much of the "riot grrrl" subculture, a feminist punk-rock movement that

emerged in the Pacific Northwest in the early 1990s. While at Evergreen, Brownstein began to focus more seriously on playing music, while still maintaining her interest in acting and taking part in an improvisational comedy group. Inspired by the music and liberal social politics of bands such as Bikini Kill, Bratmobile, and Heavens to Betsy, she formed her own band, Excuse 17, in 1993.

During her brief time at Western Washington University, Brownstein had met future bandmate Corin Tucker, then a member of the two-woman band Heavens to Betsy, after the duo had performed at a gallery in downtown Bellingham. Tucker was also attending the Evergreen State College, and she and Brownstein began playing music together as a side project. In 1994, they recorded their first album under the name Sleater-Kinney, adding Scottish-born Australian drummer Laura (sometimes spelled Lora) Macfarlane to the mix. Notably, while Brownstein and Tucker both played guitar, the group had no bass player, either at first or later on; instead, both women tuned their guitars to D-flat, one and one-half steps lower than standard, and Brownstein usually played lead guitar while Tucker played rhythm. Both provided vocals as well, although in that respect Tucker usually took the lead.

## SLEATER-KINNEY

Sleater-Kinney's self-titled debut album received some positive critical attention upon its release in 1995, which was also the year that Excuse 17 broke up. The band's next few albums, including *Call the Doctor* (1996), *Dig Me Out* (1997), and *The Hot Rock* (1999), cemented the group's reputation as a tough punk band that not only rocked but also spoke truth to power, addressing such issues as consumerism and gender inequality. In 1997, Macfarlane was replaced by drummer Janet Weiss, cofounder of the Portland indie-rock band Quasi.

The band surprised some fans and critics with their 2005 album, *The Woods*. Released on the Sub Pop label, the album moved further away from the simple beats and rhythms of punk to looser, more adventurous sounds associated with "classic rock" luminaries such as Led Zeppelin, Jimi Hendrix, Deep Purple, and Black Sabbath. Kyle Ryan wrote in a review for the *AV Club* (24 May 2005) that "*The Woods . . .* mak[es] the band's other albums seem half-baked by comparison. Sleater-Kinney might have set the bar impossibly high for its subsequent albums."

Brownstein continued to tour and record with Sleater-Kinney until 2006, when the band announced they were going on "indefinite hiatus." Brownstein did not return to the music scene for another four years; in 2010, she announced on NPR's *All Songs Considered* blog that she had formed a new band, Wild Flag, which included Weiss as well as former Helium front woman Mary Timony. The group's first album, *Wild Flag* (2011), was also their last. "We had a fun run, but all the logistics started seeming not quite worth it," Brownstein told Simon Vozick-Levinson for *Rolling Stone* (20 Mar. 2014).

### PORTLANDIA

Brownstein met Fred Armisen, her future *Portlandia* collaborator, in 2003, when Armisen, a Sleater-Kinney fan, invited the band to a *Saturday Night Live* after-party. Armisen and Brownstein quickly became friends and kept in touch. Because they lived on opposite sides of the country—New York and Portland, respectively—they decided to collaborate on a sketch-comedy project in order to spend more time together. That project was a series of satirical online sketches released under the name ThunderAnt. With the help of Lorne Michaels, the longtime producer of *Saturday Night Live* and other NBC comedy programs, they pitched their comedy show to IFC.

*Portlandia* premiered in 2011 and quickly became a cult and critical success. Shot on location, the show, much of which is improvised, parodies various niche cultures and movements in Portland, such as hipsters, overly well-intentioned liberals, and those inclined to demand über-local and organic products in often absurd and hyperbolic ways. Characters have included dumpster divers, bicycle-rights activists, humorless feminist bookstore owners, and animal-rights activists who untie a dog from a pole outside of a restaurant so that it can be "free."

What Brownstein and Armisen target and parody on the show comes, at least to a degree, from looking within themselves. Before joining the cast of *Saturday Night Live*, Armisen was also in a band, and he is familiar with various niche groups and the rules that sprout around the arts and music scenes. Having gone through this herself, Brownstein told Margaret Talbot for the *New Yorker* (2 Jan. 2012), "When you're indoctrinated into a scene, there's this pride that comes with being accepted and understood by people you admire. But the flip side of that is this almost stifling sense of democracy. You put yourself down, to overcompensate for the embarrassment of riches or the little attention you get." Worse than that, Brownstein told Talbot, was "the elitism that passes itself off as inclusiveness." She explained, "The rules are so esoteric, so hard to follow, that no one else could fit in. And what you'll never admit to yourself is that you don't *want* other people to fit in." This attitude, Talbot points out, is precisely what *Portlandia* often parodies.

Yet the show, for all its satirical jabs at Portland's various subcultures, is not bitter or mean spirited. "I don't feel outside these situations at all," Brownstein assured de Barros. "This is the world I grew up in. I'm not saying, 'Oh, those people.' I *am* those people." *Portlandia* is, in fact, somehow sweet, albeit in a strange and at times very awkward way. Nearly every sketch on the show features both Armisen and Brownstein, often as a couple—romantic or just friends—and the dynamic between them, more often than not, holds the scene together and gives it its heart.

Due to its popularity and devoted following, the show has launched several books cowritten by Brownstein and Armisen: *Portlandia: A Guide for Visitors* (2012), *The Portlandia Activity Book* (2014), and *The Portlandia Cookbook: Cook Like a Local* (2014). In addition, Brownstein has said in interviews that she is working on a memoir.

### RETURN TO ROCK

In October 2014, Sleater-Kinney released all seven of their previous albums as a remastered limited-edition vinyl box set called *Start Together*, named after the first track on their 1999 album, *The Hot Rock*. The box set included a seven-inch record marked "1/20/15" and a brand new single called "Bury Our Friends." The day before the box set was released, the band confirmed that the single was from a new full-length studio album, *No Cities to Love*, and that the date January 20, 2015, was the album's scheduled release date.

In an e-mail to NPR, as reported by Robin Hilton for the organization's *All Songs Considered* blog (20 Oct. 2014), Brownstein explained the band's original decision to go on hiatus: "I feel like creativity is about where you want your blood to flow. . . . Maybe after *The Woods* that blood had thinned; we felt enervated, the focus had become disparate and diffuse. We drifted apart in order to concentrate on other elements of our lives and careers. Sleater-Kinney isn't something you can do half-assed or half-heartedly. We have to really want it. And you have to feed that hunger and have the energy to." After nearly a decade, the band announced a tour in support of the new album, scheduled to begin in February 2015.

## PERSONAL LIFE

Brownstein briefly dated Sleater-Kinney co-founder Corin Tucker while in college; the band's debut album was recorded while the two were visiting Australia to celebrate Tucker's graduation. After they broke up, Brownstein, then twenty-one, was involuntarily outed by an article in *Spin* magazine that made reference to their relationship and erroneously identified her as a lesbian. "Only because it seems so culturally important to be able to say who you are: I definitely identify as bisexual," she later told Aaron Mesh for Portland's *Willamette Week* (3 Nov. 2010). Brownstein, who is normally reticent about her personal life, explained, "Right now, in terms of the political climate, and with a number of young gay suicides . . . and with so many politicians still being so aggressively against gay marriage, it is hard not to at least identify in a way that lets people know, 'It is OK whoever you are.'"

According to multiple interviews, Brownstein and Armisen share an incredibly close yet platonic friendship. "We never did [hook up]," Brownstein said to Rachel Rosenblit for *Elle* magazine (9 Jan. 2012). "The love affair we started was Thunder-Ant, and that blossomed into a full-blown relationship. So I think we sort of dodged a bullet. It's one of the most intimate, functional, romantic, but non-sexual relationships we've ever had."

## SUGGESTED READING

Brownstein, Carrie. "Q&A: Carrie Brownstein on Writing Her Memoir, *Portlandia*'s Fourth Season, and the Future of Sleater-Kinney." Interview by T. Cole Rachel. *Stereogum*. SpinMedia, 6 Jan. 2014. Web. 21 Oct. 2014.

de Barros, Paul. "Carrie Brownstein: The Northwest's Funny Girl." *Seattle Times*. Seattle Times, 3 Mar. 2012. Web. 21 Oct. 2014.

Hilton, Robin. "Sleater-Kinney Reunites, Announces New Album." *All Songs Considered*. NPR, 20 Oct. 2014. Web. 21 Oct. 2014.

Mesh, Aaron. "Mock Star: Carrie Brownstein Is Making Fun of You." *Willamette Week*. Willamette Week, 3 Nov. 2010. Web. 21 Oct. 2014.

Rosenblit, Rachel. "*Portlandia*'s Comedy Chemistry." *Elle*. Hearst Communications, 9 Jan. 2012. Web. 21 Oct. 2014.

Talbot, Margaret. "Stumptown Girl." *New Yorker*. Condé Nast, 2 Jan. 2012. Web. 21 Oct. 2014.

Vozick-Levinson, Simon. "Carrie Brownstein's Life after Punk." *Rolling Stone*. Rolling Stone, 20 Mar. 2014. Web. 21 Oct. 2014.

## SELECTED WORKS

*Sleater-Kinney*, 1995; *Call the Doctor*, 1996; *Dig Me Out*, 1997; *The Hot Rock*, 1999; *All Hands on the Bad One*, 2000; *One Beat*, 2002; *The Woods*, 2005; *No Cities to Love*, 2015

—Dmitry Kiper

# Madison Bumgarner

**Born:** August 1, 1989
**Occupation:** Baseball player

With his astounding pitching performance during the 2014 Major League Baseball (MLB) postseason, the San Francisco Giants' six-foot-five, 235-pound left-hander Madison Bumgarner etched his place among baseball's all-time October greats. That year he was named most valuable player (MVP) of both the National League Championship Series (NLCS) and the World Series, after almost singlehandedly leading the Giants to a third World Series title in five years. He was also a pivotal member of the Giants' 2010 and 2012 World Series–winning teams. In five career World Series appearances, Bumgarner has a perfect 4–0 record with a 0.25 earned-run average (ERA) and has allowed just one run in thirty-six innings.

Chosen in the first round of the 2007 MLB Draft by the Giants, Bumgarner is known for his unique crossfire delivery and for a pitching repertoire that includes a blistering four-seam fastball and a cut fastball that "slides across the strike zone like a greased marble," Michael Powell wrote for the *New York Times* (30 Oct. 2014). Since making his major-league debut in September 2009, he has earned three all-star selections and one Silver Slugger Award (given to the best hitter at his respective position). In 2014, he was named *Sports Illustrated*'s Sportsman of the Year and the Associated Press Male Athlete of the Year for his postseason heroics.

## EARLY LIFE

Madison Kyle Bumgarner was born on August 1, 1989, in Hickory, North Carolina. He spent his childhood and adolescence fewer than ten miles away in an area known as Bumtown, so named after the many German immigrants with the same surname who have lived there since the early 1700s. He grew up in a log cabin that was built by his father, Kevin, who works as a manager for a wholesale food distribution company. His mother, Debbie, is an accountant for the soft-drink giant PepsiCo. Bumgarner has two older half brothers, Lou and Will, from his mother's first marriage. He also had a half sister, Dena, who died suddenly at the age of thirty-six in 2010 after accidentally overdosing on the painkiller oxycodone.

Though neither of his parents were distinguished athletes, Bumgarner was born with preternatural baseball talent. His first word, coincidentally, was "ball," and by age four, he was already competing against children in older age divisions. From age six to age nine, Bumgarner played baseball at the Granite Falls Recreation Center. He was banned from playing there after age nine, however, when he joined an elite Amateur Athletic Union (AAU) team, the ten-and-under Catawba Valley Storm. In 1999 he led the Storm to the North Carolina AAU state championship.

Bumgarner's parents divorced when he was ten years old. His parents shared joint custody of him until he turned eleven, at which point his mother was granted sole custody. Nevertheless Bumgarner remained close to his father, a part-time college umpire who helped oversee his baseball development. During his youth, the two would spend two hours a day at the baseball field working on various drills. In an interview with Cody Dalton for the Newton, North Carolina, *Observer News Enterprise* (19 June 2013), Bumgarner said that his father taught him "a lot about the game," "how to respect the game," and "a lot about life."

## HIGH SCHOOL CAREER

At South Caldwell High School in Hudson, North Carolina, Bumgarner was a four-year starting pitcher on the varsity baseball team. He started seriously thinking of pursuing a professional baseball career as a sophomore, when his fastball was consistently clocked at 90 miles per hour. After beginning a weight-training regimen, Bumgarner added more velocity to his fastball, which "was so good he had virtually no need for another pitch," according to Tom Verducci for *Sports Illustrated* (9 Dec. 2014). The summer after his sophomore season, he joined an elite travel team, the Sedalia Dirtbags, which furthered his baseball development.

Bumgarner first appeared on the radar of major-league scouts during his junior year at South Caldwell High, when he posted a 12–2

Eltiempo 10/CC0 1.0

record with a 0.99 ERA and led his team to the Class 4A state finals. He went on to establish himself as one of the top pitching prospects in the state as a senior, when he went 11–2 with a 1.05 ERA and 143 strikeouts in 86 innings. Bumgarner, who, despite throwing left-handed, bats and does virtually everything else right-handed, also put up remarkable numbers as a hitter, batting .424 with eleven home runs and thirty-eight runs batted in. He led South Caldwell to a 31–3 record and the Class 4A state title and was named North Carolina's Gatorade Player of the Year.

During Bumgarner's senior season baseball scouts and agents hounded him to such an extent that his father built a wall around the school's bullpen so he would be able to warm up before games without getting distracted. Among those who saw him play was Pat Portugal, then an area scout for the San Francisco Giants. Bumgarner impressed Portugal with not only his pitching and hitting prowess but also his unflappable demeanor and his makeup, which was "off the charts," as Portugal told Verducci. "You don't ever think you're looking at a Hall of Famer, but I was thinking that with Madison. I've never done that. But he was that special."

## SAN FRANCISCO GIANTS

Bumgarner signed a letter of intent to attend North Carolina University, but he ultimately turned down a scholarship to that school to enter the 2007 MLB Draft. Despite his coveted status, some scouts still expressed reservations about his unconventional delivery, which is characterized by a slight torso twist followed by a sweeping crossfire release, and his lack of an effective breaking ball. Those concerns notwithstanding, the Giants drafted Bumgarner as the tenth overall pick and provided him a contract that included a signing bonus of $2 million.

After being drafted Bumgarner reported to the Giants' Instructional League team in Scottsdale, Arizona. Despite having a seemingly bright baseball future ahead of him, he contemplated quitting baseball within a week after arriving because of acute homesickness. "I was out there by myself," Bumgarner recalled to Verducci. "I had no idea what to expect . . . this lifestyle . . . was so different from what I was used to." Undaunted, he persevered through the remainder of his one-month-long Instructional League stint and rapidly ascended the Giants' farm system.

In 2008 Bumgarner was invited to the Giants' annual spring-training camp. There, team instructors altered his delivery slightly, shortening his arm and shoulder action. The changes hampered Bumgarner's performance, and after struggling in his first three starts with the Augusta GreenJackets, the Giants' low A affiliate, he reverted to his high school delivery. Bumgarner began complementing his four-seam and cut fastballs with two secondary offerings, a curveball and a changeup, and he was dominant the rest of the season for the GreenJackets. He tied for the South Atlantic League lead in wins (15) and led the league in both ERA (1.46) and strikeouts (164).

## WORLD SERIES DEBUT

Bumgarner was assigned to the high A San Jose Giants of the California League to open the 2009 season. After impressing in five starts with the club, he was promoted to the Connecticut Defenders of the Eastern League, the Giants' AA affiliate. Bumgarner appeared in twenty games for the Defenders, going 9–1 with a 1.93 ERA, before earning his first call-up to the majors on September 8, 2009, as an injury replacement for Tim Lincecum. At twenty years and thirty-eight days, he became the youngest player in the majors and the youngest starting pitcher for the Giants since the franchise moved from New York to San Francisco in 1958. He pitched 5 1/3 innings, allowing two runs on five hits, and earned a no-decision in a 4–3 Giants loss to the San Diego Padres.

After making three more appearances for the Giants in 2009, Bumgarner was offered the chance to compete for the team's fifth-starter job at the 2010 spring-training camp. Reeling from his half sister's death, he performed poorly and was assigned to the AAA Fresno Grizzlies in the Pacific Coast League to open the 2010 season. However, his stay in Fresno was brief. Bumgarner made fourteen starts for the club before being recalled by the Giants on June 26. He stayed with the team for the remainder of the season, going 7–6 and posting a 3.00 ERA in eighteen starts.

Bumgarner rounded out a dominant Giants' pitching rotation that helped the team capture its first National League (NL) West Division title since 2003 and its first World Series championship since 1954. It was during the 2010 playoffs that Bumgarner began to establish his big-game reputation. In his World Series debut, he pitched 8 scoreless innings in a 4–0 win over the Texas Rangers in game four. He became the youngest rookie pitcher to have a scoreless start of 6 or more innings in World Series history. The victory gave the Giants a 3–1 lead in the series, which the team won in five games. "Madison is a special talent. . . . What he's been through already at his young age and how he has handled it is pretty remarkable," Giants manager Bruce Bochy told Cody Dalton.

## RISE TO THE ELITE

Over the next two seasons, Bumgarner posted records of 13–13 and 16–11, respectively, as he solidified his place in the Giants' rotation. In April 2012 the Giants rewarded Bumgarner by signing him to a six-year contract extension worth $35 million. That year the Giants finished first in NL West with a 94–68 record and returned to the World Series, sweeping the Detroit Tigers in four games to win a second World Series title in three years. Bumgarner started game two of the series, pitching 7 scoreless innings and striking out 8. In doing so, he was the first pitcher with 15 scoreless innings to begin his World Series career since Bruce Hurst in 1986.

After showing flashes of his potential in his first three full major-league seasons, Bumgarner enjoyed a breakout year in 2013, when he established career bests with a 2.77 ERA, 199 strikeouts, and a 1.03 walks plus hits per inning pitched (WHIP) rate in thirty-one starts. He finished with a 13–9 record, pitched over 200 innings for the third straight season, and was selected to his first career all-star team. During that season Bumgarner explained to Dalton, "I'm not a big goal-setter. . . . The only thing I try to do is go out there every game of the year and make sure we have a chance to win when I'm done pitching."

Despite Bumgarner's emergence as a bona fide ace, the Giants, hampered by a rash of injuries, stumbled to a 76–86 record. However, the team returned to championship form in 2014. That year Bumgarner further bolstered his status as one of the best left-handed pitchers in the game. He went 18–10 with a 2.98 ERA in thirty-three starts and set career highs in innings (217.1) and strikeouts (219). One of the best hitting pitchers in league, Bumgarner hit two grand slams during the season, tying a major-league record. He earned his second career all-star selection, received his first career Silver Slugger Award, and finished fourth in the voting for the NL Cy Young Award.

## OCTOBER LEGEND

In 2014 Bumgarner helped the Giants to a second-place finish in the NL West with an 88–74 record; the team earned one of the two NL wild-card positions. He garnered national attention for his performance during the 2014 postseason, which "was the stuff of instant legend," Verducci wrote. Bumgarner pitched a four-hit shutout against the Pittsburgh Pirates in the NL Wild Card Game and then pitched 7 2/3 shutout innings against the St. Louis Cardinals in game one of the NLCS. He was named NLCS MVP after setting a postseason record with 26 2/3 consecutive scoreless innings on the road.

Bumgarner proved to be the difference for the Giants in the 2014 World Series, which saw him burnish his reputation as "the best postseason pitcher on the planet," as Michael Powell declared. Bumgarner won games one and five of the series against the Kansas City Royals as a starter, then pitched 5 shutout innings in relief on just two days' rest in game seven to clinch the Giants' third World Series title in five years. He was named World Series MVP after finishing with a 2–0 record, a save, and an astonishing 0.43 ERA in 21 innings. Bumgarner's five-inning save was the longest in World Series history and his 0.43 ERA was the lowest in a single World Series by a pitcher with at least 15 innings since Sandy Koufax's 0.38 mark in 1965. Meanwhile, he set a record for innings pitched in a postseason with 52 2/3.

For his historic postseason performance, Bumgarner was named *Sports Illustrated*

Sportsman of the Year and Associated Press Male Athlete of the Year. "He thinks and believes he's the best on the field when he's out there," Giants starting pitcher Tim Hudson said of his teammate to Anthony DiComo for MLB.com (21 Oct. 2014). "And any great pitcher throughout the history of the game, when they take that mound, they've got to believe the other team doesn't have a chance in heck to beat them. He's one of those guys."

In 2015 Bumgarner earned his third consecutive all-star selection, after reaching the midseason break with a record of 9–5 and 3.33 ERA. In June of that year he recorded a career-high fourteen strikeouts against the San Diego Padres and his one-thousandth career strikeout against the Colorado Rockies.

## PERSONAL LIFE

Bumgarner, who is known for his humble, down-home demeanor, married his high school sweetheart, Ali Saunders, in 2010. The couple lives on a sprawling, 140-acre farm in Dudley Shoals, North Carolina.

## SUGGESTED READING

Dalton, Cody. "Giant Strides: Bumgarner Reflects on His Career, Future." *Observer News Enterprise* [Newton, NC]. Observer News Enterprise, 19 June 2013. Web. 11 July 2015.

DiComo, Anthony. "MadBum Brings Unique Delivery, Experience for Giants in Game 1." *MLB.com*. MLB Advanced Media, 21 Oct. 2014. Web. 11 July 2015.

Powell, Michael. "A Visit to Madison Bumgarner County, and a Proud Father's Home." *New York Times*. New York Times, 30 Oct. 2014. Web. 11 July 2015.

Verducci, Tom. "2014 Sportsman of the Year: Madison Bumgarner." *Sports Illustrated*. Time, 9 Dec. 2014. Web. 11 July 2015.

—Chris Cullen

# Nolan Bushnell

**Born:** February 5, 1943
**Occupation:** Engineer and entrepreneur

Video game pioneer Nolan Bushnell is the legendary founder of the video game company Atari and the Chuck E. Cheese Pizza Time Theatre franchise. His career began in 1972 when he invented *Pong*, one of the earliest and most iconic arcade video games. The ingenious simplicity of *Pong*, which was essentially table tennis on a screen, made it an instant hit with gamers. *Pong*'s governing principle—matching risk to reward—can also be used as a metaphor for Bushnell's tumultuous career. "Good players knew that the hardest shot was the one you hit off the tip of the paddle—that gave you the maximum angle," Bushnell told John Seabrook for the *New Yorker* (30 Jan. 2012). "But, of course, hitting it off the tip made it easy to miss the ball." In his profile of Bushnell for *Inc.* magazine (1 Apr. 2009), Max Chafkin suggests that it is Bushnell's insatiable desire to be the entrepreneur with the million-dollar idea—rather than the unremarkable CEO—that has led him from outrageous fortune to relative poverty and back again. To say that Atari was a success would be an understatement. "During Atari's peak years, it wasn't just synonymous with videogames," Harry McCracken wrote for *Time* magazine (27 June 2012). "It was the archetypal Silicon Valley success story, period." The company set the standard for the budding video game industry. Early hires included Steve Jobs and Steve Wozniak—the two men who went on to found Apple Computer and in turn, define the ethos of modern day Silicon Valley. (They offered Bushnell a one-third share of Apple for $50,000 in 1976, but he declined. Apple, worth about $483.15 billion in May 2014, is now the most valuable company in the world, according to *Forbes*.) Chuck E. Cheese was another spectacular success for Bushnell until 1983, when he bet it all on a company called Androbot just as the video game industry took a nose dive. The fallout ruined Bushnell financially. Since then, Bushnell has had his hand in over twenty start-ups. While some of them have been successful, others have not, and none have reached the heights of Atari or Chuck E. Cheese, which now thrives under new management. Bushnell told Chafkin that he keeps a prototype of an Androbot android called Topo in his office as a reminder of his biggest failure and that running a business can have disappointing and devastating consequences, "but at the same time," Bushnell observed, "creating stuff is neat."

## EARLY LIFE AND EDUCATION

Bushnell was born on February 5, 1943, in the small town of Clearfield on Utah's Great Salt Lake. His mother was a schoolteacher and his father owned a small cement contracting business. When he was ten years old, he impressed his parents by replacing a broken tube on the family's television set and began going door-to-door as the neighborhood TV repairman. As Chafkin pointed out, television sets were not cheap in the 1950s and cost the equivalent of a

Tech Cocktail/Wikimedia

month's salary for many families, but even as a child, Bushnell was a shrewd businessman. He charged fifty cents for a service call—the going rate was five dollars—but made a profit charging for parts. "I would mark the hell out of the tubes," he told Chafkin. "I could make 15 bucks in an hour."

Bushnell's dad died when Bushnell was fifteen, and Bushnell briefly took over his cement business. He graduated from Davis High School in 1961 and enrolled at Utah State University but transferred to the University of Utah in 1963. Bushnell studied electrical engineering and worked summers as a barker at Lagoon Amusement Park north of Salt Lake City where he managed a game in which customers threw baseballs at a pyramid of milk bottles. "In some ways, my whole career has been about monetizing what I learned running those games," Bushnell told Ethan Watters for Wired (1 Oct. 2005). The carnival weighted the bottles at the bottom of the pyramid, making them more difficult to topple. Bushnell recalls switching the weighted bottles to the top for customers he saw as underdogs, making the whole pyramid crumble more easily. When an underdog won quickly, he told Watters, stronger customers paid even more to prove they could do the same. "It was my job to extract the most dollars from those people while helping them have a good time," Bushnell said. "That was my MBA."

## ATARI

Bushnell graduated from the University of Utah in 1968, and moved to Silicon Valley to work for an electronics company called Ampex, where he met an engineer named Ted Dabney. Together, the men created a video game called *Computer Space*, based on another game called *Spacewar!* that Bushnell had snuck into his school's computer lab to play when he was in college. They licensed the game to an arcade game company called Nutting Associates. *Computer Space* became the first commercially sold, mass-produced video game in the world in 1971 and made $3 million in sales. It even appears in the 1973 science fiction movie *Soylent Green* "as a symbol of the future," Elaine Jarvik for the University of Utah's *Continuum* magazine (Spring 2013) wrote. But Bushnell and Dabney had disagreements with the owners of Nutting over gaming rights, so the men took their *Computer Space* earnings and in 1972 launched their own company. They called it Atari after a move in a Japanese board game called *Go!*

With only five hundred dollars in capital, Bushnell and Dabney created their second game that same year. It was called *Pong*, and it was based on an existing game called *Odyssey*. (Magnavox, the company that produced *Odyssey*, later sued Atari. The case was settled out of court.) *Pong*, which was designed by Atari engineer Allan Alcorn, was simple but addictive. Players batted a white square back and forth across a dotted white line. "I had to come up with a game people already knew how to play, something so simple that any drunk in any bar could play," Bushnell said later, as quoted by Tony Long for *Wired* magazine (29 Nov. 2010). Bushnell and Dabney built a wooden cabinet for the game, attached a coin box and took it to a bar called Andy Capp's in Sunnyvale, California. At the time, the game didn't even have a name (or instructions), but the management at Andy Capp's called a few days after the delivery to report that *Pong* was jammed with one hundred dollars worth of quarters. The two men built more machines, and the games proved to be so popular that Bushnell and Dabney lowballed the profit margin when they pitched the game to Bally, a pinball manufacturing company, to make their success seem more plausible. Bally still didn't believe them. Atari ended up manufacturing and selling the game itself, and in 1975, the company came out with a consumer version called *Home Pong*.

## CHUCK E. CHEESE PIZZA TIME THEATRE

By that time, Bushnell was a very wealthy man, and Chafkin suggests that he developed a flashy persona—he was rarely seen without his trademark pipe and blazer—to hide the fact that he felt unequipped to deal with Atari's astronomical success. "I felt absolutely alone," he told Chafkin. By 1976, Atari was making $40 million a year in sales.

Bushnell wanted to take the company public, but instead sold it to Warner Communications for $28 million. Before the sale, Bushnell had developed an idea for a franchise of pizza parlor video game arcades. Video games were traditionally marketed to bars, arcades, and pool halls, and Bushnell reckoned that the market was ripe for a more family-oriented venue. As Chafkin explained, Bushnell's original concept for Chuck E. Cheese was as a subsidiary of Atari, guided by the same principle as when old Hollywood studios used to own movie theaters. It was simply a "means of distribution," Chafkin wrote. "As far as Bushnell was concerned, he was starting the new Disney."

Of course, the reality of the enterprise was a bit different. Bushnell opened his first venue in San Jose in 1977. It had arcade games and pizza for kids—wine and beer for parents—and its mascot was Chuck E. Cheese, a singing, dancing, cigar-chomping rat based on Bushnell himself. Warner Communications immediately ordered Bushnell to shut the place down. "They thought it was the stupidest idea ever," Bushnell told Chafkin. When he refused, Warner agreed to sell him back the idea for $500,000. From 1979 to 1984, Chuck E. Cheese opened more than two hundred locations around the country and twice landed on *Inc.* magazine's list of fastest-growing public companies.

Bolstered by his success, Bushnell leveraged his stock in Atari (before he was forced out completely in 1978) and Chuck E. Cheese to secure a $23 million loan from Merrill Lynch to launch a company called Androbot that would make and sell personal robots. He also decided to launch a video game division of the company called Sente—which, as Chafkin points out, is the only move that beats "atari" in *Go!*—as well as a start-up incubator called Catalyst Technologies in 1983. The same year, the video game bubble burst, leaving Atari (without Bushnell) and Chuck E. Cheese, which lost more than $81 million, in the lurch. Bushnell was just about to take Androbot public, but Merrill Lynch was investing cautiously after two unsuccessful IPOs. The bank pulled out of the deal and demanded its money back. Androbot collapsed and Bushnell resigned as the CEO of Chuck E. Cheese as the franchise filed for bankruptcy. Chuck E. Cheese later merged with a competitor. Today, without Bushnell, it continues to thrive.

## OTHER SUCCESSES AND FAILURES

Throughout the 1980s, Bushnell was involved in more than a dozen start-ups. Etak, a 1985 electronic navigation system for cars that stored maps on cassette tapes was a success, while Bushnell's idea for a console that translated music into psychedelic images on a TV screen was not. Through it all, lawyers for Merrill Lynch came collecting, and in 1997, Bushnell was forced to sell his $5 million mansion in Woodside, California. In the early 2000s, Bushnell founded a successful company called uWink that developed industrial gaming consoles. A few years later, he made plans for a chain of uWink Media Bistros, which were restaurants reminiscent of the old arcades, where people could meet and play touch screen games together. The business plan looked promising, but in another brush with bad luck, uWink Media Bistros were launched just as the 2008 recession hit. The California-based restaurants enjoyed some fleeting success before closing for good a few years later. In April 2010, Bushnell returned to Atari as a member of the board of directors and was given the title non-executive director of Atari.

More recently, Bushnell has assumed the role of a tech sage. He has been openly critical of the gaming industry's predilection for more and more violent games. In 2011, he and several other tech entrepreneurs were the subject of a documentary called *Something Ventured* and in 2013, he released a book with Gene Stone about fostering creatives in the workplace called *Finding the Next Steve Jobs: How to Find, Hire, Keep, and Nurture Creative Talent.*

## PERSONAL LIFE
Bushnell met his wife Nancy at a bar that was around the corner from the Atari offices. The couple has eight children. Bushnell's daughter, Alissa Bushnell, is his public relations representative. He lives in Los Angeles.

## SUGGESTED READING
Chafkin, Max. "Nolan Bushnell Is Back in the Game." *Inc.* Mansueto Ventures, 1 Apr. 2009. Web. 6 Oct. 2014.

Isaacson, Walter. "The Birth of *Pong.*" *Slate.* Slate Group, 7 Oct. 2014. Web. 20 Oct. 2014.

Jarvik, Elaine. "The Impresario." *Continuum: The Magazine of the University of Utah.* U of Utah Alumni Assoc., Spring 2013. Web. 7 Oct. 2014.

Long, Tony. "Nov. 29, 1972: *Pong,* A Game Any Drunk Can Play." *Wired.* Condé Nast, 29 Nov. 2010. Web. 16 Oct. 2014.

McCracken, Harry. "Atari at 40: Catching Up with Founder Nolan Bushnell." *Time.* Time, 27 June 2012. Web. 7 Oct. 2014.

Seabrook, John. "Re-Start: Nolan Bushnell and Anti-Aging Games." *New Yorker.* Condé Nast, 30 Jan. 2012. Web. 6 Oct. 2014.

Watters, Ethan. "The Player." *Wired.* Condé Nast, Oct. 2005. Web. 6 Oct. 2014.

—Molly Hagan

# Garrett Camp
**Born:** 1978
**Occupation:** Entrepreneur

Garrett Camp is a tech entrepreneur whose most notable ventures are the website StumbleUpon and the mobile ride-sharing application Uber. Camp developed StumbleUpon as a graduate student at the University of Calgary in 2001. He is currently the chair of StumbleUpon, having stepped down as the CEO in May 2012 to devote time to other ventures, including the phenomenally successful Uber app. Camp founded the latter company with entrepreneur Travis Kalanick in 2008. As of 2015, Uber was available in more than two hundred cities in fifty-three countries, and investors valued the company at over $18.2 billion. In 2014, Camp raised $50 million to launch a "start-up studio" called Expa.

## EARLY LIFE AND EDUCATION
Camp was born in 1978 and grew up in Calgary, Alberta, Canada. His mother, an artist, and his father, an economist, teamed up to design and build homes when Camp was a child. He attended a small elementary school and middle school—each with only 150 students and one class for each grade. His high school had more than fifteen hundred students. "It was a big change," he told Patricia R. Olsen for the *New York Times* (22 Oct. 2011). Camp graduated from high school in 1996 and enrolled at the University of Calgary to pursue a degree in electrical engineering. During his junior year, he studied speech-recognition technology through an internship with telecommunications company Nortel Networks. He also took classes at Concordia University. Camp earned his bachelor's degree in 2000 and stayed at the University of Calgary to complete his master's degree in software engineering.

In 2001, he and a few of his classmates came up with an idea for a company that would support a personalized home webpage, Camp explained to Michael McCullough for *Canadian Business* magazine (21 Sept. 2011). "The initial idea was, let's try so that every time you open up your home page it's a new page, just for you," he said. They decided to call the company StumbleUpon, a name that recalled the intermittent pleasures of leafing through a magazine, he told Olsen. Camp and his friends—Geoff Smith, Justin LaFrance, and Eric Boyd—bought the domain name for their company in 2001 and began to build a prototype. Things moved quickly after that, perhaps a little too quickly, he admitted to Olsen. "If I had it to do over, I might have finished school first, then devoted all my time to StumbleUpon instead of dividing my time between the two," he said. "In the end, however, it was probably good to take the time I did. From the papers I read in grad school, I learned what researchers were finding about collaborative systems, which was helpful in designing our product."

## STUMBLEUPON

StumbleUpon is an exploratory search engine that allows users to find (or rather, "stumble upon") different websites according to their own interests. "I'm interested in sites that help people find information and filter what's available. The Internet is so big that no one can stay on top of everything," he explained to Olsen. Camp and his friends completed the website prototype in 2002. For the following three years, Camp worked part time on the website while going to class. In 2005, just as Camp was finishing his thesis, the site had more than half a million users. One of those users, an angel investor named Brad O'Neill, invited Camp to Silicon Valley in December 2005 to discuss the company's future. Camp told McCullough that he was not actively looking for funding, but with the help of O'Neill and his friends, Camp raised more than $1.5 million in two weeks. (The site itself began earning revenue by charging websites to appear on the site.) In 2007, Camp moved to San Francisco to be closer to Silicon Valley.

That same year, Camp and the other cofounders realized that they had to either raise more money or sell StumbleUpon to a larger company—a common crossroads for tech start-ups. Camp told McCullough that auction website eBay offered Camp and his partners at StumbleUpon the best price and the most flexibility in terms of a partnership. In 2007, eBay officially acquired StumbleUpon for $75 million. Camp and his team worked independently of eBay's human resources and payroll, though at times this division seemed unclear. For instance, Camp

Bloomberg/Getty Images

told April Joyner for *Inc.* magazine (July/Aug. 2011) that StumbleUpon was looking to hire a database administrator at a time when eBay had put a freeze on all hires. "And I was like, 'Sure, eBay has a hiring freeze, but how can you stop us from hiring the one critical position we need to keep the site running?'" he recalled. "About a year in, after the acquisition, we started realizing it wasn't as exciting," he told a staff reporter for *Inc.* (9 May 2012). "When you're a start-up, everyone has stock options, everyone is energized. If you don't take a risk, the status quo will continue."

"When you have the right level of flexibility and the right level of incentives, that's when things can grow and develop well," he told Jeanette Borzo for the *Wall Street Journal* (15 Nov. 2010). Camp and his team felt creatively stunted by the corporate atmosphere of eBay. "If things are too rigid, people get frustrated. If they are really flexible—but there is no motivation to go out on a limb—things don't happen." In 2008, Camp began discussing the possibility of a buyback with eBay executives and some previous investors, including Ram Shriram. After months of negotiations, Camp organized a group of investors to buy the company back in 2009. The split from eBay was largely amicable, and it appeared to do wonders for StumbleUpon. The company significantly picked up its pace within nine months of becoming independent. Camp told Joyner that each month the site had about three hundred million "stumbles," or page recommendations, when they left eBay. By the summer of 2011, they were averaging one billion. In 2012, Camp stepped down as CEO of StumbleUpon. He was replaced by the company's chief financial officer Mark Bartels and currently serves as the company's chair.

## A NEW CONCEPT

Uber is similar to a taxi service: users are able to contact the nearest driver—professional drivers associated with Uber in a given city—through a mobile app. Once the driver accepts the rider, the app is able to tell the driver where the rider is going, illustrate the car's route, and estimate a time of arrival. Uber also sets fare prices. Credit card information is kept on file, and receipts are emailed to the rider. The app also allows for splitting a cab and has different services (UberBLACK, UberSUV, among them) for upscale or larger vehicles.

Uber began in 2008. Kalanick had just sold his second start-up, a company called Red Swoosh to Akamai Technologies for $20 million, and Camp and Kalanick were trying to hail a cab in Paris on a snowy evening. According to the company's official origin story, the idea for Uber was born that night. But as Kara Swisher reported for *Vanity Fair* (Dec. 2014), Uber's birth was a bit more complicated. Camp and Kalanick were in Paris for an annual European tech conference called LeWeb. After their unsuccessful attempt to procure a car, they discussed the idea for Uber with a few other entrepreneurs. Among the other start-up ideas, the concept that would become Uber did not stand out. However, Camp was stuck on the idea. When he returned to the United States, he bought the domain name UberCab.com and was determined to bring Kalanick, a divisive personality and a daredevil, in on the project. "I knew such a big idea would take a lot of guts, and he impressed me as someone who had that," Camp told Swisher.

## LAUNCHING UBER

Kalanick was initially resistant; he later told Swisher that after the failure and then lackluster performance of his first two start-ups, he was a little gun-shy. However, by the summer of 2010, Camp had assuaged his fears, and they launched UberCab in San Francisco with a few cars, a few employees, and a bit of seed money. The company was starting to gain traction—in August 2010, angel investor Chris Sacca endorsed the service in a tweet—but in October of that year, Camp and

Kalanick received a cease-and-desist order. The San Francisco Municipal Transportation Agency and the California Public Utilities Commission objected to the company's use of the word "cab" when it did not have a taxi license. Thus, UberCab became Uber. The tiff gave Kalanick—whom Swisher described as "pugnacious"—a chance to pick a fight. He told Swisher that his stance was a "principled confrontation," and he continues to duke it out with local transportation authorities. Uber has also come under fire for its surge pricing, which charges riders higher fares at peak times. Kalanick dismisses those criticisms. "It's classic Econ 101," he told Swisher. Kalanick is the CEO of the company and (for better or worse) its public face. Camp serves as the company's chair.

## EXPA

In 2014, Camp launched his latest endeavor: Expa, a company that invests in and nurtures start-up ventures. Its investors include Virgin founder Sir Richard Branson, Google board member Ram Shriram, Hewlett Packard CEO Meg Whitman, WordPress founder Matt Mullenweg, Behance founder Scott Belsky, and Timothy Ferriss, the author of *The Four Hour Workweek* (2007). Camp serves as CEO. He described the company's first project, Reserve. com, to Adam Lashinsky for *Fortune* magazine (28 Oct. 2014) as a "digital concierge" service. Reserve is the brainchild of Joe Marchese, the founder of an advertising company called TrueX, and Greg Hong.

The app, which will compete directly with another reservation app called OpenTable, allows users to make reservations at exclusive restaurants for a five-dollar fee. Like Uber, the app keeps credit card information on file—and with the option to include a predetermined tip, diners can simply walk out after a meal, having already paid for it. A private rating system allows both servers and diners to rate each other—just like Uber. The service is being beta tested in New York, Los Angeles, San Francisco, and Boston.

## SUGGESTED READING

Camp, Garrett. Interview by Jeanette Borzo. "The Perils of Being the Little Fish." *Wall Street Journal*. Dow Jones, 15 Nov. 2010. Web. 27 Jan. 2015.

Camp, Garrett. Interview by April Joyner. "Buying Back the Company." *Inc*. Mansueto Ventures, July/Aug. 2011. Web. 27 Jan. 2015.

Camp, Garrett. Interview by Adam Lashinsky. "An Uber Founder Tables a New Idea." *Fortune*. Time, 28 Oct. 2014. Web. 27 Jan. 2015.

Camp, Garrett. Interview by Michael McCullough. "Stumbling Upon Success." *Canadian Business*. Rogers. 21 Sept. 2011. Web. 27 Jan. 2015.

Olsen, Patricia R. "The Start-Up Advantage." *New York Times*. New York Times, 22 Oct. 2011. Web. 27 Jan. 2015.

"StumbleUpon CEO Steps Down." *Inc.* Mansueto Ventures, 9 May 2012. Web. 27 Jan. 2015.

Swisher, Kara. "Man and Uber Man." *Vanity Fair*. Condé Nast, Dec. 2014. Web. 27 Jan. 2015.

—Molly Hagan

David M. Benett/Getty Images

# Duncan Campbell

**Born:** 1972

**Occupation:** Artist

Duncan Campbell is an Irish artist known for his highly original and thought-provoking film installations, which combine archival materials with new footage and employ documentary and narrative film techniques to examine a wide range of subjects. Campbell, an alumnus of the Glasgow School of Art, was relatively unknown outside of art circles until 2014, when he was awarded the Turner Prize—one of Europe's most prestigious visual arts awards—for his film *It for Others* (2013), which investigates the relationship between objects and culture. The prize is awarded annually to a British contemporary artist who is under fifty years old.

Campbell's other films include *Falls Burns Malone Fiddles* (2004), an examination of Northern Irish teens in the 1970s and 1980s; *Bernadette* (2008), a portrait of the Irish political activist Bernadette Devlin McAliskey; *Make It New John* (2009), about the American automobile manufacturer John DeLorean; and *Arbeit* (2011), which looks at the 2008 global financial crisis through the life and career of German economist Hans Tietmeyer. The esteemed art critic Richard Dorment, writing for the London *Telegraph* (29 Sept. 2014), called Campbell "a consummate filmmaker with a ferocious intelligence, dry wit, and a terrier-like tendency to keep on worrying his subject."

## EARLY LIFE AND EDUCATION

Duncan Campbell was born in 1972 in Swords, a northern suburb of Dublin, Ireland. Along with his four siblings, Campbell grew up in an artistic, enterprising family. In 1967, his parents, Patrick and Veronica, founded a catering company, Campbell Catering. Campbell Catering later took over the Bewley's café chain and helped transform it into Ireland's leading tea and coffee supplier. The company was eventually acquired by the American food service giant Aramark for €64.5 million in 2004.

Campbell inherited his talent for art from his parents. In the early 2000s, his father, a lifelong arts enthusiast, launched a successful second-act career as a sculptor. Patrick Campbell set up a studio in Florence, Italy, and began showcasing his work at exhibitions in Europe and America. He went on to land a number of high-profile commissions, including the official bust of the former president of Ireland Mary McAleese.

Campbell attended Sutton Park School, an exclusive, independent secondary school in Dublin. It was there that his artistic talent became evident. By that time, Campbell was already "exceptionally good," as his father recalled to Liz Kearney for the *Irish Independent* (12 Apr. 2014), "and not just in terms of design, but he was also very good at drawing."

After graduating from Sutton Park School, Campbell enrolled at the National College of Art and Design in Dublin. He studied there for a year before transferring to the University of Ulster, in Belfast, Northern Ireland, where he earned a bachelor of fine arts degree in 1996. He then completed a master's degree in fine arts at the prestigious Glasgow School of Art, in Scotland, in 1998.

## EARLY CAREER AND *FALLS BURNS MALONE FIDDLES*

Upon completing his formal studies, Campbell remained in Glasgow to pursue his career as an artist. In contrast to multicultural hubs like Dublin and London, Glasgow was "a more economical place to work," as Campbell told Kearney, and the city boasted a thriving arts and music scene. In 1999 Campbell cofounded the Glasgow-based artist-run radio station "Radiotuesday," which broadcast a wide range of music and experimental sound recordings.

In addition to Radiotuesday, which built a strong local following, Campbell's other early creative endeavors included producing knitted renditions of nightclub posters and making videos using pages torn from fashion magazines. In 2002 he contributed a visual segment to Glasgow-based artist Luke Fowler's multimedia compilation, *Shadazz 4: Evil Eye Is Source*, which featured footage of rundown underpasses and roadside trash.

Campbell's first solo show was held at the Transmission Gallery in Glasgow in 2003. For the show, he produced a video work, called *Falls Burns Malone Fiddles* (2003), which offered a further look at urban decay. The thirty-four-minute film examines poor and working-class youth of West Belfast during the Troubles in the 1970s and 1980s. It is narrated by actor Ewen Bremner, best known for portraying Spud in *Trainspotting* (1996), and uses images culled from two Belfast-based community photographic organizations: Belfast Exposed and Community Visual Images. Those organizations, Campbell explained to Tobi Maier in an interview with the Italian art magazine *Mousse* (Apr. 2009), "were set up to counteract Belfast's image as seen through the prism of the mainstream media."

According to Campbell, *Falls Burns Malone Fiddles* is influenced heavily by the work of Irish avant-garde writer Samuel Beckett, and the film's title references Beckett's 1951 novel *Malone Dies*. In the film, Bremner's off-screen, stream-of-consciousness narrator goes through a sweeping range of emotions as he tries to tackle multiple narratives in relation to the archival images that unfurl across the screen. Campbell mixes in on-screen animations, diagrams, and symbols to deliberately blur the reality of the presented images. *Falls Burns* "looks at the production of alternative narratives, along with the terms on which they are narrated," he explained, as quoted on the Arts Council Collection website.

## *BERNADETTE* AND *SIGMAR*

Campbell's next video work, *O Joan, no . . .* (2006), also takes its influence from Beckett. The twelve-minute film features a female narrator letting out a variety of nonverbal sounds, from sighs to squeals to shrieks, in reaction to a series of black abstract images intermittently illuminated by disparate light sources. Martin Herbert, in an article about Campbell's early video works for the English art magazine *Frieze* (Apr. 2008), called *O Joan, no . . .* a "sparse, agitatedly poetic and darkly comic film" and commented that it "enlarges Campbell's formal vocabulary by nodding to a continuum of early Modernist cinematic experimentation with the barely representational and onomatopoeic."

Campbell next turned his attention to provocative historical subjects. In 2008 he released *Bernadette*, an experimental, thirty-seven-minute portrait of Bernadette Devlin McAliskey, the controversial Irish activist and politician. Drawing from a wide range of archival materials, including interviews, speeches, news clips, and articles, the film chronicles McAliskey's life and political career as seen through the slanted lens of the media. "I made it explicit that you are not going to find out everything about her [in the] film," Campbell told Vanessa Thorpe for the *Guardian* (11 Oct. 2014), adding, "It is not 'a truth' and it questions the idea there are truths out there to be discovered."

Later in 2008 Campbell was awarded the Bâloise Art Prize at the Statements sector of the prestigious Art Basel fair in Switzerland. That year also saw him release a short film, *Sigmar*, which pays homage to the experimental German artist Sigmar Polke. Described by Campbell to Maier as an "antidote" to *Bernadette*, the ten-minute film offers an interpretation of abstract details from select Polke paintings through the use of animation, documentary footage, guitar music, and fragments of surreal German-language narration.

## MAKE IT NEW JOHN AND ARBEIT

Campbell's next two films, *Make It New John* and *Arbeit*, were released in 2009 and 2011, respectively. The former looks back at the glorious rise and ignominious fall of the late American car manufacturer John DeLorean, best known as the creator of the iconic DeLorean DMC-12, a stainless steel sports car with gull-wing doors. The film, which runs fifty minutes, tells the story of DeLorean, the creation of the DMC-12, and the workers of DeLorean's failed Belfast car plant, and it is set against the turbulent backdrop of Northern Ireland in the 1980s. Like Campbell's previous works, *Make It New John* combines archival footage with new material, including imagined scenes of DeLorean factory workers conversing with each other.

The thirty-nine-minute *Arbeit* presents a biographical account of German economist Hans Tietmeyer, a former head of the Deutsche Bundesbank and one of the architects of the European Economic and Monetary Union. Through the prism of Tietmeyer's life, Campbell examines the decline of the Euro in the wake of the 2008 global financial crisis. *Arbeit* is composed almost entirely of black-and-white photographs set to "an engrossing and psychologically nuanced monologue," Max Andrews wrote in a review of the film for *Frieze* (Jan./Feb. 2012). Andrews concluded, "*Arbeit* is not only a devastating morality tale, and a rebuke to Euroskepticism told from the confounding point of view of a banker, but a thesis on amnesia, hindsight, the ontological status of the image, and an uncertain future."

## IT FOR OTHERS

In 2013 Campbell was one of three artists chosen to represent Scotland at the fifty-fifth Venice Biennale, a major contemporary art exhibition held once every two years in Venice, Italy. There, he showcased his film *It for Others*, which was inspired by Chris Marker and Alain Resnais's 1953 French essay film *Les statues meurent aussi* (*Statues Also Die*), about the colonial commercialization of African art. Campbell used Marker and Resnais's work as a base for his film, which is "about how you can understand certain histories through objects," as he was quoted as saying by Roslyn Sulcas for the *New York Times* (1 Dec. 2014).

*It for Others* runs fifty-four minutes and is divided into three sections. The opening section focuses on Campbell's failed efforts to procure the African artifacts used in Marker and Resnais's film from the British Museum. Forced to use reproductions, Campbell uses the experience to delve into the controversial issue of the repatriation of objects. He expands upon the subject in the film's final two sections, which include a dance sequence choreographed by Michael Clark that explores ideas espoused in Karl Marx's seminal 1867 anticapitalist tome *Das Kapital* and a chronicle of a 1971 image of Irish Republican Army (IRA) member Joe McCann, often referred to as "the Che Guevara of the IRA." "All my art is very aware of propaganda and in some instances I don't have a problem with art that has a contingency, a certain purpose in the world," Campbell explained to Thorpe. "But [*It for Others*] is like a snapshot of a thought process that is continuing. My thinking on it is evolving."

Despite its deliberately complex and open-ended nature, *It for Others* was mostly well received by the art cognoscenti. Dorment commented, "What sets Campbell apart from most contemporary filmmakers is not only the nimble camerawork and a lightness of touch that belies his seriousness of purpose, but his relentless doubting, a constant sense he's not sure, that he wants to know more, that he needs to see the subject from another angle."

## TURNER PRIZE

Among those impressed with *It for Others* were the judges for the 2014 Turner Prize. The film was shortlisted for and eventually won the prize, which is worth £25,000, or around $39,000. Campbell was the fifth graduate from the Glasgow School of Art to have won the prize in the previous ten years. The Turner Prize judges called *It for Others* "an ambitious and complex film which rewards repeated viewing," as quoted by Mark Brown for the *Guardian* (1 Dec. 2014).

In the wake of his triumph, Campbell told Brown that he would use his prize money on "boring" things like rent, food, and studio space. He has not ruled out following other former Turner Prize winners such as Steve McQueen, director of the Oscar-winning film *12 Years a Slave* (2013), into feature filmmaking, though he has reservations. "I make a film as long as it needs to be and the traditional, industrial model of how to produce a film would have to open up to some extent for it to work for me," he told Thorpe.

In December 2014, the same month Campbell won the Turner Prize, the Irish Museum of Modern Art (IMMA) hosted the first major Irish show of his work. In addition to the IMMA, Campbell's work has been displayed in numerous other solo and group exhibitions at venues around the world.

## PERSONAL LIFE

Campbell lives and works in Glasgow, where his studio is based. He is the father of two children.

## SUGGESTED READING

Dorment, Richard. "Turner Prize 2014: 'There's Only One Artist Here.'" *Telegraph*. Telegraph Media Group, 29 Sept. 2014. Web. 9 Aug. 2015.

Herbert, Martin. "Duncan Campbell." *Frieze*. Frieze, Apr. 2008. Web. 9 Aug. 2015.

Kearney, Liz. "Campbell's Coup . . . Making Off with the Turner Prize." *Independent*. Independent.ie, 12 Apr. 2014. Web. 9 Aug. 2015.

Maier, Tobi. "History through Peripheries." *Mousse Magazine*. Mousse Magazine, Apr. 2009. Web. 9 Aug. 2015.

Sulcas, Roslyn. "Innovative Filmmaker Wins Turner Prize for Art." *New York Times*. New York Times, 1 Dec. 2014. Web. 9 Aug. 2015.

Thorpe, Vanessa. "Turner Prize Favorite on Film, Marx and the Art of Doing Things Differently." *Guardian*. Guardian News and Media, 11 Oct. 2014. Web. 9 Aug. 2015.

## SELECTED WORKS

*Falls Burns Malone Fiddles*, 2003; *O Joan, no . . .*, 2006; *Bernadette*, 2008; *Sigmar*, 2008; *Make It New John*, 2009; *Arbeit*, 2011; *It for Others*, 2013

—Chris Cullen

# Lizzy Caplan

**Born:** June 30, 1982
**Occupation:** Actor

Lizzy Caplan has enjoyed an unusually long career for an actor who is only thirty-two years old. As a teenager, she landed her first role in the short-lived television series *Freaks and Geeks* (1999–2000), which has since become a cult favorite. She went on to appear in a number of films, including comedian Tina Fey's hit *Mean Girls* in 2004. She excelled at playing what Stephen Rodrick for *Rolling Stone* (25 Aug. 2014) called an "anti-manic pixie dream girl." It was an appealing persona, but one that Caplan nonetheless felt impeded by.

In 2012, Caplan landed her breakthrough role in the Showtime television series *Masters of Sex* (2013–), about the pioneering sex therapists William Masters and Virginia Johnson. The pair—who were married for nearly twenty years—began working together on a groundbreaking study in 1957 that culminated in the publication of their major book, *Human Sexual Response*, in 1966. Their work was instrumental in changing American attitudes toward sex, particularly sexual pleasure experienced by women. They also famously performed research on one another—an interesting twist that perhaps made the adaptation of their story for modern television inevitable.

The show, which has been well received by audiences and critics alike, is based on the 2009 biography *Masters of Sex* by Thomas Maier. Masters is played by Welsh actor Michael Sheen. Caplan, who was nominated for the 2014 Emmy Award for outstanding lead actress in a drama series for her performance in *Masters of Sex,* was immediately drawn to the project—though she never thought that she would portray Johnson. "There hasn't been one day that has gone by in those three years that I have not been thinking about this job," Caplan told Rodrick. "I don't remember a time before Virginia Johnson."

## EARLY LIFE AND *FREAKS AND GEEKS*

Elizabeth Anne Caplan was born on June 30, 1982, and raised in a Jewish family living in Los Angeles, California. The youngest of three children, her father is a lawyer; her mother died of an illness when Caplan was thirteen. She connects the traumatic event with her early desire to become an actor. "Strangely, from that age on I thought the only reason why I could even attempt to be an actress was because this horrible thing happened to me," she told Rodrick. "Like something dark and terrible had to happen in order to earn your stripes as a human being and be able to be an actress. I don't know where I got that from." Caplan attended a performing arts high school in Los Angeles and studied piano before beginning to take drama classes. By fifteen, she was auditioning in Hollywood.

Auditioning was its own kind of growing-up process, Caplan recalled to Scott Huver for *Los Angeles Confidential* magazine (Sept. 2014). She and fellow young actor Lindsay Sloane, who later scored a role on the television series *Sabrina, the Teenage Witch* in 1996, were of-

Jeff Vespa/WireImage/Getty Images

ten told that they did not have the right "look." However, at seventeen, Caplan landed a cameo role on the Judd Apatow–helmed NBC comedy series *Freaks and Geeks* about teenagers coming of age in the 1980s. Though the show only lasted one season, it went on to become a cult classic, launching the writing and directing career of Apatow, as well as the acting careers of Seth Rogen, James Franco, and Jason Segel. Caplan's role was only intended to last one episode, but Apatow and fellow creator Paul Feig found her so charming that they decided to write her character into the story line. "There was something unique about her performance," Apatow told Rodrick. "So we brought her back again."

### "WHO'S THAT GIRL?"

After *Freaks and Geeks*, Caplan appeared in a slew of made-for-television movies and television shows, including *Undeclared* (2001), a *Freaks and Geeks*–like take on college, and *Smallville* (2001–3), a coming-of-age story about Superman's alter ego Clark Kent. In 2003, she was given a role on the Fox sitcom *The Pitts*, but the show was canceled after seven episodes. The following year, Caplan played the sarcastic goth girl Janis Ian in the hit comedy *Mean Girls*, which starred Lindsay Lohan and Rachel McAdams. In the movie, Caplan's character befriends Lohan's Cady Heron, a new girl and misfit. Together they hatch a plan to ruin Regina George (McAdams),

the school's most popular girl and Janis's former best friend. Caplan's character remains a fan favorite, but *Mean Girls* did not launch Caplan's career like it did those of her costars. After the movie was released, she did not work for a full year.

As Rodrick wrote of this period of her career, Caplan won "quiet acclaim playing the role of 'who's that girl?' in shows and movies that disappeared." She was charming, but her material was ultimately forgettable. In 2008, she secured a role on the vampire television series *True Blood* on HBO. Caplan still recalls her traumatic second day on set when she was required to do her first nude scene. She had spent weeks obsessing over her body, she told Rodrick, but the reality of her situation really hit home when she entered her dressing room. "I walked into my dressing room, and where your clothes are hanging on a rack was just one pair of underwear," she said.

When Caplan was in her twenties, she was candid with reporters and spoke with a certain bravado—perhaps to mask her own insecurities about her career. Speaking with reporter Gerri Miller of *American Jewish Life* magazine (Sept./Oct. 2005) when she was twenty-three, Caplan blithely described her preferred mode of working as "one for the soul, one for the dough," meaning balancing one indie production and one more mainstream project. Though the sentiment is not uncommon among actors, it was a strange comment to make for someone who was struggling to gain a foothold in either capacity.

### PARTY DOWN

In 2009, Caplan landed a part in the Starz sitcom *Party Down* (2009–10), about a group of wannabe actors working for a catering company. Like *Freaks and Geeks*, the show—which also starred Adam Scott, Jane Lynch, and Megan Mullally—was cancelled before it found its fan base. It was off the air after two seasons, though it remains a cult classic. Caplan played a struggling comedian named Casey Klein. Scott, who interviewed Caplan for *Interview* magazine (July 2013), recalled having to convince Caplan to stay on for a second season. "It's scary to sign a six-year contract for something that you don't necessarily know about. And yet I did that most every year," Caplan told Scott. "I've done a lot of failed pilots. But it's different when you have in your mind *Party Down*. There was something about that job—and I think this is the same for you—where it's like, 'Oh, this is what it could be like.'" Scott agreed, suggesting that the cast worked so well together as an ensemble that "we had this sort of gang mentality of it being us against the world." That cohesion, many critics agree, came together in the final product. Though *Party Down* was short-lived, it remains one of Caplan's best comedic performances.

After appearing in a supporting role in the film *Hot Tub Time Machine* (2010), Caplan reunited with Scott for the dark and raunchy comedy *Bachelorette* (2012), which inevitably drew comparisons to the previous year's hit *Bridesmaids* (2011). Though she had a starring role alongside Kirsten Dunst and Isla Fisher and the digital-first release quickly reached number one on iTunes, the film ultimately received mixed reception following its theatrical release.

## MASTERS OF SEX

Caplan's fond memories of *Party Down* made her interested in doing another television show, though she later admitted to Scott that it was hard to find a script she liked. "I'm extra harsh on pilot scripts, which is difficult because pilots, generally, are not that great. You have to imagine the whole series instead of just that one script, and I have a really hard time doing that," she said.

After the cancellation of *Party Down*, Caplan received the pilot for an hour-long period drama called *Masters of Sex*. She expected not to like it—she was primarily a comedic actor, after all—and was surprised when she did. She met with the show's creator, Michelle Ashford, and several of its producers, but she kept her enthusiasm in check. "I thought that I didn't stand a chance of getting it because people just don't see me in that way," she told Scott. She gave a strong audition—it was three hours long—for an English director named John Madden, who directed the show's pilot. Caplan was comfortable with him, she told Scott, because he was not familiar with American television actors or the roles that she had played in the past. Though Caplan still did not think she would get the part, Sarah Timberman, the show's executive producer, later told Huver, "After we saw her read some of the material in the pilot, we couldn't imagine anybody else in this role." Caplan, she added, is "a force of nature—and Virginia Johnson certainly was. They're very well suited to each other. It just feels like this role was something of a calling for her."

Caplan told Scott that performing in the show is immensely satisfying but also "legitimately scary every week." The show features some graphic sex scenes, but unlike other cable television shows that merely titillate, *Masters of Sex*, it could be said, really gives the act its due. "In its stylish pilot, *Masters of Sex* initially comes off a bit like *Mad Men with Benefits*: fetishistic fun with a historical pedigree," Emily Nussbaum wrote in her review of the show for the *New Yorker* (7 Oct. 2013). "But over the first six episodes, the show deepens by degrees, becoming more poignant, and more surprising, too. It begins to acknowledge some of the unsettling implications of the doctor's work and lets characters who start as entertaining cartoons gain complexity, taking the plot in new directions." Of Caplan, she adds: "For all the show's appeal, none of this would work without Lizzy Caplan, the swizzle stick in the show's erotic cocktail. . . . She's chilled out and self-possessed, the type of woman who turns everything she says into an intelligent come-on, even when that's not her intent."

In 2014, Caplan teamed up with Apatow, Rogen, and Franco once more for the comedy film *The Interview*, in which Franco and Rogen play celebrity journalists hired to assassinate North Korean dictator Kim Jong-un. The film attracted an unexpected media storm and controversy when North Korea issued threats, condemned the plot of the movie, and, according to the Federal Bureau of Investigation, allegedly hired a group of hackers to leak the personal emails of Sony Pictures executives. Sony pulled the movie only to release it for online purchase and in select theaters on Christmas Day.

## PERSONAL LIFE

Caplan dated *Friends* actor Matthew Perry for six years before the couple parted ways in 2012. Long avoiding permanency—such as buying a house or a car—Caplan has happily begun to make a home for herself in Los Angeles. "Now I'm putting down roots, and that's nourishing me in ways that are surprising. In the past, I would have downplayed it because the idea of beginning to get what I've worked for would overwhelm me and I'd have to pooh-pooh it. But now I can safely say that I'm enjoying it in the moment," she told Kathryn Hudson for *Elle Canada* (29 Sept. 2014).

## SUGGESTED READING

Caplan, Lizzy. Interview by Adam Scott. *Interview*. Interview, July 2013. Web. 27 Jan. 2015.

Hudson, Kathryn. "*Masters of Sex*'s Whip Smart and Hilarious Lizzy Caplan." *Elle Canada*. Transcontinental Media, 29 Sept. 2014. Web. 27 Jan. 2015.

Huver, Scott. "Lizzy Caplan on 'Funny' 'Masters of Sex' Sex Scenes & More." *Los Angeles Confidential*. Niche Media, Sept. 2014. Web. 27 Jan. 2015.

Miller, Gerri. "Mean Girl No More." *American Jewish Life*. Genco Media, Sept./Oct. 2005. Web. 27 Jan. 2015.

Nussbaum, Emily. "Private Practice." Rev. of *Masters of Sex*. New Yorker. Condé Nast, 7 Oct. 2013. Web. 27 Jan. 2015.

Rodrick, Stephen. "The Liberation of Lizzy Caplan." *Rolling Stone*. Rolling Stone, 25 Aug. 2014. Web. 27 Jan. 2015.

## SELECTED WORKS

*Freaks and Geeks*, 1999–2000; *Mean Girls*, 2004; *Party Down*, 2009–10; *Hot Tub Time Machine*, 2010; *Bachelorette*, 2012; *Masters of Sex*, 2013–; *The Interview*, 2014

—Molly Hagan

# Ashton Carter

**Born:** September 24, 1954
**Occupation:** US Secretary of Defense

A theoretical physicist and medieval historian by training, Ashton Carter is the twenty-fifth US Secretary of Defense and is widely considered to be one of the most knowledgeable individuals to hold that position since its inception. As head of the Defense Department, which had a 2014 annual budget in excess of $600 billion, Carter oversees a workforce of more than three million civilians and military personnel.

The Defense Department faces a number of foreign policy challenges all over the world, including the threat of Islamic militants in the Middle East. President Barack Obama nominated Carter for the post in December 2014 and believes Carter, who has thirty years of government experience and possesses considerable academic and political skills, is more than qualified to face the international and domestic challenges of the position. Helene Cooper et al. reported for the *New York Times* that Carter "once compared working in Washington to 'being a Christian in the Coliseum. You never know when they are going to release the lions and have you torn apart for the amusement of onlookers'" (5 Dec. 2014).

## EARLY LIFE AND EDUCATION

Ashton Baldwin Carter was born in Philadelphia, Pennsylvania, on September 24, 1954. His father, William Stanley Carter, was a psychiatrist and neurologist; his mother, Anne Baldwin Carter, was an English teacher. By the time he was enrolled in Abington High School in Pennsylvania, he was already outstripping his classmates academically. He enjoyed studying medieval histories as well as discarded electrocardiograms (EKGs), which he collected while working at a local hospital. He was a member of the lacrosse, cross-country, and wrestling teams in high school, and in his spare time he enjoyed working through calculus problems. "He was a bit of a geek, but he knew his way around and people liked him," Carter's former high school classmate Rick Williams told Sally Jacobs for the *Boston Globe* (4 Feb. 2015). "He was a totally independent guy who was self-motivated."

After graduating from high school with honors in 1972, Carter entered Yale University, where he earned bachelor of arts degrees in both physics and medieval history and graduated summa cum laude in 1976. During his sophomore year at Yale, he received a perfect score in an advanced physics course taught by physicist Robert Adair who then mentored Carter at a summer fellowship at Chicago's Fermi National Accelerator Laboratory and the following year at the Brookhaven National Laboratory. After earning a Rhodes scholarship, Carter attended England's Oxford University where he earned his doctorate in theoretical physics in 1979. While at Oxford, he developed a friendship with American physicist Sidney D. Drell, who was involved with the problem of arms control. Carter's doctoral adviser, Sir Christopher Llewellyn Smith, recalled to Jacobs, "Ash got to talking to Sid over coffee about arms control so I think mentally he was starting to move in that direction."

## EARLY CAREER IN GOVERNMENT

Carter began his career in government in 1980 when he served as a missile-system analyst in the International Security and Commerce Program through the congressional Office of Technology Assessment. The following year he worked for both Secretaries of Defense

United States Department of Defense

Brown and Weinberger as a technology and program analyst on several programs including missile defense and nuclear command and control. From 1982 to 1984 Carter worked as a research fellow for the Center for International Studies at the Massachusetts Institute of Technology (MIT).

While at MIT he wrote a report for the Office of Technology Assessment, published in 1984, which challenged the proposal made by President Ronald Reagan in 1983 that the United States should put its efforts into building a space-based missile defense program, the goal of which would be to deter a nuclear attack on the United States by the Soviet Union. The program, which was dubbed "Star Wars" by the press, was popular and controversial. Carter's report proved that the notion was neither feasible nor practical. As reported by Tom Wicker in his Opinion piece for the *New York Times* (11 May 1984), Carter wrote that there was "a consensus among informed members of the defense technical community" that a working program was "so remote that it should not serve as the basis of public expectation or national policy."

## HARVARD UNIVERSITY AND THE CLINTON ADMINISTRATION

Carter left government work in 1984 when he became an assistant professor at Harvard University's Kennedy School of Government. He was promoted to associate professor in 1986,

and in 1988 he became both full professor and associate director of the school's Center for Science and International Affairs, which became known as the Belfer Center in 1997. Carter maintained a close working relationship with this arm of the university for many years, and he would ultimately serve as the Center's director from 1990 to 1993, a promotion that was in part, many believe, a result of his pragmatic approach to thorny political problems. "Ash is basically pragmatic, not an ideologue," Belfer Center director Graham Allison explained to Jacobs. "The way reality works, owls sometimes kill hawks. But I'd say that the owl comes closer to Ash in that he does not have predictable views. He lives on facts and analysis."

In 1993 Carter joined the Clinton administration's Department of Defense when he was hired to serve as assistant secretary of defense for international security policy. In addition to contributing to the Defense Policy Board, the Defense Science Board, and the Secretary of State's International Security Advisory Board, Carter was involved in strategic affairs and nuclear weapons policy, which included the treaty that removed old Soviet nuclear weapons from the newly independent nations of Ukraine, Kazakhstan, and Belarus. Carter also took part in the negotiations with North Korea when the regime removed all international inspectors from the country in 1994 to prevent their learning of the country's efforts to develop small-caliber nuclear arms. Cooper reported that Carter once explained that this period when he and other members of the US government were negotiating with North Korea "may have been the closest we came to conflict with North Korea since the end of the Korean War."

In 1996 Carter returned to the Kennedy School and for the next thirteen years he served as Chair of International Relations, Security, and Science as well as a Ford Foundation professor of science and international affairs. From 1998 through 2000, however, Carter also served as a senior advisor to the US Department of State on North Korea policy review.

## THE OBAMA ADMINISTRATION

Because Carter had gained a reputation during his time with the Clinton administration for expertise in science and defense policy as well as for speaking his mind despite potential conflict with his superiors, many were not surprised when he returned to government in April 2009. During President Barack Obama's first term Carter served as undersecretary of defense for acquisition, technology, and logistics (ATL) until 2011. In this job, which is the number three position in the Pentagon, he reformed the Defense Department's policies to enable more rapid development and procurement of necessary equipment, such as the KC-46 tanker, thousands of mine-resistant ambush protected vehicles known as MRAPs, and innovative new protective gear for all US troops. He also saved taxpayer money by implementing the Better Buying Power program at the Defense Department, which outlined for the Department's workforce the application of more considered and prudent purchases.

In August 2011 President Obama nominated Carter to replace Deputy Secretary of Defense William J. Lynn. Carter is reportedly respected by both Democrats and Republicans alike, which might account for his unanimous confirmation to the position the following month. Despite the financial constraints put in place by the across-the-board spending cuts, Carter ensured that all military and civilian personnel within the Defense Department received any and all necessary resources. He left the Defense Department in December 2013 to return to civilian life, serving as a consultant, public speaker, and lecturer.

## SECRETARY OF DEFENSE

On December 5, 2014, President Obama nominated Carter to succeed Secretary of Defense Chuck Hagel, whose resignation was announced on November 24. As secretary of defense, Carter would be charged with addressing the increasing threat in the Middle East from the militant fundamentalist Islamic group known as the Islamic State and often referred to as ISIS or ISIL. He would also be in charge of supervising the end of the US military's operation in Afghanistan, where it still has approximately 10,000 troops stationed to help the Afghan military. Cooper reported that when President Obama announced the Carter nomination, he explained to the country that "Ash [Carter] is rightly regarded as one of our nation's foremost national security leaders. . . . He was at the table in the Situation Room, he was by my side in navigating complex security challenges."

On February 12, 2015, with a 93–5 vote, the Senate overwhelmingly confirmed Carter to the position of secretary of defense. A few days after being sworn in on February 17, he visited Afghanistan to oversee operations there. "We're looking for success in Afghanistan that is lasting, the lasting accomplishment of our mission here and how to do that," Carter said during his visit, according to Michael Schmidt for the *New York Times* (20 Feb. 2015). "And the best way to do that is precisely what I'm here to assess." Secretary of Defense Carter also closely monitors the Iraqi-led operations to push ISIS out of Iraq's major cities, which had been previously secured at considerable cost by US troops during the war in Iraq. In addition to national security concerns, Carter is also looking to reinvigorate the relationship between the academia, industry, and government, an association that had a proven track record of developing technological innovations during the twentieth century. He believes in getting some of the best young minds of the current generation to work in government. According to Walter Pincus for the *Washington Post* (27 Apr. 2015), Carter said in a speech he delivered at Stanford University, "I'm in the position now of needing to attract to military service a generation of people who grew up entirely in the Internet age, whose memories of 9/11 are either faded or dim or nonexistent, and attract them to the mission of national security."

## PERSONAL LIFE

Ashton Carter is married to the former Stephanie DeLeeuw. He has two adult children, William and Ava, with his first wife, Ava Clayton Spencer. Carter is the author of eleven books and over one hundred articles on a wide variety of subjects relating to science, technology, national security, and management. He has received numerous awards throughout his career in government, including the Department of Defense Distinguished Public Service Medal, which he won five times between 1994 and 2013; the 1998 Defense Intelligence Medal; and the 2013 Joint Distinguished Civilian Service Award from the Chairman and Joint Chiefs of Staff.

## SUGGESTED READING

"Ashton Carter Fast Facts." *CNN.com.* CNN, 18 Feb. 2015. Web. 5 Aug. 2015.

Cooper, Helene, et al. "In Ashton Carter, Nominee for Defense Secretary, a Change in Direction." *New York Times.* New York Times, 5 Dec. 2014. Web. 5 Aug. 2015.

Jacobs, Sally. "For Ashton Carter, a Perennial Search for Balance." *Boston Globe.* Boston Globe Media Partners, 4 Feb. 2015. Web. 5 Aug. 2015.

Jaffee, Greg, and Loveday Morris. "Defense Secretary Carter: Iraqis Lack 'Will to Fight' to Defeat Islamic State." *Washington Post.* Washington Post, 24 May 2015. Web. 5 Aug. 2015.

Pincus, Walter. "At the Pentagon, Carter Looks to a Bygone Era as a Way to the Future." *Washington Post.* Washington Post, 27 Apr. 2015. Web. 5 Aug. 2015.

Schmidt, Michael S. "Ashton Carter, Defense Secretary, in Afghanistan for Security Talks." *New York Times.* New York Times, 20 Feb. 2015. Web. 5 Aug. 2015.

—Christopher Mari

# Safra A. Catz

**Born:** December 1961
**Occupation:** Business executive

Jay Mallin/Bloomberg via Getty Images

"Despite her high-profile post . . . very little has been written about Safra Catz except that she prefers not to be written about," claims an article in the spring 2007 issue of the Wharton School of Business's alumni magazine. The publicity-shy Catz became the co-chief executive officer of the Oracle Corporation, a Silicon Valley software giant, in September 2014. Previously, she had served as a stalwart presence at the company for some fifteen years, moving up the ranks steadily and shaping its path. She has often been regarded as the closest adviser of Oracle's iconoclastic cofounder, Larry Ellison. "Catz's title has never been particularly meaningful," Adam Lashinsky wrote for *Fortune* magazine (10 Sept. 2009). "Her real job is making sure the entire organization follows the policies that Larry Ellison sets."

"There's no difference between Safra and Larry," Mark Barrenechea, a former Oracle executive, told Rochelle Garner for *Bloomberg* (18 Dec. 2006). "One's just at the microphone and the other is behind the curtain." That loyalty has paid off handsomely for Catz, who has overseen dozens of acquisitions for Oracle during her tenure, including a $10.3 billion hostile takeover of rival PeopleSoft in 2005. She is routinely included at or near the top of lists of the world's most powerful and highest-paid female executives. In 2013 she made $43.6 million to lead all chief financial officers (CFOs), male or female, in earnings, marking the first time a woman has achieved that distinction.

## EARLY YEARS AND EDUCATION

Safra Ada Catz was born in 1961 in the Israeli town of Holon. Her mother, Judith, had survived the Holocaust as a child by sheltering with Ukrainian partisans. Once the Nazis had been defeated, Catz's mother traveled to the United States, where she learned English and studied speech pathology before visiting Israel during her junior year of college and deciding to settle there. In Israel Judith met and married "Leonard" Arieh Catz, and the couple had two daughters. After both Catz and her younger sister, Sarit, who later became a professional comedian, were born and their father had served in the Six Day War in 1967, the family moved to Brookline, Massachusetts, where Catz's mother worked as a speech therapist and her father became a physics professor at the University of Massachusetts Boston.

After graduating from Brookline High School, Catz enrolled at the University of Pennsylvania's Wharton School of Business, earning her undergraduate degree in 1983. She joined the school's fencing team and became known for her fierce attacks and determination despite having no prior experience in the sport.

Catz remained at the University of Pennsylvania for law school, transferring to Harvard University for her final year of study. During a summer internship on Wall Street, however, it dawned on her that the investment bankers at the firm were better compensated and more powerful than the attorneys, and after she earned her doctorate in 1986 she decided to pursue business instead of law.

## LAUNCHING A BUSINESS CAREER

The year Catz graduated she accepted a job at Donaldson, Lufkin & Jenrette (DLJ), a respected investment bank that had been founded in 1959. Catz had long been interested in computers, and she was excited by the potential she saw in the early software industry. She made that her focus, taking on high-profile technology industry clients such as Symantec. "She didn't know software from hardware from jellyfish," Thomas Greig, her supervisor at DLJ, told Chris O'Brien and Elise Ackerman for the *San Jose Mercury News* (25 Jan. 2004). "But that did not deter her."

Catz quickly earned a reputation as a tireless worker, spending countless hours on the phone with clients and crisscrossing the country by plane. In 1997 she transferred to Silicon Valley in California, to be closer to the high-tech companies she was representing. Among those was Oracle, which specialized in developing computer hardware systems and software products. Coworkers remember that she often spoke admiringly of Oracle's visionary cofounder Ellison, and, indeed, the two even dated for a time.

Although she spent years nurturing DLJ's technology clients, Catz was troubled by the dotcom bubble of the late 1990s, and she started to consider leaving the banking world. Serendipitously, Ellison offered a solution.

## JOINING ORACLE

In April 1999 Catz joined Oracle as a senior vice president. Initially, her presence puzzled others at the company. No one really knew the role of the seemingly mysterious woman ensconced in a small, nondescript office near Ellison's. Shortly after she was hired, she attended a meeting at which the easily distracted Ellison fidgeted and grumbled, eventually getting up to leave the room altogether. To everyone's shock, Catz grabbed his arm and sternly admonished him to sit back down. To their further surprise, he readily complied. "No one else at Oracle could do that," one of the executives who had been in the room later told Lashinsky.

Catz quickly rose through the ranks of the company, becoming an executive vice president within six months and joining the company's board of directors in 2001. In 2004 she was elevated to copresident, a title she held for more than a decade, first sharing the post with former

Wall Street analyst Charles Phillips and then with Mark Hurd, a former executive at the technology company Hewlett-Packard.

In 2005 Catz was concurrently appointed Oracle's interim CFO, further solidifying her position as a figure with deep influence in the organization. Earning the approval of some company insiders and the ire of others, she became responsible for taking control of Oracle when Ellison vacationed. "Safra allows Larry to work thirty hours a week but have the effectiveness of a CEO who works one hundred hours a week," a source told Lashinsky.

## MANAGEMENT STYLE

Throughout Catz's tenure she focused on mergers and acquisitions, and she oversaw some of the most important transactions in the company's history. Among the most buzzed-about was the hostile takeover of rival PeopleSoft, a company Ellison had been eyeing for years. Catz urged him to act after PeopleSoft announced its merger with rival JD Edwards in June 2003. Oracle's initial offer of just over $5 billion was rejected, but after eighteen months of acrimony and backbiting, a $10.3 billion agreement was reached by 2005 that transformed Oracle into the second-largest producer of business management software in the world. Federal regulators conducted an antitrust investigation of the deal and attempted to block the takeover but were unable to stop it.

That successful purchase, as Garner wrote, "began a $20 billion buying spree of twenty-seven companies, making Oracle a single source for three types of software: databases; business management systems; and middleware, or software that connects computer servers." Among those companies was Sun Microsystems, which Oracle acquired in early 2009, shocking industry insiders by beating rival IBM with a cash offer of nine dollars and fifty cents per share—$5.6 billion total minus Sun's cash and debt.

Catz has been known to always drive a hard bargain during such deals. "When we do acquisitions, we decide what we want. We decide what fills a hole. And if the price is too high, our alternative is the $5 billion we spend on [research and development] every year," she told attendees at one conference, as reported by Cory Johnson and Jack Clark for *Bloomberg News* (1 Oct. 2014). "We're not well known for overpaying, because at Oracle we always have an alternative."

Despite the juggernaut status that Oracle achieved in the wake of so many acquisitions, Catz has refused to rest on her laurels or to allow others at the company to do so. "We're number one in database, we're number one in middleware, but we're number two in applications," she said, as quoted by Johnson and Clark. "At Oracle, silver medal is first loser." After several years serving as copresident, she resumed her other role as Oracle's CFO in 2011.

In September 2014 Ellison announced his intention to step down as CEO of the company that he had helmed for more than three decades. His two copresidents, Catz and Hurd, continued their partnership, this time as co-CEOs. Hurd would focus on sales, marketing, and strategy, Ellison explained, while Catz would devote her time to finance, manufacturing, and legal matters. The change in leadership came as no surprise to industry observers, and the division of labor was widely thought to be a wise one. Catz's formidable focus on finance and hard data had long been acknowledged. "I come from Wall Street, and you'll never see me do a Power-Point because I'm all about Excel spreadsheets," she once said, as quoted by Lashinsky. "If it's not in the numbers, I don't care how strategic it is, it doesn't play out."

## ADDITIONAL POSITIONS AND PERSONAL LIFE

Catz was appointed to the board of directors of the financial services company HSBC Holdings in 2008. She is a lecturer at the Stanford Graduate School of Business, where she teaches courses on mergers and acquisitions. She is married to Gal Tirosh, an Israeli writer who stayed at home to raise the couple's sons, Daniel and Jonathan, and to coach their soccer teams. Catz has said that she would not be able to pursue her career so assiduously without his help.

Coworkers rarely discuss Catz on the record with journalists for fear of attracting her censure, but those who have often comment that her personality easily pivots between charmingly friendly and coldly dismissive. She has maintained that working in the technology industry as a female executive has special requirements. In a speech at the May 2005 Women's High-Tech Coalition conference Catz asserted, "You have to be better. You have got to work harder, work longer, be louder."

## SUGGESTED READING

Dorbian, Iris. "Oracle CFO Safra Catz Is Highest-Paid Woman Exec." *CFO Magazine*. CFO, 29 July 2014. Web. 4 Dec. 2014.

Garner, Rochelle. "Oracle's Catz, Ellison Heir, Gets Credit for Growth Strategy." *Bloomberg*. Bloomberg, 18 Dec. 2006. Web. 4 Dec. 2014.

Johnson, Cory, and Jack Clark. "Oracle CEO Catz Rips SAP and Misfit Deals." *Bloomberg News*. Bloomberg, 1 Oct. 2014. Web. 4 Dec. 2014.

Kim, Eugene. "Meet New Oracle Co-CEO Safra Catz, the Highest-Paid Female Executive in the World." *Business Insider*. Business Insider, 18 Sept. 2014. Web. 4 Dec. 2014.

Lashinsky, Adam. "Oracle's Enforcer—Safra Catz." *Fortune*. Time, 10 Sept. 2009. Web. 4 Dec. 2014.

O'Brien, Chris, and Elise Ackerman. "Oracle's Powerful Mystery Woman, Safra Catz." *San Jose Mercury News*. San Jose Mercury News, 25 Jan. 2004. Web. 4 Dec. 2014.

—Mari Rich

# Mark Cerny

**Born:** 1964
**Occupation:** Video game designer

Mark Cerny is a legend among gamers. He joined the early video game company Atari—whose former employees included Apple founder Steve Jobs—at the age of seventeen, and at eighteen created the classic arcade game Marble Madness. He went on to develop games for Sega, and, in the early 1990s, served as the president of Universal Interactive Studios. With Universal, he oversaw the development of the games *Crash Bandicoot* and *Spyro the Dragon*, both of which proved instrumental in the success of Sony's first PlayStation console. Cerny is the quintessential software guy, a visionary designer praised for using his prescient understanding of emerging technologies to create new and exciting games. But after Sony's 2006 launch of its third-generation console, the PlayStation 3, proved disastrous, the company hired Cerny instead as a hardware guy—the lead architect for the PlayStation 4. "When PlayStation 3 wrapped, we all started to do post-mortems. It was pretty brutal, frankly," Cerny told Cade Metz for *Wired* magazine (7 Nov. 2013). Foremost among the console's problems, Cerny recalled, was that it was "very, very difficult" for designers to make games for the console. "I just couldn't stop thinking that maybe there was a different path. Maybe there was a hardware that could be made where it would be natural to make the games."

The PlayStation 4, which was released in November 2013, was $200 cheaper than its predecessor and simply designed. The PlayStation 3 launched with only twelve available games; the PlayStation 4 launched with twenty-two and added another ten before 2014. In designing the system, Cerny consulted with sixteen Sony-owned design studios and another sixteen studios that were not associated with the company. Cerny, a designer himself, understood the importance of quality gaming in selling consoles. With the advent of smartphones, tablets, and similar devices, old standards like PlayStation have had to work harder to keep their audience. "Game partners are going to be as crucial as any of the particulars of the hardware," tech analyst and gaming consultant Scott Steinberg told Metz. "Cerny's roots go back thirty or forty years, and he understands what's going on here. This isn't just a technical play."

## EARLY LIFE AND EDUCATION AT ATARI

Cerny was born in 1964 and was raised in Berkeley, California. His father worked as a lecturer in nuclear chemistry at the University of California, Berkeley, and when Cerny was five years old, he taught himself to code on the school's CDC 6400 mainframe computer. When he was thirteen, he began taking math and science classes at the university, and at sixteen he enrolled full time. Outside of the classroom, Cerny, an avid *Dungeons and Dragons* player, was developing a passion for arcade games. The 1970s saw the birth of classic arcade games like *Pong* and *Space Invaders*, which would serve as precursors for the console games of the 1980s. Cerny discovered *Space Invaders* at a local arcade in 1978, the year of its release, and, by his own account, quickly became one of the game's top players. A few years later, a man named Craig Kubey was researching a book about arcade games and contacted Cerny. "He was touring the arcades looking for hotshot players, visiting game companies and interviewing game creators," Cerny told Simon Parkin for the *MIT Technology Review* (20 Aug. 2013). "I was looking for a way to turn my hobbies into a job, and Kubey agreed to mention me to Atari during one of his interviews."

Katsura Cerny/Wikimedia

Atari was the brainchild of Nolan Bushnell, a man who is often referred to as the godfather of video games for his role in the development of *Pong* in 1972. The young company essentially defined the gaming industry in terms of how video games are designed, manufactured, and marketed. Bushnell was also one of Silicon Valley's first young tech titans. He prided himself on sticking to his creative ideals and, years before Apple offered the directive, thinking differently. A few weeks after Cerny met Kubey in 1982, Bushnell asked the seventeen-year-old Cerny to join Atari's elite group of fifteen programmers. "[I]t was an amazing place," Cerny told Douglas C. Perry for the gaming website *IGN* (12 Mar. 2004). "We were all expected to be designers as well as programmers—in fact, there were no dedicated designers!" Cerny enjoyed the flexibility and creative atmosphere at Atari, although by the time he arrived, the company was already beginning to flounder under inconsistent management.

Amid all of his success, Cerny never found time to complete his college degree. It was a bitter pill for his parents to swallow—both of them, as well as Cerny's brother and four of his stepsiblings, have PhDs. Years after taking the job at Atari, Cerny told Parkin, his parents made peace with his lack of formal education "when it became clear [he] could make enough money in games to support [himself]."

The first game Cerny worked on at Atari was an arcade classic called *Major Havoc*, released in 1983. When Cerny was eighteen, the company asked him to create his own game. The result was *Marble Madness*. The game was more sophisticated than other Atari offerings; players used a trackball to navigate the on-screen marble through Escher-like mazes. When the game was 80 percent complete, Atari installed a *Marble Madness* machine in a local arcade so Cerny could watch people play the game. The testing phase was standard procedure at Atari, though two out of every three games never made it beyond that initial stage. *Marble Madness*, by contrast, was an instant hit. Bolstered by his success, Cerny quit his job at Atari to work as an independent game developer.

## WORK AT SEGA AND UNIVERSAL INTERACTIVE STUDIOS

Cerny quickly found that working on both the software and hardware for a game was too much for one person, and after eighteen months on his own, he moved to Tokyo, Japan, to work for Sega in 1985. After working at Atari, Sega was a corporate culture shock. "At Atari it was all about creativity; if the concept wasn't 100 percent original, you couldn't make it," Cerny told Parkin. "Sega was about shoveling the titles out the door. We made forty games, but by my judgment, only two were really worth playing." Console games, or video games that could be hooked up to a television and played at home, were quickly overtaking arcade games as the preference of gamers in the 1980s. During his time with Sega, Cerny worked on console games like *Missile Defense 3-D* and *Shooting Gallery* and began developing an online games network, years before most of the world would know what the word "online" even meant. Crucially, he also learned the Japanese language. In 1993, Cerny moved back to California, where he founded and managed the Sega Technical Institute, and oversaw the development of *Sonic the Hedgehog 2*, sequel to the million-copy-selling *Sonic the Hedgehog*, for Sega Genesis.

After leaving Sega, Cerny briefly joined the games team at a company called Crystal Dynamics, where he developed games for the 3DO, a CD-based console. Ultimately, however, the 3DO hardware could not compete with Nintendo and Sega. Cerny left the company in 1994 to become the vice president of Universal Interactive Studios, where he later served as president. Cerny told Neil Long for the online gaming magazine *Edge* (27 June 2013) that his new position gave him unprecedented power. "Universal didn't understand the games business," Cerny said, and as a result, he was handed "a big bag of money" with "no

supervision." In this role, Cerny is credited with giving the studios Naughty Dog and Insomniac their start. Cerny, who despite his managerial role was still programming and designing, began working with Naughty Dog to develop a game called *Crash Bandicoot* and with Insomniac to create *Spyro the Dragon*, both for Sony's new console, the PlayStation.

## CERNY GAMES AND THE METHOD

Toward the end of his time with Crystal Dynamics, Cerny found out that Sony was developing a new console. Thanks to his Japanese connections and his fluency in the language, he was able to finagle one of the very first PlayStation software development kits. He was the first non-Japanese designer to have the tools to develop games for the inaugural PlayStation. Crystal Dynamics ultimately failed to make the jump to PlayStation, but after Cerny's move to Universal, he and his team developed a series of successful games for the PlayStation and PlayStation 2, including *Crash Bandicoot* in 1996, which became the first PlayStation's top-selling franchise. In 1998, Naughty Dog and Insomniac left Universal to work more closely with Sony, and Cerny founded his own consultancy called Cerny Games. Around the same time, Cerny first shared his method for developing and testing games. A refinement of the Atari testing process, Cerny's method—gaming insiders call it "the Method," Metz wrote—has become standard procedure in the industry. When he is working on a game, Cerny focuses first on developing what he calls a "publishable first playable," he told Metz. "We don't know if a game is something someone is going to be interested in or not. It makes a lot of sense to just build a piece of it first—but that piece needs to be representative. You can't just hack something together."

Cerny then subjects his first playable to rigorous testing. In the 1990s, he used to literally pull gamers off the street, put them in a room full of gaming consoles, and tape record their play. Cerny even started putting up cardboard dividers so players would not be distracted by one another. Today, Cerny's method is a bit more sophisticated. Gamers play games in specially designed rooms while Cerny and his team watch them behind a two-way mirror. "He doesn't talk to the player at all," Andrew House, the head of Sony Computer Entertainment, the Sony subsidiary that oversees PlayStation, told Metz. "He just watches what they do and how they play the game. I remember him, quite literally, phoning game designers changes on the fly, back to the team in LA, just based on what he was seeing." Cerny applied the same principles of his method—collaboration and flexibility—to his job as the lead architect for the PlayStation 4, to successful results.

In July 2014, Wesley Yin-Poole reported for Eurogamer.net (14 July 2014) that Cerny had turned his attention back to games and was at work on a new game for the PS4 platform. Cerny referred to the game as an indie title even though it has full funding. He appreciates the smaller team that he's working with and the opportunity to try what he calls "more concept-based work."

Cerny met his wife at a friend's wedding in the early 1990s when he was working for Sega in Japan. The couple live in Los Angeles with their two cocker spaniels.

## SUGGESTED READING

Long, Neil. "A Brief History of Mark Cerny: From Atari to Becoming One of PlayStation's 'Three Musketeers.'" *Edge*. Future, 27 June 2013. Web. 20 Oct. 2014.

Metz, Cade. "Exclusive: The American Who Designed the PlayStation 4 and Remade Sony." *Wired*. Condé Nast, 7 Nov. 2013. Web. 20 Oct. 2014.

Parkin, Simon. "The Man Who Drew Up Sony's Next Game Plan." *MIT Technology Review*. MIT, 20 Aug. 2013. Web. 20 Oct. 2014.

Perry, Douglas C. "Interview with Mark Cerny." *IGN*. IGN, 12 Mar. 2004. Web. 20 Oct. 2014.

Yin-Poole, Wesley. "PS4 System Architect Mark Cerny Working on a New Indie Game." *Eurogamer.net*. Eurogamer.net, 14 July 2014. Web. 22 Oct. 2014.

—Molly Hagan

# Charli XCX

**Born:** August 2, 1992

**Occupation:** Singer-songwriter

Charli XCX had her first taste of international fame after penning and guesting on one of the top hits of 2013, Icona Pop's infectious "I Love It." A year later she notched the first number-one hit on the Billboard Hot 100 with her guest appearance on rapper Iggy Azalea's multiplatinum "Fancy." But it was not until the release of "Boom Clap," the lead single from the soundtrack of the 2014 romantic drama *The*

*Fault in Our Stars*, that the British songwriter finally took center stage. Charli's first song as a lead artist—a self-penned tune that she had not even planned on recording—has become her biggest solo hit to date, selling over one million copies in the United States and becoming certified platinum by the Recording Industry Association of America in September 2014.

However, the success is not what has been most important to Charli. "My sound is pop. I never wanted to write a hipster record or a cool record," she told Jose D. Duran for the *Miami New Times* (3 June 2013). In an interview with Lauren Nostro for *Complex* (6 Mar. 2013), she explained, "I've wanted to write good pop music, beautiful pop music—not just throwaways. I've always wanted to make it sound luscious and beautiful and cinematic."

## EARLY LIFE AND EDUCATION

Charlotte Emma Aitchison was born to Shameera and Jon Aitchison on August 2, 1992, in Cambridge, England. An only child, Aitchison, nicknamed Charli, grew up in the middle-class suburb of Stevenage, Hertfordshire, with her mother, who was born in Uganda to Indian parents, and her Scottish father, an entrepreneur.

Charli made her performing debut at age four, when she sang an a cappella rendition of Aqua's pop hit "Barbie Girl" for a cruise ship talent show. While attending Bishop's Stortford College, she honed her singing chops while developing a passion for performance art. She was a fan of the popular British all-girl pop quintet the Spice Girls. "Me and my friends would all have Spice Girls dress ups, and I'd make my friends sing songs I'd written," she told Sarah Walters for the *Manchester Evening News* (27 Mar. 2015). She has also cited Britney Spears as another early musical inspiration.

Her father exposed her to the Sex Pistols and other punk rock music. Charli has credited MySpace with helping her discover French electronica. "All of the Ed Banger artists really inspired me to begin making music," she told Olivia Estrada for *Status* (6 Oct. 2014). "It was a sound that I'd never heard before but was so fascinated by."

## GETS DISCOVERED ON MYSPACE

Charli was already writing songs at age ten, after receiving a Yamaha keyboard as a birthday present. Four years later she recorded her debut disc, *14*, with financing from her father. By early

Eva Rinaldi (CC BY-SA 2.0)

2008 Charli had uploaded several tracks to her MySpace account.

Charli's MySpace recordings eventually caught the ear of an East London party promoter, who invited her to perform at his warehouse raves. Despite being underage, Charli received permission from her parents, who also drove her to her gigs, where the sixteen-year-old unveiled her stage name: Charli XCX. "The XCX stands for 'Kiss Charli Kiss,'" she explained to Billy Johnson Jr. for *Yahoo! Music* (13 Dec. 2014). "It used to be my old MSN screen name and I kinda just panicked when I had to come up with an artist name."

Charli quickly became a fixture on East London's rave scene. During a gig at the pub Coach and Horses, Charli, who was being courted by major record labels, impressed Ed Howard, an A&R (artists and repertoire) executive from the UK division of Atlantic Records. "This little girl, she gets up on a chair in the middle of the room, with a microphone, her iPod plugged into the stereo, with a wig on," he recalled to Amos Barshad for *Grantland* (26 June 2013). "And she was amazing: rolling around the floor, stomping around the crowd. It was like performance art." In 2010 Charli accepted a recording contract with Asylum Records, a subsidiary of Atlantic Records.

In 2010, while preparing for A-levels (international college entrance exams), Charli collaborated with various Los Angeles–based producers on her major-label debut, but she connected with Ariel Rechtshaid, with whom she cowrote the dark synth-pop ballad "Stay Away" in two hours.

Charli spent the next two years honing her pop sound. During this period she attended London's prestigious Slade School of Fine Art before dropping out her second year to pursue music full-time. In June 2011, a month after its exclusive UK release, "Stay Away" was named best new track by Pitchfork Media. She duplicated that feat in November with the synth-laden electro-pop song "Nuclear Seasons." Charli also worked closely with Grammy-nominated Swedish producer Patrik Berger, whose beats formed the basis for two tracks: "You're the One" and "I Love It."

## BREAKS THROUGH WITH "I LOVE IT"

Although Charli ended up recording "You're the One" herself, she decided that "I Love It" was not right for her album. Berger presented the demo to another act that he was producing, Icona Pop. The Swedish female duo instantly fell in love with the tune and recorded their own version, while still keeping Charli's vocals on the track.

Despite being released in Sweden in May 2012, "I Love It" did not become a hit in the United States until the song appeared on a January 2013 episode of the HBO sitcom *Girls*. Ten days after the episode aired, "I Love It" cracked the Billboard Hot 100 chart, where it peaked at number seven. The song also reached the top of the Billboard Hot Dance/Electronic Songs chart.

By then, Charli's singing career was in full swing. The US version of her debut EP (extended play), *You're the One*, had been digitally released in June 2012. Along with the title track, which was named one of the best songs 2012 by *Billboard*, the disc contained "Nuclear Seasons" as well as remixes of both tunes. Later that month, she put out *Heartbreaks and Earthquakes*, a mixtape of original material and covers, including Drake's "Dreams Money Can Buy."

Charli spent the spring and summer of 2012 on the road. In addition to performing at the South by Southwest music festival in Austin, Texas, she opened for the American singer Santigold and the British rock band Coldplay on several North American tour dates. The UK and Australian editions of Charli's EP hit the shelves in September, followed by the November release of another mixtape, *Super Ultra*.

## RELEASES MAJOR-LABEL DEBUT

*True Romance*, Charli's highly anticipated major-label debut, was released in April 2013, with a majority of the album's tracks coming from her previous *You're the One* EP, as well as her 2012 mixtapes. In a review of the album for *Spin* (18 Apr. 2013), Puja Patel wrote: "Britney, she is not, but her collage of pop dreams, electro flash, and diary-rage lyrics could very well create a new generation of pop stars, one in which being a weirdo is a necessity." *True Romance* earned a best new music accolade from *Pitchfork* (25 Apr. 2013), and Marc Hogan noted in a review for *Pitchfork* that "Charli XCX's approach to pop is similarly postmodern . . . pulling from moody 80s synth-pop, sassy turn-of-the-millennium girl groups, and state-of-the-art contemporary producers to create something distinctive and immediately memorable."

Despite the critical acclaim, the album spent only one week in the top five of the Billboard Heatseekers Albums chart. Charli was quick to point out that *True Romance* did not accurately represent her. "I was conscious of trying to be cool throughout making it," she shared with Rachael Dove for the *Daily Telegraph* (15 Feb. 2015). "But I didn't feel like it was totally me." By June 2013 Charli had already begun work on her sophomore disc, reuniting with Berger. At the time she had become frustrated at being expected to recreate the success of their Icona Pop hit. "I got kind of caught up in the whole idea of writing a hit—it made me hate pop music for a while and unable to write any good songs," she explained to Kyle Anderson for *Entertainment Weekly* (25 Aug. 2014). Nevertheless, the two successfully cowrote five of her second album's thirteen tracks, trading in the 1980s synth pop of his previous effort for a 1990s aggressive, guitar-driven sound. Other collaborators included Rivers Cuomo, the front man for Weezer, and Rostam Batmanglij, the guitarist for Vampire Weekend.

## TOP OF THE CHARTS

Charli's collaborations were not just limited to her own music. In early 2014, the Grammy-nominated producers the Invisible Men approached her about writing the chorus for a song by Australian rapper Iggy Azalea. "At the time it had no name and no hook, just Iggy's verses. I just went in and did my thing, which is just shouting into a microphone for twenty minutes, and it just came together," she told Rob LeDonne for the *New York Times Magazine* (7 July 2014). Released in February 2014, "Fancy" considerably raised Charli's profile. In a review for *Rolling Stone* (21 Feb. 2014) Joe Gross declared that "Charli XCX's earworm hook holds it all down."

The song was equally well received by the public, spending seven consecutive weeks at the top of the Billboard Hot 100 and giving Charli the first number-one of her career. Accolades also included two Grammy Award nominations (for record of the year and best pop duo/group performance) and the award for top rap song at the 2015 Billboard Music Awards. Charli appeared alongside Azalea in the accompanying video, which was inspired by the 1995 comedy film *Clueless*.

However, it was not until the release of the techno-pop inspired "Boom Clap" on April 11, 2014, that Charli became a full-fledged artist in her own right. After cowriting the song with Berger during the *True Romance* sessions, the track was presented—but rejected—for Hilary Duff's upcoming album. Charli decided to record the song, which appeared on the soundtrack for *The Fault in Our Stars* (2014), a film adaptation of John Green's 2012 novel of the same name. "Boom Clap" topped Billboard's Pop Songs chart—her first number-one hit as a lead artist—and also became her first top-ten single in the United Kingdom, reaching number six on the Billboard Official UK Singles chart. Charli performed the song live at the preshow for the 2014 MTV Video Music Awards, where she was nominated in the artist to watch category.

Following the success of "Boom Clap," Charli's sophomore disc was released in mid-December 2014. *Sucker*, which also contained the single "Boom Clap," cracked the top thirty of the Billboard Hot 200, aided by her second single, the electro-punk-infused "Break the Rules," which reached the top thirty of the Billboard Pop Songs chart. The album's third single, "Doing It," features English singer Rita Ora and peaked at number eight on the Billboard Official UK Singles chart.

## PERSONAL LIFE

In August 2015 Charli XCX officially put down roots in Los Angeles, purchasing a 1920s Tudor-style home in the Hollywood Hills. That same month she announced plans to design a collection for online retailer Boohoo. The singer revealed that she has synesthesia, a neuropsychological condition that enables her to see music and sounds as colors.

## SUGGESTED READING

Anderson, Kyle. "Charli XCX on Her New Album 'Sucker' and Getting Angry at Pop Music: An EW Q&A." *Entertainment Weekly*. Entertainment Weekly, 25 Aug. 2014. Web. 25 Aug. 2015.

Barshad, Amos. "Building the Imperfect Pop Star." *Grantland*. ESPN Internet Ventures, 26 June 2013. Web. 25 Aug. 2015.

Charli XCX. "Charli XCX Talks Debut Album, Internet Haters, and Writing Icona Pop's 'I Love It.'" Interview by Lauren Nostro. *Complex*. Complex Media, 6 Mar. 2013. Web. 25 Aug. 2015.

Dove, Rachael. "Charli XCX Interview: 'I Realised That I Just Wanted to Be a F——ing Boss.'" *Telegraph*. Telegraph Media Group, 15 Feb. 2015. Web. 25 Aug. 2015.

Duran, Jose D. "Charli XCX Talks Pop: 'I Never Wanted to Write a Hipster Record.'" *Miami New Times*. Miami New Times, 3 June 2013. Web. 25 Aug. 2015.

Estrada, Olivia. "Feisty Monarchy." *Status*. Status Magazine, 6 Oct. 2014. Web. 25 Aug. 2015.

LeDonne, Rob. "British Phenom Charli XCX on Sudden Success, Singing with Iggy Azalea and What Made Madonna Special." *New York Times Magazine*. New York Times, 7 July 2014. Web. 25 Aug. 2015.

—Bertha Muteba

# Solina Chau

**Born:** 1961
**Occupation:** Business executive

Solina Chau is a business executive and venture capitalist. Working with Hong Kong tycoon Li Ka-shing, the richest man in Asia, Chau serves as the director of the Li Ka Shing Foundation, which funds philanthropic efforts to improve health care and education worldwide. She also cofounded the Hong Kong–based venture capital firm Horizons Ventures in 2002 and remains its public face. Horizons Ventures has invested in a number of high-tech firms, including Skype, Facebook, Spotify, and Waze, and the company is now closely affiliated with the Li Ka Shing Foundation, having made more than $350 million cumulative investments together.

## EARLY LIFE AND EDUCATION

Solina Chau Hoi Shuen, the daughter of a Hong Kong businessman, was born in 1961. Chau began her education at the prestigious Diocesan Girls' School (DGS), one of the oldest girls' schools in Hong Kong. As a student, she was elected junior house captain, or chief of the student association, according to a staff reporter for *Want China Times* (18 Dec. 2013). She graduated in 1978. Chau went on to study economics at the University of New South Wales in Sydney, Australia.

Culturally, college life in Sydney was a far cry from the disciplined life she had led at the DGS, although a number of her DGS classmates were studying at the university as well. But she nevertheless embraced life in the "unforgettable city," she told Winnie Kong and Helen Wong, two DGS students, in an interview for the Diocesan Old Girls' Association website in February 2002. Of her decision to study economics and embark on a career in business she told them: "I have never consciously chosen a particular career path; choice is always a luxury! I believe I am good at doing business, especially good at weighing pros and cons and calculating the odds."

## BEIJING ORIENTAL PLAZA

After college Chau worked in London, and in the late 1980s, she met a woman named Debbie Chang, a cousin of Tung Chee-hwa, a businessman who later became the first chief executive of Hong Kong from 1997 to 2005. Chau and Chang became roommates and business partners, and in 1993, they collaborated on Chau's first major project, the construction of the Oriental Plaza, a retail and office complex in downtown Beijing near Tiananmen Square. Chau won the contract to build on behalf of one of Tung's firms. Tung had convinced the Hong Kong tycoon Li Ka-shing to invest $2 billion in the project, making him the Oriental Plaza's lead investor; Chau earned a $51.6 million commission from the project.

It was around this time that Chau and Li were introduced and were reportedly often seen eating breakfast together at the Deep Water Bay Club House at the Hong Kong Golf Club, which was minutes from both of their homes. (By this time, Chau and Chang were living in a house a mere five-minute drive from Li's mansion.) At the time, the Oriental Plaza, a complex that now includes office buildings, an upscale hotel, luxury apartments, and a shopping mall, was the largest

China Photos/Getty Images North America

civil property development project in all of Asia. In 2002, Chau told Kong and Wong that the Beijing Oriental Plaza Development Project was "the most significant moment in my career life."

The development of the Oriental Plaza was not without controversy or complications. In 1994, the Beijing city government had a dust-up with McDonald's, the ubiquitous American fast food chain, after it evicted the restaurant from its location where the plaza was to be built. The restaurant had snagged the real estate when prices were low after the 1989 Tiananmen Square massacre, signing a twenty-year lease. After only two years in operation, the city asked the franchise to leave. The incident was significant, Anne-Marie Broudehoux wrote in her book *The Making and Selling of Post-Mao Beijing* (2004), because it shook the confidence of foreign businesses, calling "into question the willingness of the Chinese government and its state-owned entities to live up to the terms of the contracts they signed with overseas investors." According to Broudehoux, "The McDonald's incident—which could have had disastrous consequences for the future of foreign investment in the Chinese capital—revealed just how much the city government was willing to forfeit to insure the realization of Oriental Plaza."

The same year, Prime Minister Li Peng halted the project because it had not gained proper permissions from the central Chinese government, but in April 1995, while preparations were underway to officially submit the plaza's proposal, it was discovered that Li Ka-shing had paid Beijing's mayor Chen Xitong up to $37 million in kickbacks for ordering the removal of residential neighborhoods to make way for the plaza. The mayor was forced to step down after twelve years in office and was sentenced to sixteen years in jail in 1997 for fraud and dereliction of duty. The State Council officially approved the construction of the Oriental Plaza in 1996, more than three years after Chau had won the commission for Tung's firm.

## TOM GROUP AND HORIZONS VENTURES

In 1999, at the height of the Internet boom, Li Ka-shing and Chau cofounded a Chinese-language media company called Tom.com, now known as Tom Group, as a joint venture with Hutchison Whampoa, Cheung Kong Holdings, and other key investors. With Li's help, the company was listed on the Hong Kong Stock Exchange in 2000. The move made her the second-richest woman in Hong Kong after her $38,650 initial investment grew to be worth more than $1.6 billion. Tom Group is headquartered in Hong Kong and has more than two thousand employees in twenty cities. Tom Group has business interests in e-commerce, publishing, and entertainment and is the market leader in mainland China, Taiwan, and Hong Kong.

Chau and her partner Chang founded a venture capital firm called Horizons Ventures in 2002. Li joined the firm through his own Li Ka Shing Foundation in 2004. "Mr. Li does not participate in day-to-day review and the selection work," Chau told Shu-Ching Jean Chen for *Forbes* (12 Mar. 2014). "He loves disruptive innovations and sees it as kind of predictive lenses into the future. He loves to meet and geek with the founders and CEOs of companies within our 'disruptive' portfolio to understand their concepts and missions." (The term "disruptive" in reference to technology or business was first coined by Harvard professor Clayton M. Christensen. It means to innovate in such a way as to displace previous technologies or industries.) Unlike most venture capital firms, Horizons Ventures does not raise a pool of funds for various investments; Chau and Chang evaluate companies on a case-by-case basis and then invite Li to invest in those companies.

## TECHNOLOGY INVESTMENTS

In order to avoid competing with Tom Group, most of the technology companies Horizons Ventures has invested in are located overseas, particularly in the United States and Israel. Since its founding, Horizons Ventures has made a number of successful investments in notable Internet and mobile companies. In 2005, Li Ka-shing invested in Skype, the video-messaging application, before it sold for $2.5 billion to eBay the next year. In 2007, Chau personally pitched Li the social-networking website Facebook, which was, at the time, still considered an upstart company in competition with MySpace. Li decided to invest $120 million (for a 0.8 percent stake) in the company five minutes into Chau's presentation.

According to one banker who has worked with Horizons, as quoted by Paul J. Davies for the London *Financial Times* (23 Feb. 2014), the Facebook investment established the firm as a supporter of young, hip companies. "Out on the West Coast, when I talk about Li Ka-shing and Horizons, everyone knows who it is and there's this idea of quality and success," the banker said. "If I talk about the Korea National Pension Fund, for example [one of the world's biggest investment funds], people look at me blankly." He added, "Early stage companies want these quality backers because it means other investors will then do less due diligence."

In 2009, Li invested $7.5 million in Siri, a personal assistant application, which was acquired by Apple in 2010. Other notable investments include the music-streaming site Spotify and a $300,000 investment in Summly, an application that uses artificial intelligence to summarize large amounts of text, which was founded by a sixteen-year-old entrepreneur. Summly was acquired by Yahoo! in 2013 for an estimated $30 million.

## PERSONAL LIFE

In 1996, Chau founded the HS Chau Foundation. The foundation has spearheaded a number of "Project Tomorrow" initiatives to promote and fund educational opportunities, particularly for women in China. Chau is also a director at the nonprofit Li Ka Shing Foundation, which is closely affiliated with Horizons Ventures and raises funds to improve access to education and health care worldwide. In 2014, *Forbes* magazine ranked Chau as the eighty-second most powerful woman in the world, citing the impressive success of her investment portfolio.

Outside of the office, Chau is a voracious reader—finishing, on average, a book a week—though she rarely reads novels. "For the past ten years, I need to fly to Beijing for business every week and hence spending at least six hours of idle time on the plane," she explained to Kong and Wong. "I am determined that I will not waste a single minute of my time, so I read during the flight time." She also enjoys golfing, collecting art, and boxing, which she called "a very good intense cardiovascular exercise for strength and concentration," in her interview with Kong and Wong. Chau's personal relationship with Li is very close; several reporters have referred to Chau as Li's "confidante," although it also has been suggested that the two are romantically involved. Li's wife died in 1990. Chau is thirty-three years Li's junior.

## SUGGESTED READING

Broudehoux, Anne-Marie. *The Making and Selling of Post-Mao Beijing.* New York: Routledge, 2004. Print.

Davies, Paul J. "Li Ka-shing's Horizons: The Name behind Big-Ticket Tech Start-Ups." *Financial Times.* Financial Times, 23 Feb. 2014. Web. 17 Feb. 2015.

Flannery, Russell. "Li Ka-Shing's Midas Touch." *Forbes.* Forbes.com, 7 Mar. 2012. Web. 17 Feb. 2015.

Kong, Winnie, and Helen Wong. "Solina H S Chau—Class of '78." *DOGA.org.hk.* Diocesan Old Girls' Assoc., Feb. 2002. Web. 17 Feb. 2015.

Shu-Ching Jean Chen. "Li Ka-shing and Horizons Ventures: The Making of a Venture Powerhouse." *Forbes.* Forbes.com, 12 Mar. 2014. Web. 17 Feb. 2015.

"Solina Chau: The Woman behind HK Tycoon Li Ka-shing." *Want China Times.* WantChinaTimes.com, 18 Dec. 2013. Web. 17 Feb. 2015.

—Molly Hagan

# Roy Choi

**Born:** February 24, 1970

**Occupation:** Chef and food truck owner

Korean American chef Roy Choi is "the hipster god of the LA food scene," according to Tony Case for *Adweek* (15 June 2014). Choi is the head chef and co-owner of Kogi BBQ, a gourmet food truck company based in Los Angeles, California. Since launching Kogi in 2008, Choi has been credited with pioneering Korean Mexican fusion cuisine and for spearheading an American food truck movement that has changed Americans' perceptions about street food. Described by Katy McLaughlin for the *Wall Street Journal* (8 Jan. 2010) as "part flavor-fusion visionary, part classi-cally trained chef, part street rebel," Choi is known particularly for his now-famous Korean-style taco, Kogi's signature dish, which draws heavily on his multicultural Los Angeles roots. The success of Kogi has allowed Choi, who was named among the best new chefs in America by *Food & Wine* magazine in 2010, to build a culinary empire that includes the Los Angeles restaurants Chego, the A-Frame, and Sunny Spot. In 2014 he became a partner in the Los Angeles–based Line Hotel.

Ann Larie Valentine/Wikimedia

### EARLY LIFE AND EDUCATION

Roy Choi was born on February 24, 1970, in Seoul, South Korea, to a South Korean father, Soo Myung, and a North Korean mother, Ja Nam. Choi's parents had met in 1967 while they were both living in Los Angeles. After marrying, they returned to Korea for a brief time before permanently returning to Los Angeles in 1972, when Choi was almost two years old. They settled in the city's hard-working Koreatown neighborhood, where Choi spent much of his early childhood.

Choi's parents tried their hand at a number of businesses while he was growing up. They owned a liquor store in Koreatown and sold jewelry door-to-door before opening a Korean restaurant in Anaheim, California, in 1978. The restaurant was called Silver Garden, the Eng-lish translation of the name of Choi's younger sister, Eun-Jung, who was born that same year (her Anglicized name is Julie). It specialized in hot pot–style dishes prepared by Choi's mother, who by then had established a legendary reputa-tion among the Los Angeles–area Korean com-munity for her kimchi, a traditional Korean dish typically made with fermented cabbage, herbs,

and spices. "She had flavor in her fingertips," Choi told Terry Gross in an interview for NPR's *Fresh Air* (7 Nov. 2013). "She had this connec-tion and this innate ability to capture flavor in the moment."

Choi's culinary education began at home and continued at Silver Garden, where he observed his mother meticulously prepare for the day's lunch and dinner service. Silver Garden ini-tially thrived, at one point serving two to three hundred customers a night, but the restaurant folded after three years when its neighborhood declined. Still, the restaurant helped Choi foster a lifelong appreciation and passion for food.

Though Choi's family often struggled to make ends meet, they eventually turned their fortunes around and became wealthy as purveyors of high-end jewels. They opened a small storefront in Garden Grove, in northern Orange County, and moved into a mansion previously owned by legendary baseball pitcher Nolan Ryan in the gated, predominantly white enclave of Villa Park, located about ten miles away. Choi moved eight times before he turned thirteen.

### COLLEGE YEARS AND ADDICTION STRUGGLES

Throughout high school, Choi struggled to come to terms with his racial identity. He rebelled, straying from home, experimenting with alcohol and drugs, and joining a gang of neighborhood toughs called the Grove Street Mob. It was this troublesome behavior that led his high-achieving parents to send him to Southern California Military Academy in Signal Hill for his freshman year of high school in an effort to rehabilitate him. However, he switched to Villa Park High and graduated in 1988.

Following high school, Choi attended nearby California State University, Fullerton, where he earned a bachelor's degree in philosophy in 1993. He then enrolled at Fullerton's Western State College of Law but dropped out after only a semester. Directionless, Choi turned to various vices to entertain himself. In his early twenties he dabbled in crack cocaine and developed a ferocious gambling addiction, one that ultimately led him to hit bottom. Though his gambling exploits began auspiciously, sometimes bringing him upwards of ten thousand dollars a night, Choi's luck eventually ran out, and it was not long before he was stealing from his parents and pawning his possessions to feed his addiction.

Choi's gambling addiction came to a head sometime in 1994, when his parents forcibly dragged him out of a Los Angeles poker parlor. He spent several weeks recovering in his family's home before landing an entry-level job at an investment banking firm. His investment banking career proved to be short-lived, as his penchant for self-destructive behavior once again got the best of him; with his newfound earnings, he began drinking heavily at nightclubs around Los Angeles.

A turning point for Choi came in 1995, while half-drunkenly watching an episode of Emeril Lagasse's Food Network show *Essence of Emeril*. Finding himself entranced by the boisterous New Orleans–based chef, Choi came to the realization that cooking was his true calling in life. "Emeril saved my life," he told McLaughlin. He explained to Danielle Bacher for *Men's Journal* (Oct. 2014), "Sometimes when you're around something so closely, you don't notice it. I was around food my whole life, but it was something too close to me."

## CULINARY INSTITUTE OF AMERICA AND COOKING CAREER

In the winter of 1996, Choi enrolled at the prestigious Culinary Institute of America (CIA) in Hyde Park, New York. Despite being much older than his classmates, he comfortably settled into his new home and became a good student—despite his continuing independent streak. After completing a nine-month cycle of classes, Choi landed a coveted internship at Le Bernardin, a three-Michelin-star seafood restaurant in Manhattan helmed by re-

nowned French chef Eric Ripert. He worked there for eighteen weeks, during which time he "cut tuna poorly, burned things, and oversalted food so badly that he was ejected six times from the kitchen," as McLaughlin noted. That humiliating experience notwithstanding, Choi soldiered on and graduated from the CIA as the valedictorian of his class in 1998.

After completing his studies, Choi moved back west to accept a job in the desert town of Borrego Springs, California, as junior sous-chef at the AAA four-diamond-rated luxury resort La Casa del Zorro. He ran the kitchen at the resort's high-volume restaurant for about a year before becoming executive chef at the De Anza Country Club, also located in Borrego Springs. Despite his lofty title, Choi was forced to cater to the gastronomic needs of the club's members, most of whom preferred classic American cuisine to modern French fare. The experience, however, proved to be creatively stimulating, as Choi reinvented quintessential American comfort foods like meatloaf and fried chicken.

In 2001, after two years at the De Anza Country Club, Choi became the executive chef of a four-star and four-diamond Embassy Suites in South Lake Tahoe, California. Choi held that title until 2004, when, after earning several regional culinary honors, he was promoted to regional chef of the Embassy Suites properties in Northern California and the Pacific Northwest. In that role, Choi oversaw ten hotels, hundreds of staff members, and millions of dollars in annual revenue. He developed a cooked-to-order omelet bar and food program for the brand that was featured on *The Ellen DeGeneres Show*.

Choi continued his steady rise in the culinary world in 2007, when he was hired as chef de cuisine of the Beverly Hilton. He ran the kitchens of the hotel's Circa 55 and Trader Vic's restaurants and cooked for a number of high-profile events, including the Golden Globe Awards and the Grammy Awards.

## KOGI AND THE KOREAN TACO

In early 2008, after clashing with executive chef Suki Sugiura, Choi quit the Beverly Hilton to become chef de cuisine of RockSugar, an upscale pan-Asian fusion restaurant conceived by David Overton, the founder of the Cheesecake Factory. Choi helped open RockSugar Pan Asian Kitchen in Century City, Los Angeles, in June 2008, but he was fired from the 1,500-customer-a-day restaurant just three months later, after having a pressure-fueled meltdown. "I just failed," he noted to Nancy

Matsumoto for the *Atlantic* (16 July 2012), "the restaurant was too big, it became too busy, and there were these very rigid systems."

Frustrated with being unable to find a suitable chef position in a by-then recession-riddled economy, Choi considered walking away from the cooking profession altogether until Mark Manguera, a former colleague from the Beverly Hilton, presented him with the idea of a Korean barbecue taco. Transfixed by the possibilities of fusing Korean and Mexican flavors, Choi spent weeks perfecting a taco recipe that he hoped would represent the cultural diversity of Los Angeles. He became partners with Manguera, and in November 2008, the two launched the gourmet food truck company Kogi BBQ, which not only offered inexpensive Korean-style tacos but also other signature Korean Mexican dishes like kimchi quesadillas and pork-belly tortas. "These cultures—Mexican and Korean—really form the foundation of [Los Angeles]," Choi explained to Andrew Romano for *Newsweek* (2 June 2010). "Kogi is my representation of L.A. in a single bite."

Setting up shop at locations all over Los Angeles and Orange County, Kogi quickly developed a following, and within three months, the food truck was drawing hundreds of people every night. This prompted Choi and Manguera to expand from one truck to a fleet of four. The duo used the social-networking site Twitter to alert customers to the trucks' temporary, three-hour locations, which in turn generated unprecedented word-of-mouth buzz. In 2009, Kogi was hailed by *Newsweek* as "America's first viral restaurant" and became one of the most talked-about eateries in the country.

Meanwhile, Choi earned widespread acclaim for his Korean Mexican fusion cuisine and was credited with leading a food truck revolution. In 2010, he became the first food truck operator to be named one of America's best new chefs by *Food & Wine* magazine. "Kogi changed everything," Choi stated to Jeff Gordinier for the *New York Times* (17 June 2014). "We definitely created social change, on many different levels. . . . A cultural food experience that was looked at as dirty became gourmet."

## BUILDING A BRAND

As Kogi's popularity grew, so did Choi's. In 2010, Choi and his partners opened Chego, a rice-bowl restaurant in Los Angeles's Chinatown neighborhood, and the A-Frame, a Hawaiian-inspired eatery housed in a former IHOP in Culver City. Choi's third restaurant, the Caribbean-themed brunch space Sunny Spot, opened in Venice in 2011. He cofounded a coffee and smoothie shop, 3 Worlds Café, in Los Angeles's South Central district, in 2013.

In 2014 Choi partnered with the Sydell Group to open the Line, a 388-room hotel in Koreatown. There, he oversees two restaurants, Pot and the Commissary, as well as a room-service menu, a lobby bar, and a café. Pot specializes in Korean hot pots, and the Commissary focuses on dishes made with fruits and vegetables.

Choi published a memoir-cum-cookbook, *L.A. Son: My Life, My City, My Food*, under Anthony Bourdain's imprint for Ecco Books, a division of HarperCollins, in 2013. Cowritten by *L.A. Weekly* senior food writer Tien Nguyen and the director of marketing for Chego, Natasha Phan, the book features eighty-five recipes that correlate to different periods in Choi's life. *Chef*, a 2014 independent film written, directed, and starring Jon Favreau, about a chef who rediscovers his passion for food after starting up a food truck, was partly inspired by Choi. In the *Adweek* article, Favreau said Choi, who served as a coproducer and technical consultant on the film, "represents an accurate depiction of what America is now. He is the incarnation of multiculturalism."

Choi has served as a guest judge on Bravo's Emmy Award–winning cooking competition series *Top Chef* and has appeared on other television series, including Anthony Bourdain's CNN travel show *Parts Unknown*. He launched his own CNN digital series, *Street Food*, in October 2014.

Choi and his wife, Jean, have a daughter, Kaelyn.

## SUGGESTED READING

Case, Tony. "Riding Shotgun with Food Truck King Roy Choi." *Adweek*. Adweek, 15 June 2014. Web. 23 Oct. 2014.

Gordinier, Jeff. "Roy Choi, King of LA Food Trucks, Moves On to a Hotel." *New York Times*. New York Times, 17 June 2014. Web. 23 Oct. 2014.

McLaughlin, Katy. "The King of the Streets Moves Indoors." *Wall Street Journal*. Dow Jones, 15 Jan. 2010. Web. 23 Oct. 2014.

"The Rise of Chef Roy Choi, LA's New Food Revolutionary." *Men's Journal*. Men's Journal, Oct. 2014. Web. 23 Oct. 2014.

Romano, Andrew. "Thanks to Twitter, America's First Viral Eatery." *Newsweek*. Newsweek, 2 June 2010. Web. 23 Oct. 2014.

—Chris Cullen

# Emilia Clarke

**Born:** May 1, 1987
**Occupation:** Actor

Since *Game of Thrones*—the acclaimed television adaptation of George R. R. Martin's best-selling series of fantasy novels—debuted on HBO in April 2011, British actor Emilia Clarke has been singled out by fans and critics alike as one of the best parts of the epic drama for her performance as Khaleesi Daenerys Targaryen. The once-timid exiled princess of the Seven Kingdoms of Westeros, Daenerys has evolved into the Mother of Dragons, a warrior-queen who inspires her legions of followers with both her mercy and her growing power. An immediate hit for HBO, the series resonates with long-time fantasy fans as well as with viewers who had never read the books nor even been interested in the genre before, because it provides both intense violence and sexuality alongside complex political maneuvering and subtle character development.

Clarke, who was nominated in 2013 for an Emmy Award for her deft performance as the Khaleesi, well knows what the series has done for her career. "My life is unrecognisable compared to what it was," she said in an interview with Ed Cumming for the *Telegraph* (15 May 2012). "*Game of Thrones* has opened doors that were never there before. But it can be dangerous to see it in those terms, I think. It's best to take it as it comes and work as hard as you come, and hopefully the other things fall into place." Among the other things thus far falling into place: a budding movie career starring alongside such popular actors as Jude Law and Arnold Schwarzenegger and a starring role on Broadway in a theatrical production of Truman Capote's celebrated novella *Breakfast at Tiffany's*.

## EARLY LIFE AND CAREER

Emilia Clarke was born in London, England, on May 1, 1987. She and her younger brother grew up in Oxfordshire, in south central England. Her mother is an information technology executive, and her father is a highly regarded sound engineer for British theater. A love of performance came early to her, due in part to seeing a performance of *Show Boat* when she was very young, but also through the backstage access she had when she accompanied her father on his sound jobs. Her

Vera Anderson/WireImage

childhood imaginings of performing onstage as she stood before an empty theater while her father worked eventually culminated in an announcement at age ten: she wanted to become an actor. Clarke recalled her father's reaction to Emma John in an interview for the *Guardian* (27 Oct. 2013): "He told me: 'There's just one line you need to learn: Do you want fries with that?' He was trying his damndest to be realistic, show me that it wasn't Disney." Nevertheless, he agreed to take her to an open audition on London's West End, in which she discovered on the spot that she would not only have to act but sing as well. After failing to impress the producers with her versions of a folk song about a donkey and a bit of the Spice Girls, she returned home, undaunted.

After attending boarding school in Oxford, Clarke hoped to make it into the Royal Academy of Dramatic Art. When the school rejected her in 2005, she traveled the world. Upon returning home to the United Kingdom, she applied to Drama Centre London, among whose graduates are the noted actors Pierce Brosnan and Colin Firth. Thrilled to be accepted onto the waiting list, she was not entirely prepared for life at what graduates call the Trauma Center, in which aspiring young performers are challenged to go deep into their characters. They are also prepared for a world of frequent rejection. "The training definitely breaks you down, in a way that's fundamentally good," Clarke said to Brian Raftery for the *Wall Street Journal* (5 Feb. 2014). "It makes you humble to the work.

You realize you are just a part of the thing that you're creating."

Upon graduation Clarke found little in the way of acting work. She instead spent much of her time working several food-service gigs, much as her father had cautioned. She did manage to snare a walk-on part on the British television series *Doctors* in 2009 and a role in the television movie *Triassic Attack* in 2010, but her first real breakthrough came when she replaced an actor from the test pilot of HBO's new series *Game of Thrones*.

## BECOMING THE MOTHER OF DRAGONS

When Clarke's agent contacted her about auditioning for the role of Daenerys Targaryen, the aspiring actor knew absolutely nothing about Martin's best-selling series of fantasy novels, *A Song of Ice and Fire*. Before her audition with HBO executives in Los Angeles, California, she tried to learn as much as she could about the series and its dedicated fans. For her audition, she was given two scenes: one in which she stands up to her vicious older brother and the other in which she emerges from her late husband's funeral pyre with three newly hatched dragons. Clarke has said in interviews that she came to understand Daenerys from just those two scenes, as a young woman who tries to do the right thing despite the wrongs that are committed against her. "We needed an actress who could convincingly embody both the timid, voiceless Dany we first meet, and the Mother of Dragons she later becomes," noted series producers and writers David Benioff and D. B. Weiss in a jointly written e-mail to Brian Raftery for the *Wall Street Journal*. "Some of the young women could do fearful but not fearsome—one or two could do the reverse. Only Emilia nailed both."

In the first four seasons of *Game of Thrones*, Daenerys has evolved from an innocent girl unsure of her place in the world into a messianic leader who not only inspires the followers who have flocked to her but who also seems destined to reclaim the Iron Throne of Westeros, from which her insane father had been deposed. Unlike the other claimants to the throne, the Khaleesi shows an uncommon level of mercy that tempers her relentless quest to rule Westeros. Her journey—which is largely filmed separately from the rest of the major characters, because the character is presently living on a different fictional continent and trying to get home—has captivated viewers and critics alike. Clarke's Emmy nod for outstanding supporting actress in a drama series was among the sixteen nominations *Game of Thrones* received for the 2013 season. When asked by Dave Itzkoff, writing for the *New York Times* (18 July 2013), what it felt like to be nominated for an Emmy, Clarke replied: "It's a phenomenal feeling. . . . I'm shocked and surprised that I'm even vaguely near the same category as [fellow cast members] Peter Dinklage and Diana Rigg."

## TAKING ON BROADWAY AS HOLLY GOLIGHTLY

Clarke's work as the flaxen-haired Daenerys has enabled her to take on other high-caliber roles, including a turn as Holly Golightly, the troubled main character from Truman Capote's famous 1958 novella *Breakfast at Tiffany's*, in a Broadway adaptation by director Sean Mathias. Mathias, who had directed a version of the play in London in 2009, believed that Clarke was perfectly suited to his 2013 Broadway revival. Yet both director and actor were well aware of the challenges of a role made famous by the legendary Audrey Hepburn in the 1961 film adaptation and understood that audiences might not be accepting of a new face in so famous a part. Of Hepburn's iconic turn in the *Breakfast at Tiffany's* film, Clarke told Charles McGrath for the *New York Times* (7 Mar. 2013): "What you're seeing up there is perfection, and you can't mimic or copy perfection. You can take that and add it to your inspiration board, but then you want to go to the source, the novella, and break that down to its most finite part, which is that Holly is a girl who's a product of the Great Depression, the great drought. You start there, attempting to understand her world, and then you realize that the stakes were so high for her because she has to stay mysterious, and the only way she can do that is by keeping on running."

The Broadway run of *Breakfast at Tiffany's* starring Clarke received lukewarm reviews, and theatergoers did not show up in droves. (Many *Game of Thrones* fans could be found at the stage door waiting for Clarke's autograph, however.) "It was definitely . . . optimistic," Clarke said of her Broadway experience to Emma John for the *Guardian*. "A young Brit girl with no theatre experience decided to take on an iconic American role on Broadway. Maybe I should have thought that through?" Although her Broadway debut was a mixed experience, she has admitted she would love to return to the stage to perform in works by famed American playwrights such as Tennessee Williams, Clifford Odets, or August Wilson, as well as in classical works like those of William Shakespeare or Henrik Ibsen.

## NOTABLE FILM ROLES

Clarke has, by contrast, had increasing success on the big screen and appears poised to make a successful transition from television to film. She landed a part in the British film *Spike Island* (2012) and acted alongside Jude Law in *Dom Hemingway* (2013) as the daughter of the title character—a former safe cracker who attempts to reconnect with his daughter after a dozen years behind bars. She will also take on the role of Sarah Connor, made famous by Linda Hamilton a generation earlier, in *Terminator: Genisys*, which costars the original Terminator, Arnold Schwarzenegger, and is slated for release in 2015.

Above all, Clarke seeks diversity in her film work, even as *Game of Thrones* continues to thrive on television. "Maybe this is shooting for the moon," Clarke told Emma John, "but I'd like to be able to look back on my career and stand by every choice I made and say: 'Yeah, I did that for the prestige'—or 'Yeah, I did that because I needed a mortgage.' There's so much talent out there, and I want to go out and find it and work with it. That's my naive, optimistic aim."

## SUGGESTED READING

Clarke, Emilia. "Emmy Nominees: Emilia Clarke of 'Game of Thrones.'" Interview by Dave Itzkoff. *New York Times*. New York Times, 18 July 2013. Web. 20 Nov. 2014.

Clarke, Emilia. "Game of Thrones Interview: Emilia Clarke." Interview by Ed Cumming. *Telegraph*. Telegraph, 15 May 2012. Web. 20 Nov. 2014.

John, Emma. "Emilia Clarke: Out of the Dragon's Den." *Guardian*. Guardian News and Media, 27 Oct. 2013. Web. 20 Nov. 2014.

McGrath, Charles. "The Heavy Mantle of Holly Golightly." Rev. of *Breakfast at Tiffany's*, dir. Sean Mathias. *New York Times*. New York Times, 7 Mar. 2013. Web. 20 Nov. 2014.

Raftery, Brian. "Emilia Clarke, the Breakthrough Actress on 'Game of Thrones.'" *Wall Street Journal*. Dow Jones, 5 Feb. 2014. Web. 20 Nov. 2014.

## SELECTED WORKS

*Doctors*, 2009; *Triassic Attack*, 2010; *Game of Thrones*, 2011– ; *Spike Island*, 2012; *Dom Hemingway*, 2013

—Christopher Mari

# Ta-Nehisi Coates

**Born:** September 30, 1975
**Occupation:** Journalist

Ta-Nehisi Coates is an award-winning national correspondent for the *Atlantic*, a periodical for which he writes extensively on topics of cultural, social, and political importance. He also maintains a blog that is widely considered to be one of the liveliest and most engaging sections of the *Atlantic*'s website. He is the author of *The Beautiful Struggle: A Father, Two Sons, and an Unlikely Road to Manhood* (2008) and *Between the World and Me* (2015). The latter was one of six books on President Barack Obama's 2015 summer reading list. Coates's fans include prominent journalists and writers such as novelist Toni Morrison, MSNBC political commentators Rachel Maddow and Chris Hayes, and the *New Yorker*'s Hendrik Hertzberg, among others. Coates holds "a place of prominence in the stream of American thought, a perch that positions him as an ascendant public intellectual with a voice that stands out in the white noise of a wired and word-flooded era," Manuel Roig-Franzia wrote for the *Washington Post* (18 June 2014).

Jordan Michael Smith wrote for the *New York Observer* (5 Mar. 2013) that Coates "is the single best writer on the subject of race in the United States." Similarly, Chris Ip for the *Columbia Journalism Review* (Nov./Dec. 2014) called him "the most celebrated journalist writing about race today." As Ip and many other observers pointed out, "The Case for Reparations," Coates's lengthy May 2014 cover story, broke the single-day traffic record on the *Atlantic*'s website and inspired a multitude of pieces in response.

Mulling the reasons for Coates's popularity, Ip wrote, "Reporting on race requires simultaneously understanding multiple, contradictory worlds, with contradictory narratives. Widespread black poverty exists; so do a black middle class and a black president. It requires both a hypersensitivity to peoples' different lived experiences, and a frankness when telling hard truths. Reporters need to be able to see both how far America has come, and how far the country has left to go." He added, "Coates, together with others who join him, is trying to claim the frontier of a new narrative." Coates's contributions to this narrative for the *Atlantic* have included "There Is No Post-Racial America" (July/Aug. 2015) and "Color-Blind Policy, Color-Conscious Morality" (13 May 2015). "Fear of a Black President" (Sept. 2012), about President Obama's difficulties addressing race without alienating white voters, was one of his most widely read articles. Yet, while Coates does unquestionably write about race on a frequent basis, he dislikes being pigeonholed. "I think I write about America, and about things that interest me," he told Smith.

Of his purpose in tackling such difficult and often contentious topics, he told television reporter Budd Mishkin for NY1 (15 June 2015), "You have to decide how to live morally. People ask me at the end, 'How do you feel? What do you expect to happen [after writing a piece]?' I don't expect anything to happen. I just want to be judged on the side of people who said something. When it is counted up, I don't want to be one of those people who closed my ears."

## EARLY LIFE

Ta-Nehisi Coates—whose first name is derived from the ancient Egyptian word for Nubia—was born to William Paul Coates and Cheryl Waters on September 30, 1975. He was raised in a poor section of West Baltimore, Maryland. "We lived in a row house in the slope of Tioga Parkway," he wrote in his 2008 memoir, *The Beautiful Struggle*. "There was a small kitchen, three bedrooms, and three bathrooms—but only one that anybody ever wanted to use." Many journalists mention that the crime-ridden area was the setting for the gritty television drama *The Wire*; much of the show's fourth season was, in fact, filmed at William H. Lemmel Middle School, which Coates attended. In the book, Coates poetically writes of the neighborhood's ethos: "We died for sneakers stitched by serfs, coats that gave props to teams we didn't own, hats embroidered with the names of Confederate states."

Coates's family life was not an entirely conventional one. "My dad was a young man [and] he had relationships with four different women at various points," Coates explained to Terry Gross for the National Public Radio show *Fresh Air* (18 Feb. 2009). "With my mother, there were two kids. The first woman he was married to, the first wife, there were three kids. My dad hated the term stepbrother. He hated the term stepmother, stepfather, all that. We really didn't do that. He hated the term half-brother, there were no halves. We were raised to be really, really close." Coates lived with his parents and brother, while the other children lived for most of the year with

their respective mothers, although they visited each other on the weekends, and when any of the boys struggled in school or posed a disciplinary problem, he was sent to live in Coates's household for a time, so that his father, could "get the kid back on track." Reflecting on his family life, Coates recalled to Gross, "I didn't consider it particularly unusual because, quite frankly, there were a lot of kids in the neighborhood who had a similar situation, except in most cases, the father was not there."

## EDUCATION

Waters supported her sons by working as a schoolteacher. (When Coates misbehaved, she punished him by making him write lengthy essays, even when he was as young as six or seven.) Paul Coates, a Vietnam War veteran, was a member of the Black Panthers, and from the basement of the row house where he lived with Waters and their two boys, he operated a small publishing company specializing in black nationalist literature and other Afrocentric volumes. Seeking to make sense of the poverty and violence he saw every day—so different from the white, suburban life he saw depicted on television—Coates avidly read those books, and it was not until he entered Howard University, a historically black university, that he began questioning some of the more fringe beliefs they inculcated in him. In a series of posts to his Twitter account (23 Dec. 2014), he wrote:

"I was not above quoting some dumb [stuff] about 'ice people' and 'sun people.' And I was not above telling you the ancient Egyptians had helicopters and sailed to South America before Columbus. . . . [But my professors] knew that if I ever went out and said that in front of any group of well-read people, I would get my head cut off."

Before entering Howard, Coates had struggled from time to time in school, and he started his senior year with a dismal 1.8 grade point average. He wrote in his memoir, "My default position was sprawled across the bed staring at the ceiling or cataloging an extensive collection of X-Factor comic books." Coates, who often touches upon pop culture topics such as comic books in his writing, was also an enthusiastic player of the role-playing game Dungeons and Dragons. "Knowing my dad and where he was in terms of black consciousness, having a kid . . . play a game that is based in . . . Tolkien and Norse mythology sounds like a weird mix," he admitted to Gross. "But in fact, my dad appreciated the imagination that was inherent in the game. . . . He never was, you know, a sort of person that was like, I don't want you playing a white man's game or I don't want you reading a white man's book. That didn't really exist in my household."

While Paul wanted his sons to be bright and well read, he also encouraged them to interact with other boys in the community—despite the violence and criminal activity they encountered in the process. "My dad's thinking was that he was raising men . . . for all seasons," Coates told Gross. "He wanted people who were comfortable in the neighborhood, people who were exposed to things outside the neighborhood, people who could be comfortable in many different worlds."

That comfort with a wide variety of people served him well at Howard, which drew students from around the world and from every socioeconomic level and religion. Coates did not, however, graduate from Howard. He failed his British and US literature courses and, after six years of on-and-off study, he left the university in 2000 to pursue a career in journalism.

## EARLY CAREER

Coates subsequently found work at the *Washington City Paper,* then edited by the late David Carr, who went on to become a beloved figure at the *New York Times.* "If you had told me he would be a big deal, I would have said, 'Get real,'" Carr recalled to Smith in 2013. "He

was not a great speller. He wasn't terrific with names. And he wasn't all that ambitious." When not writing, Coates took a job with a food delivery service to make ends meet. After leaving the *Washington City Paper,* he bounced from job to job, working for short periods of time at *Philadelphia Weekly*, the *Village Voice*, and *Time* magazine. He left the *Village Voice* after they asked him to write a regular column on black men. "The moment you put that upon yourself—'black correspondent'—that's always with you, you never get rid of that," he told Smith.

As in Washington, Coates took food-delivery jobs to earn extra money. Concurrently, he wrote his memoir, which received admiring reviews when it was published in 2008. That year, he also sold a piece to the *Atlantic.* Rejected by several other periodicals, "This Is How We Lost to the White Man," which examined comedian Bill Cosby's controversial criticism of black men, impressed *Atlantic* editor James Bennet, who then hired Coates as a regular commentator. (Carr, a fan despite his criticism, had introduced the two, and Coates has noted the irony of his benefiting from the networking of two white men.)

## WRITING FOR THE *ATLANTIC*

Coates was assigned to write short blog posts for the *Atlantic*'s website on hip-hop (which he had grown to love while at Howard), politics, race, and other topics. He started an online book club focused on volumes about the Civil War and instituted a daily "open thread," on which his followers could discuss anything they liked. He quickly earned a reputation as a skilled moderator, introducing participants to new ways of thinking and firmly banning anyone he felt was uncivil. He was also known to be willing to broaden his own way of thinking, and he wrote in one post (20 June 2014), "I have long believed that the best part of writing is not the communication of knowledge to other people, but the acquisition and synthesizing of knowledge for oneself."

The *Atlantic* also publishes Coates's longer essays, which have become among the most popular and thought-provoking in the magazine. Media insiders predict that he will remain on the staff of the *Atlantic* for the foreseeable future, pointing out that when the *New York Times* offered him a job as a full-time op-ed columnist—one of the most coveted jobs in journalism—he turned down the offer.

Coates published his second book, *Between the World and Me*, on July 14, 2015. Written in the form of a letter to his teenaged son, the book explores America's history of racial violence and the challenges Coates faced growing up. The release had been scheduled for the fall but was moved up in response to several racially charged incidents that occurred in early 2015, including the shooting of nine African American parishioners at a church in Charleston, South Carolina, by a white supremacist. According to Benjamin Wallace-Wells, writing for *New York* magazine, novelist Toni Morrison praised Coates's work, writing, "I've been wondering who might fill the intellectual void that plagued me after James Baldwin died. Clearly, it is Ta-Nehisi Coates."

## OTHER WORK

Coates has been a visiting professor at the Massachusetts Institute of Technology—a rarity for someone without an advanced degree—and in 2014 he accepted a post as a journalist-in-residence at the City University of New York. Among his laurels are a 2013 National Magazine Award for essays and criticism, a 2014 George Polk Award, and a 2015 Harriet Beecher Stowe Center Prize for Writing for Social Justice.

## PERSONAL LIFE

Coates lives in Harlem with his wife, Kenyatta Matthews, and their son, Samori Maceo-Paul Coates.

## SUGGESTED READING

Coates, Ta-Nehisi. *The Beautiful Struggle: A Father, Two Sons, and an Unlikely Road to Manhood*. New York: Spiegel, 2008. Print.

Coates, Ta-Nehisi. "A Last Tango with Paris." *Atlantic*. Atlantic Monthly Group, 20 June 2014. Web. 14 Sept. 2015.

Coates, Ta-Nehisi. "Ta-Nehisi Coates' 'Unlikely Road to Manhood.'" Interview by Terry Gross. *Fresh Air*. NPR, 18 Feb. 2009. Web. 14 Sept. 2015.

"Fear of a Black Pundit: Ta-Nehisi Coates Raises His Voice in American Media." *Observer*. Observer Media, 5 Mar. 2013. Web. 14 Sept. 2015.

Ip, Chris. "Ta-Nehisi Coates Defines a New Race Beat." *Columbia Journalism Review*. Columbia Journalism Rev., Nov./Dec. 2014. Web. 14 Sept. 2015.

Mishkin, Budd. "One on 1 Profile: Writer Ta-Nehisi Coates Takes the Next Big Step in His Career." *NY1*. Time Warner Cable Enterprises, 15 June 2015. Web. 14 Sept. 2015.

Roig-Franzia, Manuel. "With *Atlantic* Article on Reparations, Ta-Nehisi Coates Sees Payoff for Years of Struggle." *Washington Post*. Washington Post, 18 June 2014. Web. 14 Sept. 2015.

—Mari Rich

# Ellar Coltrane

**Born:** August 27, 1994
**Occupation:** Actor

The 2014 coming-of-age film *Boyhood* received widespread critical acclaim, with a great deal of the praise lavished on previously unknown actor Ellar Coltrane. Rather than cast different actors for each stage of his main character's life, as in most films that take place over a span of several years, auteur Richard Linklater cast Coltrane at age six and filmed him and his fellow actors intermittently, for several days at a time, between May 2002 and August 2013, when Coltrane turned nineteen years old. Cast and crew devoted forty-five days altogether to film what was known on the set and in the media as Linklater's "twelve-year project."

*Boyhood*, which garnered a Golden Globe Award for best picture as well as numerous Oscar nominations, "isn't just an aesthetic gambit," according to Boris Kachka for *New York Magazine* (30 June 2014). "It's also a psychological experiment, absorbing the personalities and dramas of its stars and, twelve years later, showing them—and then the world—a fictional doppelgänger of their lives. That might feel like a small step for grown-up actors accustomed to the perils of self-exposure, but for Coltrane . . . it's a giant leap." Linklater has told journalists that it will always be unclear to him how much Coltrane shaped the movie and how much the movie shaped the young actor. Coltrane evinces little doubt that the experience of working with Linklater made a profound impact on his life. *Boyhood* "is a huge part of me," he told Kachka. "It's a gift that [he] gave me. It's kind of proof that I'm real."

Axelle/Bauer-Griffin/FilmMagic

## FAMILY LIFE AND EDUCATION

Ellar Coltrane, born Ellar Coltrane Kinney Salmon, a native of Austin, Texas, was born on August 27, 1994. He decided against using his last name professionally once filming on *Boyhood* had ended, fearing that it would feel too personal to see his family name on the screen during the credits. His father, Bruce, hailed from a wealthy and conservative New Orleans family and rebelled as a young man by becoming a professional musician. He played in Austin-based band Joe Rockhead, of which, in a widely reported coincidence, Linklater was an avid fan. (At the casting call, Coltrane occupied himself by doodling on the back of an old band poster, elevating Linklater's interest; Coltrane has joked that the director chose him only because he was a fan of his father.)

Coltrane's mother, Genevieve Kinney, was a dancer, painter, and performance artist who works with disabled individuals as an equine therapist. Her upbringing was decidedly less conventional than that of her husband; her own mother, Kathy Horton, has been described by reporters as a "hippie" who lives in a rusted school bus in Elgin, Texas. Bruce Salmon was Genevieve's second husband.

Coltrane was homeschooled by his parents until he was sixteen. He then attended a charter school for about two years before dropping out and earning a GED. His parents, he told Kachka, are "strange people, and they took a very bizarre approach to parenting, but they supported me unconditionally, which is something a lot of parents fail at."

Coltrane had acted in only a few locally shot commercials and a 2002 indie release called *Lone Star State of Mind* before trying out for the part of Mason, the main character, in *Boyhood*. (Coltrane's aunt was a model, and an agent had seen him in her agency's waiting room one day, leading to those small parts.)

## CASTING FOR *BOYHOOD*

Despite Coltrane's joking assertions that he was cast only because Linklater was an avid Joe Rockhead fan, the director has said that he ascertained almost immediately that the towheaded six-year-old was special. "I remember staring at him and wondering, *Who are you? Are you the real one?* . . . Ellar was just the most interesting of them all, kind of ethereal—a lot like now," Linklater has said, as quoted by Kachka. The director elaborated to Tara Brady for the *Irish Times* (11 July 2014): "Looking back, meeting him was the moment that made the film," Linklater asserted. "He was the interesting, arty, mysterious kid . . . Kind of poetic in his own way. A lot of charisma. Other kids were more quote-unquote 'straight.' They might have been the class president or the really popular guy at school. In a way, I was the other kids. . . . But I think Ellar was almost like the more interesting part of myself. He's the part I'd rather make a film about."

Although Linklater was indisputably drawn to Coltrane's innate qualities, Coltrane's parents did have some bearing on his casting; Linklater was encouraged by the fact that they were both artists of sorts, reasoning that they would be more willing to allow their son to commit to a lengthy and unusual film project. "The nightmare is to go four or five years in and they'll say, 'We don't think this is good for Ellar.' Artists get [the concept of] storytelling over twelve years. Money people balk and think of all the bad things that could happen. Artists tend to think of all the good things," the director explained to Kachka. (None of the actors was contractually obligated to remain with the project for the full dozen years, but all, to Linklater's great relief, remained committed to his vision.)

All of the main actors—including Ethan Hawke and Patricia Arquette, who play Mason's divorced parents, and Linklater's own daughter, Lorelei, who grew up onscreen as Mason's sister, Samantha—were required to be simultaneously available each year for a week of rehearsals, dinners, and brainstorming sessions. This was a particularly difficult feat for Hawke and Arquette, both busy with various other roles over the course of those years.

Besides the actors' schedules, the filming posed other logistical headaches. Locations for shooting had to be carefully considered based on whether the actors would be available in later years, and the annual production budget remained the same, even in the face of mounting inflation. During the later years of the project, it became difficult to find technicians who knew how to use 35-millimeter film (which had been standard in the industry when shooting began) because younger crew members were only familiar with digital cameras.

## FILMING OVER TWELVE YEARS

Coltrane has described the experience of filming annually as more akin to attending a wonderful summer camp than working. He began taking a greater hand in developing his character as the film progressed. "I became a pretty direct part of writing the dialogue," he told Michael Mechanic for *Mother Jones* (3 July 2014). "[Linklater] would have the framework of the scene and we would just have conversations, and that would become the dialogue. I never had to think about getting in character, and that's really one of [his] magic tricks. You don't really know it, and then suddenly you *are* the character."

Linklater took great care not to incorporate elements such as smoking and kissing into Mason's story until Coltrane had experienced them himself in real life, and he asked his young actor to take notes as the months between filming passed. "There is so much of myself up on the screen. Even though it is a very crafted character, it's also a lot of me," Coltrane told Christina Radish for the entertainment site *Collider* (8 July 2014). "It's hard to exactly define where I end and the character begins, or vice versa." Like Genevieve Kinney, for example, Coltrane's on-screen mother marries and divorces three times, and Coltrane's own words about *Star Wars* and Facebook were used verbatim in the film. A painting he had done appears on a wall of the set; Linklater frequently let Coltrane wear his own clothing; and a blue Toyota that Mason drives in certain scenes actually belonged to the actor. Coltrane, however, was careful to check in with the director before he made any major cosmetic changes during the year. Linklater never objected when the young actor wanted

to get piercings or new haircuts, although for one scene—when Mason undergoes a traumatic haircut at the hands of a bullying stepfather—Coltrane was asked to let his hair get longer than normal. (Because he was so relieved when his hair was finally cut on camera, Coltrane has told interviewers that Mason's distress during that scene was entirely fabricated.)

While Linklater did not allow Coltrane or Lorelei to watch the film as it was being made, seeking to save them from self-consciousness, he gave them copies to watch on their own once it was complete, counseling them to develop a relationship with the film themselves before critics and the public began weighing in and possibly tainting the experience. "It's me and I'm changing and it's me at different times and it's incredibly surreal, you know, just terrifying and beautiful and comforting and painful all at the same time," Ellar told Malina Saval for *Variety* (20 Feb. 2015). "The first time I saw the movie it was hard to even really see much of the story. It was just all about . . . the catharsis, the tenderness of seeing yourself age."

## AFTER *BOYHOOD*

During the filming of *Boyhood*, Coltrane took on minor roles in a handful of other films, including *Faith & Bullets* (2005), Linklater's *Fast Food Nation* (2006), and *Hallettsville* (2009). Still, once *Boyhood* wrapped, he spent time working for his stepfather's landscaping company and has expressed uncertainty about pursuing acting on a full-time basis.

"I want to make art," he told Saval. "The only thing in life that really gives me any peace is just being lost in the process of creating something, whether it's the film or painting and drawing, which has been a big part of my life for a long time. . . . I'm not interested in being famous or anything, but I'm definitely interested in expressing emotions, and acting and filmmaking can be great outlets for that."

Coltrane's physical appearance is sometimes compared to that of the iconic actor James Dean, and he has proven to be a popular figure with fashion editors. He has appeared in the pages of *L'Uomo Vogue* and *Paper* magazine's annual "Most Beautiful People" issue, among other periodicals, and he has signed a contract with Wilhelmina Models.

## SUGGESTED READING

Coltrane, Ellar. Interview by Michael Mechanic. "Meet the Star of *Boyhood*, the Oscar Front-runner Everybody's Talking About." *Mother Jones*. Mother Jones, 3 July 2014. Web. 4 June 2015.

Coltrane, Ellar. Interview by Steven Zeitchik. "*Boyhood*'s Ellar Coltrane Balances Fame and the Future." *Los Angeles Times*. Los Angeles Times, 21 Feb. 2015. Web. 4 June 2015.

Handy, Bruce. "Up Close and Personal with Ellar Coltrane, *Boyhood*'s Boy Wonder." *Vanity Fair*. Condé Nast, Mar. 2015. Web. 4 June 2015.

Kachka, Boris. "Ellar Coltrane Spent Twelve Years Acting for Richard Linklater. Now What?" *New York Magazine*. New York Media, 30 June 2014. Web. 4 June 2015.

Mondello, Bob. "Oh, *Boyhood*! Linklater's Cinematic Stunt Pays Off." *All Things Considered*. NPR, 11 July 2014. Web. 4 June 2015.

Shanahan, Mark. "Time Is Everything in *Boyhood*; for Arquette and Coltrane, Film Captures the Flow of Ordinary Life." *Boston Globe*. Boston Globe Media Partners, 18 July 2014. Web. 4 June 2015.

—Mari Rich

# Hafeez Contractor

**Born:** June 19, 1950

**Occupation:** Architect

Hafeez Contractor is India's most famous architect. Daniel Brook, in a profile of Contractor for the *New York Times Magazine* (19 June 2014), described him as a "luxury brand," known to many Indians simply as Hafeez. Contractor's signature style—developed since he rose to prominence in the 1980s—is glitzy and ostentatious, a strange mash-up of disparate elements like Gothic arches and Greek temples, amplified. Critics hate him, but clients love him, because his only consideration is their desire. In 2010 Contractor completed a 570-foot skyscraper in Mumbai that is the private home of Indian billionaire Mukesh Ambani. Ambani is India's richest man and a potent symbol of the country's economic rise as well as its changing mores regarding wealth. When the project was announced in 2007, Randeep Ramesh wrote for the London *Guardian* (1 June 2007), "The building, named Antilla after a mythical island, will have a total floor area greater than Versailles and be home for Mr. Ambani, his mother, wife, three children and 600 full-time staff." There is a floor

Soumik Kar/The India Today Group/Getty Images

that is entirely devoted to a home movie theater and another six devoted to car parking. Antilla also provides a bird's eye view of the famous slums of Mumbai; just one of them, a place called Dharavi, boasts a population the size of San Francisco packed into less than one square mile of space. "What defines a Contractor project," wrote Brook, "is the feeling that you are in a world apart."

In Mumbai, India's financial capital, industrialists like Ambani live side by side with some of the world's poorest people. "I used to always say something should be done about the slums," Contractor told Brook, this time for an article in *Slate* (25 Feb. 2013). "And I always used to say that the best way of [dealing with] slums was that you give them free houses, keep the land, and build on it and make money." In the 1990s, Contractor engineered a slum redevelopment policy with a populist politician named Bal Thackeray. The alliance with the controversial Thackeray (who died in 2012) showed Contractor's pragmatism and drive to do what is necessary to realize his ambitions; Thackeray was the leader of the far-right Hindu nationalist Shiv Sena party, which has been known to support violence against Muslims. Still, Thackeray and Shiv Sena were the most powerful political force in Mumbai; with Thackeray's help, Contractor was able to realize his policy in 1996. However, many suggest that Contractor's motivation was less than benevolent. Rural poverty continues to drive more and more Indians into urban areas, and cities like Mumbai are chronically short on space. The poor gather in makeshift settlements like Dharavi. Residents have little legal claim to their land, which presents a very tempting opportunity for developers. Slum residents "squat atop some of the most treasured real estate in the world but are unable to extract its value," Joshua K. Leon wrote for *Dissent* magazine (13 Mar. 2013). According to the slum redevelopment policy Contractor promoted, developers are able to raze slums to build luxury high rises if they reserve (theoretically) half of the apartments for low-income residents. Under the initial plan, any slum dweller who arrived in Mumbai before 1995 was eligible for free housing. That plan was later extended to 2000, but as of 2014, Mumbai residents remained skeptical. According to Mansi Choksi for *Al Jazeera* (12 Mar. 2014), less than 13 percent of the projects initiated under the plan had been completed in the first seventeen years. An activist named Shailesh Gandhi told Choksi, "In all these years, the scheme has failed to make any significant contributions to housing the poor because there is scope for corruption at every step."

## EDUCATION AND EARLY CAREER

Contractor was born in Mumbai (then Bombay) to a wealthy industrial Parsi family in 1950. The small Parsi community of Mumbai are Zoroastrians who migrated from Persia centuries ago and thrived as merchants and professionals under British colonialism. According to Contractor's family, his great-great-grandfather helped build the University of Baroda in Gujarat. Contractor's father died suddenly, thirteen days after he was born. Contractor never knew life under the British Raj, as India gained independence from Great Britain in 1947, but his family's business, with holdings in power plants and liquor, struggled under India's early rulers. "Private power plants would have no place in Jawaharlal Nehru's state," Brook wrote, "and alcohol would be banned in Gandhi's spiritual nation." Though the political tides would turn in time for Contractor to rebuild the family empire, as a young man, he barely made it into architecture school in Mumbai. He was inspired by his cousin, an architect named Tehmasp Khareghat. Contractor was an excellent student and worked with Khareghat while pursuing his degree, though the two cousins were quite different: Khareghat was resistant to client input, while Contractor was willing to do more to please clients. He was frustrated

with his cousin, whom he believed did not adequately market himself, and refused to expand his practice. Contractor was more ambitious. As a student at the University of Mumbai, his senior project was put on display at a contemporary art museum in Mumbai, and after graduation in 1975, he won a scholarship to study at Columbia University in New York City. He earned his master's degree in architecture in 1977. He was driven to return to India after graduation, despite the temptation to remain in New York like so many of his compatriots. He told Brook, "I said, 'Graduate in the afternoon, catch a flight in the night.' And I literally meant it. I left for my flight from the farewell dinner."

Contractor returned to his cousin's firm in India, but continued to be disappointed by the manner in which Khareghat conducted his business. "A client would tell him what she wanted," Contractor recalled to Rahul Bhatia for New Delhi's *Open Magazine* (7 Nov. 2009). "But he would tell her she was not looking at the inside flow"—and the client would move on. "I felt 'why should we practice architecture the way it is taught, when those you are practicing it for don't want you to practice it that way?'" he said. Contractor soon left to start his own firm, and his timing could not have been better. At the time, housing and building restrictions stymied Indian builders, and Contractor became a hot commodity by finding ways around them. In the 1980s, a Mumbai developer named Kirti Kedia approached him to build apartment units with footage specifications that were not going to allow the project to meet regulations—but Contractor found a way. The resulting Megh, Malhar, and Raag Towers in Mumbai all have unusual curved shapes. As Brook wrote, Contractor "had outsmarted the regulations by literally cutting corners."

## HIRANANDANI GARDENS AND INFOSYS

Contractor's first major clients, in the 1980s, were the Indian property tycoons Niranjan and Surendra Hiranandani. The brothers asked Contractor to build a luxurious community in Powai, a suburb of Mumbai, called Hiranandani Gardens. At the time, professional architects made their careers and reputations working on government projects, and avoided work with private developers like the Hiranandanis. "All the great dons would not even touch builders," Contractor recalled to Bhatia, an attitude that worked in his favor during the development boom of the

1980s. Contractor worked quickly, finding a way to accommodate every client's demands. When a client told him what they wanted, he formulated the design in his head and sketched an external design of the project by the time the meeting was over. For Contractor, then and now, the outside of the building is its selling point, and internal comfort is of lesser importance. "He understood the builders' language perfectly," Bhatia noted. "The ultimate buyers were people emerging from the stasis of socialist India, and the building had to be about aspiration." Projects like Hiranandani Gardens, which appear as one of the urban backdrops in the 2008 film *Slumdog Millionaire*, are emblematic of the rise of the new India, where such islands of luxury and stability have their own schools, stores, and infrastructure; they enjoy electricity and clean water twenty-four hours a day, in a country of chronic blackouts and food insecurity.

In 1991 India adopted significant free market reforms, opening the floodgates of foreign capital to domestic businesses. Among the beneficiaries was Infosys, a software outsourcing corporation. In the early 1990s, Contractor encountered Infosys founder Narayana Murthy dining at a restaurant in New Delhi. He introduced himself, and by the end of the conversation had convinced the billionaire to let him improve upon the Infosys headquarters in Bangalore, where he installed, at Murthy's request, a replica of I. M. Pei's glass pyramid at the Louvre in Paris. Contractor later designed elaborate, futuristic-looking campuses across India for Infosys (including one in Mumbai) that are more like cities unto themselves—with food courts, bookstores, swimming pools, and cricket pitches—than workplaces, Brook noted. At the campus outside Pune, Contractor constructed two giant orbs that house employee offices; he told Brook that he calls them "dew drops." At the Infosys corporate facility in Mysore, Contractor built a central structure that mimics St. Peter's Basilica in Vatican City.

## OTHER PROJECTS

In New Delhi, Contractor designed an office complex that houses Microsoft, KPMG, Lufthansa, and American Express. Two of his more recent projects, a condominium tower called Minerva and another called the Imperial Towers (on which Contractor worked with two other firms), are built on the sites of former slums. Contractor's soaring designs are changing the cityscape and skyline of Mumbai, and not everyone is happy about it. He has run afoul of conservationists who accuse him of sacrificing the historical and environmental well-being of the city to wealthy citizens who, as evidenced by Ambani, are more concerned with leaving their own mark than building for the public good. Contractor argues that skyscrapers are the only feasible housing solution in Mumbai, but his slum redevelopment policy has failed to adequately address the needs of Mumbai's poorest residents. In 2014, there were nearly 7 million slum dwellers in Mumbai; they have been estimated to comprise more than half the population of the city. Residents are active members of the local economy, often working from their homes to sort garbage or take in laundry. In fact, Mumbai thrives on the labor of the poor, but that labor is difficult to perform, for many, from a residential apartment. (Other architects have floated plans in which the city would build low-rise, mixed-use housing to address this problem.) Brook met a former slum-dwelling family at Imperial Towers. They were enthusiastic about their new home, despite the fact that, unlike their wealthy neighbors, they were allowed only one hour of running water a day. It is just one way that developments like Contractor's keep poor residents and wealthy residents segregated in India's cities; the slum redevelopment project in Mumbai, he told Brook, allows both classes to "enjoy their own freedom, but they don't disturb the other guy's freedom."

## PERSONAL LIFE

Contractor is married and lives in Mumbai.

## SUGGESTED READING

Bhatia, Rahul. "Deconstructing Hafeez Contractor." *Open*. Open Media Network, 7 Nov. 2009. Web. 23 July 2015.

Brook, Daniel. "The Slumdog Millionaire Architect." *New York Times*. New York Times, 19 June 2014. Web. 23 July 2015.

Brook, Daniel. "Slumdogs, Millionaires." *Slate*. Slate Group, 25 Feb. 2013. Web. 24 July 2015.

Choksi, Mansi. "India Slugfest over Mumbai Slum Votes." *Al Jazeera*. Al Jazeera Media Network, 12 Mar. 2014. Web. 25 July 2015.

Leon, Joshua K. "Make Way for High Rises: Who Benefits from Slum Demolitions in Mumbai?" *Dissent*. Dissent Magazine, 13 Mar. 2013. Web. 24 July 2015.

Ramesh, Randeep. "Indian Tycoon Builds Tower Block Home." *Guardian*. Guardian News and Media, 1 June 2007. Web. 24 July 2015.

—Molly Hagan

# Laverne Cox

**Born:** May 29, 1984
**Occupation:** Actor

Laverne Cox is well known to fans of the Netflix television series *Orange Is the New Black* for her portrayal of Sophia Burset, an inmate who works as a prison hairdresser. Sophia is a transgender woman, and her widely applauded inclusion on the show is one of very few portrayals of a transgender character in such a sensitive and realistic light on television. Cox, who often explains to interviewers that she was "assigned" a male identity at birth but never felt male, has, like the character she portrays, medically transitioned into a woman and has taken on the frequently thankless task of advocating for the transgender community. In early 2014, she famously chastised talk-show host Katie Couric for asking invasive questions about the hormonal and surgical procedures she had undergone. "The preoccupation with transition and surgery objectifies trans people," Cox said, as quoted by Katie McDonough for *Salon* (6 Feb. 2014). "And then we don't get to really deal with the real, lived experiences. The reality of trans people's lives is that so often we are targets of violence. We experience discrimination disproportionately to the rest of the community. . . . If we focus on transition, we don't actually get to talk about those things."

In mid-2014 Cox became the first transgender person ever to appear on the cover of *Time* magazine, and she has become one of the most important voices in the movement for transgender rights. "Cox's off-screen work as a trans activist contains the same depth, love, and humor that critics have celebrated in her acting—and is reaching just as wide an audience," McDonough asserted. Cox happily wears that mantle. "I always knew when I got a public platform, it was part of my job to educate people," she told Alex Morris for *Glamour* (Nov. 2014). "Being famous to just wear lovely clothes—which I *do* love doing—that's not for me."

Dominick D/Wikimedia Commons

## EARLY LIFE

Laverne Cox was born Roderick Laverne Cox in Mobile, Alabama. "I always say, 'I'm from Mobile, but I was never *of* Mobile,'" she told Matthew Breen for the *Advocate* (10 July 2014). "I was never there fully in my head." Cox has a twin brother who is a musician and artist known as M. Lamar.

The twins' parents never married, and they had no relationship with their father. Their mother, Gloria, taught in Mobile County public schools for decades and later took a post at Bishop State Community College. Gloria instilled a love of learning in her children, and Cox has recalled to interviewers that in her youth she particularly enjoyed biographies of black artists such as opera singer Leontyne Price and Arthur Mitchell, founder of Dance Theatre of Harlem. Not all of her tastes were so lofty; she was also an avid fan of such television shows as *Solid Gold* and *Fame* and enjoyed imitating the choreography while watching.

Despite some reservations about her young son's feminine mannerisms, Gloria agreed that Cox could begin taking dance lessons in third grade. As Cox frequently relates to interviewers, it was at about that time that one teacher angrily told Gloria, "Your son is going to end up in New Orleans wearing a dress if you don't get him into therapy right away," as Cox recalled in an interview with Katy Steinmetz for *Time* (29 May 2014). Narrow-minded teachers were only one of the perils facing Cox, who was regularly bullied and harassed by fellow students while in elementary school. At age eleven, in a brief fit of despair, she took an entire bottle of pills she found in the medicine cabinet. Luckily, they caused only a stomachache.

## EDUCATION AND CAREER

Determined to prove that she was better than her tormentors, Cox successfully ran for vice president of her class in seventh grade, and two years later she began high school at the Alabama School of Fine Arts in Birmingham, where she adopted an androgynous style of dressing. Upon graduating she entered Indiana University, where she studied dance and began performing in musicals and dreamed of relocating to a big city to more fully explore her gender identity. She eventually transferred to Marymount Manhattan College in New York City, where she was cast in Max Frisch's *Andorra*. Although the part was small and required no speaking, Cox drew attention for her stage presence and spot-on mannerisms. In her senior year, after being approached on the subway by a filmmaker who commented on her unusual hairstyle and vintage clothing, Cox won her first screen role. (She used her birth name in the credits and does not like to discuss the film.)

Despite having tried at times to wear boys' clothing and conform to gender norms, Cox realized that she would never be content that way. "It was a very painful process," she recalled to Morris. "I was so unhappy and thought, I either have to transition or I have to kill myself." A few years before beginning her medical transition, she began living full time as a woman. At one point she agreed to enter a beauty pageant at the Pyramid Club in the East Village section of New York. "It was the first time I'd gone full femme," she told Breen, explaining that she had never before worn a woman's swimsuit or fake breasts. "It was very freeing and very wild." Identifying as a woman came with its own set of problems, however, including being repeatedly harassed and attacked on the streets of the city.

Still, once she had gotten her first hormone shot, Cox felt able to assert aloud that she was transgender. "I never really said that before," she told Breen. "I feel like it was something I'd been running away from my whole life, something I'd been fighting and trying not to be and trying to negotiate, instead of just trying to be who I am." With her sights set on an acting career, Cox, who had earned a bachelor's degree in

theater, knew she would be facing an even more formidable fight.

## SUCCESS ON SCREEN

As Hugh Ryan wrote for *Newsweek* (17 July 2013), "Scripted roles for transgender actors are few and far between. More often than not they are limited to bit parts where they deliver a single sassy line, solicit someone for sex in a sordid alley, or die brutally during the opening credits of a police procedural." During the early stages of her career, Cox took on some of those roles—most notably with an occasional minor spot on *Law & Order*—and tried to keep in mind her acting teacher's dictum that it was her job to bring "truth and rawness" to even the most stereotypical or two-dimensional part. She often found herself competing for roles with drag queens, men who identify as male but dress like women as part of an often humorous stage persona. "I have such respect for drag queens," she told Erik Piepenburg for the *New York Times* (28 July 2011). "But what is troubling about the mainstreaming of drag, and people conflating drag and being transsexual, is that people think this is a joke. My identity is not a joke. Who I am as a woman is not a joke. This is my life."

In 2008, Cox, who was then working at a restaurant in New York City's Union Square neighborhood, got something of a big break when she was cast on the first season of VH1's *I Want to Work for Diddy*, a reality show on which contestants vied to be hired as personal assistant to hip-hop mogul Sean Combs (known at various times during his career as Diddy, P. Diddy, or Puff Daddy). The show provided a chance not only to advance her floundering acting career but to prove to a wide audience that a transgender person could be embraced by the historically homophobic hip-hop community.

While she was eliminated from competition in the sixth episode, *I Want to Work for Diddy* garnered a GLAAD Media Award in 2009 for outstanding reality program. Her participation on *I Want to Work for Diddy* led to an invitation for Cox to produce and star in a VH1 show, *TRANSform Me*. On that show, which aired in 2010, she and her team taught average female participants to make the most of their attributes—resulting in sometimes jaw-dropping "before" and "after" shots. While it enjoyed only lackluster ratings, *TRANSform Me* marked the first time an African American transgender woman had produced and starred in her own show. *TRANSform Me* was nominated for a GLAAD Media Award for outstanding reality program in 2011.

## ORANGE IS THE NEW BLACK

Because of her background on VH1, multiple journalists have quipped that Cox is not only the first-ever successful African American transgender woman on television, but one of the few—of any race or gender identity—to make the leap from reality television to massive success on a scripted show. That show is *Orange Is the New Black*, which premiered in July 2013 on Netflix. Loosely based on a 2010 memoir by Piper Kerman, the show examines life at a women's prison in upstate New York. The main character (renamed Piper Chapman for the small screen) is an upper-middle-class white woman convicted for having worked as a drug courier a decade before—a jet-setting job that in her youthful folly she had found adventurous. Chapman, a college-educated blonde, is a rarity in the prison, and the series introduces viewers to a large and diverse group of her fellow inmates, including Cox's character, Sophia Burset. Sophia (whose birth name is Marcus) is in prison for committing credit-card fraud to fund her sex reassignment surgery. Marcus—played to great effect in flashback scenes by Cox's twin brother—has the support of an understanding wife, but their son has difficulty in accepting his father as transgender, and in revenge he snitches to the police about the fraud.

Viewers and critics alike responded favorably to Sophia—and to Cox's nuanced portrayal. "No character from *Orange Is the New Black*'s stellar first season had more Netflix viewers buzzing than Sophia Burset, the prison hairdresser whose trailblazing storyline flipped the TV game on its head," Marc Snetiker wrote for *Entertainment Weekly* (8 Aug. 2014). He opined that the actor's performance gets "better and better with time" and asserted, "The combination of comedy and heartbreaking sadness that comes with a single look from Cox can't be understated." For the role, Cox was nominated for an Emmy Award in the category of outstanding guest actress in a comedy series in 2014. Although she lost to her fellow costar Uzo Aduba, she made history as the first transgender actress to be nominated for the prestigious prize.

Since joining the show, which is expected to enter its third season in mid-2015, Cox has been asked repeatedly why it is noteworthy for an actual transgender person to be playing a transgender character. In an interview for the Emerson

College publication *Emertainment Monthly* (9 Nov. 2013), she explained to Michelle Douvris and Sara Chaffee: "If the character is written the way Sophia is written, as a multidimensional character who the audience can really empathize with, all of the sudden they're empathizing with a real trans person. And for trans folks out there, who need to see representations of people who are like them and of their experiences, that's when it becomes really important."

In addition to her work on *Orange Is the New Black*, Cox has had supporting roles in several independent films and won best supporting actress at the 2013 Massachusetts Independent Film Festival for her role in director Susan Seidelman's *Musical Chairs* (2011). She has also appeared as a guest star on a number of television series and has been cast in a starring role in the CBS legal drama *Doubt*.

## ACTIVISM

When not acting, Cox, who was named a "woman of the year" by *Glamour* magazine in 2014, uses her public platform to advocate for the transgender community. "I looked around at the lives of so many trans folks—lives that are often in danger," Cox told Morris, explaining the pressing need for such activism. "The homicide rate is disproportionately high among trans people. The rate of bullying is disproportionately high. Forty-one percent of all trans people have attempted suicide, compared to 4.6 percent of the rest of the population."

Cox, who received the 2014 Stephen F. Kolzak Award from GLAAD for her work in fighting discrimination, speaks at dozens of college campuses each year, giving the presentation "Ain't I a Woman: My Journey to Womanhood." In late 2014 she hosted *The T Word*, an MTV documentary about transgender youth. She is also serving as the executive producer of a documentary film, expected to be released in 2016, about CeCe McDonald, a transgender African American woman who killed an assailant while defending herself against a violent transphobic attack and subsequently served time in a federal men's prison.

## SUGGESTED READING

Breen, Matthew. "Laverne Cox: The Making of an Icon." *Advocate*. Here Media, 10 July 2014. Web. 14 Jan. 2015.

Douvris, Michelle, and Sara Chaffee. "Sitting Down with *Orange Is the New Black* Star Laverne Cox." *Emertainment Monthly*. Emerson College, 9 Nov. 2013. Web. 26 Feb. 2015.

McDonough, Katie. "The Post-Katie Couric Shift." *Salon*. Salon Media, 6 Feb. 2014. Web. 26 Jan. 2015.

Morris, Alex. "The Advocate: Laverne Cox." *Glamour*. Condé Nast, Nov. 2014. Web. 26 Jan. 2015.

Piepenburg, Erik. "When They Play Women, It's Not Just an Act." *New York Times*. New York Times, 28 July 2011. Web. 26 Feb. 2015.

Ryan, Hugh. "Transgender Characters Get a Transformative Moment on Netflix's *Orange Is the New Black*." *Newsweek*. Newsweek, 17 July 2013. Web. 26 Jan. 2015.

Snetiker, Marc. "Here's Why Sophia Is Still the Best Character on 'Orange Is the New Black.'" *Entertainment Weekly*. Entertainment Weekly, 8 Aug. 2014. Web. 26 Feb. 2015.

—Mari Rich

# Dominique Crenn

**Born:** 1965

**Occupation:** Chef and restaurateur

Chef Dominique Crenn creates more than mere meals; she calls her dishes "poetic culinaria," and they are meant to express to her patrons her artistic ideals and philosophy of life. Her multi-course tasting menu is, in fact, presented to diners in the form of a printed poem: a small dish of sea urchin, caviar, and citrus, for example, is represented as "mellow serenades of colors licorice and orange." Her San Francisco–based restaurant, Atelier Crenn, "serves a cuisine so visually, texturally, and conceptually inventive it has both delighted and baffled critics and drawn international attention," according to a profile by Katy McLaughlin for the *Wall Street Journal* (21 July 2012).

French-born Crenn is the first female chef in the United States to have earned two Michelin stars; the venerable Michelin Guide awards restaurants zero to three stars, with a two-star establishment being deemed worthy of a special detour because of its exceptional cuisine. The stars are highly sought after by chefs because the vast majority of restaurants never receive the honor. Of San Francisco's thousands of restaurants, only seven in the entire city merited a two-star rating in 2014. Given the scarcity of women at that illustrious level, Crenn, as Ryan Sutton wrote for *Bloomberg News* (31 July 2013), "is a vital outlier in the male-dominant world of fine dining." She prefers, however, not to be thought of in those terms. "I don't want to be drawn into the gender bias," she told Kerstin Kühn for the culinary magazine *FOUR* (8 Aug. 2014). "I don't want people to look at me as female or male; I just want them to appreciate what I do."

## EARLY YEARS AND EDUCATION

Dominique Crenn was born in France in 1965. When she was eighteen months old, she was adopted by Alain Crenn, a politician, and his wife. She was raised in Versailles, just outside of Paris, and spent many summers in Brittany, where her extended family owned farmland. (In addition to his political pursuits, Alain was an avid painter, and he maintained a studio—or *atelier*—there as well; Crenn's restaurant, which is named, in part, as an homage to him, is decorated with several of his artworks.)

Alain's best friend was Albert Coquil, the food critic for the newspaper *Le Télégramme*, and Crenn, a well-behaved child, was often taken to Michelin-starred or other high-profile restaurants. She has recalled peering into the kitchen and being entranced by the chefs, resplendent in their white coats and moving as smoothly and efficiently as soldiers.

Her culinary tastes were also inspired by her time on the farm, picking potatoes in the heat of a Brittany summer. She recalls in particular being served a stew by her grandmother one day and realizing that every ingredient in it had been nurtured and harvested right there on her family's land. She told the audience at a TEDx talk she gave for Bay Area women in December 2010 that because she was so young at the time, she could not articulate the tastes and feelings the experience sparked in her. "A lot of people categorize me as a chef as being farm-to-table," she quipped, "But for me as a child it was farm-to-mouth."

Crenn's mother was also an exceptional cook who taught her daughter the pleasures of rustic home meals. When Crenn was just nine years old, her mother fell ill, and Crenn stepped in to prepare roast chicken, lamb, fresh salads, and cheese plates for the family's dinners.

Despite her obvious natural talent, when she began investigating the possibilities of apprenticing in a high-end kitchen, Crenn was repeatedly told to consider becoming a restaurant manager or member of the waitstaff instead. While she sometimes despaired of ever working in France's male-dominated culinary scene, she decided merely to defer her dream and embarked upon earning a bachelor's degree in economics and a master's degree in international business.

## STARTING A CULINARY CAREER

Sensing that it would be easier to pursue her culinary aspirations in the United States, Crenn moved to San Francisco in the late 1980s. She immediately felt at home in the city, and one day— despite having no professional training or experience— she confidently walked into Stars, the restaurant run by the legendary chef Jeremiah Tower, and asked for a job. To her surprise, Tower agreed. She went into work each day at three in the afternoon to meet with the sous-chef. "They give you a menu and a station. There's no recipe, just some guidelines," she explained to Gabe Ulla for *Eater* (13 Jan. 2012). "So, there's maybe some calamari and some other components, and they tell you to go and do the dish. Then, at 4:30, they'd come around and test it. If it didn't work out, you'd get thirty minutes to fix it. It's difficult and filled with pressure, but at the same time, you realize that that gives you the ability to be creative, understand the ingredients, and truly know the steps that go into making something work."

Crenn remained at Stars for two years and then moved on to posts at such well-regarded establishments as Campton Place, 2223 Market, and Yoyo Bistro at the Miyako Hotel. While at Yoyo, she met a group of businesspeople who were planning to open a high-end restaurant at the Intercontinental Hotel in Jakarta, Indonesia. Because the country's culinary scene was even more male-dominated than that of France, they felt that having an all-female kitchen staff would be an appealing novelty. Crenn has described her time as Indonesia's first female head chef as one of the most gratifying experiences of her life, but when civil unrest broke out in 1998, she was forced to leave the country.

Upon her return to the United States, she settled in Los Angeles and took a job as the executive chef at the Manhattan Country Club, in nearby Manhattan Beach. She left the country club after eight years to become the opening chef at Adobe Restaurant and Lounge in Santa Monica. She had remained in contact with the management of the Intercontinental Hotel, however, and when they approached her about joining their San Francisco operation in 2008, she took the opportunity.

It was at Luce in San Francisco's Intercontinental Hotel that she earned her first Michelin star, in 2009; the following year, Luce was again awarded one star, which indicates a very good restaurant with cuisine prepared to a consistently high standard. During her tenure there, *Esquire* magazine named Crenn chef of the year, and she triumphed on the popular cooking show *Iron Chef America*.

## ATELIER CRENN

In January 2011 Crenn opened her own restaurant, Atelier Crenn. "This is a very personal project for me," she explained to Ulla. "I wanted to connect [patrons] with my experiences not only with food but maybe with the people that I've met and the places that I've traveled to. I didn't want to do a fine dining with white tablecloths. I wanted something livelier. I wanted people to come, have fun, come into the kitchen, and feel comfortable. It's not fine dining, but maybe dining at its finest." The 2013 Michelin Guide gave the restaurant a coveted two-star ranking, as did the 2014 edition.

Many reviewers wax rhapsodic about Crenn's efforts, devoting paragraphs to descriptions of her signature dishes, which include "Walk in the Forest," a medley of wild mushrooms served with hazelnut praline and burnt pine meringue meant to evoke childhood strolls with her father, and a composed salad called "Jardin d'Hiver," in which miniature beets and radishes emerged from quinoa "soil" dusted with goat cheese "snow." There were occasional grumbles, with some critics finding the food pretentious or overwrought. In a review for *San Francisco Weekly* (23 Mar. 2011), for example, Jonathan Kauffman asserted, "The chef will have to resolve how to balance her food-as-art intentions with the food-as-meal expectations of patrons." He described one dish he found indicative of the problem: "A small slab of Arctic char was cooked sous-vide, garnished with a little shaved fennel, and placed on a large river rock set in a bowl. The server poured a floral tea into the bowl, and the rock was soon ringed in dry-ice fog. Lovely—except the fish was cooked fifteen degrees too rare, and served twenty-five degrees too cool, to enjoy."

Few critics found fault, however, with Crenn's habit of emerging from the kitchen to greet diners personally or her focus on treating Atelier Crenn's staff in a firm yet civil manner, with none of the screaming or browbeating common in many professional kitchens. She recalled to Ulla that as an aspiring young chef, she had once written in her journal, "I want to treat people in my kitchen with respect and understand that no matter what experience someone has, they always can bring something to the table."

For the fall of 2014, a shorter tasting menu became available at Atelier Crenn for $140, while the longer "chef's grand tasting menu" cost $220, with wine pairings available for $95 and $150, respectively.

## PERSONAL LIFE

Journalists often comment on Crenn's compelling appearance. "With her thick black hair looking rock 'n' roll mussed, her large, dark eyes rimmed in kohl, and a big scarf wrapped, city cool-girl style, around her vintage cotton army jacket, she looks less like a chef and more like a French indie actress in the vein of Charlotte Gainsbourg," Molly Watson wrote for *Elle* (17 Feb. 2011), while Anna Peirano, writing for *429* magazine (2 Nov. 2011), praised the chef's "sophisticated style and artistic energy" and opined, "She could be a painter, a musician, or an actress." Unbeknownst to most filmgoers, they might have glimpsed Crenn—or at least her cartoon doppelganger—on the big screen: the character of Colette Tatou in the animated movie *Ratatouille* (2007), set in a top-notch French restaurant, is said to be based on her.

In 2009, after suffering from a near-fatal accident while getting out of the bathtub, Crenn was moved to get a life-affirming tattoo on her forearm; it depicts a girl gazing up at a winged pig flying overhead. Based on the old saying that an unlikely event will happen "when pigs fly," that tattoo reminds her, she says, that all things are possible.

While Crenn rarely discusses her personal life with journalists, food writer Karen Leibowitz described a dinner she shared with Crenn and her partner, a woman who works as a therapist, in a 2012 issue of *Lucky Peach*. Crenn is working on her first book and has signed a contract with Houghton Mifflin Harcourt. "It won't be just another coffee table book with pretty pictures," she told Kühn, "but something that will raise issues and inspire dialogue."

## SUGGESTED READING

Bauer, Michael. "Food as an Art Form." *San Francisco Chronicle*. SFGate, 10 Apr. 2011. Web. 21 Nov. 2014.

McLaughlin, Katy. "Finding Poetry in Food (and Vice Versa)." *Wall Street Journal*. Dow Jones, 21 July 2012. Web. 21 Nov. 2014.

Sutton, Ryan. "Crenn's Brilliant Squab Triumphs in S.F." *Bloomberg News*. Bloomberg, 31 July 2013. Web. 21 Nov. 2014.

Ulla, Gabe. "Dominique Crenn on France, Fine Dining, and Chef Life." *Eater*. Vox Media, 13 Jan. 2012. Web. 21 Nov. 2014.

Watson, Molly. "Turning the Tables: Atelier Crenn's Dominique Crenn." *Elle*. Hearst Communications, 17 Feb. 2011. Web. 21 Nov. 2014.

—Mari Rich

# John Darnielle

**Born:** March 16, 1967
**Occupation:** Musician and author

John Darnielle is mostly known as the founder, guitarist, front man, and composer of the indie-rock band the Mountain Goats. His songs are smart, literary, often sad, and emotionally heavy. Darnielle has released more than a dozen albums, starting in 1991. He received a good deal of praise for his album *Tallahassee* (2002) and gained even more critical praise and popularity with *The Sunset Tree* (2005), a deeply personal album about his abusive stepfather. Sasha Frere-Jones, a music critic for the *New Yorker* (16 May 2005), called him "America's best non-hip-hop lyricist." Aside from his music career, Darnielle is also a fiction writer. In 2014 he put out his first full-length novel, *Wolf in White Van*, which received positive reviews and was long-listed for the 2014 National Book Award.

## EARLY LIFE

John Darnielle was born in Bloomington, Indiana, in 1967. Not long after that, the family moved to San Luis Obispo, California. By then, Darnielle also had a younger sister. When Darnielle was five years old, his parents—his father was an English professor and his mother a librarian—divorced. Soon after the divorce, his mother married a man who beat her as well as the children; and he continued to do so throughout their rocky marriage.

Darnielle attended Catholic school and was fascinated by religion; however, by his teenage years, his views had turned around. Although he was still was fascinated by religion, but he was no longer a believer. Darnielle, however, found solace in his imagination. He loved *The Incredible Hulk* comic books because of the Hulk's

loyalty and his ability to transform himself into a large, destructive force. In an interview with Terry Gross for the *National Public Radio* program "Fresh Air" (17 Sept. 2014), Darnielle talked about the Hulk's anger and transformation in relation to his own feelings, saying, "You wish you could make people see just how powerful it feels. You feel like if it were unleashed it would break things—and the Incredible Hulk is that, just made of flesh."

After he received a typewriter from his mother Darnielle began to write short stories and poems. In junior high school, he won a New York literary competition. According to a profile by Stephen Rodrick in *New York Magazine* (1 Mar. 2009), Darnielle's stepfather would not let him go to New York for the ceremony. Darnielle acknowledged in the profile that his stepfather "had this huge brain and great taste, and he had me listening to Randy Newman when I was 8, but he was also a monster." One day when he was fifteen, Darnielle told Rodrick he sat for three hours in a building above some train tracks and had there been a train, he would have jumped to his death. In fact, during his teenage years, Darnielle contemplated and talked about suicide a lot. He was open about it with his friends, he told Gross. Although Darnielle never attempted suicide, the overwhelming pain he was dealing with led him to severely hurt himself: for a period of time he carried razors on him and would sometimes cut himself.

He was also using drugs, namely heroin, and later crystal meth. Darnielle was a smart kid, too, but he told Gross, "Your intelligence doesn't override your desire to destroy yourself." Eventually, however, after an overdose, Darnielle decided to cut back. Later, on the advice of a therapist, he decided to help others by working as a psychiatric-nurse technician at Metropolitan State Hospital, in Norwalk, California. It was a short-term facility for adolescents. Darnielle lived on the hospital campus and enrolled at nearby Pitzer College, where he majored in English and classics.

## MUSICAL BEGINNINGS

While living and working at Metropolitan State Hospital and going to school, Darnielle bought a cheap guitar and began writing songs. He decided to record under the band name the Mountain Goats, after a lyric in a *Screamin' Jay Hawkins* song called "Big Yellow Coat." He started recording his songs, on a dual cassette recorder in his room. He would give out his songs on cassettes to friends and play local small venues. Dennis Callaci, head of Shrimper Records in California was given one of these cassettes. Callaci released the Mountain Goats' first album, a cassette-only release called *Taboo VI: The Homecoming* (1991). Darnielle continued putting out his cassette tapes and playing local music venues.

Darnielle toured the country mostly solo for years, with occasional collaborators. From 1991 to 1995 he toured with Rachel Ware, bassist and vocalist. The Mountain Goats recorded some singles, EPs, and two full-length albums, *Zopilote Machine* and *Sweden* (1995). After graduating from Pitzer in 1995 Darnielle toured Europe a few times with bass player Peter Hughes, but for the most part toured on his own.

In 2001, the independent record label 4AD offered support so that he and Hughes could record an album in a modern music studio. *Tallahassee*, an acoustic concept album about a married couple living in Tallahassee, Florida, was recorded and released in 2002. The album not only sold better than the Mountain Goats' previous albums, it also earned Darnielle some press in national media outlets, like the *New York Times* and *National Public Radio*. One of the Mountain Goats' next albums, *We Shall All Be Healed* (2004), began to depart from the lo-fi cassette recordings of just voice and guitar, and introduced piano and strings and a new kind of lushness. The songs though, were still full of sad and poetic fragments and tales.

The following album, *The Sunset Tree* (2005), told the tale of Darnielle's damaging relationship with his stepfather and was released about a year after his stepfather died. Featuring a drummer, a cellist, and a pianist, the album was widely praised in the press and hailed as one of the Mountain Goats' best. Aside from record sales, critical acclaim and an increasingly obsessive fan base, the album was significant because it was so personal. By this point Darnielle had released more than four hundred songs. In his review of the album for the *New York Times* (25 Apr. 2005), Kelefa Sanneh wrote, "The extraordinary new Mountain Goats CD is *The Sunset Tree*, and it may be Mr. Darnielle's best album so far (which is saying a lot) and his most straightforwardly autobiographical." He later adds: "The album is full of exquisite songs that overlap without quite connecting: Mr. Darnielle knows that the best albums are usually the ones you can't quite figure out."

## TOURING

On his 2006 *Get Lonely* album, Darnielle focused his lyrics on a first-person narrative of sadness and solitude. He was becoming more popular and the relationship between Darnielle and his fans continued to be a powerful one. In his profile Rodrick explored that dynamic: "Mountain Goats fans tend to have an air of sadness about them, and because Darnielle sings so openly and candidly about his own difficulties, he connects with his audience on a level that few artists are able to reach . . . . Darnielle sings about what his fans feel but can't articulate. He's their hero, but he's also their soulmate, the one person in the world who understands them."

While touring in 2007, the Mountain Goats became a trio, with Darnielle, Hughes, and drummer Jon Wurster. The trio formed the musical foundation of the band's next two albums, *Heretic Pride* (2008) and *The Life of the World to Come* (2009). The latter was a first for Darnielle, because its lyrical content was entirely inspired by the Bible. The lyrics do not preach, but rather explore the role faith can have in people's lives. Darnielle, in his hundreds of songs, had explored this area before—but had never dedicated an entire album to it. Regarding the album *All Eternals Deck* (2011), K. Ross Hoffman for the All Music Guide website wrote that Darnielle offers up "poetically cryptic songs crammed full of emphatic imperatives, lists of objects,

place names, photographic and cinematic imagery, ambiguously metaphorical melodrama, and elliptically sketched characters doomed to lives of regret, despair, terror or worse." The album continued on in the style of the Mountain Goats' later albums, full of instruments such as drums, bass, piano, and plenty of strings. The lushness, however, did not overwhelm the lyrics. The following year the band followed up with *Transcendental Youth* (2012), a similarly solid, heartfelt album.

## PUBLISHED FICTION

Darnielle's first published work, *Master of Reality* (2008), was a novella for 33 1/3, a series of short books each about popular music, focusing on a single album. Darnielle wrote about the album *Master of Reality* (1971) by the British hard rock band Black Sabbath. Unlike other books in the series, Darnielle decided to write a fictional piece about the album instead of a work of criticism and analysis. The story of the album is told by Roger Painter, a boy locked in a Southern California adolescent psychiatric center.

Darnielle followed up on the theme of an isolated young man, in his debut novel, *Wolf in White Van* (2014). The main character, teenager Sean Phillips, has had a disfiguring injury since the age of seventeen, when he shot himself in the head during an attempted suicide but survived. Now he plays a game that requires him to use his imagination, but it appears that it has real-life and quite disastrous consequences. The game, Trace Italian, is a role-playing game via mail, and it blurs the line between fantasy and reality. The story is told in reverse chronological order. The book received mostly positive reviews. In the *New York Times* (7 Nov. 2014), Ethan Gilsdorf called *Wolf in White Van* "a stunning meditation on the power of escape, and on the cat-and-mouse contest the self plays to deflect its own guilt."

## PERSONAL LIFE

Darnielle met his wife, Lalitree, in 1994. As of 2012, the couple and their son were living in Durham, North Carolina.

## SUGGESTED READING

Frere-Jones, Sasha. "The Declaimers." *New Yorker*. Condé Nast, 16 May 2005. Web. 11 Mar. 2015.

Gross, Terry. "As a Lyricist and Novelist, The Mountain Goats' Lead Man Writes About Pain." *NPR*. NPR, 17 Sept. 2014. Web. 11 Mar. 2015.

Rodrick, Stephen. "God & Worshipper." *New York Magazine*. New York, 1 Mar. 2009. Web. 11 Mar. 2015.

**SELECTED WORKS**

*Tallahassee*, 2002; *The Sunset Tree*, 2005; *Get Lonely*, 2006; *The Life of the World to Come*, 2009; *All Eternals Deck*, 2011; *Transcendental Youth*, 2012

—Dmitry Kiper

Mark Sullivan/BET/Getty Images for BET

# Davido

**Born:** November 21, 1992
**Occupation:** Recording artist and producer

Davido is an award-winning Nigerian recording artist and record producer. He and fellow acts such as Wizkid and Iyanya are a part of a new generation of Nigerian artists who are re-inventing Afropop and influencing global music trends. Centered in Nigeria, the West African music scene favors complex rhythms and combines electronic dance music (EDM), R & B, reggae, and hip-hop to create a sound that pushes those genres in new directions. Nigerian artists such as Davido evoke the iconic imagery of American hip-hop, but, as David Drake wrote for *Fader* magazine (1 Aug. 2014), "rhythmically, Nigeria's scene is leagues more advanced than its American counterpart." In the video for Davido's single "Fans Mi," featuring American rapper Meek Mill and released in summer 2015, Davido sifts through piles of cocaine and showers nearly naked women with dollar bills. (In a comedic twist at the end, the white powder assumed to be cocaine turns out to be yam flour, though in conservative Nigeria the suggestion of an illicit substance was enough to draw serious public ire.) As Drake wrote of Nigerian popular music, "It's not just an increasingly rhythmic bed that Nigeria injects into the diasporic genres of hip-hop, R & B, dancehall, and soca. It's also an omnivorous pop sensibility, uniting disparate ingredients into a vibrant creative soup."

The son of a business magnate, Davido released his debut studio album *Omo Baba Olowo* (the title means "son of a rich man" in Yoruba) on the heels of the release of his hit single "Dami

Duro" in 2012. Since then, Davido's rise has been meteoric; he is currently one of the continent's biggest stars and won the 2014 African Muzik Magazine Award for artist of the year and the 2014 BET Award for best international act: Africa. Davido is also a producer and the chief executive officer of his own record label, HKN Music, which he co-owns with his older brother, Adewale Adeleke.

**EARLY LIFE AND EDUCATION**

Davido was born David Adedeji Adeleke on November 21, 1992, in Atlanta, Georgia. His father, Deji Adeleke, is the chair of the company Pacific Energy, which has holdings in banking, power and energy, and steel. His father is also a devout Seventh-day Adventist and the founder and prochancellor of Adeleke University in Ede, Nigeria. Davido's mother, Vero Adeleke, a political science lecturer at Babcock University in Nigeria, died in 2003 when Davido was eleven years old. Davido, who was raised in Lagos, grew up listening to American rappers 50 Cent and Ja Rule. "When I was young, Nigerian music hadn't really developed as it is now," he told Adeola Adeyemo for the Nigerian entertainment and lifestyle website *Bella Naija* (4 Feb. 2012). But in the same interview, Davido also cites the influence of a Nigerian hip-hop group called Plantashun Boyz, one of the forerunners of the current Nigerian sound.

He began studying business administration at Oakwood University, a private college operated by the Seventh-day Adventist Church in Huntsville, Alabama. He dropped out after his sophomore year and returned to Nigeria to pursue a career in music. His father was less enthusiastic about Davido's musical ambitions and insisted that he finish his degree at Babcock University, a Seventh-day Adventist school, in Ogun State. Davido's father was one of the school's founders and the first chair of its board of trustees, and his mother had been a professor there. Thanks to his family's influence, the school created a new music department, and Davido was admitted as the department's first and only student in 2012. He earned his bachelor's degree in music with second-class honors in June 2015.

## OMO BABA OLOWO

Davido began recording songs while he was still a student in the United States. His group, called KB International, played a few shows, but Davido felt he had a better shot breaking into the Nigerian market. He returned to Lagos in 2010 and set up his own record label, HKN Music. (HKN stands for Hakan, which means "king of kings" in Turkish.) He also hired a manager named Asa Asika. Asika was a young promoter and though the two had known each other for many years, Davido was his "first solo project," he told a reporter for the Nigerian website *360nobs* (4 Dec. 2013). Davido also began working with producer and songwriter Shizzi.

In May 2011, Davido released his debut single, "Back When," featuring the popular Nigerian rapper Naeto C. The song was "mildly accepted by critics and was just enough to get him the attention he needed at the time," Abisola Alawode wrote for *Leadership* (29 Aug. 2014). But his follow-up single, "Dami Duro," coproduced with Shizzi and released in October of that year, was Davido's first hit. The song was an unapologetic introduction to Davido. "*Ema dami duro,*" he sings in Yoruba, "*emi omo baba olowo,*" which translates to "Don't try to stop me, I am the son of a very rich man." Davido later said that the song was inspired by an encounter with the police. "Dami Duro" was a huge club hit across the African continent and won Davido a slew of awards, including the 2012 Nigeria Entertainment Award for hottest single of the year and best new act. Davido released a popular remix of the song featuring the rapper Akon in 2012. "Dami Duro" appeared on Davido's debut album *Omo Baba Olowo* (also known as *O.B.O.: The Genesis*), released in July 2012.

Some attributed Davido's swift rise to his moneyed background. After all, Davido's chief rival Wizkid, a middle-class recording artist from Lagos, had spent years trying to break into the industry; Davido simply founded his own record company and was later accused of practicing payola, or paying radio and television stations to play his songs and videos. But Davido denies any connection between his privilege and his success. "I didn't tell God to give me a rich father, I was just lucky," he told Adeyemo. "I think people should even respect me more for trying to do my own thing because now I don't ask him for one naira." Still, his rich-kid image was pervasive enough to taint the reception of *Omo Baba Olowo,* Alawode wrote. "Despite the huge marketing budget put behind it, the album was received with mixed reviews, with many saying the record fell below expectations." Others wrote him off, Alawode added, as merely a "flash in the pan."

## SOPHOMORE ALBUM

Davido, of course, was determined to prove those critics wrong. In 2013, he released a song called "Gobe." "Gobe," Yoruba for "trouble," peaked at number one on the Nigerian music charts and was met with positive reviews. "Its instant popularity was no fluke," Alawode remarked. "By this time, the public's general opinion started to change. 'He may actually be talented,' they said." The song did spark some controversy however, after a (later determined to be fraudulent) Twitter account claiming to be the Nigerian record producer Password accused Davido of stealing his song. Indeed, Password did release an almost identical tune, also called "Gobe," in 2011, but Davido put theft rumors to rest when he revealed that he had worked with the real Password and purchased the rights to remake the song. In the summer of 2013, Davido released another monster hit called "Skelewu." Both "Gobe" and "Skelewu" were listed by the Nigerian *Premium Times* (29 Dec. 2013) among the top ten songs of 2013. "Skelewu" earned nominations for the 2014 MTV Africa Music Award for song of the year and the 2014 Nigeria Entertainment Award for best music video of the year. Many critics shared the view of music blogger Stephen Osaji, who wrote for *SoChistar* (23 Oct. 2013), "Davido keeps on proving me wrong with each new track he releases, and I find that quite annoying." Osaji added that he would "no longer undermine Davido's talent." The song also peaked at number one on the Afribiz Top 100 chart, and the music video, directed by Moe Musa, inspired a popular dance craze.

In early 2014, Davido released a Shizzi-produced single called "Tchelete (Goodlife)," a collaboration with the South African duo Mafikizolo. He also released an upbeat love song about a poor farmer who falls in love with a wealthy woman called "Aye." "Aye" was another monster hit for Davido, and, according to American music critic David Drake for *Pitchfork* (17 Dec. 2014), the song defined the Afropop sound in 2014. "Perhaps the sweetest song of devotion yet written, Davido's 'Aye' boils over with sincerity, its thicket of rhythms eventually taking shape as clean, piercing guitar lines cut through to provide a melodic counterpoint," he wrote. Davido performed the song when he headlined New York City's first African Summer Jam concert in August 2014. For *Fader* (5 Aug. 2014), Drake reported that at the end of the night, "the entire room sang 'Aye' back to his outstretched mic."

According to those who are familiar with the Nigerian music scene, artists such as Davido are perfectly poised for crossover success in the American music market. Davido has announced an upcoming collaboration with Rick Ross and released a single called "Fans Mi" featuring Meek Mill in 2015. Despite his growing international fame, "Fans Mi" was banned by the Nigerian Broadcasting Corporation, along with Wizkid's "In My Bed" and Nicki Minaj's "Anaconda," for depicting an "ostentatious lifestyle, violence, drug trafficking and indecent exposure," May Jesaro reported for Kenya's *Standard Media* (23 Aug. 2015).

## PERSONAL LIFE

Davido has one child, a daughter named Imade Adeleke, who was born in May 2015 to Sophie Momodu. In late May 2015, he bought a vacation home in Atlanta, Georgia. He also owns a home in Lekki, a seaside district in Lagos, Nigeria.

## SUGGESTED READING

Adeyemo, Adeola. "BN Saturday Celebrity Interview: 'You Can't Stop Me!' 2012's Hottest Star, Davido—the Music, the Fame, the Fans & More!" *Bella Naija*. Bella Naija, 4 Feb. 2012. Web. 11 Sept. 2015.
Alawode, Abisola. "Davido vs. Wizkid—Battle for Popularity, Ego War or Juvenile Petu-

lance?" *Leadership*. Leadership Newspaper, 29 Aug. 2014. Web. 11 Sept. 2015.
Drake, David. "Live: African Summer Jam Gets Off to a Bumpy but Bumping Start." *Fader*. Fader, 5 Aug. 2014. Web. 11 Sept. 2015.
Drake, David. "The Most Essential Nigerian Afropop Tracks of 2014." *Pitchfork*. Pitchfork Media, 17 Dec. 2014. Web. 11 Sept. 2015.
Drake, David. "Pop Music's Nigerian Future." *Fader*. Fader Media, 1 Aug. 2014. Web. 11 Sept. 2015.
Osaji, Stephen. Rev. of "Skelewu," by Davido. *SoChistar*. SoChistar, 23 Oct. 2013. Web. 11 Sept. 2015.
Vaughan, Kemi. "Wealthy Parents, Super Star Kids." *Punch*. Punch Nigeria, 6 July 2013. Web. 11 Sept. 2015.

—Molly Hagan

---

# Mo'ne Davis

**Born:** June 24, 2001
**Occupation:** Little League pitcher

Since the first Little League Baseball World Series took place in 1947, almost nine thousand players between the ages of eleven and thirteen have participated in the annual tournament, which is held every August in South Williamsport, Pennsylvania. Only eighteen of those nearly nine thousand players have been girls. Perhaps no girl has made as big an impact on youth baseball's biggest stage as Mo'ne Davis, who became a national sensation at the age of thirteen when she achieved a number of "firsts" for girls at the Little League World Series (LLWS) in 2014. As a star pitcher for the Taney Dragons of Philadelphia, Davis became the first female player not only to win a game in the Little League World Series but also to throw a shutout. She also became the first Little Leaguer, male or female, to appear on the cover of *Sports Illustrated*.

Though the Dragons' dramatic run ended just one win away from the US championship game, Davis became a household name after the tournament, appearing on talk shows and at high-profile events around the country. Despite her young age, Davis—a multisport athlete and honor-roll student at Philadelphia's Springside School and a longtime member of the Anderson Monarchs, a Philadelphia-based baseball team—has become a role model for girls for breaking

Maddie Meyer/Getty Images

down gender boundaries in baseball. "She is our generation's Billy Jean King, or a younger version of Ultimate Fighting Championship (UFC) women's champion Ronda Rousey," Gary Estwick proclaimed for AL.com (25 June 2015).

## EARLY LIFE

Mo'ne Ikea Davis was born on June 24, 2001, in Philadelphia, Pennsylvania, to Lamar Davis and LaKeisha McLean. Her parents divorced when she was a child. Since the age of six, Davis has lived with her mother, a registered nurse's assistant, and her stepfather, Mark Williams, a construction worker. She has an older brother, Qu'ran; a younger brother, Maurice; and a younger half sister, Mahogany.

From a young age, Davis favored sports above other pursuits. She shadowed Qu'ran on the football field and basketball court. She grew up just a few blocks away from the Marian Anderson Recreation Center in South Philadelphia's Graduate Hospital neighborhood. Named after the celebrated African American singer, the recreation center offered a wide array of athletic activities, including football, basketball, baseball, soccer, and swimming.

Davis's natural athletic talent was first spotted at the recreation center. Davis was seven years old when she came to the attention of the center's program director, Steve Bandura, who recognized her strong throwing arm while watching her play football with a group of older boys. Bandura invited her to attend a basketball practice at the center. Davis showed up to the practice and, after quickly picking up a complicated drill called the "three-man weave," was granted a spot on Bandura's all-boys team. During the drill, Bandura recalled to Albert Chen for *Sports Illustrated* (20 Aug. 2014), "Her turn came, and it looked like she had been doing it her whole life. I knew right then that this was someone special."

## A BORN ATHLETE

Founded by Bandura in 1995, the Anderson Monarchs are an elite, year-round travel team that plays basketball, baseball, and soccer. Bandura started the Monarchs for inner-city children whose families could not afford to pay for them to compete on suburban travel teams. Davis quickly became a standout point guard for the Monarchs, and soon after, she learned to play baseball and soccer.

As she did with basketball, Davis picked up baseball right away, despite never having previously worn a baseball glove. Because of her strong arm, her coaches made her a pitcher. She also learned how to play other baseball positions, including first and third base, shortstop, and catcher. Davis proved to be a natural on the soccer pitch as well and became a central midfielder on the Monarchs' soccer team. "She has a spatial awareness that allows her to see the soccer field and the basketball court like a chessboard," Bandura explained to Christina M. Tapper for *Sports Illustrated for Kids* (1 Dec. 2014).

Shortly after joining the Monarchs, Davis was encouraged by Bandura to transfer to a private school. She understood the importance of education from her mother, who was forced to drop out of high school at the age of sixteen when she became pregnant. After scoring high on her entrance exams, Davis transferred from Francis Scott Key Elementary School to Springside School, an all-girls school in the Chestnut Hill section of Philadelphia. Dedicated and focused, she became a perennial honor-roll student at the prestigious school and a star on its basketball and soccer teams.

## ROAD TO WILLIAMSPORT

Davis's athletic development came quickly, thanks in part to her playing almost exclusively with and against boys. Because the Monarchs lacked the funds and resources of suburban travel teams, Bandura had his teams compete in older age divisions, which also furthered Davis's development. Davis instantly won the respect of her peers with her preternatural athletic skills. In 2011 she led the Monarchs to championships in basketball, soccer, and baseball. "[People] underestimate me, but then I just come out and play my game and they see the results," Davis told Tony Fioriglio for the Norristown, Pennsylvania, *Times Herald* (22 July 2014).

Davis's journey to the Little League World Series began to take shape in 2012, when the Taney Youth Baseball Association received its Little League charter. In addition to playing year round for the Monarchs, Davis played for a Taney league team, the Wizards, which were based out of the Markward Recreation Center in Philadelphia's Center City district. After receiving its charter, Taney began to assemble an official Little League all-star team from a large pool of players from across Philadelphia. That all-star team, named the Taney Dragons, competed in district, sectional, state, and regional tournaments, for the chance to advance to the Little League World Series.

After reaching the district tournament in their first year as an official Little League team in 2013, the Dragons entered the 2014 season with higher expectations. That season Taney head coach Alex Rice, at the suggestion of Bandura, invited Davis and other Monarchs to join the team, in an effort to give them the best chance to advance to Williamsport. Not wanting to pass up a once-in-a-lifetime opportunity, Davis and six other Monarchs agreed to play on the Dragons.

By then Davis had emerged as one of the best all-around youth baseball players in Philadelphia. As a pitcher she threw blazing fastballs in the seventy-mile-per-hour range and knee-buckling curveballs, drawing comparisons to Cy Young Award–winning pitcher Clayton Kershaw of the Los Angeles Dodgers. Meanwhile, as a batter, she was able to routinely hit home runs. Because Little League pitching mounds are forty-six feet away from the plate, instead of the major-league standard of sixty feet six inches, Davis's fastball is "comparable to a Major League batter facing a 92 mph heater," Fioriglio wrote.

## MAKING LLWS HISTORY

As an inner-city team from Philadelphia, the Dragons were considered long shots to make it out of their Pennsylvania state tournament, let alone advance to the Little League World Series. Led by Davis, they proved their doubters wrong. After becoming the first Philadelphia team to win both its district and sectional tournaments, the Dragons defeated Collier Township of Allegheny to claim the state Little League championship. Davis then helped lead the Dragons to the Mid-Atlantic regional title, striking out six batters and allowing no runs on three hits in an 8–0 championship-game victory over Delaware. "She's very level, cool, poised," Alex Rice noted to Matt Breen and Melissa Dribben for the *Philadelphia Inquirer* (16 Aug. 2014). "You won't see her fall apart on the mound, you can't get to her."

With their victory over Delaware, the Dragons became the first Philadelphia team, and only the ninth from Pennsylvania, to advance to the LLWS. Meanwhile, Davis became only the fourth American girl and eighteenth overall to play in the prestigious tournament; she and Canada's Emma March became the first girls to play in Williamsport since 2004 and only the third pair of girls to play in the same tournament. During the duration of the two-week tournament, Davis lived in the same house as March, while her teammates and coaches were housed in dormitories within the Williamsport complex.

Already entering the tournament with much fanfare because of her gender and the Dragons' underdog status, Davis became a national media sensation when she threw a complete-game shutout in her team's opening-round game against the team from Nashville, Tennessee. She pitched six innings, striking out eight batters and allowing just two hits in a 4–0 victory for the Dragons. In the process, she became the first female player to pitch a shutout in LLWS history.

In the Dragons' next game against the Pearland, Texas, team Davis had an RBI-single in the first inning, helping her team to a 7–6 victory. She became only the sixth girl to get a hit in LLWS history. After losing their next two games—against the Las Vegas, Nevada, team and Chicago's Jackie Robinson West—the Dragons were eliminated from the tournament, falling just two wins shy of the US championship. That result notwithstanding, Davis and the team helped set LLWS ratings records for ESPN, the tournament's television broadcaster.

## NATIONAL CELEBRITY

In the wake of her historic LLWS performance, Davis became an overnight celebrity and the talk of the sports world. She received public plaudits from professional athletes, celebrities, and dignitaries, including basketball players Magic Johnson and Kevin Durant, baseball player Mike

Trout, football player Russell Wilson, rapper Lil Wayne, and First Lady Michelle Obama, and she was bombarded with media requests. One of those media requests came from *Sports Illustrated*, which decided to put Davis on the cover of its August 25, 2014, issue. Davis became the first Little League player and youngest athlete in history to appear on the cover of the vaunted sports magazine.

Davis also made the rounds on the national talk-show circuit, appearing as a guest on *The Queen Latifah Show* and *The Tonight Show with Jimmy Fallon*. In September 2014 she donated her LLWS jersey to the National Baseball Hall of Fame in Cooperstown, New York. Then, in October of that year, she starred in a Chevrolet car commercial directed by Spike Lee and threw out the first pitch before game four of the Major League Baseball World Series. In November she marched in the Macy's Thanksgiving Day parade with her teammates and appeared as a presenter at the Soul Train Music Awards. In December she met President Barack Obama and the First Family at the national Christmas-tree lighting at the White House.

For her achievements Davis earned role-model status and received a number of honors, including being named the 2014 Associated Press Female Athlete of the Year. At thirteen she became the youngest-ever recipient of the award. Davis was also named *Sports Illustrated for Kids*' SportsKid of the Year for 2014 and was featured on *espnW*'s 2014 Impact 25 list. "No matter who you are, you should be able to do what you like to do and what you've always dreamed of doing," she told Melissa Isaacson for *espnW* (8 Aug. 2014).

As an eighth-grader during the 2014–15 season, Davis played for Springside's girls' high school varsity basketball team and the school's middle school varsity baseball team. She also played summer baseball with the Anderson Monarchs. Despite rising to stardom for her baseball prowess, Davis considers basketball her favorite sport. She has expressed a desire to play point guard for renowned coach Geno Auriemma at the University of Connecticut and, ultimately, to one day play in the Women's National Basketball Association (WNBA).

In June 2015 Davis was drafted by the Harlem Globetrotters, the world-famous traveling exhibition basketball team. She will not have to play for the team until after she graduates from college as a result of a "Future Discovery Clause."

## PERSONAL LIFE

An avowed "sneakerhead," Davis has launched a sneaker line called M4D3 that benefits underprivileged girls. In March 2015 she released the memoir *Mo'ne Davis: Remember My Name*, which chronicles her inspirational life story.

## SUGGESTED READING

Breen, Matt, and Melissa Dribben. "Taney's Mo'ne Davis Handles Celebrity in Stride." *Philadelphia Inquirer*. Philly.com, 16 Aug. 2014. Web. 15 June 2015.

Chen, Albert. "Mo'ne Davis, Taney Take Center Stage at Little League World Series." *Sports Illustrated*. Time, 20 Aug. 2014. Web. 15 June 2015.

Davis, Mo'ne. *Remember My Name: My Story—From First Pitch to Game Changer*. New York: Harper, 2015. Print.

Estwick, Gary. "Little League Star Mo'ne Davis: The Role Model, the Kid." *AL.com*. Alabama Media Group, 25 June 2015. Web. 27 June 2015.

Fioriglio, Tony. "Little League: Taney's Mo'ne Davis Showing She Can Play with the Boys." *Times Herald* [Norristown, PA]. Times Herald, 22 July 2014. Web. 15 June 2015.

Isaacson, Melissa. "Girls Power Little League Contenders." *espnW.com*. ESPN Internet Ventures, 8 Aug. 2014. Web. 15 June 2015.

Tapper, Christina M. "SportsKid of the Year 2014: Mo'ne Davis." *Sports Illustrated for Kids*. Time, 1 Dec. 2014. Web. 15 June 2015.

—Chris Cullen

# Nina Davuluri

**Born:** April 20, 1989
**Occupation:** Miss America 2014

When Nina Davuluri was crowned Miss America on September 15, 2013, she made history as the first Indian American woman ever to triumph in the iconic pageant, which was founded in 1921. Many considered it a particularly meaningful milestone given that contestants were at one time required to be "of good health and of the white race" according to pageantry guidelines. Even as late as the 1940s, contestants had been made to fill out a questionnaire detailing how far back they could trace their ancestry.

The first Asian contestant, who hailed from Hawaii, entered the Miss America pageant in

1948, and the first Asian winner, a woman of Filipino descent, was not crowned until 2000. The pageant did not include an African American contestant until 1970 and did not crown an African American winner until 1983. At the same time, those contestants were not subjected to the same level of virulent, racist backlash that greeted Davuluri due to the rise of the Internet and the ubiquity of social media sites such as Facebook and Twitter by 2013. "If you Googled 'Miss America' [the day after the pageant], the top story was not about Davuluri's glitzy crown but the racist tweets that followed her victory," Emily Greenhouse wrote for the *New Yorker* (20 Sept. 2013). "The American public once sneered at television sets in private when they didn't like what they saw. Today, they have the Internet. On Sunday night, many disapproved of the new Miss America, and they took to Twitter."

For her part, Davuluri seemed to take such hostile responses to her victory in stride. At a press conference following the initial outpouring of vitriol, she told journalists, "I have to rise above that. I always viewed myself as first and foremost American."

## EARLY YEARS AND EDUCATION

Nina Davuluri was born on April 20, 1989, in Syracuse, New York. Her father, Koteshwara Choudhary, is a physician specializing in obstetrics and gynecology, and her mother, Sheila Ranjani, is an expert in information technology. Originally from the city of Vijayawada, in the Indian state of Andhra Pradesh, the couple came to the United States in the early 1980s after an arranged marriage. Davuluri has one older sister, Meena.

The family moved to Oklahoma when Davuluri was a child and later, when she was ten, they settled in St. Joseph, Michigan. She attended St. Joseph High School, where she participated in an impressive roster of extracurricular activities, including playing the clarinet in the high school marching band, cheerleading, joining the varsity tennis team, and competing as a member of the Science Olympiad team. She also studied ballet, tap, and jazz dance. When she visited family in India for a month each summer, she took daily lessons in traditional Indian dance. Davuluri has also confessed to being something of a "nerd" while growing up. An avid fan of the *Lord of the Rings*, the Harry Potter series, and the Star Wars films, she greatly enjoyed science fiction and fantasy.

Kevin Dooley/CC BY 2.0

One of Davuluri's high school English teachers, Bean Klusendorf, recalled to Patricia Montemurri for the *Detroit Free Press* (28 Oct. 2013), "She had a wider world perspective. She brought a maturity that we don't always see with high school students. I know her Indian heritage was important to her, and she lived in this crossroads of culture—respecting and honoring her Indian tradition and living in a very American culture." However, that balancing act was not always easy. Davuluri, one of just a handful of Indian American students at St. Joseph, has told journalists that she was often asked if she worshipped cows or if she was going to submit to an arranged marriage like her parents. Whenever she was tempted to get frustrated, she reminded herself that most people were not malicious, merely curious.

## ENTERING THE PAGEANT CIRCUIT

Inspired by her sister, who had entered the pageant circuit in an attempt to win scholarship money and had been crowned Miss St. Joseph, Davuluri entered the Miss America's Outstanding Teen competition when she was sixteen. In 2006 she was named Michigan's Outstanding Teen, and the following year she was first runner-up in the national event. In total, she garnered $25,000 in scholarship money.

Despite being a good student, when Davuluri graduated from high school in 2007, she was waitlisted at the University of Michigan, her first choice, and instead attended Michigan State University for a semester. Reapplying, she was accepted to the University of Michigan in time for the spring semester, and during her time there, she was inducted into the National Honor Society and won the Michigan Merit Award. As in high school, she also participated in numerous extracurricular activities, including pledging a sorority (Sigma Kappa) and joining Maya, the university's Indian dance troupe. In 2011, Davuluri earned her bachelor's degree with a concentration in brain, behavior, and cognitive science.

By the time Davuluri had graduated from the University of Michigan, her family had moved to Fayetteville, a village near Syracuse, New York. Intent upon earning money for graduate school, she decided to reenter the Miss America pageant system, this time as a resident of New York State. She took home the title of 2012 Miss Greater Rochester and she was the second runner-up in that year's Miss New York event.

## MISS AMERICA 2014

Faring better the following year, Davuluri won the title of 2013 Miss Syracuse and went on to triumph in the state-level pageant. Despite the state's diversity, she was the first Indian American woman ever to hold the title of Miss New York. However, a minor controversy initially overshadowed her crowning. At a celebration in her hotel room, Davuluri was reportedly heard calling Mallory Hagan, the reigning Miss America at the time and a former rival, fat. The remark was considered particularly offensive because Davuluri herself had struggled with weight gain and bulimia while in college. She denied making the comment but apologized to Hagan for any perceived offense, and the matter blew over before the national pageant.

Davuluri had never imagined making it to the stage in Atlantic City, where the Miss America pageant has famously been held since its inception (barring a brief period when it was moved to Las Vegas). "I grew up watching Miss America for years and years, and as the daughter of immigrants, I always thought to myself that I could never be that—because I didn't look a certain way; I didn't fit the model of what was up there on that screen," she told Jeff Yang for the *Wall Street Journal* (24 Sept. 2013). "And it shouldn't be about race, it shouldn't—but it is."

Despite such misgivings—and despite the worried advice of her family—she elected to perform a lively dance number that combined Bollywood moves with traditional elements dur-

ing the talent segment of the show. She chose the song "Dhoom Taana" from the 2007 Bollywood film *Om Shanti Om* and enlisted Los Angeles–based choreographer Nakul Dev Mahajan to help with the routine.

Her performance was widely praised—as was her answer during the interview segment of the competition. When asked how she felt about Asian women modifying their features with plastic surgery in order to fit Western standards of beauty, she confessed that she disagreed strongly with the practice and said, as quoted by Vi-An Nguyen for *Parade* magazine (16 Sept. 2013), "I've always viewed Miss America as the girl next door, and the girl next door is evolving as diversity in America evolves. She's not who she was ten years ago, and she's not going to be the same person come ten years down the road."

Proof of that assertion could be found right on the pageant stage; three of the five finalists for the 2014 crown were Asian, and Crystal Lee, Miss California 2013 and a former Miss Chinatown USA, ended the competition as first runner-up.

## AFTER LEAVING THE STAGE

The chorus of racist social media posts started even before the credits rolled on the televised broadcast, with many posters evincing disgust that Theresa Vail, Miss Kansas 2013 and a blond Army National Guard member with visible tattoos and a professed love of hunting, had not taken the crown. Others—most notably fellow Indians—griped that Davuluri would never have won a pageant in India, where skin-lightening products are a major business, because her complexion is too dark.

Davuluri responded gracefully, telling journalists at her press conference that the notes of support and congratulations she was receiving far outnumbered the negative messages. She soon mounted her own social media campaign, "Circles of Unity," aimed at promoting multiculturalism and reasoned dialogue. Maura Judkis wrote for the *Washington Post* (22 Sept. 2013) that regardless of public opinion, the crowning marked another turning point in American society: "People who couldn't care less about Miss America—who maybe didn't even know that the ninety-two-year-old pageant was still televised—may have found themselves tweeting to defend Davuluri's honor." Judkis concluded, "People may still question the relevance of beauty pageants with every rhinestone crown that makes its way to a new set of shiny tresses, but the conversation is beginning to change."

Davuluri spent much of 2014 traveling almost two hundred thousand miles to college campuses, civic events, and other places as well as appearing on several radio and television talk and news programs throughout the country to promote her Miss America platform, which was dubbed "Celebrating Diversity through Cultural Competency." "I want to use this opportunity to encourage positive dialogue among all Americans about the ways in which we are all unique and how that makes us stronger as a country," she explained in a press release from the Miss America Organization (19 Sept. 2013) announcing her agenda. She was also a vocal advocate for science, technology, engineering, and math (STEM) education, stressing its importance to young audiences and offering special encouragement to women, who are underrepresented in STEM–related careers. Additionally, she served as an ambassador for Children's Miracle Network Hospitals.

On September 14, 2014, Davuluri passed her crown to the winner of the 2015 Miss America title, Kira Kazantsev, a first-generation American whose parents had left Russia in the 1990s seeking a better life.

## PERSONAL LIFE

Although Davuluri had initially expressed her intention to attend medical school like her older sister, by the time her reign was over, she had changed her mind and decided upon earning a master's of business administration.

Like many Indian American parents, she explained, hers had unduly pushed her toward medicine. She says, however, that they have become more accepting of her sometimes nontraditional choices. They serve as a "living example" of learning to accept diversity, she told Alicia W. Stewart for CNN (30 Oct. 2013). "One of the hardest things that I experienced was really living the platform in my own home. And I say that because . . . I come from a very Indian household and the reality of the situation is that you simply cannot raise your children in America and expect them to be 100 percent Indian. That's not possible. And it shouldn't have to be, because we're so influenced by our peers and our community and people around us."

## SUGGESTED READING

Davuluri, Nina. "Here She Is, the Miss America You Don't Know." Interview by Alicia W. Stewart. *CNN*. Cable News Network, 30 Oct. 2013. Web. 12 Aug. 2015.

Greenhouse, Emily. "Combatting Twitter Hate with Twitter Hate." *New Yorker*. Condé Nast, 20 Sept. 2013. Web. 12 Aug. 2015.

Hunt, Geoffrey, and Rajendrani Mukhopadhyay. "More than Pretty." *ASBMB Today*. Amer. Soc. for Biochemistry and Molecular Biology, Nov. 2014. Web. 12 Aug. 2015.

Judkis, Maura. "Miss America Fights Post-Pageant Racism with a Beauty Queen's Poise." *Washington Post*. Washington Post, 22 Sept. 2013. Web. 12 Aug. 2015.

Pomarico, Nicole. "Miss America 2014 Nina Davuluri Broke Serious Barriers in 2013." *Bustle*. Bustle.com, 14 Sept. 2014. Web. 12 Aug. 2015.

Yang, Jeff. "Miss America Nina Davuluri Reveals Her Secret Life as a Nerd." *Wall Street Journal*. Dow Jones, 24 Sept. 2013. Web. 12 Aug. 2015.

—Mari Rich

# Lana Del Rey

**Born:** June 21, 1985
**Occupation:** Singer and songwriter

Writing for the influential music magazine *Pitchfork* (30 Aug. 2011), Ryan Dombal described Lana Del Rey as "old-school Hollywood glamor meets splice-friendly YouTube culture with a fair share of coquettish attitude and smoke-parlor Stevie Nicks vocals thrown in." Del Rey frequently inspires journalists to heights of pop culture–tinged metaphor. In a piece for *Nylon* (28 Nov. 2013), Melissa Giannini called her "a mishmash of Priscilla [Presley] and Ann-Margret, Jackie [Kennedy] and Marilyn [Monroe], Valencia-filtered to hazy perfection."

For a young artist whose oeuvre is still relatively small, Del Rey has proven to be an exceptionally polarizing figure in the music world. Most of the disagreement centers on her persona—whether or not it is the calculated product of a savvy team of stylists and industry insiders, and, if so, whether that detracts from the appeal of such darkly beguiling singles as "Summertime Sadness" and "Video Games." "Without straying too far off the pop grid, she's the perfect antidote to Rihanna-Gaga overload—dare we say, a skinnier Adele, a more stable Amy Winehouse?" Jacob Brown wrote for the *New York Times Style Magazine* (9 Feb. 2012). "If you were going to manufacture a star for this moment, you'd manufacture her. Some people believe that's precisely what happened."

## EARLY YEARS AND EDUCATION

Lana Del Rey was born Elizabeth Woolridge Grant on June 21, 1985, in New York, to Rob and Patricia Grant. Along with a younger brother, Charlie, she has a younger sister, Caroline, a photographer who has taken many of the stylized pictures that have characterized Del Rey's public persona. Although Del Rey has denied that her family is wealthy, her father is an entrepreneur who has enjoyed a large measure of success in his various endeavors. At one time owning a boat-building company, during the widely viewed 1977 America's Cup, he came up with the idea of using his fleet's sails as moving billboards, much to the chagrin of the tradition-bound race organizers. He had a long tenure as a star copywriter at a large advertising agency and he later founded a company that manufactured and distributed Adirondack chairs and other rustic furniture.

Because her father loved the Adirondack region, he ultimately moved his young family to Lake Placid, New York, where he became a sought-after real estate agent. Del Rey attended St. Agnes, a Catholic elementary school, and has told interviewers that she was drawn to the beauty of her local church and the mysticism of church teachings. In her early teens, she took a philosophy course and found it revelatory. "That was where I knew I'd find my people," she told Giannini. "I wanted to be around people who were asking, 'Why are we here?'" At the same time, she had also developed an early affinity for alcohol. When her parents discovered the problem, she was sent to an austere boarding school in Connecticut. By the time she graduated high school, she was sober.

Couch surfing between friends' apartments, Del Rey next studied philosophy at Fordham University in the Bronx. In her spare time she volunteered at homeless shelters and rehab programs, and she began singing in downtown Manhattan venues like Galapagos, The Living Room, and The Bitter End.

## BECOMING LANA DEL REY

While still in her senior year at Fordham, Del Rey was signed by 5 Points Records, a small indepen-

Georges Biard/Wikimedia Commons

dent label, as Lizzy Grant. Del Rey told Giannini that the label paid her $10,000, which she reportedly used to rent a trailer in a mobile home park in northern New Jersey, commuting to school by train. Her residence at the trailer park has become an integral part of her backstory, as have her reports of being estranged from her parents for years, being homeless for a time, and consorting with bikers.

In 2010, with the help of industry veteran David Kahne, known for his work with the Strokes and Regina Spektor, she hit upon the stage name Lana Del Ray and released an eponymous album titled *Lana Del Ray a.k.a. Lizzy Grant* on iTunes. (She later decided to change the spelling to "Rey.") That recording was soon pulled from distribution, and she publicly announced that she would prefer that people focus on her newer efforts, many of which she was posting on YouTube.

One of those, for the single "Video Games," went viral in 2011. Purposely grainy and amateurish-looking, the video mingled vintage shots of the famed Chateau Marmont hotel, found footage of California landscapes, and hazy shots of Del Rey. While Caryn Ganz, writing for *Rolling Stone* (20 June 2014), later decried Del Rey's use of "vintage references like they were bargain-bin lipsticks," Giannini wrote that the video served as "something the Internet generation craved near the tail end of the first decade of the new millennium." She added, "Plus, the mysterious, self-styled 'gangster Nancy Sinatra' cooing to the camera was, to say the least, compelling." In 2012, "Video Games" garnered a prestigious Ivor Novello Award for best contemporary song, cementing Del Rey's status as an artist to watch.

### BORN TO DIE

Del Rey was subsequently signed to Interscope Records and in early 2012, released the album *Born to Die*, which received decidedly mixed reviews. Its reception was not helped by the fact that Del Rey had been booked on *Saturday Night Live* shortly before its release (becoming one of only two artists to be given a performance slot on the long-running sketch comedy show prior to the release of a record with a major label), and her performance was almost universally excoriated and ridiculed. "The music is slow and full, a smoky mid-1960s cinema soundtrack, deployed pristinely, with crackling hip-hop drums setting the pace," Jon Caramanica wrote in a review of *Born to Die* for the *New York Times* (25 Jan. 2012). "On top of music like that, anything shy of full commitment would underwhelm, and over the course of this album, that's just what happens. Ms. Del Rey has an idea about her presentation, which counts for something—to some it counts for everything—but her singing still sounds like a road test."

Caramanica also weighed in on the issue of the singer's authenticity, writing, "That songwriter who used words like 'velvet' and 'exotic' in the tiki-lounge way of overemphasizing noir culture? Yep, it was a pose, cut from existing, densely patterned cloth. Just like all the other poses. And all the other cloths." Despite the failed *Saturday Night Live* performance and less-than-positive reviews, *Born to Die* made it to number two on the Billboard 200 album chart and was certified gold. One of the album's tracks, "Summertime Sadness," which was cowritten by hit-maker Rick Nowels and eventually remixed by Cedric Gervais, was downloaded more than one million times and enjoyed a rather lengthy stay in the top ten of the Billboard Hot 100 singles chart. After releasing the album *Paradise* in late 2012, she had her first taste of Hollywood fame when her song "Young and Beautiful," also cowritten by Nowels, was featured in the greatly hyped and anticipated 2013 film remake of *The Great Gatsby*, starring Leonardo DiCaprio.

### ULTRAVIOLENCE

These efforts were followed in 2014 by *Ultraviolence*, a full-length album whose title is a nod to the 1962 dystopian novel *A Clock-*work Orange*. Dan Auerbach of the Black Keys collaborated with Del Rey to produce this more stripped-down collection that veers further from the formulaic radio hit and the hip-hop influences of her previous work and includes tracks such as "West Coast" and "Money, Power, Glory" (a kind of sarcastic retort to previous criticism). In describing her new record, Del Rey told Jon Pareles for the *New York Times* (12 June 2014), "Each tune fully represents the ebbs and flows, the periods of normality mixed with this uncontrolled chaos that comes in through circumstances in my life."

Critics were somewhat more generous in their reviews of this project than they had been upon the release of *Born to Die*. Writing for *Pitchfork* (16 June 2014), Mark Richardson explained that unlike *Born to Die*, "*Ultraviolence* finds one feeling—a seedy, desperate, hyper-romanticized sense of isolation and loss—and blows it up to drive-in screen proportions." He continued, "*Ultraviolence* sounds tragic and beautiful—darkly-shaded ballads are what she was created to make, and this album is nothing but, a Concept Album from a Concept Human." With more than 180,000 copies sold in its first week of release, the album landed at number one on the Billboard 200 album chart. That same year, her haunting rendition of the classic Disney tune "Once upon a Dream" was used to great effect in the Angelina Jolie film *Maleficent* (2014).

Del Rey's songs have earned her a variety of prizes, including a BRIT Award for international breakthrough act in 2012, an MTV Europe Music Award for best alternative act in 2012, and a BRIT Award for international female solo artist in 2013.

### PERSONAL LIFE

Del Rey—already under steady fire for her perceived cultural appropriation and general reputation as a poseur—caused something of a media uproar when she told Tim Jonze for the *Guardian* (12 June 2014) that she considered the late musicians Amy Winehouse and Kurt Cobain to be personal heroes. When Jonze asked if she considered those artists' premature, drug-related deaths to be glamorous, she replied affirmatively and said, "I wish I was dead already." Cobain's daughter, Frances, responded by addressing Del Rey through social media, tweeting, "The death of young musicians isn't something to romanticize." Del Rey later blamed Jonze for asking leading questions and misinterpreting her words. As for her departure from her beginnings as

Lizzy Grant, Del Rey addressed questions regarding her identity when she told Scott Simon in an interview for National Public Radio (NPR) (21 June 2014), "Lana Del Rey is exactly who she's supposed to be: Free enough to be her own person, and that's exactly who I am. I'm not like a persona. I'm not a caricature of myself."

Named *GQ*'s 2012 Woman of the Year, Del Rey is a favorite of fashion editors and is frequently featured in glossy photo shoots. She appeared on the cover of the British edition of *Vogue* in March 2012, had her first *Rolling Stone* cover feature in 2014, and has modeled for such brands as H & M and Jaguar.

She was once engaged to marry Barrie-James O'Neill, the frontman of the alt-folk band Kassidy, but the pair split in 2014.

**SUGGESTED READING**

Brown, Jacob. "A Star Is Born (and Scorned)." *New York Times Style Magazine*. New York Times, 9 Feb. 2012. Web. 4 Nov. 2014.

Caraminca, Jon. "Dissected Long Before Her Debut." Rev. of *Born to Die*, by Lana Del Rey. *New York Times*. New York Times, 25 Jan. 2012. Web. 4 Nov. 2014.

Del Rey, Lana. "Lana Del Rey: 'I Don't Have Other People In Mind.'" Interview by Scott Simon. Natl. Public Radio. 21 June 2014. *NPR*. Web. 4 Nov. 2014.

Del Rey, Lana. "Rising: Lana Del Rey." Interview by Ryan Dombal. *Pitchfork*. Pitchfork Media, 30 Aug. 2011. Web. 6 Oct. 2014.

Giannini, Melissa. "National Anthem." *Nylon*. Nylon, 28 Nov. 2013. Web. 4 Nov. 2014.

Jonze, Tim. "Lana Del Rey: 'I Wish I Was Dead Already.'" *Guardian*. Guardian News and Media, 12 June 2014. Web. 4 Nov. 2014.

**SELECTED WORKS**

*Born to Die*, 2012; *Paradise*, 2012; *Ultraviolence*, 2014

—Mari Rich

# Mahendra Singh Dhoni

**Born:** July 7, 1981
**Occupation:** Cricketer

Mahendra Singh "M. S." Dhoni is one of India's most popular and accomplished cricketers. Widely regarded as "India's best captain ever," as the best-selling Indian novelist Chetan Bha-

gat wrote for *Time* (21 Apr. 2011), Dhoni has achieved unprecedented success in every format of the game. Cricket, the second most popular sport in the world, is divided into three major formats: Test, One Day International (ODI), and Twenty20 (T20). Test cricket is the longest and most prestigious form of the game, with matches played between two teams over five days, while ODI and T20 cricket are shorter forms, with matches taking place over a single day. Major international tournaments in each format are sanctioned by the International Cricketing Council (ICC), cricket's governing body.

As captain, Dhoni, a right-handed batsman and wicketkeeper, has helped India win the top prize in all three formats. In 2007 he led India to victory at the inaugural ICC World T20, which was held in South Africa. Dhoni also guided India to the top spot in the ICC test rankings in 2009. Then, in 2011 he led his country to triumph at the ICC Cricket World Cup, which was played in India, Sri Lanka, and Bangladesh; the tournament is the international championship of ODI cricket. In late 2014 he retired from test cricket after playing in a record ninety test matches for India.

In addition to his career with the Indian national team, Dhoni has enjoyed a successful club career with the Chennai Super Kings of the Indian Premier League (IPL), an annual Indian T20 tournament that was founded in 2008. He has

Michael Bradley/AFP/Getty Images

served as the Kings' captain since their inception and led them to IPL titles in both 2010 and 2011.

## EARLY LIFE AND EDUCATION

The youngest of three children, Mahendra Singh Dhoni was born on July 7, 1981, in Ranchi, Bihar, India, the eventual capital of the eastern state of Jharkhand. His parents, Pan Singh and Devaki Devi, hail from the northern Indian state of Uttarakhand. He has a brother, Narendra, who is a politician, and a sister, Jayanti, who is an English teacher.

Along with his siblings, Dhoni grew up in a one-bedroom apartment in Ranchi and was raised in a hard-working, middle-class family. His father was a pump operator at MECON Limited, a public-sector engineering consultancy firm; his mother was a homemaker. The family's apartment was adjacent to Ranchi's MECON Stadium, where Dhoni was first introduced to sports. Because Ranchi was not known for its cricketing prowess, Dhoni initially played soccer and badminton.

Dhoni attended Jawahar Vidya Mandir, a public school in Ranchi's Shyamali neighborhood, where he was a standout goalkeeper on the soccer team. He started playing cricket at the age of twelve after his soccer coach, Keshab Ranjan Banerjee, suggested he try his hand at wicket-keeping, the sport's equivalent of goaltending. Impressed with Dhoni's natural agility and flexibility, Banerjee felt cricket would offer him greater exposure and the best chance for a long-term athletic career. Dhoni heeded Banerjee's advice and took up the sport in earnest.

According to Dhoni, he practiced wicketkeeping for a year before playing a single match. He also worked on his batting by playing tennis ball cricket on hard grounds. At the outset, Banerjee revealed to Andy Wilson for the *Guardian* (17 Jan. 2013), Dhoni was "not that talented, he had an odd style of catching the ball," though he was "always a confident boy." Still, he was already displaying his unconventional batting style, which is characterized by a powerful uppercut swing known as "the helicopter."

In 1995, at age fourteen, Dhoni became the regular wicketkeeper for the Commando Cricket Club, which was coached by Chanchal Bhattacharya, a local sports journalist. There, he quickly developed into a force behind the stumps. As Bhattacharya recalled to M. S. Unnikrishnan for the Chandigarh, India, *Tribune* (29 Apr. 2006), Dhoni "kept wickets like a seasoned campaigner in the very first match."

Dhoni remained with Commando for three years, during which he was selected to play in the 1997–98 Vinoo Mankad Trophy Under-16 Championship. He graduated from Jawahar Vidya Mandir in 1999.

## RISE TO THE INDIAN NATIONAL TEAM

Following his stint with Commando, Dhoni played for a series of local clubs as he moved through India's wide-ranging cricket system. One of those included a team run by the company Central Coalfields Limited, a subsidiary of Coal India Limited. At eighteen Dhoni made his first-class cricket debut for Bihar in the Ranji Trophy competition of 1999–2000. (Jharkhand was part of Bihar until 2000, when it was made its own separate state.)

In 2001 Dhoni was selected to play for the East Zone in the Duleep Trophy, a domestic first-class cricket competition between teams representing the country's geographical zones. That year he moved to Kharagpur, a town in West Bengal, where he started working as a ticket collector for South Eastern Railway. He subsequently joined the railway's divisional cricket squad. Over the next three years, Dhoni played for the railway team and represented Bihar in Ranji Trophy competitions. He also continued to play for the East Zone in Duleep and Deodhar Trophy cricket tournaments.

Dhoni's ferocious batting, acrobatic wicketkeeping, and strong performances in ODI tournaments eventually caught the attention of national scouts, and in 2004 he earned a spot on the India A cricket team. Dhoni made his debut with the team in a triangular limited-over tournament in Nairobi, Kenya, in which he impressed observers by scoring two centuries. (In cricket, a century is when a player scores one hundred or more runs in one inning alone.)

## ON THE WORLD STAGE

Dhoni played in his first ODI match for India in December 2004, when he participated in the team's tour of Bangladesh. In April of the following year, he announced his arrival on the world cricket stage when, in only his fifth one-day match, he scored 148 against Pakistan in Vishakapatnam, India. The score came off only 123 deliveries, setting a record for an Indian wicketkeeper. Dhoni eclipsed that record just six months later when he scored an astonishing 183 off 143 balls during an ODI series against Sri Lanka. "I knew I had to perform to be there at the international level," he told S. Dinakar for *Sportstar* (3–9 Dec. 2005), India's leading sports weekly.

Dhoni made his test-match debut in December 2005, when he replaced Dinesh Karthik as India's test wicketkeeper. The following month he notched up his maiden century in his second test match against Pakistan, in which he scored another 148. By the spring of 2006, Dhoni, who during this time was sporting long, flowing hair, had "already achieved iconic status," according to Gopal Sharma for the Chandigarh *Tribune*. "The inimitable but flamboyant style of his batting, willingness to adapt, down-to-earth attitude and the all-pervasive grin on an unconventional visage make him a true superstar," Sharma wrote.

In 2007 Dhoni was appointed India's captain for the inaugural ICC World T20 in South Africa. At the tournament, he led a young and inexperienced team to an unlikely victory over Pakistan in the final. After demonstrating his leadership abilities, Dhoni was named captain of both the Indian ODI and test teams. He made his debut as India's full-time test captain during a test series against England in December 2008, when bowler-captain Anil Kumble retired.

## A REMARKABLE RECORD

Over the next six years, Dhoni became the most successful captain in Indian history. As captain he led India to twenty-seven wins in sixty test matches, both of which are records. He played in ninety tests overall, the most ever for an Indian wicketkeeper, and scored 4,876 runs at an average of 38 per dismissal. Under Dhoni, India reached the top spot in the ICC test rankings for the first time in December 2009. The team would hold that position for eighteen months until their tour of England in 2011.

Dhoni has also "left an indelible mark on India's one-day game, setting a benchmark that all future and past captains will be judged by," a reporter noted for *India Today* (6 Apr. 2015). As India's ODI captain, he has amassed over five thousand runs, becoming only the third Indian captain to do so. The biggest moment of his ODI captaincy came in 2011, when he led India to the ICC Cricket World Cup after defeating Sri Lanka in the final. It marked the first time in twenty-eight years that India had won the coveted championship and the first time that a country won on its home soil. In one-day cricket, Dhoni has established a reputation as one of the best batsmen and finishers in history.

Throughout his tenure as India's captain, Dhoni was known for his hands-off style of leadership. He was also known for his unflappable, stoic demeanor both on and off the field, earning him the nickname Captain Cool. "One of the things I liked about MS was, what you saw was what you got," Rahul Dravid, a legendary batsman and former teammate, told *ESPN Cricinfo* (30 Dec. 2014). "Very uncomplicated, always led by example . . . he never asked you to do anything that he himself didn't do."

In December 2014 Dhoni announced his retirement from test cricket during India's tour of Australia, citing exhaustion from playing all three forms of cricket. He has remained active in ODI cricket, captaining India at the 2015 ICC Cricket World Cup, which was held in Australia and New Zealand.

## CHENNAI SUPER KINGS AND BUSINESS INVESTMENTS

Since 2008 Dhoni has served as captain of the IPL team Chennai Super Kings. Under his leadership, the Super Kings have enjoyed more success than any other IPL team. They won back-to-back IPL titles in 2010 and 2011, and finished as IPL runners-up in 2008, 2012, and 2013. They also captured Champions League T20 titles in 2010 and 2014.

Dhoni serves as vice president of India Cements Ltd., a cement manufacturing company that owns the Super Kings. He has offered to step down from that post as well as from his Super Kings' captaincy, however, due to betting and corruption allegations that have surrounded the team.

Dhoni's other business interests include serving as co-owner of Chennaiyin FC, a soccer franchise in the Indian Super League. An avid bike enthusiast, he also co-owns a Supersport World Championship team, Mahi Racing Team India, which he founded in 2012.

Thanks to numerous endorsements, Dhoni has become the highest-earning Indian sports player and one of the highest-paid athletes in the world. In 2014 he ranked twenty-second on *Forbes* magazine's annual list of the world's hundred highest-paid athletes, with an estimated $30 million in earnings.

## PERSONAL LIFE

Dhoni married Sakshi Singh Rawat in July 2010. The couple has a daughter, Ziva, who was born in February 2015. In 2011 Dhoni was named one of the world's most influential people by *Time* magazine.

## SUGGESTED READING

Bhagat, Chetan. "Mahendra Singh Dhoni: Captain Fantastic." *Time*. Time, 21 Apr. 2011. Web. 23 Apr. 2015.

"'Dhoni Led by Example, Not Rhetoric' –Dravid." *ESPN Cricinfo*. ESPN Sports Media, 30 Dec. 2014. Web. 23 Apr. 2015.

Dhoni, Mahendra Singh. Interview by S. Dinakar. *Sportstar*. Sportstar, 3–9 Dec. 2005. Web. 23 Apr. 2015.

"How Dhoni (Almost) Got His Groove Back." *India Today* 6 Apr. 2015: 1. Print.

Sharma, Gopal. "The Dhoni Phenomenon." *Tribune* [Chandigarh]. Tribune Trust, 29 Apr. 2006. Web. 23 Apr. 2015.

Unnikrishnan, M. S. "Ranchi Rocker." *Tribune* [Chandigarh]. Tribune Trust, 29 Apr. 2006. Web. 26 May 2015.

Wilson, Andy. "MS Dhoni, the Smalltown Boy Whose India Team Transformed World Cricket." *Guardian*. Guardian News and Media, 17 Jan. 2013. Web. 23 Apr. 2015.

—Chris Cullen

# Tammy Duckworth

**Born:** March 12, 1968
**Occupation:** Politician

Tammy Duckworth was elected to the US House of Representatives in 2012, making her the first female Thai American member of Congress when she assumed office in January 2013. Along with Representative Tulsi Gabbard of Hawaii, she became one of the first female combat veterans to be elected to Congress. As she told Joshua Green about her experience serving in the Iraq War for *Esquire* (1 Oct. 2006), "I never thought we should have invaded. But I served. I went because it was my duty. And I was proud to go."

Her experience of being shot down in 2004 while serving there, which left her a double leg amputee, has given her perspective. In an interview with Andrew Goldman for the *New York Times* (15 Feb. 2013), Duckworth stated that she now considers her legs as tools, so she does not agonize over her loss any longer. In 2007, she received the Veterans Leadership

USC/Wikimedia

Award from the nonprofit Iraq and Afghanistan Veterans of America.

## EARLY LIFE AND EDUCATION

Ladda "Tammy" Duckworth was born in 1968 in Bangkok, Thailand. Her late father, Franklin G. Duckworth, was a Marine who served in World War II, the Korean War, and the Vietnam War and who traced his ancestry to fighters in the American Revolutionary War. Her mother, Lamai Sompornpairin Duckworth, is of Chinese Thai descent. Because her father worked for multinational corporations and the United Nations, Duckworth, her parents, and her brother Thomas, moved frequently. The family settled in Hawaii when Duckworth and her brother were teenagers.

After graduating in 1985 from McKinley High School in Honolulu, Duckworth attended the University of Hawaii before enrolling at George Washington University, where she earned a master's degree in international affairs in 1992. She met her future husband, Bryan Bowlsbey, through the Reserve Officers' Training Corps (ROTC) there. The two married in 1993.

In 1992, Duckworth moved to Illinois, where she entered a PhD program in political science at Northern Illinois University (NIU) and joined the Illinois Army National Guard. While there, she worked at the NIU School of Nursing. In 2002, she became the manager of Rotary International's Asia/Pacific department in the Club and District Administration Division.

## MILITARY SERVICE

Looking for opportunities to serve in combat and change the perception of women in the military, Duckworth trained as a helicopter pilot. She became the first female platoon leader of her unit and was teased by the other pilots, who called her "mommy platoon leader" for making them cocoa before winter training exercises.

In 2004, Duckworth was deployed to Iraq with the Illinois Army National Guard's 1st Battalion, 106th Aviation Regiment; she was among the first Army women to fly combat missions during Operation Iraqi Freedom. On November 12, 2004, a rocket-propelled grenade brought down the Black Hawk helicopter that Duckworth copiloted. She survived due to body armor and the efforts of her crewmates but lost both legs. In an article for *Stars and Stripes* (14 June 2005), she recalled to Leo Shane III how she saw a burst of flame and wondered why she could no longer control the pedals. "I found out later the pedals were gone, and so were my legs." She also lost partial use of her right arm, which was broken in three places, and nearly half the blood in her body.

The medics at the emergency room in Baghdad, who removed her right leg a few inches from the hip and the left leg below the knee, were surprised she was still alive. According to Rick Newman in his 2012 book *Rebounders*, one of her medics recalled how she was "propped up on one arm, saying, 'I want the status of my crew. How are my men?'" Duckworth was flown to a hospital in Landstuhl, Germany, before transferring to Walter Reed Army Medical Center in Washington, DC.

## RECOVERY AND FIRST RUN FOR CONGRESS

She spent a year at Walter Reed recovering and being fitted with prosthetic legs. During that time, Duckworth was encouraged by peer visitors, other people who had survived major injuries and been fitted with prosthetic limbs. She later became a peer visitor herself. Despite her injuries, her sense of self remained strong. "This didn't change who I am," she told Shane seven months after the explosion. "I'm an air-assault pilot. I'm not about to let some guy who got lucky with an RPG decide how to live my life." She also determined that even on a bad day, no one was shooting at her, which gave her a fearlessness she had not previously had.

She was awarded a Purple Heart, an Air Medal, and an Army Commendation Medal. She refused the option of taking medical retirement; both she and her husband remain in the Illinois Army National Guard, where she continues to drill as a lieutenant colonel.

While Duckworth was at Walter Reed Army Medical Center, still learning to navigate on her prosthetic legs, influential Illinois Democrats encouraged her to run for office. She ran for the US House of Representatives in 2006 for the Illinois Sixth District. Republican Henry Hyde, who had held the seat for sixteen terms, announced that he was retiring. Duckworth was an ideal candidate because of her military service; she could counter the usual charges leveled against Democrats as being weak in the area of national security. Her Republican opponent was Peter Roskam, a personal injury lawyer and state senator with a solid conservative record. She lost the race by two percentage points.

## SERVING VETERANS

In 2006, Duckworth became the director of the Illinois Department of Veterans Affairs. She succeeded in creating tax credits for businesses that hired veterans, and she worked on issues of veterans' health and housing. She also created the country's first 24–7 crisis hotline for veterans.

Barack Obama, whom Duckworth had met when he was a US senator, won the 2008 presidential election. He then appointed her as assistant secretary of public and intergovernmental affairs in the Department of Veterans Affairs (VA). In that role, as she told Adam Weinstein for *Mother Jones* (Sept. 2012), "I was all about admitting our failures. I was frustrated the VA had been in this culture of hiding its problems." Those problems included a nearly 25 percent rate of posttraumatic stress disorder among veterans and a 30 percent unemployment rate for veterans aged twenty to twenty-four. In addition, about one-fourth of returning vets also had traumatic brain injuries. One estimate by the Center for a New American Security holds that from 2005 to 2010 American service members and veterans committed suicide at a rate of approximately one every thirty-six hours.

Establishing the Office of Online Communications was one of Duckworth's initiatives at the VA. She also worked to assist underserved veterans, including women and American Indians. When the government was about to shut down in 2012 over the issue of raising the debt ceiling, Duckworth was at the VA. As she told Michelle Goldberg for *Newsweek* (14 May 2012), "I was sitting in my office at the VA at midnight. I'm in charge of trying to communicate to veterans that we're going to shut down the government and your access to your benefits may not happen on a timely basis. I'm getting ready to send out messages to the VA staff that, oh, by the way, you might not get to come into work tomorrow and you might not get paid." That experience deeply angered her, pushing her to run again for Congress.

## US HOUSE OF REPRESENTATIVES

In 2012 Duckworth began campaigning against Tea Party candidate Joe Walsh for the Illinois Eighth District. She won the election and joined the House of Representatives in January 2013, one of nine recent veterans to be elected to Congress. However, as she explained to Weinstein, "At the end of the day it's not about Democrats or Republicans. It's not about Obama or Romney. It's about the fact that on that day, those men carried me out when they didn't have to. They thought I was dead."

Duckworth was among eighty-eight members of Congress who in February 2013 opposed a plan for the United States Postal Service to cease Saturday deliveries. Their concern was that some Americans might not receive medicines ordered by mail in a timely manner.

In June 2014, Duckworth introduced a bill to end franking privileges for members of Congress, who do not pay for certain types of mailing in advance. From 1996 through 2008, the average annual amount that members of the House spent on postage for mass mailings to their constituents was $18.7 million. The cost does come out of the members' individual budgets after the mail has been sent, but Duckworth wanted Congress members to be held to the same standards as ordinary Americans and to pay up front.

Duckworth set a standard for personal responsibility in June 2014, returning unspent money back to the US Treasury. She had been allotted $1,232,818, known as the Members' Representational Allowance. Using those funds wisely, she was able to give back $113,918. In addition, she had the lowest salary payroll among the eighteen Illinois congressional delegates and said she only spent funds as needed. Furthermore, during the 2012 sequester, she gave the United States Treasury $10,000 of her salary.

## VETERANS HEALTH ADMINISTRATION SCANDAL

In spring 2014, when stories came to light of about forty veterans who had died due to delayed care appointments through the Veterans Health Administration facility in Phoenix, Arizona, Duckworth was not among those who called for Secretary of Veterans Affairs Eric Shinseki to resign. She did, however, want him held responsible. As she told Lynn Sweet for *Chicago Sun-Times* (11 May 2014), "I think that if this is truly happening, then he needs to fix it. So I would not support calling for him to resign. I think he needs to figure out what is happening and he should have the opportunity to fix it." She feared that Phoenix was symptomatic of difficulties throughout the system nationally.

In June 2014, Duckworth became one of the co-sponsors of the Clay Hunt Suicide Prevention for American Veterans Act. The act seeks to reform the way that the Department of Veteran Affairs handles cases of posttraumatic stress disorder and traumatic brain injury and to require annual third-party evaluations of all mental health care and suicide prevention programs at the Departments of Defense and Veteran Affairs.

The issue of substandard VA care continued to haunt Duckworth as she campaigned for a second term in the House of Representatives in 2014. Her Republican challenger, Larry Kaifesh, a colonel in the Marine Corps Reserve, noted that the issue had been going on while Duckworth was working for both the Illinois and the US Veterans Administration, though he did not directly accuse her of wrongdoing. Duckworth refuted the implication when speaking with Sally Ho for the *Chicago Tribune* (22 Sept. 2014), saying, "I was not in charge of the Veterans Health Administration, and wherever I saw problems, I certainly brought those forward."

## PERSONAL LIFE

Every November 12, Duckworth reunites with her crewmates to celebrate "alive day." She has staunchly advocated that women be allowed to serve in combat situations. As she told Goldman when he asked about women serving in combat, "If you can do it and if you're willing to lay your life down for this nation, then I don't care if you're gay, straight, black, white, yellow, male or female, good for you, thank you for serving. Go do the job." After being wounded in combat, she made it a priority to become certified to pilot small planes and earned a fixed-wing pilot's license in 2010.

Her hobbies include surfing, skydiving, and scuba diving. She is trilingual, being fluent in Indonesian and Thai as well as in English. Duckworth has resumed studies for her doctorate degree in political science at Northern Illinois University and began working toward a PhD in health and human services at Capella University. She volunteers at food banks and enjoys browsing flea markets. She and her husband live in Hoffman Estates, Illinois.

## SUGGESTED READING

Duckworth, Tammy. "Tammy Duckworth's Deadly Hot Cocoa." Interview by Andrew Goldman. *New York Times*. New York Times, 15 Feb. 2013. Web. 6 Oct. 2014.

Goldberg, Michelle. "Iraq Vet Tammy Duckworth Takes on the Tea Party." *Newsweek*. Newsweek, 14 May 2012. Web. 6 Oct. 2014.

Green, Joshua. "Illinois's Sixth Congressional District." *Esquire*. Hearst Communications, 1 Oct. 2006. Web. 6 Oct. 2014.

Ho, Sally. "Challenger Tries to Tie Duckworth to VA Health Care Scandal." *Chicago Tribune*. Chicago Tribune, 22 Sept. 2014. Web. 6 Oct. 2014.

Weinstein, Adam. "Nobody Puts Tammy Duckworth in a Corner." *Mother Jones*. Mother Jones and the Foundation for Natl. Progress, Sept./ Oct. 2012. Web. 6 Oct. 2014.

—Judy Johnson, MLS

# Josh Earnest

**Born:** ca. 1975
**Occupation:** White House press secretary

Josh Earnest is the thirtieth White House press secretary and the third person to hold that office during Barack Obama's presidency. Unlike many of his predecessors, he did not have a prior career as a journalist. Since graduating from Rice University in 1997, Earnest has worked solely in the political arena in various capacities. He has been a member of the White House staff since President Obama took office in January 2009, serving as a deputy press secretary until he was tapped by Obama to serve as White House press secretary in mid-2014. Earnest understands the importance of his high-profile position, which is to provide a clear understanding of the policies of the Obama administration to the White House press corps and the American people at large. He also knows that he must do this very effectively, particularly as the clock begins to wind down on Obama's final term in office. Earnest told Justin Sink for *The Hill* (9 July 2014), "It's my responsibility to communicate clearly to everybody what the president is doing. And if there is a missed impression, then it's my responsibility to clean that up."

Official White House Photo by Pete Souza/Wikimedia Commons

## EARLY LIFE AND EDUCATION

The oldest of his parents' three sons, Joshua Ryan Henry Earnest was born in Kansas City, Missouri, in 1975. His mother, Jeanne, is a psychologist with a private practice in Lee's Summit, and his father, Donald, is the athletic director at the Pembroke Hill School in Kansas City.

Earnest studied at the Barstow School in Kansas City on scholarship. At this private prep school, he enjoyed playing sports, particularly basketball and baseball. "He's definitely the quintessential coach's son," Adam Moore, a childhood friend and classmate, told David Goldstein for *McClatchy DC* (24 May 2012). "He has probably the best baseline jumper you've ever seen from the left-hand corner baseline. He could hit that three-pointer every time." But unlike many players in Washington politics, Earnest had little interest in the political world as a teenager; in interviews he claims all he remembers of politics growing up was tagging along with his parents when they voted in elections.

That all changed when he enrolled as an undergraduate at Rice University, where he became immersed in the political life as a political science and policy studies major. He also wrote for the campus newspaper, the *Rice Thresher*, and coordinated the campus-wide Beer Bike activity. It was through his advisor, Robert Stein, a political science professor, that he became introduced to some of the local political figures who helped him enter the political world. "You can't put a price tag on something like that," Earnest said of his former advisor in an interview with Tina Nazerian for the *Rice Thresher* (8 Apr. 2015). "Somebody who's willing to inspire you in that way, and who's willing to mentor you in that way." Earnest also gained a bit of understanding about international politics during his senior year, when a spring break trip to Israel and Gaza helped him to get some firsthand knowledge of the Israeli-Palestinian conflict.

## EARLY POLITICAL CAREER

Earnest dove immediately into politics upon his graduation from Rice in 1997, first working in the Houston mayoral race. He then worked on the campaign for Michael Bloomberg's first successful election as mayor of New York City in 2001. In that same year Earnest moved to Washington, DC, where, after having to sleep in a friend's spare bedroom for about six weeks, he would later work as a congressional aide to US congressman Marion Berry from 2002 to 2003 and as a spokesman for the Democratic National Committee from 2003 to 2006. "I drove [to DC] from Houston," Earnest said in his interview with Nazerian. "And I still remember driving around town and even driving in front of the White House at that point sort of thinking about how what a tremendous experience and honor it would be to work at the White House."

Before making it to the White House, Earnest would work on a governor's race in Florida and, beginning in 2007, on what would become a successful and historic presidential campaign: Obama's first run for the presidency. He began working on the Obama campaign as the Iowa communications director and continued in this role during the 2008 Iowa caucuses and through the 2008 Democratic National Convention, at which Obama accepted the Democratic nomination for president. Earnest remained with Obama following the start of his first term in office, which began in January 2009.

Once in the White House, Earnest served as a deputy press secretary under Robert Gibbs, Obama's first press secretary. He was subsequently promoted to principal deputy White House press secretary under Jay Carney, who served as Obama's press secretary from 2011 to 2014. As the principal deputy, Earnest was charged with monitoring all of the daily news programs—everything from morning news shows and newspapers to blogs, political talk shows, and newscasts—to see what had been said and by whom each day, as well as to pro-

vide insights on what questions the White House press corps might have for the White House press secretary on any given subject. Carney described Earnest to Goldstein as "indispensable. I depend on his judgment all the time." Earnest would occasionally serve as Carney's understudy if there were days when he was unable to attend a press briefing.

## TAKING ON A TOUGH JOB AT A TOUGH TIME

Although Obama handily won a second term as president in 2012, his Democratic party had difficulty in the 2014 midterm elections and lost control of both houses of Congress to the Republicans. At the end of May 2014 it was announced that Carney would be departing his post and would be replaced as White House press secretary by Earnest. Reports of the president's announcement of Earnest's succession to the role included positive reinforcement of his character and ability. Obama described him as "honest and full of integrity" and added that "his name describes his demeanor," as quoted by David Jackson for *USA Today* (30 May 2014).

When Earnest took on the job, he knew he had a great challenge ahead of him: conveying the president's message to the American people six years into his term in office, a point at which many members of the public—as well as the press and other politicians—are looking toward the next presidential election. Because the Twenty-Second Amendment to the US Constitution prohibits presidents of the United States from serving more than two four-year terms in office, commentators very frequently describe the president's last two years in office as a "lame duck" phase, in which the commander in chief has less political influence than previously exerted.

Shortly after taking up his new post as press secretary, Earnest explained the challenges to Sink: "We definitely are in a phase where we are looking for creative opportunities to help the president and his message break through." To that end, Earnest meets with the president's top advisors each morning, in the hopes of using their knowledge about the current issues in the news to help hone the message he presents to the press. He described the benefits of this strategy to Nazerian: "It's an opportunity for me to . . . ask the national security advisor or the president's top homeland security advisor about news that occurred overnight that's related to national security."

## UP TO THE CHALLENGE

So far in his tenure as the new press secretary, Earnest has had to field a characteristically wide variety of questions from the press on some rather volatile issues. These topics have included Obama's executive actions toward immigration, the government's investigation and response regarding the cyber attack against Sony Pictures, and Obama's comments in the wake of the attack on a kosher deli in Paris.

Earnest has been described in the media as being a more personable press secretary than his two immediate predecessors, Gibbs and Carney. He projects what some see as a friendlier presence behind the podium. During his press briefings he frequently makes mention of favorite sports teams and fields questions from many more members of the press than Carney had, who usually took the majority of his questions from front-row reporters. Seemingly uninterested in sparring with reporters or the president's political opponents to the same extent Gibbs and Carney had, he has attempted to keep the open-door policy he employed with journalists while serving as Carney's chief deputy.

Despite these efforts, Earnest has also had to endure criticisms of his job—not necessarily for the way he has done his work as press secretary but rather for the office of press secretary itself—from critics on both the left and right. Writing for *Slate* (30 May 2014), David Weigel said: "The tragedy of the White House beat, as hacks like me keep pointing out, is that the White House is forever innovating ways to make it useless. . . . What news there is gets generated by reporters acting on their own, not by anything pulled from the White House press secretary. . . . Josh Earnest's role is to dodge; to provide (hopefully viral) TV drama . . . ; to produce stories without producing news." In a similar piece for the *American Spectator* (8 Aug. 2014), Jay Homnick wrote: "I think it is time to eliminate the office of White House press secretary. There is no point in having a permanent Commender in Chief to tell us how great a job the President is doing, without regard to reality, actuality, veracity or accuracy."

## PERSONAL LIFE

Since August 2012 Earnest has been married to Natalie Wyeth, a deputy assistant secretary for public affairs at the US Treasury Department, the great-granddaughter of the famed illustrator N. C. Wyeth, and the granddaughter of the noted engineer Nathaniel C. Wyeth. They met at the Democratic National Convention in 2008, when Earnest was serving as deputy communications director for the Obama campaign and Wyeth was working as the convention's press secretary. They began dating around the time they had started working together on the president's inaugural committee; their first date was at a restaurant in Washington's Chinatown shortly after the inauguration in January 2009. "It was the first time we really interacted and socialized outside of the office," Wyeth said to Vincent M. Mallozzi for the *New York Times* (26 Aug. 2012). "I think there was instant chemistry. We got to know more about each other's lives before politics, and though our families come from different backgrounds, we have a lot of things in common and want the same things out of life."

Wyeth, a cum laude graduate of the University of Southern California, contends that she was sure Earnest was the man she would marry after their second date. "I knew it instinctively," Wyeth proclaimed to Mallozzi. "He's the kindest person I know, not just to me, but to everyone around him. And I consider myself incredibly blessed to be the person he chose to spend his life with." The couple's first child, a baby boy named Walker, was born in 2014.

## SUGGESTED READING

Goldstein, David. "Josh Earnest Went from Baseball in Kansas City to Hardball at White House." *McClatchy DC*. McClatchy DC, 24 May 2012. Web. 19 May 2015.

Homnick, Jay. "The Unimportance of Being Earnest." *American Spectator.* American Spectator, 8 Aug. 2014. Web. 21 May 2015.

Mallozzi, Vincent M. "Natalie Wyeth and Joshua Earnest." *New York Times.* New York Times, 26 Aug. 2012. Web. 19 Apr. 2015.

Nazerian, Tina. "Rice Alumnus Josh Earnest Recalls Path to White House." *Rice Thresher.* Rice Thresher, 8 Apr. 2015. Web. 19 May 2015.

Sink, Justin. "Looking for a Creative Breakthrough." *The Hill.* Capitol Hill, 9 July 2014. Web. 19 May 2015.

Weigel, David. "Jay Carney Is Retiring. Let's Not Replace Him." *Slate.com.* Slate Group, 30 May 2014. Web. 17 Apr. 2015.

—Christopher Mari

# Jennifer Eberhardt

**Born:** ca. 1965
**Occupation:** Social psychologist

Many people think that a person's racial bias has to be conscious and explicit, but social psychologist and MacArthur Fellowship "genius grant" recipient Jennifer Eberhardt knows better. For the past two decades she has been studying the way white people associate African Americans with crime. One disturbing study of hers found that a black man who looks more "stereotypically black"—for example, has darker skin and a wider nose—and has been convicted of murdering a white victim is more likely to get the death penalty than a black man with less "stereotypically black" features. Eberhardt has also found that after being shown a picture of a black man for a fraction of a second, not long enough to consciously process it, white study participants are quicker to identify a grainy, unclear image as a gun or a knife than if they had been shown a white face.

Eberhardt is an associate professor in the department of psychology at Stanford University, and she is also the codirector of Social Psychological Answers to Real-world Questions (SPARQ), which is a part of Stanford. In January 2015 Eberhardt testified in Washington, DC, at the First Public Hearing: Building Trust and Legitimacy as part of the President's Task Force on Twenty-First Century Policing. She discussed her research as well as her recommendations on the potential positive uses of body cameras by police.

## COLOR LINES

Jennifer Lynn Eberhardt was born in the mid-1960s in Cleveland, Ohio. Until about the age of twelve, Eberhardt lived in a predominantly black Cleveland neighborhood called Lee-Harvard. By the time she started junior high school, Eberhardt's family had moved to suburban Beachwood, a mostly white, relatively wealthier neighborhood. Eberhardt's father, who worked for the post office, used his savings to take his family to a neighborhood where his daughter would have better access to education and other resources. The junior high school Eberhardt attended was also mostly white, which was a change for her; she was accustomed to most of her classmates being fellow African Americans. This contributed to her fascination with faces

and race. Although her new and old neighborhoods were only a bike ride away, Eberhardt has often said in interviews, they were very different in many ways. She became fascinated by how neighborhoods that are so geographically close can be so unlike each other in racial makeup and availability of resources as well as in the actual facial characteristics of friends and neighbors.

Eberhardt told Claudia Dreifus for the *New York Times* (5 Jan. 2015) that although white people say that all black people look alike, all her white classmates looked alike to her, "which was a real handicap because I wanted to have friends but I couldn't tell who I'd met the day before," she added. "I wasn't practiced at sorting those faces." Eberhardt was referring to a real phenomenon of the biology and psychology of perception: growing up in a very racially homogenous environment, whether all black or all white or all Asian, can make it difficult for a person to consistently and significantly perceive differences in the facial features of a new group, though not all members of that group actually have the same features. Having grown up in a majority black neighborhood, Eberhardt was not initially able to accurately distinguish various features of the new, white faces she encountered. This experience had a profound effect on the eventual direction Eberhardt took in her career and research, specifically with regard to race, inequality, and the significance of facial characteristics in multiple aspects of everyday life. "The funny thing is that today, one of the things I study is face recognition," Eberhardt told Dreifus, "and maybe because that's a kind of a metaphor for race relations. Not being able to read another person's face—it symbolizes a psychological distance that makes it difficult to understand the experiences of another group." Eberhardt then added, "I think about this often in terms of tensions between the police and the community and the trouble they have in reading one another."

## EDUCATION

Eberhardt feels that another difference changing neighborhoods made was that it increased the likelihood that she would pursue a higher education. In an interview with Geoffrey Mohan for the *Los Angeles Times* (16 Sept. 2014), Eberhardt said, "I don't know if I would've gone to college if I hadn't moved." After graduating high school, she went on to attend the University of Cincinnati, in Ohio, where she initially majored in design, because she wanted to pursue a career in the visual arts. "I wanted a career that would provide a great deal of space for creativity," she said in an interview with the *Observer* journal (Jan. 2007). But Eberhardt did not get the creative and artistic satisfaction from design that she thought she would. "Every new project," she told the *Observer*, "from designing cardboard chairs to hold 200 pounds to building bird cages from wire, I greeted with a bit more misery than the last project." After she changed her major to psychology, it turned out that the very thing she was missing in studying design—having a fulfilled sense of creativity and imagination—she got from studying psychology. "I loved learning about research and later conducting studies," she added in her *Observer* interview, "each of which I greeted with even more enthusiasm than the last study."

Toward the second half of her time as an undergraduate, Eberhardt began contemplating her future and where she would go for graduate school, and during her senior year she encountered yet another period of doubt and uncertainty about her future career. As she told the *Observer*, she had heard of successful black doctors, engineers and lawyers, but she had not heard of black psychologists. She became concerned about whether that was a realistic or possible career path for her. Regardless, however, she still applied to grad schools—but only two: the University of Cincinnati, where she was a senior, and Harvard University, in Cambridge, Massa-

chusetts. Eberhardt graduated from the University of Cincinnati with a bachelor of arts degree in 1987, after which she went on to pursue her graduate education at Harvard University. She received her master's degree from Harvard in 1990 and her doctorate in 1993. There Eberhardt found out that not only could she come up with interesting ideas to investigate, she could investigate them empirically.

After getting her PhD, Eberhardt taught at Yale University as an assistant professor of both psychology and African American studies. In 1998 she moved to California and joined the Stanford University faculty, where she eventually became an associate professor in the department of psychology and codirector of Social Psychological Answers to Real-world Questions (SPARQ), a think tank that refers to itself as a "do tank" and, according to its website, "partners with practitioners in government, business, and nonprofits to craft solutions to our communities' most pressing problems."

## RACE MATTERS

Eberhardt has unveiled some fascinating and troubling findings about the association of African Americans and crime, which she believes to be one of the biggest and most persistent stereotypes in America. One study showed that people more readily associate black people with crime than white people. In this experiment, Eberhardt and her colleagues showed participants an image of an adult male with a neutral expression for a fraction of a second: some were shown the face of a white male; some were shown the face of a black male. (The experimenter did not tell the subjects what the true purpose of the test was.) After being shown a photograph for a fraction of a second, the subjects were then shown a distorted image that over time became less distorted—and turned out to be a clear image of a gun or a knife. What Eberhardt and her colleagues wanted to know was how quickly the test subjects could identify the image as a weapon—and whether it would vary depending on the photo the subjects were shown beforehand. Because the subjects saw the photo of a black or white male for only a fraction of a second, they could not consciously process what they saw. Nevertheless, it turned out that those participants who were exposed to black faces prior to seeing the stimulus were quicker to identify the blurry image as a gun or a knife than those participants who were exposed to white faces. The conclusion was not that the white participants consciously harbor racist views, but that at the very least, whether they know it or not, they more readily associate black faces with crime.

In her research on sentencing juveniles, Eberhardt found that even bringing to mind a black juvenile offender led participants to view all juveniles as deserving of more severe punishment. And in a study with registered voters, Eberhardt found that pointing out the disproportionately high incarceration rate of African Americans compared to white people made subjects more supportive of the policies that lead to this disparity, not less.

Perhaps one of Eberhardt's most disturbing findings concerns the relationship between the features of a black man convicted of murdering a white person and the resulting sentence: life in prison or death. In her experiment, rather than comparing black people to white people, she looked at differences in features among different black people. She presented to participants cropped photographs of convicted black men eligible for the death penalty. The question posed to the participants was how "stereotypically black" the faces looked, though the real question Eberhardt was pondering was whether there was a difference in the sentence (life in prison or the death penalty) handed down to those black men perceived to have a more "stereotypically black" appearance. "We told our subjects," Eberhardt told Dreifus, "to use any dimension they wanted with which to make that judgment: skin color, width of nose, thickness of lips. Interestingly, though we didn't give them clear direction of what we meant by 'stereotypically black,' there was a lot of agreement about what that was." Then Eberhardt took the pictures of those identified as looking "stereotypically black"—which according to her website turned out to mean "darker skinned, with a broader nose and thicker lips"—and looked at whether there was any correlation with what sentence they received. There was. Those black men who looked more "stereotypically black" were more than twice as likely to receive the death penalty as black men who looked less "stereotypically black." Furthermore, the findings of the conclusion were upheld even when controlling for nonracial factors, such as physical attractiveness and the severity of the crime.

## CHANGING THE SYSTEM

Putting her research to practical use, Eberhardt participated in a 2015 review of the Oakland Police Department headed by the attorney general of California. (Oakland is a city in the San Francisco Bay Area and has a substantial African American population.) Eberhardt helped to create a new training program for the department, the country's first police training program aimed at teaching officers to confront unconscious biases. Eberhardt maintains, and has said repeatedly in interview after interview, that even though many people may have unconscious racial biases, this does not mean that those biases cannot be examined and unlearned—or at least reduced.

## PERSONAL LIFE

Eberhardt is married to Ralph Richard Banks, a professor of law at Stanford University. The couple live in the San Francisco Bay Area with their three sons. Eberhardt and Banks knew one another in Cleveland when they were both in elementary school.

## SUGGESTED READING

Albrecht, Brian. "Cleveland Native Jennifer Eberhardt Awarded 'Genius Grant.'" *Cleveland.com*. Northeast Ohio Media, 19 Sept. 2014. Web. 8 Sept. 2015.

Eberhardt, Jennifer. "Perceptions of Race at a Glance: A MacArthur Grant Winner Tries to Unearth Biases to Aid Criminal Justice." Interview by Claudia Dreifus. *New York Times*. New York Times, 5 Jan. 2015. Web. 8 Sept. 2015.

Eberhardt, Jennifer. "Champions of Psychology: Jennifer Eberhardt." Interview. *Observer*. Association for Psychological Science, Jan. 2007. Web. 8 Sept. 2015.

Ho, Vivian. "California Cops Will Be Trained to Confront Unconscious Bias." *San Francisco Chronicle*. Hearst Communications, 17 Apr. 2015. Web. 8 Sept. 2015.

Mohan, Geoffrey. "Stanford's Jennifer Eberhardt Wins MacArthur 'Genius' Grant." *Los Angeles Times*. Los Angeles Times, 16 Sept. 2014. Web. 8 Sept. 2015.

—Dmitry Kiper

# Megan Ellison

**Born:** January 31, 1986
**Occupation:** Film producer

Margaret Elizabeth "Megan" Ellison is one of a handful of powerful women film producers. In 2014 she made Time magazine's list of the year's one hundred most influential people, in the category of pioneer. Her films have earned thirty-five Academy Award nominations; the three films that Ellison produced in 2013—*American Hustle*, *Her*, and *The Grandmaster*—earned an unheard of seventeen Oscar nominations. She is the first woman producer to gain two best picture nominations in the same year. Ellison funds directors who take chances, rather than taking the safe route to box office success. Of the importance of Ellison and others financing movies, Brad Pitt told Marc Graser for *Variety* (4 Mar. 2012), "There are few very strong independent financiers that are more interested in content than profit. These guys . . . like Megan Ellison are so important to what we do in the structure we are in right now." Without them, Pitt said, "harder-sell risk-taking films might not make it to the screen." Despite the risks she has taken, Ellison has produced films that have grossed more than $300 million.

**EARLY LIFE**

Born into wealth, Ellison is the daughter of Oracle's cofounder Lawrence J. Ellison, whom *Forbes* in 2014 named the third wealthiest person in the United States. Her mother, Barb Ellison, is from Oregon and was Ellison's third wife; they married after their son, David, was born. The marriage did not begin well. Ellison presented Barb with a prenuptial agreement on their wedding day. When their daughter was a year old, their divorce was finalized. However, Ellison remained in the lives of his children. A sailing fan, he missed only one major race, to attend his daughter's elementary school graduation.

Ellison graduated from Sacred Heart Preparatory School in Atherton, California, in 2004. She attended, but did not earn a degree from, University of Southern California's School of Cinematic Arts.

**BEGINNING IN FILM**

In 2006, after seeing the film *Loving Annabelle*, Ellison contacted Katherine Brooks, who had

Michael Kovac/Getty Images North America

written and directed the film, and told her that she wanted to invest in Brooks's next film. The picture was *Waking Madison*, about a young woman who attempts to cure her multiple personality disorder by spending thirty days in a room without any food. Although it was shot in 2007, it was not released until 2010, and went directly to DVD in 2011.

Ellison next invested in a Colin Firth feature, *Main Street*, in 2009; the film was shown at a few film festivals in 2010 and had a limited US release in 2011 before being released on DVD that year. The same year, Ellison produced the film *Passion Play*, which premiered in 2010 and had a limited theatrical run in 2011 but did not do well at the box office.

Ellison and her older brother, David, also a producer who attended USC, joined in 2010 to produce *True Grit*, starring Jeff Bridges and directed by the Coen brothers. David Ellison's own film company, Skydance Productions, tends to focus more on sure-thing, moneymaking films such as *Top Gun 2* and *Star Trek: Into Darkness*. Both Ellisons are interested in commercial as well as artistic success and so acquire hot properties. For rights to the *Terminator* films, the Ellison duo paid twenty million dollars; however, Megan Ellison later removed her film company from production. Her brother continued to support the franchise.

## ANNAPURNA PICTURES

On Ellison's twenty-fifth birthday in 2011, her father released more money to her following the commercially successful release of *True Grit* the year before. The rumored sum was two billion dollars. Ellison began working with Creative Artists Agency in an adjunct capacity to the firm's financial group. She then founded her own production company, Annapurna Pictures, named for the Hindu goddess of nourishment and for the Himalayan hiking trail she trekked in 2006.

Alyssa Rosenberg wrote for the *Washington Post* (20 Nov. 2014), "Annapurna Pictures movies tend to be less intrigued by the inner lives of women [than movies made by Pacific Standard, Reese Witherspoon's company], and they are more likely than Pacific Standard films to have male main characters. But the women in the movies Ellison makes never seem less than formidable and fascinating, even when they have to swipe the movie from a male co-star or lead."

Annapurna was first located in three large homes near Beverly Hills. Ellison used two as her production offices and lived in the third. In November 2013, she sold the properties for a combined total of nearly forty-seven million dollars, reaping a profit on all of the homes. A month later, she purchased a large single home and the adjoining lot, giving her nine acres of land, for thirty million dollars. Built in 1990, the home has nearly ten thousand square feet of living space and amenities such as a gym and a pool.

## INDEPENDENT MONEY

Hollywood studios are hampered by the need to produce high-grossing films that not only sell tickets but also generate sequels and merchandise. Independently wealthy producers, including Ellison, have given a new impetus to the industry. As Brad Weston, head of New Regency, told Pamela McClintock for *Hollywood Reporter* (16 May 2014), "They are infusing money into the system and giving us the ability to make more movies. It provides a full set of choices."

Cash infusions are not new; Howard Hughes was providing what some termed "dumb money" to studios early in the 1930s. Ellison's approach is different, however; she is actually interested in the craft of filmmaking and in telling a story for intelligent adults.

The kind of smart, independent films that Ellison funds have become rare. As one studio head told Graser, "At the end of the day, Hollywood is all about making money. That sounds cynical, but it's true. My hands are tied having to come up with big franchises. I can't make certain movies anymore, no matter how profitable they might become. I make movies that turn into toys."

## ZERO DARK THIRTY

*Zero Dark Thirty*, the 2012 film about the capture of Osama bin Laden, was shot in India and Jordan, with production costs running to forty-five million dollars. Ellison traveled to both countries during the shooting of the film, which was directed by Kathryn Bigelow with a script by Mark Boal. Ellison told Melena Ryzik for the *New York Times* (11 Dec. 2012) "We moved to India at the last minute because we got our permits approved there, and it looks so much more like Pakistan than shooting in Jordan." Even so, they had to use a diplomatic pouch to transport the night vision goggles for one scene; cameras were for a time stuck in customs.

Boal and Bigelow had been working on a script with an east-meets-west theme about Tora Bora and the failure to capture Osama bin Laden. When bin Laden was actually captured and killed, the two had to abandon this project, which had been well underway, and rapidly rework their plans into what would become *Zero Dark Thirty*. For Boal, the movie hinged on the woman who located bin Laden, played by Jessica Chastain.

Bigelow shot about two million feet of film footage, which is around twice as much as the average. Along with Bigelow and Chastain, Ellison wore a burqa to film a sequence in a mosque in Jordan.

The movie generated controversy because of its graphic depiction of torture during the first twenty minutes of the film. The criticism fueled a desire to see the film, leading to a successful box office run. The film received a best film award from the American Film Institute and generated enough profit to compensate for losses on previous films.

Amy Pascal, the cochair of Sony Pictures Entertainment, told Vanessa Grigoriadis for *Vanity Fair* (Mar. 2013), "Sometimes when you're a woman, people judge you a little more harshly. I think that if Megan was a guy people wouldn't be jumping on her as much."

Ellison expressed her belief in Boal by offering significant funding for a new venture he spearheads, Page 1, dedicated to making movies based on current events, as *Zero Dark Thirty* was.

## THE SONY HACK

Sony Pictures Classic was one of the Sony companies subject to a massive computer hacking episode in late 2014. Several executives' personal e-mails were hacked and made public, Amy Pascal's and Scott Rudin's among them. Those e-mails were not flattering to several people in the business, including Angelina Jolie. Ellison was also a target; Rudin referred to her as a "bipolar twenty-eight-year-old lunatic."

Ellison took the barb with grace. She stated on Twitter, where she has some 76,000 followers, that she considered herself more of an eccentric.

Mark Ruffalo, an actor who starred in the Ellison-backed 2014 film *Foxcatcher*, was nominated for a Golden Globe and an Academy Award for his role. He defended Ellison in an interview with Amy Kaufman for the *Los Angeles Times* (11 Dec. 2014), saying, "I would make 100 movies with her. I love her and she's risky and her risks pay off. There's a different kind of film being made in America because of her and they're not really inside the system. A lot of disruption is coming to light."

## THE NEXT STAGE

In January 2015, Annapurna Pictures joined with the artist Chris Milk to add a new virtual reality division, VRSE.farm. The overarching goal is to give writers a new way to tell stories and to offer filmmakers the expertise needed for computer-generated images (CGI).

The first completed work is Chris Milk's *Evolution of Verse*, which premiered at the Sundance Film Festival's New Frontier Exhibitions on January 24, 2014. In addition to being CGI-rendered, the picture is 3D virtual reality. Milk told Patrick Hipes for *Deadline.com* (22 Jan. 2015), "Megan has the most vision and foresight of any producer working in cinema today. I'm humbled and honored to be exploring the virtual reality medium alongside her. We can't wait to help our fellow filmmakers write a completely new storytelling language."

## PERSONAL LIFE

Ellison's mother began breeding horses after her divorce from Larry Ellison. Megan Ellison competed in equestrian events at the North American Young Rider Championship in 2004 after train-

ing at her mother's Wild Turkey Farm in Woodside, California.

David Geffen, who cofounded Dream-Works, is a mentor of Ellison's; she is also enamored of the films that directors Robert Altman and John Cassavetes made during the 1970s. Of Ellison's appearance on movie sets, JoAnne Sellar told Danny Leigh for the *Guardian* (13 Feb. 2013), "She's incredibly self-effacing. If you ran into her on set, you'd assume she was someone's PA [personal assistant]." Ellison is also wary of reporters and interviewers, based on what she believes is the unfair treatment her father has received at their hands. She rarely grants interviews; her Twitter account contains mainly quotations and links to clips on YouTube.

Ellison is openly gay; her longtime partner is Robyn Shapiro.

## SUGGESTED READING

Graser, Marc. "Heavy Hitters Pick Up Slack as Studios Evolve." *Variety* 426.3 (2012): 8. Print.

Grigoriadis, Vanessa. "Caution: Heiress at Work." *Vanity Fair*. Condé Nast, Mar. 2013. Web. 16 Jan. 2015.

Leigh, Danny. "Megan Ellison, the Most Powerful New Force in Hollywood." *Guardian*. Guardian News and Media, 2013. Web. 22 Jan. 2015.

Masters, Kim. "A Very Ellison Holiday Season." *Hollywood Reporter* 44 (2012): 23–24. Print.

McClintock, Pamela. "Take Note, Hollywood: the New Movie Money Is Here." *Hollywood Reporter* 420.17 (2014): 44–46. Print.

Rosenberg, Alyssa. "How Reese Witherspoon and Megan Ellison Are Changing the Movies." *Washington Post*. Washington Post, 2014. Web. 13 Jan. 2015.

Smith, Gavin. "Woman of Mystery." *Film Comment* 49.1 (2013): 36. Print.

## SELECTED WORKS

*True Grit*, 2010; *Zero Dark Thirty*, 2012; *The Master*, 2012; *The Grandmaster*, 2013; *American Hustle*, 2013; *Her*, 2013; *Foxcatcher*, 2014

—Judy Johnson

# François Englert

**Born:** November 6, 1932
**Occupation:** Physicist

François Englert is a Nobel Prize–winning physicist partially responsible for discovering the theoretical boson contribution to particle mass.

## EARLY LIFE AND EDUCATION

François Englert was born in Etterbeek, Belgium, in 1932. During World War II, he was forced to conceal his Jewish identity while living in orphanages in the Belgian towns of Dinant, Lustin, Stoumont, and finally Annevoie-Rouillon, which was liberated by US forces in 1945.

Englert attended the Université Libre de Bruxelles (ULB; Free University of Brussels) in Belgium after the war, receiving his bachelor's degree in electromechanical engineering in 1955. Englert remained at ULB to complete his master's degree in physics in 1958 and his PhD in 1959. He joined the physics department at Cornell University in Ithaca, New York, as a research associate in 1959 and became an associate professor at the university in 1960.

## CAREER IN THEORETICAL PHYSICS

In 1961, Englert returned to Belgium and joined the theoretical physics group at ULB. There, Englert collaborated with Robert Brout, a Belgian physicist whom Englert had first met when both men were part of the physics department at Cornell.

In 1964, Englert was given a full professorship at ULB, and that same year, he and Brout published a groundbreaking paper, "Broken Symmetry and the Mass of Gauge Vector Mesons," in the journal *Physical Review Letters*. In the paper, they proposed a theory regarding the existence of mass, a physical property that describes the resistance to movement and gravitational attraction among particles. Englert and Brout theorized that observations of mass were due to the fact that particles in space interacted with a field, defined in physics as a physical quantity that can be measured across space and time, and that interactions with this mass-generating field, now called a Higgs field, caused particles to display the characteristics associated with mass.

Also in 1964, University of Edinburgh physicist Peter Higgs published papers in which he reached similar conclusions to Englert and Brout. Though Higgs's research was published after Englert and Brout's article, Higgs provided a more comprehensive version of the theory and was later credited as the primary theorist on the subject. Higgs further speculated about the existence of a then-undiscovered particle, later called the Higgs boson, theoretically responsible for generating mass through its interactions with other fundamental particles.

Shortly after Higgs published his research, American physicists Gerald Guralnik and Carl Hagen and British physicist Tom Kibble published a third paper in which they reached the same conclusions as Higgs, Englert, and Brout. Much of the early research into mass-field theories were credited to Higgs, and the field and particles were thus named in Higgs's honor. Later, the physics community recognized the collective contributions of all the pioneers involved in the study. The mechanism through which the Higgs boson interacts with other particles officially became known as the Englert-Brout-Higgs-Guralnik-Hagen-Kibble mechanism, though it is generally called the Higgs mechanism for short.

In 1980, Englert and Brout became codirectors of theoretical physics at ULB, a position that Englert held until 1998. In 1983, experiments revealed the existence of new fundamental particles involved in the Higgs field, called the W and Z particles respectively, leaving the Higgs boson as the last particle needed for experimental confirmation of the Higgs mechanism.

Englert and the other pioneers of Higgs field research began receiving global recognition in the 1990s. In 2004, Englert, Brout, and Higgs shared the Wolf Prize in Physics, one of the most prestigious awards for achievement in physical research. In 2010, Brout, Englert, Higgs, Hagan, Kibble, and Guralnik jointly shared the J. J. Sakurai Prize for Theoretical Particle Physics, the most prestigious award given by the American Physical Society.

In July of 2012, experiments conducted with the Large Hadron Collider at the European Organization for Nuclear Research (CERN) in Geneva, Switzerland, revealed a signal indicating the possible presence of the Higgs boson. Definitive confirmation of this discovery was made in March of 2013, confirming the experimental validity of the Higgs mechanism.

Due to Nobel Prize conventions, only living scientists are eligible to receive the award, and only three researchers may share a single award. Brout died in 2011, thus making him ineligible for the Nobel Prize when the Higgs mechanism was experimentally confirmed in 2013. In October 2013, it was announced that Higgs and Englert would share the 2013 Nobel Prize in physics for contributions to the scientific understanding of mass.

## IMPACT

The discovery of the Higgs mechanism is considered one of the most important fundamental developments in theoretical physics of the twentieth and twenty-first centuries. Numerous features of the universe, including gravity, spatial forces between planets and stars, and the behavior of electromagnetism, have been affected by the existence of the Higgs field. The Higgs boson is so central to current theories of how the universe functions that the particle is sometimes referred to in the popular science press as the "God particle."

## PERSONAL LIFE

Englert is married to Mira Nikomarow.

## SUGGESTED READING

"Accelerated Impact: Francois Englert Wins the 2013 Nobel Prize in Physics." *Chapman Magazine*. Chapman University, 31 Jan. 2014. Web. 26 Mar. 2014.

Englert, François. "The Mass Generation Mechanism and the Scalar Boson." *Université Libre de Bruxelles*. U Libre de Bruxelles, n.d. Web. 26 Mar. 2014.

Englert, François. "Nobel Lecture: The BEH Mechanism and Its Scalar Boson." *Nobelprize.org*. Nobel Foundation, 8 Dec. 2013. Web. 26 Mar. 2014.

Englert, François. "USC Shoah Foundation Institute Testimony of Francois Englert." Interview. *USC Shoah Foundation Visual History Archive*. USC Shoah Foundation, 26 Mar. 1998. Web. 26 Mar. 2014.

Englert, F., and R. Brout. "Broken Symmetry and the Mass of Gauge Vector Mesons." *Physical Review Letters* 13.9 (1964): 321–23. Print.

Tao, Eric. "François Englert—The Other Guy behind the Higgs Mechanism." *Dartmouth Undergraduate Journal of Science*. Dartmouth U, 4 Nov. 2013. Web. 26 Mar. 2014.

"The 2004 Wolf Foundation Prize in Physics." *Université Libre de Bruxelles*. U Libre de Bruxelles, n.d. Web. 26 Mar. 2014.

## SELECTED WORKS

*Broken Symmetry and the Mass of Gauge Vector Mesons*, 1964; *Vector Mesons in the Presence of Broken Symmetry*, 1966; *From Disorder to Space-Time Geometry*, 1987; *Primordial Inflation*, 1999; *The Hidden Horizon and Black Hole Unitarity*, 2010

—Micah Issitt

# Tony Fadell

**Born:** March 22, 1969
**Occupation:** Inventor and entrepreneur

In 2001 Tony Fadell made a name for himself by helping to transform the Apple iPod into the world's most popular digital music playing device. During his nine-year tenure at Apple, Fadell was also a key player in the early development of the company's smartphone line, supervising the first three iPhone models: the original iPhone, the iPhone 3G, and the iPhone 3GS. Despite his success with Apple, Fadell has not been content to rest on his laurels. "I DON'T want the iPod to be my defining thing," he said in an interview for the *Economist* (9 Mar. 2013). "I'm all about peaking late in life."

Fadell made headlines in 2010 when he left Apple to start the home automation company Nest Labs, which has revolutionized home energy use by providing consumers with artfully designed, energy efficient, and programmable thermostats and smoke detectors. Over a four-year period his startup grew to nearly five hundred employees. In January 2014 Google acquired Nest Labs for more than $3 billion.

## EARLY LIFE

Anthony Michael Fadell was born on March 22, 1969, in Detroit, Michigan, to a mother from Detroit's working-class Polish Town neighborhood and a Lebanese American father. He moved often growing up, primarily due to his father's regional sales executive job at blue jeans manufacturer Levi Strauss. Fadell, whose mother worked as a hospital administrator, credits his grandfather, an educator and Detroit school superintendent, with sparking his early love of learning how things work and how to fix things. "I'd be 3 or 4 and he'd say, 'Change the light switch,' and I'd go off and do it," Fadell recalled to Marco della Cava for *USA Today* (11 Nov. 2013). "What all that taught me was, hey, humans built this thing, humans can fix it, humans can make it better. I'm human, so why can't I?"

Fadell's fascination with electronics began at the age of ten after taking a computer programming class during the summer. Within two years, he had bought his first computer—the Apple II Plus—with help from his grandfather as well as money he earned as a caddie and a paperboy. In his junior year at Grosse Pointe South High School, the enterprising Fadell, who had taught himself coding, cofounded an Apple reseller and software-writing firm, Quality Computers, with one of his friends.

## JOINS APPLE SPINOFF

Following graduation from Grosse Pointe South in 1987, Fadell majored in computer engineering at the University of Michigan where he and one of his college professors launched a children's educational software firm and a company that redesigned speedier microprocessors for the powerful Apple IIGS, the last in the Apple II series of personal computers. While still at Michigan, Fadell sold the latter enterprise to Apple.

After earning his bachelor of science degree in 1991, Fadell headed to California's Silicon Valley intent on joining the Apple spinoff General Magic (GM). "I wanted to work with my heroes so I just turned up at their office at 8:30 one summer morning," he recalled to Jessica Salter for the *Telegraph* (20 June 2014). "They said, 'We're not hiring.' Three months later I went back and got a job." At the time, GM was developing groundbreaking proprietary technology to power a new breed of handheld devices, also known as personal digital assistants (PDAs).

## LEAVES APPLE FOR PHILIPS ELECTRONICS

During his four years at General Magic, Fadell was promoted to lead systems architect, where he helped develop a programming language (Telescript) and an operating system (Magic Cap) that were incorporated into two PDAs: Sony's Magic Link and Motorola's Envoy. In 1995, Fadell unsuccessfully pitched a smaller, improved handheld design to Apple. He then approached other companies including Philips Electronics, whose CEO offered him the opportunity to head its newly formed mobile computing unit.

As Philips's chief technology officer and senior director of new business, the twenty-six-year-old was the division's youngest executive. He also had a brash management style. "I had

Official Leweb Photos/Wikimedia Commons

such chutzpah," he told Pamela Kruger and Katharine Mieszkowski for *Fast Company* (17 Sept. 1998). "I would never admit I was wrong. I was always questioning the direction of the company." Under Fadell, the mobile division developed Windows-based PDAs. The 1997 Velo 1 won *Businessweek*'s bronze Industrial Design Excellence Award (IDEA).

## THE ORIGIN OF THE IPOD

In 1998 Fadell was promoted to vice president of Philips's Strategy and Ventures division, which involved overseeing the company's digital audio strategy and investments. In the summer of 1999, Fadell, a former deejay, branched out on his own, launching the digital music startup Fuse. For his first project, he focused on developing a smaller, sleeker device containing an internal hard drive that was capable of storing thousands of songs. "Tony's idea was to take an MP3 player, build a Napster music sale service to complement it, and build a company around it," Ben Knauss, a former senior manager at PortalPlayer, told Leander Kahney for *Wired* (21 July 2004).

After the stock market crash in 2000, Fadell failed to obtain a new round of venture capital and decided to pitch his idea to several companies, including Philips Electronics and Seattle-based streaming media pioneer RealNetworks, who offered him a job. Fadell's stint at designing products based on the RealPlayer software program was brief, however, and he resigned after just six months, reportedly due to friction with RealNetworks CEO Rob Glaser.

## APPLE CONSULTANT

In January 2001 Fadell was contacted by Apple's head of hardware to design a portable MP3 player that could also accommodate Apple's existing iTunes music library. "The idea was '1,000 songs in your pocket'—a long-battery-life device that syncs with the Mac," Fadell shared with Max Chafkin for *Fast Company* (10 Sept. 2013). During his six-week consulting gig, Fadell, aided by Stan Ng who was Apple's hardware marketing manager, created three top-secret mockups that were based on MP3 reference designs from San Jose, California, chipset supplier PortalPlayer. The most notable and revolutionary design was for a device about the size of a cigarette case.

In March 2001 Fadell showed Styrofoam models to CEO Steve Jobs and several other Apple executives. After intentionally presenting two less promising versions—one featuring a slot for a hard drive or flash memory card and the other containing removable storage—Fadell impressed Jobs with the final model, which was hidden under a bowl at the center of the conference table. "I . . . put fishing weights in it and had graphic panels on it," he told Jon Chase for *Entertainment Weekly* (21 Oct. 2011). "Steve picked it up, said 'Hmmm, feels about right.'" This final design was approved by Jobs, who gave the team just seven months to design, build, and perfect the device in time to be ready for the holidays.

## SPEARHEADS IPOD DESIGN

In April 2001 Fadell was hired full-time to manage the Special Projects engineering team. To meet the seven-month deadline, Fadell's group worked twenty-hour days, seven days a week, closely collaborating with PortalPlayer, whose prototypes served as blueprints for Apple's device. The group tackled several mockup issues, including batteries lasting less than three hours, overly complex interfaces, and no support for playlists longer than ten songs. Jobs was actively involved, meeting with Fadell's team and PortalPlayer every two to three weeks to address issues with the player that ranged from the interface and sound quality to the size of the device's scroll wheel.

On October 23, 2001, the iPod was unveiled at Apple's corporate headquarters in Cupertino, California. While the high-resolution device was touted for its 1,000-song storage ability, easy-to-use scroll wheel, and high-capacity 5 GB hard drive, it drew criticism for its $400 price tag and its incompatibility with Microsoft computers. Apple responded with the July 2002 release of the Windows-compatible iPod and the April 2003 launch of iTunes Music Store; by June 2003 the company had sold one million iPods.

In 2004 Fadell was named vice president of iPod engineering. However, even at the time he anticipated that the iPod's success would not last. "It was inevitable something would take its place. You know, in 2003 or 2004, we started asking ourselves what would kill the iPod," Fadell confided to John Brownlee for *Fast Company* (22 Sept. 2014). "And even back then . . . we knew it was streaming. We called it the 'celestial jukebox in the sky.'"

In October 2005 Fadell was promoted to senior vice president of the iPod division. He reported directly to Jobs and supervised all aspects of the division, including the development and shipping of the original iPhone (an iPod-sized smartphone with a touchscreen).

## STARTS NEST LABS

In November 2008 Fadell resigned from Apple to spend more time with his growing family. He remained with the company as an off-site consultant to Steve Jobs while he took an eighteen-month family trip. When he returned, he focused his attention on his soon-to-be-built, smart home in Lake Tahoe, California. While researching eco-friendly gadgets, Fadell realized that they controlled half or more of the average home's energy bill. "I went through every single device in the house, thinking, 'How would you consume energy differently, how would you interface differently?'" he told David Rowan for *Wired* (3 July 2014). "I was frustrated by so many products. The first one was the thermostat. Then the smoke alarm."

In May 2010, Fadell resigned from his consultant job at Apple and partnered with fellow Apple engineer Matt Rogers to launch the jointly funded, home automation company Nest Labs, which was secretly based in a rented Palo Alto garage. Armed with a ten-person basic staff of engineers, designers, and computer scientists, Nest Labs envisioned an upscale, self-programmable, energy-saving thermostat for the iPod generation. By December 2010, with the help of outside funding from two venture capital investment firms, Nest Labs developed its first prototype, which was admittedly too large to be practical or marketable. By March 2011, the team had settled on a final design that was sleek and hockey-puck shaped. Within five months, Google had joined the company's second round of funding. In October 2011 the Nest Learning Thermostat made its debut with a touch-screen, Wi-Fi capability, and colorful backlighting.

A year later, Nest Labs, which does not disclose sales figures, unveiled a comparatively priced second-generation thermostat that was a more streamlined version of the original Nest product and compatible with 95 percent of US home heating and cooling systems. The company claimed another victory in 2012 when the US Patent and Trademark Office rejected Honeywell International's patent infringement lawsuit filed against Nest Labs. In October 2013, after securing another $80 million in third-round funding, Nest Labs expanded their product offering to include Nest Protect, a motion-controlled smoke and carbon monoxide detector. However, the device was at the center of a May 2014 recall involving 440,000 faulty units. The issue was resolved in September 2014 by providing customers with a software update.

## PARTNERS WITH GOOGLE

In January 2014, after just four years in business, Google acquired Nest Labs for $3.2 billion. Fadell was retained as CEO at Nest, and manages the company independently of Google. In January 2015, Fadell, who was still CEO of Nest Labs, was also named to head Google's faltering Glass division. Google Glass, which was first introduced in 2012, is a wearable, head-mounted computer product that was met with negative reviews from technology experts and privacy concerns from the public. Rather than completely giving up and shelving the product, Google hired Fadell to oversee the redesign and re-release of Glass.

## PERSONAL LIFE

While at Apple full-time in the early 2000s, Fadell was introduced to fellow employee Danielle Lambert, who was Apple's senior vice president of human resources at the time. After meeting in February 2002, the couple became engaged twelve weeks later and married six months after that. They live in California with their three children.

## SUGGESTED READING

Brownlee, John. "iPod Mastermind Tony Fadell on the Death of the iPod: 'You Can't Get Too Nostalgic.'" *Fast Company*. Fast Company, 22 Sept. 2014. Web. 18 May 2015.

Kahney, Leander. "Inside Look at Birth of the iPod." *Wired*. Condé Nast, 21 July 2004. Web. 18 May 2015.

Kruger, Pamela, and Katharine Mieszkowski. "Stop the Fight." *Fast Company*. Mansueto Ventures, 31 Aug. 1998. Web. 18 May 2015.

Levy, Steven. "Steve Jobs: A Wired Life—The Perfect Thing." *Wired*. Condé Nast, 25 Nov. 2011. Web. 18 May 2015.

"The Podfather, Part III." *Economist*. Economist Newspaper, 7 Mar. 2013. Web. 18 May 2015.

Rowan, David. "How Tony Fadell Brought a Touch of Apple to Google." *Wired*. Condé Nast, 3 July 2014. Web. 18 May 2015.

Salter, Jessica. "9 Tips for Success from Tony Fadell." *Telegraph*. Telegraph Media Group, 20 June 2014. Web. 18 May 2015.

—Bertha Muteba

# Anna Fenninger

**Born:** June 18, 1989
**Occupation:** Alpine ski racer

Anna Fenninger is an Austrian alpine skier who won a gold medal in the women's super giant slalom, or super-G, at the Sochi Olympics in 2014. Fenninger was identified as an elite skier at an early age, winning gold at the 2006 Junior World Championships while still a teenager, before becoming the super combined world champion in 2011. She won her first overall World Cup title a month after her Sochi victory in 2014. There are four disciplines within alpine skiing: downhill, super-G, giant slalom, and slalom. A fifth event, the combined, fuses both downhill and slalom. According to a reporter for the BBC (3 Nov. 2009), super-G "combines the speed of downhill with the more frequent turns seen in giant slalom. The course is shorter than downhill, but longer than giant slalom"—and unlike other events, there are no training runs. Skiers get only one chance to prove their speed and agility. In addition, the course at the Sochi Olympics in 2014 was one of the most difficult in recent memory, and not just because of its design. An unusually warm winter led to a dangerous and slushy slope. In the women's super-G, seven out of the first eight competitors failed to reach the finish line, and out of the total forty-nine starters, eighteen failed to reach the bottom. Florian Winkler, the man who set the course, defended his work, telling a reporter for the Agence France-Presse (16 Feb. 2014) that he intended for the course to be a challenge. "It was our goal for the course. Still fair, but you have to think a bit more. I was surprised by the number of girls who skied out. It was a day of mistakes for many," he said, adding, "I think the best handled it really well, they showed how it's done."

When racing, Fenninger dons her signature cheetah-print helmet to raise awareness for her off-the-slope passion, the Cheetah Conservation Fund (CCF) in Namibia. Fenninger got involved with the organization after her friend, a South African photographer, contacted her for support in bringing the issue to the attention of Europeans. She is now the official European ambassador for CCF. According to its website, the CCF was founded in 1990 after a surge in development in Namibia in the 1980s threatened to kill off the cheetah, the world's fastest land animal, entirely. The organization works to restore the cheetah's natural habitat and protect it from poachers. In 2014, the CCF released a calendar featuring Fenninger, as well as a mildly risqué ad in which the skier poses in a cheetah-print body suit.

### EARLY LIFE AND TRAINING

Fenninger was born on June 18, 1989, in Hallein, Austria. Skiing is Austria's national sport, and is followed with a fervor akin to football in the United States. Fenninger began to ski seriously at a very early age, and completed her secondary education at the Bad Gastein Ski Race Academy, located at one of Austria's premiere ski resorts. An early friend and fellow skiing prodigy was World Cup champion Marcel Hirscher. The two skiers, born in the same year, both felt they had great athletic expectations to live up to. "We grew up in the same region and we skied with each other a lot when we were children," Fenninger told a reporter for the website *Olympic. org.* "We went to the same school, were in the same class and we competed in races together. It's a lovely story." In an interview (conducted in German) with Herbert Lackner for *Profil* (6 Aug. 2014) an Austrian weekly, Fenninger admitted that committing herself to the sport at a young age has had its drawbacks, but while she did not get to have the experience of being a carefree young person, she has had a number of experi-

Manfred Werner/ Tsui/Wikimedia

ences that other young people will never have. On top of that, she added, her rigorous schedule makes even partying seem unappealing; she falls into bed by ten o'clock in the evening, dead tired.

### JUNIOR CUP AND WORLD CUP DEBUT

Fenninger made a splash in her debut at the Junior World Championships in Quebec in March 2006, where she won gold in the super-G and silver in downhill. She finished fifth in the slalom. Pete Rugh for *Ski Racing* magazine (5 Mar. 2006) dubbed her "the most aggressive racer of the day," having bested the super-G silver medalist, Camilla Borsotti of Italy, by eight-tenths of a second. In an interview with Rugh after her race, a stunned Fenninger said, "I didn't think I would win the super-G."

She made her FIS (International Ski Federation) World Cup debut in 2006, and in 2006 and 2007, she won back-to-back overall titles at the Europa Cup. Her early success brought with it added pressure, Fenninger told Graham Dunbar for the Associated Press (14 Mar. 2014). She made her World Championship debut in 2007 and struggled to compete in all five events, completing only one of her ten races. "I felt a bit alone there, and too young," she told Dunbar. "I had my trainers and they were new for me and I had to know how they are and how they work. Everything was new. I felt not that confident." Despite dislocating her shoulder in 2008, Fenninger managed to win five more medals at the Junior World Championships before returning to the World Championships in 2009. She placed second in the super-G and seventh in the combined. The next year, 2010, proved to be a disappointing one for Fenninger. She participated at the Olympic Games in Vancouver, but failed to place in the downhill, super-G, or combined. She briefly considered retiring, but instead, she refocused her training, and returned to the World Championships to win her first career title, beating her teammate Elisabeth Görgl in the super combined in 2011. It was the first major turning point of her career. It was also the last time she competed in all five alpine events. After 2011, in which she also won the World Cup title in giant slalom and was named Austrian sport's breakthrough star of the year, Fenninger decided to focus primarily on downhill and super-G (the speed events) and, later, giant slalom. In 2012 and 2013, she won her first and second World Cup title in giant slalom. (In an odd coincidence, all three of Fenninger's World Cup winning races between 2011 and 2013 took place on December 28.)

## SOCHI OLYMPICS

The year before the Sochi Olympics, 2013, was a strong one for Fenninger, but her Olympic Games got off to a rocky start when she placed eighth in the super combined on February 10, and went out in the downhill event on February 12. (The women's downhill event at Sochi was notable in that it was the first women's alpine event to ever end in a tie. Slovenia's Tina Maze and Switzerland's Dominique Gisin shared gold.) The women's super-G event took place on February 15. The temperature was a balmy 60-odd degrees and though the top of the course was icy, the bottom, as one Olympian described it to Rob Hodgetts for the BBC (15 Feb. 2014), was "soapy." The unseasonable conditions made certain parts of the course—namely two trouble spots, one after the initial pitch and the other at several sharp turns after a high-speed jump near the bottom—treacherous for most of the athletes that day. "You had to have the right direction coming off that [last] jump because you're landing almost to the next gate," Laurenne Ross of the United States told David Leon Moore for *USA Today* (15 Feb. 2014). Ross, who started seventh, failed to make the turns after the last jump. "I had a [radio] report that I needed to have some direction off the jump. But it was kind of unclear, because some of the girls had

gone out in the top section, too. It was so tough running early like that." Fenninger started seventeenth and might have benefitted from watching the women before her struggle with the course. Still, it was her technical prowess that got her through the run. Fenninger, Bill Pennington wrote for the *New York Times* (15 Feb. 2014), "was crisp through the choppy snow of the top section, smooth through the flat, cruising middle section, and navigated the final jump with her skis pointing in the proper direction so she could be early on the pivotal left-footed turn over the knoll that vexed so many of her competitors." Her time was 1:25.52. Fenninger beat Germany's Maria Höfl-Riesch by 0.55 seconds. Her teammate, Nicole Hosp, trailed her by 0.66 seconds to take bronze. Later, Fenninger said it was the best day of her life.

Fenninger competed in her third event, the giant slalom, three days later. Maze was the first racer out of the gate that day. Taking advantage of the new, soft snow, Maze started the day with a lead of nearly half a second. Fenninger gave two solid runs, but ultimately, it wasn't enough to catch up to Maze. Fenninger, whose two-leg time trailed Maze's by an infinitesimal 0.07 seconds, won silver.

Less than a month later, Fenninger competed in the World Cup in Switzerland in March, earning her first World Cup overall title, the sport's biggest prize, at the age of twenty-four. Her childhood friend, Hirscher, clinched the men's overall title, his third, a few days later. In their interview, *Profil*'s Lackner suggested that skiing was a solitary sport, but Fenninger disagreed. She needs the support of a team to push her and make her better, she said, and that without the team she would not be where she is now. Fenninger dates retired Austrian snowboarder Manuel Veith and loves to ride motorcycles. She plans to continue skiing for the foreseeable future, though she has studied hotel management and briefly interned as a hotel clerk. When she is not travelling for her sport, she lives on the outskirts of Salzburg.

## SUGGESTED READING

"Anne Fenninger: Austria's Alpine Amazon." *Olympic.org*. Intl. Olympic Committee, n.d. Web. 19 Oct. 2014.

Dunbar, Graham. "Fenninger Faced Pressure to Win Since Teen Years." *AP*. Associated Press, 14 Mar. 2014. Web. 19 Oct. 2014.

Hodgetts, Rob. "Sochi 2014: Austria's Anna Fenninger Wins super-G Gold." *BBC Sport.* BBC, 15 Feb. 2014. 19 Oct. 2014.

Lackner, Herbert. "Anna Fenninger: 'Schonen geht gar nicht.'" *Profil* [Austria]. News Networld Internetservice, 6 Aug. 2014. Web. 19 Oct. 2014.

Moore, David Leon. "Austria's Anna Fenninger Wins Gold in super-G; USA shut out." *USA Today.* USA Today, 15 Feb. 2014. Web. 19 Oct. 2014.

Pennington, Bill. "As Austrians Prevail, American Skiers Falter." *New York Times.* New York Times, 15 Feb. 2014. Web. 19 Oct. 2014.

Rugh, Pete. "Austrian Phenom Anna Fenninger Takes World Juniors super G." *Ski Racing.* Ski Racing, 5 Mar. 2006. Web. 19 Oct. 2014.

"Sochi Games course setter defends difficult super-G set-up." *National* [Abu Dhabi]. Agence France-Presse, 16 Feb. 2014. Web. 19 Oct. 2014.

"Winter Sports: Alpine Skiing." *BBC Sport.* BBC, 3 Nov. 2009. Web. 19 Oct. 2014.

—Molly Hagan

Gage Skidmore (CC BY 2.0)

# Gal Gadot

**Born:** April 30, 1985
**Occupation:** Actor

A former Miss Israel and model, Gal Gadot has been best known thus far in her career as the star of four films in the Fast & Furious franchise, the incredibly profitable street-racing series that has made billions of dollars worldwide since the release of its first installment in 2001. However, that was before director Zack Snyder tapped her to take on the role of Wonder Woman, the iconic comic book character who, since her debut in 1941, has become the most recognizable superheroine of all time. Despite her success as a comic book character and on a popular television show in the 1970s (portrayed by Lynda Carter), Wonder Woman has never been adapted for the big screen.

That is about to change as Gadot takes on the role in Snyder's upcoming *Batman v Superman: Dawn of Justice* (2016), costarring Ben Affleck and Henry Cavill, as well as in a standalone *Wonder Woman* film that is due out in 2017. Gadot's Wonder Woman will also serve as an integral part of Warner Bros. Studios' shared DC Comics cinematic universe, which it is developing to compete with Marvel Comics' own shared cinematic universe; Marvel has been making billions for its parent company, Disney, over several years with its feature films. Yet, despite there being a plethora of comic book film adaptations since the early 2000s, no female comic book character has yet scored box-office gold in that time. Snyder and Warner Bros. believe that Gadot's interpretation of the iconic character will change all that. Gadot told Keith Staskiewicz for *Entertainment Weekly* (10 July 2015), "I think it's about time for a female heroine to hold her own in a superhero movie. It's been too long."

## EARLY LIFE

Gal Gadot was born on April 30, 1985, in Rosh HaAyin, Israel, into an Ashkenazi Jewish family. Her parents are *sabras*, a Hebrew term meaning Jews who were born in Israel. Gadot had an active childhood, due in large part to her mother, who was a gymnastics teacher. According to anecdotes related by her mother, Gadot often craved attention. Gadot recalled of her youth to Teddy Wayne for *Interview* (22 July 2015), "Growing up I was never sitting watching TV in the afternoons. I always played ball outside in the backyard. I was a dancer for twelve years. I did tennis, basketball, volleyball, dodgeball, you name it. I was such a tomboy. I loved sports."

In Israel, every citizen, male or female, is required to serve at least two years in the Israel

Defense Forces (IDF). Gadot intended to fulfill her service but, in 2004, decided to try out for the Miss Israel pageant on a lark—and won. "That was my entrance into the modeling world," she recalled to Curt Schleier for *Forward* (2 May 2011). "I rescheduled my army time and started working as a model [for three years]."

Gadot represented Israel at the Miss Universe beauty competition, held that year in Ecuador. When she failed to make the cut to the top fifteen, she returned home to find herself in demand as a model. At age twenty she entered the IDF, where she served for two years as a gym trainer and fitness instructor for fellow soldiers. She also learned how to handle a variety of firearms, both skills that would serve her well in future film roles. Gadot reflected on her military service for Wayne: "To begin with, I hope that no country in this world will need an army. But, unfortunately, having the reality we have in Israel, it's a mandatory thing. . . . It gives you values, like giving something of yourself, your time, your energy. It gives you good discipline, because it's not about you; it's about the system. . . . It made me more responsible and mature."

After completing her service, Gadot, still unsure as to which direction she wanted to go in terms of a career, left the army to study law and international relations simply because "it felt like the right decision," as she explained to Wayne. At the same time, she was working as a model. She gained some attention in 2007, when she was featured on the cover of *Maxim* in the magazine's "Women of the Israeli Army" photo shoot, which had been done to promote tourism to Israel. She also became the face of Castro, a leading clothing brand in Israel.

## EARLY ACTING CAREER AND THE FAST & FURIOUS FRANCHISE

A casting agent from England saw Gadot's photo and wanted her to audition for the female lead in the upcoming James Bond film *Quantum of Solace* (2008). When her agent told her that he was going to set up an audition for her to become the new Bond girl, Gadot recalled to Staskiewicz for *Entertainment Weekly* (3 July 2015), "I said, 'There's no way I'm going to go; it's all in English. I'm not an actress, and I'm in school.'" At first her agent thought she was joking, but when she failed to appear at the audition, he called her and begged her to go see the casting director. She reluctantly agreed to go, despite not having learned the scenes, and was apologetic to the

casting director when she got there. Although she did not get the part, she did have several callbacks for the role. The experience made her intrigued by the thought of acting and she told her agent to keep an eye out for future roles.

Within a month, Gadot had landed the lead role on the Israeli television series *Bubot* (2007–8); within two months, she had won the part of Gisele Yashar in the fourth installment of the Fast & Furious franchise, *Fast & Furious* (2009). Her character subsequently appeared in *Fast Five* (2011), *Fast & Furious 6* (2013), and *Furious 7* (2015). In her interview with Schleier, Gadot described her character in the franchise: "In the fourth film, I was the right hand of the leader of a drug cartel in Mexico. We established in her history that she was just supporting her family. And when she had the opportunity, she helped Dom [played by series star Vin Diesel] and eventually became an ally." She added, "One of the things I like about her is that she always leaves you craving to know more about her." Along with establishing her talents as an actor, Gadot also got to show off her skills with firearms and her ability to handle a motorcycle.

Gadot looks back on her experience in those films with considerable affection, in part because of the strong friendships she forged with the series' lead actors, Vin Diesel and Paul Walker. Walker was tragically killed in a car accident on November 30, 2013, during the filming of *Furious 7*. After suspending production for a time, the cast and crew agreed to finish the film with Walker's brothers serving as stand-ins for the unfinished scenes. She said to Wayne, "It's so sad, and when I talk about it, I still get tears in my eyes, because he was a great man. He was an angel in life. He was so down-to-earth, so interested in everyone. He was a rare person. I still miss him and will miss him forever."

## BECOMING WONDER WOMAN

Although adaptations of comic books have been around for decades, films based on comic books started becoming box-office cash cows for studios beginning in the early 2000s, when the Marvel Comics characters of Spider-Man and the X-Men were adapted for the big screen. In addition to those two series, other Marvel characters, including Iron Man, the Hulk, Thor, and Captain America, have been adapted to film. Marvel has even brought them together in a shared cinematic universe, in which the actors from the various films join together, most notably in the Avengers series of films. Although DC Comics had successful films featuring such major characters as Superman and Batman over the years, its parent company, Warner Bros., had not yet put together a shared cinematic universe—until the success of its 2013 film adaptation of *Superman, Man of Steel*. Its sequel, *Batman v Superman: Dawn of Justice* (2016), will continue that shared universe, when Superman, played by Cavill, faces off against Affleck's portrayal of Batman. In this landmark film for DC Comics, Gal Gadot's Wonder Woman will also make her debut.

Despite decades of success as a comic character, Wonder Woman has had some difficulty in making it to the big screen, due in part to studio heads who believe that a female comic book character would not be able to carry a blockbuster solo film. Snyder, the director behind *Man of Steel* and its upcoming sequel, believed that the character was more than capable of carrying a film. In fact, he wanted her to play a significant part in the Superman sequel, one in which she would help form the Justice League, a team of superheroes who are the mainstays of the DC Comics universe.

By that time, Gadot had reached a point in her acting career where she felt comfortable enough, financially and professionally, to be choosier when it came to the parts she would play. "I didn't want to do the obvious role that you see in Hollywood most of the time. . . . I wanted to do something different," she told Wayne. When Snyder asked to meet her, she did not actually know what part she was auditioning for. After she read a scene from the 1994 film *Pulp Fiction*, he told her that the audition was for the role of Diana Prince, Wonder Woman's alter ego. Gadot told Staskiewicz how she was stunned at the opportunity to play Wonder Woman, "There are so many expectations for this character. It's impossible not to be a little nervous about it."

## FUTURE ROLES

After landing the part, Gadot was signed by Warner Bros. to a three-picture deal in which she would earn $300,000 per film. The deal is to include the upcoming *Batman v Superman* film, as well as a *Wonder Woman* solo film and a Justice League film, with the latter two due out in 2017. In order to prepare for the role, Gadot has undergone weight-training regiments as well as training in handling classical weapons—everything from a sword and shield to Wonder Woman's iconic magic lasso. She expressed her enthusiasm over landing the role to Wayne: "I'm so excited about this role. I feel like I've been given a huge opportunity to inspire people, not only women. And not because of me but because of who Wonder Woman is and what she stands for. There's a lot of responsibility."

Continuing to add to her repertoire and versatility as an actor, Gadot also won roles in three other films featuring high-profile actors due out in 2016. These upcoming releases include *Criminal*, a thriller costarring Ryan Reynolds and Kevin Costner; *Triple 9*, a heist film with Kate Winslet and Chiwetel Ejiofor; and *Keeping Up with the Joneses*, a suburban spy comedy with Jon Hamm, Zach Galifianakis, and Isla Fisher.

## PERSONAL LIFE

Gal Gadot has been married to Yaron Varsano, an Israeli businessman, since September 2008. For a time they owned a hotel together in Tel Aviv, Israel, but have since sold it. Gadot was a motorcycle enthusiast for a number of years; however, since the birth of her daughter, Alma, in late 2011, she has given up the hobby. Being a mother has also affected the way in which she chooses her film roles. She remarked to Wayne, "When I choose a role, I always think about whether my daughter can get something out of it when she watches the movie later after she's grown up. Or even just show her that Mommy's doing what Mommy loves to do."

## SUGGESTED READING

Denham, Jess. "Profile: Wonder Woman Gal Gadot Is a Model, Army Girl and Fast & Furious Star." *Independent*. Independent, 5 Dec. 2013. Web. 8 Sept. 2015.

Gadot, Gal. "Gal Gadot." Interview by Teddy Wayne. *Interview*. Interview, 22 July 2015. Web. 8 Sept. 2015.

Schleier, Curt. "Chatting with *Fast Five* Star Gal Gadot." *Forward*. Forward Assn., 2 May 2011. Web. 8 Sept. 2015.

Staskiewicz, Keith. "Capes of Wrath." *Entertainment Weekly* 10 July 2015: 22–30. Print.

Staskiewicz, Keith. "Gal Gadot: 'It's Impossible Not to Be a Little Nervous' about Playing Wonder Woman." *Entertainment Weekly*. Entertainment Weekly, 3 July 2015. Web. 8 Sept. 2015.

## SELECTED WORKS
*Fast & Furious*, 2009; *Fast Five*, 2011; *Fast & Furious 6*, 2013; *Furious 7*, 2015; *Criminal*, 2016; *Triple 9*, 2016; *Batman v Superman: Dawn of Justice*, 2016

—Christopher Mari

---

# Tavi Gevinson
**Born:** April 21, 1996
**Occupation:** Founder of *Rookie* magazine

Tavi Gevinson has been referred to as precocious and multitalented. Before the age of twenty, she has written, edited, and managed a highly successful online fashion magazine; acted on Broadway; and, due in large part to her online presence, has served as an inspiration for girls and young women worldwide.

When Gevinson was eleven years old she started the online blog *Style Rookie*, which by the following year had brought her fame and the admiration of fashion designers and fashion industry insiders. Within a few years she moved on to her next project, *Rookie*, an online magazine for teens and young women, of which she is still the editor-in-chief. For three consecutive years, beginning at the age of fifteen, Gevinson has landed on *Forbes* magazine's "30 Under 30: Media" list of influential young people. *Time* magazine put her on its "25 Most Influential Teens of 2014" list. In September 2014, only a few months after graduating from high school, Gevinson made her Broadway debut as one of three lead actors in the play *This Is Our Youth*. Writing for the *New Yorker* (1 Sept. 2014), Hilton Als praised the young actress when he wrote, "Whether standing stock still or dancing awkwardly, jubilantly . . . Gevinson claimed not just our attention but also our interest. From all available evidence, Gevinson . . . is a star being shaped by her own will to be seen and heard—but now as someone other than herself."

## EARLY YEARS
Tavi Gevinson was born on April 21, 1996, and raised in Oak Park, a suburb of Chicago, Illinois. She and her two older sisters, Rivkah and Miriam, were brought up by parents Steve Gevinson and Berit Engen. Engen is originally from Norway and is a weaver and Hebrew instructor. Gevinson's father is a retired high school English teacher and served as the head of the English

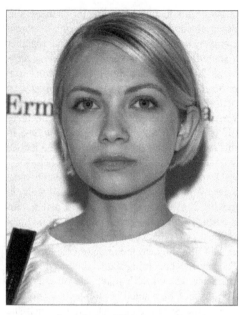

Gary Gershoff/WireImage/Getty Images

department at Oak Park and River Forest High School. He retired the year before Gevinson joined the school's freshman class.

Gevinson had mixed feelings about high school and described the look and feel of the school to Amy Larocca for *New York* magazine (10 Aug. 2014) as having a "big football field and boxy '70s design" that allowed her to pretend she was in a John Hughes movie or the cult-favorite TV show *Freaks and Geeks*. She had good friends, "the art kids," and played in various punk bands and dyed her hair turquoise. But Gevinson was also philosophical about the experience, as she said to Larocca, "I think everybody should go to high school. It's horrible, and it unites you with other people."

## STYLE ROOKIE, STYLE STAR
Unlike anyone else at her high school, however, Gevinson was the talk of the fashion world and was profiled in national publications and flown around the globe with her father to attend fashion shows and events. Before all that, however, in March 2008 at the age of eleven, Gevinson began a fashion blog she called *Style Rookie*. Unlike many fashion-obsessed young people of decades past, Gevinson had the whole of the Internet at her disposal, which she searched for forums and discussions of fashions old and new. She browsed the layouts and ads in vintage magazines and read other style blogs. For her blog, Gevinson would take posed pictures of herself in

curious outfits and write about whatever aspect of the fashion world she wished. Susie Lau, a pioneer of the personal fashion blog and creator of the blog *Style Bubble*, told Lizzie Widdicombe for the *New Yorker* (20 Sept. 2010) that Gevinson's blog stood out, and not just because of her age. In addition to having an "unusually deep knowledge of fashion history," wrote Widdicombe, Gevinson referenced movies, books, and even Greek mythology. Widdicombe observed that although there are many young, unique people in the fashion world, Gevinson stands out because she is a "rare spectacle."

Although she and her style were often referred to as "cute" by some, Gevinson was more interested in the dichotomies of a look and combining the cute with the weird and the adorable with the eccentric or the spooky and creepy. The director Tim Burton, for example, was an early inspiration.

By her one hundredth blog post, Gevinson eloquently and plainly stated her fashion philosophy, as quoted by Widdicombe, "No rules, no restrictions, no normalcy, no pleasing anyone. . . . I might only be less attracted to the entire 'chic' deal because, as a younger person, I do gravitate more towards tackier clothes. That being said, I'm twelve! I have no one to impress and I'm not concerned about wearing something flattering to my body. I will dress as ugly and crazy as I want as long as I'm still young enough to get away with it." Gevinson began attracting more readers, around 50,000 a day, and getting attention in the fashion world and the mainstream press. The blog earned her praise from *Teen Vogue* editor in chief Amy Astley and such fashion giants as designer Karl Lagerfeld.

## POPULAR APPEAL, NAYSAYERS, AND CRITICS

When pop culture first began taking note of Gevinson, she was approached to appear on *The Tonight Show* and *Oprah*, both of which she initially turned down because, as she explained to Widdicombe, the viewers those shows attracted were "not a crowd whose eyes I want on me." (She has since appeared on *Late Night with Jimmy Fallon*, *The Colbert Report*, and *The Tonight Show with Jimmy Fallon*.)

Gevinson has spoken twice at ideacity conferences (in 2010 and in 2014) in Toronto, Canada, and at the independently organized TED event, TEDxTeen in 2012 in which she talked about being a teen and "just trying to figure it out." Almost from the beginning, however, there were cynics and naysayers, some of whom questioned whether Gevinson was actually one twelve-year-old girl and not a group of adults or a single adult pulling a prank. Others, such as Museum of the Fashion Institute of Technology director Valerie Steele, tried to diminish Gevinson's accomplishments by claiming that she would not be getting the attention she was receiving if she were an adult. Other fashion writers objected to the VIP access that Gevinson received at fashion shows and events. Still others believed that Gevinson's "fifteen minutes of fame" would end soon enough and her popularity would eventually fade away. But instead she continued to evolve, focusing first on the writing of *Style Rookie*, eventually shutting the website down in 2011, moving on to online magazine editing, and then becoming an actor—all the while navigating the dramas and victories of teenage life.

### ROOKIE

In September of 2011, Gevinson launched *Rookie*, an online magazine for teenage girls that was inspired by Gevinson's love of *Sassy*, a 1990s print magazine aimed at precocious teen girls. *Rookie*, wrote Kara Jesella for *Slate* (13 Sept. 2011), unapologetically combined fashion and feminism, such as the article that appeared in its first issue: "Getting over Girl Hate" addressed how competition between women is encouraged within American popular culture.

Though *Rookie* is not the only online outlet to combine fashion and feminism, wrote Jesella, it is "the most visible." Alex Morris for *Rolling Stone* (14 Aug. 2014) summed up the popularity of Gevinson and the magazine: "*Rookie*'s popularity is such that it has created a sort of clubhouse effect, spawning an annual yearbook and a nationwide tour—in which girls crammed into ice cream parlors and record stores from Brooklyn to LA in the hopes of meeting Gevinson—and turning its petite founder into both a media juggernaut and a generational spokeswoman with friends like [actress and screenwriter] Lena Dunham . . . and [singer/songwriter] Lorde."

When Gevinson originally posted on her blog that she was looking for contributors for *Rookie*, she received 3,000 responses, according to Larocca. Perhaps the most important of those responses came from Anaheed Alani, a forty-year-old who worked for the *New York Times*. Alani had been a fan of Gevinson's blog for a while and explained to Larocca that she "found her writing and her sense of humor and her outlook on the world to be exciting, really smart."

After Alani joined Gevinson, however, they realized that they needed help with the business side of things, and that's where Alani's husband, *This American Life* radio program host and producer Ira Glass, stepped in. In addition to articles and editorials, the magazine also landed interviews with big names, including Lorde, *Parks and Recreation*'s Aubrey Plaza, *Mad Men*'s Kiernan Shipka, and screenwriter and director Sofia Coppola. Every year the magazine publishes a yearbook, which is edited by Gevinson and is a compilation of the best of the website's content from the previous year.

## BROADWAY

In September 2014, Gevinson made her Broadway debut in the Kenneth Lonergan production *This Is Our Youth*. Directed by veteran theater director Anna D. Shapiro, the play is set in the 1980s and also stars Michael Cera, best known for such films as *Superbad* (2007) and the popular television show *Arrested Development* (2003–6; 2013), and Kieran Culkin. Before moving to Broadway, *This Is Our Youth* first played Chicago's legendary Steppenwolf Theatre. Rehearsals for the play in Chicago began while Gevinson was still in her last year of high school. However, by the time the play opened on Broadway, Gevinson had graduated and moved to New York City. The play opened in New York in September 2014 and ran until January 2015, and the reviews were generally very positive. Although Gevinson had appeared in a few films, most notably *Enough Said* (2013) and the documentary *The Punk Singer* (2013), *This Is Our Youth* is undeniably her biggest acting role to date.

As the name implies, the play is about the lives of young people. All three main characters are sorting out their personal issues while trying to relate to one another in the Upper West Side Manhattan apartment of Dennis Ziegler, who is played by Culkin. Dennis sells marijuana and enjoys taking shots at his friend Warren Straub, played by Cera. Warren's father has kicked him out of their apartment, but before leaving, Warren steals $15,000 cash from his father and then comes to see Dennis, only to be made fun of for his clumsiness and ineptness with girls. The two young men make a plan that involves drugs and turning the $15,000 into more money. Warren, however, spends the stolen money in part on Gevinson's character, an eighteen-year-old Fashion Institute of Technology student named Jessica Goldman. More than relying on plot de-

vices, the play is driven by each of the characters and how all three relate to one another. Ben Brantley for the *New York Times* (11 Sept. 2014) praised director Shapiro's "sensational, kinetically charged revival" of the play and called Gevinson an "astonishingly assured actress." Brantley also observed that Gevinson "nails exactly the aggressive defensiveness of a girl who sees boys as both the enemy and salvation."

## SUGGESTED READING

Als, Hilton. "Youth Culture." *New Yorker*. Condé Nast, 1 Sept. 2014. Web. 4 May 2015.

Brantley, Ben. "Desperate Fledglings, Flung from the Nest." *New York Times.* New York Times, 11 Sept. 2014. 5 May 2015.

Larocca, Amy. "At 18, Tavi Gevinson Is a Fashion Veteran—and a Broadway Rookie." *New York Magazine*. New York Media, 10 Aug. 2014. Web. 4 May 2015.

Widdicombe, Lizzie. "Tavi Says: Fashion Dictates from a Fourteen-Year-Old." *New Yorker.* Condé Nast, 20 Sept. 2010. Web. 4 May 2015.

—Dmitry Kiper

# Donald Glover

**Born:** September 25, 1983
**Occupation:** Actor and musician

Few young celebrities can boast of having achieved success in as many different endeavors as Donald Glover, who began his career as a scriptwriter for the celebrated television sitcom *30 Rock* immediately upon graduation from New York University (NYU). He left *30 Rock* at the end of its third season to pursue other interests and quickly landed the part of Troy Barnes on the sitcom *Community*. He left after several seasons to focus on his emerging career as a rap artist. Known by his stage name Childish Gambino, Glover has released two critically and commercially successful albums as of 2014, and in 2011 he fronted the one-man live show "I Am Donald," which combined rap, comedy, and video. Glover has written numerous screenplays and has been featured in several major motion pictures. He admits the fast pace is sometimes hard on him, but he strives to do as much as he can for as long as he can. Glover told Lily Rothman for *Time* magazine (5 Dec. 2013), "I want to become something that when people hear I have a project people will be like, 'Oh, this should be

Jesse Chang/Wikimedia Commons

interesting,' without hearing the project. . . . I want to be an idea. Ideas are the only things that last. . . . I'm only interested in ideas because I feel like that's the only thing that helps us grow as humans."

## EARLY LIFE AND EDUCATION

Donald McKinley Glover, Jr. was born on September 25, 1983, at the Edwards Air Force Base in California and raised in Stone Mountain, Georgia, with his brother Stephen and his sister Brianne. His parents, Beverly and Donald Sr., were Jehovah's Witnesses and regularly served as foster parents to children in need. In their conservative household, television was severely restricted, which forced young Donald to record the audio of episodes of *The Simpsons* so that he could secretly listen to them later. Glover admits he grew up with a sense of impending dread. In an interview with Bill Jensen for the *Village Voice* (13 Apr. 2011), Glover recalled of his childhood, "I was the type of kid—I felt like I was always being blamed for things that weren't my fault. So I always wanted things to go smoothly. And growing up in the South, people didn't like me because I was black. And it took on this thing: I'm gonna be *me* so much, and be *sooo* likeable, that I will change their minds. And I know now that that's impossible. But I had to try."

Glover was a rambunctious child, prone to seeking attention from his parents and other adults by putting on plays and puppet shows. A good student, he developed an interest in the performing arts that landed him at the DeKalb School of the Arts in Georgia, where he acted in such classic musicals as *42nd Street* and *Pippin*. His success at DeKalb eventually helped to secure him a place at NYU's Tisch School of the Arts, where he studied dramatic writing with the idea of someday becoming a playwright. "NYU is like a Jurassic 5 concert—there are supposed to be black people there, but there aren't," Glover joked in his stand-up routine, as quoted by Jensen.

Glover's playwriting dreams evolved into other creative endeavors during his undergraduate years. He began performing with Hammerkatz, a NYU sketch comedy group that included his future writing partners Dominic Dierkes and DC Pierson. He also began mixing beats as a freshman and eventually took up the moniker Childish Gambino after it came up on a Wu-Tang Clan name-generator site. He also performed with the Upright Citizens Brigade, the improvisational comedy and sketch group. His teacher there passed his email address to the comedian Amy Poehler, who passed it to her friend and writing partner Tina Fey, who passed it on to David Miner, a producer for *30 Rock*. Miner subsequently contacted Glover asking him for writing samples.

## *30 ROCK* AND *COMMUNITY*

Glover's early writing—some sketches he had penned along with a pair of spec scripts for the television comedies *The Simpsons* and *Everybody Hates Chris*—impressed both Miner and Fey, who offered him a job in 2006 writing for *30 Rock*, a comedy about the behind-the-scenes antics of a late-night sketch comedy show based loosely on *Saturday Night Live*. Glover is credited with writing some of the best lines for Tracy Morgan's diva-like character, as well as for Jack McBrayer, who portrayed a network page who hails from Glover's very own Stone Mountain, Georgia. Glover also appeared on the show in several small parts, including one as a young Tracy. After three seasons on the show, Glover decided that he wanted to try other things.

He first attempted to win a spot on *Saturday Night Live* by playing President Barack Obama but was turned down. He then got a call to try out for a part on another television comedy, *Community*, a series about a group of misfits at a fictional community college in Colorado. Glover became one of the show's breakout stars by playing Troy

Barnes, a former super-cool high school quarterback who comes to embrace his nerdy side. One of the most popular aspects of *Community* was the interplay between Glover's character and the character of Abed Nadir, played by Danny Pudi, who is a film student with an obsessive knowledge of television and movies and who helps to break Troy out of his jock persona.

Glover believes that characters like Troy help African American kids step away from stereotypes. In an interview with Steve Inskeep for NPR's *Morning Edition* (15 Nov. 2011), Glover noted how "we put stereotypes on ourselves—like, everybody does that. But I think it's just a little harder for black kids to just be who they are because there are people on both sides are [sic] telling them who they are all the time. Television is telling you who you are. Like, everybody is telling you who are and who you can be and what your limits are."

## BECOMING CHILDISH GAMBINO

After five seasons on *Community*, Glover left the show to concentrate on his musical career. He released his first album, *Camp*, in 2011 under the name Childish Gambino. In 2013 he returned to the music scene with the release of his second album, *Because the Internet*. Unlike many of the clichés surrounding rap artists, Glover's Childish Gambino persona is none of these things but instead is an often insecure, nerdy kid. The humor that permeates much of his other work exists in his raps but is filtered through a persona that is unsure of his place in the world. Yet, just as in his standup work, his script writing for *30 Rock*, or his acting on *Community*, Glover is clearly giving music his all and displays an earnestness that many critics admire. Music fans have come to admire him as well: *Camp* peaked at number 11 on the Billboard 200, and *Because the Internet* peaked at number 7.

While many rappers have been dismissive of Glover's work as Childish Gambino, a number of critics have found much to admire. Jensen described Glover as representing "a new archetype of entertainer—a black nerd who can like white stuff. Not a black nerd in the over-the-top Steve Urkel or Dwayne Wayne sense, but a regular black guy who likes the same stuff white people like—but just happens to be more talented than you." In the *New York Times* (20 Feb. 2014), Jon Caramanica wrote that Glover "has been an unsteady presence in music, a carpetbagger on the surface but one with extremely serious intentions. . . . *Because the Internet* is

his first release that suggests that making music isn't just an itch for Mr. Glover, but an actual talent. He's still a clunky rapper, a stylistic literalist with a jokey tone. But the production here . . . is vastly improved."

## OTHER WORKS

Although working at a breakneck pace, Glover shows no signs of slowing down in any of his creative pursuits. He toured the United States in 2011 on the I Am Donald tour in which he rapped and performed stand-up comedy. The tour carried across twenty-three cities in just thirty-three days. He also continues to expand as an actor, guest-starring on television shows ranging from *Sesame Street* on PBS to *Girls* on HBO, and he has been featured in a number of short and feature-length films such as *The Muppets* (2011) and *Alexander and the Terrible, Horrible, No Good, Very Bad Day* (2014). His upcoming full-length films include *Magic Mike XXL* (2015), a comedy about male strippers, and the sci-fi tinged *The Martian* (2015) about a US astronaut stranded on Mars. The film is directed by Ridley Scott and stars Matt Damon. Glover also continues to pen various video shorts, screenplays, and television series, including episodes of *Live at Gotham* and *Comedy Central Presents*, as well as his 2012 special *Donald Glover Weirdo*. "You don't get to where all my heroes were without giving up a part of who you are," Glover told Jensen. "Right now, I refuse to even have a dog. No girlfriend. I don't want anything tying me down. I want to be everywhere. I don't see a limit for me. I want to do everything."

In December 2014, the US cable channel FX announced that it had ordered a pilot for the comedy series *Atlanta*, which Glover had written and would be starring in and executive producing. The story line revolves around two cousins, one of whom makes a name for himself in the Atlanta rap music industry. Glover plays the other cousin, a college dropout determined to follow the same path of success.

## SUGGESTED READING

Caramanica, Jon. "Go On, Rant and Rave: It Shows You're Real." *New York Times*. New York Times, 20 Feb. 2014. Web. 20 Nov. 2014.

Glover, Donald. "Childish Gambino Is Trying to Be a Grown-Up." Interview by Steve Inskeep. *Morning Edition*. NPR, 15 Nov. 2011. Web. 20 Nov. 2014.

Jensen, Bill. "Donald Glover Is More Talented Than You." *Village Voice*. Village Voice, 13 Apr. 2011. Web. 21 Nov. 2014.

Rothman, Lily. "A Conversation with Childish Gambino: Nostalgia, Bitcoins and Advice from Tina Fey." *Time*. Time, 5 Dec. 2013. Web. 20 Nov. 2014.

Sneider, Jeff. "'Community's' Donald Glover Joins Matt Damon in Ridley Scott's 'The Martian.'" *Washington Post*. Washington Post, 10 Oct. 2014. Web. 20 Nov. 2014.

## SELECTED WORKS

*30 Rock*, 2006–9; *Community*, 2009–14; *Alexander and the Terrible, Horrible, No Good, Very Bad Day*, 2014; *Magic Mike XXL*, 2015; *The Martian*, 2015

—Christopher Mari

# Anand Gopal
**Born:** 1980
**Occupation:** Author and journalist

In 2014 journalist Anand Gopal received stellar reviews for his nonfiction debut *No Good Men among the Living: America, the Taliban, and the War through Afghan Eyes*, which is a devastating account of the US–led war in Afghanistan. In the book—the culmination of four years of reporting—Gopal presents accounts of the fighting through the perspectives of several Taliban commanders who had not previously been interviewed by Western journalists. With their help, Gopal provides a clearer picture of the war, the people of Afghanistan, and the impact that the US–led invasion has had on that nation. In order to obtain this unparalleled access to these leaders, Gopal worked with many tribal elders throughout the country who then provided the necessary protection in order to be allowed to meet with the Taliban.

What Gopal learned from his experiences and from the people with whom he met changed the ways in which he perceived the war and Afghanistan as a whole. He told Joseph Richard Preville for the website *Turkey*Agenda (24 June 2014), "I spent many months traveling the Afghan countryside and meeting people whose views of the war were very different than my preconceived notions. For instance, I stayed for a time in a village in Kandahar with a noted tribal elder. He was something of a local don, and every day vil-

lagers would come to his house for tea or a meal. In the course of one day, an Afghan army officer, a US military patrol, and a Taliban commander all visited him to pay him respect. To survive so many years of conflict, he'd worked to maintain ties with all sides. It struck me how irrelevant, under such circumstances, the American notions of friend and foe actually were. From the Afghan villager's point of view, life was about navigating the various forces and power structures that towered over their lives." *No Good Men among the Living* has received several important accolades, including being placed on the *New York Times Sunday Book Review* list, 100 Notable Books of 2014. The book was also a finalist for the National Book Award's 2014 nonfiction prize.

## EARLY LIFE AND EDUCATION

Little has been published about the early life of Anand Gopal apart from the fact that he is of Indian descent and was born in 1980, according to the Library of Congress. (Some sources give his birthdate as 1979.) He earned his bachelor's degree from New York University (NYU) and then continued his education at the University of Pennsylvania, where he studied physics and chemistry as a graduate student.

Gopal was living in New York City on September 11, 2001, when individuals later known to be affiliated with the al-Qaeda terrorist network hijacked four commercial jet aircraft and flew two planes into the Twin Towers of the World Trade Center in New York City. Another aircraft was crashed into the Pentagon building outside Washington, DC, and the fourth jet was forced down (reportedly by passengers on the aircraft) and into a field outside Shanksville, Pennsylvania. All told, almost three thousand people were killed. In addition, the Twin Towers were destroyed and the Pentagon was severely damaged. The attacks launched the North Atlantic Treaty Organization (NATO) operations against al-Qaeda in Afghanistan later that year and would also serve as the impetus for the US–led invasion of Iraq in 2003 in order to uncover illegal weapons of mass destruction, which intelligence agencies worldwide feared would be used to fuel terrorist networks.

The experience of living through the terrorist attacks of September 11 propelled Gopal to investigate and understand this new threat by traveling to the country from which the attacks had been planned. Gopal recalled for Preville for *Turkey*Agenda: "After 2001, the United States divided the world—and Afghans—into two categories: you were either with us or against us. This artificially ordered a complex and messy battlefield, one that, over the years, has been the scene of shifting alliances and sudden turnarounds."

## JOURNALISM CAREER

To insulate himself from undue suspicion, Gopal grew a beard and studied the language before traveling to Afghanistan, which was and still is a dangerous country for foreign journalists. He first served as the Afghanistan correspondent for the *Christian Science Monitor* from February 2008 to April 2009 and then held the same position for the *Wall Street Journal* from May 2009 to February 2010. During his time in Afghanistan, Gopal sought out and attempted to interview high-ranking leaders of the Taliban, the Islamic fundamentalist movement that had spread across the country in the years after the Soviet departure from Afghanistan in 1989. The Taliban had evolved out of the mujahideen, the Islamic guerilla fighters who had fought the Soviets. From 1996 to 2001 the Taliban was the Afghan government, and the group supported and protected the al-Qaeda network led by Osama bin Laden, who authorized the September 11 attacks.

Because Gopal was a Western journalist, few Taliban leaders agreed to be interviewed by him, so it took time to build mutual trust. But when he did, Gopal was not only able to interview multiple high-ranking Taliban officials, but he also developed a sharper understanding of the complexity of relationships in Afghan life. In a December 9, 2014, interview with Justin Vogt for *Foreign Affairs*, Gopal explained, "I was very interested in reaching out to the Taliban . . . and what I found very quickly is you go and ask them questions such as, why are you fighting, what kind of state do you want to see, and you get boilerplate answers. You get propaganda." Gopal remained patient, however, and continued to meet with Taliban leaders until one day he decided to try a different method: rather than ask politically based questions, Gopal instead asked the men personal questions. "I'd say, tell me about your childhood . . . your favorite memory growing up . . . if you're in love. . . . People love to talk about themselves more than anything else. And that really got them to open up, and I was able to cultivate a relationship in this way that really lasted over two or three years. And Afghanistan's a society based on trust. And once you can establish

that kind of trust, it actually can keep you safe in many ways."

## 2014: A BREAKOUT YEAR

In September 2012, Gopal was named a Bernard L. Schwartz Fellow at the New America Foundation, a progressive nonprofit and nonpartisan public policy institute established in 1999. During his two-year fellowship, Gopal was able to complete work on his first book, *No Good Men among the Living: America, the Taliban, and the War through Afghan Eyes*, which was published in 2014. In the book he looks at the history of Afghanistan from 1979 to the present through the experiences of three Afghans: a housewife, a tribal strongman, and a Taliban leader. The housewife, Heela, endured numerous tragedies during the war, including finding her husband's body on a dirt road. She went on, however, to win a seat in Afghanistan's senate. The tribal strongman, Jan Mohammed, became the governor of the province of Oruzgan thanks in part to his connections to the US–backed Afghan president Hamid Karzai. He also received considerable amounts of money and praise from American commanders for the effective way in which he dispatched his opposition. The Taliban leader Akbar Gul was also known as Mullah Cable because of the way he brutally used cable whips. After the Taliban were removed in 2001, Gul fled to Pakistan before returning to his native country in order to open a telephone repair shop. After a time, however, he became frustrated with the corruption of the local officials and the unending US presence, and he again took up arms with the Taliban. Gopal's debut presents a divided nation in which the cities (chiefly the capital city of Kabul) are controlled by the US–backed government and the countryside is dominated by warlords and strongmen. At the end of its thirteen-year effort in Afghanistan, Gopal concludes that the United States has been unable to end the insurgency or stitch together a functioning democracy that is favorably inclined toward the West.

*No Good Men among the Living* earned many positive reviews upon its publication. Calling the book a "haunting ethnography of Afghanistan after the American invasion," a reviewer for *Publishers Weekly* (May 2014) wrote, "[Gopal] presents a stirring critique of American forces who commanded overwhelming firepower, but lacked the situational knowledge to achieve their objectives. . . . Gopal reveals the fragility of the tenuous connection between intention and destiny in a war-torn land." In the *New York Times* (25 Apr. 2014), Kim Barker proclaimed, "Gopal's book . . . is a devastating, well-honed prosecution detailing how the American government bungled the initial salvo in the so-called war on terror, ignored attempts by top Taliban leaders to surrender, trusted the wrong people, and backed a feckless and corrupt Afghan regime. The book has its flaws, minimizing the role of neighboring Pakistan in the Taliban's resurgence and letting the Taliban off too easy. But it is ultimately the most compelling account I've read of how Afghans themselves see the war."

## MIDDLE EAST COVERAGE
In addition to his acclaimed reporting from Afghanistan, Gopal has covered major events throughout the Middle East, including the revolutions in Egypt, Syria, and Libya. He has reported for periodicals such as *Harper's*, the *Nation*, the *New Republic*, and *Foreign Policy*, and he traveled to Iraq in 2014 to report on the growing power of the Islamic State of Iraq and Syria (ISIS), which is also known as the Islamic State of Iraq and the Levant (ISIL). ISIS is an Islamist fundamentalist group that controls large portions of Iraq and Syria. The group has committed numerous human rights abuses and has been condemned by the world community.

As of January 2015 Gopal is a doctoral student in sociology at Columbia University in New York City.

## SUGGESTED READING
Barker, Kim. "Hostile Climate: American Policy and Missed Opportunities in Afghanistan." *New York Times*. New York Times, 25 Apr. 2014. Web. 11 Jan. 2015.

Gopal, Anand. "Foreign Affairs Focus on Books: Anand Gopal on Afghanistan and Iraq." Interview by Justin Vogt. *Foreign Affairs*. Council on Foreign Relations, 9 Dec. 2014. Web. 27 Feb. 2015.

Gopal, Anand. "Interview with Anand Gopal on His New Book 'No Good Men among the Living: America, the Taliban, and the War through Afghan Eyes.'" Interview by Joseph Richard Preville, *Turkey*Agenda. *Turkey*Agenda, 24 June 2014. Web. 21 Jan. 2015.

Gopal, Anand. "Who Are the Taliban?" *Nation*. The Nation, 22 Dec. 2008. Web. 27 Feb. 2014.

"*No Good Men among the Living: America, the Taliban, and the War through Afghan Eyes*." *Publishers Weekly* PWxyz, May 2014. Web. 27 Feb. 2015.

—Christopher Mari

# Vijay Govindarajan
**Born:** November 18, 1949
**Occupation:** Professor, consultant, author

Vijay Govindarajan, popularly known as VG, is the Earl C. Daum 1924 Professor of International Business at Dartmouth College's Tuck School of Business, where he has worked for nearly thirty years, and was named the school's first Coxe Distinguished Professor in 2014. When *Fortune* magazine included him on their 2012 list of the fifty best business-school professors in the world, he was hailed as Dartmouth's resident "innovation guru," and General Electric (GE) named him their first professor in residence and chief innovation consultant in 2008. "In the US, there is a close collaboration between industry and academics," Govindarajan told Arthur J. Pais for the Indian news website Rediff.com (2 Nov. 2012). "I love that synergy."

During his time at GE, Govindarajan helped develop the concept of "reverse innovation," which refers to the commercial exchange between rich and poor countries. Traditionally, wealthy countries such as the United States innovate, or create new and exciting products, which they then sell to poor and developing countries with minor adjustments, taking into account the needs of those markets. Reverse innovation flips that script. Developing markets such as India are making innovative and cost-effective products by necessity for their own population, then selling those products to rich countries.

Consistently named one of the top fifty influential thinkers in the world, Govindarajan also cofounded the $300 House Project, for which he received the Hunt Institute Award for Vision in 2012. In addition to his regular column for *Businessweek*, he has also cowritten a number of books, including several best sellers; his most recent book, *Beyond the Idea: How to Execute Innovation in Any Organization* (2013), was one of a few written with fellow Dartmouth professor Chris Trimble.

Govindarajan, who was born and raised in southern India, told Ankit Khandelwal for the *Times of India* (22 Apr. 2013) that his background has had an enormous impact on his life and work. "There are so many problems in India in areas as diverse as housing, health care, and energy. People are living with very little resources. Growing up in India, I realized that innovation and proper planning is the only way to solve such problems."

## EARLY LIFE IN INDIA

Vijay Govindarajan was born on November 18, 1949, in Madras (now Chennai), India, and was raised in Annamalai Nagar, a town in the Cuddalore district of the state of Tamil Nadu. Growing up, Govindarajan looked up to his paternal grandfather, a former secretary to the maharaja of Mysore and a traditional Brahmin (a high-ranking Indian caste) who taught children of the low Dalit (untouchable) caste without pay. His grandfather made no distinction between those children and his own grandchildren, Govindarajan recalled to Pais. The education alone, doled out under a banyan tree in front of the Hindu temple every Saturday and Sunday, gave the low-caste children a tremendous leg up in the world. Several of them even returned to the village as professors. "They would fall at my grandfather's feet for giving them that opportunity for coming up in life," Govindarajan told Pais.

Govindarajan himself was one of four children (he has two brothers and a sister), but his grandfather pushed him to succeed from a young age. After Govindarajan finished fifth grade, his grandfather got the syllabus for sixth grade and made him stay inside and study while all of the other children were outside playing. "He never once said you did a great job. For him, it was always, 'You can do better!'" Govindarajan told Pais. Still, he said, "I knew he was always proud of me." Govindarajan stood first in his class until he entered Annamalai University, where he met other students from other schools who had also been first in their respective classes. But his grandfather's pushing drove him to succeed, he told Pais. "When someone has so much ambition for you, you cannot let that person down."

## EARLY CAREER AND HARVARD EDUCATION

After earning his bachelor's degree from Annamalai University in 1969, Govindarajan then received his chartered accountancy (CA) degree. He was awarded the President's Gold Medal for ranking first among accounting students in India. After beginning to work for DCM Limited, a conglomerate based in New Delhi, Govindarajan was accepted into the company's

The India Today Group/Getty Images

Senior Management Trainee Program—thanks to a bureaucratic slipup. He was the only accountant, and though he had been confident in his skills, practicing accounting from a managerial perspective completely upended his previously held views about the job. "I realized that I had been looking at accounting in isolation, whereas in reality it exists as part of management," he told Indranil Das and Nikita Garia for the business-management magazine the *Human Factor* (1 Mar. 2009). He decided that he needed to get his master of business administration (MBA) degree.

In 1974, Govindarajan traveled to the United States with only eleven dollars. Luckily, he told Pais, he was accepted into the prestigious Harvard Business School (HBS), though he struggled to adjust to American life. He was a strict vegetarian, and the only food he could identify as meatless was toast, so he ate it for every meal. Govindarajan was also very shy, which was problematic in light of the school's teaching method. "The pedagogy at HBS is case method," he told Pais. Professors offer real-world business problems to students in class and ask them to work together to solve those problems—a very interactive, extrovert-oriented method of learning. Govindarajan continued, "In India we are used to the lecture method, where the teacher gives the lecture. Students passively listen to the teacher and repeat the answers in exams. In the case method, you put your opinions to public scrutiny—180 degrees different from what I was used to." Too insecure to speak up in class, he discovered after a few months that his classmates—even the most talkative among them—felt the same way.

After the dean forced him to join a study group, Govindarajan learned to excel in this environment, and his experience at HBS inspired him to eventually become a professor himself. To address his vegetarian dilemma, the school allowed him to teach a campus cook how to prepare South Indian food. He earned his MBA in 1976 and remained at HBS to work toward his doctor of business administration (DBA) degree, during which time he won the Robert Bowne Prize for best dissertation proposal.

Govindarajan graduated with his DBA in 1978 and returned to India to teach at the Indian Institute of Management in Ahmedabad. He loved his students, but he lacked proper resources as an educator. There were no opportunities for faculty research. "After two years," he recalled to Das and Garia, "I felt if I continued in India, I am going to depreciate my intellectual capital dramatically."

## EMPHASIZING REVERSE INNOVATION

In 1980, Govindarajan accepted a teaching position at HBS. He then spent a few years as an associate professor at Ohio State University before moving to Dartmouth's Tuck School of Business in 1985. He was the school's first Indian faculty member. "I almost felt the weight of India on my shoulders," he told Pais.

GE asked Govindarajan to become the company's first professor in residence and chief innovation consultant in 2008. He spent two years with GE, during which time he helped develop the concept of reverse innovation, which he and coauthors Trimble and Jeff Immelt (CEO of GE) first introduced in an article called "How GE Is Disrupting Itself." In the article, published in the *Harvard Business Review* in October 2009, the authors describe GE's plan to spend $3 billion creating one hundred health-care innovations to reduce cost, increase access, and improve quality in the sector. The plan cited the example of two cutting-edge products, a $1,000 handheld electrocardiogram device and a $15,000 portable ultrasound machine, both of which were created for use in developing countries.

Govindarajan and his coauthors called this process reverse innovation "because it's the opposite of the *glocalization* approach," they wrote. "With glocalization, companies develop great products at home [in the United States] and then distribute them worldwide, with some adaptations to local conditions." This approach was successful when growth in wealthy nations far outpaced growth in developing countries, but this is no longer the global dynamic. For companies in developing countries, such as India, it is necessary to offer quality goods and services that are also cheap and accessible. This puts those companies at a global advantage—an advantage that US companies could benefit from if they, too, looked to address the problems of the world's poorest.

## $300 HOUSE PROJECT

In 2010, Govindarajan and environmental marketing consultant Christian Sarkar wrote a blog post for the *Harvard Business Review* in which they challenged readers to find a way for the world's poorest people to purchase and construct a house for $300. The article generated so many responses—from laymen as well as architects, engineers, and Harvard and MIT professors—that the men started a crowdsourcing website to make the challenge a reality. "What we have done is created a company with 2,500 employees and no chief executive," Govindarajan told Emmanuelle Smith for the *Financial Times* (12 Feb. 2012). "They are willing to share their ideas in an open way. It's a true open-innovation platform."

Through the website, Govindarajan and Sarkar officially established the $300 House Open Design Challenge. The competition, which was hosted by the German design company Jovoto, yielded three hundred entries that were judged by a panel of sixteen as well as the website contributors. After a handful of the best designs were chosen, winning teams further refined their plans. As of 2013, teams had begun test building in Haiti and India.

## CONTINUING TO PROMOTE INNOVATION

In 2013, Govindarajan and Northeastern University's Ravi Ramamurti wrote an op-ed piece for the *Washington Post* in which they described different ways that US hospitals could follow the example set by nine specific private hospitals in India. The hospitals pay their employees about twenty times less than hospitals in the United States, but crucially, even if they paid their staff at American rates, they would still be able to offer comparable, high-quality services at only 5 to 10 percent of the cost of the same services in the United States.

Inspired by George Orwell's dark political satire *Animal Farm* (1945), Govindarajan and

Trimble also wrote a parable about managing innovation, which they published as *How Stella Saved the Farm: A Tale about Making Innovation Happen* in 2013. "We wanted something that would be short, fun to read, with a serious message," Govindarajan told Dibeyendu Ganguly for India's *Economic Times* (18 Jan. 2013). "By using animals as characters, we've made it into a fantasy, which makes it fun to read. They [readers] think it's remote from their world, so they let their guard down and enjoy it. But then they begin to recognize the characters as people they know."

Govindarajan uses the story, about a worldly young sheep named Stella, in his one-day workshops. The parable highlights not the work of the visionary (Stella, in this case) but rather that of the larger team who executes the visionary's idea. It is, in many ways, a condensed version of the concepts illustrated in Govindarajan and Trimble's 2010 book, *The Other Side of Innovation: Solving the Execution Challenge*, Ganguly wrote. Govindarajan maintains that the hard research behind *Stella* sets it apart from other parables. "Every detail in *Stella* is based on real experiences of real organizations," he told Ganguly.

## PERSONAL LIFE

Govindarajan and his wife, Kirthi, were married in 1980. Kirthi Govindarajan has an MBA and worked as the chief of information and cost systems at a Veterans Health Administration hospital. The couple have two daughters. Their eldest, Tarunya, graduated from Dartmouth and Stanford University and works in Silicon Valley; their younger daughter, Pasy, has worked for Hasbro.

## SUGGESTED READING

Ganguly, Dibeyendu. "Why Innovation Uber-Guru Has Written a Parable *How Stella Saved the Farm*." *Economic Times*. Bennett, 18 Jan. 2013. Web. 21 Nov. 2014.

Govindarajan, Vijay. "Future Is Now: Prof. Vijay Govindarajan." Interview by Ankit Khandelwal. *Times of India*. Bennett, 22 Apr. 2013. Web. 21 Nov. 2014.

Govindarajan, Vijay. "I Almost Felt the Weight of India on My Shoulders." Interview by Arthur J. Pais. *Rediff.com*. Rediff.com, 2 Nov. 2012. Web. 21 Nov. 2014.

Govindarajan, Vijay. "Innovate Radically for Non-Consumers." Interview by Indranil Das and Nikita Garia. *Human Factor*. Planman Media, 1 Mar. 2009. Web. 21 Nov. 2014.

Govindarajan, Vijay, and Ravi Ramamurti. "Indian Hospitals Could Show US Hospitals How to Save Money without Cutting Quality." *Washington Post*. Washington Post, 1 Nov. 2013. Web. 21 Nov. 2014.

Immelt, Jeffrey R., Vijay Govindarajan, and Chris Trimble. "How GE Is Disrupting Itself." *Harvard Business Review*. Harvard Business School, Oct. 2009. Web. 21 Nov. 2014.

Smith, Emmanuelle. "The House That Students Built." *FT.com*. Financial Times, 12 Feb. 2012. Web. 21 Nov. 2014.

## SELECTED WORKS

*The Other Side of Innovation: Solving the Execution Challenge* (with Chris Trimble), 2010; *Reverse Innovation: Create Far from Home, Win Everywhere* (with Chris Trimble), 2012; *How Stella Saved the Farm: A Tale about Making Innovation Happen* (with Chris Trimble), 2013; *Beyond the Idea: How to Execute Innovation in Any Organization* (with Chris Trimble), 2013

—Molly Hagan

---

# David Graeber

**Born:** February 12, 1961
**Occupation:** Activist, professor

Scholar and writer David Graeber gained attention as one of the leaders of the Occupy Wall Street movement in 2011. He has had a dual career, publishing academic works on sociology in peer-reviewed journals while working as a political activist and writing about that aspect of his life as well. He told Gustaaf Houtman for *Anthropology Today* (Oct. 2012) that these two aspects of his career dovetail nicely, "because just as scholarship has an interest in creating a genuinely free society, everyone in the world benefits from human understanding in the largest sense." Some consider Graeber the most influential anthropologist of his time.

## EARLY LIFE AND EDUCATION

David Graeber grew up in Manhattan's Chelsea neighborhood, the son of working-class intellectuals. His mother was a garment worker who once starred in an all-women musical revue put on by the International Ladies' Garment Workers' Union; his father was a plate stripper of offset printers who had fought in the Spanish

Pier Marco Tacca/Getty Images Europe

Civil War with the Republicans, who included anarchists among their number. Graeber and his older brother grew up in New York surrounded by radicals in a cooperative apartment building sponsored by a trade union.

Because of his father's experience with anarchism as a legitimate political stance, Graeber grew up taking it seriously. "Most people don't think anarchism is a bad idea," he told Drake Bennett for *Bloomberg Businessweek* (26 Oct. 2011). "They think it's *insane*. Yeah, sure it would be great not to have prisons and police and hierarchical structures of authority, but everybody would just start killing each other. That wouldn't work, right?" He continued, "[But] it wasn't insane. I was never brought up to think it was insane." One of Graeber's earliest political memories is of carrying a sign that proclaimed "We want peace" during the turbulent 1960s. He was only seven years old. By sixteen, he was self-identifying as an anarchist.

Meanwhile, as a preteenager, Graeber became obsessed with Mayan hieroglyphics, and within a few years his original translations earned him a scholarship to Philips Academy in Andover, Massachusetts. He studied anthropology as an undergraduate at the State University of New York at Purchase; as a graduate student at the University of Chicago, he began field research that would further shape his ideas on anarchism. Graeber spent a total of twenty months in Madagascar, in 1989 and 1991, where he studied the people of Betafo,

who were descended from both slaves and nobility. After the central government abandoned the area due to the cuts imposed by the International Monetary Fund (IMF), the people made decisions by consensus. This method is also called direct action, as opposed to an elected body making decisions; Graeber refers to it as democracy without government. He wrote his dissertation on the Betafo community and completed his doctoral degree in 1996.

## DIRECT ACTION NETWORK

Graeber was part of the November 1999 protests in Seattle, Washington, where the World Trade Organization (WTO) was meeting. Nearly forty thousand activists gathered to stand against global free trade as it had been conceived. Although the protest did not result in specific changes, the umbrella group that organized it, which came to be called the Direct Action Network (DAN), formed branches across the country, including in New York, where Graeber remained active. That branch has become one of the most successful of the network; its working groups address an array of issues such as corporate bureaucracy, police brutality, and the prison system.

DAN is an attempt at direct democracy, rather than a hierarchical organizational structure. The group as a whole has a loose set of principles favoring nonviolence, direct democracy, and international solidarity. Many of its members have protested on global as well as national issues. The DAN groups work toward consensus, Graeber explained to Francesca Polletta for *Social Policy* magazine (Summer 2001), "because that way people are never forced to do anything they didn't consent to. Real freedom would have to be based on consent." Such a democratic process leads to a greater sense of unity among the members, particularly if they are contemplating an action that could lead to being arrested.

Graeber has been involved with other protests as well, including Philadelphia and New York demonstrations at the Republican National Conventions in 2000 and 2004, respectively; the Group of Eight Summit protest in Genoa, Italy, in 2001; the Summit of the Americas protest in Quebec City, Quebec, also in 2001; and the 2010 tuition protests in London.

## ADVENTURES IN ACADEME

Graeber taught at Yale University from 1998 to 2005. He was never considered for tenure, and his contract, which would have moved him from assistant to associate professor, was not renewed in 2005, sparking protests and a wave of support. He remained at Yale for another two years. In response to criticism, Yale merely stated that most junior faculty did not receive tenure. Thomas Blom Hansen, a friend of Graeber's who teaches at Stanford University, explained the difficulty to Bennett: "There was an issue about his personal style, whether he was respectful enough to various senior people both in the department and at the university. He's not someone who is known to be very pliable. I don't think anyone doubts that he's a major figure in his field. But he's not really interested in the humdrum daily life of administration that constitutes an increasing part of our life in the academic world."

No universities in the United States or Canada responded to some twenty applications he sent out, hoping to remain in North America. However, foreign universities expressed interest. In 2008, Graeber became a lecturer and then a reader at Goldsmiths College at the University of London. He accepted a position in 2013 at the London School of Economics and Political Science.

### DEBT: THE FIRST 5,000 YEARS

In his book *Debt: The First 5,000 Years*, published in 2011, Graeber argues against the notion of a pure barter economy leading to a monetary one purely for the sake of convenience, as Adam Smith posited. Rather, money was a way to pay taxes and tribute in Egypt. Societies without money used gifts as a way to gain favor or to repay a favor, relying on an intricate net of obligation and kinship. A money- and debt-based economy undermines that in favor of an impersonal market, according to Graeber.

In *Debt*, Graeber traces the role of debt and of people who lend money, who are often portrayed as evil. Rulers throughout history have used debt, in his view, to finance government (especially wars) and to keep people in subjection. That course of action generally led to major revolts, such as the French Revolution. Graeber argues for debt cancellation, or a jubilee, which ancient civilizations such as Assyria and Babylon used to forestall rebellion. "It would be our way of reminding ourselves that money is not ineffable, that paying one's debts is not the essence of morality, that all these things are human arrangements and that if democracy is to mean anything, it is the ability to all agree to arrange things in a different way," he wrote.

To Graeber's way of thinking, a jubilee is a more palatable method than either inflation or austerity measures to prevent a major financial crisis. He told Houtman, "Money isn't petro-

leum. It's not like there's only so much of it, so if you give it to me you have to take it from someone else. A debt can be cancelled just by making it unenforceable." Although *Debt* has received critical acclaim in both Germany and Great Britain, it has attracted less attention in the United States. In 2012 the book received the prize for best book of the year from the Society for Cultural Anthropology. Shortly before its publication, however, Graeber became involved in a game-changing gathering.

### OCCUPY WALL STREET

In July 2011, *Adbusters*, a Canadian magazine, called for a movement to occupy Wall Street, the financial center of the United States, on September 17. Graeber had published a short piece in the Vancouver-based magazine wondering what could trigger a Western protest to match those that had occurred in Egypt and Spain. In June, four people had shown up in New York for a protest.

The group New Yorkers Against Budget Cuts provided much of the hard work for the Occupy Wall Street protest. Graeber, who spent six weeks with the protesters planning the event, told Houtman that he viewed the movement as a way "to give voice to the widespread feeling in America that the system is so hopelessly corrupt it's basically no longer legitimate, that the political class has been bought and sold and cannot even address the problems ordinary people face."

Protesters gathered in Zuccotti Park, a thirty-three-thousand-square-foot pedestrian park in New York City, halfway between the site of the World Trade Center and Wall Street. Their purpose was to challenge the fact that 1 percent of the population controls vast amounts of wealth and concomitant power. More specifically, people were upset at the amount of debt—in the form of student loans, mortgages, and credit cards—being carried and the influence of money in political life.

The protesters considered themselves part of a broader global movement that included Spain's Indignants, a political protest movement that began in 2011 as the Indignant People's March, and the people who fomented the Arab Spring. People from Greece, Spain, and Egypt were part of those helping with plans for Occupy Wall Street. According to Graeber, the US protesters were the most radical; many were anarchists, opposed to government of any sort and clearly against the capitalist system.

Like the people of Madagascar whom Graeber had studied, the protesters of Occupy Wall Street reached decisions by consensus, relying on a General Assembly (GA) where issues such as how to keep warm on cool fall evenings in the park could be addressed. Graeber refers to this as horizontal organization, rather than the vertical organization of most hierarchical structures. Horizontal leadership has no leaders, no political parties, and no list of demands. Although the protest lasted for nearly two months, Graeber spent only three days there, not wanting celebrity status or an overt leadership role that would nullify his ideas of direct democracy.

Graeber is undaunted by the lack of change in most people's lives following the 2011 demonstrations on Wall Street. He explained to Jo Lateu for the *New Internationalist* (Jan. 2014), "Moments of global revolutionary ferment, like we saw in 1968 or 2011, tend to result in chaos or even regression in the years immediately following, but plant seeds that gradually transform everything."

One significant gain was New York's city council passing a resolution against granting personhood to corporations and their call for Congress to do the same. The movement also created bonds with immigrant-rights groups and unions.

## PERSONAL LIFE

Graeber believes that anarchism is more about practice than theory. "To be an anarchist, for me, is to do that self-consciously, as a way of gradually bringing a world entirely based on those principles into being," he said to Lateu. He began learning to drive a car for the first time in 2011, when he was fifty years old.

## SUGGESTED READING

Bennett, Drake. "David Graeber, the Anti-Leader of Occupy Wall Street." *Bloomberg Businessweek*. Bloomberg, 26 Oct. 2011. Web. 26 Nov. 2014.

Berrett, Dan. "Intellectual Roots of Wall St. Protest Lie in Academe." *Chronicle of Higher Education*. Chronicle of Higher Education, 16 Oct. 2011. Web. 26 Nov. 2014.

Graeber, David. "David Graeber on Acting Like an Anarchist." Interview by Jo Lateu. *New Internationalist*. New Internationalist, Jan. 2014. Web. 26 Nov. 2014.

Graeber, David. "The Occupy Movement and Debt: An Interview with David Graeber." Interview by Gustaaf Houtman. *Anthropology Today* 28.5 (2012): 17–18. Print.

Polletta, Francesca. "'This Is What Democracy Looks Like': A Conversation with Direct Action Network Activists David Graeber, Brooke Lehman, Jose Lugo, and Jeremy Varon." *Social Policy* Summer 2001: 25–30. Print.

Sanneh, Kelefa. "Paint Bombs." *New Yorker*. Condé Nast, 13 May 2013. Web. 26 Nov. 2014.

Shea, Christopher. "A Radical Anthropologist Finds Himself in Academic 'Exile.'" *Chronicle of Higher Education* 19 Apr. 2013: A14–15. Print.

## SELECTED WORKS

*Toward an Anthropological Theory of Value*, 2001; *Fragments of an Anarchist Anthropology*, 2004; *Lost People: Magic and the Legacy of Slavery in Madagascar*, 2007; *Debt: The First 5,000 Years*, 2011; *The Democracy Project*, 2013

—Judy Johnson, MLS

---

# Ariana Grande
**Born:** June 26, 1993
**Occupation:** Singer and actor

While many young singers, such as Selena Gomez and Miley Cyrus, have made their way to the top of the pop charts in the last decade, few seem to have done so with the speed and the power of Ariana Grande, who has topped the charts with two back-to-back hit albums, *Yours Truly* (2013) and *My Everything* (2014). Not very long ago Grande was spending the majority of her time acting in various Nickelodeon channel sitcoms, but that all changed when her debut single "The Way" became one of the most cheerful hits of 2013. Despite being in just her early twenties, she has been hailed as the heir apparent to such powerhouse pop singers as Mariah Carey and Whitney Houston. Many commentators believe that her tremendous and sudden critical and commercial success is due to the fact that her music enjoys a widespread appeal. "Her music isn't only directed at teens," Carissa Tozzi, entertainment director of *Seventeen*, told Jim Farber for the *Daily News* (14 Aug. 2014). "People can appreciate it in their twenties, thirties, forties or whatever age."

Although Grande has been performing since she was a young girl (she even appeared on Broadway as a teenager), she understands that her newfound success as a pop singer has elevated her to an entirely different level of fame, one in which every aspect of her personality is scrutinized. Despite this reality, she believes she remains fundamentally unchanged by these achievements. She told Craig McLean for the *Telegraph* (17 Oct. 2014), "I'm still the same person I've been since I was four years old. Literally. Obviously, I'm a mature adult. But I'm still the same girl. I'm still Ariana from Boca who loves musical theatre, who loves her family, who loves the beach, who loves animals."

## EARLY LIFE

Ariana Grande-Butera was born into an Italian American family in Boca Raton, Florida, on June 26, 1993. Her father, Edward Butera, is a graphic designer, and her mother, Joan Grande, is the chief executive officer of Hose-McCann Communications, a company founded by her late maternal grandfather that builds communications equipment for the US armed forces. She has a half brother, Frankie, who is her senior by about ten years.

Although her childhood was mostly pleasant in her upper-class hometown, she had a difficult time as her parents' marriage staggered and eventually ended in divorce. Of that experience, she recalled to McLean, "Being in the middle of it was so stressful. And of course being made up of both of them—I was like, 'Hey, if they both dislike each other's attributes so much, what am I to like about me? I'm made from these two people and I'm caught in the middle of all this fighting.' It was traumatic."

As her parents' marriage ended, Grande grew closer to her mother. One of the bonds mother and daughter shared—along with Frankie—was a love of musical theater. At age eight Grande won the title part in the local Little Palm Family Theater production of *Annie*. Unwilling to leave her daughter alone during rehearsals and due to the company's house rules that stated that parents could not remain backstage or in the theater, Joan Grande decided to audition for a role and won the part of Daddy Warbucks's maid. By 2008 Grande—who by this point had dropped her father's surname in favor of her current stage name—was living in New York City with her mother and brother, having earned a role in *13*, a Broadway musical about a young adult's adjustment to a new state and school.

Melissa Rose/Flickr/Wikimedia Commons

## GETTING EXPOSURE THROUGH TELEVISION

Although her role in *13* earned her a National Youth Theatre Association Award, Grande's agents believed—despite her commitment to singing and performing—that she would have a better chance of an eventual career in music if she went to Hollywood and pursued acting. "They told me I need[ed] to build a fan base," she told Farber. "They said, 'No one's going to buy an R&B album from a fourteen year old.'"

Grande subsequently moved to Los Angeles. Before long she had secured a role on the Nickelodeon sitcom *Victorious*, which ran from 2010 to 2013. The show focused on a group of teens at a performing arts high school. However, Grande was not particularly happy working as just an actor. Of this period, she told McLean, "I was adjusting to these new things—red carpets, and people wanting pictures with me, and people taking pictures of me when I didn't know they were being taken. There was a lot of weird superficial nonsense that sprouted from it that I definitely wasn't used to. It was very weird. I just really liked performing."

In order to keep singing, Grande performed at a number of sporting events and sang on all of the soundtracks for *Victorious*. Around the time that she turned eighteen, she finally got her heart's desire: a recording contract with Republic Records. Her new manager was none other than Scooter Braun, the veteran responsible for making Justin Bieber a star. Not entirely giving up on acting, though, Grande later appeared as the same character, Cat Valentine, in the short-lived spinoff series *Sam & Cat* (2013–14), which costarred Jennette McCurdy of *iCarly*.

## POP SENSATION

The millions of Twitter followers who had been fans of her work on Nickelodeon certainly did end up playing a role in her breakthrough into the music world. Grande simultaneously burst onto the pop charts in 2013 when she scored a top-ten hit on the Billboard Hot 100 chart with her debut single "The Way." The song, featuring Mac Miller, was taken from her first album, *Yours Truly*, which had been produced by legends such as Babyface and Harmony Samuels. The album stylistically harkens back to the 1990s, drawing comparisons to the best records of that era from such gifted vocalists as Whitney Houston and Mariah Carey. But when asked about the possibility of her individuality as an artist getting lost in such parallels, Grande has confidently responded that she is not concerned. "It's a blessing to get the comparison. . . . It's an incredible compliment but it doesn't worry me, because when you listen to my album as a whole, you get to know me," she said in an interview with Sowmya Krishnamurthy for *Rolling Stone* (11 Sept. 2013).

A commercial success, *Yours Truly* would spawn other hit singles, including "Baby I" and "Right There," and received considerable praise from critics. In a review for the *Los Angeles Times* (6 Sept. 2013), Mikael Wood wrote, "What 'Yours Truly' lacks in thrills, it replaces with charm: this might be the most inviting pop record of 2013, with a bubbly ebullience that makes even its most familiar moves feel fresh."

### MY EVERYTHING

After putting together a quick EP titled *Christmas Kisses* for the 2013 holiday season and performing "The Way" and "Right There" for ABC's *Dick Clark's New Year's Rockin' Eve with Ryan Seacrest*, Grande returned to the studio to produce a proper follow-up to her debut. Despite being a self-proclaimed "micromanaging workhorse," as she explained to Lizzy Goodman for *Billboard* magazine (15 Aug. 2014), Grande relinquished some of that control for the sake of elevating her newest effort. "Everything that I was trained to try and was absolutely positive I would hate, I tried," she added. Her second album, *My Everything*, dropped in mid-2014

and became one of the mainstays of the summer season, beginning with its debut single "Problem," which was a smash hit. Indicative of the clout and respect she had already garnered in the industry, the song also featured popular rapper Iggy Azalea.

The album itself went on to top the Billboard charts that year and was certified double platinum. Its commercial success was due in part to its all-star cast of music producers, including Max Martin, Shellback, Ryan Tedder, and Benny Blanco, as well as vocal cameos by Big Sean and Nicki Minaj. Again, Grande's musical efforts met with considerable critical praise. Writing for *Rolling Stone* magazine (26 Aug. 2014), Rob Sheffield proclaimed, "*My Everything* is where the 21-year-old Nickelodeon starlet grows up. It's a confident, intelligent, brazen pop statement, mixing bubblegum diva vocals with EDM break beats." Fresh off of such positive reception of the album, later that year Grande joined other high-profile artists, including Taylor Swift, Maroon 5, and Sam Smith, on the road for iHeartRadio's annual Jingle Ball Tour.

## PERSONAL LIFE

In 2013 Grande experienced a painful feud and estrangement with her father. The following year she mourned the loss of her grandfather to cancer; he had been an important figure in the singer's life, and she had disrupted her promotional obligations to sit by his bedside. "He was the patriarch of my family, our rock. He will always be my favorite person," she said to Farber.

In interviews Grande has often described herself as an animal lover and activist. After becoming a vegan, she abstains not only from eating animals but also animal products, such as milk and cheese. In 2014 the youth division of the People for the Ethical Treatment of Animals named her the sexiest vegan celebrity. Although she accepted the award, she hardly considers herself a sex symbol but rather a role model for young people with creative ambitions. "I don't feel confident in my sexuality—or in my fashion," Grande remarked to Farber. "It's just not in my mind. I think of music first. I want people to listen instead of look and judge."

Although she was raised Roman Catholic, Grande has said that she broke with the Catholic Church because of its unwillingness to change its traditional teachings on marriage in the wake of the growing acceptance of same-sex marriage in the secular world. Much of her stance stems from her brother's experience living as a gay man. She and her brother began exploring other belief systems and came to embrace Kabbalah, the ancient Jewish tradition of mystical interpretation of biblical scripture. She explained her interest in Kabbalah to McLean: "You have to take a second and breathe and reassess how you want to approach or react to a situation or approach an obstacle, or deal with a negative person in your space. That takes a lot of self-control and practice and, I guess, willpower."

## SUGGESTED READING

Farber, Jim. "Ariana Grande Owes Her Stardom to Singing, Not Sex Appeal." *Daily News.* NYDailyNews.com, 14 Aug. 2014. Web. 19 May 2015.

Goodman, Lizzy. "*Billboard* Cover: Ariana Grande on Fame, Freddy Krueger and Her Freaky Past." *Billboard.* Billboard, 15 Aug. 2014. Web. 19 May 2015.

McLean, Craig. "Ariana Grande: 'If You Want to Call Me a Diva I'll Say: Cool.'" *Telegraph.* Telegraph, 17 Oct. 2014. Web. 19 May 2015.

Sheffield, Rob. Rev. of *My Everything*, by Ariana Grande. *Rolling Stone.* Rolling Stone, 26 Aug. 2014. Web. 19 May 2015.

Wood, Mikael. "Review: Ariana Grande's Charmingly Retrograde 'Yours Truly.'" Rev. of *Yours Truly*, by Ariana Grande. *Los Angeles Times.* Los Angeles Times, 6 Sept. 2013. Web. 19 May 2015.

—Christopher Mari

# Amy Gutmann

**Born:** November 19, 1949
**Occupation:** College president

Amy Gutmann is a respected scholar who has published widely on the topics of access to higher education and health care, identity politics, and the role of ethics in public affairs. For several years she was affiliated with Princeton University, where she was the founding director of the University Center for Human Values, and in 2004 she became the president of the University of Pennsylvania.

Thanks to policies enacted by Gutmann, most University of Pennsylvania students will earn their degrees without the significant debt incurred by many students at other such institutions. Admitted students whose parents earn under $40,000 a year attend at no cost, and the

Stuart A Watson/Wikimedia Commons

school has replaced the loan portion of its financial aid packages with grants, which do not have to be repaid. Some journalists have pointed out that although Gutmann herself once struggled financially, those days are far behind her; her yearly salary is now estimated at $2.8 million, making her one of the highest-paid university presidents in the country.

## EARLY YEARS

Amy Gutmann was born on November 19, 1949, in the New York City borough of Brooklyn. Her father, Kurt Gutmann, had fled Nazi Germany as a college student in 1934, suspecting that the country would soon be facing dramatic changes. Kurt convinced his parents and four siblings to leave Germany with him, and they settled in Bombay, India. Gutmann often tells interviewers that her father's foresight and courage in making the move have been a great source of inspiration.

Kurt opened a metal foundry in Bombay, which became Mumbai in 1995, and ultimately remained in India for more than a dozen years. An avid photographer, he vacationed in the United States in 1948 and met a young woman named Beatrice in New York City. After a whirlwind courtship of just a few months, Kurt and Beatrice married. They lived briefly in India, but as soon as they were able to sell the foundry they moved to New York City, where their only child, Amy, was born.

The family eventually settled in Monroe, New York, a small town about an hour north of New York City. Kurt started a scrap-metal business in the nearby town of Middletown. Despite his efforts, money was always tight, and the family did without many of the things others took for granted, like vacations and new vehicles. Still, Gutmann has been unstinting in her praise for both of her parents. "[They were] just extraordinary people," she told Nicole Weisensee Egan for the *Philadelphia Daily News* (15 Oct. 2004)."And they were terrific parents. My father cared about his family and his business and he was a real intellectual as well. He would come back from the scrap mills with books for me." Gutmann recalls that her father once lugged home an entire set of encyclopedias that he had purchased for her. The couple regularly assured their daughter that they would do whatever it took to see that she got a good education.

## EDUCATION

Kurt, however, did not live to see his daughter graduate from college; he died of a heart attack when she was a junior in high school, in 1966. Beatrice subsequently found work as a secretary at Monroe-Woodbury High School, where her daughter later became class valedictorian. Because money was even tighter after her father died, Gutmann considered only less expensive public colleges. However, her family doctor, who had taken a personal interest in the bright teen, encouraged her to apply for a scholarship to Radcliffe College. (One of the so-called Seven Sisters colleges, Radcliffe was affiliated with Harvard University and fully integrated into the university in 1999.)

As the doctor predicted, Gutmann, who had been the president of her high school math team, won a full scholarship and became the first person from her school ever to enroll at the prestigious college. While she initially considered majoring in math, she changed her focus after taking a course in political philosophy and becoming deeply interested in the importance of education in a democracy and the role of ethics in public affairs. She took part in peaceful student protests against the Vietnam War and learned, as she told Adam Bryant for the *New York Times* (18 June 2011), that conforming did not feel as important in college as it had in high school. "Interestingly, when I got there I realized that fitting in [didn't mean] conforming," she said. "It was having bold ideas and taking risks, smart risks, and branching out beyond one's comfort zone."

Gutmann graduated from Radcliffe magna cum laude in 1971, and the following year she earned a master's degree in political science from the London School of Economics. In 1976 she earned a PhD in political science from Harvard.

## UNIVERSITY POSTS

Gutmann began teaching at Princeton University in New Jersey the same year she earned her doctoral degree. She ultimately remained at the Ivy League institution until 2004, working her way through the academic and administrative ranks. She was made a full professor in 1987 and in 1990 became the founding director of the University Center for Human Values, whose goal is to bring together an interdisciplinary group of academicians interested in important ethical issues in private and public life.

Among her other important titles at Princeton were director of graduate studies (1986–88), director of the program in political philosophy (1987–89), dean of the faculty (1995–97), academic advisor to the president (1997–98), and provost (2001–04). Among her missions as provost was to boost the school's standing in the area of African American studies, and in a widely publicized coup she convinced the prominent black scholars Cornel West and Kwame Anthony Appiah to leave Harvard and join her faculty.

Gutmann has enjoyed a similarly stellar reputation since assuming the presidency of the University of Pennsylvania in 2004, where she also holds the titles of Christopher H. Browne Distinguished Professor of Political Science in the School of Arts and Sciences and Professor of Communication in the Annenberg School for Communication. In her inaugural address, she outlined what she calls the Penn Compact, an ambitious vision statement that mapped out her goals of improving access to the school for bright, qualified applicants, encouraging cross-disciplinary work between its departments, and better connecting the university to the surrounding community and the world. "I believe passionately in the pursuit of knowledge for its own sake," she asserted in the speech. "But I also believe that universities have a responsibility to use knowledge to serve humanity."

In addition to establishing the school's no-loan policy, which guarantees that students from families making less than $40,000 a year attend free of charge and that financial aid packages include grants rather than loans, she has amassed a string of other accomplishments. Under her leadership, the school raised $4.3 billion during its "Making History" campaign, increased green space on its campus by 25 percent, and launched new centers for nanotechnology, medical research, and other fields.

The university announced in 2012 that Gutmann signed a contract to remain in her post until at least 2019. "My parents overcame enormous obstacles so I feel tremendously fortunate to be able to give back to our society and the world," she told Egan. "And the way I can do it best is to lead a great university. Because I think there's nothing more important for the future of democracy than higher education."

## SCHOLARSHIP

Gutmann is renowned for her scholarship on issues relating to the role morality plays in political life and the importance of education to a successful democracy. She has written or co-written more than a dozen books on those topics, including *The Spirit of Compromise: Why Governing Demands It and Campaigning Undermines It* (2012). In the book, which was listed as one of the best academic volumes of the year by *Choice* magazine, Gutmann and co-author Dennis Frank Thompson assert that a refusal to compromise on the part of elected officials has led to congressional gridlock and diminished public trust in government, and they suggest ways to remedy the situation.

Among her other well-regarded books are *Democratic Education* (1987), in which she calls upon parents, teachers, and the state to equip students with the knowledge and skills to uphold democracy, and *Color Conscious: The Political Morality of Race*, which she co-wrote in 1996 with Appiah and which examines the place of race in politics and in moral life.

## PERSONAL LIFE, AWARDS, AND OTHER APPOINTMENTS

In 2009 President Barack Obama named Gutmann the chair of the Presidential Commission for the Study of Bioethical Issues, and in 2014 she was elected chair of the Association of American Universities. Her many honors include the Harvard University Centennial Medal (2003), the Carnegie Corporation Academic Leadership Award (2009), and designation by the editors of *Newsweek* in 2011 as one of the "150 Women Who Shake the World."

Gutmann is a member of the American Academy of Arts and Sciences and the National Academy of Education, and she holds a W. E. B. DuBois Fellowship at the American Academy of Political and Social Science. She has received several honorary degrees, including doctor of laws degrees from both the University of Rochester and Columbia University and a doctor of letters degree from Wesleyan University.

Gutmann is married to Michael W. Doyle, the Harold Brown Professor of Law and International Affairs at Columbia University. Their daughter, Abigail Gutmann Doyle, is an associate professor of chemistry at Princeton.

## SUGGESTED READING

Bryant, Adam. "Welcoming the Wild Ideas of the Week." *New York Times*. New York Times, 18 June 2011. Web. 26 Nov. 2014.

Egan, Nicole Weisensee. "New President to Take Reins at University of Pennsylvania." *Philadelphia Daily News* 15 Oct. 2004. Print.

Gutmann, Amy. "Time for More Women to Lead Our Schools." *Washington Post*. Washington Post, 22 Feb. 2013. Web. 26 Nov. 2014.

Gutmann, Amy. "Inaugural Address." University of Pennsylvania, Philadelphia. 15 Oct. 2014. Address.

O'Neill, James M. "From a Humble Start to Top of the Ivy League Gutmann's Focus on Access Reflects Debt Owed, She Says." *Philadelphia Inquirer*. Philadelphia Media Network, 23 Jan. 2004. Web. 26 Nov. 2014.

Schawbel, Dan. "Penn's Amy Gutmann on Building a Successful Career." *Forbes*. Forbes.com, 11 July 2012. Web. 26 Nov. 2014.

Snyder, Susan. "For Penn, Gutmann's Tenure Is Proving Golden." *Philadelphia Inquirer*. Philadelphia Media Network, 17 Sept. 2012. Web. 26 Nov. 2014.

## SELECTED WORKS

*Liberal Equality*, 1980; *Democratic Education*, 1987; *Democracy and the Welfare State*, 1988; *Ethics and Politics: Cases and Comments*, 1990; *Color Conscious: The Political Morality of Race*, 1996; *Democracy and Disagreement*, 1996; *Identity and Democracy*, 2003; *Why Deliberative Democracy?*, 2004; *The Spirit of Compromise: Why Governing Demands It and Campaigning Undermines It*, 2012

—Mari Rich

# Hakuhō Shō

**Born:** March 11, 1985

**Occupation:** Sumo wrestler

Hakuhō Shō is a Mongolian *rikishi*, or sumo wrestler, whom many have touted as the best competitor in the sport's long and storied history. As of November 2014, Hakuhō was one championship away from becoming the winningest rikishi of all time. Sumo is a highly ritualized Japanese sport. The earliest written records of sumo date back to the eighth century, when it was introduced as a component of the ceremonies performed in the imperial court. Sumo was used as a means of military training in the late twelfth century, but was also considered a dedication to the gods. Everything from a wrestler's training life to his physical appearance carries with it its own religious significance according to the mythology of the sport. Rikishi wear their hair in a top-knot, the shape of which denotes their rank, as does their *kesho-mawashi*, the embroidered apron high-ranking rikishi wear before they compete. The loincloths they wear during matches are called *mawashi*. Referees dress in silk robes and gesture with war fans. They even carry daggers, a nod to the days in which a bad call meant instant seppuku—a gruesome ritual suicide by disembowelment. Sumo became the country's national sport in the seventeenth century, and today, sumo culture in Japan resembles that of American football, with fan blogs, commentary, and commercial player contracts. The business is complex, but the objective is simple. Opponents stand on a raised block of clay about two feet high and twenty-two feet across. Rice-straw bales demarcate the *dohyo*, or the circle in which the fighting takes place. Wrestlers try to push their opponent out of the *dohyo*—which is purified by a Shinto priest before each tournament—or knock them off balance, getting them to touch the mat with any part of their body other than the soles of their feet. Most matches are seconds long, which is why rikishi value their incredible size. Hakuhō stands six feet four inches tall, and weighs a relatively lithe 350 pounds. Some rikishi weigh closer to 600 pounds.

Hakuhō was promoted to *yokozuna*, or grand champion—sumo's highest rank—in 2007. The title holds more symbolic weight than a black belt in karate or even an Olympic gold medal because it is so rare. "In 265 years, sixty-nine men have been promoted to *yokozuna*," Brian Phillips wrote for the sports website *Grantland* (5 Nov.

FourTildes/Wikimedia Commons

2014). Hakuhō is only the fourth non-Japanese wrestler to achieve yokozuna status, though recent years have seen an influx of foreigners in the sport. Despite a number of changing mores—most notably, a movement to train female sumo wrestlers—sumo's ancient ranking system persists. There are six divisions in the sport. The highest two divisions are *Juryo* and *Makuuchi*. Once a rikishi reaches this echelon (the lower of the two divisions being *Juryo*) they are called *sekitori*. *Sekitori* are the real professionals, and unlike lower-ranked rikishi, they draw a salary. Rikishi of any rank can be promoted or demoted according to their match record, except for yokozuna like Hakuhō. Yokozuna can never be demoted, only encouraged to retire. Promotions are recommended by the prestigious Yokozuna Deliberation Council and carried out by the Japan Sumo Association.

Rikishi are traditionally forbidden from showing emotion during their matches, but this is not a problem for the stoic Hakuhō. Hakuhō eschews celebrity culture (unlike other sumo wrestlers) in favor of tradition, harkening back to sumo's mythological roots. From his unusually graceful entrance into the ring, flanked by a *tachimochi*, or attendant, who carries his sword, and a *tsuyuharai*, or dew sweeper, who clears his path, to his prodigious rivalry with Asashōryū Akinori, Hakuhō's rise and reign has been the stuff of legend.

## EARLY LIFE AND TRAINING

Hakuhō Shō is not the wrestler's real name, but his *shikona*, or formal ring name. Hakuhō was born

Mönkhbatyn Davaajargal on March 11, 1985, in the capital city of Ulaanbaatar, Mongolia. His father, Jigjidiin Mönkhbat, is a retired wrestler who won a silver medal at the 1968 Olympic Games in Mexico City. Jigjidiin was a force in Mongolian wrestling, a style of fighting that is similar to sumo with a history just as long. In Mongolia, wrestling, Peter Geoghegan wrote for the London *Independent* (10 Sept. 2014), is "a national obsession." As a child, Hakuhō was skinny but dreamed of becoming a rikishi and "growing as big as a house," according to Phillips. He went to Tokyo in October 2000, but at 137 pounds, no trainer wanted anything to do with him. Traditionally, novices have already entered a *heya*, or a training stable, by the time they are fifteen. Hakuhō was fifteen—and he knew a lot about sumo—but he had no experience and was deemed too old to start.

On his last day in Tokyo, another Mongolian rikishi persuaded the master of the Miyagino heya to accept Hakuhō as an apprentice. In a heya, room and board are provided "in return for a somewhat horrifying life of eating, chores, training, eating, and serving as quasi-slaves to their senior stablemates," Phillips wrote. Novices train under one or more coaches, or *oyakata*. A young trainee begins his day around 4:30 in the morning, as the lowest ranked or unranked rikishi wake first. At morning practice, wrestlers complete exercises to strengthen and improve flexibility in their lower bodies. *Shiko*, the exaggerated and forceful stomping of one foot and then the other, strengthens muscles, while *matawari*, an exercise in which wrestlers sit with legs splayed and touch their chest to the floor, stretches. In another practice known as *teppo*, rikishi toughen up their hands by repeatedly striking a wooden pole with an open palm. Trainees also engage in practice matches and a drill called *butsukari-geiko*, in which wrestlers hurl themselves at one another in an attempt to push each other out of the *dohyo*. Practices at the heya are completely silent—only the coaches are allowed to speak.

A few hours later, young trainees prepare breakfast for everyone at the heya and then clean up afterward. Meals are built around a traditional stew called chankonabe and supplemented with bowls of rice and glasses of beer. Chankonabe is a caloric elixir of chicken (or fish or beef) with cabbage, egg and bean sprouts. The sportswriter Franz Lidz tried one variation of the brew, writing for *Slate* (30 Nov. 2004) that it was "the most exuberantly revolting meal of my life." Hakuhō shared his sentiment. "I ate a lot of [chankonabe]. I've eaten so much I've thrown up," Hakuhō told a reporter as quoted by the Malaysian *Star* (8 June 2007). "My senior sumo wrestlers forced me to eat. That was more difficult than our sumo training." Practices that Americans might refer to as hazing abound in heya culture. In one widely publicized case in 2007, a teenage novice collapsed and died after being beaten by his stable master and stablemates. Rikishi eat breakfast at about noon, and after multiple helpings of chankonabe, take a long nap to slow their digestion and gain weight. In total, they consume about ten thousand calories a day. An afternoon practice and dinner round out the day.

## PROFESSIONAL CAREER

Hakuhō's *shikona*, Hakuhō Shō, means "white Peng." According to Chinese mythology, Peng is a giant bird that transforms from a giant fish, Kun. Hakuhō won his first *basho*, or tournament, in May 2006 at the age of twenty-one. Sumo is a year-round sport. Wrestlers compete in six grand tournaments, *honbasho* or simply *basho*, which are held every two months. Hakuhō was quickly recognized as a sumo prodigy, and the reigning champion of the sport, Asashōryū Akinori, became his most serious rival. "Until Hakuhō came along," Phillips wrote of Asashōryū, "he was, by an enormous margin, the best wrestler in the world." Asashōryū, coincidentally, is also from Mongolia, but in almost every other way, he and Hakuhō were polar opposites. Phillips described Asashōryū—whose name means "morning blue dragon"—as the physical embodiment of sumo's uneasy union with modernity. Asashōryū "was hotheaded, unpredictable, and indifferent to the ancient traditions of a sport," Phillips wrote. He was made a *yokozuna* in 2003, and in many people's eyes, besmirched the title's legacy. He picked fights with his opponents outside the ring, yelled at the referee, and gloated when he won. Sometimes, he showed up to tournaments in a business suit—tradition dictates that rikishi wear a kimono and sandals—other times he showed up drunk. Asashōryū flouted nearly every revered tradition in sumo, while Hakuhō appeared to be tradition incarnate. Phillips wrote that people say Hakuhō is "more Japanese than the Japanese."

Early in Hakuhō's career, Asashōryū was the clear top dog in the rivalry, but as the years went by, it was Hakuhō who gained the upper hand. Hakuhō was promoted to *yokozuna* in 2007, and for the next three years, the two *rikishi* faced off in their prime. In 2009, Kevin Gray, writing for the sports website *Bleacher Report* (24 Jan. 2009), called them the "Nadal and Federer of the sumo world," a reference to Rafael Nadal and Roger Federer, who share one of the most famous rivalries in the history of tennis. Sometimes, their bouts turned ugly, like in 2008, when Asashōryū gave Hakuhō "an extra shove after hurling him down in a tournament," Phillips wrote. Still, when Asashōryū retired unexpectedly amid scandal in 2010, it was Hakuhō who had won the last seven of their matches, making his lifetime record against Asashōryū 14–13.

Hakuhō told a reporter for the *Malaysian Star* (8 June 2007) that he feels pressure to win. "As a yokozuna, you can't lose," he said. "A god can't lose." After Asashōryū retired, Hakuhō rarely did lose. Of watching him compete in 2014, Phillips wrote: "What the others are doing in the ring is fighting. Hakuhō is composing a little haiku of battle." He is graceful but his strength is uncanny. He has tossed 400-pound men out of the dohyo like they were rag dolls. Hakuhō demolished his old adversary's formidable record, and in 2010, went on a sixty-three-match winning streak, tying a record set in the 1780s for the second longest streak in sumo history. Hakuhō is poised to become the greatest rishiki of all time. As of November 2014, he had won thirty-one *makuuchi*—the highest professional sumo division—championships—one championship short of the all-time record.

## SUGGESTED READING

Geoghegan, Peter. "Grunt and Grapple: Mongolia's Passion for Wrestling Fights Off Lures of Booming Economy." *Independent* [London]. 10 Sept. 2014. Web. 20 Nov. 2014.

Gray, Kevin. "Sumo: Confident Asashoryu Faces Hakuho in Last Day Showdown in Tokyo." *Bleacher Report*. Bleacher Report, 24 Jan. 2009. Web. 20 Nov. 2014.

"Hakuhō Ready to Make Debut as Sumo's Newest Grand Champion." *Star* [Malaysia]. Star Publications, 8 June 2007. Web. 20 Nov. 2014.

Lidz, Franz. "From Soup to Guts: Sumo Wrestlers Fatten Up on Chankonabe." *Slate*. Slate Group, 30 Nov. 2004. Web. 20 Nov. 2014.

Phillips, Brian. "Sea of Crises." *Grantland*. ESPN Internet Ventures, 5 Nov. 2014. Web. 20 Nov. 2014.

—Molly Hagan

# Margaret Hamburg

**Born:** July 12, 1955

**Occupation:** Commissioner of the US Food and Drug Administration

Margaret Hamburg made her reputation as New York City's crusading health commissioner in the 1990s by reducing the city's skyrocketing tuberculosis rates through an innovative intervention program. She has since become the twenty-first commissioner of the US Food and Drug Administration (FDA), overseeing the safety of the nation's food and drug supplies. Only the second woman to hold the position, Hamburg began serving under President Barack Obama in May 2009 and has since sought to modernize the FDA's approach to regulation and widen its purview, as more and more of the United States' food and drugs come from a globalized market. Of the FDA's work, Margaret Hamburg remarked to Geng Ngarmboonanant in an interview for the *Politic* (2 Mar. 2013), "I think that there is a necessary and appropriate level of government regulation. Sound, smart regulation by the FDA not only promotes and protects the health and safety of the public, but it supports industry by ensuring clear standards and a level playing field, promoting meaningful innovation, and enhancing trust and confidence in the products it produces."

## EARLY LIFE AND EDUCATION

Margaret Ann Hamburg was born on July 12, 1955, in Chicago, Illinois, the daughter of distinguished physicians who also served as professors at Stanford Medical School. Her mother, Beatrix McCleary, was the first black woman to attend Vassar College, as well as the first to graduate from the Yale School of Medicine. Her father, David Hamburg, is of Jewish ancestry and has held several prestigious positions, including president of the National Academy of Sciences' Institute of Medicine from 1975 to 1980. (Both Hamburg and her parents are members of the Institute of Medicine; she became one of its youngest members upon her election in 1994.) "I grew up right on the Stanford campus, surrounded by many friends and families that were related to the field of medicine . . . so it was always part of part of my experience," Hamburg recalled for the National Library of Medicine's 2003–5 exhibition *Changing the Face of Medicine* (14 Oct. 2003). "But because it was so much a part of my experience, I did have to go through the re-thinking: Is this something I really want to do, or was I just raised to think that of course I would be a doctor?"

Hamburg graduated from Henry M. Gunn Senior High School in Palo Alto, California, in 1973. As a teenager she spent a semester as an intern at the famed British primatologist and anthropologist Jane Goodall's research station in Tanzania. She attended Harvard University from 1973 to January 1978, earning a bachelor's degree in psychology, and continued her studies at Harvard Medical School.

After receiving her medical degree in 1983, Hamburg took a medical residency at the Cornell University Medical College–associated New York Hospital (now NewYork-Presbyterian Hospital) in New York City, where she had her first exposure to the then-emerging AIDS epidemic. "I was taught that the era of infectious disease threats was over with the advent of antibiotics and vaccines and good sanitation practices—and that the future of medicine was chronic disease—and then watched this initially mysterious and devastating disease emerge, with no one knowing the cause, what to call it, or how to treat it," Hamburg told Ngarmboonanant. About her time at the New York Hospital, she continued, "I saw a lot of AIDS patients but I wasn't able to offer them anything. I also saw how this medical disease was causing so much disruption in a variety of social, legal, and political issues." It was this experience that convinced her to pursue a career in public health policy.

### EARLY CAREER

Hamburg completed her residency in 1986. She then moved to Washington, DC, where she worked as a special assistant to the director at the US Department of Health and Human Services' Office of Disease Prevention and Health Promotion. This was followed by another position as special assistant at the National Institutes of Health's (NIH) National Institute of Allergy and Infectious Diseases (NIAID) in nearby Bethesda, Maryland, where her main focus was on AIDS research. "I remember going with [NIAID director] Anthony Fauci to a meeting with AIDS activists in Greenwich Village," Hamburg recalled in an interview with Susan Berfield for *Bloomberg Businessweek* (19 May 2014). "We weren't sure if we would be welcomed or have things thrown at us. It opened my eyes to the fact that if you want to make a difference on serious, complex problems, you have to be willing to sit down with everyone, think and act in new ways, and keep your eye on what the goals are."

### NEW YORK CITY HEALTH COMMISSIONER

In 1990 Hamburg left the NIAID, where she had recently been made assistant director for science policy, to serve as New York City's deputy commissioner for family health services during the administration of Mayor David Dinkins. Within a year, she had been tapped to take over as commissioner of the New York City Department of Health, a position she would hold until 1997, through part of the administration of Mayor Rudolph Giuliani. Just thirty-six years old at the time of her appointment, Hamburg was the youngest health commissioner in the city's history. While the city health commissioner's duties are wide ranging and include everything from providing clinical services to ensuring the environmental health of the city's eight million residents, Hamburg's main task was to help control New York's then-spiraling rates of AIDS and tuberculosis (TB), which had been spurred on in large part by needle sharing among drug addicts. In order to prevent the spread of these diseases, Hamburg supported the implementation of a controversial needle-exchange program, which allowed addicts to exchange their used needles for clean ones.

Tuberculosis was a particular problem in the 1990s, with outbreaks of new drug-resistant strains making the disease the leading infectious cause of death among New York City residents. Treatment entailed daily medication for a period of up to two years, and stopping the medication prematurely only led to increased drug resistance. In order to combat this threat, Hamburg sent workers to patients' homes, or to find homeless patients on the streets, to make sure they followed their drug regimens. She even had Dinkins take a test after he met with someone who later tested positive for tuberculosis. "She took care of me like a newborn," the former mayor recalled to Gardiner Harris for the *New York Times* (11 Mar. 2009). "She's the kind of person you figure can do almost anything." Hamburg's hard work paid off; between 1992 and 1997, the city's tuberculosis rates declined by 46 percent, and the most resistant strains decreased by 86 percent. This innovative TB initiative became a model for tackling tuberculosis infections worldwide.

In addition to these accomplishments, Hamburg improved health services for women and children and, in the years prior to the terrorist attacks of September 11, 2001, oversaw the nation's first public health bioterrorism program. Her work as New York's health commissioner drew the attention of the administration of President Bill Clinton. In 1993 she was Clinton's first choice to head his newly created post of AIDS coordinator, but she declined the position because she was expecting her first child at the time. Four years later, in 1997, she accepted Clinton's invitation to serve as assistant secretary for planning and evaluation at the Department of Health and Human Services, where she worked on the nation's preparedness to respond to national health threats ranging from flu pandemics to terrorist attacks.

## THE NUCLEAR THREAT INITIATIVE

In 2001 Hamburg became a founding member of the Nuclear Threat Initiative (NTI), developed by media mogul Ted Turner and former US senator Sam Nunn to reduce the threat of weapons of mass destruction around the world. Hamburg was eager to work in the area of naturally occurring biological threats, though she originally intended to do so for only a year in order to devote some time to her family. However, in the wake of the September 11, 2001, terrorist attacks on New York City and Washington, DC, the group's work took on an added urgency. In a May 2003 speech to graduating students at Bowdoin College, Hamburg remarked, as quoted by Randy James for *Time* magazine (12 Mar. 2009), "I believe that in this age of terror, the only thing that can stop a small group of committed individuals is a large group of committed individuals. Only all of us acting together, with wise policies and sound judgments, can make our world safer."

Hamburg served as the NTI's vice president for biological programs from 2001 to 2005, addressing the dangers of bioterrorism as well as issues such as flu pandemics. She relinquished the position in 2005 to become a senior scientist at the NTI. "I stepped down from an executive role and became a senior scientist when my daughter said, 'Why can't I have a normal mother who doesn't talk about anthrax all the time?'" Hamburg said to Berfield. "I had been there for a while. As a senior scientist, I had a very flexible

schedule, I was on lots of committees and one corporate board."

## THE FOOD AND DRUG ADMINISTRATION

Hamburg left the Nuclear Threat Initiative in 2009 when she was nominated by President Barack Obama to head the Food and Drug Administration, a $2 billion agency that oversees the safety of the nation's food and drug supplies. The FDA's influence is considerable, accounting for the regulation of roughly a quarter of every dollar spent on various products in the United States. When Hamburg took over as FDA commissioner, the agency had suffered through a series of scandals in recent years, including the deaths of a number of people who had consumed tainted peanut products, as well as too-close ties to the pharmaceutical industry that caused the FDA to approve medicines later proved to be harmful.

From her earliest days in office, Hamburg has tried to make the FDA as robust an agency as possible in order to safeguard the country's food and medical supplies. "Strengthening FDA's programs and policies will help us protect the safety of the food supply, give the public access to safe and effective medical products, find novel ways to prevent illness and promote health, and be transparent in explaining our decision making," she said, as quoted on the FDA's official website (17 Jan. 2014). "A strong FDA is an agency that the American public can count on."

The FDA's various responsibilities include regulating certain tobacco products (since 2009), studying the rise of antibiotic resistance in humans, protecting the nation's food supply from harm, controlling disease outbreaks, and approving drug trials. Hamburg has also helped broaden the FDA's reach internationally by meeting with foreign officials to improve the safety of food and drugs shipped from overseas. (As of 2014, approximately 80 percent of US seafood, 50 percent of fresh fruit, and 20 percent of vegetables are imported, as are 40 percent of completed drugs and 50 percent of medical devices.) Shortly after her first official visit to China, Hamburg said, as quoted by Alicia Mundy for the *Wall Street Journal* (6 Oct. 2010), "[Chinese food and drug regulators] have a growing recognition that the Chinese export brand is at risk if they don't take better care with the safety of the food and drug supplies they are sending to us."

Because the FDA is a fact-based regulatory organization, Hamburg is often faced with the prospect of having to pull drugs off the market after scientific studies demonstrate that the medicine either does not work as initially believed or could in fact be dangerous to consumers. "One of the things that's really hard is when you have to make a decision about a product that held great potential, and patients and their families were hoping this would be the answer," Hamburg told Berfield. "But then the data show it doesn't work. Saying no is very, very tough." She described one such case, involving a cancer drug called Avastin: "The FDA had given [Avastin] tentative approval with the requirement that the company manufacturing it continue to do studies. The data did not support that approval, and I had to withdraw it. That was a decision I had to make myself, and it was one that was being scrutinized by patients and doctors who thought the drug was helping them."

## PERSONAL LIFE

Margaret Hamburg is married to Peter Fitzhugh Brown, a hedge-fund manager and researcher in artificial intelligence who was instrumental in persuading her to accept both the New York job and the position of FDA commissioner. Prior to the latter, the couple had to either sell or forfeit several hundred thousand dollars' worth of stocks, stock options, and hedge-fund holdings in various drug companies in order to avoid any conflict of interest.

Hamburg and Brown have two children, Rachel and Evan. Hamburg was the first New York City health commissioner to give birth while in office, and her name is listed on her children's birth certificates twice, both as their mother and as the commissioner.

## SUGGESTED READING

"Dr. Margaret Hamburg." *Changing the Face of Medicine*. Natl. Lib. of Medicine, 14 Oct. 2003. Web. 15 Sept. 2014.

Hamburg, Margaret. "How the FDA Chief Deals with Disappointed Patients and E-Cigarettes." Interview by Susan Berfield. *Bloomberg Businessweek*. Bloomberg, 19 May 2014. Web. 15 Sept. 2014.

Hamburg, Margaret. "The Woman in Charge: Margaret Hamburg." Interview by Geng Ngarmboonanant. *Politic*. Yale U, 2 Mar. 2013. Web. 15 Sept. 2014.

Harris, Gardiner. "Ex–New York Health Commissioner Is FDA Pick." *New York Times*. New York Times, 11 Mar. 2009. Web. 15 Sept. 2014.

James, Randy. "Obama's FDA Pick: Margaret Hamburg." *Time*. Time, 12 Mar. 2009. Web. 15 Sept. 2014.

"Meet Margaret A. Hamburg, MD, Commissioner of Food and Drugs." *US Food and Drug Administration*. Dept. of Health and Human Services, 17 Jan. 2014. Web. 15 Sept. 2014.

Mundy, Alicia. "FDA Chief Focuses on Antibiotic Resistance." *Wall Street Journal*. Dow Jones, 6 Oct. 2010. Web. 15 Sept. 2014.

—Christopher Mari

# Victor Davis Hanson

**Born:** September 5, 1953
**Occupation:** Historian and scholar

Victor Davis Hanson is one of America's preeminent historians, highly regarded for his exhaustive studies on the history of warfare and agriculture, military history, foreign affairs, and the ancient world. He has received a host of honors for his work, including the National Humanities Medal, which was presented to him by President George W. Bush in 2007. He is perhaps best known for his book *Carnage and Culture* (2001), which was published just prior to the terrorist attacks of September 11, 2001, but the book argued forcefully for the military superiority of Western nations throughout history.

Hanson remarked in a biographical article by Robert Messenger for the National Endowment for the Humanities website: "I don't see enough people standing up to defend the West. We don't realize how tenuous its legacy is and how it has to be transmitted from generation to generation. . . . The legacy of the West is a guidance system through the natural perils of human nature and behavior." Among his many books is *The Savior Generals*, published in 2013.

## EARLY LIFE AND EDUCATION

The son of a school administrator and one of California's first female judges, Victor Davis Hanson was born in Selma, California, on September 5, 1953. He and his brothers were the fifth successive generation to be raised on the family's forty-three-acre orchard and vineyard farm. Hanson's parents taught all of their sons the value of hard work and imbued them with an understanding of the changelessness of the human condition. "I see my whole career as integrated. I grew up on a farm and inherited a tragic view from my parents and grandparents," Hanson remarked to Messenger. "Studying the classics for eight years, both here and abroad, and teaching them for twenty years, all reiterated the sense that human nature was unchanging and the human ordeal predictable. Whether it was working on a farm or reading Sophocles or Thucydides, the message kept being reiterated in different ways: Nothing really changes."

For a time, Hanson contemplated becoming an attorney, but as an undergraduate at the University of California, Santa Cruz, he became immersed in the classics, avidly absorbing the works of the ancient Greeks and Romans. He earned his bachelor's degree with the highest honors in 1975 before traveling to Athens, Greece, to continue his studies at the American School of Classical Studies from 1978 to 1979. He returned to the United States to earn his doctorate in the classics at Stanford University in 1980.

Unable to find work as a classicist and feeling a responsibility to his family farm following his grandfather's death, Hanson returned to farming full time from 1980 to 1984. During this period, the Italian classicist Emilio Gabba read and admired Hanson's dissertation and offered to publish it. *Warfare and Agriculture in Classical Greece* was published in 1983 and found considerable praise among classicists, who admired how Hanson demonstrated the flaws in the then-prevailing theory that invading armies systematically uprooting orchards and vineyards had brought about famine in the Greek city-states. Hanson knew from personal experience how difficult it is to uproot vine systems with modern technology and understood that it would be nearly impossible for ancient peoples to have done so with less developed tools.

## WORKING AS AN EDUCATOR

When the price of raisins collapsed in 1984, Hanson took on additional employment at California State University, Fresno, where he first began teaching Latin and later helped to found the college's classics department. "CSU Fresno has a high number of minority students and poor kids. We had to make the argument to a Hispanic kid that he should invest a thousand hours a year in Greek when he nevertheless had student loans to pay and a job to work, and when his family couldn't see any correlation between reading Aeschylus and success," he remarked to Messenger. "But the basic skills one needs to be successful in society are not always vocational. You

will succeed or fail by the degree to which you reason, speak, and write well. The Greeks give us a blueprint for such mastery."

In 1991, Hanson received the distinguished American Philological Association Award for Excellence in the Teaching of Classics at the College Level, which is presented annually to the best undergraduate educators of Greek and Latin in the United States. In addition to teaching at California State University, Fresno, he was a visiting classics professor at Stanford University from 1991 to 1992 and the visiting Shifrin Professor of Military History at the US Naval Academy in Annapolis, Maryland, from 2002 to 2003. He serves as the Martin and Illie Anderson Senior Fellow in Residence in Classics and Military History at the Hoover Institution, Stanford University, and as the Wayne and Marcia Buske Distinguished Fellow in History at Hillsdale College. In this latter capacity, he teaches courses in both classical culture and military history. He told Neal Conan in an interview for NPR (10 May 2010) that there is a very great need to teach military history, a subject often overlooked at American universities: "We can learn from history and try to avoid wars in the future by learning what causes them in the past."

## MAJOR THEMES AND WORKS

Hanson has been steadily publishing books since the early 1980s. *The Western Way of War* (1989) sold particularly well and helped to establish his reputation as a notable historian of farming, the ancient world, and the practice of warfare—subjects not often covered by modern historians. His books have earned numerous recognitions: *Fields Without Dreams: Defending the Agrarian Idea* (1996) was named the Bay Area Book Reviewers nonfiction winner of the year; *The Land Was Everything: Letters from an American Farmer* (2000) was named a notable book of the year by the *Los Angeles Times*; and *Carnage and Culture* was a *New York Times* Best Seller that sought to explain why Western nations had so often prevailed in warfare. In it, Hanson used nine landmark battles from the classical period to the modern age to bolster his thesis. In a review of *Carnage and Culture* for the *New York Times* (12 Aug. 2001), Geoffrey Parker wrote that Hanson "more than makes his case that 'technology, capital, the nature of government, how men are mustered and paid, not merely muscular strength and the multitude of flesh, are the great levelers in conflicts between disparate cultures, and so far more often determine which side wins and which loses—and which men are to die and which to live on.'"

Another of Hanson's notable books is *A War Like No Other* (2006), which describes the epic series of pitched battles between the Greek city-states of Athens and Sparta that occurred from 431 BCE to 404 BCE and are known collectively as the Peloponnesian War. In this work, he describes a side of the ancient Greeks—revered today for their democratic and philosophical ideals—that is often glossed over: their ruthlessness and brutality in warfare. Reviewing *A War Like No Other* for the *Washington Post* (15 Jan. 2006), Tracy Lee Simmons called Hanson "one of our premier military historians" and noted that the book "demonstrates the care of an avid, meticulous scholar whose learning can be worn lightly because it's so assured. He has also become a formidable journalist in recent years, which has prompted him to produce prose that is starkly appealing, direct, and accessible to the common, curious reader."

In *The Savior Generals*, he demonstrates the value of independent thinking and good leadership found in five ancient and modern military commanders—Themistocles, Belisarius, William Tecumseh Sherman, Matthew Ridgway, and David Petraeus—whom Hanson believes saved their forces from utter defeat. By linking figures from the distant past to a general such as Petraeus, who masterminded the troop surge in Iraq to turn around a failing war effort, Hanson again presses his point that history not only has much to teach our modern world but could also help to prevent many mistakes in future wars or even to prevent war entirely. In a review for the *Wall Street Journal* (23 May 2013), Mark Moyar called Hanson "one of his generation's most notable historians" and wrote of *The Savior Generals*: "Although his portraits come from the military realm—ranging from the classical period to the current day—they illustrate eternal verities that arise in all types of endeavor, and they capture attributes associated with master strategists in all walks of life, such as a disregard for conventional wisdom and an intuitive grasp of the big picture."

## OTHER WRITINGS AND AWARDS

Hanson has received numerous awards and honors throughout his long career. He received a fellowship from the National Endowment for the Humanities at the Center for Advanced Studies in the Behavioral Sciences in Stanford, California, from 1992 to 1993 and was an Alexander Onassis fellow in 2001. He was the recipient of the Eric Breindel Award for opinion journalism in 2002, the National Humanities Medal in 2007, and the Bradley Prize in 2008. Additionally, he earned the Wriston Lectureship at the Manhattan Institute in 2004 and the Nimitz Lectureship in Military History at the University of California, Berkeley, in 2006.

The author, coauthor, or editor of more than twenty books, he has also written hundreds of pieces for such publications as the *Claremont Review of Books*, the *Daily Telegraph*, the *International Herald Tribune*, the *Los Angeles Times*, the *New York Post*, the *New York Times*, the *Wall Street Journal*, the *Washington Post*, and the *Wilson Quarterly*. He has written a weekly column for the online edition of the *National Review* since 2001 and a syndicated weekly column for Tribune Media Services since 2004. Hanson's books also include *The Father of Us All* (2010), a collection of essays about ancient and modern warfare, and the historical novel *The End of Sparta* (2011), which described the Epaminondas invasion through the eyes of an ordinary farmer.

## SUGGESTED READING

Hanson, Victor Davis. Interview by Neal Conan. "Hanson on War: 'The Father of Us All.'" *NPR Books*. NPR, 10 May 2010. Web. 27 Jan. 2015.

Messenger, Robert. "Awards and Honors: 2007 National Humanities Medalist—Victor Davis Hanson." *NEH.gov*. National Endowment for the Humanities, n.d. Web. 27 Jan. 2015.

Parker, Geoffrey. "'Carnage and Culture': Explaining Western Military Dominance." *New York Times*. New York Times, 12 Aug. 2001. Web. 27 Jan. 2015.

Simmons, Tracy Lee. "The Greek Way of War." *Washington Post*. Washington Post, 15 Jan. 2006. Web. 27 Jan. 2015.

## SELECTED WORKS

*Warfare and Agriculture in Classical Greece*, 1983; *The Western Way of War*, 1989; *Fields Without Dreams: Defending the Agrarian Idea*, 1996; *The Land Was Everything: Letters from an American Farmer*, 2000; *Carnage and Culture*, 2001; *A War Like No Other: How the Athenians and Spartans Fought the Peloponnesian War*, 2005; *The Father of Us All*, 2010; *The End of Sparta*, 2011; *The Savior Generals*, 2013

—Christopher Mari

# Bobby Holland Hanton
**Born:** 1984
**Occupation:** Stunt performer

Although he says people usually do not believe him when he tells them about what he does for a living, Bobby Holland Hanton is not bothered. He knows that he has appeared in dozens of movies along with—technically in place of—such stars as Daniel Craig, Christian Bale, Ryan Reynolds, Channing Tatum, Jake Gyllenhaal, and Chris Hemsworth. He has portrayed everyone from James Bond to a list full of superheroes. His years of training and expertise have made him one of the most in-demand and versatile stunt doubles for hit films and renowned directors. On the job, Hanton has jumped from one rooftop to another, fallen one hundred feet, and been hit by both people and cars—usually several times in one day—saving the actors the anxiety, trouble, and possible injury or death if they were to perform these dangerous feats themselves. After breaking into the film industry in a major way as Craig's stunt double in *Quantum of Solace* (2008), Hanton has gone on to assume roles in a wide range of films, including *Inception* (2010), *Harry Potter and the Deathly Hallows: Part 1* (2010) and *Part 2* (2011), *Green Lantern* (2011), *The Dark Knight Rises* (2012), *Skyfall* (2012), and *Thor: The Dark World* (2013). Adding to his repertoire, he also became a spokesperson for Dove Men+Care in 2012.

Imeh Akpanudosen/Getty Images

which made him more in tune with his physicality, Hanton was ready for the challenge and accepted the job. As part of the acrobatic shows he participated in, he performed high-diving stunts from thirty feet. After finishing his stint as a performer at Legoland, he landed occasional commercial work requiring his acrobatic and gymnastic skills and continued appearing in live shows. From there, he began his unexpected journey toward the film stage.

## GROWTH NOT STUNTED

Bobby Holland Hanton grew up in Portsmouth, England. Around the age of four, Hanton took up gymnastics, competing for England in the under-seventeen category. His mother, Jane, regularly took him to gymnastics practice, sacrificing her own time, and he has always been grateful, he told Ruth Scammell for the Portsmouth *News* (26 June 2012). When he later progressed from the gym mats to Hollywood explosions and chase scenes, she has requested that he not "tell her anything if it's too dangerous," he added.

Leaving the sport at the age of seventeen, at least in part, according to Elizabeth Holmes for the *Wall Street Journal* (13 Nov. 2012), because he had grown too tall, Hanton then played semi-professional soccer for Fareham Town. One day, he noticed a newspaper ad that altered his life's direction; Legoland Windsor Resort, a theme park in England, was looking for acrobatic performers. Thanks to his training in gymnastics,

## SIX REQUIREMENTS OF BEING A STUNT DOUBLE

Hanton heard from former gymnast friends about the United Kingdom stunt performers' union register—a directory published by the Joint Industry Stunt Committee (JISC), whose aim is to maintain standards and safety in the profession—and became intrigued. He learned that there were about twelve disciplines to choose from and that in order to get on the register and be considered for work as a stunt performer, he had to qualify in at least six categories.

As he explained to Nick Collias for Bodybuilding.com (5 Nov. 2012), from around the age of twenty-one, he dedicated the next few years to training in between working to finance his mission: "It was difficult, because basically you have to fund it yourself, and you have to find the time yourself. . . . So I worked in live shows, and on my days off I would go and train and inject all of my money into that." Like his friends,

Hanton already had a head start with gymnastics—and he knew how to high dive and use the trampoline—but the rest was fairly new. Ultimately, after years of hard work, he qualified with the following skills: swimming, kickboxing, gymnastics, trampoline, scuba diving, and ten-meter high diving.

## HOLLYWOOD BECKONS

At the age of twenty-three, before he was officially finished with his training, Hanton got word from a stunt coordinator of an audition for a performer about six feet tall (Hanton is six feet one) with acrobatic skills. It was for the new Bond film *Quantum of Solace*, starring Craig. There were not many people on the stunt register with the acrobatic, gymnastic, and spatial awareness skills that Hanton possessed, but securing the role was still not easy. He had to endure five difficult auditions with the stunt coordinator and the fight team that involved various assault courses and prove that he was good on the ropes.

He got the job, which meant he had to put his training on hold. On the other hand, being Craig's stunt double in a Bond film proved to be a kind of training in itself. For that film, his first, Hanton had to do a stunt that, years later, he would describe as one of the most dangerous he has ever done: a rooftop chase scene involved jumping from building to building, about 130 feet above ground. In an interview with Ryan Joseph for *Esquire* (30 Oct. 2012), he expressed how invaluable this first experience was: "I learned a lot and had to in the six-month period that I worked on that movie. I'm sure if you speak to any stunt performer from the UK, the biggest stunt job you could ask for is to double in a James Bond movie. . . . It kick-started my stunt career, and I've been working solid. But that will always be one movie that will stick out in my mind."

After following this role over the next four years with other impressive gigs in such films as *Inception*, *Harry Potter*, and *Green Lantern*, Hanton experienced one of his other proudest scenes in the Batman film *The Dark Knight*, which starred Bale. Yet again, this stunt involved great heights. "On *The Dark Knight Rises*, when I was Bruce Wayne, I had to climb out of the prison he's in and jump, miss the landing, fall one hundred feet, and slam into the opposite wall," he told Melia Robinson for *Business Insider* (12 Sept. 2013). "It was one of my first ever high-falls, a one-hundred-footer, which is quite a nice feat to achieve for a stunt performer." Putting on the Batman suit was a proud moment in itself; he described it to Hugh Blackstaffe for the website *One Room with a View* (17 June 2014) as a "dream come true."

## DOUBLE IN DEMAND

Although Hanton has become a successful stunt man, he has been sure to credit the team that surrounds him: stunt and fight coordinators, other stunt professionals, and the actors. Being a good stunt performer, Hanton often says, is not about doing something only once—whether it is a jump, a fall, taking a punch to the head, or being thrown out of a moving car—but about being able to do it over and over again. For a single stunt, a director might require many takes. He is also—sometimes painfully—aware that if he wants to have a long career in stunt work, he has to be able to get up, perhaps a bit bruised, and get back to work; then, when that project is over, he has to be able to move on to the next film in as good a shape. It can be physically wearing, he told Joseph: "If I'm getting smashed into a wall, I jam my arm . . . the next day I'm hitting the same exact point, people don't realize—you only see it once. But you do it six, seven, maybe ten times."

Hanton not only stays in excellent physical shape throughout the year, following a strict diet and exercise regimen (except for the one day a week he reserves for downtime and occasional sweets), but he also has to change his shape depending on the actor he will be doubling. Although Craig was somewhat muscular for the 2006 Bond film *Casino Royale*, he was quite lean for *Quantum of Solace*. This meant that Hanton, who is very muscular, had to get leaner; to achieve that physique, he swam routinely. When he was Reynolds's stunt man for *Green Lantern*, he had to bulk up, focusing on his upper body. As Bale's stunt man for *The Dark Knight Rises*, he had to focus on his biceps and maintain a lean, yet muscular, physique. For *Thor: The Dark World*, he tried to get even bigger, like the lead actor Hemsworth, who is a bit taller and naturally big and muscular. Hanton had to do a lot of upper-body circuit training to increase muscle mass (he gained about twelve pounds for the role). The physical training for Thor was, overall, one of the hardest he has had to deal with to date. In addition to training and exercise, Hanton is hyper aware of what he eats, which changes depending on what kind of shape he needs to be in for a particular movie.

## UPS AND DOWNS OF A DOUBLE LIFE

Hanton is often asked if he ever gets scared before a big stunt. Despite his ample training and experience, on at least one occasion he has admitted to feeling some anxiety. As he told Collias, "I can't speak for everyone, but I'm going to be honest and say there are a lot of stunts we do that do scare me. But then that scared part gets overridden with adrenaline and I say, 'Let's do this. I know I can do this.'" He went on, "Once it is safe and done, it is such a wonderful feeling to know that something people think is not possible can be done. Don't get me wrong, we get knocks and bruises, and it doesn't always go as planned, but that is part of what we signed up for. The buzz side of it, and the adrenaline side of it, totally overrides the worry of getting injured."

The job does at times provide moments of levity as well, Hanton says. For example, he told Scammell, "It can be quite funny. You're fighting in a wig and tache and the tache starts coming off. You think, 'I can't believe this is my job.'" The irony is, Scammell points out, that many others cannot believe it either. When Hanton tells people that he is a professional stunt performer, they usually think he is kidding. Or, as he stated to Scammell, "They think it's a wind-up." In reality, he has been part of stellar stunt crews in blockbuster films that have garnered multiple awards and nominations. Hanton was part of the stunt team for *Skyfall* that was honored in 2013 with a Screen Actors Guild Award for outstanding action performance by a stunt ensemble in a motion picture.

## PERSONAL LIFE

When it comes to his personal life, Hanton explained to Robinson that he appreciates being able to live his dream while maintaining his privacy: "I like that I can go to work with amazing people, do a job that I love, and as soon as it's finished, I can go home and it's just me. When actors become big, they can't really be themselves anymore." On those rare days when he does not hit the gym and relaxes instead, he also enjoys visiting friends and family as well as getting a full eight hours of sleep.

## SUGGESTED READING

Davis, Noah. "Confessions of Hollywood's Leading Stunt Double." *Details*. Condé Nast, 1 Oct. 2013. Web. 24 Oct. 2014.

Hanton, Bobby Holland. "Here's What It's Like Being the Stunt Double behind Batman, Thor, and James Bond." Interview by Melia Robinson. *Business Insider*. Business Insider, 12 Sept. 2013. Web. 24 Oct. 2014.

Hanton, Bobby Holland. "Man behind the Masks: *Skyfall* Stuntman Bobby Holland Hanton." Interview by Nick Collias. *Bodybuilding.com*. Bodybuilding.com, 5 Nov. 2012. Web. 24 Oct. 2014.

Hanton, Bobby Holland. "Q&A: Secrets of the Bond Stuntman." Interview by Ryan Joseph. *Esquire*. Hearst Communications, 30 Oct. 2012. Web. 24 Oct. 2014.

Hanton, Bobby Holland. "12 Rounds with Bobby Holland Hanton." Interview by Hugh Blackstaffe. *One Room with a View*. One Room with a View, 17 June 2014. Web. 24 Oct. 2014.

Holmes, Elizabeth. "Building a Body for Bond, Batman and More." *Wall Street Journal*. Dow Jones, 13 Nov. 2012. Web. 24 Oct. 2014.

Scammell, Ruth. "The Name's Hanton, Bobby Holland Hanton!" *News* [Portsmouth, England]. Johnston, 26 June 2012. Web. 24 Oct. 2014.

## SELECTED WORKS

*Quantum of Solace*, 2008; *Inception*, 2010; *Harry Potter and the Deathly Hallows: Part 1*, 2010; *Harry Potter and the Deathly Hallows: Part 2*, 2011; *Green Lantern*, 2011; *The Dark Knight Rises*, 2012; *Skyfall*, 2012; *Thor: The Dark World*, 2013; *Jupiter Ascending*, 2015

—Dmitry Kiper

# Neil Harbisson

**Born:** July 27, 1982
**Occupation:** Artist and activist

Imagine being an artist who cannot see color—Neil Harbisson, such a person, was born with achromatopsia, a hereditary disease that prevents one from seeing color. Therefore, Harbisson spent the first part of his artistic career painting in black and white. However, he eventually had a device implanted into his head—which he calls an "eyeborg"—that translates colors into sound, allowing him to "see" color. He is considered by some to be the first cyborg artist. "At the beginning, I felt that I was wearing a device but slowly the software started to feel more and more as an extension of my senses," he explained to Scott Simon for NPR's *Weekend Edition* (11 Jan. 2014). "And there was a point where I couldn't differentiate the software from my brain. I started to dream in color so my brain was reproducing the sound of the software. And I started to feel that the antenna was no longer a device that I was wearing but a part of my body."

## EARLY LIFE AND EDUCATION

Harbisson was born in Belfast, Ireland, but raised in a coastal town in Catalonia, Spain. His mother is Spanish and an amateur artist. He was born with achromatopsia, meaning he could see in greyscale only. Before his diagnosis, at age eleven, his parents thought he was merely confusing his colors or was unable to differentiate between them. He associated colors with ideas; in his childhood, for example, he considered pink to be a hippie girl and blue as an intelligent boy he knew. He was teased at school—one of his memories is of being given a red pen but being told that it was blue, causing him to write his paper in the wrong color ink.

As an adolescent, Harbisson wore only black and white clothing, wanting an altogether colorless world, and thought of finding and moving to an island without color. He soon realized his efforts were useless. As he told Guy Raz for NPR's *TED Radio Hour* (7 Mar. 2014), "If you think about chemistry, there's importance in the color of the material. And color is also in literature. You find color in every book. Every three or four pages, you find the name of a color. Even with things that have nothing to do with color like Yellow Pages or Bluetooth or the green card or James Brown. Brown is in his name. It's everywhere."

Harbisson went to Dartington College of Arts in Devon, England, to study experimental music composition, with thoughts of becoming a concert pianist. While there, however, he heard Adam Montandon, the founder of HMC Media-Lab, speak about cybernetics. He approached Montandon after the lecture and told him of his limitations. On the train ride back to his home, Montandon puzzled over how to create color via sound waves and cybernetics.

## BECOMING A CYBORG

In 2004, Harbisson was fitted with a device that transmits light into higher and lower frequencies of sound. The frequencies of light waves correspond to color from infrared to ultraviolet. The first color he saw with his device was red, on a

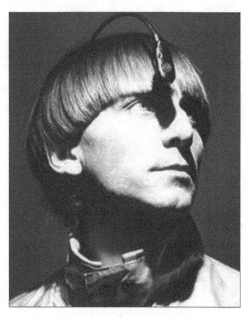

Dan Wilton/The Red Bulletin/Wikimedia Commons

sign; red became his favorite color for years. The early device, which he developed with Montandon, processed only six colors; later he was able to hear 360 hues of color. His device included an antenna he wore attached to his head, which in turn was attached to headphones and a computer. Later he began using pressure through bone conduction to sense color. For the first five weeks, he had headaches from the sounds that colors produced. It took him about five months to distinguish the colors represented by sounds.

Harbisson spent a year trying to persuade hospital administrators in Barcelona, where he lives, to agree to surgically implant the device. Most thought he was joking; he ended up discussing the matter with the bioethics team. In 2013, Harbisson's device was implanted using three screws, two of them to support the electronic chip and antenna and one to transmit the sound. He began to dream in color, a signal to him that the device was working.

Harbisson does not regard the implanted device as unnatural, citing both other creatures with antennae and dolphins, which communicate through bone conduction. He believes humans can use other senses that are in nature to enhance their abilities without becoming robots. As he told Simon, "To create technology and then apply it to ourselves is something only humans can do, so I feel much more human now that I have technology in me."

## THE CYBORG FOUNDATION

In 2010, Harbisson cofounded the Cyborg Foundation with his childhood friend Moon Ribas. Located in Barcelona, the Cyborg Foundation exists to develop further cybernetic extensions and enhancements. Experiments include the "earborg," which modifies sound into color, and a "speedborg," which uses an electronic earring to allow the wearer to detect movement. Another project is 360-degree sensory extension, allowing the wearer to sense movement behind his or her body using vibrations. The foundation also donates eyeborg software.

Harbisson hopes for increased use of these kinds of modifications, citing a sensor that could enable blind or sight-impaired people to read without Braille. As he told Stuart Jeffries for the *Guardian* (6 May 2014), "We'll start with really simple things, like having a third ear on the back of our heads. Or we could have a small vibrator with an infrared detector built into our heads to detect if there's a presence behind us." He also foresees using his own blood circulation to charge the antenna of his device. Currently, he recharges via a USB port at the back of his head.

One of the nonprofit's stated goals is to protect cyborg rights. These rights include being able to go shopping or to attend a film without suspicion of illegal activity. Harbisson was kicked out of Harrods, the famous London department store, because he was deemed a security threat. He was not welcome at movie theaters, where he was suspected of bootlegging films with his device. He battled to have his device included as part of his passport photograph. He successfully contended that because he considers the eyeborg part of his body, it should be part of his official photo. As Harbisson told Raz, "I don't feel that I'm wearing technology. And I don't feel that I'm using technology. I feel that I am technology. I feel like the antenna is a part of my body, which is an unusual feeling, but it makes sense. When you've been wearing it for so long, your body just accepts this as a part of you."

## WORKING IN COLOR

After Harbisson began to hear color, he began to paint the sounds. As he explained in an interview for the *New York Times* (27 Nov. 2013), "Since I hear color, I paint music and play colors. I use canvases as scores and colors as notes. My works are based on transposing colors to sound and sounds to color. The colors of my paintings are invisible to me and silent to the viewer.

Therefore, the artwork lies somewhere between both perceptions."

A painting begins with the first note of a piece, which Harbisson places in the center of the canvas. He then adds color note by note, with the final note being a kind of frame for the entire canvas. The colors correspond to frequencies of light. For example, the frequency of a note between F and F-sharp is always red. When Harbisson painted Ludwig von Beethoven's "Für Elise," it came out predominately in pinks and purples.

Transposing notes to color has increased Harbisson's knowledge and appreciation of music. He hears much of Wolfgang Amadeus Mozart's music as yellow, because of all the G notes, but Justin Bieber, who uses many Ds and Es, is pink. He has extended his range of color perception to include ultraviolet and infrared frequencies; the latter is his favorite color, because of its low humming sound.

Hearing color has given him a new appreciation for the works of artists such as Mark Rothko and Andy Warhol, whose work produces a clear sound. He finds works by Diego Velázquez and Edvard Munch disturbing; because these artists use many shades in the same color family, the sound becomes muddy and threatening. He has also found that cities are not gray but that each has a particular hue that matches them. For example, he hears Lisbon as yellow turquoise and Madrid as amber terra-cotta.

Harbisson has also done portraits of famous people, finding surprising correspondences. For example, he noted that actress Nicole Kidman and Britain's Prince Charles sound the same around the eyes. He sometimes will create audience portraits at a concert. He has discovered that skin is not black, tan, or white; all skin colors are somewhere on the scale of orange.

## THE CYBORG FOUNDATION'S TECHNOLOGY AND INFLUENCE

Cyborg modifications have applications for the arts. For example, Ribas, a choreographer, is developing what she calls "seismic sense." She wears a device that connects to online seismographs, allowing her to sense earthquakes, which she then turns into performance art in real time. Ribas moves in the direction of and in time to the earthquake, while Harbisson creates music and light to accompany her movements.

The short film about Harbisson and Ribas's company, entitled *Cyborg Foundation*, by Rafel Duran Torrent, was the grand jury prizewinner at Sundance Festival's Focus Forward Filmmaker Competition in 2013. The honor included a $100,00 cash prize.

Harbisson also hopes to inspire people to use mobile technology in new ways. For example, he has created an application compatible with smartphone cameras that allows the camera to analyze color and then, through the phone's speaker, change the color into sound.

The work that Harbisson and Ribas do raises questions for others. As Jonathan Jones, writing for *Guardian* (27 Aug. 2014) asked, "Is the day just round the corner when art lovers will sit in darkened rooms feeling art vibrate inside their skulls? Will such experiments introduce a totally new sensuality, as we explore remote regions of emotion and poetry made possible by technology?"

## PERSONAL LIFE

Harbisson's bedroom is painted in black and white; because these colors are silent, he can sleep well. The floors are red, the lowest note on the scales. Green, a middle tone, is the color of his door. Harbisson told *CNN* (10 Sept. 2012), "The way I dress has also changed. Before, I used to dress in a way that looked good, now I dress in a way that sounds good. If I'm happy I dress in a major chord. If I'm sad I dress in a minor chord." In 2014, Harbisson became the first person ever to conduct an orchestra using color only—members of Barcelona's Palau de la Música choir and the Catalan Quartic String Quartet sang and played notes based on the colors Harbisson presented to them.

## SUGGESTED READING

"Art and Technology." *New York Times*. New York Times, 27 Nov. 2013. Web. 31 Dec. 2014.

Curtis, Sophie. "Colour-Blind Artist Conducts Choir Using Colour Alone." *Telegraph*. Telegraph Media Group, 10 Feb. 2014. Web. 31 Dec. 2014.

Harbisson, Neil. "Painting by Ear." *Modern Painters* 20.5 (2008): 70–73. *Academic Search Complete*. Web. 31 Dec. 2014.

Harbisson, Neil. Interview by Scott Simon. "Wearable Sensor Turns Color-Blind Mind into 'Cyborg.'" *Weekend Edition*. NPR, 11 Jan. 2014. Web. 31 Dec. 2014.

Harbisson, Neil. Interview by Guy Raz. "Extrasensory." *TED Radio Hour*. NPR, 7 Mar. 2014. Web. 31 Dec. 2014.

Lee, Jennifer 8. "A Surgical Implant for Seeing Colors through Sound." *New York Times*. New York Times, 2 July 2012. Web. 31 Dec. 2014.

—Judy Johnson, MLS

# Kevin Hart
**Born:** July 6, 1979
**Occupation:** Comedian and actor

Kevin Hart is widely described as one of the most popular comedians working today. Because he stands approximately five feet four, he is also consistently described as short or diminutive, and he uses that trait—along with a furious, swaggering physicality—to great comic effect. Much of his work is self-deprecating. "He is self-effacing, humble, and eager to make jokes about his height, love life, and friendships," Dwight Brown wrote for the *Huffington Post* (3 July 2013). Those jokes have fueled something of an empire. Since getting his start during amateur comedy hours in Philadelphia-area clubs, Hart has starred in several big-budget films, including *Think Like a Man* (2012), *About Last Night* (2014), and *Ride Along* (2014), and his live tours, which are recorded for theatrical and DVD release, have earned millions of dollars. For example, *Laugh at My Pain*, which he distributed in AMC Theaters in 2011, made nearly $8 million at the box office and sold exceptionally well on DVD, and his 2012 world tour, *Let Me Explain*, brought in a total of more than $30 million.

Brown opined that one day Hart will be mentioned in the same breath as such legendary black comedians as Richard Pryor and Eddie Murphy and wrote, "Filling thirty thousand seats at Madison Square Garden [as he did during the *Let Me Explain* tour] is a step in the right direction for a young man who's done a superb job building a fan base that's addicted to his brand of urban culture [and] lightweight humor." While he has a loyal African American fan base, a significant percentage of his audience is white. "You make yourself broad," he told Amy Wallace for *GQ* (May 2014). "You make yourself appealing. 'Hey, y'all, I'm cool with everybody.' That's my message."

Eva Rinaldi/Wikimedia Commons

## EARLY LIFE AND EDUCATION

Kevin Hart was born on July 6, 1979, and grew up in Philadelphia, Pennsylvania. He and his older brother, Robert, were raised by their mother, Nancy. Their father, Henry, was a cocaine addict who cycled in and out of prison, and Nancy kicked him out of the house for good when her boys were young. Nancy, who worked as a systems analyst at the University of Pennsylvania, was notoriously strict. Hart says that he first understood the power of humor when he was able to avoid a spanking by making her laugh. She ensured that Hart stayed off the sometimes rough streets of North Philadelphia by enforcing strict homework rules and making him join the swim team. "I am who I am today because of my mother," Hart told Wallace.

Nancy was also strict about monitoring her sons' media consumption, forbidding them to view anything rated R or that contained cursing. Hart discovered that his aunt and uncle were much more lenient with his cousins, and he frequently went to their home to watch Eddie Murphy specials. He began parroting the comedian's lines, and by his mid-teens had earned a reputation as a class clown. "I was the guy on the swim team entertaining the bus on the way to the meets," he recalled to Jonah Weiner for *Rolling Stone* (25 Oct. 2012).

After graduating from George Washington High School, Hart briefly attended both Temple University and the Community College of Philadelphia. Despite his mother's disappointment, he found that he was not cut out for college. (He has quipped that it takes true effort to fail a basic-level quiz at a community college, but that he managed to do so repeatedly.)

Hart found work at a Philadelphia shoe store, and between customers he entertained his coworkers with jokes and funny stories. They encouraged him to perform during an open-mic comedy night at a local club—a night that launched his career, albeit not immediately.

## EARLY COMEDY CAREER

Describing his first time on a stage, Hart told Jessica Gross for the *New York Times Magazine* (20 June 2014), "I will never forget it. I was really nervous, but I jotted down four or five topics. I talked about how perverts grind on people to get to the back of the bus. I talked about getting robbed by a midget, who head-butted me instead of hitting me. . . . It was awful." Still, he continued, "There were only about seventeen people in the audience, and six of them were with me, so it wasn't bad. I was able to maintain some confidence."

Hart preserved, appearing whenever he got the chance and feeling lucky if he was paid twenty-five dollars for a show. Although skeptical, his mother agreed to cover his monthly rent for one year while he tried to break into the business. One night at a comedy club, he met Keith Robinson, a relatively successful comic who took Hart under his wing. The two men frequently drove to New York City to visit such venues as Dangerfield's and Caroline's, so that Hart could learn from more-established talents. He continued to perform wherever he could. "It was six-hour drives to comedy clubs in East Bubbles——, getting no money," he recalled to Weiner. "I performed at a strip club in Atlantic City called Sweet Cheeks. I performed in a bowling alley while people were f——ing bowling." His audiences, however, continued to grow, particularly after Hart followed Robinson's advice to stop modeling himself on Murphy and other comedians and start basing his work on his own life. (One popular bit that resulted from that counsel describes Hart's drug-addicted father attending a school spelling bee while high and rooting as though it were a sporting event. His addled cheer—"All right, all right, all riii-iiight!"—has become something of a catchphrase for Hart.)

Hart eventually signed with a manager and began meeting with television networks. He signed a development deal with ABC for $225,000 and moved to Los Angeles; after giving his mother some of the windfall, by his own admission, he squandered the rest. "That's why I have so much respect for money now," he told Wallace.

## TELEVISION AND FILM

Hart got an important break in 2002 when he was cast in the Judd Apatow series *Undeclared*, about a group of college dorm mates. (Somewhat against type, Hart played a serious and religious student named Luke.) That show proved short-lived, but Hart next landed his own ABC program, *The Big House*, portraying a spoiled Malibu college student who is sent to live with working-class relatives in Philadelphia after his father is imprisoned for embezzling. That show, which he taped in 2004, was canceled unceremoniously before it ever aired. The network had flown Hart to the "upfronts," a star-studded event at which new shows are introduced to possible sponsors, but a few minutes before he was scheduled to appear on the stage, he was told of the cancellation. He has never forgotten the indignity of the situation, particularly because it was a factotum in a headset, rather than a network executive, who informed him of the change in plans. That year he appeared in *Soul Plane*, a little-seen movie that critics universally panned. Writing for *USA Today* (27 May 2004), Claudia Puig asserted, "*Soul Plane* is such a sorry raunchfest that when a main character announces in a key scene, 'I'm not running out like I always do,' one is tempted to shout, 'But I am!' and then bolt from the theater."

Hart has since had better luck on both the large and small screens. After a string of small parts in such movies as *The 40-Year-Old Virgin* (2005), *Scary Movie 4* (2006), and *Little Fockers* (2010), in 2012, he landed a major role in *Think Like a Man*, a comedy about the romantic misadventures of four couples. While most critics found the movie predictable and trite, Hart got good reviews for his engaging performance. That trope has followed him throughout his film career. Critics have bemoaned the formulaic nature of *Grudge Match* (2013), a boxing picture starring Robert De Niro and Sylvester Stallone; *Ride Along*, a buddy-cop comedy costarring the rapper and actor Ice Cube; the romantic comedy *About Last Night* (2014); and the sequel *Think Like a Man Too* (2014)—while still praising Hart's comedic chops.

Hart's latest television project, a spoof reality show called *The Real Husbands of Hollywood*, premiered in 2013 and was renewed for a third season in 2014. It has ranked as the number-one sitcom on cable television among adults eighteen to forty-nine years old, and most critics agree that it would attract even more viewers if it did not air on the niche BET (Black Entertainment Television) network.

## CONCERT PERFORMANCES AND OTHER PROJECTS

Although critics may disagree about the merits of Hart's film and television work, few disagree about the power of his live performances. He has filled arenas all over the world—including New York City's Madison Square Garden—with thousands of fans, and sales of his concert DVDs have made him a millionaire many times over. His DVDs include *I'm a Grown Little Man*, originally recorded in 2006 and released widely in 2009; *Seriously Funny* (2010), which was shot in front of a Cleveland audience; *Laugh at My Pain*, which cost $750,000 to shoot and edit and which made $8 million when distributed to movie theaters and even more on DVD; and *Let Me Explain* (2013).

Hart has long owned his own company, Hartbeat Productions, through which he financed his last two concert movies and created *The Real Husbands of Hollywood*. ABC is reportedly planning an upcoming series based on his life that will be produced under Hartbeat's auspices. Also in the works is a website that he envisions will include videos, games, music, and more. Hart, who hosted the MTV Video Music Awards in 2012, announced the news of the Internet venture to his ten million Twitter followers by writing, "Operation take over the entertainment world is officially in session!" Stand-up comedy, he told Wallace, has "put me in a position to own, to do, to get."

## PERSONAL LIFE

Hart married Torrei Hart in 2003. They have a daughter, Heaven Lee, born in 2005, and a son, Hendrix, born in 2007. (Heaven's middle name is spelled Leigh by some sources.) The couple divorced in 2011. Their split seemed amicable until early 2014, when Torrei announced that she would be appearing on a VH1 reality show called *Atlanta Exes* and intimated that Hart's current fiancée, model-actress Eniko Parrish, had been partially responsible for the failed marriage. Hart struck back via social media, tweeting, "I guess giving a woman over 20k a month and still being there for her and being an incredible father isn't enough!"

While Hart has been accused of misogyny because his act often includes jokes that play upon stereotypes of women as bossy, strident, and manipulative, his defenders point out that he makes fun of himself just as often. Outside of the spotlight, Hart has been a generous philanthropist, giving hundreds of thousands of dollars to his struggling former school district in North Philadelphia and to Hurricane Sandy relief organizations, among other causes.

## SUGGESTED READING

Brown, Dwight. "Kevin Hart: Let Me Explain." *Huffington Post*. TheHuffingtonPost.com, 3 July 2013. Web. 26 Nov. 2014.

Gross, Jessica. "Kevin Hart: 'I Don't Need Therapy.'" *New York Times Magazine*. New York Times, 20 June 2014. Web. 26 Nov. 2014.

Itzkoff, Dave. "Life Sends Lemons? Make Comedy." *New York Times*. New York Times, 30 Aug. 2012. Web. 26 Nov. 2014.

Rapkin, Mickey. "The Many Sides of Kevin Hart's Heart." *Elle*. Hearst Communications, 16 Jan. 2014. Web. 26 Nov. 2014.

Wallace, Amy. "Walking Tall with Kevin Hart." *GQ*. Condé Nast, May 2014. Web. 26 Nov. 2014.

Weiner, Jonah. "Kevin Hart: Hot Superstar Stand-Up." *Rolling Stone*. Rolling Stone, 25 Oct. 2012. Web. 26 Nov. 2014.

## SELECTED WORKS

*The 40-Year-Old Virgin*, 2005; *Little Fockers*, 2010; *Laugh at My Pain*, 2011; *Think Like a Man*, 2012; *Let Me Explain*, 2013; *About Last Night*, 2014; *Ride Along*, 2014

—Mari Rich

# Sally Hawkins

**Born:** April 27, 1976
**Occupation:** Actor

"Small, wiry, with expressive, highly mobile eyes and mouth that appear almost too large for her face, [Sally] Hawkins hates the limelight yet keeps finding herself shoved into it," a reporter for the online British entertainment magazine *Metro* (14 Nov. 2012) wrote. "She's an intense, febrile presence on stage and screen, and there are regular articles suggesting she's on the cusp of a break-out Hollywood career." Hawkins has lent her talents to such well-received films as Mile Leigh's *Happy-Go-Lucky* (2008), for which she won a Golden Globe as best actress in a comedy or musical, and Woody Allen's *Blue*

Obenson/Wikimedia Commons

*Jasmine* (2013), which garnered her an Academy Award nomination for best supporting actress. She was introduced to an even wider audience the following year, when she appeared in *Paddington* (2014), a big-budget screen adaptation of the children's book series.

Yet despite her work with Allen and her star turn in *Paddington*—which *Entertainment Weekly* reporter Esther Zuckerman characterized on January 19, 2015, soon after its release, as "a critical darling with a respectable box office haul to boot"—Hawkins has denied interest in becoming a player in the American movie industry. "I've always known I'm not typical Hollywood fodder," she told the *Metro*, "which is useful, since Hollywood can eat you up and spit you out. Don't get me wrong: I'd love the chance to work with someone like Paul Thomas Anderson. But I do know what I want and Hollywood is not what I want."

## EARLY YEARS AND EDUCATION

Sally Cecilia Hawkins was born on April 27, 1976, in Dulwich, an area of South London, England. She has one older brother. Her parents, Jacqui and Colin Hawkins, write and illustrate children's books. Trained as graphic designers, they married in 1968 and in 1979 they hit upon the idea of creating books together. Among their most popular volumes have been *Fairytale News*, in which classic stories are rendered tabloid-style; *Dance of the Dinosaurs*, a whimsical bedtime tale; and the *Fingerwiggles* series, novelty books that allow a child to insert fingers through each page in order to simulate an elephant's trunk or a puppy's paws, for example.

"Stories were integral to our upbringing—making up stories and seeing my parents create something from nothing with such strong characters on the page," Hawkins told an interviewer for PBS in 2007. "My Dad acts out a character's part before he draws it, and both my parents . . . see if it works and fits, and if the rhythm is right. It really did spark something in me and especially that creativity, the ability to step into someone's shoes like that. I owe them everything for that. They make it up and I get it given to me on a page."

Hawkins, who attended James Allen's Girls' School, in Dulwich, was an anxious child who stammered and sometimes had trouble reading. She dislikes discussing the topic, but told John Preston for the *Telegraph* (22 Apr. 2010), "[At times] I flip lines, and sight-reading is terrifying. But it's not as if it cripples me, which I know it does with some people."

When she began appearing in primary school plays, it opened a new world for her. "Something just went click inside me," she recalled to Preston. "Suddenly I wasn't shy anymore. Instead I felt confident and happy. I can remember the enormous sense of relief it gave me. I loved the feeling of making people laugh. That was just lovely, the best thing ever. It also unlocked language for me and made me realize the power of words."

Hawkins attended the Royal Academy of Dramatic Art (RADA) where she learned a variety of acting techniques. "I took every course I could. I was like a sponge," she told Alex Simon for *Venice* magazine (Nov. 2012). "It was a fabulous introduction to all these different techniques: Stanislavski System, and the Method, and all these phenomenal and unusual texts." She began finding work soon after graduating in 1998. In 1999, for example, she appeared on the British television series *Casualty*, and in 2000 she had a guest turn on another hospital drama, *Doctors*. She got her big break, however, in 2002, the year she established a close working relationship with director Mike Leigh. She had initiated the connection by writing to his casting director, Nina Gold, to introduce herself while still a student.

## WORK WITH MIKE LEIGH

Leigh is renowned for his unusual method of directing: rather than working with a firm script, he outlines a scenario for his actors and allows them to develop their characters slowly, over the course of months—creating their backstories, envisioning their mannerisms, and improvising their dialogue. "Mike's way of working makes complete sense to me because you're creating these real people and the worlds in which they live," Hawkins told Amy Raphael for the *Telegraph* (29 Mar. 2008). "He has to be very secure that you not only know the character's history, but also what they had for breakfast that morning, what books they're reading, what they're watching on the television. You're chomping at the bit to go and when he releases you, it's like a spring. It's like stepping into a different life that is already set up."

In 2002 Leigh cast Hawkins in *All or Nothing*, which follows the lives of a group of working-class residents at an apartment complex in South London; she played Samantha, an unemployed young woman with a perpetual scowl and voracious sexual appetite. They worked together again in 2004, on *Vera Drake*—a film about an abortionist in 1950s London, where Hawkins portrayed an upper-middle-class girl who has been raped.

Although those first two parts were relatively small, Hawkins played the lead in Leigh's *Happy-Go-Lucky* (2008), about Poppy, a cheerful schoolteacher whose unshakeable optimism is considered annoying by some. The movie—and Hawkins's performance—was widely lauded. "Poppy is one of the most difficult roles any actress could be assigned," Roger Ebert opined in his October 23, 2008, review for the *Chicago-Sun Times*. "She must smile and be peppy and optimistic at (almost) all times, and do it naturally and convincingly, as if the sunshine comes from inside. That's harder than playing Lady Macbeth. This is her star-making role." He concluded, "I will deliberately employ a cliché: She is a joy to behold."

The role won Hawkins a slew of international awards, including a Golden Globe. Emphasizing her discomfort with the world of Hollywood, she has told interviewers that while giving her acceptance speech at the high-wattage ceremony, she became befuddled upon seeing Tom Cruise from the podium.

## WORK WITH WOODY ALLEN

In addition to Leigh, Hawkins has worked twice with director Woody Allen. In 2007 she had a minor part in Allen's little-seen *Cassandra's Dream*, a crime drama starring Colin Farrell and Ewan McGregor. In 2013 she appeared alongside Cate Blanchett in *Blue Jasmine*, a film about a spoiled socialite (Blanchett), forced to take refuge with her working-class sister, Ginger (Hawkins), after her husband is imprisoned for a Bernie Madoff–like Ponzi scheme. Echoing sentiments expressed by many other reviewers, Mark Kermode wrote for the London *Guardian* (28 Sept. 2013), "Equally at home in comedy and drama, Hawkins is the perfect counterpoint to Blanchett's intensity, and it's her warmhearted character with whom the audience builds the strongest bond." The role of Ginger earned Hawkins—who had been worried when considering the part about accurately replicating an American accent—an Academy Award nomination for best supporting actress.

Hawkins is grateful for the chance to work repeatedly with directors of Leigh's and Allen's caliber. "Working with people you know is just so much easier whoever you are," she explained to Matt Mueller for the London *Independent* (19 Nov. 2014). "Everyone has their quirks, and I know Woody and Mike find it easier to work with people who understand how they work and think. It cuts a lot of time and awkwardness out."

## OTHER ROLES

In addition to her work with Leigh and Allen, Hawkins has taken on a wide variety of other screen projects. In 2002, for example, she appeared in a television miniseries adaptation of Sarah Waters's novel of 1890s-era music halls and lesbian affairs, *Tipping the Velvet*. She then played Mary Shelley in the 2003 television movie *Byron* and had a small role in the 2004 crime thriller *Layer Cake*. A Sarah Waters novel figured in her career again in 2005, when she starred as Sue Tinder, a thief who falls in love with her intended mark, in the miniseries adaptation of *Fingersmith*. Proving her comedic chops, she was featured in four episodes of the sketch show *Little Britain* from 2003 to 2005; in one sketch that received particular media attention, another character vomited on her.

Hawkins's other noteworthy screen projects include the 2005 miniseries *Twenty Thousand Streets under the Sky*; the 2006 television movie *Shiny Shiny Bright New Hole in My Heart*, in which she starred as a woman addicted to shopping; the 2007 *Masterpiece Theater* production of Jane Austen's novel *Persuasion*, in which she portrayed Anne Elliot; the 2009 coming-of-age drama *An Education*, set in 1960s London; and the 2010 comedy *It's a Wonderful Afterlife*.

In 2010, Hawkins starred in *Made in Dagenham*, a film based on a true incident in which female factory workers walked out of an auto plant in 1968 to protest sexual discrimination. Critics praised Hawkins for elevating the material. Roger Ebert wrote in his November 23, 2010, review: "The unexpected thing about *Made in Dagenham* is how entertaining it is. That's largely due to director Nigel Cole's choice of Sally Hawkins for his lead."

Following turns in film adaptations of *Jane Eyre* (2011) and *Great Expectations* (2012), Hawkins helped bring another classic to life on the big screen with the 2014 hit *Paddington*, based on Michael Bond's classic children's books about a bear cub from Peru who travels to London in search of a home and is taken in by a kindly family. Hawkins played Mrs. Brown, the mother of the family, and critics praised her performance. In 2014 she was cast as Eleanor, Duchess of Gloucester, in the miniseries *The Hollow Crown*; her episodes are expected to air in 2016.

Throughout her career, Hawkins has also appeared on the London stage in such productions as *Romeo and Juliet* in 1998, *The Cherry Orchard* in 1999, and *Constellations* in 2012. She made her Broadway debut in a 2010 revival of George Bernard Shaw's *Mrs. Warren's Profession*.

## PERSONAL LIFE

Hawkins lives in southwest London. She has joked to interviewers that if she is still single when she is thirty-five, she has a pact with friend and comedian James Corden that they will marry.

Of her fame, Hawkins has noted: "Because I'm small, I can hide in a big coat, and I've got lots of hair which I use as a kind of a helmet," she told Mueller. "I'm still thrown when I am recognized. But when it happens, I find it really lovely. At least people don't throw things or shout at me."

## SUGGESTED READING

Chang, Justin. "'Happy' Brit Feels Most Comfortable with Leigh at Her Side." *Variety*. Variety Media, 8 Dec. 2008. Web. 4 Feb. 2015.

Hoggard, Liz. "Sally Hawkins: 'You Only Do Good Work When You're Taking Risks.'" *Independent*. Independent Digital News and Media, 10 Nov. 2012. Web. 4 Feb. 2015.

Mueller, Matt. "Actress on New Film *Paddington*, and Performing Opposite a Bear's Head on a Stick." *Independent*. Independent Digital News and Media, 19 Nov. 2014. Web. 4 Feb. 2015.

Preston John. "Sally Hawkins Interview." *Telegraph*. Telegraph Media Group, 22 Apr. 2010. Web. 4 Feb. 2015.

Raphael, Amy. "Sally Hawkins: Life as Mike Leigh's Muse." *Telegraph*. Telegraph Media Group, 29 Mar. 2008. Web. 4 Feb. 2015.

Ryzik, Meena. "An Anxious Sally Hawkins, Onstage and in Auditions." *New York Times*. New York Times, 10 Jan. 2014. Web. 4 Feb. 2015.

## SELECTED WORKS

*All or Nothing*, 2002; *Vera Drake*, 2004; *Persuasion*, 2007; *Happy-Go-Lucky*, 2008; *It's a Wonderful Afterlife*, 2010; *Made in Dagenham*, 2010; *Blue Jasmine*, 2013; *Paddington*, 2014

—Mari Rich

# Maura Healey

**Born:** February 8, 1971
**Occupation:** Attorney General of Massachusetts

Early in the race for Massachusetts attorney general, Maura Healey may have seemed an unlikely choice for the position. An attorney and former professional basketball player who had never before run for office, Healey faced older and more politically experienced opponents both within and outside of her own party, a challenge she willingly acknowledged. "I come into this race as an underdog," she told Eric Levenson for *Boston.com* (26 Aug. 2014). "I've been an underdog my whole life. I'm a five-foot-four point guard in a big person's game." Nevertheless, Healey, who had gained significant practical experience working under her predecessor, Attorney General Martha Coakley, was confident in her ability to serve the commonwealth and its residents. In November 2014, Massachusetts voters affirmed their belief in her capabilities, electing her to the position with more than 60 percent of the vote.

The first openly gay person to serve as attorney general anywhere in the United States, Healey has an impressive record when it comes to civil rights issues, having played a crucial role in the first state challenge of the 1996 Defense of Marriage Act (DOMA) during her tenure as chief of the civil rights division of the attorney general's office under Coakley. Civil rights remained a key concern as Healey began her term in office, as did issues such as consumer protection, economic development, and public health. "I want to lead an attorney general's office . . . that is bold and innovative when it comes to addressing problems and needs of people in the state," she explained to Shira Schoenberg for the *Republican* (29 Dec. 2014).

## EARLY LIFE AND EDUCATION

Maura Tracy Healey was born on February 8, 1971, to Jerome and Tracy Healey. Although her parents were originally from northeastern Massachusetts, the family settled in the southern New Hampshire town of Hampton Falls, where Healey and her four younger siblings grew up on a large property that had once been a farm. Her father, an officer in the US Navy who later worked for the US Public Health Service and the Environmental Protection Agency, served for a time on the Hampton Falls board of selectmen; her mother worked as a school nurse.

As a child, Healey developed a love of sports, particularly basketball. Following her parents' divorce, her mother married Edward Beattie, a coach at Winnacunnet High School. Beattie became Healey's coach when she joined the girls' basketball team at the school. A talented player, Healey broke numerous high school records and continued to excel upon joining the Harvard University women's basketball team following her enrollment at the university in 1988. After graduating with a bachelor's degree in government in 1992, Healey traveled to Europe to serve as point guard for UBBC Wustenrot, an Austrian professional basketball team. She spent two years abroad, returning to the United States in 1994.

Although Healey's basketball career may initially seem to have little in common with her later legal and political work, she has noted that it in fact shaped her outlook on the role laws play in the lives of ordinary people. "I'm a product of Title IX and a beneficiary of Title IX, which was a federal law that made possible great gains for girls and women in athletics," she explained to Charlotte Robinson for the *Huffington Post* (13 Mar. 2014). "Because of that law I was ultimately able to play college basketball, Division I, and ultimately have a professional basketball career. So I think that the kind of laws we have are terrifically important." In 1995, Healey enrolled in the Northeastern University School of Law to pursue a law degree. She graduated from Northeastern in 1998 and was soon admitted to the bar.

## EARLY CAREER

Healey began her career in law working as a clerk for A. David Mazzone, a judge for the US District Court for the District of Massachusetts. At the time, Mazzone was well known for overseeing the cleanup of the highly polluted Boston Harbor, a project he had spearheaded since issuing a ruling on the subject in the mid-1980s. Healey had the opportunity to assist Mazzone in this project, in addition to numerous other legal matters.

After a year with Mazzone, Healey joined the Boston office of the law firm Hale and Dorr, where she worked primarily in commercial litigation. She also represented various sports teams, including the Boston Red Sox, and took on pro bono work. In 2004, Healey spent several months working as a special assistant district attorney for Middlesex County. In that role, she tried a wide variety of cases on behalf of the Commonwealth of Massachusetts.

In 2006, Healey's father died after a battle with cancer. His death prompted Healey to think about what she wanted to do with her career,

which up to that point had been less devoted to public service than she would have preferred. "I thought, Maura, life is too short," she told Scot Lehigh for the *Boston Globe* (2 Feb. 2014). "Get off the stick." Having decided to take her career in a new direction, she left Hale and Dorr—by then known as WilmerHale—in early 2007 to take a position with the Massachusetts attorney general's office. Under Attorney General Martha Coakley, Healey served as chief of the office's civil rights division from 2007 to 2012. During that time, she oversaw numerous civil rights cases dealing with issues such as education, privacy, and health care.

## CHALLENGING DOMA

One of Healey's major accomplishments as chief of the civil rights division concerned the Defense of Marriage Act (DOMA), the controversial 1996 federal law that defined marriage as the union between one man and one woman and, though not prohibiting same-sex marriage in individual states, effectively barred same-sex couples who were legally married from receiving federal benefits such as Social Security, veteran's benefits, and retirement savings. With Healey's assistance, Coakley in 2009 filed a lawsuit against the US Department of Health and Human Services on behalf of the Commonwealth of Massachusetts, the first state to challenge the law, arguing that the portion of DOMA defining marriage was unconstitutional. A US Court of Appeals justice later ruled in favor of the commonwealth.

Although DOMA was ultimately struck down in 2013, when the US Supreme Court ruled it unconstitutional in *United States v. Windsor*, Healey's work in *Massachusetts v. United States Department of Health and Human Services* was a significant stepping stone toward that ruling. For Healey, it was proof that progress was possible. "I know at the time I argued that case, the majority of Americans were not supportive of marriage equality, and even the president and the Justice Department were standing behind DOMA," she explained to Robinson. "But I also know that eventually that changed, and we did prevail. . . . Things can change, but it requires perseverance, resolve, and that's certainly a commitment I'm going to continue."

In early 2012, Healey took on the role of chief of the office's public protection and advocacy bureau. Overseeing more than one hundred staff members, she supervised investigations in numerous divisions of the office, including the consumer protection and civil rights divisions. She later served briefly as chief of business and labor but resigned from the position in October 2013.

## POLITICAL CAMPAIGN

By late 2013, Coakley was approaching the end of her second term as attorney general and planning to run for governor of Massachusetts in the 2014 election. With the role of attorney general needing to be filled, Healey decided to run for the office. Although she had no political experience and had never run a campaign before, Healey's years of work in the attorney general's office had given her significant experience in dealing with the types of issues the attorney general typically handles. Though initially an underdog, she defeated lawyer and former state senator Warren Tollman by a wide margin to win the Democratic nomination in the primary.

Healey's reputation soon changed from that of a little-known political newcomer to an up-and-coming progressive star, and she gained endorsements from many Massachusetts politicians, political and social organizations, and newspapers. "Healey has a firm grip on how to deploy the powers the office indisputably has—and to tend to the basic duties of that office," a writer for the *Boston Globe* (1 Sept. 2014) remarked in the paper's official endorsement. "Meanwhile, her unusual biography—she played professional basketball in Europe before attending law school—and her audacious performance in debates hint at a level of imagination and creativity that would serve her well." As that endorsement suggests, Healey's prior career in professional sports proved to be an unexpected asset; one of Healey's early campaign ads even likened her goal of dealing with tough challenges as attorney general to her demonstrated ability to defeat much larger players as a five-foot-four point guard.

On November 4, 2014, Healey defeated Republican nominee John B. Miller in the state election, winning approximately 62 percent of the vote. Her election was particularly notable not only because of her status as a political outsider but also because she was the first openly gay individual elected to the position of attorney general in the United States. Healey took office on January 21, 2015.

## ATTORNEY GENERAL

In the months after taking office, Healey positioned herself as a strong proponent of numerous causes, including both broad issues and concerns specifically affecting Massachusetts. One major issue of concern to Healey was the heroin and prescription opioid crisis facing much of the state, where a substantial increase in drug overdoses and drug-related crime had prompted many residents to call on the state to take action. Upon taking office, Healey established a task force within the attorney general's office charged with addressing that issue, proposing that the office work to address both the misuse of legal prescription drugs and the trafficking of heroin. While many politicians and law enforcement officials have traditionally sought to end drug crises by arresting and incarcerating those who use the drugs, Healey positioned herself as a proponent of a more treatment-based approach, viewing the opioid crisis as more of a public health issue than a criminal one.

Healey likewise sought to address controversial issues such as the opening of casinos in Massachusetts, where casino gambling was legalized in 2011, and the Boston 2024 Olympic bid proposed in 2014. Building on her years as chief of the office's civil rights division, Healey also worked extensively in that realm, particularly in the areas of women's and gay rights. Ultimately, she prioritizes addressing the needs of the people of Massachusetts above all. "At the end of the day, people are coming to you with problems," she told Steve LeBlanc for the Associated Press (28 Dec. 2014). "Our job is to help solve those issues."

## PERSONAL LIFE

Healey met her partner, Gabrielle Wolohojian, while they were both working for Hale and Dorr. Since 2008, Wolohojian has served as a justice in the Massachusetts Appeals Court system. The two live in the Charlestown neighborhood of Boston.

Although Healey has told journalists that she does not intend to allow her status as the United States' first openly gay attorney general to affect her decision making, she is well aware that she fills an important role for her lesbian, gay, bisexual, and transgender (LGBT) constituents. "To the extent that it may make some young LGBT kid out there be less afraid or not wonder about what's going to happen to him or her, or make them feel like they can be anything they want to be, or do anything they want to do, that's great," she told LeBlanc.

## SUGGESTED READING

Graff, E. J. "The Unstoppable Maura Healey." *Boston*. Metrocorp, Aug. 2015. Web. 31 Aug. 2015.

LeBlanc, Steve. "AP Interview: Healey Eager to Step into AG Role." *Washington Times*. Washington Times, 28 Dec. 2014. Web. 31 Aug. 2015.

Lehigh, Scot. "A Strong Early Prospect for AG Race." *Boston Globe*. Boston Globe Media Partners, 2 Feb. 2014. Web. 31 Aug. 2015.

Levenson, Eric. "Pro Basketball Star-Turned-Attorney General Hopeful Maura Healey Can Still Ball." *Boston.com*. Boston Globe Media Partners, 26 Aug. 2014. Web. 31 Aug. 2015.

"Maura Healey for Attorney General." *Boston Globe*. Boston Globe Media Partners, 1 Sept. 2014. Web. 31 Aug. 2015.

Robinson, Charlotte. "Maura Healey Talks Historic Campaign for Attorney General in Massachusetts." *Huffington Post*. TheHuffingtonPost.com, 13 Mar. 2014. Web. 31 Aug. 2015.

Schoenberg, Shira. "Incoming Attorney General Maura Healey Sets Priorities: Child Protection, Drug Addiction, Gambling Issues on List." *Republican*. MassLive, 29 Dec. 2014. Web. 31 Aug. 2015.

—Joy Crelin

# Marillyn Hewson

**Born:** 1953

**Occupation:** Chairman, president, and CEO of Lockheed Martin

Marillyn Hewson is the Chairman, president and chief executive officer of Lockheed Martin, the world's largest aerospace and defense contractor.

## BACKGROUND

Marillyn Hewson was born in 1953 in Junction City, Kansas. Her father was a civilian working for the army; her mother, Mary Adams, was a member of the Women's Army Corps. Her father died when she was nine, leaving her mother to raise five young children on her own.

In order to support the family, Hewson's mother bought an apartment building and rented out its four small apartments. She focused on teaching her children to be independent and to overcome obstacles and difficult situations. She remained active in her children's lives, taking a job at the cafeteria in their school so she could be near them, serving as a room mother, and involving herself in scouting activities. She was also active in local politics. Hewson credits her mother with teaching her determination, resilience, leadership, and the importance of service.

Hewson attended the University of Alabama, where she earned a bachelor of science in business administration in 1977 and a master of arts in economics in 1979. After graduation, she joined the Bureau of Labor Statistics as an economist.

## EARLY YEARS AT LOCKHEED

In 1983 Hewson began working at Lockheed Corporation (now Lockheed Martin) in its Marietta, Georgia, plant. Hired as a senior industrial engineer, she was responsible for analyzing systems and processes for building aircraft, such as the C-5B Galaxy transport plane, the C-130 Hercules, and the C-141 StarLifter.

In 1985 Hewson was one of five employees chosen for the plant's management development program. The program gave her hands-on training in procurement, finance, and shop-floor supervision. She rose rapidly through the ranks, earning promotions to a series of management positions. From 1993 to 1995 she was the director of operations control. In 1995 she became the director of commercial practices. Later that year, she moved to Fort Worth, Texas, to take the position of director of consolidated material systems and advanced sourcing.

Promoted to vice president of internal audit in 1998, Hewson moved away from the operations side to the boardroom. Her responsibilities involved reporting to the board of directors and executive officers about company-wide issues. This move also brought her to Lockheed's headquarters in Bethesda, Maryland.

## CORPORATE ASCENSION

In 2000 Hewson became the vice president of global supply-chain management. This was soon followed by her promotion to senior vice president of corporate shared services in May 2001, which made her one of eight senior vice presidents reporting directly to the CEO and chairman. She was responsible for centralizing human resources, payroll, and procurement functions while maintaining good relations with the unit managers who were losing these responsibilities. Hewson was appointed general manager of logistics services in 2006 and became the executive vice president of global sustainment one year later. From 2008 to 2010, she was the president of systems integration, and from 2010 to 2013, she was the executive vice president of electronic systems.

In January 2013 Hewson became the CEO and president of Lockheed Martin, following the sudden resignation of Christopher Kuba-sik, the man who had been expected to take over. In 2014 Hewson also became Lockheed Martin's chairman.

As CEO and president, Hewson has helped restructure the company and expand its core business beyond its traditional defense base. With the US Department of Defense cutting defense spending, Lockheed Martin downsized significantly, closing numerous facilities and cutting staff from 146,000 in 2009 to 115,000 by 2014. At the same time, the company moved to increase its business in the commercial sector, among international customers, and in the renewable energies markets. Within her first year as CEO and president, Hewson managed to make significant employee reductions and increase profits at the same time.

## OTHER RESPONSIBILITIES AND HONORS

Hewson served as a member of the board of Carpenter Technologies from 2002 to 2006 and was chairman of the board of Sandia Corporation from 2010 to 2013. She joined the boards of E. I. du Pont de Nemours in 2007, Lockheed Martin in 2012, and the National Geographic Education Foundation in 2013.

Hewson was named one of *Fortune*'s fifty most powerful women in business every year from 2010 to 2014. For two consecutive years, *Forbes* magazine included her on its list of the world's one hundred most powerful women, ranking her thirty-fourth on the list in 2013 and twenty-first in 2014. She also received a 2013 Responsible CEO of the Year Award from *CR Magazine* for her commitment to sustainability, which was reflected by Lockheed Martin's "A" rating for carbon performance and for joining the Dow Jones Sustainability Index.

## IMPACT

Over the course of her career, Hewson has become one of the world's most powerful women in business. Not only is she at the helm of a multibillion-dollar global organization, but she is restructuring it during difficult economic times and reshaping it to rely less on its traditional products and to expand into new markets that will ensure its continued prominence in the global security and aerospace fields in the future.

## PERSONAL LIFE

Hewson married a fellow University of Alabama student, James Hewson, in 1975. They have two sons. When the children were young, Hewson's husband chose to be their primary caregiver, which accommodated the family's needs as they moved eight times during Hewson's rise through the ranks of Lockheed Martin. Hewson and her husband live in Potomac, Maryland.

## SUGGESTED READING

Aitoro, Jill R. "Marillyn Hewson: Inside Out." *Washington Business Journal.* Amer. City Business Jours., 1 Feb. 2013. Web. 21 July 2014.

Attwood, Ed. "Interview: Lockheed Martin's Marillyn Hewson." *ArabianBusiness.com.* Arabian Business, 23 May 2014. Web. 21 July 2014.

Censer, Marjorie. "After Nearly 30 Years with Lockheed, Hewson Is Named Chief Executive." *Washington Post.* Washington Post, 13 Nov. 2012. Web. 21 July 2014.

Hewson, Marillyn A. "A Mother's Resilience." *Politico.* Politico, 19 Sept. 2013. Web. 21 July 2014.

"Marillyn A. Hewson." *Lockheed Martin.* Lockheed Martin, 18 July 2014. Web. 21 July 2014.

"Marillyn Hewson Honored with Responsible CEO of the Year Award." *Lockheed Martin.* Lockheed Martin, 25 Sept. 2013. Web. 21 July 2014.

—Barb Lightner

# Tom Hiddleston
**Born:** February 9, 1981
**Occupation:** Actor

Since the early 2000s, Marvel Studios has become one of the most successful production houses in the United States thanks to its ability to transfer popular comic book characters—including Iron Man, Captain America, and Thor—from the printed page to the big screen. These interconnected films, collectively known as the Marvel Cinematic Universe and distributed by parent company Walt Disney Studios Motion Pictures, have grossed more than $7 billion worldwide at the box office. The Marvel films make up the highest grossing franchise in American film history, when not considering inflation.

According to many critics and moviegoers, that success is due in part to the acting talents of Tom Hiddleston, who delivered a star-making turn as Loki, the legendary Norse god of mischief. Hiddleston's charismatic, tortured villain was the main antagonist in the films *Thor* (2011) and *The Avengers* (2012) and played a large role in *Thor: The Dark World* (2013). Hiddleston is a respected Shakespearean actor who has already worked with such noted directors as Kenneth Branagh (who directed *Thor*), Woody Allen, and Steven Spielberg. Writing for the *New York Times* (6 Nov. 2013), Roslyn Sulcas described Hiddleston as "a classically trained British actor of the most classic kind, and the latest in a long line of British performers to move with remarkable dexterity between Serious Theater and mass-market cinematic fame."

Benjamin Ellis/Wikimedia

## EARLY LIFE AND EDUCATION
The middle child of Diane and James Hiddleston, Thomas William Hiddleston was born on February 9, 1981, in Westminster, London, England, and grew up in Oxford. His mother, a former stage manager, came from a comfortably secure English family. His father was raised in a working-class section of Glasgow, Scotland, and worked himself through Newcastle University, ultimately becoming a managing director of a pharmaceutical company. Hiddleston's older sister, Sarah, is a journalist. His younger sister, Emma, is an actress who has worked in British television. In interviews, Hiddleston has described his sisters as his best friends.

Although his parents divorced when he was thirteen, Hiddleston has described his childhood as being very happy. He spoke of his boyhood to Richard Godwin in an interview for the *London Evening Standard* (18 Oct. 2013): "I was always concerned about wasting time. I don't ever want to look back and think: 'Why wasn't I doing something or making something?' I used to read obituaries obsessively. They always started with a birth date and maybe the county where the subject was raised—and then the life would start at twenty-five. What happened to those twenty-five legitimate years of good living time?"

Hiddleston's interest in acting developed slowly. He began first thinking seriously of pursuing it as a profession after seeing a production of Ibsen's *John Gabriel Borkman* as a young teenager. He also enjoyed acting in school. Because of his fa-

ther's success in business, Hiddleston was able to receive a quality education, entering Eton College, the exclusive British boarding school, at age thirteen. During his time at Eton, he acted frequently, including in a production of R. C. Sherriff's World War I drama *Journey's End*, which was critically acclaimed when it was performed at the Edinburgh International Festival. Following the success of that production, Hiddleston was certain he would make acting his career. Upon graduating from Eton, he studied Latin and Greek at the University of Cambridge and worked in the school's drama club. It was there that he was spotted by a talent agent, who promised to find him paid acting work during school vacations.

## JOBBING ACTOR
While still attending Cambridge, Hiddleston worked on various television projects, including the made-for-television films *The Life and Adventures of Nicholas Nickleby* (2001) and *The Gathering Storm* (2002), among others. After graduating with honors from Cambridge, he decided not to go straight into acting but rather to study drama at the prestigious Royal Academy of Dramatic Arts, where he felt he could hone his craft. "I thought, 'I'm not trained, and I've been lucky,'" Hiddleston told Sulcas. Those years away from professional acting, however, kept him from securing the types of roles that seemed so easily attained while at Cambridge. "I kept a diary, with all the details of every audition," he recalled to Sulcas. "After about

three months, I had to stop, because it was a catalog of failure, a long list of jobs I had failed to get."

His first theatrical film role came in 2007, when he played a teenager named Oakley in Joanna Hogg's *Unrelated*, which also featured his sister Emma. Other parts followed, including the role of John Plumptre in the television movie *Miss Austen Regrets* (2008), the role of William Buxton in the two-episode second series of the British television show *Cranford* (2009), and the voice of naturalist Charles Darwin in the television documentary *Darwin's Secret Notebooks* (2009). He also found some success on the British stage, including most notably in a 2007 production of William Shakespeare's *Othello*.

Through his theatrical work, Hiddleston eventually came into contact with the famed director and actor Kenneth Branagh, with whom he would later work in a West End production of Anton Chekhov's *Ivanov* (2008) and on the BBC television series *Wallander* (2008, 2010). For a time, Hiddleston also continued to seek roles in Hollywood, with little luck. "You would turn up for every audition, and there would be a line of identical tall, blond twenty-nine-year-olds," he recalled to Sulcas. "It was incredibly stressful. I didn't sleep and I didn't get any parts."

## BREAKING OUT AS LOKI

Then Hiddleston received a call from Branagh, who was about to direct *Thor*, the big-budget film adaptation of the Marvel comic-book series about the legendary Norse god of thunder. Branagh suggested Hiddleston try out for the lead role. He did and quickly made the shortlist, along with Chris Hemsworth, to whom the role would eventually go. The studio, however, was so impressed by Hiddleston's dedication—he not only knew his lines but had also put on 25 percent more muscle for the role—that they offered him the role of the film's chief antagonist, Loki, the Norse god of mischief and Thor's brother in the comic book. Both being great lovers of Shakespeare, Branagh and Hiddleston decided to shape Loki's personality out of the motivations of many of the Bard's greatest characters, drawing on the wiliness of Iago and the ambitions of Macbeth, among others.

Critics cheered Hiddleston's take on the famed comic-book character, often proclaiming the actor to be the best part of the Marvel Studios films in which he has appeared thus far. In a review of *Thor: The Dark World* for NPR (7 Nov. 2013), for example, Ian Buckwalter noted, "Hiddleston remains the single greatest asset at Marvel's disposal, a complicated baddie played by a fine actor with a blend of wounded malice and impish glee." Hiddleston's performance also impressed Branagh, as well as his onscreen colleagues. Chris Hemsworth, who portrays Thor, believes Hiddleston adds a particular vulnerability to a role that in other hands would have simply been a charismatic one-note villain; Natalie Portman, who plays scientist Jane Foster, has said that Hiddleston's background as a Shakespearean actor and his attention to detail added to the texture of the films. Of his breakout role, Hiddleston told Godwin, "I've got to be honest. Loki is the thing that has opened me up beyond audiences who come to the Donmar [Warehouse theater]. I've had a riot playing him. If you're going to be a god, you may as well be the god of mischief, right?"

## OTHER ROLES

Critics have singled out many of Hiddleston's other performances for praise, even when his roles are minor ones. He has been commended for his work as Captain Nichols in Steven Spielberg's World War I epic *War Horse* (2011) and for his turn as the great American writer F. Scott Fitzgerald in Woody Allen's comedy *Midnight in Paris* (2011). Other roles include a charming former RAF pilot who romances Rachel Weisz's character in the postwar drama *The Deep Blue Sea* (2011) and an ancient vampire in Jim Jarmusch's *Only Lovers Left Alive* (2013). In the latter film, Hiddleston's character, Adam, is estranged from his longtime lover, a two-thousand-year-old fellow vampire named Eve (Tilda Swinton), and is living as a reclusive genius musician in a drab section of Detroit, Michigan. Adam is depressed and seems on the verge of suicide when Eve returns from the life she has been living in Tangier. In his review of *Only Lovers Left Alive* for the *Philadelphia Inquirer* (25 Apr. 2014), movie critic Steven Rea wrote, "Swinton, her hair white and long and her eyes tired and kind, and Hiddleston, moody and resigned, are wonderful—delivering their lines with the dry sighs of a desert breeze."

Hiddleston has completed work on two films due in 2015: *Crimson Peak*, directed by Guillermo del Toro, and *High-Rise*, directed by Ben Wheatley. He has also been signed to play famed country singer Hank Williams in the biopic *I Saw the Light*, also scheduled for release in 2015. Although he has played a wide variety of roles, Hiddleston has yet to portray a contemporary character on film. In an interview with Amy Nicholson for the

*Village Voice* (9 Apr. 2014), he expressed his desire for such a "normal" role: "I think it's really difficult to make a good romantic comedy. I'd love to play them; they just don't tend to come my way at the moment. I'm taking it as a compliment one way or another, but it's very much an ambition of mine to wear jeans."

## PERSONAL LIFE

Hiddleston has been a supporter of the United Nations Children's Fund (UNICEF) since January 2013, when he traveled with UNICEF UK to Guinea. He has also donated shoes to the Small Steps Project, a UK–based international children's charity that holds an annual celebrity shoe auction to raise funds. In 2013, Hiddleston's shoes commanded £4,500 at auction—the year's highest bid, topping the winning bid for Rolling Stones front man Mick Jagger's shoes by nearly eight thousand pounds.

## SUGGESTED READING

Buckwalter, Ian. "Turns Out One Does Simply Walk into More *Thor.*" Rev. of *Thor: The Dark World*, dir. Alan Taylor. *NPR.* NPR, 7 Nov. 2013. Web. 9 Oct. 2014.

Godwin, Richard. "Faking Bad: Meet Hollywood's Nicest Villain, Tom Hiddleston." *London Evening Standard*. Evening Standard, 18 Oct. 2013. Web. 9 Oct. 2014.

Nicholson, Amy. "Tom Hiddleston Threatens to One Day Play a Normal Guy." *Village Voice*. Village Voice, 9 Apr. 2014. Web. 9 Oct. 2014.

Rea, Steven. "Tender Undead: Only Lovers Left Alive." Rev. of *Only Lovers Left Alive*, dir. Jim Jarmusch. *Philly.com.* Interstate General Media, 25 Apr. 2014. Web. 9 Oct. 2014.

Sulcas, Roslyn. "Thor's Nemesis Makes Some Thunder: Tom Hiddleston Gets Mythic for *Thor: The Dark World.*" *New York Times*. New York Times, 6 Nov. 2013. Web. 9 Oct. 2014.

## SELECTED WORKS

*Thor*, 2011; *Midnight in Paris*, 2011; *The Deep Blue Sea*, 2011; *War Horse*, 2011; *The Avengers*, 2012; *Only Lovers Left Alive*, 2013; *Thor: The Dark World*, 2013

—Christopher Mari

# Jules A. Hoffmann

**Born:** August 2, 1941
**Occupation:** Biologist

Jules A. Hoffmann is one of three immunologists who shared the 2011 Nobel Prize in physiology or medicine for crucial discoveries regarding the cellular and molecular function of the immune system in fruit flies, including the discovery of the role of Toll-like receptors in immune defense.

## BACKGROUND

Jules Alphonse Hoffmann was born on August 2, 1941, in Echternach, Luxembourg. His father, Jos Hoffmann, was a high school teacher and amateur entomologist, and Hoffmann has said that his interest in insects stemmed from participating in his father's entomological field excursions. Hoffmann published his first research paper, on the waterbug, at age seventeen.

Hoffmann attended the University of Strasbourg in France, where he earned his bachelor's and master's degrees in biology and zoology. Hoffmann conducted his PhD research at the Institute of Zoology of the French National Research Agency (CNRS) under Professor Pierre Joly, studying the endocrine development and reproduction of grasshoppers. Hoffmann completed his PhD in 1969, focusing on the origin of blood cells in grasshoppers via blood-forming tissues within grasshopper circulatory systems.

In 1973, Hoffmann conducted postdoctoral research in Marburg, Germany, working with biochemist Peter Karlson. Karlson's team identified the steroid hormone ecdysone, which is involved in the endocrine control of the molting process in grasshoppers.

## CAREER IN IMMUNOLOGY

Hoffmann's interest in immunology was inspired by CNRS studies indicating that insects suffered from no microbial infections following organ transplants, suggesting the existence of an innate mechanism to counter infection. In 1978, Hoffmann became the director of a newly established laboratory of endocrinology and immunology of insects at CNRS. Hoffmann's laboratory focused on two areas of research: the study of endocrine processes in reproduction and development and the study of microbial defense in certain insect species.

Danièle Hoffmann, Hoffmann's wife and a fellow immunologist, conducted postdoctoral research with Hans Boman in Stockholm, Sweden, where Boman's team discovered the antimicrobial peptide hormone cecropin. Boman's research inspired new avenues of research at Hoffmann's CNRS laboratory, including a shift from studying grasshopper and moth immunity to working with various species of flies. In 1988, Hoffmann's laboratory, under the leadership of researcher Jean-Luc Dimarcq, discovered the hormone diptericin, which is essential in antibacterial defenses. Another researcher in Hoffmann's laboratory, Jean-Marc Reichhart, was the primary researcher in a series of experiments to clone diptericin and study the activation of the hormone in fruit flies, or *Drosophila*. In 1992, *Drosophila* geneticist Bruno Lemaitre became the laboratory's primary specialist in fruit fly genetics and immunology.

In 1994, Hoffmann's laboratory identified several antimicrobial peptides, including defensin. Working with Boman's team, researchers discovered that the "fat body cells" of fruit flies were the source of many of the most important antimicrobial hormones. Hoffmann helped to organize a project through the Human Frontiers in Science Programme (HFSP) to create a cooperative venture to combine research from five laboratories working on insect antimicrobial properties.

Hoffmann's team made the critical discovery that the Toll gene, formerly believed to be active only in embryonic development, was crucial in immune defense. The mechanism for the immune function of Toll involves the presence of Toll-like receptors (TLR) on the surface of cells that are responsible for allowing the immune system to recognize potential pathogens and initiate an immune response. These discoveries became part of a 1996 research paper published in the journal *Cell*, of which Lemaitre was the first author.

Over the next decade, the function of TLRs in mammalian immunity allowed for crucial breakthroughs in the development of medical treatments for immune system disease. This led to increasing honors for the research teams involved in the discovery of the TLR mechanisms. Hoffmann served as president of the French National Academy of Sciences from 2005 to 2008 and, in 2011, shared the Shaw Prize, the most prestigious scientific award offered by Hong Kong, with American immunologists Bruce Beutler and Ruslan M. Medzhitov, for their col-

lective contributions to the understanding of immune system genetics.

In 2011, it was announced that Hoffmann, Beutler, and Canadian immunologist Ralph M. Steinman would share the 2011 Nobel Prize in physiology or medicine for their pioneering research into the nature of innate and acquired immunity. Steinman's receipt of the award became controversial following his death in 2011, as Nobel Prizes are traditionally awarded only to living scientists. Steinman received the award posthumously because his nomination came before his death.

The choice of Beutler also became controversial when a group of scientists argued to the Nobel Prize committee that the contributions of Medzhitov and other scientists were more significant than Beutler's contributions to the field. Shortly after the Nobel Prize was awarded, several media outlets, including *Science Insider* and *Lab Times*, reported on an emerging controversy challenging whether Hoffmann was deserving of the Nobel Prize. Criticisms of the Nobel Prize for Hoffmann came primarily from Lemaitre, who claimed that Hoffmann had little involvement in the CNRS research that led to the discovery of TLR mechanisms. Defenders of Hoffmann argued that Hoffmann was the appropriate winner as the leader of the lab and the chief spokesman for all of the laboratory's research, including Lemaitre's pioneering TLR studies.

## IMPACT

The discovery of the Toll gene and TLRs was instrumental in the development of antimicrobial agents essential in combating infectious disease and addressing ongoing issues in organ replacement procedures.

## PERSONAL LIFE

Hoffmann's wife, Danièle Hoffmann, is an immunologist who was Hoffmann's first doctoral student at CNRS and completed her PhD in 1978. Hoffmann and his wife have two children and four grandchildren.

## SUGGESTED READING

Enserink, Martin. "Nobel Prize for Immunologists Provokes Yet Another Debate." *Science*. AAAS, 16 Dec. 2011. Web. 27 Mar. 2014.

Garwood, Jeremy. "Borrowed Plumes." *Lab Times* 10 Feb. 2012: 26–33. Print.

Hoffmann, Jules A. "Nobel Lecture: The Host Defense of Insects: A Paradigm for Innate Immunity." *Nobelprize.org*. Nobel Foundation, 7 Dec. 2011. Web. 27 Mar. 2014.

Hoffmann, Jules A. "Autobiography of Jules A. Hoffmann." *Shaw Prize*. Shaw Prize Foundation. 28 Sept. 2011. Web. 27 Mar. 2014.

"Jules A. Hoffmann." *IBMC*. U de Strasbourg, n.d. Web. 27 Mar. 2014.

"Jules A. Hoffmann PhD." *Gairdner*. Gairdner, 2011. Web. 27 Mar. 2014.

—Micah Issitt

# Elizabeth Holmes

**Born:** February 3, 1984

**Occupation:** Founder and CEO of Theranos

Steve Jennings/Getty Images North America

At the age of thirty, Elizabeth Holmes became the youngest self-made female billionaire in the world. She founded Theranos, a company that performs laboratory tests inexpensively, revolutionizing medical testing. As Holmes explained to Matthew Herper for *Forbes* (2 July 2014), "What we're about is the belief that access to affordable and real-time health information is a basic human right, and it's a civil right." Theranos is a privately held company headquartered in Palo Alto with more than seven hundred employees. By 2014 the company had received nearly $400 million from investors. Blood and other diagnostic laboratory testing is an industry that generates about $75 billion in revenue each year. Theranos was valued at $9 billion in 2014; Holmes owns 50 percent of the company, giving her a net worth of $4.5 billion dollars. She was named to the Forbes 400, *Forbes* magazine's list of the richest people in the United States, in 2014; she was one of only three women of the twenty-seven newly listed wealthy. She is listed as coinventor on eighty-two patent applications in the United States and nearly two hundred patent applications in other countries. Holmes is passionate about putting potentially lifesaving information into the hands of patients. She told Caitlin Roper for *Wired* (18 Feb. 2014), "By testing, you can start to understand your body, understand yourself, change your diet, change your lifestyle, and begin to change your life."

## EARLY LIFE AND EDUCATION

Holmes was born in 1984 in Washington, DC. Noel, her mother, was a congressional committee staff member, working on defense and foreign policy on Capitol Hill. Her father, Christian Holmes IV, has worked for agencies such as the US Agency for International Development (USAID). His work influenced Holmes; as a young person, she saw pain and loss that could have been prevented had diseases been detected early. She has one younger brother, Christian.

When Holmes was eight, the family traveled to Cincinnati, Ohio, where a hospital at University of Cincinnati Medical Center was named for her great-great-grandfather, the first Christian Holmes, a physician who had emigrated from Denmark. She became inspired to become a doctor but could not stand the sight of blood. Both her mother and grandmother fainted at the sight of long medical needles. She told Ken Auletta for the *New Yorker* (15 Dec. 2014), "I really believe that if we were from a foreign planet and we were sitting here and said, 'O.K., let's brainstorm on torture experiments,' the concept of sticking a needle into someone and sucking blood out slowly, while the person watches, probably qualifies."

Holmes grew up in Houston, Texas, after her father took a private-industry job with Tenneco in 1993 when she was nine years old. He spent two weeks of each month in China for several years. He found tutors for his children to learn Mandarin because they were fascinated by the work their father had done in China. While she was still in high school, Holmes completed three years of Mandarin at Stanford University, despite being told that the university did not accept high school students. She convinced the faculty to allow her to enroll in the classes after successfully passing a phone interview conducted in Mandarin.

Holmes also began her first business while still in high school. Struck by the lag in Chinese universities' information technology systems, she sold C++ compilers to Chinese universities. In 2001 Holmes entered college at Stanford, which named her a President's Scholar and gave her three thousand dollars for research. The grant allowed her to begin her work with Channing Robertson, a chemical engineer and dean of Stanford's engineering school. As a freshman, she talked her way into lab work with PhD students, attending research group meetings with them by the end of that year. Knowing Mandarin proved helpful when she took an internship in Singapore at the Genome Institute during the summer between her freshman and sophomore years of college. There, she worked on testing for the severe acute respiratory syndrome, or SARS, a virus that had caused an outbreak in China that year.

## FOUNDING A COMPANY

In 2003, when Holmes was nineteen and a sophomore at Stanford University, she went to Robertson. She had taken his seminar on advanced drug delivery during her first year at Stanford. She suggested that they join forces to start a new company. She showed him the patent application for the wearable patch she had invented and explained her idea to blend the drug-delivery system with monitors to see what was happening in the blood to determine the efficacy of the drug. (The patent was approved in 2007.) She thought of adding a microchip so that information about the patient could be communicated to doctors and other health care professionals. Robertson commented to Roger Parloff for *Fortune* (12 June 2014), "I kind of kicked myself. I'd consulted in this area for thirty years, but I'd never said, here we make all these gizmos that measure and all these systems that deliver, but I never brought the two together." Holmes convinced Robertson to spend one day each week as a technical advisor; he eventually retired from Stanford and worked full time for Theranos. The company's name is a blend of the words therapy and diagnosis.

A semester later, in March 2004, Holmes dropped out of Stanford to focus on Theranos;

she had already been skipping classes consistently to develop her ideas. Her parents gave her the money that they would have spent on her education. As Holmes's mother explained to Parloff, "What do you want for your children? You want them to do something they're passionate about. To follow their dream. To help people. To change the world. So we said, 'Of course. Go do this.'"

Holmes kept quiet about her work, preventing any competitor from getting a jump on her idea. For a decade she worked on building both software and hardware. Beginning in 2005, Theranos partnered with GlaxoSmithKline and Pfizer as they tested drugs in clinical trials. This work allowed Theranos to refine its systems and to catch the toxic effects of drugs that were undergoing testing before patients could be harmed.

Holmes has a humanitarian vision, as she explained to Parloff. "This is about being able to do good. And it's about being able to change the health care system through what we believe this country does so well, which is innovation and creativity and the ability to conceive of technology that can help solve policy challenges."

## DISRUPTING THE SYSTEM

Doctors in the United States perform nearly ten billion tests annually at a cost of about $73 billion. Physicians base some 70 percent of their diagnoses on these lab results. Blood testing has not been substantially changed, however, since the clinical labs—such as Quest Diagnostics and Laboratory Corporation of America—began in the 1960s and 1970s, making diagnostic laboratory testing a ripe industry for disrupting.

Using one-thousandth of the amount of blood required for traditional lab tests, Theranos allows for blood testing to be done with minimum loss of blood. This technology is a boon for cancer patients, the elderly, small children and infants, and patients taking blood thinners. The finger stick does not require a needle and syringe; the small vial that contains the blood is called a nanotainer. In addition, Theranos technology can alert physicians to patients' adverse drug reactions; currently, more than one hundred thousand people die annually from such reactions in the United States.

Holmes estimates that between 40 and 60 percent of patients ordered to have blood tests refuse to do so. This refusal may be because of a fear of needles and pain or because of cost or inconvenience. Using a small sample of twenty-five to fifty microliters, Theranos can run about seventy different tests. Traditional methods to achieve the same results would require several vials of blood, each with a three-thousand- to five-thousand-microliter sample.

Theranos can perform more than two hundred different diagnostic tests, with a goal of being able to do more than one thousand of the most commonly ordered tests. Results are available to patients within four hours rather than the more common wait of several days for results. The fact that Theranos tests cost less helps patients who are uninsured or underinsured and has the potential to save national insurance programs such as Medicare and Medicaid billions of dollars each year. For example, the typical cost for a cholesterol check in 2014 was around fifty dollars; the Theranos cholesterol test cost less than three dollars. Because transparency is also one of Holmes's goals, Theranos publishes the list of prices on its website.

In 2013 Holmes announced a deal with Walgreens, the largest retail pharmacy in the United States, to place Theranos testing centers in its drugstores; her goal is to have a Theranos "wellness center" within five miles of most people in the United States. Doing so will eliminate the need for patients to take time off work to have blood tests run during normal business hours because Walgreens stores are open until late in the evening. Some are twenty-four-hour stores. Walgreens, which has more than eight thousand stores in the United States, began rolling out the Theranos centers in California and Arizona. It has a goal of expanding into Europe with its European partner, Alliance Boots.

Holmes told Auletta, "My own life's work in building Theranos is to redefine the paradigm of diagnosis away from one in which people have to present with a symptom in order to get access to information about their bodies to one in which every person, no matter how much money they have or where they live, has access to actionable health information at the time it matters."

## BOARD OF DIRECTORS

Despite her youth, Holmes has won over a number of influential people who serve on the board of her company. Former US secretary of state Henry Kissinger told Parloff, "I can't compare her to anyone else because I haven't seen anyone with her special attributes. She has iron will, strong determination. But nothing dramatic. There is no performance associated with her. I have seen no sign that financial gain is of any interest to her. She's like a monk. She isn't flashy.

She wouldn't walk into a room and take it over. But she would once the subject gets to her field."

Holmes has convinced a number of prestigious persons to serve on the board of Theranos, including former US senators Bill Frist and Sam Nunn, former US secretary of defense William J. Perry, and retired US Marine Corps general James Mattis. Theranos board member and former US secretary of state George P. Schultz was the first one to be wowed by Holmes; through him, she met and interviewed most of the rest.

Holmes's younger brother, Christian Holmes V, who is two years her junior and a graduate of Duke University, is a director of commercial operations for Theranos.

## PERSONAL LIFE

Holmes's uncle died of skin cancer that had mutated into brain cancer. She told Michelle Quinn for *San Jose Mercury News* (15 July 2014), "You look at something like that and it doesn't make sense. If it was caught in time, it's a completely manageable condition." His death was among the factors that led to her decision to change medicine. Holmes is a vegan, drinking juices throughout her sixteen-hour workdays. She does not own a television set and has not taken a vacation in a decade. She does not date, joking that she is married to Theranos. Like Steve Jobs, one of her personal heroes, she dresses exclusively in black.

## SUGGESTED READING

Auletta, Ken. "Blood, Simpler." *New Yorker*. Condé Nast, 15 Dec. 2014. Web. 9 Feb. 2015.

Herper, Matthew. "Bloody Amazing." *Forbes*. Forbes.com, 2 July 2014. Web. 9 Feb. 2015.

Parloff, Roger. "This CEO Is Out for Blood." *Fortune*. Time, 12 June 2014. Web. 9 Feb. 2015.

Quinn, Michelle. "Meet Elizabeth Holmes, Silicon Valley's Latest Phenom." *San Jose Mercury News*. San Jose Mercury News, 15 July 2014. Web. 9 Feb. 2015.

Roper, Caitlin. "This Woman Invented a Way to Run 30 Lab Tests on Only One Drop of Blood." *Wired*. Condé Nast, 18 Feb. 2014. Web. 9 Feb. 2015.

—Judy Johnson

# Michelle Howard
**Born:** April 30, 1960
**Occupation:** US Navy admiral

On July 1, 2014, Michelle J. Howard became the first woman to be promoted to the rank of four-star admiral in the United States Navy. Her promotion gave her the title of vice chief of naval operations, the second highest-ranking officer in the Navy. While the US Army and the US Air Force have each named four-star female officers, Howard is the first woman—and the first African American woman, more specifically—to hold the post in the Navy's 239-year history.

The Navy first allowed women to serve on combat ships and to fly fighter jets in 1993, but Howard has been breaking boundaries for women in the military since she graduated from the US Naval Academy in 1982. Her previous achievements include being the first African American woman to serve as a three-star officer in the US military and to command a US Navy ship. In April 2009, as the leader of counterpiracy operations in the Gulf of Aden in the Arabian Sea, Howard oversaw efforts to rescue cargo ship Captain Richard Phillips after his vessel was captured by Somali pirates. The event eventually became the subject of an Academy Award–nominated 2013 film titled *Captain Phillips*, starring Tom Hanks. Howard—or rather an actor playing Howard—does not appear in the film, though a female voice on the ship's radio identifies herself as the admiral.

In her current position, Howard is second-in-command to Admiral Jonathan W. Greenert. Her job responsibilities cover "the whole scope of the Navy," she told Elena Schneider for the *New York Times* (11 July 2014). In addition to day-to-day operations, Howard has contended with increasing instances of sexual assault in the Navy as well as the service's lack of women. Women account for only 18 percent of service members in the Navy.

## EARLY LIFE AND EDUCATION

Michelle Janine Howard, whose father was an Air Force master sergeant, was born on April 30, 1960, and moved frequently across the United States throughout her childhood. Celebrated for surmounting obstacles tied to her gender, she told Rachel Martin for NPR's *Morning Edition* (10 Oct. 2014) that the color of her skin was an earlier and larger hurdle to clear. "My first

Monica A. King/Wikimedia Commons

negative initiation to being black was in kindergarten when kids started to call me the n-word on the playground," she said. "And I'm running home crying. And my father's like, you've got to toughen up. This is the country you live in." Of growing up as a minority during the height of the civil rights movement, Howard added, "You have a series of things that happen to you growing up that people who are in the majority don't experience. They don't experience driving across country as a family and not being able to get a hotel and sleeping in the car." On one such drive across the country, Howard's father sat the family down at a restaurant where he knew they would not be served as a form of protest. "It gives you an awareness of politics at a very young age," she told Martin.

Howard was twelve when she decided she wanted to serve in the US Navy, mainly after viewing a documentary about the service academies that captured her imagination. "The leadership, the marching around, the uniforms, all appealed to me," she told Schneider. Caught up in her excitement, she was devastated when her brother pointed out her failure to notice that there were not any women included in the taping; at the time, women were not allowed to enroll in the US Naval Academy in Annapolis, Maryland. Howard's mother told her that if the ban was still in place when she graduated from high school, they would sue the government to have it removed. Meanwhile, later on school nights, she was captivated by the unique career achievements represented by the female African American character of Lieutenant Uhura on the popular television series *Star Trek*.

Howard was inspired by her mother's determination and unwavering support of her goal, but by the time she graduated from Gateway High School in Aurora, Colorado, in 1978, a lawsuit was no longer necessary. The law had been changed to allow women to enroll in the US Naval Academy when Howard was sixteen. She became a member of the third freshman class that included female students, but among that class of 1,363 students, she was one of only seven African American women. She graduated in 1982. Of her time as a student, Howard told Schneider, "There were angry men at Annapolis, but we got through it." In 1998, Howard graduated from the Army's Command and General Staff College with a master's in military arts and sciences.

### EARLY CAREER

According to retired Brigadier General Wilma L. Vaught, who joined the Air Force in 1957, Howard embarked on her career at an ideal time in the military's history. "She was a junior officer when breakthroughs were happening in the 1980s and then she was at the midlevel when there were openings for more challenging positions," Vaught said, as quoted by Schneider. "She couldn't have hit it any better." Still, as a young midshipman, colleagues recalled that Howard was unassuming. She was quiet and diminutive—standing at about five feet tall—but she quickly established herself as intelligent and hardworking.

After graduating from the Naval Academy, Howard served aboard the USS *Hunley*, though the submarine tender rarely left the pier. She then volunteered for a tour aboard the USS *Lexington*, an aircraft carrier, to gain more experience. The decision, said one colleague, is indicative of Howard's nature. "The whole body of her career work is that she was going to the hard places, doing the harder things," retired Rear Admiral Sonny Masso told Sam Fellman for the *Navy Times* (4 Jan. 2014). Serving aboard the *Lexington*, Howard received the Secretary of the Navy/Navy League Captain Winifred Collins Award for outstanding female leadership in 1987.

In 1990, Howard was the chief engineer aboard the USS *Mount Hood* before serving in Operation Desert Shield (the US–aided defense of Saudi Arabia against Iraqi forces) later the same year, and Operation Desert Storm (the US attack on Iraq) in 1991. Howard took on the role of first lieutenant aboard the USS *Flint* in July 1992. In January 1996, she became the executive officer of USS *Tortuga*, which was deployed to the Adriatic Sea as part of Operation Joint Endeavor. The US–led operation, set in motion in 1995, was part of an effort to keep the peace in Bosnia, formerly the Republic of Yugoslavia. Later the same year, the *Tortuga* served in West Africa.

### PROMOTION AND DISTINGUISHED SERVICE

Howard became the first African American woman to command a ship in the US Navy when she took command of the USS *Rushmore* on March 12, 1999. From May 2004 to September 2005, she was the commander of the Amphibious Squadron Seven, where she oversaw tsunami relief efforts in Indonesia and security operations in the North Arabian Gulf. In 2009, Howard was working in Washington, DC, as the senior military assistant to Secretary of the Navy Donald Winter. In April, she was transferred to the USS *Boxer*, a deck assault ship that was patrolling the Gulf of Aden in the Arabian Sea, where she oversaw one thousand Marines and ran the international Combined Task Force 151, which included several warships. The Gulf of Aden, situated between Yemen and Somalia, is a vital thoroughfare for sea trade, but as Somalia suffered from civil war, drought, and a lack of effective government, the gulf became a dangerous pass known as "Pirate Alley." Desperate Somalis were known to chase after cargo ships in skiffs, holding the crews for ransom.

During Howard's first week on the job, a group of Somali pirates attacked and boarded the US containership *Maersk Alabama* about three hundred miles off the coast of Somalia. The ship's captain, Richard Phillips, was taken hostage on a lifeboat. It was the first seizure of an American ship by pirates in nearly two hundred years; there was no set protocol to respond to the situation, but Howard had to act and give orders quickly to save Phillips's life. She mobilized thousands of US and international personnel and a team of Navy SEALs who received an order from President Barack Obama to shoot to kill if Phillips's life was threatened. The hostage situation lasted for four days. "Time was unfolding in clock seconds, and I just felt the weight of each tick," Howard recalled to Larry Keller for *Success* magazine (20 June 2013). "The [lifeboat] is getting closer to shore—how are we going to get the pirates to stop trying to go to shore? You realize you're on this time line that's pretty compressed to get this guy home safe."

On April 12, Navy SEAL snipers shot and killed three of the pirates while a fourth was captured. At the time, Howard did not realize the magnitude of the story of the rescue circulating back in the United States. When she returned to speak to the Congressional Black Caucus in Washington, DC, she told Keller, she received a standing ovation when she walked into the room. "People were stopping me, and it was all because of *Maersk Alabama*," she said.

In February 2013, Howard received the Chairman's Award at the NAACP Image Awards, and in January 2014, she was a guest of First Lady Michelle Obama at President Obama's State of the Union address. Later that year, in July, Howard was promoted to the rank of four-star admiral at a ceremony at the Women in Military Service for America Memorial at Arlington National Cemetery. In her speech, she related how she had called to order a woman's set of four-star shoulder boards. The woman on the other end of the line checked the system and told her that, as Howard had predicted, such a decoration did not exist in the company's inventory. The company had some custom-made, "and you folks are seeing the first set," she told the crowd, as quoted by Dan Lamothe for the *Washington Post* (1 July 2014). While some critics have questioned whether Howard has received such promotions mainly because of her race and gender, Colonel Krewasky A. Salter, a former teacher of Howard's at the US Army Command and General Staff College, stated, "Admiral Howard is all about capability, not that she's a woman or that she's African American," as quoted by Schneider.

## PERSONAL LIFE

Howard married US Marine Wayne Cowles in 1989 after having met him as a security officer on her first tour. A year after their wedding, they were both deployed in Operation Desert Storm. After Cowles retired, he quit his civilian jobs to move with his wife whenever she was transferred. "He got a little grief from his former Marine Corps buddies who called him 'camp follower,'" Howard recalled to Tara Bahrampour for *Glamour* magazine (Oct. 2014), "and he'd say, 'Hey, you guys are just jealous.'" Howard's civilian interests include reading and

trout fishing, an enthusiasm she inherited from her mother.

## SUGGESTED READING

Bahrampour, Tara. "Meet the Highest-Ranking Woman in U.S. Naval History." *Glamour*. Condé Nast, Oct. 2014. Web. 10 Feb. 2015.

Fellman, Sam. "Howard's Path to Navy History." *Navy Times*. Gannett, 4 Jan. 2014. Web. 26 Feb. 2015.

Howard, Michelle. "A Phone Call Helped Navy's First Four-Star Woman Embrace Her Path." Interview by Rachel Martin. *Morning Edition*. NPR, 10 Oct. 2014. Web. 26 Feb. 2015. Transcript.

Keller, Larry. "Michelle Howard: Uncharted Waters." *Success*. Success Magazine, 20 June 2013. Web. 26 Feb. 2015.

Lamothe, Dan. "Adm. Michelle Howard Becomes First Four-Star Woman in Navy History." *Washington Post*. Washington Post, 1 July 2014. Web. 26 Feb. 2015.

Schneider, Elena. "A Four-Star Female Admiral Makes History for the Navy." *New York Times*. New York Times, 11 July 2014. Web. 26 Feb. 2015.

—Molly Hagan

# Hu Shuli

**Born:** 1953
**Occupation:** Founder, Caixin Media

Hu Shuli is a Chinese journalist who is best known as the founding editor of the biweekly magazine *Caijing* (the name translates to "finance and economics"). In China, every act of journalism—even a report about a natural disaster—is a politically dangerous act. In 2015 the nonprofit organization Reporters Without Borders ranked China number 176 out of 180 countries on its World Press Freedom Index. As of April in the same year, the organization reports, there were twenty-nine journalists in Chinese prisons. Hu founded *Caijing* in 1998, and by 2009, she had amassed a slew of monikers that spoke to her toughness and resolve in running a hard news operation within an oppressive regime. In an article for the *New Yorker* (20 July 2009), Evan Osnos called her "a female Godfather," after the Mafia boss famously portrayed by Marlon Brando in the film *The Godfather* (1972). David Ignatius of the *Washington Post* referred to

World Economic Forum/Wikimedia Commons

## EARLY LIFE AND CULTURAL REVOLUTION

Hu Shuli was born in 1953 in Beijing. Journalism is in her blood: Her maternal grandfather, Hu Zhongchi, was a well-known translator (he was one of the first translators of Pearl S. Buck's 1931 novel, *The Good Earth*) and the editor of the Shanghai newspaper *Shen Bao.* His brother, Hu Yuzhi, founded a publishing house that published the work of Lu Xun, one of the most famous writers of China's modern age, as well as translations of books by American journalist Edgar Snow and novelist John Steinbeck. Hu's aunt ran a children's newspaper. Her mother, Hu Lingsheng, was a senior editor at the Communist Party newspaper *Workers' Daily* in Beijing, and her father, Cao Qifeng, worked for a trade union.

Hu's parents named her Shula after a Soviet martyr, but she changed her name to Shuli, a more popular name, in the 1970s. Hu was an outspoken child, a trait that distressed her parents. "I was not very disciplined," she told Osnos. "I always spoke about what I was thinking." She attended an elite middle school, where students were allowed to read foreign books that were banned elsewhere, including novels by J. D. Salinger, Jack Kerouac, and Aleksandr Solzhenitsyn.

Hu was thirteen when China's Cultural Revolution began. The revolution was an attempt to purge Chinese culture of any tendency or artifact considered bourgeois by the Chinese government. Schools were suspended, and students—of which Hu was one—joined groups of Red Guards that destroyed churches and art suggestive of China's prerevolutionary past. Hu's intellectual family was blacklisted: her mother was placed under house arrest, and her father was demoted. Hu travelled around the country as a Red Guard until she was sixteen, at which point she, like millions of other young Chinese people, was sent to the countryside to work on a farm. (Hu's sister, Cao Zuyoa, wrote a book about the mass relocation and its effect on her generation called *Out of the Crucible.*) Hu tried to read when she could, but the task was almost impossible in the face of China's changing mores. "It was a very confusing time," she told Osnos. "We lost all values."

her as China's "avenging angel." More than one member of the foreign press has called her "the most dangerous woman in China." Her tactics for getting out the news, and divining the hazy line drawn by the Chinese government between what is fit to print and what is not, are delicate, but her rhetoric is blunt: "If it's not absolutely forbidden," she told Osnos, "we do it."

In 2009 Hu left *Caijing* to found a company called Caixin Media, where she continues to speak truth to power, if only in subtle ways. Adi Ignatius wrote in *Time* (21 Apr. 2011), that in February 2011, Hu's magazine ran a commentary about the unrest in Egypt. One parallel between the Egypt and China was made clear: "Autocracy creates turbulence," the article said. "Democracy breeds peace."

Hu has won a number of awards for her work. In 2003 she was named editor of the year by the *World Press Review*, and in 2007 she received the Louis Lyons Award for conscience and integrity in journalism from the Nieman Foundation at Harvard University. In 2011 Hu and her team won the Shorenstein Journalism Award from Stanford University. She won Taiwan's Hsing Yun Journalism Award the same year, and the Missouri Honor Medal for distinguished service in journalism in 2012. In addition to her position as editor in chief at Caixin, Hu is also the dean of the School of Communications and Design at Sun Yat-sen University in Guangzhou.

## EDUCATION AND EARLY CAREER

Hu spent two years on the farm before joining the Army, where she was assigned a post at a rural hospital in Jiangsu Province. She worked as a nurse's assistant for eight years while teaching herself English in her spare time. In 1978, when Hu was about twenty-five years old, Chinese colleges opened their doors again. She gained entry to the People's University in Beijing, where she studied journalism. Her classes focused on journalism in service of Communist ideals; when she wrote her dissertation on how the *New York Times* covered the assassination attempt on President Ronald Reagan in 1981, she received a poor grade, David Barboza wrote for the *Times* (18 Apr. 2005), because she failed to tie her interpretation to Marxist theory. After graduation, Hu joined the staff of *Worker's Daily*. In 1985 she was assigned to the newspaper bureau in Xiamen, a city that the government was using to test-drive a free-market economic model. Hu, a champion networker, quickly made friends with local government officials, including Xiamen's vice-mayor, Xi Jinping. Like many of Hu's early contacts, her acquaintance with Xi would prove to be very powerful: Xi became the president of the People's Republic of China in 2012.

In 1987 Hu won a fellowship from the World Press Institute, and spent five months in St. Paul, Minnesota. She marveled at the size of the city's newspaper in comparison to the then-four-page *Worker's Daily*. (When she returned to China, she pushed the paper to accept advertising and expand.) She interned for *USA Today* before returning to Beijing, less than a year before the Tiananmen Square movement in 1989. Chinese students were angry about growing wealth inequality, and took to the streets that spring to protest. The government tolerated the protests, which inspired a huge swath of the Chinese population to join the fray. The government declared martial law in late May, but the brutal crackdown came on June 3, 1989. Hundreds of thousands of troops descended on the square; in less than twenty-four hours, anywhere from several hundred to two thousand civilians (the toll remains unclear) were dead. Hu visited the square the night of June 3. "I went to the street, then went back to the office and said, 'We should cover this,'" she recalled to Osnos. But the newspaper had already received its marching orders: they were not to publish anything about it.

## SEEC AND *CAIJING* MAGAZINE

Many reporters who had spoken out about the Tiananmen Square massacre were jailed, but Hu was only suspended for eighteen months. She used the time to write a book, *Behind the Scenes at American Newspapers*, which examines the relationship between the American government and the press and challenges Chinese journalists to emulate that relationship in China. Hu began working as an international editor at the *China Business Times* in 1992, during a period of economic and market reform in China. She met an influential group of men who had studied business in the United States and who wanted to set up a Chinese stock market. They called themselves the Stock Exchange Executive Council (SEEC). In 1998, Wang Boming of the SEEC contacted Hu with a business proposition. He was starting a magazine called *Caijing*, and he wanted Hu to be its editor. It was a good deal, similar to business partnerships at some American news outlets: Wang agreed to give her full editorial control and an annual budget of about half a million dollars, Osnos reported—"enough to prevent reporters from taking bribes." Wang "and his reform-minded allies in the government saw the magazine as an extension of their determination to modernize the economy," Osnos wrote. *Caijing* became one of only a handful of publications in China with private funding.

Hu's magazine printed its first issue in April 1998. In it, her team exposed a crooked real estate company, angering state censors. She was testing the waters, Osnos wrote. "Each story refined Hu's calculation of how far she could push."

## SARS REPORTING AND THE LUNENG INCIDENT

In 2003 one of *Caijing*'s reporters travelled to Hong Kong, where she was baffled to see people wearing surgical masks covering their noses and mouths. Newspapers in the neighboring Guangdong Province were allowed to carry only soothing stories about a new virus under control, but Hu took the story into her own hands. "I bought a lot of books about breathing diseases, infections, and viruses," she recalled to Osnos. Through the World Health Organization (WHO), Hu and her team eventually identified the virus as severe acute respiratory syndrome (SARS). *Caijing* published several weeks of supplements about SARS, in addition to the magazine, before the government stepped in—but the story was already circulating. The reports that were run earned Hu international acclaim. She later told Keiko Yoshioka for Osaka, Japan's *Asahi Shimbun* (18 Apr. 2013), "I decided to run the stories because they concerned life-and-death matters." The information was not always easy to get, she told Yoshioka: "As a result of questioning several hospitals by our reporting team, we learned that the authorities had told the hospitals to keep the matter a secret."

Hu did not face any punishment for her SARS reporting, but in 2007, when she ran a report about the shady dealings of a conglomerate called Luneng, the government ordered her to destroy the story. *Caijing* was forced to recall the paper from the newsstands and delete it from its website. "The staff in *Caijing*'s Shanghai office are said to have torn up issues by hand," Osnos wrote.

Hu was deeply humiliated by the Luneng incident, telling Osnos that she considered it the magazine's "largest disaster." Osnos offered one explanation for why she might feel that way, as suggested by a source close to *Caijing*, who said that "revealing the attempt to profit wildly from the privatization deal had come too close to implicating the children of senior Party leaders" who make up a significant number of China's business leaders, "a taboo that trumps even reformists' desire for a more open press." Another Chinese journalist, the former editor in chief of *Southern Metropolis Daily*, echoed this sentiment and even suggested that *Caijing*'s ties to powerful businessmen have protected its journalists, while journalists from other publications are jailed. "*Caijing*'s topics haven't affected the fundamental ruling system, so it is relatively safe," he told Osnos. "I am not criticizing Hu Shuli, but in some ways *Caijing* is just serving a more powerful or relatively better interest group."

## CAIXIN MEDIA

After an editorial dispute with Wang, Hu resigned as the editor in chief of *Caijing* in November 2009. One hundred and forty of her reporters left with her. In December, Hu founded Caixin Media with a group of private investors. The first issue of their flagship title, *Century Weekly* (known as *Caixin Weekly* as of April 6, 2015), was published in January 2010. As of 2015 Caixin Media published four magazines, and had expanded into television programs, websites, mobile apps, and books. In 2011 *Century Weekly* uncovered a horrific practice in the Hunan province, in which rural parents could not afford, under the country's more relaxed one-child policy, to pay for the proper permissions on their second child. The children are seized, like property, and put in orphanages, *Century Weekly* reported. Some are put up for adoption abroad. There are plenty such stories to be reported in China, Hu told a group of students at the Chinese University in Sha Tin. As quoted by Verna Yu for the *South China Morning Post* (27 Sept. 2012), she said, "There are just too few platforms for rational voices."

## PERSONAL LIFE

Hu studied economics as a Knight Journalism Fellow at Stanford University in 1994, and earned her executive MBA degree from Fordham University and the China Center for Economic Research at Peking University in 2002. Her husband, Miao Di, is a film professor at the Communication University of China in Beijing. The couple met in college and were married in 1982.

## SUGGESTED READING

Barboza, David. "Pushing (and Toeing) the Line in China." *New York Times*. New York Times, 18 Apr. 2005. Web. 14 Apr. 2015.

Hu, Shuli. "Interview Hu Shuli: China Still Has Not Compiled a Common Dream." Interview by Keiko Yoshioka. *Asahi Shimbun*. Asahi Shimbun, 18 Apr. 2013. Web. 12 Apr. 2015.

Ignatius, Adi. "The 100 Most Influential People in the World 2011: Hu Shuli." *Time*. Time, 21 Apr. 2011. Web. 12 Apr. 2015.

Osnos, Evan. "The Forbidden Zone." *New Yorker*. Condé Nast, 20 July 2009. Web. 12 Apr. 2015.

Yu, Verna. "Journalist Hu Shuli Sees Ample Scope for Investigative Stories." *South China Morning Post*. South China Morning Post, 27 Sept. 2012. Web. 12 Apr. 2015.

—Molly Hagan

# Ryan Hunter-Reay

**Born:** December 17, 1980
**Occupation:** Race car driver

Ryan Hunter-Reay is the most successful American driver in open-wheel racing. He is best known for being the first American to win the Indianapolis 500 since Sam Hornish Jr. in 2006. "That's where all the heroes were," Hunter-Reay told Matt Baker for the *Tampa Bay Times* (26 Mar. 2015). "I remember watching [the Indianapolis 500] as a kid thinking, this is it. That is the top level of motorsports. That's where I want to be one day." Though he is only thirty-three years old, Hunter-Reay's career has been a bumpy ride. He entered his first open-wheel season in 2003, but was unable to secure a steady ride until Andretti Autosport, a team owned by former professional racer Michael Andretti, signed him in 2010. "It's a pretty intense and pressure-packed career," Hunter-Reay told Becky Randel for *South Florida Business and Wealth* magazine (26 Sept. 2014). "There is a lot of corporate money involved. Just like business, people want results and they deserve them. When the results do come, it's an amazing feeling of relief—even sometimes more so than the celebration."

Hunter-Reay also won the IndyCar Series Rookie of the Year in 2007. He was the IZOD IndyCar Series champion in 2012, and he has twice won the Excellence in Sports Performance Yearly (ESPY) Award for best driver.

## EARLY LIFE AND EDUCATION

Hunter-Reay was born on December 17, 1980, in Dallas, Texas, and grew up in Fort Lauderdale, Florida. He developed a love for water and the ocean, and when he was four or five years old, he began fishing with a close group of friends that he keeps today. "We were miles offshore by ourselves fishing as early as 13 or 14," he told fellow racer, Hélio Castroneves in an interview for *Venice: Fort Lauderdale's Magazine* (16 Jan. 2015). Hunter-Reay also developed a love for motor sports; he remembers watching the Indy 500 on television and idolizing racers like Bobby Rahal, who won the race in 1986, and Al Unser Jr., who won in 1992 and 1994. He used to watch the race with his father every Memorial Day weekend, plastic race cars in hand. "My dad was a gearhead—he loved cars. I grew up loving cars as well," Hunter-Reay told Don Markus for the *Baltimore Sun* (20 May 2013). "He took me to a few races as a fan, and that's where it started." Like a lot of Indy hopefuls, Hunter-Reay got his start racing go-karts. He was a six-time national karting champion, and in 1999, he was the Skip Barber Formula Dodge national champion. Though his racing often interfered with his education, he attended Fort Lauderdale's Pine Crest School for elementary and middle school, and graduated from Cardinal Gibbons Catholic High School in 2000, having worked out a deal with the principal that allowed him to miss two days each school week if he made up the work.

## EARLY CAREER

In 2000 Hunter-Reay won the Barber Dodge Pro series Rookie of the Year Award, and in 2002 he won three races in the Toyota Atlantic Series. He

Jim Spellman/WireImage/Getty Images

won a race in each of his first two open-wheel seasons in 2003–4, where he earned his first win with the Champ Car World Series at Surfers Paradise in Queensland, Australia. After his win, Hunter-Reay bounced from team to team; he had just lost a third ride before the 2006 season, and unable to compete in open-wheel racing, he raced sports cars and even worked as a test-car driver for Rick Hendrick's NASCAR team. "I just got into anything I could, whenever I could," he told Jim Peltz for the *Los Angeles Times* (19 Apr. 2013), "and worked my way back into open-wheel racing." Midway through the racing season in 2007, Bobby Rahal, one of Hunter-Reay's childhood idols, signed him to Rahal Letterman Racing, which Rahal owns with late night talk show host David Letterman. Hunter-Reay drove in six races for the team and in three of the races finished in one of the top ten positions. He also raced the Indianapolis 500 for the first time. "Nothing can prepare you coming up on that driver entrance stage and you see 350,000 to 400,000 people in one place," he told Markus. "Being the first time, it was overwhelming. It blew me away, the enormity of the event. It's still the single-day biggest sporting event in the world." Hunter-Reay's sixth-place—for which he was named the Indy 500 Rookie of the Year—was his best finish until 2014.

Hunter-Reay continued to race with Rahal Letterman Racing through 2008, but in 2009, the team's sponsor dropped out, leaving them in the lurch. Hunter-Reay then signed a six-race deal with Vision Racing, a team owned by Tony George, the former CEO of IndyCar from 1990 to 2004. In 2010, Hunter-Reay got his big break; he landed a ride with Andretti Autosport, one of the best teams in IndyCar, before the season began. Still, Hunter-Reay knew he was in a precarious position. He knew he would need a big win to secure enough sponsorship money to finish out the racing season. It was in 2012 he pulled out a career-making victory at the Toyota Grand Prix at Long Beach. The win was "pivotal," he told Peltz. He finished out the season with a flourish, clinching the season championship. Hunter-Reay told Peltz, "My entire career has been career instability. It's been jumping from team to team. So being a champion offers a shot at career stability."

## 2014 INDY 500 VICTORY

Hunter-Reay re-signed with Andretti Autosport in 2012, and expectations for him were high going into the 2013 Indy 500, but he was bested in the last three laps by driver Tony Kanaan. Hunter-Reay finished third and going into the 2014 racing season there was less hype surrounding him. In an interview with Chris Estrada for *NBC Sports* (22 May 2014), he expressed confidence going into the ninety-eighth Indianapolis 500 race telling Estrada, despite a poor qualifying round, "There's a bit of a gut feeling." The race came down to Hunter-Reay and Brazilian racer Hélio Castroneves, a three-time Indy 500 champion, trading the lead three times—one last, risky pass pushed the race in Hunter-Reay's favor. He won by 0.060 seconds, the second-closest finish in the race's history. (The closest race happened in 1992, when Al Unser Jr. beat Scott Goodyear by 0.043 seconds to win his first Indy.) "I'm a proud American boy, that's for sure," Hunter-Reay told Jenna Fryer for the *Huffington Post* (25 May 2014) immediately after the race. "I've watched this race since I was sitting in diapers on the floor in front of the TV. My son did it today. He watched me here. I'm thrilled. This is American history, this race. This is American tradition."

## PHILANTHROPY AND PERSONAL LIFE

Hunter-Reay created a charitable foundation called Racing for Cancer, after his mother, Lydia, died of colon cancer in November 2010. The foundation has raised more than $2 million; Hunter-Reay hopes to use the funds to build a comprehensive cancer treatment facility in South Florida. He drives IndyCar's No. 28 DHL Honda in memory of his mother and the twenty-eight million people currently living with cancer.

Hunter-Reay is married to Rebecca "Beccy" Gordon. She and Hunter-Reay met at the Toyota Grand Prix in Long Beach in 2004. The couple live in Fort Lauderdale with their son, Ryden, born in 2012.

## SUGGESTED READING

Baker, Matt. "For Ryan Hunter-Reay, Racing Is the American Way." *Tampa Bay Times*. Tampa Bay Times, 26 Mar. 2015. Web. 11 Apr. 2015.

Estrada, Chris. "After 2013 Near-Miss, Hunter-Reay Confident Ahead of This Year's Indy 500." *NBC Sports*. NBC Sports, 22 May 2014. Web. 12 Apr. 2015.

Fryer, Jenna. "Ryan Hunter-Reay Wins 2014 Indianapolis 500." *Huffington Post*. TheHuffingtonPost.com, 25 May 2014. Web. 11 Apr. 2015.

Hunter-Reay, Ryan. "Road Tested." Interview by Hélio Castroneves. *Venice: Fort Lauderdale's Magazine* Winter 2014: 128–33. Print.

Markus, Don. "Once a Fan of the Indy 500, Ryan Hunter-Reay Hopes to Win It Sunday." *Baltimore Sun*. Baltimore Sun, 20 May 2013. Web. 11 Apr. 2015.

Peltz, Jim. "Long Beach Has Special Meaning for Ryan Hunter-Reay." *Los Angeles Times*. Los Angeles Times, 19 Apr. 2013. Web. 11 Apr. 2015.

—Molly Hagan

# Nyjah Huston
**Born:** November 30, 1994
**Occupation:** Skateboarder

In the world of street skateboarding, a sport known for its young superstars, Nyjah Huston has achieved an unprecedented level of success. With a methodical and merciless style, Huston has wowed the skateboarding world with his uncanny ability to make the most difficult tricks and maneuvers seem effortless. He has been doing so practically from birth: he landed his first sponsorship at the age of seven, and by 2006, at age eleven, he had become the youngest competitor in the history of the X Games, the world's preeminent extreme-sports event. Sporting waist-length dreadlocks, Huston became a regular and highly visible presence in skateboarding films and at major competitions around the world.

After breaking free from an overbearing father, Huston took control of his career and started realizing his potential. He won his first major title, the inaugural Street League Skateboarding (SLS) championship, in 2010, and captured his first-ever X Games gold medal in 2011. Huston has since become a dominant force on the SLS tour and a mainstay on the X Games podium. In 2014 he won every contest he entered, helping him solidify his status as "the best skateboarder alive," per Nate Scott for *USA Today* (10 Sept. 2014).

In addition to participating in professional competitions, Huston has filmed six full-length videos, which have featured him performing tricks that have continually redefined what is possible in skateboarding. With more than $2 million in career prize money, he is the highest-earning street skateboarder of all time.

## EARLY LIFE

Nyjah Imani Huston was born on November 30, 1994, in Davis, California, to an African American father, Adeyemi, and a white mother, Kelle. His parents, who had started dating in junior high school, were free-spirit adherents of Rastafarianism, a lifestyle centered on natural living. They followed a strict vegan diet and habitually listened to reggae music. Along with his siblings, Huston was raised vegan and home-schooled. He has two older brothers, Ahbi and Jahmai; a younger brother, Kiade; and a younger sister, Isha.

Huston also grew up immersed in skateboarding culture. He was introduced to skateboarding through his father, an avid skateboarder who was eager to share his passion for the individualized sport, which he felt meshed well with the Rastafarian way of life. According to Elena Bergeron for *ESPN The Magazine* (30 May 2013), Huston started pushing one of his father's skateboards around the family home "dump-truck style" at the age of two and first learned how to skate at age five.

Unlike his brothers, who were more comfortable skating among friends, Huston took to skateboarding in earnest. Meticulous, disciplined, regimented, and preternaturally talented, he would spend hours on end perfecting tricks and maneuvers. Huston's unflinching dedication was nurtured by his father, who drove him each day to local skate parks. When Huston was seven, his father bought and renovated a run-

John Sciulli/WireImage/Getty Images

down skate park in Woodland, California. The family-owned skate park, renamed Frontline, dramatically accelerated Huston's skateboarding development. As Huston put it to Bergeron, "If you're in an environment where you have a perfect skate park every single day, you're naturally gonna get good if you love to do it."

## RISE TO SKATEBOARDING PROMINENCE

Huston's career first took off in 2001, when skateboarder Reese Forbes took notice of him while visiting a skate park in Milpitas, California. Recognizing his enormous potential, Reese helped Huston, as well as his brother Ahbi (also a talented skateboarder), land endorsement deals with his then-sponsor Element Skateboards. The two joined the Irvine, California-based company's Twigs skateboarding team, which featured young riders.

By 2004 Huston was regularly winning amateur contests around the country and appearing in Element-sponsored skateboarding videos. His first major video spot, a Twigs team project called *Tricks*, was released in 2005. That same year Huston won the Tampa Am, the top amateur competition in the country. Just ten years old at the time, he defeated competitors two and three times his age. Huston, who by then had dreadlocks down to his waist, called the win "one of the bigger things that I've accomplished in my career," in an interview with Adam Salo for ESPN Action Sports (27 July 2011).

Huston turned professional at age eleven in 2006. As skateboarding's youngest professional, he began competing on the high-profile Dew Tour, which features the world's best skateboarders. He finished second at two Dew Tour events before competing at the 2006 X Games in Los Angeles, where he placed eighth in the street skateboarding competition. At eleven years and 246 days, Huston became the X Games' youngest-ever competitor. Around this time, Don Bostick, president of World Cup Skateboarding, skateboarding's official governing body, predicted to Matt Higgins for the *New York Times* (17 July 2006): "If he can make it through his teen years, I think he's the future of street and park skateboarding."

## FALLOUT WITH FATHER

The only thing standing in the way of Huston's fast-rising success was his father. As his son's full-time manager, Adeyemi Huston was in charge of all his finances, negotiating his contracts and obligations with sponsors and choosing what competitions he entered. He had dedicated himself fully to his son's career and relentlessly pushed him to succeed, which included making him practice when he was sick and largely sheltering him from the outside world. Constantly vying for his father's approval, Huston acquiesced to his demands. "The combination of Nyjah trying to perfect himself and please his dad at the same time created a super talent that is almost uncanny," Huston's mother told Ian Michna for *Jenkem* magazine (28 Apr. 2014).

In 2006 Adeyemi moved his entire family to a twenty-six-acre farm in Puerto Rico, in an effort to further withdraw them from society. Purchased with Huston's prize earnings, the farm had such an unreliable plumbing system that it often broke in harsh weather conditions, forcing the family to carry heavy buckets of clean water from a holding tank in order to perform everyday household chores. Not long after the move to Puerto Rico, Huston's family began to dissolve.

While Huston and his father attended a skateboarding competition in Barcelona, Spain, in 2008, his mother fled Puerto Rico with his siblings and moved back to California. She filed for divorce from Adeyemi and, ultimately, won custody of Nyjah in 2010. In the interim between the divorce proceedings, however, Huston continued to live with his father. As he explained to Bergeron, "Because my dad was my manager, I was kind of the one child out of all my brothers and sisters who didn't kind of have a choice."

By 2009 Huston had been dropped by his sponsors Element and éS footwear as a result of his father's cantankerous relationship with them. That year he started his own board company, I&I Skateboards, with his father, and began skating in professional contests for them. The venture proved to be short-lived, however, and nearly bankrupted Huston, who had launched the company with his earnings. In an interview with *Transworld Skateboarding* (May 2012), he said, "As cool as it is to have your own company, it's hard at the same time. . . . Eventually, I just wanted to focus on the skateboarding again to be the best that I could be."

## REEMERGENCE AS STREET SKATEBOARDING SUPERSTAR

By the end of his parents' divorce proceedings in 2010, Huston had amassed hundreds of hours of independent skateboarding footage featuring him developing and performing new tricks. His father, nonetheless, refused to return the footage to him, permanently damaging their relationship. Huston moved back to California to live with his mother, who became his new manager. He has since had little contact with his father but has credited him with playing an integral role in his development as a skateboarder.

Despite the family drama, Huston remained a steady presence and strong performer in professional skating competitions. Most notably, he notched second-place finishes at the Maloof Money Cup and X Games, in 2008 and 2009, respectively. However, once Huston moved in with his mother, "everything just fell into place," as he told Bergeron. Skating with a newfound sense of freedom, he blossomed into a superstar.

In 2010 Huston again finished as runner-up at both the Maloof Money Cup and X Games before competing at the first-ever SLS contest, held in Glendale, Arizona. Founded by professional skateboarder and MTV reality star Rob Dyrdek, SLS features the world's top street skateboarders competing for lucrative cash prizes at events held in arenas around the country. The first professional league established for street skateboarding, SLS runs at a much faster pace than traditionally run skateboarding competitions, using an instant-scoring technology called ISX to score tricks as they happen. As opposed to the chaotic nature of jam sessions, the Street League format forces skaters to strategize their runs with a wide array of tricks. "I think it is the best format," Huston opined in the *Transworld Skateboarding* interview. "I see it as a good middle ground between a jam session and a one-minute run because you can fall and still have a chance to win."

In Glendale, Huston beat out some of the world's top skateboarders, including Paul Rodriguez and Chris Cole, to win the inaugural event of the Street League tour. He placed third in two other tour events, earning enough contest points to win the 2010 SLS Super Crown World Championship.

## HIGHEST-EARNING STREET SKATEBOARDER

Thrust back into the spotlight, Huston returned to Element and landed a sponsorship deal with the footwear company DC Shoes. With two of the biggest names in skateboarding backing him, he won almost every contest he entered in 2011. He won the first three events of the second SLS season, ultimately finishing second overall in the tour championships, and he captured his first X Games gold medal in the street skateboarding event.

At the first event of the 2011 SLS tour in Seattle, Washington, Huston became the first skateboarder ever to complete a backside 270 noseblunt-slide, a trick that earned him a score of 9.9, the highest in SLS history. "He's good at everything," Dyrdek asserted to Bernie Wilson for the Associated Press (26 Aug. 2011). "He has an immense amount of control and technicality that's far superior to most guys." Huston again earned attention in the run-up to that year's third SLS stop in Glendale when he cut his signature dreadlocks, a move many viewed as a symbolic break from his past. "I didn't want to be thought of as the kid with dreadlocks for my whole life," he explained to Wilson. "I felt the time was right."

Also in 2011, Huston released his first solo video reel, titled *Rise & Shine*. Released through Element on iTunes, the highly anticipated production was honored three times at the fourteenth annual Transworld Skateboarding Awards, winning awards for best street, best video part, and readers' choice. In an article for that publication (May 2012), Kevin Duffel called *Rise & Shine* "quite possibly the best video part of all time." In 2013, Huston's released his sixth full-length video, *Fade to Black*, produced by DC Shoes.

Huston won his second SLS series championship in 2012. The following year, SLS partnered with the X Games to launch the first-ever world tour for professional street skateboarding. Huston won four of the 2013 tour's seven events, which included winning street skateboarding gold medals at X Games held in Brazil, Spain, and the United States. He finished second overall for the 2013 SLS Super Crown World Championship.

Huston returned with a vengeance in 2014, when he put together the first perfect season in SLS history. In addition to winning his third SLS world championship, he competed at the 2014 X Games in Austin, Texas, where he captured his sixth career street skateboarding gold medal. By the end of the 2014 season, he had won the most prize money of any skateboarder in history, with more than $2 million in earnings.

## PERSONAL LIFE

As SLS makes a push to become a mainstream recognized sport, Huston is regarded as its "biggest star," Scott wrote. He has released two signature shoes, the Nyjah S and the Nyjah Vulc, with DC Shoes, and an apparel collection with his clothing sponsor Asphalt Yacht Club. Lowell Taub, who represents Huston at the entertainment behemoth Creative Artists Agency, said to Bergeron, "We truly think that Nyjah, if he's not already, is poised to become the face of his sport the way that Shaun White is the face of snowboarding."

Huston owns a two-story home in Huntington Beach, California. His honors include being named best male action sports athlete at both the 2013 and 2014 ESPY Awards.

## SUGGESTED READING

Bergeron, Elena. "Eighteen at Last."*ESPN The Magazine*. ESPN Internet Ventures, 30 May 2013. Web. 2 Feb. 2015.

Higgins, Matt. "Navigating a Pro Career and the Preteen Scene." *New York Times*. New York Times, 17 July 2006. Web. 2 Feb. 2015.

Huston, Nyjah. "Nyjah Huston." Interview by Kevin Duffel. *Transworld Skateboarding* May 2012: 106–9. Print.

Scott, Nate. "Nyjah Huston, Rob Dyrdek and the Quest for a National Skateboarding League." *USA Today*. USA Today, 10 Sept. 2014. Web. 2 Feb. 2015.

Wilson, Bernie. "Huston, 16, Closing in on $1M in Prize Money." *AP Regional State Report–California* (2011). *Newspaper Source Plus*. Web. 17 Feb. 2015.

—Chris Cullen

# Susie Ibarra

**Born:** November 15, 1970
**Occupation:** Composer and percussionist

Susie Ibarra is a jazz percussionist and composer, but that description does not accurately capture the breadth of Ibarra's work—spanning free jazz, electronica, and Filipino folk music—as a musical artist. "A global rhythmist at heart . . . Ibarra forges drumming that extends beyond boundaries, beyond cliché, and beyond our common understanding of what a drummer's role is and ultimately can be," Ken Micallef wrote for *Modern Drummer* magazine (1 Dec. 2010). Ibarra's musical style varies widely. Ibarra described her work to Lance Hahn in an interview for the now defunct Asian American pop culture magazine *Giant Robot* (2004). "My trio is electro-acoustic experimental music with a chamber vibe. My quartet is jazz. And I have a Filipino trip-hop band, too, S.I. Electric Kulintang, in which I explore the nature of trance music and its relation to grooves." Ibarra founded the latter group, Electric Kulintang, with her husband, Roberto J. Rodriguez, a Cuban American percussionist and composer. Kulintang is a traditional Filipino gong ensemble, consisting of a row of eight small gongs, and it has a long and varied history that spans the Asian continent. Ibarra brings contemporary improvisational techniques—the techniques she uses when playing jazz drums—to kulintang.

Like one of her idols, the free jazz composer Sun Ra, Ibarra's work blurs the lines separating disparate styles of music, performance, and art. But establishing herself in the male-dominated jazz culture was not always easy. "It's hard to be totally alone and a woman on the jazz scene," she told David Yaffe for the *New York Times* (30 May 1999). "But I know that I must have a strong love of music, because I had to go through a lot. Sometimes, professional musicians have either vibed me out or made passes at me. I tried to shrug it off, but it can be discouraging whether you have a teacher or a famous musician hitting on you." Other female musicians have shared similar stories, she added, "but for every tough situation I have had more situations with people who are way above that and are about the music."

After over two decades of performances, Ibarra has established herself as a mainstay of the avant-garde jazz scene. Ibarra received the 2008 Asian Cultural Council/Rockefeller Fellowship and the New York Foundation for the Arts Fellow Award for music and sound in 2010. Ibarra has taught at Bennington College in Bennington, Vermont, since 2012.

## EARLY LIFE AND EDUCATION

Ibarra was born on November 15, 1970, in Anaheim, California, and spent part of her early childhood in Iowa, but grew up in Houston, Texas. Both of her parents were raised in Manila, the capital of the Philippines. Her parents were not professional musicians, but her father, a surgeon, learned to play the piano by ear during World War II. Ibarra considers her mother, who entered medical school at the age of sixteen, to be her role model. "My mother's not a musician, but she's always loved music," Ibarra told Dave Mandl for the *Wire* magazine (1 June 2002). "She's the one who had us all learn piano." (Ibarra is the youngest of five children. She has three brothers and one sister.) Ibarra started playing piano when she was four years old and studied classical music until she was fourteen. As a child, she explored her family's vast record collection, which included albums from Ella Fitzgerald, Doris Day, and Count Basie. She bought her first record, Michael Jackson's iconic *Off the Wall* (1979), when she was thirteen. In high school, Ibarra saw a local punk band and fell in love with the idea of being a drummer. She split the cost of her first kit with her mother. Ten days later, Ibarra joined a hardcore punk band called Devil Donkey. Her lifestyle was far from that of a punk rocker, however. She continued to play piano and organ at church on weekends. "I guess the most outrageous thing I had in high school was a perm," she told Thurston Moore in an interview for *Index* magazine (Apr. 2001).

Ibarra, who was also a visual artist, studied drawing and painting at the Glassell School of Art in Houston and Otis Art Institute of Parsons School of Design in Los Angeles. In the late 1980s, she won a scholarship to study art at Sarah Lawrence College in Bronxville, New York. Music was her hobby, she recalled to Mandl, though she practiced drumming frequently. "It was just something I loved to do, so I brought my drums up," she said. "I couldn't practice in my room, so I'd go to [sic] science department nearby and practice there." She attended her first New York concert in 1988. The band was the Sun Ra Arkestra, led by jazz composer and musician Sun Ra. Ibarra had first heard Sun Ra on a Disney soundtrack—producer Hal Willner's *Stay Awake: Various Interpretations of Music from Vintage Disney Films* (1988)—for which Sun Ra and his band covered the song "Pink Elephants on Parade" from the movie *Dumbo.* Ibarra dragged a few friends to the concert where Sun Ra's set had a profound impact on her and, indeed, changed the course of her life. She approached the Arkestra's drummer, Buster Smith, and began taking drumming lessons with him and his brother Marvin. Under Smith's tutelage, she eventually dropped out of art school to pursue music full time.

## EARLY JAZZ CAREER

Ibarra studied music at the New School for Jazz and Contemporary Music. In the early 1990s, she began studying brush technique with the late Vernel Fournier, one of the most celebrated brush drummers in jazz. She also studied with Milford Graves, an iconic free jazz drummer, who is credited with revolutionizing the form in the 1960s. ("Free jazz," a concept popularized in the late 1950s by artists such as Sun Ra, refers to the style of a musician's improvisation. Free jazz could be considered a movement within jazz itself, like bebop or hard bop, but free jazz musicians do not observe the rules that govern those styles. Much like abstract visual artists, free jazz musicians improvise their own rules in performance.) Ibarra first encountered Graves's music in 1990 through the album *Love Cry* (1967) and his work with the New York Art Quartet. Graves clearly had global influences, Ibarra told Hank Shteamer for *Time Out* magazine (4 June 2013). "I loved his unique way of mixing traditional drumming with avant-garde and jazz. I also loved how he mixed influences of South Asian, Asian, African, West African, and American music in his drumming," she said. "You could hear this in his playing all wrapped up and delivered through powerful and explosive music." She studied extended techniques—a term used to describe any nonstandard technique of drumming to achieve a particular sound—with Graves for nearly three years.

Trumpeter Dave Douglas, who worked with Ibarra on an improvised orchestral suite called *Blue Latitudes* in 2006, told Sean P. Fitzell for the American Composer's Orchestra website, "Susie Ibarra is a unique synthesis of all the music she has played, and that flexibility and experience has a lot to do with what she brings to the music. . . . She has a sense of focused intensity that is rare and musically expressive."

In 1993 through 1998, Ibarra began playing with the bassist William Parker and joined his revolving, big-band ensemble, Little Huey Creative Music Orchestra, as well as his In Order to Survive ensemble. From 1996 to 1999, Ibarra played with a quartet led by the late saxophonist and composer David S. Ware. Despite her small size, Ibarra is known as a particularly physical drummer. For this reason, she thrived in Ware's ensemble, though it took some of her male cohorts a while to square her muscular style of play with her gender. Ibarra recalls playing a London festival with the Ware quartet where the director saw her and assumed that she was the group's pianist. "Then, even after I played, he told me that he was amazed that I could produce those sounds onstage," she recalled to Yaffe.

## NOTABLE RECORDINGS

In 1992, Ibarra formed a duo with the Israeli tenor saxophonist and bass clarinetist Assif Tsahar. (Tsahar was also Ibarra's first husband.) They recorded an album called *Home Cookin'* in 1998. The album features live sets from the Knitting Factory in Brooklyn, as well as the multi-instrumental "Dream Songs," which were recorded in the couple's living room. A reviewer for the *All about Jazz* website (1 June 1999) called *Home Cookin'* "one of the best records of the year." Ibarra also recorded a live album called *Drum Talk* (1998) with one of her mentors, the drummer Denis Charles. Micallef called the record, on which both musicians played drums, "a free-jazz landmark." Ibarra, who was by this time coming into her own as a jazz icon, formed the Susie Ibarra Trio with pianist and harpist Cooper Moore and violinist Charles Burnham. They released their first album, *Radiance*, in 1999. Ibarra served as the leader and sole composer on the album, though *Radiance* also included an "inventive reading" of the Jimi Hendrix song "Up from the Skies," as Derek Taylor wrote in a review for *All about Jazz* (1 Dec. 1999). It was the first time Ibarra had taken the lead on a project—an event that fans had been anticipating for a long time. "It's wonderful to have the opportunity to hear her in a setting completely of her own design," Taylor wrote. "As might be expected by listeners familiar with her prolific percussive talents the end result is something more than a little magical."

The Susie Ibarra Trio teamed up with Tsahar, clarinetist Chris Speed, trumpeter Wadada Leo Smith, and accordionist Pauline Oliveros for their next album, *Flower after Flower*, released in early 2000. Oliveros, who has been a prolific musician since the 1950s, is a pioneer of what she calls "deep listening." "She was so ahead of her time," Ibarra told Moore. "She was one of the few women who was seen as a serious composer." Ibarra met Oliveros in 1996 at a residency at Mills College in Oakland, California, where Oliveros teaches. In 2002, Ibarra formed a trio with pianist Craig Taborn and violinist Jennifer Choi to record *Songbird Suite*. The early 2000s were prolific years for Ibarra; she collaborated with the indie rock band Yo La Tengo on their 2000 album *And Then Nothing Turned Itself Inside Out* and recorded *Black Narcissus* with the trio Mephista (which includes pianist Sylvie Courvoisier and electronic musician Ikue Mori) in 2002. In 2003, she released *Tone Time*, a studio improvisation record, with bassist Mark Dresser. In 2004, Ibarra, Choi, Taborn, and Smith released *Folkloriko*, and Mephista released a record called *Entomological Reflections*. Ibarra's *Drum Sketches* came out in 2007.

## FILIPINO KULINGTANG

In the early 1990s, Ibarra started studying and playing Javanese and Balinese gamelan, two very different percussion-based styles of music, and Filipino kulintang gong music. She played gigs around New York City in Central Park and at the Metropolitan Museum at world music events. She studied kulintang with Danongan "Danny" Kalanduyan and later studied tablas with Samir Chatterjee. In 2002, Ibarra was invited to a world music and jazz festival in Detroit called the Concert of Colors Festival. She was opening for Ray Charles, and she wanted to do something special. She decided to test-run her new ensemble, a kulintang-based quartet called Electric Kulintang. Ibarra was pleased with the result and officially founded the group—as a duo with her husband, Rodriguez—the same year. In 2004 and 2005, Ibarra and Rodriguez traveled to the Philippines to conduct a number of field recordings. They captured kulintang music in the province of Maguindanao, as well as the stylings of Kalanduyan's family in Mindanao. The duo released an album called *Dialects* featuring recordings from that trip in 2006, the same year that they first performed their suite, "7,000

Mysteries" in New York City. (The Philippines is made up of more than seven thousand islands.) The performance combined Ibarra's field recordings with live improvisation and computer distortion. "The result is a sort of aural tapestry," Peter Catapano wrote for the *New York Times* (18 Feb. 2006). "At times, beats that would be welcome in a laid-back club predominate. But the grooves come and go and melt away to near-abstraction. A full palette of environmental sounds—what Mr. Rodriguez calls 'the music of life'—emerge and recede: motorbikes, children's cries, flip-flops scraping on pavement."

In 2002, Ibarra began a collaboration with Pulitzer Prize–winning poet, Yusef Komunyakaa. They worked on a chamber opera called *Shangri-La*, about American and European sex tours in Southeast Asia. It was first performed in New York City in 2005. Ibarra released a solo album called *Drum Sketches* in 2007. Electric Kulintang has also released a sound poem (a collaboration with Komunyakaa) called "War Horses" (2008), an electronic record called *Drum Codes* (2011), and a DVD of a surround-sound performance with seven Filipino indigenous tribes called *Hidden Truths: Prayer for a Forgotten World* (2012). "I guess if I had to ask if there are any themes or threads that run through [my music], I would say it's all coming from a common language," Ibarra told Todd Lee for *Azine* (9 Nov. 2009). "A musical language that I have been slowly developing over the years from influences, interests, and experiences."

## PERSONAL LIFE

Ibarra's first marriage, to duo partner Tsahar, ended in divorce in 1999. The two, who were married for seven years, started a record label called Hopscotch. Tsahar later told Daniel Piotrowski for *Jazz Times* (1 June 2003) that he and Ibarra had grown up together musically. "Old love—you always have something for it, in music and in romance," he said, "but creativity is never looking back."

Ibarra married Rodriguez in 2002. Ibarra founded Song of the Bird King, a multimedia art and environmental company devoted to preserving the music and culture of indigenous communities, in 2009.

## SUGGESTED READING

Catapano, Peter. "Bang a Gong (or Eight) in a Pan-Cultural Fusion." *New York Times*. New York Times, 18 Feb. 2006. Web. 4 Sept. 2014.

Fitzell, Sean P. "Susie Ibarra: Exploring Aural-Visual Symbiosis." *AmericanComposers.org*. American Composer's Orchestra, n.d. Web. 4 Sept. 2014.

Ibarra, Susie. Interview by Lance Hahn. *Giant Robot*. Giant Robot Magazine, 2004. Web. 4 Sept. 2014.

Ibarra, Susie. "Filipina-American Percussionist Susie Ibarra." Interview by Todd Lee. *Azine*. Asian American Movement Ezine, 9 Nov. 2009. Web. 4 Sept. 2014.

Ibarra, Susie. Interview by Ken Micallef. *Modern Drummer* 1 Dec. 2010: 46–57. Print.

Ibarra, Susie. Interview by Thurston Moore. *Index* 1 Apr. 2001. 58–64. Print.

Yaffe, David. "Susie Ibarra: Holding Her Own among All the Guys." *New York Times* 30 May 1999: 22. Print.

## SELECTED WORKS

*Drum Talk* (with Denis Charles), 1998; *Radiance* (with Susie Ibarra Trio), 1999; *Dialects* (with Electric Kulintang), 2006; *Drum Sketches*, 2007

—Molly Hagan

# Julia Ioffe

**Born:** 1982
**Occupation:** Journalist

Russian-born Julia Ioffe was based in Moscow for three years as a correspondent for the *New Yorker* and *Foreign Policy*. She was a senior editor at the *New Republic*, a position she left in December 2014. Ioffe is so respected and influential that she was one of a dozen journalists President Barack Obama consulted in September 2014 before announcing new plans to escalate US military efforts against the Islamic State (ISIS). She has written on a variety of topics, particularly Russian politics, US foreign policy, and culture. Her position on immigration has been influenced by her family's status as political refugees. "My family got to move to America not because we followed some strict, unchanging law etched into a granite tablet somewhere, but because there was a political will in Washington to push for us, and because that political will dovetailed perfectly with American's foreign policy priorities at the time," Ioffe wrote for the *New Republic* (27 Nov. 2014), "American immigration law is perhaps one of the most mercurial sets of laws we have. It is not set in stone, nor has it ever been. Historically, it has depended on racism, trade priorities, and geopolitical considerations, just as it does today."

## EARLY LIFE AND EDUCATION

Ioffe's father, Michael, was born in Russia and immigrated to the United States. He trained as a mathematician and became a computer programmer. He also refereed recreation league and college soccer games on nights and weekends until he tore his meniscus. When she was in high school, Ioffe sometimes accompanied her father to games, preparing to become a referee herself. As she recalled in an article for the *New Republic* (16 June 2014), "Up in those bleachers, I would hear him tooting his whistle, explaining what his freshly acquired English couldn't yet. On the field, he wasn't an immigrant struggling to keep a family of four afloat on one small salary, but just one of the guys on the pitch, the guy who knew at least this one thing better than them."

Through family members who came to the United States as refugees in the 1970s and 1980s, Ioffe's family arrived in the United States in 1990, when she was seven and her parents were thirty. The previous year some fifty-six thousand Russian Jews had come to the United States. They settled near the relatives who had served as guarantors for them during the immigration process. Over the next few years, about sixty extended family members arrived and lived within a fifteen-mile radius of Ioffe's family home in Maryland. Despite their voluntary departure, her parents romanticized Russia. Ioffe was intrigued by and fell in love with the country.

At Princeton University, Ioffe studied Soviet history. She was preparing for law school when she realized her mind did not work well for law. When she considered what she was good at, she identified writing papers as a strength. In 2004 she traveled to Russia to research for her thesis. The *New Yorker* was at that time looking for a fact-checker who knew Russian, so she began her journalistic career in the summer of 2005. For a time, she worked as an editor for the website Big Think before moving to the Knight Foundation Case Studies Initiative at the Columbia University Graduate School of Journalism.

## BEGINNING A CAREER

In 2009, Ioffe received a Fulbright scholarship to travel to Moscow for nine months, which turned into three years. She lived on the same street and in the same building as her great-grandmother had, passing the elementary school where she attended first grade every day before her family moved to the United States. She referred to herself as a rare breed, a Russian repat, or repatriot. However, she retained her United States citizenship, and her passport gave her the freedom to leave.

She began writing for *Russia!* magazine in 2009. By 2010 she had contributed to Radio Free Europe/Radio Liberty's Russia Service, *Foreign Policy* magazine, the *New Republic*, and the *New Yorker*. Because of her outspoken criticism of Russian president Vladimir Putin in an article she had written for *Foreign Policy* (16 Mar. 2010), she was not permitted to interview Vladimir Churov, the chair of the Russian Central Elections Committee, on the broadcast program "Face to Face." After reading her article, Churov cancelled the interview, which was to have focused on key regional elections, the topic of Ioffe's article.

Rather than replace Ioffe with someone more acceptable to Churov, the producer cancelled the show. "It's definitely flattering for a journalist to be so hated, but I was disappointed that I wouldn't get to interview Churov," she said to K. Bjorklund for Radio Free Europe/Radio Liberty (23 Mar. 2010). "I was really looking forward to asking him why he came into the office in overall hunting fatigues the week before the election."

## THE DECEMBRISTS

In December 2011, Ioffe was in Moscow covering a story about the country's parliamentary elections, in which the United Russia party claimed victory. She heard about a protest planned for a section of the city known as Chrstye Prudy on December 5. At first she did not plan to attend, expecting few people would take part. Drawn to the boulevard despite herself, Ioffe was astonished to find some six thousand protesters demanding Putin step down. "Something about this election, the cynicism and ham-fistedness with which it was carried out, the euphoria when, despite the apparent fraud, United Russia failed to get even 50 percent, made the barricades an attractive option for a cohort that has long been written off as politically inactive," Ioffe wrote in an article for the *New Yorker* (5 Dec. 2011). Five days later at a second protest, even more people let their opposition to Putin's reelection be known. On Christmas Eve, about one hundred thousand people in Moscow protested.

Prior to Putin's inauguration as president in May 2012, about seventy thousand people again peacefully protested in Moscow. In contrast to the previous protest, however, the police had largely blocked entrance to the square where the protest was to be held. The scene quickly became violent; Ioffe took a chunk of concrete in her leg and several hundred protesters were arrested. She left Russia in September.

## THE SNOWDEN AFFAIR

Ioffe returned to the United States in 2012 and accepted a position with the *New Republic*. About her return to the United States, she wrote for that magazine (24 Sept. 2012), "I will miss how tough Moscow makes you, and how miserable, and the way it teaches you to hunt out and savor the good. I will miss the dizzying happiness born of those moments. In three years, I've never seen anyone crying in the street."

In 2013, Edward Snowden, a contractor for the US National Security Administration, began leaking classified documents indicating a US government program of mass surveillance. Realizing he could be tried and sentenced as a traitor, Snowden subsequently fled to Russia and was ultimately granted temporary asylum in that country. President Obama cancelled his scheduled bilateral summit with Putin as a result of Snowden's receiving asylum. Invited to speak on MSNBC's *The Last Word with Lawrence O'Donnell*, Ioffe was astounded to be treated rudely and not allowed to make her points as an expert on Russia. She later accused O'Donnell of "mansplaining" Russian politics to her in an article for the *New Republic* (8 Aug. 2013).

## LEAVING THE *NEW REPUBLIC*

Like many print journals, the venerable *New Republic*, which had been in print since 1914, faced financial difficulties. In March 2012 a new chapter began when Chris Hughes, a cofounder of Facebook, became the new owner and editor in chief. Ioffe was one of two women he hired to bring women's voices to the magazine.

In 2014, however, Hughes and the magazine's new chief executive officer Guy Vidra, a former Yahoo News executive, decided to dramatically reorganize the magazine as a digital media company with an expanded Manhattan office. Many staffers were dismayed at the decision; longtime editors Franklin Foer and Leon Wieseltier resigned. Within days, more than twenty other top editors, including Ioffe, tendered their resignations.

Hughes put out a statement for the press indicating he was sad at the loss but excited about the new direction of the magazine. While his home was full of books and leather furniture, he also was a techie; some observers felt he was not fully at home in either world. After submitting her resignation from the magazine, Ioffe told Ben Terris for the *Washington Post* (14 Dec. 2014), "I noticed he had all this photography hanging everywhere, and I said something to him about it, that I liked it. And he whispers conspiratorially, 'It's all from Art.com! I'm so cheap!'"

According to Emily Heil for the *Washington Post* (5 Dec. 2014), Ioffe posted about her decision to leave the magazine on Facebook, writing, "The narrative you're going to see Chris and Guy put out there is that I and the rest of my colleagues who quit today were dinosaurs, who think that the Internet is scary and that Buzzfeed is a slur. Don't believe them. We're not afraid of change. We have always embraced it." In January 2015, Ioffe announced that she would be joining the *New York Times Magazine* as a contributing writer.

## SUGGESTED READING

Bjorklund, K. "'You Wrote Nasty Things about Putin.'" *Radio Free Europe/Radio Liberty*. RFE/RL, 23 Mar. 2010. Web. 30 Jan. 2015.

Heil, Emily. "'Mass Resignations' at the New Republic follow Editors' Departure." *Washington Post*. Washington Post, 5 Dec. 2014. Web. 30 Jan. 2015.

Ioffe, Julia. "I'm an Immigrant in America Thanks to Executive Action—Just like Many of Your Ancestors Were." *New Republic*. New Republic, 27 Nov. 2014. Web. 30 Jan. 2015.

Ioffe, Julia. "My Dad Could Have Prevented Pepe's Red Card." *New Republic*. New Republic, 16 June 2015. Web. 30 Jan. 2015.

Ioffe, Julia. "What I Will (and Won't) Miss About Living in Moscow." *New Republic*. New Republic, 24 Sept. 2012. Web. 30 Jan. 2015.

Terris, Ben. "Chris Hughes: From Savior to Villain at the New Republic." *Washington Post*. Washington Post, 12 Dec. 2014. Web. 30 Jan. 2015.

—Judy Johnson

# Atifete Jahjaga
**Born:** April 20, 1975
**Occupation:** President of Kosovo

Atifete Jahjaga was sworn in as the first female president of Kosovo on April 7, 2011, at the age of thirty-five. Kosovo, a country comparable in size to the state of Delaware, is located in southeastern Europe between Serbia and Macedonia. Jahjaga is Kosovo's fourth president and also its youngest. Since taking office, the former police officer and deputy director of the national police has targeted the country's widespread corruption and high crime rate—in a December 2014 survey, the Transparency International Corruption Perception Index, a Berlin-based watchdog group, reported that Kosovo and Albania are the two most corrupt states in southeastern Europe. Jahjaga has also worked to normalize relations with Serbia, Kosovo's bitter enemy, and mend the centuries-old ethnic tensions that are still brewing between the ethnic Albanians and the ethnic Serbs in northern Kosovo. (In 2009, a year after Kosovo declared its independence from Serbia, the ethnic Serbs boycotted the national election and held their own.) But foremost in the minds of many Kosovans, Jahjaga has lobbied for Kosovo to join the European Union, followed by NATO (North Atlantic Treaty Organisation) and the United Nations. Former US secretary of state Hillary Clinton threw her support behind Jahjaga in this endeavor in 2012. "We are Europeans," Jahjaga said at a conference at the German Council on Foreign Relations, or DGAP (Deutsche Gesellschaftfür Auswärtige Politik e.V.), in 2013. "Our identity is European." She added: "The European path for Kosovo is irreversible."

## EDUCATION AND EARLY CAREER

Jahjaga was born on April 20, 1975, in Rashkoc, in the district of Gjakova in western Kosovo. She attended primary and secondary school in Kosovo's capital city of Priština. She went on to study with the faculty of law at the University of Priština in 2000. In 2006, Jahjaga received her postgraduate certificate in police management and penal law from the University of Leicester in the United Kingdom, and in 2007, she received a postgraduate certificate in crime science from the University of Virginia. According to the Kosovo government's official website, Jahjaga is currently pursuing a master's degree

AFP/Getty Images

in international relations at Priština; she has participated in professional and research programs at the George C. Marshall European Center for Security Studies in Garmisch-Partenkirchen, Germany, the National Academy of the FBI, and the US Department of Justice.

Jahjaga began working with the Kosovo police force shortly after it was established in 2000. She served as a regional police officer, and was promoted to several other positions within the organization including assistant deputy director of the Kosovo Police, assistant head of human resources, special executive assistant to the deputy commissary for the administration of the Kosovo Police, head of the training department, assistant deputy commissary of the PK Border Police, and assistant deputy commissary of the Kosovo Police for personnel and training. In February 2009, she became the deputy general director of the police of Kosovo.

## A BRIEF HISTORY OF KOSOVO

Though Kosovo is the youngest country in Europe, its roots extend back to the days of the Roman Empire. To truly comprehend the struggles of its modern populace, one must go back to that time. Kosovo was settled by ethnic Serbs in the seventh century. The Kingdom of Serbia, with Kosovo at its heart, flourished until around 1389 when Kosovo fell to the Ottoman Empire, ushering in five centuries of Turkish rule; the anniversary of the Battle of Kosovo that year remains an important date for Serbs. Under the Ottomans, a number of Albanians migrated to the region, and by the nineteenth century, Albanians had become the dominant ethnic group in Kosovo, as remains the case today. (Kosovo's ethnic Albanians, however, insist that they were the true first settlers of Kosovo; they claim to be descended from an ancient Illyrian group that inhabited the Balkans prior to the seventh century.) The Ottomans ruled over Kosovo until the First Balkan War in 1912, after which Kosovo was ceded to Serbia. In 1918, the multiethnic state of Yugoslavia was established with great hopes, but it was dismembered in 1941, and reconfigured as the communist Federal Republic of Yugoslavia after World War II in 1945.

The Yugoslav constitution deemed Kosovo an autonomous province in 1974, but in 1987, Slobodan Milošević, a Serb, was elected President of the Federal Republic of Yugoslavia. He oversaw a Serb nationalist revival, and in 1989—the six-hundredth anniversary of the Battle of Kosovo—stripped Kosovo of its autonomous status. Milošević did his best to eradicate any Albanian influence from Kosovo throughout the 1990s while Kosovars (another name for Kosovo's ethnic Albanians) embraced the Democratic League of Kosovo (LDK), a pro-Albanian political party, holding their own parallel elections. In 1997, Albanian guerrillas—part of the Kosovo Liberation Army (KLA)—launched an armed uprising. In response, Milošević began a genocidal campaign against Kosovo's Albanian population. Hundreds of thousands of people became refugees; thousands more were raped, tortured, and murdered. The war ended in 1999, when NATO intervened, bombing Serbian forces for nearly eighty days. Until 2008, Kosovo was administered by peacekeepers from the United Nations. It officially declared its independent statehood—recognized by the United States and many countries in the European Union, but not Serbia—on February 17, 2008.

## ELECTION AS PRESIDENT

In 2007, United Nations special envoy Martti Ahtisaari submitted a proposal called the Ahtisaari Plan to the international body. The plan outlined the creation of an independent Kosovo focusing on maintaining the peace between Kosovo's ethnic Albanians, who make up about 90 percent of the country's population, and its ethnic Serbs. The Ahtisaari Plan also stipulated a period of international supervision until the fall of 2012, in the form of an international civilian representative, to ensure that both groups could participate equally in the newly formed government. When Kosovo officially declared its independence from Serbia in 2008, they did so pledging to erect a government and constitution in keeping with the Ahtisaari principles. The country's first elections were held the same year. Kosovo operates as a democratic republic; its president, a largely ceremonial role, serves as the head of state and its more powerful prime minister serves as the head of government. Kosovo's prime minister is Hashim Thaçi, a former political leader with the KLA, who was elected in 2008.

Jahjaga assumed the office of president in April 2011, a week after the courts ruled her predecessor's election by parliament to be unconstitutional. Behgjet Pacolli, a Swiss Kosovan construction tycoon, resigned in accordance with the ruling just two months after taking office in February. Jahjaga's ascension to the post surprised many, including Jahjaga herself. "I never thought until yesterday that I would take a high political office, but I was ready to serve my country," she told a reporter for the Agence France-Presse (8 Apr. 2011) after taking her oath of office. As the deputy director of the police force, Jahjaga was not associated with any of the three main political parties, though she enjoyed a good reputation. She was celebrated as a consensus interim candidate, and was elected with eighty votes (only 100 of the 120 members of parliament were present). Her election, or appointment, a reporter for the *Economist* (8 Apr. 2011) wrote, headed off a potential crisis. "If [the political leaders] had not agreed on a new president new general elections would have been in the offing, just a few months after the last round."

The *Economist* further reported, based on the account of former president Pacolli, that Jahjaga's name was pulled from an envelope in a meeting that included himself, American ambassador Chris Dell, Prime Minister Thaçi, and opposition party leader, Isa Mustafa. "Pacolli likes to spin many stories," a source told the *Economist* in response to the report. "The three leaders discussed many names and agreed on one. This is Kosovo, not the Oscars." Still, the nature of Jahjaga's election gave many pause and led opposition leaders to call for her resignation. The presidency itself carries little significance—and without a political party to support Jahjaga, the *Economist* argued, no real power—but these hindrances have served her well. At least, the

*Economist* wrote in 2011, "foreigners in Kosovo can now meet a leader without fear of being accused of giving succour" to Thaçi, who has been accused of war crimes.

As president, Jahjaga oversaw the passage of an amendment to compensate victims of rape from the Kosovo War. Serb forces systematically raped Albanian women during the conflict; those victims are now entitled to health, housing, and employment benefits. Jahjaga's term ends in 2016.

## RELATIONSHIPS WITH SERBIA AND WESTERN EUROPE

About a year before Jahjaga took office, the heads of state from Serbia and Kosovo met to discuss a handful of logistical issues, such as how to regulate border traffic, with Lady Cathy Ashton, an EU foreign policy representative. The tentative relationship between the two countries, the *Economist* suggested (2 Feb. 2013) is less about true reconciliation than it is about their mutual desire to enter to the European Union. In February 2013, Jahjaga met with Serbian president Tomislav Nikolić in Brussels. "This meeting is symbolic," Jahjaga told Arbana Vidishiqi for Radio Free Europe/Radio Liberty (5 Feb. 2013), "but also an important one, because this is a first meeting between the presidents of the Republic of Kosovo and the Republic of Serbia." The talk paved the way for a landmark deal brokered by Thaçi and Serbian leader Ivica Dačić on April 19, 2013. Both countries agreed to sign the Brussels Agreement, which stipulated, among other things, that neither would try to block the other's campaign to enter the European Union, and also that Serbs in northern Kosovo would have their own police and appeal court. "Our two neighboring countries have been forced to share a past and will be forced to share a future," Jahjaga said after taking office in 2011, as quoted by the Agence France-Presse. "As we cannot change the past, we will build a future learning from past mistakes."

## PERSONAL LIFE

Jahjaga's native language is Albanian, but she is also fluent in English and Serbian. She lives with her husband, Astrid Kuçi, in Priština.

## SUGGESTED READING

Agence France-Presse. "Kosovo Swears in Top Woman Cop as Leader." *Australian.* Australian, 8 Apr. 2011. Web. 9 Jan. 2015.

"Kosovo's New President: Election by Envelope?" *Economist*. Economist, 8 Apr. 2011. Web. 9 Jan. 2015.

"Kosovo Wants to Contribute to Europe." *German Council on Foreign Relations (DGAP)*. DGAP, 24 Oct. 2013. Web. 8 Jan. 2015.

"Serbia and Kosovo: Inching Closer." *Economist*. Economist, 2 Feb. 2013. Web. 9 Jan. 2015.

"Serbia and Kosovo Reach EU-Brokered Landmark Accord." *BBC News*. BBC, 19 Apr. 2013. Web. 9 Jan. 2015.

Vidishiqi, Arbana. "Interview: Kosovo President on 'Symbolic But Important' Talks with Serbian Counterpart." *Radio Free Europe/Radio Liberty*. RFE/RL, 5 Feb. 2013. Web. 9 Jan. 2015.

—Molly Hagan

Renée James (CC BY-SA 4.0)

# Renée James

**Born:** 1964
**Occupation:** Business executive

When Renée James was named president of Intel Corporation in 2013, her appointment was a clear sign of the many changes the forty-five-year-old computer hardware manufacturer was seeking to make to both its core businesses and its corporate culture. James, a longtime employee of the company, had a background in business rather than hardware, and her years of spearheading various software initiatives for Intel proved useful as the company sought to expand its reach far beyond the computer chips for which it had become known. Attempting to move into a new area of business is often a risky proposition, but for James, the risk of failure is just another challenge to overcome. "When you're doing something that you think—that you know—is a breakthrough, you cannot obsess about the possibility of failure," she explained to Mike Rogoway for the *Oregonian* (3 Oct. 2009) "Is [failure] possible? Yeah. Not that likely." In addition to overseeing Intel's expansion into new realms of computer technology, James became a key figure in Intel's attempt to increase the diversity of its workforce, helping to implement corporate policies and external programs geared toward attracting women to technological fields.

In July 2015, James announced via a memo to all Intel employees that she would be leaving the company at the end of the year. Unlike many such announcements, which often provide vague reasons for the individual's departure, James's made her intentions clear: her tenure as president of Intel had encouraged her drive to lead, and she sought to obtain a position as chief executive officer elsewhere. Despite her plan to leave the company, James reassured Intel's workforce that she would remain in her role for several months to manage the transition and that her departure from Intel was occurring on good terms. "Intel has been my second family," she wrote in her memo (2 July 2015). "It is an amazing company that has changed the way people live their lives, and I am proud to have contributed to that in a meaningful way."

## EARLY LIFE AND EDUCATION

Renée J. James was born in 1964. She grew up in Los Gatos, California. A sizable town in northern California, Los Gatos later became one of the towns within the Silicon Valley region, known for its many high-tech companies. After graduating from high school, James enrolled in the University of Oregon, where she majored in political science. She was also a member of the university's track team. She completed her bachelor's degree in 1986 and went on to obtain a master of business administration degree from the University of Oregon in 1992.

After completing her bachelor's degree, James took a job with Bell Technologies, a computer company specializing in Unix systems and based in Fremont, California. The company was acquired by the Intel Corporation in the spring of 1989 and ultimately absorbed into that larger company. James went with it, beginning a productive career with Intel that would span three decades.

## INTEL

By the time James joined the company in the late 1980s, Intel had two decades of experience as a noted manufacturer of computer hardware, particularly semiconductor chips. Intel was founded in 1968 by California engineers Robert Noyce and Gordon Moore, with the financial assistance of early venture capitalist Arthur Rock. Noyce and Moore soon recruited engineer Andrew "Andy" Grove, who later held several major positions within the company.

During its early years, Intel produced memory chips and microprocessors that were then incorporated into the computers and similar devices produced by other companies. Major users of Intel hardware during the company's first few decades of existence included IBM, then the premier producer of business and personal computers. Although Intel was successful in its niche, the company often struggled when attempting to expand its business into areas such as software and consumer electronics. Nevertheless, the company established a pattern of acquiring companies working in areas in which Intel hoped to develop a foothold. This policy brought James to the company through the acquisition of Bell Technologies and continued throughout her tenure, with Intel exploring new opportunities while continuing to focus on its core microprocessor business.

## EARLY CAREER

After joining Intel, James found herself working directly for Grove, who by then was the company's chief executive officer. Her official position was that of technical assistant, a position implemented throughout the highest levels of Intel's management and designed to benefit both executives and assistants. As Grove's technical assistant, James carried out a number of tasks typical for executive assistants, but she also assisted Grove with technology, such as helping him prepare multimedia presentations. In working closely with the company's leader, James learned not only about the management of Intel but also about business and technology in general. "He's a fabulous mentor," she told Poppy Harlow and Lauren Said-Moorhouse for CNN

(24 Jan. 2014) of Grove. "I learned more about thinking, about industry structures and strategy, and [about] 'what's the real issue?' from him than I'll learn from anybody."

James remained with Grove for several years, and her title eventually changed to chief of staff to reflect her many responsibilities. She ultimately adopted elements of Grove's leadership strategy upon her advancement to higher positions within the company, including his notable use of red pens. For his part, Grove, who remained CEO until his resignation for health reasons in 1998, considered James highly capable and has told reporters that he hoped she would one day hold one of the highest positions at Intel. "Renée has an incredible ambition to do things and succeed and then do something harder and succeed," he told Rogoway. "It's a driving ambition and it makes her undertake high-risk things. And it's not that she doesn't worry about the bumps. . . . But she takes them on."

Over the subsequent years, James took on a number of different roles within Intel. During the 1990s she contributed to Intel's efforts to establish itself as a software company as well as to the company's short-lived Internet application hosting service. For a time she oversaw the productive relationship between Intel and Microsoft, which used Intel chips in its personal computers. James was named general manager of the software and services group in 2005 and executive vice president of the company in 2012. During her time as head of software and services, Intel acquired several notable software companies—including Wind River, McAfee, and Telmap—in order to expand its reach and offerings.

## PRESIDENT OF INTEL

In May 2013, James was appointed president of Intel. Filling the second-highest position in the company, she reported solely to new CEO Brian Krzanich, who replaced former CEO Paul Otellini the same day. As president, James was responsible for overseeing a host of projects, including Intel's efforts to establish a foothold in the tablet market and break into wearable consumer technology. In addition to the company's manufacturing and software operations, she contributed to the operation and development of departments such as human resources and training. James's work as president was in many ways consistent with Intel's previous strategy of exploring new options, even when there was no guarantee of success. "We have a tolerance for risk taking," James explained to Rogoway of Intel's philosophy in 2009. "We have a tolerance for taking measured risks and betting. It's not a tolerance for failure." This risk-tolerant attitude meshed well with the company's overall goal of prioritizing innovation and creating new streams of revenue.

One of James's additional priorities as president was improving the diversity of Intel's workforce, particularly in regard to gender. Although she preferred to focus on her accomplishments and future goals rather than her gender, she acknowledged that her status as the first woman to hold one of Intel's top roles put her in a key position to speak out about women in the workplace. "I realize that I'm a role model, and so I feel more of a responsibility to give back to other women who are facing similar challenges," she explained to Harlow and Said-Moorhouse. Although James played an important role in Intel's diversity initiatives following her appointment, in many ways, such initiatives were the latest in a series of attempts to address the issue. "We've been working on diversity for a long time now," she told T. V. Mahalingam for India's *Economic Times* (13 Feb. 2015). "But in ten years of working on it—asking our managers to make our workforce diverse and inclusive—we've not made as much progress. We've stayed flat over a decade." In light of this difficulty, Intel implemented new training programs dedicated to improving workplace culture, invested $300 million in training and recruiting programs for women and other underrepresented groups, and supported programs designed to foster interest in science, technology, engineering, and mathematics (STEM) among girls and young women.

## NEW OPPORTUNITIES

On July 2, 2015, James released a memo announcing her plan to leave Intel. As some commentators noted, the notice did not use the vague language featured in many such correspondence; rather, James was clear about her desire to "pursue an external CEO role" following her departure from Intel. She announced that she would remain with Intel for the remainder of the year in order to assist with the transition. Many commentators and reporters tried to surmise where James would land as CEO, and although by early fall 2015 James's next step still remained unknown, it seemed clear that the "driving ambition" Grove identified in her will propel her on her way. "When [Krzanich] and I were appointed to our current roles, I knew then that being the leader of a company was something that I

desired as part of my own leadership journey," she wrote in her memo. "Now is the right time for me to take that next step."

## PERSONAL LIFE

James is married and has two sons. She and her family live primarily in Portland, Oregon. James also has a home near Intel's headquarters in Santa Clara, California.

## SUGGESTED READING

Caulfield, Brian. "Intel: The Biggest Software Company You've Never Heard Of." *Forbes*. Forbes, 9 May 2012. Web. 31 Aug. 2015.

Hardy, Quentin. "Renée James, President of Intel, Is Leaving the Company." *New York Times*. New York Times, 2 July 2015. Web. 31 Aug. 2015.

Harlow, Poppy, and Lauren Said-Moorhouse. "Can Wearable Technology Reverse Intel's Declining Fortunes?" *CNN*. Turner Broadcasting System, 24 Jan. 2014. Web. 31 Aug. 2015.

James, Renée. "Letter to Employees by Intel President Renée James." *Intel*. Intel, 2 July 2015. Web. 31 Aug. 2015.

Mahalingam, T. V. "The Global IT Industry Needs More Women, Says Intel's President Renée James." *Economic Times*. Bennett, 13 Feb. 2015. Web. 31 Aug. 2015.

Rogoway, Mike. "Rewriting the Rules: Intel's Software Chief Challenges Convention." *Oregonian*. Advance Digital, 3 Oct. 2009. Web. 31 Aug. 2015.

Takahashi, Dean. "How Intel's New President Renée James Learned the Ropes from the Legendary Andy Grove." *VentureBeat*. VentureBeat, 2 May 2013. Web. 31 Aug. 2015.

—Joy Crelin

# N. K. Jemisin

**Born:** September 19, 1972
**Occupation:** Author and blogger

N. K. Jemisin is a speculative fiction writer and blogger. An African American woman, Jemisin has been an outspoken advocate for minority voices in the science fiction and fantasy genres, which have long been dominated by white male authors and formulaic, pseudo-European landscapes. In 2013 Jemisin proposed a reconciliation among sci-fi and fantasy writers. Using Australia's public efforts to overcome its own racist policies and attitudes as an analogy—she was speaking at a convention in Melbourne—Jemisin suggested opening dialogue among fans and writers in respect to the genre's oppressive past. Science fiction's relationship with politics has a rich and celebrated history. From George Orwell's *1984* to the work of Afro-futurist writers like the late Octavia Butler, science fiction authors have been using speculative worlds to explore the problems of the past and present for years—but contemporary, commercial writing is stuck in a rut, Jemisin has argued. "The genre can go many, many more places than it has gone," Jemisin told Laura Miller for *Salon* (9 Nov. 2011). "Fantasy's job is kind of to look back, just as science fiction's job is to look forward. But fantasy doesn't always just have to look back to one spot, or to one time. There's so much rich, fascinating, interesting, really cool history that we haven't touched in the genre: countries whose mythology is elaborate and fascinating, cultures whose stories we just haven't even tried to retell."

Jemisin's own stories explore themes of cultural conflict and oppression. She uses the genre to "wrench historical and cultural themes out of their familiar settings and hold them up in a different light," Miller wrote. In Jemisin's debut novel, *The Hundred Thousand Kingdoms* (2010), the protagonist, Yeine, is a brown-skinned woman from a matriarchal society in which men are denigrated as the weaker sex. Politics between gods and humans, ancient mythologies, romance, and betrayal make the novel, which is over four hundred pages long, a truly sprawling epic that defies genre. The book, the first in Jemisin's *Inheritance Trilogy*, won the 2011 Locus Award for best first novel and was nominated for Hugo and Nebula awards, two of the most prestigious prizes in the genre. Her duology, *The Dreamblood*, was published in 2012. Jemisin is also a contributor to the antiracist blog *Angry Black Woman* and the feminist blog *Alas, A Blog*. She is also a founding member of the Boston writers group BRAWLers.

## EDUCATION AND EARLY WRITING CAREER

Nora K. Jemisin was born in Iowa City, Iowa, on September 19, 1972. She grew up in Mobile, Alabama, but spent summers with her father, a visual artist, in New York City. When she was nine, the Ku Klux Klan lynched a black teenager named Michael Donald around the corner from her grandmother's house. "I remember my grandmother sitting in her den with a shotgun across her knees while I cracked pecans at her feet," Jemisin said in her guest of honor speech at the Australian science fiction and fantasy convention Continuum on June 8, 2013. Jemisin had no idea what was going on, though the moment has stuck with her. "She told me the gun was just an old replica; she'd brought it out to clean it. I said 'OK, Grandma,' and asked whether she'd make me a pie when I was done," she recalled. As a child, Jemisin considered herself a tomboy, and prided herself on resisting anything feminine, from ballet to unicorns, although she loved reading science fiction. At eleven, she wrote on the *Fantasy Café* blog (19 Apr. 2012), she had a minor identity crisis after shunning Steven R. Boyett's 1983 novel *Ariel* because it had a "girly" cover. About to set the book down, "I clearly remember thinking, *but I'm a girl*," she wrote. Little did she realize that the childhood conundrum—particularly the tricky question of what it means to be a woman—would continue to inform her work in unexpected ways.

Jemisin earned her bachelor's degree in psychology from Tulane University in New Orleans in 1994. She went on to study counseling at the University of Maryland at College Park, where she also began writing science fiction. Jemisin told Miller that, in her first novel, she caught herself carrying out some of the genre's well-worn tropes. She wrote in the third person, and her main character was a man. "I was thinking it had to have a quest in it," she added, "with a MacGuffin of Power being brought to a Place of Significance." The story didn't pan out, so she set it aside. She wrote two novels during that time and sent them to a publishing house. Both were rejected. Not realizing that this is an incredibly common experience among writers, Jemisin was crushed. Unsure of her next move, she attended the Viable Paradise (VP) workshop, a one-week tutorial on the ins and outs of professional writing life, in 2002. The people at VP suggested that she start writing short stories. For Jemisin, it was a daunting prospect. "I had written nothing but novels and I could not think short," she told a journalist for the Oakland-based sci-fi magazine *Locus* (18 Aug. 2010). "But as I had the sense knocked into me at VP, I realized stories and novels are different but complementary art forms, and there are reasons to learn from both. Writing short stories could improve my novel writing. So I thought, 'Why not?'" Soon, Jemisin realized that she loved short fiction, and she cites the work of Ursula K. Le Guin, author of the seminal young adult fantasy novel *A Wizard of Earthsea* (1968) as an influence.

Jemisin's first published short stories—"Too Many Yesterdays, Not Enough Tomorrows" and "Red Riding Hood's Child"—appeared in the speculative fiction magazine *Ideomancer* in 2004 and the erotic magazine *Fishnet* in 2005, respectively. Her story "The You Train" was published in the sci-fi weekly *Strange Horizons* in 2007 and received an honorable mention in the twenty-first collection of *The Year's Best Fantasy and Horror* that year. In 2008 her story "Playing Nice with God's Bowling Ball," first published in the (now defunct) online magazine *Jim Baen's Universe*, received an honorable mention in the twenty-sixth *Year's Best Science Fiction*. One of Jemisin's most famous stories, "Non-Zero Probabilities," was a Hugo (2010) and Nebula Award (2009) finalist. Published in *Clarkesworld* magazine, the story is about a hypothetical New York City in which characters' fates are governed by good and bad luck. After reading it, the science fiction novelist Lettie Prell told Jeremy Jones of *Clarkesworld* (1 Apr. 2010), "I'm excited to read more from her, for her voice has matured and also her insights, and a more poetic prose that nevertheless maintains the unique voice I first noticed and admired."

### THE INHERITANCE TRILOGY AND OTHER WORK

Jemisin based her sprawling fantasy, *The Inheritance Trilogy*, on the ancient Mesopotamian *Epic of Gilgamesh*, which pits wily gods against hapless humans. In the world of *The Hundred Thousand Kingdoms* (2010), the first novel in the trilogy, one human family has managed to enslave several of the gods to use for their own purposes. The book's protagonist, Yeine, is estranged from her family (the one that captured the gods) but must return to their city, called Sky, after her mother's mysterious death. Jemisin wrote the first draft of *The Hundred Thousand Kingdoms* from the third-person perspective of different characters, a common trope in fantasy. There was also a heavy emphasis on the quest structure. But when it came to time to rewrite, Jemisin decided to chuck all of that out the window. "I thought, 'I'm just going to write the way I *feel* like writing,'" she told *Locus*, even if that meant that the book "might not be epic fantasy anymore." She refocused the story on her protagonist, letting Yeine tell her own story in a stream-of-consciousness narrative. She handed the draft off to her agent thinking that the book would never find a publisher. Ten days later, Jemisin's agent called to

tell her that the book would go to auction—there were multiple offers. "I was at work that day," Jemisin recalled to Locus, "and that whole day she was giving me phone calls, and I would have to close the door to my office and scream."

"Convoluted without being dense, Jemisin's engaging debut grabs readers right from the start," a journalist for *Publishers Weekly* (1 Mar. 2010) wrote in a starred review of *The Hundred Thousand Kingdoms*. "Multifaceted characters struggle with their individual burdens and desires, creating a complex, edge-of-your-seat story with plenty of funny, scary, and bittersweet twists." *The Hundred Thousand Kingdoms* made Jemisin a star in the science fiction and fantasy world. The book was nominated for a slew of prizes, including the coveted Nebula Award for best novel in 2010, leading Paul Goat Allen of *Fantasy* magazine (1 Apr. 2011) to describe Jemisin's "ascension to the fantasy fiction stratosphere" as "meteoric." The trilogy's second book, *The Broken Kingdoms*, was published in 2011 to more acclaim, though Jemisin said it was tough to start. "*The Broken Kingdoms* was challenging at first because I kept trying to write the same kind of story that I'd done in *The Hundred Thousand Kingdoms*. But then I realized it can't be that kind of story," Jemisin told Jones. Instead of following the powerful family in Sky, the book, set ten years after the first, takes place in Shadow, the city beneath the palace. The third book, *The Kingdom of Gods*, was published in 2012 and focuses on Sieh, a trickster child-god introduced in *The Hundred Thousand Kingdoms*.

In 2012, Jemisin published two novels—*The Killing Moon* and *The Shadowed Sun*—comprising the duology, *The Dreamblood*. The stories take place in a fantasy realm modeled on ancient Egypt. Her book *The Fifth Season*, which has been slated for publication in August 2015, will be the first volume of *The Broken Earth*. Jemisin lives in the Brooklyn borough of New York City, where she also works as a career counselor.

### SUGGESTED READING

Allen, Paul Goat. "Feature Interview: Sky's (Not) the Limit: The Ascension of N. K. Jemisin." *Fantasy*. Fantasy, 1 Apr. 2011. Web. 17 Nov. 2014.

"The Hundred Thousand Kingdoms: Review." *Publishers Weekly*. PWxyz, 1 Mar. 2010. Web. 17 Nov. 2014.

Jemisin, N. K. "Continuum GoH Speech." Continuum. Ether Centre, Melbourne. 8 June 2013. Speech.

Jemisin, N. K. "Don't Fear the Unicorn." *Fantasy Café*. Fantasy Café, 19 Apr. 2012. Web. 17 Nov. 2014.

Jones, Jeremy L. C. "Peculiar Notes of Contradiction: A Conversation with N.K. Jemisin." *Clarkesworld*. Wyrm, 1 Apr. 2010. Web. 17 Nov. 2014.

Miller, Laura. "If Tolkien Were Black." *Salon*. Salon Media, 9 Nov. 2011. Web. 17 Nov. 2014.

"N. K. Jemisin: Rites of Passage." *Locus*. Locus, 18 Aug. 2010. Web. 17 Nov. 2014.

## SELECTED WORKS

*The Hundred Thousand Kingdoms*, 2010; *The Broken Kingdoms*, 2011; *The Kingdom of Gods*, 2012; *The Killing Moon*, 2012; *The Shadowed Sun*, 2012

—Molly Hagan

---

# Abigail Johnson

**Born:** December 19, 1961
**Occupation:** Business executive

In the fall of 2014, Abigail Johnson ascended to the position of chief executive officer (CEO) of Fidelity Management and Research (FMR), the parent company of financial services firm Fidelity Investments. A privately held company, Fidelity was founded by her grandfather, Edward C. Johnson II, in 1946 and later run by her father, Edward C. Johnson III. Johnson's appointment to the position not only ensured that the company would remain under the family's leadership but also called attention to the Johnson family's history of deep involvement in the firm's operations. "Minding the store is just what we do," Johnson explained to Geoffrey Smith for *BusinessWeek* (7 July 2002).

Having first worked for Fidelity during the summer before her freshman year of college, when she worked the phone lines and assisted the company's customers, Johnson joined the family business full time in 1988, initially taking on a position as an analyst. Over the following decades, she worked in several of the company's divisions before moving to the role of president in 2012. As CEO, Johnson is determined to improve Fidelity's operations and help the company expand into areas to meet the needs of investors throughout the United States. "Every day you have to get up with new energy and new ideas to contribute to pushing the organization forward," she told Moira Forbes for *Forbes* (1

Nov. 2013). The task is a daunting one, but in many ways, it is a challenge for which Johnson has been preparing her whole life.

## EARLY LIFE AND EDUCATION

Abigail Pierrepont Johnson, known to those around her as Abby, was born on December 19, 1961, in Boston, Massachusetts. One of three children born to Edward and Elizabeth Johnson, she has a brother named Edward and a sister named Elizabeth. Her mother was involved in the arts and the preservation of historic landmarks in Boston, while her father, known as Ned, was an employee and later head of Fidelity Investments, a financial services company founded by his father, Edward Johnson II. The Johnson family had a long history in the Boston area, and Fidelity Investments was a key player in the city's financial industry. As a child, Johnson was intrigued by her parents' work. "You want to know what your parents do all day when you're working your butt off at school," she explained at the entrepreneurship summit TiECON East, as quoted by Stephanie N. Mehta for *Fortune* (2 June 2014).

Johnson attended Shady Hill School and Buckingham Browne and Nichols, private day schools in Cambridge, Massachusetts. She went on to enroll in Hobart and William Smith Colleges in Geneva, New York, where she studied art history. She completed her bachelor's degree in 1984. Johnson later pursued graduate studies in business at Harvard University, earning her master of business administration in 1988.

As one might expect from her family's deep involvement in financial services, Johnson began her career in finance early in life, spending the summer before college answering phones and taking instructions from Fidelity's clients. "I was responsible for filling out the forms to correctly put in order the transactions that they were requesting," she told Forbes. "It was a pretty basic job. But it gave me an appreciation of what it was like to be responsible for really important things in people's lives and making sure that they were always done accurately and correctly."

## EARLY CAREER AT FIDELITY

After completing her bachelor's degree, Johnson moved to New York and worked for a time as a research associate at the management consulting firm Booz Allen Hamilton. She later returned to Boston. Johnson rejoined Fidelity as an analyst in 1988, initially focusing on the Fidelity Select

© Brian Snyder/Reuters/Corbis

Industrial Equipment Portfolio fund, and spent the next decade managing various mutual funds for the firm. Funds for which she was responsible during that period included the Fidelity Dividend Growth Fund and the Fidelity Trend Fund. Despite her status as the daughter of the CEO, she was reportedly subject to much of the same scrutiny as the other employees at her level, and her decisions as a fund manager were judged based on their merits rather than on her last name.

Fidelity Management and Research Company, the parent company of Fidelity Investments, was founded in 1946 by Johnson's grandfather, Edward Johnson II. The company was privately held and family owned from the start, and by 2014, 49 percent of the company remained in the hands of the Johnson family; the other 51 percent of the company was owned by its employees. Johnson's father joined the business as an analyst in 1957 and took on the role of CEO in 1977. Although the firm primarily specialized in mutual funds—actively managed funds that invest in multiple stocks, bonds, or other securities—Ned Johnson worked to introduce new products and innovations during his tenure as CEO. Under his leadership, Fidelity became a leading provider of retirement funds and also introduced affordable options for middle-class investors.

Unlike many large companies, Fidelity generally shies away from acquisitions. "We don't have a public currency that would make any [major] acquisition viable," Johnson explained to Mehta. "Everyone in the company understands this. We build stuff ourselves and over the long term that's been very good." Nevertheless, the company consists of numerous divisions, including its individual, workplace, and institutional investing groups as well as its philanthropic branch, Fidelity Charitable, and Fidelity Labs, a technology-focused division devoted to innovation. The Fidelity Management and Research Company also owns a number of additional businesses and previously owned the Community Newspaper Company, which published various small newspapers in Massachusetts.

## MANAGEMENT

In 1994, while still working as a portfolio manager, Johnson was named associate director of Fidelity Management and Research; she later rose to the role of director. After nearly a decade of managing funds, she took on increased responsibility in the company, serving as a manager of equity investment systems and later as director of the company's equity division. Johnson became president of Fidelity's mutual fund division in 2001 and four years later took the reins of the Fidelity Employer Services Company, a branch dedicated to building retirement plans for external companies as well as providing various other workplace services.

Observers both within and outside the company had long speculated about whether Johnson would one day succeed her father as CEO of Fidelity, and in 2012 her promotion to president became a clear signal that she was, in fact, being groomed for the job. As president, Johnson went from working with smaller groups within the company to overseeing its many divisions. "I had to learn to communicate to very different types of groups of managers with different orientations, different priorities," she told Forbes. "And that was a real leadership challenge."

As president, Johnson faced the difficult task of shepherding Fidelity through a period of competition and economic instability. Although one of the United States' largest mutual fund companies, Fidelity was not producing results that matched the triumphs of previous decades. Some investors had become increasingly cautious about the stock market following the global recession that began in 2007, while others sought out investment options that Fidelity did not offer. The firm was notoriously slow to begin offering access to exchange-traded funds (ETFs), investment vehicles similar to mutual funds but traded on the open market, for example. Nevertheless, Johnson was determined to weather such challenges and expand Fidelity's reach in a steady, goal-driven manner. "I demand pretty aggressive goal setting and a commitment to measured progress towards those goals because I don't like surprises," she explained to Forbes. "I don't even like good surprises."

## CEO

In October 2014, Ned Johnson released a memo to Fidelity's employees announcing that he was retiring from the position of CEO. He named Johnson as his successor and noted that he would remain active in the company in the role of chair. "Along with our senior team, we will work together to strengthen Fidelity's industry leadership and to innovate in ways that enhance the experience we provide to our customers," he wrote in his memo, as quoted by Benjamin Snyder for *Fortune* (13 Oct. 2014).

In many ways, Johnson is considered quite similar to her predecessor; father and daughter are both intensely private people, making few public appearances and rarely granting interviews to journalists. In other ways, however, Johnson is a significant departure from her father, particularly in terms of management style. Observers within the company have noted that while her father focuses on slow, gradual improvement, Johnson takes a different approach. "Sometimes you can gradually improve things," she explained to Smith. "But sometimes, they don't work, and you've just got to just say: Let's grind this baby to a halt."

Many of the challenges the company faced when Johnson became president in 2012 remain sources of concern for Fidelity, and she has devoted herself to reducing costs, expanding into new or little-explored areas, and working closely with the heads of the company's various divisions. As a privately held company, Fidelity is far less beholden to external forces such as stockholders, who could potentially lead the call for new leadership or new business strategies, than its publicly traded counterparts. At the same time, Johnson has long argued against letting the company become too secure in its standing. "No matter how senior you get in an organization, no matter how well you're perceived to be doing, your job is never done," she told Forbes in 2013. "Every day you get up and the world is changing, your customers are expecting more from you. Your competitors are putting pressure on you by doing more and trying to beat you here and beat you there."

## PERSONAL LIFE

Johnson met her husband, Christopher J. McKown, the cofounder of Iora Health, while they were working for Booz Allen Hamilton. They married in June 1988. Johnson and McKown have two daughters and live primarily in Milton, Massachusetts, in a home that once belonged to Johnson's grandparents.

## SUGGESTED READING

Condon, Christopher. "Abby Johnson, the Rarely Seen Face of Fidelity." *Washington Post*. Washington Post, 23 Oct. 2013. Web. 31 Aug. 2015.

Forbes, Moira. "7 Career Lessons from Billionaire Abigail Johnson." *Forbes*. Forbes.com, 1 Nov. 2013. Web. 31 Aug. 2015.

Goodway, Nick. "Abigail Johnson: The $1,600,000,000,000 Woman." *Independent*. Independent.co.uk, 30 Aug. 2012. Web. 31 Aug. 2015.

McLaughlin, Tim. "Fidelity's Abigail Johnson to Head All Main Operations." *Reuters*. Thomson Reuters, 28 Aug. 2012. Web. 31 Aug. 2015.

Mehta, Stephanie N. "One-on-One with Abby Johnson, Fidelity's Ultra-Private President." *Fortune*. Time, 2 June 2014. Web. 31 Aug. 2015.

Smith, Geoffrey. "Fidelity: Here Comes Abby." *BusinessWeek*. Bloomberg, 7 July 2002. Web. 31 Aug. 2015.

Snyder, Benjamin. "Abigail Johnson Named CEO of Fidelity Investments." *Fortune*. Time, 13 Oct. 2014. Web. 31 Aug. 2015.

—Joy Crelin

# Kevin Johnson

**Born:** March 4, 1966

**Occupation:** Mayor of Sacramento; former professional basketball player

Kevin Johnson, a former player in the National Basketball Association (NBA) and the mayor of Sacramento, California's capital city, is among a select group of athletes who have made a successful transition into the world of politics. An undersized point guard known for his fiery, competitive attitude, explosive quickness, and never-say-die playing style, the six-feet-one Johnson enjoyed a standout thirteen-year NBA career, spending all of it—with the exception of part of his rookie season—with the Phoenix Suns. During his tenure in the league, he earned a number of honors and helped transform the Suns into a perennial playoff contender. He retired from basketball in 2000 as one of the most accomplished and popular players in Suns history.

Following his retirement, Johnson worked briefly as a television broadcaster before returning to his hometown of Sacramento to become a community activist and businessman. He oversaw the expansion of St. HOPE (Helping Others Pursue Excellence), a nonprofit community development organization he founded in 1989. After leading numerous successful revitalization efforts in Sacramento, Johnson, a Democrat, entered the political arena and ran for mayor of Sacramento in 2008. In November of that year, he defeated two-term incumbent Heather Fargo in a runoff election to become the fifty-fifth mayor in the city's history. In the process, he became the first native Sacramentan, and the first African American to win election to the office. He was reelected to a second term in 2012. Johnson is a "force to be reckoned with," Sam Amick wrote for *USA Today* (13 Mar. 2014), "a pint-sized point guard who packed serious punch and whose days of running the underdog team have only continued in his current role."

## EARLY LIFE

Kevin Maurice Johnson was born on March 4, 1966, in Sacramento, California. An only child, he was primarily raised by his maternal grandparents, George and Georgia Peat, in the hardscrabble Sacramento suburb of Oak Park. Though active throughout his life, Johnson's mother was only sixteen years old when he was born and initially not prepared to take on the responsibility of raising him. His biological father, Lawrence Johnson, died in a freak drowning accident in Sacramento when Johnson was three.

Johnson's grandfather, a sheet-metal worker, stepped in as a father figure and taught him the importance of hard work, education, and giving back to others. "You know in the Bible, the good Samaritan? My grandfather was a modern-day version of that," Johnson told Kurt Streeter for the *Los Angeles Times* (4 Oct. 2014). Early on, Johnson learned a love for sports and competition from his grandfather, who introduced him to the game of chess, and his mother, who was an accomplished softball player and a national roller-skating champion.

Dianna Miller/Wikimedia Commons

Johnson's first passion was baseball, which he started playing at the age of seven. Growing up a fan of the Oakland Athletics, he dreamed of becoming a professional baseball player. It was at roller skating, however, that Johnson first distinguished himself as an athlete. Taking after his mother, he raced competitively throughout junior high school and competed in two national roller skating championships.

## HIGH SCHOOL AND COLLEGE CAREER

By the time he entered Sacramento High School in 1979, Johnson had given up skating to focus on baseball. An exceptional switch-hitting shortstop, he became a standout on the school's varsity baseball team. During his freshman year, Johnson started playing basketball, after his friends convinced him to go out for the junior-varsity team. Though initially taking up the sport for conditioning purposes, Johnson proved to be a natural and emerged as one of the top point guard prospects in the country. As a senior and varsity team captain, he averaged 32.5 points in scoring to lead all California high school players.

Johnson was courted by college basketball powerhouses all over the country, but he chose to remain close to home, enrolling at the University of California at Berkeley (UC Berkeley). At the time of Johnson's arrival, the school was not known for its basketball prowess, posting nonwinning records in nine of its previous ten seasons. Undaunted, Johnson promised to turn around California's basketball fortunes. "Part of the reason was I knew it had a tradition somewhere along the way," he told

Jeff Faraudo for the *San Jose Mercury News* (25 Jan. 2007), "and I wanted to be part of reviving it."

As a four-year starting point guard for the Golden Bears, Johnson fulfilled his aspirations. He set all-time school records for points (1,655), assists (521), and steals (155), and was a two-time All-Pac-10 Conference First Team selection. During his junior season, he led UC Berkeley to a landmark victory over rival UCLA, ending a twenty-five-year, fifty-two-game-losing streak against the school. He also helped Cal secure a berth in the National Invitation Tournament (NIT), marking the school's first postseason appearance in twenty-six years. He again carried the school to the NIT as a senior.

Prior to his senior season, Johnson, who had played sparingly on Cal's baseball team as a freshman, was selected by his long-time favorite Oakland Athletics in the twenty-third round of the 1986 Major League Baseball (MLB) Draft. That summer, he participated in several workouts with the Athletics and appeared in a game with their farm team in Modesto, California. However, he ultimately opted against professional baseball in favor of basketball, after deeming the latter sport a safer career choice. In 1992, Johnson became the first Golden Bears men's basketball player to have his jersey retired.

## NBA CAREER

In the spring of 1987, Johnson, who earned a bachelor's degree in political science from UC Berkeley, was selected by the Cleveland Cavaliers as the seventh overall pick in the NBA Draft. Though expected to contend for the team's starting point guard spot, he received only limited playing time in Cleveland, serving primarily as a backup to veteran Mark Price. After appearing in fifty-two games with the Cavaliers, Johnson was dealt to the Phoenix Suns in a multiplayer trade.

For Johnson, landing in Phoenix proved fortuitous. In his first month with the team, in April 1988, he averaged nearly thirteen points and nine assists in twenty-eight games, good enough to earn him Rookie of the Month honors. The Suns finished the 1987–88 season with just twenty-eight wins, but enjoyed a twenty-seven-game improvement the following season, when Johnson averaged 20.4 points per game and 12.2 assists in eighty-two games. He was named the NBA's Most Improved Player, and led the Suns to the Western Conference finals, beginning a stretch of thirteen consecutive playoff appearances for the team.

Over the next ten seasons of his career, Johnson became one of the best point guards in the NBA, as the Suns developed into one of the league's most formidable teams. He again averaged over twenty points and ten assists during the 1989–90 and 1990–91 seasons, making him one of five players in NBA history to accomplish the feat in three consecutive seasons. The Suns earned another trip to Western Conference finals in 1989–90, but did not advance to the NBA Finals until the 1992–93 season, when they finished with a league- and franchise-best 62–20 regular-season record. In the finals, the Suns lost to the twice-defending champion Chicago Bulls in six games. Johnson solidified his reputation as a dogged competitor in game three of the finals, when he played an NBA-record sixty-two minutes and put up twenty-five points in a 129–121 triple-overtime victory over the Bulls.

Johnson achieved legendary status during the second round of the 1994 NBA playoffs, when he threw down an improbable one-handed dunk over the Houston Rockets' seven-foot center Hakeem Olajuwon. The Suns lost that series, but Johnson's dunk would go down in history as one of the most memorable in basketball history. Johnson retired after the 1997–98 season, but made a brief comeback towards the end of the 1999–2000 season to replace injured Suns point guard Jason Kidd. After playing in six regular season and nine postseason games, he retired for the second and final time.

Johnson finished with career averages of 17.9 points and 9.1 assists per game. He was named to three NBA All-Star teams (1990, 1991, and 1994) and earned four All-NBA Second Team selections (1989–91 and 1994). He averaged at least eighteen points and nine assists per game in seven different seasons, the third-most in history, ranks fifth all-time in career assists per game among former players, and holds numerous Suns franchise records. In 2001, Johnson was inducted in the Suns Ring of Honor and had his number seven retired.

Often overshadowed by other point guards of his era, which included Hall of Famers Michael Jordan, Magic Johnson, and John Stockton, Johnson is regarded as "one of the most underrated players in league history," according to Sam Amick. Paul Westphal, who served as head coach of the Suns from 1992 to 1995, said of his former player to Marcus Crowder for California Magazine (Win. 2009), "People kind of know he was real good, but I don't think they know how good." In 2014 Johnson was named among ten finalists for that year's Naismith Memorial Basketball Hall of Fame class.

## COMMUNITY ACTIVIST

After retiring from basketball, Johnson joined NBC as an in-studio analyst for the *NBA on NBC*. He held that role during the 2000–2001 NBA season, after which he returned to Sacramento to focus on his business interests and non-profit group, the St. HOPE Corporation. Johnson spent the next several years expanding St. HOPE, which he had originally founded in 1989 as an after-school program called the St. HOPE Academy. "It just grabbed me," he explained to Kurt Streeter, "this idea that something had to be done to help my community."

In 2003 St. HOPE's development division opened a 25,000 square-foot mixed-use space in Oak Park's commercial district called the 40 Acres Art Gallery and Cultural Center. Also that year, Johnson established St. HOPE Public Schools, a prekindergarten through grade twelve charter school system that serves approximately two thousand students in four schools, one of which includes Sacramento High School (now Sacramento Charter High School). The schools are aimed at improving students' grades, standardized test scores, and graduation rates. In 2008 the St. HOPE Leadership Academy Charter School opened in New York's Harlem neighborhood.

## MAYOR OF SACRAMENTO

In March 2008, emboldened by his success as a community activist and businessman, Johnson decided to join the race for mayor of Sacramento. "My goal was always to be more than a basketball player," he told Eric Bailey for the *Los Angeles Times* (2 June 2008). Johnson campaigned on a theme of hope and change similar to that of President Barack Obama, and expressed a vision of helping to create "a city that works for everyone," while strongly advocating for a pro-business agenda and education reform. Despite his political inexperience and running into heated controversies surrounding his business affairs and personal life, he defeated his opponent, two-time incumbent Democrat Heather Fargo, in a runoff election in November 2008 with 58 percent of the vote.

As the fifty-fifth person, first native Sacramentan, and first African American to be named to the post, Johnson hit the ground running. He overhauled the city's governance structure and implemented plans to combat homelessness, spur the arts, and foster economic development. He also spearheaded a series of education reform initiatives. Johnson's zealousness for change was not always well received, however, and a referendum he proposed to broaden mayoral powers was promptly quashed. "I was just full of energy and wanted to get things done. I was going 100 miles an hour," he explained to Streeter. "I had to learn that in politics, it does not work like it does in sports."

In June 2012 Johnson won reelection to a second mayoral term in a landslide against three competitors. During his second term, he won national attention for successfully orchestrating a deal that kept the Sacramento Kings from relocating to Seattle, Washington. He also pushed through a plan to build a new $448 million basketball arena for the team in Sacramento, with approximately $255 million in public funding.

Johnson's political profile increased in 2014, when he was voted president of the US Conference of Mayors, a national nonpartisan organization, and served as a spokesman for the NBA players union on the Donald Sterling racism scandal.

Johnson has been married to Michelle Rhee, a former Washington, DC, schools chancellor, since 2011. In addition to his political responsibilities, he serves as president and CEO of the Kevin Johnson Corporation.

## SUGGESTED READING

Bailey, Eric. "Ex-NBA Star Finds Politics Can Be a Rough Game Too." *Los Angeles Times*. Los Angeles Times, 2 June 2008. Web. 19 Nov. 2014.

Crowder, Marcus. "The Dogged Competitor." *California*. Cal Alumni Association, 2009. Web. 19 Nov. 2014.

McPeek, Jeramie. "Kevin Johnson: The Spirit of Giving." *Suns*. NBA Media Ventures, Dec. 1995. Web. 19 Nov. 2014.

Streeter, Kurt. "Ex-Basketball Star Kevin Johnson Is Back Holding Court in His Hometown." *Los Angeles Times*. Los Angeles Times, 4 Oct. 2014. Web. 19 Nov. 2014.

—Chris Cullen

# Travis Kalanick

**Born:** August 6, 1976

**Occupation:** Business executive, entrepreneur

"Uber CEO Travis Kalanick is so headstrong, so enthusiastic, and so combative that he is at risk of seeming like a parody of today's tech entrepreneur," Christine Lagorio-Chafkin wrote for *Inc.* magazine (July–Aug. 2013). Kalanick heads the company Uber, which allows consumers to hire a private car or to arrange a shared ride using a simple mobile-phone application.

Although Uber has met continual resistance from city transportation officials, received numerous complaints about price gouging, and drawn criticism from women's rights advocates after multiple drivers have been accused of sexually assaulting riders, the company is thriving. As of early 2015 it was operating in some two hundred cities all over the world and was valued by financial industry insiders at more than $40 billion. Uber vehicles have become so ubiquitous in many urban centers that the word itself has been more broadly adopted: much as to "Google" something now means to search for it online, several economists are referring to "Uberized" markets—those in which services such as food delivery and home cleaning can be quickly and easily summoned through a mobile application or website. Kalanick does not discount the notion of Uber becoming a player in those other markets. "If we can get you a car in five minutes, we can get you anything in five minutes," he asserted to Kara Swisher for *Vanity Fair* (Dec. 2014).

## EARLY YEARS AND EDUCATION

Kalanick was born on August 6, 1976, and grew up in the Los Angeles neighborhood of Northridge, located in the San Fernando Valley. His father, Don, was an engineer, and his mother, Bonnie, worked in ad sales for the *Los Angeles Daily News*. Some observers have pointed out that Kalanick, who learned computer coding in sixth grade, has since demonstrated the tech savvy of Don in combination with Bonnie's deal-closing abilities.

Kalanick has a brother, Cory, now a firefighter, as well as two half sisters. As a young boy, Kalanick reportedly dreamed of becoming a spy. His ambitions turned to business early on, however. He received a 1580 out of 1600 on his Scholastic Aptitude Test (SAT), and while still in his teens, he launched an SAT-tutoring service dubbed the New Way Academy, whose flagship offering was a course called "1500 and Over." With the bravado that almost everyone who has ever interviewed him mentions, he has claimed that his first client improved his test score by a remarkable four hundred points.

After high school Kalanick entered the University of California, Los Angeles (UCLA), where he majored in computer engineering and joined the Computer Science Undergraduate Association. It was in a UCLA dorm room that Kalanick met fellow students Michael Todd and Vince Busam, who would set him on his way to the next phase of his life as an entrepreneur.

## FIRST TECH VENTURE

Todd and Busam had embarked on a side project called Scour, a file-sharing service that allowed users to search for videos, movies, and images from their peers and to download them. Cobbled together by a small group of fledgling computer engineers, the service quickly attracted a few million users—including Shawn Fanning, who later went on to found the peer-to-peer file-sharing service Napster.

Scour quickly outgrew Busam's dorm room, where the group of young tech entrepreneurs gathered to work, so they moved to an apartment nearby. In 1998 Kalanick dropped out of school to join the company as a full-time employee. (Because of the major role he played in Scour's early success, he is generally described as a co-founder; he was awarded stock and did not take a salary for a year, collecting unemployment benefits instead.) Even with the larger working quarters, it was a decidedly bootstrap operation. The company's dozen employees crowded into the unit's living room or bedrooms, and if one wanted to use the microwave to heat lunch, he had to ask the others to power down their monitors lest a fuse blow. Placed in charge of marketing and business development, Kalanick came up with several attention-getting campaigns—once hiring individuals to hang bottles of personal lubricant on the doorknobs of dorm rooms along with stickers reading, "Do not enter, SX in progress." (SX stood for Scour Exchange.)

Scour's massive early success was followed by an equally massive downfall. In 2000 the company was sued for a whopping $250 billion by a group of major entertainment companies, including the Motion Picture Association of America, the Recording Industry Association of America, and the National Music Publishers Association, who did not appreciate their content being shared so freely. In response, Scour declared Chapter 11 bankruptcy and had its assets divided in court.

## REDSWOOSH

While Kalanick went through a brief period of depression, spending some fourteen hours a day in bed during the court proceedings, he soon began planning what he termed his "revenge business." Along with Todd, later in 2000 he launched RedSwoosh, forgoing a regular salary and living at home with his mother. This time, instead of allowing the sharing of content they did not have the rights to, the pair built RedSwoosh as a way to deliver web content cheaply to users by allowing them to share bandwidth.

Turning RedSwoosh into a success was no easy feat. A potential investor was killed in the terror attacks of September 11, 2001; Kalanick and Todd had a major falling out that left ill feelings on both sides; the company ran into serious trouble with the Internal Revenue Service after it stopped withholding payroll taxes; and at one point almost the entire engineering team quit en masse. Undaunted, in 2006 Kalanick moved operations to Thailand to save money, and the following year the company was acquired by Akamai Technologies for a reported $23 million ($19 million in stock and $4 million in earnouts). "He would get up in the morning with nobody on his team, and he still made it in the

end," a former employee told Alyson Shontell for *Business Insider* (11 Jan. 2014). "It's inspirational in a lot of ways that when things got tough and he was down to nothing, he still kept going."

Kalanick used his newfound wealth to invest in other companies and to travel; within the first year he had visited Spain, Japan, Greece, Hawaii, France, Australia, and Senegal, among other locales. In late 2008 he attended LeWeb, a cutting-edge conference founded by a pair of French entrepreneurs that attracted digital innovators and tech visionaries from around the world.

## FOUNDING UBER

Also at LeWeb was Garrett Camp, the founder of StumbleUpon, a content-aggregating site. Camp related a story of spending eight hundred dollars to hire a private driver on New Year's Eve, and he had been brainstorming ways to bring down the price of limo services ever since. "We were jammin' on ideas," Kalanick recalled to Andy Kessler for the *Wall Street Journal* (25 Jan. 2013). When asked what the next big idea would be, Camp replied, "'I just want to push a button and get a ride. . . . Travis, let's go buy ten Mercedes S-Classes, let's go hire twenty drivers, let's get parking garages, and let's make it so us and a hundred friends could push a button and an S-Class would roll up, for only us, in the city of San Francisco, where you cannot get a ride,'" as quoted by Kalanick. He explained, "This wasn't about building a huge company, this was about us and our hundred friends."

Despite his assertions that the service was destined to be only a small enterprise, Kalanick's entrepreneurial zeal made that an unlikely prospect. Uber launched in San Francisco as an iPhone app in June 2010, allowing users to summon nearby cars from limousine companies or private owners who had been prescreened by the company. Using the app, a rider could track the car's progress, learn the driver's name, and later rate the level of service. (In turn, drivers could rate passengers as well.)

Four months later, in what was soon to become a pattern in almost every city in which Uber launched, Kalanick was served with a cease-and-desist order by the California Public Utility Commission and the San Francisco Municipal Transportation Agency. "Given my background," Kalanick told Kessler, recalling his experiences at Scour, "this was like homecoming." After consulting with attorneys, who assured him that Uber was operating within the law, Kalanick refused to halt operations. In what also became a pattern, the brouhaha in San Francisco quickly faded, thanks in some part to Kalanick's savvy use of social media to generate public support among riders.

## LEGAL CHALLENGES

Rollouts in other major American cities—including New York, Boston, Chicago, Seattle, and the District of Columbia—soon followed. Most, like San Francisco, unsuccessfully tried to block Uber from operating in their locales. But, as Kalanick told Lagorio-Chafkin, "Uber riders are the most affluent, influential people in their cities. When we get to a critical mass, it becomes impossible to shut us down." Lagorio-Chafkin wrote that Uber was part of a new age of innovation, calling it "Silicon Valley's cult of disruption taking on city hall." She continued, "Consider that on your phone, you can purchase luggage (say, on Amazon), find someone to carry said luggage (TaskRabbit), rent an apartment for a couple of days (Airbnb), and hail a luxury sedan (you get the picture). But when the luggage retailer doesn't pay state sales tax, the employment provider doesn't pay minimum wage, the renter doesn't hold the lease, and the sedan driver doesn't charge a fixed rate? The government is pissed."

One of the groups railing the loudest against Uber is composed, unsurprisingly, of drivers of conventional taxis and their representatives. Once, after receiving a cease-and-desist letter from a taxi commission, Kalanick displayed it on Instagram (12 Oct. 2013) with the caption: "Charming greeting card from a taxi cartel representative."

In addition to interference by government officials and transportation commissions, other problems soon began to plague the company. Its practice of surge pricing—charging more during periods of peak use in order to draw more Uber drivers into service—regularly draws ire from users, for example. Uber attracted particular vitriol for its use of surge pricing in the wake of Hurricane Sandy and the 2014 Sydney hostage crisis. Although Kalanick explains that raising fares is the only way to achieve a balance between supply and demand at busy times, the company announced in mid-2014 that it would stop the practice during extreme weather events and other disasters.

## GROWTH IN SPITE OF SCANDAL

Uber also came in for public opprobrium after multiple drivers were accused of sexual assault and rape by female passengers. In one exceptionally high-profile case, an Indian woman accused an Uber driver in New Delhi of raping her in late 2014, and she subsequently sued Uber, which her lawsuit slammed as the "modern-day equivalent of electronic hitchhiking" for failing to adequately ensure passenger safety. The company apologized and promised to introduce such features as an in-app emergency button but defended its system of background checks on drivers.

The website Buzzfeed.com caused a stir in November 2014 when it released a report that an Uber senior vice president had been overheard making comments suggesting that Uber get revenge on members of the press who are critical of the company by investigating their private lives and publicizing the details. Uber quickly disavowed the remarks and issued an apology from the executive.

Nevertheless, Uber is valued at more than $40 billion. Al Ramadan, Christopher Lochhead, and Dave Peterson explained in an editorial for *Fortune* magazine (11 Dec. 2014), "Uber's latest valuation is partly driven by how quickly the company is expanding abroad, but it also reflects a growing global market for on-demand transportation." They continued, "Despite [its many] problems, Uber's lead is so large and its value has grown so quickly, it would have to stumble badly to lose the battle for supremacy in this new space."

## PERSONAL LIFE

Kalanick is dating violinist Gabi Holzwarth. The couple met at a party hosted by venture capitalist Shervin Pishevar, who had hired Holzwarth to play violin at the event and introduced the two. Holzwarth credits Kalanick's devotion and support for helping her recover from the eating disorder bulimia.

## SUGGESTED READING

Kessler, Andy. "Travis Kalanick: The Transportation Trustbuster." *Wall Street Journal*. Dow Jones, 25 Jan. 2013. Web. 10 Mar. 2015.

Lagorio-Chafkin, Christine. "Resistance Is Futile." *Inc*. Mansueto Ventures, July–Aug. 2013. Web. 10 Mar. 2015.

Shontell, Alyson. "All Hail the Uber Man! How Sharp-Elbowed Salesman Travis Kalanick

Became Silicon Valley's Newest Star." *Business Insider*. Business Insider, 11 Jan. 2014. Web. 10 Mar. 2015.

Swisher, Kara. "Man and Uber Man." *Vanity Fair*. Condé Nast, Dec. 2014. Web. 10 Mar. 2015.

Velasco, Schuyler. "Can Uber Afford to Have This Many Enemies?" *Christian Science Monitor*. Christian Science Monitor, 18 Nov. 2014. Web. 10 Mar. 2015.

—Mari Rich

# William Kamkwamba

**Born:** August 5, 1987
**Occupation:** Inventor

Erik (HASH) Hersman/Wikimedia Commons

"William Kamkwamba's story is uniquely inspiring," Helene Gallis wrote for *World Watch Magazine* (July/Aug. 2010), a publication devoted to issues of global sustainability. "He stakes out a path that hopefully many will follow, both in developing and in developed countries. Most importantly, he represents an image of Africa and Africans that rejects the pity and guilt commonly invoked by most news stories out of the continent. In fact, he represents the opposite—and may simultaneously be offering solutions to poverty, degradation, starvation, aid dependency, and corruption."

Kamkwamba earned this level of approbation for building a windmill. Given that many other people have completed the same task, it may not initially seem like adequate reason for such high praise. Kamkwamba, however, built his working windmill when he was just fourteen years old, using found materials from the scrapyard in his Malawian village and with no guide other than an old textbook. He had dropped out of school because his family lacked the small tuition fee, and overcame great odds to teach himself engineering. Consider also that Malawi was then in the midst of a severe famine that left Kamkwamba and many of his fellow villagers starving, and it becomes abundantly evident why he is considered such a noteworthy figure.

After building that windmill—the first ever to be erected in his village—and rising to fame, Kamkwamba expanded his goals and his influence. He has given numerous talks and presentations to global audiences, earned an engineering degree from Dartmouth College, written an autobiography, *The Boy Who Harnessed the Wind: Creating Currents of Electricity and Hope* (2009), and launched the Moving Windmills Project, a nonprofit organization that supports a wide variety of rural economic development and education projects in his native country. "All things are [made] possible," he wrote in his book, "when your dreams are powered by your heart."

## EARLY LIFE

William Kamkwamba was born on August 5, 1987, in Dowa, Malawi. His parents, Trywell and Agnes Kamkwamba, raised him and his six sisters on the family farm in the village of Masitala, located in the Malawian region of Wimbe. There they grew maize and sometimes tobacco. Meat was scarce, and Kamkwamba learned how to craft animal traps from whatever materials he could find. Malawian culture is imbued with strong elements of storytelling and belief in sorcery; as Kamkwamba wrote in his autobiography, "Before I discovered the miracles of science, magic ruled the world."

The village enjoyed few modern amenities. A small television and VCR in a thatched hut served as a movie theater on those occasions when power was available, and Kamkwamba and his friends fashioned their toys from discarded beverage cartons, bottle caps, and other scraps. Homes had no electric lights, and people went to bed early to avoid burning expensive kerosene lamps or candles. At his primary school in Wimbe, however, Kamkwamba developed a deep interest in how cars, batteries, and radios worked, and he thought of becoming a scientist one day.

In 2001 a severe drought hit Malawi, resulting in the worst famine the country had suffered in decades. The Kamkwamba family subsisted on a single meal a day, with only a small handful of *nsima*, a traditional porridge, for each of them. For one Christmas meal, Kamkwamba considered himself lucky to be served a rubbery square of boiled goat skin to gnaw on. Kamkwamba was devastated to learn that, because of the famine, his parents could no longer afford the required fees for him to attend the local school, which cost 1,200 kwacha—about eighty dollars. He was forced to drop out.

Determined to get an education despite his dire circumstances, Kamkwamba began frequenting the local library, stocked with books donated from the United States. Although he knew only basic English, he studied diagrams and pictures. He found an old eighth grade textbook called *Using Energy* whose cover particularly intrigued him. "[It] featured a long row of windmills—though at the time I had no idea what a windmill was," he wrote in *The Boy Who Harnessed the Wind*. "All I saw were tall white towers with three blades spinning like a giant fan." They reminded him of the toy pinwheels he had fashioned from sticks and old plastic water bottles. "But the fans on this book were not toys," he wrote. "They were giant beautiful machines that towered into the sky, so powerful that they made the photo itself appear to be in motion. I opened the book and began to read."

## BUILDING A WINDMILL

Inspired by the book, Kamkwamba set about building a small prototype dynamo, which proved successful. This was followed by a five-meter-tall windmill constructed out of a broken bicycle, a tractor fan blade, and an old shock absorber, with a tower constructed of slender blue gum trees. Its circuit breaker was made from nails, wire, and magnets. "Going to the scrapyard began to replace school in my mind," he recalled in his autobiography. "It was an environment where I learned something each day. I'd see strange and foreign materials and try to imagine their use." Piece by piece, he adapted the assortment of junk he found into the parts needed to produce a working wind turbine.

Despite some initial mishaps—including damaging his father's battery-powered radio when he tested the bicycle-wheel dynamo by cramming its wires into the radio's socket—Kamkwamba was finally ready to put his creation to work. Dozens of neighbors gathered around, many of them jeering mockingly. They believed that the boy they had seen constantly picking through trash at the scrapyard was crazy. As the wind picked up, and the blades spun rapidly, however, the light bulb hooked up to the dynamo began to glow. "It was glorious light, and it was absolutely mine," Kamkwamba wrote. "I threw my hands in the air and screamed with joy." Soon, the villagers who had mocked him were lined up outside his home to see the electric light that now illuminated many of its rooms and to pay a small fee to charge their mobile phones.

Kamkwamba's inventiveness did not stop there. He hooked the windmill up to a car battery, allowing the energy to be stored and used as needed. Eventually he extended the tower to twelve meters to increase the blades' wind exposure above the tree line. He also later built a second windmill to power an irrigation pump for the whole village.

## INTERNATIONAL RECOGNITION

In 2006 word of Kamkwamba's initiative reached the world outside of Wimbe thanks to Hartford Mchazime, the head of the nongovernmental organization (NGO) that had sponsored Kamkwamba's community library. Mchazime had seen the windmill and alerted journalists to the story. Kamkwamba was particularly excited when Everson Maseya, a Radio One host he had listened to for years, came to interview him. A story in the Malawi *Daily Times* headlined "School Dropout with a Streak of Genius" was equally thrilling. Mchazime did more than simply drum up media attention, however, and led the drive to return Kamkwamba to school. Mchazime collected money for school fees and lobbied the Malawi Ministry of Education to place Kamkwamba at the Madisi Secondary boarding school.

Kamkwamba's story began to spread, and came to the attention of the organizers of the Technology, Entertainment, and Design (TED) conference series. He was invited to speak at a 2007 TED Talk in Tanzania. Before giving his talk, "How I Built a Windmill," which he delivered somewhat nervously in halting English, Kamkwamba had never been on an airplane or used a computer. Tom Reilly, one of the TED organizers, realizing the young man had never experienced the Internet, showed him how to conduct a Google search. Unsurprisingly, he chose to look up windmills. "In one second, [Tom] had pulled up five million page results—pictures and models of windmills I'd never even imagined," Kamkwamba wrote. Acknowledging the incongruity of accessing the Internet for the first time at a conference attended by some of the world's greatest scientists and technology pioneers, he joked, "They could have put a blinking sign over my head and charged admission."

The TED presentation proved popular, and Reilly helped attract support for Kamkwamba's goals to further his education and continue to improve his village. Kamkwamba was accepted at the African Bible College Christian Academy in Lilongwe, Malawi, and worked to improve his English. In 2008 Kamkwamba joined the inaugural class of the African Leadership Academy, a school founded to develop promising students from throughout Africa. Thanks to his work there, by the time he gave his second TED Talk, "How I Harnessed the Wind," in 2009, Kamkwamba had gained a large measure of confidence and increased his commitment to creating social change.

### THE BOY WHO HARNESSED THE WIND

Another watershed moment occurred in 2009 when Kamkwamba and coauthor Bryan Mealer published the best-selling book *The Boy Who Harnessed the Wind: Creating Currents of Electricity and Hope*, documenting his journey out of poverty. The work earned near universal praise from reviewers. "*The Boy Who Harnessed the Wind* [is] an autobiography so moving that it is almost impossible to read without tears," Kate Vander Wiede wrote for the *Christian Science Monitor* (15 Oct. 2009). "The infectious enthusiasm, heartbreaking tragedy, and final triumph make for an unforgettable story of success in the face of overwhelming odds." The book was later adapted into an illustrated children's book as well.

In the wake of the publicity from *The Boy Who Harnessed the Wind*, several US schools approached Kamkwamba offering admission and scholarships. He ultimately chose Dartmouth's Thayer School of Engineering for its wide-ranging liberal arts program and close sense of community. He majored in environmental studies and earned his bachelor's degree in 2014.

### WILLIAM AND THE WINDMILL

In 2013 Kamkwamba's life was profiled in the award-winning documentary *William and the Windmill*, and the same year he was named to *Time* magazine's list of thirty world changers under thirty. He also established the nonprofit Moving Windmills Project, which supports economic development and education projects in Malawi. The group's efforts have included providing wind and solar power for villages, distributing antimalarial netting for beds, building a drip irrigation system, installing running water in villagers' homes, providing fertilizer and seeds to local farmers, establishing scholarships so that no child is turned away from school for lack of funds, and stocking local libraries. Kamkwamba also provided uniforms and equipment to the Wimbe United soccer team, an investment that boosted the local economy and has helped keep young men out of trouble by focusing on sports.

Kamkwamba's interests beyond windmills and community improvement include computers, cameras, and other technology, as well as animals and action movies.

### SUGGESTED READING

Childress, Sarah. "A Young Tinkerer Builds a Windmill, Electrifying a Nation." *Wall Street Journal*. Dow Jones, 12 Dec. 2007. Web. 29 Jan. 2015.

Gallis, Helene. "Sustainable Entrepreneurship in Africa." *World Watch Mag.* Worldwatch Inst., July/Aug. 2010: 12–17. Web. 29 Jan. 2015.

Kamkwamba, William, and Bryan Mealer. *The Boy Who Harnessed the Wind: Creating Currents of Electricity and Hope*. New York: Morrow, 2009. Print.

Levinson, Cynthia. "William Kamkwamba's Electric Wind." *Faces* Oct. 2011: 10. Print.

Morozov, Evgeny. "Thought Leaders for the Internet Era." *Foreign Policy*. FP Group, 30 Nov. 2009. Web. 29 Jan. 2015.

Wulff, Jennifer. "The Power of One." *Dartmouth Alumni Mag.* Dartmouth Alumni Mag., Sept./ Oct. 2011. Web. 29 Jan. 2015.

—Mari Rich

# Kim Kashkashian

**Born:** 1952

**Occupation:** Violist

Kim Kashkashian is an internationally recognized viola player who has performed professionally for four decades. As a big proponent of the viola, she is known for her active role in creating new musical compositions for the instrument. The viola, not to be mistaken for a violin, is tuned one-fifth of an octave lower and is one-seventh longer than a violin. In 2012 Kashkashian received a Grammy Award for best classical instrumental solo for her album *Kurtág and Ligeti: Music for Viola* (2012). "Her technique is masterful—and her tone is instantly arresting for its warmth, austere purity, and concentrated intensity," wrote Edith Eisler for *Strings* (Aug.–Sept. 2000).

She has worked with such composers as Arvo Pärt (whose music is often used by documentary makers and film producers) and Luciano Berio (a composition faculty member who conducted an evening of musical theater at Julliard in 1967). Kashkashian has appeared as a soloist with orchestras all over the world, including Berlin, New York, and London. She has also appeared in recital at the Metropolitan Museum of Art in New York, at the New England Conservatory's Jordan Hall, and in cities such as Paris and Tokyo. Kashkashian has performed and recorded with acclaimed musicians, such as the cellist Yo-Yo Ma and violinists Daniel Phillips and Gidon Kremer.

## EARLY LIFE AND EDUCATION

Kim Kashkashian was born in 1952 in Detroit, Michigan. She started playing the violin at the age of eight, even though she initially wanted to play the clarinet. Kashkashian's family could not afford to rent a clarinet, so Kashkashian's mother insisted she play the instrument they had available, which was a violin her cousin was no longer using. Kashkashian began her studies with violist Ara Zerounian, a teacher in the Detroit public schools, and then at the age of twelve, she began studying the viola at the Interlochen Arts Academy in northern Michigan. That was when she first tried playing the viola, the range of which is closer to the clarinet. She then went on to attend preparatory school at the Peabody Institute at Johns Hopkins University, a conservatory and a university preparatory school

Bagoum/Flickr/Wikimedia Commons

in Baltimore, Maryland. In her first year she studied with violist Walter Trampler, but during her second year at school, Trampler left and she began to study with violist Karen Tuttle. Kashkashian also studied at the Philadelphia Musical Academy (later renamed the University of the Arts).

## PROFESSIONAL DEBUT

Kashkashian began her professional performing career primarily playing chamber music; however, she told Eisler, she wanted to "develop [her] solo abilities," and she figured the best way to do that was to enter competitions. In 1981 she received second prize at the Lionel Tertis viola competition in England and third prize at the ARD International Competition in Munich, Germany. After placing third at ARD, she was invited to perform at several concerts and festivals; each new performance led to another opportunity. She explained to Eisler, "I developed certain musical contacts in Europe, and one of them eventually changed the direction of my life." One of the concerts Kashkashian played was broadcast over the radio and was heard by Manfred Eicher of ECM Records. Once he heard her musical performance, he offered to record her. That connection would continue to benefit Kashkashian throughout her career.

Kashkashian has performed on dozens of albums, playing solo or with orchestras, quartets, and duets. She signed with ECM (Edition of Contemporary Music) Records in 1984 after she was featured on the album *Mozart: Sinfonia Concertante, Mozart Violin Concertos 1–5 and Sinfonia Concertante in E Flat*, released by DGG (Deutsche Grammophon Gesellschaft) Records, and on the album *Divertimento*, released by Sony. In 1986 she released her first album, *Romances and Elegies for Viola and Piano*, on ECM Records and featuring pianist Robert Levin. After signing with ECM Records, Kashkashian was in high demand. In 1987, to make it easier to fulfill her busy performing schedule in Europe, she moved to Germany, though she still continued to perform in the United States.

## EARLY COLLABORATIONS

The next years would prove to be productive ones for Kashkashian, who became prolific in her recording output. In 1988 Kashkashian put out her next album, *Hindemith: Sonatas for Viola and Piano and Viola Alone*, also featuring pianist Robert Levin. In 1989 she appeared on the album *Shostakovich: String Quartet No. 15; Gubaidulina: Rejoice!* as part of a string quartet, featuring Kashkashian on viola, Yo-Yo Ma on cello, and Gidon Kremer and Daniel Phillips on violin. That album was released by CBS Records (Columbia Broadcasting System, Inc.), as was Kashkashian's next quartet album, *Schubert: Quartet No. 15, D. / 887 Mozart: Adagio and Fugue K.546*, which featured the same musicians. That same year the same group, minus Phillips, appeared as a trio on *Divertimento, K. 563*, featuring compositions by Wolfgang Amadeus Mozart, the famous Austrian composer of classical operas, symphonies, and concertos.

In 1991 Kashkashian released another album on ECM Records, *Linda Bouchard: Pourtinade/ Paul Chihara: Redwood / Dmitri Shostakovich: Viola Sonata, Op. 147–Kim Kashkashian*, featuring pianist Robert Levin and percussionist Robyn Schulkowsky. The album *Lachrymae* (1993), featured Kashkashian alongside the Stuttgart Chamber Orchestra; Dennis Russell Davies conducted the concert, which featured compositions by Paul Hindemith, Benjamin Britten, and Krzysztof Penderecki. Next came *Giya Kancheli: Vom Winde Beweint; Alfred Schnittke: Konzert für Viola und Orchester* in 1994, featuring the works of two composers, Giya Kancheli's *Mourned by the Wind* and Alfred Schnittke's *Liturgy for Solo Viola and Orchestra*. That same year she did a duet album with famed jazz and classical pianist Keith Jarrett, titled *Bach: 3 Sonaten für Viola da Gamba und Cembalo*,

which featured three J. S. Bach compositions for viola and harpsichord. *Hommage à R. Sch.: György Kurtág, Robert Schumann* (1995) had compositions performed by Kashkashian, Levin (on piano), and the Swiss German clarinetist Eduard Brunner. She also released the album *Abii Ne Viderem* with the Hillard Ensemble. Her next album was *Mozart: The Five Violin Concertos* (1996), an orchestra performance conducted by Nikolaus Harnoncourt, with Kashkashian on viola and Gidon Kremer on violin.

## BRAHMS, BARTÓK, AND MOZART

In 1997 Kashkashian released two records on ECM, *Caris Mere, Kancheli: Caris Mere for Soprano and Viola*, with clarinetist Eduard Brunner, soprano Maacha Deubner, and saxophonist Jan Garbarek; and *Brahms: Sonaten für Viola und Klavier*, which consisted of Sonatas no. 1 and no. 2, by Brahms, for clarinet (or viola) and piano, with Levin on piano. The recordings of the sonatas won Kashkashian and Levin the Edison Music Award, an annual Dutch music prize awarded for outstanding achievements in the music industry.

After her win, Kashkashian put out two more albums in 2000. The first, *Kim Kashkashian Plays Béla Bartók, Peter Eötvös, György Kurtág*, was recorded with the Netherlands Radio Chamber Orchestra, with Peter Eötvös conducting. The second was *Luciano Berio: Voci*, a collection of folk and traditional songs, played with the Vienna Radio Symphony Orchestra. In 2001 she was awarded the Cannes Classical Award for a premiere recording by a soloist with an orchestra for her album *Bartók, Eötvös and Kurtág, Concerto for Viola and Orchestra*.

Also in 2001 Kashkashian, along with cellist Yo-Yo Ma and violinist Gidon Kremer, released an album titled *Mozart*. Then in 2002 she released the album, *Tigran Mansurian: Monodia*. The following year Kashkashian released another album, *Hayren: Music of Komitas and Tigran Mansurian*. Then came two consecutive works featuring the music of Mozart. In 2006, on Universal Records, Kashkashian released *Mozart: Violin Concerto No. 5; Sinfonia Concertante K. 364, Mozart: The Five Violin Concertos*, played with the Vienna Philharmonic Orchestra, and in 2007 she and violinist Gidon Kremer collaborated on *Mozart: Kegelstatt-Trio; Duos for Violin and Viola*.

## GAINING RECOGNITION

Also in 2007 Kashkashian released *Asturiana: Songs from Spain and Argentina*, with Robert Levin on piano. Kashkashian and Levin arranged and performed the songs on this album. They created a wide variation of selections with up-tempo songs, mellow lullabies, and songs of various moods and feelings. Stephen Eddins, in an undated review for *AllMusic.com*, wrote, "The transcriptions are inventive and imaginative, with the vocal lines idiomatically adapted for the viola's expressive capabilities." Eddins continued, "Kashkashian is a remarkable violist who brings vibrancy to everything she plays, and these relatively straightforward songs are no exception."

Two years later came the album *Neharot* (2009), a collection of instrumental music by Israeli and Armenian composers; the album also featured the accompaniment of the Boston Modern Orchestra Project, the Kuss Quartet, and the Munich Chamber Orchestra. Eddins observed that Kashkashian's "passionate investment in this material is evident in the focused intensity of her performances." The album received high praise all around, including praise from National Public Radio host Robert Siegel, who, in his review for *All Things Considered* (4 Sept. 2009), said, "I was amazed to find myself blown away by the title track."

In 2010 Kashkashian also put two records out: *Fauré: Trio Op. 120; Quartet Op. 15 No. 1*, with the Beaux Arts Trio, as well as *Madhares*, playing the music of Austrian composer Larcher with the Quatuor Diotima quartet, pianist Till Fellner, and Dennis Russell Davies conducting the Munich Chamber Orchestra. That same year Kashkashian launched Music for Food, a concert series to help relieve food insecurity in the Boston, Massachusetts, area.

Two years later Kashkashian put out the solo viola record *György Kurtág, György Ligeti: Music for Viola* (2012) on ECM. For her performance on that album, Kashkashian received the 2012 Grammy Award for best classical instrumental solo album. Elizabeth Oka wrote for the *Huffington Post* (20 May 2013), "In this album, Kashkashian acts like a programmer, thinking about the gradual build towards a climax. She shapes the album around dramatic intent."

In 2014, *Tre Voci* or three voices, a trio album featuring Kashkashian on viola, Marina Piccinini on flute, and Sivan Magen on harp, was released. It took the trio a few years to release an album—the group had formed in 2010—but the wait appeared to be worth it. The album featured works by the composers Claude Debussy, Sofia Gubaidulina, and Tōru Takemitsu. The combination of flute, harp and viola was unusual, to be sure, but Kashkashian has always embraced novel ways of thinking about music.

## TEACHING POSITIONS

Kashkashian has taught at a variety of conservatories and universities, including the University of Indiana at Bloomington, Mannes College of Music in New York, and Hochschule für Musik Freiburg and the Hochschule für Musik Hanns Eisler Berlin, both in Germany, where she resided for more than a decade. In September 2000 she moved back to the United States and began teaching viola and chamber music at the New England Conservatory in Boston, Massachusetts.

## PERSONAL LIFE

Kashkashian lives in a suburb outside of Boston. She has a daughter, Areni.

## SUGGESTED READING

Eisler, Edith. "Profile: Violist Kim Kashkashian." *Strings*. Strings, Aug.–Sept. 2000. Web. 22 May 2015.

Kappes, John. "Violist Kim Kashkashian Debuts with Cleveland Orchestra on Bartók." *Cleveland.com*. Northeast Ohio Media, 28 May 2008. Web. 22 May 2015.

Ramey, Corinne. "Kim Kashkashian: An Explorer's Mind." *Strings*. Strings, Mar. 2013. Web. 22 May 2015.

Siegel, Robert. "Kim Kashkashian's Vocal Viola." Rev. of *Neharot*. *All Things Considered*. NPR, 4 Sept. 2009. Web. 22 May 2015.

## SELECTED WORKS

*Mozart: Sinfonia Concertante, K. 364, Violin Concerto No. 1 Sinfonia Concertante, Mozart Violin Concertos 1–5 and Sinfonia Concertante in E Flat*, 1984; *Brahms: Sonaten für Viola und Klavier*, 1997; *Bartók, Eötvös and Kurtág, Concerto for Viola and Orchestra*, 2001; *Asturiana: Songs from Spain and Argentina*, 2007; *Neharot*, 2009; *György Kurtág, György Ligeti: Music for Viola*, 2012

—Dmitry Kiper

# Sam Kass

**Born:** 1980

**Occupation:** Chef and health advocate

Sam Kass wears many hats, and they are not all chef's toques. Kass became a personal chef as well as a friend and nutrition adviser to President Barack Obama's family in 2005, when Obama was still a relatively unknown US senator. After Obama was elected president, the Obamas asked Kass to come along with them to Washington, DC. From the beginning of 2009 until the end of 2014, Kass served not only as the Obama family's personal chef in the White House but also as one of the most high-profile promoters of First Lady Michelle Obama's healthy-eating and exercise initiatives. Until 2014 Kass was the executive director of Michelle Obama's Lets Move! campaign and a senior policy advisor for nutrition policy.

Even in Chicago, before ever knowing that he would one day be working for the president and the first lady, Kass was an active advocate promoting healthy eating and criticizing diets rich in fats, salt, preservatives, processed food, and high fructose corn syrup and lacking in fruits and vegetables. Kass has received media attention not only for his advocacy and apparent closeness with the Obama family but also for his shaved head and good looks. The political website the *Hill* named Kass to its "50 most beautiful" people list in 2013. Kass was also named to *Fast Company* magazine's list of the most creative people of 2011.

## EARLY LIFE AND EDUCATION

Sam Kass grew up in the Hyde Park neighborhood of Chicago, Illinois. From an early age he was passionate about sports. For a part of his elementary school education and throughout high school, Kass attended the University of Chicago Laboratory Schools, where his father, Robert, was a teacher. His mother, Valentine Hertz Kass, was involved in science education and programming. (Robert Kass was later the fifth-grade teacher of Malia Obama, one of Barack and Michelle Obama's two daughters.)

Kass's focus on sports was serious: he had big dreams of playing professional baseball. After graduating high school in 1998, he went on to play center field at a community college in Kansas City, after which he transferred to the University of Chicago, where he played right field

NBC/NBCUniversal/Getty Images

for the Maroons from 2001 to 2003 and earned a .366 career batting average. He is ranked third in the school's history for career stolen bases, with thirty-six.

At the University of Chicago, Kass began to develop another passion, one that altered the direction of his life. He had a summer job at a Chicago restaurant called 312, where he first found a real fascination with food. His last semester of college was spent abroad, in Vienna, Austria, where aside from his studies he worked at an upscale restaurant—and he ended up training there under the supervision of master chef Christian Domschitz from 2003 to 2004. Kass received his bachelor's degree in US history from the University of Chicago in 2004.

After he finished his training at the Viennese restaurant, Morwald im Ambassador, Kass returned to his native Chicago, where be found work as a line cook at the Mediterranean restaurant Avec. There, he worked under chef Koren Grieveson, and proved that he was a capable and talented cook. Aside from Vienna, Kass had also traveled around the world to study not only cooking but food production. According to a profile by Jacob Weisberg for *Vogue* (22 Jan. 2014), Kass spent time in Italy making wine, in Mexico working with Zapatista farmers, and in New Zealand working as a private chef. Although he enjoyed working alongside fellow chefs, Kass told Weisberg that he also noticed how little attention the chefs were paying to the "implications of what we were putting on the plate." It was at this time that Kass began to become interested in the links between food and politics.

## COOKING FOR THE OBAMA FAMILY

In Chicago Kass started his own company, Inevitable Table, working as a private chef at the homes of various clients. He had already been a friend of the Obama family by the time Michelle Obama asked him for his help as a chef. (In fact, according to Weisberg, Kass had known the Obamas since his high school days growing up in Hyde Park.) Her husband, then Senator Barack Obama, was often away from home in Washington, DC, or elsewhere around the country, and Michelle was having a hard time as a full-time working mother raising two little girls. Because she was extremely busy, the family diet suffered as a result, leading to the consumption of a lot of takeout food and precooked meals. Kass took a look at the Obama family's cupboards and eating patterns and decided it was vital to change everything around: According to Jennifer Steinhauer in an article for the *New York Times* (28 Aug. 2014), Kass got rid of the "offending" foods in the Obamas' pantry and began cooking wholesome, healthy meals consisting of whole grains and plenty of steamed vegetables.

As many profiles have pointed out, this was great luck not only for the Obama family but also for Kass, in terms of the opportunities that lay around the corner. Michelle Obama got the benefit of help in the kitchen and a healthy diet for the family, and her little girls took a liking to Kass, following him around the kitchen and watching him chop and stir and steam. Barack Obama, of course, also had national aspirations. "My hunch is that President Obama at that point needed someone like Sam; it helped him to be able to focus on campaigning for the presidency," chef Dan Barber, a friend and mentor to Kass, told Weisberg. "Sam being there as a cook, as a presence in the household—someone Michelle could be buddies with and the kids could adore—created a happy family life while he was away from home. I imagine Obama feels indebted for how Sam filled the void." Barack Obama and Kass went on to form a special bond, almost like a family, often compared to that of an uncle and nephew or even father and son.

## FOOD FOR THOUGHT

In Chicago Kass was involved in advocacy and education on the topic of health and nutrition. Most notably, as a volunteer, he was one of the primary organizers of an event called "Rethinking Soup" at the Jane Addams Hull-House Museum. The event provided a healthy soup for free and presented informative lectures on the cultural, environmental, and economic aspects of food production. At a "Rethinking Soup" event in May 2008, Kass took on the National School Lunch Program. According to a text of his speech quoted by Tara Parker-Pope in an article for the *New York Times* (29 Jan. 2009), Kass gave a brief history of the school lunch program, pointing to its creation by the government in 1946, soon after World War II. By the time of his speech in 2008, the program was serving about one hundred thousand public and nonprofit private schools and feeding twenty-eight million children across the United States every day. Kass expressed his support for the goals of the program, but he did express his concerns about what the students were being fed—and why.

He went on to describe another "vital role" of the lunch program: to absorb the kinds of food being overproduced as a result of government subsidies, particularly beef, pork, and dairy. He then pointed out that the very program that is supposed to feed America's children is actually providing them with poor nutrition. Between 80 and 85 percent of schools, he said, fail the most basic government standards for the percentage of fat in those meals. Kass then expressed concern over the color additives, preservatives, and high fructose corn syrup present in those school lunches and their potential to impact the students' ability to learn and, secondly, the threat of such a diet to students' physical health in the long term, drastically increasing the risk of obesity and diabetes.

## MOVING TO THE WHITE HOUSE

After Barack Obama was elected president in November 2008, Kass's life changed in a big way. The Obama family asked him to come to Washington, DC, to continue working for them as their personal chef. Knowing that such an opportunity would open doors for his advocacy, Kass was thrilled to take on the role in the nation's capital. Kass joined the White House kitchen staff as the assistant chef in charge of family meals under Executive Chef Cristeta Comerford soon after Obama's inauguration in January 2009. Whereas Comerford served as the head chef for various White House functions and state dinners, Kass cooked personally for the Obamas' family dinner. Kass has always avoided specific questions about what the Obamas eat for dinner, saying jokingly that it is "classified," but he has provided occasional details: whole grains, fish, or chicken (sometimes steak) and always vegetables, usually green vegetables. He developed a good sense of what they liked and what they did not like and what he wants to make, so he did not have to await their order; he just made them good, home-cooked meals.

But if Kass had only been the president's family chef, he would not have gotten nearly the amount of coverage and attention as he did for his advocacy work. In 2010 he became a food-initiative coordinator and then became the executive director of Michelle Obama's Let's Move! initiative, which promotes healthy eating and exercise as a way of life. Even in his first year at the White House, Kass was already involved in matters outside of the kitchen. "Behind the scenes," Rachel L. Swarns wrote for the *New York Times* (4 Nov. 2009), "he attends briefings on child nutrition and health, has vetted nonprofits as potential partners for White House food initiatives, and regularly peppers senior staff about policy matters." Even then, wrote Swarns, "Kass has emerged as one of the most high-profile promoters of Michelle Obama's healthy living agenda."

## COOKING UP POLICY

As a promoter of that agenda, Kass went on to be even more in the public eye, talking to Elmo (the Muppet) about nutritious school lunches in a video promoting the Healthy, Hunger-Free Kids Act, discussing the new federal nutritional guide MyPlate and demonstrating how to cook a healthy lasagna on the *Today* show, and even working with the retail giant Walmart to reduce the sodium, sugar, and fat content in Walmart's private-label products and to lower the cost of fruits and vegetables in Walmart grocery stores. Walter Scheib, who had been a chef at the White House for eleven years under President Bill Clinton and President George W. Bush, praised Kass for doing such important policy work in an interview with Nancy Benac for the Associated Press (20 Feb. 2012). "It's way overdue that chefs be involved in that component," he said.

After seven years on the White House staff, Kass announced that he was leaving his post and moving to New York City to live with his wife. He planned to continue his advocacy work in New York. President Obama lauded Kass's many achievements during his time at the White House in a statement announcing Kass's departure (8 Dec. 2014): "From constructing our Kitchen Garden to brewing our own Honey Brown Ale, Sam has left an indelible mark on the White House. And with the work he has done to inspire families and children across this country to lead healthier lives, Sam has made a real difference for our next generation."

## PERSONAL LIFE

In August 2014, Kass married Alex Wagner at Blue Hill at Stone Barns in Tarrytown, New York. The Obama family attended the wedding service. Wagner is a political commentator and the host of *Now with Alex Wagner* on MSNBC. The couple live in New York City.

## SUGGESTED READING

Steinhauer, Jennifer. "Sam Kass, the Obamas' Foodmaster General." *New York Times*. New York Times, 28 Aug. 2014. Web. 9 Feb. 2015.

Swarns, Rachel L. "A White House Chef Who Wears Two Hats." *New York Times*. New York Times, 3 Nov. 2009. Web. 9 Feb. 2015.

Thompson, Krissah, and Tim Carman. "Sam Kass, Chef to the Obamas, Is Leaving the White House." *Washington Post*. Washington Post, 8 Dec. 2014. Web. 9 Feb. 2015.

Weisberg, Jacob. "The Talk of the Town." *Vogue*. Condé Nast, 22 Jan. 2014. Web. 9 Feb. 2015.

—Dmitry Kiper

# Liya Kebede

**Born:** March 1, 1978
**Occupation:** Model and actor

Ethiopian supermodel Liya Kebede appears frequently on the runway and in the pages of glossy fashion magazines. She made history in 2003 as the first black woman ever signed to represent the cosmetics giant Estée Lauder, in a deal worth a reported $3 million. Such high-profile contracts are widely considered the peak of achievement for models, and Kebede remains one of the only women of color ever to reach that lofty—and lucrative—level. Veteran modeling agent James Scully told *New York* magazine (9 May 2008) that Kebede reminded him of the actress and model Grace Kelly, claiming, "Models work for years to develop the poise, grace, and style that she came to the business already equipped with!"

Despite her great beauty and professional success, many consider Kebede's greatest achievements to be her work as an activist and philanthropist. She served from 2005 to 2011 as a Goodwill Ambassador for Maternal, Newborn and Child Health for the World Health Organization (WHO) and has also launched an eponymous charitable foundation, which works to expand maternal health services in her native country and throughout Africa.

Kebede has also tried her hand at acting from time to time with some success. She is the head of her own fashion line called Lemlem; the company provides employment to people in Ethiopia, helps preserve the traditional art of weaving, and encourages other businesses to invest and manufacture in Africa. Named one of the one hundred most influential people of 2010 by *Time* magazine and a 2013 Glamour Woman of the Year, Kebede seamlessly combines the worlds of fashion and philanthropy, embodying much more than just good looks.

## EARLY YEARS AND EDUCATION

Liya Kebede was born on March 1, 1978, in Addis Ababa, Ethiopia. She has four brothers. Their father was a successful airline executive, but Kebede frequently points to their mother as a source of particular inspiration, describing the older woman as a no-nonsense person unafraid to roll up her sleeves to get things done and able to dole out sensible advice. "My mother is an exceptional woman. I count my successes possible because of her love and encouragement," Kebede told Nick Remsen for *Vogue* (23 Apr. 2014). "She taught me so many lessons—from giving my best effort in all aspects of work to approaching life with both appreciation and humor. The single most important thing she taught me was to take the time to serve others and to go the extra mile, in particular, for those who have had less opportunities and fewer chances."

Kebede enjoyed reading and watching movies as a child. While a student at the Lycée Guebre-Mariam, an exclusive high school in Addis Ababa that attracts an international student body, she came to the attention of a French film director. He introduced Kebede to one of his compatriots, a modeling agent, and she began working as a model simply as a way to pay for her education. After completing her studies, she moved to France and then to the United States to begin her modeling career in earnest.

## MODELING CAREER

Although Kebede at first took minor catalog modeling jobs for various retailers, in 1999 she

Nicolas Genin/Wikimedia Commons

debuted on the runway for the fashion houses Ralph Lauren and BCBG Max Azria. Her relatively rapid success defied the norm for minority models, who generally struggle to gain the popularity of their white counterparts. Scully, who helped bring Kebede to prominence, told Guy Trebay for the *New York Times* (8 Apr. 2003) that many designers "will tell you black girls don't move merchandise." Another agent told Trebay, "Fashion is about the right moment and every season you have to have the new moment and the new girls. But there is no black moment. There is not now and there never will be."

Despite that entrenched bias, in 2000 designer Tom Ford chose Kebede to walk the runway wearing his new collection for the fashion brand Gucci. That show is widely considered to be a turning point in her career, as the brand's iconic status helped propel Kebede to international attention. Another career-making break came in May 2002, when Carine Roitfeld, the editor of the *Vogue Paris* magazine at the time, featured Kebede on the cover and devoted much of the entire issue to her. An editorial in the magazine referred to the model as "a disco princess, priestess of rap, relaxed nomad, and soul sister."

Kebede went on to a string of additional high-profile assignments, appearing in further international editions of *Vogue* as well as other fashion magazines, such as *Harper's Bazaar* and *Glamour*. She worked with some of the most in-demand photographers in the world, including

Patrick Demarchelier, Mario Testino, and Steven Meisel and modeled for Calvin Klein, Burberry, Fendi, Marni, and Chanel, among other brands.

Kebede caught the eye of executives at Estée Lauder, and in early 2003 it was announced that she would be the new "face" of the multimillion-dollar brand. Patrick Bousquet-Chavanne, the president of the company, described Kebede's hiring as an exceptionally wise move. "Not only is she helping us to communicate with a wider audience as our first ethnic model," he told Trebay, "She has a kind of beauty that brings fashion to the brand." Other endorsements followed, and Kebede was signed to campaigns for luxury brands like Tiffany & Co. as well as more mass-market ones like the Gap. By 2007 *Forbes* magazine ranked her among the highest-paid supermodels in the world.

## ACTIVISM AND PHILANTHROPY

In 2005 Kebede was named one of the World Health Organization's goodwill ambassadors, a position in which celebrities help raise public awareness of important global health problems and solutions. In that role she has focused on women's and children's health issues, drawing attention to maternal death and childhood mortality especially. "I have always felt committed to women's causes and the maternal health issue in particular spoke to me after I had my two children," she explained to Lauren Said-Moorhouse for *CNN World: African Voices* (18 Sept. 2014). "I was stunned when I first learned that a woman was dying every minute in my home country and other developing nations from complications of pregnancy and childbirth."

In addition to touring and speaking on behalf of WHO, in 2005 Kebede established the Liya Kebede Foundation. The group works with local aid organizations across Africa to train health care professionals in obstetrics and neonatal care. When the foundation opened a maternity center in the town of Awassa (also called Awasa or Hawassa), Ethiopia, to name just one of its initiatives, the number of healthy births in the area doubled in just a year.

In 2007 Kebede was reappointed as a WHO ambassador. She also founded her own clothing label Lemlem (which means "to flourish or bloom" in Amharic) as a way to combine fashion with social activism in support of local African economies. Focusing first on children's clothing, the line branched out into adult fashions as demand increased. "The core of our collection is handwoven and made with handspun thread,"

Kebede told Said-Moorhouse, explaining that some pieces incorporate fabric traditionally used for Ethiopian wedding dresses. "Supporting Ethiopian weavers and their craft has remained our central mission and we're proud we can sell a beautiful product while also helping these artisans thrive."

## ACTING

Kebede appeared in small parts in a handful of films, including the Nicholas Cage thriller *Lord of War* (2005) and *The Good Shepherd* (2006), a spy drama that starred Matt Damon, Angelina Jolie, and Robert De Niro, before taking on a major role. In 2009 she took on her first leading part, starring in the biopic *Desert Flower* as Waris Dirie, a model from Somalia who used her fame as a platform to campaign against female genital mutilation. Reviews of both Kebede's performance and the picture itself were uneven. After *Desert Flower* was released in the United States, Gary Goldstein wrote for the *Los Angeles Times* (18 Mar. 2011), "A lovely performance by Ethiopian supermodel-actress Liya Kebede as supermodel-activist Waris Dirie works wonders to elevate this uneven, occasionally awkward but often absorbing film." Writing for the *Jerusalem Post* (5 Nov. 2010), on the other hand, Hannah Brown opined, "Kebede . . . is as beautiful as any female lead in the history of movies, but she doesn't quite capture the spark that must have motivated the fiercely driven and independent Waris."

Kebede's other film appearances include *Day of the Falcon* (2011), a period piece set in the Arab world at the start of the oil boom; *Capital* (2012), a financial thriller; *The Best Offer* (2013), an Italian picture about a reclusive art collector; the fantasy-horror flick *Innocence* (2013); and *Samba* (2014), a film about a Senegalese immigrant to France.

Meanwhile, Kebede's philanthropic activities continued to develop alongside her acting career. In 2014, for example, she collaborated with jewelry designers Monique Péan and David Yurman to create pieces whose proceeds would go directly to her foundation.

## PERSONAL LIFE

Kebede met her husband, Kassahun (known as Kassy), a financier, in 1999, while both were visiting their native Ethiopia. They enjoyed a whirlwind courtship that included a safari in Kenya and were married in 2000. They settled in

New York City and have one son, Suhul, and one daughter, Raee.

When she is not working, Kebede, reportedly cares little about what she wears. "I don't think much about it," she confessed to Cathy Horyn for *Town & Country* (Oct. 2003). "I just open the closet and get a bottom and then a top, and that's it."

## SUGGESTED READING

Ballentine, Sandra. "Liya Kebede on How to Raise a Global Citizen." *Condé Nast Traveler*. Condé Nast, 19 Aug. 2014. Web. 16 Oct. 2014.

Connor, Katie L. "Liya Kebede: A Woman Apart." *Marie Claire*. Hearst Communication, 20 Jan. 2011. Web. 16 Oct. 2014.

Horyn, Cathy. "Liya's World." *Town & Country*. Hearst Communications, Oct. 2003. Web. 16 Oct. 2014.

Remsen, Nick. "Liya Kebede Reflects on Her New Jewelry Partnership with David Yurman, Motherhood, and Life's Lessons." *Vogue*. Condé Nast, 23 Apr. 2014. Web. 16 Oct. 2014.

Said-Moorhouse, Lauren. "Step into a Supermodel's Shoes with Liya Kebede." *CNN*. Cable News Network, 18 Sept. 2014. Web. 16 Oct. 2014.

Savacool, Julia. "More Than a Pretty Face: Liya Kebede." *Marie Claire*. Hearst Communication, 14 May 2007. Web. 16 Oct. 2014.

Trebay, Guy. "A Black Model Reaches the Top, A Lonely Spot." *New York Times*. New York Times, 8 Apr. 2003. Web. 16 Oct. 2014.

—Mari Rich

Fanny Schertzer/Wikimedia

# Duncan Keith

**Born:** July 16, 1983
**Occupation:** Hockey player

As Scott Burnside wrote for the ESPN website (18 May 2014), Chicago Blackhawks defenseman Duncan Keith is "one of the game's most deceptive players, regularly anticipating opposing teams' passes, knocking them down or intercepting them and starting a rush the opposite direction." Keith made his National Hockey League (NHL) debut with the Blackhawks in the 2005–6 season and has since become the linchpin of the team's defense. Known not only for his shutdown defense but also for his prowess on offense, Keith put his all-around skills on full display in the 2009–10 season, when he finished second among NHL defensemen in assists (55) and points (69). That season, he won the Norris Trophy for the league's best defenseman and helped lead the Blackhawks to their first Stanley Cup since 1961. He captured another Stanley Cup title with the Blackhawks in 2013 and won his second career Norris Trophy in 2014. Keith has led the Blackhawks in ice time every season of his career and led the NHL in that category in both 2010–11 and 2011–12, helping him establish a reputation as arguably the most physically fit player in the league. He has also earned two all-star selections and has won two Olympic gold medals with Canada's national team.

## EARLY LIFE

Duncan Keith was born on July 16, 1983, in Winnipeg, Canada. He has an older brother, Cameron, and a younger sister, Rebecca. When Keith was two years old, his family moved to Fort Frances in northwestern Ontario after his father, Dave, became an assistant branch manager with the Canadian Imperial Bank of Commerce. Keith's mother, Jean, was a nurse's aide.

Growing up just two blocks away from Fort Frances's east-end outdoor ice rink, Keith cultivated an early passion for hockey. He learned how to skate at age four and began playing ice hockey competitively soon thereafter. He also took both power- and figure-skating lessons. Keith's mother, who drove him each day to early-morning practices, recalled to John Paul Byrne for *Okanagan Life* magazine (7 Jan. 2011), "Duncan always wanted to be the first one on the ice." At age seven Keith started playing for the Fort Frances Times Tigers in the novice division; before long, he moved on to the atom and peewee levels. He initially played forward before switching to defense when he was about ten years old.

## JUNIOR AND COLLEGE HOCKEY

When Keith was fourteen, his family moved to Summerland, British Columbia. About a year later, they settled in nearby Penticton, a city known for its rich hockey tradition. Keith played his final two years of minor hockey there on a bantam team.

At sixteen Keith won a spot on the Penticton Panthers (now the Penticton Vees), an elite junior team in the British Columbia Hockey League known for developing numerous NHL players. When Keith joined the Panthers, he was only five feet nine and less than 140 pounds, but he made up for his small size with his exceptional skating ability, quickness, and speed. In three seasons as a defenseman with the Panthers, Keith amassed 226 points (78 goals and 148 assists) in 163 games, helping lead the team to consecutive Interior Division titles in 1999–2000 and 2000–2001.

After graduating from Penticton Secondary School in 2001, Keith won an athletic scholarship to Michigan State University, where he played on the hockey squad under legendary coach Ron Mason. As a freshman Keith earned 15 points in forty-one games, ranking him fourth among team defensemen. Around this time, Mason said of Keith to Kyle Woodlief for *USA Today* (8 Jan. 2002), "He's got great hands and the kind of skills you just can't teach."

Keith played in fifteen games for Michigan State as a sophomore before returning to British Columbia to join the Kelowna Rockets in the Western Hockey League (WHL). In thirty-seven games with the Rockets during the 2002–3 season, he posted 46 points and a remarkable goal differential of plus 32.

## CHICAGO BLACKHAWKS

Before the 2003–4 season, Keith signed a three-year entry-level contract with the Blackhawks, which had selected him in the second round of the 2002 NHL Entry Draft, ignoring concerns about his size. Keith was assigned to the Norfolk Admirals, the Blackhawks' affiliate in the American Hockey League (AHL), to further develop his game and build before entering the NHL. Keith spent the entire 2003–4 and 2004–5 seasons with the Admirals, during which he tallied a total of 51 points in 154 regular-season games.

Keith lost his opportunity for a roster spot on the Blackhawks in 2004–5 because of the NHL lockout, which resulted in the cancellation of the entire season. Nevertheless, he cracked the Blackhawks' lineup in the 2005 training camp and made his NHL debut on October 5, 2005, against the Anaheim Ducks. He quickly established himself as one of the Blackhawks' best-conditioned players. Blackhawks general manager Stan Bowman told Burnside that Keith was "an incredibly fit athlete. . . . He's sort of like a cyclist in terms of his aerobic ability. That's why he plays so many minutes."

Pairing with another talented young defenseman, Brent Seabrook, during the 2006–7 season, Keith played in all of the Blackhawks' eighty-two regular season games and led the team in ice time for the second consecutive year. One month into the season, the Blackhawks fired head coach Trent Yawney and replaced him with Denis Savard. Despite Yawney's early-season dismissal, Keith credited the coach with teaching him how "to play proper D[efense] and what it took," according to Neil Stevens for the Canadian Press (11 Jan. 2008).

## A WORKHORSE DEFENSEMAN

By the start of the 2007–8 season, Keith had grown to six feet one and bulked up to 190 pounds. Solidifying his standing as the Blackhawks' workhorse, he again played in all eighty-two games and led the team in ice time, averaging more than twenty-five minutes per game. He also led the team and ranked second among NHL defensemen with a plus-30 goal differential, helping him earn his first career all-star selection. Anchored defensively by Keith and Seabrook and bolstered offensively by rookie phenoms Patrick Kane and Jonathan Toews, the Blackhawks compiled a winning season for the first time in six years, narrowly missing the playoffs.

High expectations surrounded the Blackhawks' young nucleus of talent entering the 2008–9 season, for which Keith was designated one of the team's two alternate captains. Consequently, after the Blackhawks struggled to a 1–3 start, Savard was fired and replaced with Joel Quenneville, formerly head coach of the Colorado Avalanche. Under Quenneville, who favored a high-tempo, attacking brand of hockey, Keith elevated the offensive side of his game. He posted 44 points in seventy-seven games and led the Blackhawks with a career-high goal differential of plus 33. Meanwhile, the Blackhawks finished second in the division, earning their first playoff berth since 2002.

## TOP DEFENSEMAN AND THE BLACKHAWKS' RESURGENCE

Two months into the 2009–10 season, the Blackhawks secured Keith for the long term by signing him to a thirteen-year contract extension worth $72 million, the largest in team history. Armed with his new contract, Keith took his game to another level, and he and Seabrook formed the most formidable defensive pairing in the league. In eighty-two games, Keith recorded career highs in a number of categories, and he placed second among league defensemen in assists (55) and points (69). For his performance, he was awarded the Norris Trophy.

Thanks to Keith's shutdown defense, the Blackhawks made the playoffs for a second consecutive year, defeating the Nashville Predators, the Vancouver Canucks, and the San Jose Sharks in the first three rounds of the playoffs before facing the Philadelphia Flyers in the Stanley Cup Finals. The Blackhawks won the series in six games to earn the franchise's first Stanley Cup title in forty-nine years.

Keith, who famously had seven teeth knocked out by an errant puck in the Western Conference Finals, played a significant role in the Blackhawks' title run, posting 2 goals and 15 assists in twenty-two postseason games. "Keith offers a heady mix of high-end speed, smart reads, and courage without any noticeable holes," Michael Farber wrote for *Sports Illustrated* (14 June 2010) during the Stanley Cup Finals.

## SECOND NORRIS TROPHY AND STANLEY CUP WINS

After the Blackhawks suffered through first-round playoff exits in 2011 and 2012, the team returned to championship form in 2012–13. In the lockout shortened season, Keith recorded 27 points in forty-seven games and helped lead the Blackhawks to a league-best regular-season record. The Blackhawks won their second Stanley Cup in four seasons after defeating the Boston Bruins in the 2013 Stanley Cup Finals.

Keith confirmed his status as one of the NHL's best defensemen in 2013–14. In seventy-seven games that season, he led all league defensemen with 5 assists and finished second among defensemen with 61 points. The Blackhawks advanced to the playoffs for the sixth consecutive season but lost to the Los Angeles Kings, the eventual Stanley Cup champions, in seven games in the Western Conference Finals.

After the conclusion of the Stanley Cup playoffs, Keith won his second career Norris Trophy, becoming the third Blackhawks defenseman to win the award more than once. He entered the 2014–15 season as the only active NHL defenseman with multiple Norris Trophies. Individual achievements notwithstanding, Keith explained to Shawn Roarke for NHL.com (24 June 2014), "What means the most to me is to be part of an organization that treats its players so well, and I think when you have that team success with great teammates, everyone looks better individually."

## PERSONAL LIFE

Keith married Kelly-Rae Kenyon, a fellow Penticton resident, in July 2011. The couple has a son, Colton, who was born in May 2011. They divide their time between homes in Chicago and British Columbia. Keith has represented Canada's national team in three international competitions, winning a silver medal at the 2008 Ice Hockey World Championships in Quebec City and Halifax, Canada, and capturing gold medals at the 2010 and 2014 Olympic Winter Games in Vancouver, Canada, and Sochi, Russia, respectively.

## SUGGESTED READING

Burnside, Scott. "Who Is the Real Duncan Keith?" *ESPN*. ESPN Internet Ventures, 18 May 2014. Web. 22 Oct. 2014.

Byrne, John Paul. "Duncan Keith: Slam Dunc." *Okanagan Life*. Okanagan Life Magazine, 7 Jan. 2011. Web. 22 Oct. 2014.

Farber, Michael. "A Cup Most Unkind." *Sports Illustrated* 14 June 2010: 50–54. Print.

Roarke, Shawn. "Keith Wins Norris Trophy for Second Time." *NHL.com*. NHL, 24 June 2014. Web. 22 Oct. 2014.

Woodlief, Kyle. "Spartans' Keith Finally Settles in One Place." *USA Today*. Gannett, 8 Jan. 2002. Web. 22 Oct. 2014.

—Chris Cullen

# Key & Peele

**Occupation:** Comedy duo

**Keegan-Michael Key**
**Born:** March 22, 1971

**Jordan Peele**
**Born:** February 21, 1979

The comedy duo Keegan-Michael Key and Jordan Peele have stated several times in interviews that their Comedy Central sketch show, *Key & Peele*, would not have been possible, or at least would not have been as accepted and popular, if it were not for the election of President Barack Obama. Both Key and Peele, like Obama, have black fathers and white mothers, and the way they explore race has become one of the show's staples. Since its first season in 2012, the show has proven itself to be not only funny, but also smart and insightful. It has also grown immensely popular online, with a total of more than 600 million views for their sketches, which include "East/West College Bowl," "Obama Anger Translator," "Auction Block," "Soul Food," and "Liam Neesons and Bruce Willy." The series is not a typical sketch comedy show. Each skit is shot like a film, and the actors, Key and Peele, truly disappear into their characters. In 2012 they were declared *Entertainment Weekly*'s Entertainers of the Year, and in 2014 *Time* magazine put them on its Most Influential People list.

## EARLY DAYS

Keegan-Michael Key was born in 1971 in Michigan to a white mother and black father. He was given up for adoption; the couple who adopted him was also a white woman and a black man. Key grew up in Detroit. As an adult, Key came to know his birth mother and the two developed a close relationship. Growing up, Key was very aware of the fact that he was adopted and that brought feelings of doubt and not being wanted, even though his adoptive mother "tirelessly worked most of her life to build up [his] self-esteem," he told Gross. In an interview with Alyssa Rosenberg for the website *ThinkProgress* (15 Feb. 2012), Key said he was raised a Christian, and that he also later studied Buddhism and a bit of Hinduism. At the time of the interview he said he considered himself a "spiritual Christian." Peele, on the other hand, said he was not religious.

Jordan Peele was born in 1979 in New York City, where he was raised by a single mother. As

Jason LaVeris/FilmMagic/Getty Images

he told Terry Gross on the National Public Radio interview program *Fresh Air* (20 Nov. 2013), he saw his father "once a month, once every couple of months" until he was six years old, when his father walked out of his life completely. Peele never saw him again—and never really knew him, he added. Later in his life Peele discovered that his father had many other children with various women "across the country and other countries." Peele, the product of a black father and a white mother, grew up in New York, a racially diverse city, but from a young age he was aware of how complicated the issue of racial identity could be and how fluid it is—an awareness that he shares with Key.

## CODE-SWITCHING

Though they grew up in different cities and under different circumstances, Key and Peele were both products of interracial relationships and from an early age had a desire to transcend the various limited views of race they saw reflected around them. It was that desire that pushed them both into acting—and ultimately into comedy. "I think the reason I went into theater, ultimately, was because that was one of those multicultural groups. Because you identify with other people that share similar passions to you, so it didn't matter how much melanin was in their skin," Key told Gross. "That clan is born out of love and passion as opposed to born out of some sense of obligation to belong to a certain group. [. . .] That's what salvaged my life, I think, in

high school." Peele pointed out that growing up biracial, they both did "a fair amount
of code-switching." Although in linguistics
"code-switching" refers to switching between
multiple languages or dialects within a single
conversation—for example, using Spanish or
even "Spanglish" words in a conversation in
English—Peele meant code-switching in a different sense: switching dialects based on context. As an example, Peele said that when he and
Key are hanging out with each other, they speak
in a "more casual black dialect." He added that
"that's our comfort zone when we're making
each other laugh." Many people, young and old,
engage in various forms of code-switching, but
Key and Peele's awareness from a young age of
the necessity of adapting their self-presentation
to different social contexts was one of the things
that led them to acting.

## ACT ONE

Peele moved from New York City to Chicago,
where he perfected his performing skills at Im-
provOlympic and Second City Chicago. He also
worked on his improvisational comedy chops in
Amsterdam, the Netherlands, at Boom Chicago
Theater. On a trip back to Chicago, he met Key
for the first time through their mutual involvement in Second City, and the two soon became
friends. Peele then returned to the United States
to appear in the FOX sketch comedy show
*MADtv*, where he was a regular for five seasons,
starting in 2003. Peele appeared as an actor in
the show's skits for 94 episodes and wrote for 29
episodes. Key started out at Second City Detroit
and then also moved to Second City Chicago,
where he received awards for both his writing
and his acting. In 2004 Key also joined *MADtv*,
where he was a regular for six seasons. Key acted in 107 episodes and wrote for 22 episodes.

## MOVING ON

Key and Peele were certainly indebted to the
experience they gained on *MADtv*, though when
deciding to do a show of their own it was also
a lesson in what they did not want to do. On
the show, Key and Peele banter onstage about
a topic and present filmed shorts and sketches
related to the topic. The sketches themselves are
not done in front of a studio audience, but are
instead produced with attention to detail, like
a movie, and focus more on their acting. The
actors do not play to the camera or try to get a
cheap laugh but come off fully invested in their
characters. The variety of characters they take on

is staggering. Key and Peele play seemingly every type of person—from gay to straight, young
to old, masculine to feminine—and also a variety of races and ethnicities, from Latino to black
to Asian to Indian to Italian to American Indian.
But in their sketches they do not play general
descriptions of people or stereotypes; they play
individuals, and if some individuals act in stereotypical ways, that is an aspect of their individuality, something to be explored.

Aside from *MADtv*, according to James Walcott of *Vanity Fair* (13 Oct. 2014), Key and Peele
were also influenced by quite a variety of shows:
the nearly all-black skit show *In Living Color*,
the experimental *Mr. Show*, comedian Martin
Lawrence's sitcom *Martin*, and comedian Dave
Chappelle's Comedy Central sketch comedy
show *Chappelle's Show*.

## A SHOW OF THEIR OWN

*Key & Peele* premiered on Comedy Central in
2012. The fact that they were on Comedy Central and that their sketch comedy show took on
issues of race in humorous and challenging ways
initially led to frequent comparisons to *Chappelle's Show*. Emily Nussbaum, in her column
for the *New Yorker* (30 Sept. 2013), admitted
that she had initially misjudged the series. It all
started with the skit "Obama Anger Translator,"
in which Jordan Peele plays the cool and calm
President Barack Obama, addressing the nation in a steady and cerebral manner, whereas
Keegan-Michael Key plays Luther, his "anger
translator." Obama is sitting, talking about his
policy and diplomatically addressing various
partisan difficulties he has had. Luther "translates" Obama's careful, tactful responses to his
detractors into exclamations of frustration—at
times yelling or stomping around the room,
fuming. In her piece about the show, Nussbaum
called that skit "smart" and "cathartic," but she
also labeled it a "one-joke gag." As amusing as
it is, it is not a subtle piece of comedy. But then
one day, writes Nussbaum, she discovered "Pizza Order," the first skit about Wendell (Peele),
an obese adult nerd whose room is full of action figures. He calls a pizza restaurant to place
an order, and ends up "gauging the room" and
ordering three large pizzas, all for himself. So
far, Nussbaum writes, it simply appears to be a
"fat joke." But that is what *Key & Peele* is so
good at—misdirecting the viewer into thinking the skit is about one thing when it is about
something else entirely. The pizza guy (Key) on
the phone ends up being interested in "Claire,"

who he thinks is a woman but is actually one of Wendell's action figures; he declares his love for her with increasing passion as Wendell tries to dissuade him. As Nussbaum points out, it is difficult to summarize skit plots (and there is "nothing more numbingly Soviet"), but the skit ends with a twist that muddies the traditional comedy dynamic of the straight man and the butt of the joke. "Key and Peele's biracialism is central to their comedy," Nussbaum writes, "but in a far different way than I'd imagined: it is expansive, not constricting, a Golden Ticket to themes rarely explored on television. Like many of the best, most transgressive comics, they treat human behavior as a form of drag, shape-shifting with aggressive fluidity."

Key and Peele took on code-switching in the show's very first skit, in which they played two guys on the street talking on their cell phones who deepen their voices and make them more "urban" and "hard" once they become aware of one another's presence. Viewers, of course, see plainly what they are doing. Once one of the guys finally walks away, the other guy says into his cell phone (in a drastically more effeminate voice) that he "almost got mugged." Another way Key and Peele explore race is via various forms of "contest": between, for example, Martin Luther King and Malcolm X, between jazz singer Bobby McFerrin and comedy actor Michael Winslow, and between two guys at a soul food place trying to "out-order" each other by going for the most bizarre and unappetizing dishes—in a skit that gets more absurdist by the moment (one ends up ordering "donkey teeth").

## OTHER WORK

Although best known for their Comedy Central series, Key and Peele have also appeared together in the FX drama *Fargo*, in 2014, a series based on the Coen brothers' film of the same name. In the series, Key and Peele play FBI agents named Pepper and Budge. Together they also have various projects in development, including a film based on the "Substitute Teacher" sketch, as well as the films *Keanu* and *Police Academy*.

## SUGGESTED READING

Gross, Terry. "For Key and Peele, Biracial Roots Bestow Special Comedic 'Power.'" *NPR*. NPR, 20 Nov. 2013. Web. 29 Jan. 2015.

Nussbaum, Emily. "Color Commentary." *New Yorker*. Condé Nast, 30 Sept. 2013. Web. 29 Jan. 2015.

Rosenberg, Alyssa. "The Essential Comedians for the Age of Obama: A Conversation with Keegan-Michael Key and Jordan Peele." *ThinkProgress*. Center for Amer. Progress Action Fund, 13 Feb. 2012. Web. 29 Jan. 2015.

Walcott, James. "How Keegan-Michael Key and Jordan Peele Have Broken the Comedy-Duo Mold." *Vanity Fair*. Condé Nast, 13 Oct. 2014. Web. 29 Jan. 2015.

—Dmitry Kiper

# Dennis Kimetto

**Born:** January 22, 1984
**Occupation:** Long-distance runner

In the world of sports, Kenya has long been known as a hotbed of elite distance runners. Scientists have proposed such factors as genetic predisposition, body type, and diet to explain the country's incredible distance-running prowess. While many of those proposals have been subject to heated debate, Dennis Kimetto has made a strong case to support them. In a matter of just a few years, Kimetto has risen to become arguably the best marathoner in the world. He had been barely eking out a living as a subsistence farmer when, in 2008, a chance encounter with fellow compatriot and champion marathoner Geoffrey Mutai helped launch his running career. He first made a name for himself in 2012, when he set a world record in the twenty-five-kilometer road race. That year Kimetto also made his marathon debut at the Berlin Marathon, where he set another world record for the fastest debut in history. In 2013 he recorded course-record victories at both the Tokyo and Chicago marathons.

Kimetto gained worldwide prominence, however, in 2014, when he won the Berlin Marathon in a world-record time of 2:02:57. He shattered the previous record by twenty-six seconds and became the first person to break the hallowed 2:03 barrier. In interviews Kimetto has credited his meteoric success not only to talent but also to hard work and determination. Speaking with Christopher Kelsall for *Athletics Illustrated* (23 Feb. 2015), he explained, "Whether poor or rich, people must be able to have that motivation and go for it."

## EARLY LIFE AND EDUCATION

Dennis Kipruto Kimetto was born on January 22, 1984, in Kamwosor, a rural village in what is today Elgeyo Marakwet County. His parents, James and Alice, worked as subsistence farmers on a small landholding near the town of Kapngetuny. Along with his six siblings, Kimetto grew up helping his parents with farm work, as they struggled to provide for the family. "We did not have a lot of money," he told Anita Tejwani for *Inspiration Unlimited eMagazine* (25 Feb. 2015). "But together we were always happy."

Like many young Kenyans, Kimetto began running out of necessity. He made two round trips each day to Kamwosor Primary School, which was located approximately four kilometers from his home; he would run to school in the morning, run home for lunch, and then return to school for afternoon classes. Kimetto's first running competitions came in the form of school races, which he usually won; his parents, in their formative years, were runners for their schools in national races. Financial constraints, however, prevented Kimetto from pursuing his running talent and ultimately forced him to drop out of school in the seventh grade.

Kimetto did not start fostering dreams of a professional running career until his teenage years. After watching fellow compatriot Paul Tergat, a former marathon world-record holder, narrowly lose out to the Ethiopian distance runner Haile Gebrselassie in the ten-kilometer event at 2000 Olympic Games in Sydney, Australia, he became inspired to follow in his footsteps. "I thought, perhaps I could run at that level," he told Andy Edwards for the International Association of Athletics Federations (IAAF) website (29 Sept. 2014).

## FROM FARMER TO RUNNER

For Kimetto, running professionally offered him a chance "to escape the poverty," as he put it to Motunde Smith for the sports news e-magazine *Athletics Africa* (21 Nov. 2014). It would be years, however, before he realized his running ambitions. After leaving school, Kimetto continued to work on his family's farm, growing maize and raising cattle. He also took on menial jobs outside of his village, such as planting and weeding people's farms, to earn extra income for his family. In his spare time, Kimetto trained on his own, running on trails and dirt roads in and around his village. Still, he covered only short distances, running approximately four miles a day.

A turning point for Kimetto occurred in 2008, when he serendipitously encountered Geoffrey Mutai during one of his runs. At the time, Mutai

Boris Streubel/Bongarts/Getty Images

was emerging as one of Kenya's best distance runners and leading an elite training group about eight kilometers from Kapngetuny. Impressed by Kimetto's flowing, effortless stride, Mutai invited him to join his group, which also included the burgeoning Kenyan marathoner Wilson Kipsang. Kimetto took up Mutai's offer, but he continued to divide his time between farming and training.

When Kimetto first started training with Mutai's running group, he struggled to keep up with the elite runners. Nevertheless, after deciding to focus on his running career full-time, he eventually reached their level. "He is patient, and he has the passion and the enthusiasm to really train and be at the top," Wilson Kipsang said of Kimetto to Joe Battaglia, writing for *Running Times* (24 Sept. 2014). Though initially putting a financial strain on his family, Kimetto's decision to become a full-time runner was encouraged by his parents. "My father said, 'train as well as you can and go for it, you can change your life,'" he recalled to Edwards.

## FIRST ROAD RACES AND MARATHON DEBUT

Kimetto entered his first competitive distance races in 2011. He enjoyed immediate success, winning eleven domestic races that year, including the Nairobi Half Marathon, with a time of 1:01:30. Kimetto's performance in the Kenyan capital helped him land a contract with

Volare Sports, a Netherlands-based athlete-management company run by Gerard Van de Veen. As part of Volare Sports' elite stable of athletes, which include Mutai and Kipsang, Kimetto began competing in more high-profile distance events.

Kimetto's first race outside of Kenya came in February 2012, when he competed at the Ras Al Khaimah Half Marathon in Dubai, United Arab Emirates. "I felt scared, seeing runners like Wilson Kipsang alongside me," he admitted to Edwards. "Nobody knew who I was." To the surprise of many, Kimetto won the prestigious race in a time of 1:00:40. Less than two months later he won the Berlin Half Marathon, under the name Denis Koech, finishing one second ahead of fellow Kenyan Wilson Kiprop, with a personal-best time of 59:14.

In May 2012 Kimetto followed up that performance with a record-breaking first-place finish at the Big 25 Berlin, a twenty-five-kilometer road race that has been held annually since 1981. His time of 1:11:18 was thirty-two seconds faster than the record set by Ugandan-born Samuel Kosgei in 2010. In his interview with Anita Tejwani, Kimetto called the win "a milestone in my life."

Berlin also served as the setting for Kimetto's marathon debut, which was nothing short of remarkable. At the 2012 Berlin Marathon, which was held in September of that year, he placed second in the 26.2-mile (42-kilometer) race with a time of 2:04:16, finishing just one second behind Mutai. Though some commentators alleged that Kimetto deliberately let his mentor win, his time was the fastest marathon debut in history on a record-eligible course.

## COURSE RECORDS AT TOKYO AND CHICAGO

Following his marathon debut, Kimetto began competing regularly on the World Marathon Majors (WMM) circuit. Founded in 2006, the WMM is a race series comprising six of the largest and most prestigious marathons in the world: Tokyo, Boston, London, Berlin, Chicago, and New York City. Runners earn points for finishing in the top five in any of the WMM qualifying races, which also include the IAAF World Championships Marathon and the Olympic Marathon. At the end of each annual scoring cycle, the top male and female point-earners split a million-dollar prize purse.

Kimetto ran in his second career WMM event at the Tokyo Marathon in February 2013. De-

spite unfavorable weather conditions, he won the race in a course-record time of 2:06:50, beating defending champion Michael Kipyego by eight seconds. His course record was improved to 2:05:42 by Kenyan Dickson Chumba in 2014.

That October Kimetto made his North American debut at the Chicago Marathon. Despite being little more than two months removed from a bout of malaria, he cruised to his second career victory with a then personal-best time of 2:03:45, seven seconds ahead of third-place finisher and compatriot Emmanuel Mutai (no relation to Geoffrey Mutai). Kimetto's winning time shattered the marathon's previous course record of 2:04:38, set by Ethiopia's Tsegaye Kebede in 2012, and fell just twenty-two seconds short of the world record, established by Kipsang at the Berlin Marathon two weeks earlier. Kimetto received a $100,000 purse for winning the event and a $75,000 bonus for setting a course record.

Following the Chicago Marathon, Kimetto used part of his winnings to purchase a car and construct a four-bedroom home for his family in Eldoret, the largest town and county seat of Uasin Gishu, located about thirty-seven miles (sixty kilometers) from Kamwosor. It is also home to an IAAF high-performance training center. "What really motivates me to be a fighter is the fact that I come from a humble background," he explained to Joe Battaglia. "I try to really make sure that I achieve my best so that I can assist my family."

## MAKING HISTORY IN BERLIN

In April 2014 Kimetto competed at the Boston Marathon, which had been cut short a year earlier due to a terrorist attack near the finish line that killed three people and injured hundreds more. Because of its point-to-point and largely downhill layout, the course, which begins in Hopkinton, Massachusetts, is often susceptible to strong, performance-aiding tailwinds. As a result, the course has been deemed ineligible for marathon records by the IAAF. That status notwithstanding, Kimetto entered the race hoping to win. He dropped out around the thirty-five-kilometer-mark, however, due to a hamstring injury.

After his disappointing performance in Boston, Kimetto set his sights on recovering in time for the Berlin Marathon in September 2014. In only the fifth marathon of his career, he rebounded in a big way by shattering the marathon world record with a time of 2:02:57, improving Kipsang's previous record by twenty-six seconds. He was pushed for most of the race by Emmanuel Mutai, who placed second with a time of 2:03:13, the second-fastest marathon time in history. With his record-breaking time, Kimetto, who averaged an astonishing four minutes, forty-one seconds per mile, became the first person to break the 2:03 barrier in the marathon. It marked the sixth time in fewer than a dozen years that a men's marathon world record was achieved on Berlin's notoriously fast and flat course.

Kimetto's historic win came with a combined purse of approximately $154,000. He was also in strong contention to take home the lucrative prize of $500,000 for the 2013–14 WMM series, but he narrowly lost the title to Wilson Kipsang, who surpassed him in the final standings by one point after winning the 2014 New York City Marathon.

On April 26, 2015, Kimetto made his debut at the London Marathon, where he went head to head with Kipsang, the event's defending champion. In a surprise turn of events, neither world record-holder Kimetto nor London reigning champion Kipsang won the race, coming in at 2:05:50 and 2:04:47 (third and second), respectively, behind fellow Kenyan Eliud Kipchoge's 2:04:42. Periodic rain made the course somewhat more difficult, and Kipchoge did not break either Kipsang's course record or Kimetto's world record.

Despite losing London, Kimetto's "aim is to run on [a] high level for a long time," as he stated in his interview with Christopher Kelsall. He has announced plans to compete at the 2015 IAAF World Championships in Beijing, China, and the 2016 Olympics in Rio de Janeiro, Brazil.

## PERSONAL LIFE
Kimetto continues to train outside of Kapngetuny with Geoffrey Mutai and his other Kenyan running partners. "We follow a rigid code," he told Motunde Smith. "We know what we're doing every day from Monday to Sunday, every week. The program changes every week. But we always stick to it, all of us."

When he is not training, Kimetto continues to devote time to farming. Like his mentor, he has helped foster the careers of young local athletes. He has also led charitable efforts in his Kenyan community, using money earned from winnings and appearance fees to build churches and schools.

Kimetto lives in Eldoret with his wife, Caroline, and their son.

## SUGGESTED READING
Battaglia, Joe. "From Poverty to Podium." *Running Times*. Rodale, 24 Sept. 2014. Web. 2 Apr. 2015.
Edwards, Andy. "Marathon World Record-Holder Kimetto Warns Rivals to Expect a Decade of His Marathon Virtuosity." *IAAF*. International Association of Athletics Federations, 29 Sept. 2014. Web. 2 Apr. 2015.
Kimetto, Dennis. Interview by Christopher Kelsall. *Athletics Illustrated*. Athletics Illustrated, 23 Feb. 2015. Web. 2 Apr. 2015.
Smith, Motunde. "It Was the Poverty That Made Me Run." *Athletics Africa*. YSMedia, 21 Nov. 2014. Web. 2 Apr. 2015.

—Chris Cullen

# Phil Klay
**Born:** 1983
**Occupation:** Author

Phil Klay won the 2014 National Book Award for fiction for *Redeployment*, his debut collection of short stories told from soldiers' perspectives about the war in Iraq. A US Marine Corps veteran who served in Iraq's Anbar Province, Klay came to the material with a sense of urgency, wanting to relate the experiences of those who served in one of America's most controversial wars. Unlike some other veterans who become authors, Klay did not write as much about his own personal experiences as he did the experiences of people he knew while stationed there. *Redeployment* became a collection of first-person narratives when he realized there was not one story about Iraq but rather multiple stories that sometimes overlapped. All were true and all were relatable human experiences. When the collection was published in early 2014, Klay was lauded as an up-and-coming author by a number of critics. In an interview with a reporter for the *Financial Times* (21 Mar. 2014), Klay was asked what it meant to him to be a writer. He responded, "I hope it means getting readers to deeply, empathetically engage with experiences unlike theirs and thereby broaden their understanding of their fellow humans."

## EARLY LIFE AND EDUCATION
Phil Klay was born in 1983, in White Plains, New York. His mother, Marie-Therese F. Klay, is now the director of public sector develop-

J. Countess/Getty Images

posed to the war in Iraq, expressed considerable dismay that he would join the military. Despite this, he underwent his six months of training and prepared for the possibility of being shipped overseas. When asked why he felt he needed to enlist, Klay explained to Ruby Cutolo for *Publishers Weekly* (14 Mar. 2014): "I like the ethos of the military and the idea of joining an institution in which, at the very least, everyone who signs up believes in something."

## FROM US MARINE CORPS TO AN MFA

Upon his graduation from Dartmouth in 2005, Klay was commissioned a second lieutenant in the US Marine Corps. He served as a public affairs officer in Iraq's Anbar Province from January 2007 to February 2008. He ultimately attained the rank of captain before being honorably discharged from the Marines in 2009. Although he was in Iraq during a period of intense fighting, he readily admits that he was not directly a part of it; much of his time was spent interacting not only with the media, but also with engineers, medics, Iraqi police, and various marine units. He was also writing stories and taking photos. Klay was involved with communicating with service members' families in the states, and much of what he saw in Iraq stayed with him after he returned home. He recalled arriving in New York City and marveling at the fact that everything seemed so thoroughly normal, that nothing in anyone's demeanor seemed to indicate that the country was at war in the Middle East.

ment of a nonprofit health organization located in Boston, Massachusetts; his father, William D. Klay, also lives in Boston and is the retired senior credit officer of Citibank's office in London, England.

Growing up, Klay never anticipated becoming a writer, but he was always a passionate reader. In interviews he has noted that many of the works by authors he was exposed to in high school continue to influence him today. In an interview with the *Financial Times*, Klay recalled some of his early influences: "Certainly, my exposure in high school to writers like Flannery O'Connor, Shūsaku Endō, Fyodor Dostoevsky, and Graham Greene was formative."

Klay's family holds a longstanding belief in public service. His mother's father, Thomas R. Byrne, served as ambassador to Norway from 1973–76 and to Czechoslovakia from 1976–78; his father volunteered in the Peace Corps from 1971–73. An older brother served as a US Marine and a younger brother served in the US Army Reserve. It likely came as little surprise to the family then that Klay decided to go to Officer Candidate School (OCS) while studying English literature, creative writing, and history at Dartmouth College in New Hampshire. He understood that with the nation at war in Afghanistan and Iraq, the lives of millions all over the globe would be affected, and he felt he needed to make a contribution to the effort. Many of his professors, however, particularly those who were op-

The war and the experiences he had overseas remained with him after his discharge. He began writing about Iraq, first as part of his master of fine arts program at New York's Hunter College and then when he attended the Veterans Writing workshop at New York University (NYU), a program created by Ambassador Jean Kennedy Smith and NYU. "People have expectations about what your return means, and there are dominant modes for thinking about war experiences and what those experiences mean—and they're not sufficient," he remarked to Cutolo. "Writing is the best way that I know to think about something, because you put it down, and you put it under pressure, and you examine this idea that you have." Klay worked with Roy Scranton, Jake Siegel, and Matt Gallagher, who would all become published authors, which he found helped him to hone his writing considerably, as did working with civilian writers he met in his MFA program. Each group, in different ways, enabled him to come closer to the truth he wanted to convey and gave the stories an authenticity he believes would not have been possible without their insights.

Klay's fiction and nonfiction writing began to appear in prestigious publications, including the *New York Times*, *Newsweek*, the *Daily Beast*, and *Tin House*, among others. With the help of his editor Andrea Walker as well as his fellow writers, he began crafting a series of short stories, all first-person narratives related to his war experiences. The final stories he selected after four years of research and revision would form his debut collection, *Redeployment*. In an interview with NPR (6 Mar. 2014), Klay explained, "I decided very early on it was going to be all first-person narratives. . . . I wanted to have very different viewpoints, very different experiences, just so the reader could kind of think about what they were trying to say and how they clash with each other. There's not a single narrative about this war." And I didn't want to come and say, you know, this is how it was. This is what Iraq was."

### REDEPLOYMENT

*Redeployment* has twelve stories, each with its own narrator. While many of the stories describe the challenges veterans face when they return home, other stories are about the experiences of soldiers in active duty. In "Prayer in the Furnace," a chaplain tries to deal with soldiers overwhelmed by relentless violence. In "Money as a Weapons System," an officer in the Foreign Service who longs to do something meaningful as the leader of a reconstruction team, contends with waste, political infighting, and outright incompetence. "Ten Kliks South" centers on a nineteen-year-old artilleryman who has yet to kill anyone, while "Bodies" looks at the life of a Mortuary Affairs soldier who is charged with recovering the bodies of soldiers killed in action. Together, these stories and others provide an overarching view of the war and its repercussions.

Klay received outstanding reviews for *Redeployment*. A critic for *Kirkus Reviews* (1 Jan. 2014) called Klay's debut a "sharp set of stories . . . about US soldiers in the Iraq and Afghanistan wars and their aftermaths, with violence and gallows humor dealt out in equal measure. . . . A no-nonsense and informed reckoning with combat." In the *New York Times* (26 Feb. 2014), Michiko Kakutani proclaimed: "Gritty, unsparing, and fiercely observed, these stories leave us with a harrowing sense of the war in Iraq as it was experienced, day by day, by individual soldiers. . . . Mr. Klay has a radar-sharp ear for how soldiers talk—a potent mix of bravado, sarcastic humor, macho posturing, and military jargon—and he's adept, too, at delineating the deeper emotions that lie beneath the swagger."

In early 2014 Klay was named one of the National Book Foundation's "5 Under 35" honorees. Each year five writers under the age of thirty-five are chosen by previous National Book Award winners and finalists. Later that year he was named the winner in the National Book Award's fiction category. When interviewed by Rebecca Rubenstein for the National Book Foundation and asked how he felt about being a finalist for award, he replied, "Thrilled and overwhelmed. I worked on the book for four years, and just to have something that for years you'd only shared with friends out in the world is a strange enough feeling. I never imagined that [*Redeployment*] would get the reception it has."

### PERSONAL LIFE

In February 2014 Phil Klay married his longtime girlfriend, Jessica Alvarez, whom he met while they were both studying at Dartmouth. After graduating from Dartmouth, Alvarez went on to receive her law degree at New York University and has worked as a law clerk for Edgardo Ramos, a judge on the US District Court for the Southern District of New York. She then became an associate at a New York City law firm. Klay and Alvarez live in Brooklyn, New York. Klay has said that his next novel will not be about the Iraq war.

Unlike many writers who begin working directly on the computer, Klay prefers to write longhand first, and then he types up what he's written onto his computer and revises continually. He follows this by sending drafts to friends who help him revise. He tends not to write just at home: he also writes in public places throughout the city such as public libraries, museums, parks, and coffee shops.

### SUGGESTED READING

Cutolo, Ruby. "War Is Hell: Phil Klay." *Publishers Weekly*. PWxyz, 14 Mar. 2014. Web. 2 June 2015.

"Jessica Alvarez and Phil Klay." *New York Times*. New York Times, 9 Feb. 2014. Web. 4 June 2015.

Kakutani, Michiko. "The Madness of War Told in the First Person." *New York Times*. New York Times, 26 Feb. 2014. Web. 2 June 2015.

Klay, Phil. "Transcript: Reminder from a Marine: Civilians and Veterans Share Ownership of War." *NPR Books: Author Interviews.* NPR, 6 Mar. 2014. Web. 3 June 2015.

Labrise, Megan. "Phil Klay." *Kirkus Reviews*. Kirkus Media, 10 Mar. 2014. Web. 2 June 2015.

"'Redeployment' Author Phil Klay on the Music That Helps Him Write." *Financial Times*. Financial Times, 21 Mar. 2014. Web. 2 June 2015.

Turrentine, Jeff. "In Phil Klay's 'Redeployment,' Engrossing Short Stories about the Iraq War." *Washington Post*. Washington Post, 6 Mar. 2014. Web. 2 June 2015.

—Christopher Mari

Steindy/Wikimedia Commons

# Jürgen Klinsmann

**Born:** July 30, 1964

**Occupation:** Coach of the US men's national soccer team

When Jürgen Klinsmann was hired to replace Bob Bradley as head coach of the US men's national soccer team in 2011, he arrived amid much fanfare. Described by Bill Saporito for *Time* (12 June 2014) as "the US's first rock-star soccer coach," Klinsmann, a German native, first made his mark as a player before transitioning to coaching. A two-time German Footballer of the Year (1988, 1994), he enjoyed a highly decorated, seventeen-year professional club career as a striker that included stints with seven teams in Europe's top four soccer leagues. He was also a longtime member and former captain of the German national team, playing with the team in three World Cups (1990, 1994, and 1998) and other major international tournaments. He retired from playing professional soccer after the 1998 World Cup.

Klinsmann's first coaching job came in 2004 when he was named head coach of the German national team. He led the team for two years, during which he helped revamp the German soccer system. Two years after leading Germany to a surprising third-place finish at the 2006 World Cup, Klinsmann was hired to coach the country's most prominent club team, FC Bay-

ern München (also known as Bayern Munich), which he coached for one season.

As coach of the US men's national team (US-MNT), Klinsmann has implemented a coaching philosophy that combines European and American influences. Known for his unconventional methods and candid demeanor, he led the team to record-breaking seasons in 2012 and 2013 and helped to advance the team to the knockout stage at the 2014 World Cup. Since 2013 he has also served as technical director for the US Soccer Federation.

## EARLY LIFE AND EDUCATION

The second of the four sons of Siegfried and Martha Klinsmann, Jürgen Klinsmann was born on July 30, 1964, in Göppingen, West Germany. His father, who died in 2005, was a baker and gymnastics instructor, and although Klinsmann's father put him in a compulsory gymnastics program, he gravitated toward soccer early on and began honing his skills by kicking a ball around in the gym where his father taught.

Klinsmann first started playing organized soccer when he was eight and according to several accounts was overwhelmed with fear in his first organized games. Nevertheless, he soon dedicated himself to the sport, spending countless hours after school kicking a ball against his family's garage door. At nine, he showed a glimpse of his superstar potential when he scored sixteen goals in a single forty-minute game.

When Klinsmann was fourteen, his family moved to Stuttgart and he joined the youth soccer program sponsored by the Stuttgart Kickers, a professional club. Klinsmann's first professional contract was with the Kickers when he was sixteen. His father only allowed him to sign with the club after Klinsmann promised to earn a baking certificate as a backup profession.

Intending to fulfill his promise, Klinsmann apprenticed at his family's bakery before receiving his baking diploma in 1982. He has credited his father with teaching him the value and importance of hard work. "Our region . . . that's just in the DNA," he explained to Kevin Baxter for the *Los Angeles Times* (26 Apr. 2014). "For me it was just normal to be doing two things, three things. Going to school, working and training."

## THE GOLDEN BOMBER

Early into Klinsmann's three-year tenure with the Kickers, he worked with a sprinting coach to improve his strength and stamina. That work helped transform him into a fearless player with a knack for scoring: during the 1983–84 season, Klinsmann scored 19 goals in 35 matches.

In 1984 Klinsmann signed with VfB Stuttgart, a club that plays in the top tier of the German football league system. In five seasons with VfB Stuttgart, Klinsmann solidified his reputation, amassing 79 goals in 156 contests. He helped lead the club to the German Cup finals in 1987 and the Union of European Football Associations (UEFA) finals in 1989. Klinsmann's best season came in 1987–88, when he led the division with nineteen goals and was voted German Footballer of the Year.

Following the 1989 UEFA Cup, Klinsmann left Germany to play in other countries. "I needed to go and explore," he told Baxter. He signed a contract with Italy's top league, the Milan-based FC Internazionale Milano (commonly known as Inter) later that year. After amassing forty goals in three seasons, he relocated to Monaco to play for the club FS Monaco in France's first division, where he stayed for two seasons before moving on to the Tottenham Hotspur FC of the English Premier League in 1994.

During the 1994–95 season Klinsmann scored twenty-one goals in forty-one games and was named English Footballer of the Year. He won widespread popularity in England for his charismatic personality and earned the nickname "the Golden Bomber" for his blonde hair and scoring prowess.

Klinsmann returned to Germany in 1995 to play for FC Bayern Munich, where he remained for two seasons. During that time, he led the club in scoring, helped capture the 1996 UEFA Cup, and won the 1997 division title. Klinsmann split the 1997–98 season with Italy's UC Sampdoria and the Tottenham Hotspur. By the end of his seventeen-year club career, he had scored a total of 226 goals in 506 matches.

## GERMAN NATIONAL TEAM

While playing for various professional clubs, Klinsmann was also a member of the German national team, Deutscher Fussball-Bund (DFB; the "Mannschaft"), "the country's most revered institution," Mark Ziegler wrote for *U-T San Diego* (7 June 2006). He debuted with the team in 1987 and played with them at the 1988 Winter Olympics in Seoul, South Korea, where they captured the bronze medal. He became a pivotal member of three World Cup teams, leading West Germany to victory in 1990. He then led the German team in scoring with five goals at the 1994 World Cup, where they advanced to the quarterfinals; afterward, he was named German Footballer of the Year for the second time of his career. As captain at the 1998 World Cup, Klinsmann again helped his team reach the quarterfinals. With three goals in the tournament, he became the first player to score at least three goals in three consecutive World Cups. Klinsmann also competed for Germany at the 1992, 1996, and 1998 UEFA European championships, leading the team to victory in 1996. He finished his national team career with 47 goals in 108 appearances. He retired from playing both club and international soccer in 1998.

## COACHING

Klinsmann's future seemed destined for coaching when in the summer of 2004 the German soccer association hired him to coach the German national team. Despite having no prior coaching experience, Klinsmann brought a fresh approach to the then-struggling team, which had gone winless at the 2004 European championships. Shortly after being hired, he said, "We need to question every single ritual and habit," as quoted by Ziegler. "And we need to do it continuously, and not just in soccer."

Klinsmann's approach included integrating coaching philosophies he was exposed to as a player with ideas learned from working with the US national team and observing different US sports. One of the biggest changes Klinsmann implemented was switching Germany's playing style from defensive to offensive. Though marking a major break from tradition, the change proved beneficial with the team finishing third at the 2006 World Cup. Klinsmann was named German Coach of the Year.

Klinsmann left the German national team in 2006 to spend more time with his family. Nevertheless, he was lured back into coaching in 2008 when he agreed to coach his former team, Bayern Munich. Klinsmann's tenure with the team was brief and tumultuous, however, and he was fired after one season for clashing with team management over his aggressive, attacking style of play.

## US NATIONAL TEAM

In July 2011 Klinsmann was hired to replace Bob Bradley as coach of the US national team, becoming the first foreign-born US coach since 1995. After turning down offers from the United States Soccer Federation (USSF) in 2006 and 2010, Klinsmann agreed to a three-year deal worth $7.5 million. In an article for *Sports Illustrated* (11 June 2012), Sunil Gulati, the president of the USSF, told Grant Wahl, "Jürgen connects with people. . . . Selling people on the game without necessarily trying to sell in the typical sense."

As was the case with the German national team, Klinsmann was expected to breathe new life into the US team, which had for too long lagged behind the world's best soccer teams. Klinsmann immediately instituted a faster, offensive style of play for the team and instilled a European mentality by preaching urgency and accountability. He also introduced innovative training practices and a litany of regular blood and cardiorespiratory fitness tests to maximize on-field performance. "I want competition. I want people to push from behind, for everybody not to feel safe, because that drives them," he explained to Saporito.

Klinsmann's methods at first seemed to have little effect, with the team posting four losses, one win, and one draw in its first six matches. The team won their next five matches, however, among them a 1–0 victory against Italy. It was their first win against Italy, a four-time World Cup champion.

## RECORD-BREAKING SEASONS AND 2014 WORLD CUP

In 2012 Klinsmann guided the United States to a 9–2–3 record, its best to date, and they fared even better the following year with sixteen wins and a win at the 2013 Confederation of North, Central American, and Caribbean Association Football (CONCACAF) Gold Cup. The US national team then qualified for the 2014 World Cup, and in December 2013, Klinsmann was awarded a four-year contract extension and was named USSF's technical director.

In the run-up to the 2014 World Cup, Klinsmann was heavily criticized for saying that his team had no realistic chance of winning the tournament. He faced more criticism when he left Landon Donovan, the most accomplished US soccer player in history, off the team's roster. The team was eliminated by Belgium, 2–1 in the round-of-sixteen match, which saw US goalkeeper Tim Howard make a World Cup record sixteen saves.

In the first five games of the 2015 season, Klinsmann led the team to a 2–2–1 record. As the USSF technical director, he has set in motion ambitious long-term initiatives to overhaul the entire US soccer system in efforts to make it more competitive worldwide.

## PERSONAL LIFE

Klinsmann, who is fluent in German, Italian, French, and English, resides in Newport Beach, California, with his wife and two children.

## SUGGESTED READING

Baxter, Kevin. "U.S. Coach Jürgen Klinsmann Is Ready for World Cup to Begin." *LA Times*. Los Angeles Times, 26 Apr. 2014. Web. 27 Mar. 2015.

Saporito, Bill. "Stars, Stripes and Soccer." *Time*. Time, 12 June 2014. Web. 27 Apr. 2015.

Wahl, Grant. "Now Is the Time In Soccer When We Dance." *Sports Illustrated* 116.24 (2012): 52–56. Print.

Ziegler, Mark. "The Face of Germany." *U-T San Diego*. Union-Tribune, 7 June 2006. Web. 27 Mar. 2015.

—Chris Cullen

# Jørgen Vig Knudstorp

**Born:** November 21, 1968
**Occupation:** CEO of LEGO Group

When Jørgen Vig Knudstorp succeeded Kjeld Kirk Kristiansen as CEO and president of the LEGO Group in 2004, the Denmark-based global toy behemoth was on the precipice of collapse. Founded in 1932 by Kristiansen's grandfather, Ole Kirk Kristiansen, LEGO—a portmanteau of the Danish phrase "leg godt," meaning "play well"—had enjoyed decades of prosperity before faltering in the late 1990s and early 2000s due to unsuccessful brand extensions and an increasingly tech-based toy industry.

The first non-family member to head LEGO, Knudstorp, a former McKinsey & Company consultant, took charge of the company when it was losing nearly a million dollars per day. Undaunted, he immediately initiated a renewed focus on the company's core products and put in place other initiatives to ensure its long-term survival. Under Knudstorp's careful hand and guidance, LEGO went from being on the verge of bankruptcy to enjoying a nearly fourfold increase in revenue from 2004 to 2014. In 2014, LEGO became the world's largest toymaker after experiencing a dramatic increase in sales from products inspired by its hit film, *The LEGO Movie*, released that year. Addressing LEGO's future in the digital age, Knudstorp told Andrew Ward for the *Financial Times* (17 July 2011) that "kids are always going to want to run after a soccer ball and build things with LEGO bricks." He added, "LEGO is all about imagination and creative problem solving and those are crucial skills for children everywhere."

## EARLY LIFE AND EDUCATION

Jørgen Vig Knudstorp was born on November 21, 1968, in Fredericia, a town on the eastern part of the Jutland peninsula in central Denmark. He was raised in the Fredericia suburb of Snoghoj, located forty miles from LEGO's global headquarters in Billund. Knudstorp's father was an engineer, and his mother was a kindergarten teacher; he inherited his father's analytical skills and his mother's creative bent and interest in design.

Knudstorp, like countless other children, loved playing with LEGOs growing up. His early affinity for the colorful interlocking plastic

WIS Bernard/Paris March Archive

bricks was facilitated by his parents, who forbid him from playing with electronic toys. This household edict contributed to a "very good LEGO upbringing," as Knudstorp said to Ward. LEGOs equipped Knudstorp with creative thinking and problem-solving skills that would prove invaluable later in his business career.

After graduating from Fredericia Gymnasium in 1987, Knudstorp initially followed in his mother's footsteps and pursued a career in education. He spent eighteen months working as a kindergarten teacher before enrolling at Aarhus University, in Aarhus, Denmark, to study business. Knudstorp has credited his experience as a kindergarten teacher with giving him lasting lessons about leadership. "If you can be a leader with kindergarten children," he told Ward, "you can be a leader anywhere."

After earning a bachelor's degree in economics, Knudstorp pursued postgraduate studies. He received a master of science degree and a PhD in economics and management, also from Aarhus University, in 1995 and 1998, respectively. He also completed an executive MBA program at the prestigious Cranfield School of Management in the United Kingdom and did some course work at the Massachusetts Institute of Technology in the United States.

## MCKINSEY & COMPANY

Upon completing his PhD, Knudstorp was hired to work as a management consultant at the prestigious global consulting firm McKinsey & Company. He spent three years with the firm in Paris, France, where he learned the ins and outs of running a company. During this time Knudstorp also taught in the business and economics department at Aarhus University, winning the department's "Golden Pointer" award for best lecturer in 2001.

By 2001, Knudstorp was leading all of McKinsey & Company's recruitment activities in Europe. Still, he remained dubious about his long-term future in the consulting business, instead believing he would ultimately return to a career in academia. Those plans were put on indefinite hold, however, when Knudstorp was contacted by a recruiter about a job with the LEGO Group. Excited by the prospect of returning to his home country to work for one of its most iconic companies, Knudstorp successfully interviewed with LEGO, and in September 2001, he began his tenure at the company as director of strategic development. "The encounter with LEGO group became a crossroads for me, even though I didn't quite want to admit it to begin with," Knudstorp told Bjørg Tulinius for the Aarhus University website (25 Sept. 2014).

## CEO OF LEGO GROUP

At LEGO, Knudstorp quickly rose through the ranks. As director of strategic development, he traveled to LEGO entities all over the world, acquiring firsthand knowledge about all aspects of the company. He also met regularly with LEGO president and CEO Kjeld Kirk Kristiansen and other members of the company's executive management team. Knudstorp noted to Tulinius that he "got a 360 degree view of the whole company," enabling him to "develop a strategic perspective."

Knudstorp assumed a greater role in LEGO's day-to-day operations in April 2003, when he was promoted to acting chief financial officer (CFO). By then, he was already being groomed to replace Kristiansen, who had served as LEGO's top executive since 1979. Impressed with his genuine nature, analytical skills, and financial expertise, Kristiansen overlooked Knudstorp's relative inexperience in management and promoted him to the position of CEO and president in September 2004, making Knudstorp only the fourth CEO in the history of the LEGO Group and the first from outside the Kristiansen family.

At the time of Knudstorp's appointment, LEGO was in midst of the worst crisis in its history. Operating under the motto "Only the best is good enough," LEGO had developed a long-standing reputation for making exceptional, high-quality toys that fostered creativity and imaginative play in children. With the launch of its signature interlocking bricks in the 1950s, LEGO quickly became one of the most profitable and respected toy brands in the world; it was named the toy of the twentieth century by both Fortune magazine and the British Association of Toy Retailers at the turn of the millennium. Nevertheless, LEGO's profits began to falter in the 1990s, as the company struggled to find its place in a toy industry that was being rapidly transformed by technology. In efforts to modernize the brand, LEGO diversified its products to include children's clothing and accessories, video games, and theme parks. The strategy proved to be a failure, and in 1998, the company suffered the first financial loss in its history.

## BACK TO THE BRICK

LEGO's financial troubles came to a head in 2004, when the company posted over $300 million in losses for the previous year. "We had a dress rehearsal of the world financial crisis: a strong decline in sales and a massive increase in our indebtedness," Knudstorp said to James Delingpole for the *Daily Mail* (18 Dec. 2009). As the iconic toymaker's newly appointed leader, Knudstorp was immediately charged with turning around the company, which had become a prime takeover target. One of Knudstorp's first actions was to implement a strategy that emphasized going back to basics, focusing on the company's core LEGO brick products instead of money-sapping diversification efforts. He also overhauled LEGO's corporate culture, replacing its "nurturing the child" mission statement with one that was primarily geared toward bottom-line-oriented financial growth. Knudstorp introduced performance-based pay for managers and cut the development time for new products in half, from two years to twelve months. "We needed to build a mind-set where nonperformance wasn't accepted," he told Nelson D. Schwartz for the New York Times (5 Sept. 2009).

During the early stages of his turnaround efforts, Knudstorp ran LEGO "like a ruthless private equity firm," Andrew Ward noted. To restore profitability, he sold off all of LEGO's non-core products, including its four theme parks and videogames development division, and jettisoned more than a thousand employees. He also shifted some of LEGO's production from Billund to lower-cost facilities in Mexico and the Czech Republic and reduced the number of pieces, or "components" in LEGO-speak, used in LEGO products by nearly half, from 12,900 to 7,000.

Knudstorp's efforts paid immediate dividends. In 2005, LEGO posted a net profit of $87 million and revenues of $1.2 billion—a 12 percent increase from the previous year. The company would increase its profits considerably over the next nine years, with net income surging 35 percent to a record $993 million in 2012. That same year, LEGO overtook Hasbro to become the second-largest toymaker in the world.

Knudstorp helped generate continuous sales growth during this period by expanding into Asian markets for the first time and overseeing the development of numerous new product lines and concepts, many of which were conceived from fact-finding sessions with LEGO's legion of rabid fans. Among these were toy construction sets centered on the iconic superhero Batman, the mythical underwater city Atlantis, Italian luxury sports cars, structures designed by American architect Frank Lloyd Wright, and the *Indiana Jones*, *Pirates of the Caribbean*, and *Lord of the Rings* film franchises. A globally successful product line aimed specifically at girls, LEGO Friends, was launched in 2012.

## MOVING INTO THE FUTURE

Knudstorp's long-term vision for LEGO is geared toward maintaining a careful balance between tradition and innovation. While keeping LEGO firmly rooted in its iconic plastic bricks, Knudstorp has also led projects aimed at strengthening the company's place in the digital realm in order to keep it relevant in the age of computer games. One of those projects was *LEGO Universe*, a massively multiplayer online game that was globally distributed by Warner Bros. Interactive Entertainment and launched in October 2010. However, the project, which took three years to develop, was discontinued after only a year due to unsatisfactory revenue.

Another joint venture with Warner Bros. proved to be much more successful. In 2014, LEGO made its first foray into the feature-film business with the theatrical release of *The LEGO Movie*, a 3-D computer-animated adventure comedy directed and cowritten by Phil Lord and Christopher Miller. Distributed by Warner Bros. Pictures and featuring a star-studded cast of voice actors, the film was both a critical and a major commercial success,

earning nearly $470 million in global box-office receipts. Thanks to that performance and sales from associated merchandising, LEGO overtook Barbie maker Mattel as the world's biggest toymaker, after reporting an 11 percent rise in sales and a 14 percent rise in net profits in the first half of the 2014 fiscal year.

Riding on the coattails of the success of *The LEGO Movie*, Knudstorp and his management team announced that LEGO would be developing a television series in the reality competition format, intended to launch in 2015. A *LEGO Movie* sequel has also been announced and is expected to be released in 2017. While LEGO's rejuvenated focus on digital expansion has been met with resistance from some traditionalists, Knudstorp has maintained that the company continues to keep its core values and rigorous quality standards intact. He told Tulinius, "We're holding on to our values: that there should be an aha-experience in every product, and that LEGO is about teaching children that they can do things themselves."

As head of LEGO, Knudstorp oversees more than eleven thousand employees worldwide. By 2014, LEGO had produced enough components for every person on Earth to own ninety-four bricks. According to Knudstorp, LEGO has never had to recall a single brick.

## PERSONAL LIFE

Knudstorp serves on the boards of the LEGO Foundation and the IMD School of Management and is an adjunct professor at the Copenhagen Business School. He was selected to join the World Economic Forum's Young Global Leaders network in 2006 and was the recipient of Aarhus University's distinguished alumnus award in 2014. He and his wife, Vanessa, a medical doctor, have four children.

## SUGGESTED READING

Delingpole, James. "When Lego Lost Its Head—and How This Toy Story Got Its Happy Ending." *Daily Mail Online*. Associated Newspapers, 18 Dec. 2009. Web. 18 Nov. 2014.

Schwartz, Nelson D. "Turning to Tie-Ins, Lego Thinks beyond the Brick." *New York Times*. New York Times, 5 Sept. 2009. Web. 18 Nov. 2014.

Tulinius, Bjørg. "The Aarhus University Distinguished Alumnus 2014: Jørgen Vig Knudstorp." *Aarhus University*. Aarhus U, 25 Sept. 2014. Web. 18 Nov. 2014.

Ward, Andrew. "A Brick by Brick Brand Revival." *FT.com*. Financial Times, 17 July 2011. Web. 18 Nov. 2014.

—Chris Cullen

# Chanda Kochhar

**Born:** November 17, 1961

**Occupation:** Managing director and CEO of ICICI Bank

Chanda Kochhar is the first female CEO of India's ICICI Bank and one of only a handful of female CEOs of large financial institutions worldwide.

## EARLY LIFE AND EDUCATION

Chanda Deepak Kochhar was born Chanda Roopchand Advani on November 17, 1961, in Jodhpur, the second-largest city in the Indian state of Rajasthan. One of three children, she grew up in Jaipur, Rajasthan's capital. Her father, Roopchand Advani, was the principal of Malaviya Regional Engineering College (now Malaviya National Institute of Technology), and her mother worked as a clothing designer.

Unlike many traditional Indians, Kochhar's father was a strong advocate of female education and encouraged all of his children, male and female alike, to strive for a career. Kochhar attended the St. Angela Sophia School until the tenth grade. She was an avid sports player who enjoyed lawn tennis and basketball.

Kochhar's father died when she was thirteen, and her family moved to Mumbai three years later. Kochhar attended Jai Hind College, earning a bachelor's degree in 1982, and went on to study cost accountancy at the Institute of Cost and Works Accountants of India (ICWAI). She would later earn a master's degree in management studies from the University of Mumbai's Jamnalal Bajaj Institute of Management Studies.

## RESHAPING A BANK

After graduating from ICWAI in 1984, Kochhar began working at the Industrial Credit and Investment Corporation of India Ltd. (ICICI) as a management trainee in the projects department. Her job responsibilities included project appraisal and monitoring in the paper, cement, textile, and pharmaceuticals industries. She also had to make on-site visits to factories, as ICICI at that time was a development finance institution involved in corporate lending. At the time, finance was very much a male-dominated industry, and it was not unusual for Kochhar to meet people who doubted that a woman could inspect factory equipment.

K. V. Kamath, then CEO and managing director of ICICI, was the one who had hired Kochhar, and he also became her mentor. She rapidly assumed greater responsibilities and worked with every division of the organization. In 1993, when ICICI was preparing to enter the commercial banking field, Kochhar was part of the core group who set up the bank, devised its retail and corporate strategy, and then implemented that strategy. ICICI became ICICI Bank the following year, and Kochhar was promoted to assistant general manager of corporate banking. In 1996, in addition to becoming the deputy general manager, she was charged with setting up and leading the infrastructure industry group.

In 1998, Kochhar was appointed general manager of ICICI's major client group, newly formed to handle the bank's top two hundred clients. As general manager, she was responsible for marketing products from across the bank's holdings, which required building cross-divisional teams and cross-selling to some of India's largest companies. She was assigned responsibility for the strategy and e-commerce divisions of ICICI in 1999, while still managing the major client group.

In 2000, when ICICI Bank decided to enter the retail business, Kochhar was tapped to set it up. She has said in interviews that this was a turning point in her career. Under her leadership, ICICI became India's largest retail financer within five years. Kochhar rapidly took on even greater responsibilities, becoming the executive director of the retail banking business on April 1, 2001. In April 2006, she was named the deputy managing director, overseeing both the corporate and retail banking businesses. In October of the same year, she also became the head of the international business. She was named joint managing director and chief financial officer one year later, in October 2007, on the eve of a global financial crisis.

Kochhar became the chief executive officer and managing director of ICICI Bank in May 2009, following Kamath's retirement from the position. One of her first actions as CEO and managing director was to create a five-year strategy that shifted the bank's goals from growth to consolidation. Kochhar led ICICI through the financial crisis, with the bank emerging relatively unscathed and with stronger assets and market capitalization. By early 2014, ICICI Bank had assets of more than $98 billion, making it India's largest private-sector bank and the second-largest bank in the country.

From November 11, 2008, to June 24, 2009, Kochhar served as independent director of the government-owned Oil and Natural Gas Corporation Limited, India's largest petroleum exploration and production company. She has also served on several committees and councils, including the US–India CEO Forum, the UK–India CEO Forum, and the Prime Minister's Council on Trade and Industry.

Kochhar has received numerous awards and recognitions. She has been ranked on *Fortune*'s list of the most powerful women in business since 2005 and *Forbes*'s list of the one hundred most powerful women in the world since 2009. She has helped ICICI garner multiple awards for excellence in retail banking. In 2010, the Asian Business Leadership Forum awarded her its Woman of Power Award, and in 2011, the government of India awarded her the Padma Bhushan, a recognition granted to people who have made great contributions to the country. In 2011, she was given the Global Leadership Award by the US–India Business Council.

### IMPACT

In her decades-long career at ICICI, Kochhar has helped transform a relatively small financial intuition into the largest retail financer in India. Under her direction, ICICI Bank became the country's largest private bank and the second-largest bank overall.

### PERSONAL LIFE

Kochhar is married to wind-energy entrepreneur Deepak Kochhar, whom she met in business school. They have a daughter, Aarti, and a son, Arjun, and reside in Mumbai.

### SUGGESTED READING

"Chanda D. Kochhar: Money Monitor." *India Today.* Living Media India, 12 Mar. 2010. Web. 16 July 2014.

Leahy, Joe. "Profile: Chanda Kochhar." *Financial Times.* Financial Times, 30 Jan. 2009. Web. 16 July 2014.

Punj, Shweta. "Turnaround Tsarina: Chanda Kochhar." *Business Today.* Living Media India, 18 Sept. 2011. Web. 16 July 2014.

Sharma, Saurabh. "Chanda Kochhar Visits MNIT after 4 Decades." *Times of India.* Bennett, 22 Oct. 2012. Web. 16 July 2014.

Singh, Yoshita. "SBI's Bhattacharya, ICICI's Kochhar among Forbes' Most Powerful Women." *Business Today.* Living Media India, 28 May 2104. Web. 16 July 2014.

—Barb Lightner

# Sarah Koenig

**Born:** July 1969

**Occupation:** Journalist, host of *Serial* podcast

Sarah Koenig is "the world's first superstar podcaster," Stephen Colbert declared about the award winning journalist when she appeared as a guest on his now-defunct Comedy Central show, *The Colbert Report*, in December 2014. Koenig is the cocreator, executive producer, and host of the podcast *Serial*, a twelve-episode, nearly nine-hour-long series that revisited the real-life case of Adnan Syed, a Pakistani American who was convicted of the 1999 murder of his former girlfriend, high school student Hae Min Lee. Debuting in October 2014, *Serial* won instant critical acclaim and quickly became a global phenomenon; it has been downloaded more than 76 million times since its debut, making it the most popular podcast in history. Propelled by Koenig's "deep, nuanced, shoe-leather reporting" and her "strikingly casual, immersive and transparent" storytelling style, as Ernest Londoño called it in the *New York Times* (12 Feb. 2015), *Serial* has been credited with helping to redefine podcasting and long-form journalism in the digital age. In addition to hosting *Serial*, Koenig, who began her career as a newspaper reporter, has served as a producer on the popular radio program *This American Life* since 2004.

### EARLY LIFE AND EDUCATION

Sarah Koenig was born in July 1969 and grew up on Long Island, New York. Along with her older sister, Antonia, Koenig comes from a family of distinguished writers. Her father, Julian Koenig, was a legendary advertising executive and writer. He was responsible for creating some of the most original and innovative campaigns in advertising history, including the Think Small and Lemon ads for the Volkswagen Beetle and Timex's "It takes a licking and keeps on ticking"

Mike Coppola/Getty Images for Peabody Awards

slogan. He was also credited with coining the name Earth Day for the national environmental holiday.

When Koenig was a child, her parents divorced. In 1980 her mother, the former Maria Eckhart, who was born in Tanzania and grew up in England, married Peter Matthiessen, a renowned author, naturalist, and onetime Central Intelligence Agency agent. One of the founders of the prestigious literary magazine the *Paris Review*, Matthiessen was the only writer ever to win the National Book Award for both nonfiction (*The Snow Leopard*, 1978) and fiction (*Shadow Country*, 2008).

Matthiessen's circle of friends included some of the most famous and influential writers of the twentieth century, including James Jones, George Plimpton, William Styron, and Kurt Vonnegut, among others. Growing up around such esteemed literary and intellectual minds, Koenig learned at an early age "that conversation was so highly prized as a thing to do and to engage in in a real way," as she told Jennifer Landes for the *East Hampton (New York) Star* (24 Dec. 2014). "I didn't understand how great that was and how rare it was in some ways."

After graduating from Concord Academy, a coed, independent boarding and day school in Concord, Massachusetts, Koenig attended the University of Chicago. She earned a bachelor's degree in political science in 1990. Afterward, she moved to New York to pursue a career as an actor.

## JOURNALISM CAREER

Koenig spent several years acting in New York theater productions and taking on a variety of odd jobs to make ends meet. In 1993, after coming to the realization that she needed "a proper job," as she put it to Marina Fang for the University of Chicago's *Chicago Maroon* (2 Mar. 2015), she applied for a reporting job at the *East Hampton Star*, her hometown newspaper. Despite never having written for a school newspaper, Koenig told Fang that she had always been enamored with the "romanticized" notion of being a reporter.

Koenig worked at the *East Hampton Star* for about a year and a half, during which she covered local news and "learned a ton, all the basics," as she noted to Landes. She then moved to Moscow, Russia, to work as a reporter for ABC News. Koenig, who also studied Russian history and literature in college, worked for the station only briefly before moving on to work for the Moscow bureau of the *New York Times*.

After about a year and a half at the *Times*, Koenig returned to the United States and started working as a reporter for the *Concord Monitor* in New Hampshire. At the *Monitor*, she primarily covered national, state, and local elections, most notably George W. Bush's 2000 presidential campaign. Following her stint at the *Monitor*, Koenig went to work for the *Baltimore Sun*. One of her first reporting jobs at the *Sun* included covering the disbarment of the late criminal defense attorney M. Cristina Gutierrez, who represented Syed at his first trial.

## *THIS AMERICAN LIFE* AND THE MOVE TO RADIO

It was while working at the *Monitor* and *Sun* that Koenig started writing freelance stories for *This American Life* (*TAL*), a weekly hour-long radio program hosted and produced by Ira Glass. Impressed by her stories, after receiving her application Glass offered her a job as a producer on the show, which specializes in narrative nonfiction pieces. Koenig accepted Glass's offer and joined *TAL* as a producer in January 2004. Commenting on her move to radio, she explained to Fang, "I loved working at newspapers, but my heart was never really in the stories I was doing. . . . So I think it was more that I just wanted to do a different kind of work."

Since joining *TAL*, Koenig has produced a wide variety of stories. In 2006 she won a Peabody Award for coproducing an episode titled "Habeas Schmabeas," which examined inmates at the United States' notorious Guantanamo Bay prison in Cuba. Another acclaimed episode, "Switched at Birth," which Koenig produced in 2008, told the story of two girls who were accidentally switched at birth at a hospital in Wisconsin in 1951. Koenig, a resident of State College, Pennsylvania, documented Penn State University's party school reputation in 2009 and covered the school's reaction to the Jerry Sandusky child-abuse scandal in 2011. She also covered stories close to home, looking at the life and legacy of her distinguished father in "Origin Story" and sharing her mother's rules of conversation in "The Seven Things You're Not Supposed to Talk About," episodes that aired in 2009 and 2013, respectively.

It was in 2013 that Koenig and fellow *TAL* producer Julie Snyder began brainstorming ideas for a *TAL* spin-off series. In contrast to *TAL*, which features several stories over the course of its hour-long run time, Koenig and Snyder hoped to create a podcast that would follow a single story over multiple episodes. "I like getting lost in the world of a story for a really long time," Koenig told Fang. "I like that kind of reporting . . . and that's what I was hoping we could recreate with the podcast, just kind of create that world for people."

## SERIAL

Koenig floated around possible story ideas for months until Rabia Chaudry, a friend of Syed's family, approached her about the possibility of reexamining Syed's murder case. Intrigued, she spent more than the next year investigating the case, interviewing various people who were involved and pouring over hundreds of pages of court documents. Along with Snyder, Koenig then roughly plotted out twelve episodes for the podcast, which they called *Serial* in a nod to British novelist Charles Dickens, the undisputed master of the serialized novel. "Structuring the arc of the season before you know how the story ends [was] very challenging," she admitted to Mellissa Locker for *Time* (30 Oct. 2014).

Though Koenig had to face the loss of both her father and stepfather in 2014, she also got the chance to witness the fruit of her labor late that year when the first season of *Serial* premiered in October and ran until December. It reconsidered the case of Syed, who, at age nineteen in 2000, was convicted of murdering his former girlfriend, Lee, a seventeen-year-old high school senior at Baltimore County's Woodlawn High School. Lee, a South Korean–born immigrant, was found strangled to death in a seedy Baltimore park in early February 1999, several weeks after she and Syed broke up. Syed, an honors student at Woodlawn with no prior criminal record, was found guilty of first-degree murder, robbery, kidnapping, and false imprisonment. He was sentenced to life in prison, despite there being no physical evidence linking him to the crime and no eyewitnesses to the actual murder. From the beginning, he has maintained his innocence.

Each of *Serial*'s twelve episodes, which were released weekly on Thursdays and varied from thirty minutes to an hour in length, explored different aspects of the Syed case, which was riddled with numerous holes, inconsistencies, and unanswered questions. Two weeks before *Serial*'s debut, Glass, who served as an editorial adviser for the podcast, explained to Julia Lurie for *Mother Jones* (19 Sept. 2014) that they wanted to give listeners "the same experience you get from a great HBO or Netflix series, where you get caught up with the characters and the thing unfolds week after week, but with a true story, and no pictures."

## GLOBAL PHENOMENON

*Serial* became an immediate sensation upon its debut. It was the number-one podcast on iTunes two weeks before it premiered and went on to hold the top spot on the iTunes rankings for over three months; it became the fastest podcast to reach five million downloads and streams in iTunes history. Critics also widely lauded the series. Locker called *Serial* "a compelling, if not addictive, series." Meanwhile, in a review for the London *Telegraph* (14 Nov. 2014), Darren Richman likened the podcast to David Simon's groundbreaking and similarly novelistic HBO crime-drama series *The Wire*. Richman further asserted that "Listening to the show is like watching one of cinema's great documentaries but knowing there'll be another instalment in a week's time."

In addition to winning the enthusiastic support of critics, *Serial* won legions of fans and celebrity followers. Its popularity was such that it spawned several companion podcasts, its own discussion forum on the news and entertainment website Reddit, and numerous parodies. Much of its success and popularity was attributed to Koenig, whose intimate, conversational storytelling style gave listeners a window into "her frustrations, doubts and random thoughts about the case," Londoño wrote. He added, "Listening to her is like hearing a riveting story from a close friend over drinks."

At the same time, *Serial* was criticized by some media observers for its treatment of race, for withholding information for narrative effect, for being biased in favor of Syed, and for having an ambiguous ending. Koenig, however, has insisted that all of her reporting was strictly objective and that whatever information was withheld was done so for ethical reasons. She added that there was never any intention to neatly wrap up an ongoing case, which took a new turn in February 2015, when Syed was granted an appeal hearing by the Maryland Court of Special Appeals. In an interview with Taffy Brodesser-Akner for *New York Times Magazine* (26 Nov. 2014), Koenig asserted, "I don't feel a responsibility to make [*Serial*] the kind of entertainment that you would get on some TV drama. . . . That's not what I do. I'm a reporter."

In April 2015 *Serial* became the first-ever podcast to be honored with a Peabody Award. As of mid-2015, it had been downloaded over 76 million times, making it the most successful podcast in history to date. A second season of *Serial*, which will focus on a different case, is expected to begin airing in the fall of 2015.

**PERSONAL LIFE**

Koenig lives in State College, Pennsylvania, with her husband, Ben Schreier, who teaches English and Jewish studies at Penn State. The couple has two children, Ava and Reuben. In addition to appearing on *The Colbert Report*, Koenig has been featured in a number of prominent publications, including the *New York Times*, the *Guardian*, the *Wall Street Journal*, and *Time*, the latter of which named her one of the world's most influential people in 2015.

**SUGGESTED READING**

Gamerman, Ellen. "*Serial* Podcast Catches Fire." *Wall Street Journal*. Dow Jones, 13 Nov. 2014. Web. 10 July 2015.

Koenig, Sarah. "Sarah Koenig Can't Promise a Perfect Ending to *Serial*." Interview by Taffy Brodesser-Akner. *New York Times Magazine*. New York Times, 26 Nov. 2014. Web. 10 July 2015.

Koenig, Sarah. "*This American Life* Channels *True Detective* in a New Podcast." Interview by Julia Lurie. *Mother Jones*. Mother Jones

and the Foundation for Natl. Progress, 19 Sept. 2014. Web. 10 July 2015.

Koenig, Sarah. "Uncommon Interview: *Serial*'s Sarah Koenig (A.B. '90)." Interview by Marina Fang. *Chicago Maroon*. Chicago Maroon, 2 Mar. 2015. Web. 10 July 2015.

Landes, Jennifer. "Sarah Koenig Catches Lightning with Her *Serial* Podcast." *East Hampton Star* [NY]. East Hampton Star, 24 Dec. 2014. Web. 10 July 2015.

Locker, Melissa. "*Serial*: Sarah Koenig on the Addictive New Podcast from *This American Life*." *Time*. Time, 30 Oct. 2014. Web. 10 July 2015.

Londoño, Ernest. "Hooked on the Freewheeling Podcast *Serial*." *New York Times*. New York Times, 12 Feb. 2015. Web. 10 July 2015.

—Chris Cullen

# Susan Gregg Koger

**Born:** ca. 1985

**Occupation:** Cofounder and chief creative officer of ModCloth

Susan Gregg Koger is the creative force behind ModCloth, a clothing company that has become, according to Dhani Mau for the widely read website Fashionista (5 Aug. 2013), "practically synonymous with that sort of twee, retro, 'indie' look we all know—a look that's beloved by lots of ladies, who all now have a go-to place to get it affordably." In an article for the *New York Times* (11 Sept. 2013), Marisa Meltzer praised Gregg Koger's "perpetually girlish, improvisational aesthetic" and wrote, "Playfulness has become a ModCloth hallmark. . . . Bold, whimsical prints, like bicycles, town houses, sailboats, elephants and gingham, are popular—all a world away from the sleek silhouettes and elaborate makeup of Fashion Week."

In 2010 ModCloth was named America's Fastest Growing Retailer by *Inc.* magazine and one of the fifty most innovative firms in the world by the editors of *Fast Company*. In 2013 it recorded more than $100 million in revenue and has attracted a solid stream of venture capital. Those facts are all the more remarkable considering that Gregg Koger started the company while still in high school and turned her attention to it on a full-time basis right after graduating from college. In subsequent years she frequently landed on thirty-under-thirty lists of such publications as *Forbes* and *Refinery29*. "Never apologize for your age," she told a reporter in 2013 for the lifestyle site *Design Sponge*, describing the best piece of advice she ever received. "Age doesn't mean you know everything. Be aware of what you don't know and be curious, but don't look at your age or lack of experience as a negative; it can allow you to approach an industry from a different point of view."

## EARLY YEARS AND EDUCATION

Susan Gregg Koger was born Susan Gregg around 1985 and raised in a South Florida suburb. (Some sources list Davie, in Broward County, as her hometown.) She has one half sister almost two decades her senior; she was thus essentially raised as an only child in what she has characterized as a peaceful and organized household. She enjoyed reading and other solitary pursuits. She also relished playing dress-up. Her grandmother had once worked in a department store, and she maintained a closet filled with vintage treasures, including a 1960s-era leopard-print coat, which Gregg Koger donned during a basement fashion show she mounted with her cousins.

As a teen Gregg Koger earned pocket money as a clerk at a gift shop in the local mall, and when not working or studying, she haunted the local thrift shops—an activity her mother and grandmother also enjoyed. That hobby became vital to her when she was accepted into Carnegie Mellon University, in Pittsburgh, Pennsylvania, in 2002. "In South Florida, I didn't have a coat growing up, I didn't really have sweaters. I think I saw snow once before I moved to Pittsburgh, and when I started looking for winter wear I realized that there was just so much great stuff in South Florida because all the retirees come down and they unload," she recalled to Mau. "I started finding this great stuff and I couldn't pass it up." Among her favorite early finds was an orange wool coat from the 1960s, appropriate for Pennsylvania's chilly weather. Unable to say no to appealing garments—even those that did not fit her properly—Gregg Koger soon found her closet overflowing.

During the summer before college, Gregg Koger's high school sweetheart, a young tech whiz named Eric Koger, suggested that she make a website on which to sell some of her excess clothing and helped her get started. "I thought it sounded like a really fun project, and I just totally got bitten by the entrepreneurial bug," she told Mau. "It was just such a fun process to source the products and then to create a story around [the pieces] and photograph them and merchandise them and describe them." She has told journalists that one moment in early 2003, when she discovered that her first garment—a vintage bowling shirt—had sold, marked her birth as an entrepreneur.

## MODCLOTH'S ROCKY START

Gregg Koger and Koger ran their fledgling business out of her dorm room at Carnegie Mellon, where he had also enrolled. In their junior year they rented a house in the neighborhood of Squirrel Hill in which to live and work, and during school breaks, they returned to the thrift shops of Florida to replenish their inventory. Eventually they discovered that they could not meet the demands of their growing customer base with only one-of-a-kind vintage pieces, so they took time off from school to attend a major fashion trade show in Las Vegas, where they found a handful of independent designers creating quirky retro items.

In 2005, too young to compete in their own school's entrepreneurs' contest, they instead entered Colorado State University's Venture Adventure, where they failed to impress the judges despite the steadily increasing popularity of their website. They performed poorly, as well, during an elevator-pitch event sponsored by the MIT Enterprise Forum, where they were advised that their written business plan was not up to par. Still, the competitions introduced them to a wide entrepreneurial network, through which they ultimately met helpful publicists and investors.

Gregg Koger, who majored in business and German, graduated with a bachelor's degree in 2006 and began devoting herself to ModCloth, as she and Koger had named the business, on a full-time basis. By then the site was attracting some 70,000 unique shoppers a day and earning a reported $90,000 in annual revenue. When the couple married shortly after graduation, the bride began using the name Susan Gregg Koger.

Gregg Koger focused on expanding ModCloth further. Doing so required her to take personal loans and use her credit cards. "I asked myself, 'What's the worst that could happen?' I'd go bankrupt, which would remain on my credit report for 10 years," she recalled to Karen Schwartz for *Marie Claire* (21 Feb. 2014). "I was in my early 20s, so it didn't seem so bad. Once I thought it through, it still seemed like a risk worth taking."

## A COMMUNAL CLOTHING COMPANY

Early on Gregg Koger discovered a way to circumvent one major roadblock: manufacturers who insisted that the company commit to buying hundreds of units of one garment. Unsure of whether a particular item would sell in that large a quantity, she went directly to her customers to ask them. "Almost immediately, responses came in. Not only was it an incredibly effective way to gauge order numbers, it was also a powerful tool for engagement," Gregg Koger told Schwartz.

One of ModCloth's hallmarks as a company has been that ability to engage with and connect to its customers on a deeper level. "[People were always] interested in being able to come to Mod-Cloth to interact with the community and feel like they're part of something that's bigger than just a fashion retailer, so we've been extremely social and extremely community-centric from the beginning," Gregg Koger explained to Mau. The company still runs a Be the Buyer survey that asks whether or not a particular item should be made available for sale, and other popular interactive features have included a Make the Cut contest, in which users vote for which up-and-coming designers ModCloth will sign; a style gallery where shoppers can post pictures of themselves in their new outfits; a blog written by Gregg Koger; and a virtual tour of the founder's closet. "Other fashion brands ignore that your customer isn't just into fashion," Gregg Koger said to Meltzer. "We've always wanted her to come to the site even if she doesn't have a dollar to spend." She continued, "A lot of our growth as a social company is that I've been part of the demographic and psychographic of the company. . . . We're constantly throwing stuff against the wall. You can have a gut feeling, test it out, see how well it does, and go from there." In July 2015 ModCloth boasted well over 2.2 million followers on Pinterest, 1.2 million likes on Facebook, 136,000 Twitter followers, and 379,000 followers on Instagram.

Much customer loyalty has been engendered by Gregg Koger's commitment to carrying a wide range of sizes, her pledge not to employ Photoshop as the vast majority of other fashion companies do, and her use of an exceptionally diverse group of models, including a transgender person. "I'm not saying the 'traditional' model body type isn't beautiful—it absolutely is—but so are the myriad of other body types that exist," she told Kylie McConville for the web publication *Elite Daily* (30 Apr. 2015). In 2015 Mod-Cloth's fastest-growing segment was the plus-size category, which the company has plans to expand.

## GROWING PAINS AND INTROSPECTION

After rapid expansion in the late 2000s through 2013, ModCloth experienced slow growth and two rounds of layoffs in 2014, bringing the total number of employees down to about 300 from 450. Eric Koger, who had earned an MBA at Carnegie Mellon, stepped down as CEO of ModCloth in early 2015. He was replaced by Matthew A. Kaness, former chief strategy officer for Urban Outfitters whom the couple had known and admired for years.

In a February 2015 article by Hilary Burns for *Bizwomen*, Gregg Kroger described 2014 as a year of introspection as she and others pondered the best course for the company to take. "First and foremost, we are an incredible lifestyle brand, and that's where we're going to focus our energy and efforts." Still, Gregg Koger remains optimistic about the company's future, especially given the inspiring feedback she has received from customers so far and new initiatives to come. "You're going to see exciting stuff in 2015," she said.

## PERSONAL LIFE

After they wed, Susan Gregg Koger and Eric Koger bought a home in the Pittsburgh neighborhood of Friendship. By 2015 the couple was living in San Francisco. Gregg Koger travels frequently for work and splits her time between ModCloth's offices in San Francisco, Los Angeles, and Pittsburgh.

## SUGGESTED READING

Gregg Koger, Susan. "Biz Ladies Profile: Susan Gregg Koger of ModCloth." *Design\*Sponge*. Design\*Sponge, Apr. 2013. Web. 10 July 2015.

Mau, Dhani. "How Susan Koger Built Mod-Cloth's $100 Million Empire from Her College Dorm." *Fashionista*. Breaking Media, 5 Aug. 2013. Web. 1 June 2015.

McConville, Kylie. "I Want Your Job: Susan Koger, Cofounder and CCO Of ModCloth." *Elite Daily*. Elite Daily, 30 Apr. 2015. Web. 1 June 2015.

Meltzer, Marisa. "ModCloth Is Selling an Era They Missed Out On." *New York Times*. New York Times, 11 Sept. 2013. Web. 1 June 2015.

Reeger, Jennifer. "Company Blends Old-School Style, New-School Sales." *Pittsburgh Tribune-Review*. Trib Total Media, 27 Feb. 2011. Web. 1 June 2015.

Schwartz, Karen. "ModCloth Cofounder Susan Gregg Koger on Taking Risks: 'What's the Worst That Could Happen?'" *Marie Claire*. Hearst Communications, 21 Feb. 2014. Web. 1 June 2015.

—Mari Rich

# Elizabeth Kolbert

**Born:** July 6, 1961
**Occupation:** Journalist and author

*New Yorker* staff writer Elizabeth Kolbert is an acclaimed and respected science writer, exploring deeply the role of humankind in creating climate change and its dire consequences already taking place—as well as the bigger ones to come, including the possible extinction of up to 50 percent of the Earth's species by the end of the twenty-first century, more extreme climates (dryer droughts, wetter and more disastrous storms), and perhaps just as unnervingly, unpredictable changes. Aside from her articles in the *New Yorker*, Kolbert has published two well-received books on the topic, *Field Notes from a Catastrophe: Man, Nature, and Climate Change* (2006) and *The Sixth Extinction* (2014). For the latter she received a great deal of critical praise: the book was selected as one of the *New York Times Book Review*'s 10 Best Books of 2014 and won the 2015 Pulitzer Prize for general nonfiction.

## EARLY LIFE AND EDUCATION

Elizabeth Kolbert was born July 6, 1961, in New York, New York. Her father, Gerald, was an ophthalmologist, and her mother, Marlene, went on to become the president of the Mamaroneck (New York State) Board of Education. Kolbert spent her early years in the New York City borough of the Bronx, after which she and her family moved to Larchmont, New York, a village in the town of Mamaroneck, in Westchester County, about twenty miles northeast of Manhattan. Kolbert grew up in Larchmont and attended Mamaroneck High School, where she was the editor of the school newspaper, the *Globe*.

Upon graduating high school, in 1979, she attended Yale University, in New Haven, Connect-

SLOWKING/ GFDL v1.2 https://www.gnu.org/licenses/old-licenses/fdl-1.2.html

icut, where she studied literature. After receiving her bachelor's degree in 1983, Kolbert studied at the University of Hamburg, in Germany, on a Fulbright scholarship. At this point she began working for the *New York Times*, as a stringer, on occasion writing stories about travel and Germany's nuclear weapons.

After about a year, Kolbert returned to the United States where she worked for the *New York Times* business section as a "copygirl," after which she joined the paper's metro desk, which covers the New York metropolitan region. In 1988 she became the *New York Times* Albany bureau chief, reporting on politics in the state capital. Four years later Kolbert was promoted to the paper's national desk, for which she covered the 1992 and 1996 presidential elections. She became the *New York Times* "Metro Matters" columnist in 1997 before leaving the paper in 1999 to join the *New Yorker* magazine as a staff writer.

## WRITING FOR THE *NEW YORKER*

Although at the *New Yorker* Kolbert had to write different kinds of articles than she had at the *New York Times*, her initial assignments were reminiscent of her national political beat at the paper. She covered New York City politicians and others who had national appeal or significance. For example, she wrote about Hillary Clinton's run for a Senate seat, and the hostility and issues she had to deal with, and later she profiled Clinton as a working senator. Kolbert profiled New York City mayor Rudolph Giuliani in the aftermath of the September 11, 2001, terrorist attacks. She also wrote about Fire Chief William Feehan, Democratic congressman Charles Rangel, and New York State governors George Pataki and Michael Bloomberg. She also profiled personalities not directly affiliated with politics, such as the Reverend Al Sharpton, television talk-show host Regis Philbin, and former *New York Times* executive editor Howell Raines. These profiles were collected in a book published in 2004 titled *The Prophet of Love: And Other Tales of Power and Deceit.*

The attention the book received in the press was generally positive. A review in *Publishers Weekly* (14 May 2004) called it a "collection of graceful and perceptive articles." The reviewer observed that Kolbert's best political articles—in the first part of the book, titled "Politics"—were on the post–September 11 atmosphere of New York City, particularly the profiles of Mayor Giuliani and Fire Chief Feehan. As for the second part of the book, titled "Impolitics," Kolbert, wrote the reviewer, "trains her considerable intelligence and wit" on various New York personalities.

Kolbert had first become interested in issues concerning the environment and the climate in 1989, when she was in her late twenties, after she read Bill McKibben's book *The End of Nature* (1989), which became a classic, groundbreaking work about climate change. After about two years at the *New Yorker*, Kolbert found herself in Greenland on assignment. She spent about a year there doing research on a process known as ice coring, which allows scientists to get chronological data on changes in climate over long periods of time. In an interview with Yale University's online magazine *Environment 360* (11 Mar. 2009), Kolbert described that experience as "very, very eye-opening." Although she had a great interest in global warming and was familiar with some of the science, she did not have a deep enough understanding of the facts or enough direct experience with the effects of climate change, and she was concerned that this significant topic was barely talked about.

From her experience in Greenland came a three-part series of articles titled "The Climate of Man." The first article in the series was published in the April 25, 2005, issue of the *New Yorker.* The subtitle was "Disappearing islands, thawing permafrost, melting polar ice. How the earth is changing." The science is in, wrote Kolbert, and the impact of global warming is undeniable. The following year, she published her first book on the topic.

## FIELD NOTES FROM A CATASTROPHE

For her book *Field Notes from a Catastrophe*, Kolbert traveled all over the world, namely areas significantly impacted by climate change: for example, the island of Shishmaref, Alaska, where some people were leaving their homes because there was not enough ice around to protect them against storms; Canada's Northwest Territories, where some indigenous hunters were battling warmer weather and changing wildlife patterns; and the Netherlands, where floods and rising sea levels are a major concern. In the Netherlands, Kolbert met with companies working on creating homes and roads that can handle flooding. The effect of climate change is worldwide, wrote Kolbert, from England to Oregon and South Africa, not just Iceland and Greenland. Aside from her "field trips," Kolbert went to laboratories and observatories, talked to many climate scientists, and even met with those who, in her opinion, are "standing in the way" of any substantive change or progress on the issue; the latter was a reference specifically to then-president George W. Bush.

*Field Notes from a Catastrophe* received many excellent reviews. Anushka Asthana, for the *Guardian* (12 Aug. 2007) observed, "Kolbert presents the arguments in an utterly compelling and convincing manner." Mariana Gosnell, for the *New York Times* (16 Mar. 2006), wrote, "In language that is clear, if somewhat dry, she examines the major pieces of the story, shedding light on some insider concepts of climatologists." Kolbert won the 2006 Lannan Literary Fellowship for nonfiction for the book.

Three years after the publication of the book, in an interview with Yale University's *Environment 360* website, Kolbert was asked why she thinks the American public not only does not know much about the nature of climate change but also considers it a low priority. Kolbert pointed out that climate change has been described as a "slow-moving catastrophe," which means that when one finally feels the grave effects of such a catastrophe in one's "own life, then it's way too late." That is why, said Kolbert, it is also a difficult problem for the "political system to deal with."

## THE SIXTH EXTINCTION

In her third book, *The Sixth Extinction: An Unnatural History* (2014), Kolbert continued to dig into the science and themes she discussed in her previous book. She leads with the premise that human beings are causing climate change, but what effect is that having on other living and organic life? By the end of the twenty-first century, she notes, scientists estimate between 20 and 50 percent of all living species will be extinct. In the book, she states that since life on Earth began about 3.8 billion years ago, there have been five mass extinctions. The dinosaurs, as well as approximately three-fourths of all plant and animal species, went extinct 66 million years ago—after an asteroid six miles in diameter collided with the planet—in what was the last of the five mass extinctions. Kolbert makes clear, however, that modern extinctions are happening and are a result of human activity. Various ecosystems are being wrecked by the warming of the atmosphere and the oceans. In fact, the oceans, Kolbert writes, have absorbed about one-third of the carbon dioxide humans have put out. Because the oceans have become warmer, more ocean water evaporates, making the air (which is already warmer) even moister, which causes some regions to experience increased flooding, mudslides, and rainstorms. On the other hand, regions that are prone to droughts are experiencing longer droughts, because warm air absorbs whatever heat is left in the soil. Kolbert covers a great deal more consequences, including how various species that carry diseases (such as mosquitoes), natural pests (such as bark beetles), and bacteria and viruses are spreading farther, beyond their natural habitats.

Terry Gross, the host of National Public Radio's interview program *Fresh Air* (12 Feb. 2014), asked Kolbert what Gross herself said sounds like a "horrible question"—though it was clearly for the purposes of continuing an informed discussion: "I live in the city. What impact does it have on my life if coral reefs can't grow anymore and if they start declining because of the acidification of the oceans?" Kolbert provided two answers. For one, human beings are undoing the natural beauty of the world, a beauty that has taken millions of years to develop. On a personal note, however, Kolbert said, "I guess my answer would be we're not sure. . . . We haven't done this before. You don't get to sort of see this experiment run over and over again. So we're doing, it's often said, a massive experiment on the planet, and we really don't know what the end point's going to be."

*The Sixth Extinction* earned Kolbert the 2015 Pulitzer Prize for general nonfiction and a great deal of critical praise. Former vice president Al Gore, a well-known advocate for action on climate change, called her book "powerful" in the pages of the *New York Times* (10 Feb. 2014). He also called the book "timely, meticulously researched and well-written." Nicholas Lezard for the *Guardian* (13 Jan. 2015) concluded his review by pointing out that "Kolbert's book is not, thankfully, as depressing as you might think. She has a good grip on her subject and uses a light touch when it is most needed. The main thing is that what she says is necessary to know."

## PERSONAL LIFE

In 1991 Kolbert married John Kleiner, who was an assistant professor of English at Williams College, a liberal arts school in Williamstown, Massachusetts. That year Kleiner received his PhD in literature from Stanford University, in California, and went on to become a professor of English at Williams College. The couple lives in Williamstown and has three children.

## SUGGESTED READING

Gore, Al. "Without a Trace." *New York Times Sunday Book Review*. New York Times, 10 Feb. 2014. Web. 6 Aug. 2015.

Kolbert, Elizabeth. Interview. "A Reporter's Field Notes on the Coverage of Climate Change." *Environment 360*. Yale University, 11 Mar. 2009. Web. 6 Aug. 2015.

Kolbert, Elizabeth. Interview by Terry Gross. "In the World's 'Sixth Extinction,' Are Humans the Asteroid?" *Fresh Air*. National Public Radio, 12 Feb. 2014. Web. 6 Aug. 2015.

## SELECTED WORKS

*The Prophet of Love*, 2004; *Field Notes from a Catastrophe*, 2006; *The Sixth Extinction*, 2014

—Dmitry Kiper

# Maxim Kontsevich

**Born:** August 25, 1964
**Occupation:** Mathematician

Russian-born mathematician Maxim Kontsevich has made contributions to mathematics and theoretical physics that have been internationally recognized. An educator as well as a researcher, he has taught as a visiting professor at Princeton University, Harvard University, Rutgers University, and the University of Miami, among other positions, and was a professor for two years at the University of California at Berkeley. He has held a permanent professorial position at the Institut des Hautes Études Scientifiques (IHES), or Institute of Advanced Scientific Studies, in France since 1995. Kontsevich's pioneering work in areas such as string theory has received widespread acclaim, furthering his reputation as a highly influential thinker. His major awards include the 2012 Shaw Prize in Mathematical Sciences, the 2012 Fundamental Physics Prize, and the 2014 Breakthrough Prize in Mathematics, the three of which brought him a total of $7 million in award money.

## EARLY YEARS AND INFLUENCES

Maxim Lvovich Kontsevich was born on August 25, 1964, in Khimki, Russia, a suburb of Moscow. He and his older brother, Leonid, grew up in a household where knowledge and learning were highly valued. His mother was an engineer and his father was a researcher at the Institute of Oriental Studies of the Russian Academy of Sciences, where he developed the Kontsevich system for transcribing the Korean language into the Cyrillic alphabet, which is still in use.

Kontsevich grew up in a home full of books, half of which were in Chinese or Korean, according to his autobiography written for the Shaw Prize Foundation (17 Sept. 2012). His older brother was the earliest major influence on his growing interest in physics and mathematics, which began in earnest when Kontsevich was around ten or eleven years old. He read his brother's copies of the mathematics and physics magazine *Kvant*, which was aimed at high school students and kept him informed on current research and unsolved problems, along with popular books on mathematics. He also began participating in mathematics competitions around this time.

Kimberly White/Getty Images

Kontsevich was quickly marked as an advanced learner due to the rapid pace of his studies. From the ages of thirteen to fifteen he took special additional courses for gifted children, including in his main interests of physics and mathematics, which were taught by university students. At the age of sixteen he received second place in a national math competition, and as a result received admittance to Moscow State University without having to take an entrance exam. According to his Shaw Prize autobiography, Kontsevich was also exempt from taking regular undergraduate classes due to his demonstrated achievement during his high school and supplementary education. Instead he moved directly to graduate level courses and research seminars, which proved greatly influential in shaping his knowledge and theoretical approach to mathematics.

At Moscow State University Kontsevich had many brilliant, encouraging professors, most notably his tutor Israel Moiseevich Gelfand, a major figure in the world of mathematics. "His weekly seminar," Kontsevich wrote in his autobiography in reference to Gelfand's class, "was completely unpredictable, and covered the whole spectrum of mathematics. Outstanding mathematicians, both Soviet and visitors from abroad, gave lectures. In a sense, I grew up in these seminars. . . . The interaction with theoretical physics remains vitally important for me even now."

## UPWARD TRAJECTORY

Kontsevich's education blended seamlessly into his professional career as he began pursuing further research projects. In 1983, just three years after starting his university studies, he published his first paper at the age of nineteen (with coauthor A. A. Kirillov), titled "Growth of the Lie Algebra Generated by Two Generic Vector Fields on the Line." In 1985 he left Moscow State University for a position on the staff of the Institute for Information Transmission Problems in Moscow, which is a part of the Russian Academy of Sciences. Three years later he took another professional step that would set him on the path to international recognition. In 1988 he traveled abroad—to Poland and France—for the first time and wrote what he modestly refers to in his Shaw Prize autobiography as "a short article concerning two different approaches to string theory." Soon after, Kontsevich was invited to take a temporary research residency at the Max Planck Institute for Mathematics in Bonn, Germany, in 1990.

At the end of his three-month stay in Bonn, Kontsevich attended an informal annual meeting of mathematicians, where, he noted for the Shaw Prize Foundation, "the latest hot results were presented." He was intrigued by an opening lecture given by British mathematician Michael Atiyah on the work of theoretical physicist Edward Witten, and immediately began developing a model to prove Witten's conjecture regarding the complex subject of "matrix models and the topology of moduli spaces of algebraic curves." In a matter of days Kontsevich had a project outline prepared and presented it to Atiyah and other colleagues. As a result, the Max Planck Institute invited him to return for a full year position to pursue his ideas. Remaining in Germany, he enrolled as a student at the University of Bonn and earned his doctorate in 1992, with his thesis successfully establishing the proof for Witten's conjecture. Those results were officially published as a paper the same year to great critical acclaim.

Kontsevich's impressive introduction to the international stage of mathematics immediately led to a variety of opportunities as a visiting lecturer and researcher. Over a period of three years he served as a visiting professor at the University of Bonn, Harvard University, and the Institute for Advanced Study at Princeton University. Meanwhile he continued to conduct research on concepts including Vassiliev invariants, quantum cohomology, and Feynman diagrams. His early career was already marked by several awards, including the 1992 Otto Hahn Medal and the 1992 Prix de la Mairie de Paris for mathematics. Then, in the spring of 1993, Kontsevich began to develop the idea of homological mirror symmetry, a significant discovery and explanation not only for mathematics but for theoretical physics as well that would become the ongoing main focus of his research.

## HOMOLOGICAL MIRROR SYMMETRY

Kontsevich's discovery of homological mirror symmetry represented the "opening of a grand new perspective" according to his Shaw prize autobiography. As with other problems he has worked on, mirror symmetry can be directly related to mathematical issues present in string theory, a complex physics hypothesis that asserts, basically, that everything in the universe is made up of infinitesimally small "strings" and that there are more than the standard three dimensions. Though by his own admission Kontsevich frequently jumps to various new subjects, from abstract algebra to finite fields, mirror symmetry has been a comparatively steady focus of his research.

In 1993 Kontsevich accepted a professorship at the University of California, Berkeley. He left the post within two years after getting an offer to become a tenured professor in France at the renowned Institut des Hautes Études Scientifiques. He would go on to become chair of the mathematics department at IHES. He simultaneously continued to take visiting positions, including at the University of Miami and, since 1997, a chair post at Rutgers University. In 1997 he also won both the Henri Poincaré Prize and the Prize of the International Congress of Mathematical Physics, and the following year he received the 1998 Fields Medal from the International Mathematical Union.

Kontsevich has attended and presented his work at many conferences all over the world throughout his career, including the International Congress of Mathematical Physics, the International Congress of Mathematicians, the Conference on Current Geometry, and the Latin American Colloquium on Algebra. By 2002, having received more recognition and more awards, he frequently presented multiple times a year throughout the world. Kontsevich has continued to be an in-demand lecturer. His list of published papers grew at the same time, with his results frequently acknowledged as important and well calculated.

## LATER CAREER AND AWARDS

With Kontsevich's ever increasing visibility in the international mathematics community came continued professional recognition through awards and honors. In 2008 he and Witten were presented with the Crafoord Prize by the Royal Swedish Academy of Sciences for, as the official press release announced, "their important contributions to mathematics inspired by modern theoretical physics." Four years later Kontsevich received the 2012 Shaw Prize in Mathematical Sciences, for his "pioneering works in algebra, geometry, and mathematical physics and in particular deformation quantization, motivic integration, and mirror symmetry." The prize came with an award of $1 million. That year he was also one of nine winners of the inaugural Fundamental Physics Prize created by Russian investor Yuri Milner; that achievement carried a $3 million reward. Two years later Kontsevich won another inaugural prize, the 2014 Breakthrough Prize in Mathematics, which was financed by Milner and Mark Zuckerberg, founder of the social media company Facebook, and also came with a $3 million incentive. Kenneth Chang, writing for the *New York Times* (23 June 2014) noted that Kontsevich's career has been "unusually lucrative" compared to that of typical mathematicians, while Milner himself told Chang that Kontsevich is "a well-deserving individual. He really sits in the middle between physics and mathematics."

While Kontsevich may be unusual among mathematicians in having achieved rapid professional and financial success, he remains committed to his work. He even told Chang he was "a bit embarrassed" at the amount of prize money he has won. In his autobiographical statement for the Shaw Prize in Mathematical Sciences, Kontsevich provided a brief, comprehensive summary of his own view of his research focus over the years, including the assertion that "The interaction during the last two decades between mathematics and theoretical physics has been an amazing chain of breakthroughs. I am very happy to be a participant in this dialogue, not only absorbing mathematical ideas from string theory, but also giving something back."

Kontsevich has been married to his wife, Ekaterina, since 1993. Their son was born in 2001. He and his family live in France.

## SUGGESTED READING

Chang, Kenneth. "The Multimillion-Dollar Minds of 5 Mathematical Masters." *New York Times*. New York Times, 23 June 2014. Web. 8 Dec. 2014.

Kontsevich, Maxim. "Autobiography of Maxim Kontsevich." *ShawPrize.org*. Shaw Prize Foundation. 17 Sept. 2012. Web. 8 Dec. 2014.

O'Connor, J. J., and E. F. Robertson. "Maxim Lvovich Kontsevich." *History.mcs. St-Andrews.ac.uk*. U of St. Andrews, July 2009. Web. 8 Dec. 2014.

—Dmitry Kiper

---

# Christopher Kostow

**Born:** 1976
**Occupation:** Chef

Christopher Kostow, of the Restaurant at Meadowood in California's Napa Valley, is one of the youngest chefs ever to receive three Michelin stars as well as one of the few American-born three-star chefs. According to its fact sheet, a three-star rating from the popular guidebook—which is compiled by a select group of professional food reviewers—indicates a restaurant with "exceptional cuisine where diners eat extremely well, often superbly. Distinctive dishes are precisely executed, using superlative ingredients. Worth a special journey."

Most visitors to this restaurant, which is part of the luxurious Meadowood resort, concede that the experience is, indeed, superb. In a review for the *San Francisco Chronicle* (18 Feb. 2010), critic Michael Bauer, who awarded the restaurant the paper's top ranking, asserted, "From start to finish, [Kostow] commands the kitchen, creating dishes you won't find on any other menu, served in a dining room awash with elegance and good taste." He went on to laud such items as an "artful arrangement of cannelloni, stuffed with sweetbreads on a creamed spinach puree, bejeweled with dots of butter-braised turnips, delicate leaves of miner's lettuce, hedgehog mushrooms, slices of truffles and a truffle broth poured on tableside."

Despite such undeniably rarified fare, Kostow has said that he wants to correct the Napa Valley's reputation as a place only for the wealthy. He told a writer for *Art Culinaire* (22 Sept. 2010), "We're very successful [at Meadowood] in creating a juxtaposition between exceptionally refined food and a very personable environment. We could very easily become a restaurant that could become pretentious. I think especially in this day and age as we move towards the democratization of food, that you can't do that and you shouldn't want to do that."

## EARLY YEARS

Kostow was born in 1976 and raised in Highland Park, Illinois, a suburb north of Chicago. His father was an attorney, and his mother, an elementary school teacher. He has one older brother and one younger. The family loved to visit restaurants, and Kostow grew up eating frequent Italian, Mexican, and German meals from the hole-in-the-wall establishments his parents favored. Among his fondest memories is going fishing with his father in Ontario, Canada. They would bring along a bag of cornmeal and a supply of lard and fry what they caught in a skillet, right on the spot.

When Kostow was fourteen, he took a job at Ravinia, a summer music festival in Chicago, working as a cashier at the event's food court. When he noticed that the cooks seemed to be having more fun than the other workers, he asked to be transferred to kitchen duty. "I relished the environment—the fast pace and loud music along with the order and control," he wrote in his 2014 book, *A New Napa Cuisine*. "Although I would not return to cooking for many years, my love of restaurants was born during those summers slaving over a deep fryer and a griddle."

Kostow attended Hamilton College in upstate New York, earning a degree in philosophy in 1999. He admits that most people consider his course of study an unusual one for an aspiring chef, but he wrote in his book, "Studying philosophy did teach me to absorb a lot of information with a critical eye and then use that information in a singular and personal manner. . . . [In cooking] I am confronted with different flavor memories and techniques—some created, most borrowed—and whether or not I am successful is driven by my ability to retain this information, distill it through my lens, and create (on my best days) something that is uniquely my own."

## THE START OF A PROFESSIONAL CULINARY CAREER

Upon graduating from Hamilton, Kostow chose not to pursue culinary school, believing that the cost of tuition would be better spent paying his living expenses while seeking internships and low-wage kitchen jobs that would

Robin Marchant/Getty Images North America

provide him with practical experience. Moving to California, he sent his resume to Trey Foshee, an award-winning chef at the restaurant George's at the Cove. After several calls and visits, Foshee finally agreed to give the persistent applicant a chance. "I found myself being led into my first professional kitchen. It was hot, small, and cramped, full of hulking cooks and cast-iron pans," Kostow wrote in his book. "To a philosophy student and dilettante, it looked like a blacksmith's foundry." Foshee set Kostow to work shucking oysters and plating desserts.

On New Year's Eve in 2000, Kostow has recalled, he was directed to decorate the dessert plates with spun-sugar ornaments the pastry chef had spent weeks making. Halfway through, he realized that he had forgotten to do so. Although he was certain he would be fired, Foshee forgave the error, and Kostow ultimately remained at the La Jolla restaurant for three years, working his way through the various stations in the kitchen. When not at the restaurant, Kostow haunted the public library, reading books by Jacques Pépin and Julia Child. He also purchased *Chez Panisse Café Cookbook* by Alice Waters from a local store, photocopied the pages, and then exchanged it for another. He repeated the process numerous times, gaining access to lavish books he would not otherwise have been able to afford.

## A STAR IS BORN

When he had learned all he could from Foshee, Kostow traveled to France, spending time in Montpellier, Salon-de-Provence, Juan-les-Pins, and Paris. It was a grueling time, and he briefly considered abandoning his culinary aspirations. He refocused on his goals, however, after being hired as a sous-chef at San Francisco's Campton Place to work under the Swiss-born chef Daniel Humm, who granted him an unusual amount of creative freedom and autonomy in the kitchen.

In early 2006, after Humm had moved to the East Coast, Kostow left Campton Place to become the chef at Chez TJ, a Mountain View, California, restaurant housed in a tiny Victorian-era building. Going home each day to a trailer parked behind the kitchen, Kostow brought a high level of passion and pride to the job, determined to cultivate and source the best ingredients to establish a positive reputation for a restaurant located in a place unfamiliar to many people. That year Michelin sent reviewers to the San Francisco Bay area for the first time, and to Kostow's surprise, Chez TJ garnered a one-star rating, indicating "a very good restaurant in its category, offering cuisine prepared to a consistently high standard." The following year, the establishment was awarded a second star, marking it as "worth a detour." Soon patrons from around the country were arriving at Chez TJ to sample homey but sophisticated dishes.

## THE RESTAURANT AT MEADOWOOD

Flush with the success of taking Chez TJ from zero stars to two, Kostow considered a move to an even larger stage. In 2008 he found that stage at Meadowood, a 250-acre luxury resort in California's Napa Valley. Surrounded by vineyards, the resort boasted a spa, a golf course, tennis courts, croquet lawns, and a restaurant that had already been awarded two stars.

With a kitchen four times the size of the one at Chez TJ and a staff twice as large (including several cooks he had brought with him from Mountain View), Kostow set out to earn the Restaurant at Meadowood a third star. After being named one of the best new chefs of 2009 by *Food & Wine* magazine, he succeeded in earning that third star in late 2010, making the Restaurant at Meadowood one of only two outside of New York to hold the distinction at the time—the other was Thomas Keller's legendary French Laundry in Yountville, California. As of late 2014, it remained one of only nine three-star dining establishments in the entire country.

"Dinner at Meadowood is a decidedly less buttoned-up affair than at other three-stars. From the moment you walk through the thick wooden doors, you're struck with the sense of being in a home," Chris Ying wrote for *Bon Appétit* (4 June 2014). Ying went on to praise his meal's "moments of unfettered luxury," such as the spiny-tail lobster "wrapped in *lardo*, topped with caviar, and set in a spoonful of rich pork stock."

Veteran and respected chefs experienced in working with Napa Valley cuisine have also lauded Kostow's approach and his ability not only to work with traditionally great recipes and ingredients, but to create original interpretations to elevate those ingredients. "Many have marveled at the bounty of the Napa Valley, but so few have found a way to continue discovering that bounty over and over, presenting it in a thoughtful, innovative, and fresh way," Keller said, as quoted by Matt Villano for *Napa Sonoma* magazine (Jan. 2015). "I am always struck by Chris Kostow's curious demeanor and humble reverence for the land around him." Kostow does indeed make ample use of the land's bounty, sourcing fresh ingredients from the garden adjacent to the resort as well as from the land that is managed in conjunction with the local St. Helena Montessori School.

## CELEBRITY, AWARDS, AND COMMUNITY

Although Kostow frequently tells interviewers that he does not seek celebrity, he agreed to appear on one 2010 episode of the televised culinary competition *Iron Chef America*. Facing off against well-known chef Cat Cora, he won the contest, which involved making a series of oat-based dishes. "TV is a double-edged sword," he told Carolyn Jung for the blog *FoodGal.com* (1 Sept. 2010). "It has raised awareness among the populace about what we do. But there's a false sense about it. People think we run around all day competing in the kitchen. In some ways, it demeans what we do. I take this all with a grain of salt."

In addition to his Michelin stars, Kostow has achieved several other honors, including being named a 2012 regional champion by the editors of *Time*. In 2013 he was named best chef in the western United States by the James Beard Foundation, and Meadowood appeared second on *Bon Appétit* magazine's list of the twenty most important restaurants in the country. Of such accolades, Kostow told Amy McKeever for the Napa Valley edition of the online publication

*Eater* (24 July 2013) that he wants the restaurant to be the kind of place "that people come to enjoy. Not a restaurant people come to check it off a list." He continued, "So yes, those awards help drive business, but they'd better not create your identity."

Remaining true to his vision, Kostow has also collaborated with local farmers and artists, fostering a sense of community. Most recently, he partnered with ceramics artist Richard Carter to produce a line of rustic ceramic tableware that is available to the public.

## PERSONAL LIFE

Kostow and his wife, Martina, a public relations consultant he met at a food festival, married in 2011. They have one daughter, Daisy. Martina is of Thai descent and often prepares traditional Asian dishes for family meals. They have a dog, Charlie (one of an unusual breed known as a Thai ridgeback), and live in St. Helena.

Travels have taken Kostow to Mexico to peruse farmers' markets and Abu Dhabi to cook camel meat. He even overcame his fears to write his first cookbook in 2014. Throughout everything, Kostow remains devoted to cooking itself. "I love the sound of a knife on a cutting board and the aggressive music blasting through the sound system—just as I did when frying chicken and drinking Franzia during my summers at Ravinia," he wrote in his book. "Call it arrested development, or a heightened degree of self-awareness, but then—as now—there is nothing on earth that I would rather do. Although I wasn't aware of it at the time, when I entered that first kitchen, I would never really leave."

## SUGGESTED READING

Arnold-Ratliff, Katie. "Regional Champion: Christopher Kostow Wants to Change How We See—and Taste—the Napa Valley." *Time* 10 Dec. 2012: 56–58. Print.

Bauer, Michael. "Meadowood Chef Christopher Kostow Gets 4 Stars." *San Francisco Chronicle*. Hearst, 18 Feb. 2010. Web. 6 Apr. 2015.

Kostow, Christopher. *A New Napa Cuisine*. Berkeley: Ten Speed, 2014. Print.

McKeever, Amy. "Christopher Kostow on Revitalizing Meadowood and the Power of Slow Expansion." *Eater*. Vox Media, 24 July 2013. Web. 6 Apr. 2015.

Villano, Matt. "The Chef, the Storyteller." *Napa Sonoma*. Diablo, Jan. 2015. Web. 6 Apr. 2015.

Ying, Chris. "Chef Christopher Kostow Stealthily Masters Napa Valley." *Bon Appétit*. Condé Nast, 4 June 2014. Web. 6 Apr. 2015.

—Mari Rich

# John Kovac
**Born:** ca. 1970–71
**Occupation:** Physicist and astronomer

Physicist and astronomer John Kovac received considerable international attention in March 2014, when the research group he was leading at the South Pole announced that they had discovered telltale evidence of cosmic inflation—the theory that the universe, shortly after the beginning of the big bang more than 13.8 billion years ago, had expanded faster than the speed of light for a brief instant. Kovac had already received numerous awards for his work in cosmology, including a 2011 Alfred P. Sloan Research Fellowship and a CAREER Award, presented to him in 2013 by the National Science Foundation (NSF). He had also organized a number of meetings and symposia on astrophysics from Antarctica, had authored more than thirty scholarly publications, and was considered one of the leaders in the field of cosmology, which studies among other things the cosmic microwave background (CMB) radiation left over from the big bang.

The Kovac group's discovery was widely hailed as a triumph for science. If correct, it would help researchers better understand not only the origins and history of the early universe but also the structure and physical laws that exist in it today. Kovac's discovery, however, was dealt a crippling blow in January 2015, when another group of researchers announced that what he and his team had discovered was not a twisting pattern produced by the origin of the universe but simply galactic dust. Kovac remains undaunted by this setback, however, and believes the work he continues to do at the South Pole will produce new insights into the origins and workings of the universe. He told Joel Achenbach for the *Washington Post* (17 Mar. 2015): "I'm not invested in any particular answer here. I think as an experimentalist that's the right attitude to take.... You've got to be really strict and say, whatever the universe says, I'm going to be equally happy. It's probably going to be a more spectacular answer than whatever your notions were going in."

## EARLY LIFE AND EDUCATION

John M. Kovac was born in the early 1970s. He and his three siblings were raised in Temple Terrace, Florida, outside Tampa, where the family moved when he was seven years old. Both his mother, Sharon "Midge," and his father, Mike, dean of the University of South Florida College of Engineering from 1986 to 1999, encouraged his love of the sciences. Kovac attended Roman Catholic schools in the Tampa area, graduating from Corpus Christi Catholic School and Jesuit High School. His experience at these institutions provided him with an education he continues to value. "[They] were really formative for me," Kovac said, as quoted by Jerome R. Stockfisch for the *Tampa Tribune* (19 Mar. 2014). "They gave me a great education in science." In high school, Kovac led the math club, served as an editor of the yearbook, and wrestled for the school team. His teachers remember him best for his intelligence and congeniality. "He was well-liked, he had a great sense of humor. He was a really bright, well-rounded kid," Bill Eggert, one of Kovac's former science teachers at Jesuit High School, told Jerome R. Stockfisch (24 Mar. 2014). "He wasn't intimidating with his smarts. He was very well-adjusted."

Following his high school graduation in 1988, Kovac earned his bachelor's degree from Princeton University in 1992 and then went on to earn his doctorate at the University of Chicago, under the supervision of John E. Carlstrom, in 2004. Since high school Kovac had been interested in the idea of cosmic inflation. This theory, initially put forth by Alan Guth, sought to explain both why no exotic particles predicted by the big bang theory are left in the universe and why the universe appears uniform, instead of chaotic. Rapid inflation, according to Guth's theory, would have smoothed out the universe's rough edges as well as watered down all of the exotic particles beyond detectable levels. For his graduate work, Kovac decided to make cosmic inflation his main topic of investigation.

## COSMIC BACKGROUND RADIATION

For his graduate work, Kovac studied CMB radiation, which is the thermal radiation (heat) left over from the big bang. CMB radiation provides insights into the creation, structure, and continuing expansion of the universe. Specifically, Kovac detected the first polarization of the CMB with the Degree Angular Scale Interferometer (DASI), a telescope at the NSF's Amundsen-Scott South Pole Station in Antarctica. (Radio astronomers like to work at the South Pole because its low temperatures and clear, dry air provide the best terrestrial conditions for their observations.) For his work in CMB polarization, which demonstrated that CMB waves tended to polarize, or vibrate slightly more in one direction than the other, Kovac was presented with the Grainger Fellowship.

Kovac went on to serve as a postdoctoral research fellow at the California Institute of Technology (Caltech) in Andrew Lange's group, which was also based in the South Pole. (All told, Kovac has spent a great deal of time in Antarctica, making twenty-four trips to the South Pole for scientific observation. In the early 1990s he spent fourteen straight months there.) His goal was to detect gravitational waves stemming from inflation, which would build on the discoveries he had described in his thesis. Gravitational waves had been an object of intense study for astronomers since Arno Penzias and Robert Wilson accidently discovered CMB radiation in the 1960s, for which they won the Nobel Prize in Physics in 1978. If gravitational waves from inflation exist, scientists believe they would twist the direction of polarization by squeezing space one way and stretching it in another. This would make any map of the sky appear to be filled with spiraling arrows. Among the instruments he used for his early research was the Background Imaging of Cosmic Extragalactic Polarization (BICEP1), which was part of a coordinated effort at the South Pole to detect polarization of the CMB.

## HUNTING FOR PROOF OF COSMIC INFLATION

The BICEP1 instrument, which made its observations from 2006 to 2008, was the first stage in looking for cosmic inflation. Kovac, who around this time began serving as an associate professor at Harvard University, was one of the leaders of this team, along with Jamie Bock at Caltech, Clem Pryke at the University of Minnesota, and Chao-Lin Kuo at Stanford University. Beginning in 2010 Kovac led the team working on the program's second telescope, BICEP2, which studied the early expansion of the universe until 2012. The Keck Array, considered the third phase of the program, began operating in 2011 and is expected to continue to do so until 2016. BICEP3, another telescope, was added to the program in the summer of 2014–15.

In 2014 Kovac's team announced that their instruments had detected gravitational waves—the

first real proof of Guth's theory of cosmic inflation. The announcement was made at a briefing
at the Harvard-Smithsonian Center for Astrophysics and in a publication in the *Astrophysical
Journal*, but Kovac had also met with Guth at his
office at the Massachusetts Institute of Technology (MIT) prior to the official announcement to
deliver the good news personally. "It was a very
special moment, and one we took very seriously
as scientists," Kovac remarked to Dennis Overbye for the *New York Times* (17 Mar. 2014).

According to their reports, the Kovac team's
telescopes had uncovered gravitational waves,
the rippling evidence in space-time that the
universe had undergone violent expansion at
speeds exceeding the speed of light when it had
existed for just one-trillionth of a trillionth of a
trillionth of a second. The Kovac group's findings might not only prove Guth's theory, which
had been the backbone of theoretical cosmology
for more than thirty years, but also suggest that
the universe might simply be part of a larger
cosmos—an endless number of universes that
extend infinitely and whose ultimate reaches
would be unknown to humankind. It is a mind-
blowing concept to many, especially when one
considers that the known universe contains at
least 225 billion galaxies and expands outward
almost some 13.8 billion light-years. If the Kovac group's findings were correct, not only was
the concept of a multiverse possible, but they
would also lend credence to the theory that the
four fundamental forces of the universe—gravity, electromagnetism, and strong and weak nuclear forces—constituted a single unified force
that many physicists believe controlled the universe in its earliest times. The news of Kovac's
findings surprised and pleased much of the scientific community, which had not expected the
theory of cosmic inflation to be proved in their
lifetimes. MIT cosmologist Max Tegmark remarked, "If this stays true, it will go down as
one of the greatest discoveries in the history of
science," as quoted by Dennis Overbye.

## FORGING AHEAD AFTER
## DISAPPOINTMENT

Unfortunately, almost from the start, critics suggested that the Kovac group's findings were too
good to be true. Some believed that the work
outlined by the BICEP2 team had not accounted
fully for another possible explanation for the polarization they observed—galactic dust, which
also tended to polarize light. The group countered that they had used good data to estimate
the amount of dust in the skies over Antarctica
and believed they still had enough evidence to
suggest they were seeing gravitational waves
caused by cosmic inflation. In January 2015
astronomers looking at data from the European
Space Agency's Planck satellite confirmed the
Kovac group's worst fears: there was far more
galactic dust over the South Pole than they had
realized. The ripples they saw were not evidence of cosmic inflation but simply galactic
dust. There had been no discovery, no proof of
Guth's theory. Alan Lightman wrote in *Popular
Science* (14 Apr. 2015) of the bitter end to the
BICEP2 team's story: "It's not that the Kovac
group did sloppy work. . . . In their ardor to con-
firm what would have been one of the greatest
scientific discoveries of the century, they had not
sufficiently considered the possible competing
effects of galactic dust—effects that other scientists had worried about at the time."

As for Kovac and his fellow researchers, they
have returned to their observations in Antarctica
but are not seeking to affirm evidence of cosmic inflation. They remain committed solely to
discovering scientific truths. When asked if the
team's new observations taken with BICEP3
will prove cosmic inflation, Kovac told Joel
Achenbach, "That's going to depend on what the
universe has to say. The power of our data is going to keep getting better."

## PERSONAL LIFE

Kovac and his wife, Saskia, have one son, Jack.
The family lives in Massachusetts.

## SUGGESTED READING

Achenbach, Joel. "A Year Later, BICEP2 As-
tronomer Is Upbeat as He Hunts for Elusive
Big Bang Signal." *Achenblog*. Washington
Post, 17 Mar. 2015. Web. 19 May 2015.

Lightman, Alan. "Nothing but the Truth." *Popular Science*. Popular Science, 14 Apr. 2015.
Web. 19 May 2015.

Overbye, Dennis. "Space Ripples Reveal Big
Bang's Smoking Gun." *New York Times*. New
York Times, 17 Mar. 2014. Web. 19 May
2015.

Stockfisch, Jerome R. "Tampa Education In-
spired Head of Big Bang Team." *TBO (Tampa
Bay Online)*. Tampa Tribune, 19 Mar. 2014.
Web. 19 May 2015.

Stockfisch, Jerome R. "Teachers, Fellow Students Knew John Kovac Would Make a Mark in Science." *TBO*. Tampa Tribune, 24 Mar. 2014. Web. 19 May 2015.

—Christopher Mari

# Sarah Kramer

**Born:** June 27, 1968

**Occupation:** Cookbook author and blogger

Cookbook author Sarah Kramer became a vegan, avoiding all animal products, during the mid-1990s. Her cookbooks, with their wit, common sense, clever illustrations, and inventive recipes have become a source of wisdom for many in the vegan community.

## EARLY LIFE

Born on June 27, 1968, in Regina, Saskatchewan, to parents who founded Saskatchewan's first professional theater company in 1966, Sarah Kramer spent much of her childhood traveling with the company. Although her father, Ken, was from western Canada, her mother, Sue, was British, so trips to England were also part of her travel experiences. In addition, members of her father's family had a vacation home on Maui, so the family sometimes escaped Saskatchewan's cold winters by heading to Hawaii.

Kramer's mother was a vegetarian and raised Kramer and her younger brother to adhere to the lifestyle, even though their father enjoyed meat. After Kramer's mother died when Kramer was ten years old, her father continued to provide vegetarian meals for her and her brother, Ben. Speaking of her mother's dedication to vegetarianism to Leonie Cooper for the *Guardian* (6 Feb. 2008), Kramer recalled, "I didn't get to have a long intellectual conversation about it, but she loved animals, and thought that eating them was wrong and passed that down to me."

As a young woman Kramer was into the usual diversions of adolescents, particularly the punk-music scene. She traveled with friends to various music venues and to places such as Las Vegas.

## GOING VEGAN

As she grew older Kramer continued a vegetarian lifestyle. Although she ate eggs and dairy, she did not taste meat until she was thirteen years old, despite peer pressure from classmates.

Stranded during a camping trip with a friend, Kramer ate pepperoni, which she was able to eat because it did not resemble an animal. After that, she occasionally ate meat, though she felt it was wrong to do so.

At seventeen Kramer moved out of her father's house. Food was unimportant to her; she spent her money on alcohol and cigarettes, punk-rock venues, and rent. She did not know how to cook, so she ate a great deal of Japanese noodles.

In 1988 Kramer moved to Victoria, British Columbia. At a yard sale she purchased two cookbooks that she remembered her mother using—Frances Moore Lappé's *Diet for a Small Planet* (1971) and Laurel Robertson's *Laurel's Kitchen* (1976). Slowly she learned to cook and to bake bread. She also became interested in issues related to sustainability and began avoiding products tested on animals.

The lifestyle she had followed, coupled with poor eating habits, took its toll in poor health. Diagnosed with chronic fatigue syndrome, Kramer read everything she could about the disease and determined that a vegan lifestyle might improve her health. She cut sugar, alcohol, and caffeine from her diet, as well as all animal products. As she stated in her book *La Dolce Vegan! Vegan Livin' Made Easy* (2005), "For me, veganism is about thinking outside of your own needs, seeing a world beyond yourself and opening your heart up to compassion, empathy, and understanding. . . . It's a compassionate lifestyle choice that I made to feel comfortable being myself."

## A LIFE-CHANGING TRIP

Following a trip to Memphis, Tennessee, to visit Graceland, Elvis Presley's home, Kramer and her roommates headed for New Orleans to investigate the punk-music scene there. Unfortunately, they were assaulted, and their money and car were stolen. Kramer had expected to be shot and killed; their assailant had a gun, but he only hit her with it.

Hurt but alive, Kramer was rushed to a local hospital and accepted the care of complete strangers, who arranged housing and provided clothing. Eventually Kramer's stepmother wired money so that she and her friend could get home. Police found the stolen car, but it had been set afire.

The robbery kick-started Kramer's life. She went into therapy to process what had happened, and she developed a new appreciation for life. Having been surrounded by creative people in her childhood, she also wanted to share her creativity. Writing a cookbook seemed the perfect solution.

## COOKBOOKS FOR CHRISTMAS AND MORE

During the mid-1990s Kramer and her friend Tanya Barnard were seeking an inexpensive, personalized idea for holiday gifts. Kramer had just received a computer as a wedding gift; Barnard suggested they use it to create a cookbook, which became *How It All Vegan! Irresistible Recipes for an Animal-Free Diet* (1999). Using Microsoft Publisher, they created a fifty-page cookbook that friends and family loved. As a result, they did a second printing of one thousand copies, selling the book via the Internet and at punk-rock concerts. When that print run was exhausted, Kramer sent a proposal to Arsenal Pulp Press. Within days, she was offered a contract. The book won *VegNews*'s 2003–4 Veggie Award for best new vegetarian cookbook.

Because of her assault in New Orleans, Kramer feared doing a book tour and traveling. However, doing so allowed her to regain her confidence as she met kind and like-minded people. Reviewers commented favorably on *How It All Vegan!*. As Maria Burgos wrote for *Vegetarian Times* (Apr. 2005), "Kitschy '50s-style photographs and a modern, attractive layout make the book easy to read. Can't-miss sections include vegan substitutions, environmentally friendly household cleaners, animal treats, and homemade cosmetics. There's also a vegan ingredient guide to help you read the labels in store-bought goods."

Kramer next published *The Garden of Vegan* (2002). After completing the book with Kramer, Barnard pursued a nursing career. Initially uncertain if she could continue to create cookbooks on her own, Kramer did just that, with *La Dolce Vegan!* in 2005. Also that year, *VegNews* named her its favorite cookbook author. In 2008 Kramer wrote *Vegan à Go-Go!*, focusing on how to travel well as a vegan. These books included recipes from not only Kramer but also readers, as well as travel tips and ways to make travel simpler. In 2012 Kramer released an app for iPhone and iPad, GoVegan! with Sarah Kramer, which includes a shopping list, tips, and recipes. As Kramer put it to Leonie Cooper, *Vegan à Go-Go!* fulfills a need since "people get in a panic because they want to make miso gravy but don't have their cookbooks with them."

## PERSONAL LIFE

Kramer married Gerald Anderson (better known as Gerry Kramer) in 1996; she rode a vintage Vespa motor scooter to their wedding in Las Vegas. Together they own Tattoo Zoo, a vegan-friendly tattoo parlor, founded in 1994, located in Victoria, British Columbia. The Kramers have worked on Canadian horror films such as *Binge & Purge* (2002), *Meat Market 3* (2006), and *The Dead Inside* (2005), all written and directed by Brian Clement. She also enjoys photography.

Kramer is a breast-cancer survivor; she closed Sarah's Place, a vegan curio store, to undergo treatment after a unilateral mastectomy. However, she has since reopened her store. Her story was featured in a 2014 *New York Times* blog about breast-cancer survivors. She wrote, "I keep waiting to be torn-up about only having one breast, but it hasn't happened yet. It doesn't even look that weird to me. My husband Gerry said the other night: 'You are still you. I thought you'd look weird with your breast missing but you don't.' . . . And he's right. I'm still me." In 2015 she began studying to become an Aquafit instructor, hoping to work with other breast-cancer survivors in a program offered through the YWCA.

## SUGGESTED READING

Blumenthal, Raena. "Fun Vegan Vittles." *E: The Environmental Magazine* 13.5 (2002): 60. *Academic Search Alumni Edition*. Web. 6 Mar. 2015.

Burgos, Maria. "In Good Conscience." Rev. of *How It All Vegan! Irresistible Recipes for an Animal-Free Diet*. *Vegetarian Times* 330 (2005): 74. Web. 6 Mar. 2015.

Cooper, Leonie. "The Garden of Vegan." *Guardian*. Guardian News and Media, 6 Feb. 2008. Web. 6 Mar. 2015.

## SELECTED WORKS

*How It All Vegan! Irresistible Recipes for an Animal-Free Diet*, 1999; *The Garden of Vegan*, 2002; *La Dolce Vegan! Vegan Livin' Made Easy*, 2005; *Vegan à Go-Go!*, 2008.

—Judy Johnson, MLS

# La Roux

**Born:** March 8, 1988

**Occupation:** Singer

Elly Jackson, better known under her stage name La Roux, is a critically acclaimed electronic pop music artist. Her first album, *La Roux* (2009), featured such popular singles as "Bulletproof," "Quicksand," and "In for the Kill." Very much influenced by the sounds of 1980s pop music, her popularity grew in the United States in 2010, the year she won a Grammy Award for the album and toured successfully. The tour had to be cut short for personal reasons, however, and Jackson disappeared from the public eye for about four years.

The debut of La Roux's second album, *Trouble in Paradise* (2014), marked a new beginning exhibiting new influences, especially disco music. Though not unanimously praised, the album was still a welcome return for some critics, and especially for fans who had waited half a decade for Jackson's return to making music. The album peaked at number twenty on the Billboard 200 chart.

## EARLY LIFE AND EDUCATION

Eleanor Kate "Elly" Jackson was born on March 8, 1988, in London, England, and grew up in the city's Brixton district. Her mother is the actor Trudie Goodwin, and her father also acted as well as played guitar. Jackson has an older sister, Jess. In an interview with Benji Wilson for the *Daily Mail* (20 Nov. 2009) Jackson said her parents did not tell her what career to pursue except to discourage her from becoming an actor, primarily because they felt there were "so few jobs out there." Jackson had a stable childhood with her parents and older sister, living in the same house throughout those years. She grew up hearing a lot of varied music at home from her parents' record collection, and she developed an obsession with music and the record industry at a young age.

Jackson became particularly fascinated by folk-inspired artists such as Joni Mitchell and Nick Drake, centered around the acoustic guitar and unadorned vocals. She also named Carole King as an early inspiration. By the time she was eight years old, Jackson already had an electric guitar and loved to play it. She told Wilson that she was "such a show-off," as she and a friend played the songs of 1950s rock-and-roller Buddy

Man Alive!/Wikimedia Commons

Holly, even convincing their teacher to let them perform for the class. "I think the class thought it was pretty cool," she recalled to Wilson.

Her secondary school education, starting with middle school, was a very different experience. She attended a strict religious school where she had to wear a uniform and had a hard time getting along with the teachers. "I just couldn't wait to leave," she told Wilson. She preferred to pursue a music career, a decision her family supported though they insisted she complete her education so she could have other options. She was admitted to a sixth-form college, and there she began to attend rave parties. The club scene would eventually deeply shape the direction of her musical endeavors.

## FORMING LA ROUX

In 2004, at the age of sixteen, Jackson was attending a party in Brixton when she made the connection that would spark her rise to success. As the rave began to wind down, someone handed her a guitar. Her playing attracted the attention of another clubber, who recommended that Jackson get in touch with one of his friends, a record producer. That friend turned out to be Ben Langmaid, who had established himself in the 1990s dance music scene as a DJ and had produced several successful projects. After being introduced to Jackson he was indeed highly interested in working with her.

At the time Jackson met Langmaid she still had long hair, like a 1960s female folk singer, and played mostly acoustic music and sang folk-inspired songs. But a change took place as she delved deeper and deeper into electronic dance music with the influence of Langmaid. The two officially began working together in 2006. Although they initially experimented with an acoustic direction under the name of Automan, soon they stepped away from attempting to make any kind of folk music and instead relied on influences such as David Bowie, Prince, and The Knife. Langmaid continually pushed Jackson to challenge herself: "He could see there was something in there that he wanted to get out," she told Gerrick D. Kennedy for the *Los Angeles Times* (14 July 2010), "I'd never done the bold singing. He'd say 'Go cover "Call Me" from Blondie and be back in a week.'"

Soon after, Jackson cut off her long hair and styled her new shorter hairdo into what would become her signature look, a 1980s-inspired quiff. Her bright red hair also inspired the duo to adopt the name La Roux, French for "the Red One," which Jackson came across in a baby names book. Jackson had decided early on that her stage persona would be an androgynous character sporting jackets of loud colors, big shoulder pads, and other flashy styling, similar to the looks cultivated by fashion icon musicians such as Bowie and Prince.

## LA ROUX AND COMMERCIAL SUCCESS

After four years of perfecting their songs and style, Jackson and Langmaid were ready to release their music. La Roux's first single "Quicksand," released in 2008, immediately brought the group media attention, earning positive reviews and making the charts the following year. Also in 2009 the group opened for singer Lily Allen on her tour of the United Kingdom. Although Langmaid shared songwriting credits with Jackson, he did not appear on stage and left all interviews and publicity to Jackson. The group's next single, "In for the Kill," reached number two on the UK Singles chart and made the European Hot 100 Singles chart, and La Roux's popularity continued to grow throughout Europe.

Later in 2009 the single "Bulletproof" debuted at number one on the UK Singles chart, and also brought La Roux increasing attention in the United States. The group's first album, *La Roux* (2009), contained all three hit singles, and its release would go on to further push the group's popularity in an upward trajectory. The

album reached number two in the United Kingdom and number seventy on the US Billboard 200 chart, and was nominated for the 2009 Mercury Prize. The following year the group gained further popularity in the United States, particularly after making a notable appearance at the Coachella music festival in April 2010 as part of a successful tour. With this exposure, "Bulletproof" reached number six on the Mainstream Top 40 (Pop Songs) Billboard chart. In February 2011 the success of *La Roux* was solidified when it won the best electronic/dance album Grammy Award.

For the most part the album was well received by critics and fans of electronic music. It was notable for its paradoxical mix of classic 1980s-style synthesizers and artificial drums with a contemporary and even futuristic sound. Jackson's vocals were always at the forefront of the songs, and her androgynous look and hairdo were commented upon by reviewers nearly as much as the music itself. Most notably in the group's music videos she stood out as woman who was not portrayed in a hypersexual way and who seemed to be in control. "While style is a large part of La Roux's substance, it never feels slick, and that's due to Jackson's voice as much as it is the group's intentionally stiff sounds—in fact, it's the way that her vocals interact with those sounds that makes these songs so dynamic," wrote Heather Phares for All Music Guide. Phares went on to call the album "a standout, not just among the many other '80s revivalists, but the entire late-2000s pop landscape."

## SPLIT WITH LANGMAID

After a good deal of touring, Jackson and Langmaid decided to take a break and focus on making their next record. The pressures of fame were beginning to weigh on the twenty-one year old Jackson, and she developed anxiety issues and suffered panic attacks. Stepping back from the stress of touring and focusing instead on new material seemed like a natural step. Jackson was planning to play actual instruments on the new album, particularly guitars. She also wanted to bring in other musical influences, such as reggae and especially disco.

Langmaid, however, did not support Jackson's new vision for La Roux. In an interview with Tim Jonze for the *Guardian* (24 May 2014), Jackson said Langmaid would not consider several songs that she had written, and that "the artist that I'd decided to be, Ben didn't agree with."

On top of those artistic differences were personal issues between the two; the extremely close bond they had shared during the making of the first record had drifted apart. Jackson began to have a closer professional relationship with her engineer, Ian Sherwin, with whom Langmaid did not get along. Before the album was finished Langmaid left the group, leaving La Roux to be Jackson's solo project. Sherwin took over Langmaid's duties, and, as Jackson remarked to Jonze, "A few hours after Ben departed, we were back in the chairs working."

Meanwhile Jackson's anxiety issues grew worse. Eventually she found she had completely lost her ability to sing. This led her to consult various medical experts to find a cure, but they had little success. She canceled more gigs and pushed back the release of the second album. Finally she visited Andy Evans, a performance anxiety specialist, and after two years of therapy she was able to overcome the problem. She had a comeback performance at the 2013 Coachella festival, at which she teased some of her new material, before retreating from the public eye once again to finally finish her follow-up album.

### TROUBLE IN PARADISE

Five years passed between the release of La Roux's first album and her appropriately titled sophomore release, *Trouble in Paradise* (2014). The album was notable for its shift to a new musical direction. The influence of the 1980s was still strong, but with Jackson in full artistic control it incorporated noticeable reggae themes and a major disco influence. In an interview with Nick Murray for *Rolling Stone* (6 June 2014) she discussed her influences during the making of the new record: "It's specific sounds of specific songs like 'Shame Shame Shame' by Shirley & Company or 'Clean Up Woman' by Betty Wright or 'Love Me Tonight' by Fern Kinney or 'I Need You Tonight' by Punkin Machine. It's specific tracks, that I feel particularly inspired by, it's something to do with the way they feel, the way they sound." Jackson further differentiated *Trouble in Paradise* from its predecessor, telling Murray, "It's a lot warmer, it's a lot sexier. . . . I can't think of a better way to explain it. I wouldn't say it's more playful, but it's playful in [a] different way. It's cheekier—I would say it's musically cheekier. And I think it's got a lot more groove because it's all kind of performance based."

La Roux's record reached number twenty on The Billboard 200 chart in 2014, number six on the UK Albums chart, and number one on the US Dance/Electronic Albums chart. *Trouble in Paradise* was met with mostly positive reviews, with many critics approving of the stylistic shift and calling it an improvement on *La Roux*. Jackson embarked on a tour to support the album in 2014 using a full band rather than synthesizers and backing tracks.

### PERSONAL LIFE

Jackson lives in London. Although she has frequently been asked about her sexuality due to her androgynous image, she has refused to answer whether she is gay, straight, or bisexual, only saying that those labels do not matter to her and that she wants to keep her private life private. She has also gained media attention for her outspoken critical comments about other celebrities and the state of the music industry.

### SUGGESTED READING

Jonze, Tim. "La Roux: 'I Don't Get Fame.'" *Guardian*. Guardian News and Media, 24 May 2014. Web. 5 Feb. 2015.

Murray, Nick. "La Roux on Sexier, Cheekier New Album 'Trouble In Paradise.'" *Rolling Stone*. Rolling Stone, 6 June, 2014. Web. 5 Feb. 2015.

Wilson, Benji. "The Other Side of La Roux." *MailOnline*. Associated Newspapers, 20 Nov. 2009. Web. 5 Feb. 2015.

—Dmitry Kiper

# Eddie Lacy

**Born:** June 2, 1990
**Occupation:** Football player

In recent years the National Football League (NFL) has transitioned to an increasingly quarterback-driven game. However, Eddie Lacy of the Green Bay Packers is among a select group of running backs who is helping reverse that trend. A workhorse with a bruising rushing style, the five-foot-eleven, 234-pound Lacy, who enjoyed a standout college career at the University of Alabama, emerged as one of the best power runners in the NFL in his first two professional seasons. In 2013 he led all NFL rookies and set Packers franchise records with 1,178 rushing yards and eleven rushing touchdowns, en route to becoming the Associated Press (AP) NFL Offensive Rookie of the Year. He also earned a Pro Bowl selection and was named to the AP All-Pro Second Team. During the 2014 season, Lacy again eclipsed the 1,000-yard rushing mark and helped the Packers win a second consecutive National Football Conference (NFC) North Division title.

## EARLY LIFE

The third of four children, Eddie Darwin Lacy Jr. was born on June 2, 1990, in Gretna, Louisiana, a suburb of New Orleans located on the west bank of the Mississippi River. He has two older brothers, Donovan and Darion, and a younger sister, Brittany. His father, Eddie Sr., an operating-room technician, met his mother, Wanda, a nurse, while both worked at the F. Edward Hebert Hospital in New Orleans.

Although neither of his parents had been athletes, Lacy developed a passion for playing football at an early age, thanks in part to the influence of his brothers, who both played the sport. He started playing Pop Warner football at six and further honed his skills in street pickup games with neighborhood friends. A running back from the moment he stepped on the gridiron, Lacy routinely ran over and through defenders whenever he played, despite his relatively small size. "Sometimes, when he ran with the football," Elizabeth Merrill wrote for *ESPN the Magazine* (16 Nov. 2012), "people would stop and videotape him."

Lacy loved playing football but has said that he never enjoyed watching the sport. Instead of spending his weekends watching college football and NFL games, he preferred doing activities outside. "Sitting down watching TV, watching football," Lacy told Paul Imig for Fox Sports Wisconsin (19 Dec. 2014), "it was definitely not one of my interests." Because of his aversion to televised football, Lacy grew up with little knowledge of NFL teams and players.

## HARDENED BY HURRICANE KATRINA

In 2005, Lacy enrolled at Helen Cox High School, at the time, a new public school in nearby Harvey, Louisiana. He made the varsity football team as a freshman, but his first prep season was interrupted by Hurricane Katrina, which slammed into the Gulf Coast in August of that year. The hurricane, which caused more than $100 billion in damage, killed nearly two thousand people, and displaced more than one million, destroyed Lacy's childhood home and forced his family to move to a series of temporary lodgings. Lacy's family first evacuated to a

Gabriel Cervantes (CC BY 3.0)

hotel in Beaumont, Texas, then moved in with an aunt in Baton Rouge, Louisiana, where they shared a three-bedroom home with five other families, before relocating about 30 miles south to the town of Geismar. In Geismar, they found a temporary residence through an online house-sharing program before eventually settling into a trailer.

After being faced with the prospect of having to play for the freshman squad at Geismar's Dutchtown High School, Lacy persuaded his parents to let him live with his football coach in Gretna so he could continue attending Helen Cox High School. He became a starter and standout for the school's football team, which played an abbreviated schedule as a result of the hurricane. Poor grades, however, forced Lacy to move back with his parents before the start of his sophomore year.

Distraught over having to leave his childhood friends, Lacy became depressed and withdrawn. To escape his grief, he turned to football, which "was my way to cope with everything I had built up inside," as he explained to Ben Reiter for *Sports Illustrated* (4 Sept. 2014). Lacy finished the final three years of his prep football career at Dutchtown High, where he learned how to "run angry" under Coach Benny Saia. He earned first-team all-state honors as a junior, when he rushed for 1,800 yards and twenty-six touchdowns. He eclipsed the 1,000-yard mark again as a senior, despite playing in only seven games due to injuries. "He'd run over you. He'd run around you. . . . He could do it all. He was the total package," Saia told Tyler Dunne for the Milwaukee, Wisconsin, *Journal Sentinel* (13 July 2013).

## UNIVERSITY OF ALABAMA

Lacy was recruited by football powerhouses all over the country, but none more so than the University of Alabama and the University of Tennessee. He ultimately chose the former over the latter because of its caliber of players and for the opportunity to play under renowned coach Nick Saban. "The only way you can get better," Lacy told Allen Wallace for *Scout* (23 Feb. 2009), "is to play against the best and that's what I felt would happen at Alabama." The running back was in danger of failing to qualify academically for Alabama, but earned good enough grades in summer school to restore his eligibility.

In the fall of 2009 Lacy joined a crowded Crimson Tide backfield that included sophomore sensation Mark Ingram Jr. and fellow freshman phenom Trent Richardson. As a result, he redshirted during the 2009 season, at the end of which Ingram won the Heisman Trophy and Alabama won the NCAA (National Collegiate Athletic Association) Bowl Championship Series (BCS) national title. Still, Lacy became a standout practice player, earning the nickname "Circle Button"—a reference to the button one has to push on a Sony PlayStation controller to have a player make a spin move in the Madden NFL video game—for his uncanny ability to spin away from and elude defenders.

As Alabama's number-three back during the 2010 season, Lacy rushed for 406 yards and six touchdowns in twelve games. He served as a complementary back to Ingram and Richardson and was a regular contributor on special teams. Despite early-season trouble handling the football, Lacy added another dimension to the Alabama's running game and offered fans a glimpse of what was to come in the 2011 Capital One Bowl, when he made two impressive touchdown runs during the team's 49–7 blowout victory over Michigan State University.

After Ingram departed school for the 2011 NFL Draft, Lacy teamed with Richardson to shoulder the majority of the rushing workload for the Crimson Tide during the 2011 season. He appeared in twelve games and finished second on the team with 674 yards on ninety-five carries. Anchored by its formidable running game, Alabama returned to championship form, going 12–1 and winning a second BCS title in three years with a 21–0 victory over Louisiana State University.

Lacy underwent surgery for turf toe following the BCS title game but recovered in time for the 2012 season. Richardson left for the NFL, and Lacy entered the 2012 season as Alabama's primary back. He did not disappoint. He rushed for 1,322 yards and seventeen touchdowns in fourteen games, and earned first-team All-Southeastern Conference honors. He helped Alabama post a 13–1 record and repeat as national champions as they obliterated Notre Dame, 42–14, in the 2013 BCS title game. He received the game's most valuable player (MVP) award, after rushing for 140 yards and scoring two touchdowns.

## GREEN BAY PACKERS

Lacy, who majored in consumer science, decided to forgo his final year of college eligibility and enter the 2013 NFL Draft. Many analysts rated Lacy as the best running back in the draft. Some, however, questioned both his durability and love for the game. Consequently, Lacy slipped to the second round before being selected by the Packers with the sixty-first overall pick. He was the fourth running back chosen in the draft, after Giovani Bernard, Le'Veon Bell, and Montee Ball. "I know a lot of teams questioned how much I love football because I don't talk about it 24/7," Lacy explained to Dunne. "But I feel like it's not how much you know about it or how much you watch it. It's all about production . . . You put me on the field and I'll contribute." In 2013, he signed a four-year contract with the Packers worth $3.4 million.

## RECORD-SETTING ROOKIE SEASON

Lacy's NFL career got off to a slow start. In his professional debut, on September 8, 2013, he rushed for a modest forty-one yards on fourteen carries in the Packers' 34–28 opening-day loss to the San Francisco 49ers. He then suffered a concussion on his first carry in the Packers' week-two game against the Washington Redskins. The injury sidelined him for the rest of that game and the following one, against Cincinnati Bengals.

After being given an extra week to recover during the Packers' bye week, Lacy returned to the field with a smarter and safer rushing strategy, which paid immediate dividends. He rushed for 1,127 yards over the Packers' thirteen regular-season games, the second-most in the NFL over that span. He finished his rookie season with 1,178 rushing yards on 284 attempts and eleven rushing touchdowns, all of which were Packers franchise rookie records. He also led all rookies in rushing yards and rushing touchdowns, and finished eighth in the league overall in that category.

Lacy's record-breaking achievements helped carry the Packers into the postseason, as they finished first in the NFC North Division with an 8–7–1 record. Though the Packers lost to the 49ers, 23–20, in the NFC wildcard playoff game, Lacy was recognized for his regular-season performance. He was named the AP Offensive Rookie of the Year, receiving thirty-five votes from a nationwide panel of fifty sportswriters. He also received AP All-Pro Second Team honors and was selected to the NFC Pro Bowl squad, as an injury replacement for Minnesota Vikings running back Adrian Peterson. After the season, Johnathan Franklin, a fellow Packers rookie running back in 2013 who suffered a severe and, ultimately, career-ending neck injury during a week-twelve game against the Minnesota Vikings, told Ben Reiter about Lacy, "He can run, he's strong, he's smart, he can block—I believe he can be one of the greatest to play this game. As long as he lasts."

## 2014 AND 2015 SEASONS

In 2014, Lacy built upon his outstanding rookie campaign and solidified his place among the league's elite power runners. That season he started all sixteen games and surpassed the 1,000-yard rushing mark for the second consecutive year, with 1,139 yards, which was good for seventh in the league. He also notched nine rushing touchdowns, tied for third in the league, and made forty-two receptions. He became the fifth player in Packers history to record back-to-back 1,000-yard rushing seasons and only the fourth running back in franchise history to record at least 1,000 rushing yards and forty receptions in the same season. Meanwhile, the Packers repeated as NFC North Division champions with a 12–4 record. They advanced to the NFC Championship Game, where they squandered a sixteen-point halftime lead, losing to the Seattle Seahawks, 28–22, in overtime.

Lacy entered the 2015 season as one of the most underpaid running backs, relative to performance, in the league. He holds Packers franchise records for the most rushing yards (2,317) and the most total touchdowns (24) for a player's first two seasons. Since 2013, he ranks seventh in the league in rushing yards and fourth in rushing touchdowns.

## PERSONAL LIFE

During the NFL off-season, Lacy resides in Gonzales, Louisiana. In the spring of 2014, he used part of his rookie signing bonus to build a four-bedroom home for his family in Geismar. The home is located less than ten minutes away from their trailer. "I have peace in a sense that I know that my parents are now more comfortable than they were in the past," Lacy said to Ryan Wood for the *Green Bay Press-Gazette* (24 Oct. 2014).

## SUGGESTED READING
Dunne, Tyler. "Packers Rookie Running Back Lacy Has Burden to Carry." *Milwaukee Journal Sentinel*. Journal Sentinel, 13 July 2013. Web. 18 Aug. 2015.

Imig, Paul. "Packers' Lacy Doesn't Watch, Follow Football But Does 'Play It Pretty Good.'" *Fox Sports Wisconsin*. Fox Sports Interactive Media, 19 Dec. 2014. Web. 18 Aug. 2015.

Merrill, Elizabeth. "Home and Away." *ESPN the Magazine*. ESPN Internet Ventures, 16 Nov. 2012. Web. 18 Aug. 2015.

Reiter, Ben. "Packers Running Back Eddie Lacy Is Primed for a Breakout Season." *Sports Illustrated*. Time, 4 Sept. 2014. Web. 18 Aug. 2015.

Wood, Ryan. "Homecoming: The House That Eddie Lacy Built." *Greenbaypressgazette.com*. Press Gazette Media, 24 Oct. 2014. Web. 18 Aug. 2015.

—Chris Cullen

# Jhumpa Lahiri
**Born:** July 11, 1967
**Occupation:** Writer

Jhumpa Lahiri won the 2000 Pulitzer Prize for fiction for *Interpreter of Maladies* (1999), her first published collection of short stories. Additional awards she has earned include a Guggenheim Fellowship in 2002 and Barnard College's Young Alumna of the Year Award in 2004. President Barack Obama appointed her to the President's Committee on the Arts and Humanities in February 2010. She joins the Lewis Center for the Arts at Princeton University as professor of creative writing in 2015, where she will teach workshops in fiction and translation. Speaking to Julia Leyda for *Contemporary Women's Writing* (Jan. 2011) about the importance of the

David M. Benett/Getty Images Europe

written word, Lahiri said, "Literature allows us to suspend our everyday reactions and takes us to places, literally and figuratively, we wouldn't have gone to otherwise. That, to me, is one of its greatest triumphs."

## EARLY LIFE AND EDUCATION

Amar and Tia Lahiri immigrated to Great Britain from India in 1964; Nilanjana Sudeshna Lahiri was born in London three years later, on July 11, 1967. ("Jhumpa" is a nickname—a common phenomenon in Bengali culture, where people have "good names" for public use and "pet names" for private use.) Lahiri's parents moved to the United States in the wake of the Immigration and Nationality Act of 1965, which abolished the quotas that had previously favored western European immigrants, and found work first in Massachusetts and then in Rhode Island. Amar was a librarian at the University of Rhode Island; Tia, who has master's degrees in Bengali literature and drama, taught. Lahiri's sister, Simanti, was born in 1974.

When it was time for Lahiri to begin kindergarten, she did not speak any English. Her mother sent her to school anyway, knowing that she was bright and would pick up the language. This was also when Lahiri's pet name became her public name; her teacher could not pronounce Nilanjana, so her mother told the teacher to call her Jhumpa instead. "When I entered the American world as a child, I endlessly had to ex-

plain to people how to say my name and how to spell it and what it meant," Lahiri said to Adam Langer for *Book* magazine (Sept.–Oct. 2003). "I really felt my name was causing people pain on some level."

Lahiri showed an interest in good writing from an early age. "We read a lot in our house," her mother told Langer. "Everybody was reading something all the time, and whenever I read something, I like other people to know about it. So, every time I read a good novel or a good short story, I would read it aloud and Jhumpa always showed a lot of interest." Lahiri's favorite books as a child included books with orphans for heroes, such as L. M. Montgomery's *Anne of Green Gables* (1908), and stories about pioneers, such as the books of Laura Ingalls Wilder. She also loved the character Jo March in *Little Women* (1868–69), by Louisa May Alcott, and the siblings in C. S. Lewis's *The Lion, the Witch, and the Wardrobe* (1950).

At South Kingston High School, Lahiri was coeditor of the school newspaper and played flute in the marching band. After school, she worked at the Kingston Free Library, shelving books. She graduated in 1985 and went on to attend Barnard College, a women's institution. Because English was her favorite class and she enjoyed writing, she decided to major in English. Early literature interested her, so she also minored in Latin and studied Greek. After completing her bachelor's degree in English, she then earned master's degrees in English, creative writing, and comparative studies in literature and the arts, followed later by a doctorate in Renaissance studies, all from Boston University.

## FINDING HER WAY

Lahiri initially thought she would remain in academia, but she soon changed her mind. "Everybody was railing against all the writers I had read and loved as an undergraduate and had revered so deeply," she told Leyda. "They were being relegated to the past, to the dead white man camp, and there was an expectation that I, as a young woman of color, should despise them. But I couldn't. It wouldn't be true to myself to look at it that way, and that was one of the reasons I stepped away from academics in general—I just couldn't participate in that." She considered a career in publishing; in the late 1990s she had an unpaid internship at *Boston* magazine, where she was not encouraged to write.

The idea of becoming a writer was at first frightening. "Writing felt like such a bold thing to do," Lahiri told a reporter for *Writing* magazine (1 Apr. 2006), "I was almost afraid to even try. But when I read books such as *A Portrait of the Artist as a Young Man*, *Lolita*, and the works of Shakespeare, I wanted to know: How did these writers do what they did?" She had the opportunity to discover the answer when she received a fellowship to the Fine Arts Work Center in Provincetown, Massachusetts, for 1997–98. There she crafted the nine tales, loosely based on her own family, that would become her first short-story collection, *Interpreter of Maladies*.

## INTERPRETER OF MALADIES

Rarely does a first book receive the attention that Lahiri's did. *Interpreter of Maladies* earned her the 2000 Pulitzer Prize for fiction and the 2000 Hemingway Foundation/PEN Award, and *New Yorker* magazine named the collection the year's best debut. Not understanding that a first book was eligible for a Pulitzer, Lahiri was deeply surprised when she received the call from a publicity intern at her publishing company. She called her mother, crying, and told her it was all because of her parents that she won the award. "A lot of people ask me how I felt when I heard she won it," Tia Lahiri told Langer. "I tell them I felt as though I was holding a star in my fist. It was like I was reaching for something and a star came."

The success of Lahiri's first collection brought her into the spotlight, an uncomfortable place for her. While many in India were thrilled at her success, others criticized her for not portraying Indians in a more positive manner. Still others did not appreciate a woman who had not been born in India writing about the culture. She was variously considered not Indian enough and not American enough.

Lahiri shrugs off the attention. "I've never written for anyone other than myself," she told Teresa Wiltz for the *Washington Post* (8 Oct. 2003). "No matter what people say or expect, at the end of the day, they're not the one in the room with me, writing." She added, "I've always never loved anything more than sitting quietly in a room by myself, imagining things."

## MORE WRITING, MORE AWARDS

In 2003, Lahiri published her first novel, *The Namesake*. She told Edward Nawotka for *Publishers Weekly* (7 July 2003), "I found working on the novel both more forgiving and more demanding. I felt I could write and write and write—scenes, passages, things that went in or helped me understand the book, or maybe things that were just contributing. It let me move around more among different perspectives, but it was more overwhelming, because for every change I made in the novel, I had one hundred pages I would have to toss. It took all of these years to learn to work in that larger form."

Lahiri's guide while writing the novel was Thomas Hardy, the British writer whom she considers to be her favorite novelist, citing his sense of place, his ability to draw characters, and his economy of words. *The Namesake* earned numerous honors, including an entry on the *New York Times*' list of 100 Notable Books of the Year, and was a finalist for the Los Angeles Times Book Prize. It was adapted into a film in 2006.

Lahiri's second collection of short stories, *Unaccustomed Earth*, was published in 2008. It won the Frank O'Connor Short Story Award and the Vallombrosa-Gregor von Rezzori Prize. Lahiri is gratified by the response to her work; she told Felicity Wood for *Bookseller* magazine (4 Oct. 2013), "Being nominated for prizes is humbling; it's not something one expects so it's overwhelming. Whatever happens from either prize, it's already a wonderful recognition. . . . We have to be happy that books are being talked about and discussed."

## THE LOWLAND

Published in 2013, Lahiri's second novel, *The Lowland*, was shortlisted for both the National Book Award for fiction and the Man Booker Prize. Set in India and Rhode Island during the 1960s and 1970s, the story revolves around two brothers and two marriages. Lahiri wanted to understand the political movements that occurred during the years in which the novel's action takes place.

Lahiri worked on the novel for five years. She explained the plot's origins to Wood: "The starting point was both a family story and a political story. I heard about an execution that happened close to my paternal grandparents' house during the repression of the Naxolite movement in Calcutta, where two brothers were killed in front of their parents. I had an image of someone being killed, and I knew that in the real-life version they'd both been killed. So I started thinking about just one person, but then a brother entered into the dynamic and then the wife they both have in common."

## LITERATURE OF THE OTHER

When Lahiri's first collection of short stories appeared, a few other women of Indian descent, including Anita Desai, Chitra Banerjee Divakaruni, and Bharati Mukherjee, were publishing works on the Indian immigrant experience. Those women, however, had been born in India. Lahiri straddled both worlds, born in the West but frequently visiting Calcutta with her family. "A new generation of writers . . . were coming of age who were trying to be American or pass as American or not pass or whatever," she told Leyda, "but who didn't really have any other place to call home."

Lahiri is identified with the post-1965 generation, one of the children whose parents came to the United States in the wave of Asian immigration that followed the passage of that year's Immigration and Nationality Act. In 1960, only twelve thousand immigrants were from India; by 1970, that number had jumped to fifty-one thousand, and it has since continued to climb.

The post-1965 influx of immigrants meant a huge increase in interest in the immigrant experience and the nature of living between worlds. However, Lahiri does not like the term "immigrant fiction." "If certain books are to be termed immigrant fiction, what do we call the rest? Native fiction? Puritan fiction? This distinction doesn't agree with me," she told an interviewer for the *New York Times Book Review* (8 Sept. 2013). "Given the history of the United States, all American fiction could be classified as immigrant fiction. . . . From the beginnings of literature, poets and writers have based their narratives on crossing borders, on wandering, on exile, on encounters beyond the familiar. The stranger is an archetype in epic poetry, in novels. The tension between alienation and assimilation has always been a basic theme."

## PERSONAL LIFE

Lahiri became a United States citizen when she was eighteen. She lives in Brooklyn with her husband, journalist Alberto Vourvoulias-Bush, whom she married in Calcutta in 2001, and their children, Octavio and Noor. She and her husband read aloud to their children nightly. Lahiri also studies Italian and has begun reading to the children in that language. Her own reading follows a rhythm; in summers, she reads contemporary works, while during the winter she reads older literature.

## SUGGESTED READING

Lahiri, Jhumpa. "An Interview with Jhumpa Lahiri." Interview by Julia Leyda. *Contemporary Women's Writing* 5.1 (2011): 66–83. Print.

Lahiri, Jhumpa. "Highs and Lows." Interview by Felicity Wood. *Bookseller* 4 Oct. 2013: 26–27. Print.

Lahiri, Jhumpa. Interview. *New York Times Book Review* 8 Sept. 2013: 8. Print.

Lahiri, Jhumpa. "Pulitzer Winner Finds Much in a Name." Interview by Edward Nawotka. *Publishers Weekly* 7 July 2003: 49. Print.

Langer, Adam. "A Daughter's Journey." *Book* Sept.–Oct. 2003: 52–55. Print.

Wiltz, Teresa. "The Writer Who Began with a Hyphen." *Washington Post* 8 Oct. 2003: C1. Print.

## SELECTED WORKS

*Interpreter of Maladies*, 1999; *The Namesake*, 2003; *Unaccustomed Earth*, 2008; *The Lowland*, 2013

—Judy Johnson, MLS

# Donna Langley

**Born:** February 3, 1968
**Occupation:** Media executive

As chairman of Universal Pictures, Donna Langley has been the driving force behind such popular films as *Mamma Mia!* (2008), starring Meryl Streep; the Jason Bourne franchise, starring Matt Damon; and the films of comedy director Judd Apatow. After cutting her teeth at New Line Cinema, where she oversaw the wildly popular Austin Powers comedies of the late 1990s and early 2000s, Langley joined Universal Pictures in 2001 as the senior vice president of production. Langley has risen through the ranks as the film industry has undergone dramatic changes—a steep drop in DVD sales has translated into lower production costs. The financial finagling, taken up in earnest by Universal in 2013 when the company was sold to Comcast, is only a part of the job, Langley insists. Regarding Hollywood and the film industry, Langley admitted to Felicia Taylor for CNN (9 Oct. 2012): "There is a superficial side to it . . . We are all creating a fantasy after all, every day. That is what we do. But the people behind the scenes, they are people who are going to work every day . . . these are all people who are so passionate about what they are doing."

## EARLY LIFE AND CAREER

Langley was born in Staines, England, and raised on the Isle of Wight, located in the English Channel. Her parents, John and Ann Langley, still live in Newport. Langley is the only member of her family who was adopted. "It always made me feel really special," she told Taylor. "I felt like I was chosen." Growing up, Langley was a dancer and loved swimming and water sports. She attended Lake Middle and Carisbrooke High Schools in Newport and Kent College, where she studied art history. After graduating, she lived in London but was intrigued by tales of Hollywood—"a far-off place, in a distant land," she joked to the *Hollywood Reporter* (5 Dec. 2012). Langley had come of age loving films about social issues, such as Oliver Stone's *Salvador* (1986) and *A Dry White Season* (1989) about South African apartheid; so, in 1991, when she was twenty-two years old, she moved to Los Angeles to try her hand in the film business. Her intention, she told the *Hollywood Reporter* (7 Dec. 2011), was "to work in production somewhere," but her first job was not with a studio. She worked as an unpaid intern with a literary agency during the day and as the hostess at the swanky LA nightclub, the Roxbury, at night. The ultraexclusive club—which was memorably parodied by *Saturday Night Live* players Will Ferrell and Chris Kattan in the 1998 comedy *Night at the Roxbury*—catered to Hollywood elite, and through her job, Langley met Mike De Luca, a producer who was then the president of production at New Line Cinema and famous for his work on *American History X* (1998), *The Social Network* (2010), and *Captain Phillips* (2013). De Luca offered her a job at the film studio, where Langley started as an intern but quickly earned an assistant position. She continued to work her way up the ladder at New Line and considers De Luca one of her mentors. "The thing I admire about Mike is he's able to stay connected to his gut instinct," she told the *Hollywood Reporter*. "And his batting average is as good or better as the people doing more traditional number crunching."

Joe Scarnici/Getty Images North America

## NEW LINE CINEMA

As a junior executive at New Line, Langley was the driving force behind a certain script that other studios had passed on. She showed the script to her boss, and soon after, New Line began production on a film by *Saturday Night Live* comedian Mike Myers called *Austin Powers: International Man of Mystery*. A parody of the James Bond franchise, the film was released in 1997 and launched a franchise with recurring characters including the over-the-top Powers and his nemesis Dr. Evil (both played by Myers). The first Powers film was a success, and its sequel, *Austin Powers: The Spy Who Shagged Me*, was one of the highest grossing films of 1999. *Austin Powers in Goldmember* (2002) completed the trilogy. "It really was just such a tremendous sort of validation of my taste, in a way." Langley told CNN for a segment that aired October 9, 2012. "And that was first time that really happened to me."

## UNIVERSAL STUDIOS

In 2001, Langley moved to Universal Studios, becoming the senior vice president of production, in which capacity she reported to vice chairs Scott Stuber and Mary Parent. The first project she green-lighted was the Paul Greengrass drama *United 93* (2006) about one of the planes that was hijacked by al-Qaeda terrorists on the morning of September 11, 2001. The same year, she oversaw Alfonso Cuarón's dystopian thriller *Children of Men*, and in 2007, she cemented her relationship with Judd Apatow with commercial and critical hit *Knocked Up*. Of Apatow, Langley told Diane Garrett for *Variety* (30 July 2007), "I take zero credit for what Judd is doing. . . . I just get out of his way." The years 2007 and 2008 were two of the most profitable in Universal's history thanks to Langley, who also oversaw the thriller *The Bourne Ultimatum* (2007) and the musical *Mamma Mia!*, one of the studio's most profitable films ever.

Langley was promoted to president of production in 2005 and was named cochair in 2009, when Universal ousted both chairman Marc Shmuger (who was replaced by Adam Fogelson) and cochairman David Linde. At the time, Michael Cieply for the *New York Times* (24 Oct. 2009) reported that the shake-up was part of a larger trend in the industry toward fewer management positions in lean times. "The cuts have been part of Hollywood's general effort to reduce production as revenue, particularly from DVD sales, falls," he wrote. Five years later, in an interview with the *DGA (Directors Guild of America) Quarterly* in the summer of 2014, Langley confirmed the shift, saying that the industry had changed "radically." Studios rely on ticket and, more recently, video-on-demand sales to boost revenue. This change, she adds, is reflected in the amount of money studios are willing to spend to make a film.

Langley's subsequent years with the studio have garnered some major hits—most notably the Academy Award–winning adaptation of *Les Misérables* (2012), a horror flick called *The Purge* (2013), and *Fast and Furious 6* (2013). The year 2012 was the best year in Universal's one-hundred-year history, but Langley has also overseen a handful of duds that have cost Universal millions. The movie *Battleship* (2012), based on the popular board game, failed to live up to its hype and earned only a lackluster profit for the studio. Another film, *47 Ronin* (2013), a samurai flick starring Keanu Reeves failed to break even, and *R.I.P.D.* (2013), a comedy about undead cops fighting supernatural crimes starring Ryan Reynolds and Jeff Bridges, recouped only a tiny fraction of its $130 million production cost. To mitigate the inevitable box office bombs, Langley has a few highly anticipated upcoming projects. A new Jason Bourne movie is expected to be released in 2016, and Jurassic World, a sequel to the iconic 1993 Steven Spielberg film Jurassic Park, is slated for summer 2015. In 2012, Langley secured the film rights to the best-selling erotic novel Fifty Shades of Grey—the film is scheduled for a 2015 release.

## PROMOTION TO CHAIRMAN

In 2013, Philadelphia cable company Comcast bought NBCUniversal for $16.7 billion and hired Jeff Shell, a television executive with no film-production experience, to take over the business end of Universal Film Entertainment in September of the same year. Shell extended Langley's contract with Universal through 2017, expanding her position to include worldwide marketing and overseas production. Her cochair, Fogelson, was fired. As Brooks Barnes for the *New York Times* (26 Jan. 2014) put it, "Universal makes money, but not enough." In 2013, according to Barnes, the studio had an operating cash flow of $291 million on revenue of about $4 billion. "I'm sure there are detractors who wonder why I'm not gone, but I have a pretty unique ability to tune out a lot of the chaos," Langley told Barnes. "I keep my head down, and I do the work." Langley is not afraid to make big decisions, either. In October 2013, she fired James Schamus, the head of Universal's art-film centered Focus Features, just as the studio's *Dallas Buyer's Club* (2013) started gaining Oscar buzz. (The film won three Academy Awards including best lead actor for Matthew McConaughey and best supporting actor for Jared Leto.)

In her current position, Langley is one of only two women in Hollywood with the power to greenlight major movies. (The other is Amy Pascal, the cochair of Sony Pictures Entertainment and chairman of Sony Pictures Entertainment Motion Picture Group.) Still, her record of supporting women filmmakers has been inconsistent, and her argument for hiring an overwhelming number of male directors toes a familiar line. "In my own experience, when we have an open directing assignment of any kind, not just the big films, I would say it is the exception, not the rule, that there is a woman in the group of directors that we are interviewing," she told the DGA. Still, Langley and Universal have a few women-helmed projects slated for release in 2015 and 2016, including a film called *Unbroken*, based on the 2010 book by Laura Hillenbrand about Olympian Louis Zamperini who was taken prisoner in World War II, directed by Angelina Jolie. As for her interest in women's issues outside of the film industry, Langley told Jordyn Holman for *Variety* (7 Oct. 2014) that she works as a mentor to women leaders through the global Vital Voices mentorship program. In the summer of 2014 she traveled to Qatar and vowed to help the nonprofit organization boost their exposure in Hollywood circles.

## PERSONAL LIFE

Langley received Women in Film's Crystal Award for Excellence in Film in 2010. She is married to Ramin Shamshiri, an architectural and interior designer. They have two young sons, Paolo and Adello. Langley told Taylor that she is happy with her decision to put off having kids until after she was forty years old. "I think I am a better mother having done it a little bit later in life and having got to a point where my career was really on solid footing," she said. Langley and her family live in the Los Feliz neighborhood of Los Angeles.

## SUGGESTED READING

Barnes, Brooks. "Chairwoman of Universal Expands Her Portfolio." *New York Times*. New York Times, 26 Jan. 2014. Web. 10 Nov. 2014.

Cieply, Michael. "Scene Stealer: The Skinnier Look of Studio Management." *New York Times*. New York Times, 25 Oct. 2009. Web. 10 Nov. 2014.

Garrett, Diane. "Universal Exec Makes Daring, Diverse Choices." *Daily Variety* 296.21 (2007): A19. *Associates Programs Source*. Web. 17 Nov. 2014.

Holman, Jordyn. "Donna Langley Provides Resources and Mentorship to Women in Vital Voices Program." *Variety*. Variety Media, 7 Oct. 2014. Web. 10 Nov. 2014.

Taylor, Felicia. "Making It as a Female Movie Mogul in Hollywood." *CNN*. Cable News Network, 9 Oct. 2012. Web. 10 Nov. 2014.

Taylor, Felicia. "No Easy Answers." *DGA Quarterly*. DGA, Summer 2014. Web. 10 Nov. 2014.

—Molly Hagan

# Robert Lanza

**Born:** February 11, 1956
**Occupation:** Scientist

"I may be the only person who's had the [Catholic] Church, the pope, and a couple of presidents condemn my work," scientist Robert Lanza joked to Pamela Weintraub for *Discover* magazine (19 Aug. 2008). Lanza, who has also written about a cosmological theory called "biocentrism," is

Robert Lanza/Wikimedia Commons

a pioneer and longtime champion of embryonic stem cell research, a regenerative human therapy that could one day utilize cloned human stem cells to cure diseases. Lanza is the most public face of the controversial research, and his celebrity has made him the target of religious groups that criticize him for "playing God."

Despite a rough childhood, Lanza performed his first significant experiment at the age of fourteen; was awarded a Fulbright scholarship; and studied with scientific luminaries such as Jonas Salk, who discovered and developed the first polio vaccine, and B. F. Skinner, the famous Harvard behaviorist. In 2000 he became the first person to successfully clone an endangered animal, an Indian bison, and he developed a cross-species cloning technique that would allow scientists to bring back extinct species, such as the woolly mammoth, by modifying the DNA of closely related species. In 2011 he obtained FDA approval for a clinical trial in which human embryonic stem cells were transplanted into human patients with vision loss caused by degenerative diseases. In 2014 the experiment yielded unexpected positive results. Lanza has won a number of awards during his career, and in 2014 he was named one of *Time* magazine's hundred most influential people in the world. He has served as the chief scientific officer of biotech company Advanced Cell Technologies (ACT; now Ocata Therapeutics) since 1999.

## EARLY EXPLORATION AND THE CHICKEN EXPERIMENT

Lanza was born on February 11, 1956, and grew up in the gritty Roxbury section of Boston. As a child he saved money collecting and returning golf balls at a nearby club to send for a mail-order baby squirrel monkey that he saw advertised in the magazine *Field and Stream*. The animal was one of his few companions. His father was a professional gambler, and he did not get along with his mother, who often barred him and his four siblings from the house during the day, allowing them to return only for dinner and sleeping. Lanza's next-door neighbors, a woman named Barbara and her husband, Eugene O'Donnell, were much more of a family to him. Still, most of the time, Lanza was left to his own devices. He usually spent that time in nature. "I would go up in trees and catch little screech owls in their holes," he told Weintraub. "I'd go on long excursions trying to figure out how the universe worked. Even at that early age, I was in awe and wonder of the world."

In the Stoughton public schools, Lanza was placed in remedial classes—students were labeled A, B, or C, according to their aptitude for learning. Lanza was a C. However, his fifth-grade teacher recognized his interest in science and animals. She encouraged him to enter a project in the school science fair. He won second place, but more important, he gained confidence in his academic abilities. His neighbor Barbara taught him science in eighth grade and arranged for him to enroll in honors biology in high school, a class that was open only to A-level students. Lanza's resentful classmates accused him of receiving special treatment, and he was determined to prove them wrong. He set out to win the school science fair as a freshman—only seniors won the competition—with a project that used the genetic code, which had been cracked only three years before in 1966. His plan, he explained to Weintraub, was to alter the genetic makeup of an albino chicken to make it pigmented. His teacher thought the idea was crazy, but O'Donnell helped him gather the necessary components of the experiment—the chicken eggs and syringes and penicillin from the hospital. Lanza based his experiment on an article he found in the medical library at Harvard. In the end he won the state science fair and a slew of other awards. Over the course of his experiment, the crafty fourteen-year-old had wiled his way into the Harvard Medical School building and befriended Stephen Kuffler, then

chair of neurobiology at the university, and graduate student Josh Sanes, the future director of Harvard's brain center. The men helped Lanza repeat his experiments in a formal lab setting. He published the results in the science journal *Nature* in 1974.

## WORK WITH DR. CHRISTIAAN BARNARD

After high school Lanza enrolled in the University Scholars Program at the University of Pennsylvania in Philadelphia. As a university scholar, Lanza could take any class he wanted, even as an undergraduate. He began taking classes in the medical school in 1975, when he was nineteen. He became interested in heart transplants and contacted Christiaan Barnard, a South African surgeon who performed the first successful human-to-human heart transplant in 1967. Barnard invited Lanza to study in South Africa. "It was fascinating but horrific," he recalled to Weintraub. "Some of the heart transplant patients had run out of their immunosuppressive drugs. . . . Their bodies were rejecting the organs and they were dying with their families all around them." He returned to Philadelphia with a handful of papers he had authored with Barnard but a diminished interest in surgery. Heart transplants, a concept that had once seemed so earth-shattering, had become "conventional," he told Weintraub.

Lanza received his bachelor's degree in 1978 and his MD degree in 1983. After graduation he moved to Los Angeles, California, to reevaluate his life and the universe. This period of self-reflection later resulted in his theory called "biocentrism."

## CELLULAR BIOLOGY AND DIABETES

After a few years Lanza contacted Patrick Soon-Shiong, a professor at the University of California, Los Angeles (UCLA). Lanza wanted to find a cure for diabetes, and Soon-Shiong was working on one that involved transplanting insulin-producing cells called "islets." "The hurdles there were similar to those we faced with heart transplants: overcoming a shortage of tissue and preventing rejection," he told Weintraub. One of Lanza's first patients taught him an important lesson about transplants, Lanza recalled. The man had to have his pancreas removed, but instead of throwing away the glands, Lanza extracted insulin-producing cells and injected them back into the man's portal vein. The cells settled in his liver. "It made a lasting impression on me because what it meant was that if you could deliver a person's own cells, you would eliminate the risk of rejection, and you could give the patient insulin-producing cells without the need for insulin injections for the rest of his life," he told Weintraub.

In 1990 Lanza was approached by Bill Chick, the president of BioHybrid Technologies in Shrewsbury, Massachusetts. Though Lanza did not know it at the time, Chick, a lifelong diabetic, was dying. He hired Lanza to work at BioHybrid Technologies because he was interested in Lanza's ideas about encapsulating islet cells and thought that, if Lanza could perfect the method, it might save him. While Lanza was working on the project, the Roslin Institute in Edinburgh, Scotland, successfully cloned an adult sheep named Dolly. It was an epiphany for him, Lanza told Weintraub, explaining, "If you can create an embryo genetically identical to the adult—that is, a clone—you can harvest immune-compatible cells to replace any tissue you might want without fear of rejection." Lanza applied this revelation to his work with Chick. "My idea was to clone the sick individual, not for reproduction but for therapy," he told Weintraub. "The stem cells produced through this therapeutic cloning would, like other embryonic stem cells, be capable of developing into many cell types and serve as a repair system for whatever part of the body required replenishment at the time. You solve the rejection problem, and you have unlimited amounts of tissue." Lanza wanted to test his theory on Chick, but Chick refused.

## STEM CELL RESEARCH AND CLINICAL TRIAL

After Chick's death in 1998, Lanza was at a crossroads. He could leave Massachusetts and find work elsewhere, but he had already bought an entire island in Clinton and he did not want to leave. As fate would have it, Lanza, who was by this time interested in the medical possibilities of cloning and stem cells, discovered that ACT was down the road from BioHybrid Technologies. When he asked the company for a job, they accepted on one strange condition—they asked him to collect the signatures of all the Nobel laureates living in the United States who supported embryonic stem cell research. At the time it was unclear whether the National Institutes of Health would even allow the research that ACT and Lanza wanted to pursue. ACT was an agricultural company that had researched cloning animals. With Lanza, its new focus would be human therapy, and company officials knew that the shift would ruffle feathers. They were right. Lanza told Weintraub that, after he began working with ACT, he feared for his life. "At one point we had bodyguards here. There was a bombing up the street . . . I didn't think I would be alive for more than a few years."

Despite the constant threat—and a lack of funding thanks to the conservative policies of President George W. Bush's administration—the company made significant progress in their work. In 2011 Lanza and ACT gained FDA approval for a clinical trial for human patients with Stargardt disease, a hereditary condition, and age-related macular degeneration (AMD). For such patients, the trouble lies in their retinal pigment epithelium (RPE) cells. As RPE cells die, the person slowly goes blind. Lanza and his team obtained permission to cultivate RPE cells from embryonic stem cells. That July doctors at UCLA injected the first two patients with Lanza's RPE cells. The trial yielded the first-ever paper published concerning human embryonic stem cells transplanted into human patients. In October 2014 Lanza and his colleagues published a follow-up report in the science journal the *Lancet*. The article provided strong evidence for the efficacy of using stem cells to treat Stargardt disease and AMD.

"Our goal was to prevent further progression of the disease, not reverse it and see visual improvement," Lanza told Alice Park wrote for *Time* (14 Oct. 2014). "But seeing the improvement in vision was frosting on the cake." The success of the trial was one of the biggest science news stories of the year and a major breakthrough for stem cell research.

## BIOCENTRISM

In 2007 Lanza published an article called "A New Theory of the Universe" in *American Scholar*. In it, he outlined his own cosmological view of the world called biocentrism, a view that places consciousness and biology at its center. Lanza teamed with astronomer and author Bob Berman to write a book about biocentrism called *Biocentrism: How Life and Consciousness Are the Keys to Understanding the True Nature of the Universe* (2009). Biocentrism is the idea that observable reality is subjective—that each living organism is the center of its own "sphere of reality," as Lanza argues in his original essay. But, as the authors write in the book, biocentrism has much broader implications. "Life creates the universe," they write, "instead of the other way around." The theory is also a critique of modern physics, which, Lanza wrote, has lost its way in its attempts to "resolve its conflicts by adding and subtracting dimensions to the universe like houses on a Monopoly board." (Lanza was referring to the perceived inelegance of string theory.) Still, Lanza uses quantum mechanics, a theory in physics, to support his conclusions, which verge on the poetic. "The trees and snow evaporate when we're sleeping. The kitchen disappears when we're in the bathroom," Lanza writes. "The universe bursts into existence from life, not the other way around as we have been taught. For each life there is a universe, its own universe. We generate spheres of reality, individual bubbles of existence. Our planet is comprised of billions of spheres of reality, generated by each individual human and perhaps even by each animal."

## PERSONAL LIFE

Lanza lives alone on a ten-acre private island in Clinton, Massachusetts. His house is decorated with dinosaur fossils. Asked why, he told Emily Nathan for the London *Financial Times* (16 Jan. 2015), "You know how some people collect oil paintings, or watercolors? I just want to feel life. You look at something and it feels alive . . . and it reminds you that there's a lot more to life in the world than only us."

## SUGGESTED READING

Lanza, Robert. "Fighting for the Right to Clone." Interview by Pamela Weintraub. *Discover*. Kalmbach Publishing, 19 Aug. 2008. Web. 7 Apr. 2015.

Lanza, Robert, and Bob Berman. *Biocentrism: How Life and Consciousness Are the Keys to Understanding the True Nature of the Universe*. Dallas: BenBella, 2009. Print.

Nathan, Emily. "Controversial Cloning Pioneer Robert Lanza on His Private Island." *Financial Times*. Financial Times, 16 Jan. 2015. Web. 8 Apr. 2015.

Park, Alice. "Stem Cells Allow Nearly Blind Patients to See." *Time*. Time, 14 Oct. 2014. Web. 8 Apr. 2015.

—Molly Hagan

# Sergey Lavrov

**Born:** March 21, 1950
**Occupation:** Diplomat

Sergey (sometimes spelled Sergei) Lavrov is Russia's foreign minister, a role equivalent to the secretary of state in the United States. A career diplomat, Lavrov is known as a negotiator who "does not suffer fools," explained Timothy Heritage for *Reuters* (6 Aug. 2012) and generally does as he pleases. In 2003, when Lavrov was a Russian envoy to the United Nations (UN), he openly disregarded the UN's smoking ban at its headquarters in New York City and said that then Secretary General Kofi Annan "doesn't own this building." Despite his prickly persona, Lavrov seems to command a grudging respect from his international colleagues. "He is very smart. He also does know UN procedure very well. He can be very nice and practical," former secretary of state Madeleine Albright said of him, as quoted by Adam Taylor for the *Washington Post* (14 Mar. 2014), before adding, "And he can be the opposite."

Lavrov assumed his current office on March 9, 2004, after serving as Russian representative to the UN for ten years. He was reappointed as foreign minister in 2008 and 2012. Lavrov's distaste for American intervention overseas started during his time with the UN, and his fierce loy-

Mikhail Evstafiev/Wikimedia Commons

alty to Russia has made for a rocky relationship between the two countries. Most recently, Lavrov has clashed with the United States over Syria's bloody civil war as well as Ukraine's revolution and Russia's subsequent annexation of the former Soviet state. As Susan B. Glasser wrote in her profile of Lavrov for *Foreign Policy* (29 Apr. 2013), the "hard-drinking, hard-charging" Lavrov "has come, more than anyone perhaps aside from [Russian President Vladimir] Putin himself, to personify Russia's return to the world stage." Despite his combative demeanor, Glasser wrote that Lavrov's "relentless willingness to take on the United States globally, to challenge, whenever and wherever possible, America's view of itself as the indispensable power . . . has earned him admirers among his often more tactful counterparts."

## EDUCATION AND EARLY CAREER

Sergey Viktorovich Lavrov was born in Moscow on March 21, 1950. His father was Armenian and his mother was an ethnic Russian from Georgia. He attended the Moscow State Institute of International Relations (MGIMO) where he held the prestigious position of secretary of the Komsomol, the Leninist Young Communist League. He graduated with a degree in Asian Studies in 1972, after which he spent four years working for the Soviet embassy in Sri Lanka where he learned to speak Sinhalese. (He also speaks English and French.) In 1976 Lavrov returned to the Soviet Union to work in the Department of International Organizations of the Soviet Foreign Ministry. In 1981 he moved to New York City to work at the Soviet mission at the United Nations. Colleagues recall his brash intelligence but also his elaborate drawings during meetings. "He was a great doodler, but his mind was always spinning away," Charles A. Duelfer, former deputy head of the UN weapons inspectors program in Iraq in the 1990s, told David M. Herszenhorn and Michael R. Gordon for the *New York Times* (16 Sept. 2013).

After the fall of the Soviet Union in 1991, Lavrov served as Russia's deputy foreign minister from 1992 to 1994, and in 1994 he replaced Yuli M. Vorontsov as the Russian ambassador to the UN. In his role as ambassador, Lavrov vehemently opposed the 1999 NATO bombing of Serbia during the war in Kosovo, and more recently, Lavrov has voiced his opposition to any international recognition of a sovereign Kosovo.

In November 2002, Lavrov and the remaining UN Security Council agreed that Iraq should be given one final chance to account for its weapons of mass destruction (which were later determined not to have existed at all), and Security Council Resolution 1441 was issued stating that Iraq and its government must comply with the UN or face "serious consequences." The United States, with the support of the United Kingdom, invaded Iraq several months later in March 2003, claiming that the resolution gave them the right to do so. Russia and France disagreed, and the rift between the United States and Russia was further exacerbated. The ultimate failure of the United States in Iraq is, however, a favorite talking point for Lavrov.

## POST-COLD WAR RELATIONS WITH THE UNITED STATES

Glasser reported that Lavrov once discussed with former secretary of state Condoleezza Rice the night of the Soviet Union's dissolution and Mikhail Gorbachev sudden resignation as president on December 25, 1991. Lavrov remarked, "Just like that, fifteen separate states were born." As Rice explained to Glasser, Lavrov "didn't know what country he represented anymore." Rice applied that intense feeling of uncertainty to what she knew of Lavrov's character and that it was "a way to explain Sergei: He was intensely pro-Russian. And Russia was trying to find out where it fit after the Soviet Union." Lavrov, cognizant of the country's humiliating fall from power in the 1990s, began pursuing a new "Russian assertiveness," which Glasser suggested most often manifested itself in Lavrov saying no to proposals put forth by the United States. This proclivity to reject US-backed plans earned him the nickname, "Mr. Nyet," the same name that had been given to his Cold War predecessor, former foreign minister Andrei Gromyko.

In 2008 David Remnick, editor in chief of the *New Yorker*, suggested in an interview with Lavrov for the Council on Foreign Relations (24 Sept. 2008) that the United States and Russia had reverted back to an adversarial, Cold War relationship. Lavrov insisted that this is not the case; however, in response to President Putin's 2013 announcement that Russia's foremost endeavor in the world was "balancing," Glasser asked Lavrov, "What . . . are you balancing if not the United States?" Lavrov did not answer. Glasser points out, however, that in August 2008, Russia invaded the small former Soviet republic of Georgia. Georgian leaders had expressed sympathy with Western ideals and an interest in joining the European Union (EU) and NATO. Relations between the United States and Russia further soured when, as reported by Glasser, Lavrov suggested to Secretary of State Rice that Russia and the United States work together to overthrow Georgia's democratically elected president.

Lavrov, observers say, is driven more by pragmatism than idealism and by building Russia up rather than tearing the United States down (although he is not above the latter to serve the former). After the invasion of Georgia, the two countries agreed to "reset" their relationship. In an effort to symbolize the US commitment to starting over in its relationship with Russia, Secretary of State Hillary Clinton presented Lavrov with a gift of a "reset" button, but due to a botched translation, the button actually read "overcharged."

In 2011, during the surge of demonstrations and riots in the Arab world that was later dubbed the Arab Spring, Russia's UN ambassador Vitaly Churkin broke with the Russian tradition of "nyet" and abstained from a vote on a US-backed resolution to authorize a no-fly zone in Libya. Unfortunately, as Glasser explained, the hoped-for reset of Russian-US relations ended there. Lavrov furiously insisted that Russia had never supported US military intervention in Libya, and to prove his point, drew a hard line on Syria.

## CONFLICT IN SYRIA

Despite widespread protests from within Russia against the reelection of Vladimir Putin as president (after he served as Russia's prime minister), Putin was mysteriously swept into office in 2012 by an overwhelming portion of the vote. The fraudulent election and Putin's worrisome domestic policies (including his ban on "gay propaganda" as well as a ban on the adoption of Russian children by US families) made international headlines as Lavrov and Secretary of State Clinton negotiated an appropriate response to the escalating conflict in Syria. In 2011 and 2012, street protests fueled by the Arab Spring became an all-out civil war between antigovernment forces and the regime of President Bashar al-Assad. Benjamin Bidder for *Der Spiegel* (7 Feb. 2012) reported on the statement released by UN secretary general Ban Ki Moon that called Assad's violence against his own citizens "totally unacceptable" and that "no government can commit such acts against its people without its legitimacy being eroded." Lavrov hesitated to publically condemn Assad's regime, which fur-

ther dispelled any friendly relations with Clinton. "Over time it just stopped working," a senior US official told Glasser of the relationship. "It was part personal, part substance."

At a meeting of the UN Security Council in 2012, Russia and China vetoed a resolution that would impose sanctions on Syria, halt the delivery of Russian weaponry, and would allow for military intervention. Clinton resigned her post the same year and was replaced by former US senator John Kerry, who took up continued negotiations with Lavrov. In 2013, the two men brokered a tentative deal in which Syria would relinquish its chemical weapons to avoid an attack. The UN-led removal of Syria's chemical weaponry was completed in 2014, though there have been subsequent reports to the contrary. The conflict continues and is complicated by ISIS (Islamic State of Iraq and Syria) militants and the US-led airstrikes against them.

## PERSONAL LIFE

In February 2015, the Moscow arts magazine *Russkiy Pioner* (Russian Pioneer) published a series of Lavrov's poems that were inspired by the American Beat movement. The first poem, "One for the Road," takes place in New York City and was written in 1989. "One for the Road 2," was written in 1996. Lavrov has reportedly published three books of poems in Russia, and he was asked to write the official anthem for his alma mater, the Moscow State Institute of International Relations.

Lavrov and his wife have one daughter.

## SUGGESTED READING

Bidder, Benjamin. "Kremlin's Tough Top Diplomat: Russian Foreign Minister Is Nobody's Fool." *Der Spiegel*. Spiegel Online, 7 Feb. 2012. Web. 12 Feb. 2015.

Glasser, Susan B. "Minister No: Sergei Lavrov and the Blunt Logic of Russian Power." *Foreign Policy*. Graham Holdings, 29 Apr. 2013. Web. 10 Feb. 2015.

Heritage, Timothy. "Russia's Lavrov Perfects the Art of Saying 'Nyet.'" *Reuters*. Thomson Reuters, 6 Aug. 2012. Web. 23 Feb. 2015.

Herszenhorn, David M., and Michael R. Gordon. "Veteran Diplomat Fond of Cigars, Whiskey, and Outfoxing US." *New York Times*. New York Times, 16 Sept. 2013. Web. 10 Feb. 2015.

Lavrov, Sergey V. "A Conversation with Sergey Lavrov." *Council on Foreign Relations.* Council on Foreign Relations, 24 Sept. 2008. Web. 24 Feb. 2015.

Taylor, Adam. "Sergei Lavrov: The Russian Foreign Minister the US Loves to Hate." *Washington Post.* Washington Post, 14 Mar. 2014. Web. 10 Feb. 2015.

—Molly Hagan

# Jennifer Lee

**Born:** 1971

**Occupation:** Film writer, director

Relative to her experience, Jennifer Michelle Lee has made an incredibly outsized impact in film. In an industry where just four percent of directors are women and very few of those have blockbuster hits, Lee is the cowriter and codirector of *Frozen* (2013), Walt Disney Animation Studio's monster hit about the unbreakable bonds of sisterly love. By 2014, the computer-animated feature had generated more than $1 billion at the global box office and had become the highest grossing animated motion picture of all time. In addition to its commercial success, *Frozen* also won a pair of Oscars in 2014 for best animated feature film and best original song for the now classic "Let It Go."

*Frozen*'s success is a remarkable turn for Lee. The first female director at Disney, she came to film after a career in book publishing and to directing with only a few screenwriting credits to her name, including the 2012 animated Disney film *Wreck-It Ralph*. Since winning her Oscar, Lee has been asked to cowrite and codirect a sequel to *Frozen* and to write the screenplay for the beloved children's novel *A Wrinkle in Time* by Madeleine L'Engle. Lee, who in interviews frequently marvels at her own journey, believes that the best way for women to succeed in the film industry is by being able to do many things well. She told Terry Flores for *Variety* (10 June 2014), "My only advice would be to tackle the business from all sides. . . . Not meaning you have to do it all but really understanding all the angles and producing and working with actors. I think it makes fantastic connections and builds that collaboration."

Vera Anderson/WireImage

## EARLY LIFE AND EDUCATION

The younger daughter of Sav Rebecchi and Linda Lee, Jennifer Rebecchi (who now uses her mother's maiden name) grew up in Barrington, Rhode Island, in 1971. She and her older sister, Amy Leigh Kaiser, were very close growing up. When their parents divorced, the girls moved with their mother to East Providence, Rhode Island, where they attended East Providence High School. Both girls then studied at the University of New Hampshire. Kaiser earned a degree in education (and is now an English teacher at a high school in Chappaqua, New York), and Lee graduated in 1992 with a degree in creative writing.

Despite being close growing up, the sisters became somewhat estranged during their college years. They did not bond again until shortly after the death of Lee's boyfriend who was killed in a boating accident when she was twenty years old. Lee recalled to Sean Flynn for the *Newport Daily News* (17 Feb. 2014), "It's like I'd lost her, and then all of a sudden we kind of arrived at the same place together. And then from that moment on, she was like my champion. She was always there for me. . . . Having to lose each other and then rediscover each other as adults, that was a big part of my life."

The sisters moved to New York City in 1992 with the idea of getting teaching positions, but neither wound up in education at that point. Amy spent some time working in the Associated Press's accounting department while Lee worked as a graphic artist for the famed publisher Random House where she designed audiobook and DVD covers. Growing unsatisfied with her career, she applied in 2001 for and was accepted into the Columbia University School of the Arts graduate film program where she became particularly fascinated with independent films and the French New Wave films of the 1950s and 1960s. "We were very driven—because we were paying for it!" Lee recalled of her time at Columbia to Jill Stewart for *LA Weekly* (15 May 2013). "We knew hard work." Lee received her MFA in film from Columbia in 2005.

## EARLY CAREER

While at Columbia Lee met and became friends with fellow classmate Philip Johnston, through whom she would establish contacts in the film industry. She also began to earn a reputation as a writer of socially conscious screenplays. Her career was launched while still at Columbia when in 2004 she won top honors at the Columbia University Film Festival for her screenplay, *Hinged on Stars.* In 2006 Lee received her first film option, and the following year Leonardo DiCaprio's production company, Appian Way, optioned her next film, *The Roundup.* In March 2011, Lee received a call from Johnston asking her to come to Burbank, California, to help him complete the screenplay for *Wreck-It Ralph*, a computer-animated Disney movie about a video game villain who decides to break from his programming and become a hero. After completing work on *Wreck-It Ralph* in 2012, Disney executives, impressed with her work, asked Lee to stay on to help them adapt Hans Christian Andersen's famed story "The Snow Queen" into a computer-animated film. Unfortunately for the studio, the film had been stalled in development for some time. Lee began working with director Chris Buck to see if she could help adapt it; she quickly became completely enamored with the nineteenth-century tale.

## *FROZEN*

*Frozen,* as originally imagined, was more of an action-adventure story than it was a traditional Disney animated musical, so Lee began to work with the animators and the husband-and-wife songwriting team of Robert Lopez and Kristen Anderson-Lopez to reimagine the tale with more music and more comedic elements. Things began to click when the character of the Snow Queen evolved from being one of pure evil into a frightened girl unable to control her

frost-making powers. Disney creators knew they had a hit on their hands after Lee conceptualized the two main characters as sisters rather than enemies: Elsa, the tortured soul afraid of her powers, and Anna, the spunky younger sister unwilling to give up on her sister. As Lee rewrote the story and Lopez and Anderson-Lopez continued to hone the musical score, Lee was asked to co-direct the film alongside Buck as well as coauthor it. For Lee, the key dynamic in the film was the relationship between the two sisters and how their love for one another—not the romantic love of a handsome prince or a dashing hero—would help save the day. Lee told Nichole LaPorte for *Fast Company*: "[Anna] goes from having a naive view of life and love . . . to the most sophisticated and mature view of love, where she's capable of the ultimate love, which is sacrifice."

Although *Frozen* maintained many motifs from past Disney animated feature films—princesses and magic, handsome princes and goofy sidekicks—it reimagined many of these elements in bold new ways and provided many twists to what at first seemed like a traditional plot. The core change came from the dynamic between the two sisters. Their relationship provided the main emotional draw for viewers while animators sought to provide previously unimagined worlds inside a Disney film. Reviewing the film for the *New York Times* (26 Nov. 2013), Stephen Holden wrote, "[The film's] gleaming dream world of snow and ice is one of the most visually captivating environments to be found in a Disney animated film. There are moments when you may feel that you are inside a giant crystal chandelier frosted with diamonds."

*Frozen* impressed audiences of all ages and garnered numerous awards. In addition to its two Oscars, the film won the 2014 Golden Globe for Best Animated Feature Film, the 2014 British Academy of Film and Television Arts (BAFTA) award for best animated film, and the 2014 Critics Choice award for Best Animated Feature.

## UPCOMING PROJECTS

After the end of the awards season, Lee was an in-demand talent in Hollywood. She, Chris Buck, the songwriting team of Lopez and Anderson-Lopez, and all of the voice actors learned they would be reuniting to complete the sequel *Frozen Fever*, which is currently slated to be a short film and will feature new songs. The film is scheduled to debut in 2015 before Disney's live-action *Cinderella*. In addition to this, Lee plans to work on a new project with Buck.

As she told Flores, "We're actually going to start from scratch. It'll be something completely brand new. Those are our marching orders. Start over with what you're passionate about."

One of the things Lee is passionate about is adapting a screenplay for one of her favorite books from childhood, Madeleine L'Engle's *A Wrinkle in Time*, which is a sci-fi tale first published in 1962 about children who go off in search of their scientist father who is lost in time and space. Studio executives are reportedly enamored with Lee's take on the narrative, which is the first book in a five-book series and could lead to a new film franchise for Disney. While no director has been attached to the film, some in the media have speculated that Lee may direct the project as well. No release date for the film has yet been set.

Lee married Robert Joseph Monn in 1999, with whom she had a daughter, Agatha, in 2003. The couple later divorced.

**SUGGESTED READING**

Flores, Terry. "'Frozen's' Jennifer Lee Melts Glass Ceilings." *Variety*. Variety Media, 10 June 2014. Web. 3 Dec. 2014.

Flynn, Sean. "Is It Her Time to Shine?" *Newport Daily News*. Edward A. Sherman Publishing, 17 Feb. 2014. Web. 3 Dec. 2014.

Graser, Marc, and Dave McNary. "'Frozen' Director Jennifer Lee to Adapt 'A Wrinkle in Time' for Disney." *Variety*. Variety Media, 5 Aug. 2014. Web. 3 Dec. 2014.

Holden, Stephen. "From the Heat of Royal Passion, Poof! It's Permafrost." *New York Times*. New York Times, 26 Nov. 2013. Web. 3 Dec. 2014.

LaPorte, Nicole. "How 'Frozen' Director Jennifer Lee Reinvented the Story of the Snow Queen." *Fast Company*. Mansueto Ventures, 28 Feb. 2014. Web. 3 Dec. 2014.

Stewart, Jill. "Jennifer Lee: Disney's New Animation Queen." *LA Weekly*. LA Weekly, 15 May 2013. Web. 3 Dec. 2014.

**SELECTED WORKS**

*Wreck-It Ralph*, 2012; *Frozen*, 2013; *Frozen Fever*, 2015

—Christopher Mari

# Kawhi Leonard

**Born:** June 29, 1991
**Occupation:** Basketball player

San Antonio Spurs small forward Kawhi Leonard is considered one of the brightest young talents in the National Basketball Association (NBA). Since being drafted by the Spurs out of San Diego State University in 2011, the six-foot-seven Leonard has quietly grown into one of the best all-around players in the league. After showing gradual improvement in his first three NBA seasons, he broke through in the 2014 NBA Finals, when he earned most valuable player (MVP) honors as the Spurs won their fifth NBA championship.

A superior defender and versatile offensive threat, Leonard has long been regarded as the heir apparent to the Spurs' so-called Big Three of power forward Tim Duncan, shooting guard Manu Ginobili, and point guard Tony Parker. According to Ian Thomsen for NBA.com (31 Jan. 2015), Leonard is "the Spurs' best defender and as versatile as anyone on their team offensively."

**EARLY LIFE**

Kawhi Anthony Leonard was born on June 29, 1991, to Mark Leonard and Kim Robertson in Los Angeles, California. When he was one year

SD Dirk/Wikimedia Commons

old, his family moved to Moreno Valley, about an hour's drive east of Los Angeles. Leonard's parents divorced when he was five, after which he was raised primarily by his mother in Moreno Valley.

Despite his parents' divorce, Leonard remained close with his father, who owned and ran a car wash business in Compton, in southeast Los Angeles. His father ingrained in him the value of hard work and introduced him to sports. During the summer months, Leonard usually accompanied his father to work, helping him hand wash cars "until he could see his face in the reflection," Jeff Goodman wrote for Fox Sports (2 June 2014). "It was hard work," Leonard recalled to Goodman. "But I loved it."

Leonard carried his work ethic to basketball, which he started playing at a young age. He worked tirelessly to improve his shooting skills and kept in shape throughout the year by running up and down hills. Leonard's assiduousness helped compensate for what has been described as unimposing physical size and moderate athletic ability as a youth. As his uncle Dennis Robertson put it to Chris Mannix for *Sports Illustrated* (13 Nov. 2014), "I don't think anyone looked at him growing up and said, 'That kid is going pro.'"

**FINDING SOLACE AMID TRAGEDY**

During his freshman and sophomore years, Leonard attended Canyon Springs High School in Moreno Valley. As a freshman he was a standout wide receiver and safety on the school's football team, but he did not play basketball after missing tryouts. After his freshman year, Leonard quit football to focus solely on basketball. He played basketball at Canyon Springs for only one season before transferring to Martin Luther King High, in nearby Riverside, as a junior. "I believed I could play in the NBA," Leonard asserted to Mannix. "I was focused on that."

Leonard's basketball future was already looking bright when, on January 18, 2008, his father was shot and killed at his Compton car wash. Finding out the news while riding home from a high school basketball game, Leonard was devastated. "I felt like the world stopped," he told Goodman. On the day after his father's murder, Leonard scored seventeen points in a loss to rival Compton Dominguez. The murder, which was believed to be gang-related, remains unsolved, but Leonard has said that he has no desire to learn the identity of the killer.

Following his father's murder, Leonard found solace on the basketball court. Already a superb defender and rebounder, he worked hard to broaden his offensive game, spending all his time after school practicing drills and perfecting his shooting mechanics at an array of local gyms. "From Day One he was driven to be great," his high school coach, Tim Sweeney, noted to Mannix. "He already had all the intangibles. . . . He worked as hard as any player who came through here."

Leonard's hard work paid off. As a junior he drew interest from several schools, but none more so than San Diego State University. Leonard committed to San Diego State before the start of his senior season, during which he blossomed into an all-around talent. He averaged 22.6 points, 13.1 rebounds, 3.9 assists, and 3.0 blocks; led his team to a 30–3 record and the CIF-Southern Section Division I-AA title; and was named California Mr. Basketball. Despite being recruited by a number of the nation's top basketball programs, Leonard kept his commitment to San Diego State, which guaranteed him an opportunity to compete for a starting position.

**SAN DIEGO STATE**

Prior to arriving in San Diego, Leonard told his uncle that he would play two years of college basketball before going professional. His bold prediction proved true as he emerged as one of the top players in the nation.

During his freshman season in 2009–10, Leonard started thirty-three of thirty-four games and led the Aztecs in scoring (12.7 points per game) and rebounding (9.9 per game). He had an even more impressive sophomore campaign, averaging 15.5 points and 10.6 rebounds in thirty-six games. He helped lead the Aztecs to a school-record thirty-four wins and a second consecutive Mountain West Conference title, and he was the driving force behind the school's first National Collegiate Athletic Association (NCAA) Sweet Sixteen appearance. He was named a second-team all-American by the Associated Press and was a finalist for both the Wooden and Naismith Awards.

During his two years at San Diego State, Leonard separated himself from his peers with his relentless drive and "coachability." "What's rare about Kawhi is his work ethic and his desire to get better," San Diego State assistant coach Justin Hutson told Thomsen. "He listens to coaching and he applies it." Leonard's dedication was such that he would wake up each day at five o'clock in the morning to work out before class; on some occasions, he even brought his own lamps with him to illuminate the court when the gym lights were turned off.

## SAN ANTONIO SPURS

Staying true to his word, Leonard left San Diego State after his sophomore season to join the professional ranks. He was chosen as the fifteenth overall pick in the 2011 NBA Draft by the San Antonio Spurs, who acquired his draft rights after trading guard George Hill to the Indiana Pacers. Wanting to add a bigger body to their talented but aging and relatively undersized lineup, the Spurs traded for the six-foot-seven Leonard hoping he would play the small-forward position in their system, which emphasizes a team-first mentality and relies heavily on constant ball and player movement. "Kawhi had all the attributes we were looking for," Spurs head coach Gregg Popovich explained to Mannix.

Despite primarily playing power forward in college, Leonard immediately bought into the Spurs' plan for him and won over coaches with his willingness to learn. After the draft, he spent three days working with Spurs assistant Chip Engelland to iron out kinks in his shooting mechanics. Leonard's work with Engelland was interrupted, however, by the 2011 NBA lockout, which began one week after the draft and lasted 161 days. Undaunted, he continued to work out on his own and entered his rookie season with a much-improved shot.

During the abbreviated 2011–12 NBA season, shortened from eighty-two to sixty-six games, Leonard eased into a complementary role alongside the Spurs' veteran superstars Duncan, Ginobili, and Parker. He averaged 7.9 points, 5.2 rebounds, and twenty-four minutes in sixty-four games, starting in thirty-nine. He shot 37.6 percent from three-point range, a noticeable improvement from his 25 percent average in college, and he added a new dimension to the Spurs' with his defensive versatility. He was named to the NBA All-Rookie First Team and finished fourth overall in the NBA Rookie of the Year voting.

The Spurs compiled an NBA-best 50–16 regular-season record and won their third Southwest Division title in four seasons. They advanced to the Western Conference Finals but lost to the Oklahoma City Thunder.

## FUTURE OF THE FRANCHISE

Prior to the 2012–13 season, Gregg Popovich predicted that Leonard was "going to be a star" and would eventually become "the face of the Spurs," as quoted by Sean Deveney for the *Sporting News* (2 Sept. 2012). Popovich's foresight proved true as Leonard showed flashes of his "star" potential in his second NBA season, despite missing twenty-four games with a knee injury. In the fifty-eight games in which he appeared, Leonard saw his playing time increase to thirty-one minutes per game, as a result of injuries that limited Duncan, Ginobili, and Parker. He finished third on the team in scoring, averaging 11.9 points per game; it marked the first time that anyone other than one of the Big Three finished in the top three since 2003.

Leonard's play was pivotal in the Spurs winning a third consecutive Southwest Division title and advancing to the NBA Finals. The Spurs lost to the Miami Heat in a dramatic seven-game series. In the finals, Leonard averaged 14.6 points, 11.1 rebounds, and 2 steals, while regularly defending the Heat's superstar forward, the four-time MVP LeBron James, widely regarded as the toughest defensive assignment in basketball.

The Spurs felt Leonard's impact even more during the 2013–14 season, in which he recorded career highs in most statistical categories. In sixty-six games, he averaged 12.8 points, 6.3 rebounds, 2 assists, 1.75 steals, and 29.2 minutes, while shooting 52.2 percent from the field and 37.9 percent from three-point range. Regularly tasked with defending opposing teams' best players, Leonard continued to solidify his status as one of the league's best and most versatile defenders and was named to the NBA All-Defensive Second Team for the first time. "There are not many guys in this league who can defend multiple positions at a high level," Oklahoma City Thunder head coach Scott Brooks stated to Mannix. "He's one of them."

## 2014 NBA FINALS MVP

Leonard burst into the national consciousness during the 2014 NBA Finals. The Spurs finished with a league-best 62–20 record and advanced to face the Miami Heat in an NBA Finals rematch.

Despite having minimal impact in the first two games of the series, Leonard emerged as a star in the final three games after being encouraged by Popovich to be more aggressive on offense. He scored a career-high twenty-nine points in the Spurs' blowout victory over the Heat in game three. He followed that performance with twenty- and twenty-two-point outputs in games four and five, which the Spurs won in convincing fashion to capture their fifth NBA championship. "He's a great learner and super competitive, has a drive to be the best that's really uncommon in our league," Popovich said of Leonard after the Spurs' championship-clinching game-five win, as quoted by Associated Press (15 June 2014).

After averaging 17.8 points and 6.4 rebounds on 61.2 percent shooting in the series, while guarding James, Leonard was named the NBA Finals MVP. He became the second-youngest recipient of the prestigious award, behind only Magic Johnson. He also became one of six players in history to win the award without earning an all-star selection during the regular season.

Leonard entered the 2014–15 season hoping to take a leadership role with the Spurs. Despite being hampered early in the season by conjunctivitis and a hand injury, he continued to distinguish himself as the franchise's next leader. By the end of the regular season, in April 2015, he was leading the team with a career-high 16.5 points per game and the NBA with 2.5 steals per game. He will be a restricted free agent in the summer of 2015 but has expressed his desire to remain with the Spurs.

## PERSONAL LIFE

Following the example set by Duncan, Ginobili, and Parker, Leonard has exemplified the Spurs' team-first values both on and off the court. He is known for his quiet demeanor and selfless nature and for shunning the spotlight. He has won attention around the league for his extremely large hands, each of which measure more than eleven inches from thumb to pinkie. Leonard's hand size, coupled with his seven-foot-three wingspan, has helped him become one of the NBA's most disruptive defenders.

Leonard resides in San Antonio. During the off-season he holds a youth basketball clinic in his hometown of Moreno Valley.

## SUGGESTED READING

Goodman, Jeff. "Father's Memory Helps Drive Aztecs Star." *FoxSports.com*. Fox Sports Interactive Media, 2 June 2014. Web. 23 Mar. 2015.

Mannix, Chris. "Need He Say More? Kawhi Leonard's Evolving Game Speaks for Itself." *Sports Illustrated*. Time, 13 Nov. 2014. Web. 23 Mar. 2015.

Thomsen, Ian. "Time to Lead Fast Approaching for Soft-Spoken Leonard." *NBA.com*. NBA Media Ventures, 31 Jan. 2015. Web. 23 Mar. 2015.

Young, Jabari. "Spurs' Leonard through His Family's Eyes." *San Antonio Express-News*. Hearst Communications, 20 Sept. 2014. Web. 23 Mar. 2015.

—Chris Cullen

# Lawrence Lessig

**Born:** June 3, 1961

**Occupation:** Professor and political activist

Lawrence Lessig is an influential legal scholar and political activist known for his efforts to reform US copyright and campaign finance laws. A prominent faculty member at Harvard University, Lessig is also the cofounder of the Creative Commons nonprofit organization, which promotes an alternative copyright system. In 2014 he founded the Mayday PAC, a political action committee devoted to electing reform-minded legislators to battle corruption. Federal judge Richard Posner, a mentor of Lessig's, called him "the most distinguished law professor of his generation," as quoted by John Heilemann in *New York* magazine (30 May 2005).

Lessig's deeply held views—about the future of the Internet, copyright law, and government corruption—are often at odds with legal precedent and the prevailing attitudes of the political establishment, but that does not prevent him from steadfastly pursuing his goals. He confronts overwhelmingly large social problems with the mind of an academic but the idealism of an evangelist, and does not settle for token progress. "Lessig does not separate his intellect from his emotions," wrote Evan Osnos for the *New Yorker* (13 Oct. 2014). "When Lessig seeks a way to reorder the world to function better, he favors fundamental fixes."

## EARLY LIFE AND EDUCATION

Lessig was born on June 3, 1961, in South Dakota and grew up in Williamsport, Pennsylvania, in a religious and politically conservative family. As a young child Lessig sang in church and attended a summer camp for choirboys. Lessig was then invited to study at the school that ran the summer camp, the American Boychoir

School (then known as the Columbus Boychoir School) in New Jersey. Lessig was an excellent student—both musically and academically—and was eventually appointed head boy.

Lessig claims that he suffered sexual abuse at the hands of the school's music director, Donald Hanson. Although Lessig moved back to Williamsport to attend high school, he finagled a position on the Boychoir School's board of directors and had a hand in Hanson's forced resignation. Still, he kept his experience largely secret until 2002, when he represented a fellow former Boychoir student and victim and eventually helped overturn New Jersey's laws on the immunity of nonprofits in sexual abuse cases.

As a teenager, Lessig idolized his Republican father and was a member of the National Teen Age Republicans in high school. His interest in libertarian politics led him to run the campaign of a state senate candidate, an effort that failed. He attended the University of Pennsylvania with the aim of becoming a businessman, and earned a degree in economics and one in management from the Wharton School of Business in 1983. Lessig then entered Trinity College at Cambridge University in England, where he unexpectedly stayed for three years to study philosophy, graduating with a master's degree in 1986. His time abroad radically changed his outlook. The controversial policies of conservative British prime minister Margaret Thatcher helped temper Lessig's once staunchly right-wing views, but his sister Leslie told Steven Levy for *Wired* magazine (Oct. 2002) that the change was more significant than that. "He came back a different person," she said. "His views of politics, religion, and his career had totally flipped." However, the libertarian ideal of freedom remained an important concept to Lessig. "I still think I'm a libertarian," Lessig told Osnos, "It's just that I understand the conditions in which liberty can flourish."

When he returned to the United States, Lessig shifted his interest to law, and briefly studied at the University of Chicago Law School before transferring to Yale Law School, where he became especially interested in constitutional law. He earned his juris doctor in 1989, and subsequently clerked for Judge Richard Posner on the United States Court of Appeals for the Seventh Circuit, who became his mentor. "He was terrific, a tremendous worker who had a ferocious intensity," Posner told Levy. Lessig also clerked for Supreme Court Justice Antonin Scalia, where he was the conservative justice's liberal foil, in

Joi Ito/Wikimedia Commons

1990 and 1991. After passing the bar exam Lessig began teaching at University of Chicago Law School, where he studied political change in Eastern Europe.

## INTELLECTUAL PROPERTY IN THE INTERNET AGE

Lessig's conversion from scholar to cyberlaw evangelist began in the early 1990s. As a visiting professor at Yale University in 1995, he taught a class called Law and Cyberspace. He became fascinated by the developing Internet and its potential effect on the law—and vice versa. Recognizing that the field was largely unexamined, he began to focus on Internet law and theorized that restrictive coding had the potential to limit the otherwise near-total freedom of the Internet. Soon he was recognized as the issue's leading expert.

Lessig began writing a book about cyberspace law in 1996, when he accepted a fellowship at Harvard Law School. In 1997 he was appointed a professor at Harvard Law School as the leader of the Berkman Center for Internet and Society. In 1998, Lessig worked with Judge Thomas Penfield Jackson as a technical adviser on the antitrust case *United States vs. Microsoft*, and though he was eventually removed from the case it helped establish his expertise on intellectual property. Lessig published his book, *Code and Other Laws of Cyberspace*, in 1999, essentially laying the groundwork for so-called cyberlaw.

"*Code* was an academic book," Lessig told Levy. "There's an argument about how cyberspace is changing and how commerce will change cyberspace. And there's a frustration with libertarians who are oblivious to the sense in which it's regulatable. But it wasn't yet a movement." It would soon become a movement, however, one spearheaded by Lessig's increasing activism.

Lessig began to campaign against the Copyright Term Extension Act (also called the Sonny Bono Act), which was passed in 1998 and extended US copyright terms to prevent many works from entering the public domain. The law angered Lessig and other proponents of the public domain because it defeated their view of a copyright's actual purpose: to protect property only long enough to encourage innovation before giving way to free and equal access. According to Lessig, as paraphrased by James Surowieki for the *New Yorker* (21 Jan. 2002), the framers of the US constitution drew a distinction between physical property (things) and intellectual property (ideas). Lessig asserted that overprotection of copyrights allows corporations to monopolize artistic and intellectual culture—potentially destroying the fruitful atmosphere of innovation made possible by the Internet.

"It doesn't have to be like this," Lessig wrote of intellectual property rights in the digital era in an op-ed for the *Wall Street Journal* (11 Oct. 2008). "We could craft copyright law to encourage a wide range of both professional and amateur creativity, without threatening [an artist's] profits. We could reject the notion that Internet culture must oppose profit, or that profit must destroy Internet culture."

## CREATIVE COMMONS AND FURTHER ACTIVISM

In 2000 Lessig left Harvard to join the faculty of Stanford Law School, where he would found the Stanford Center for Internet and Society. In 2001, he cofounded an alternative, not-for-profit copyright system called Creative Commons. It was intended to allow creators of various types of media to obtain more flexible license for their work, allowing specific property rights to be maintained or waived. In this way creative works could be more easily shared, reused, and reworked, promoting the development of cultural content free of the control of established distributors such as the music industry or software companies.

Lessig published another book on intellectual property, *The Future of Ideas: The Fate of the Commons in a Connected World*, in 2002. The same year, he argued in the Supreme Court case *Eldred vs. Ashcroft*, an attempt to overturn the Sonny Bono Act, but lost, a setback that dimmed his belief that his goals were achievable. As he told Osnos, the conclusion he drew from the court's decision was that certain copyrights might never expire "so long as Congress is free to be bought to extend them again." Lessig began to become more involved in the activist movement, coining the idea of "Free Culture" and joining the boards of groups such as the Free Software Foundation (FSF) and the Digital Universe project. In 2006 he was also elected as a member of the American Academy of Arts and Sciences.

In 2007, due to the prompting of his computer programmer friend Aaron Swartz, a fellow Internet freedom activist, Lessig began to recognize a connection between the copyright issues he continued to struggle with and the influence of political corruption. Lessig respected Swartz and considered him like another son, so when Swartz challenged him—arguing that efforts against laws like the Sonny Bono Act would never succeed in the face of systemic government corruption—Lessig listened. "[I]t kind of terrified me to imagine myself spending the rest of my life tinkering on the margins of the small arguments," he told Osnos. By 2008 Lessig had made up his mind to sidetrack his copyright work in order to take on the political system.

## CAMPAIGN FINANCE REFORM

After briefly considering a run for political office, Lessig chose instead to pursue an activist campaign against government corruption. And instead of focusing on taking down corrupt politicians themselves, he positioned his work as a crusade to change the self-rewarding system that allows and enables their bad behavior on multiple cultural levels. Meanwhile, he returned to Harvard as the Roy L. Fruman Professor of Law and Leadership and the director of the Edmond J. Safra Center for Ethics in 2009.

Lessig formed the Change Congress organization with the goal of getting politicians to pledge to work to reform campaign finance laws. When that did not take off, he experimented with the idea of holding a new constitutional convention to combat what he saw as deep-rooted problems with the system of government. Throughout these projects he attempted to remain bipartisan: "The single most salient feature of the government that we have evolved is not that it discriminates in favor of one side and against the other. The single most salient feature is that it discriminates against all sides in favor of itself," Lessig wrote in his 2011 book *Republic, Lost: How Money Corrupts Congress—and a Plan to Stop It*.

In 2013, Swartz, who faced federal charges for illegally downloading millions of academic articles, committed suicide, an event that deeply affected Lessig. "I'm only now understanding exactly how crazy his death made me," Lessig told Osnos. On the one-year anniversary of Swartz's death, Lessig walked 190 miles across the state of New Hampshire to draw attention to campaign finance reform. His followers numbered only several dozen, but later the same year, he launched the Mayday PAC (political action committee) with former Republican political consultant Mark McKinnon. The PAC had the ironic purpose of raising money in order to fund efforts to eradicate money from politics. The group's aim is to support the election of reform-minded candidates and ultimately shape federal campaign finance policy. Its chosen candidates fared poorly in the 2014 congressional elections, though it hopes to play a more influential role by 2016.

## PERSONAL LIFE

Lessig met his wife, Bettina Neuefeind, a public-interest lawyer, at the University of Chicago. The couple has three children: Tess, Teo, and Willem.

## SUGGESTED READING

Heilemann, John. "The Choirboy." *NYMag.com*. New York Media, 30 May 2005. Web. 16 Mar. 2015.

Houdek, Alesh. "Has a Harvard Professor Mapped Out the Next Step for Occupy Wall Street?" *Atlantic*. Atlantic Monthly, 16 Nov. 2011. Web. 16 Mar. 2015.

Lessig, Lawrence. "In Defense of Piracy." *Wall Street Journal*. Dow Jones, 11 Oct. 2008. Web. 16 Mar. 2015.

Levy, Steven. "Lawrence Lessig's Supreme Showdown." *Wired*. Condé Nast, Oct. 2002. Web. 16 Mar. 2015.

Osnos, Evan. "Embrace the Irony." *New Yorker*. Condé Nast, 13 Oct. 2014. Web. 16 Mar. 2015.

Surowiecki, James. "Righting Copywrongs." *New Yorker*, Condé Nast, 21 Jan. 2002. Web. 16 Mar. 2015.

—Molly Hagan

# Jenny Lewis

**Born:** January 8, 1976
**Occupation:** Musician

Unlike many child actors, who are never able to top their childhood success, Jenny Lewis switched from acting to pursuing a musical career in the 1990s and has since become a beloved indie musician. She is celebrated by her fans for her confessional, soul-searching songwriting and her polished yet unpredictable pop music. She first gained attention as the lead singer and contributing songwriter for Rilo Kiley, a band she cofounded with her then boyfriend Blake Sennett, before pursuing other projects and a solo career. She produced three critically revered solo albums and worked in a duo, Jenny and Johnny, with her longtime boyfriend, Johnathan Rice. "Jenny is a great record maker," Lenny Waronker, the Warner Bros. Records executive who also helped with her third solo album, *The Voyager*, told Matt Diehl for Billboard (28 July 2014). "She's more than a voice and a good songwriter; she's a big musical brain capable of almost anything. She's always going to make something special, real and a little unexpected."

## EARLY LIFE

When Jenny Lewis was born in Las Vegas, Nevada, in 1976, her mother, Linda, and father, Eddie Gordon, were working as nightclub performers in an act called Love's Way. Because of their parents' hectic road schedule, she and her sister spent much of their time living in hotel rooms and being supervised by a babysitter who also worked as a female Elvis impersonator. But things soon changed. Lewis recalled in an interview with Kelly McGivers for NPR (19 July 2014): "My parents divorced when I was three years old. . . . The band broke up and the marriage dissolved, and my mother, my sister and I moved to Southern California. And I didn't see my dad a lot growing up; he was on the road a lot. I'd see him every couple years."

Lewis's unusual and often difficult childhood and family background would become a major influence on her personality and career.

pinkbelt/CC BY 2.0

Her mother, herself the child of a dancer and a vaudeville performer, moved with her daughters to Van Nuys, in the San Fernando Valley. She worked as a waitress because she could not find any theatrical work. Unable to make ends meet, the family soon found themselves on welfare. Their fortunes changed, however, when a talent agent spotted the redheaded Lewis at her preschool and offered to represent her as a child actor.

### WORKING AS A CHILD ACTRESS

Represented by the noted children's agent Iris Burton, who also guided the early careers of actors Fred Savage and brothers River and Joaquin Phoenix, Lewis soon found herself working steadily, in commercials for products like Jell-O and Corn Pops, as well as in minor roles on such hit television shows as *The Golden Girls*, *Growing Pains*, *Roseanne*, *Baywatch*, and *Mr. Belvedere*. She also acted in feature films like *The Wizard* (1989), *Troop Beverly Hills* (1989) and *Pleasantville* (1998). She quickly had become the breadwinner of the family, something she realized at an extraordinarily young age. "Eight years old," Lewis said to Jeff Himmelman for the *New York Times Magazine* (24 July 2014). "I remember the moment. That's a pretty big thing for a kid to realize. And I remember the power in that." Income from her acting allowed the family to purchase two homes in California,

one in Sherman Oaks, the other a townhouse in North Hollywood.

Through her teen years Lewis lived the life of a child actor, both sheltered and privileged. She was tutored on the sets and spent time hanging out with fellow child actors like Corey Haim, who introduced her to hip-hop music through a mix tape with the Beastie Boys on one side and Run-D.M.C. on the other. Because she earned the family's income, she found she could do whatever she wanted, even as a teenager, so long as she was able to perform. Despite going through a wild period, she enjoyed acting very much and later would claim it helped prepare her for her eventual career as a musician. But she also found the parts she was getting were extremely limited. "I was the best friend," she explained to Himmelman. "I was the friend, forever. I wanted the big, juicy roles, and they didn't come to me."

### RILO KILEY

Before long, Lewis came to realize that music was her true calling, and singing her passion. Lewis told Himmelman for the *New York Times* (24 July 2014) of her musical influences as a teenager: "I felt like hip-hop was my music, it was like my outsider music . . . but then my mom started answering our phone, 'Yo, what's up.' She was hearing me talk to my friends. I was like, 'No, mom, don't cop the hip-hop talk.' I was like, Wait, I've got to find something else, because my mom is starting to get into A Tribe Called Quest, and this is weird. So then I started listening to indie rock, basically." An early outlet came when Lewis formed her own high school band, a Jimi Hendrix cover group called Soulfish, in which she was the lead singer. Meanwhile, her relationship with her mother deteriorated, leading to the loss of the properties and wealth she had accumulated through her acting career.

When she was seventeen, Lewis met another former child actor, Blake Sennett, with whom she began writing songs. The two also dated, maintaining a volatile but productive relationship. In 1998 they formed a band, Rilo Kiley, along with Pierre de Reeder and Dave Rock, and began pursuing music seriously. In 2001 Rock was replaced by Jason Boesel and the band released its debut full-length studio album, *Take-Offs and Landings*. Lewis and Sennett's romantic relationship ended around the time their second album, *The Execution of All Things* (2002), was released, but they continued to tour and record together.

As Rilo Kiley began to make a name for themselves among indie rock fans, Lewis also branched out with other collaborations. Most notably, she joined the group The Postal Service, led by indie star Ben Gibbard of Death Cab for Cutie. The group's debut album, *Give Up*, would go on to sell more than a million copies and be certified platinum after its release in 2003. Lewis began to attract attention as a star in the making, and she took on a more prominent role as the lead figure in Rilo Kiley, handling the majority of the vocals after previously splitting the role with Sennett. The band's third album, *More Adventurous* (2004), was a creative step forward and brought more mainstream attention. As a group, Rilo Kiley soon became critically acclaimed as indie rock artists. Their music was featured on numerous television shows, including in episodes of *The O.C.*, *Buffy the Vampire Slayer*, *Grey's Anatomy*, *Weeds,* and *Dawson's Creek*, as well as in several films. Although tensions within the band began to surface, Lewis acknowledged the importance of their work and its influence on her. "Through my partnership with Blake, I found a voice within myself that I didn't know I had," she told Himmelman. "It sounds kind of cheesy, but I figured out who I was."

### RABBIT FUR COAT AND ACID TONGUE

Despite being the lead singer and a contributing songwriter for Rilo Kiley, Lewis felt trapped within the group's dynamic. In 2006 she released her first solo album, *Rabbit Fur Coat* (supported by the musical duo the Watson Twins), in part to prove that she could do something on her own after Sennett made a record under his own name. Although the album was not as great a commercial success as *Give Up*, it proved popular in indie circles and outperformed Rilo Kiley's records on the charts while demonstrating her abilities as a singer and songwriter of music written in the gospel and Southern styles. Meanwhile, Rilo Kiley released their major label debut, *Under the Blacklight* (2007), before going on hiatus. It would prove to be their last album.

*Rabbit Fur Coat*'s success and Rilo Kiley's break enabled Lewis to put together a follow-up solo record, *Acid Tongue* (2008). It featured a string of special guests, including Elvis Costello and Chris Robinson of the Black Crowes, as well as her father, with whom Lewis reestablished a relationship. He had been playing in lounges in Alaska when Lewis resumed contact with him and asked him to work on her album. She was able to forgive him for not being around during her childhood. Also at work on that recording was her boyfriend, Johnathan Rice, with whom she would go on to record *I'm Having Fun Now* (2010) as Jenny and Johnny. *Acid Tongue* received even better press than her solo debut. Writing for the *New York Times* (29 Sept. 2008), Jon Caramanica called it a "jaunty, loose-limbed follow-up," and noted that "Ms. Lewis, also the frontwoman for Rilo Kiley, is unwrapped here, emboldened in her songwriting and more flexible in her voice."

### THE VOYAGER

Although Lewis was carving out a solo career for herself, she would not release another album until 2014. This was due in large part to the life changes she faced in the interim: her father died in 2010 and Rilo Kiley officially broke up in 2011. During this period she also began suffering from insomnia for the first time in her life, at one point not sleeping for five nights in a row. She found it difficult to write about her father's death as well as the other emotional turmoil she was experiencing. It was only with the help of Ryan Adams, a singer-songwriter, musician, and producer well known for his roots-rock influences, that Lewis was able to complete work on her third solo album, *The Voyager* (2014). In order to ensure that Lewis would not tinker with her work too much, Adams told her not to listen to the music she had just recorded but to push on to the next take or the next song. Along the way he also gave her some songwriting advice. "We all dug in," Adams told Diehl. "Past the point where I press 'Record,' my job is to get people excited. Jenny was very much ready for that ride. Her songs were horses; we just kicked down the fence and watched them blast off across the horizon."

Remarkably, after all the insomnia and writer's block Lewis had endured, they completed work on the album in just a week and a half at Sunset Sound studio in Los Angeles. Also at work on *The Voyager* were Beck, who produced the single "Just One of the Guys," Benmont Tench of Tom Petty and the Heartbreakers, Lou Barlow of Sebadoh and Dinosaur Jr., the Watson Twins, and a number of other musicians, including Johnathan Rice. Once again Lewis's efforts were met with critical praise, with reviewers applauding the album's growth beyond the rootsy sounds of her previous solo releases as well as the thoughtful lyrics.

## SUGGESTED READING

Anderson, Kyle. "Jenny Lewis." *Entertainment Weekly* 8 Aug. 2014: 68. Print.

Caramanica, Jon. "Critics' Choice; Love or Die: Will We Ever Learn? Jenny Lewis—'Acid Tongue'." *New York Times*. New York Times, 29 Sept. 2008. Web. 7 Aug. 2015.

Diehl, Matt. "Jenny Lewis on Rocking Out, Ryan Adams and Saying Goodbye to Rilo Kiley." *Billboard*. Billboard, 28 July 2014. Web. 7 Aug. 2015.

Himmelman, Jeff. "Could Jenny Lewis Have Been a Hip-Hop Star If Her Mom Hadn't Said 'Yo' So Much?" *New York Times*. New York Times, 24 July 2014. Web. 7 Aug. 2015.

Himmelman, Jeff. "The Jenny Lewis Experience." *New York Times Magazine*. New York Times, 24 July 2014. Web. 7 Aug. 2015.

McEvers, Kelly. "Rainbow in the Dark: Jenny Lewis on Staring Down Sadness." *NPR Music*. NPR, 19 July 2014. Web. 7 Aug. 2015.

## SELECTED WORKS

*Take-Offs and Landings* (with Rilo Kiley), 2001; *More Adventurous* (with Rilo Kiley), 2004; *Rabbit Fur Coat* (with the Watson Twins), 2006; *Acid Tongue*, 2008; *I'm Having Fun Now* (with Jenny and Johnny), 2010; *The Voyager*, 2014

—Christopher Mari

# Patricia Lockwood

**Born:** April 27, 1982
**Occupation:** Poet

Patricia Lockwood has published well-received collections of poetry, in addition to poems published individually in literary journals. However, her fame and her following is largely the result of her innovative use of the social media platform Twitter, which she joined in 2011 and where she gained more than thirty thousand followers. She has even been called the poet laureate of Twitter. As Adam Plunkett wrote for *New Yorker* (29 May 2014), "She's made for the medium. It rewards her particular talents for compression, provocation, mockery, snark."

Many of Lockwood's Twitter followers go on to read her other poetry, which is considerably more complex than a brief Twitter post, propelling her to the forefront of a wave of poets breaking new ground and bringing poetry to new audiences. Most notably, her prose poem "Rape Joke," published online in 2013, became a viral sensation and catapulted her to widespread recognition. As Lockwood told Jesse Lichtenstein for *New York Times Magazine* (28 May 2014), "The idea about readers being too lazy to read poetry—they just need an in, a voice they can trust."

## EARLY LIFE

Lockwood was born in 1982 and lived in the Midwest during her childhood. Her father, Greg Lockwood, married her mother, Karen, when they were teenagers. Greg served in the Navy on a nuclear submarine, where he became deeply religious. He became a Lutheran minister before converting to Catholicism, eventually becoming a priest despite being married. This unusual religious background, among other family quirks, would significantly shape Lockwood's early years. As she told Lichtenstein, "Catholicism is very beautiful. When your father is a priest, it's invested with extra authority, and your father is invested with extra authority." Her father's role as priest gave her a sense of it being natural to perform publicly. As a teenager, Lockwood belonged to "God's Gang," a Christian youth group whose members sometimes spoke in tongues.

Lockwood's family moved often around the St. Louis and Cincinnati areas during her childhood; she attended six different Catholic schools. By the time Lockwood was in fourth grade and writing haiku, her mother intuited that she would become a writer. As a result of the frequent moving, Lockwood decided in eighth grade to distinguish herself with humor, while also beginning to write seriously. By the time she was sixteen, she was at work on a manuscript attempting to connect Roman Catholicism to Greek myths. Also around this time she lost her faith.

Although she had planned to attend St. John's College in Annapolis, Maryland, Lockwood did not attend college at all. Her father told her the Christmas before she planned to go that they could not afford to send her. Rather than attempt to get financial aid or apply elsewhere, she got a short-lived job at a bookstore and started posting her poetry online.

Lockwood explained the impact of her lack of higher education to Lichtenstein, suggesting that it allowed her to focus exclusively on honing her skill with words: "If you looked at my brain, it would be like those taxi drivers who have one huge lobe that just contains directions, except for me it would be metaphors. I felt like I had a freak ability." In addition, she viewed not attending college as a way to extend her time of reading anything she wanted to read, without being bound by a curriculum. She followed her own interests and instincts for learning.

## THE POWER OF TWITTER

Lockwood's writing began to attract attention on poetry message boards, including from fellow amateur writer Jason Kendall. The two began corresponding, eventually met, and were married within two years, when Lockwood was twenty-one. They moved in together and supported each other's efforts to begin literary careers. Lockwood wrote a novel, which attracted some interest from significant New York City literary agents, establishing her first contacts in the publishing world.

However, the book's difficult subject matter—allegedly involving incest—meant it was never released. Lockwood turned to other projects. She read and wrote prodigiously while Kendall, who set aside his own writing to support her talent, earned money at newspaper jobs. The couple moved frequently, while constantly sending poems to various journals. Eventually they began to be accepted by publications such as *Poetry* and *The New Yorker*, slowly raising Lockwood's profile.

Lockwood opened a Twitter account in 2011, and by her own admittance did not fully understand the platform at first. But within weeks she had developed a comedic style of blurring the lines between social media and poetry that would become her signature. Around the same time a scandal was building around politician Anthony Weiner over his sending sexual material via text message, and the term "sexting" (a combination of sex and texting) was born. Lockwood took the idea and began a long-running series of humorous, absurdist sext poems published on Twitter.

She used the sext form to make fun of the sexualization of women in the larger culture and establish a surrealist viewpoint. "I write tweets pretty quickly, because the longer you work over a tweet, the worse it is," Lockwood told Lauren O'Neal for *Rumpus* (3 Jan. 2014). "If the elements don't arrive at you all at once and lock themselves into place with an audible and satisfying *snap*, a lot of times those pieces don't *want* to fit." One of the additional advantages of publishing online, she found, was that people could respond in real time—feedback and fandom were immediate. She soon had thousands of followers, including many teenagers just beginning to be exposed to poetry and literature.

## *BALLOON POP OUTLAW BLACK*

In 2012 Lockwood's first poetry collection, *Balloon Pop Outlaw Black*, was published. She considered it a book of poems meant to be seen and read on the page, rather than to be read aloud. It placed on *The New Yorker*'s best books list that year; the following year it was the best-selling small press poetry book by a living poet. Much of the collection is concerned with the cartoon character Popeye, whom Lockwood thought of as a pictograph, instantly recognizable.

Lockwood described the collection to Chris Randle for *Hazlitt* (9 January 2013) as "my crazy book. That was a book that I just sort of sat down and over a year-and-a-half period just blazed out. I think that everyone has a crazy book where they're too isolated, they don't have enough money, and they're in a weird small dark apartment, and they're not going outside enough, and they're just every morning going to the computer and blazing out this book." One unusual influence during the writing of the poems for the collection was the work of Laura Ingalls Wilder. Lockwood was struck by Wilder's attention to details and to descriptive passages, for example noting instructions for how to build a house. That sequencing of construction directly inspired one of the collection's poems, "The Cartoon's Mother Builds a House in Hammerspace."

Lockwood further learned the power of social media when Kendall, at age thirty, needed cataract surgery on both eyes, which the couple couldn't afford. On the advice of friends, Lockwood put up a PayPal account linked to her Twitter feed, where she explained the $10,000 shortfall between the cost of the surgery and what insurance would cover. Within twelve hours, the money was pledged by her fans. Lockwood was stunned.

Kendall's five surgeries left him slow to heal and the couple without steady financial support. They returned to Kansas City to live with Lockwood's family, and Lockwood focused attention on her next project. As with the sexts, controversial current events would provide a spark, along with her nonstop wit. "I'm verbally incontinent—anything just pours out of me," she told Lichtenstein. "My father's that way. He doesn't worry about it. My mother does. I got both. I say just the worst things the English language is capable of, and then later on I lie awake at night thinking, Oh, Tricia, you've done it again."

## "THE RAPE JOKE" AND *MOTHERLAND FATHERLAND HOMELANDSEXUALS*

In 2012 Lockwood began writing a poem based on her own experience of rape by her then boyfriend at the age of nineteen. However, she filed the poem away unpublished. Then the stand-up comedian Daniel Tosh did a piece on rape jokes, igniting a widespread debate about rape and humor and inspiring Lockwood to finish her work, which she titled "Rape Joke." When it was published in July 2013 on the website *The Awl* it was met with immediate acclaim for the way it invokes both the absurdity of joking about rape and actual humor at the same time. Lockwood tweeted a message to her Twitter followers, "The real final line of 'Rape Joke' is this. You don't ever have to write about it. But if you do, you can write about it any way you want."

The poem cemented Lockwood's growing reputation—it was reprinted in the 2014 edition of *Best American Poetry*—and prompted an outpouring of responses on the Internet, as well as many personal messages from women who had also experienced rape. The *New York Times* invited Lockwood to participate in a panel with other writers and artists on the subject of social issues. During the discussion, Lockwood responded to the question of obligation to address social issues in work, saying, "I would never tell artists that they had to address social issues in their work. . . . Tell them, instead, that these questions are difficult, that the story is missing something without them, that they are another dimension, and then see what happens."

Lockwood's second poetry collection, *Motherland Fatherland Homelandsexuals*, was released in June 2014 and contains "Rape Joke." The *New York Times* named it as one of its one hundred notable books of 2014. In contrast to the first book, it included poems written to be performed aloud. It also included a more open exploration of the subject of sex. It made a difference in how Lockwood was viewed and written about, which initially surprised her. As she told Hilary Lawlor for *Electric Literature* (18 July 2014), "I'm seen in a much more gendered way. More specifically, like a young sexual poet, which is really funny to me, actually, because what I was doing in that book was following a theme."

In a starred review, *Publishers Weekly* (28 April 2014) stated that Lockwood "continues to develop a poetics that interrogates those categories to which societies pledge allegiance: nation, gender, nature, and sexuality." Lockwood herself voiced her desire to speak to a new generation of diverse readers, stating during the *New York Times* panel that "there is a specific chill that outsiders, women, minorities experience from books their whole lives: a frost, a separation, a pane of glass. I felt a sudden fierce desire to not contribute to that."

## PERSONAL LIFE

Lockwood met Jason Kendall when she was nineteen and he was twenty; they were married when she was twenty-one. Lockwood rarely drives, claiming that she is not a safe driver. She considers herself a slow reader and a slow writer, assets giving her the ability to carefully consider words and their relationships to each other.

## SUGGESTED READING

Lichtenstein, Jesse. "The Smutty-Metaphor Queen of Lawrence, Kansas." *New York Times Magazine*. New York Times, 28 May 2014. Web. 6 Aug. 2015.

Lockwood, Patricia. "The Rumpus Interview with Patricia Lockwood." By Lauren O'Neal. *Rumpus*. Rumpus, 3 Jan. 2014. Web. 6 Aug. 2015.

Plunkett, Adam. "Patricia Lockwood's Crowd-Pleasing Poetry." *New Yorker*. Condé Nast, 29 May 2014. Web. 6 Aug. 2015.

"Race, Class, and Creative Spark." *New York Times*. New York Times, 27 Nov. 2014. Web. 6 Aug. 2015.

—Judy Johnson

# Mia Love

**Born:** December 6, 1975
**Occupation:** Politician

Mia Love made history in 2014 when she became the first black female Republican to be elected to Congress. The daughter of immigrants fleeing political violence in Haiti, she is also the first Haitian American to be elected to Congress. She has also received attention for her Mormon faith and her steadfast opposition of "big government," placing her as an upcoming Republican star for many conservatives.

Love first rose to prominence during an unsuccessful run for Congress in 2012, during which she gave a notable speech at the Republican National Convention. As her national profile grew, she increasingly became a polarizing figure. Many Republicans held her as a counterargument to allegations that their party appealed exclusively to white men, while many Democrats criticized her views. Yet even as Love gave rise to many conversations about race, gender, and politics, she remained committed to her goals. As she wrote for Utah's *Deseret News* (1 Mar. 2015), "Instead of looking to Washington, we need to look within. It's time for Washington to trust the American people." She elaborated, "And we, in turn, should use the opportunity to advance the conservative principles that have lifted more people out of poverty, fueled more freedom, and driven more dreams than any other set of principles in the history of the world."

## EARLY LIFE AND EDUCATION

Love was born Ludmya Bourdeau on December 6, 1975, in Brooklyn, New York, to a Haitian couple who had recently come to the United States to escape the violence of Haiti's dictatorship under the Duvaliers. Her parents left Haiti with nothing more than ten dollars, and it was only after Love was born that the whole family gained US citizenship under the immigration law of the time. Love explained her parents' experience of the American dream to Ross Winston for *Newsweek* (29 Oct. 2014), claiming that "when they finally became US citizens, they had studied the Constitution, American history, they learned the English language. And when they pledged allegiance to the American flag for the first time, they meant every word of it and understood what they were saying." That reality later shaped Love's ideas on immigration.

The family moved to Norwalk, Connecticut, when Mia was five, as her mother had relatives there among the city's fairly large Haitian community. Her mother worked as a nurse in a retirement home, and her father worked odd jobs; both placed great emphasis on making one's own way in life through hard work rather than relying on others. Again, Love's family background would go on to deeply influence her personal and political beliefs.

Love attended Norwalk High School, where she was in choir and color guard and developed an interest in theater. Following graduation she attended the University of Hartford to study musical theater at the Hartt School. She earned a bachelor of fine arts in 1997, taking classes in theater, dance, and voice with the intention of pursuing a career on Broadway. After college she took a job as a flight attendant

U.S. Congress/Wikimedia Commons

while deciding whether to seriously pursue a performing career.

## CONVERSION TO MORMONISM AND MARRIAGE

The Bourdeau family was Roman Catholic, and it was a surprise when her older sister Cynthia converted to Mormonism. Her parents were initially suspicious of the Church of Jesus Christ of Latter-day Saints (LDS church) and asked Love to investigate her sister's situation. After discovering that Cynthia had been helped by Mormon missionaries, she began to further research the LDS church and became intrigued by what she found. Love attended church services herself and was won over by the messages she heard, particularly the call for a husband to love his wife as Christ loved the church. As she told Winston, "The commitment I saw that these people had to their spouses and families—it wasn't about being married for now but for all eternity. That was really cool to me." Soon she too was baptized in the LDS church.

In 1997 she decided to move to Salt Lake City to be closer to the Mormon Tabernacle there. She reconnected with Jason Love, a fellow Mormon whom she had first met while he was on a mission in Connecticut. The two went hiking with friends around Labor Day in 1998, and their relationship quickly grew. Their first solo date was at a firing range, where Jason was impressed by Mia's adventurousness. They were engaged within two months.

After wedding plans were in place, Love received a call from Broadway producers of the musical *Smokey Joe's Café*, who wanted her for a lead role, but she turned down their offer in favor of her marriage. As she explained to Winston, "I was making a choice to be with somebody for eternity. There was really no choice." Love taught music and acting after her marriage and was involved for a time in community theater but soon focused on motherhood.

## ENTERING POLITICS

Love had been raised in a Republican household but became more interested in politics through her husband's activity. Her active involvement in politics began when the couple bought a house in a new development in Saratoga Springs, Utah. The warm, shallow lake nearby was a breeding ground for midges, and the relentless swarms bothered everyone in the community. In 2002 neighbors approached Love, who was known for her assertive personality, to ask her to confront the developers about the problem. One week after she took up the issue, the area was sprayed for bugs. People in the community began to see Love as a can-do activist.

In 2003 Love ran for and won a seat on the city council of Saratoga Springs, motivated by a US Supreme Court case about potentially eliminating the phrase "under God" from the Pledge of Allegiance. During her time on the city council, the budget deficit shrank from $3.5 million to $779,000.

When Love ran for mayor of Saratoga Springs in 2009, she won with 60 percent of the vote, becoming the first black mayor in Utah. She reveled in her political roles, telling Jennifer Steinhauer for the *New York Times* (30 Oct. 2012), "They wanted someone who could get things done, and I am known for that." She helped guide the city through a financial crisis and a major population boom while building a reputation for following strictly conservative policies influenced by the Tea Party movement. When Saratoga Springs citizens wanted money for a library, she allocated $10,000 and suggested that if the people really wanted a library, volunteers would fund the rest.

## RUNNING FOR CONGRESS

In 2012 Love decided to run for the US House of Representatives seat in Utah's Fourth District. She faced off against Jim Matheson, a veteran Democrat and son of a former Utah governor who was highly popular despite the state's generally conservative voting base. National Republican groups began supporting Love in hopes of finally defeating Matheson, whom they viewed as vulnerable. The heated campaign quickly got ugly, and Love's Wikipedia page was even filled with racist and sexist slurs. Attack ads questioned Love's background and credentials, with some allegedly spreading false information.

The widespread attention to the Utah congressional election boosted Love into the national spotlight, not least because her race and gender were seen by many as in opposition to her Republican values. While some Democrats attacked this supposed conflicting identity, Republicans elevated Love as representative of the new face of their party. She gave a high-profile speech at the 2012 Republican National Convention, where fellow Mormon Mitt Romney was nominated for president. When Romney formed a Black Leadership Council for his campaign, Love was one of the members.

Love's primary campaign message was against big government. As Betsy Woodruff reported for *National Review* (12 Nov. 2012), Love remarked to voters on the campaign trail, "You will never be successful being handcuffed and dependent on government." She favored eliminating federal subsidized student loans and grants for local law enforcement, as well as reducing the roles of the Department of Education and the Department of Energy.

Despite the support of Romney and other prominent Republicans, Love lost the 2012 election, but by a slim margin of fewer than three thousand votes. When she ran again in 2014, Matheson had announced his retirement. Her new opponent was Doug Owens, a lawyer from Salt Lake City. Love raised more than five times more campaign money as Owens did, although much of it came from donors living outside Utah. Running on essentially the same platform as in 2012, Love won the 2014 election with 50 percent of the vote to Owens's 47 percent.

Before her win, according to Ross, Love told her husband that if elected, her message to her new colleagues would be, "My job is to make every single one of you less powerful. Let's get to work."

## POLITICAL POSITIONS

Sworn into office on January 6, 2015, Love got busy at once. She joined the Congressional Black Caucus, a traditionally liberal group that she declared on the campaign trail she would work to dismantle from within. In February she delivered a rare freshman speech to the House on health-care reform, calling for a repeal of the Affordable Care Act.

Love carried a deeply conservative record into office, with views in line with the Tea Party's brand of conservatism. She favored major cuts to established federal programs and departments. She was appointed to the House Financial Services Committee, which covers banking, public housing, and insurance. According to Matt Canham, writing for *Salt Lake Tribune* (21 Nov. 2014), she stated, "The important work done by this committee over the next two years will have a direct impact on ensuring that our nation's economy continues to improve. For me, this mission begins with clearing away harmful regulatory burdens that keep our businesses from creating jobs and getting Utahns back to work." Love's first choice for an appointment had been the Energy and Commerce Committee, which has broad jurisdiction in a number of areas, but the Republican leadership decided not to put any freshman representatives there.

Love's speeches often reference the experiences of her parents in coming to the United States legally. Love opposes amnesty for people living illegally in the United States, making clear her zero-tolerance stance toward those immigrants. She has voiced support for securing the nation's borders, identifying illegal immigrants, and determining a policy for dealing with them.

Love never perceived her race as an issue, believing that skin color is not a barrier unless a person chooses a victim mentality. She told Ross, "I'm no victim. I'm perfectly comfortable in my skin. My parents always told me, In order for people to see you as an equal, you need to act as an equal and be an equal, not make excuses for what you look like. I'm proud of having the skin color I have. It's a feature I'm not ashamed of."

### PERSONAL LIFE

Love and her husband, Jason, have two daughters, Alessa and Abigail, and a son, Peyton.

### SUGGESTED READING

Curtis, Mary C. "Mia Love Is Black, Mormon, Republican and Blowing People's Minds." *Washington Post*. Washington Post, 12 Nov. 2014. Web. 1 Apr. 2015.

Love, Mia "Big Government Needs to Get Out of the Way, Give Americans a Chance to Rise." *Deseret News*. Deseret News, 1 Mar. 2015. Web. 1 Apr. 2015.

Moyer, Justin Wm. "Meet Mia Love. You'll Be Seeing a Lot More of the Republicans' First Black Congresswoman." *Washington Post*. Washington Post, 5 Nov. 2014. Web. 1 Apr. 2015.

Ross, Winston. "Mia Love Tries to Be the First Black Republican Woman in Congress." *Newsweek*. Newsweek, 29 Oct. 2014. Web. 1 Apr. 2015.

Will, George. "From Utah, with Love." *Human Events*. Eagle Publishing, 22 Sept. 2012. Web. 1 Apr. 2015.

Woodruff, Betsy. "Mia's Marathon." *National Review*. National Review, 12 Nov. 2012. Web. 1 Apr. 2015.

—Judy Johnson

# Rick Lowe

**Born:** ca. 1961

**Occupation:** Artist and activist

Rick Lowe—the winner of a 2014 John D. and Catherine T. MacArthur Foundation Fellowship, informally referred to as a "genius grant"—is best known for Project Row Houses (PRH), a nonprofit organization that he started in 1993 with several other artists. The MacArthur Foundation described PRH, located in one of Houston's oldest African American neighborhoods, as "an unusual amalgam of arts venue and community support center." Other observers have found it difficult to describe his work in such succinct terms. "Nestled in Houston's Third Ward are six blocks chock full of art. Art you can touch, art built with slats and nails, art that people live in and live with. It's work that takes the shape of a neighborhood," Kriston Capps wrote for *CityLab* (19 Sept. 2014). "Since its founding in the early 1990s, the program—or artwork, or conceptual project—has grown from twenty-two houses along a block-and-a-half to more than seventy buildings spread around the neighborhood. 'Social sculpture' is the term Lowe uses to describe Project Row Houses. It's as good as any. Project Row Houses defies easy categorization."

"Rick pioneered a form of art that had no name," PRH's executive director, Linda Shearer,

SLOWKING/ Courtesy of the John D. and Catherine T. MacArthur Foundation

explained to Claudia Feldman for the *Houston Chronicle* (16 Sept. 2014). "Now his concept is taught in undergraduate and graduate art programs. It's called 'creative place making' and 'social practice.' What's remarkable is that Rick was on this track of socially engaged art and developing community long before anybody thought about it."

Lowe, however, has told interviewers that he dislikes the term "social practice," finding it bland and nondescript. He also has reservations about "place making." "I think the biggest problem with that term is the way it's being utilized in the framework of community building," he said to Nicole Audrey Spector for *Guernica* (25 Sept. 2014). "Placemaking focuses on the *place*—its physical attributes. My work focuses on the people who comprise that place and how they fit within the context of the making of the place." Lowe further explained to Spector that he sees the challenge as one of putting the needs of the residents of lower-income communities first instead of improving a neighborhood's physical attributes primarily to allow for its gentrification. "A lot of investment in creativity and in the creative class is about creating a place that seems hip and cool, where people will go out in the evenings and have their lattes on the weekends. That's about generating economic investment. That's needed and that's fine, but there has to be a way in which we can do that while bringing people up in the neighbor-

hood who are already there, rather than pushing them out."

## EARLY LIFE AND EDUCATION

Rick Lowe was born about 1961. (Although his exact date of birth is not readily available, he was fifty-three years old when he received his 2014 MacArthur Foundation grant.) The eighth-born of twelve children, he was raised in rural Russell County, Alabama. His father was not a consistent presence in the family's day-to-day life, and Lowe and his siblings spent most of their time helping their mother work in the cotton and peanut fields. "I always tell people that I felt like [we] were the last sharecroppers in the world," he told Spector. "Most people stopped in the late '60s, but we sharecropped until 1975." Lowe said that he had little to no exposure to art during his early childhood.

In high school, he sometimes drew, creating maps or sketches of the presidents for social studies projects. Still, he never considered art a serious pursuit, preferring to focus instead on playing basketball. His athletic prowess won him admission to Alabama State University, but once there he realized he had little interest in competing with elite college players.

He subsequently transferred to Columbus College, in Georgia, and realizing that art might be a viable course of study for him, he declared that as his major. "I wasn't at the same level as my classmates, but I worked hard at it," he recalled to Spector. "My professors introduced art to me as something that could transform people's lives. I was interested in that because I always felt like there was a need for people to speak about the kinds of conditions in which I grew up. There were things that nobody really talked about." Working as a busboy and dishwasher to pay his tuition, Lowe began creating artwork dealing with police brutality, homelessness, and other social issues.

## EARLY ART CAREER

Lowe did not graduate from college, taking the advice of a professor who told him, "You're a doer. You should go out into the world and do it," as he said to Feldman. Initially, he moved to the Mississippi Gulf Coast, where one of his brothers had settled, and he found a job at an ice cream storage plant to support himself while he created his art.

Wanting to be in a large city, Lowe moved to Houston in 1984. He took art classes at Texas Southern University (TSU) and met a community of fellow black artists, including Bert Long, Bert Samples, Jesse Lott, Floyd Newsum, George Smith, and James Bettison. The group often discussed the intersections of art and community, social justice, and basic human needs, and those concerns began to increasingly inform Lowe's paintings.

In 1990 a group of high school students visited Lowe's studio, and one said, as quoted by Spector, "Your stuff shows what's happening in our neighborhoods, but we don't need people showing us what's happening. We know what's happening. We need solutions. If you're an artist and you're creative, why can't you create a solution?" Lowe has said that the student's critique was among the most valuable of his career, and it marked a turning point for him. He realized that while his work had been spurring discussion, he wanted it to enact positive change.

## PROJECT ROW HOUSES

When Lowe came across a group of row houses in Houston that became Project Row Houses, he realized that he had a chance to put his philosophy into action. He was inspired in his new mission by John Biggers, a Houston painter known for vibrant public murals depicting African American community life, and Joseph Beuys, a German artist who posited that everyone shapes their world on a constant basis and thus everyone is in some sense an artist.

The houses—narrow, rectangular structures built in a style known as "shotgun," with one room leading directly into the next—were located in Houston's Third Ward, an historic African American neighborhood. Erected in the 1930s, they were in poor repair, with some occupied by drug dealers and users. With the help of the group of artists he met at TSU, along with community activists and volunteers he recruited, Lowe began work. "It was messy in the beginning," he admitted to Spector. "We didn't have a clear objective of what we were trying to do. We just started to secure the houses, clean them up, and clear the land. As we did that, people from the neighborhood were stopping by."

Lowe realized that the residents of the Third Ward themselves could give the best advice about shaping the project. An influx of young, disenfranchised visitors led to the creation of arts-education programs. When older people praised those efforts but wondered why some of the buildings weren't being used as actual housing, Lowe started the Young Mothers Residential

Program, to provide shelter and support to single mothers seeking better lives for their families.

Among Project Row Houses' other initiatives are maintaining studio space for established and emerging artists; holding regular marketplaces for local craftspeople; launching an incubation program that has thus far supported the creation of a food co-op and radio station; mounting LIVE at the Eldorado Ballroom, a concert series hosted at an historic ballroom donated to the organization; and building ZeRow House (2009–10)—a prototype for small, affordable, sustainable housing—with the cooperation of students from Rice University, who entered the innovative structure in the US Department of Energy's Solar Decathlon in 2009.

In 2003 Row House Community Development Corporation (Row House CDC) was established as a separate 'sister' corporation to PRH. Its aim is to provide affordable community housing while preserving the culture, architecture, and history of the Third Ward, and it now manages dozens of low-income rental units.

## OTHER PROJECTS

Lowe has worked on several community-based social sculpture projects around the country as well as internationally. From 1996 to 1999 Lowe helped spearhead the Watts House Project, in Los Angeles, which was based largely on PRH and which revitalized the area around the well-known Watts Towers. In 2006 he was deeply involved in a collaborative rebuilding effort in New Orleans called Transforma Projects after Hurricane Katrina. His other work includes *Trans.lation: Vickery Meadow*, which celebrated the cultural diversity of a Dallas neighborhood, Vickery Meadow, whose thirty thousand residents hail from all over the world, speaking some twenty-seven different languages. For the project in 2013 and 2014, Lowe facilitated a series of pop-up markets at which people could buy or sell wares from their native countries, organized craft workshops, and built galleries to attract art lovers who might not otherwise visit the formerly crime-ridden three-square-mile area.

In 2014 Lowe started a multiyear residency with the Asian Arts Initiative's Pearl Street Project, a revitalization program in Philadelphia's Chinatown area. His project for the residency will take inspiration from community input collected by artist and architect Walter Hood to create new work with a focus on Pearl Street. Lowe's residency is funded by the Pew Center for Arts and Heritage.

In addition to his community-based social sculpture projects, Lowe has exhibited his art at about a dozen museums and galleries both in the United States and abroad since 1993. These include the Phoenix Art Museum; Museum of Contemporary Arts, Los Angeles; the Contemporary Arts Museum Houston and the Museum of Fine Arts, Houston; Kumamoto State Museum in Kumamoto, Japan; and the Zora Neale Hurston Museum in Eatonville, Florida.

## MACARTHUR GRANT AND OTHER HONORS

In September 2014 the MacArthur Foundation announced that they were naming Lowe a 2014 MacArthur Fellow, an honor that came with a $625,000 no-strings-attached cash prize. In the wake of the announcement—widely considered a pinnacle in any artist's career—he fielded numerous offers. He subsequently accepted a ten-day residency at the University of California, Berkeley, and served as a visiting scholar at Auburn University.

Lowe has previously served as a Loeb Fellow at the Harvard Graduate School of Design from 2001 to 2002, a visiting artist at the Otis College of Art in Los Angeles in 2010, and an artist-in-residence at MIT's Community Innovators Lab in 2012. Lowe's other honors include the American Institute of Architects Keystone Award (2000); the Heinz Award (2002), given in memory of the late US senator John Heinz; the United States Artists Booth Fellowship in Architecture and Design (2009); and Creative Time's Leonore Annenberg Prize for Art and Social Change (2010).

In November 2013 President Barack Obama appointed Lowe to the National Council on the Arts, whose members advise the chair of the National Endowment for the Arts. His appointment will run until 2018. "I think it's meaningful to have someone like me on the National Council on the Arts, someone with a community-oriented agenda who oftentimes is not really heard in the art world," Lowe told Spector.

## SUGGESTED READING

Capps, Kriston. "How a Houston Housing Project Earned a MacArthur Grant." *CityLab*. Atlantic Monthly Group, 19 Sept. 2014. Web. 27 June 2015.

Dela, Sasha. "Project Row Houses: An Interview with Rick Lowe." *Temporary Art Review*. Temporary Art Review, 1 Oct. 2013. Web. 27 June 2015.

Feldman, Claudia. "Houston Artist Rick Lowe Wins MacArthur Fellowship." *Houston Chronicle*. Hearst Newspapers, 16 Sept. 2014. Web. 27 June 2015.

Glentzer, Molly. "Houston's MacArthur Fellow Keeps Churning Out 'Social Practice' Projects." *Houston Chronicle*. Hearst Newspapers, 27 Dec. 2014. Web. 27 June 2015.

Johnson, Patricia C. "Rick Lowe's World: A Work in Progress." *Houston Chronicle*. Hearst Newspapers, 23 Jan. 2005. Web. 27 June 2015.

Kimmelman, Michael. "In Houston, Art Is Where the Home Is." *New York Times*. New York Times, 17 Dec. 2006. Web. 27 June 2015.

Miranda, Carolina A. "What Rick Lowe's MacArthur Grant Win Means for Art and Social Practice." *Los Angeles Times*. Los Angeles Times, 19 Sept. 2014. Web. 27 June 2015.

Spector, Nicole Audrey. "Rick Lowe: Heart of the City." *Guernica*. Guernica, 25 Sept. 2014. Web. 27 June 2015.

—Mari Rich

# Lois Lowry

**Born: March** 20, 1937
**Occupation:** Young-adult novelist

Writer Lois Lowry has received multiple awards for the more than forty young-adult novels and children's books she has penned over many decades. In addition to two Newbery Medals in 1990 and 1994, she received the Margaret A. Edwards Award for lifetime achievement in writing for young adults in 2007.

Lowry writes books that are considered realistic fiction as well as fantasy works, and she believes that her books emphasize the importance of the interdependence between humans and their environment. Perhaps her best-known title, the dystopian novel *The Giver* (1993) has simultaneously remained a staple on the required-reading lists of junior high schools throughout the country while also falling at number eleven on the American Library Association's list of the one hundred most-challenged books from 1990 to 1999 and at number twenty-three from 2000 to 2009. Despite today's increasing popularity of dystopian novels available for young adults, including such series as the *Hunger Games* and

*Divergent*, many have credited *The Giver* as the first of its kind.

Though Lowry has maintained that she has never intentionally inserted messages into her books, she has also emphasized the sense of both accountability and fulfillment that she feels in regard to writing for young readers. "Early on I came to realize something. . . . That is, kids at that pivotal age, twelve, thirteen, or fourteen, they're still deeply affected by what they read, some are changed by what they read, books can change the way they feel about the world in general. . .I think writing for kids is profoundly important," she told Lucas Kavner for the *Huffington Post* (5 Oct. 2012).

## EARLY LIFE AND EDUCATION

Because her father, Robert Hammersberg, was a career US Army officer and dentist, Lois Lowry has described herself as a military brat. Her mother, Katherine, took care of the family. Born in Honolulu, Hawaii, Lowry was an introverted child and a fervent reader. In addition to her older sister, Helen, she has a younger brother, Jon.

The family moved often due to her father's military assignments. When World War II began, Lowry's mother moved the family back to her parents' home in Pennsylvania. Lowry attended schools there and in New York. In an interview with Meghna Chakrabarti and Anthony Brooks for WBUR's *Radio Boston* (7 Jan. 2013), she explained the significance of this regular movement upon her eventual growth as a writer: "I think that's one of the things that contributed to making me such an observer. I was always the new kid, plunged into new circumstances." With Helen's help, she taught herself to read at an early age and, by the age of eight or nine, she knew that she wanted to be a writer.

After the war ended, she attended junior high school in Tokyo. On her thirteenth birthday, her father surprised her with a portable Smith-Corona typewriter—a rare gift for young girls at that time. At seventeen, she entered Brown University to study writing but left two years later to marry Donald Grey Lowry, an officer in the Navy. Four children—two girls and two boys—quickly followed.

Lowry later returned to college to finish her education, receiving her bachelor of arts degree in 1972 from the University of Southern Maine. While attending graduate school and while her children were still young, she began writing nonfiction articles and short stories. Her first success allowed her to pay for a housekeeper so

Kenneth C. Zirkel/Wikimedia Commons

that she could spend more time writing. Following her divorce in 1977, writing became a necessary means of financial support.

## EARLY SUCCESSES

Although her first published works were for adults, Lowry soon realized that her true calling was as a writer of young-adult fiction. In 1977, she published her first novel for young adults at the suggestion of an editor at Houghton Mifflin who had seen a short story of hers in the women's magazine *Redbook*. Based on Helen's tragic early death from cancer, *A Summer to Die*, a semiautobiographical story about a young girl's loss of her older sister, won the International Reading Association's Children's Book Award in 1978.

Lowry began her first series in 1979, introducing readers to Anastasia Krupnik, the outspoken and introspective young protagonist who tackles everyday problems and adventures in a Boston suburb. Anastasia became the focus of eight more books and her little brother, Sam, also had multiple works written about him.

Throughout these initial publishing ventures, Lowry continued to hone her craft, relying upon her own unique writing process. She begins with her characters, followed by the plot, which is driven by a key incident. The characters respond to the various events of the book, sometimes surprising Lowry and providing unexpected plot twists. In her speech delivered at the 2001 Zena Sutherland Lecture and reprinted in *Horn Book*

*Magazine* (Mar./Apr. 2002), Lowry explained, "It's much too glib, too falsely self-deprecating, to say that the character takes over. I don't lose control. I have, after all, created the character. What he does, or she does, is entirely dependent upon me. But it happens in a subliminal way and sometimes takes me by surprise. I want it to. I love those surprises, wait for them, yearn for them." Only after she has finished writing the novel, she assigns the title.

## ACHIEVING CRITICAL ACCLAIM WITH *NUMBER THE STARS*

In 1989, after learning the detailed history of the years that her longtime friend spent as a child living in Denmark during Nazi occupation, Lowry published *Number the Stars*. Set in World War II and focused on the Danish resistance to the Holocaust, the book follows the story of a young girl whose family is involved in helping transport Jewish families to neutral Switzerland.

In addition to gaining insight about the everyday details from her friend's memories of the time, Lowry also traveled to Denmark herself, where she spoke to members of the resistance and walked the city of Copenhagen and the surrounding countryside. In an article for *Reading Teacher* (Oct. 1990), in which she described her process for writing the novel and her need to experience Denmark itself, she wrote, "I went to the place in Copenhagen where the Resistance fighters had been executed. When I saw that the Danes still place flowers there each day, after close to fifty years, it reinforced my admiration for them and my need to tell their story."

The novel won a Newbery Medal the next year, Lowry's first. However, despite the serious tone of novels such as *Number the Stars*, Lowry has never been interested in teaching life lessons through her writing. As she explained to Jessica Gross for the *New York Times Magazine* (1 Aug. 2014), "I have no wish to insert messages into my books or to be didactic. And I think, ultimately, most books fail if they try to do that. Those were the books of my childhood, trying to teach moral lessons to children. It never worked."

## *THE GIVER*

Lowry's second Newbery Medal came in 1994 for *The Giver*. The book has sold more than twelve million copies worldwide. Some parents have attempted to ban the novel, believing that it is inappropriate for the intended age level for a variety of reasons. In defense of her work, Lowry told Sohrab Ahmari for the *Wall Street*

*Journal* (20 June 2014), "The best way to prepare [children] for the world that they face is to present what the possibilities are and to let them be scared of what might happen." She continued, "I think that's really what literature does in every realm. You rehearse your life by reading about what happens to other people."

The idea for the novel originated from Lowry's increased meditation upon the concept of memory after visiting her elderly parents in a nursing home. While her mother sadly recalled the details of Helen's death, her father could not remember his daughter's name or her passing. By the time Lowry returned home, she had begun to formulate the plot for *The Giver*, a story in which a civilization entrusts all of their memories, good and bad, to one person, known as the Receiver of Memory. While this individual struggles with the knowledge of humanity's capacity for both good and evil, as well as such concepts as the beauty of color, the rest of the community lives ignorantly in a black-and-white world defined by sameness, receiving daily injections of medication to ensure that they will never remember otherwise.

Although widely recognized as a dystopia, Lowry has explained that she did not have this intention in mind when beginning the book. In an interview with Anita Silvey for *School Library Journal* (1 June 2007), she stated, "Only gradually did I begin to understand that I was not creating a utopia—but a dystopia. I slowly understood that I was writing about a group of people who had at some point in the past made collective choices and terrible sacrifices to achieve a level of comfort and security."

In 1998, five years after publication of *The Giver*, Lowry released the memoir *Looking Back: A Book of Memories*. With this book, Lowry hoped to provide insight into the origins of her influential story ideas for both children and adults.

## AND THEN THERE WERE FOUR

*The Giver* eventually became the first in a quartet that includes *Gathering Blue* (2000), *Messenger* (2004), and *Son* (2012). Lowry had not initially planned any sequels, but many readers found the ending of *The Giver* too ambiguous for their tastes. "I never felt it necessary to spell out the details, even in my own mind. But as an optimist, I thought the boys were still alive," she explained, as quoted by Ilene Cooper in *Booklist* (1 June 2012). In response to many readers' letters, Lowry continued the saga of the dystopian world.

Kira, a girl trusted with the history of her community, is the protagonist of *Gathering Blue*. The book, considered a kind of companion, was not a sequel to *The Giver*, though some of the same story lines were pursued. In the final pages, a boy is mentioned. Lowry initially called him Jonas, the protagonist of *The Giver*; however, her editor asked her to remove the name so as not to confuse those who may not have read the book's predecessor.

*Messenger* united the two books through the character of Matty. When Lowry completed that novel, she believed that the story had ended. Once again, however, readers began sending letters, asking about the infant Gabriel from *The Giver* and what had become of him. *Son* was her attempt to answer these questions and bring the three worlds together. Lowry was aware that in telling the story of Gabriel's mother, Claire, searching for her lost son, she was using material from her own life. Lowry's own son, Grey, a US Air Force fighter pilot, had been killed in a crash in 1995. She was a grieving mother, just as Claire was.

*The Giver* has also been translated into more than a dozen languages and adapted into other forms, including a stage play. The Lyric Opera of Kansas City and the Minnesota Opera commissioned an opera based on the book as well. The work, which Susan Kander composed, premiered in January 2012. Two years later, the book became a film, starring Jeff Bridges and Meryl Streep.

## PERSONAL LIFE

Lowry's first marriage ended when she was forty. Shortly after, she met insurance agent Martin Small, with whom she shared thirty years before his death in 2011. She enjoys photography as well as writing, and some of her photos have been used as the covers for her novels, including *Number the Stars* and *The Giver*. While her permanent residence is in Massachusetts, she also has a summer home, an eighteenth-century farmhouse, in Bridgton, Maine.

## SUGGESTED READING

Ahmari, Sohrab. "'When People Choose, They Choose Wrong.'" *Wall Street Journal*. Dow Jones, 20 June 2014. Web. 8 Dec. 2014.

Cooper, Ilene. "Another Look At: Lois Lowry's Giver Quartet." *Booklist* 1 June 2012: 91. Print.

Lowry, Lois. "Interview with Lois Lowry, Margaret A. Edwards Award Winner." Interview by Anita Silvey. *School Library Journal*. School Lib. Jour., 1 June 2007. Web. 8 Dec. 2014.

Lowry, Lois. "Lois Lowry on Giving Up 'The Giver' to Hollywood." Interview by Jessica Gross. *New York Times Magazine*. New York Times, 1 Aug. 2014. Web. 8 Dec. 2014.

Lowry, Lois. "Lois Lowry, 'Son' and 'The Giver' Author, Reflects on Dystopian Novels, Psychopaths and Why Kids Make the Best Audiences." Interview by Lucas Kavner. *Huffington Post*. TheHuffingtonPost.com, 5 Oct. 2012. Web. 8 Dec. 2014.

Lowry, Lois. "The Remembered Gate and the Unopened Door." *Horn Book Magazine* Mar./Apr. 2002: 159–77. Print.

## SELECTED WORKS

*A Summer to Die*, 1977; *Anastasia Krupnik*, 1979; *Number the Stars*, 1989; *The Giver*, 1993; *Gathering Blue*, 2000; *Messenger*, 2004; *Son*, 2012

—Judy Johnson

---

# Rich Lowry

**Born:** August 22, 1968
**Occupation:** Editor

Since 1997, Rich Lowry has been the editor of the *National Review*, one of the foremost magazines of news and opinion dedicated to conservative political values. He has been a sought-after voice of American conservative thought for almost two decades. In the *National Review*, as well as in his twice-weekly syndicated newspaper column and in appearances on television opinion programs, Lowry argues forcefully for core conservative values, including a strong military, decisive responses to threats to the US homeland, lower taxes, less government regulation, and support for the free-market system. He and his fellow conservatives are also defenders of traditional Judeo-Christian values and Western culture, the concept of American exceptionalism, and individual rights, and they excoriate the concepts of multiculturalism and moral relativism as being harmful to democratic societies as a whole.

Gage Skidmore/CC BY SA 2.0

## EARLY LIFE AND EDUCATION

Richard A. Lowry was born on August 22, 1968, in Arlington, Virginia, where he and his older brother were raised. His mother was a social worker; his father was an English professor. Lowry was an outdoorsy, high-spirited kid, and while not a troublemaker, he recalls that he was a considerable contrarian—a personality trait that he believes led to his development into a political conservative. His fascination with American politics began in 1984, when he started watching *Firing Line* (1966–99), the political talk show hosted by William F. Buckley Jr. Buckley, who died in 2008, was an influential conservative intellectual who first shot to fame in 1951 with the publication of his book *God and Man at Yale*. In 1955, Buckley founded the *National Review*, a news and opinion magazine crucial to shaping the conservative movement in the United States in the second half of the twentieth century, and served as its editor for decades.

Lowry began reading the *National Review* in the back of his high school classroom shortly after watching *Firing Line* for the first time. He also became a staunch supporter of President Ronald Reagan, a Republican who served in office from 1981 to 1989. Reagan advocated such conservative viewpoints as supply-side economics and forceful economic, military, and political competition with the Soviet Union in an effort to break Soviet domination over Eastern Europe and spur democratic reform within

the Soviet empire. Reagan left office with sky-high approval ratings, due in part to the surging US economy and the collapse of the Soviet Union (which ceased to exist at the end of 1991). Reagan remains a touchstone among modern political conservatives in the United States, including Lowry.

Lowry attended the University of Virginia, where he earned a bachelor's degree in English and history in 1990. During his undergraduate years, Lowry admits he was a poor student, spending more time working on the college's conservative newspaper, the *Virginia Advocate*, than attending to his studies. Many of his staunchly conservative articles angered his fellow students; a member of the student council even called his mother to tell her that she had raised a "fascist." "The advantage of being a conservative journalist on campus—because political correctness can be so suffocating and so humorless—[is that] you get to be kind of the rebels that are kind of fun and raise hell and have some laughs in the process," Lowry recalled to George Gurley for the *New York Observer* (15 Dec. 2003).

## WORKING FOR THE *NATIONAL REVIEW*

Following his graduation from the University of Virginia, Lowry secured a position as a research assistant to Charles Krauthammer, the syndicated conservative opinion columnist whose work appears in the *Washington Post*, among other outlets. In 1992, Lowry entered and tied for second in a young writers contest sponsored by the *National Review*. His work in the contest earned him the attention of the magazine's editors, who ultimately hired him as an articles editor in 1994. He subsequently served as the magazine's national political correspondent, working out of Washington, DC, where he covered both the administration of President Bill Clinton (1993–2001) and the US Congress.

In 1997 the *National Review*'s founder, William F. Buckley, tapped Lowry to become the magazine's new editor, replacing John O'Sullivan, who had been editing the magazine for about a decade. Although Lowry was just twenty-nine years old at the time, Buckley saw Lowry's youth as beneficial to the magazine, as Buckley had founded it when he himself was just twenty-nine. At the time of Lowry's promotion to editor, Buckley told the *New York Times* (5 Nov. 1997), "I'm very confident that I've got a very good person." The magazine's staff seemed pleased with the selection as well. "He's just an all-American guy. The thing that Rich brings to the magazine—which is kind of rare in its history—is normality," *National Review* contributor Richard Brookhiser said to Gurley.

Beginning as editor of the *National Review* during Clinton's second term, Lowry took the president to task for a number of issues, including his involvement with Monica Lewinsky, a White House intern with whom Clinton had an affair. He was also extremely critical of Clinton's handling of issues related to terrorism. Lowry believes that Clinton underestimated the threat of the al-Qaeda terrorist network, headed by Osama bin Laden, and that his inaction was in part responsible for the terrorist attacks of September 11, 2001, which occurred just months after Clinton left office.

## LEGACY: PAYING THE PRICE OF THE CLINTON YEARS

Lowry's first book was a searing indictment of the Clinton administration and of Clinton himself. Published in 2003, *Legacy: Paying the Price of the Clinton Years* became a *New York Times* Best Seller. In it, Lowry depicts Clinton as beset by scandals of his own making and intimately involved in cover-ups of misdeeds. Over the course of the book, Lowry also attacks what he sees as Clinton's ineffectual responses to acts of terrorism, including the first World Trade Center attack in New York in January 1993, the Oklahoma City bombing in 1995, the bombings of US embassies in East Africa in 1998, and the attack on the USS *Cole* in 2000. He argues that Clinton's tepid responses to these attacks emboldened bin Laden and al-Qaeda and laid the groundwork for the September 11 attacks. In the *American Spectator* (Dec. 2003/Jan. 2004), Dick Morris wrote of *Legacy*: "Lowry's most interesting discussion centers on Clinton's record between the foul lines, on the playing field of American politics. It is there, in the realm of public policy, not of personal misconduct, that Lowry makes his most provocative arguments about the failures of the Clinton administration. In foreign affairs and national security, Lowry lays out a damning case of presidential neglect, shortsightedness, and half-measures. . . . Assessing the Clinton years without focusing on their culmination on September 11 would be like discussing Harding and Coolidge without mentioning the stock market crash that took place, like September 11, early on their successor's watch."

## AUTHOR OF FICTION AND NONFICTION

Lowry's next book was a novel, *Banquo's Ghosts* (2009), which was a political thriller he coauthored with Keith Korman. In it, they describe a rogue CIA agent who has decided that the only way to eliminate the threat of Iran's fledgling nuclear program is to assassinate that program's chief scientist. He enlists the aid of a drunken, left-leaning journalist who has been given access to Iran's nuclear facilities because he is known as something of an apologist for the Iranian government's policies. In the *National Review*, Otto Penzler (20 Apr. 2009) declared *Banquo's Ghosts* "a true thriller—a fine novel by authors who understand the difference between good and evil and are unashamed to take a position on the side of the former."

Lowry's most recent book is *Lincoln Unbound: How an Ambitious Young Railsplitter Saved the American Dream—and How We Can Do It Again* (2013), a biography of the sixteenth US president and the first Republican one, who led the country during the Civil War. Lowry shows Abraham Lincoln as above all a political striver and a self-made man, someone with the individualism and can-do spirit that embody American values—especially for a political conservative like Lowry. The review in *Kirkus Reviews* (15 May 2013) proclaimed: "To discover what Lincoln truly believed, Lowry . . . confines himself largely to Lincoln's pre-presidential career, explaining how the backwoods boy of little schooling and negligible property early on identified with the Whigs rather than the Jacksonian Democrats who captured so many of his similarly situated peers. . . . Some readers are bound to accuse Lowry of nudging Lincoln into the author's own preferred categories of belief, but they'll be hard-pressed to find any violation of the historical record."

## OTHER WORK

In addition to editing the *National Review*, Lowry writes about and comments on global and domestic politics, as well as American values and cultural issues in a wide variety of media outlets. He appears on a number of Fox News Channel programs as a political commentator and has been a guest on long-running and popular political talk shows such as *Meet the Press* and *The McLaughlin Group*. He has also written for the *New York Times*, the *Washington Post*, the *Wall Street Journal*, the *Los Angeles Times*, *Time*, and *Politico*.

Lowry also has his own twice-weekly syndicated column with King Features, in which he discusses, for example, his reactions to decisions made by the administration of President Barack Obama and issues of the day such as the status of undocumented immigrants, same-sex marriage, and race relations.

## SUGGESTED READING

Gurley, George. "Power Punk: Rich Lowry." *Observer*. Observer Media, 15 Dec. 2003. Web. 14 July 2015.

"Lincoln Unbound." *Kirkus Reviews*. Kirkus Reviews, 28 Apr. 2013. Web. 14 July 2015.

Morris, Dick. "One Eye in the Mirror." Rev. of *Legacy: Paying the Price for the Clinton Years*, by Rich Lowry. *American Spectator* Dec. 2003/Jan. 2004: 72–73. Print.

"National Review Changing Editor." *New York Times*. New York Times, 5 Nov. 1997. Web. 14 July 2015.

Penzler, Otto. "On Our Side." Rev. of *Banquo's Ghosts*, by Rich Lowry and Keith Korman. *National Review* 20 Apr. 2009: 52–53. Print.

## SELECTED WORKS

*Legacy: Paying the Price for the Clinton Years*, 2003; *Banquo's Ghosts* (with Keith Korman), 2009; *Lincoln Unbound*, 2013

—Christopher Mari

# Andrew Luck

**Born:** September 12, 1989
**Occupation:** Football player

When Andrew Luck began his professional career with the Indianapolis Colts in 2012, he was considered the most polished college quarterback to enter the National Football League (NFL) in decades. The number-one overall pick in that year's NFL Draft, Luck would have likely been the first pick in 2011 had he not decided to finish his academic career at Stanford University. That decision proved to be the right one for Luck, who succeeded Peyton Manning as quarterback of the Colts after the NFL legend was cut from the team following multiple career-threatening surgeries. Despite facing enormous pressure to fill the shoes of Manning, the most beloved athlete in Indianapolis history, Luck quickly lived up to the team's lofty expectations.

Jeffrey Beall/Wikimedia Commons

Luck passed for more yards (12,957) in his first three seasons than any quarterback in NFL history. He also led the Colts to the playoffs in each of his first three seasons and was named to three consecutive Pro Bowls (2012–14). In the process Luck became "the model for the modern quarterback: a combination of size, agility, and arm strength, to go with a mental acumen capable of processing the NFL's increasingly complex offensive system," Reeves Wiedeman wrote for *Men's Journal* (Sept. 2014). Comparing Luck to his contemporaries, Wiedeman continued, "At 6-foot-4 and 240 pounds, Luck is bigger than Colin Kaepernick and as fast as Cam Newton, with an arm as strong as Russell Wilson's."

## EARLY LIFE AND EDUCATION

Andrew Austen Luck was born on September 12, 1989, in Washington, DC. His father, Oliver, was a former two-time All-American quarterback at West Virginia University who had been selected in the second round of the 1982 NFL Draft by the Houston Oilers (later renamed the Tennessee Titans). Oliver Luck spent five seasons with the Oilers, serving mostly as a backup quarterback, before retiring from the NFL in 1986. He then became a lawyer and dabbled in politics. Luck's father met his wife, Kathy, while both were pursuing law degrees at the University of Texas at Austin in the 1980s.

Luck had an itinerant, multicultural upbringing. When he was just one year old, his family moved to Frankfurt, Germany, where his father, then fresh off an unsuccessful run for West Virginia's second congressional district, accepted a job as general manager of the Frankfurt Galaxy in the World League of American Football (WLAF). Luck's family moved to London, England, in 1996 when his father became president of the WLAF, which was later rebranded as NFL Europe. Luck's three younger siblings, sisters Mary Ellen and Emily and brother Addison, were all born in Europe.

Along with his siblings, Luck was brought up immersed in European customs and traditions. He seldom watched television growing up and traveled extensively throughout Europe with his family. As Luck put it to Wiedeman, "I didn't get the American pop-culture education." He did develop an early passion for one of Europe's most cherished pastimes: soccer. Luck played the sport throughout his youth and grew up attending games at such famed venues as London's Wembley Stadium and the Rheinstadion in Düsseldorf, Germany. Luck credits soccer with helping him develop the footwork and balance necessary to play quarterback, while visiting numerous stadiums ignited his interest in architecture.

## THE MAKINGS OF A QUARTERBACK PRODIGY

Luck did not start playing football until the age of twelve, when his father relocated the family to Houston, Texas. He joined a Pop Warner team coached by his father and started out as a defensive end and running back before being selected as quarterback due to his throwing ability. Luck described his father's coaching style to Michael MacCambridge for *Indianapolis Monthly* (2 Oct. 2012), saying, "He was oddly relaxed about a lot of things, football-wise. He didn't make me go out there and do drills for hours on end and hit the perfect target. I think he realized I was having fun playing the position."

When Luck entered Stratford High School, he focused exclusively on playing quarterback. Though Stratford had a highly competitive football program, Luck became the school's starting varsity quarterback as a sophomore, winning over head coach Eliot Allen with his physical ability, remarkable football acuity, and spotlight-shunning humility. In his three seasons as Stratford's starting varsity quarterback, Luck amassed 7,139 passing yards and 53 touchdowns, to go along with 2,085 rushing yards. He also shined academically and graduated as covaledictorian of his class with a perfect 4.0 grade-point average. "Everybody wants to talk about what he can do athletically," Eliot Allen told Austin Murphy for *Sports Illustrated* (13 June 2011). "But with Andrew, the it factor is his knack for making people better, making them want to follow him."

Luck was recruited by dozens of colleges with top-ranking football teams all over the country, but he opted to enroll at Stanford University for the intellectual challenge. He chose the school despite the fact that its football program had not posted a winning season since 2001. Nevertheless, Luck had been impressed by the win-at-all-costs mentality of the school's second-year head coach, the former NFL quarterback Jim Harbaugh.

After being redshirted his freshman year, Luck won Stanford's starting quarterback spot in the spring of 2009. He went on to become one of the most-decorated quarterbacks in Stanford history. In three seasons as the Cardinals' signal caller, Luck set school records for total offense (10,387 yards), touchdown passes (82), completion percentage (67.0), and wins by a quarterback (31), among others. In 2010 and 2011, he received the Maxwell Award as the top collegiate player in the nation as well as Pac-12 Conference Player of the Year and first-team All-America honors. He was also the Heisman Trophy runner-up in both of those years, in which Stanford finished with 12–1 and 11–2 records, respectively.

Despite being the consensus choice to be selected first in the 2011 NFL Draft, Luck, who had led the Cardinals to a 2011 Orange Bowl victory, opted to return to Stanford for his redshirt junior season. The decision was met with backlash from the media, who questioned if it was worth passing up millions of dollars and risking injury. "I didn't agonize over the pros and cons," Luck, who took out a multimillion-dollar insurance policy, noted to MacCambridge, adding that he thought he "could get better at football and would feel more comfortable taking that next step."

## NEW FACE OF THE COLTS

After answering his critics with another record-breaking season at Stanford, Luck fortified his standing as a once-in-a-generation talent. As was widely expected, he was selected by the Indianapolis Colts with the first overall pick in the 2012 Draft. The Colts decided on Luck after parting ways with their longtime franchise quarterback Peyton Manning, who had missed the entire 2011 season due to a severe neck injury. Without Manning the Colts had suffered through a disastrous 2–14 season, after which team owner Jim Irsay fired general manager Chris Polian and head coach Jim Caldwell. Polian and Caldwell were replaced, respectively, by Ryan Grigson and Chuck Pagano, who jettisoned more than half of the Colts' roster. Luck was to be the new centerpiece they would build around.

Following the draft, Luck returned to Stanford to complete his degree in architectural design. When Luck first reported to the Colts in June 2012, he wasted little time convincing the team's new brass that he was their quarterback of the future. On Luck's first day of practice, as Pagano recalled to Andy Benoit for *Sports Illustrated* (8 Sept. 2014), he "started calling out plays. . . . using terminology no one had learned yet, doing things that everybody who'd been through the whole off-season didn't know yet." In July 2012 Luck signed a fully guaranteed four-year contract with the Colts worth $22 million.

Luck's ability to process and store information quickly accelerated his learning curve entering the 2012 season. Handling more offensive responsibilities than most first-year quarterbacks, Luck enjoyed a sterling rookie campaign. He started all sixteen games and set NFL rookie records for most passing yards in a season, (4,374) and most passing yards in a game (433). He also set numerous Colts franchise records, including most rushing touchdowns by a quarterback (5).

Luck immediately galvanized a young and inexperienced Colts team that was forced to play much of the year without Pagano, who was diagnosed with leukemia four weeks into the season. Rallying under the mantra "Chuckstrong," the Colts enjoyed a nine-game improvement from the previous season, going 11–5 and returning to the playoffs after a one-year absence. Seven of the Colts' wins were fourth-quarter, come-from-behind efforts orchestrated by Luck, who was rewarded at the end of the season by being named to his first career Pro Bowl.

## BUILDING HIS LEGACY

Following the 2012 season, Pagano resumed his regular head coaching duties. The team also brought in Pep Hamilton, one of Luck's former coaches at Stanford, as offensive coordinator. Under Hamilton, Luck transitioned from a two-tight-end offensive attack built around the

play-action passing game to a run-heavy, ball-control offense that relied on maximizing time of possession.

For the precocious Luck, the transition was seamless. Starting all sixteen games again for the Colts during the 2013 season, he passed for 3,822 yards and scored 23 touchdowns. He also cut his interception total to nine (after throwing eighteen as a rookie), improved his completion percentage (from 54.1 to 60.2), and rushed for a career-best 377 yards. He became the first quarterback in NFL history to throw for more than 8,000 yards in his first two seasons. Under the guidance of Luck, the Colts overcame a rash of injuries to again finish at 11–5 en route to an American Football Conference (AFC) South division title and second consecutive playoff berth.

Luck added three more fourth-quarter comebacks to his resume during the regular season, but he saved his best late-game heroics for the postseason. In the AFC wild-card playoff round, he led the second-biggest playoff comeback in NFL history, rallying the Colts from a seemingly insurmountable twenty-eight-point deficit to beat the Kansas City Chiefs, 45–44. Commenting on Luck's uncanny ability to elude pressure and extend plays, Colts receiver T. Y. Hilton, who caught the game-clinching touchdown against the Chiefs, told Benoit, "With Andrew, the play is never over. You just keep working and he'll find you." Although the Colts lost to the New England Patriots in the AFC divisional round, 43–22, Luck earned a trip to his second straight Pro Bowl.

## 2014 SEASON

Luck showed further development in 2014. That year he was forced to adjust to yet another new offensive system. Hamilton installed a pass-oriented spread offense featuring multireceiver sets to accommodate for the Colts' ineffective running game. The offense gave Luck more presnap responsibility at the line of scrimmage, allowing him to change protections or call audibles based on opposing teams' defensive alignments.

Luck responded to the Colts' trust in him by posting the best numbers of his still-young career. During the 2014 season he led the NFL with forty touchdown passes and finished third in the league with a franchise-record 4,761 passing yards, while posting a 61.7 completion percentage and a 96.5 quarterback rating. He also broke Manning's franchise record for the most three-hundred-yard pass games in a season, with ten, and was selected to his third straight Pro Bowl. He led the Colts to their third consecutive eleven-win season and second straight AFC South title. In the playoffs Luck helped the team overcome the Manning-led Denver Broncos in the AFC divisional playoff round to advance to the AFC Championship Game, where the Colts were again eliminated by the Patriots.

By the end of the 2014 season, Luck had amassed 12,957 career passing yards, the highest total ever by a quarterback in his first three seasons, and eighty-six career touchdown passes, second only to Dan Marino for the most in a player's first three years. According to Pagano, Luck is already "on track to be one of the best ever to play the game," as he asserted to Benoit. Hamilton, meanwhile, said of Luck to Ashley Fox for ESPN.com (16 Jan. 2015): "I think he's gotten to the point where he's consistently controlling football games and making plays that a lot of quarterbacks can't do. He's gotten better as he's gained experience in this league. He's a little ahead of schedule."

### PERSONAL LIFE

Luck, who is known for his cerebral and unassuming nature, is one of football's most unique personalities. He has gained attention around the league for his unusual aversion to traditional trash talk, instead complimenting opponents after they hit or sack him. Luck is a voracious reader, enjoys gourmet food, and remains an avid soccer fan.

### SUGGESTED READING

Benoit, Andy. "Best of Luck." *Sports Illustrated.* Time, 8 Sept. 2014. Web. 26 Feb. 2015.

Fox, Ashley. "Colts Hand Keys to Andrew Luck." *ESPN.* ESPN Internet Ventures, 16 Jan. 2015. Web. 26 Feb. 2015.

MacCambridge, Michael. "Andrew Luck: Are You Prepared for the Most Dramatic Transition in Colts History?" *Indianapolis Monthly.* Indianapolis Monthly, 2 Oct. 2012. Web. 26 Feb. 2015.

Murphy, Austin. "Man with a Plan." *Sports Illustrated* 13 June 2011: 66–77. Print.

Wiedeman, Reeves. "Andrew Luck: A QB with Brains, Brawn, and a Big Arm." *Men's Journal.* Men's Journal, Sept. 2014. Web. 26 Feb. 2015.

—Chris Cullen

# Loretta Lynch

**Born:** May 21, 1959
**Occupation:** United States Attorney General

Loretta Elizabeth Lynch took office as the eighty-third United States attorney general on April 27, 2015, a position to which President Barack Obama had nominated her the previous November. When he nominated Lynch as attorney general, Obama said she "might be the only lawyer in America who battles mobsters and drug lords and terrorists, and still has a reputation for being a charming people person." She also served as special counsel to the prosecutor of the International Criminal Tribunal for Rwanda, prosecuting those accused of genocide; in that role, she investigated charges of false testimony and witness tampering at the tribunal. Lynch is also the first sitting attorney general to use Twitter.

### EARLY LIFE AND EDUCATION

Born in Greensboro, North Carolina, Lynch was the second of three children. Her father, Lorenzo, is a fourth-generation Baptist pastor who supported the famed 1960 attempts to integrate a Woolworth's lunch counter in Greensboro. Her mother, Lorine, who picked cotton and worked in a laundry and summer camp when in high school to save money for college, became a librarian. According to Reena Flores for *CBS News* (17 June 2015), President Barack Obama said of Lynch's parents, "They are her biggest cheerleaders." He cited the scrapbooks her mother kept on Lynch, which she produced when her daughter was being investigated before becoming a United States attorney. He continued, "The agent later told Loretta that she probably wasn't a threat to America because if she were, her parents would have documented it in some way."

The family moved to Durham, North Carolina, when Lynch was six. She first encountered racism in elementary school. When she scored high on a standardized test, administrators demanded she retake the test, thinking she had cheated. Despite her mother's protestations, Lynch retook the exam and scored even higher.

She stuffed envelopes for her father's unsuccessful run for mayor, but did not become involved in civil rights causes. Instead, she focused on her schoolwork, earning the highest marks of any student in her high school. How-

Lonnie D. Tague/USDOJ Photo

ever, because Durham schools had been deseg-regated by court order only seven years earlier, some faculty members believed the school was not ready for an African American student as valedictorian. She shared the honor with two other students, one white and one black.

In 1981 Lynch received her bachelor of arts degree, cum laude, from Harvard College, where she was also on the cheerleading squad. Three years later she graduated from Harvard Law School, where she was a member of the Harvard Black Law Students Association. She also served as an advisor for the first year moot court competition and as a member of the Legal Aid Bureau.

While at Harvard, Lynch cofounded a chapter of the African American sorority Delta Sigma Theta with Eric Holder's future wife, Sharon Malone. The sorority was founded at Howard University in 1913; justice, empowerment and community service are its key tenets.

## EARLY CAREER

Lynch began her law career at the Wall Street law firm of Cahill Gordon & Reindel, where she worked from 1984 to 1990. She was one of three African American women in the office, and Lynch and the other two referred to themselves as "the triplets." In 1990 Lynch became a federal prosecutor for the Eastern District of New York. She headed the district's Long Island office for several years in the mid-1990s before serving as

US Attorney Zachary W. Carter's chief assistant starting in 1998.

## UNITED STATES ATTORNEY

In 1999 President Bill Clinton appointed Lynch as United States attorney for the Eastern District of New York. With 160 attorneys under her authority, Lynch oversaw federal prosecutions in Brooklyn, Long Island, Queens, and Staten Island. She served in that position until 2001.

One of Lynch's most important cases was that of Abner Louima, which went to trial in 1999. Louima, a Haitian immigrant, had been sodomized with a broom handle by a New York police officer, Justin Volpe, two years earlier. In her handling of the case, Lynch was determined to focus on the issue of police brutality, not race.

A year after Volpe was convicted and went to prison, Lynch addressed a luncheon of the Association of Black Women Attorneys. As Amy Davidson reported for the *New Yorker* (15 Dec. 2014), Lynch said, "We live in a time where people fear the police. But we must also understand that when people say they fear the police, as bad as that is, they are also expressing an underlying fear, that when they are confronted with the criminal element in our society they will have no one to call upon to protect them. And that feeling of vulnerability and utter helplessness is the worst feeling that we can inflict upon fellow-members of our society." Lynch has made it a point to maintain good relationships with police departments.

After her term as a US attorney, Lynch became a partner in the law firm of Hogan and Hartson. In 2003 she was also appointed as director of the Federal Reserve Bank of New York. Attorney General Eric Holder appointed her to his advisory committee in 2010.

That year, President Obama appointed Lynch to be United States attorney for the eastern district of New York once again. The district has tried more terrorism cases since 2001 than any other office. Obama praised Lynch for her handling of terrorists who planned to bomb the New York subway and the Federal Reserve Bank when he appointed Lynch to replace Eric Holder as attorney general in November 2014.

## NOMINATION AS ATTORNEY GENERAL

The waiting period for Lynch's confirmation was unusually long: 166 days elapsed before the Senate approved the nomination with a vote of fifty-six to forty-three. The delay was in part because her nomination occurred just after the election that gave the Senate majority to the Republicans. The Democrats, as outgoing majority, agreed to wait until the new senators arrived, but once they did, the delay went on. Only two other attorneys general waited longer, one under Woodrow Wilson and the other under Ronald Reagan. The delay was not about Lynch's qualifications. Rather, the combination of factors included the Senate's insistence on dealing with other issues first, such as an anti–human trafficking bill with a controversial rider related to abortion funding, and an attempt by the Republicans to use her nomination as leverage to fight Obama's attempts at immigration reform.

When Lynch was to appear before the Senate for confirmation hearings, members of the sorority Delta Sigma Theta, wearing the crimson and cream that are its colors, came to support her. Her father was in the gallery of the Senate on the day of the vote.

On April 27, 2015, Vice President Joe Biden made official Lynch's position as eighty-third attorney general. As Sari Horwitz reported for the *Washington Post* (27 Apr. 2015), Lynch commented, "I'm here to tell you, if a little girl from North Carolina—who used to tell her grandfather in the fields to lift her up on the back of his mule so she could 'see way up high granddaddy'—can grow up to become the chief law enforcement officer of the United States of America, we can do anything."

## BEGINNING AS ATTORNEY GENERAL

Lynch's first official visit after her investiture was to the city of Baltimore, where tensions were running high between police and members of the community following the death of Freddie Gray, a twenty-five-year-old African American man who died while in police custody. She visited not only the University of Baltimore campus but also the police station. She praised the police officers, some of whom had worked double shifts during the unrest following Gray's death.

Ron Weich, dean of the University of Baltimore's law school, told Carrie Johnson for NPR's *Morning Edition* (6 May 2015), "I think it speaks volumes that the attorney general's first visit is to Baltimore. I think she's saying that she wants to be at the forefront of efforts to heal this community." The Justice Department she heads began investigating whether any civil rights laws were broken in the Gray case. More broadly, the entire police department of the city may be examined, as was that of Ferguson, Missouri, during earlier demonstrations involving

the death of an African American man shot by a white police officer.

Within the first month on the job, Lynch also handed down billions of dollars in fines to Wall Street firms accused of manipulating currency markets.

As a US attorney for the Eastern District of New York, Lynch had gathered evidence for then-attorney general Eric Holder against executives of FIFA, the international soccer organization, who were charged with racketeering, money laundering and wire fraud, among other crimes. Lynch was then placed in the unusual situation of presiding over the arrest of those very leaders against whom she had built a case.

While some countries, such as Russia, have expressed concern that the United States is overreaching in the FIFA case, others are pleased. Thabiso Sithole, a sportscaster from South Africa, told Matt Apuzzo and Sam Borden for the *New York Times* (29 May 2015), "It was interesting, from this side, that there's a woman calling the shots for the United States, and a black woman at that"—especially, he added, since soccer is "such a boys' club."

## MAKING IT OFFICIAL

All of these accomplishments took place before her formal swearing-in on June 17, 2015. She took the oath of office, which Supreme Court Justice Sonia Sotomayor administered, using Frederick Douglass's Bible. Lynch told those attending, "Over 200 years ago, we decided what kind of a country we wanted to be. We have not always lived up to the promises made. Yet we have pushed ever on, and with every challenge we get a little bit closer."

The same evening as Lynch's formal investiture, a single shooter killed nine African Americans who were at a prayer meeting at Emanuel African Methodist Episcopal Church in Charleston, South Carolina. The Justice Department began determining whether charges of domestic terrorism or hate crime should be added to the murder charges against the accused. Only a day after Lynch was sworn in, 243 people in seventeen districts were charged with Medicare fraud in the largest nationwide sweep in history. A combined effort of the attorney general's office and the Department of Health and Human Services, it was led by the Medicare Fraud Strike Force. About $712 million in false billings were uncovered.

Continuing her connections to police departments in light of eroding trust following police brutality incidents in a number of cities, Lynch began convening roundtables with law enforcement officers. Six cities in different parts of the nations were selected for the pilot program. She told officials in Birmingham, Alabama, "Through conversations like this one, I want to highlight the innovative ways you all are strengthening police-community relations and to think about how the steps you're taking can be translated into other jurisdictions. I am hopeful that these vital conversations will help guide the transformative change we would all like to see nationwide."

## PERSONAL LIFE

Lynch is married to Stephen Hargrove, a master control operator at *Showtime*. Hargrove has two children from a previous relationship. Lynch plays tennis to handle her stress.

## SUGGESTED READING

Apuzzo, Matt. "Nominee for Attorney General Less an Activist Than Holder." *New York Times*. New York Times, 13 Jan. 2015. Web. 23 June 2015.

Apuzzo, Matt, and Sam Borden. "FIFA Charges Instantly Earn Loretta Lynch Global Recognition." *New York Times*. New York Times, 30 May 2015. Web. 23 June 2015.

Clifford, Stephanie. "Loretta Lynch, a Nominee for Attorney General, Is Praised for Substance, Not Flash." *New York Times*. New York Times, 8 Nov. 2014. Web. 5 June 2015.

Flores, Reena. "Obama Imagines a 'Mortified' Lynch at Her Swearing-in as AG." *CBS News*. CBS, 17 June 2015. Web. 22 June 2015.

Horwitz, Sari. "Loretta Lynch Is Sworn In as Attorney General." *Washington Post*. Washington Post, 27 Apr. 2015. Web. 10 June 2015.

Sisneros, Henri. "Issues for a New U.S. Attorney General." *Utah Bar Journal* 28.2 (2015): 40–43. Print.

—Judy Johnson, ML

# Thuli Madonsela

**Born:** September 28, 1962
**Occupation:** Public protector of South Africa

Thuli Madonsela is South Africa's public protector. As described by Alexis Okeowo for the *New York Times Magazine* (16 June 2015), Madon-

© AP/Corbis

sela's role "falls somewhere between a government watchdog and a public prosecutor." Her office, which was created to investigate and report on government corruption, was established in the 1996 post-apartheid South African constitution. She is the third person and the first woman to hold the post. She was appointed by South African president Jacob Zuma after he was elected in 2009. The year before she came on the job, the office of the public protector handled almost nineteen thousand cases; under Madonsela, within five years the office was handling double that number.

In 2014, the same year she was named to *Time* magazine's list of the world's "100 Most Influential People," Madonsela presented the findings of an eighteen-month investigation of Zuma. In what would come to be called the Nkandla report, Madonsela revealed that the president had used over $20 million in taxpayer funds to renovate his sprawling estate near the town of Nkandla in the province of KwaZulu-Natal. The report spawned a backlash from Zuma's powerful political party, the African National Congress (ANC). For South Africans, the ANC is a "democratic beacon," Okeowo wrote—the party that shaped post-apartheid South Africa, led for years by the late Nelson Mandela. The ANC has been in power in South Africa for more than two decades. Under the party's leadership, the country has made significant strides. "The lives of the bottom 20 percent have changed since apartheid,"

Jonny Steinberg, a South African professor at Oxford, told Okeowo. "And all of these changes have been delivered directly by the state." Still, in recent years, the country has suffered from sluggish economic growth, chronic electricity blackouts, local corruption, and a national unemployment rate of 25 percent—50 percent for young people. Accusations of cronyism and, as Okeowo reported, a mishandling of the AIDS crisis have further contributed to the party's declining public favor under the Zuma administration. But Madonsela's work illustrates the difficulty of reforming the ANC or removing it from power. In many ways, her continuing struggle with Zuma—and what it says about the power and perceived importance of her office—is the story of a country still reckoning with its past. "The work here has exposed fault lines in our democracy," Madonsela told Okeowo of her report. "It's got people talking about what kind of democracy we have—and what kind of democracy we deserve."

## EARLY LIFE AND EDUCATION

Thulisile Nomkhosi Madonsela was born on September 28, 1962, in Soweto, a township in the sprawling city of Johannesburg. (Mandela lived in Soweto until his arrest the same year Madonsela was born.) Her mother worked as a maid. Her father was an electrician who later started a taxi business. She has two sisters and one brother. Madonsela was a bright student and attended school in the neighboring country of Swaziland because her parents did not want her to study at the apartheid-era schools for black children. She loved comic books and, as a student at Evelyn Baring High School, aspired to be a lawyer. Her father, who wanted her to be a nurse, refused to pay for her higher education. Still, as Madonsela revealed in a letter to her sixteen-year-old self for *Oprah Magazine South Africa* (26 Apr. 2012), academics buoyed her self-esteem and engendered pride in her family members, friends, and church: "I know you are socially awkward, plagued by a nagging feeling of being unloved and ugly," she wrote, but "you will excel, academically, throughout your life and this will bring you to where you are right now."

Madonsela's good grades earned her a scholarship to the University of Swaziland, where she began working with the black trade union movement. Her brother, Musa, was an anti-apartheid activist, and their work often brought police officers knocking on the door of their family

home. Madonsela earned her bachelor's degree in 1987 and graduated with a law degree from the University of the Witwatersrand (Wits) in Johannesburg in 1990. The ban on the ANC was lifted—and Mandela was freed—the same year. Mandela was elected president of the ANC in 1991. During this historic moment in South Africa's history, Madonsela served as a legal advisor for the ANC and helped draft the country's new constitution. "It was once-in-a-lifetime," she recalled to Okeowo.

## EARLY CAREER AND PUBLIC PROTECTOR

In the early 1990s, along with her role in the new government, Madonsela was a research fellow and part-time lecturer at Wits Law School, and she continued her work with trade unions. For about a decade starting in 1994, she moved through positions of increasing responsibility with the Independent Electoral Commission and the Department of Justice. She was working for the South African Law Reform Commission, an independent organization that works with the South African Parliament and local legislatures, when President Zuma appointed her public protector in 2009. (Candidates for the job are culled from public nominations. Finalists are interviewed by members of Parliament, who then recommend one finalist to the president.)

Madonsela approached her job with a zeal the office had not seen before. Her first major case came in 2011, when she issued a report on the national commissioner of the South African Police Service, Bheki Cele. Madonsela and her team alleged that Cele had made unlawful deals with a well-connected property company to secure sites for police headquarters in Pretoria and Durban, on the eastern coast. Cele and the government agreed to a highly inflated rate on ten-year leases for the buildings, without putting the project out to bid. While Madonsela found no evidence of criminality, in her report she said that Cele's conduct was "improper, unlawful, and amounted to maladministration." A week after releasing the report, police raided her office, looking, Aislinn Laing reported for the *Telegraph* (28 July 2012), "for documents Miss Madonsela had refused to allow Mr. Cele to see." Newspapers reported rumors that Madonsela was under investigation for corruption herself, but she refused to succumb to public pressure and held a press conference to announce that she was continuing her investigation. Cele was a powerful ally of Zuma's, but in 2012 Zuma, in what many viewed then as the biggest scandal of his presidency, sided with Madonsela and fired Cele. In 2014, Cele was appointed minister of agriculture, forestry, and fisheries. After the release of the Nkandla report, he criticized Madonsela in *Beeld*, an Afrikaans daily, as quoted by the South African *City Press* (7 Apr. 2014), saying, "She must stop acting like she is God."

The Cele investigation won Madonsela many supporters in South Africa and abroad; in 2011, the South African newspaper the *Daily Maverick* named Madonsela "South African Person of the Year." Liang reported that about a quarter of annual state spending (around $3.5 billion) is wasted in kickbacks and maladministration. In South Africa, the term for this kind of corruption is "tenderpreneurship," or the practice of awarding government contracts to companies owned by government officials or their families or friends. In 2012, the BBC followed Madonsela as she investigated one case involving a primary school on the rural Eastern Cape. The school opened in 2008, but in 2012, the school had still not received money for desks or chairs. The case is indicative of the kind of work Madonsela does on a daily basis. "I was particularly concerned about the ordinary administrative wrongs against ordinary people," she told Okeowo of her attitude upon taking the job. "I wanted to position the office so that any *gogo dlamini*, any old lady, in the middle of nowhere in South Africa knows where to go when they feel they've been wronged by the state."

### THE NKANDLA REPORT

In March 2014, less than two months before national elections, Madonsela released the Nkandla report—culled from nearly two years of investigation and formally titled *Secure in Comfort*—regarding the financing of President Zuma's sprawling estate in the KwaZulu-Natal Province. Madonsela reported, as quoted by Alan Cowell for the *New York Times* (19 Mar. 2014), that Zuma "benefitted unduly" from state-funded improvements to his home made for the stated purpose of improving security. These improvements included an amphitheater, a helipad, a cattle enclosure, and a visitor center; a swimming pool was officially described as "firefighting equipment," Cowell reported, "to justify the cost." (Madonsela officially released the report in 2014, but a draft of it was leaked to South Africa's *Mail and Guardian* newspaper in late 2013.) Madonsela called on the president to return the money.

She faced swift retribution for her report from politicians, church leaders, and anti-apartheid organizations, some of whom went so far as to accuse her of being racist toward ANC voters. The deputy minister of defense, Kebby Maphatsoe, even accused her of being a CIA agent. "I was sad that people would stoop that low," she told Okeowo of Maphatsoe's comments. "It was the saddest moment of my career. That is the ANC that I grew up loving." The report hurt Zuma's public image, but he has yet to address it in any serious way, though he made jokes about it in Parliament in May 2015. He was elected to a second term in 2014.

### BACKLASH

In March 2015, the State Security Agency announced that it was conducting an investigation into accusations that Madonsela is a CIA agent. In April, Parliament denied her request for an expanded budget—according to Okeowo, Madonsela's office had settled some twenty-one thousand of twenty-nine thousand of its most recent cases but required a larger staff to complete the rest. Her request was denied, and Mathole Motshekga, the ANC chair of a parliamentary justice committee, accused her of wasting taxpayer money. Her race, gender, and age have made her job more difficult, she told Okeowo. Parliament has criticized her high salary—though her male predecessor was paid the same amount. After the release of the Nkandla report, she faced a barrage of criticism, including insults about her physical appearance. "I have felt the way some of the people talk down to me," she said. "There's internalized racism by black people themselves, who would feel, 'I can take an order from a white person, I can take orders from a male, but really I'm not used to taking orders from a black woman.'"

However, Madonsela has never shown any signs of backing down from her commitment to responsible government, writing to her sixteen-year-old self for *Oprah Magazine*: "Today, you are the nation's Public Protector—a very responsible position that helps curb excesses in the exercise of public power while enabling the people to exact justice for state wrongs. You had the privilege of playing some role in bringing about change in this country. . . . Above all, remember that love is everything and don't forget to forgive yourself and others."

## PERSONAL LIFE

She has two children, a daughter named Wenzile Una and a son named Mbusowabantu "Wantu" Fidel.

## SUGGESTED READING

Cowell, Alan. "Report Faults South African Leader for State-Funded Work on Home." *New York Times*. New York Times, 19 Mar. 2014. Web. 2 Aug. 2015.

Laing, Aislinn. "Thuli Madonsela: South Africa's Anti-Corruption Watchdog Raises the Nation's Hopes." *Telegraph*. Telegraph Media Group, 28 July 2012. Web. 2 Aug. 2015.

Okeowo, Alexis. "Can Thulisile Madonsela Save South Africa from Itself?" *New York Times*. New York Times, 16 June 2015. Web. 30 July 2015.

Page, Samantha. "Thuli Madonsela's Letter to Her 16-Year-Old Self." *Oprah Magazine South Africa*. Associated Media, 26 Apr. 2012. Web. 30 July 2015.

"South Africa Police Chief Bheki Cele in 'Unlawful Deal.'" *BBC News*. BBC, 14 July 2011. Web. 2 Aug. 2015.

"Thuli Madonsela Must Stop Acting Like She Is God—Bheki Cele." *News24*. 24.com, 7 Apr. 2014. Web. 2 Aug. 2015.

—Molly Hagan

# Martin Makary

**Occupation:** Surgeon and health care commentator

Doctor Marty Makary is a researcher, health reform advocate, and author of the best-selling book *Unaccountable: What Hospitals Won't Tell You and How Transparency Can Revolutionize Health Care* (2012). He has published more than 150 articles in medical journals and has written articles about his views and research findings for popular publications like *Newsweek* and the *Wall Street Journal*. In 2013 he was named one of "20 Most Influential Leaders in American Healthcare" by *Health Leaders Magazine*. Makary is the chief of minimally invasive surgery and a surgical director at the Johns Hopkins Pancreas Multidisciplinary Cancer Clinic. He is also an associate professor of health policy and management at the Johns Hopkins Bloomberg School of Public Health.

Keith Weller/Wikipedia

## EDUCATION

Martin "Marty" Adel Makary studied biology at Bucknell University, in Lewisburg, Pennsylvania, from which he received a bachelor of arts degree in 1993. He then went on to study medicine at Thomas Jefferson University in Philadelphia, Pennsylvania, from which he received his medical degree in 1998. That year he also received a master's degree in public health (MPH) from Harvard University in Cambridge, Massachusetts. Makary then did his residency in general surgery at Georgetown University Medical Center in Washington, DC. After finishing his residency at Georgetown in 2003, Makary did a fellowship in cancer surgery at Johns Hopkins University, where he focused on gastrointestinal (GI) surgery and surgical oncology.

## EARLY LESSONS

During his first day as a student at one of Harvard Medical School's teaching hospitals, Makary experienced something that would stick with him for the rest of his life and influence his thinking about patient safety, as he recounted in his book, *Unaccountable: What Hospitals Won't Tell You and How Transparency Can Revolutionize Health Care*, as well as many articles and interviews.

In a *Wall Street Journal* (September 21, 2012) article titled "How to Stop Hospitals from Killing Us," Makary recounted the events of that first day: "Wearing a new white medical coat that was still creased from its packaging, I walked the halls marveling at the portraits of doctors past and present. On rounds that day, members of my resident team repeatedly referred to one well-known surgeon as 'Dr. Hodad.' I hadn't heard of a surgeon by that name." Makary didn't know what to make of the situation—until a fellow student told him what "Hodad" stood for: Hands of Death and Destruction. "Stunned," Makary wrote, "I soon saw just how scary the works of his hands were. His operating skills were hasty and slipshod, and his patients frequently suffered complications. This was a man who simply should not have been allowed to touch patients. But his bedside manner was impeccable (in fact, I try to emulate it to this day). He was charming. Celebrities requested him for operations. His patients worshiped him. When faced with excessive surgery time and extended hospitalizations, they just chalked up their misfortunes to fate. Dr. Hodad's popularity was no aberration. As I rotated through other hospitals during my training, I learned that many hospitals have a 'Dr. Hodad' somewhere on staff (sometimes more than one)."

This unnerving experience led to a realization about why this persisted. Because the importance of a doctor's reputation is so crucial to his or her livelihood, whistleblowers, whether they be doctors or nurses, risked being targeted by the accused doctor or hospital. "I've seen whistleblowing doctors suddenly assigned to more emergency calls," Makary wrote, "given fewer resources or simply badmouthed and discredited in retaliation. For me, I knew the ramifications if I sounded the alarm over Dr. Hodad: I'd be called into the hospital chairman's office, a dread scenario if I ever wanted a job. So, as a rookie, I kept my mouth shut."

But his experience with regard to patient safety was not entirely negative. Makary also learned from positive role models, such as patient safety advocate Lucian Leape, who was his professor at Harvard. Upon arriving at Johns Hopkins, where he did his fellowship in cancer surgery, Makary was influenced by the example of doctor Peter Pronovost, who developed a checklist for the intensive care unit (ICU). That checklist would serve as a precedent for the operating room checklist Makary would go on to create.

## THE CHECKLISTS

After implementing the operating room checklist at Johns Hopkins, Makary published data showing those checklists worked to improve patient safety. This data would become the basis of doctor, author, and fellow advocate Atul Gawande's book *The Checklist Manifesto: How to Get Things Right* (2009), which quickly became a best seller. The reasoning for the checklist, even aside from convincing studies, was clear. If, for example, pilots in the US Air Force, who started using checklists decades ago, were using a checklist to make sure everything was in order before flying an incredibly complex piece of machinery (a plane), then doctors should also use a checklist before operating on the human body, which was at least as complex. In other words, if doctors and hospitals had any hope of lowering fatality rates and improving patient outcomes, they had no choice but to use the checklist, which according to studies Makary published lowered postoperative infection rates. Some of the items on the list—very basic things clearly in the best interests of patients—include washing hands, regularly sterilizing IV lines, communicating clearly before and during the operation, and checking off of duties by nurses. A variation of this checklist was later adopted by the World Health Organization.

Makary would go on to create other checklists, which are available on his website, Unaccountablebook.com. He created three checklists for patients: general medical, surgical, and cancer. The general medical checklist addresses questions concerning how to pick your primary care doctor, what questions to ask your doctor after a new diagnosis, whether to get a second opinion (always a good idea, Makary says), how to go about finding a doctor for a second opinion, and what questions to ask your doctor about taking medication. For questions about surgery, he offers opinions on what kinds of questions to ask about whether you need surgery, whether you should use your regular hospital for that surgery, whether you should have a recommended surgery for chronic back pain, and similar topics. As for cancer, his advice includes what questions to ask if diagnosed with cancer, what to ask if offered the opportunity to take part in a medical trial, and what questions to consider with regard to alternative therapies.

## TRANSPARENCY PLEDGES

Makary also developed a six-item Transparency Pledge for healthcare providers and an eight-point Transparency Pledge for hospitals, both of which are also available on his website. The latter includes disclosing to patients conflicts of interest, addressing medical errors as soon as they occur, offering patients a procedure video (if possible) after the operation, and measuring hospital safety. The pledge for healthcare providers includes openly sharing the patient's medical record with the patient and reporting hazards that can harm the patient to the hospital, among other things.

In the *Wall Street Journal* article, as well as in various interviews, Makary points out that before going to a restaurant, people often look up ratings on Yelp or Zagat or some other resource—and a restaurant's health grade is often prominently displayed on its front window—whereas if people want to make life-or-death decisions about what hospital or what doctor to use for a serious treatment or surgery, they often have to rely on arbitrary factors, like proximity or a recommendation founded not on evidence but on reputation or a doctor's personality. An example Makary cites in the article as well as in his book is one of public reporting: in the early 1990s, New York hospitals were required to report heart surgery death rates. That led patients to be better informed—the death rates varied from 1 percent to 18 percent, a significant difference—and it also led hospitals with poor records to improve. As a result, writes Makary, in six years death rates declined by 83 percent overall. One doctor, for example, was simply ordered to stop doing heart surgery, because his death rate was significantly affecting the hospital's overall death rate.

## UNACCOUNTABLE

In his book, *Unaccountable: What Hospitals Won't Tell You and How Transparency Can Revolutionize Health Care*, and many subsequent interviews, Makary made the case that if medical errors were a disease, they would be one of the leading killers of Americans, not far behind heart disease, which is number one, and cancer, which is number two. At least 210,000 patients die in the United States every year because of medical errors and at least ten times that number are hurt in one way or another—unnecessary treatment, sloppy surgery, or surgery on the wrong side of the body (the wrong leg or wrong breast), for example. Aside from the human toll, there is also the financial aspect: Makary argues that tens of billions of dollars are spent annually on these mistakes, either in additional care, insurance costs, or legal costs for doctors and hospitals.

In an interview with *ProPublica* (September 18, 2012), a political investigative journalism publication, Makary was asked why these problems persist and what the barriers are to increasing transparency. With regard to the former, he said, "There's been a corporatization of health care where we have a system where we tell the hospitals to fill the beds, so the hospital administrators fill the beds. We tell the doctors to do more procedures, so they do more procedures. For patients, we create a notion that more care is better care, and so they demand more care. Everyone is doing their job. The problem is we have good people working in a bad system." And as far as the biggest barriers to change, he highlighted "complacency and blind trust." More specifically, he said, "The complacency is embodied in the traditions of medicine. Medicine has its own culture, values, vocabulary, and justice system. Part of that culture is that we only listen to ourselves. There's a tremendous amount of appropriate respect for tradition and hierarchy, like in the military. . . . That's the greatest challenge now in the system, asking the questions of how we can cut the giant costs of health care, which is funding unnecessary overtreatment, medical mistakes." And as for "blind trust," that's how the public often sees doctors and health-care professionals, which he says is not the public's fault, because they often don't have access to data that could lead them to make an informed decision. The biggest hope we have, said Makary, is in the future generation—new doctors. "They have little tolerance for secrecy and demand transparency."

## RESEARCH INTERESTS AND EXPERTISE

According to the Johns Hopkins Medicine website, Makary's research interests include operative risk assessment in the elderly, cancer therapy, minimally invasive surgery, health services research, occupational safety, diabetes, and obesity.

His expertise, accrued over a period of higher education that lasted ten years and continued during and after his climbing up the ranks at Johns Hopkins, includes various abdominal and pancreatic surgeries as well as surgical oncology, transplant surgery, and minimally invasive procedures.

Makary lives in Washington, DC.

## SUGGESTED READING

Allen, Marshall. "Why Patient Harm Is One of the Leading Causes of Death in America." *ProPublica*. ProPublica, 18 Sept. 2012. Web. 18 Nov. 2014.

Landro, Laura. "Hospital Horrors." *Wall Street Journal*. Dow Jones, 3 Oct. 2012. Web. 18 Nov. 2014.

Makary, Marty. "How to Stop Hospitals from Killing Us." *Wall Street Journal*. Dow Jones, 21 Sept. 2012. Web. 18 Nov. 2014.

—Dmitry Kiper

---

# Kate Mara

**Born:** February 27, 1983
**Occupation:** Actor

Aaron Mentele/Wikimedia Commons

After years of working as a jobbing actor in mostly supporting roles in film and television, Kate Mara came into her own in 2013, when she took on the part of the ambitious but morally compromised reporter Zoe Barnes on Netflix's critically acclaimed political drama *House of Cards*. Her portrayal of Barnes—which won her rave reviews from critics and fans alike—also earned her an Emmy nomination in 2014 for outstanding guest actress in a drama series. "I just wanted to be a part of something that I felt was helping me grow as an actor," Mara remarked in an interview with Scott Huver for *Manhattan* magazine (24 Apr. 2014). "Luckily, *House of Cards* is exactly what I wanted. Every day I would go to work knowing I was going to be challenged in some way, or that I would have to be on my toes."

Mara's high-profile performance has since helped to open up new opportunities for her: she has costarred with Johnny Depp in the big-budget sci-fi thriller *Transcendence* (2014) and was offered a role alongside Matt Damon in the film *The Martian* (2015), which is based on the critically acclaimed bestselling novel of the same name. In the summer of 2015, she will appear as Sue Storm, also known as the Invisible Woman, in *Fantastic Four*, the highly anticipated reboot of the film adaptation of the long-running Marvel comic book series.

## EARLY LIFE

One of four siblings (including her sister, Rooney, who is also a successful actor), Kate Mara was born to Chris and Kathleen Mara on February 27, 1983, in Bedford, New York. She hails from National Football League royalty on both sides of her family: her maternal great-grandfather, Art Rooney Sr., founded the Pittsburgh Steelers, and her paternal great-grandfather, Tim Mara, founded the New York Giants.

Because of her family's business success, she could have chosen any path in life. Mara, however, fell in love with the idea of acting at a young age. A shy girl who found pretending to be other people an enjoyable escape, she became convinced that someday she would become an actor—something her parents were not particularly sure she should do. In an interview with Gill Pringle for the *Independent* (25 Apr. 2014), Mara recalled, "I was nine years old when I started 'the campaign,' and fourteen when I got an agent. That's five years of a lot of conversations. I did a lot of really bad community theater so I think I proved I was very serious about it. I would leave misspelt notes on my mother's pillow all the time."

After an endless series of auditions, Mara's first professional acting gig came on an episode of *Law & Order* in 1997. Aside from her film debut in *Random Hearts* (1999) with Harrison Ford, she primarily landed roles on television shows, such as *Madigan Men* and *Ed* in 2000 and *Law & Order: Special Victims Unit* in 2001. Her work was steady enough that she felt comfortable deferring her entrance into the Tisch School of the Arts at New York University. She saw little reason to learn how to become an actor when she was already working in the field, and the social parts of college held little appeal for her. She told Pringle, "School was not something I enjoyed, especially the social aspect of it, so college to me just sounded like a more intense social experience that I was not excited about. I don't regret that in any way, even if a lot of my friends were shocked that I didn't want to go to college."

## EARLY HOLLYWOOD CAREER

At nineteen, Mara moved to California, hoping that her relocation to the West Coast would help further advance her career. She quickly earned more television work alone, appearing in 2003 on such series as *Everwood*, *Nip/Tuck*, *Cold Case*, and *Boston Public*. In 2004, she appeared in roles on such shows as *CSI: Miami*, *CSI: Crime Scene Investigation*, and *Jack & Bobby*.

Despite interest from the television world, further film roles continued to elude her until she won a supporting part as Heath Ledger's teenage daughter in *Brokeback Mountain* (2005), which many critics now see as her breakout role. The next year saw more promise in her television potential as she appeared in several episodes of the hit Fox thriller *24*. She followed these performances with more supporting roles—usually as a girlfriend, wife, or daughter—in such films as *We Are Marshall* (2006), starring Matthew McConaughey; *Shooter* (2007), starring Mark Wahlberg; and *127 Hours* (2010), starring James Franco. In an interview with Patricia Sheridan for the *Pittsburgh Post-Gazette* (3 Feb. 2014), Mara remarked of her varied supporting roles: "I don't find it super-appealing to just play likable characters. I am interested in doing all of it, and it doesn't bother me to think an audience is probably not going to like me very much. If they don't and you are playing an unlikable character, well, you are just doing your job well."

In 2011, Mara's sister, Rooney, who had followed her to Hollywood, shot to fame with her portrayal of Lisbeth Salander, the main character in the US film adaptation of Stieg Larsson's popular 2005 novel *The Girl with the Dragon Tattoo*. "Now I have someone who's in the club with me," Mara said of Rooney to Huver. "There was such a long period of time when I didn't have that. It's really rare to have a sibling going through the same, or very, very similar, experiences as you: similar stresses and joys and uncertainties. . . . I don't take it for granted at all."

While her sister was making the film in Sweden, Mara visited the set and met the film's director, David Fincher. After Fincher was hired by Netflix to adapt the BBC political drama *House of Cards* for Netflix, he realized that Kate was perfect for a role he had in mind.

## HOUSE OF CARDS

The American adaptation of *House of Cards* tells the story of a sharp, devious congressman named Francis Underwood (played by Kevin Spacey) who seeks to gain greater power for himself by any means necessary after being passed over for an important position in the president's cabinet. In the series, Mara portrayed Zoe Barnes, a determined but morally ambiguous reporter who gets intimately involved with Underwood. Mara was thrilled by the idea of playing Zoe and especially of working with Fincher, who had done so much to advance her sister's career. Although she does not consider herself on the same moral page as Zoe, Mara felt some sympathy toward the character and was attracted to the idea of playing such a bold role. She told Amanda Dobbins for *Vulture* (9 Feb. 2014), "Obviously, I do not agree with a lot of the s—— that she does. The stuff that I connected with was the human, emotional stuff. Her ambition."

During the course of the show, Zoe has an affair with Underwood, who is married to the almost equally formidable Claire (played by Robin Wright), in order to get inside information on what is going on in Washington. While Zoe is smart, she is also a bit naïve and fails to truly grasp what her involvement with the duplicitous Underwood might mean. The chance to play such a complicated character, with such a solid cast, on an experimental show that released all of its episodes all at once through an online streaming platform rather than over a season on a cable or network television channel was a once-in-a-lifetime opportunity for Mara. She also took the job knowing, from the very beginning, that her character's part in the storyline only lasted into the first episode of the second season. In her interview with Sheridan, she recalled, "I was just thrilled to be working with David Fincher and the cast. You know, Kevin Spacey and Robin Wright are two people that I've always wanted to work with. The expectation of it doing well and that sort of thing was just the cherry on top. It could have failed miserably, and sure that would be disappointing, but the experience of working with those people and the challenge of that is really why I got involved."

## A FUTURE IN FILM

Since departing the show after its second season, Mara has developed her film career. In 2014, she appeared in *Transcendence* as the leader of an antitechnology extremist group that seeks to undermine the plans of a scientist, played by Johnny Depp, to further advance the field of artificial intelligence. Although a critical and commercial disappointment, the film has not prevented Mara from securing other roles in big-budget movies. She has worked on four films scheduled for release in 2015, including *Captive*, a thriller about a single mother taken hostage in her apartment; *The Martian*, a film based on the best-selling novel by Andy Weir and directed by Ridley Scott about an astronaut (played by Matt Damon) who becomes trapped on Mars and must survive until a rescue mission can reach him; and *Man Down*, a postapocalyptic thriller about a war veteran's (played by Shia LaBeouf) search for his family.

Most notably, she will star in *Fantastic Four*, in which she will play one of four ordinary human beings who gain superpowers through an accidental exposure to radiation. The movie, based on the Marvel comic that began in 1961 and directed by Josh Trank, is a reboot of a lackluster two-film series by 20th Century Fox that began in 2005. Trank's interpretation of the series—from casting choices to leaked plot points—has already divided fans of the well-loved comic. "The whole thing will be different than anything I've ever done," Mara said to Huver of her experience on *Fantastic Four*. "I really loved Josh Trank's take on it, and I'm a fan of his last film, *Chronicle*, which was like an antisuperhero movie—really dark, which is what I like. I like things that are rooted in reality and that are dark and not what you expect. And I think that that's probably what *Fantastic Four* will be."

As Mara gains more opportunities and her star continues to rise, she has been asked about plans for her future and whether she has awards in mind. Reiterating her commitment to simply finding roles that make her happy to wake up and go to work, she emphasizes her desire to live in the present, telling Jamie Lincoln for *Interview* magazine (17 Apr. 2014), "I definitely have goals and dreams and things like that for my future, but I'm just more comfortable living in the right now and taking every day as it comes."

## PERSONAL LIFE

While Mara believed she had a destiny outside of football from a young age, her love of the game, which always brought her large family together, remains strong—she has a clause in her contract allowing her to leave a film set so that she can attend any Super Bowl game in which the Giants or Steelers are playing. This development was inspired by the disappointment she felt after having to miss the Steelers' Super Bowl win in 2006 because of the *24* filming schedule. For the most part, Mara avoids talking about her personal life, claiming that her career is a much more interesting topic. However, often preferring to stay in or catch a movie, the self-professed homebody and vegan enjoys exercising and taking her dogs for walks.

## SUGGESTED READING

Dobbins, Amanda. "Investigating Kate Mara: A Walk with *House of Cards*' Star Reporter." *Vulture*. New York Media, 9 Feb. 2014. Web. 26 Feb. 2015.

Huver, Scott. "Lady Luck." *Manhattan*. Modern Luxury, 24 Apr. 2014. Web. 26 Feb. 2015.

Mara, Kate. "Kate Mara, the On-Screen Radical." Interview by Jamie Lincoln. *Interview*. Interview, 17 Apr. 2014. Web. 26 Feb. 2015.

Mara, Kate. "Patricia Sheridan's Breakfast with . . . Kate Mara." Interview by Patricia Sheridan. *Pittsburgh Post-Gazette*. Pittsburgh Post-Gazette, 3 Feb. 2014. Web. 26 Feb. 2015.

Pringle, Gill. "House of Cards' Kate Mara: 'It is Complicated Being Compared to My Sister Rooney.'" *Independent*. Independent Digital News and Media, 25 Apr. 2014. Web. 26 Feb. 2015.

## SELECTED WORKS

*Brokeback Mountain*, 2005; *24*, 2006; *We Are Marshall*, 2006; *Shooter*, 2007; *127 Hours*, 2010; *House of Cards*, 2013–14; *Transcendence*, 2014; *Captive*, 2015; *Fantastic Four*, 2015; *The Martian*, 2015

—Christopher Mari

# Marc Márquez
**Born:** February 17, 1993
**Occupation:** Motorcycle road racer

Spanish motorcycle racer Marc Márquez is said to be a friendly guy off of the track, but as he told John F. Burns for the *New York Times* (31 Aug. 2014), "When helmet goes on, Marc is no more nice. Racing is racing. And I race, always, to win." And win he does. Márquez, who celebrated his twenty-first birthday in 2014, is the youngest champion in the history of elite motorcycle racing, and his aggressive and, some say, reckless technique is redefining the sport. In April 2013 he was the youngest winner of a premier class motorcycle Grand Prix and the youngest world champion in November of the same year. He was the first rookie to win the MotoGP world title since American Kenny Roberts, who accomplished the feat over thirty-five years ago in 1978. His nicknames include the Smiling Assassin, Marc the Magnificent, and Marc the Maniac. "Marc always rides at the limit," Dani Pedrosa, Márquez's Honda teammate, told Burns. "It seems like he's crashing all the time, but he's not crashing."

Elite motorcycle road racing is divided into three classes, each with a corresponding sized bike: MotoGP, Moto2, and Moto3. MotoGP, the class in which Márquez races, is considered the premier category, reserved for only the best racers and fastest machines. MotoGP riders race with prototype machines manufactured by Ducati, Yamaha, and Honda exclusively for racing. Márquez races for Honda. His father gave him a dirt bike when he was four years old (a Yamaha, he admits), and he began racing just a few years later. Under the tutelage of 1999 Moto3 world champion Emilio Alzamora, Márquez rose through the ranks to enjoy a record-smashing MotoGP rookie season in 2014. But Márquez was a hero in Spain long before that. Motocross is enormously popular in Spain; as early as 2012, Márquez's second season of Moto2, he told Dennis Noyes for *Cycle World* (26 July 2012), "There are times when I wish I could just be a normal person so I could go out with my friends without having to stop for pictures and autographs. On the other hand," he added, "when so many people know and admire you, you realize you are doing something right, and that it is worthwhile." Ever since he was a teen, Márquez has exhibited the more intangible qualities of a popular global superstar.

Juan Mabromata/AFP/Getty Images

Some have even compared him to the swaggering Italian world champion Valentino Rossi, one of the sport's biggest celebrities. But Márquez has already established his own distinct brand of likability: he is humble in interviews yet ruthless on the track, coy—when a reporter asked him which woman he would take out on a date if he had his choice, he said his mother—yet surprisingly candid about his own hopes and fears. "He has that one-in-a-billion ability to live life at two speeds," Mat Oxley wrote for *Motor Sport* magazine (1 Feb. 2014), "combining zoom-lens focus on the details with perfect peripheral vision, fully seeing and understanding everything that's going on around him."

## EARLY LIFE IN CEVERA

Márquez was born on February 17, 1993, in Cervera, a small town about sixty miles outside of Barcelona, Spain. His father, Julià Márquez, worked in construction, and his mother, Roser Alentá, works as a secretary for a logistics company. (Márquez's brother, Álex, who is three years his junior, is also a motocross champion. In 2014, Álex won the Moto3 world title, making him and his brother the only pair of siblings to ever win world championships in the same year.) Julià was also a member of the local motorcycle club, the Moto Club Segre. The young Márquez would often accompany his father to enduros, or long-distance, off-road races, though there was no indication that he would grow up to race like his father. "Marc was so small," his mother told Maria Guidotti for *Cycle World* magazine (12 Nov. 2014), "that we had to make fruit shakes to help him grow." When he was four years old, his father bought him a dirt bike. Márquez learned to race on dirt tracks, "acclimatizing to riding with the front tire tucked and the rear tire slewing sideways," Oxley wrote. Motorcycle legends like American Grand Prix racer Wayne Rainey and Australian world champion Mick Doohan, Oxley points out, learned the same way. Márquez was a born risk-taker, but he has also been described as a very smart child. "He had fast reactions, and eyes that took in everything," Luis Capdevila, a family friend, told Mike Nicks for the London *Independent* (30 Aug. 2013). "If you gave him advice he absorbed it immediately."

When he was eight years old, Márquez won a $4,500 scholarship from the Spanish motorcycle federation. The money helped his family buy him a new bike and equipment, but the cost of competing was still more than the family could comfortably afford. Soon, however, Márquez was discovered by former world champion Emilio Alzamora, who was then working for Monlau Competicion, a facility that nurtures young riding talent. Alzamora took an interest in Márquez in 2004, becoming his mentor and later, his manager.

## EARLY RACING CAREER

Márquez cut his teeth on the Catalan and Spanish National Championships, competing in his first Catalan Championship in 2000 and winning his first championship in 2001. In 2002, Márquez switched to road racing and won the Open RACC 50cc championship; the following year, he moved up to the 125cc class and finished second overall. In 2004, Márquez competed in the 125cc class in the Catalan Championships, and went on to win the 125cc Catalan crown both that year and the following year. In 2007 he moved up again, this time to the 125cc CEV Championship, where he finished ninth overall. Márquez made his world championship debut in Portugal in 2008, and two months later, he finished third at the British Motorcycle Grand Prix at Donington Park. He was fifteen years old. In 2010, Márquez broke his collarbone in a crash in Jerez, Spain; he was back on his bike three weeks later, and scored his first victory in the 125cc Moto3 class in June in Italy. Márquez went on a five-race winning streak (he won a total of ten races that year) and took his first world title at the end of the season.

In 2011 Márquez moved into the 600cc Moto2 class, but failed to score a single point in the first three rounds of the season. He won the fourth race and seemed to be headed for another world title when a bad crash in practice before a race in Malaysia derailed his plans. Márquez won seven races that year, coming in second, but an injury that he sustained in the crash persisted. According to Gary Rose for the BBC (10 Nov. 2013), Márquez damaged the muscle that controls rotation of the eyeball. He was plagued with vision problems that put him out of commission for the end of the 2011 season and much of the 2012 preseason. In January 2012, he underwent eye surgery, and was back on his bike two months later. He made a strong comeback, winning his first race in Qatar thanks to a controversial last-lap pass on Swiss rider Thomas Lüthi. His style continued to draw criticism even as Márquez racked up victories. By season's end, he had won nine races and appeared on the podium fourteen times. He was named the 2012 Moto2 world champion. At this point in his career, it was a foregone conclusion that the young prodigy would move up to the 1000cc MotoGP class, but his contract with Repsol Honda in July 2012 made it official.

## MOTOGP WORLD CHAMPION

Márquez made it to the podium in his debut race in Qatar, and became the youngest rider to post the fastest lap in the premier class. He won his second race and became the youngest rider to ever win a MotoGP race. Márquez went on to break nearly every single record to be had in the class: he is the first rookie to win four consecutive races; he is the winningest rookie, as well as the first rookie to appear in the top three sixteen times, the first rookie to qualify on pole (the track position reserved for the rider with the best qualifying time) nine times, and the first rookie to amass 334 season points. Most importantly, Márquez became the first rookie since Roberts in 1978 to win the MotoGP World title. He is the youngest rider ever to achieve the feat. He also stands alongside Rossi and England's Mike Hailwood and Phil Read as only the fourth rider in history to win world titles in every class.

After his history-making rookie season, Márquez broke his leg in a training accident in February 2014. By late March he was back on his bike for the season's first race in Qatar. He won the race and went on to win the next nine of the season. He was gunning for a record eleventh consecutive win in Brno in the Czech Republic, but he was beaten by his teammate, Dani Pedrosa. Still, his winning streak gave him the edge he needed to clinch a second consecutive world title three races before the season's end.

To characterize Márquez's style as merely reckless ignores the uncanny level of control he exerts over his bike—though he does consistently take his machines to their limit, which has its own consequences. In 2013, Oxley points out, Márquez was the second most frequent crasher in the MotoGP class. All of those crashes—including one particularly nasty tumble in Italy at 175 miles an hour—came in practice. "In other words, Márquez uses practice to try new ideas and push the boundaries, and sometimes those experiments go wrong," Oxley wrote. In addition to his lack of concern for his own physical well-being—and, some riders have argued, the physical well-being of others (he racked up more penalty points than any other rider in 2013)—Márquez has revived some old cycling techniques and created some new ones to give himself a competitive edge. Like the elite riders of the 1980s and 1990s, Márquez employs sliding, sacrificing the longevity of his tires to assert more control over his bike. He also uses his elbows to safeguard against crashes. Most riders wear plastic elbow pads. Márquez has to wear specially made magnesium sliders, but even those rarely last more than one race.

Márquez's life off the track is a lot like that of any other twenty-one-year-old. He vacations with family and friends, and though speed may not scare him, the ocean does. If he is on a beach and the water is clear, he is okay, he told Matthew Birt for *MCN* (8 Aug. 2014). "But when I go out a bit further I get scared. I keep thinking something is going to come and take me." Until very recently, Márquez and his brother still lived with their parents—where they shared a room and slept in bunk beds—but in 2014, Márquez moved to the tiny European state of Andorra.

**SUGGESTED READING**

Birt, Matthew. "Marc Márquez: 'I Prefer Bikes to Girls.'" *MCN*. Bauer, 8 Aug. 2014. Web. 14 Dec. 2014.

Burns, John F. "Marc Márquez Continues Dominance with British Grand Prix Win." *New York Times*. New York Times, 31 Aug. 2014. Web. 14 Dec. 2014.

Guidotti, Maria. "Márquez MotoGP: A Family of Champions." *Cycle World*. Bonnier, 12 Nov. 2014. Web. 14 Dec. 2014.

Nicks, Mike. "Fearless Kid Marc Márquez Leaves MotoGP Legends Standing." *Independent* [London]. Independent.co.uk, 30 Aug. 2013. Web. 14 Dec. 2014.

Noyes, Dennis. "Spanish Flyer: Marc Márquez Is the Teenage Heir to Spain's Grand Prix Racing Throne." *Cycle World*. Bonnier, 26 July 2012. Web. 14 Dec. 2014.

Oxley, Mat. "All Arms and Elbows." *Motor Sport*. Motor Sport, 1 Feb. 2014. Web. 14 Dec. 2014.

Rose, Gary. "Marc Márquez: MotoGP Champion Is Motorcycling's Smiling Assassin." *BBC*. BBC, 10 Nov. 2013. Web. 14 Dec. 2014.

—Molly Hagan

# Catherine Martin

**Born:** January 26, 1965
**Occupation:** Costume and production designer

"When Shakespeare said 'clothes maketh the man,' what he was really saying was that the way you present yourself—by adorning yourself, by costuming yourself every morning—speaks reams about who you are, and about how you view your place in the world," Catherine "CM" Martin, the Academy Award–winning costume and production designer told Channon Hodge in a video for the *New York Times* (31 Dec. 2013). With her husband and collaborator, director Mark Anthony "Baz" Luhrmann, Martin has been, as Maggie Bullock wrote for *Elle* magazine (3 May 2013), "conjuring—and, more to the point, managing—a distinctive brand of madcap genius for some 25 years." The couple's best-known films include Shakespeare's *Romeo + Juliet* (1996) set in a gritty modern-day Verona; *Moulin Rouge!* (2001), about the famous Parisian nightclub of the same name; and most recently, an epic reimagining of F. Scott Fitzgerald's most famous Jazz Age novel, *The Great Gatsby* (2013), filmed in 3-D. Luhrmann's visions are strange and sometimes overwhelming. In his movies, turn-of-the-century can-can dancers sing David Bowie songs, and even the excesses of America's quintessential fictional playboy, Jay Gatsby, are amplified: the colors are brighter, the parties are larger, and the flappers, with their arms around bottles of champagne the size of a man, swing from the chandeliers. If Luhrmann dreams

Cindy Ord/Getty Images Entertainment/Getty Images

it, Martin told Bullock, she has the formidable task of making it happen. "Baz is the author, the one who generates the kernel of the idea," she said, "and I'm an applied artist." Actor Nicole Kidman, who starred in *Moulin Rouge!* and Luhrmann's 2008 epic *Australia*, had a different take. "You can't divide them, CM and Baz. They blur—he helps her; she helps him," she told Bullock.

## EARLY LIFE AND EDUCATION

Catherine Martin was born on January 26, 1965, in Lindfield, a suburb of Sydney, New South Wales, Australia. Her mother is French, her father, Australian. They met at the Sorbonne in Paris, where she was studying mathematics and he was studying eighteenth-century French literature. Martin and her brother grew up in Sydney but spent a lot of time with their art-loving grandparents, who lived in the Loire Valley in France. Martin demonstrated an early desire to learn to sew. She was fascinated with how clothes were constructed, but also why people wore them, and what it said about their lives. "I was really interested in the history of fashion, and in social history, as long as I can remember," she told Philippa Hawker for the *Sydney Morning Herald* (26 Dec. 2014).

Martin attended North Sydney Girls High School. At fifteen, Martin was making her own dresses. While working as an usher at a movie theater in Lindfield, she dreamed of Hollywood.

Martin studied visual arts at the Sydney College of the Arts and pattern-cutting at East Sydney technical college, while working odd jobs making costumes for stage productions and costume companies in Sydney. She finished her degree at Sydney's National Institute of Dramatic Art (NIDA) in 1988.

## PARTNERSHIP WITH LUHRMANN BEGINS

While at NIDA, Martin met Luhrmann, an opera director and former NIDA student. Her mentor and former professor, Peter Cooke, took credit for bringing the two together. "[Luhrmann] came to me and said, 'I need a designer,' and I said, 'You need Catherine Martin,' because she was so fabulously literate, and inspirational," Cooke recalled to Caroline Overington for the *Sydney Morning Herald* (26 Mar. 2002). "She used colour and imagery and form in a really remarkable way." The two hit it off immediately, though their romance and their working partnership developed more slowly than Martin would have liked, she told Bullock. Luhrmann, on the other hand, told Bullock that he knew that their relationship—both as collaborators and as spouses—was "meant to be." In 1988 Martin and Luhrmann collaborated on their first project, an opera called *Lake Lost* with composer Felix Meagher and dramatist Wendy Harmer, for Australia's Bicentennial. They built a large swimming pool with a small island in the Melbourne television studio in which the opera was staged.

## *LA BOHÈME*

In 1990 Martin and Luhrmann were asked to stage *La Bohème*, Giacomo Puccini's epic tale of love and loss set in nineteenth-century Paris, for Opera Australia. Luhrmann had a unique vision for the opera: he wanted to set it in 1957 instead. He was inspired, visually, by the playful sense of place in the 1953 movie *Roman Holiday*, starring Audrey Hepburn, but also by the brooding shadows of American film noir and the romantic spirit of French film star Gérard Philipe. The show became the Sydney Opera House's biggest hit. The process of making *La Bohème* introduced Martin to people whom she would continue to work with throughout her career, but it also brought their work to the attention of a much larger audience. It served as a stepping stone to the couple's work in film, though Luhrmann's *La Bohème* enjoyed a long life of its own. In 1993 the opera was staged at the Sydney Opera House and recorded for television, starring Cheryl Barker and David Hobson, and in 2002, it moved to Broadway in New York City. *New York Times* theater critic Ben Brantley deemed it a "rapturous reimagining" of the Puccini's story and praised Luhrmann and Martin for finding "the visual equivalent of the sensual beauty and vigor of the score" (9 Dec. 2002). In 2003 Martin won the Tony Award for best scenic design for her work on the Broadway production.

## STRICTLY BALLROOM

Martin and Luhrmann made their first feature film in 1992. *Strictly Ballroom*, an outrageous romantic comedy about a champion ballroom dancer, was inspired by Luhrmann's mother, who taught ballroom dancing. Luhrmann actually wrote the story in 1984 and presented it as a stage play; it won best production at a youth drama festival in Slovakia in 1986.

Martin and Luhrmann decided to adapt the story for film in 1988 and finally amassed enough funding to begin filming in 1991. It was their first foray into the film world, and according to Martin, it was no walk in the park. "The production probably wanted to fire me for the first month or so, because everyone thinks they can do better than a 25-year-old girl," she told Hawker, referring to her age at the time. "And I just stuck to my guns and kept going. Kept working hard." Martin created a delightfully gaudy spectacle on the production's miniscule budget, working with sequins and chicken feathers.

After the film was dropped by a cinema in Australia—an executive refused to screen it because he felt it would not make any money—*Strictly Ballroom* premiered at the Cannes Film Festival in 1992. It received a fifteen-minute standing ovation and ignited a bidding war among major film distributors. The film is one of the highest grossing in Australian cinema history and became a cult classic in the United States. It was nominated for thirteen Australian Film Institute (AFI) Awards and won eight, including one, for Martin, for best production design. It was nominated for a Golden Globe for best picture (musical or comedy) in 1993. Martin also won two British Academy of Film and Television (BAFTA) Awards for her work on the film, for costume design (with Angus Strathie) and best production design. In 2014 Martin and Luhrmann adapted the movie back to the stage in *Strictly Ballroom: The Musical*. It premiered at the Sydney Lyric Theater.

## ROMEO + JULIET

*Strictly Ballroom* launched Luhrmann's career as a filmmaker and brought him to Hollywood to direct his second film, a modern-day interpretation of *Romeo + Juliet* (1996) starring teen idols Leonardo DiCaprio and Claire Danes. The Verona of the film is best described as an urban, dystopian Miami. The Capulets and Montagues are warring street gangs, and the virginal (and soon-to-be deceased) Juliet appears at a costume party wearing white angel's wings. The film is a manic mash of genres and styles, grating to some, though even its critics appear to appreciate its visual merits. "When the film cooks up a thousand-candle bier for Juliet, it moves fully into the garish realm of rock video, but many of its small touches actually show a droll restraint," Janet Maslin wrote for the *New York Times* (1 Nov. 1996). "And when a tropical storm at the beach mirrors the action in its fury, Mr. Luhrmann briefly but successfully achieves what the whole film is after: a visual universe fully in tune with the characters' ageless passions." Martin received her first Academy Award nomination for best art direction for the film in 1997. She won a BAFTA for best production design in 1998.

## MOULIN ROUGE! AND THE GREAT GATSBY

In 2001 Luhrmann and Martin released their most extravagant film to that date, a musical called *Moulin Rouge!*, about a can-can dancer named Satine (Nicole Kidman) in fin-de-siècle Paris. Martin responded to Luhrmann's vision with aplomb. She designed four hundred unique showgirl costumes for the dancers, who performed to a version of Nirvana's "Smells like Teen Spirit," and created a look for Kidman in the mold of classic screen sirens like Greta Garbo, Marlene Dietrich, and Marilyn Monroe. The costumes even inspired trends in retail. Martin, along with her team, won two Academy Awards for their work on *Moulin Rouge!*, which was the first musical since Disney's *Beauty and the Beast* (1991) to be nominated for best picture. Martin went home with statues for best art direction and best costume design and dedicated both awards to Luhrmann.

Luhrmann and Martin next tackled *Australia*, an epic origin story of their home country starring Nicole Kidman and Hugh Jackman, released in 2008. Despite sweeping views of the outback, the film was poorly received.

In the early 2010s Luhrmann focused his lens

on an age of opulence similar to the one he had captured in *Moulin Rouge!* Working with Martin and his former Romeo, Leonardo DiCaprio, Luhrmann undertook the daunting task of adapting *The Great Gatsby* for film in 3-D. The hedonism of the 1920s, which came to an abrupt end with the stock market crash of 1929, Martin told Bullock, seemed a fitting subject in the wake of the crash in 2008. Still, many criticized the film as a celebration of Gatsby's excesses, rather than a critique of them, as they were presented in Fitzgerald's novel. As had proven true in the past, when critics found fault with the film, they stopped short of its design. In her video interview with Hodge, Martin describes taking a lyric passage of the book, in which narrator Nick Carraway observes the breeze lifting the women's dresses, and translating it into the costumes for the introductory shot of Gatsby's love, Daisy Buchanan (Carey Mulligan). Accordingly, Martin designed Mulligan's gauzy, white gown with petal cut-outs that captured the "kinetic energy" that she felt in Fitzgerald's text, she said. "You have to express the feeling," she told Hodge, "not the actuality." Martin won her third and fourth Oscars for *Gatsby*—making her the winningest Australian in the Academy Awards' history—for best costume design and best production design.

## OTHER PROJECTS AND PERSONAL LIFE

In addition to her work in film, Martin has worked in the fashion industry since the early 1990s. She has styled photo shoots for Australian *Vogue*, directed fashion shows, and worked with the haute couturier Chanel. She also runs a homewares and interior-design business, and in 2013 Martin and Luhrmann were asked to design the interiors of the historic Saxony Hotel in Miami, Florida.

Martin and Luhrmann were married in a ceremony that took place on the stage of the Sydney Opera House in 1997. Martin wore a white tuxedo inspired by a similar outfit worn by model and actress Bianca Jagger when she married Mick Jagger of the Rolling Stones in 1971. The technical director of the opera house officiated the wedding and made his entrance by swooping "in on a high wire, wearing an angel costume, complete with tutu," Bullock wrote. The couple have two children: Lillian, born in 2003, and William, born in 2005. They live in New York City and Sydney.

## SUGGESTED READING

Brantley, Ben. "Sudden Streak of Red Warms a Cold Garret." *New York Times*. New York Times, 9 Dec. 2002. Web. 15 Apr. 2015.

Bullock, Maggie. "Baz Luhrmann's Leading Lady." *Elle*. Hearst Communications, 3 May 2013. Web. 14 Apr. 2015.

Corliss, Richard. "The Baz Bohème." *Time*. Time, 21 Dec. 2002. Web. 15 Apr. 2015.

Freeman, Hadley. "Can-Can Do." *Guardian*. Guardian News and Media, 7 Sept. 2001. Web. 15 Apr. 2015.

Hawker, Philippa. "Catherine Martin Is Strictly Sensational." *Sydney Morning Herald*. Fairfax Media, 26 Dec. 2014. Web. 15 Apr. 2015.

Martin, Catherine. "Clothes and Character: Dressing Gatsby." Interview by Channon Hodge. *New York Times*. New York Times, 31 Dec. 2013. Web. 14 Apr. 2015.

Overington, Caroline. "Two Oscars, but Only One Baz." *Sydney Morning Herald*. Fairfax Media, 26 Mar. 2002. Web. 15 Apr. 2015.

—Molly Hagan

# Virgilio Martínez Véliz

**Born:** August 31, 1977
**Occupation:** Chef

In the twenty-first century Peru has grown into one of the top gastronomic locations in the world. This popularity is largely thanks to a new generation of talented homegrown chefs like Virgilio Martínez Véliz, whose flagship restaurant Central, in Lima's Miraflores district, has pushed the boundaries of Peruvian cuisine. A protégé of the noted Peruvian celebrity chef and restaurateur Gastón Acurio, Martínez worked in kitchens all over the world before opening Central in 2009. In the tradition of chefs like René Redzepi of Denmark's Noma restaurant, he takes inspiration from local flora and fauna for his cuisine, which is devoted to showcasing rare and unfamiliar Peruvian ingredients. Martínez's forward-thinking approach to food has helped Central earn a reputation as one of the most influential restaurants in the world. In 2013 the restaurant debuted at number fifty on the highly coveted World's 50 Best Restaurants list, produced annually by the British trade magazine *Restaurant*. It rose to number fifteen on the list in 2014.

Martínez has opened three other restaurants: Senzo, in Cusco, Peru, and the sister restaurants Lima and Lima Floral, in London, England. Lima, which serves contemporary Peruvian cuisine in a casual setting, is the first Peruvian restaurant in Europe to earn a star in the prestigious Michelin guide. Martínez is the cofounder of Mater Iniciativa, a project dedicated to exploring the culinary potential of previously unknown products from Peru's different ecosystems. "Peruvian food is so much more than just ceviche at the beach," he told Howie Kahn for the *Wall Street Journal* (4 Mar. 2015).

## EARLY LIFE

Virgilio Martínez Véliz was born on August 31, 1977, in Lima, Peru. As in other Hispanic countries, Peruvian names are traditionally listed with the given name followed by the father's surname and then the mother's maiden name. Martínez's father, Raúl, is a banking lawyer, and his mother, Blanca, is an architect and painter. He has an older brother, Raúl, and two younger sisters, Malena and Maria Paz.

Some of Martínez's earliest memories involve food. A skateboarder in his youth, he fondly remembers buying from local food vendors while coasting on the streets of Lima. "We'd buy the greatest fruit," he recalled to Kahn, "and put together salads on the street." Martínez grew up eating traditional Peruvian specialties such as ceviche—raw fish marinated in citrus juice and spices—and *anticuchos*, grilled beef heart kebabs. A product of a privileged upbringing, he also often ate out at high-end restaurants, which would sometimes be the only place for him to talk to his busy father.

By the time he reached his teens, Martínez was eyeing a career as a professional skateboarder, but a serious shoulder injury abruptly ended those plans. Martínez strongly considered becoming an architect like his mother, but was ultimately persuaded by his father to go to law school. Martínez's father "wanted [him] to make money," he told Debbie Yong for the Singapore *Straits Times* (17 Apr. 2012), adding, "The image of success that I had from a young age was to be a lawyer."

## FINDING HIS CALLING

Martínez attended law school for three years before dropping out to pursue a career as a chef. During his time in law school, he channeled his passion for food by voraciously reading cook-

Central Restaurante/Wikimedia Commons

books. It was after reading British chef Marco Pierre White's groundbreaking cookbook, *White Heat* (1990), which revolutionized people's perceptions about fine dining, that Martínez became determined to enter the culinary world. Martínez's decision was met with vehement opposition from his father, who reportedly did not speak to him for two years as a result. "I always knew I was going to be a cook, I just didn't know when," Martínez told Yong.

In the mid-1990s, when Martínez embarked on his cooking career, Peru was known more for its violent and unsafe reputation than its cuisine. The country was devoid of cooking schools and its cuisine—a hodgepodge of indigenous, Spanish, Italian, African, Japanese, and Chinese influences—was largely unheralded. "I wasn't proud as I am now" of Peruvian food, Martínez admitted to Tom Sietsema for the *Washington Post* (20 Jan. 2012).

Martínez attended the prestigious culinary school Le Cordon Bleu, studying at locations in Ottawa, Canada, and London. After receiving his culinary diploma, he honed his cooking skills in kitchens around the world. Martínez worked at the upscale Ritz hotel in London before doing stages at a series of Spanish restaurants, including the late famed chef Santi Santamaria's Can Fabes, a now-defunct three-Michelin-star Catalan restaurant in Sant Celoni, Spain. He also worked at André Soltner's legendary French restaurant Lutèce in New York, which closed in 2004 after forty-three years.

## ASTRID Y GASTÓN

It was in 2004 that Martínez first approached Gastón Acurio about working at Acurio's acclaimed flagship restaurant, Astrid y Gastón. Widely credited with putting Peruvian cuisine on the map, Acurio had first opened Astrid y Gastón in Lima in 1994 as a French brasserie before gradually transforming the restaurant into one that served only modern and innovative Peruvian fare. Acurio eventually opened dozens of restaurants throughout Latin America and the rest of the world, helping to usher in a new cuisine called *Novoandina* ("New Andean"), which combined modern cooking techniques with ingredients from Peru and other Andean countries.

Impressed with Martínez's talent and passion, Acurio, who similarly dropped out of law school to become a chef, immediately offered him a chef position at Astrid y Gastón. Martínez worked there briefly before being tapped to open an outpost of the restaurant in Bogota, Colombia, in February 2005; he later led the restaurant's expansion to Madrid, Spain. As an executive chef for Astrid y Gastón, Martínez, under the guidance of Acurio, learned how to combine his global culinary influences with Peru's wide range of unique ingredients.

Martínez's desire to fully explore Peru's vast food culture came after a two-month training stage at the Four Seasons Hotel in Singapore in 2005. During this time Martínez became a habitué of the city's famous hawker, or street food, centers, whose creativity and diversity inspired him to return to Peru on a culinary exploration of the country's most remote regions. As he told the California-based Indian chef Geeta Bansal for her *OC Weekly* food blog *On the Line* (6 May 2013), "I started to travel around Peru to identify products and get to know people. This process led to the creation of my cuisine."

## CENTRAL RESTAURANT

In 2009 Martínez ventured on his own to open Central, a modern Peruvian restaurant in the fashionable Miraflores district of Lima. The two-story, eighty-seat restaurant is located just two blocks from the Pacific Ocean. Despite launching the $1.5-million venture without any outside financing, Martínez still turned to family members for assistance: his mother was responsible for the sleek design of the restaurant, sister Malena left her job as a physician to oversee

its tea program, and sister Maria Paz, a fashion designer, conceived employee attire and table linens. His wife, Pía León, serves as the restaurant's chef de cuisine

Described by Michael Slenske for *W Magazine* (Nov. 2012) as a "glass-and-stone-walled jewel box," Central has a contemporary ground-floor dining room adjacent to a glass-walled kitchen. It also has an upstairs space featuring a library stocked with reference books and indigenous ingredients, a temperature-controlled chocolate cabinet, an extensive wine cellar, a rooftop herb garden, and a reverse-osmosis water purification system. Central derives its name from the idea of a gastronomic headquarters for Martínez and his team.

During Central's first two years of operation, Martínez continually developed, tested, and perfected new recipes, with ingredients from all over Peru. Most of his foraging forays were concentrated in Peru's Cusco region, the epicenter of the Inca Empire and home of the world-famous Machu Picchu ruins. There, he began working with local farmers, anthropologists, and scientists, in order to gain a better understanding of the region's products and ancient agricultural history. He noted to Kahn, "We didn't have a plan when we started Central other than auteur cuisine with lots of ego . . . . But coming [to Cusco] changed my whole outlook. The answers and the emotions are all here, in our history."

## RISE TO INTERNATIONAL PROMINENCE

After a rocky start, in which Central was even forced to shut down for several months due to permit issues, Martínez "emerged with a locally sourced, tightly edited, artfully plated, and wholly delicious ten-course tasting menu dubbed Experience Origin," Slenske wrote. The menu, which changes frequently, evokes Peru's geographical diversity, from its dry coastal areas bordering the Pacific Ocean to its tropical rain-forests in the Amazon and high plains in the Andes Mountains; printed on high-quality fabric, it lists each course with its corresponding geographical region and altitude. As Sietsema put it, "To dine at Central . . . is to taste-test much of Peru."

Martínez's dishes are characterized by their unusual ingredients. Among them are a dish called Extreme Altitude containing chuño, a frozen dehydrated potato from the Andes, and *cushuro*, a caviar-shaped bacteria that grows in high-altitude Andean lakes; Red Jungle, featuring arapaima, a white-fleshed fish indigenous to the Amazon River, served alongside an Andean cactus fruit called airampo, a rainforest fruit called *huito*, and palm hearts; and a dessert, Mountain Range and Forest, comprising cacao, powdered coca leaf, edible clay, and cherimoya, another fruit from the Andes. In his interview with Bansal, Martínez said, "My food is very visual, to me landscapes, feelings, romance, emotions are very important. I believe my cuisine is very close to nature but in an artistic way."

Martínez's innovative cuisine instantly won the attention of the global food cognoscenti. In 2013 Central debuted on *Restaurant* magazine's prestigious annual World's 50 Best Restaurants list, coming in at number fifty. Then, in 2014, the restaurant jumped thirty-five places to number fifteen on the list. That year also saw Central voted the top restaurant in Latin America by Latin America's 50 Best Restaurants Academy. Meanwhile, Central was selected as the best restaurant in Peru by the Peruvian food guide *Summum* three years in a row, from 2012 to 2014.

## MATER INICIATIVA AND OTHER RESTAURANTS

In 2012 Martínez teamed up with his sister Malena to found the research organization Mater Iniciativa. The organization painstakingly catalogues every ingredient Martínez and his team bring back from foraging expeditions around Peru, which alone has hundreds of types of corn and four thousand varieties of potatoes. Mater's day-to-day operations are overseen by Malena, who works with a group of chefs and researchers to gain a comprehensive understanding of the products.

In addition to Central, Martínez has launched three other restaurant ventures. In 2012 he opened Senzo, a fine-dining restaurant located in the Palacio Nazarenas hotel in Cusco. Like Central, Senzo, which is headed by Mexican executive chef Karime López, has its own herb garden, uses locally sourced Peruvian ingredients, and offers haute cuisine dishes "true to Virgilio's vision," Bansal noted.

Also in 2012 Martínez partnered with Venezuelan brothers Gabriel and Jose Luis Gonzalez to open Lima, a contemporary yet casual Peruvian restaurant located in the Fitzrovia neighborhood of London. Featuring inventive interpretations of traditional Peruvian dishes like suckling pig and octopus, the eighty-seat restaurant became the first Peruvian restaurant in Europe to earn a Michelin star in 2013.

Martínez and the Gonzalez brothers opened Lima's sister restaurant, Lima Floral, in London's Covent Garden district, in 2014. The restaurant, which seats seventy, expands on the culinary concept established at Lima and includes a basement bar specializing in cocktails made with pisco, Peru's national spirit.

Both Lima and Lima Floral source many of their ingredients from the United Kingdom, but the more unusual products still come from Peru. Revenues from both ventures fund Mater Iniciativa, whose future headquarters in Peru will feature "a recipe lab, space for bench science, a comprehensive seed bank, dorms for visiting researchers and chefs and a restaurant with an uninterrupted 360-degree view of the Andes," according to Kahn. "I have two full-time jobs," Martínez told Kahn. "Finding edible things that have existed here forever, since before the Incas, and introducing them to a modern-day audience."

## PERSONAL LIFE

Martínez spends the majority of his time at Central with his wife Pía, whom he married in May 2013. He frequently travels to food conferences around the world as an ambassador for Peruvian cuisine.

## SUGGESTED READING

Kahn, Howie. "Chef Virgilio Martínez Takes Peruvian Cuisine to New Heights." *Wall Street Journal.* Dow Jones, 4 Mar. 2015. Web. 6 Mar. 2015.

Martínez Véliz, Virgilio. "Geeta Bansal Interviews Virgilio Martínez, Peru's Newest Chef Star." Interview by Geeta Bansal. *OC Weekly.* OC Weekly, 6 May 2013. Web. 20 Feb. 2015.

Sietsema, Tom. "Postcard from Tom: Review of Central Restaurante in Lima, Peru." *Washington Post.* Washington Post, 20 Jan. 2012. Web. 20 Feb. 2015.

Slenske, Michael. "Dispatch: Lima and Cusco in Peru." *W Magazine.* Condé Nast, Nov. 2012. Web. 6 Mar. 2015.

Yong, Debbie. "Virgilio Martínez to Open Peruvian Eatery in London." *Straits Times.* Singapore Press, 17 Apr. 2012. Web. 6 Mar. 2015.

—Chris Cullen

# Elizabeth McCracken

**Born:** September 16, 1966
**Occupation:** Author

Writer Elizabeth McCracken has achieved success with each of her publications, and she most recently won the Story Prize in March 2015 for her 2014 collection *Thunderstruck*. As Jill Menkes Kushner put it for *Literary Review* (Winter 1997), her work "offers the comfort of known feelings and the opportunity to appreciate the uniqueness of how those feelings are expressed, through original characters who offer a fresh view of familiar territory."

McCracken has received a number of awards for her work, among them a 1998 Guggenheim Fellowship and grants from both the Michener Foundation and the National Endowment for the Arts. In 2010, she joined the faculty at the University of Texas at Austin, where she holds the James Michener Chair of Fiction. Because her characters are often misfits—tattoo artists, giants, a woman still writing to family and friends long dead—McCracken is sometimes compared to southern gothic writers such as Eudora Welty and Flannery O'Connor. Asked for advice to young writers, she told Brendan Dowling for *Public Libraries* (Mar.–Apr. 2001), "When you're writing, save all your ambition for the page. Being too career ambitious will make you more fearful in your work. Be willing to break your own heart."

## EARLY LIFE

McCracken was born in Brighton, Massachusetts, on September 16, 1966, to Natalie and Samuel McCracken. Her mother descended from a family of Jewish rabbis; her father was a Presbyterian. Both of McCracken's parents were academics and writers, though not of fiction. Her mother was a writer and editor for Boston University; her father was an assistant to the provost of Boston University and a writer. Her older brother, Harry, became a writer as well. The family moved to Portland, Oregon, when McCracken was nine months old, returning to the Boston area after a subsequent stay in London.

The family moved five times before McCracken was seven, an experience that taught her not to try to follow the latest in pop culture to fit in with her peers; rather, she was interested in catching the attention of adults, who were

Ullstein Bild/Ullstein Bild/Getty Images

interested in the past. By the time McCracken entered high school, most of her wardrobe was vintage clothing.

Both parents were in accord in a preference for their own childhood years. The music and games of the 1940s, the era in which her parents grew up, were a part of McCracken's upbringing in 1970s Boston. Instead of losing her heart to teen idols, McCracken's favorite singer was Bing Crosby. She says both parents were "nostalgians," and reared their children to be as well. In fact, McCracken was so attuned to World War II that she was largely unaware of the Vietnam War.

The McCrackens often visited Des Moines, Iowa, when their daughter was growing up. McCracken's maternal grandmother was an activist and lawyer whose grandfather was the first ordained rabbi in Des Moines. As McCracken wrote for an interview in *Writer* (Mar. 2005), "I come from a family of unbelievable eccentrics on both sides. Not always as physically quirky as they are in my fiction, but certainly in terms of personality." She grew up hearing stories of family members long dead, some of whom ended up in her fiction.

## EDUCATION AND PROFESSION

On her fifteenth birthday, McCracken began working at the Newton, Massachusetts, public library, shelving fiction. She remained for seven years, eventually moving to the circulation desk.

McCracken earned a bachelor's degree in English from Boston University and later obtained a master's of fine arts degree from the prestigious Iowa Writers' Workshop at the University of Iowa. While in Iowa, she was able to visit her maternal grandmother often.

McCracken earned a master's degree in library science from Drexel University in 1993 and worked as a librarian for ten years. As she explained to Dowling, "I didn't want to teach five sections of composition a semester, which was the kind of job I would've gotten had I been very lucky. Some writers have no trouble working jobs they hate and then coming home to write. Not me. I wanted my 'money' job to be something as gratifying as writing. I didn't want to have to scramble for work."

## FIRST FICTIONS

Because there were amateur and professional writers in both her parents' families, none of her relatives considered becoming a writer an odd occupational choice. The stories that McCracken had written at the Iowa Writers' Workshop became part of her first collection, *Here's Your Hat, What's Your Hurry?* (1993). Further work on those stories occurred during her two years as a fellow at Provincetown's Fine Arts Work Center in 1990 and 1992. The published collection garnered the American Library Association's Notable Book Award in 1994.

McCracken also began her first novel, *The Giant's House* (1996), while at the Provincetown Fine Arts Work Center. She then took a position as a librarian in Somerville Library, near Boston. The job allowed her time to finish the novel, which features a young librarian, Peggy, as the narrator who befriends a young giant and falls in love with him, despite a fifteen-year age difference.

The book won a place on the 1996 *Granta* magazine's Best Young American Novelists list. The novel was also a finalist for the National Book Award in fiction. In addition, Barnes and Noble gave her the Great New Writers Award, which recognizes the American author of a first novel who was featured in the company's Discover program. The critical and popular success of the novel helped garner McCracken the job of visiting writer at the Iowa Writing Festival in 1997 and at Western Michigan University the following year.

After the success of *A Giant's House*, McCracken left her library job, but she later returned to it two days a week. As she explained to Sybil Steinberg and Michael Coffey for *Publishers Weekly* (6 Aug. 2001), "As a writer, you're essentially alone, and you're necessarily the most important person in the world. That's not psychologically healthy. . . . For a librarian, though, there's a fuller spectrum. People come in and say 'I need this' or 'I need that.' . . . I love the sheer randomness of it."

## MINING THE PAST

McCracken's interest in the past has informed her novels, as she told *Harper's Bazaar* (Sept. 2001), "Twice I've meant to write novels that take place in the present. Both times I came up with a contemporary plotline and then got waylaid by the back story. The present is best explained by the past, after all. If you're lucky, your childhood is largely plotless, as mine was. Even now, I stink at plot. I blame my happy, uneventful childhood."

A love of Abbott and Costello comedy routines, which she watched as a child, as well as her membership in a chapter of a Laurel and Hardy society, led to her second novel. *Niagara Falls All Over Again* (2001) is the story of two vaudeville performers. The work is first-person autobiographical fiction, based loosely on a great uncle. On her drive to Provincetown's Fine Arts Work Center, McCracken "wrote" the first twenty pages in her head. She heard it clearly in the voice of Mose Sharp, half of a vaudeville comic act. When published, the book won the PEN New England Award.

## MEMOIR AND MORE STORIES

McCracken lived as an academic nomad, taking fellowships and teaching opportunities that came her way. She had accepted her status as a single woman when, at age thirty-five, she met Jonathan Edward Carey Harvey at a party at Barnes and Noble. The two married and continued the wandering life in Ireland, Berlin, and Denmark, with teaching duties in Iowa City between traveling. On their second trip to France, McCracken became pregnant, but the boy was stillborn in 2006.

Both parents were heartsick, but they wanted another child. They left France, determined never to return; McCracken was offered a job at Skidmore College in Saratoga Springs. In 2007 a healthy baby, Augustus, joined the family. Later, the couple's daughter, Matilda, was born.

McCracken began writing a memoir on the loss of her first child; it was published in 2008. She took the title, *An Exact Replica of a Fig-*

ment of *My Imagination* (2008), from a sign she had seen at a reconstruction of Fort George in Schuylerville, New York. As she explained early in the work, "I don't want to wear my heart on my sleeve or put it away in cold storage. . . . I don't feel the need to tell my story to everyone, but when people ask, *Is this your first child?* I can't bear any of the possible answers."

The book received Publishers Weekly's designation as one of the best books of 2008. As reviewer Deborah Donovan wrote for *Booklist* (1 Aug. 2008), "McCracken manages to limn her poignant story with touches of humor, empathy toward those who struggled to express their awkward sympathy, and, ultimately, hope, in the form of the baby asleep in her lap as she types, one-handed."

Her 2014 collection *Thunderstruck* contained two new stories, plus seven revised tales that had been published previously in literary magazines. One of the stories, "Juliet," revisits McCracken's familiar ground of libraries, examining the responses of librarians to the murder of a patron. The book won the annual Story Prize, which carries a $20,000 award, in March 2015.

## FRIENDS, INFLUENCES, AND THOUGHTS ON WRITING

McCracken was at the Provincetown Fine Arts Work Center at the same time as fellow writer Ann Patchett. The two became and have remained close friends and writing partners. Other writers who have influenced McCracken include Charles Dickens, Carson McCullers, Grace Paley, and Studs Terkel.

McCracken claims she writes because she is unqualified for any other job. She told Sarah Anne Johnson in an interview for *Writer* (Mar. 2006), "Quite seriously, I became a writer because of the lack of requirements for the job. I am clumsy, careless, and my mind wanders. I like to gossip. I like to play God. I often don't care what other people think. I don't like to brush my hair very often. I like to eat while I work. I hate commuting." She does not subscribe to the idea of required daily writing. As she told *Provincetown Arts* (2005–6), "It's important not to believe that you're failing as a writer because you failed to put in your three hours that day. There are enough reasons you can find to loathe yourself, and that's a bad one to add to the mix."

## SUGGESTED READING

Donovan, Deborah. Rev. of *An Exact Replica of a Figment of My Imagination: A Memoir*, by Elizabeth McCracken. *Booklist* 1 Aug. 2008: 25–26. Web. 8 Apr. 2015.

Kushner, Jill Menkes. "Elizabeth McCracken: Perspectives on Romance and Loss." *Literary Review* (1997): 342–45. Web. 31 Mar. 2015.

McCracken, Elizabeth. "Be Willing to Break Your Own Heart: An Interview with Elizabeth McCracken." By Brendan Dowling. *Public Libraries* Mar.–Apr. 2001: 91. Web. 23 Mar. 2015.

McCracken, Elizabeth. "Sentimental Journey." *Harper's Bazaar* Sept. 2001: 308. Web. 23 Mar. 2015.

McCracken, Elizabeth. "Thinking in Metaphor: An Interview with Elizabeth McCracken." By Sherry Ellis. *Provincetown Arts* (2005–6): 118–20. Web. 23 Mar. 2015.

Steinberg, Sybil, and Michael Coffey. "A Priest and a Rabbi Walk into a Bar." *Publishers Weekly* 6 Aug. 2001: 56. Web. 31 Mar. 2015.

## SELECTED WORKS

*Here's Your Hat, What's Your Hurry?*, 1993; *The Giant's House*, 1996; *Niagara Falls All Over Again*, 2001; *An Exact Replica of a Figment of My Imagination*, 2008; *Thunderstruck*, 2014

—Judy Johnson, MLS

---

# Dinaw Mengestu

**Born:** June 30, 1978
**Occupation:** Novelist and writer

Several critics have described Dinaw Mengestu as a writer of the "immigrant experience" in the United States, but his novels tackle subject matter that is much broader and deeper than that assessment indicates. While the immigrant experience factors into his fiction—he was born in Ethiopia and raised in Illinois—his books are really about memory, identity, relationships, and how fluid and unstable they are. He has won much praise for his novels, which include *The Beautiful Things That Heaven Bears* (2007), *How to Read the Air* (2010), and *All Our Names* (2014). In 2010, the *New Yorker* named him to its "20 under 40" list of talented writers to watch, and in 2012 he received a fellowship from the MacArthur Foundation, commonly referred to as the "genius grant."

## EARLY LIFE

Dinaw Mengestu was born in Addis Ababa, Ethiopia, in 1978. Two years later, he, his mother, and his sister immigrated to the United States, joining his father, who had already left Ethiopia during a period known as the Red Terror. (In 1974, a communist revolution in Ethiopia led to the overthrow of Emperor Haile Selassie and then to widespread instability, chaos, and violence. Mengestu's father had relatives who were part of the new government, but other family members were strongly opposed to communism, and this endangered his life. For example, his father's brother was arrested and then killed.) The family settled in Peoria, Illinois. The city is the headquarters of the manufacturing company Caterpillar, where Mengestu's father worked. (Peoria would later serve as a setting in some of Mengestu's fiction.)

The family moved to Forest Park, a suburb of Chicago, when Mengestu was about eight years old. Growing up in Forest Park, Dinaw experienced racial and ethnic diversity and integration. He and his family felt welcome at the neighborhood Baptist church. Mengestu's friends were from a variety of places. In an interview with Kevin Nance for the *Chicago Tribune* (21 Mar. 2014), Mengestu recalled that one of his best friends was Vietnamese, another one was Colombian, one was German American, and another one was half-black and half-Mexican. "So we all had multiple identities," he told Nance. "None of us were just one thing or another. We were all of us aware that if you went to one person's house, you had Vietnamese food, or if you went to another person's house, you had tortillas. At my house you had Ethiopian food. It was a remarkably eclectic childhood."

## BEATING THE SYSTEM

The racial and cultural climate Mengestu experienced in Forest Park was seemingly the polar opposite of his experience in high school. He attended Fenwick High School in Oak Park, Illinois, a private Catholic school where students were more divided along racial lines. "It was overwhelmingly white, and the minorities who were there were mostly African American. I was neither white nor 'African American' in that sense, which was more problematic," he told Nance. "You were reacting to kids who were sometimes openly racist, but on the other side, you were different from the black kids as well because of your name and your cultural history.

Andrew Toth/Getty Images North America

That's when I started thinking of myself as being more than 'black' or 'American,' but as being a product of Ethiopia."

At the age of fourteen, he began to learn more about Ethiopian culture and politics, and he even wore the country's colors and symbols as part of his outfit. As a result of being teased for his "otherness," Mengestu decided, consciously or not, to embrace it and learn more about it. In an interview with Mike Thomas for the *Chicago Sun-Times* (20 Oct. 2012), Mengestu said he experienced open racism in high school, with some students often calling him racial slurs during freshman year within earshot of the teachers; he told Thomas the teachers said and did nothing—or pretended not to hear. Mengestu admitted to Thomas that even before starting high school and experiencing its racially tense environment, he was an angry young man. But the way he was treated in high school certainly did not help matters. He even got in a few fights.

Being teased and feeling isolated, Mengestu withdrew into himself. By his junior year, his "rage," he told Thomas, began to subside: he became calmer and less invested in his fashion "protestations." One of his closest friends was a kid named Aamer Madhani, who was an early literary influence on him and recommended books to Mengestu. Mengestu began to read more, particularly J. D. Salinger and beat writers such as Jack Kerouac, Lawrence Ferlinghetti, and Gregory Corso. The beats' bohemian "rejection of normative values," Mengestu said, made him want to do the same. He started writing in his journal, even in class. Mengestu graduated from Fenwick High School in 1996.

## WRITING AROUND THE CLOCK

Mengestu attended Georgetown University in Washington, DC. His creative writing teacher during his junior year, Norma Tilden, in an interview with Thomas for the *Chicago Sun-Times*, said Mengestu at the time struck her as "extremely personable and warm," and his prose seemed to her elegant and straightforward and impressed her "from the very first page." Tilden added that she was also impressed by his "alertness to the sounds and rhythms of American English as we hear it spoken now." Around this time, in 1999, the *New Yorker* magazine issued its first "20 under 40," a list of highly promising writers under the age of forty. During his time at Georgetown, Mengestu worked at the university library and thus had a chance to read a lot, including a great variety of contemporary literature. When that *New Yorker* list came out, he read many of the writers on it. He already had the desire to be a writer and even fantasized about how amazing it would be if he were to make that list one day—but he did not even know if the magazine would do another one. (The magazine did, putting out the list annually from then on.)

Mengestu graduated from Georgetown with a bachelor's degree in 2000. He went on to attend the School of the Arts Writing Program at Columbia University in New York City, from which he graduated with a master's degree in 2005. The following year, he received a fellowship in fiction from the New York Foundation for the Arts, and in 2007 the National Book Foundation named him to its list of "5 under 35." In the summer of 2010 Mengestu did indeed make the *New Yorker*'s "20 under 40" list.

## A NEW VOICE

Mengestu's debut novel, *The Beautiful Things That Heaven Bears* (2007) received nearly unanimous praise. The book's central character, Sepha Stephanos, fled his native Ethiopia as a teenager as a result of the military coup that shook the country in 1974. The book covers a period of eight months in Stephanos's life and is set in the Logan Circle neighborhood in Washington, DC. The book is about memory, pain, displacement, friendship, and romantic feelings. He spends time with his best friends, Congo Joe and Ken the Kenyan, with whom he has certain

"rituals," frequent traditions that provide comfort to people who have been displaced: going to a certain bar or hanging out in Stephanos's store to drink whiskey and play trivia games about African dictators—about which they have great knowledge.

In his review for the *New York Times* (25 Mar. 2007), Rob Nixon wrote, "Mengestu has a fine ear for the way immigrants from damaged places talk in the sanctuary of their own company, free from the exhausting courtesies of self-anthropologizing explanation. He gets, pitch perfect, the warmly abrasive wit of the violently displaced and their need to keep alive some textured memories—even memories that wound—amid America's demanding amnesia." Another major aspect of the book is the relationship between Sepha and Judith, a white woman who moves into the predominantly black (and rapidly gentrifying) neighborhood of Logan Circle. Another friendship, which most reviewers found to be fascinatingly deep and beautiful, is between Sepha and Judith's biracial daughter, Naomi, to whom he often reads from Fyodor Dostoevsky's classic novel *The Brothers Karamazov*. Writing for the *Washington Post* (11 Mar. 2007), Christopher Byrd called *The Beautiful Things That Heaven Bears* "an assured literary debut by a writer worth watching."

## SUBSEQUENT NOVELS

Readers and reviewers were watching and waiting for Mengestu's second novel, but *How to Read the Air* (2010) did not garner the widespread praise accorded to Mengestu's debut. The book is narrated by thirty-three-year-old Jonas Woldemariam, born and raised in Peoria, Illinois, by his Ethiopian parents. The book has alternating chapters: one narrative line chronicles his three-year marriage to a woman in New York City, the other chronicles his parents' relationship, particularly the trip—a belated honeymoon—his parents took to Nashville, Tennessee, while Jonas's mother was pregnant with him. Jonas imagines what his parents thought and did when he was not there to witness it, which is part of the theme of the book: Jonas, as an adult, works at a refugee center where he writes back stories for refugee applicants—stories in which he exaggerates, embellishes, fills in gaps, dramatizes, and so on. The implicit, and sometimes explicit, theme of the book becomes how individuals construct and reconstruct their identities and personal histories.

In his mixed review of the novel for the *Guardian* (31 Dec. 2010), James Lasdun wrote the book's structure was "ably handled if a touch formulaic" and observed that a big problem in the book is the passive way in which Jonas approaches both his life and the narrative. Lasdun called the book an "unevenly impressive novel." In a review for the *New York Times* (8 Oct. 2010), Miguel Syjuco also offered a mixed review, in conclusion calling Mengestu a "remarkably talented" writer while in the same sentence saying he looks forward "to watching the author's gaze expand to the world beyond his own experience." A few weeks after Syjuco's review came out, in an interview with Anne Shulock for the *Rumpus* (19 Oct. 2010), Mengestu called that critique "ridiculous." He argued that he is not writing directly from his own experience but about Africans living in America, people caught between two countries. To him, Mengestu said, that is not "just a subject." He argued, "The sense that you 'move beyond' the African immigrant experience, as if that experience could somehow be completed or fulfilled—if I wrote forty more novels, I will not have done justice to the diversity and range that's possible." Two years later, he was selected as a 2012 MacArthur Fellow, which came with a grant of $500,000.

In his third novel, *All Our Names* (2014), Mengestu continued his exploration of memory and identity. The book has two narrators. The first narrator, Isaac, tells his story of leaving Ethiopia, his home country, and going to college in Uganda in the early 1970s. The second narrative takes place in the Midwest, where Isaac comes to college as a foreign exchange student. That part is narrated by Helen, his social worker. The narratives ultimately converge, not just in time but also in theme—the search for love and understanding. In his review of the novel for the *New York Times* (19 Mar. 2014), Malcolm Jones said of Mengestu's first two novels, "Good as they were, those books now look like warm-up acts." *All Our Names*, which Jones called a "beautiful novel" and said "the story is so straightforward but at the same time so mysterious that you can't turn the pages fast enough, and when you're done, your first impulse is to go back to the beginning and start over."

Mengestu and his wife, Anne-Emanuelle, live in Paris, France, with their two young sons, Gabriel and Louis-Selassie.

## SUGGESTED READING

Byrd, Christopher. "Exile on P Street." Rev. of *The Beautiful Things That Heaven Bears*, by Dinaw Mengestu. *Washington Post*. Washington Post, 11 Mar. 2007. Web. 27 Jan. 2015.

Jones, Malcolm. "Cultural Exchange." Rev. of *All Our Names*, by Dinaw Mengestu. *New York Times*. New York Times, 19 Mar. 2014. Web. 27 Jan. 2015.

Lasdun, James. Rev. of *How to Read the Air*, by Dinaw Mengestu. *Guardian*. Guardian News and Media, 31 Dec. 2010. Web. 27 Jan. 2015.

Mengestu, Dinaw. Interview by Anne Shulock. *Rumpus*. Rumpus, 19 Oct. 2010. Web. 27 Jan. 2015.

Nance, Kevin. "Dinaw Mengestu on 'All Our Names.'" *Chicago Tribune*. Chicago Tribune, 21 Mar. 2014. Web. 27 Jan. 2015.

Nixon, Rob. "African, American." Rev. of *The Beautiful Things That Heaven Bears*, by Dinaw Mengestu. *New York Times*. New York Times, 25 Mar. 2007. Web. 27 Jan. 2015.

## SELECTED WORKS

*The Beautiful Things That Heaven Bears*, 2007; *How to Read the Air*, 2010; *All Our Names*, 2014

—Dmitry Kiper

---

# Idina Menzel

**Born:** May 30, 1971

**Occupation:** Actor, singer-songwriter

Idina Menzel is well known to Broadway aficionados for her star turns in the hit musicals *Rent* (1996–97) and *Wicked* (2003–5). She appeals to an entirely different demographic as well: the legions of youngsters who were introduced to her in 2013 through the blockbuster animated Disney film *Frozen*, in which her character, Elsa, belts out the anthem "Let It Go," a paean to embracing personal power and freeing oneself from the restrictions of the past. The song, reminiscent of the equally poignant "Defying Gravity" that she sang on stage during her tenure as Elphaba the witch in *Wicked*, leapt to number nine on *Billboard*'s Hot 100 chart in mid-March 2014, marking the first time any performer had both a top-ten single and a Tony Award to his or her credit. (Menzel earned her Tony in 2004 for her portrayal of Elphaba.) "Let It Go" won the Oscar for best original song in 2014, and the

Walter McBride/Getty Images North America

full soundtrack topped the Billboard 200 album chart for several weeks.

So ubiquitous did the song become on the radio, and so frequently did young fans upload videos of themselves belting the tune on various social media sites, that Menzel has jokingly told journalists that she feels she should apologize to parents. As of mid-2014, fans had posted some sixty thousand cover versions on YouTube, where they had collectively been viewed more than sixty million times. Yet despite its popularity among amateur singers, most critics agree that the song's power is strongly tied to Menzel's impressive vocal abilities. "The sound she creates when she belts in her high soprano register is a primal cry embedded in her being that insists that we listen and pay attention," Stephen Holden wrote for the *New York Times* (17 June 2014).

## EARLY YEARS AND EDUCATION

Idina Menzel was born on May 30, 1971, and grew up in Syosset, New York, a hamlet near Long Island's North Shore. Her family name was spelled "Mentzel," but she dropped the *t* when she began performing, feeling that the name was easier to pronounce without it. Her unusual first name means "gentle" in Hebrew. Menzel's father, Stuart Mentzel, worked in the garment industry selling pajamas, and her mother, Helene, was a therapist. They divorced when Menzel was a teen. She has a younger sister, Cara.

A perennial favorite in school productions, Menzel starred in an elementary school version of *The Wizard of Oz*, on which *Wicked* is loosely based. While she would eventually study classical music, she always loved soul and R&B artists such as Aretha Franklin and Etta James, and the first album she ever owned was the soundtrack to the film *A Star Is Born* (1976), starring Barbra Streisand. At about age fifteen, Menzel began earning money by singing at local weddings and bar mitzvahs. "I'd drive myself illegally with my junior license to the Temple Beth Shalom ballroom and work with all these older men," she told Boris Kachka for *New York* magazine (31 Oct. 2005). "I grew up kind of fast. I had to come in with this huge repertoire."

Menzel attended New York University's Tisch School of the Arts. There, in the city, away from Long Island's wedding circuit, she performed with rock bands in downtown venues such as the Bitter End and CBGB. She graduated with a bachelor of fine arts in 1993.

## "TANGO: MAUREEN"

In January 1996, at the Off-Broadway New York Theatre Workshop (NYTW) in Manhattan's East Village, a new rock musical by the name of *Rent* had its official premiere, and Menzel was in the cast. The musical was a loose adaptation of the Giacomo Puccini opera *La Bohème*; the original setting, Paris's Latin Quarter in the 1840s, was transformed into gritty 1990s New York, and instead of focusing on a tubercular seamstress and her artist friends, *Rent* centered on a dancer with human immunodeficiency virus (HIV) and her compatriots.

Menzel portrayed Maureen Johnson, a bisexual performance artist dating a lesbian lawyer. The musical received a great deal of media buzz when its young creator, Jonathon Larson, died from an undiagnosed aortic aneurysm the night before the Off-Broadway premiere. Given the show's theme of dying artists, some journalists found a bleak romanticism in Larson's unexpected death.

Many fans attended the show multiple times, and as demand for tickets grew, the production moved to Broadway's Nederlander Theatre in early 1996. There, it received rapturous reviews. Writing for the *New York Times* (14 Feb. 1996), Ben Brantley called Menzel and her costars "performers of both wit and emotional conviction." He continued, "Along with George C. Wolfe and Savion Glover's *Bring in da Noise, Bring in da Funk*, this show restores spontaneity and depth of feeling to a discipline that sorely needs them. People who complain about the demise of the American musical have simply been looking in the wrong places." In addition to serving as Menzel's big break, the show also brought her into contact with her future husband, Taye Diggs, who played Benjamin Coffin III, Maureen's landlord and former boyfriend.

*Rent* closed in 2008, after a remarkable twelve-year run. By that time, Menzel had already left to take on a variety of other projects, including Manhattan Theatre Club's performance of *The Wild Party* (2000), *Summer of '42* (2000) at Connecticut's Goodspeed Opera House, a New York City Center Encores! production of *Hair* (2001), and a Broadway adaptation of *Aida* (2001). She also released a solo synth-rock album, 1998's *Still I Can't Be Still*, for which she wrote all of the tracks with bassist Milton Davis.

## WICKED

In 2003, Menzel debuted as Elphaba opposite Kristin Chenoweth's Glinda in *Wicked*, which was based on Gregory Maguire's novel *Wicked: The Life and Times of the Wicked Witch of the West* (1995), a revisionist version of the classic 1939 film *The Wizard of Oz*—itself a retelling of L. Frank Baum's 1900 tale. The work, which takes place before Dorothy lands in Oz and focuses on the lives of the two "good" and "bad" witches, posits that Elphaba, deemed "wicked" because of her green skin and dubious parentage, is actually misjudged. Menzel's big number, "Defying Gravity"—the end of which she belted out while suspended high above the stage—was, like "Let It Go," a powerful ballad about living without limits. While her appeal to younger audiences would reach feverish heights with *Frozen*, even then Menzel was becoming an object of adoration for many preteen girls, who crowded the stage door each night to tell her how much they identified with her misunderstood character.

During this time, Menzel continued to pursue a solo career. Although her previous solo album had sold fewer than twenty thousand copies, she did not give up on the idea of being a successful recording artist in her own right. In 2004, dropped by the company that had produced *Still I Can't Be Still*, she self-produced and released *Here*, which ultimately sold even fewer copies.

Menzel remained with *Wicked* until 2005. Although the show was originally critically panned and some critics bemoaned Menzel bringing a pop-music sensibility to the "Great White Way," *Wicked* has remained a fan favorite and top grosser, and Menzel earned a Tony Award for the role. She also secured a lasting place in Broadway legend when, during a matinee performance on the day before she was scheduled to leave the show, she fell through a trapdoor and fractured a rib; the next night, she appeared, clad in a tracksuit, to say farewell and join briefly in the final scene, unwilling to disappoint the fans she knew had come to see her rather than an understudy.

## ON THE SCREEN

In addition to reprising the role of Maureen in the 2005 film version of *Rent*, Menzel has several other on-screen appearances to her credit. She had a small part as a bridesmaid in the independent romantic comedy *Kissing Jessica Stein* (2001) and a more pivotal role in the Disney musical *Enchanted* (2007), which starred Amy Adams and Patrick Dempsey; ironically, Menzel was one of the few main actors in the film who did not sing. (A duet was written for her and costar James Marsden but did not appear in the final film.)

Menzel also made occasional guest appearances on such television series as *Rescue Me* (2004), *Kevin Hill* (2005), and *Private Practice* (2009). The latter two series starred Diggs, who was for several years the more high-profile of the couple. "I'd walk down the red carpet with Taye and nobody knew who I am; they'd push me aside," Menzel told Kachka. That indisputably changed in 2010, when she began appearing on the popular television show *Glee* as Shelby Corcoran, the biological mother of Rachel Berry, one of the main characters. In addition, her third studio album, *I Stand*, was released on the Warner Bros. label in 2008 and saw significantly more success than her previous efforts, reaching number 58 on the Billboard 200 chart.

Menzel's newfound celebrity with non-Broadway audiences was cemented by her role in the animated film *Frozen*, in which her character, Princess Elsa, has the power to turn anything into ice. Menzel herself got an unexpected boost in name recognition when actor John Travolta mangled the pronunciation, mistakenly calling her "Adele Dazeem" while introducing her performance of "Let It Go" at the 2014 Oscars ceremony. Of her single's unprecedented success in the charts, Menzel told Suzy Evans for *Billboard* magazine (24 Mar. 2014), "People say Broadway actors can't cross over, but it seems society is ready to accept a theater person singing a song on the radio." She added, "People have often closed doors because they didn't think we were capable of a hit song or some kind of pop-culture moment."

After a hiatus from Broadway, Menzel's next high-profile role came in 2014 with *If/Then*, in which she starred as Elizabeth, a newly divorced urban planner from Phoenix who hopes to find career satisfaction and romance in Manhattan. When asked by Jesse Green for *Elle* (19 Feb. 2014) about her return to Broadway, Menzel emphasized her appreciation for the stage that has always welcomed her: "It's where I feel the most understood, most at home. . . . Whether it will run like *Wicked*—I don't let myself have those expectations. I've already had lightning in a bottle more than once." In a review of the show for the *New York Times* (30 Mar. 2014), Ben Brantley wrote, "In *Wicked* . . . Menzel played Elphaba, a green-skinned outcast who discovered her inner power—and the highest human decibel level Broadway had known since [Ethel] Merman. Though in *If/Then* she keeps tight reins on the volume until a smashing climactic lament in the second act, young theatergoers who identified with her Elphaba will probably identify with her Elizabeth, too, now that they're a bit older."

### PERSONAL LIFE

Menzel and Diggs dated for several years after meeting on the set of *Rent*. They married in early 2003 and had a son, Walker, in 2009. In 2010, the couple founded the charity camp A Broader Way, which is dedicated to providing arts programs for young girls from urban communities. Discussing the intersection of her life and work, Menzel told Dave Itzkoff for the *New York Times* (20 Feb. 2014), "You can't be the vulnerable, transparent, raw person required to be an artist, and then cover that stuff up and meet the world with some kind of armor on."

Menzel has been open about the difficulties of juggling fame and family life. "We work at it," she told a reporter for *People* (20 Apr. 2013). "I'm not going to glamorize it or glorify it—we go through tough times like everybody else, but we love each other very much." Still, it came as something of a shock to members of the public, particularly those who had been fans since the couple's *Rent* days, when they announced their split in late 2013, after a decade of marriage.

### SUGGESTED READING

Evans, Suzy. "Idina Menzel's Fairy Tale Journey: From Broadway to *Frozen* and a 'Gorgeous' Note from John Travolta." *Billboard*. Billboard, 24 Mar. 2014. Web. 7 Oct. 2014.

Holden, Stephen. "Big Voice, Defying Gravity: Idina Menzel at Radio City Music Hall." Rev. of concert by Idina Menzel. Radio City Music Hall, New York. *New York Times*. New York Times, 17 June 2014. Web. 7 Oct. 2014.

Itzkoff, Dave. "A Woman at a Crossroads: Idina Menzel's Role in *If/Then* Is Not Such a Stretch." *New York Times*. New York Times, 20 Feb. 2014. Web. 7 Oct. 2014.

Kachka, Boris. "Something Wicked This Way Comes." *NYMag*. New York Media, 31 Oct. 2005. Web. 7 Oct. 2014.

Menzel, Idina. "Idina Menzel: Back on Broadway." Interview by Jesse Green. *Elle*. Hearst Communications, 19 Feb. 2014. Web. 7 Oct. 2014.

### SELECTED WORKS

*Rent*, 1996–97; *Wicked*, 2003–5; *Enchanted*, 2007; *Glee*, 2010–13; *Frozen*, 2013; *If/Then*, 2014

—Mari Rich

# Ingrid Michaelson

**Born:** December 8, 1979
**Occupation:** Singer-songwriter

Ingrid Michaelson went from virtual unknown to indie-pop sensation in 2007 when her single "The Way I Am" was featured in an Old Navy television commercial. By that time her catchy, upbeat songs had also become a staple on the popular ABC drama *Grey's Anatomy*. What makes Michaelson's seemingly overnight success so compelling is the fact that she has refused to sign with a major record label, choosing instead to license her music. "It's all outsourced through me, so I'm the one making the decisions. No one tells me what songs to sing or what artwork to use," she explained to Stuart Husband for the *Daily Mail* (13 Feb. 2010). "I have ownership of what I do."

Since then, Michaelson's music has been featured in several popular television shows, including *One Tree Hill*, *So You Think You Can Dance*, *Parenthood*, and *Pretty Little Liars*. Michaelson has also self-released six albums under her own Cabin 24 Records label, most recently *Lights Out* (2014), which includes the crossover single "Girls Chase Boys"—a top-ten hit on Billboard's Adult Top 40 and Hot Rock Songs charts, as well as her highest-charting single since "The Way I Am." Equally popular is the accompanying video featuring Michaelson dressed in a man's suit, backed by a group of dancing men wearing makeup and hot pants—a gender-bending take on the 1988 video for Robert Palmer's Grammy-winning song "Simply Irresistible."

## EARLY YEARS

Ingrid Ellen Egbert Michaelson, a Staten Island, New York, native, was born on December 8, 1979, to Elizabeth (Egbert) and Carl Michaelson. She credits her composer father and her mother, a sculptor, art teacher, and former director of the Staten Island Museum, with introducing her to various genres of music and supporting her interest. Ironically, the one genre her father typically refused to listen to, believing that all of the songs essentially sounded the same, was pop music. "My dad only listened to classical music and I watched a lot of old Bing Crosby-Fred Astaire-Ginger Rogers-Rosemary Clooney movies and we would listen to that, and then the Beatles," Michaelson told Jon Ferguson for *LancasterOnline* (4 Mar. 2010). "I had melody driven into my brain."

Michaelson was four when her parents enrolled her and her brother in piano lessons. After two years of training at Manhattan's prestigious Third Street Music School, the seven-year-old Michaelson attended the Dorothy Delson Kuhn Music Institute at Staten Island's Jewish Community Center, where she studied under vocal coach Elizabeth McCullough. She also honed her performing skills as a member of the Kids on Stage program, which she first joined when she was nine. At age fifteen or sixteen she left the city-funded theatrical troupe and stopped taking piano classes but continued with voice lessons.

## ABANDONING THEATER FOR MUSIC

Following her 1997 graduation from the highly competitive Staten Island Technical High School, Michaelson studied theater at Binghamton University's Harpur College of Arts and Sciences in Vestal, New York. Focusing mainly on studying theater, she struggled with the fundamentals of music. "I was terrible at the theory, but I had a great ear," she told Bill Werde for *Billboard* magazine (12 Jan. 2008). Active on campus, she also joined several student organizations, including Binghamton's theater repertory company; the sketch comedy troupe the Pappy Parker Players; and the Binghamtonics, the school's oldest co-ed a cappella group.

© Paul A. Hebert/Press Line Photos/Corbis

After earning her bachelor's degree in theater in 2001, Michaelson auditioned for several stage roles. It took nearly a year before she was offered the role of Ellie Cratchit in a touring production of *A Christmas Carol*. During her theatrical run, Michaelson, feeling unfulfilled by acting, finally turned to songwriting. "It was an outlet, something I could always create. I didn't have to wait for someone else to tell me I fit the role," she told Michael Norman for Cleveland.com (15 June 2010).

## LAUNCHING A MUSIC CAREER

Still living with her parents, in 2002 Michaelson began pursuing a music career, writing and performing her own songs during open mike nights at the Muddy Cup, a Staten Island coffeehouse where she was employed as a barista. Her gigs also included performances at New York City–area coffee shops and various small venues, including the Bitter End. Three years later, Michaelson self-released her first album, *Slow the Rain* (2005), online through the label she had founded to ensure creative control over her music, Cabin 24 Records. However, the piano-driven debut went largely unnoticed.

Weekend recording sessions at the Manhattan studio where her friend worked as a tech resulted in Michaelson's more upbeat, folksy album *Girls and Boys* (2006), which she made available to the public via the popular social networking site MySpace. "I learned pretty quickly that just because you're playing at a good venue doesn't mean people are going to come and see you," she told Devan Sipher for the *New York Times* (18 Dec. 2007).

Michaelson's sophomore effort caught the attention of Lynn Grossman, founder of the Los Angeles–based licensing, publishing, and management firm Secret Road. "I listened to her song 'Breakable' about forty times in a row, and I completely fell in love with the song," Grossman told Sipher. In October 2006 the two met face-to-face at the annual week-long CMJ Music Marathon, a New York City–based festival for up-and-coming artists. After deciding to work together, Michaelson became anxious to see her songs playing on the small screen.

Her wish was fulfilled a month later when "Breakable" was used in the episode of *Grey's Anatomy* that aired on November 16, 2006. The following year, two other tracks from her album were featured in the series: "The Way I Am" and "Corner of Your Heart." At the request of the show's musical director, Michaelson wrote "Keep Breathing," which was showcased in the intense closing minutes of the May 17, 2007, season finale, which had more than twenty million viewers. Michaelson and the song's lyrics were subsequently among the most searched items on Google Trends. Satisfied with this commercial success, by June she had left her job as director for a children's theater company.

## BREAKING THROUGH WITH OLD NAVY
Michaelson's mainstream breakthrough came in September 2007, when the music supervisor for the Old Navy clothing chain decided to use "The Way I Am" for its fall advertising campaign. That same month, Michaelson rereleased *Girls and Boys* after signing a distribution deal with Original Signal Records.

The popularity of the Old Navy ad helped the album sell thousands more copies and reach the top spot of Billboard's US Top Heatseekers chart. "The Way I Am" achieved platinum status, selling more than 1.5 million copies. In November 2007 Michaelson's video for the single received heavy rotation on VH1 as part of the music channel's monthly series *You Oughta Know*, which showcases artists on the rise.

In March 2008 Michaelson headlined the fourth annual Hotel Café tour alongside Sara Bareilles, before serving as the opening act for Jason Mraz in Europe. Later that year, in the midst of working on her next full-length record, she released the EP *Be OK*, a compilation of covers, previously unreleased tracks, and live songs that she recorded as a tribute to her fans. Michaelson, whose mother was battling cancer, gave a portion of the proceeds from sales to the nonprofit initiative Stand Up to Cancer. She also donated all earnings from necklaces she personally designed for her tour, which kicked off in her hometown of Staten Island.

For her highly anticipated follow-up album, *Everybody* (2009), Michaelson drew inspiration from her latest breakup. *Everybody* peaked at number eighteen on the Billboard 200, becoming Michaelson's highest-charting album to date. In September 2009 she embarked on a headlining tour of North America and Europe.

## FINDING A MATURE VOICE AND SOUND
Michaelson remained on the road in the spring of 2010 as part of a tour she headlined with Mat Kearney. In September she partnered with Mom + Pop Music to digitally release the single "Parachute," which she cowrote with Marshall Altman. The song was a top-five dance hit for British singer Cheryl Cole.

With *Human Again* (2012), another release on Cabin 24 Records and Mom + Pop Music, Michaelson gravitated toward a more mature, grandiose sound. Orchestral strings are featured throughout several of the album's tracks, including the haunting "Ghost," the drum-driven "Fire," and the empowering "Do It Now." Encouraged by producer David Kahne, Michaelson pushed herself vocally, singing with the same range and energy of her live performances. This power is evident in the ballads "Always You" and "Keep Warm." Grossman commented on Michaelson's artistic growth on her fourth project in an interview with Jill Menze for *Billboard* magazine (23 Jan. 2012), saying, "She wanted to move beyond perceptions of her fitting perfectly into the singer/songwriter or the ukulele-based, perfect-music-to-sell-a-product genres."

To promote the record, which debuted at the top of Billboard's Independent Albums chart, Michaelson spent most of the year touring across North America, Europe, and Australia.

## TURNING PERSONAL TRAGEDY INTO MUSIC
The year 2013 proved to be personally challenging for Michaelson. Not only had her mother's cancer returned, but her father was also battling an illness and her beloved dog passed away. While caring for both of her parents, Michael-

son was diagnosed with Graves disease as well as a severe case of acid reflux, which affected her singing voice and forced her to stop work on her new album.

When Michaelson returned to the recording studio, she adopted a different approach. "In the past, I've always written all the records myself and I've worked with one producer, and this time around, I just needed help, I needed a village," she told Scott Mervis for the *Pittsburgh Post-Gazette* (22 May 2014). "I wrote with a whole bunch of friends and some people I didn't know, which was scary. . . . I just felt like I needed many different people to help me up out of this hole I was in." Collaborators included Kearney; her bassist, Chris Kuffner; Nashville songwriter Trent Dabbs; as well as producers Jacquire King and Busbee.

Released in April 2014, *Lights Out* is Michaelson's most personal effort to date. "A lot of what I wrote about in the past was just straight up love and I have no problem admitting that," she told Sophia Hollander for the *Wall Street Journal* (31 July 2014). This album is "more about coming to terms with losing people and your mortality," she added. The ballad "Afterlife," which was inspired by her mother's cancer battle, most reflects that theme. On August 30, 2014, after an unsuccessful bone marrow transplant, Michaelson's mother lost her battle with cancer.

## PERSONAL LIFE

Michaelson married musician Greg Laswell in August 2011. The couple lived in Brooklyn and worked together on some of Michaelson's projects. In February 2015 the couple announced that they were separating.

In addition to several other side projects, Michaelson serves as host of *Little Kids. Big Questions*, a comedic web series supported by actor Rainn Wilson. She also moonlights as a member of the Army of 3 cover band, whose debut EP was released in 2013.

## SUGGESTED READING

Ferguson, Jon. "For Singer-Songwriter Ingrid Michaelson, It's All about the Melody." *LancasterOnline*. LNP Media Group, 4 Mar. 2010. Web. 27 Apr. 2015.

Hollander, Sophia. "Ingrid Michaelson's Breakout Moment." *Wall Street Journal*. Dow Jones, 31 July 2014. Web. 27 Apr. 2015.

Husband, Stuart. "The DIY Diva: Singer Ingrid Michaelson Calls Her Own Tune." *Daily Mail*. Associated Newspapers, 13 Feb. 2010. Web. 27 Apr. 2015.

Mervis, Scott. "Ingrid Michaelson Brings in Lots of Voices for Bigger-Sounding 'Lights Out.'" *Pittsburgh-Post Gazette*. PG, 22 May 2014. Web. 27 Apr. 2015.

Sipher, Devan. "Singing Her Way from Obscurity to Fame on the Internet." *New York Times*. New York Times, 18 Dec. 2007. Web. 27 Apr. 2015.

Werde, Bill. "Ingrid Michaelson: The Way She Is: The End of the Old Music Business? Or the Face of the New One?" *Billboard*. Billboard, 12 Jan. 2008: 24–26. Print.

## SELECTED WORKS

*Slow the Rain*, 2005; *Girls and Boys*, 2006; *Be OK*, 2008; *Everybody*, 2009; *Human Again*, 2012; *Lights Out*, 2014

—Bertha Muteba

# Ezra Miller

**Born:** September 30, 1992
**Occupation:** Actor

In the early 2010s actor Ezra Miller gained a fan following and critical acclaim for his portrayals of very different alienated teens in such indie films as *Another Happy Day* (2011), *We Need to Talk about Kevin* (2011), and *The Perks of Being a Wallflower* (2012). After those performances brought him significant mainstream attention, he went on to expand his résumé with roles such as a suitor in the period piece *Madame Bovary* (2014), an awkward intern in the comedy *Trainwreck* (2015), and an abused subject of a psychological study in the drama *The Stanford Prison Experiment* (2015). In a profile of Miller for *Interview* (Apr. 2011), fellow actor Kate Bosworth asked if he had any fear of the dark roles for which he was becoming known. "No!" Miller responded, "That's what I yearn for. It's what I want."

Before long Miller cemented his position as an up-and-coming star, poised to make a leap into big-budget blockbusters. In 2014 he landed the role of the iconic DC Comics superhero the Flash in a big-screen adaptation set to be released in 2018. In 2015 he was reportedly cast in the upcoming movie *Fantastic Beasts and Where to*

© Joe Stevens/Retna Ltd./Corbis

*Find Them*, the first in a planned trilogy of films based on a spinoff of the hugely popular Harry Potter series of books by J. K. Rowling.

### EARLY LIFE AND EDUCATION

Ezra Miller was born on September 30, 1992, in Wyckoff, New Jersey, where he was raised alongside his two older sisters. His father, Robert S. Miller, was a publishing executive who worked for Workman Publishing and Hyperion Books; his mother, the former Marta Koch, was a modern dancer. His father was Jewish, and Miller grew up considering himself Jewish and spiritual. He has credited his artistic qualities to his mother, from whom he developed a love of music. At an early age, he discovered a passion for opera, particularly the works of Mozart, such as his 1791 opera *The Magic Flute*, while taking singing lessons to overcome a strong stutter. This eventually led him to appreciate classical masters such as Bach, Beethoven, and Handel as well as more contemporary artists such as Tupac Shakur, David Bowie, Kurt Cobain, and Neil Young. His singing earned him a residency at the Metropolitan Opera in New York City while he was still in elementary school.

At age eight Miller performed at Lincoln Center in New York City in the US premier of *White Raven*, Philip Glass's 1991 opera about the voyages of the celebrated Portuguese explorer Vasco da Gama, with a libretto by Luísa Costa Gomes. During that opera's performance, he was hoisted into the air, where, as he recalled to Jada Yuan for *New York* magazine (9 Jan. 2012), "I conducted the orchestra. With one grand, sweeping gesture, I brought up the sun. It was the most profound ego boost that an eight-year-old could possibly receive." The experience of being shuttled back and forth between New Jersey and New York City to perform at major theatrical events gave Miller a considerable ego at an early age. Miller told Bosworth: "I was a cocky kid, and I felt like I was an adult at, like, nine, you know? I think that's because my parents always treated me as an adult."

Miller continued to be affiliated with the Metropolitan Opera Children's Chorus until he reached puberty and his voice changed. Although devastated by his inability to continue singing, he discovered acting as a new creative outlet. He dropped out of Hoboken's Hudson School in his junior year—supposedly because of a dream in which Ludwig van Beethoven told Miller he wanted to give up on music after writing only four symphonies. He described his fateful interpretation of the dream to Yuan: "I think it's about how it's the responsibility of every artist to make sacrifices and seemingly irrational decisions in order to carve out their little pebble of work to put on the big, like, art kingdom that everyone's been building for so long."

### EARLY FILM ROLES

Miller soon landed significant acting roles in both film and television. He appeared in a five-episode arc on the television show *Californication* in 2008. He also scored a leading role as an alienated teen who attends boarding school and films the accidental drug-induced deaths of twin sisters in *Afterschool* (2008). The film's director, Antonio Campos, told Yuan, "I could just tell he was special. He was a lot smarter . . . more sensitive. He wasn't afraid to make a fool of himself." Other roles in film and television soon followed. He appeared on television in *Law & Order: Special Victims Unit* in 2009 and *Royal Pains* in 2009 and 2010 and on the big screen in *City Island* (2009), *Beware the Gonzo* (2010), and *Every Day* (2010).

Miller's next standout work came in 2011, when he played an angry, smart, drug-addicted teenager named Elliot in *Another Happy Day*, which was one of the more noted films at that year's Sundance Film Festival. In the film, Miller's character is forced to confront all the broken figures in his family: his self-absorbed parents and his equally troubled siblings. In one scene he spits in the face of his mother, played by El-len Barkin. In an interview with Mickey Rapkin for *Details* (1 Dec. 2011), Miller described how he prepared for such a highly charged scene: "That particular action was written in the script. . . . When Ellen and I were first getting to know each other, we were well aware that this was in our future. We did a substantial amount of personal, emotional buffering so that we could feel comfortable."

## BREAKOUT PERFORMANCES

Many film critics and fans describe Miller's work as the title character in *We Need to Talk about Kevin* (2011) as being his breakout per-formance. In the film—which was directed by Lynne Ramsay and based on the 2003 novel of the same name by Lionel Shriver—Miller por-trays an alienated teenager who, just prior to his sixteenth birthday, goes on a killing spree in his high school not unlike such real-life tragedies as the 1999 Columbine shootings. The tension of the film centers on the relationship between Miller's character Kevin and his mother (played by Tilda Swinton), who gave up a career she en-joyed in order to be a mother. Miller told Bo-sworth: "Basically, Kevin explores a mother who held within herself a deep resentment of the child. We see Kevin over the course of his life become more and more of a monster. And her resentment grows stronger until there's this explosion of rage and they're at war. That per-formance was entirely about finding all of the anger and the resentment inherent to mother and child. It's just a scary truth. And it's a very old story that's entirely under-told. It's too dark. Too dirty."

Also considered among Miller's breakout performances was his supporting role in the 2012 film adaptation of *The Perks of Being a Wallflower*, the hugely popular novel by Stephen Chbosky first published in 1999. In the film, which was written and directed by the novel's author, Miller played Patrick, the gay stepbroth-er of Emma Watson's character, Sam. As high school seniors, the duo befriend a lonely fresh-man named Charlie (played by Logan Lerman), who has struggled to make friends since the death of his best friend a year ago. Despite the controversial nature of the novel, with its frank depictions of teenage sexuality, drug use, alien-ation, and depression, Chbosky ensured that his film adaptation hewed closely to the source.

Miller was a big fan of Chbosky's novel and initially had his doubts about being part of an ad-

aptation of a work he identified so closely with. However, after meeting the author, Miller's hesi-tation turned into enthusiasm. "Steve made this film the same way he wrote the book, as an act of giving in full generosity. He opened up about his own plight and revealed his own teen struggles just so other people could have a reference," he told Erika Berlin for *Rolling Stone* (11 Oct. 2012). "I think Steve looked so deeply into himself and wrote a story that's so personal that a charac-ter like Patrick touches something universally accessible. . . . Who knows what he'll do or what he'll be? We can all kind of recognize those characters, and I think there's something really cool about that." To add to the authenticity of the performances, Miller and the rest of the cast lived together and bonded like real high school friends. The experience even inspired the for-mation of two different bands, in which Miller played percussion.

## MAINSTREAM ATTENTION

After the critical success of *We Need to Talk about Kevin* and *The Perks of Being a Wallflow-er*, Miller was well established as a portrayer of alienated teens. Yet rather than continue in that thread, he used his new level of recognition to take on a variety of drastically different roles. He ventured into period drama with the 2014 film adaptation of Gustave Flaubert's classic 1856 novel *Madame Bovary*, in which he plays one of Madame Bovary's suitors. He explored comedy with a supporting role in *Trainwreck* (2015), directed by Judd Apatow and written by comedian Amy Schumer, who also stars. Miller was also acclaimed for his work in *The Stanford Prison Experiment*, a 2015 drama based on the notorious 1971 psychological study at Stan-ford University that pitted young male students against one another in a simulated prison situa-tion. In a review for *USA Today* (14 July 2015), Brian Truitt, who praised the film for its almost documentary-style realism, called attention to Miller's great turn as prisoner 8612, which he praised for providing "exceptional and powerful moments of breakdown."

These performances further increased Mill-er's star power, leading studios to target the young actor for major franchise roles. In 2014 the Warner Brothers studio announced that Mill-er had been chosen to portray the film version of the Flash, one of DC Comics' most popular superhero characters, in a standalone film set to be released in 2018. Also anticipated was a cam-eo by Miller in *Batman v. Superman: Dawn of*

*Justice* (2016), intended to set up the live-action cinematic universe of DC Comics and its iconic superhero team the Justice League, of which the Flash is a member. In June 2015 Miller was in talks to play Kredan, an American magician, in *Fantastic Beasts and Where to Find Them*, the first spinoff of the Harry Potter series based on the books by J. K. Rowling.

## PERSONAL LIFE
Miller has identified himself as queer, though not gay, saying that he has had relationships with various people regardless of sex or gender. He also voiced his preference for young people to avoid being tied down in single relationships before they are ready. An advocate of marijuana use, he was arrested for possession while filming *The Perks of Being a Wallflower*.

## SUGGESTED READING
Berlin, Erika. "Q&A: Ezra Miller on the Perks of Being in 'Wallflower.'" *Rolling Stone*. Rolling Stone, 11 Oct. 2012. Web. 11 Aug. 2015.
Bosworth, Kate. "Ezra Miller." *Interview*. Interview, Apr. 2011. Web. 11 Aug. 2015.
Dodds, Eric. "Ezra Miller Reportedly in Talks for Role in *Harry Potter* Spinoff." *Time*. Time, 25 June 2015. Web. 11 Aug. 2015.
Truitt, Brian. "Review: Hard Times in 'Stanford Prison.'" *USA Today*. USA Today, 14 July 2015. Web. 11 Aug. 2015.
Yuan, Jada. "We Need to Talk about Ezra." *New York*. New York Media, 9 Jan. 2012. Web. 11 Aug. 2015.

## SELECTED WORKS
*Another Happy Day*, 2011; *We Need to Talk about Kevin*, 2011; *The Perks of Being a Wallflower*, 2012; *The Stanford Prison Experiment*, 2015

—Christopher Mari

# Maryam Mirzakhani
**Born:** May, 1977
**Occupation:** Mathematician

In August 2014 the International Mathematical Union announced that Maryam Mirzakhani, an Iranian-born professor of mathematics at Stanford University in California, had won the prestigious Fields Medal, long considered the Nobel Prize of mathematics. Like her fellow

© Courtesy: Maryam Mirzakhani/Corbis Images

three recipients that year, Artur Avila, Manjul Bhargava, and Martin Hairer, Mirzakhani was under forty, as required by the prize's rules, but she was the only woman among them—and the only female mathematician ever to be so honored by the International Mathematical Union. She had been recognized primarily for developing a general formula for calculating the number of closed geodesic curves on theoretical objects known as Riemann surfaces—curved surfaces similar to those found on a doughnut or a sphere.

While many mathematicians consider her work pure mathematics, without real-world applications, some scientists see it having potential implications in quantum field theory, which looks at how the universe came into existence, as well as in other areas of physics, engineering, material science, cryptography, and prime numbers. Although a very confident mathematician, Mirzakhani is particularly humble about her considerable accomplishment and has stated that she has little desire to be the female representative of modern mathematics. Having declined most interviews about her award, she remains dedicated to her mathematical research, which continues to be her one abiding passion. In an interview with Erica Klarreich for *Quanta Magazine* (12 Aug. 2014), Mirzakhani described her mathematical research as akin to writing a novel: "There are different characters, and you are getting to know them better." She continued,

"Things evolve, and then you look back at a character, and it's completely different from your first impression."

## EARLY LIFE AND EDUCATION IN IRAN

Maryam Mirzakhani was born in Tehran, Iran, in May 1977, shortly before the Iranian Revolution (1978–9) that would see the overthrow of the shah and the implementation of an Islamic Republic under Ayatollah Ruhollah Khomeini. Her early childhood, during which she dreamed of becoming a writer, was spent under the shadow of the Iran-Iraq War (1980–88). During these years she read every book she could get her hands on, including histories, novels, and biographies of notable women like Helen Keller and Marie Curie.

The war ended as she entered middle school; she had won a spot at the Farzanegan middle school for girls in Tehran thanks to her scores on a placement test. There she met her best friend, Roya Beheshti, who is now a mathematics professor at Washington University in St. Louis. The girls shared each other's interests, including a love of reading, and frequently spent their time after school rummaging through the crowded bookstores on a busy street in Tehran near Mirzakhani's home. Because the booksellers discouraged browsing, the girls picked what they would read at random. "Now, it sounds very strange," Mirzakhani told Klarreich. "But books were very cheap, so we would just buy them."

Despite having difficulty in mathematics for a time during middle school, Mirzakhani had developed an interest in the subject by the time she entered the Farzanegan high school for girls, thanks in part to her older brother. In an interview with the Clay Mathematics Institute (2008), Mirzakhani recalled, "My older brother was the person who got me interested in science in general. . . . My first memory of mathematics is probably the time that he told me about the problem of adding numbers from one to one hundred. I think he had read in a popular science journal how Gauss solved this problem. The solution was quite fascinating for me. That was the first time I enjoyed a beautiful solution, though I couldn't find it myself." She was also encouraged to pursue mathematics by her school's principal, who sought to give her female charges the same opportunities as their male counterparts. One of these opportunities included having her students compete to secure a place on Iran's historically male International Mathematical Olympiad team. In 1994, as seventeen-year-

olds, both Mirzakhani and Beheshti made the team; Mirzakhani won a gold medal that year. In 1995, at the next Olympiad, she achieved a perfect score.

Upon her graduation from high school, Mirzakhani attended Sharif University of Technology in Tehran, where she continued to be fascinated by various fields of mathematical study and inspired by her fellow budding mathematicians. As an undergraduate, she enjoyed attending reading groups and problem-solving sessions with her classmates. In 1999 she graduated with a bachelor's degree in mathematics and moved to the United States to continue her education.

## EDUCATION IN THE UNITED STATES

Mirzakhani studied for her doctorate in mathematics at Harvard University in Cambridge, Massachusetts. While she enjoyed her time there, she found her fellow graduate students were often confused by the fact that she had received an advanced education in Iran as a woman. She recalled in her interview with the Clay Mathematics Institute, "As a graduate student at Harvard, I had to explain quite a few times that I was allowed to attend a university as a woman in Iran. While it is true that boys and girls go to separate schools up to high school, this does not prevent them from participating say in the Olympiads or the summer camps."

Her undergraduate experience had been primarily in the mathematical fields of combinatorics (the branch of math that studies the combinations of finite sets of objects) and algebra. While she had enjoyed complex analysis and hyperbolic geometry, she knew little of the subjects but grew fascinated with them, particularly the area of Riemann surfaces, after attending an informal seminar held by Curtis T. McMullen, a noted mathematician who had won the Fields Medal in 1998. McMullen became Mirzakhani's thesis advisor, overseeing her work on the surfaces of geometric structures and their deformations. "She had a sort of daring imagination," McMullen told Klarreich. "She would formulate in her mind an imaginary picture of what must be going on, then come to my office and describe it. At the end, she would turn to me and say, 'Is it right?' I was always very flattered that she thought I would know."

Riemann surfaces can be divided into three groups: hyperbolic, parabolic, and elliptic surfaces. In her doctoral thesis, which she completed in 2004, Mirzakhani developed a formula that calculated the number of closed geodesic curves (saddle-shaped lines going across the curving surface) found on a hyperbolic (doughnut-shaped with two or more holes) surface with a very large genus (or number of holes). As Riemann objects are abstract and cannot be constructed in normal space, their angles and distances are only calculable through a specific set of equations. Her thesis was so original and startling that its results generated three papers published in the three major mathematical journals: the *Annals of Mathematics, Inventiones Mathematicae*, and the *Journal of the American Mathematical Society*. When asked about the most satisfying part of working in mathematics during her interview with the Clay Mathematics Institute, Mirzakhani responded, "Of course, the most rewarding part is the 'Aha' moment, the excitement of discovery and enjoyment of understanding something new, the feeling of being on top of a hill, and having a clear view."

## WINNING THE FIELDS MEDAL

Upon earning her doctorate, Mirzakhani served as both an assistant professor of mathematics at Princeton University in New Jersey, and as a Clay Mathematics Institute research fellow from 2004 to 2008. In 2008 she became a full professor of mathematics at Stanford University. Three years later, along with University of Chicago mathematician Alex Eskin, Mirzakhani submitted a paper explaining the monumental proof of the rigidity of complex geodesics and their closures in moduli space.

It was while at Stanford that she learned, the next year, that she had earned the Fields Medal, which is officially known as the International Medal for Outstanding Discoveries in Mathematics. The medal had been established in 1936 to recognize the contributions mathematicians make to the sum of human knowledge and was unofficially named for Canadian mathematician John Charles Fields after he provided a significant endowment from his estate. Mirzakhani was presented with the award in Seoul, South Korea, on August 13, 2014, at the International Congress of Mathematicians; she became the first Stanford professor to earn the award since Paul Cohen had done so in 1966.

While the public at large was surprised to learn that Mirzakhani was the first woman to receive the Fields Medal, her colleagues and fellow mathematicians who knew of her contributions to geometry and dynamical surfaces were not as surprised. "What's so special about Maryam, the thing that really separates her, is the originality in how she puts together these disparate pieces," Steven Kerckhoff, one of Mirzakhani's collaborators and a fellow mathematics professor at Stanford, told Bjorn Carey for a Stanford University press release (12 Aug. 2014). "That was the case starting with her thesis work, which generated several papers in all the top journals. The novelty of her approach made it a real tour de force."

Many news outlets commented on the fact that Mirzakhani had become the first woman to win the most prestigious mathematics prize in the world. It was an achievement especially notable because men still earn approximately 70 percent of the advanced degrees in mathematics.

## AWARDS AND OTHER ACCOMPLISHMENTS

Mirzakhani has received several awards for her work, including a merit fellowship from Harvard University in 2003, the 2013 Ruth Lyttle Satter Prize from the American Mathematical Society, and the Clay Research Award in 2014. She has been invited to lecture and give talks at several different universities. Her papers have been published in many prestigious scientific journals, including, as previously mentioned, the *Annals of Mathematics* and the *Journal of the American Mathematical Society*.

When asked if she has a particular method for coming up with new mathematical proofs, Mirzakhani told Carey, "I don't have any particular recipe." She continued, "It is the reason why doing research is challenging as well as attractive. It is like being lost in a jungle and trying to use all the knowledge that you can gather to come up with some new tricks, and with some luck you might find a way out." She prefers to work on her mathematical proofs on huge pieces of paper, filling the pages of equations with doodles and other relevant sketches. Some of her current work includes better understanding of translation surface and their orbits.

Mirzakhani is married to Jan Vondrak, a theoretical computer scientist associated with the IBM Almaden Research Center, in San Jose, California. The couple has a young daughter named Anahita.

## SUGGESTED READING

Carey, Bjorn. "Stanford's Maryam Mirzakhani Wins Fields Medal." *Stanford News*. Stanford U, 12 Aug. 2014. Web. 15 Jan. 2015.

Chang, Kenneth. "Top Math Prize Has Its First Female Winner." *New York Times*. New York Times, 12 Aug. 2014. Web. 15 Jan. 2015.

Klarreich, Erica. "A Tenacious Explorer of Abstract Surfaces." *Quanta Magazine*. Quanta Magazine, 12 Aug. 2014. Web. 15 Jan. 2015.

"Interview with Research Fellow Maryam Mirzakhani." *Clay Mathematics Institute: Annual Report* (2008): 11–13. Web. 15 Jan. 2015. PDF file.

—Christopher Mari

# Maya Moore

**Born:** June 11, 1989
**Occupation:** Basketball player

Danny Karwoski/Wikimedia Commons

The Minnesota Lynx superstar Maya Moore is one of the most decorated female basketball players of all time. A versatile six-foot forward known for her all-around offensive and defensive skills, tireless work ethic, and humble demeanor, Moore has won championships at every level of her career. She won three Georgia state high school championships and two National Collegiate Athletic Association (NCAA) titles as a record-breaking player at the University of Connecticut, better known as UConn, before being selected by the Lynx with the top pick of the 2011 Women's National Basketball Association (WNBA) Draft. Moore continued her winning ways at the professional level, leading the Lynx to their first WNBA titles in 2011 and 2013. She also won a gold medal as a member of the US women's basketball team at the 2012 Olympic Games in London, England.

A three-time WNBA All-Star starter, Moore earned Rookie of the Year honors in 2011 and was named the WNBA's Most Valuable Player (MVP) in 2014. She was also the 2013 WNBA Finals MVP. Moore also has a combination of talent and charisma, and as Joan Niesen wrote for *Grantland* (5 Dec. 2012), "She is, without a doubt, the league's present; its brightest star, its biggest talent."

## EARLY LIFE

Maya April Moore was born on June 11, 1989, in Jefferson City, Missouri. An only child, she was raised by her mother Kathryn Moore, who named Maya after poet laureate Maya Angelou. Her biological father, Michael Dabney, a star guard for Rutgers University in the mid-

1970s, deserted the family before she was born. Moore would reconnect with her father as an adult but has preferred not to discuss the subject in interviews.

Moore's mother introduced Moore to sports early on. Kathryn had played volleyball at Occidental College in Los Angeles, California. When Moore was three, her mother mounted a toy basketball hoop on a bedroom door in their apartment to keep her occupied while she cooked dinner. Not long afterwards, her mother signed her up for gymnastics. The sport, however, proved to be too slow for Moore, who preferred to play basketball in the family driveway. "I was a basketball junkie," she admitted to Niesen.

A crystallizing moment for Moore occurred on June 21, 1997, when the WNBA began its first season. Moore, who had received a pair of league-sanctioned basketballs from an uncle for her eighth birthday, began following the league and its star players in earnest, bolstering her passion for the game. Around this time, Moore quit gymnastics in order to play Amateur Athletic Union (AAU) basketball. She joined the Jefferson City Basketball Club, and as an eight-year-old, started at guard on a ten-and-under team.

Moore played basketball in Jefferson City until the age of eleven, when her mother, a Sprint employee, moved with Moore to Charlotte, North Carolina, to accept a higher-paying job with the company. The two remained in Charlotte for one year before relocating to Lawrenceville, Georgia, a suburb of Atlanta.

## HIGH SCHOOL PHENOM

In Georgia, Moore blossomed into the top basketball prospect in the nation. At fourteen she got her first taste of being a champion when her AAU team, the Georgia Magic, won the national championship. Moore attended Collins Hill High School in Suwanee, Georgia, where she was a highly decorated basketball player. As a four-year starting guard-forward, she led the Eagles to a 125–3 record, three Georgia Class 5A titles, and the 2007 National Championship, and she finished as the school's all-time leader in points (2,664) and rebounds (1,212). Following her junior and senior seasons, Moore won the Naismith Prep Player of the Year Award, becoming only the second player to win the award twice. She was also a four-time first-team All-America selection.

Moore's prep career was rivaled only by her success on the AAU circuit. As a member of the Georgia Metros, a team she joined the summer after her freshman year, she captured four national AAU championships. Metros director Charles Huddleston told a reporter for the Danbury, Connecticut, *News-Times* (19 Mar. 2008) that Moore is "the kind of player that wants the ball in her hands when the game is on the line." Equally adept in the classroom, Moore graduated from Collins Hill High with a 4.0 grade-point average.

## STAR AT UCONN

After her junior year at Collins Hill, Moore committed to the University of Connecticut in Storrs. She chose UConn over her other top college choices so she could play for renowned coach Geno Auriemma, who is credited with helping to set the standard for excellence in women's college basketball. Under Auriemma, a famously demanding perfectionist, Moore knew she would be pushed to her full potential.

Moore became a starter in the eighth game of her freshman season after junior guard Kalana Greene suffered a season-ending knee injury. Moore proceeded to have "the most magnificent freshman campaign in women's hoops history," Kelli Anderson wrote for *Sports Illustrated* (17 Nov. 2008). Setting a UConn freshman single-season record with a team-best 17.8 points per game average, Moore led the Huskies to a 36–2 record and a berth in the NCAA Final Four for the first time since 2004. She was named Big

East Player of the Year, becoming the first freshman, male or female, to receive the honor.

Named a captain before her sophomore season, Moore would lead the Huskies to consecutive undefeated, national championship seasons as a sophomore and junior in 2009 and 2010 and another Final Four appearance as a senior in 2011. From 2008 to 2010, the Huskies won ninety consecutive games, the longest winning streak for a men's or women's team in college basketball history. Moore won three consecutive Wade Trophies as the nation's best player from her sophomore through senior seasons, becoming the first player to ever win the award three times. She also became the second women's basketball player to be named an Associated Press First-Team All-American four times.

Moore finished her career at UConn with 150 wins, the most by any player in NCAA history. She also finished as UConn's all-time leading scorer, with 3,036 points, the fourth-highest total in NCAA history. She is the only women's basketball player in Division I history to amass 2,500 points, 1,000 rebounds, 500 assists, 250 steals, and 150 blocks. Moore graduated from UConn as a sports media and promotion major and with a 3.67 GPA.

## MINNESOTA LYNX AND WNBA ROOKIE OF THE YEAR

By the time she finished her storied career at UConn, Moore was already heralded as one of the greatest players in women's basketball. Consequently, she became arguably the most coveted prospect in WNBA history. The Minnesota Lynx, who had won the number-one selection in the draft lottery after compiling the second-worst record in the league for the 2010 season, considered Moore a surefire franchise player who would help them get over the hump. The Lynx franchise selected Moore with the top pick in the 2011 WNBA Draft.

Moore joined the Lynx team, which already featured three WNBA All-Stars: guard-forward Seimone Augustus, point guard Lindsay Whalen, and power forward Rebekkah Brunson. Despite being forced to transition from power forward, the position she mostly played in college, to small forward, Moore lived up to the enormous hype surrounding her professional debut. The only WNBA rookie to start all thirty-four games during the 2011 season, she averaged 13.2 points, 4.6 rebounds, and 2.6 assists, and helped propel the Lynx to a league- and franchise-best 27–7 record. The Lynx lost only one playoff game en route to their first WNBA championship.

At the end of the season, Moore was named Rookie of the Year, making her the second player to receive that honor and win a WNBA championship in the same season. She was also the first rookie to be voted a starter for the WNBA All-Star Game since 2002. Geno Auriemma called his former pupil "one of those great athletes who is able to block everything out except what's important," as he told Phil Ervin for *Fox Sports North* (6 Sept. 2013).

## SECOND WNBA TITLE

In May 2011 Moore became the first female basketball player to sign an endorsement deal with Nike's Jordan Brand. That prestigious affiliation only bolstered Moore's profile entering the 2012 season, in which she improved her numbers in every major statistical category. During her sophomore campaign Moore averaged 16.4 points, 6.0 rebounds, and 3.6 assists per game and guided the Lynx to the league's best record for the second straight year as they again finished 27–7. The Lynx returned to the WNBA Finals, but they ultimately failed to defend their title, losing to the Indiana Fever in four games. Moore earned All-WNBA Second Team honors for the first time in her career.

Prior to the 2013 season, Moore overhauled her diet in an effort to drop weight and add more explosiveness and quickness to her game. The new diet regimen, which included cutting back on dairy products and refined sugar, paid immediate dividends. In 2013 she led the Lynx and finished third in the WNBA in points per game (18.5) and became the first player to lead the league in both three-point field goals (72) and three-point field goal percentage (45.3). She was named an All-Star starter for the second time and earned her first All-WNBA First Team selection. Towards the end of the season, Moore said to Ervin, "I just never want to stop working, stop getting better, stop being hungry."

Moore helped the Lynx finish with the league's best record for the third consecutive year, finishing 26–8. The Lynx swept through the playoffs with a 7–0 record and won their second WNBA title in three seasons. Moore was named WNBA Finals MVP after averaging twenty points per game in the Lynx's three-game sweep of the Atlanta Dream. During the Lynx's customary trip to the White House, President Barack Obama acknowledged Moore's many previous visits to the executive mansion by joking that she had her own wing there.

## LEAGUE MVP

Moore was named a team captain for the 2014 season, which saw her emerge as the WNBA's best player. She led the WNBA in scoring for the first time, averaging a career-high 23.9 points per game. She also averaged career-highs in minutes (34.7), steals (1.9), and rebounds (8.1) per game, good for second, fifth, and eighth in the league, respectively. Moore had a WNBA-record twelve games of thirty or more points, including a career-high forty-eight points in a double-overtime victory over the Atlanta Dream. Following a thirty-plus point outburst against the Tulsa Shock, Shock head coach Fred Williams called Moore "the Michael Jordan of this league," as quoted by Pat Borzi for the *New York Times* (17 Aug. 2014).

Moore's stellar all-around play anchored a Lynx team that was forced to contend with injuries sustained by starters Rebekkah Brunson and Seimone Augustus. Led by Moore, the Lynx finished second in the Western Conference with a 25–9 record. They advanced to the Western Conference finals but lost to the Phoenix Mercury in three games.

Despite failing to reach the WNBA Finals for a fourth consecutive season, Moore was recognized for her efforts and won the 2014 WNBA MVP Award after being the runner-up for the award the previous season. She also earned her third career All-Star selection and second straight All-WNBA First Team selection. One of the WNBA's most durable players, Moore has never missed a game in her career. "The great thing about Maya is, much like Michael Jordan when he played, there is such a burning inner drive to be the best, that Maya doesn't see herself as a player who has peaked, with nothing to learn," Lynx head coach Cheryl Reeve explained to Mirin Fader for *SLAM* magazine (28 Oct. 2014). "Even though she's young and accomplished a lot, there's still more she can do."

## INTERNATIONAL COMPETITION AND CHARITABLE WORK

In addition to her WNBA career, Moore has played club basketball overseas with now-defunct Ros Casares Valencia in Spain and the Shanxi Xing Rui Flame in China. She led Ros Casares to both the Euroleague and Spanish League championships in 2012 and the Shanxi

Flame to their first Women's Chinese Basketball Association titles in 2013 and 2014.

Moore has also represented the United States in various international competitions since high school. She won gold medals as a member of the US women's basketball team at the 2012 Olympic Games and the 2010 and 2014 World Championships. She is one of only eight players to have earned an NCAA championship, a world championship, an Olympic gold medal, and a WNBA title.

As one of the most popular players in the WNBA, Moore has made it a point to give back to fans and the community. She has hosted an annual day camp for girls in the Twin Cities area called the Maya Moore Academy and worked with the NBA's Hoop Troop program.

## SUGGESTED READING

Anderson, Kelli. "Ready for Moore?" *Sports Illustrated.* Time, 17 Nov. 2008. Web. 27 Feb. 2015.

Ervin, Phil. "Lynx's Maya Moore Proves Even the Best Can Get Better." *Fox Sports.* Fox Sports Interactive Media, 6 Sept. 2013. Web. 28 Jan. 2015.

Fader, Mirin. "Inner Drive." *SLAM.* Enthusiast Network, 28 Oct. 2014. Web. 28 Jan. 2015.

Niesen, Joan. "Such Great Heights." *Grantland.* ESPN Internet Ventures, 5 Dec. 2012. Web. 28 Jan. 2015.

—Chris Cullen

# Ronald D. Moore

**Born:** July 5, 1964

**Occupation:** Television screenwriter and producer

After spending a decade as a fan-favorite screenwriter and producer on various Star Trek television series and films, Ronald D. Moore challenged television viewers' perceptions of science fiction with his reimagined *Battlestar Galactica* series, which provided a sober look at the challenges of a postapocalyptic world. In the series, human beings are pitted against their creations, a race of robots called Cylons, which have, since their development decades earlier, evolved into android versions that are virtually indistinguishable from real humans and are overcome by a religious fanaticism to destroy their creators. The show's dark themes and morally ambiguous

characters proved tremendously popular with both fans and television critics. During its four-year run, the series was considered one of the best shows on television and earned Moore and the cast several awards, including a Peabody, a Hugo, and an Emmy.

Moore returned to television in 2014 as executive producer of two new series: *Helix*—about a group of scientists racing against the clock to solve the mystery behind an unknown disease outbreak—and *Outlander*—about a young married woman from the mid-twentieth century thrown back in time to Scotland in the year 1743. Both shows have become smash hits and were renewed for second seasons, proving that science fiction has a wide appeal, despite widely held beliefs to the contrary. Looking back on his success with *Battlestar Galactica*, Moore told Adam Rogers in an interview for *Wired* (17 Dec. 2013): "I would be very happy if the show proved that you can take the genre seriously, that it doesn't have to be just silly and escapist—you can play it honestly and play the characters truthfully. And that there's an appetite for that approach."

## EARLY LIFE AND EDUCATION

Ronald Dowl Moore was born on July 5, 1964, in the small town of Chowchilla, California. In elementary school he became fascinated with science fiction, primarily through two classic television series produced in the 1960s:

*Star Trek*, starring William Shatner and Leonard Nimoy, and *The Wild Wild West* starring Robert Conrad and Ross Martin. As Moore recalled to Rogers: "I watched both in syndication in the '70s. *Wild Wild West* was really interesting, that combination of genres—a Western and secret agent, and they dabbled in the occult and paranormal. I really wanted to do a new version for CBS. I still think it's a great property. Someday I hope to go back to it."

As a child, he wrote science fiction–inspired stories about dinosaurs fighting in World War II and enjoyed building models, including a detailed replica of *Star Trek*'s famed spaceship, the USS *Enterprise*. A high school football quarterback, he went to Cornell University on a Navy Reserve Officers' Training Corps (ROTC) scholarship to study political science. While there, he was a member of the Kappa Alpha Society, a fraternity and literary society. He eventually dropped out of college and moved to Los Angeles, California, in the hopes of writing screenplays for the film industry, but he had little luck at first. In 1989, he sold a spec script to *Star Trek: The Next Generation*, a Star Trek spinoff series that had begun airing in 1987. His script ultimately became the third-season episode "The Bonding."

### THE NEXT GENERATION AND DEEP SPACE NINE

Soon after selling his first script, Moore secured a spot on the writing staff of *Star Trek* and before long he became a fan-favorite scriptwriter for *The Next Generation*, as well for a second spinoff series, *Star Trek: Deep Space Nine*, which debuted in 1993. His character-driven stories were known for their challenging takes on war, loss, and conflicting emotions. He also became somewhat infamous for killing off characters, most notably Captain James T. Kirk, who had been played by William Shatner in the original series and in numerous Star Trek films, including the one in which he met his demise, *Star Trek: Generations* (1994). "It's weird," Moore said to John Hodgman for the *New York Times* (17 July 2005), as he recalled working on the film script with fellow writer Brannon Braga. "[Kirk] was my childhood hero, and I killed him. What does that mean? What does that say about me?"

During his time working on *The Next Generation*, Moore was promoted to producer and

ultimately cowrote the well-received series finale "All Good Things" in 1994, for which he, Braga, and director Winrich Kolbe won the 1995 Hugo Award for best dramatic presentation. On *Deep Space Nine*, he served as supervising producer under Rick Berman and Michael Piller and used his longtime love of the Navy to provide a more realistic view of the fictional ships of Starfleet. He penned the teleplays for the episode "The Search, Part I," which introduced the space station's ship the USS *Defiant*, and for the thirtieth-anniversary episode "Trials and Tribble-ations," which used state-of-the art visual effects to splice characters from the original series seamlessly into a *Deep Space Nine* time-travel storyline. For their work on "Trials and Tribble-ations," Moore, his cowriters, and director Jonathan West were nominated for the 1997 Hugo Award for best dramatic presentation.

### STAR TREK: VOYAGER AND OTHER PROJECTS

By the time of the *Deep Space Nine*'s finale in 1999, Moore had been promoted to coexecutive producer of the series and was going to begin work on his next series, *Star Trek: Voyager*, which had first aired in 1995 and was in its fifth season when he joined the show.

Moore did not last long as a coexecutive producer on *Voyager*, and he left the series with writing credits on only two episodes. Having come from *Deep Space Nine*, he was dismayed with the way *Voyager* was being produced. The show's premise was that the USS *Voyager* had been accidently stranded in a distant part of the galaxy and that it would take decades for them to return home. All along the return route, the crew faced with all kinds of menaces and had only limited supplies to rely on. Yet, no matter the perils the ship encountered, by the next week's episode all the damage to the ship had been miraculously repaired. Moore's complaints about this lack of reality fell on deaf ears, and he left *Voyager* after a few months.

For the first time in a decade, he was on his own. In 1999, shortly after leaving *Star Trek*, Moore worked as a consulting producer on the fantasy series *Good vs Evil* before becoming the coexecutive producer of the science-fiction series *Roswell*, about teenage aliens. He worked on *Roswell* until the series ended in 2002. He then briefly served as executive producer of the HBO series *Carnivàle*

(2003), about a magical carnival of the 1930s, for which he wrote three episodes.

## REIMAGINING *BATTLESTAR GALACTICA*

Moore's biggest success, however, came when he was tapped to work alongside producer and screenwriter David Eick to revive *Battlestar Galactica*, a 1978 television series about a "ragtag fugitive fleet" of space-faring humans looking for a lost colony called Earth. The original show, which had frequently been derided during its initial run as a rip-off of *Star Wars*, had gathered a cult following in the decades since its cancellation. Many people, including original series star Richard Hatch, believed the series could be revived and its original storyline continued. Moore, however, was unsure, until he went back and watched the original series and saw the potential in a story about a handful of humans surviving the end of their civilization. "When I watched the original pilot," Moore said to Hodgman, "I knew that if you did *Battlestar Galactica* again, the audience is going to feel a resonance with what happened on 9/11. That's going to touch a chord whether we want it to or not. And it felt like there was an obligation to that. To tell it truthfully as best we can through this prism."

Rather than continue the original series, Moore and Eick decided to start the story over and recast the main characters with new actors. They also reimagined the humans' enemies, the Cylons, as a race of robots created by human beings that had evolved into androids that were indistinguishable from ordinary humans. A sense of paranoia ran through the new show's storyline—anyone could be a Cylon—which led to widespread distrust. The surviving humans were often shown as being morally ambiguous, and the Cylons were inspired by a religious fanaticism that compelled them to wipe out their human creators. Moore dubbed the approach "naturalistic science fiction" because it reflected the real-world concerns of the post–September 11 era regarding security, religion, and the ethics of warfare. The new *Battlestar Galactica*, which premiered as a miniseries in 2003, proved so popular with fans and critics that a series began airing in 2004. Before long, critics were hailing it as one of the best shows on television, and longtime fans, who had been wary of any changes to the original premise, were eagerly climbing on board. The show received a Peabody Award in 2005, and Moore was nominated for the 2007 Emmy Award for outstanding writing for a drama series.

The show completed four full seasons before ending its run in 2009. While the series finale was controversial to some fans, who were unhappy with how some parts of the show's mythos were explained, many fans and critics were pleased with the result and agreed with Mary McNamara who, in a review for the *Los Angeles Times* (20 Mar. 2009), proclaimed: "It's hard to imagine a more visually and thematically satisfying finale. . . . All is finally revealed, though in a way that leaves the door open for hours of satiated, as opposed to angry and agitated, speculation, not to mention a whole new round of term papers." In the New Jersey *Star-Ledger* (20 Mar. 2009), Alan Sepinwall wrote: "The finale expertly blended all the things that made the series so wonderful: action, great performances in service of well-rounded characters, contemporary politics placed in futuristic settings, and a healthy dose of spirituality." Moore's reimagined series also spawned two prequel spinoffs, *Caprica* (2010), for which Moore served as executive producer, and the television movie *Battlestar Galactica: Blood and Chrome* (2012), which Moore did not script or produce.

## RETURN TO TELEVISON: *OUTLANDER* AND *HELIX*

After overseeing several pilots that failed to go to series and producing the 2011 television movie *17th Precinct*, Moore returned to television in 2014 as producer of two new series: *Outlander*, based on Diana Gabaldon's series of time-travel romance novels, and *Helix*, a science-fiction series created by Cameron Porsandeh that centers on a group of scientists grappling with an unknown viral outbreak in a remote research facility in the Arctic. When asked by Lesley Goldberg of the *Hollywood Reporter* (12 Feb. 2014) how he manages to balance work on two series simultaneously, Moore responded: "*Outlander* really takes the lion's share of my time. *Helix* has Steve Maeda, who is the showrunner and deserves the lion's share of the credit. . . . I helped get it up on its feet and helped develop the initial mythology, and I'd come into post every once in a while and cut some things and help out, but he's really the guy."

Both series have become popular with viewers and critics and each has been renewed for a second season. *Outlander*, which Moore had been inspired to take on because his wife is a fan of the books, has been a breakout hit for the Starz network, and *Helix* has set records for the Syfy Channel in the live-plus-three and live-plus-seven categories, which measure how many viewers have watched an episode on DVR within three or seven days of its initial broadcast, respectively.

## PERSONAL LIFE

Moore was married to Ruby Moore from 1995 to 2003. In 2004, he married Terry Dresbach, who has worked as a costume designer for *Carnivàle* and *Outlander*. Moore has three children, Robin, Roxy, and Jonathan.

## SUGGESTED READING

Goldberg, Lesley. "Ron Moore on Adapting 'Outlander,' 'Helix's' Future and Taking on James Bond." *Hollywood Reporter*. Hollywood Reporter, 12 Feb. 2014. Web. 13 Oct. 2014.

Hodgman, John. "Ron Moore's Deep Space Journey." *New York Times*. New York Times, 17 July 2005. Web. 13 Oct. 2014.

McNamara, Mary. "'Battlestar Galactica' Finale Is Satisfying—So Say We All." *Los Angeles Times*. Los Angeles Times, 20 Mar. 2009. Web. 13 Oct. 2014.

Rogers, Adam. "The Man Who Rescued *Battlestar Galactica* Is Back on TV." *Wired*. Condé Nast, 17 Dec. 2013. Web. 13 Oct. 2014.

Sepinwall, Alan. "Battlestar Galactica, 'Daybreak, Part 2': There Must Be Some Kind of Way Out of Here." *Star-Ledger*. New Jersey On-Line, 20 Mar. 2009. 13 Oct. 2014.

## SELECTED WORKS

*Star Trek: The Next Generation*, 1987–94; *Star Trek: Deep Space Nine*, 1993–99; *Roswell*, 2000–2; *Battlestar Galactica*, 2003–9; *Helix*, 2014–; *Outlander*, 2014–

—Christopher Mari

# Alicia Munnell

**Born:** December 6, 1942
**Occupation:** Economist

Economist Alicia Munnell is the Peter F. Drucker Professor of Management Sciences at the Carroll School of Management at Boston College. From 1995 to 1997 she served as a member of the President's Council of Economic Advisors and before that, from 1993 to 1995, she was the assistant secretary for economic policy for the US Department of Treasury. Munnell, who is also the director of the Center for Retirement Research at Boston College, specializes in the economics of retirement. In 2014 she coauthored a book called *Falling Short: The Coming Retirement Crisis and What to Do about It*, in which she wrote about the looming Social Security deficit and the poor state of private retirement pensions. Due to a complex slew of factors both political, such as the movement toward the privatization of retirement funds through 401(k) plans, and empirical, namely the sheer number of baby boomers dropping out of the workplace and drawing Social Security benefits, Munnell and the Center for Retirement Research found that 52 percent of workers "will not have a retirement income near their former standard of living," as compared to 31 percent of workers in 1983, economist Jeff Madrick wrote for the *New York Review of Books* (5 Mar. 2015). "People are not going to have enough money when they stop working," Munnell told Deirdre Fernandes for the *Boston Globe* (30 Nov. 2014). "We need to fix this. It's really important."

Munnell has always been interested in the economics of retirement, but she cut her teeth at the Federal Reserve Bank of Boston, commonly known as the Boston Fed. There she coauthored an influential study that found racial discrimination in mortgage lending in Boston. The paper made her an enemy of the New England banking industry and likely cost her a chance to take over as president of the Boston Fed in 1994. But Munnell, who has authored or coauthored more than twenty books throughout her career, has never been one to curb her speech for political gain. "I'm less of a bomb-thrower the older I get," she told Fernandes. "But if I see something I don't agree with, I still speak out."

## EDUCATION AND EARLY CAREER

Alicia Haydock Munnell was born on December 6, 1942, to Walter Haydock and Alicia Wildman Haydock Roux. Haydock was a private investor, and Munnell's grandfather was a respected psychiatrist in New York City. She and her siblings grew up in Manhattan, where Munnell attended the exclusive Spence School, an all-girls preparatory school on the Upper East Side. She graduated with her bachelor's degree in economics from Wellesley College as a member of Phi Beta Kappa in 1964 and earned her master's degree from Boston University in 1966. (In 1985 the university named Munnell to its Academy of Distinguished Alumni.) Munnell earned her PhD in economics, specializing in Social Security and private pension plans, from Harvard University in 1973.

She began working for the Federal Reserve Bank of Boston after graduation. In 1984 she became senior vice president and director of research of the Boston Fed. She was one of only a few women serving in such a powerful position at the organization; she recalled lighting up cigars in meetings (even though she did not smoke) to prove that she could fit in with her male colleagues. During her time with the Boston Fed, Munnell amassed a body of scholarly work regarding Social Security and pensions, and she addressed mortgage lending and racial discrimination in Boston in a 1992 paper called "Mortgage Lending in Boston: Interpreting HMDA Data."

Data from the 1990 Home Mortgage Disclosure Act (HMDA) "showed substantially higher denial rates for black and Hispanic applicants than for white applicants," Munnell and her fellow authors wrote. African Americans and Hispanics were "two to three times as likely to be denied mortgage loans" as white applicants, and "high-income minorities in Boston were more likely to be turned down than low-income whites." The paper was roundly criticized by the banking industry and was the subject of an extended critique in *Forbes* magazine. But Munnell's interpretation of the HMDA data, over twenty years after it was published, turns out to have been not only accurate but indicative of a nationwide trend. Both Wells Fargo and Bank of America paid out huge settlements in cases alleging racial discrimination in mortgage lending, and in a 2014 article for the *Atlantic*, Ta-Nehisi Coates compiled a number of studies that identified systematic racism against African Americans and Hispanics in US housing policy over the previous thirty-five years.

## CLINTON ADMINISTRATION AND BOSTON COLLEGE

President Bill Clinton appointed Munnell as the assistant secretary for economic policy at the Treasury Department in 1993. She began serving her post as assistant-secretary designee in late January and went up for confirmation in Congress in March. Chris Byron, writing for *New York* magazine (29 Mar. 1993), speculated that Republicans would block her confirmation because of another paper she wrote in 1992 called "Current Taxation of Qualified Pension Plans: Has the Time Come?" In the paper, Munnell proposed a one-time, 15 percent tax on existing private pension funds, arguing that the special provisions accorded employer-sponsored pension plans hurt the national budget and benefited only a small, privileged few.

Despite her unpopular point of view, Munnell was confirmed in her post. In 1995 she was the top choice to replace John P. LaWare on the Board of Governors of the Federal Reserve System, but Senate Republicans, who had gained the majority with the 1994 elections, vowed to block her nomination. President Clinton instead named her to serve on the Council of Economic Advisors. She served in that post until 1997, when she returned to Boston to take a faculty position at Boston College. She founded the school's Center for Retirement Research in 1998.

## FALLING SHORT

In 2014 Munnell, with Charles Ellis, an investment consultant, and Andrew Eschtruth, the associate director for external relations at the Center for Retirement Research, published a book called *Falling Short: The Coming Retirement Crisis and What to Do about It.* The book addresses a multifactorial problem: American workers are retiring earlier and living longer; workplace pensions are disappearing in favor of private retirement plans; and health-care costs are rising. "Social Security replacement rates (the portion of preretirement income it provides) are being gradually reduced," Munnell wrote, as quoted by Michael Hiltzik for the *Los Angeles Times* (14 Nov. 2014). "On the private employer side, traditional pensions are rapidly disappearing, replaced by 401(k) plans." These changes "shift all risks and responsibilities from the employer to the individual, and most of us are not well prepared for this burden."

*Falling Short* is a guide for people looking to retire, but the authors' advice can be broken down into three basic solutions. First, the authors suggest working longer. Legally raising the minimum retirement age from sixty-two to sixty-four years could help, but choosing to delay retirement until the age of seventy can increase Social Security checks by 76 percent. Of course, working longer is easier said than done. As Teresa Ghilarducci, the author of *When I'm Sixty-Four: The Plot against Pensions and the Plan to Save Them* (2008), told Helaine Olen for *Slate* (2 Mar. 2015), "Working longer is a retirement plan like winning the lottery or dying earlier is a retirement plan. Being able to work longer is not a plan"—thanks to health issues and age discrimination that can force older employees out of the work force—"It's a hope."

Still, if one is able, waiting to retire gives workers more time to save on their own—the second solution. That may seem obvious, but the third solution is even more so: learn to live on less, the authors write. For many, the last solution might be the most feasible, depending on one's age. The authors calculate that if a worker began saving for retirement at the age of twenty-five, that worker would need to save 12 percent of his or her income to comfortably retire at sixty-five. If that same worker waited until age forty-five to start saving, they would need to set aside 35 percent of their annual income.

## FURTHER THOUGHTS ON RETIREMENT
In addition to outlining those three steps, Munnell's book advances several other thoughts on personal and government responsibility with respect to retirement. She is a big proponent of the reverse mortgage, a financial arrangement in which one can take equity from one's home to pay for retirement. (She serves on the board of Longbridge Financial, a reverse-mortgage company in New Jersey.) She also advocates for automatic enrollment in pension plans. British workers operate under a similar system, in which one has to opt out rather than opt in to employer-sponsored pension plans. "Only half of American workers participate in some kind of employer-sponsored pension plan," a reporter for the *Economist* noted in an article about *Falling Short* (29 Nov. 2014). "Auto-enrollment boosts participation by 40 percentage points."

*Falling Short*, Munnell told Hiltzik, is a compilation of her research over the previous fifteen years. In addition to advice for individuals, Munnell writes about her ideas for Social Security. She does not support any cuts to current benefits, but she does advocate for raising the average federal income tax—from 19 percent to 23.6 percent—to more equitably distribute the burden of the "legacy debt," money paid out to the generation that fought in World War I and suffered through the Great Depression. (Right now, that debt is being shouldered by workers making less than $117,000.) As Hiltzik rightly points out, most Americans will have little control over their retirement plans as they get older—many choices about retirement will be made by one's employer, even as employers are paying out less in retirement benefits. "Americans have not been facing up honestly to their prospects in retirement,"

Hiltzik warned. But "*Falling Short* will help them do so."

## PERSONAL LIFE
As a teenager Munnell made her society debut at the Debutante Assembly and New Year's Ball in New York City in 1960. She married Thomas Clark Munnell, a Harvard graduate who went on to become an investment banker, in 1963, during her junior year of college. They had two sons, T. Clark Munnell Jr. and Hamilton H. Munnell. They later divorced, and Munnell later married Henry S. Healy, an attorney. She lives in Boston.

## SUGGESTED READING
Byron, Christopher. "Alicia in Wonderland." *New York* 26.13 (1993): 16–17. Print.

Fernandes, Deirdre. "A Warning on Realities of Work, Retirement." *Boston Globe* 30 Nov. 2014. Web. 9 July 2015.

Hiltzik, Michael. "The Hard Truth about Americans' Retirement Options." *Los Angeles Times*. Los Angeles Times, 14 Nov. 2014. Web. 13 July 2015.

Madrick, Jeff. "The Rocky Road to Taking It Easy." *New York Review of Books*. NYREV, 5 Mar. 2015. Web. 13 July 2015.

Olen, Helaine. "The Semi-Retirement Myth." *Slate*. Slate Group, 2 Mar. 2015. Web. 9 July 2015.

"Work, Save, Move: How to Fix America's Pension System." *Economist*. Economist Newspaper, 29 Nov. 2014. Web. 9 July 2015.

—Molly Hagan

# Elvira Nabiullina
**Born:** October 29, 1963
**Occupation:** Chair of the Central Bank of Russia

As chairperson of the Central Bank of Russia, Elvira Nabiullina heads the central bank of a Group of Eight (G8) country, one of the eight leading advanced economies in the world. In 2014, Russia had the world's tenth-largest economy, with a gross domestic product (GDP) of nearly $2 trillion, according to figures released by the International Monetary Fund (IMF). Although Russia has since been suspended from the G8, which is now known as the Group of Seven (G7), her milestone stands.

Gleb Shchelkunov/Kommersant Photo
via Getty Images

A longtime political adviser to Russian president Vladimir Putin, Nabiullina was appointed to the post of chairperson in 2013 and has presided over a troubled period for Russia's economy. By the time of the annual Saint Petersburg International Economic Forum in June 2015, Russia was deep into a recession precipitated by falling oil prices, an unstable ruble (the Russian unit of currency), and Western sanctions imposed in the wake of Russia's 2014 annexation of Crimea, formerly part of Ukraine.

Many observers feel the situation will remain dismal for the foreseeable future. Although the editors of *Forbes* (26 May 2015) listed Nabiullina at number 71 on their 2015 list of the world's one hundred most powerful women, they also wrote, "In December [2014], the Bank of Russia spent billions of dollars to bump up interest rates and stabilize the ruble, but Russia's economic future still looks bleak." Similarly, Paul Sonne and Andrey Ostroukh wrote for the *Wall Street Journal* (17 June 2015), "The government has embarked on a vast $35 billion program to combat the economic crisis, bailing out banks and state enterprises in need. Still, the picture remains far from rosy. Russia's industrial output fell 5.5 percent in May from the previous year. . . . The recession is deepening, with analysts predicting a 4.5 percent economic contraction for the second quarter." Even Nabiullina herself warned that conditions would be difficult to mitigate. "In light of new realities and adverse external trends it would not be realistic to expect too rapid a development of the banking sector," she told Stefanie Linhardt in an interview for the industry publication the *Banker* (May 2015).

## CHILDHOOD AND EDUCATION

Elvira Sakhipzadovna Nabiullina was born on October 29, 1963, in Ufa, the capital city of the Republic of Bashkortostan, near the Ural Mountains. She is the older of two siblings in a family of ethnic Tatars. (After the Uzbeks, the Tatars are the second-largest non-Slavic ethnic group in the former Soviet Union, numbering more than six million.) Her father was a truck driver, and her mother was a factory worker. Russian journalists often proudly refer to her relatively humble background in order to highlight how far her innate intelligence and hard work have taken her.

A stellar student with a particular aptitude for math, Nabiullina reportedly earned the fondness of her classmates by freely allowing them to copy her homework. She was also an avid student of French and an inveterate reader, devouring books by such authors as Fyodor Dostoevsky, Franz Kafka, and Leo Tolstoy. She also enjoyed poetry and still lists among her favorites Paul Verlaine—many of whose works she can still recite in the original French, according to her husband—and Anna Akhmatova, whose first husband was executed by Soviet secret police and whose third (common-law) husband perished in a gulag labor camp. (Russian journalists often mention Nabiullina's fondness for Verlaine, finding an appealing irony in the idea of a serious-minded economist enjoying French poetry; fewer mention Akhmatova, whose work was frequently censored by the Stalinist government.)

In the early 1980s Nabiullina studied economics at Moscow State University (MSU), which at the time was officially known as M. V. Lomonosov Moscow State University of the Order of Lenin, the Order of the October Revolution and the Order of the Red Banner of Labour. Considered one of the finest schools in Russia, MSU boasts nearly a dozen Nobel laureates among its graduates, including former Soviet president Mikhail Gorbachev, physicist and activist Andrei Sakharov, and famed writer Boris Pasternak.

At MSU Nabiullina "majored in the history of economic thought, which was less dominated by Soviet ideology than other specialties of the social science," as Evgenia Pismennaya wrote for *Bloomberg Business* (12 June 2013). Although her program mainly focused on works by Karl Marx and Vladimir Lenin, she also had the opportunity to study otherwise-restricted texts by such Western economists as Robert Higgs and Joan Robinson, to which many observers attribute her relatively liberal views; according to a longtime friend, Pismennaya reported, "Nabiullina has described herself as a liberal economist, one with no hint of radicalism."

In 1985, while still a student, Nabiullina joined the Communist Party. However, disillusioned by the slow pace of reform under Gorbachev, she later renounced her affiliation and, according to Pismennaya, "quit the party by slipping her membership card under the door of the party's office on campus." Nabiullina graduated in 1986 and earned a PhD in economics from MSU in 1990, although some sources claim that she never defended her dissertation.

## EARLY CAREER

In 1991, just as the Soviet Union was collapsing, Nabiullina took a job working under Yevgeny Yasin, the father of a college friend, at the Soviet Science and Industry Union (now the Russian Union of Industrialists and Entrepreneurs). She remained at the organization until 1994, when Sergei Vasilyev, then deputy minister of the economy under President Boris Yeltsin, tapped her for the position of deputy head of the Ministry of Economy's Economic Reform Department. Nabiullina became head of the department in 1996, thanks in part to Yasin, who by then had been appointed minister of the economy; the following year she was made Yasin's deputy minister, replacing Vasilyev.

Following Russia's 1998 economic crisis, in which the nation defaulted on more than $40 billion in domestic debt, the government of acting prime minister Sergei Kiriyenko was disbanded. Nabiullina left public service to become deputy chairperson of the board of Promtorgbank, which was owned by a member of the Russian Union of Industrialists and Entrepreneurs. Industry insiders have pointed out that this was her only tenure at a bank, rather than a government body, lobbying group, or research organization, and that it lasted for less than a year. Finding herself less suited to straightforward banking than to her previous analytical work, Nabiullina soon left Promtorgbank for the post of executive director of the newly established Eurasian Ratings Service, Russia's first debt rater.

In 1999 Nabiullina left the Eurasian Ratings Service to become vice president of the Center for Strategic Research, a research group founded by economist German Gref. In preparation for succeeding Yeltsin as president, then–prime minister Vladimir Putin had hired the group to draft the economic program for his first presidential term. In 2000, when an appreciative Putin made Gref minister of economic development and trade, Nabiullina became his first deputy minister. She held that post until 2003, when she took over as president of the Center for Strategic Research.

When Gref left the government in 2007 for a position at the large state-run lender Sberbank, Putin tapped Nabiullina to replace him as minister. Less than a year later, Russia, like much of the world, faced a severe financial crisis, and Nabiullina helped devise an emergency lending scheme that Putin has since credited with limiting the extent of damage. She subsequently helped draft numerous laws regulating various state functions, including more transparent procurement policies and more efficient social programs. In 2012 she was named aide and economic adviser to the president.

## CENTRAL BANK OF RUSSIA

While it was apparent that Putin held Nabiullina in high esteem, some were shocked when on March 7, 2013, he nominated her as head of the Central Bank of Russia. Describing the reaction to her selection, Douglas Busvine wrote for *Reuters* (22 Mar. 2013), "In an era when central bankers have come to be seen as the high priests of global finance, creating money out of nothing, Putin's choice of the soft-spoken former economy minister delivered as big a surprise to Kremlin watchers as did the election of Pope Francis to the world's 1.2 billion Roman Catholics."

Many had hoped that Aleksei Ulyukayev, a deputy chairman of the bank who had exhibited a strong sense of independence and a willingness to stand up to the Kremlin, would be named. "[Nabiullina] is often seen as a close political ally of Putin," Ivan Tchakarov, a chief economist at Russia's Renaissance Capital investment bank, told Andrew E. Kramer for the *New York Times* (12 Mar. 2013). "This will certainly be perceived by markets as a signal that the central bank of Russia in the future will be much more subject to pressure. This is a blow to the independence of the central bank." Kramer pointed out that Putin's nomination of Nabiullina, "despite a consensus among global economic policy planners that countries with independent central bankers tend to do better economically over the long term," would be particularly worrisome for global investors.

## RUSSIA'S FINANCIAL CRISIS

Despite critics' objections, Nabiullina's appointment was confirmed, and she ascended to the post in June 2013. Her tenure as governor of the Central Bank of Russia has often been troubled. In late 2014, in the midst of a recession precipitated by falling oil prices, the value of the ruble plummeted to historic lows. Nabiullina made the risky decision to drastically increase interest rates, from 10.5 percent to 17 percent, in an attempt to bring down inflation. Later the same day, the bank promised not to institute capital controls, and the currency market slowly began to recover.

At the end of January, the bank began to gradually roll back the interest rate, starting with a reduction of two percentage points. In a *New York Times* article published on January 30, 2015, the day the first reduction was announced, Kramer quoted Nabiullina as saying, "Today's decision is intended to balance the goal of curbing inflation and restore economic growth." By mid-June, the interest rate was at 11.5 percent, and inflation, while still high, had dropped to 15.3 percent from a peak of 16.9 percent in March.

In an interview conducted by Geoff Cutmore for CNBC (18 June 2015), Nabiullina claimed that inflation was likely to fall below 7 percent over the next twelve months and reiterated her ultimate goal of reaching 4 percent inflation. "Our mandate is different from the mandate of the Federal Reserve System," she said. "Our fundamental mandate is price stability, and through price stability, we are creating conditions for a stable economic growth. . . . What we're facing right now is a very obvious goal to reduce inflation. The inflation reduction in itself or maintaining it at a low level is the most important factor of the investment environment and a stable economic growth." Nabiullina also told Cutmore that the events of the past year—including foreign sanctions, falling oil prices, a wildly fluctuating currency, and continual interest-rate adjustments—had all had an impact on the way she will approach policy decisions in the future. "These kind[s] of changes . . . teach everybody a lesson," she said.

## PERSONAL LIFE

Nabiullina has been awarded several state honors, including two Orders of Merit for the Fatherland, second class (2002) and first class (2006). She is married to Yaroslav Kuzminov, who was one of her professors at MSU. He has since become the rector of the National Research University Higher School of Economics, one of Russia's preeminent research universities. The couple has one son and one daughter.

## SUGGESTED READING

Busvine, Douglas. "Special Report: Inside Putin's Central Bank Surprise." *Reuters*. Thomson, 22 Mar. 2013. Web. 22 July 2015.

Kramer, Andrew E. "Extending His Sway, Putin Names Loyalist to Head Russian Central Bank." *New York Times*. New York Times, 12 Mar. 2013. Web. 22 July 2015.

Nabiullina, Elvira. "CNBC Interview: Russia Central Bank Governor, Elvira Nabiullina." Interview by Geoff Cutmore. *CNBC*. CNBC, 18 June 2015. Web. 23 July 2015.

Nabiullina, Elvira. "Elvira Nabiullina: Q&A." Interview by Stefanie Linhardt. *Banker* May 2015: 72–73. Print.

Pismennaya, Evgenia. "Putin's Central Banker Nabiullina Recites Verlaine as Regulator." *Bloomberg Business*. Bloomberg, 12 June 2013. Web. 22 July 2015.

Pismennaya, Evgenia, and Ilya Arkhipov. "The Central Banker Who Saved the Russian Economy from the Abyss." *Bloomberg Business*. Bloomberg, 25 Mar. 2015. Web. 22 July 2015.

Sonne, Paul, and Andrey Ostroukh. "Russia's Struggling Economy Clouds St. Petersburg Economic Forum." *Wall Street Journal*. Dow Jones, 17 June 2015. Web. 22 July 2015.

—Mari Rich

# Kumail Nanjiani

**Born:** February 21, 1978
**Occupation:** Comedian

Kumail Nanjiani is a comedian and actor best known for his role on the HBO television show *Silicon Valley*. The half-hour comedy satirizes tech culture, and follows the trials and tribulations of a start-up company called Pied Piper. Nanjiani plays a coder named Dinesh, who is forever locked in a battle of one-upmanship with fellow coder Gilfoyle, played by Martin Starr. The show, which is in its third season, has been well received, garnering Golden Globe and Emmy nominations for outstanding comedy series. Nanjiani was born and raised in Karachi, Pakistan, and attended college in the United States. He once had a fear of public speaking, but after graduating from college he decided to pursue a career in stand-up comedy. He spent years performing in Chicago, where he debuted his hit one-man show *Unpronounceable* (2007), but honed his act and image in the alternative comedy scene in New York City. In 2011 Nanjiani appeared on his first episode of the IFC comedy *Portlandia* and landed a supporting role on the TNT legal dramedy *Franklin and Bash* (2011–14). In addition to his role on *Silicon Valley*, Nanjiani hosts two podcasts—*The Indoor Kids*, about video games, and *The X-Files Files*, about the popular science fiction television show—and premiered a documentary-style Comedy Central show called *The Meltdown with Jonah and Kumail* (based on a show the comedians host live in Los Angeles) in 2014.

## EARLY LIFE AND EDUCATION

Nanjiani was born on February 21, 1978, in Karachi, Pakistan. He was raised in a very religious Shiite family. Sex and sexuality were taboo—Nanjiani recalls being devastated by his first tinge of attraction to supermodel Cindy Crawford—but as an adolescent, he spliced clips from pornography into VHS tapes of popular movies. "I hope my dad never watched *Roger Rabbit* when I wasn't around," he joked to Ann Marie Baldonado for National Public Radio's *Fresh Air*. Though he considers Karachi his home, and cherishes his childhood memories there, he admits that it was not a safe place to live for a Shiite Muslim (a religious minority in Pakistan). One summer, his parents sent him and his younger brother to visit their aunt in Singapore. He found out years later that the trip was planned because his father had received a note threatening to kidnap his oldest son—Nanjiani—for ransom. (Such kidnappings, targeting well-off families, have become commonplace.) He moved to the United States when he was eighteen. His father, a psychiatrist, moved the family and his practice to New Jersey five or six years later. Nanjiani recounts his first solo trip through US customs in his show *Unpronounceable*. The official read the name on his passport and told him it was "unpronounceable." "Not, 'I can't pronounce that,' or 'How do you pronounce that? Just—'Nope, sorry,'" he recalled. He later told Shereen Nanjiani, a Scottish broadcaster who is also his second cousin, for BBC Radio Scotland (1 Sept. 2012) that his first weeks in the United States were

some of the worst of his life. The loneliness, he said, "was like . . . drowning." He successfully used humor to navigate the unfamiliar terrain. "I never felt funny before that," he told Shereen Nanjiani.

Nanjiani attended Grinnell College, a small liberal arts school in Grinnell, Iowa, where he grappled with the absurdities of US culture and—unexpectedly—the nature of his faith. As a freshman, he was studying computer science and trying to find time throughout the day to pray. But then he began taking philosophy classes and experienced, as he recalls in his show, an existential crisis that eventually led him to embrace atheism. Nanjiani graduated with a dual degree in computer science and philosophy in 2001, the same year he decided to pursue a career as a professional comedian. It was also the same year as the September 11 terrorist attacks on the World Trade Center, after which the country experienced a virulent spasm of racism against Muslims, or anyone who appeared Middle Eastern or South Asian. Nanjiani considered joining a tour of Muslim comics that performed for primarily Muslim audiences, but decided that it was at odds with the kind of comic he wanted to be.

## EARLY CAREER AND
## *UNPRONOUNCEABLE*

As a stand-up, Eric Konigsberg described Nanjiani in the *New York Times* (30 Oct. 2009) as "slightly absurdist and occasionally free-form." His humor, informed by his interests in pop culture and video games, is observational, Nanjiani told Baldonado, but was not, early on, particularly personal. "I realized [there] was a big part of who I was that I wasn't talking about," he said. He decided to write a show that would be the story of his life. "And I gave myself a few months to write it, and it was really hard, but it was also really, really gratifying. And it actually helped me come to terms with a lot of stuff that had been plaguing me and stuff that had been confusing to me," he said. His one man show *Unpronounceable,* directed by Paul Provenza, debuted at the Lakeshore Theater in Chicago in 2007. In many ways, the show was Nanjiani's first big break; it received rave reviews and he went on to perform it in Los Angeles and New York City, where he moved in 2007. Andrew Marantz wrote for *Time Out New York* (27 Mar. 2008), "At times, the monologue is funny; at other times it's incisive and harrowing. But Nanjiani is most adept during the moments it's both: He has that rare ability to make painful material hilarious." Nanjiani's parents, however, were concerned that the show denigrated the family and their faith. When they read it, they were relieved to see that it did neither of these things, though they still requested that their son stop performing it. He obliged, a decision that he still feels conflicted about.

Nanjiani opened for comedian Zach Galifianakis's national tour in 2008, and began writing for a show called *Michael and Michael Have Issues,* starring comedians Michael Showalter and Michael Ian Black, on Comedy Central. The show was the first time Nanjiani acted outside of performing stand-up. All of the writers were required to appear on the show and Nanjiani auditioned to play himself four times. He began appearing as a guest on different comedy shows, including *The Colbert Report,* on which he played a Guantanamo Bay detainee named Omar (or as the joke turns out, Homer, who is actually from Greece) who lives under Colbert's desk. In July 2009 Nanjiani appeared at the Just for Laughs comedy festival in Montreal, attracting the attention of television network producers. He sold a sitcom to NBC based on his own life—as is a common rite of passage for successful comedians—though it was not picked up. "Every guy who does stand-up has a sitcom idea and a script," Pete Holmes, a comedian and *New Yorker* cartoonist, told Konigsberg. "We all hustle doing a little bit of everything—sketch comedy, Internet, videos. But it's an incredible time right now. It still feels really small—and

then every few months another person gets on a sitcom." Despite his growing visibility—or perhaps because of it—Nanjiani kept up the grueling schedule of a full-time stand-up, performing nearly every night in at least one club, sometimes two. "If I go four or five nights without getting onstage, I have a hard time being in the moment," he told Konigsberg in 2009.

## TELEVISION CAREER

In 2011 Nanjiani landed a supporting role on the TNT legal comedy-drama *Franklin & Bash,* starring Mark-Paul Gosselaar and Breckin Meyer. For three seasons—the show was canceled during its fourth season in 2014—Nanjiani played a lawyer named Pindar "Pindy" Singh. He began appearing on the IFC sketch show *Portlandia,* starring *Saturday Night Live* alum Fred Armisen and Carrie Brownstein of the band Sleater-Kinney, in 2011. In 2013 he filmed a Comedy Central stand-up special called *Beta Male,* and landed a starring role on the new HBO comedy series *Silicon Valley.* The show was created by Mike Judge, the writer of *Beavis and Butt-head* and the 1999 cult classic *Office Space,* and premiered to enthusiastic reviews in April 2014. It follows an awkward-yet-brilliant young techie named Richard (Thomas Middleditch) who works for a Google-like corporation called Hooli and lives in an "incubator" that is really a drab ranch house owned by a once-successful pot-smoking entrepreneur (T. J. Miller) hoping to get in on the next big thing by offering up rooms rent-free to his incubatees. Nanjiani's character, Dinesh, also lives in the incubator, as does Dinesh's frenemy, Gilfoyle. Both sign on to work with Richard when Richard realizes the extraordinary value of a data compression app he has been working on. The clueless crew celebrates their success at first—until they realize that they must learn to navigate the treacherous road available to tech start-ups in Silicon Valley. "Like any good satire, *Silicon Valley* makes itself easy to understand in context," Matt Zoller Seitz wrote for *New York Magazine*'s *Vulture* blog (4 Apr. 2014). "This story is not ultimately about coding or apps, or even the incredibly specific personality types who inhabit the world of high technology. It's about start-up entrepreneurs who have great ideas but no business sense, and are therefore ripe for exploitation by people who've been around the block."

## PERSONAL LIFE

Nanjiani started dating Emily Gordon, a non-Muslim from North Carolina, in 2007. About eight months into their relationship, she got very sick and went into a coma for eight days. Nanjiani was distraught and told his parents about his relationship with Gordon—which was significant considering that they had wanted him to enter an arranged marriage with a Muslim woman. When his family realized how serious he was, they embraced the relationship and encouraged the couple to get married. After Gordon was well, they did so and moved to New York, though they did not tell their new friends that they were married until a few years later. When the couple was first married, Gordon worked as a marriage counselor, but she eventually quit her job to work with Nanjiani. The two are writing a movie about their origin story with the help of comedy writer Judd Apatow, and they cohost the podcast *The Indoor Kids*. Gordon is also a producer on *The Meltdown with Jonah and Kumail*. They live in Los Angeles.

## SUGGESTED READING

Baldonado, Ann Marie. "For Comedian Kumail Nanjiani, Getting Personal Is Complicated." *NPR*. NPR, 10 June 2015. Web. 3 Aug. 2015.

Konigsberg, Eric. "It's Not a Bad Time to Be Funny in the City." *New York Times*. New York Times, 1 Nov. 2009. Web. 3 Aug. 2015.

Marantz, Andrew. "An Angel Gets His Wings." *Time Out New York*. Time Out, 27 Mar. 2008. Web. 3 Aug. 2015.

Nanjiani, Kumail. "Kumail Nanjiani: Extended Interview." By Shereen Nanjiani. *BBC Radio Scotland*. BBC, 1 Sept. 2012. Web. 3 Aug. 2015.

Seitz, Matt Zoller. "Seitz: *Silicon Valley*'s Version of Machismo Is Hilarious, and Feels New." *Vulture*. New York Media, 4 Apr. 2014. Web. 3 Aug. 2015.

## SELECTED WORKS

*Franklin & Bash*, 2011–14; *Silicon Valley*, 2014–; *The Meltdown with Jonah and Kumail*, 2015–

—Molly Hagan

# Andris Nelsons

**Born:** November 18, 1978
**Occupation:** Conductor

Andris Nelsons is one of the youngest conductors to ever serve as the music director of the world-renowned Boston Symphony Orchestra (BSO). The six-foot-two, Latvian-born maestro is known for his athletic style; observers say that he lunges and leans his way through each performance with an awkward grace. Whatever his unorthodox style, it works. Alex Ross wrote of Nelsons in an article for the *New Yorker* (1 Dec. 2014), "Every time I've seen him conduct . . . he has set off brushfires of intensity." Many other critics have joined in the praise, and Nelsons has become widely recognized as one of the premier talents in a new generation of conductors.

Even among the wave of younger conductors taking over from the previous generation, Nelsons has seen an unusually rapid rise to the top of the orchestral music world. Appointed the director of the Latvian National Opera while in his mid-twenties, he took over the directorship at the City of Birmingham Symphony in England at the age of twenty-nine. Appearances with other major orchestras throughout Europe and the United States followed. His position as one of the world's top conductors was cemented when he was named the successor to James Levine at the BSO, becoming the organization's youngest director in over a century at the age of thirty-four. A music director's job is both administrative and artistic, as they are responsible for an orchestra's repertoire, its overall artistic direction, and for building a relationship with its audience. Such critical duties are typically entrusted to maestros with many years of experience. But Nelsons embraces these responsibilities. For him, music is much more than a job. "Music is something so mystical, so unexplainably a thing you cannot put in the rules or boundaries," Nelsons told Jeff Lunden for NPR's *All Things Considered* (26 Sept. 2014). "It speaks about our feelings, about questions of life and death. It goes absolutely beyond any kind of rules."

## EARLY LIFE AND EDUCATION

Nelsons was born in Riga, Latvia, which was then a part of the Soviet Union, on November 18, 1978. His mother and stepfather were choir conductors and music teachers, and his father

Boston Globe/Getty Images

was a cellist, so he grew up surrounded by music. But Nelsons truly caught the music bug after his parents took him to see the Richard Wagner opera *Tannhäuser* when he was five years old. "I looked at the conductor—of course with the eyes of a five-year-old I didn't understand what he was doing—but I thought it's probably amazing and a very important responsibility because he raises his hands and people start to play. And I thought it's magic in a way," Nelsons told Andrea Shea for the Boston *ARTery* (26 Sept. 2014).

Growing up, Nelsons attended music school, where he learned piano and began playing trumpet. He also seriously studied singing, though he focused on the trumpet at the Emil Darzins School of Music and the Latvian Academy of Music. As a teen, he played for the Latvian National Opera Orchestra, but he harbored ambitions of conducting. He tried his best to learn by reading and developing his own technique, though as he told Shea, "It's not a thing you can learn in four walls isolated." He began to study conducting with Alexander Titov at the Rimsky-Korsakov Conservatoire in St. Petersburg, Russia, and took master classes with other established conductors such as Neeme Järvi and Jorma Panula.

A breakthrough occurred when Nelsons attended a concert in Riga conducted by Mariss Jansons, the director of the Oslo Philharmonic of Norway and one of the most respected conductors in the world. At the intermission, Nelsons

was asked to fill in for a sick trumpet player, an invitation that he eagerly accepted. He then traveled to Berlin, Vienna, and Munich just to watch Jansons conduct, and the older maestro gladly allowed Nelsons to observe his technique. By 2002 Nelsons was taking private lessons in conducting with Jansons as his mentor.

## EARLY CONDUCTING CAREER

Nelsons ended his trumpet career with the Latvian National Opera when he was appointed music director and principal conductor of the organization in 2003. He first conducted Wagner's *Der Ring des Nibelungen*, or "Ring Cycle," an epic comprised of four operas and seen as a major production for any group, at the age of twenty-six. As his reputation grew he earned more guest conducting appearances across Europe, including both opera and concert positions. Among these were collaborations with the Tonhalle-Orchestra Zürich in Switzerland, the Symphonieorchester des Bayerischen Rundfunks in Munich, the BBC Philharmonic Orchestra, and the Bavarian Radio Symphony Orchestra.

In 2006 Nelsons became the director of the Nordwestdeutsche Philharmonie in Herford, Germany, and in 2007 he first appeared with the Deutsche Oper in Berlin conducting Giacomo Puccini's classic opera *La Bohème*. During the next two years, he made debut performances with a number of top-tier orchestras, including the Berliner Staatsoper, the Vienna State Opera, Pittsburgh Symphony, the Cleveland Orchestra, and the Orchestre National de France in Paris. Though he has worked with many musicians in many cities, Nelsons prizes his relationship with his players and conducts with a deft hand. "It's not absolute leadership," he told Ulrike Mertens and Gabriel Sànchez Zinny for *FOCUS* magazine (2009). "The music does the leading, so it should be the composer who is the leader. It's not good for a conductor to say 'I'm the leader' in an excessively egoistic sense."

In October 2007, Nelsons succeeded Sakari Oramo as the music director of the City of Birmingham Symphony Orchestra (CBSO) in Birmingham, England. He won the appointment after a single private performance with the orchestra. Nelsons thrived with the CBSO, making several highly regarded recordings of works by composers such as Pyotr Ilyich Tchaikovsky and Richard Strauss. Critic Tom Service remarked in an article for the *Guardian* (30 July 2010), "The connection between him and his players is among the most special I've seen anywhere."

Nelsons continued to travel in addition to his work with the CBSO, further expanding his international profile. In October 2009, he made his debut with the New York Metropolitan Opera and became a regular guest conductor. Other regular appearances included with the Royal Concertgebouw Orchestra in Amsterdam, the Berlin Philharmonic, the Vienna Philharmonic, and the Leipzig Gewandhaus Orchestra, while he had notable performances at the Lucerne Festival in Switzerland and the Bayreuth Festival in Germany.

By 2013, Nelsons was one of the most in-demand conductors available, and rumors abounded that he would accept a position with the Berlin Philharmonic in 2018. But in the summer of 2013, Nelsons announced that he would officially conclude his contract with the CBSO in 2015 after accepting the directorship of the Boston Symphony Orchestra.

## THE BOSTON SYMPHONY ORCHESTRA

The Boston Symphony Orchestra (BSO) is both world-renowned and locally beloved. Levine, Nelsons's predecessor, resigned in 2011 after his tenure was plagued by health problems, and the organization spent several years searching for the right replacement conductor; writing for *Boston* magazine (26 June 2013), Matthew Reed Baker compared the Boston community's interest in the search to its obsession with its sports figures. Mark Volpe, the managing director of the BSO, told Lunden that Nelsons was the board of directors' and the musicians' unanimous choice. "This guy—the music's kind of oozing out of not just his hands, but his whole body," Volpe said of the conductor.

Nelsons had made his guest debut with the BSO in March 2011, conducting Gustav Mahler's *Ninth Symphony* at Carnegie Hall, and had several subsequent appearances that convinced many that he would be a good fit. His acceptance of a five-year contract offer was met with great fanfare; the city of Boston officially declared his signing to be "Andris Nelsons Day," and in addition to completing dozens of interviews Nelsons even threw out the first pitch at a Red Sox baseball game at Fenway Park. In stark contrast to Levine's aloof demeanor, Baker described Nelsons's personality in the face of the media frenzy as "warm, thoughtful, and most importantly, *accessible*."

Nelsons made his official debut as the BSO's fifteenth music director in September 2014. He played to a full house, but the performance was also filmed for a national televised broadcast. Nelsons's eclectic program began with the overture to Wagner's *Tannhäuser*, followed by excerpts from operas by Wagner, Pietro Mascagni, and Puccini and concluding with Italian composer Ottorino Respighi's "Pines of Rome." The performance was well reviewed, including by Jeremy Eichler for the *Boston Globe* (29 Sept. 2014), who reflected, "Nelsons's youth, his immersive podium style, and his fundamental openness will help the orchestra reach new audiences. Yet for this new era to reach its full potential, he will also need to add to this mix a boldness of artistic and institutional vision commensurate with his willingness to take risks onstage. . . . The future of this partnership should be very bright indeed."

The BSO hopes that Nelsons will prioritize Boston and make the orchestra his chief focus. (Many music directors, like Levine and even Nelsons in the past, hold several posts, which can potentially produce conflicts.) Bostonians hope that his youth and enthusiasm will revitalize the BSO, and by his own account, Nelsons is up to the challenge. After his first season, he planned a European tour with the BSO and new recordings. He explained to Baker his vision for the future, including his openness to exploring a wide repertoire, from the Germanic, Slavic, and French classics to American and contemporary works. "Some people like music from an emotional point of view, and others like it more analytic and intellectual, and to fulfill both is the expectation. Personally I am very emotional-orientated. I feel you have to [be] emotionally fulfilled," he told Baker. "It's like food for our soul. We feed people with our music."

## PERSONAL LIFE

Nelsons is married to Latvian soprano Kristine Opolais. They met in 2003 at the Latvian National Opera, where Opolais was a member of the ensemble. The two share a love of Italian composer Puccini and continue to work together on occasion. "It is easy when I'm singing with him," Opolais told Charlotte Cripps for the *Independent* (16 Aug. 2013) of being conducted by her husband. "I don't even have to look at him because we feel each other." The couple has a daughter named Adriana.

## SUGGESTED READING

Cripps, Charlotte. "Opera's Double Act: Kristine Opolais and Andris Nelsons." *Independent.* Independent.co.uk, 16 Aug. 2013. Web. 26 Feb. 2015.

Lunden, Jeff. "New Boston Symphony Music Director Andris Nelsons: 'It's Not a Job—It's Life." *All Things Considered.* NPR, 26 Sept. 2014. Web. 26 Feb. 2015.

Nelsons, Andris. Interview by Ulrike Mertens and Gabriel Sànchez Zinny. *FOCUS Magazine.* Egon Zehnder, 2009. Web. 26 Feb. 2015.

Nelsons, Andris. "Q&A: New BSO Maestro Andris Nelsons." Interview by Matthew Reed Baker. *Boston Magazine.* Metrocorp, 26 June 2013. Web. 26 Feb. 2015.

Ross, Alex. "Brushfires: Andris Nelsons Energizes the Boston Symphony." *New Yorker.* Condé Nast, 1 Dec. 2014. Web. 26 Feb. 2015.

Service, Tom. "What Makes a Great Conductor? Just Watch Andris Nelsons." *Guardian.* Guardian News and Media, 30 July 2010. Web. 26 Feb. 2015.

Shea, Andrea. "Becoming Andris Nelsons: A Young Maestro's Journey to Boston." *ARTery.* WBUR, 26 Sept. 2014. Web. 16 Feb. 2015.

—Molly Hagan

Manfred Werner (Tsui)/Wikimedia Commons

# Anna Netrebko

**Born:** September 18, 1971

**Occupation:** Opera singer

Many journalists wax rhapsodic about Anna Netrebko. "She has everything," Jessica Duchen wrote for the *Independent* (6 Nov. 2006), "a glorious voice—high-set, lyrical, extremely expressive; terrific acting—the more dramatic, the better; and the sweet yet sultry looks of Audreys Tautou and Hepburn, glamorous and vulnerable at the same time." Netrebko is also often likened to the legendary soprano Maria Callas, a comparison she regularly brushes off. She told Melissa Whitworth during an interview for the *Telegraph* (19 Feb. 2006), "I don't see why people should compare us. First, I have absolutely nothing in common with Maria Callas. I adore her, she is the goddess, but we have a different voice and a different personality." Critic Charles McGrath agreed with those sentiments, writing for the *New York Times Magazine* (2 Dec. 2007), "[The comparison] is both a high compliment

and a bit of a stretch. Callas was more intense, more forceful and also more tortured. On the other hand, Callas never appeared on a music video. Netrebko has a whole DVD of them." That 2004 DVD, *Anna Netrebko: The Woman, the Voice,* outsold similar releases by pop stars like Britney Spears and Beyoncé, and featured the soprano floating in a swimming pool, clad in a sultry swimsuit.

Like the aforementioned pop stars, Netrebko has sold out entire stadiums. Tickets for her performance in Verdi's *La Traviata* (*The Fallen Woman*) at the 2005 Salzburg Festival were reportedly scalped for $7,000 each. She is featured regularly in fashion magazines such as *Elle* and *Vogue* and has signed endorsement deals with a wide variety of brands, including Chopard jewelry and Vöslauer mineral water. The subject of at least two unauthorized biographies in Europe, the singer is also a fixture in the pages of tabloids around the world.

Netrebko's blend of virtuosity and widespread fame makes her something of a divisive figure in the opera world. "Her admirers thrill to her robust stage presence and plush, vibrant tone; they celebrate her distinctive fashion sense and crave details about her glamorous private life," David Mermelstein wrote for the *Wall Street Journal* (19 Sept. 2012). "Her detractors insist that her celebrity compromises her artistry. . . . Yet Ms. Netrebko's star power remains undisputed."

## EARLY YEARS AND EDUCATION

Anna Netrebko was born on September 18, 1971, in Krasnodar, a city in southwestern Russia. She has told interviewers that the area was largely bereft of cultural attractions. Her late mother, Larisa, was a telecommunications engineer, and her father, Yuri, is a geologist of some renown. She has one older sister, Natalya. The family was comfortable financially and lived in a house that was considered relatively large by neighborhood standards. It had a grape arbor in the backyard, and Netrebko's parents often threw large parties at which Yuri served his homemade wine.

Netrebko's parents loved music but rarely listened to anything classical. They took her to concerts and plays whenever possible, however, and Netrebko remembers enjoying the performances greatly. She began taking piano lessons when she was six but soon lost interest in playing. She fared better at age seven, when she joined a children's choir and was deemed talented enough to be a soloist. "I was constantly doing house concerts with my friends," she told Duchen. "Whenever my parents had a party, we'd announce, 'And now, a concert,' and they'd all go, 'Oh, not again!'"

At age sixteen Netrebko moved to St. Petersburg with the vague idea of becoming an actress. When she saw the amount of competition in the field, she switched her focus instead to her other talent—singing. For two years Netrebko studied at a music college and then applied to the highly regarded conservatory in St. Petersburg. "I said to myself: 'O.K. I will try. Maybe they will take me, and if not the worst that can happen is I will go home and be in the operetta,'" she recalled to McGrath.

To earn pocket money while she studied, Netrebko found work as a janitor at the famed Mariinsky Theatre in St. Petersburg. The job gave her the opportunity to watch ballet and opera rehearsals, and it also gave rise to an enduring Cinderella story that has clung to Netrebko no matter how many times she has disavowed it. The tale holds that Valery Gergiev, the artistic director of the Mariinsky, heard her singing as she scrubbed the stage floor on hands and knees and was so enchanted that he invited her to join the opera company on the spot. In reality, Netrebko formally auditioned for Gergiev—and that successful audition took place only after she had entered and won Russia's prestigious Glinka Vocalists' Competition in 1993 and completed her conservatory studies.

## CAREER BEGINNINGS

In 1994 Netrebko was cast as Barbarina in a Mariinsky production of Mozart's *Le Nozze di Figaro* (*The Marriage of Figaro*), and to her surprise, she was quickly promoted to the starring role of Susanna. The following year, Gergiev took a risk by awarding her the part of Lyudmila when the Mariinsky toured San Francisco with Mikhail Glinka's *Ruslan and Lyudmila*. "It was a big, big role and it was a big success," Netrebko told Duchen of her US debut. "So that was where my international career started."

Netrebko was soon considered one of the Mariinsky's leading soloists. In addition to Susanna and Lyudmila, her roles included Rosina in *The Barber of Seville*, Amina in *La Sonnambula* (*The Sleepwalker*), Lucia in *Lucia di Lammermoor*, Gilda in *Rigoletto*, Violetta Valery in *La Traviata*, and Mimi and Musetta in *La Bohème*.

Most music journalists mark 2002 as a turning point in Netrebko's career. That year, she sang the role of Donna Anna in Mozart's *Don Giovanni* at the Salzburg Festival, a preeminent event held each year in the city of Mozart's birth, and her performance was widely lauded. That same year she made her Metropolitan Opera debut in a lavishly staged production of Prokofiev's *War and Peace*, earning solid reviews for her portrayal of Natasha and sparking the interest of New York City's opera fans.

Peter Gelb, the Metropolitan Opera's general manager, began following Netrebko's career, and after seeing her perform in Austria a handful of times, he approached her to perform regularly with his company. She quickly became one of the company's biggest box office draws, singing such parts as Adina in *L'Elisir d'amore*, Antonia in *Les Contes d'Hoffmann*, Juliette in *Roméo et Juliette*, and the title roles in *Manon* and *Anna Bolena*, among many others.

## LATER ROLES

Reviewing Netrebko's performance in a 2005 production of *Rigoletto*, Anthony Tommasini echoed sentiments often expressed by music critics awed by her voice, acting ability, and physique. He wrote for the *New York Times* (12 Dec. 2005): "Ms. Netrebko is not a generic bright-voiced lyric coloratura but a dusky-toned soprano with a sizable sound. Expressivity comes first in her artistry. . . . During the early scene in which she speaks of the mysterious young man who has been following her home from church, her lovely body and luminous voice quivered with yearning." Her costar in the production was Mexican tenor Rolando Villazón, with whom she has worked often over the course of her career.

As she reached middle age she began taking on darker, more dramatic roles, making a transition from ingenue parts often collectively called the "inas" in reference to many of the characters' names. In 2014, for example, she portrayed Lady Macbeth in Verdi's operatic version of the Shakespeare play. "Her Lady Macbeth is causing a sensation at the Metropolitan Opera, winning roars from audiences . . . and rave reviews," Michael Cooper wrote for the *New York Times* (5 Oct. 2014). He noted that Netrebko's "willingness to take risks" as she expanded her repertoire has been met with praise from many critics.

In addition to Austria, New York City, and her native Russia, Netrebko has performed at such iconic venues as the Teatro alla Scala in Milan and the Royal Opera House in London. Netrebko is signed as of 2014 to an exclusive contract with the record label Deutsche Grammophon and has released several well-received live performances and compilation albums, including *Anna: The Best of Anna Netrebko* in 2009.

## PERSONAL LIFE

Netrebko once dated Italian bass-baritone Simone Alberghini. She later had a relationship with the singer Erwin Schrott, with whom she has a son, Tiago. Causing much confusion in the press, she often referred to Schrott as her husband, although most sources state that a wedding never actually took place. Still, the two were often called opera's "golden couple," and fans eagerly followed news of their romance. Although they separated in 2013, they remained friends and have continued to perform together from time to time. In 2014 Netrebko was engaged to tenor Yusif Eyvazov.

Well known as an enthusiastic shopper, Netrebko particularly loves fashion brands such as Escada, Louis Vuitton, and Marc Jacobs. Her musical tastes are reported to extend to pop and hip-hop, and she has confessed to being an avid fan of British singer Robbie Williams. When she is not traveling to perform, Netrebko makes her home with her sister and Tiago on the Upper West Side of Manhattan, not far from the Metropolitan Opera House at Lincoln Center.

## SUGGESTED READING

Duchen, Jessica. "Anna Netrebko: A Rare Jewel from the East." *Independent*. Independent, 6 Nov. 2006. Web. 29 Oct. 2014.

McGrath, Charles. "A New Kind of Diva." *New York Times Magazine*. New York Times, 2 Dec. 2007. Web. 29 Oct. 2014.

Mermelstein, David. "So Long, Ingénues." *Wall Street Journal*. Wall Street Journal, 19 Sept. 2012. Web. 29 Oct. 2014.

Scheinin, Richard. "Diva Anna Netrebko Travels the Superstar and the Mommy Tracks." *Oakland Tribune*. Inside Bay Area, 9 June 2009. Web. 29 Oct. 2014.

Shengold, David. "Wild Thing." *Opera News*. Opera News, 1 Nov. 2003. Web. 29 Oct. 2014.

Whitworth, Melissa. "Cinderella Soprano." *Telegraph*. Telegraph Media Group, 19 Feb. 2006. Web. 29 Oct. 2014.

Woolfe, Zachary. "The Diva, Defined: Netrebko Has Arrived." *New York Times*. New York Times, 23 Sept. 2011. Web. 29 Oct. 2014.

## SELECTED WORKS

*Ruslan and Lyudmila*, 1995; *Don Giovanni*, 2002; *Rigoletto*, 2005; *Anna: The Best of Anna Netrebko*, 2009; *Macbeth*, 2014

—Mari Rich

# Neymar

**Born:** February 5, 1992
**Occupation:** Soccer player

The Brazilian soccer star Neymar is a forward for Futbol Club (FC) Barcelona, the captain of the Brazilian national team, and one of the most popular and beloved soccer players in the world. Ranked the sixth best active player by the *Guardian* in 2013 despite his relative youth, he was also hailed by Jason Gay for the *Wall Street Journal* (19 May 2014) as the "prince of Brazilian soccer, one of the most electric and creative players in the modern game." Neymar has often drawn comparisons to Pelé, arguably the greatest soccer player of all time, for his mesmerizing dribbling skills and technical abilities. Indeed, Pelé himself and other stars such as Lionel Messi have praised Neymar's potential to be the best player in the world.

Neymar began his career in 2003, when, at age eleven, he joined the youth team of Santos FC, one of Brazil's most successful soccer clubs.

In 2009, at age seventeen, he turned professional and made his debut with Santos's first team. He quickly proved himself a top player and helped lead the team to sustained success, becoming a celebrity in the process. He was named South American Player of the Year in both 2011 and 2012. In 2013, after being courted for years by some of Europe's top clubs, Neymar left Santos to sign with FC Barcelona. As a member of the Brazilian national team, Neymar played an instrumental role in leading Brazil to the semifinals of the 2014 World Cup, which was hosted by his home country.

## EARLY LIFE

Neymar da Silva Santos Júnior was born on February 5, 1992, in Mogi das Cruzes, São Paulo, Brazil. He is the older of two children; his sister, Rafaella, is about four years younger. Neymar's father, Neymar Sr., was a former professional soccer player. A few years after Neymar was born, his father retired from professional soccer and moved the family back to his hometown of São Vicente, where he worked three jobs to make ends meet for the family.

It was in São Vicente that Neymar's illustrious soccer career took root. Given his first ball by his mother at the age of two, Neymar first started practicing dribbling drills and techniques in the family kitchen before graduating to the streets. In street games, he usually played against older neighborhood children, oftentimes using sandals as goals and nothing more than a rock as a ball.

Like many other Brazilian soccer players, Neymar also honed his skills playing *futsal*, a brand of soccer that is played indoors on a hard surface with a smaller ball. It was not long before he "developed an instinctive feel for the ball, as if it were an extension of his body," David Hytner wrote for the *Guardian* (1 June 2013). Neymar credited futsal for teaching him "how to dribble with more speed" and giving him "a better, more concentrated view of the game," as he told Janet Tappin Coelho for the *Daily Mail* (27 June 2014).

## SOCCER PRODIGY

Neymar played for local futsal teams before gaining his first experience on a large soccer pitch with Portuguesa Santista, a club based in the nearby coastal city of Santos. The club's coach, Roberto Antonio dos Santos, recognized Neymar's potential while watching him play soccer on the beach in São Vicente. Noticing similarities between the young player and Pelé's

Raul Sifuentes/STR/Latin Content WO/Getty Images

onetime heir apparent, Robinho, dos Santos asserted to Coelho, "I knew instantly that the boy would give a lot of trouble to opposing teams."

Neymar did just that, and by age eleven, he was being heavily courted by teams all over Brazil. In 2003 he and his family moved to Santos to further his soccer career. He eventually caught the attention of scouts from Santos FC, a club that plays in the Campeonato Paulista, one of Brazil's top professional soccer leagues. Neymar entered Santos's renowned youth system and quickly rose through the ranks of the club, where Pelé had famously begun his professional career almost fifty years earlier. Closely monitoring Neymar's burgeoning career and development as a soccer player was his father, who became his manager and advisor.

In 2006, at age fourteen, Neymar was granted an opportunity to play in Europe for Spanish soccer juggernaut Real Madrid, one of the most popular and successful clubs in the world. He and his father were subsequently flown to Madrid, where he trained with the club's youth team. Blown away by Neymar's dribbling abilities and technical prowess, the club offered him a lucrative contract. However, Neymar grew homesick after only a few weeks in Spain and ultimately turned down their offer, opting to continue his development in Brazil with Santos. "We thought he had to grow up in Brazil," his father explained to Sam Borden for the *New York*

*Times* (9 July 2012). "That was the first serious choice we had to make."

## TURNING PROFESSIONAL

Neymar's decision to remain in Brazil proved to pay off. He turned professional in 2009, when he was seventeen, and in March of that year he made his debut with Santos's first team. In his rise up Santos's junior ranks, Neymar had distinguished himself as a prolific goal-scorer at the striker position with preternatural ball-handling skills, and he was already being hailed as a future superstar in Brazilian soccer. One month after Neymar's professional debut, Pelé predicted that the newcomer would surpass his own soccer achievements. In his first season with Santos, he scored fourteen goals in forty-eight matches.

After performing solidly for Brazil's under-seventeen squad at the 2009 U-17 World Cup, Neymar was expected to make an even greater impact for Santos during the 2010 season. He did not disappoint, scoring an impressive forty-two goals in sixty matches. He led Santos to the Campeonato Paulista regional championship, and was named best player of the tournament after notching fourteen goals in nineteen games. He also helped Santos win the 2010 Copa do Brasil, or Brazilian Cup, Brazil's national championship.

Early into the 2010 season, Neymar began sporting his signature flamboyant mohawk hairstyle. The style quickly caught on with Brazil's rabid soccer fans, thousands of whom began copying the look. Neymar took his growing celebrity in stride: "My objective is to entertain," he told Hytner. "That is the Brazilian mentality when it comes to football."

Neymar's emergence as one of Brazil's brightest and most beloved young stars led to calls for him to be included on the country's 2010 World Cup squad. Despite a popular petition, Neymar was left off the team by manager Dunga, who felt he had yet to prove himself in international play. After Brazil was eliminated from the tournament, new coach Mano Menezes called Neymar up to the Brazilian national team for a friendly match against the United States in August 2010. In his national team debut, Neymar scored on a header. He then turned down another offer to join a prestigious European soccer club, this one from Chelsea FC of the English Premier League.

Neymar's growing clout in Brazilian soccer came with pitfalls. During his first two seasons with Santos, he became known almost as much for his temper as for his talent on the soccer pitch. One of Neymar's most notorious episodes came in September 2010, when he had a much-publicized run-in with team manager Dorival Júnior after not being allowed to take a penalty kick in a match. In retaliation to the snub, Neymar verbally harangued Dorival in front of his teammates and the crowd. Though Dorival demanded that the player receive a fifteen-day suspension, Brazil's soccer board instead fired Dorival. Neymar later publicly apologized for the incident, telling Coelho that "it was the worst day of my life" and claiming he had learned from the mistake.

## INTERNATIONAL SUPERSTAR

Neymar redeemed himself with Brazilian soccer fans in 2011, when he helped Santos defend their league championship and win the Copa Libertadores, South America's premier club tournament, for the first time since 1963. In December of that year, Neymar led Santos to a runner-up finish at the 2011 FIFA (Fédération Internationale de Football Association) Club World Cup. He was named South American Player of the Year for 2011.

During the 2012 season, Neymar guided Santos to their third consecutive league title and led them to victory in the Recopa (Winner's Cup) Sudamericana tournament. That season also saw Neymar reach a career milestone: on his twentieth birthday, he scored his one hundredth professional goal. He was again named South American Player of the Year. He also continued to shine for the Brazilian national team, scoring three goals in the 2012 Olympics as the team advanced to the finals, where Brazil lost to Mexico, 2–1.

Neymar solidified his status as an international icon in February 2013, when he became the first Brazilian player to appear on the cover of *Time* magazine. In his profile of Neymar for that publication (4 Mar. 2013), Bobby Ghosh described the Brazilian star as "a Messi-class talent" with "an unaffected effervescence to his game." Though his 2013 season was largely dominated by discussion of his inevitable transfer to a European club, Neymar helped Santos reach their fourth consecutive Campeonato Paulista final. He also led Brazil to victory at the 2013 Confederations Cup, in which he scored four goals.

After much speculation, Neymar left Santos in May 2013 to sign with FC Barcelona. The Spanish powerhouse reportedly paid Santos a transfer fee of €57 million (around $78.8 million). The transfer, however, quickly became embroiled in controversy after it was revealed that much of the fee went to Neymar and his family. Nevertheless, Neymar started training with his new Barcelona teammates, which included superstar Lionel Messi.

In his first season with Barcelona, Neymar scored fifteen goals in forty-one games, but his performance was largely hampered by various injuries. Barcelona nonetheless won the 2013 Supercopa de España, or Spanish Super Cup, and finished as runners-up in both La Liga and the Copa del Rey, Spain's top club competitions.

## 2014 WORLD CUP

As Neymar learned to gel with his Barcelona teammates, he prepared for the biggest competition of his life: the 2014 World Cup. Because the tournament was to be held in Brazil for the first time since 1950, Neymar faced enormous pressure to lead his national team to a record sixth World Cup title and first since 2002. In the run-up to the Cup, he shot down much-hyped comparisons to Pelé, telling Gay, "I am just a boy who wants to play soccer."

Wearing Brazil's iconic number ten jersey, Neymar lived up to expectations, scoring four goals and one assist in five World Cup matches. His sterling World Cup performance ended abruptly, however, after he suffered a broken vertebra during Brazil's 2–1 victory over Colombia in the quarterfinals. Though the injury did not require surgery, Neymar was sidelined for the remainder of the tournament. Brazil struggled in his absence and was defeated by eventual World Cup champion Germany, 7–1, in the semifinals. Neymar was named captain of the Brazilian national team in September 2014.

In August 2014 Neymar returned to training with Barcelona after recovering from his back injury. In his second season with the Spanish club, he returned to top form and teamed up with Messi and Luis Suárez to form the best attacking trio in the world. In April 2015, the trio, known in Spain as "MSN," surpassed one hundred goals for the 2014–15 season, breaking a Barcelona club record. Neymar and company were also on track to win La Liga, the Copa del Rey, and the UEFA Champions League competitions, the so-called treble of European soccer.

## PERSONAL LIFE

Neymar is one of the most visible and heavily marketed athletes in the world. He holds sponsorship deals with dozens of companies, among them Nike, Panasonic, Volkswagen, Unilever, and Red Bull. According to *Forbes* magazine, he was the sixteenth highest-paid athlete in the world in 2014, with $33.6 million in earnings. He is a fashion and style icon in Brazil, and has been known to enjoy partying although he does not drink alcohol.

Neymar has a son, David Lucca da Silva Santos, born in August 2011, from a previous relationship.

## SUGGESTED READING

Borden, Sam. "A Soccer Prodigy, at Home in Brazil." *New York Times*. New York Times, 9 July 2012. Web. 18 May 2015.

Coelho, Janet Tappin. "Brazil's New Golden Boy: How Neymar Survived a Near-Fatal Car Crash as an Infant to Become the Star of the World Cup." *Daily Mail*. Associated Newspapers, 27 June 2014. Web. 18 May 2015.

Gay, Jason. "Brazil's Neymar on the Weight of the World Cup." *Wall Street Journal*. Dow Jones, 19 May 2014. Web. 18 May 2015.

Ghosh, Bobby. "Game Changer: Why Is Soccer Superstar Neymar Still Playing in Brazil?" *Time*. Time, 4 Mar. 2013. Web. 18 May 2015.

Hytner, David. "Neymar: The Brazil and Barcelona Phenomenon Prepares to Face England." *Guardian*. Guardian News and Media, 1 June 2013. Web. 18 May 2015.

—Chris Cullen

# Phebe Novakovic
**Born:** 1958
**Occupation:** Business executive

Phebe Novakovic is the chief executive officer (CEO) of the US defense contractor General Dynamics. Novakovic, who received her master's degree in business administration (MBA) from the Wharton School of Business at the University of Pennsylvania, was an operations officer with the Central Intelligence Agency (CIA) and a special assistant to the US secretary of defense before joining General Dynamics in 2002. In 2014 *Fortune* magazine ranked her as one of the fifty most powerful women in business. She is one of the highest-paid female CEOs in the United States (in 2013 her annual salary was about $19 million), and, as reported by Carola Hoyos for the London *Financial Times*

Bloomberg/Getty Images

(3 Jan. 2013), she is among an elite handful of women taking executive leadership roles in the defense industry.

Loren Thompson, a consultant to General Dynamics and a member of the think-tank Lexington Institute told Hoyos that the US defense industry was experiencing "a revolutionary demographic shift that may soon make women the dominant gender among senior executives," though Thompson suggested that it would mean little in terms of policy. "To be successful in the defense industry, women must conform with the same numbers-driven performance criteria that men face," he said. To underscore the pressure to perform at the top of their professions, Hoyos cited a 2004 study conducted by professors Michelle Ryan and Alex Haslam at Exeter University in England. They studied the one hundred largest companies in the United Kingdom and concluded, according to Hoyos, "women are more likely to be appointed to leadership positions that are associated with an increased risk of criticism and failure." No one is more aware of this than Novakovic who, during her time with General Dynamics, has had to reconcile the needs of her company's shareholders with the fundamental changes taking place in the defense industry.

## EDUCATION AND GOVERNMENT CAREER

Novakovic is of Serbian descent. She graduated from Smith College in Northampton, Massachusetts, in 1979, which was also the year she went to work as an analyst for the McLean Research Center where she performed operational analyses on department of defense weapon systems. From 1983 to 1986 Novakovic served as an operations officer in the CIA. She left the intelligence agency to pursue her MBA, which she earned from the University of Pennsylvania's Wharton School of Business in 1988. In 1992, at the beginning of the Clinton administration, Novakovic joined the Office of Management and Budget (OMB), which is a governmental agency in the executive branch that reports directly to the president. Novakovic worked for the OMB until 1997 when she became the deputy associate director for US national security and was responsible for managing the budgets of the US Department of Defense and various intelligence agencies. In a speech that Secretary of Defense William Cohen gave on January 24, 2000, he thanked his team, including Novakovic. "I have depended upon . . . wise counsel and judgment," he told the assembled crowd, "counsel and judgment like that of Phebe Novakovic, an invaluable Special Assistant to me and [Deputy Secretary of Defense] Dr. Hamre."

## EARLY CAREER WITH GENERAL DYNAMICS

Novakovic left the department of defense in 2001, and in 2002 she took a position as the vice president of strategic planning at General Dynamics, a defense and aerospace contractor based in Falls Church, Virginia. General Dynamics is the oldest defense contractor in the United States. It was founded in 1899 as the Electric Boat Company and was the first submarine builder in the Western Hemisphere. The company officially became General Dynamics when it began manufacturing tanks, missiles, and warships in 1952. Following the Cold War, the company began selling off its military businesses until Nicholas Chabraja, a former trial lawyer, took over the company in 1997. As CEO he oversaw the increase in business that resulted from increased military spending after the September 11 terrorist attacks in 2001, and in 2002 Chabraja personally recruited Novakovic with the expectation that she would one day be a leader in the company.

In 2005 Novakovic was promoted to senior vice president of planning and development, and in May 2010 she was named executive vice president of General Dynamics and head of the corporation's Marine Systems Group. The Marine Systems Group includes three companies: Bath Iron Works, Electric Boat, and NASSCO (National Steel and Shipbuilding Company). Also in 2010, Novakovic was elected to the board of directors at Abbott Laboratories, an American pharmaceutical company.

As head of Marine Systems, Novakovic delivered four ships to the US Navy in 2010, and she negotiated a $1.8 billion deal for two destroyers. In May 2012 she was named president and chief operating officer (COO) of the corporation. The promotion, company sources agreed, was seen as the next logical step toward her ultimate promotion to CEO. "This will be an opportunity for Phebe to broaden her operational experience across the company, which should be good preparation for the next step up," RBC investment analyst Rob Stallard told Andrea Shalal-Esa for Reuters (8 Mar. 2012). It was an open secret that Novakovic was being groomed to succeed CEO Nicholas Chabraja, the man who has been credited with making the company profitable after its post–Cold War slump.

## CEO OF GENERAL DYNAMICS

Chabraja ceded his position as CEO to former Chief of Naval Operations Jay Johnson in 2009, and Novakovic took over from Johnson on January 1, 2013. A few weeks after taking office, investors absorbed the news that the company had recorded a $2 billion loss in the fourth quarter of 2012. Jay Hancock for the *Washington Post* (6 Dec. 2014) reported that one analyst called the number "eye-watering." However, the blow to the company was softened by Novakovic's response. When the news of the loss was made public, General Dynamics' stock began to fall in response, but it rebounded later the same day after Novakovic spoke with analysts. As Shalal-Esa reported for Reuters on January 23, 2013, Novakovic reassured investors that General Dynamics would "stick to our knitting" in 2013 "and do what we know how to do." Michael Lewis, managing director of the Silver Group, an advisory firm, told Jill R. Aitoro for the *Washington Business Journal* (24 Jan. 2013) that Novakovic "did an excellent job" because "the stock was down 5 percent at the open [but] after her candid remarks on fixing the business, the stock [was] up slightly."

Novakovic took the opportunity to be honest with the company's shareholders—a rarity in such earnings calls. She shared her disappointment with the numbers and was frank about the performance of particular businesses under the General Dynamics umbrella, adding, as quoted by Aitoro, "I . . . believe that the acquisition process at GD is somewhat broken, and I will not venture back into that market until we have re-established the discipline in this process." She went on to say that "some of the acquisitions that we've made I'm not a particular fan of, and had I been consulted, wouldn't have been done."

## 2013: A YEAR OF LEARNING

Still, Novakovic's first year as CEO was not a banner one for General Dynamics, particularly in their combat systems group, which had a loss in revenue that was down 23.4 percent from 2012. Novakovic attributes the losses—a $1.4 billion shortfall from projected revenue—to a combination of two factors: General Dynamics lost about $500 million as a result of the 2013 government shutdown and sequestration, and army spending slowed and smaller contracts were awarded. "I think the most profound lesson learned here is that we had unprecedented and unforeseen behavior by our Army customer, all for good and valid reasons," Novakovic told Aitoro for a January 22, 2014 *Washington Business Journal* article. "But their reaction to the changes in their funding stream [was] not anticipated by us." General Dynamics lost another $500 million when a large international order—the details of which were not revealed—was delayed. The loss spelled a larger shift in US military spending that Novakovic readily acknowledged at the beginning of 2014. Of the previous year she told Aitoro, "We've got a year of learning under our belts."

## GENERAL DYNAMICS DIVERSIFIES

But even before Novakovic took over as CEO in 2013, it was clear that the company had anticipated potential future losses. In 2011 for example, General Dynamics acquired a health data firm called Vangent. "They saw that their legacy defense market was going to be taking a hit," market research analyst Sebastian Lagana told Hancock. "And they knew [proposed] legislation was . . . going to inject funds into the health-care market." The passage of the Affordable Care Act made health care a "growth market," as Harvard professor Steve Kelman told Hancock, and government cuts (as evidenced by the fiscal plight of General Dynamics) decreased the government's defense budget. General Dynamics isn't the only defense contractor shifting resources toward health care: Lockheed Martin reassigned its existing missile-defense software to a hospital tool that helps identify sepsis, a potentially fatal bodily reaction to infection.

Kelman also identified cybersecurity as another growth market in the United States and one in which General Dynamics already was involved with. In 2012 they acquired a computer security company called Fidelis Security Systems and renamed it General Dynamics Fidelis Cybersecurity Solutions. Edward Timmes was hired to head its cyber systems division. General Dynamics' move toward cybersecurity is seen as more closely related to General Dynamics' original corporate focus than is health care, though it will likely put the company in direct competition with Silicon Valley firms. "Warfare is going digital," Tom Captain, an aerospace and defense consultant told the *Economist* (19 July 2014), and Novakovic, like Chabraja before her, continues to look for ways to diversify the company. As Loren Thompson wrote for *Forbes* magazine (26 Nov. 2012), "As I told a reporter long ago, Boeing makes planes, Raytheon makes missiles, General Dynamics makes money."

## PERSONAL LIFE

Novakovic is married to David Morrison. Morrison, who is recently retired, is a former chief lobbyist for the Boeing Corporation.

## SUGGESTED READING

Aitoro, Jill R. "General Dynamics' Phebe Novakovic on Combat Systems: 'What Made Us So Wrong?'" *Washington Business Journal.* American City Business Journals, 22 Jan. 2014. Web. 10 Jan. 2015.

Aitoro, Jill R. "General Dynamics Stock Bounces Back on CEO Phebe Novakovic's Candor." *Washington Business Journal.* American City Business Journals, 24 Jan. 2013. Web. 10 Jan. 2015.

Hancock, Jay. "Federal Contractors Now Find Opportunities for Growth in Healing, not War." *Washington Post.* Washington Post, 6 Dec. 2014. Web. 10 Jan. 2015.

Hoyos, Carola. "The Women Piloting an Industry." *Financial Times.* Financial Times, 3 Jan. 2013. Web. 10 Jan. 2015.

Shalal-Esa, Andrea. "Charge, Government Spending Cuts Hammer General Dynamics Results." *Reuters*. Thomson Reuters, 23 Jan. 2013. Web. 15 Jan. 2015.

Shalal-Esa, Andrea. "UPDATE 2—General Dynamics Names Phebe Novakovic President." *Reuters*. Thomson Reuters, 8 Mar. 2012. Web. 10 Jan. 2015.

Thompson, Loren. "General Dynamics Begins 2013 with New Leader, Changing Business Mix." *Forbes.* Forbes, 26 Nov. 2012. Web. 10 Jan. 2015.

—Molly Hagan

# Chris O'Dowd

**Born:** October 9, 1979
**Occupation:** Actor

Thanks to his star turn as a geeky slacker in the popular British sitcom *The IT Crowd* (2006–10, 2013), Chris O'Dowd was already widely known in the United Kingdom by the time he was introduced to American audiences. Catapulting him to relative Hollywood fame was the Judd Apatow–produced, surprise hit film *Bridesmaids* (2011), which showed movie-goers that an ensemble cast comprised largely of women was just as capable of gross-out comedy as one made up of only men. In *Bridesmaids*—whose stand-out scene involves a bridal party suffering the effects of food poisoning while trying on gowns in a chichi boutique—O'Dowd portrays Nathan Rhodes, a sensible and affable police officer who falls in love with the picture's flighty main character. *Bridesmaids* allowed the actor to "showcase what he was best at—the quieter character comedy that doesn't rush at jokes head-on; O'Dowd as the everyguy not so much getting the girl as bumbling his way towards her," wrote Stuart McGurk in a cover feature for *GQ* (Apr. 2014).

O'Dowd followed that big-screen success with other films, including *Friends with Kids* (2011), *The Sapphires* (2012), *This Is 40* (2012), *Calvary* (2014), and *St. Vincent* (2014)—as well as with a memorable performance on the HBO series *Girls*. Perhaps closest to his heart of all recent projects is the semiautobiographical series that he writes titled *Moone Boy*, which has aired on Britain's Sky 1 TV since 2012. Taking the story to another medium, O'Dowd has also cowritten a series of children's books based on the protagonist, Martin Moone (played by David Rawle), a young boy who must contend with a chaotic homelife and an imaginary friend, played by O'Dowd, who gives him dubious advice. "Martin is me but, thanks to David, he's much more charming than I was at that age," O'Dowd said, as quoted by Keith Watson for the online British entertainment magazine *Metro* (17 Feb. 2014).

## EARLY YEARS

Chris O'Dowd was born on October 9, 1979, in Sligo, Ireland. He grew up in nearby Boyle, a picturesque town in County Roscommon, with an older brother and three sisters. His father, Sean, is a graphic designer while his mother, Denise, is a counselor and psychotherapist. The couple separated when O'Dowd was of college age.

O'Dowd's siblings delighted in playing pranks on him. He also describes himself as having been a rather awkward teenager. "Six foot, I had a massive nose and ears," he explained to Genevieve Roberts for the *Independent* (4 Dec. 2011). "Acne. I looked like I had a perm. No one would dance with the hunchback in the corner." Sports, however, provided a pathway to social acceptance. O'Dowd was an avid player of the Irish team sport known as Gaelic football. For years he represented Roscommon in the Gaelic Athletic Association (GAA), proving himself especially admirable as a goalkeeper during the 1997 Connacht Minor finals against County Mayo.

## EDUCATION AND THE ACTING BUG

Unsure of his future career path, O'Dowd studied politics and sociology at University College in Dublin, thinking he might become a political speechwriter. "I like orators," he told Craig McLean for the *Telegraph* (11 Apr. 2014). "I liked listening to Churchill, or Kennedy. And there's loads of Irish ones. . . . The idea of being a rabble-rouser is something I've always been attracted to." He did not excel in his studies, however. "I didn't drop out but I went to exams and, honest to God, there were times when I didn't even know what they were about. It was one of those situations," he explained to Hadley Freeman for the *Guardian* (18 May 2012).

Despite his academic difficulties, O'Dowd found one aspect of college he particularly enjoyed: appearing in student plays. He subsequently attended the London Academy of Music and Dramatic Art (LAMDA) but did not earn a degree, leaving after eighteen months. As the program focused more on traditional dramatic

Karwai Tang/WireImage/Getty Images

training, he appreciated the experience but did not care for the approach—and he did not foresee becoming a comedic actor. "I found it so absurd that we did all of our classes through the workings of Shakespeare. It felt so out of date," he told Benji Wilson for the *Daily Mail* (9 Apr. 2011).

At one point O'Dowd took a job at a call center in London, where one of his tasks involved raising money for endangered animals. When people showed little interest in saving the bats or newts he had been told to discuss with them, he began making up creatures, such as a "tiger swan," that might prove more appealing. "The tiger swan was essentially a swan with the markings of a Bengal. . . . And then I would tell people this and they would say, 'I've just never heard of it.' And I'd be like, 'Well, it's endangered,'" he recalled to Terry Gross for National Public Radio's *Fresh Air* (29 May 2014). So successful were his various ruses that he reportedly raised £440, 000 in one year.

## BREAKING THROUGH WITH *THE IT CROWD*

At the same time, O'Dowd was tenacious about looking for acting jobs, and soon he began building a roster of credits. From 2003 to 2005 he appeared regularly on the medical soap opera *The Clinic*, which aired on an Irish network. During that time, he landed roles in two films: *Vera Drake* (2004) and *Festival* (2005). In the latter film, he worked with his future sitcom costar, Richard Ayoade.

In 2006 O'Dowd and Ayoade were tapped to star in a new British television show titled *The IT Crowd*, whose creator, Graham Linehan, had already experienced success in Europe with the popular sitcom *Father Ted*. Airing on Britain's Channel 4, the new sitcom featured O'Dowd as Roy Trenneman, a lazy tech-support worker confined to the basement of a large corporation along with his nerdy and socially awkward coworker, Maurice Moss (played by Ayoade). O'Dowd's friend from his LAMDA days, Katherine Parkinson, played their less technologically savvy manager, Jen Barber, who attempted to serve as a guide for her geeky employees when it came to navigating the world outside of the basement.

Quickly becoming a cult favorite, audiences continued to tune in to follow the antics of the three quirky characters. Roy's standard phone greeting—"Have you tried turning it off and on again?"—became something of a catchphrase among the show's many fans. Building on this success and exposure, O'Dowd also won roles in other television projects, such as *The Amazing Mrs. Pritchard* (2006), *Roman's Empire* (2007), and *FM* (2009).

In 2010 O'Dowd appeared as a Lilliputian military man in a big-budget version of *Gulliver's Travels*, starring the comedians Jack Black and Jason Segel. Despite its well-known cast, which also included Emily Blunt, the picture did exceptionally poorly at the box office and was excoriated by critics. O'Dowd was philosophical about the disastrous reception of the film, telling Gross, "I mean, to be honest, when you're starting your career out, you don't mind so much. And you don't know that things aren't going to be great because there's so many great people involved, you presume, oh, they're going to fix this in some stage by magic or something."

## BRIDESMAIDS AND MORE

O'Dowd starred next in the 2011 British television miniseries *The Crimson Petal and the White*. Later that year, he got the chance to redeem himself in Hollywood when, thanks to the fact that director Paul Feig was a great fan of *The IT Crowd*, he appeared in *Bridesmaids* as the loveable cop Nathan Rhodes. The blockbuster comedy, which also starred *Saturday Night Live* veterans Kristen Wiig and Maya Rudolph, "introduced droves of women to a new kind of

leading man," as Maggie Pehanick wrote for *Entertainment Weekly* (17 May 2011).

Following the massive critical and box-office success of *Bridesmaids*, O'Dowd became something of a regular in Apatow films, including *Friends with Kids* and *This Is 40*. While beginning the project of writing and acting for *Moone Boy*, he also got the chance to work with another big name in the entertainment industry, Lena Dunham, signing on to do a series of guest spots on the her HBO hit *Girls*. In a handful of 2012–13 episodes he portrayed Thomas-John, a venture capitalist who enters into a surprising relationship with one of the main characters.

In between these various ventures, O'Dowd starred in *The Sapphires*, a feel-good picture about a group of Aboriginal Australian singers who entertain US troops during the Vietnam War. Both the film as a whole and O'Dowd's performance as the girls' manager received solid nods from critics. "You could call it an Aussie *Dreamgirls*. I'd call it a blast of joy and music that struts right into your heart," Peter Travers wrote for *Rolling Stone* (21 Mar. 2013). "If you've seen him as the cop in *Bridesmaids* and on Lena Dunham's *Girls*, you know this guy is a wicked scene-stealer. But his performance as Dave is award-caliber, killer funny and alert to every nuance." Though his run on *The IT Crowd* had essentially ended in 2010, he returned to the basement for a special series' finale episode that aired in 2013.

O'Dowd has received equally fine reviews for his more recent work, including the dance comedy *Cuban Fury* (2014) and the Bill Murray-helmed *St. Vincent*. He has expressed the difficulty of comedic roles as well as an increased desire to avoid being typecast. "As time goes on, you realize your limitations," he told McGurk. "The one thing I do have against comedy is sometimes it feels like you really do need to produce a joke at the end of everything." In mid-2014 he proved his dramatic versatility, starring in a Broadway revival of John Steinbeck's classic novel *Of Mice and Men* alongside James Franco and Leighton Meester. He was nominated for both Drama Desk and Tony Awards for his portrayal of Lennie, a slow-witted but kind-hearted character. O'Dowd has also continued to write and star in *Moone Boy*, which has won an International Emmy.

## PERSONAL LIFE

O'Dowd has been married to Dawn Porter, a television presenter and journalist, since 2012.

After the wedding she changed her name to Dawn O'Porter. In early 2015 the couple had a baby boy, whom they named Art. They have a home in Los Angeles.

## SUGGESTED READING

Freeman, Hadley. "Chris O'Dowd: From *The IT Crowd* to Hollywood." *Guardian.* Guardian News and Media, 18 May 2012. Web. 11 May 2015.

McGurk, Stuart. "The King O'Comedy." *GQ.* Condé Nast, Apr. 2014. Web. 11 May 2015.

O'Dowd, Chris. "Chris O'Dowd Interview: 'Fame Hasn't Changed Me. But It's Changed Everybody around Me.'" By Craig McLean. *Telegraph.* Telegraph Media Group, 11 Apr. 2014. Web. 11 May 2015.

O'Dowd, Chris. "From the Screen to Broadway: Chris O'Dowd Takes On 'Of Mice and Men.'" Interview by Terry Gross. *Fresh Air.* Natl. Public Radio, 29 May 2014. Web. 11 May 2015. Transcript.

O'Dowd, Chris. "An Interview with Chris O'Dowd, the Homeless Tony Nominee." By Barbara Hoffman. *New York Post.* NYP Holdings, 17 May 2014. Web. 11 May 2015.

Travers, Peter. "*The Sapphires.*" Rev. of *The Sapphires*, dir. Wayne Blair. *Rolling Stone.* Rolling Stone, 21 Mar. 2013. Web. 11 May 2015.

## SELECTED WORKS

*The IT Crowd*, 2006–10, 2013; *Bridesmaids*, 2011; *Friends with Kids*, 2011; *The Sapphires*, 2012; *This Is 40*, 2012; *Girls*, 2012–13; *Moone Boy*, 2012– ; *St. Vincent*, 2014

—Mari Rich

# Alexis Ohanian

**Born:** April 24, 1983

**Occupation:** Internet entrepreneur and activist

A year after graduating from college, Alexis Ohanian and his former college dorm mate, Steve Huffman, founded Reddit, the self-described "front page of the Internet." The social networking site and community board began to grow in popularity and, within a year, had become one of the fifty most popular websites. In 2006 Ohanian and his fellow cofounder sold the site to the publishing giant Condé Nast. Ohanian

Alec Perkins, Hoboken, USA/Wikimedia Commons

became a multimillionaire at the age of twenty-three. But he continued to be involved with the site for three years and would later, in the fall of 2014, return as chairman. He also wrote the best-selling book *Without Their Permission: How the 21st Century Will Be Made, Not Managed* (2013), went on to found and cofound various tech companies, and has passionately advocated for Internet freedom. He has twice appeared on the Forbes Thirty under Thirty list.

## EARLY YEARS

Alexis Ohanian was born on April 24, 1983. He was raised in Columbia, Maryland, by his mother, Anke, a night-shift pharmacy technician, and his father, Chris, a travel agent. When Ohanian was ten years old, his parents bought their first computer. The PC was primarily for their son, who became obsessed with it. Although on occasion he would break it, he would repair it himself as well. At that time, in 1993, the Internet was not ubiquitous, and at first the Ohanians did not have an Internet connection. When they did finally get one, much to their son's delight, it worked via a dial-up modem, which was slow but still provided a connection to the rest of the world.

Ohanian was a big video-game enthusiast. He particularly loved *Quake II*, so he created a website, his first, which was a fan page for that video game. As he writes in *Without Their Permission*, he was thrilled by the "power" of being able to attract real people to see his fan site—his online creation. "I could build something from my suburban bedroom," he wrote, "and millions (okay, well, hundreds) of people all over the world could see just how much I loved a video game. That's how I got interested in making websites. There was no turning back." He also launched FreeAsABird.org, through which he designed custom websites for small nonprofit organizations, free of charge. Although he was only a teenager, nobody questioned Ohanian's age. He would e-mail the organization with a pitch to help, and no one had any idea how old he was.

Ohanian also held various paying part-time jobs during high school, including working for two-and-a-half years as a waiter at Pizza Hut. But it was his job for a company called Sidea that would go on to make the biggest impact. His job for Sidea involved doing software and hardware demonstrations at a booth at a CompUSA store. With the aid of a big computer monitor and a headset microphone, young Ohanian made presentations—every half hour, regardless of audience presence or attentiveness—about computer products current at the time. In *Without Their Permission*, Ohanian points out that that was genuinely a "fabulous way for me to start public speaking." Speaking to a room full of people, or a room with a few people, or an empty room day after day proved to be an invaluable lesson.

## LEARING TO DISRUPT

Ohanian was a big kid. The tallest boy in class, as a young teen he was also overweight, weighing around 260 pounds. In school he stood out, but he was not exactly popular with the "cool" kids or the opposite sex. But that did not seem to bother him much. He had his group of friends. "I cared too much about video games and computers," he writes in *Without Their Permission*, "to realize how not cool I was." In the world outside of school, however, he was presumed to be older just because of his size. He recounts an amusing story of one day, while working at CompUSA, being approached by a man shopping for a mouse for his computer. Although there were no significant differences between them, Ohanian suggested the color of one mouse as being a bonus "feature." Amused, the man gave him his business card and offered him a job in sales. "I didn't have the heart to tell the man I was only fourteen," Ohanian writes. After years of being overweight, Ohanian in his junior year decided to cut out junk food and soft drinks and to start exercising. He lost nearly sixty pounds as

a result.

Another important lesson came from observing his father. For about three decades, his father had been a travel agent, but then his industry began to encounter turbulence—first a bit, then a lot. Because Ohanian was so fascinated by and good with computers and knew his way around the Internet, he understood all too well how people's ability to book their own plane tickets and hotel rooms dramatically affected his father's ability to make a living. His father, according to Ohanian's autobiography, adapted to the circumstances by switching his business model: his specialty became first-time and business travelers. Ohanian was privy to all these changes and developments because his father would openly discuss them during dinner. The lesson for Ohanian was simple and straightforward: "The Internet was a powerful tool, and I wanted to be sure I knew how to use it. The free market is ruthless. But it has to be. It's up to us to make the most of it." In other words, "disruptions" (to one's plans or business model) happen all the time, but to be ahead of the game it is best to be the one doing the disrupting.

## REDDIT: THE ORIGIN STORY

When, in the fall of 2001, Ohanian arrived at the Hancock House dorm on the University of Virginia campus, he had plans of becoming an immigration lawyer. He was also as enthusiastic about video games as he had ever been. That first day, across the hall from his dorm room, Ohanian noticed a fellow student playing the racing game *Gran Turismo*, and was instantly thrilled that someone at college was playing a video game. He and the other young man, Steve Huffman, instantly bonded over video games and would go on to be become best friends. Because these two young students would later create Reddit, one of the most popular websites on the Internet, this story would often be told and retold in many subsequent profiles and interviews.

Another part of this "origin story" is how Ohanian decided he did not want to become a lawyer after all. When he sat down to take the LSAT, the law school admissions exam, he chose not take the test, but instead walked out. Ohanian needed to think—and probably eat—so he went to a local Waffle House, which is where he decided he has no desire whatsoever to attend law school or be a lawyer. He would later call this moment an epiphany. He decided what he did want to do was start a company with his best friend, engineering student Steve Huffman.

## THEIR FIRST STARTUP

During the summer between junior and senior year, Ohanian attended an international technopreneurship (technology entrepreneurship) conference in Singapore, an island country in Southeast Asia. He had been invited to attend the conference by Mark White, one of his favorite professors. By that point Ohanian and Huffman had already thought up a business idea, and in Singapore Ohanian shared the idea with his professor: MyMobileMenu, a service that allows users to order from restaurants on their phones. Professor White loved the idea and agreed to help. But this was in 2004, quite some time before the proliferation of smartphones.

In the spring of 2005, Paul Graham gave a talk called "How to Start a Startup" before an audience in Cambridge, Massachusetts. In the crowd were college seniors Ohanian and Huffman, who had decided to attend over their spring break. Ohanian had no idea who Graham was, but Huffman surely did, the latter being the more tech-savvy of the two. After the talk Ohanian and Huffman approached Graham, asking to pitch him their business idea in exchange for a drink; Graham liked what he heard about MyMobileMenu and asked them to interview for Y Combinator, then a new company that trained and funded startups. The two could not have been more thrilled, but after the interview came some bad news: Graham told them Y Combinator would not support their idea but wanted to support them as entrepreneurs, so they needed to come up with a new plan. Upon their next meeting, Graham told them, as Ohanian recalled to Christine Lagario-Chafkin for *Inc.* magazine (June 2012), "You guys need to build the front page of the Internet." Ohanian and Huffman then went to work, with the help of the Y Combinator program. "We built Reddit in three weeks," Ohanian told Lagario-Chafkin. The site launched in 2005, and by the following year, due to its enormous potential and popularity, it was purchased by the publishing giant Condé Nast for an undisclosed sum (reportedly Ohanian received as much as $20 million). At twenty-three Ohanian was a multimillionaire.

The same year that they launched Reddit, Ohanian graduated from the University of Virginia with a bachelor's degree in history and commerce—with a concentration on management and international business—as well as a minor in German. Huffman graduated with an engineering degree.

## OTHER PROJECTS

After Condé Nast bought Reddit, Ohanian stayed on as a product manager but left that post in 2009 to pursue other projects and interests. That year he gave a popular TEDIndia talk about how the organization Greenpeace, in their campaign against the Japanese government allowing the practice of killing humpback whales, launched a campaign to name a whale to personalize the project and how Reddit users voted for Mister Splashy Pants—a name Greenpeace at first resisted and then embraced. In 2010 Ohanian volunteered for three months as a fellow in Yerevan, Armenia, for Kiva, a nonprofit organization that attempts to help people around the world through microloans. Upon returning to the United States, Ohanian resumed his entrepreneurial journey with Huffman, starting Breadpig, what he calls a "sidekick-for-hire," which publishes web comics as well as "other geeky novelties," according to his autobiography. Starting in 2010 Ohanian served as Y Combinator's ambassador to the East for three years. Also in 2010 he joined Hipmunk, a travel website Huffman founded, for which Ohanian primarily did prelaunch marketing and design. Ohanian is also an investor in dozens of startup companies.

Ohanian's book, *Without Their Permission: How the 21st Century Will Be Made, Not Managed* (2013), received publicity blurbs from the likes of statistician Nate Silver, Y Combinator partner Garry Tan, and Zappos.com CEO Tony Hsieh. A combination of memoir, guide on how to create a great startup, and manifesto on Internet freedom, it went on to become a *Wall Street Journal* business best seller.

## ACTIVISM

In 2011 Ohanian used his influence and expertise to campaign against two congressional bills that had the potential to stifle Internet freedom: the Stop Online Piracy Act (SOPA) and Protect IP Act (PIPA). The opposition to these two pieces of proposed legislation came from both parties, as well as many average people and tech giants, including Wikipedia, Yahoo, Mozilla, and many others. As reported by Hayley Tsukayama for the *Washington Post* (5 Sept. 2012), Ohanian has pointed out how bipartisan the opponents of PIPA and SOPA were: "Republicans want to keep the open Internet safe from big government. Democrats want to keep it safe from big corporations. I say we agree to agree and move ahead. It was so successful because we literally had the Tea Party next to the MoveOn.org guys at these meetings. They don't often hang out together."

A couple years later Ohanian spoke out against paid prioritization of the Internet, the concept that Internet service providers (ISPs) should be allowed to charge higher rates for priority website access during times of peak web traffic. Ohanian and other advocates of net neutrality argue that the free, open Internet has facilitated innovation and startup growth and that government regulation of ISPs is needed to ensure that those conditions continue.

In June 2014 Ohanian became a partner at Y Combinator, and that November he returned to Reddit full-time as chairman after the company's CEO resigned. Ohanian lives in the New York City borough of Brooklyn. He has a cat named Karma.

## SUGGESTED READING

Koidin Jaffee, Michelle. "The Voice of His Generation: Reddit Co-Founder Alexis Ohanian Fights for a Free and Open Internet." *University of Virginia Magazine*. U. Va. Alumni Assn., Fall 2014. Web. 2 Dec. 2014.

Lagorio-Chafkin, Christine. "How Alexis Ohanian Built a Front Page of the Internet." *Inc.* Mansueto Ventures, 30 May 2012. Web. 2 Dec. 2014.

Ohanian, Alexis. *Without Their Permission.* New York: Grand Central, 2013. Print.

Schulman, Michael. "Founder of Reddit and the Internet's Own Cheerleader." *New York Times*. New York Times, 22 Nov. 2013. Web. 5 Dec. 2014.

Tsukayama, Hayley. "Alexis Ohanian, Reddit Co-Founder and Web Advocate." *Washington Post*. Washington Post, 5 Sept. 2012. Web. 2 Dec. 2014.

—Dmitry Kiper

# John Oliver

**Born:** April 23, 1977
**Occupation:** Comedian

When the premium television network HBO announced in 2013 that it was developing a weekly comedy news program hosted by British-born comedian John Oliver, many in the media were skeptical that the program would be a success. Oliver had become well known as a correspondent on Comedy Central's *Daily Show with Jon*

David Shankbone/CC BY 3.0

*Stewart*, and that program, along with its satirical counterpart *The Colbert Report*, seemed to have a monopoly on timely, televised political humor. The weekly schedule and notoriously difficult timeslot of the proposed program raised additional doubts regarding its relevance and ability to capture audiences. For Oliver, however, such difficulties presented a welcome challenge. "I was attracted to that dead spot late on Sunday night on HBO, which is the prime-est real estate that there is," he told David Carr for the *New York Times* (16 Nov. 2014). "I loved the idea that we could build something and that we would live or die by our attempt."

Following its premiere on April 27, 2014, *Last Week Tonight with John Oliver* proved not only popular among HBO subscribers but also capable of sparking national conversations about the controversial issues it spotlights. Nevertheless, Oliver insists he is not a journalist and that his program is not intended to be a serious source of news. "We certainly hold ourselves to a high standard and fact-check everything, but the correct term for what we do is 'comedy,'" he explained to Carr.

## EARLY LIFE AND EDUCATION

John William Oliver was born on April 23, 1977, in Erdington, a suburb of Birmingham, England. The oldest of four children, he grew up north of London. Oliver's parents, Jim and Carole, were both educators; Carol was a music teacher, while

Jim worked as a social worker and went on to serve as a school principal. His parents at times struggled in their roles as educators during the administration of conservative prime minister Margaret Thatcher, and Oliver has told interviewers that witnessing those struggles helped shape his political outlook.

As a child, Oliver was an avid fan of soccer and a supporter of the Liverpool Football Club, and he dreamed of one day playing professionally. He and his father bonded over their mutual love of the sport, and Oliver has noted that sporting events played a significant role in their relationship. "You see your dad express joy and sorrow in a way you haven't seen before, and you learn also to project all human feelings onto something that doesn't matter," he told Scott Raab for *Esquire* (1 July 2013).

After graduating from the Mark Rutherford School in Bedford, England, Oliver enrolled in Christ's College, Cambridge, where he studied English. He quickly became friends with fellow Cambridge student Richard Ayoade, who would go on to star in the Channel 4 sitcom *The IT Crowd*. The two friends focused on comedy while at Cambridge, becoming active members of the Cambridge Footlights Dramatic Club. That organization, for which Oliver and Ayoade served as vice president and president, respectively, was known for having nurtured the talents of numerous British comedy greats, including several members of the comedy group Monty Python and the comedy and science-fiction writer Douglas Adams. Oliver graduated from Christ's College in 1998, having settled on pursuing a career in comedy.

## EARLY CAREER

In the years after graduating from Christ's College, Oliver worked to establish himself as a comedian in London, where he shared an apartment with Ayoade for a time, and throughout the United Kingdom. Although he often struggled financially and spent much of his time performing stand-up comedy in what he described to David Kamp for *Vanity Fair* (Feb. 2015) as "situations of profound discomfort," he has noted in interviews that he was very happy during that period of his life and never even considered the possibility of giving up. His parents were very supportive of his career path, although his thwarted childhood dream of playing professional soccer was the source of some lingering disappointment. "My dad . . . said to me, 'You know, you've worked hard and it's going well, but you do understand that I wanted you to play for Liverpool?'" he told Raab. "I said, 'Yeah, I know, Dad. We're both disappointed. Please understand that we share this sense of failure.'"

In addition to performing stand-up at comedy clubs, Oliver began to make a name for himself at the Edinburgh Festival Fringe, a large performing arts festival in Scotland. After appearing in a group performance in 2001, he performed a solo show the following year and later became a regular fixture at the festival. He appeared in single episodes of various British television shows as himself and as an actor, and in 2005 he made the first of many guest appearances on the BBC Two comedic panel show *Mock the Week*. Oliver frequently collaborated with friend and fellow comedian Andy Zaltzman, with whom he performed two-person stand-up acts and also starred in various radio programs, including the political comedy show *Political Animals* and the fiction series *The Department*. The two began recording a comedy podcast, *The Bugle*, in 2007.

## THE DAILY SHOW

In 2006, after nearly a decade in comedy, Oliver was invited to audition for a correspondent position on the American television program *The Daily Show with Jon Stewart*, having been brought to the attention of the show's producers by popular British comedian Ricky Gervais. Oliver, who had never been to the United States before, flew to New York to audition and was soon hired as the satirical news program's British correspondent.

*The Daily Show* had been part of Comedy Central's weekday programming since its debut in 1996. Originally hosted by Craig Kilborn, the show took on a more political tone after comedian and television personality Jon Stewart took over as host in 1999. By the time Oliver joined the program in 2006, *The Daily Show* had become well known for skewering United States politics, particularly during election seasons. For Oliver, who joined the writing staff in 2007, the show provided a "crash course" in American politics and culture, he told David Usborne for the *Independent* (7 Apr. 2010), as well as in *The Daily Show*'s particular brand of humor. He credits Stewart in particular as a mentor and commented to Brian Hiatt for *Rolling Stone* (26 Sept. 2014), "There is nothing so far that he has not taught me."

Oliver's work as a *Daily Show* correspondent was well received by critics during his tenure, and he and the rest of the show's writing staff were nominated for the Emmy Award for outstanding writing for a variety series every year between 2008 and 2014, winning three times, in 2009, 2011, and 2012. Perhaps Oliver's biggest test, however, came in June 2013, when he began an extended run as guest host while Stewart was directing the film *Rosewater* (2014). Oliver's tenure as host proved he was more than capable of filling such a role, setting the stage for his success as host of his own program following his departure from *The Daily Show* later that year.

## LAST WEEK TONIGHT

In April 2014, Oliver's new program, *Last Week Tonight with John Oliver*, premiered on the premium television network HBO. A humorous news program in the vein of *The Daily Show*, *Last Week Tonight* differs from its predecessors in a number of crucial ways, most notably in its weekly rather than daily schedule and its focus on events and issues that are topical and relevant but perhaps not breaking news. Each episode of the show consists of multiple segments and usually features one particularly long segment in which Oliver provides an in-depth take on a single issue. Such segments, which are often reminiscent of investigative pieces aired on traditional news programs, have focused on issues ranging from net neutrality to the practice of civil forfeiture.

Although many critics were skeptical about the show's prospects when it was first announced, *Last Week Tonight* met with an overwhelmingly positive response following its premiere and was popular among HBO subscribers as well. A second season of the show began in February 2015. Perhaps more notable than the show's critical acclaim or popularity, however, are the far-reaching effects its in-depth segments have had on the general public. Although HBO programs are generally available only to subscribers, clips from *Last Week Tonight* have frequently gone viral after being posted to video-sharing sites such as YouTube, introducing viewers worldwide not only to Oliver's humorous take on various issues but also, at times, to the very issues themselves. Oliver's segment on net neutrality, for example, has been credited with raising significant public awareness of the otherwise little-understood issue. Yet despite *Last Week Tonight*'s demonstrated ability to inform and perhaps even spark change, Oliver remains adamant that the show should not be considered a legitimate journalistic endeavor. "We are making jokes about the news and sometimes we need to research things deeply to understand them," he told Carr, "but it's always in service of a joke." In 2015 *Last Week Tonight with John Oliver* won the Writers Guild Award for best comedy/variety series.

## OTHER WORK

Oliver became well known in the United States after joining the cast of *The Daily Show*, and his newfound fame afforded him numerous opportunities as a comedian and an actor. In addition to performing stand-up comedy throughout the United States, he recorded the 2008 stand-up special *John Oliver: Terrifying Times* and has made guest appearances on a variety of talk shows and comedy programs. He made his first film appearance as an actor in the 2008 Mike Myers film *The Love Guru* and the following year took on a recurring role in the NBC comedy series *Community*, playing community college professor Ian Duncan. Oliver has found success as a voice actor as well, lending his voice to the films *The Smurfs* (2011) and *The Smurfs 2* (2013) as well as to episodes of various animated series, including *Gravity Falls* in 2012, *Rick and Morty* in 2013, and *The Simpsons* in 2014.

## PERSONAL LIFE

Oliver met his wife, Kate Norley, while filming a *Daily Show* piece at the Republican National Convention in 2008. Norley, a former US Army combat medic who attended the convention with her veterans' advocacy group, helped Oliver, who had entered off-limits areas of the convention center, hide from the security guards pursuing him. The two married in 2011.

In 2009 Oliver obtained his green card, the culmination of a long and stressful process that rendered him acutely aware of flaws in the United States' immigration procedures. "If it's this difficult for me—and I have almost all the help and privileges I could have, to help me navigate the system—then clearly the immigration system is broken and barbaric," he explained to Oliver Burkeman for the *Guardian* (7 June 2013). However, despite his difficulties in securing permanent residency and his career poking fun at some of the more absurd and infuriating aspects of American culture and politics, Oliver considers his adopted country home and himself an American, an attitude that manifests in his use of words such as "I" and "we" when discussing issues facing the United States. "I think I'm entitled to say 'we' now," he told Carr. "I'm not going anywhere. This is my home."

## SUGGESTED READING

Burkeman, Oliver. "John Oliver: A Very British Coup." *Guardian*. Guardian News and Media, 7 June 2013. Web. 30 July 2015.

Carr, David. "John Oliver's Complicated Fun Connects for HBO." *New York Times*. New York Times, 16 Nov. 2014. Web. 30 July 2015.

Helmore, Edward. "From Our Own Correspondent." *Guardian*. Guardian News and Media, 23 July 2007. Web. 30 July 2015.

Hiatt, Brian. "20 Things You Learn Hanging Out with John Oliver." *Rolling Stone*. Rolling Stone, 26 Sept. 2014. Web. 30 July 2015.

Kamp, David. "John Oliver Is Horrified by Massages and Is a 'Committed Coward': What You Should Know about the Host of *Last Week Tonight*." *Vanity Fair*. Condé Nast, Feb. 2015. Web. 30 July 2015.

Raab, Scott. "John Oliver: The ESQ&A." *Esquire*. Hearst Communications, 1 July 2013. Web. 30 July 2015.

Usborne, David. "Made in Manhattan: John Oliver on Taking Satire Stateside." *Independent*. Independent.co.uk, 7 Apr. 2010. Web. 30 July 2015.

## SELECTED WORKS

*Mock the Week*, 2005–6; *The Daily Show with Jon Stewart*, 2006–14; *Community*, 2009–14; *Last Week Tonight with John Oliver*, 2014–

—Joy Crelin

---

# Joshua Oppenheimer

**Born:** September 23, 1974
**Occupation:** Film director

Documentarian Joshua Oppenheimer found acclaim in the film world in 2012, when his genre-defying documentary *The Act of Killing* won multiple awards and honors at film festivals around the world. The film was released in theaters the following year to general acclaim. Executive produced by legendary directors Errol Morris and Werner Herzog, *The Act of Killing* examines the 1965 genocide in Indonesia, in which as many as 2.5 million people were brutally tortured and murdered. Through an innovative combination of interviews with some of the perpetrators and their boasting and recreation of the murder scenes, Oppenheimer

Daisysun777/Wikimedia Commons

created something uniquely startling. In 2014 the film was nominated for an Oscar and won the best documentary award at the British Academy of Film and Television Awards, among other honors. That year Oppenheimer also released a companion film called *The Look of Silence* and received the MacArthur fellowship.

## EARLY SEEDS

Joshua Oppenheimer was born in Austin, Texas, on September 23, 1974. He grew up in Washington, DC, and Santa Fe, New Mexico. According to an early profile by Marios V. Broustas, writing for the Harvard *Crimson* (5 June 1997), Oppenheimer was raised in a "politically charged family." His mother, Carol, was a labor lawyer; she said politics were a frequent topic of discussion at the dinner table. Oppenheimer's father was a political science professor, and his stepfather was also a labor lawyer. "We've always talked about politics in our home and tried to figure out the best way to make changes," Carol Oppenheimer told Broustas.

## REBEL WITH A CAUSE

While he was studying filmmaking at Harvard University, Oppenheimer took part in and even led many protests around campus. In the fall of 1995, according to Broustas, Oppenheimer, who is gay, joined in a protest against Kenan Professor of Government Harvey C. Mansfield Jr. for antigay comments he had made at a prominent trial and for his opposition to women's studies, among other issues. The group of protesters called attention to their cause by holding up ironic signs sporting slogans such as Keep Harvard White, Keep Harvard Rich, and Keep Harvard Male. More than a year later, Oppenheimer helped to lead a protest during a speech at the Institute of Politics against the Christian conservative political activist Ralph Reed. Oppenheimer and the other protesters dressed as nuns and then kissed on cue: men with men, and women with women. The protesters were removed by police, and Oppenheimer told Broustas that he filed a complaint with Harvard University officials after the incident, because the protesters' free speech rights were violated. He did not pursue the complaint, however, because of the amount of time he was devoting to his thesis film project. Oppenheimer also served as the political chair of what came to be called the Bisexual, Gay, Lesbian, Transgendered and Supporters Alliance.

As a student Oppenheimer also began infiltrating neo-Nazi groups in England and the United States (his family had fled Nazi Germany) and various prominent conservative Christian groups that sought to turn gay people straight by such extreme methods as electroconvulsive therapy. The goal of these infiltrations was not only to monitor whatever efforts these groups were making, but also to collect information and interview various group members for his documentaries.

He received his bachelor of arts degree in filmmaking in 1997. International filmmaker Dusan Makavejev served as his adviser for his thesis, *The Entire History of the Louisiana Purchase* (1998), a documentary film that combines documentary footage, home movies, archival footage, and even fiction in an exploration of the growth of the US heartland and various fringe political and spiritual movements that have arisen there. Thus, even during the early stages of his career, Oppenheimer was exploring the concept and significance of documentary, film, and genre. He later obtained a PhD from the University of the Arts, London.

### THE GLOBALIZATION TAPES

The roots of Oppenheimer's award-winning documentary, *The Art of Killing*, lie in interviews conducted for his previous film, *The Globalization Tapes* (2003). This documentary, which he began working on around 2001, focused on the efforts of plantation workers in Indonesia to organize a union. Even though there

were many good reasons for workers to unionize and seek better treatment—for example, the herbicide they were spraying was seriously damaging their health—they were afraid to do so. It was in understanding why they were afraid that Oppenheimer would stumble onto his next big project. These workers had relatives (aunts, uncles, cousins, parents, and grandparents) who had been killed by the Indonesian government from 1965 to 1966 as part of a mass genocide that resulted in the death of at least half a million people, possibly more than two million. The then-new government that took over in 1965 came to power in a military coup backed by the United States, which led to a dictatorship and political corruption that continues to the present day. That government began to torture and kill people deemed to be enemies of the state, namely communists or communist sympathizers, intellectuals, ethnic Chinese people, and various activists, including those in the trade union movement and the women's rights movement. Many of those Oppenheimer interviewed asked if he could find information on missing friends and relations, whom they assumed were probably killed in the genocide. These people told Oppenheimer that the perpetrators of the mass murders—who were recruited from the civilian population—would speak openly and even proudly about their deeds, feeling they had nothing to hide. That turned out to be true in a way Oppenheimer could not have imagined. He ended up learning not only who had died, but also how they had been killed.

### THE ACT OF KILLING

Oppenheimer worked on *The Act of Killing* for nearly a decade, interviewing dozens of those who were in the death squads, and in the film he decided to focus on two men who are, or at least appear to be, quite different: Anwar Congo, who is thin and grey-haired with a grandfatherly charm, and Herman Koto, who is fat and flamboyant and fond of cross-dressing. Congo is undeniably the main focus of the documentary, and viewers watch him talk of how he murdered more than a thousand people and even watch him recreating those murders with actors and extras and makeup. By allowing Congo to perform and discuss the reenactments—and letting the viewers see behind the scenes—Oppenheimer made a new kind of documentary film.

Part of the focus of the documentary, inevitably, is on the death squad members' obsession with American films, particularly with the actors

Marlon Brando, Al Pacino, and John Wayne, as well as the films of the rock-and-roll star Elvis Presley. Oppenheimer has said in various interviews that he does not seek to blame all that violence on movies; he does not hold Hollywood films or actors responsible. Instead, he seeks to examine the relationship between those movies and the violence and sadistic showmanship they inspired. Thus, the name of the documentary has multiple meanings.

*The Act of Killing* is a highly complex examination of the dark side of human nature, the nature of violence, and the notions of "good" and "evil." "The paradox of the film is that what appears to be a sign of a lack of conscience, or lack of remorse, as seen through Anwar, is the opposite," Oppenheimer told Drew Fortune in an interview for the *Onion*'s AV Club (30 July 2013). "It's a sign of humanity. It's a sign that he knows what he did was wrong, and he's trying to avoid thinking about it and recognizing it. The tragedy is that once you've corrupted yourself by killing one person and [getting] away with it, then it's justified." He then added, "If called upon, you have to kill again, because if the government says, 'Now kill these people,' for much the same reasons, if you don't do it, it's tantamount to admitting it was wrong the first time." Another paradox of the directing experience for Oppenheimer was that the more time he spent with the killers, the more he saw their humanity; at no time did he believe what they did was right or justifiable, but he did see them as people and not as evil monsters. On the other hand, frequent exposure to stories of grotesque and violent mass murders, filming reenactments, and visiting actual sites where the murders took place had a substantial psychological effect on Oppenheimer. He would often have nightmares or trouble sleeping.

## CRITICAL RECEPTION

Upon the release of the documentary, first in film festivals and then to movie theaters around the world, in 2013, great reviews began pouring in. In a review for the *New Yorker* (15 July 2013), Jonah Weiner wrote that "Oppenheimer has captured something remarkable: the rupture between the stories Congo has always told himself and the counter-narrative he's long held at bay." He then added that viewers will exit the film "stumbling, sickened, and stunned." Writing for the *New York Times* (18 July 2013), A. O. Scott called the documentary "inventive, profoundly upsetting and dismayingly funny." A reviewer for the online magazine *Slate* (18 July 2013), Dana Stevens, wrote, "*The Act of Killing* is among the most profound, formally complex, and emotionally overpowering documentaries I've ever seen." Stevens elaborated, "It's also, by turns and sometimes at once, luridly seductive and darkly comic and physically revolting—a movie that makes you want to laugh and cry and retch and run out of the theater, both to escape the awful things the film is showing you and to tell everyone you know that they need to see it, too."

## THE LOOK OF SILENCE

Oppenheimer followed up *The Act of Killing* with *The Look of Silence*. Whereas the former focused on the genocide from the perspective of the killers, the latter focused on the victims. One such victim, Ramli, was deemed an enemy of the state; he was first stabbed and later taken away by the death squad and tortured with a machete until he bled to death. In 2004 Oppenheimer had filmed the story of his murder told by the men who took part in it. In *The Look of Silence*, he shows the telling of that story to Adi, Ramli's younger brother. As with Oppenheimer's previous documentary, the name of the film itself is multilayered: it both describes how Adi reacts to the story of his brother's murder (with stone-cold silence) and the fact that Adi, an optometrist, questions his brother's murderers while conducting an eye exam or letting them try on eyeglasses. Adi is not vengeful; he simply wants closure. In a review of the film for the *Telegraph* (28 Aug. 2014), Robbie Collin called *The Look of Silence* "an essential companion piece to Oppenheimer's earlier film; another astonishing heart-of-darkness voyage into the jungle of human nature."

## PERSONAL LIFE

Joshua Oppenheimer lives in Copenhagen, Denmark. He is a partner at Final Cut for Real, a Danish company devoted to producing creative documentaries, and a reader for the Department of Photography and Film at the University of Westminster in England.

## SUGGESTED READING

Broustas, Marios V. "Oppenheimer Commands Non-Linear Universe." *Harvard Crimson.* Harvard U, 5 June 1997. Web. 16 Mar. 2015.

Collin, Robbie. Rev. of *The Look of Silence*, dir. Joshua Oppenheimer. *Telegraph*. Telegraph Media, 28 Aug. 2014. Web. 16 Mar. 2015.

Oppenheimer, Joshua. "Joshua Oppenheimer and the Atrocity Exhibitionists." Interview by Nathan Reese. *Interview*. Brant Publications, n.d. Web. 16 Mar. 2015.

Oppenheimer, Joshua, and Werner Herzog. "Joshua Oppenheimer and Werner Herzog on *The Act of Killing*." Interview by Drew Fortune. *AV Club*. Onion, 30 July 2013. Web. 16 Mar. 2015.

Stevens, Dana. Rev. of *The Act of Killing*, dir. Joshua Oppenheimer. *Slate*. Slate, 18 July 2013. Web. 16 Mar. 2015.

Weiner, Jonah. "The Weird Genius of 'The Act of Killing.'" Rev. of *The Act of Killing*, dir. Joshua Oppenheimer. *New Yorker*. Condé Nast, 15 July 2013. Web. 16 Mar. 2015.

## SELECTED WORKS

*The Entire History of the Louisiana Purchase*, 1998; *The Globalization Tapes*, 2003; *The Act of Killing*, 2013; *The Look of Silence*, 2014

—Dmitry Kiper

# Kevyn Orr

**Born:** May 11, 1958

**Occupation:** Emergency manager of Detroit

In March 2013, Kevyn Orr was appointed by Michigan governor Rick Snyder to the position of emergency manager of Detroit, the culmination of a long period of economic decline for the city. Following Orr's appointment, legislation was approved granting the emergency manager complete control over city finances. Governor Snyder approved Orr's recommendation that Detroit file for bankruptcy in July 2013—thus enacting the largest municipal bankruptcy filing in American history.

## BACKGROUND

Kevyn Orr was born on May 11, 1958, in Fort Lauderdale, Florida. His father was a minister and his mother worked for the Broward County school system. After graduating from Nova High School, Orr enrolled at the University of Michigan, where he earned a bachelor's degree in 1979. Orr then enrolled in the University of Michigan Law School, where he earned his law degree in 1983.

After law school, Orr was hired by the Miami-based law firm Sterns, Weaver, and Miller. In 1991, he joined the Federal Deposit Insurance Corporation, taking a position with the Resolution Trust Corporation (RTC), where he gained significant experience in bankruptcy law. The RTC—an entity owned by the United States government—was charged with mitigating debts pertaining to the savings and loan crisis of the 1980s and 1990s, during which over 30 percent of savings and loan associations in the United States collapsed. After the RTC's duties were fulfilled in 1995, Orr was appointed as the Justice Department's deputy director of the Executive Office for United States Trustees. In 2001, Orr was selected to become a partner at Jones Day, an international law firm based in Washington, DC. While at Jones Day, Orr played an integral role in litigating the bankruptcy filing of the automaker Chrysler.

## MANAGING DETROIT'S DEBT CRISIS

In March 2013, city officials in Detroit, Michigan, filed a declaration of financial emergency. Facing a budget deficit of over $300 million and estimated debts of over $18 billion, officials concluded that the city would be unable to continue meeting its pension obligations and would be forced to cease providing paychecks to municipal employees. The city's financial ruin was the culmination of decades of financial mismanagement, political corruption, ongoing commitments to thousands of pension plans, and the decline of the city's automobile industry.

After Orr's appointment as the emergency manager of the city of Detroit on March 14, 2013, the city of Detroit officially filed for bankruptcy on July 18, 2013. The filing – the largest of its kind in American history – was approved by US Bankruptcy Judge Steven Rhodes on December 3, 2013.

In February 2014, Orr's office submitted Detroit's Chapter 9 plan of adjustment, including offers of compensation to the city's creditors and bondholders. The plan also included a proposed 34-percent cut in the pension checks of retired city workers and a 10-percent cut in the pension checks of retired police officers and firefighters.

In his role as emergency manager, Orr also developed other strategies to address the city's debts, formulating a disclosure statement outlining various policy recommendations. Orr estimated that approximately $6 billion of the city's debt was related to health care commitments. His analysis also suggested that $3.5 billion was owed to pensioners and $2 billion was owed to municipal bondholders. One option that was rejected by Orr early on was the idea of a federal or state bailout for the city of Detroit, which Orr feared would set a dangerous precedent for other cities in the United States facing financial challenges.

In a deal reached by Orr and Snyder prior to the city's bankruptcy filing, the Michigan Local Emergency Financial Assistance Loan Board agreed to lease Detroit's Belle Isle as a state park for a period of thirty years. The deal will save Detroit an estimated $6 million annually in operating costs. Other policy initiatives under consideration by city officials include increased privatization of public utilities, such as the city's water systems, sewage, and trash collection. Throughout Detroit's financial crisis, several initiatives were proposed by creditors, including that revenues be raised through the sale of the Detroit Institute of Arts collection of fine art, which has an estimated value of hundreds of millions of dollars. Instead, local and national private foundations were approached to contribute money in lieu of selling the art or making severe cuts to city pensions. In January 2014, nine foundations, including the Ford Foundation and the Kresge Foundation, made pledges exceeding $300 million to the effort.

In addition to policy initiatives, Orr has worked with city officials to encourage nationwide businesses to relocate to Detroit, thereby spurring citywide economic growth and development. Low real estate and labor costs resulted in the arrival of several information technology companies to downtown Detroit in late 2013 and early 2014.

As part of the task of moving Detroit beyond its bankruptcy filing, Orr and his staff undertook negotiations with fourteen of the city's labor unions, as well as negotiations with the city's public safety unions, which represent police officers and firefighters. A tentative collective bargaining agreement, aimed at moving beyond the city's emergency policies involving pay cuts and wage freezes for city workers, was reached in April 2014.

In May 2014, Orr's office published its first post-bankruptcy city budget. The budget included cuts to numerous city departments, including the general funds of the police and fire departments. Meanwhile, the efforts by Orr and other city officials aimed at revitalizing the city's economy through investments in its technology sector appear to be making strides. A 2013 report cited a 15-percent annual increase in tech industry employment in Detroit, with 10 percent of all employment in the metro area being tech-related.

## IMPACT

In the months following Detroit's approved bankruptcy filing, Orr oversaw the process of adjusting the city's massive debts and satisfying some of its most crucial financial responsibilities. The process was highly contentious, as cuts to public services and benefits to public employees were required in order to generate increases in available liquidity with which to pay off creditors. Following his appointment as emergency manager, Orr was expected to remain in the role for a period of eighteen months, as he and his colleagues in the city government work to reestablish Detroit's fiscal foundations.

## PERSONAL LIFE

Orr's wife, Donna Neale, is a surgeon at Johns Hopkins Hospital in Baltimore, Maryland. Married since 2004, the couple has two children.

## SUGGESTED READING

Davey, Monica. "Bankruptcy Lawyer Is Named to Manage an Ailing Detroit." *New York Times*. New York Times, 14 Mar. 2013. Web. 9 May 2014.

"Facts on Kevyn D. Orr." *Detroit Free Press*. Detroit Free Press, 24 Mar. 2013. Web. 9 May 2014.

Finley, Allysia. "Kevyn Orr: How Detroit Can Rise Again." *Wall Street Journal*. Wall Street Journal, 2 Aug. 2013. Web. 9 May 2014.

Fletcher, Michael A. "The Man Who Is Trying to Save Detroit." *Washington Post*. Washington Post, 20 July 2013. Web. 9 May 2014.

Helms, Matt. "One Year Later: Kevyn Orr Confident of Detroit Rebound from Bankruptcy." *Detroit Free Press*. Detroit Free Press, 24 Mar. 2014. Web. 9 May 2014.

Yaccino, Steven. "Detroit's Emergency Manager Offers Dire Report on City." *New York Times*. New York Times, 12 May 2013. Web. 9 May 2014.

—Joshua Pritchard

# Evan Osnos

**Born:** December 24, 1976
**Occupation:** Author

After spending eight years as a journalist living in Beijing, China, Evan Osnos wrote *Age of Ambition: Chasing Fortune, Truth, and Faith in the New China* (2014). The book, which was a finalist for the Pulitzer Prize, won the National Book Award for nonfiction in 2014. Along with the Pulitzer, it is the most prestigious literary award in the United States. He has written for National Public Radio's (NPR's) *This American Life* and Public Broadcasting System's (PBS's) *Frontline*. His awards include a Mirror Award for profile writing, the Livingston Award for Young Journalists, and the Asia Society's Osborn Elliott Prize for excellence in journalism on Asia. He also serves as a fellow of the Brookings Institution and a member of the Council on Foreign Relations. For four years he wrote the *Letter from China* blog for the *New Yorker*'s website. Currently he is the Washington, DC, correspondent for the *New Yorker*, covering foreign affairs and politics. His shorter works have been anthologized in *The Best American Science and Nature Writing* (2010) and in *The Best Spiritual Writing* (2012).

Slowking (GFDL v1.2)

## EARLY LIFE AND EDUCATION

Evan Lionel Richard Osnos was born on December 24, 1976, in London, England. Osnos's parents, Peter and Susan, had met in Vietnam, where his mother was working for Lawyers Military Defense Fund and his father was a journalist for the *Washington Post*. Peter Osnos was later assigned to Moscow; he and his wife traveled to London, where their son was born. Peter Osnos was in Moscow for four years and then returned to the United States before moving to London for two years. When the Osnos family moved back to the United States, they lived in New York and Connecticut. Osnos's mother was a consultant to nonprofit organizations and foundations. His father helped to found the publishing house PublicAffairs Books, a member of the Perseus Books Group, where he was editor-at-large. Osnos has an older sister named Katherine.

After the move to Connecticut, Osnos played hockey with the Greenwich Blues as a way to get to know people. He explained to Bill Slocum for *Greenwich Magazine* (May 2014), "I think in

a funny way, the experience of playing hockey was the first time I began to feel at home in my body. I realized you could go out in the world and you weren't going to be dashed to pieces. You weren't quite as fragile as you thought you were." He attended Greenwich High School, where he wrote for and became coeditor-in-chief of the school newspaper, the *Beak*.

He went on to Harvard University; during college he was an intern at the *Chicago Tribune*. Osnos became interested in China because of a class he took at Harvard focused on the 1989 demonstrations at Tiananmen Square. The contrast with what was the usual information about China— events that had taken place hundreds of years before—intrigued Osnos, as did the fact that the major participants were college students his age. Of the Tiananmen protests, Osnos told Slocum, "It was kind of this free-form energy, which had been pent up for decades when China was at its lowest, most poverty-stricken, socialized, kind of lethargic condition. Now it was bursting out." He studied Mandarin Chinese and traveled to China to study there for one semester and one summer during college. He graduated from Harvard magna cum laude in 1998 with a degree in political science.

## EARLY CAREER AT THE *CHICAGO TRIBUNE*

In 1999 Osnos became a metro reporter for the *Chicago Tribune*. One of his first assignments was to profile a young lawyer running for office—Barack Obama. It was the first and only election Obama ever lost. Commenting on Obama's speeches at that time, Osnos told Slocum, "He hadn't figured out yet how to structure his narrative. You sort of had the feeling of a very talented athlete at a very new sport."

In June 2001 Osnos became the paper's New York correspondent. He then went to Iraq at the time of the United States' invasion as a journalist embedded in the Marines, traveling to Iraq via Kuwait. He remained from March 2003 until February 2005. He was in Karbala when the city unexpectedly erupted in violence. The destruction and the battles took a toll on Osnos. He told Slocum, "I remember sitting in Baghdad, feeling it was ultimately, tragically, a story about the decomposition of a country. It was painful to see." At the same time he continued to be drawn to a country that was reinventing itself for the twenty-first century: China.

## ON TO CHINA

In June 2005 Osnos became the *Chicago Tribune*'s China foreign correspondent, living in Beijing and reporting on events there. He eventually became bureau chief. While living in China, he accepted the fact that the Chinese government had bugged his phones; he made it a point to keep his office open to the government so that any search, electronic or physical, would involve no surprises.

He began traveling throughout China and Southeast Asia in 2006, seeking to discover the environmental and global impacts of China becoming the workshop to the world. He focused on three areas: timber, oil, and cashmere. His three-part story "China's Great Grab" won the 2006 Sigma Delta Chi Award for newspaper foreign correspondence. For Osnos, however, the award was not the biggest success. As a direct result of the segment on timber, he told Jim Poyser for *Quill* (June/July 2007), Illinois lawmakers proposed the Illegally Logged Wood Act, "a bit that would make Illinois the first state in the nation to ban the sale of products of illegal timber."

Speaking to Brian Lamb for C-SPAN (31 May 2007), Osnos praised the newspaper for maintaining a news bureau in a foreign city, which is an expensive proposition and no longer done as frequently as in earlier years. "They need the day-to-day coverage and they need intensely local coverage. But, they also want something to put on the paper every day that shows people

that there is a much wider world beyond what they're reading about their neighborhoods. And, people respond to it."

Osnos was part of the team at the newspaper that won a 2008 Pulitzer Prize for investigative reporting on product safety. Later that year he left the *Chicago Tribune* and became the China correspondent for the *New Yorker*, where he maintained a regular blog, *Letter from China*, as well as writing articles for the magazine's print edition. Osnos wrote about other areas of East Asia as well. In 2012 he won the Overseas Press Award for his article "The Fallout" (17 Oct. 2011). The piece concerns the disaster at the nuclear plant in Fukushima, Japan.

## AGE OF AMBITION

Osnos explained to Charlie Rose for MSNBC's *Charlie Rose Show* (14 May 2014) that he sees two levels of ambition in China. There is the national ambition that is reported in Western newspapers. He explained, "The one that's harder to see, the one that you see on the ground when you live in China and you talk to people, is the ambition in their personal lives and their private lives and then their families, which is to transform themselves through this economic metamorphosis that the country is going through."

Osnos regards 1978 as a pivotal year for China. The Chinese premier at that time, Deng Xiaoping, freed the people from the Marxist purity that had led to its economy being worse than that of North Korea. The Chinese Communist Party remained in control, and the Marxist rulers, such as Mao Zedong, were still revered. But land was no longer owned collectively, and people were free to start businesses.

Osnos explained his view of his reporting on China to Lamb: "My role is to try to write the stories that otherwise don't get a whole lot of attention whether it's a little village in Southern China that produces paintings at an astronomical rate or if it's the way that Chinese young people are using the Internet to find romance."

Some Chinese publishers contacted Osnos about publishing the book in China, where there is a substantial market for books by Western authors. Ultimately, Osnos decided against the idea, because of the significant cuts that would have to be made to the book due to censorship. He did agree to publish the full work in Taiwan, so that many Chinese readers would still have access to it.

*Age of Ambition* won the National Book Award for nonfiction in 2014, beating out several writers favored to win, including Roz Chast, John Lahr, Anand Gopal, and Edward O. Wilson. The book also gained attention when it was one of seventeen books that President Obama bought at an independent bookstore, Politics and Prose, to celebrate "Small Business Saturday" at the end of November 2014.

## BROADENING HIS FOCUS

Osnos's genuine interest in people, which led him to take a bus trip through Europe with a Chinese tour, is evident in his profiles of people, including a series on Chinese artist and dissident Ai Weiwei for the PBS news program *Frontline*. Osnos's wife commented on his method of writing to Slocum, "He approaches things with a huge amount of research and thought. He doesn't do anything off the cuff. Like anyone who performs at a very high level, there is a mix of talent and incredible brute force."

Although Osnos clearly maintains an interest in China, he is enlarging his areas of expertise as a political writer. Articles that he has for the *New Yorker* since his return from China and reassignment as a correspondent for national and international affairs cover subjects such as Vice President Joe Biden, the expense of the 2014 midterm elections, and Samantha Power, the United States ambassador to the United Nations and an influential advisor to President Obama.

## PERSONAL LIFE

Osnos married Sarabeth Berman, an executive at the nonprofit Teach for All, in July 2011 at Boston's Museum of Science. Although he had known her sister at Harvard, the two met in 2008 at a brunch in Beijing and again later the same day at a lake. Berman had gone with friends to skate; Osnos was going to play ice hockey. Berman told Vincent Mallozzi for the *New York Times* (8 July 2011), "The first time I met him I thought he was this very athletic guy. I came to find out that he brushes off his ice skates and his hockey stick every other year." Osnos flew to New York to surprise Berman, who had gone there for work, in fall 2010; he proposed at Riverside Park, kneeling in the mud. The couple left China in mid-2013, eager to reconnect with friends and family back in the United States. Explaining his return to the United States, Osnos said he realized he had responsibilities to people that he could not fulfill from the other side of the world.

## SUGGESTED READING

Mallozzi, Vincent M. "Sarabeth Berman, Evan Osnos." *New York Times*. New York Times, 8 July 2011. Web. 9 Sept. 2015.

McClurg, Jocelyn. "'Redeployment' Wins Big at National Book Awards." *USA Today*. Gannett, 19 Nov. 2014. Web. 9 Sept. 2015.

Osnos, Evan. "Evan Osnos of the *New Yorker* on His Book 'Age of Ambition: Chasing Fortune, Truth and Faith in the New China.'" Interview by Charlie Rose. *Charlie Rose*. Charlie Rose, 14 May 2014. Web. 9 Sept. 2015.

Osnos, Evan. "Q&A with Evan Osnos." Interview by Brian Lamb. *C-SPAN*. Natl. Cable Satellite, 31 May 2007. Web. 9 Sept. 2015.

Poyser, Jim. "Winner: Evan Osnos, 'Chicago Tribune.'" *Quill* 95.5 (2007): 23. Print.

Slocum, Bill. "Human Interest." *Greenwich Magazine*. Greenwich Magazine, May 2014. Web. 9 Sept. 2015.

—Judy Johnson

---

# Mel Ottenberg
**Occupation:** Stylist

Mel Ottenberg is best known as the stylist who has crafted pop star Rihanna's look. That makes him "something of a game-changer," as Faran Krentcil wrote for *Elle* (25 Oct. 2013). "He is, after all, the one responsible for millions of teens around the world suddenly (and fervently) gluing fake pearls onto their sunglasses and Mickey Mouse ears onto their headbands." Indeed, the singer's clothing frequently receives as much attention as her music. "It might be safe to say that no one is more idolized or copied than Rihanna, who has absolutely perfected the seapunk-urban-luxury-bad-gal style," Leila Brillson asserted for *Refinery 29* (23 Apr. 2013). "And, New York–based Ottenberg—the stylist who has helped Rihanna hone her sartorial statement—is one of the pioneering forces responsible for this very recognizable style. There is no one that understands the essence, that *je ne sais quoi*, of Rihanna quite like him."

Although working as Rihanna's stylist is demanding—Ottenberg has had to hire one assistant just to deal with Rihanna-related matters—Ottenberg holds several other posts as well. Notably, since 2013, he has served as the fashion director of the German cultural magazine *032c*. In a profile for the *New York Times*

(28 May 2014), Matthew Schneier pointed out that most "stylists tend to split between celebrity and editorial camps," making Ottenberg, who chooses to keep a foot in both worlds, something of a rarity. "Working with [Rihanna] is really fulfilling," the stylist explained to Schneier, "but it's just one part of what I do. There's definitely a divide."

## CHILDHOOD AND EDUCATION

Little has been published about Ottenberg's earliest years. His father, Ray, was a lawyer by training who later took over the family's bakery. Ottenberg's bakery, overseen by Ray and his brother Lee, is a Washington, DC, institution that was founded in the 1860s by their great-grandfather Isaac, a German immigrant who delivered his hand-kneaded rolls and rye bread with a horse-drawn cart. Although the bakery became an enormous and thriving business, with multiple plants, hundreds of employees, and numerous institutional accounts, Mel Ottenberg had little interest in joining the family company. (He has told interviewers, however, that his first paying job was answering the office phone as a teen.)

Instead, Ottenberg was deeply interested in fashion and art from a young age. "I went to the Corcoran [School of the Arts and Design] every weekend for years and years, taking drawing classes and painting classes," Ottenberg recalled to Helena Andrews for the *Washington Post* (3

Steve Mack/FilmMagic/Getty Images

June 2014). "My best friend's mom always had *Vogue* and it was such a different world. I'd never really seen something like that, you don't experience that in DC and it sort of transported me into fashion. At ten years old I was obsessed."

In his early teens, he began sneaking out to local clubs, where, as he told Andrews, "There were kids wearing real fashion and I would go and just be in awe. The style that I was really influenced by wasn't so much the status quo, it was more of the underground stuff. I wasn't lacking for any cool style inspiration." While attending the Edmund Burke School, a progressive private institution with a diverse student body, he cultivated an idiosyncratic style that included Junior Gaultier shirts, red jeans, Doc Martens boots, and a closely cropped Caesar haircut. Despite the attempts of his circle of friends to enliven the fashion scene, the District of Columbia was not the most style-conscious place to grow up, he has admitted. "Maybe it's not the last word in fashion, I'll put it that way," he told Andrews. "I'm still biased because I love it so much, but it's definitely not the fashion capital."

Upon graduating from the Edmund Burke School in 1994, Ottenberg entered the Rhode Island School of Design, earning a bachelor's degree in fashion design from the highly regarded college in 1998. He loved the town of Providence and the region's frequent snowfalls, and he credits the school with instilling in him a strong work ethic. At that point he was deeply focused on becoming a clothing designer, rather than a stylist. (Distinct from the job of clothing designer, being a stylist involves choosing the clothing, accessories, and overall look of the models used in editorial photo shoots or performing that same function for an individual, as Ottenberg does for Rihanna.) "You just sort of have to find your way," he told Rachel Raczka for the *Boston Globe* (11 June 2014). "In school, I would never, never have given a second thought to styling. I just sort of fell into it. I think it's really good to study and learn things . . . whether or not you think it's going to be your final destination in a career."

## EARLY CAREER

Not long after graduating, Ottenberg met Amsterdam-born photographer Matthias Vriens-Mcgrath, who was making a name for himself doing shoots for such periodicals as *i-D*, the *Face*, *Vogue Hommes International*, and *Interview*. Ottenberg later began working as a stylist for those same publications. His first editorial assignment, he has told interviewers, was for a 2001 issue of the *Face*, which featured a mustachioed model sporting artfully ripped T-shirts and jeans—many items drawn from his own closet. "I laugh when I think about myself prepping for shoots in the beginning," he recalled to Daria Radlinski for an article posted on the website of the clothing company Opening Ceremony. "I didn't have a cell phone! Sometimes I didn't have electricity either. I worked from home and my friend Stacy . . . was my assistant." He continued, "I would print out pictures of the collections I found online and make these little collages and fax them to places, because people used to fax."

Once, he has recalled, a fire broke out in his apartment building the night before one of his first professional shoots. Firefighters broke the windows, scattering shoes and jewelry everywhere in the process. Expected in Los Angeles at eight o'clock in the morning, Ottenberg spent the night trying to organize his soot-filled apartment and pack the items needed for the job. (In the end, he made it to California and counted the shoot a great success.)

Ottenberg steadily racked up other assignments, working with such edgy photographers as Terry Richardson and David LaChapelle, contributing to a wide array of magazines, and styling such stars as Pamela Anderson, whom he placed naked in a giant glass terrarium. In 2009, he found himself at the center of something of a controversy. Then acting as a personal stylist for John Galliano, he was charged with creating an outfit for the British designer to wear at the end of the show featuring his cruise collection. Galliano wanted to look, he reportedly told Ottenberg, like the Artful Dodger from the 1968 film adaptation of Charles Dickens's novel *Oliver Twist*. (In past years, he had dressed as a foppish pirate or matador.) According to a young assistant who had been working with Ottenberg, the stylist purchased a $2,000 pair of oversized boots and spent another $1,000 on coarsely woven pants. Despite those expenditures, Ottenberg was unhappy. Feeling that the ensemble lacked the authenticity Galliano desired, he ordered the assistant to approach a homeless man on the street and offer to purchase the clothing from his back. Ottenberg has vehemently denied the assistant's account, but many media commentators have cited the tale as proof of the fashion world's astonishing insularity and cluelessness.

## WORKING WITH RIHANNA

Ottenberg was presented with a daunting challenge when the popular singer Rihanna was scheduled to perform, along with seventy-five backup dancers, at the halftime show of the 2011 National Basketball Association's All Stars game in two days' time, and she needed a stylist. Although he was reluctant to take on a high-profile assignment on such short notice, Ottenberg ultimately agreed, dressing the singer in a vintage Dolce & Gabbana bustier, fringed shorts, and Chanel boots.

The two got along well, and Rihanna hired Ottenberg to style that year's Loud tour. "To see it opening night, to see it live and to see the fans freaking out and singing along, I was hooked," he told Schneier. "I was like: 'This is cool. This is something different. You can do something with this. You can start trends. This is something people will talk about.'" Their work together drew widespread attention when the video for the hit single "We Found Love" was released in fall 2011. The widely watched video garnered a Grammy Award for best short-form music video and an MTV Video Music Award as video of the year. "The wardrobe is echt Ottenberg," Schneier wrote, "some fashion, including, notably, pieces from emerging and under-the-radar designers like Komakino and Forfex, but also heaps of well-worn vintage, much of it from close to home." (Ottenberg has told interviewers that many of the pieces belonged to his longtime boyfriend, fashion designer Adam Selman, who now also works regularly with Rihanna.)

Ottenberg and Selman are also responsible for one of the most-buzzed-about dresses Rihanna—or any celebrity, for that matter—has worn in recent years. Made of little more than sheer netting and 230,000 Swarovski crystals, the gown fully exposed the singer's entire body (except for one area covered by a small thong undergarment). She donned it to accept the 2014 Fashion Icon Award from the Council of Fashion Designers of America (CFDA). While observers were used to seeing Rihanna display her body—she caused a firestorm on Instagram, for example, for repeatedly showing her nipples—many were stunned at this level of exposure, and some opined that her behavior was inappropriate for a respected red-carpet event. For his part, Ottenberg told Katharine K. Zarrella for Style.com (3 June 2014), "I'm with her all the time, so my shock gauge is off." He went on, "This was the perfect night do to something fun, and I wanted her to have something great that you couldn't find anywhere else in the world."

The stylist and the singer are often photographed together and enjoy a good professional relationship, but Ottenberg is quick to correct anyone who assumes that the two are close friends. As he explained to Schneier, "I'm part of the hired help."

## OTHER ACTIVITIES

In addition to Rihanna, Ottenberg has worked with such stars as Cate Blanchett, Chloë Sevigny, and James Franco. In 2013, he was named fashion director of the Berlin-based magazine *032c*, a biannual publication focused on art and fashion. His editorial work continues to appear in other periodicals, including such mainstream titles as *Harper's Bazaar*, *GQ*, and the *New York Times*, and he has been responsible for lauded advertising campaigns for Nike and Dior.

Ottenberg designed costumes for two little-seen films: *The Heart Is Deceitful above All Things* (2004) and *Angel* (2005). In 2013, he appeared as himself on the Rihanna-produced reality show *Styled to Rock*, which aired for one season on the Bravo network. Alongside singer Pharrell Williams and model Erin Wasson, he judged a group of aspiring designers hoping to create clothing for Rihanna and other music stars, and while he tends to dislike being in front of the camera, he told interviewers that he found it gratifying to help young designers. When not traveling on assignment, Ottenberg works in a spacious studio in downtown Manhattan, on Canal Street.

## SUGGESTED READING

Andrews, Helena. "Washingtonian Mel Ottenberg Is the Man Responsible for the 'Naked Dress.'" *Washington Post*. Washington Post, 3 June 2014. Web. 27 Feb. 2015.

Brillson, Leila. "The Man behind RiRi's Style Dishes on Tour Outfits and Why Being Nude Rocks." *Refinery 29*. Refinery 29, 23 Apr. 2013. Web. 27 Feb. 2015.

Krentcil, Faran. "Stylist Mel Ottenberg Had to Coax Rihanna into Her Tom Ford Met Ball Gown." *Elle*. Hearst Communications, 25 Oct. 2013. Web. 27 Feb. 2015.

Raczka, Rachel. "How to Style an Icon." *Boston Globe*. Boston Globe Media Partners, 11 June 2014. Web. 27 Feb. 2015.

Schneier, Matthew. "Rihanna's Style Has a Name: Mel Ottenberg." *New York Times*. New York Times, 28 May 2014. Web. 27 Feb. 2015.

Zarrella, Katharine K. "Mel Ottenberg and Adam Selman Talk Rihanna's Scandalous CFDA Look." *Style.com*. Condé Nast, 3 June 2014. Web. 27 Feb. 2015.

—Mari Rich

# Mari Pangestu

**Born:** October 23, 1956

**Occupation:** Minister of tourism and creative economy of Indonesia

Mari Pangestu is an economist who has served since 2011 as the Republic of Indonesia's minister of tourism and creative economy, a newly created position at the time. Previously Indonesia's minister of trade, Pangestu has established herself as one of the country's leading economists. "When she makes a suggestion, leaders stop to listen," Rod Morehouse, former president of the Australia Indonesia Business Council, told Sacha Passi for *Southeast Asia Globe* magazine (15 Feb. 2013). He added, "She has huge intellectual capacity and the ability to get on with all whom she meets. Couple this with the fact that she comes from one of the rising economic powers of the future, [and] her ability to shape the world is not one that many would question."

Pangestu has served as a member of the Indonesian cabinet since 2004 and has been instrumental in developing policies that have strengthened Indonesia's economy through international trade. She is also the first ethnic Chinese Indonesian to hold a cabinet position in the Indonesian government. Indonesia's Chinese population is small but wealthy, which has bred resentment among the larger population. A series of riots in May 1998 specifically targeted ethnic Chinese, prompting many to flee the country, but Pangestu refused to leave. "Everybody has been affected by this incident. But I feel that my place is here in Indonesia," she told Michael Shari for *Businessweek* (18 June 1998) at the time. "In my own way, I know I should try to contribute to rebuilding this country."

## EARLY LIFE AND EDUCATION

Mari Elka Pangestu was born in Jakarta on October 23, 1956, to Evi Elka Pangestu and Pang

Fabrice Coffrini/AFP

Lay Kim. She has two brothers, Tikki Pang Pangestu and Pingki Elka Pangestu. She attended preschool in Berkeley, California, where her father was studying economics. Her family moved back to Jakarta when she was in primary school, and her father worked as an economics professor at the University of Jakarta before taking a position at the Australian National University (ANU) in Canberra in 1966. He was recruited by the influential economist Heinz Arndt to launch the university's Indonesia Project, now a major research center. Pangestu was only nine years old at the time and recalls playing hide-and-seek in the academic buildings where she would later build her own career as an economist.

Growing up, however, Pangestu wanted to be a doctor. She began her undergraduate studies at ANU but did not decide to study economics until her sophomore year. She earned a bachelor's degree with honors in economics in 1978; two years later she completed her master's degree in economics, also at ANU. Her master's thesis was titled "Direct Foreign Investment in the ASEAN [Association of Southeast Asian Nations] Countries."

She considered staying at ANU to pursue her doctorate, but at Arndt's urging, she decided to go abroad instead. "Heinz convinced me to go to the USA because he thought it would widen my horizons," she said in September 2011, delivering that year's Heinz W. Arndt Memorial Lecture at ANU. "He was right." Pangestu earned

her PhD from the University of California, Davis in 1986. Her dissertation was titled "The Effect of Oil Shocks on a Small Oil Exporting Country: The Case of Indonesia."

## ENDING THE SUHARTO REGIME

Indonesia, the world's fourth-most populous country, has a turbulent history, but it is uniquely poised to assert itself as a global economic force. The nation endured Japanese occupation during World War II and declared its independence from the Netherlands in 1945. The leader of the independence movement, Sukarno, became the country's first president in 1949. In 1965, however, Sukarno was overthrown by Major General Suharto in a bloody coup that resulted in more than 1.5 million Indonesian citizens dead or imprisoned. Suharto imposed his own authoritarian rule until he fell from power in 1998 after a financial crisis rocked the country and left approximately 20 million Indonesians in poverty.

Pangestu, who at the time was the executive director of the Center for Strategy and International Studies (CSIS), a Jakarta think tank, was an unlikely key player in Suharto's fall. As an academic for the World Bank, she researched Indonesian monopolies linked to Suharto and their negative effects on the country's fragile economy. Organizations such as the International Monetary Fund (IMF) and the World Bank had banded together to lend Indonesia $43 billion after the 1997 financial crisis, but Pangestu's research "heavily influenced the International Monetary Fund's decision to call for an end to these monopolies as a precondition for extending aid," according to Shari. Suharto failed to implement the aid package and proposed a plan to cut fuel subsidies to remedy the situation. The decision incited violent riots that forced his resignation.

## ACADEMIC CAREER AND MINISTRY OF TRADE

Pangestu had joined CSIS as a research associate in 1986, the same year she became a lecturer at the University of Indonesia at Jakarta. In 1987, she became the deputy director of the university's Inter University Center, and from 1992 to 1998 she served as the program coordinator of the Pacific Economic Cooperation Council (PECC). As executive director of CSIS in 1997, she was an outspoken critic of former Suharto.

Pangestu was appointed minister of trade in 2004 by the country's first directly elected president, Susilo Bambang Yudhoyono. She created the ministry from Indonesia's former Ministry of Industry and Trade and saw her appointment as an opportunity to implement the reforms she had been advocating as an academic. As trade minister, Pangestu worked to attract foreign investment in Indonesia and improve the country's infrastructure in order to expand its export market. She might have pursued her objectives a bit too zealously for some, however; in a cabinet reshuffle in 2011, she was named the minister of tourism and creative economy instead.

## MINISTER OF TOURISM AND CREATIVE ECONOMY

Michael Buehler, an associate research fellow at the Asia Society, told Passi that the decision to reappoint Pangestu was more political than pragmatic. "Her removal from the [trade] ministry to become minister of tourism was clearly a demotion," he said. "The 2011 reshuffle was determined by party and personal loyalties and not driven by an assessment of the performance of ministers." According to Passi, Pangestu's successor, Gita Wirjawan, is "effectively backtracking from Pangestu's longstanding push for free trade and delivering a blow to Indonesia's reputation in 2012 as one of the world's most enticing emerging markets."

Tourism is a major part of Indonesia's current growth strategy, and incoming travel has grown consistently over the past seven years and "faster than in all other regions in the world" between 2011 and 2013, according to Sara Schonhardt for the *New York Times* (29 Apr. 2013). Still, the country's crumbling ports and airports present a particularly daunting hurdle. In response to this, Pangestu has chosen to promote sixteen specific destinations outside of Bali that already have strong infrastructure. In her role as minister of creative economy, Pangestu is also interested in, among other goals, developing and promoting a culinary scene in Indonesia. "What we call 'culinary diplomacy' or 'soft-power diplomacy' can be so powerful. Whether it is your food, your fashion, your film, or your music, it's a really strong way to develop understanding between countries and to promote your country," she told Stephen Green for *Margin* (5 June 2014), the official magazine of ANU's College of Business and Economics. "That's one of the reasons that tourism and creative industries have been put together—they are so closely linked."

## WORLD TRADE ORGANIZATION

In 2013, Indonesia nominated Pangestu for the position of director general of the World Trade Organization (WTO). The WTO is an international body that oversees the rules of trade between nations and reserves the right to effectively veto domestic laws in member states when it comes to matters of international trade. Though members largely embrace free trade, there is little agreement on how best to facilitate it. "I don't underestimate the difficulties of finding common ground," Pangestu told Howard Schneider for the *Washington Post* (25 Jan. 2013). "If it was easy we would have completed negotiations long ago. It is such a more complex world."

Pangestu, who worked as a consultant to the WTO negotiating trade talks in 2005 and 2008, argued that the WTO should make more concentrated efforts to enable the flow of goods from country to country within a multinational supply chain. She was also eager to broker a potentially unpopular multilateral deal on agriculture. Indonesia has been hit hard by food shortages and price hikes on food in the past, the root cause of which can be found abroad, Pangestu told Paige McClanahan for the *Guardian* (25 Mar. 2013). "Western farm subsidies have artificially depressed world food prices, triggering a decline in production and a fall in global food stocks," McClanahan wrote, paraphrasing Pangestu. "Meanwhile, developing countries' panic-driven restrictions on food exports have exacerbated incipient food crises."

Nine candidates competed to replace Pascal Lamy of France as the WTO's director general. Pangestu and four others advanced to the first round of the election. Pangestu "probably ha[d] the most extensive academic knowledge of trade of any candidate for the position," Dylan Matthews wrote for the *Washington Post* (2 Apr. 2013), but she lacked popular support. Eventually, Pangestu and two others withdrew due to lack of support from the 157 WTO member states. Roberto Azevêdo of Brazil won the appointment and began his first term on September 1, 2013.

## PERSONAL LIFE

Pangestu has received numerous honors and awards over the course of her career, most recently an honorary doctorate from Australian National University. She has also written numerous books on the subjects of poverty, trade reform, and regionalism. In 1992 she helped establish Yayasan Sejati, a foundation that supports environmental and sociocultural initiatives.

Pangestu's husband, Adi Harsono, has a degree in nuclear physics and works in the oil and gas industry. The couple have two sons, Raymond Bima and Alexander Arya.

## SUGGESTED READING

Green, Stephen. "MC for the Creative Economy." *Margin*. Australian Natl. U, 5 June 2014. Web. 24 Nov. 2014.

Matthews, Dylan. "One of These 9 People Will Lead the World Trade Organization." *Washington Post*. Washington Post, 2 Apr. 2013. Web. 24 Nov. 2014.

McClanahan, Paige. "Doha Trade Talks Critical to Stop Food Price Spikes, Says WTO Hopeful." *Guardian*. Guardian News and Media, 25 Mar. 2013. Web. 16 Nov. 2014.

Pangestu, Mari. "A Talk with Indonesia's Mari Pangestu." Interview by Michael Shari. *Bloomberg Businessweek*. Bloomberg, 18 June 1998. Web. 24 Nov. 2014.

Passi, Sacha. "Rebel with a Cause." *Southeast Asia Globe*. Southeastern Globe Communications, 15 Feb. 2013. Web. 24 Nov. 2014.

Schneider, Howard. "The Behind-the-Scenes Campaign in Davos: Who Will Run the World Trade Organization?" *Washington Post*. Washington Post, 25 Jan. 2013. Web. 24 Nov. 2014.

Schonhardt, Sara. "Seeing Tourism as Crucial, Indonesia Tries to Step Up Its Game." *New York Times*. New York Times, 29 Apr. 2013. Web. 24 Nov. 2014.

—Molly Hagan

# Peng Lei

**Born:** ca. 1971

**Occupation:** Cofounder of Alibaba Group

Peng Lei, who sometimes goes by Lucy Peng, is a founding partner of Alibaba, China's largest e-commerce company. Alibaba is an online marketplace similar to Amazon in the United States and has grown to become one of its most formidable rivals. Its initial public offering (IPO) on the New York Stock Exchange in 2014 became the largest in history, valuing the company at $25 billion. Alibaba was founded in a tiny Hangzhou apartment by an English teacher named Jack Ma in 1999. Ma began growing Alibaba in 2002, when he set up an online marketplace akin to eBay called Taobao, which means "search-

ChinaFotoPress/Getty Images

ing for treasure" in Chinese. It was the first of Alibaba's myriad acquisitions; its holdings now include everything from a small shopping website called Tmall to a professional soccer team. In 2005 American company Yahoo bought a 40 percent stake of Alibaba. In 2012 American director Porter Erisman—who worked with the company from 2000 to 2008—released a documentary called *Crocodile in the Yangtze*, chronicling Alibaba's extraordinary rise. "Quarter after quarter, year after year, Alibaba has delivered blockbuster growth," David Barboza wrote for the *New York Times* (6 Sept. 2014). Peng, who many now call Ma's "right hand," was one of Alibaba's first recruits. She was an economics teacher with no tech experience, but her background was unimportant to Ma, who wanted employees to share his vision. As the creator of Alibaba's human resources department, Peng is the guardian of that vision.

## EDUCATION AND EARLY CAREER

Peng, who is in her forties, was born in Hangzhou, Zhejiang Province, in eastern China. She studied at Hangzhou Business College and, upon graduation in 1994, began teaching economics at Zhejiang Finance College. She married a man named Sun Danyu in 1997. (The two divorced for a short period and then remarried, though the dates are unclear.) In 1999, after five years of teaching, Peng quit her job to join her husband and an English teacher named Jack Ma, who was starting an Internet company. Ma had been introduced to the World Wide Web on his first trip to the United States in 1995. Upon his return to Hangzhou, he set up one of China's first Internet companies: China Pages, an online directory of Chinese businesses seeking foreign customers. He teamed with VBN, an early American Internet provider. One of his partners, Yu Xiaohong, recalled to Barboza, "At that time, the concept of the Internet was foreign to the Chinese people—people had no idea and no reaction when we introduced them to the idea." China Pages was on the road to success, but in 1996, Ma was pressured into forming a joint venture with Hangzhou Telecom—effectively handing over the reins of his company to the Chinese government.

Alibaba's rate of growth has been exponential since it opened for business in 1999. In 2000 Peng began building a corporate culture that has sustained Alibaba with few growing pains. "The core competence of a company is people, and the core competence of people is the art of employment," Peng told Cao Kezhen and Wang Rui for the China Entrepreneur Club website (9 Sept. 2014). "Your ideas can be copied, but the closeness of relationships cannot be copied, and the art of recruitment and training cannot be copied."

## THE LEGEND OF ALIBABA

"Everyone knows the story of Alibaba," Ma told Barboza, referring to the Arabian folk tale "Alibaba and the Forty Thieves." "He's a young man who is willing to help others." Indeed, Alibaba favored poor villagers to thieves; in many ways, Ma saw his company Alibaba in the same ideological vein. The company's mission has been similar to that of China Pages—to connect Chinese businesses and overseas customers—though Alibaba is much more than a simple directory. Ma's goal in building an e-commerce site was to empower small businesses—and he certainly has done that. On September 17, 2014, CNBC visited what is known as a "Taobao village" in Beishan, one of many Chinese "farming communities transformed thanks to new job opportunities created by Alibaba's consumer-to-consumer site of the same name." In another Taobao village, an underemployed farmer with a seventh-grade education became a millionaire selling yarn on Alibaba.

As Scott Cendrowski reported for *Fortune* magazine (17 Sept. 2014), Ma chose his original seventeen partners based on shared values rather than tech experience—this metric has proved

extraordinarily successful for Alibaba. Ma held the company's first meeting in his apartment in Hangzhou on February 21, 1999. Based on early reports, Alibaba functioned in much the same way as young Silicon Valley tech firms function—that is to say, unglamorously. A former Goldman Sachs banker named Shirley Lin recalled her visit to the company's "office." "I went up to the apartment, where they were all working 24/7. . . . The whole place stank—all those instant noodles. Jack's ideas were not entirely original—they had been tried in other countries. But he was completely dedicated to making them work in China," she told Barboza, adding, "I was moved by what I saw." Goldman Sachs invested $5 million in the company a month later. Soon after that, the company secured $20 million from Masayoshi Son of Japan's Softbank. Ma shared most of the windfall with his cofounders.

## BUILDING A CORPORATE CULTURE

Peng was initially hired to sort through résumés, though she came to be one of the architects of Alibaba's corporate culture. By 2000, Alibaba had more than one hundred employees but no official corporate framework, so Peng and Ma began developing a charter that later became known as the "Six Core Values." Ma's outlook focuses on honesty and employee satisfaction. In his own interview with Cao and Wang for the China Entrepreneur Club website (9 Sept. 2014), Ma emphasized taking risks over making profits, adding, "clients come first, personnel comes second, stockholders third." In 2003 Peng applied the core values to performance assessment through a system of her own design. She offered an example to Cao and Wang. "What is teamwork? An example of teamwork is airing opinions as fully as possible before a decision is made and adhering to the decision in behaviors and words," she said. "Each value, including our interpretation [of] leadership . . . is described as concrete deeds." Still, she quickly realized that managers were using her value system to blame subordinates. Peng revamped her system—as she has continued to do at every stage of the company's growth—making it more difficult for higher-ups to punish their employees with value judgments. Peng has begun tailoring the company's six values to the distinct structures of Alibaba's subsidiaries. She calls it "subculture building," she told Cao and Wang.

Citing inspiration from a movie that Ma encouraged the staff to watch in 2005, Peng said that she sees Alibaba's HR department as the ideological guardian of the company. "My ideal is to find a way to touch individuals' souls, to stimulate them and the team and help the company grow," she told Cao and Wang. "We need HR to have a soul." This ethos is also reflected in Alibaba's training program, "Eternal Lakeside," a nod to the name of the apartment complex in which Alibaba began. When executives from other companies join Alibaba, they spend an entire month learning about the company's history and outlook before entering the business side of operations. As far as fostering employee performance, Peng also introduced a concept she calls "meeting of souls," in which employees meet to discuss one another's performance. (She has criticized American businesses for their lack of "soul.") For all of her enthusiasm for the company, and the spirit it embodies, Peng was not so convinced of Ma's idealistic vision when she started with Alibaba. "I just enjoyed the process of doing something with a group of enthusiasts," she told Cao and Wang.

## ALIPAY

Alibaba also owns Alipay, an online payment system similar to PayPal. Peng served as the chief executive of Alipay from 2010 to 2013. When Ma stepped down as CEO in 2013, Peng was named CEO of Alibaba's Small and Micro Financial Services Group. Under Peng's guidance, Alipay and Alibaba's microfinancing division reached respective valuations of $60 billion and $50 billion. Since 2011, Peng has run an entity called Ant Financial, a successful outgrowth of Alipay, and since June 2014, she has been the "chief people officer" of Alibaba Group Holding.

## ALIBABA AND WOMEN

In the United States, Alibaba has been praised for the diversity of its staff. One-third of Alibaba's founding partners are women, as are eight of the thirty partners who control managing decisions. By contrast, as of 2014, the number of women working as vice presidents or higher at Facebook was 23 percent. Alibaba's employees attribute the number of women working for the company to the number of female founders. "It's not that they are looking specifically for women—it just grew naturally," former employee Jasper Chan told Charles Clover for the *Financial Times* (12 Dec. 2014). "A lot of the people who were around at the beginning were women." Alibaba has also adopted a number of

female-friendly policies such as providing lead aprons (to protect against computer radiation) for pregnant employees. Still, former and current employees agree that both men and women work very hard at the ever-expanding company. "We do joke that Ali uses women like they are men, and uses men like they are dogs," a former employee told Clover. "I feel I grew a lot during my time with Alibaba, especially working under pressure and building up my endurance." Alibaba's culture and Peng's drive have allowed her to succeed in what has become a model company for the growth of the Chinese economy. As she told Cao and Wang, "China has the greatest potential in the world to be the birthplace of a great company. Sure, I do daresay that company [is] Alibaba."

## SUGGESTED READING

Barboza, David. "The Jack Ma Way." *New York Times*. New York Times, 6 Sept. 2014. Web. 17 May 2015.

Cendrowski, Scott. "Alibaba's Maggie Wu and Lucy Peng: The Dynamic Duo behind the IPO." *Fortune*. Time, 17 Sept. 2014. Web. 17 May 2015.

Clover, Charles. "Women of 2014: The Women of Alibaba." *Financial Times*. Financial Times, 12 Dec. 2014. Web. 17 May 2015.

Epstein, Gady. "Alibaba's Jack Ma Fights to Win Back Trust." *Forbes*. Forbes.com, 23 Mar. 2011. Web. 26 May 2015.

Yoon, Eunice. "Inside a Taobao Village." *CNBC*. NBC Universal, 17 Sept. 2014. Web. 18 May 2015.

—Molly Hagan

# Chelsea Peretti

**Born:** February 20, 1978
**Occupation:** Comedian

In September 2013, comedian Chelsea Peretti was introduced to television audiences as Gina Linetti, the self-centered and outspoken office administrator on the Fox comedy series *Brooklyn Nine-Nine* (2013–). But as those familiar with her stand-up, writing work, and guest appearances in numerous television shows are well aware, she is no newcomer to the world of comedy. An actor and writer since childhood, Peretti began performing stand-up comedy at venues such as the Upright Citizens Brigade Theatre after graduating from college and over the years made a name for herself in both New York and Los Angeles. An established television writer, she contributed to comedy shows such as *The Sarah Silverman Program* and *Parks and Recreation* as well as to various web series and podcasts. The role of Gina, however, took her career to another level as *Brooklyn Nine-Nine* earned critical praise as well as various awards. Still, Peretti remains devoted to her stand-up roots; her first hour-long comedy special, *Chelsea Peretti: One of the Greats*, premiered on Netflix in November 2014 to significant critical acclaim.

## EARLY LIFE AND EDUCATION

Chelsea Vanessa Peretti was born on February 20, 1978, in Oakland, California. Her parents, a lawyer and a teacher, divorced when she was one. They shared custody of Peretti and her older brother, Jonah, who grew up splitting their time between Oakland and the nearby city of El Cerrito. Jonah would go on to cofound the news website the *Huffington Post* and later found the website BuzzFeed.

Peretti attended Chabot Elementary School in Oakland, where she befriended and sometimes carpooled with future *Brooklyn Nine-Nine* costar Andy Samberg. Although Peretti had not yet developed the ambition to be a comedian, her anecdotes of her time in school reflect the offbeat sense of humor that would characterize her

Jason LaVeris/FilmMagic/Getty Images

later work. "In elementary school, people would consider me weird," she told Kimberly Chun for *SFGate* (12 June 2014). "The cool girl was Pocahontas for Halloween—I was an old man one year and a tarantula another year. Dare I say I was ahead of my time?"

As a child, Peretti became involved in the performing arts, appearing in plays at San Francisco's American Conservatory Theater and taking classes at the theater's Young Conservatory. She maintained an interest in both acting and writing in high school and, remaining true to her comedic nature, wore an elaborate gown and carried a parasol to her high school graduation. Ultimately she chose to study writing at Barnard College, a New York City college affiliated with Columbia University. While at Barnard, Peretti performed improvisational comedy and worked for a time as an intern for the television sketch comedy show *Saturday Night Live* (*SNL*), where she had the opportunity to observe the behind-the-scenes workings of television comedy. She graduated from college with a degree in English in 2000.

## EARLY CAREER

Peretti began her career after college as a freelance writer, contributing to such publications as the *Village Voice*. She soon began performing stand-up comedy at various clubs in New York, including the well-known Upright Citizens Brigade Theatre. Her early forays into comedy also involved several collaborations with her brother, including one known as the Rejection Line, a phone number that single New Yorkers, and others, could give out to overly aggressive would-be suitors. Upon calling the number, the caller would be greeted with the recorded message, "Unfortunately, the person who gave you this number does not want to talk to you or speak to you again. We'd like to take this opportunity to officially reject you," as quoted by Oliver Burkeman in the *Guardian* (3 May 2002).

Around the same time the pair also started the satirical website Black People Love Us, published online in 2002. The website, ostensibly the creation of a white couple named Sally and Johnny and featuring testimonials from their many African American friends, called attention to racial microaggressions in a humorous manner. Black People Love Us went viral soon after its publication, garnering significant media attention.

In 2004, Peretti formed the performance group Variety SHAC, along with musician Shonali Bhowmik and comedians Andrea Rosen and Heather Lawless. "We wanted to work together but we weren't really [getting booked for] shows on the same nights because people tend to put on one female [comedian] per show," she told Lisa Medchill for the *Observer* (10 July 2007) of the group's origins. "It's actually considerate because otherwise we might step on each other's tampon jokes." The members of Variety SHAC performed together on stage and also made short comedy films, many of which were posted on the Upright Citizens Brigade website.

## TELEVISION AND THE INTERNET

After several years of performing in New York, Peretti moved to Los Angeles, where she continued to perform stand-up and also established herself as a comedy writer versatile enough to master both television and the Internet. Her first stint writing for television came when she was hired to join the creative crew of *The Sarah Silverman Program*. She had also created two new series of web videos, titled *All My Exes* and *Making Friends*, which she wrote and starred in. The former concept involved humorous, scripted "interviews" with fake exes about why the relationship ended, while the latter presented a comedic take on the difficulty of establishing friendships in New York City. By 2011 she was contributing to scripts for the hit primetime show *Parks and Recreation*, adding to her opportunities to experience different people's tastes in comedy. As an actor, she made guest appearances in numerous television shows and began lending her voice to the Adult Swim (Cartoon Network) animated program *China, IL* that same year. Never straying too far from her Internet platform, in 2012, she launched the podcast *Call Chelsea Peretti*, in which she responds to calls and e-mail messages from listeners.

In 2013, Peretti returned to *SNL* not as an intern but as a guest writer, contributing to sketches for two episodes while also writing for and appearing on the *Kroll Show*. An avid user of the social-networking site Twitter, she has made a name for herself with her frequent, humorous tweets, and in 2013 her account, @chelseavperetti, was included in *Time* magazine's list of the best Twitter feeds of the year. She has explained to journalists that while she is aware that no online content can truly be removed from the Internet, she does curate her tweets carefully, at times deleting those that she deems insufficiently funny. Of her interest in Internet-based comedy, Peretti told Jeremy

Popkin for the comedy blog *Splitsider* (30 Sept. 2013), "I've actually always been interested in the medium because I've done all kinds of different stuff on the Internet, and I just think that more and more it is just the world that we live in." She explained, "What has always drawn me to the Internet is the immediacy of it. In the same way as stand-up, you can write a joke and do it that night onstage and get instant reactions. . . . You can have an idea and put it out instantly and it's just so gratifying."

As she became better known as a stand-up comic, television writer, and actor, Peretti was increasingly thrust into the spotlight, a change that she believed had come at the right time in her life. "[I]'m really, really happy it didn't happen right out of college for me, because I feel like I know who I am so much more now than I did then," she explained to Popkin. "I feel like I have a certain confidence that comes from working really hard over the years and it feels great."

## *BROOKLYN NINE-NINE*

In September 2013, Peretti entered a new stage of her career with the premiere of the comedy series *Brooklyn Nine-Nine* on Fox. The show, which stars Peretti's childhood friend Samberg as Detective Jake Peralta, follows the adventures and mishaps of the police detectives and other employees of a fictional precinct of the New York Police Department (NYPD). Peretti plays Gina Linetti, the self-centered, dance-loving, and smartphone-addicted assistant to the precinct's captain, Raymond Holt (Andre Braugher).

Drawn to the show because of the presence of creators Dan Goor and Michael Schur, who had previously worked on *Parks and Recreation*, Peretti initially auditioned for the role that became tough detective Rosa Diaz, ultimately played by Stephanie Beatriz. While she did not get that part, the showrunners decided to write the role of Gina specifically for her, incorporating elements of Peretti's personality and comedy persona into the character. Peretti enjoys playing the character, who, in many ways, serves as a foil to the others in the precinct. "Because she's not a detective, she's able to say things that no one else could really say because . . . she doesn't have a ton of fear of personal ramifications or losing her job," she told Popkin. "I mean, when it comes down to it, she is scared of that, but she gets to kind of really say all her thoughts without much of a filter so that's fun to play comedically."

*Brooklyn Nine-Nine* was received well by critics during its first season and in January 2014 won the Golden Globe Award for best television comedy series. In between filming, Peretti traveled nationally for her American Treasure stand-up tour that same year. A second season of *Brooklyn Nine-Nine* aired beginning in September and culminated with an episode in which Captain Holt is promoted to a position in the NYPD's Department of Public Relations and thus forced to leave the precinct, taking Gina with him. Despite the characters' departures from the precinct, however, *Brooklyn Nine-Nine*'s showrunners confirmed in interviews that both Braugher and Peretti would return in the show's third season, which was scheduled to premiere in the fall of 2015.

### ONE OF THE GREATS

Midway through the second season of *Brooklyn Nine-Nine*, Peretti released her first hour-long stand-up special, *Chelsea Peretti: One of the Greats*. In an interview with Phil Davidson for *Splitsider* (26 Sept. 2014), Peretti discussed the thought process behind the special's title. "I think it's an overblown statement but at the same time I feel like women are frequently seen as guests in the comedy world—you know, a kid sister of the 'real comedians,'" she explained. "I like the idea of positioning myself as legendary rather than trying to fit in."

A production of the video-streaming service Netflix, the special blends older comedic material with new jokes and addresses topics such as modern technology, gender stereotypes in comedy, and texting with dogs. Peretti played an active role in the editing of the special, determining which jokes were worthy of inclusion. "I'm very passionate about anything where I get to have some creative control," she told Davidson.

### PERSONAL LIFE

Peretti has been in a relationship with fellow comedian and actor Jordan Peele, the costar of the Comedy Central sketch show *Key and Peele*, since 2013. She lives in Los Angeles, California.

### SUGGESTED READING

Burkeman, Oliver. "New Tactic in the Dating Game." *Guardian*. Guardian News and Media, 3 May 2002. Web. 4 Sept. 2015.

Chun, Kimberly. "Chelsea Peretti Brings Stand-Up Show from 'Brooklyn' to SF." *SFGate*. Hearst Communications, 12 June 2014. Web. 4 Sept. 2015.

Frank, Aaron. "Chelsea Peretti: The Comedy of Awkwardness." *LA Weekly*. LA Weekly, 15 May 2013. Web. 4 Sept. 2015.

Peretti, Chelsea. "Chelsea Peretti on *Brooklyn Nine-Nine*, Writing for *SNL*, and Her New Netflix Special." Interview by Phil Davidson. *Splitsider*. Awl, 26 Sept. 2014. Web. 4 Sept. 2015.

Peretti, Chelsea. "Chelsea Peretti Talks TV, Twitter, and What She Wants in a Boyfriend." Interview by Anna Breslaw. *Heeb*. Heeb Media, 19 Dec. 2011. Web. 4 Sept. 2015.

Peretti, Chelsea. "Talking to Chelsea Peretti about *Brooklyn Nine-Nine*, *Parks and Rec*, and the Differences between NY and LA Standup." Interview by Jeremy Popkin. *Splitsider*. Awl, 30 Sept. 2013. Web. 4 Sept. 2015.

### SELECTED WORKS

*China, IL*, 2011–15; *Kroll Show*, 2013–15; *Brooklyn Nine-Nine*, 2013–; *Chelsea Peretti: One of the Greats*, 2014

—Joy Crelin

# Jonah Peretti

**Born:** January 1, 1974
**Occupation:** Founder of *BuzzFeed*

Jonah Peretti is the founder of the news and pop culture website *BuzzFeed*. Once a subject of ridicule in media circles, *BuzzFeed* has matured into one of the most financially successful news sites on the Internet. It has shifted its focus away from vacuous lists and articles, as in "The 40 Greatest Dog GIFs of All Time," toward more serious news. Its reasons for doing so, however, have less to do with journalistic ideal and more to do with growing a readership. *BuzzFeed* was a pioneer of a controversial yet increasingly common finance model known as native advertising, which is a term that essentially means that, while some of the site's listicles are original content (like the aforementioned dog GIFs), others are paid advertising content, like the Pillsbury-sponsored, "10 Things You Never Knew You Could Do With a Crescent Roll."

Peretti, who has a master's degree in network science, has been fascinated by the spread of in-

Max Morse/Wikimedia Commons

of California, Santa Cruz, where students were not assigned grades, and talked his way into upper-level classes, the most memorable of which were in the History of Consciousness program. As a senior he was taking graduate courses in critical theory and Lacanian psychoanalysis. He spent each summer teaching, and graduated with a degree in environmental studies in 1996. After graduation, Peretti moved to New Orleans, Louisiana, where he taught computer classes for students in grades six through twelve. He worked with his students to develop projects that combined education and technology in innovative ways. Peretti wrote a number of papers on the subject, which brought him, three years later, to study for his master's degree at the Media Lab at the Massachusetts Institute of Technology (MIT). He intended to continue studying educational technology but instead shifted his focus to network theory.

## EARLY INTERNET SUCCESS

In 2001, while working on his thesis at MIT, he tried to order a pair of Nike shoes customized with the word "sweatshop" stitched on them. The company refused to honor his request, but Peretti continued to correspond with the company via e-mail to convince them to make the shoes. He forwarded the e-mail exchange to ten friends, and it became an Internet sensation, and he was soon invited to appear on NBC's *Today Show*. It was the early days of the Internet and the concept of "going viral" had yet to be culturally adopted. Peretti was intrigued by the attention, observing to Rowan, "The only force propelling the message was the collective action of those who thought it was worth forwarding."

After MIT, Peretti took a job with Eyebeam, an art and media center in New York City, where he met a Columbia University professor named Duncan Watts and viral video star Ze Frank, both of whom would later play important roles at *BuzzFeed*. During this time Peretti also teamed up with his sister Chelsea to create a handful of web projects with the aim of again going viral. The first was the New York Rejection Line, a site that encouraged users to give out a certain phone number to unwanted suitors. The second project was a site called Black People Love Us! about a (fictional) culturally tone-deaf white couple. Each new project offered Peretti a new insight into the web and what people were interested in reading. "I thought, if there's this massive shift happening in the way content and ideas spread, what does that mean?" he told Rowan. "The best

formation on the Internet since its early days. He developed *BuzzFeed* shortly after cofounding the *Huffington Post* with Ken Lerer and Arianna Huffington in 2005 as an experiment to study how data moves from person to person across the web. For Peretti, quality is less important than reach, and *BuzzFeed* derives a vast majority of its traffic through social media sites like Facebook and Twitter, which has allowed him to radically expand the site and elevate its content. Peretti hired Ben Smith of *Politico* as *BuzzFeed*'s first editor-in-chief in 2011, and he has since lured away reporters from the *Guardian*, *Rolling Stone*, and the *New York Times*. In 2013 Peretti hired Pulitzer Prize–winning journalist Mark Schoofs, formerly of the nonprofit news source ProPublica, to head the site's investigative team.

## EARLY LIFE AND EDUCATION

Peretti was born in Oakland, California, on January 1, 1974. His mother taught at the University of California, Berkeley, and his father is a public defender. His sister, Chelsea Peretti, is a stand-up comedian and appears on the Fox sitcom *Brooklyn Nine-Nine*. Peretti, according to David Rowan for *Wired* magazine (2 Jan. 2014), was a "super-talkative" child but had difficulty learning how to read. It turned out that Peretti was dyslexic. "It wasn't fun," Peretti told Rowan of his early years, "but having a brain that works slightly differently gives you a different perspective." He attended the University way was to make things, and track them as they spread." He traced the spread of his work using a program he developed called ForwardTrack.

## HUFFINGTON POST

In 2003, Watts introduced Peretti to Kenneth Lerer, a former America Online (AOL) executive and wealthy tech entrepreneur. Lerer asked Peretti to help him create a website called Stop the NRA, which supported the Clinton-era assault weapons ban. The site failed to gain much political traction despite gathering about 150,000 signatures. (Lerer donated the domain to the Brady Campaign to Prevent Gun Violence two years later.) The two men were looking for another project when Lerer met with Arianna Huffington, a Greek American columnist and socialite who was once married to former Republican congressman Michael Huffington. Lerer and Huffington were interested in creating a liberal alternative to the *Drudge Report*, a popular website helmed by conservative commentator Matt Drudge. With Huffington's contacts and Peretti's technical expertise, they reasoned, such a website might prove to be a successful business venture.

The *Huffington Post* was launched in 2005. In an interview with Felix Salmon for *Matter* (11 June 2014), Peretti marveled at how quickly the site evolved. "A great way to learn about the Internet is to build one of the biggest sites on the Internet," he said. "It's hard to remember how much we've all changed, because we've changed so much." The *Huffington Post* functioned as a news aggregation site with an accompanying blog. It trafficked in political news stories and gossip penned by other sources, while Huffington, Eric Alterman wrote for the *New Yorker* (31 Mar. 2008), called upon her "alarmingly vast array of friends and connections" to write guest posts about a variety of topics.

## TECHNIQUES TO SUCCESS

The *Huffington Post*'s enthusiastic hoard of commentators and a technique known as search-engine optimization propelled the site's early success, as did the headline-stylings of the late Andrew Breitbart, a conservative commentator who went on to work as an editor at *Drudge*. At the time, Peretti recalled to Salmon, he was trying to figure out how to make the site both "contagious and sticky." A "sticky" site draws loyal readers back every day with new content, Peretti explained to Salmon. Contagion was trickier, but with the novelty of celebrity-penned

content—not to mention celebrity tweets—on the horizon, Peretti found an important component of the perfect gateway post. He went out of his way to streamline celebrity written content on the *Post* so that, as he explained to Salmon, "it had all the things that blogs were supposed to have so that people who knew about blogging would see it and say, 'Oh, [*Seinfeld* creator] Larry David is blogging.' Not, 'Larry David's doing some weird new thing that Arianna Huffington invented.'" In short, the *Huffington Post*'s strategy was two-pronged: the Larry Davids brought readers to the site, while Breitbart's click-bait headlines kept them coming back for more.

Much of the site's most-trafficked content, Peretti found, never appeared on the homepage because it was trashier than the image the site originally presented. "Peretti called it the 'mullet strategy'—business in front, party in the back—a metaphor that grated on some of his colleagues," Andrew Rice wrote for *New York* magazine (7 Apr. 2013). As the *Huffington Post* grew a large enough audience to compete with major new outlets, Huffington tried to reign in Peretti's tendency to "party." As Peretti later told Rice, "*Huffington Post* was very focused on being a successful media company. And so there wasn't that much freedom to play." Peretti left the company shortly before it was acquired by AOL for $315 million in early 2011.

## BUZZFEED

Peretti launched *BuzzFeed* as a side project with John S. Johnson, his old boss at Eyebeam, while he was still working at the *Huffington Post* in 2006. The early site boasted no writers or editors; it was simply an algorithm that collected potentially viral stories from across the web. The stories were chosen based on the number of views and shares it had. Partner websites could use *BuzzFeed* to see which posts were popular, and in exchange, they allowed *BuzzFeed* to install a programming code that would analyze their traffic. As of 2013, over two hundred sites ran the program, giving *BuzzFeed* a treasure trove of data about how people read and share articles. It is the site's analytic power—not its content—that continues to draw Silicon Valley, while traditional news outlets struggle to find funding. What began as an experiment proved wildly successful by what Rice called "an obvious truth: People like upbeat, even childlike content." By making the site the party Arianna Huffington tried to distance herself from, *BuzzFeed* was, ironically, able to win some real journalistic credibility. Of course, Peretti's prestigious hires didn't save the site from accusations of plagiarism in 2012. The online news website *Slate* found that a number of *BuzzFeed*'s most popular items were lifted from other sites including Reddit and Pinterest. In 2014, *BuzzFeed* came under fire again for quietly deleting some 4,000 old posts. In media circles, *Slate*'s Will Oremus explained (14 Aug. 2014), "retracting a story is viewed as a serious blow to one's journalistic credibility—and to do so without notifying readers is a cardinal sin." Peretti however, seemed less concerned. Tech companies, he explained to Oremus, delete things that are broken or just not quite up to current standards. "If you look at that era of *BuzzFeed* through the lens of newspaper or magazine journalism, you would say [deleting those posts] was a strange decision," he said. "We just didn't and don't look at that period of *BuzzFeed* as being a journalistic enterprise."

## PERSONAL LIFE

Peretti and his wife, Andrea Harner, live in the Park Slope neighborhood of Brooklyn, New York, with their twin boys.

## SUGGESTED READING

Alterman, Eric. "Out of Print." *New Yorker.* Condé Nast, 31 Mar. 2008. Web. 16 Mar. 2015.

Oremus, Will. "One Viral Media Company That Isn't Evil, Just Misunderstood." *Slate.* Graham Holdings, 14 Aug. 2014. Web. 16 Mar. 2015.

Rice, Andrew. "Does *BuzzFeed* Know the Secret?" *New York.* New York Media, 7 Apr. 2013. Web. 16 Mar. 2015.

Rowan, David. "How *BuzzFeed* Mastered Social Sharing to Become a Media Giant for a New Era." *Wired.* Condé Nast UK, 2 Jan. 2014. Web. 16 Mar. 2015.

Salmon, Felix. "*BuzzFeed*'s Jonah Peretti Goes Long." *Matter.* Medium, 11 June 2014. Web. 16 Mar. 2015.

—Molly Hagan

# Saul Perlmutter

**Born:** September 22, 1959
**Occupation:** Physicist

Saul Perlmutter is one of three astrophysicists awarded the 2011 Nobel Prize in Physics for his contributions to the discovery that the universe is in a state of accelerating expansion.

## BACKGROUND

Saul Perlmutter was born in Champaign-Urbana, Illinois, the second of three children born to Daniel and Felice (née Davidson) Perlmutter. Perlmutter's maternal relatives were Jewish immigrants from Romania. In 1963, Perlmutter's family relocated to Philadelphia, Pennsylvania, where his father took a position at the University of Pennsylvania, eventually becoming professor emeritus in chemical and biomolecular engineering, while his mother became a professor emeritus of sociology at Philadelphia's Temple University.

Perlmutter's family lived in Philadelphia's West Mount Airy neighborhood and he attended Germantown Friends School. Perlmutter went on to attend Harvard University, graduating in 1981 with a degree in physics. He was then accepted as a graduate student in the physics department at the University of California, Berkeley, working in the Lawrence Berkeley National Laboratory (LBNL) under Richard A. Muller. Perlmutter completed his PhD in 1986 and remained at the university to complete postdoctoral research.

## SUPERNOVAS AND UNIVERSAL ACCELERATION

While completing his PhD at Berkeley, Perlmutter helped to design software and other equipment for an automated telescope that researchers hoped to use to study supernovas, which are massive stellar explosions that produce bright flashes of light visible from Earth. The Berkeley Automatic Supernova Search (BASS) was established in 1984, and the team found their first supernova in 1986.

Since the 1930s, scientists hoped to use supernovas to study the rate of expansion of the universe and developed a hypothesis that was based on the idea that the observable universe was generated from a "big bang" and had been expanding since. Until the 1990s, the prevailing theory was that the universal expansion was decelerating. By the 1980s, scientists had been able to determine the precise amount of light emitted by various types of supernovas. For instance, Type Ia supernovas produce light five billion times brighter than the sun when they occur. Using this value, astronomers can estimate the distance from Earth to a supernova through the intensity of light observed from the event. Further, because the universe is expanding, over time the light from a supernova "shifts" as the nova moves. Given sufficient data on this "red shift," scientists are able to measure the rate at which the universe is expanding.

Working with BASS team member Carlton Pennypacker, Perlmutter used a wide-field camera to search multiple galaxies (ten thousand or more) each night in hopes of capturing sufficient data from supernovas to begin calculating the rate of universal expansion. The Supernova Cosmology Project was founded in 1988 and became a cornerstone for Berkeley's Center for Particle Astrophysics.

In 1994, Perlmutter's team began working with the newly established High-Z Supernova Search Team, founded by Australian National University physicist Brian Schmidt. In 1997, while analyzing a batch of results, Perlmutter's team reached the conclusion that the expansion of the universe was accelerating, contrary to the prevailing theory of a decelerating universe. Simultaneously, the High-Z Supernova Search Team reached the same conclusion in a study led by team member Adam Riess. Perlmutter's team delivered the results of their study at a January 1998 meeting of the American Astronomical Society and published the details of their findings in 1999. The confirmation of the acceleration hypothesis by two independent teams led to general acceptance of the theory within the scientific community.

To explain why the universe is accelerating, astronomers hypothesize the existence of a mysterious force called dark energy that is driving the expansion of the universe. Since 1998, Perlmutter's team at the LBNL and other teams around the world have been continuing their research to gain a better understanding of how dark energy functions in the universe.

## RECOGNITION AND SUPPORT

Recognition of Perlmutter's achievement began shortly after the publication of the team's findings. In 2002, Perlmutter won the E. O. Lawrence Award in Physics from the US Department of Energy, and he was named California Scientist of the Year in 2003. In 2006, Perlmutter, Schmidt, and Riess shared the Shaw Prize in Astronomy, from the Hong Kong–based Shaw Prize Foundation.

Also in 2006, Perlmutter's team was successful in obtaining NASA support for the Super-Nova/Acceleration Probe (SNAP), which forms part of the Joint Dark Energy Mission (JDEM) a collaborative international effort to gain further information about dark energy. In 2011, it was announced that Perlmutter, Riess, and Schmidt would share the Nobel Prize in Physics for their discovery of accelerated expansion and contributions to the physical understanding of the universe.

## IMPACT

The accelerating universe hypothesis has led to a vast expansion in physics research as astronomers and physicists attempt to refine existing evidence and postulate about the potential existence of dark energy. The acceleration hypothesis is one of a relatively small number of experimental discoveries that violate the standard physical model of the universe.

## PERSONAL LIFE

Saul Perlmutter is married to Laura Nelson, an anthropologist working out of California State East Bay. The couple has one child, a daughter named Noa Nelson Perlmutter.

## SUGGESTED READING

"Autobiography of Saul Perlmutter." *Shaw Prize*. Shaw Prize Foundation, 12 Sept. 2006. Web. 28 Mar. 2014.

Chiao, Raymond Y. *Visions of Discovery: New Light on Physics, Cosmology, and Consciousness*. Cambridge: Cambridge UP, 2011. Print.

Fazeli-Fard, Maggie. "It's Not Rocket Science." *Monthly*. East Bay Monthly, Dec. 2011. Web. 29 Mar. 2014.

Mason, Betsy. "Scientist Discovers the Genuine Dark Side." *Contra Costa Times*. Contra Costa Times, 3 July 2006. Web. 29 Mar. 2014.

"Nobel Lecture: Measuring the Acceleration of the Cosmic Expansion Using Supernovae." *Nobel Prize*. Nobel Media, 8 Dec. 2011. Web. 29 Mar. 2014.

Panek, Richard. *The 4 Percent Universe: Dark Matter, Dark Energy, and the Race to Discover the Rest of Reality*. Boston: Houghton, 2011. Print.

Sanders, Robert. "Saul Perlmutter Awarded 2011 Nobel Prize in Physics." *News Center Berkeley*. UC Regents, 4 Oct. 2011. Web. 29 Mar. 2014.

—Micah Issitt

# Phoebe Philo

**Born:** 1973
**Occupation:** Fashion designer

Phoebe Philo is a British fashion designer who made her true debut at the helm of Céline in 2010. Céline is a fashion house owned by the French luxury conglomerate LVMH, itself a luxe marriage between Louis Vuitton and Moët Hennessy. Philo was lauded as the creative director of Chloé in the early 2000s, and since taking over at Céline in 2008, she has reinvented the brand to reflect her own classic, minimal tastes. She rejects novelty with a fervor that could be described as feminist. Marco Gobbetti, Céline's chief executive officer, told Robert Murphy for the *Wall Street Journal* (25 Mar. 2015), "Céline is a brand for women . . . not a man's fantasy of women."

Founded by Céline Vipiana in 1945, Céline started out as a children's shoe boutique. The company began making bags and separates for women in the 1960s and for years after was considered serviceably chic but perhaps a bit stuffy.

Mike Marsland/Getty Images

Michael Kors served as creative director from 1997 to 2004, but after his departure, the brand struggled to distinguish itself from other luxury labels. Executives at Céline approached Philo, who had taken a two-year hiatus from the fashion world to have her second child, in 2008. At her first show, Philo stunned the fashion world with her tasteful restraint, ushering in a new era of minimalism. "There's this incredible mystique about Phoebe," Lisa Armstrong, fashion editor at the *Telegraph*, told Alice Rawsthorn for the *New York Times Style Magazine* (25 Feb. 2010). "She's this cool London girl who always did the right thing at the right time at Chloé and walked away from it at the absolute height. Everyone talked about her first Céline show as if it was the second coming. The atmosphere in that room was electric. We were all waiting to see what she would do."

## EARLY LIFE AND EDUCATION

Phoebe Philo was born in 1973 in Paris, France. Her parents are British, and the family returned to England before Philo turned two. Philo and her two siblings grew up in Harrow, a suburb of London. Her father is a property manager, and, Philo told Rawsthorn, he is "of the school that you need one pair of shoes, one pair of pants, one of everything and you only buy another one when it falls apart." Her mother, who worked as a graphic designer and an art dealer, has always been more interested in clothes. She recalls her mother going to her parent-teacher meetings at school in an Yves Saint Laurent coat and jeans in the rain.

While Philo has never enjoyed shopping, she was always particular about what she wore. At the age of ten, she reworked her school leotard to make it look like something Madonna might wear. "My mother used to dress me in quite good-taste clothes, and I really wanted things that were sparkly and spangly and trashy and nasty. I don't know if I ever chose fashion, it was just there in me," Philo told Alexandra Shulman in an interview during the 2014 British *Vogue* Festival in London, as quoted by Hattie Crisell for *New York* (30 Mar. 2014). Her parents eventually bought her a sewing machine when she was fourteen.

After high school, Philo finished a foundation course at Wimbledon College of Art before enrolling at Central Saint Martins College, a prestigious design school in London. As a student she was inspired by brands like Helmut Lang and Jil Sander, both of which defined the radical minimalist aesthetic of the 1990s. While Philo has described her college tastes as "experimental," she told Rawsthorn, "I've always been attracted to the wilder things, but not when it comes to my own work. I've always had a sense that if I can't wear it, what's the point?"

## EARLY CAREER WITH CHLOÉ

After graduating in 1996, Philo joined Stella McCartney, her former Central Saint Martins classmate and the daughter of former Beatles star Paul McCartney, to work on her first collection at the iconic French label Chloé in Paris. McCartney, then just twenty-five years old, replaced Karl Lagerfeld as creative director of the brand that year. Lagerfeld, who was then in his sixties, was displeased by the choice, sniping to *Women's Wear Daily*, as quoted by Amy M. Spindler for the *New York Times* (22 Apr. 1997), "Let's hope she is as gifted as her father."

McCartney and Philo were under enormous pressure to impress with the label's spring/summer collection for 1998. "We were very young and it was fun," Philo recalled to Rawsthorn, "but there was a lot of work to be done." Chloé, founded in 1952, has always aimed its designs at fashionable young women. In the 1960s and 1970s, during the height of Lagerfeld's career with the label, Chloé outfitted sexy, feminine stars like Brigitte Bardot, Grace Kelly, and McCartney's mother, Linda. McCartney's first collection, inspired by her glamorous London friends, was a continuation of that tradition and featured of-the-moment supermodels Naomi Campbell and Kate Moss. Her designs for Chloé were romantic and bohemian—not at all of the masculine, structured shape that would define Philo's later career.

In 2001 McCartney left to start her own label. Philo stayed at Chloé and succeeded McCartney as creative director that same year. "At Chloé, it was very clear from the beginning that there was a Chloé aesthetic, and my job was to continue doing that," Philo told Shulman. As the head of Chloé, Philo designed frilly, vintage-inspired pieces and baby-doll dresses, favoring fabrics like chiffon, and chunky heels. She also designed the outrageously popular Paddington bag (a squashy, cylindrical satchel with long, sturdy straps and an oversized padlock). "It was widely understood that the secret of Chloé's turnaround had been Philo's ability to identify what the label's young customers might like to wear even before they'd realized it for themselves," Su-

sannah Frankel wrote for the *Independent* (16 July 2011).

Under Philo, Chloé—true to its roots—was playful and girlish but also, some journalists appeared to suggest, a bit vapid. "If Ms. Philo's message is resonating at the moment it is perhaps because it isn't much of a message at all. Unlike, say, a Tom Ford, she does not attach her personal tastes to some larger ideology about the way women should comport themselves," Ginia Bellafante wrote for the *New York Times* (13 Apr. 2004). In 2004 the British Fashion Council honored her with the prestigious designer of the year award for the first time at the British Fashion Awards.

## REINVENTING CÉLINE

Exhausted from taking care of her first child and commuting back and forth between Paris and London, Philo left Chloé in 2006. For the next two years she focused on her young family, essentially removing herself from the fashion world. "I got back to basics . . . I really stepped out of fashion. I didn't look at the collections, didn't read magazines, didn't buy much," she confided to Rawsthorn.

By 2008, however, when she was approached by executives at Céline, she was itching to return to the chaotic but rewarding world of deadlines and runways. "I hadn't ever thought much about Céline before I was approached," Philo told Frankel, "but then I looked at everything they were doing and it felt very irrelevant." This reality appealed to Philo—it meant she could wipe the slate clean and rebuild the brand in her own image. As Vanessa Friedman wrote for the *Financial Times* (8 Oct. 2010), the idea that a designer would deign to totally reimagine an existing house "is something of a fashion apostasy," but Philo has successfully used aspects of Céline as it used to be—conservative yet alluring and thoroughly Parisian—to make something new. She recognized the potential of the brand but was firm about the terms of her employment: she would remain in London, working out of a studio in Cavendish Square, and she would exercise total design control.

The older, wiser Philo has a philosophy—though true to form, she hates to verbalize it—and a vision that dictates everything from the precise tailoring of a suit to the spacing of the label's spare logo. "I wanted something that felt honest, that was a mixture of what I want to wear and how I want to live," she told Friedman. "I felt it needed to be quite simple and very real."

Among her most popular designs are her collarless shirts, creamy camel coats, leather T-shirts, silk pants, and famously fur-lined Birkenstocks. Her structured leather handbags are among the most coveted—and most expensive—in the industry. A single piece from the label can cost thousands of dollars, but Philo insists that each one is built to last. As for an overarching philosophy, which she was criticized for lacking at Chloé, her designs suggest that women should "comport themselves" the way Philo does—powerfully and without compromise.

Céline does not have a Twitter account or post photos on Instagram. The label does not sell clothes online, and during Philo's short tenure, the company has closed more stores than it has opened. Nevertheless, Philo was once again presented with the British designer of the year award in 2010 before being named one of *Time* magazine's one hundred most influential people in 2014. In early 2015 one of Céline's advertising campaigns featured the eighty-year-old writer Joan Didion. Didion is an unlikely fashion model, but like Céline she is cool, precise, and detached.

## PERSONAL LIFE

Philo met Max Wigram, a London art dealer, in 2000. The couple married in 2004, though they maintained a two-city relationship—Wigram based in London and Philo in Paris with Chloé—even after the birth of their daughter, Maya, that same year. After moving back to London and instituting a break from work, she had a second child, a son named Marlowe, in 2007. Five years later, Philo had her third child, a son named Arthur. She and her family live in London, though Céline is based in Paris.

Additionally, Philo has always maintained a desire to stay out of the public spotlight, practicing a kind of minimalism in her dealings with the media as well. She explained to Crisell that she has an "innate fear of fame" and prizes her anonymity on the streets of London where she lives. She would prefer to let her designs speak for themselves. "It's never been important to me that my name is above shop windows," she told Frankel, "and I get a lot of comfort out of having something I can stand behind. Let Céline be the name and the front of it, and I just quietly come to work every day and get on with it. It's nice. It fits."

## SUGGESTED READING

Bellafante, Ginia. "At Chloé, Sales Are Up, and the Designs Are Easy." *New York Times*. New York Times, 13 Apr. 2004. Web. 20 July 2015.

Crisell, Hattie. "Phoebe Philo on Creative Freedom at Céline, Her 'Innate Fear of Fame,' and More." *New York*. New York Media, 30 Mar. 2014. Web. 20 July 2015.

Frankel, Susannah. "Phoebe Philo: The British Fashion Designer Who Is Leading the Pack." *Independent*. Independent Digital News, 16 July 2011. Web. 20 July 2015.

Friedman, Vanessa. "Lunch with the *FT*: Phoebe Philo." *Financial Times*. Financial Times, 8 Oct. 2010. Web. 20 July 2015.

Murphy, Robert. "The House That Céline Built." *Wall Street Journal*. Dow Jones, 25 Mar. 2015. Web. 20 July 2015.

Rawsthorn, Alice. "Phoebe Philo's Third Act." *New York Times Style Magazine*. New York Times, 25 Feb. 2010. Web. 20 July 2015.

Spindler, Amy M. "Stella McCartney: Ready for Chloé." *New York Times*. New York Times, 22 Apr. 1997. Web. 20 July 2015.

—Molly Hagan

# Clifford Pickover

**Born:** August 15, 1957
**Occupation:** Futurist and writer

"My primary interest," Clifford Pickover told David Jay Brown for the blog *Mavericks of the Mind* (19 Nov. 2011), "is in finding new ways to continually expand creativity by melding art, science, mathematics and seemingly disparate areas of human endeavor. I seek not only to expand the mind but to shatter it." Pickover is a molecular biologist by training and the author of over forty books of popular science and science fiction, including three tomes in the Sterling Milestones series (produced by Sterling Publishing), for which he is well known: *The Math Book: From Pythagoras to the 57th Dimension* (2009), *The Physics Book: From the Big Bang to Quantum Resurrection* (2011), and *The Medical Book: From Witch Doctors to Robot Surgeons* (2012). The longtime IBM researcher has been named in numerous patents for computer technology inventions. He designed visual puzzles and brainteasers as the Brain Boggler columnist for *Discover* magazine and has previously served as the associate editor of the journals *Computers and Graphics, Computers in Physics,* and *Theta.* Pickover is voraciously intelligent and somewhat eccentric. His interviews are littered with references to art and literature, and his outlook is quasi-mystical. Unlike many scientists, Pickover is interested in theology and has penned a handful of books about God and science. He is also a futurist and is just as happy discussing the mind-melting possibilities of an infinite universe as he is discussing mathematical forms. "Consider this," he mused in an interview with Cynthia Magriel Wetzler for the *New York Times* (18 Feb. 2007). "By the laws of chance alone it is probable that replicas of our Earth and configurations of atoms just like yours, or variants of you, exist somewhere else in an infinite cosmos. It is likely that right now you have green eyes and fangs and are kissing someone who speaks an exotic Etruscan-Slovenian blend in some other pocket of the universe."

Pickover may not be as well known as popular scientists such as astrophysicist Neil deGrasse Tyson or evolutionary biologist Richard Dawkins, but he has a strong online following. He appears on countless personal blogs and tweets to his thousands of followers several times a day. Like any good teacher, Pickover derives his popularity from his ability to capture his readers' imagination. Pickover embraces the creative aspects of science and discovery—even when they occasionally undermine his credibility—and cites science fiction as an inspiration in his scientific work. Science fiction, Pickover told Brown, "is a literature of change" because its subjects are "poised on the edge of what is and what might be."

### EARLY LIFE AND EDUCATION

Pickover was born on August 15, 1957, in Ocean, New Jersey. His father, Merwin, worked as an electrical engineer, and his mother, Virginia, was a teacher. Pickover expressed an early and extreme love for anatomy and biology. "While growing up in New Jersey, my bedroom featured plastic anatomical models of the heart, brain, head, eye, and ear," he told Carter Bowles for the blog *Trending Sideways* (15 Nov. 2012). "My walls were covered with posters of organ systems rendered in exquisite precision." He also fell in love with writing and words and devoured science-fiction stories such as Henry Hasse's 1936 short story "He Who Shrank," one of his favorites, which explores a world of multiple universes.

Biology was Pickover's favorite subject in high school. He also became interested in science writing after reading *The Unexpected Hanging and Other Mathematical Diversions* (1969) by Martin Gardner, who wrote logic puzzles for *Scientific American.* (Pickover would later dedicate his book *The Math Book* to Gardner, who is now deceased.) He enrolled in the class of 1979 at Franklin and Marshall College in Lancaster, Pennsylvania, and completed a bachelor's degree in biology. Pickover then pursued his doctoral degree at Yale University, earning his PhD in molecular biophysics and biochemistry there in 1982.

### IBM AND FRACTALS

Pickover was hired as a researcher by the IBM Thomas J. Watson Research Center in 1982, where he has worked for over three decades. He is currently the editor in chief of the *IBM Journal of Research and Development.* Through his work at IBM, Pickover first encountered fractals, which are infinitely repeating irregular geometrical patterns. A mathematician at IBM named Benoît Mandelbrot discovered fractals in the mid-1970s. Pickover was riveted when he heard Mandelbrot speak several years later. Fractals, which branch outward like tree branches, appear everywhere in nature—in weather systems, coastlines, and even organs in the human body. Mandelbrot said that one can create a fractal by taking a smooth shape, like a triangle, and breaking it down into pieces over and over again, in endless repetition. (In mathematics, this is known as iteration.) Fractals are also unique in their self-similarity, which means that each section of a fractal shape looks the same from up close and far away. Fractal geometry forever changed the way mathematicians saw the natural world. It also revolutionized computer graphics and special effects. For the first time, designers could construct irregular shapes such as mountains and landscapes using a computer.

Computers made exploring fractals easy—iteration achieved through the click of a button—and visually stimulating. In the early 1990s Pickover used an IBM Power Visualization System to create fractal patterns. He hoped that the graphics would bring with them mathematical inspiration. "Sometimes I consider myself a fisherman," he told Mark Frauenfelder for *Wired* magazine (May–June 1993). "Computer programs and ideas are the hooks, rods, and reels. Computer pictures are the trophies and delicious meals." He continued, "A fisherman does not always know what the waters will yield; however a fisherman may know where the fishing is good, where the waters are fertile, what type of bait to use. Often the specific catch is a surprise, and this is the enjoyment of the sport."

## POP–SCIENCE BOOKS

Pickover wrote about fractals, computer graphics, and puzzles in his first book, *Computers, Pattern, Chaos, and Beauty: Graphics from an Unseen World* (1990). The book's structure is scattered, with different sections discussing different aspects of visual computing. "There are no propositions, proofs, or purely mathematical sections, but understanding all of the material requires knowledge of algebra, trigonometry, calculus, differential equations, complex variables, and various special functions and analysis techniques," Sam Hobbs wrote in a positive review for the now-defunct computer magazine *C/C++ Users Journal* (Sept. 1991). "However, just as the book covers a wide range of topics, material is discussed at widely different levels of mathematical sophistication."

His first book might have been fairly technical, but the majority of Pickover's books could be categorized as popular science. He is known for exploring intriguing ideas—fractals, black holes, madness, time travel—in an irreverent way. His books are often a collage of quotes, illustrations, brainteasers, and text. For example, in *Time: A Traveler's Guide* (1998), Pickover divides each chapter into two parts. The first part follows the fictional story of a music museum curator, his alien assistant, and a human woman. The second part describes the underlying science of the first, cleverly demonstrating the relationship between fiction and reality. *Strange Brains and Genius: The Secret Lives of Eccentric Scientists and Madmen* (1999) and *Archimedes to Hawking: Laws of Science and the Great Minds behind Them* (2008) are more straightforward. Pickover is a collector of quotes and anecdotes from famous thinkers, and his trove of tidbits is on full display in these books. A reviewer for *Kirkus* (1 May 1998) wrote of *Strange Brains and Genius*, "The second to last chapter is entitled, 'Curiosity Smorgasbord,' and that is indeed how the whole book feels—a collection of profiles, anecdotes, interviews, and factoids."

## MILESTONES, PUZZLES AND SCI-FI

Pickover's best-known works are three tomes on three different fields of science that he wrote for the Sterling Milestones series: *The Math*

*Book* (2009), *The Physics Book* (2011), and *The Medical Book* (2012). In 2011 Pickover won the Neumann Prize from the British Society for the History of Mathematics (BSHM) for *The Math Book*. The structure of the books complements Pickover's tendency to be discursive in his writing, and his collection of "fun facts" only makes the educational material more interesting and not, as with some of his other work, more confusing. Alex Knapp, in a glowing review of *The Physics Book* for *Forbes* magazine (25 Oct. 2011), wrote, "[Pickover's] language is conversational and extremely accessible, all without sacrificing accuracy." He concluded, "This is a terrific book for anyone interested in physics, from casual readers to Nobel Laureates."

Pickover likes to include illustrations and brainteasers in many of his books. (He even runs the website Reality Carnival, which is a compilation of brain-twisting facts, paradoxes, and bad jokes about math and science.) At various points during his career, Pickover has been in charge of developing puzzles for major science magazines. He was the Brain Strain columnist at *Odyssey* magazine and the Brain Boggler columnist for *Discover* for many years. He is also the author of several science-fiction novels, including *Egg Drop Soup, Sushi Never Sleeps, Liquid Earth*, and *The Lobotomy Club*, all published in 2002 as Pickover's Neoreality series. Each book explores a reality closely related, yet totally different, from the one we know. Religion, or some manner of spirituality, and fractals are recurring themes. In *The Lobotomy Club*, a group of believers perform brain surgery on one another in order to experience religious visions. In *Sushi Never Sleeps*, Pickover imagines a "fractal society" in which living things exist in different size scales.

Pickover is a prolific writer and a savvy marketer, but occasionally, his books are turned down for publication. The determined Pickover simply self-publishes them and uses thinly veiled quotes from his rejection letters as pull quotes.

## INVESTIGATIONS OF THE SPIRITUAL AND PARANORMAL

Pickover's scientific interests are sometimes steeped in mysticism. "I believe the universe has facets we'll never truly understand . . . but at heart I'm skeptical about ESP, telepathy [*sic*], precognition, haruspicy, cephalomancy, and other paranormal phenomena until we have very conclusive scientific results," Pickover told Brown. Nevertheless, he lists these very subjects as among the most pressing scientific inquiries of the day. He is also interested in a creature known as a DMT machine elf. DMT (dimethyltryptamine) is a psychedelic drug that produces hallucinatory visions in those who take it. (Speaking with Brown about the subject, Pickover claimed never to have had a "drug-induced psychedelic experience" himself.) DMT users have reported visiting strange creatures that exist in a world of machines and fractal patterns. Pickover writes a lot about those elves, and his 2005 book *Sex, Drugs, Einstein, & Elves: Sushi, Psychedelics, Parallel Universes, and the Quest for Transcendence*, is dedicated to them. Pickover is a respected thinker, but his enthusiasm for the paranormal has somewhat diminished his scientific reputation.

Pickover has also written extensively about science and theology. He discusses mathematics and religion in *The Loom of God: Mathematical Tapestries at the Edge of Time* (1997), and in *The Paradox of God and the Science of Omniscience* (2002), he explores the concept of an omniscient, omnipresent, and omnipotent being, which knows all things, is everywhere at all times, and is all-powerful.

Pickover lives in Yorktown Heights, New York.

## SUGGESTED READING

Bowles, Carter. "Cliff Pickover Brings Medical Science to Life with 'The Medical Book.'" *Trending Sideways*. Bowles, 15 Nov. 2012. Web. 30 Apr. 2014.

Brown, David Jay. "Clifford Pickover." *Mavericks of the Mind*. Brown, 19 Nov. 2011. Web. 1 May 2014.

Frauenfelder, Mark. "Fishing: Mark Frauenfelder Pulls Up Clifford Pickover's Startling Imagery." *Wired*. Condé Nast, May–June. 1993. Web. 30 Apr. 2014.

Knapp, Alex. Rev. of *The Physics Book*, by Clifford Pickover. *Forbes*. Forbes.com, 25 Oct. 2011. Web. 1 May 2014.

Rothstein, Edward. "Finding the Universal Laws That Are There, Waiting . . ." *New York Times*. New York Times, 10 Jan. 2004. Web. 30 Apr. 2014.

Wetzler, Cynthia Magriel. "Celebrating Those Who Leave Some of Themselves in Their Work." *New York Times*. New York Times, 18 Feb. 2007. Web. 30 Apr. 2014.

## SELECTED WORKS

*Computers, Pattern, Chaos, and Beauty: Graphics from an Unseen World*, 1990; *Archimedes to Hawking: Laws of Science and the Great Minds behind Them*, 2008; *The Math Book: From Pythagoras to the 57th Dimension*, 2009; *The Physics Book: From the Big Bang to Quantum Resurrection*, 2011; *The Medical Book: From Witch Doctors to Robot Surgeons*, 2012; *The Book of Black: Black Holes, Black Death, Black Forest Cake and Other Dark Sides of Life*, 2013

—Molly Hagan

# Pitbull

**Born:** January 15, 1981
**Occupation:** Rapper

As a Cuban American who raps in both Spanish and English, Pitbull has successfully created music that appeals to multicultural audiences, defying convention in a historically African American genre. Pitbull's early success came through his collaborations with rapper/producer Lil Jon, whose pioneering crunk sound resulted in the bass-heavy, party tracks "Culo" (2004), "The Anthem" (2008), and "Krazy" (2008).

In 2009 Pitbull capitalized on the burgeoning Eurodance movement (characterized by a disco beat, synthesizers, and a four-on-the-floor groove), successfully transitioning to the pop world with his breakthrough solo hit "I Know You Want Me." With nine studio albums under his belt and a stream of high-profile collaborations with Ne-Yo, Jennifer Lopez, Chris Brown, and Ke$ha, among others, Pitbull has remained a pop music fixture. In response to the claims that he has become overexposed, the rapper told Leila Cobo for *Billboard* (8 Oct. 2010), "You always have to be relevant. I've never been a traditional artist. I'm a survivor."

## EARLY LIFE

Pitbull was born Armando Christian Pérez on January 15, 1981, to Cuban expatriates in Miami, Florida. His mother, Alysha Acosta, came to the Magic City in the early 1960s, as part of Operation Peter Pan, a mass evacuation of more than fourteen thousand children whose parents opposed Fidel Castro's communist regime. When Pitbull was four, his parents, both of whom struggled with addiction, split up. He

Kevin Winter/Getty Images for Clear Channel

moved frequently with his mother, who juggled various jobs as a house cleaner, telemarketer, and fast-food manager.

Pitbull was long estranged from his father, José Antonio Armando Pérez Torres, a small-time hustler and drug dealer who occasionally took him to the local tavern and encouraged him to recite the works of Cuban independence leader José Martí. He was bitten by the performing bug, telling Nischelle Turner for *CNN* (20 June 2014) that "being able to move a bar full of people over one poem, it was definitely mind-blowing for me." He added, "It also showed me what my mom, my mother has always told me. The pen is mightier than the sword."

## LAUNCHING HIS RAP CAREER

However, by his early teens, Pitbull chose to follow in his charismatic father's footsteps by selling drugs—a decision that put him at odds with his mother. "He's the one who put the hustle in my blood," he told Simon Vozick-Levinson for *Rolling Stone* (14 Nov. 2012). When Pitbull was sixteen, his mother kicked him out of the house, and he briefly lived with a foster family in Roswell, Georgia, before moving back home. Following a stint at South Miami Senior High School, Pitbull, a fan of rappers Nas and the Notorious B.I.G., attended Miami Coral Park Senior High School, where his drama teacher, Hope Martinez, first witnessed his ability during a freestyle rap battle.

Impressed by his talent, Martinez helped Pitbull land a role as a music video extra for hip-hop artist DMX. During filming, Pitbull won a freestyle contest against a member of DMX's crew, attracting the attention of Def Jam Records executive Irv Gotti, who advised him to start writing his own songs. After graduating in 1999, Pitbull launched a rap career, adopting the evocative stage name because the tenacious dog breed is "too stupid to lose," he explained to Teresa Wiltz for the *Washington Post* (25 July 2004). "They're basically everything that I am." The budding Cuban American performer also made the unique decision to rap in both English and Spanish.

## LEARNING THE INDUSTRY ROPES

Pitbull's demo found its way into the hands of Luther "Luke" Campbell, former front man for the controversial Miami rap group 2 Live Crew and founder of Luke Records. After signing with Jullian Boothe of Miami-based Slip-N-Slide Records, in 2001, Pitbull toured the United States with Campbell and appeared on his solo track "Lollipop" (2001). The veteran rapper also served as a mentor to his young protégé. "From Luke, I learned how to do everything on my own . . . how to be independent and basically work around the labels," Pitbull told Soren Baker for the *Los Angeles Times* (29 Dec. 2005).

Pitbull's "Lollipop" collaboration caught the attention of the Diaz brothers, music producers who subsequently introduced him to Robert Fernandez, the head of an artist development agency. With his Luke Records contract expiring, Pitbull worked with Fernandez to create more radio-friendly music. Fernandez also introduced Pitbull to Atlanta-based rapper and producer Lil Jon, a pioneer of the southern-flavored party rap known as crunk. In addition to offering Pitbull a track ("Pitbull's Cuban Ride Out") on his 2002 double-platinum album *Kings of Crunk*, Lil Jon also convinced director John Singleton to include the newcomer's song "Oye" on the *2 Fast 2 Furious* soundtrack (2003).

## M.I.A.M.I.

Pitbull generated local buzz with the release of his street compilations or mixtapes, *Unleashed Vol.1* (2002) and *Unleashed Vol. 2* (2003). His hometown tribute song "Welcome 2 Miami"—a remix of Jermaine Dupri's "Welcome to Atlanta"—gained heavy airplay on the city's popular Power 96 radio station (WPOW). Pitbull's hustle started paying off; in November 2003 he signed a long-term deal with New York–based independent label TVT Records, also home to Lil Jon.

Pitbull's full-length studio debut, *M.I.A.M.I.*, an acronym for "money is a major issue" as well as a nod to his home city, was released in late August 2004. The disc, which incorporated Latin hip-hop, crunk, reggaeton, and dancehall rhythms, featured numerous appearances by Lil Jon, most notably the catchy lead single "Culo." Pitfall's ode to the female posterior became his first crossover hit, peaking at number eleven on the Billboard Hot Rap Songs chart and number thirty-two on the Billboard Hot 100. By April 2005, *M.I.A.M.I.* had achieved gold status and spawned three dance singles that charted on the Billboard Rhythmic Top 40: "Back Up," "Dammit Man," and "Toma," another Lil Jon collaboration.

## FINDING HIS POLITICAL VOICE

Also in April, Pitbull announced that he was partnering with music moguls Sean "P. Diddy" Combs and Emilio Estefan to launch Bad Boy Latino, where he would oversee the label's artists-and-repertoire division. The first release under the new label was *Money Is Still a Major Issue* (2005), a collection of Pitbull's remixes and unreleased tracks (or B-sides). By the summer Pitbull had joined Eminem's Anger Management tour.

The Cuban American rapper's political voice was increasingly on display. He was among several Latin American musicians who participated in recording "Nuestro Himno," a Spanish version of the "Star Spangled Banner" that was broadcast on Spanish-language radio stations in late April 2006, to coincide with pro-immigration May Day demonstrations. As a member of Voto Latino's Artist Coalition, Pitbull helped register young Latino Americans to vote via text messaging.

Politics also found its way into Pitbull's music. In July 2006, after Fidel Castro transferred power to his younger brother Raoul, the rapper penned "Ya se acabó," which translates to "It's over." The song, entirely performed in Spanish, was ultimately not included on his sophomore effort, *El Mariel* (2006), which he titled after the 1980 boatlift that brought more than one hundred thousand fellow Cuban refugees to Florida over six months. While that record yielded party-oriented tracks such as "Bojangles" and "Ay Chico (Lengua Afuera)," it also featured songs that tackled weightier issues, including the

antidrug song "Come See Me"; "Blood Is Thicker than Water," which contains a verse protesting the Iraq War; and the somber "Raindrops," in which he mourns the passing of his formerly estranged father, to whom the album is dedicated. *El Mariel* went on to sell more than two hundred thousand copies in the United States and ranked number two on the Billboard Top Rap Albums chart, like its predecessor.

## SWITCH UP

For his third album, the rapper switched gears, from the signature reggaeton sound of his previous records to a mix of techno, hip-hop, and crunk. While *The Boatlift* (2007) boasted two popular singles—"The Anthem" and "Go Girl"—Pitbull blamed disappointing record sales on the lack of promotion by TVT, which also barred the disgruntled rapper from appearing on fellow musicians' records. (After failing to block Miami-based Slip-N-Slide Records from releasing *Welcome to the 305*, a collection of unreleased Pitbull songs recorded in 2001 and 2002, TVT was ordered to pay Slip-N-Slide over nine million dollars in damages.) In February 2008 TVT declared bankruptcy and was acquired by digital music distributor the Orchard that July. After the bankruptcy filing, Pitbull was successful in his bid to be released from his recording contract.

Pitbull resurfaced with another Lil Jon–produced track, "Krazy," which was released by the Orchard in October 2008. By the following February the single had amassed more than a half million units in digital downloads and reached the top twenty of the Billboard Hot Digital Songs and Hot Rap Songs categories. Shortly after the song's release, Pitbull signed a deal with Sony Music Latin to distribute his Spanish-language records. He then decided to partner with Polo Grounds/RCA to release his English-language albums through Sony's RCA/J Records and his own imprint, Mr. 305 Records.

## REACHING LATIN AND INTERNATIONAL AUDIENCES

Pitbull followed up his gold record with the multiplatinum hit "I Know You Want Me," first released in February 2009 by independent electronic label Ultra Records, as part of a "one-off" deal. By August, digital sales for the single, which combined reggaeton with Eurodance rhythms, totaled 1.7 million downloads. It also became his first major international hit, topping the singles charts in Belgium, France, the Netherlands, and Spain. Both "Krazy" and "I Know You Want Me" were included on Pitbull's major-label debut, *Rebelution* (2009), whose title encapsulated his industry struggles. "*Rebelution* stands for a fighter. I feel like I've been fighting in music and creating new ways and new opportunities to make things work even when people thought it wouldn't," he shared with Mariel Concepcion for *Billboard* (22 Aug. 2009). The album became the second to top the Billboard Rap Albums chart; it also yielded Pitbull's second top-ten hit on the Hot 100: the platinum single "Hotel Room Service."

Pitbull's music started gaining wider acceptance among the Latino community. At the 2009 Billboard Latin Music Awards, he took home Latin digital download artist of the year honors. His first foray into the Spanish-language market proved successful; *Armando* (2010), a tribute to his late father, peaked at number two on the Billboard Latin Albums chart and earned gold status. Pitbull further raised his international profile in 2010 with guest appearances on the multiplatinum hit Enrique Iglesias's "I Like It" and Usher's "DJ Got Us Fallin' in Love."

## POP DOMINATION

Pitbull set his sights on a pop crossover with his sixth studio album, *Planet Pit* (2011), for which he adopted the new moniker Mr. Worldwide. To ensure a plethora of radio-friendly hits, he assembled an all-star lineup of top producers (Afrojack, DJ Buddha, Soulshock, Dr. Luke, and David Guetta) and high-profile collaborators (Iglesias, Ne-Yo, Chris Brown, and T-Pain). It paid off: *Planet Pit* became Pitbull's highest-charting US album to date, peaking on the Billboard 200 at number seven and eventually being certified gold. Its success was propelled by the Ne-Yo collaboration "Give Me Everything," Pitbull's first Hot 100 chart-topper, and the T-Pain collaboration "Hey Baby (Drop It to the Floor)," his third top-ten song. Pitbull was featured on Jennifer Lopez's number-three dance hit "On the Floor." That year he was named the urban artist of the year at Premio Lo Nuestro, the longest-running Latin music awards show.

For his follow-up, *Global Warming* (2012), the rapper applied the same formula, with more modest results. The album spawned the platinum, top-ten hit "Feel This Moment," featuring Christina Aguilera, as well as the double-platinum "Don't Stop the Party" and "Back in Time," both top-twenty singles. Pitbull scored his second number-one single with "Timber," a country-tinged duet with Ke$ha and the lead track from his *Meltdown EP* (2013). He joined forces again with Lopez for "We Are One," the 2014 FIFA World Cup theme song and the second single from his eighth studio album, *Globalization* (2014), which also yielded the top-ten hit "Time of Our Lives," another collaboration with Ne-Yo. Pitbull's *Dale* (2015) was his first Spanish-language album in five years. Speaking of the creative process, Pitbull explained to Cobo, "Every track has its own way of coming together."

## OTHER VENTURES

In May 2007 Pitbull branched out into television, serving as host and executive producer of the half-hour sketch comedy/variety series *Pitbull's La Esquina*, which was shot in Miami's Little Havana neighborhood and aired on Mun2, NBCUniversal's bilingual cable channel.

With more than twenty million Twitter followers and over two million Instagram subscribers, Pitbull has also managed to parlay his celebrity into a strategic partnership with Playboy Enterprises and endorsement deals with Kodak, Chrysler, Bud Light, Dr. Pepper, Voli Vodka, and Zumba Fitness, which has designed workout programs set to his music. In addition to having a partial stake in Sheets Energy Strips, Ecolo-Blue water-filtration system, and the Miami Subs Grill sandwich chain, Pitbull has launched a line of fragrances and sunglasses.

## PERSONAL LIFE

The unmarried father of six is notoriously private about his personal life, although he has publicly advocated for charter-school education because three of his children are enrolled in them.

## SUGGESTED READING

Baker, Soren. "A Natural to Use Bilingual Rap." *Los Angeles Times.* Los Angeles Times, 25 Nov. 2011. Web. 30 June 2015.

Cobo, Leila. "Pitbull Crosses Over with Two New Albums." *Billboard.* Billboard, 8 Oct. 2010. Web. 30 June 2015.

Concepcion, Mariel. "Miami Rapper Pitbull Ready for *Rebelution.*" *Billboard* 22 Aug. 2009: 29. Print.

Turner, Nischelle. "CNN Spotlight: Pitbull." *CNN.* Cable News Network, 2 June 2014. Web. 30 June 2015.

Vozick-Levinson, Simon. "Pitbull's Global Hustle Can't Be Stopped." *Rolling Stone*. Rolling Stone, 14 Nov. 2012. Web. 30 June 2015.

Wiltz, Teresa. "Hustling to the Beat." *Washington Post*. Washington Post, 25 July 2004. Web. 30 June 2015.

## SELECTED WORKS

*M.I.A.M.I.*, 2004; *Money Is Still a Major Issue*, 2005; *El Mariel*, 2006; *The Boatlift*, 2007; *Rebelution*, 2009; *Armando*, 2010; *Planet Pit*, 2011; *Global Warming*, 2012; *Globalization*, 2014

—Bertha Muteba

# Ai-jen Poo

**Born:** ca. 1974

**Occupation:** Labor organizer and activist

In 2014, when Ai-jen Poo, director of the National Domestic Workers Alliance, was awarded a John D. and Catherine T. MacArthur Foundation fellowship, the organization cited her "compelling vision of the value of home-based care work [that] is transforming the landscape of working conditions and labor standards for domestic or private-household workers" and praised her for creating "a vibrant, worker-led movement."

The editors of *Time* magazine had recognized

David Shankbone/Wikimedia Commons

her work in 2012, naming her one of the most influential people in the world. In the April 18, 2012, issue of the magazine, Gloria Steinman was effusive in her praise: "Once in a while, there comes along a gifted organizer—think of the radical empathy of Jane Addams or the populist tactics of Cesar Chavez—who knows how to create social change from the bottom up," Steinman wrote. Lauding the fact that Poo had helped spearhead the passage of the nation's first Domestic Workers' Bill of Rights, which entitles domestic workers in New York State to overtime pay, one day off per week, and three days of paid leave per year, Steinman continued, "Ai-jen Poo has done this by showing the humanity of a long devalued kind of work. This goes beyond organizing to transforming."

Despite such accolades, Poo is widely recognized as a humble person who prefers the spotlight to be on the National Domestic Workers Alliance, rather than on herself. "[Awards are] really recognition of both the importance of domestic work in society today and the significance of domestic workers organizing, advocacy and leadership in the social change arena," she told Nathalie Alonso for *Columbia College Today* (Fall 2012). "I feel proud to be a part of a movement that inspires so many people."

## EARLY YEARS AND EDUCATION

Ai-jen Poo was born in Pittsburgh, Pennsylvania. (Some reputable sources describe her, however, as a native of New Haven, Connecticut.) Her parents had emigrated from Taiwan as graduate students; her father, Mu-ming Poo, is a molecular neurobiologist, and her mother, an oncologist. She has one sister, Ting Poo, a film editor.

In his native country, then led by Chiang Kai-shek, Mu-ming had been a pro-democracy activist, and Poo was deeply influenced by his activities. (He now teaches and conducts research at the University of California, Berkeley.) She was even more deeply influenced by her mother, who ran the household with no domestic help whatsoever, despite studying for a PhD in chemistry, working initially as a lab technician, and learning English. "I don't remember ever seeing her sit down and take a break or watch a movie or do anything for herself," Poo told Barbara Ehrenreich for *T Magazine* (1 May 2011). "She was always exhausted."

Poo attended the academically rigorous Phillips Academy in Andover, Massachusetts. Her propensity for activism was evident early on, and she once skipped an address by President George H. W. Bush (himself a Phillips alum) in order to take part in a pro-choice rally. Upon graduating from the school in 1992, Poo, who was considering becoming a professional potter, entered Washington University in St. Louis, Missouri. After a year there, she transferred to Columbia University in New York City, excited to be in one of the cultural capitals of the world.

She soon switched her focus from pottery and art to women's studies. "When I got to Columbia, the women's studies department offered the opportunity to explore the intellectual work that had been done around women's rights and how gender has shaped our world and our history," she explained to Alonso. Columbia, on the Upper West Side of Manhattan, had long been known for its tradition of student activism and volunteerism, and Poo fit right into that environment. She was arrested in 1995 for blocking one of the city's major bridges during a protest against police brutality, and the following year she took part in campus-wide protests demanding more culturally diverse classes.

While in college Poo also began volunteering at the New York Asian Women's Center, which ran a shelter for victims of domestic abuse, and she was involved with the Committee Against Anti-Asian Violence (CAAAV), which hired her as a paid staff member upon her graduation from Columbia in 1996.

### FIGHTING FOR DOMESTIC WORKERS

While working at the CAAAV, Poo spearheaded a project to organize Asian immigrant women working in low-paying service jobs. It was an era in which several of New York City's garment factories were closing their doors and firing the predominantly female laborers; many of those whose immigration paperwork was in order became home health-care aides, while the undocumented among them flocked to restaurant kitchens, beauty parlors, and casual maid services. None of those situations was enviable: the women typically worked at least twelve hours per day and still remained below the poverty line.

Although the project began with Asian women—mainly Filipina workers—Poo quickly saw the need to branch out into a citywide, multi-ethnic effort. She was particularly moved by one Jamaican woman who approached her after hearing of her work. The woman had been lured to the United States as a teen, believing she could work as a live-in nanny and maid while attending school. Instead, her employers kept her busy from sunrise until late into the night, with no time to attend high school. Even worse, she never saw a dime of her promised wages: the couple employing her claimed they were sending the checks straight to her parents, but because they restricted her access to mail, she could never be certain that they were actually doing so. After almost two decades, she finally escaped with the help of one of the couple's children. "'I don't want to live in a society where people can treat others like that," Poo recalled to Ehrenreich. "And I certainly don't want to raise my own children in a society that doesn't value everyone's humanity."

In 2000, with the help of coworkers from CAAAV, Poo created and was lead organizer of Domestic Workers United, which in 2007 became an affiliate of a larger umbrella group, the National Domestic Workers Alliance (NDWA). Soon after its formation, Poo became the director of the NDWA.

### A BILL OF RIGHTS FOR DOMESTIC WORKERS

Poo and her staffers made dozens of trips to Albany to lobby New York State lawmakers to enact legislation protecting the rights of low-wage domestic workers. They were generally accompanied by large groups of the workers, who donned matching shirts and gathered on the steps of the New York State Capitol building to make their voices heard. After Assemblyman Keith Wright (D-Manhattan) and Senator Diane Savino (D-Brooklyn/Staten Island) introduced such a bill into the state legislature in 2004, some of the workers were invited to share their life stories. Among the most moving, Poo has recalled, was that of an elderly Colombian woman who worked for more than one hundred hours per week, cooking, cleaning, and providing child care for a family of six. For that, she was paid about three dollars per hour—money she used in part to buy insulin for her own child. Living in a sewage-filled basement, she was fired suddenly with no severance pay and no other job lined up. Other workers told harrowing stories of withheld pay, sexual harassment, and similar such indignities.

"The work that nannies, home health-care aides, and housekeepers do represents the 'wild west,'" she explained to Joann Weiner for the *Washington Post* (18 Sept. 2014). "You never quite know what you'll get. Maybe you'll get an employer who will give you time off when you're sick, provide a couple of weeks of paid vacation, pay you overtime when you work well over 40 hours a week and pay for your health insurance. Or, maybe you'll get an employer who forces you to work for up to 100 hours a week, docks your pay when you're sick and gives you no days off during the year." She continued, "Even worse, a bad employer might be one who engages in human trafficking or commits sexual assault."

On November 29, 2010, the state's Domestic Workers' Bill of Rights took effect, three months after Governor David Paterson signed it. The law, which was the first of its kind in the nation, entitles domestic workers in New York State to overtime pay, one day off per week, three paid days off a year after one year with the same employer, and inclusion in the state's Human Rights Law, which protects against sexual harassment and discrimination. The law applies even to undocumented workers. "It was a breakthrough moment," Poo told Alonso. "We forced the state of New York to recognize domestic work as real work that deserves inclusion and protection, and reversed a legacy of exclusion and discrimination." Since passage of the New York law, Hawaii, California, and Massachusetts have followed suit, and other states have organized taskforces or taken other steps toward enacting similar legislation.

## CARING ACROSS GENERATIONS

In recent years Poo has turned her attention to the issues surrounding elder care and the estimated three million home-care providers in the United States. "They help our loved ones eat and bathe while providing emotional support and human connection," she wrote for the *Guardian* (29 Sept. 2014), pointing out that such workers earn an average of less than ten dollars per hour. Citing the fact that by 2035 there will be 11.5 million Americans over the age of eighty-five, she wrote, "We've now entered a new era, where our collective failure to account for family care work has become untenable."

Poo elaborated to Weiner, "Our society should support keeping people in their homes or providing for community-based care, rather than putting the elderly into nursing homes, which provide the most expensive form of care. I'd like to see another 2 million quality jobs in home care, where domestic workers are earning a living wage and have some economic security." To that end, in 2011 Poo spearheaded a new organization called Caring Across Generations, for which she is a codirector. The organization

is devoted to encouraging a cultural shift in the way Americans feel about aging, multigenerational relationships, and caregiving; advocating for effective government policies; and building a platform for multigenerational civic engagement. She has also written a book on the topic, *The Age of Dignity: Preparing for the Elder Boom in a Changing America* (2015).

In 2014 Poo was awarded a fellowship by the John D. and Catherine T. MacArthur Foundation, which came with a stipend of $625,000 to be used to further her cause. She has been named to *Time* magazine's list of the world's 100 most influential people in the world and *Newsweek*'s 150 Fearless Women list, both in 2012. In 2013 she was selected to be a World Economic Forum Young Global Leader. Her many other honors and awards include an Alston Bannerman Fellowship for Organizers of Color (2009) and an American Express NGen Leadership Award (2011).

## PERSONAL LIFE

Poo, who has also mounted initiatives to fight human trafficking and lobby for immigration reform, has on her upper right arm a tattooed image of a tiger—her Chinese zodiac sign. "Fear often gets in the way of our taking risks necessary to make real change in the world," she told Alonso. "The tattoo is a reminder to draw upon my inner tiger and to be courageous in the face of uncertainty in the service of a vision for a better world."

Poo moved to Chicago in June 2014. She commutes to work in Manhattan.

## SUGGESTED READING

Alonso, Nathalie. "The Home Front." *Columbia College Today*. Columbia College Today, Fall 2012. Web. 15 Feb. 2015.

Ehrenreich, Barbara. "The Nannies' Norma Rae." *T Magazine*. New York Times, 1 May 2011. Web. 15 Feb. 2015.

Poo, Ai-jen. "America's Most Invisible Workforce Is the One We Need the Most." *Guardian*. Guardian News and Media, 29 Sept. 2014. Web. 15 Feb. 2015.

Shah, Angilee. "Ai-jen Poo: The Rock Star of Community Organizing." *Dame Magazine*. Dame Media, 24 May 2012. Web. 15 Feb. 2015.

Swarns, Rachel. "A Capstone in a Career Spent Fighting for the Rights of Domestic Workers." *New York Times*. New York Times. 21 Sept. 2014. Web.15 Feb. 2015.

Weiner, Joann. "MacArthur Fellow Ai-jen Poo on Why She Fights for the Rights of Domestic Workers." *Washington Post*. Washington Post, 18 Sept. 2014. Web.15 Feb. 2015.

—Mari Rich

# Ruth Porat

**Born:** 1957

**Occupation:** CFO and executive vice president of Morgan Stanley

Ruth Porat became the chief financial officer (CFO) at Morgan Stanley in 2010. Considered in 2013 for the position of deputy secretary at the United States Department of Treasury under Secretary of the Treasury Jack Lew, Porat withdrew her name in order to remain at Morgan Stanley where she has been employed since 1987. Sources indicate that although Porat has said she wants to work in Washington at some point, she was not pleased with the level of attack that Lew endured during his Senate confirmation. She has assisted companies such as Amazon, Priceline, and eBay in their initial public offerings (IPO). As one of the most powerful women on Wall Street, she advised President George W. Bush and Congress on government bailouts for AIG, Fannie Mae, and Freddie Mac following the 2008 financial crisis. In 2011 she was listed among *Forbes* magazine's one hundred most powerful women in 2011. In 2014 she was named vice chair of the prestigious Economic Club of New York. She is vice chair of Stanford University's board of trustees, on the Bretton Woods Committee, and on the New York Metropolitan Museum of Art's business committee. In addition, she is a board member of both the Council on Foreign Relations and the Brookings Institution's Hutchins Center on Fiscal and Monetary Policy.

## EARLY LIFE AND EDUCATION

Porat was born in Sale, England. Porat's father, Daniel, later moved from England to Cambridge, Massachusetts, where he taught physics at Harvard University. The family then moved to California when Porat was ten, and Daniel spent the next twenty-six years or so as a research engineer for the Stanford Linear Accelerator Center at Stanford University. Porat's mother, Frieda, is a psychologist and is president of a management consulting firm. Her example made it clear to Porat that a woman could have both a career and a successful

Craig Barritt/Getty Images North America

marriage. Her father treated Porat and her brother alike, assuming that Porat would be good at math and have a career.

Because both parents worked, Porat learned to be self-motivated at a young age. As she stated in Barsh and Cranston's *How Remarkable Women Lead* (2009), "When I got home from school, nobody was ever there. I had to do everything on my own. To me, it was obvious that I would work." She graduated from Stanford in 1979 with a degree in economics and international relations, noting how few women were majoring in economics. She then went to the London School of Economics and Political Science, receiving her master's degree in industrial relations in 1981.

For two years she worked for Price Waterhouse, a public accounting firm, before obtaining a master's in business administration from the Wharton School at the University of Pennsylvania. She worked for a time at the Department of Justice in Washington, DC, but the world of business mergers and acquisitions interested her. The challenge of devising a strategy, followed by being able to bring companies together, led her to Morgan Stanley.

## MORGAN STANLEY

Porat joined Morgan Stanley's mergers and acquisitions division in 1987, before the stock market crashed. Despite the hard work and grueling schedule, she was exhilarated to be making deals that regularly made the front page of *The*

*Wall Street Journal*. She worked with several senior members of Wall Street firms and learned how they conducted themselves, setting her an example to follow in her own rise to the top.

When Porat was a second-year associate, a client contacted Morgan Stanley and made clear the expectation that a woman would make the presentation for their product, because women were the primary consumers and a woman's point of view was needed. Although Porat had never been in a boardroom or made a presentation, she was assigned the task and loved it.

In 1993 Porat left Morgan Stanley to join a mentor at Smith Barney. She knew at once it had been a mistake, but she remained at Smith Barney, heading the financial sponsors group, for two years before she returned to Morgan Stanley and took a nonmanagerial position. She did so only after being reassured that she was not being made a public example for leaving. She also was given assurance that there would be opportunity for advancement.

In 2000, Porat moved to London to lead Morgan Stanley's technology investment banking division and returned to the United States a year later, and in 2003 she was named vice chairman of investment banking. Although Porat had little experience in the financial services sector, she was also tapped to lead the financial institutions group (known as FIG) for Morgan Stanley in 2006. Some were surprised by her appointment, but as Derek Kirkland, her predecessor at the FIG, explained to the *Wharton Alumni Magazine* (Spring 2007), "Ruth thoroughly understands the company and [investment banking]."

Porat held both posts until December 2009, and on January 1, 2010, Porat became Morgan Stanley's chief financial officer (CFO).

## FISCAL CRISIS

Fannie Mae (the Federal National Mortgage Association), a publicly traded mortgage company, and Freddie Mac (the Federal Home Loan Mortgage Association), which handled the secondary mortgage market, were government-sponsored enterprises. Fannie Mae was founded in the 1938 as part of Franklin Roosevelt's New Deal in an attempt to widen opportunities for home ownership. It developed into a mixed ownership company in the 1950s and then became a shareholder-owned company in 1968, following the passage of the Housing and Urban Development (HUD) Act. Freddie Mac was established in 1970 to deal with the secondary mortgage market. The two companies

went into conservatorship as a result of the 2008 financial crisis.

Porat played multiple roles following the crisis: she worked directly with Morgan Stanley to assist banks globally to regain firm financial footing; she also co-led a group that in 2010 advised Secretary of the Treasury Hank Paulsen and the White House on handling Freddie Mac and Fannie Mae bailouts, as well as assisting the New York Federal Reserve in dealing with the insurance company AIG (American International Group).

Porat explained to Jeffrey Garten for the Yale University School of Management (19 June 2014) the broad lessons learned from the crisis, especially that "events move far too quickly during a crisis and what you're dealing with is typically, as we called it back then, the least-worst option. There are no good options in the midst of a crisis." She also learned that time is the enemy when dealing with a crisis.

As Susanne Craig of the *New York Times* (10 Nov. 2010) reported, Lee Sachs, a former aide to Treasury Secretary Timothy Geithner, said Porat possessed a "recognition and understanding of the public policy and political implications, positive and negative, of various courses of action." These qualities served her well in dealing with the crisis. Porat was also pleased to announce in 2010 that Morgan Stanley was not part of the United States Securities and Exchange Commission's investigation of collateral debt obligations.

Morgan Stanley emerged stronger afterward. It purchased Citigroup's wealth management assets and became the largest wealth management group in the United States with more than $2 trillion in client assets. Morgan Stanley boasted an 87 percent increase in earnings for the third quarter in 2014 due to increased client activity.

## WORKING FOR WOMEN

Considered one of the most important women in finance, Porat is using her influence to help other women achieve leadership roles. She promoted the passage of national paid family leave legislation to enable women to have children without feeling pressured to leave the workforce. Speaking in April 2014 to a Japan Society event in Manhattan, she noted that women comprise only 15 percent of executive officer positions and only 5 percent of CEOs at Fortune 500 companies. Porat stated that although the percentages were better than they had been half a century earlier, "they're not where they should be, and, in fact, I would say they are an embarrassment."

Throughout her career, Porat's mentors were men because there were not any women in senior positions to show her the way. She has made it a point, therefore, to assist younger women by training and coaching them to rise in the company. One aspect of her coaching is to never assume that hard work will be noticed and will reflect positively on you.

Porat advocates for a balanced mix of work life and personal life and cites her mother's example of successfully mixing a career with a loving family. Porat fears too many women defer having families or leave their careers early because they cannot find this balance.

## PERSONAL LIFE

Porat married Anthony Paduano, then a law student, in December 1983. They have endowed an undergraduate scholarship and a graduate fellowship at Stanford University. They both graduated from the London School of Economics and Political Science. The couple also renovates and sells apartments in New York City.

Porat is the mother of three children and is a two-time breast cancer survivor who continued working after her 2001 diagnosis, assuming that work would help her heal. Porat keeps a note on her desk written by her three sons during the 2008 crisis with AIG when Porat was rarely home. As she told Ben White for Politico.com (22 July 2014), "On one of those nights where we were working through the night, I came home and my three boys left me a little note because they knew I'd at least come home and shower. In their own words, three different personalities underscored how very proud they were and how important they thought the work was."

## SUGGESTED READING

Craig, Susanne. "Dealbook: A Female Wall St. Financial Chief Avoids Pitfalls That Stymied Others." *New York Times*. New York Times, 9 Nov. 2010. Web. 18 Nov. 2014.

DeCambre, Mark. "Porat to Sit Tight." *New York Post*. NYP Holdings, 29 Mar. 2013. Web. 22 Oct. 2014.

"A Deft Touch for Capital Markets Good and Bad: Ruth Porat, WG '87." *Wharton Alumni Magazine: 125 Influential People and Ideas* (Spring 2007): 52. Web. 19 Nov. 2014.

Lacapra, Lauren Tara. "Morgan Stanley's Ruth Porat: The Lack of Women Leaders Is 'An Embarrassment.'" *Business Insider*. Business Insider, 3 Apr. 2014. Web. 19 Nov. 2014.

"Tapping Potential: Encouraging Women's Empowerment in the US & Japan." *Japan Society*. Japan Society, 2 Apr. 2014. Web. 19 Nov. 2014.

"The 25 Most Powerful Women in Finance: No. 3, Ruth Porat." *American Banker*. SourceMedia, 18 Sept. 2013. Web. 29 Oct. 2014.

White, Ben. "Getting There: Ruth Porat: 'The Most Powerful Woman on Wall Street.'" *Politico*. Politico, 22 July 2014. Web. 1 Nov. 2014.

—Judy Johnson, MLS

# Petro Poroshenko

**Born:** September 26, 1965
**Occupation:** President of Ukraine

Since being elected president of Ukraine in May 2014, Petro Poroshenko—a former businessman once known as the Chocolate King because much of his fortune has come from sweets—has been confronted with an escalating civil war in the eastern part of his nation. Pro-Russian separatists in that region have sought to break away from Ukraine at a moment when the Ukrainian government is seeking closer ties with Europe and the West. Poroshenko and other leaders believe that this separatist movement is being supported covertly by the Russian government, led by President Vladimir Putin. Putin has looked to bring Ukraine deeper into the Russian sphere of influence, as it had once been part of the former Soviet Union. Yet Poroshenko—and a wide majority of Ukrainians—wish not only to maintain their nation's independence but also to reshape their country into a modern, free-market democracy. In an interview with Lally Weymouth for the *Washington Post* (25 Apr. 2014) conducted shortly before he became president, Poroshenko said: "People should understand that this is not just a problem of Ukraine. This has broken the whole postwar global security situation." He continued, "The Budapest memorandum of 1994 . . . guaranteed the territorial integrity and sovereignty of my country when we voluntarily gave up the third-largest nuclear arsenal in the world. We received a security guarantee but it is simply not working."

## EARLY LIFE AND EDUCATION

Petro Oleksiyovych Poroshenko was born on September 26, 1965, in the city of Bolhrad, which is located outside Odessa in the southwestern part of Ukraine. He was raised in the central region of Vinnytsya and is a member of Ukraine's Orthodox Church. Ukraine was then part of the Union of Soviet Socialist Republics (USSR), the communist empire that encompassed fifteen republics and was controlled by a totalitarian government located in Moscow, Russia. When the Soviet Union collapsed under economic and political pressures in 1991, Ukraine was given its independence.

Poroshenko, who was a young man during the last years of the Soviet Union, studied international economic relations at the Taras Shevchenko National University of Kyiv from 1982 to 1989; his studies, however, were interrupted by his required military service from 1984 to 1986. Between 1989 and 1992 he served as a postgraduate student assistant in the Department of International Economic Relations at the Taras Shevchenko National University.

## EARLY CAREER IN BUSINESS AND POLITICS

In 1993 Poroshenko took advantage of an opportunity to purchase Ukraine's state-owned confectionary plants. Very quickly the profits from his corporation, Ukrprominvest, earned him the nickname the Chocolate King. His success in sweets enabled him to expand his holdings into construction and media outlets, most

Sascha Steinbach/Getty Images Europe

notably Channel 5 TV, which is a very influential broadcast station in Ukraine. Unlike many other oligarchs whose wealth derived from buying up interests in the former holdings of the Soviet Union, Poroshenko appears to have had no illegal dealings. Orysia Lutsevych, a research fellow with Chatham House's Russia and Eurasia program, told reporters Luke Hardin and Oksana Grytsenko for the *Guardian* (23 May 2014): "His business looks legitimate. It wasn't built on corrupt trade in gas and oil with Russia. . . . He was never involved in any big scandals."

Poroshenko was the CEO of Ukrprominvest from 1993 until 1998, when he decided to run for a seat in the Verkhovna Rada, the lower house of Ukraine's national legislature. Although he ran as a Social Democrat, within two years he formed his own Solidarity Party and then subsequently cofounded the Party of Regions, which was the party of Viktor Yanukovich, who would serve as president of Ukraine from February 2010 to February 2014. By 2002 Poroshenko had parted ways with Yanukovich to join with Viktor Yushchenko—Yanukovich's chief rival—to form the Our Ukraine Party. Despite his shifting political allegiances, Poroshenko remained a member of Verkhovna Rada, serving as deputy head of the National Bank Council of Ukraine from 2000 to 2004 and as head of the Committee on Budget Issues from 2002 to 2005.

In 2004, alongside fellow reformers Viktor Yushchenko and Yulia Tymoshenko, Poroshenko became one of the key leaders of the Orange Revolution—the series of nonviolent protests that ultimately prevented Yanukovich from rigging the presidential election in his favor. In a runoff with Yushchenko that was watched closely by international and national observers, Yanukovich was handily defeated. Under President Yushchenko, Poroshenko served as secretary of the National Security and Defense Council of Ukraine in August 2005. He did not, however, remain in the post long. Charges of corruption were thrown around by various cabinet ministers, particularly between the supporters of Poroshenko and Yulia Tymoshenko, who was then serving as prime minister, over the privatization of state-controlled corporations. The president, in response, dismissed his entire cabinet. As a result, the united leadership of the Orange Revolution collapsed.

Though out of a cabinet job, Poroshenko remained close to Yushchenko, who is godfather to his daughters. He also remained in politics, being reelected to the Verkhovna Rada, where he worked as head of the Committee on Finance and Banking Activity from 2006 to 2007. He served as head of the National Bank Council of Ukraine from 2007 to 2012. He also served as minister of foreign affairs from 2009 to 2010, under President Yushchenko, and as minister of economic development and trade in 2012, under Viktor Yanukovych, who was elected president in 2010. As economic minister he negotiated trade deals and worked to acquire loans from the International Monetary Fund (IMF).

## THE MAIDAN PROTESTS

A major rift in the fabric of Ukrainian political life opened up in December 2013, when President Yanukovich failed to sign a trade deal with the European Union (EU), which Poroshenko, as his nation's foreign minister, had helped to write. Many Ukrainians, particularly younger citizens, wanted closer ties with the West and feared the outsized influence the Russian government, under Vladimir Putin, exerted on Yanukovich. When Yanukovich did not sign the trade deal, citizens took out their frustrations in public protests across the country but particularly in the Maidan Nezalezhnosti, Kyiv's "Independence Square." During the protests Poroshenko—who was in favor of closer ties to Europe and a supporter of the protests both politically and financially—went to the Maidan to attempt to calm the situation by addressing the crowd atop a bulldozer parked between the protesters and police. He was shouted down shortly before the protesters attempted to storm the presidential headquarters in the city. While the police dispersed the student protesters, the protests themselves continued throughout the country. According to various news reports, roughly one hundred people were killed over a two-day period in February 2014, mostly by government snipers opening fire on protestors.

On February 22, 2014, Yanukovich fled Ukraine, taking up his exile in Russia, where he is said to have been granted citizenship. Despite the bloodshed, the protests were considered a success. In his interview with Lally Weymouth, Poroshenko recalled how the organizers of the Maidan won: "You know why we won? Because we were united. There was no difference between the rich and poor people. No difference between people from the west and from the east. There was no dispute between the leaders of the Maidan. We can win only when we are united. Otherwise, Viktor Yanukovych would still be here."

## RUNNING FOR PRESIDENT

The Ukrainian legislature quickly called for new presidential elections to be held on May 25, 2014. Poroshenko immediately threw his hat into the ring, as did his old colleague and sometime rival Yulia Tymoshenko. Poroshenko ran on a platform calling for better ties to Europe and the West, both economically and politically, and widespread reform to end the rampant corruption in his country. He vowed to not only sign the EU trade agreement that the former president refused to sign but also to help modernize Ukraine with loan guarantees from the United States, the EU, and the IMF. "We aren't just talking about just financial support. We're talking about the modernization of my country and zero tolerance for corruption. We cannot survive if we give corruption any chance. Corruption can only exist with an umbrella from the top," Poroshenko told Lally Weymouth. "We need investors to say, 'We trust these guys, and I can try some investments there.' Ukraine is a huge opportunity for investment—foreign, local, even Russian."

In the midst of the 2014 presidential election, however, the shaky Ukrainian political system was dealt another staggering blow when the people of Crimea overwhelmingly voted to break away from Ukraine and to join Russia in a referendum considered dubious by international observers. Two days after the vote in March, Putin signed a bill into law that annexed Crimea. Poroshenko—and most of his countrymen—were outraged. In eastern Ukraine, pro-Russian separatists continued to destabilize the region by seizing control of government buildings in Kharkiv, Donetsk, and Luhansk in April. By May, Donetsk and Luhansk had declared their independence following referendums—although, as with Crimea, the Ukrainian government did not recognize their independence from Ukraine.

## PRESIDENT OF UKRAINE

On May 25, 2014, Poroshenko, as a nonpartisan candidate, handily defeated his next nearest rival, Tymoshenko, and avoided a runoff. After his inauguration on June 7, he vowed to fight for the return of Crimea and to maintain the territorial integrity of Ukraine against pro-Russian separatists and the estimated nine thousand Russian troops he believes are in Ukraine (as of January 2015) and supporting the separatists. In a speech quoted by David M. Herszenhorn for the *New York Times* (6 Apr. 2015), Poroshenko declared: "They started an aggression, they went to war, trying to impose federalization with iron and blood. I will not allow this to happen. Ukrainian people will not allow it to happen."

Although Putin has denied these allegations, Western powers have lined up in support of Ukraine by imposing strict economic sanctions on Russia in the hopes of forcing the Russian government to end its support of the pro-Russian separatists in Ukraine. In June 2014 Poroshenko signed the landmark trade deal with the EU that his predecessor had refused to sign the prior year. A month later severe EU sanctions were put in place against Russia's massive oil companies and banks. In an interview with the *Wall Street Journal* (20 Jan. 2015), Poroshenko told reporters Thorold Barker and Alan Cullison that he believes the sanctions imposed on Russia are working but that he remains in close contact with Putin. "It seems to me that the Ukrainian question is very emotional for [Putin]," he said during the interview. "If you ask if I trust him, my answer would be no."

Beginning in September 2014 Poroshenko worked with various partners to broker a peace deal between the Ukrainian government and the separatists. The deal, however, did not last long and Ukrainian troops and separatists have clashed continually into 2015. According to the United Nations, as of January 2015, more than 4,700 people had been killed in the fighting in eastern Ukraine. By March that number had jumped to approximately 6,000. More than 1.5 million people have been internally displaced or have fled the country. According to a report filed by Eleanor Beardsley for the National Public Radio (NPR) (25 Feb. 2015), one French analyst believes "the separatists and their Russian allies have no intention of stopping the fight." In the same report US secretary of state John F. Kerry described the separatists as an extension of the Russian military.

For his part Poroshenko has vowed not to negotiate with terrorists. He has also expressed a desire to reform his country's government through the decentralization of power and to resist any efforts to "federalize" the country—a Russian proposal that would give a degree of political autonomy to the areas of eastern Ukraine controlled by the separatists. Poroshenko believes any federalization plan would ultimately destabilize the government and fracture the country's unity.

## PERSONAL LIFE

As of 2014 Poroshenko was worth an estimated $1.3 billion. He met his wife, Maryna Anatoliivna Poroshenko, now a cardiologist, at a disco during his student days. The couple have four children: Oleksiy (b. 1985), Yevheniya and Oleksandra (b. 2000), and Mykhailo (b. 2001).

## SUGGESTED READING

Barker, Thorold, and Alan Cullison. "Ukraine President Petro Poroshenko: 'Sanctions Are Working' on Russia." *Wall Street Journal.* Dow Jones, 20 Jan. 2015. Web. 7 Apr. 2015.

Beardsley, Eleanor. "France Warns Russia and Its Allies Not to Advance on Ukrainian Port City." *NPR.* NPR, 25 Feb. 2015. Web. 9 Apr. 2015.

Harding, Luke, and Oksana Grytsenko. "Chocolate Tycoon Heads for Landslide Victory in Ukraine Presidential Election." *Guardian.* Guardian News and Media, 23 May 2014. Web. 7 Apr. 2015.

Herszenhorn, David M. "Ukrainian Leader Is Open to a Vote on Regional Power." *New York Times.* New York Times, 6 Apr. 2015. Web. 9 Apr. 2015.

"Petro Poroshenko." *Petro Poroshenko, President of Ukraine: Official Website.* Ukraine, n.d. Web. 7 Apr. 2015.

Poroshenko, Petro. "Interview with Ukrainian Presidential Candidate Petro Poroshenko." Interview by Lally Weymouth. *Washington Post.* Washington Post, 25 Apr. 2014. Web. 7 Apr. 2015.

—Christopher Mari

# Laurene Powell Jobs

**Born:** November 6, 1963
**Occupation:** Business executive

Laurene Powell Jobs, the widow of Apple founder Steve Jobs, is, according to Ryan Mac of *Forbes,* the richest woman in Silicon Valley and one of the richest women in the world, with a net worth of about $15 billion in 2014. Though she is far less famous than her late husband, Powell Jobs has been working quietly for years as a philanthropist and an advocate for education reform through a business she founded in the early 2000s called Emerson Collective. The organization, whose name references the 1888 Ralph Waldo Emerson essay "Self-Reliance," encourages social reform through entre-

Neilson Barnard/Getty Images North America

preneurship. Prior to Emerson Collective, Powell Jobs cofounded College Track, a nonprofit group that provides afterschool programs and tutoring to college-bound low-income students. Through College Track, she became involved in immigration reform, and in 2013 she commissioned a thirty-minute documentary by the Academy Award–winning filmmaker Davis Guggenheim called *The Dream Is Now*, which advocates for the rights of young, undocumented immigrants.

Powell Jobs may be emerging as a major figure in philanthropy, but according to Laura Arrillaga-Andreessen, a fellow philanthropist and lecturer at Stanford, she still prefers to keep most of her giving anonymous. "If you total up in your mind all of the philanthropic investments that Laurene has made that the public knows about," Arrillaga-Andreessen told Peter Lattman and Claire Cain Miller for the *New York Times* (17 May 2013), "that is probably a fraction of 1 percent of what she actually does, and that's the most I can say."

Jobs, who died of pancreatic cancer at the age of fifty-six on October 5, 2011, was criticized during his lifetime for his lack of interest in philanthropy. He notoriously refused to sign the Giving Pledge, initiated by billionaires Warren Buffet and Bill Gates, in which wealthy people promise to give away more than half of their fortune when they die. Powell Jobs has not signed the pledge either. "Whether someone signs something is not what's important," she told Lattman and Cain Miller. "It's what they do and how they do it that matters." Most

of Powell Jobs's fortune is in Apple and Disney stock, and she is the largest shareholder in the Walt Disney Company with over 130 million shares inherited from her late husband. (Jobs owned Pixar Studios, which was acquired by Disney in 2006.)

## EARLY LIFE AND EDUCATION

Powell Jobs was born on November 6, 1963, and was raised in West Milford, New Jersey. Her father was a pilot in the Marine Corps who died when Powell Jobs was young. According to Steve Jobs biographer Walter Isaacson, Powell Jobs's father was leading a crippled plane in for a landing. When the crippled plane hit his, he continued flying away from a residential area rather than eject in time to save himself, and he died in the resulting crash in Santa Ana, California. Powell Jobs's mother eventually remarried, and although the marriage was unhappy, her mother felt she could not leave because she had no way to support herself and her four children. "The lesson I learned was clear, that I always wanted to be self-sufficient," Powell Jobs explained to Isaacson. "I took pride in that. My relationship with money is that it's a tool to be self-sufficient, but it's not something that is a part of who I am."

Powell Jobs earned degrees in political science and economics from the Wharton School of Business at University of Pennsylvania in 1985. After graduation, she worked for the investment banking company Goldman Sachs as a fixed-income trading strategist reporting directly to Jon Corzine, who became a US senator in 2001 and governor of New Jersey in 2006. Powell Jobs found the work at Goldman Sachs unsatisfying, however, and she quit after three years in order to move to Florence, Italy, where she lived for the next eight months. When she returned to the United States, Powell Jobs enrolled as a graduate student at the Stanford Graduate School of Business in California.

## MARRIAGE TO STEVE JOBS

In October 1989, Steve Jobs, who six months earlier had been named Entrepreneur of the Decade by *Inc.* magazine, was speaking at the Stanford Graduate School of Business, and Powell Jobs, who had arrived late, was seated in a reserved seat next to him before he was called to speak. "I looked to my right, and there was a beautiful girl there, so we started chatting while I was waiting to be introduced," Jobs told Isaacson. Jobs was supposed to have a business dinner that evening, but instead he decided that he would rather spend time with the woman he had just met. The two went out to dinner that night, and Jobs proposed a few months later on January 1, 1990. Powell Jobs accepted, but in holding with Jobs's infamously hot-and-cold personality, Jobs didn't mention marriage again for months. In September 1990, Powell Jobs moved out of Steve Jobs's house, and there followed an unusual period of indecision for Jobs before he presented his fiancée with a ring in October. They were married in a Zen Buddhist ceremony at the Ahwahnee Hotel at Yosemite National Park on March 18, 1991. The couple moved to Palo Alto, California, and raised three children and another daughter named Lisa Brennan-Jobs who was born in 1978 following a relationship Jobs had with Chris-Ann Brennan.

Though Jobs's personality was tempestuous, Isaacson reports that his marriage to Powell Jobs was not. Jobs admitted to Isaacson that he could be a selfish man, and that often he did not appreciate his wife as much as she deserved to be appreciated. "Laurene had to deal with that, and also me being sick," he said in one emotional interview with Isaacson before his death. "I know that living with me is not a bowl of cherries."

## COLLEGE TRACK

After graduating from Stanford with her MBA in 1991, Powell Jobs cofounded a natural foods company called Terravera. (As a student she had spent time working in marketing at the juice company, Odwalla.) Terravera specialized in ready-to-eat organic meals, which were then sold to stores throughout northern California. As her children grew older, however, her role in the company diminished, and in 1995, she began volunteering as a mentor to students at Carlmont High School in Belmont, California, through a program called AVID (Advancement via Individual Determination). She saw that in their freshman year, minority students were often placed in remedial classes. As a result, smart students languished in classes taught at one level or more below their ability. "If you're a kid who has taken algebra in middle school and gotten an A and are put in ninth grade in a pre-algebra class, it can make you very angry," she told Carolyne Zinko for the *San Francisco Chronicle* (8 June 2008). "Given that you're going to high school 45 minutes away, your parents are working two jobs, parental involvement is needed and there's one counselor per 1,600 students, you feel stuck. This is why kids get disenfranchised." Disturbed by what she saw, Powell Jobs and colleague Carlos Watson founded a mentorship organization called College Track in 1997.

(Watson is also the founder of the for-profit education firm, Achieva.)

College Track helps low-income and minority students obtain scholarships and apply to college, but as Powell Jobs suggests, it was born out of a very specific situation at Carlmont in East Palo Alto. The problem began in the 1970s, when the predominantly white Carlmont High began bussing in students from a nearby district. Lacking adequate student records, these new students—who were mostly poor and Hispanic—were placed in the wrong classes. Socioeconomic, cultural, and language gaps between teachers and students didn't help the situation, and by the early 1990s, tensions were regularly boiling over. One teacher, LouAnne Johnson, wrote a book about Carlmont called *My Posse Don't Do Homework* (1993), which inspired the 1995 film *Dangerous Minds* starring Michelle Pfeiffer. Two years after *Dangerous Minds* premiered, College Track, which was at first housed in warehouse space in East Palo Alto, opened its doors to 35 students. By 2008, the program was mentoring 350 students out of three Bay Area campuses and was boasting a $3 million annual operating budget. By 2014, the program was operating in Los Angeles, New Orleans, and Aurora, Colorado. Selected students begin the program during the summer after their eighth grade year, and for the next four years they spend a minimum of nine hours a week being tutored and volunteering and participating in extracurricular activities. According to the *New York Times* in 2013, College Track has mentored over 1,400 students, 90 percent of whom have gone on to college.

## IMMIGRATION REFORM

In 2013 Powell Jobs participated in her first television interview since her husband's death in order to talk about immigration reform and a decade-old piece of legislation called the Dream Act that was designed to help children of undocumented immigrants gain citizenship. Powell Jobs, who is passionate about immigration reform, felt helpless as these students were unable to obtain citizenship and were also unable to acquire federal and state funds to help them go to college based on their immigration status. In December 2012, Powell Jobs commissioned Davis Guggenheim to make a short film about immigration and the Dream Act called *The Dream Is Now* (2013). (Guggenheim's previous films include *An Inconvenient Truth* in 2006 and *Waiting for Superman*, a documentary about the public education system, in 2010.) In spring 2013, Guggenheim and Powell

Jobs—along with some of the families featured in the film—travelled to Washington, DC, to screen *The Dream Is Now* for members of Congress. Although the Dream Act had not achieved the votes necessary to pass beyond the senate, President Barack Obama's administration took steps in 2012 to implement one of its proposals: deferred deportation for children of unauthorized immigrants through the Deferred Action for Childhood Arrivals (DACA) program, which is implemented through the Department of Homeland Security (DHS). "Despite the setbacks and the sometimes obstreperous political processes, once we are committed to working in a field where we can help advance knowledge or more equal opportunity, we cannot quit," Powell Jobs told Lattman and Cain Miller. "I am so motivated by the stories of their students and their families, and I don't give up because they don't give up."

## PHILANTHROPIC AND POLITICAL INTERESTS

Powell Jobs has served on the boards of New America Foundation, Teach for America, and Achieva. She is a member of the board at Ozy Media and her alma mater, Stanford University. In 2005, she co-led a $20 million fundraising campaign for the nonprofit Global Fund for Women. She has also donated money to environmental causes, Hillary Clinton's 2008 presidential campaign, and is currently one of the top donors to Ready for Hillary, a super PAC supporting a Clinton presidential run in 2016. In 2010 President Barack Obama asked Powell Jobs to serve on the White House Council for Community Solutions, and in January 2012, largely due to Powell Jobs's work with Emerson Collective, First Lady Michelle Obama asked her to sit in the presidential box during the State of the Union address.

Powell Jobs is reportedly dating Adrian Fenty, education reformer and former Washington, DC, mayor. She lives in Palo Alto with her children.

## SUGGESTED READING

Isaacson, Walter. *Steve Jobs*. New York: Simon, 2011. Print.

Lattman, Peter, and Claire Cain Miller. "Steve Jobs's Widow Steps onto Philanthropic Stage." *New York Times*. New York Times, 17 May 2013. Web. 16 Oct. 2014.

Mac, Ryan. "Meet Silicon Valley's Richest Woman: Laurene Powell Jobs." *Forbes*. Forbes, 7 Mar. 2012. Web. 16 Oct. 2014.

Zinko, Carolyne. "Laurene Powell's Educational Startup Gets Sidelined Kids Back onto the College Path." *SFGate*. San Francisco Chronicle, 8 June 2008. Web. 17 Oct. 2014.

—Molly Hagan

# Chris Pratt

**Born:** June 21, 1979
**Occupation:** Actor

In 2014, after years of playing the lovable goofy sidekick in various films, but most notably on the NBC sitcom *Parks and Recreation* (2009–15), Chris Pratt officially joined the A-list in Hollywood with his star-making turn as the roguish Peter "Star-Lord" Quill in the film adaptation of the little-known Marvel comic book series *Guardians of the Galaxy*. The commercial and critical success of this spacefaring film has led to increased interest in Pratt, who will next appear as one of the lead actors in the newest installment of the Jurassic Park franchise, *Jurassic World* (2015), before returning to the role of Quill in the announced *Guardians* sequel. Harvard University's Hasty Pudding Theatricals organization even named him its man of the year for 2015.

Despite all of the praise and comparisons to Harrison Ford's own star-making performance as Han Solo in the original *Star Wars* (1977), Pratt, who grew up in a working-class family and took a rather unusual route to the screen, remains humble yet hopeful that he can continue to make acting his life's work. "I want this to be my job forever," he said to Cara Buckley for the *New York Times* (24 July 2014). He added that he wanted his career in television and films to be like "a regular job where you work it till the job is done, and then you retire, and you live the good life until the good Lord comes and takes you."

## EARLY LIFE AND CAREER

The youngest of three children, Christopher Michael Pratt was born in Virginia, Minnesota, on June 21, 1979. When he was just three, his father, Dan, moved the family to rural Alaska, where the elder Pratt hoped to make his fortune mining gold. After four years in Alaska, the Pratt family moved to Washington State, where they settled in a small town just north of Seattle called Lake Stevens. There, Dan found work in

Mingle Media TV/Wikimedia Commons

construction remodeling houses, while Chris's mother, Kathy, took a job at the local Safeway.

During his youth, Chris enjoyed fishing and hunting (he bought his first gun at twelve with money he had earned from babysitting), performing in school assemblies, and wrestling on his school team. A good-times guy with a genial personality always looking to get a laugh, he never appeared serious enough to many adults about either himself or his future. "My high school wrestling coach reminds me about this time I came into his office and he said, 'Chris, what do you want to do with yourself?'" Pratt said to Clark Collis for *Entertainment Weekly* (11 July 2014). "I was like, 'I don't know, but I know I'll be famous and I know I'll make a s——ton of money.' I had no idea how. I'd done nothing proactive. It was as dumb as someone saying, 'I'll probably be an astronaut. I'm sure I'll stumble into an astronaut suit and end up in space one day.'"

After high school, Pratt took some acting courses at a local community college but dropped out halfway through the first semester to move with a friend to Hawaii, where he lived in a van on the beach. In Maui he found a job waiting tables with the Bubba Gump Shrimp Company. He also managed to make a Hollywood connection when he served the actress Rae Dawn Chong one day and asked her to put him in a film she was directing. "I was like, 'You're in the movies, right? I always wanted to be in

the movies,'" he recalled to Collis. "She said, 'You're cute. Do you act?'" To which he reported responding, "'Put me in a movie!'"

The film—a horror comedy titled *Cursed Part III*—was never released, but it brought Pratt to Los Angeles and gave him the opportunity to audition for roles in television. At age twenty-three he quickly landed a role as a high school athlete on the television series *Everwood* (2002–6). Following the end of that show's run, he snagged a part as a young political activist on the last season of *The O.C.* (2006–7). In addition to taking on small roles in television movies and theatrical films, he started honing his voice acting skills in cartoons like *The Batman* (2008).

### PARKS AND RECREATION AND OTHER CHARACTER ROLES

Pratt's breakout television role came on the popular half-hour network sitcom *Parks and Recreation*, which stars Amy Poehler, an alumnus of the long-running sketch comedy show *Saturday Night Live*. For seven seasons, beginning in 2009, Pratt portrayed Andy Dwyer, the show's goofy, dimwitted, but loveable slacker. The show's creators initially planned for Pratt's character to be featured in a brief arc as the boyfriend of another character, but they were so impressed with his work that they asked Pratt to stay on. Poehler and the rest of the staff had been floored by Pratt's improvisational skills, something that many of them had been trained to do while working with various sketch comedy troupes. Co-creator Michael Schur told Drew Magary for *GQ* (Dec. 2014), "When we have new directors on the show, I'll say, 'He's gonna roll into the set about twelve minutes before the scene starts shooting. He'll come not knowing what scene it is. He won't have read his lines. . . . By the time you're done with the scene, he will have done it eight different ways with eight great performances, and you'll have an embarrassment of riches.'" Debuting to mixed reviews, the show went on to earn critical acclaim as well as several Emmy nominations.

As Andy, Pratt was overweight and goofy—what many casting directors would describe as a typical character actor type. But when Pratt tried out for the more dramatic role of real-life Oakland A's player Scott Hatteberg in the Brat Pitt–led film *Moneyball* (2011), he decided to work out and lose the weight—and landed the role. Despite determinedly shedding the pounds, Pratt's character in that film was much like his other roles: a friendly, somewhat naïve charmer. After gaining the weight back and once again relying upon his innate sense of humor for the Channing Tatum film *10 Years* (2012), he then decided to try out for Kathryn Bigelow's film about the real-life killing of Osama bin Laden, *Zero Dark Thirty* (2012). He would play a member of the Navy SEALs team that found and killed the terrorist mastermind. Not only did he get the role, but it enabled him to see his acting in a whole new way. "Before 'Zero Dark Thirty,' I had played a different version of kind of the same person in every movie," he told Buckley. "It's been a bit of a survival mechanism my whole life to kind of play the dummy, and get laughs, and goof around."

### 2014: A BREAKOUT YEAR

In 2014 Pratt achieved further success by playing another loveable, humorously naïve character, but this time he only lent his voice—as Emmet Brickowski, the main character in the feature-length animated film *The Lego Movie*. A surprising critical and commercial smash, the witty and multidimensional film grossed more than $250 million in the United States alone.

But it would be Pratt's second film of the year—the live-action adaptation of the lesser-known Marvel comic book series *Guardians of the Galaxy*—that would cement his reputation as a charismatic leading man. Initially, Pratt had little interest in playing the film's main character, Peter Quill (also known as Star-Lord), who had been kidnapped from Earth as a child and grows up among alien cultures in outer space, using his wits to survive. He had been burned twice before seeking sci-fi roles—once trying out for the main character in James Cameron's *Avatar* (2009) and then again for the role of Captain James T. Kirk in J. J. Abrams's 2009 reboot of the *Star Trek* series. In both auditions, he was told he did not possess that indefinable "it factor" that the directors were looking for.

Oddly enough, the casting director for *Guardians*, Sarah Finn, kept suggesting a screen test for Pratt for the Quill role to the film's director, James Gunn. Gunn, however, could not get past the idea that Finn was asking him to test the fat guy from *Parks and Recreation*. Yet, within moments of finally meeting Pratt, Gunn knew they had found their Peter Quill. Gunn asked Pratt if he had any questions. "I said, 'Of course I have questions! Marvel's not going to let me read the script. . . . Do I have any questions? How long

do you have?'" Pratt recalled to Collis. "He was like, 'That's what Peter Quill would say.'"

### BECOMING A SUPERHERO

The role secured, Pratt began working out to lose the weight he had again gained for the Vince Vaughn comedy *Delivery Man* (2013). In an interview with Kaleem Aftab for the *Independent* (30 July 2014), he explained the drive behind his most drastic transformation: "If I was playing James Bond, I would learn how to do a British accent. . . . So it made sense that when I started doing this role that that was the thing that I was most concerned with. I need to look like a superhero."

When the film was announced by Marvel Studios—which has spearheaded the film adaptations of more famous comic book characters such as Thor, Iron Man, and Captain America—many observers thought *Guardians* would be a rare misstep for a studio that had been churning out hits. Yet despite the relative obscurity of the source material, *Guardians* proved to be a huge success, generating more than $770 million in worldwide box office receipts and earning rave reviews from critics, who not only admired its mix of action and comedy, but also the work of its lead actor. In a review of the film for National Public Radio (NPR) (31 July 2014), Linda Holmes wrote that Peter Quill is "very much a Marvel hero, but Pratt—a tremendously charismatic actor whose work as the huge-hearted and slightly foggy-headed Andy Dwyer on *Parks and Recreation* foreshadowed some of what he's doing here—gives him both a shaggier charm and a much more specifically comedic carriage than most Marvel heroes."

With his star increasingly rising in the film world, the time also came for Pratt to say goodbye to his longtime acting home and family on the set of *Parks and Recreation*. A regular staple of NBC's now dwindling prime-time comedy block on Thursday nights, the show moved to Tuesday nights and began its final season in January 2015.

### PERSONAL LIFE

Pratt has been married to the comedic actor Anna Faris since 2009. The couple met on the set of the film *Take Me Home Tonight* in 2007, which sat on the shelf for several years before being released in 2011. Their son, Jack, was born prematurely in 2012 and spent a month in the hospital before being allowed to come home; he has since grown into a healthy child. In interviews,

Pratt has credited his son's birth to strengthening his religious faith as well as the bond he shares with Faris. "It restored my faith in God, not that it needed to be restored, but it really redefined it," Pratt told ABC News (31 July 2014). "The baby was so beautiful to us, and I look back at the photos of him and it must have been jarring for other people to come in and see him, but to us he was so beautiful and perfect."

In addition to signing a contract with Marvel to do another *Guardians* film, Pratt will also star in *Jurassic World*, the fourth film in a sci-fi series that began in 1993 with *Jurassic Park*. While he enjoys acting, Pratt would ultimately like to have a presence behind the camera as a writer and director.

## SUGGESTED READING

Aftab, Kaleem. "Chris Pratt: From *Parks and Recreation* to *Guardians of the Galaxy*." *Independent*. Independent Digital News and Media, 30 July 2014. Web. 15 Jan. 2015.

Buckley, Cara. "Goofy Guy Takes a Galactic Leap." *New York Times*. New York Times, 24 July 2014. Web. 15 Jan. 2015.

Collis, Clark. "How Chris Pratt Went from Zero to Hero." *Entertainment Weekly*. Entertainment Weekly, 11 July 2014. Web. 15 Jan. 2015.

Holmes, Linda. "'Guardians of the Galaxy': Let's Hear It for F.U.N." Rev. of *Guardians of the Galaxy*, dir. James Gunn. *NPR*. NPR, 31 July 2014. Web. 15 Jan. 2015.

Magary, Drew. "Everything (Chris Pratt Does) Is Awesome Parts 1–41." *GQ*. Condé Nast, Dec. 2014. Web. 15 Jan. 2015.

Snierson, Dan. "'Parks and Recreation': Inside the Futuristic Farewell Season—and Final Days on Set." *Entertainment Weekly*. Entertainment Weekly, 13 Jan. 2015. Web. 15 Jan. 2015.

## SELECTED WORKS

*Everwood*, 2002–6; *Parks and Recreation*, 2009–15; *Moneyball*, 2011; *Zero Dark Thirty*, 2012; *The Lego Movie*, 2014; *Guardians of the Galaxy*, 2014; *Jurassic World*, 2015

—Christopher Mari

# Lynne Ramsay

**Born:** December 5, 1969
**Occupation:** Director

Lynne Ramsay is a director, cinematographer, and screenwriter best known for her films *Ratcatcher* (1999), *Morvern Callar* (2002), and *We Need to Talk about Kevin* (2011).

## BACKGROUND

Lynne Ramsay was born on December 5, 1969, in Glasgow, Scotland. She attended Napier College in Edinburgh, Scotland, where she studied photography. She next enrolled in the National Film and Television School in Beaconsfield, England, focusing her studies on direction and cinematography. When she entered the school, she had only ever shot still photography and had never worked with moving images. Ramsay has stated that her inexperience with film was frustrating at first, but her time at the National Film and Television School helped her develop a confidence in her cinematography.

Ramsay graduated from the school in 1995. Her senior short film, *Small Deaths*, consists of three vignettes that depict difficult moments in the life of a young girl. The short went on to win the Jury Prize for best short film at the 1996 Cannes Film Festival. She directed two more short films—*Kill the Day* (1996), about a heroin addict in prison, and *Gasman* (1998)—before transitioning to full-length features. The latter short film, about a brother and sister who experience family conflict at a Christmas party, won Ramsay her second Jury Prize at Cannes.

## RATCATCHER

The success of her short films enabled Ramsay to move into directing features. Disappointed by the scripts presented to her, she decided to write her own screenplay about growing up in Scotland. The screenplay became her first feature, *Ratcatcher* (1999).

*Ratcatcher* is a coming-of-age tale set in a poverty-stricken housing development in working-class Glasgow in 1973. The film reflects the limited economic opportunities Ramsay saw growing up in Glasgow, but she has stated that it is not autobiographical. Although the film never received a wide release in theaters, it earned acclaim from critics in both the United Kingdom and the United States. Ramsay also received several awards for the film, including the Carl Foreman Award for most promising newcomer in British film at the British Academy of Film and Television Arts (BAFTA) Awards and the award for best director at the Chicago International Film Festival.

### MORVERN CALLAR

For her next project, Ramsay chose to adapt a film from existing source material for the first time. She selected Scottish author Alan Warner's 1995 novel *Morvern Callar*, about a girl who uses her boyfriend's suicide as an opportunity to publish his manuscript under her own name. The film of the same title was released in 2002 to largely positive reviews. The lead actress, Samantha Morton, won the British Independent Film Award for best actress, and the film received awards at several film festivals.

### WE NEED TO TALK ABOUT KEVIN AND OTHER WORK

Ramsay's next film project, an adaptation of author Alice Sebold's novel *The Lovely Bones* (2002), never came to fruition due to creative differences. Ramsay had read the unfinished manuscript prior to its publication and signed a deal to write and direct a film adaptation, but after the novel became a bestseller, the studio wanted her to direct a more faithful adaptation than what she was planning. Ramsay left the project and was replaced by director Peter Jackson, whose adaptation of the novel was eventually released in 2009.

After her plans for *The Lovely Bones* fell through, Ramsay was hired by BBC Films to direct an adaption of the 2003 Lionel Shriver novel *We Need to Talk about Kevin*. Ramsay began working on the script in 2006, and the film went through several rewrites to lower production costs. Filming began in Stamford, Connecticut, in April 2010. The film documents the fallout after a boy kills several of his classmates and explores the causes of the tragedy. The film premiered at the Cannes Film Festival in May of 2011, earning high praise from critics. Ramsay was nominated for the BAFTA Award for best director for her work, and *We Need to Talk about Kevin* won the London Critics Circle's award for British film of the year.

In 2012 Ramsay directed the short film *Swimmer* (2012), about a young man who swims past various people as their thoughts and exchanges are heard. The film won Ramsay the BAFTA (British Academy of Film and Television Arts) Award for best short film. Also in 2012 it was announced that Ramsay was slated to direct the western *Jane Got a Gun*. However, on the first day of shooting in March 2013, it was announced that Ramsay had quit the production.

### IMPACT

In a short amount of time, Ramsay has become one of the most celebrated independent directors in the film industry. She is selective in her choice of films to direct, prioritizing her vision over quantity. Throughout her career she has received numerous awards while continuing to explore the personal themes that attract her.

### PERSONAL LIFE

Ramsay married musician Rory Stewart Kinnear in 2002. The two collaborated on the script for *We Need to Talk about Kevin*.

### SUGGESTED READING

Bailey, Andy. "Gutter Jewel: Lynne Ramsay Finds Beauty in 'Ratcatcher.'" *Indiewire*. SnagFilms, 13 Oct. 2000. Web. 26 Feb. 2014.

Chew-Bose, Durga. "Lynne Ramsay Frames the Picture." *Interview*. Interview, 2011. Web. 26 Feb. 2014.

Child, Ben. "Lynne Ramsay Rebuts *Jane Got a Gun* Lawsuit." *Guardian*. Guardian News and Media, 11 Nov. 2013. Web. 26 Feb. 2014.

Kois, Dan. "Lynne Ramsay Is Back. Finally." *The 6th Floor*. New York Times, 13 Jan. 2012. Web. 26 Feb. 2014.

"Ramsay, Lynne (1969–)." *BFI Screenonline*. British Film Institute, n.d. Web. 26 Feb. 2014.

### SELECTED WORKS

*Ratcatcher*, 1999; *Morvern Callar*, 2002; *We Need to Talk about Kevin*, 2011

—Patrick G. Cooper

# Claudia Rankine

**Born:** 1963
**Occupation:** Poet, professor

Claudia Rankine is a genre-defying, award-winning poet. Raised in Jamaica and educated in the United States, where she still lives, Rankine has taken on such complicated topics as race and identity in her poetry, and made them palpable and personal. Her collection *Citizen: An American Lyric* earned her the 2014 National Book Critics Circle Award in poetry. Her work has been published in various journals, such as *Boston Review*, *TriQuarterly*, and the *Poetry Project Newsletter*. In 2013 she was elected a chancellor of the Academy of American Poets. Rankine is the Henry G. Lee Professor of English at Pomona College in Claremont, California.

## EARLY LIFE, EDUCATION OF A POET

Claudia Rankine was born in Jamaica in 1963 and spent her early childhood in that country's capital and largest city, Kingston. At the age of seven, she moved to the Bronx in New York City and was educated at Catholic schools. She attended Williams College in Williamstown, Massachusetts, where she received a bachelor's degree in literature in 1986. At Williams she studied with the poet Louise Glück. Glück was a major influence in getting Rankine to consider writing poetry where the poems are interconnected, a sort of book-length project as opposed to a collection of separate stand-alone poems. Rankine then went on to study poetry on a graduate level at Columbia University in New York City, where she earned her MFA in 1993. At Columbia she received guidance from the poets Dan Halpern and Henri Cole. She also studied under the poet Robert Hass at the University of California at Berkeley.

## FIRST FOUR BOOKS

From the start of her career, Rankine has dealt in her poetry with the issues of modern American society, particularly those facing women and African American people. As she told the *Pomona College Magazine* (Fall 2006), "the lyric—the poem—is deep feelings about personal issues" that "break down the barriers between issues in the world." Rankine's first book of poems was titled *Nothing in Nature Is Private* (1995), which she described for the African American Literature Book Club (AALBC) website as existing "in the experience of Black, Jamaican, person, woman in a bruised world." The book received the Cleveland State Poetry Prize. Her second book of poems, *The End of the Alphabet* (1998), Rankine wrote for the AALBC website, "makes a kaleidoscopic journey through the will to existence."

After another three years, she put out her third collection, titled *Plot* (2001), a postmodern meditation on pregnancy and life, full of conversations and dreams. Again after three years, Rankine had another book published, a series of prose poems titled *Don't Let Me Be Lonely: An American Lyric*. The book combined poetry,

John Lucas/Wikimedia Commons

essays, and images, much as her next collection would a decade later. That next collection would hit a nerve, tapping into the zeitgeist in a way that was unlike anything she had previously published.

## CITIZENS DIVIDED

It took ten years for Rankine to publish her next book, *Citizen: An American Lyric* (2014), which had the same subtitle as her previous book; like that previous book, it is a poetic work that incorporates various approaches and styles. Scheduled for release in October 2014, the book arrived in stores amid an atmosphere where race, crime, class, and the killing of unarmed black men by police were once again a part of the national conversation—or rather often a part of many different conversations. After police shot Michael Brown, an unarmed black man, in August 2014 in Ferguson, Missouri, protests and unrest broke out in that small city. Brown being shot came soon after the July death of Eric Garner, a black man in Staten Island, New York City, who died not long after he was placed in a chokehold by a police officer. In these two cases, and in similar cases, police officers faced no serious consequences, which only fueled the outrage nationwide among people sympathetic to the families of the deceased, black American communities, and all those frustrated with the persistent pattern of such violence.

About a week after the killing of Michael Brown, Rankine found herself in the area. This was not her plan from the beginning. Months prior she had been invited by the Pulitzer Foundation to show "Situation Videos" she had made with her husband, filmmaker and photographer John Lucas. Rankine's plans were to stay in St. Louis, but once the Brown shooting grabbed national headlines, she decided to see Ferguson for herself. She went to the city and talked to its primarily black residents about how they felt, asking them about their experience and frustrations.

The relevance of *Citizen: An American Lyric* to the sociopolitical climate of the 2010s and the national conversations about race was evident even on the book's cover: a photograph featuring a floating image of a "hoodie," or hooded sweatshirt—but only the hood. To many this may have instantly recalled Trayvon Martin, another unarmed young black man who was killed in Florida in 2012 by an armed member of a neighborhood watch group—a man who received no jail time for the shooting. However, the image on the cover was, in fact, more than twenty years old, created in 1993. The image seems to say many things, including that what some may see as new developments—for example, the stereotyping of black youths wearing hoodies as being criminals or troublemakers or police killings of unarmed black men across the United States—are in fact not new at all and have been going on for decades or even centuries, in one way or another.

## DISLOCATING THE READER

*Citizen*, essentially, is a series of interconnected poems concerned with the slight or subtle racism that is all too common for many black people in everyday life. The beginning of the book lays out in second person ("you") various such racist incidents that have happened to Rankine or friends of hers. They are all true stories. A complete stranger cannot understand why "you" care that he has "just referred to the boisterous teenagers in Starbucks as niggers." Or one coworker says to another that "being around black people is like watching a foreign film without translation." Another passage recalls an incident in Catholic school when a white girl asks "you" to cheat off your test. Looking back, questions of race boil to the surface, such as when Rankine writes: "You never really speak except for the time she makes her request and later when she tells you you smell good and have features more like a white person. You assume she thinks she is thanking you for letting her cheat and feels

better cheating from an almost white person." In an interview with Meara Sharma for *Guernica* magazine (17 Nov. 2014), Rankine said she used second person in part because not all the incidents happened to her, but most importantly she used it because the use of "you" in the prose poems "disallowed the reader from knowing immediately how to position themselves." The reader will assume who is black and who is white, Rankine said, but she wanted the reader to be the one to make that assumption. In her interview with Sharma, Rankine explained that she could only have written the book in the spirit of poetry and not, for example, in a more straightforward mode, like that of a journalistic essay. Rankine said her goal was "openness" and not "arguing a point." For her, she said, poetry is about "creating an environment."

In the book Rankine also addresses Trayvon Martin's death, as well as events such as the 2006 World Cup and Hurricane Katrina. Rankine also spends some time on African American tennis star Serena Williams, citing, for example, five controversial (and apparently inaccurate) calls made against her in 2004 at the US Open semifinal. The absurdity of the calls, as told by Rankine, seems surreal. Throughout *Citizen*, Rankine offers different insights to the reader by focusing on real-life interactions with microscopic precision and grace. At the end of the book, Rankine concludes, "This is how you are as a citizen. Come on. Let it go. Move on." The taste that sentiment is meant to leave behind is bittersweet: irony mixed with reality.

## ACCOLADES

*Citizen* received widespread glowing reviews. The book, wrote Dan Chiasson for the *New Yorker* (27 Oct. 2014), "conducts its business, often, with melancholy, but also with wit and a sharable incredulity." Holly Bass wrote for the *New York Times* Sunday Book Review (24 Dec. 2014), "The writing zigs and zags effortlessly between prose poems, images and essays. This is the poet as conceptual artist, in full mastery of her craft." The book, Bass concluded, "throws a Molotov cocktail at the notion that a reduction of injustice is the same as freedom." *Citizen* earned her the 2014 National Book Critics Circle Award in poetry.

Rankine is also the recipient of fellowships from the Academy of American Poetry, the National Endowment for the Arts, and the Lannan Foundation. In 2013 she was elected as a chancellor of the Academy of American Poets, and in 2014 she received a Lannan Literary Award.

## OTHER PURSUITS

Besides writing poetry, Rankine often collaborates on other literary and dramatic pursuits. Rankine's play *The Provenance of Beauty: A South Bronx Travelogue* premiered in 2009 at New York's Foundry Theater; she also coauthored the play *Existing Conditions* with playwright and performance artist Casey Llewellyn. She has produced various videos in collaboration with her husband, John Lucas, including "Situation One." As of late 2014 she was working on a project fusing the events in Ferguson with elements of Greek tragedy.

Rankine has coedited numerous anthologies, including A*merican Women Poets in the Twenty-First Century: Where Lyric Meets Language* (2002), *American Poets in the Twenty-First Century: The New Poetics* (2007), and *The Racial Imaginary: Writers on Race in the Life of the Mind* (2014). Her poems have been included in the anthologies *Great American Prose Poems: From Poe to the Present* (2003), *Best American Poetry* (2001), and *The Garden Thrives: Twentieth Century African-American Poetry* (1996).

Between 1994 and 2006, Rankine taught at the University of Houston, Case Western Reserve University, and Barnard College. She has been the Henry G. Lee Professor of English at Pomona College, in Claremont, California, since 2006.

## SUGGESTED READING

Bass, Holly. Rev. of *Citizen: An American Lyric*, by Claudia Rankine. *New York Times*. New York Times, 24 Dec. 2014. Web. 9 Apr. 2015.
Chiasson, Dan. "Color Codes." *New Yorker*. Condé Nast, 27 Oct. 2014. Web. 9 Apr. 2015.
Rankine, Claudia. "Blackness as the Second Person." Interview by Meara Sharma. *Guernica*. Guernica, 17 Nov. 2014. 9 Apr. 2015.
Ulin, David. "Poet Claudia Rankine Ruminates on the Body Politic in 'Citizen.'" *LA Times*. Los Angeles Times, 9 Oct. 2014. Web. 15 Apr. 2015.

## SELECTED WORKS

*Nothing in Nature Is Private*, 1995; *The End of the Alphabet*, 1998; *Plot*, 2001; *Don't Let Me be Lonely: An American Lyric*, 2004; *Citizen: An American Lyric*, 2014

—Dmitry Kiper

# Diane Rehm

**Born:** September 21, 1936
**Occupation:** Radio host

Radio personality Diane Rehm has been on the air since 1979. Produced at the radio station WAMU in Washington, DC, her self-titled call-in talk show is distributed by National Public Radio (NPR) to almost two hundred other stations. Broadcast live on weekday mornings, it draws more than 2.4 million listeners each week. Rehm, who is instantly recognizable in person because of her distinctive voice and cloud of silvery hair, enjoys a diverse audience, who widely consider her to be a welcome voice of reason. "Talk radio can be a very belligerent place, very loud, very male," fellow radio personality Michel Martin said for the NPR program *Tell Me More* (28 Sept. 2009). "But all along, Diane Rehm has been proving that one doesn't have to have the loudest voice to carry the biggest impact." Rehm herself has said, as quoted by Paul Farhi for the *Washington Post* (25 Sept. 2009): "Civil dialogue has a role in our world. . . . No matter how loud and angry the voices become, if we persist with voices of kindness and caring, this country will continue to be the strong and decent country that everyone has believed it to be."

In addition to her calm and reasonable demeanor, Rehm is admired for her sharp intelligence. The first half of her two-hour program is typically devoted to a newsworthy issue or current event, while the second is given over to a wide-ranging assortment of other subjects (anything from the state of American poetry to personal finance), and Rehm is consistently well informed, no matter what the topic. "What is remarkable about Ms. Rehm is the detailed knowledge she displays on subjects as various as those that might be found in the *Encyclopaedia Britannica*," Stanley Fish wrote in an op-ed for the *New York Times* (19 Apr. 2006), asserting that listeners could learn more from one episode of *The Diane Rehm Show* than by sitting through a college lecture. "[She] really is smarter than most of her guests, but that is something you realize only after many hours of listening. Her brilliance is never thrust upon you. It just shines."

## CHILDHOOD

Rehm was born on September 21, 1936, in Washington, DC, to Wadie and Eugenie Aed,

The Washington Post/Getty Images

Christian Arab immigrants from Turkey. Wadie and his two brothers owned a grocery store, and Eugenie remained at home to care for Diane and her older sister. Her mother suffered from frequent headaches and bouts of depression, and Rehm believes that she would have been diagnosed with a mental illness by modern standards. Although she behaved in an outwardly charming manner to others, Eugenie was physically and verbally abusive to her daughters. Rehm has recalled being beaten with belts, wooden spoons, shoes, and a metal spatula. At other times Eugenie withdrew, refusing to speak to her daughters for weeks.

Still, Rehm, who attended William B. Powell Elementary School, remembers spending occasional happy times with her mother. Eugenie grew wonderful flowers and fruit in the family's yard, cooked delicious meals, and sewed coats and dresses rivaling anything found in Washington's stores. Some of Rehm's favorite moments were spent listening to radio dramas and mysteries with her mother.

In the summer when Rehm was nine years old, a man approached her on the playground. He chatted with her for a while and the next day contacted her parents; he identified himself as a congressman and said that their young daughter had the potential to go into show business. He convinced Wadie and Eugenie to leave Rehm alone with him at a downtown motel, where Rehm alleges that he sexually molested her. She has never revealed the name of the man.

## MARRIAGE AND FAMILY

After Rehm earned her diploma from Roosevelt High School, she was expected to marry someone from the Arab community and devote herself to homemaking, rather than attend college. In the meantime, she took a low-level job with the city highway department, where she particularly enjoyed one of her duties: using the department's two-way radio to dispatch service trucks.

When she was nineteen Rehm married George Hamaty, who was eight years her senior and a member of a prominent Arab American family. She unhappily tried settling into the role of subservient wife. When her mother passed away just a few months after the wedding, and her father died of a heart attack within the year, Rehm saw her chance to leave Hamaty. Divorce would have been unthinkable had they been alive. "It would have brought shame on them and they would have done everything in their power to see to it that I continued in the marriage," Rehm explained in her 1999 memoir, *Finding My Voice*. The couple separated in 1958 and divorced in the spring of the following year.

Rehm found living on her own for the first time in her life both scary and exciting. She took a secretarial job at the US State Department to support herself, and there she met John Rehm, an attorney whom she has described as one of the most brilliant people she ever encountered. The couple married in the winter of 1959, not long after her divorce from Hamaty was finalized.

Rehm soon had two children, David and Jennifer, and again tried settling into the life of a Washington housewife. Reeve Lindbergh, reviewing Rehm's memoir for the *Washington Post* (21 Oct. 1999), wrote: "With absolute dedication, and with a kind of instinctive expertise, Rehm pursued her first adult vocation as 'homemaker,' as did most of the women she knew. She raised her children enthusiastically, kept house diligently and did volunteer work. . . . She also accompanied her husband to official functions, played the piano, took courses in fashion modeling, and designed and created most of her own and her children's clothes."

## THE DIANE REHM SHOW

Eventually Rehm, who sometimes chafed at her lack of a college degree, took an enrichment course at George Washington University called

New Horizons for Women, aimed at helping students understand how feminism could impact lives. She was encouraged by her classmates to explore working in radio, and she soon found the courage to volunteer at WAMU. Scheduled to help out with administrative tasks, Rehm, then thirty-seven years old, instead found herself on the air her very first day at the studio, filling in for a sick program host. Her guest was a representative from the Dairy Council, and Rehm has joked to interviewers that one of the hardest things she has ever done is to fill ninety minutes of airtime with questions about milk and cheese. It helped that she was used to attending so many events with her husband; asking questions, she had learned, was a good way of facilitating connections and putting people at ease.

Within months, Rehm was hired as an assistant producer of the morning program *Kaleidoscope*, a post she kept for two years. Wanting to try her hand at television production, she left WAMU briefly, but in 1979 she returned, this time as the host of *Kaleidoscope*. In 1984, in recognition of her skill and popularity, the program's name was changed to *The Diane Rehm Show*. Initially, she had the help of just one part-time volunteer, and she served as her own producer.

Eventually, as her audience share increased, she was able to hire a paid producer, and in 1995 WAMU began distributing the show nationally. Rehm herself raised the $250,000 needed to go national, but by then she had attracted several high-profile supporters, including fellow broadcaster Larry King and book publisher Simon & Schuster.

Her guests have since included high-level political figures such as Madeleine Albright and Jimmy Carter, Nobel Prize laureates, Supreme Court justices, best-selling authors, movie stars, and people from almost every other field of human endeavor imaginable. Speaking to Bill Clinton in 2000, she became the first radio talk show host ever to conduct an interview in the Oval Office with a sitting president. "Her guests are always top-drawer, just the people you would want to hear on the topic," Fish wrote. "She treats them with a blend of courtesy and firmness that elicits precise and nuanced answers."

## RECOGNITION AND CHALLENGES

Rehm's work has earned her a string of honors, including designation as the 1999 Washingtonian of the Year by the editors of *Washingtonian* magazine; being named a fellow of the Society of Professional Journalists in 2000; the 2003 Calvary Women's Services Hope Award, honoring her contributions to women in need; the 2003 National Organization for Women's Susan B. Anthony Award; a 2009 Peabody Award; and a 2013 National Humanities Medal, awarded, as the official citation read, "for illuminating the people and stories behind the headlines. In probing interviews with pundits, poets, and presidents, Ms. Rehm's incisive, confident, and curious voice has deepened our understanding of our communities and our culture."

Despite such accolades, Rehm's career has not always gone smoothly. In the mid-1990s, her voice began audibly deteriorating. She sounded tremulous and sometimes had difficulty finishing a sentence. She visited several doctors and therapists and was given conflicting diagnoses and suggested remedies, including that she was breathing incorrectly, that she had acid reflux, and that she should try meditation. Gradually, the situation grew so serious that it sounded as if she were being strangled while trying to speak. Although she still enjoyed the strong support of audiences and station managers, she was forced to take a leave of absence. Finally, in 1998 she was diagnosed with spasmodic dysphonia, a neurological condition in which the vocal cords spasm involuntarily. She began receiving regular injections of botulinum toxin directly into her vocal cords as treatment. Though the treatment only partially relieved the symptoms, she returned to the show and has received honors for her work in raising awareness about the condition.

In addition to *Finding My Voice*, Rehm has written *Toward Commitment: A Dialogue about Marriage*, coauthored with her husband in 2002, and *Life with Maxie*, a 2010 memoir about her relationship with her cherished long-haired Chihuahua. John Rehm died on June 23, 2014, after suffering for years with Parkinson's disease; nine days prior to his death, John had decided to stop eating and drinking in order to end his own life. The couple had been married for fifty-four years. Rehm has been outspoken about understanding and honoring her husband's decision, and is supportive of the right to die.

## SUGGESTED READING

Farhi, Paul. "After 30 Years, NPR's Diane Rehm Finally Gets to Be the Guest." *Washington Post.* Washington Post, 25 Sept. 2009. Web. 1 Nov. 2014.

Fish, Stanley. "Radio Days." *New York Times.* New York Times, 19 Apr. 2006. Web. 1 Nov. 2014.

Martin, Michel. "Here's to You, Diane Rehm." *Tell Me More.* Natl. Public Radio (NPR), 28 Sept. 2009. Web. 11 Aug. 2014.

Masters, Kim. "She's Got America By the Ear; WAMU's Diane Rehm Goes National With Her Air of Civility Intact." *Washington Post.* Washington Post, 11 July 1995. Web. 1 Nov. 2014.

Radcliffe, Donnie. "Diane Rehm at Home: A Room of Her Own." *Washington Post.* Washington Post, 22 May 1997. Web. 1 Nov. 2014.

Weeks, Linton. "Diane Rehm Finds a Voice of Her Own." *Washington Post.* Washington Post, 23 Aug. 1999. Web. 11 Nov. 2014.

—Mari Rich

# Tom Reiss

**Born:** May 5, 1964
**Occupation:** Writer

## BACKGROUND

Tom Reiss was born in New York City on May 5, 1964, and is the son of an American father and French mother. He spent his early childhood in the New York City neighborhood of Washington Heights before his family moved to Texas in 1968 to accommodate his father's profession as a neurosurgeon for the United States Air Force. Reiss's family relocated to Springfield, Massachusetts, at the conclusion of his father's military service.

During his time in Springfield, Reiss was fascinated by stories shared with him by his great-uncle Lolek, who, like many of his relatives, was a German Jew who had survived and fled the Nazi takeover of Germany in the 1930s. As a teenager, Reiss's primary literary influences included Dashiell Hammett, Raymond Chandler, and James M. Cain.

Reiss attended Longmeadow High School in Longmeadow, Massachusetts, before enrolling at the prestigious Hotchkiss School, in Lakeville, Connecticut. He went on to pursue an undergraduate degree in journalism at Harvard University, graduating in 1986. After Harvard, Reiss attended the University of Houston in order to learn from famed American author Donald Barthelme, who was with the university's creative writing program.

After leaving Texas, Reiss moved to Germany, where he worked as both a travel writer and a journalist investigating the emerging phenomenon of neo-Nazism.

## WRITING CAREER

Reiss coauthored his major work, *Führer-Ex: Memoirs of a Former New-Nazi* (1996) with famed former neo-Nazi Ingo Hasselbach. Hasselbach had been an active member of the neo-Nazi movement in his native East Germany for over twenty years before renouncing his allegiance in 1993. Part memoir, part biography, *Führer-Ex* is considered one of the first major undercover investigations of the European neo-Nazi movement of the late twentieth century.

The genesis of Reiss's second major book came while he was working as a travel writer for the venerated travel publisher Condé Nast. While writing a piece about the economic and cultural effects of the late 1990s oil boom on Baku, the capital of Azerbaijan, he came across the story of Lev Nussimbaum (1905–42), a Russian-born Jew who as a young man fled the Bolshevik Revolution.

Reiss's profile of Nussimbaum's story would become his 2005 book *The Orientalist: Solving the Mystery of a Strange and Dangerous Life.* Reiss traveled to nearly a dozen foreign countries to reconstruct Nussimbaum's story, which included interactions with European fascist intellectuals, pan-Islamists, and revolutionary terrorists.

In 2006, Reiss began research on the famed French Revolutionary War general Thomas-Alexandre Dumas. Dumas, the son of a white French nobleman and an enslaved African, achieved fame as the highest-ranking person of color ever to serve in a continental European army.

Reiss attributed his interest in the topic to his mother's admiration of the nineteenth-century French novels *The Three Musketeers* and *The Count of Monte Cristo*, written by Dumas' son, Alexandre Dumas, who based some of his work on his father's experiences. Reiss's painstaking research for the book took him to France, Egypt, and the Caribbean.

*The Black Count: Glory, Revolution, Betrayal, and the Real Count of Monte Cristo* was published in September 2012 and was immediately heralded as the most comprehensive analysis of Dumas's life to date. Reiss received praise from readers and critics alike for his use of engrossing narrative and for his depth of historical detail.

Reiss earned widespread acclaim for the work. In addition to being included on the *New York Times* list of "100 Most Notable Books of 2012," *The Black Count* was also nominated for an NAACP Image Award. Furthermore, the book earned Reiss the 2013 PEN/Jacqueline Bograd Weld Award for Biography as well as the 2013 Pulitzer Prize for Biography or Autobiography.

## IMPACT

Tom Reiss tackles ornately detailed historical topics in much of his work and includes an engrossing flair of the detective novels that entertained him as a teenager. His fascination with narratives of risk and overcoming tumultuous circumstance is derived from the pride he takes in the stories of his own ancestors and the bravery they exhibited in escaping Nazi oppression.

Reiss often speaks of his lack of interest in conducting research in archives or libraries, opting instead to acquire material through an exploration of the society and cultures experienced by the topics of his work and through detective work in castle towers and locked safes.

The passion with which Reiss reinvigorates ancient histories is what has made him one of the foremost historians and one of the preeminent biographers in the United States.

## PERSONAL LIFE

Tom Reiss lives with his wife and two daughters in New York City.

## SUGGESTED READING

Brawarsky, Sandee. "The Many Lives of Lev Nussimbaum." *Jewish Journal.* Tribe Media, 7 Apr. 2005. Web. 11 June 2014.

Charney, Noah. "Tom Reiss: How I Write." *Daily Beast.* Daily Beast, 14 Aug. 2013. Web. 11 June 2014.

Damrosch, Leo. "The Third Musketeer." *New York Times.* New York Times, 14 Sept. 2012. Web. 11 June 2014.

Hasselbach, Ingo, and Tom Reiss. "How Nazis Are Made." *New Yorker* (1996): p. 36. Web. 11 June 2014.

Kazimova, Nikki. "Books: Fingerprints of a Legend." *Transitions Online.* Central and Eastern European Online Library, 8 February 2011. Web. 6 June 2014.

Shea, Dean. "The Rumpus Interview with Tom Reiss." *Rumpus.* Rumpus, 28 Feb. 2013. Web. 11 June 2014.

## SELECTED WORKS

*Führer-Ex: Memoirs of a Former Neo-Nazi,* 1996; *The Orientalist: Solving the Mystery of a Strange and Dangerous Life,* 2005; *The Black Count: Glory, Revolution, Betrayal, and the Real Count of Monte Cristo,* 2012

—John Pritchard

# Shonda Rhimes

**Born:** January 13, 1970
**Occupation:** Writer and producer

Shonda Rhimes made history in 2014 when she became the first writer and producer to have three shows airing back-to-back on prime-time television. The block of *Grey's Anatomy* (2005), *Scandal* (2012–), and *How to Get Away with Murder* (2014–) on the ABC television network dominates programming on Thursday nights. Rhimes has received three Emmy nominations for her work and was chosen in 2007 as one of *Time*'s one hundred most influential people. As an African American woman, Rhimes has found herself in headlines due to her race and gender, but she has been outspoken about not letting either define her or her work.

Asked what made Shonda Rhimes so successful, Kerry Washington, star of *Scandal*, told Sandra Gonzalez for *Entertainment Weekly* (4 May 2012), "In life and in art, we sometimes want to categorize something or someone as good or bad. And I think the truth is usually somewhere in the gray area. Shonda is courageous in her writing because she's not afraid of the gray area. She's not afraid of the complexities."

Rhimes received an honorary doctorate from her alma mater, Dartmouth, where she was commencement speaker, in 2014. In recognition of her work, she also received the 2014 Sherry Lansing Leadership Award for women in the entertainment industry and was inducted into the National Association of Broadcasters Hall of Fame in April 2015. She made her acting debut on Fox's *The Mindy Project*, playing herself.

## EARLY LIFE AND EDUCATION

Shonda Lynn Rhimes was born on January 13, 1970, in Chicago, Illinois. Her mother, Vera, who earned a PhD after her children were grown, was a teacher; her father, Ilee, was the chief information officer at University of Southern California. Rhimes is the youngest of six children; she has

Barry King/Getty Images North America

two brothers and three sisters. When she was a child, the family had "book Sundays," during which each person would spend much of the day reading. Discussing her reading habit, Rhimes told *Redbook* (18 Mar. 2013), "As a child, I spent about 85 percent of my time with my nose buried in a book. . . . I read *Little Women* every time I break up with a guy. I've been turning to Meg, Jo, Beth, and Amy for heartbreak solace since I was 13 and found out the guy I liked was interested in someone else. I'd go home and cry to my sisters, and then I'd read Louisa May Alcott. There's some profound comfort in that book for me—Jo becomes a writer and finds her heart in a most unexpected place. Above all, we learn what Jo has always known: No matter who the guy is or how great he is, no one loves you like your sisters."

Rhimes initially thought she would become a novelist and wanted to be the next Toni Morrison. Before she was able to write, she spoke stories into a tape recorder; her mother wrote them down for her. As Rhimes told Colleen Leahey for *Fortune* (10 Oct. 2013), her father's encouragement was to tell her, "The only limit to your success is your own imagination." She went on to say, "I'm sure there are barriers. I have just chosen not to acknowledge them."

When she was ten, Rhimes began attending a Catholic elementary school. Even at that stage of life she had a rich imagination, pretending her real family was arriving soon from Paris to take

her to the Sorbonne. She also worked as a candy striper in a local hospital.

In 1991 Rhimes graduated from Dartmouth College with a degree in English literature. There she wrote for the college newspaper and was part of the theater department. She took an entry level writing job at the advertising firm McCann Erickson. Because she disliked the job, she applied to film school, having heard it was more difficult to get into than Harvard Law School; the idea appealed to her competitive nature. She earned a master of fine arts degree at University of Southern California's School of Cinematic Arts (USC). She also received the Gary Rosenberg Writing Fellowship while there.

**BEGINNING**

Rhimes began working in film as a research director on the 1995 film *Hank Aaron: Chasing the Dream*. She wrote a screenplay called *Human Seeking Same*, which was never made into a movie, but its sale garnered some attention. Rhimes next wrote the script for the HBO television movie *Introducing Dorothy Dandridge* (1999). *Introducing Dorothy Dandridge* starred Halle Berry, who won a Golden Globe Award for her performance. Rhimes also wrote the 2002 film *Crossroads*, starring singer Britney Spears; the movie was a critical failure, but had moderate box office success. With the profits from *Crossroads*, Rhimes bought a home in Beachwood Canyon.

In 2004 Rhimes wrote the screenplay for the film *Princess Diaries 2: Royal Engagement*. For the project she worked with producer Debra Martin Chase. Rhimes and Chase had first met when Rhimes was still at USC and she had an internship at Mundy Lane Entertainment, a production company owned by actor Denzel Washington. Chase told Lacey Rose and Mary Rozzi for *Hollywood Reporter* (8 Oct. 2014), "When you're young, you tend to be a bit myopic in being totally led by passion, but she wasn't afraid to have a sense of the marketplace. She didn't think that that was contrary or undermining art to have a sense of what would sell and what wouldn't." When Rhimes wrote the script for *Princess Diaries 2*, both women made it a priority to add a black princess, played by Raven-Symoné, in the script.

**GREY'S ANATOMY**

In the early 2000s Rhimes developed an interest in writing long-form stories for television. After writing a pilot in 2003 that was not picked up, she began the project that would propel her into mainstream success. The medical drama *Grey's Anatomy* premiered on ABC on March 27, 2005. It follows surgical staff at a fictional hospital in Seattle, Washington, and stars Ellen Pompeo as Meredith Grey. Although she did not deliberately write their race into the characters, she chose strong actors and ended up with a multicultural show and a racially diverse cast. By 2015, *Grey's Anatomy* had won a Golden Globe Award (2007), for best television series in a drama and multiple Primetime Emmy Awards, including a win in 2006 for outstanding casting for a drama series.

Rhimes was sometime accused of not following the usual Hollywood protocol for a new writer; she was not afraid to express her opinion regarding edits and changes about the script. She explained to Lola Ogunnaike for *Essence* (March 2012), "Grey's was my first job working in television, so it didn't occur to me they could fire me. How could they? I'm the writer. I'm the only person who knows what will happen on the show. I was fearless because it didn't occur to me to be afraid. And that fearlessness saved me. Fear tightens you up and confuses you and makes you react in ways that you shouldn't, in ways that may be a detriment to your vision even if they are totally in line with what someone else is thinking." Even so, Rhimes was paired with veteran showrunner James Parriott.

### PRIVATE PRACTICE

After her Golden Globe win in 2007, Rhimes generated a spinoff series, *Private Practice*, which premiered in 2007 and starred Kate Walsh as Addison Montgomery, a neonatal surgeon. The show focuses on Walsh's character—who plays the ex-wife of Derek Shepherd on *Grey's Anatomy*—and is set at the fictional Seaside Health and Wellness clinic in Santa Monica, California. On May 3, 2007, *Private Practice* aired as part of a two-parter, that started with a *Grey's Anatomy* episode and carried over to the premiere episode of *Private Practice* and attracted 23 million viewers. In an interview with Lynette Rice for *Entertainment Weekly* (14 Sept. 2007) Rhimes said "I really want *Private Practice* to have its own identity." She added: "I really don't want it to be Grey's 2.0."

After six seasons, *Private Practice* completed its last episode. Unlike *Grey's Anatomy*, *Private Practice* never received an Emmy or Golden Globe; it did, however, win awards from the American Latino Media Awards (ALMA) and Broadcast Music, Inc. Film & TV Awards (BMI).

### MORE HITS

Rhimes's commercial success gave her more license than many writers and producers in Hollywood to create her shows. As she told Ogunnaike, "I don't know if I call it power. I call it freedom. I've earned the right to be trusted. We make our show the way we want as long as we stay in the budget."

*Scandal*, starring Kerry Washington, premiered in April 2012 and became the first network series with a black female protagonist since 1975. Washington stars alongside actors Darby Stanchfield, Tony Goldwyn, Guillermo Diaz, and Bellamy Young. *Scandal* is loosely based on the career of Judy Smith, a political crisis manager and former deputy press secretary under George H. W. Bush. Washington's character, Olivia Pope, plays a former White House communications director who starts her own crisis management firm.

With each season, the show has increased its audience; by spring 2013, more than eight million people watched it, making it the premier drama on any network at ten p.m., for the coveted eighteen to forty-nine-year-old demographic. It also became a social media event, with about 190,000 tweets sent during the show. In 2014, *Scandal* received a Golden Globe nomination and won a Primetime Emmy. Due to continued success and confident in her work, Rhimes stopped taking notes from the network; not long after, the network stopped giving notes.

*How to Get Away with Murder*, for which Rhimes was an executive producer, debuted in 2014 and was an instant hit. Created by writer Peter Nowalk, the show stars Viola Davis as Annalise Keating, a brilliant criminal defense professor who becomes involved in a murder plot. Davis stars alongside actors Billy Brown and Tom Verica.

In a September 18, 2014, review of *How to Get Away with Murder*, Alessandra Stanley for the *New York Times*, wrote: "When Shonda Rhimes writes her autobiography, it should be called 'How to Get Away With Being an Angry Black Woman.'" Rhimes, now the center of a very public conversation, told Eliana Dockterman for *Time* (8 Oct. 2014) "I find race and gender to be terribly important; they're terribly important to who I am," Rhimes said. "But there's something about the need for everybody else to spend time talking about it. . . that pisses me off."

The show speaks for itself, garnering a Golden Globe nomination in 2015. Davis told Lacey Rose and Mary Rossi for *Hollywood Reporter* (17 Oct. 2014), "Shonda is a black woman, and I understand that that's a part of what people want to write about when they write about her. But here's the thing: After you write about that, write about something else. Write about her vision, write about her courage, write about her talent, write about the fact that she's been able to achieve something that very few people have been able to achieve. Write about that."

## SHONDALAND

Rhimes created her own production company, Shondaland, in 2004, which she uses to encourage other writers. They then move from one show to another with her. As she told Lacey Rose and Mary Rossi, "Most writing staffs have this crazy high turnover, and then everyone's really miserable, and I don't understand that. I don't know why you don't grow people to then be able to take over as you. That's how I can have more shows." Rhimes runs Shondaland with partner Betsy Beers, who serves as executive producer on Rhimes's series.

Rhimes and ABC signed a deal in 2014 that linked the two until 2018. Both *Grey's Anatomy* and *Scandal* are considered "the network's two most valuable series." Paul Lee, ABC Entertainment's president, told T. L. Stanley for *Adweek* (2 June 2014), "She's at the very top of her game, and we have no doubt that she's setting a standard on ABC that others will be trying to emulate for years to come. We're thrilled to be in business with her."

In January 2015, ABC announced it would purchase a new pilot from Shondaland: a crime thriller entitled *The Catch*, produced by Rhimes and written by Jennifer Schuur. In March 2015 the show cast Damon Dayoub and Mireille Enos in its lead roles.

## PERSONAL LIFE

In the light of her personal reevaluation after the destruction of the World Trade Center, Rhimes decided to adopt a child. Nine months later, when she was thirty-two, she adopted Harper, named for novelist Harper Lee, and became a single mother. She subsequently adopted two more girls: Emerson Pearl in 2012 and Beckett, via a surrogate, in 2013. Rhimes keeps in touch with the same three girlfriends she has had for decades; they and her sisters keep her grounded. Discussing her ambition, she told Leahy,

"There's nothing wrong with being driven. And there's nothing wrong with putting yourself first to reach your goals."

## SUGGESTED READING

Alter, Charlotte. "Shonda Rhimes: 'Anyone Who Tells You They Are Doing It All Perfectly Is A Liar.'" *Time*. Time, 9 June 2014. Web. 2 Feb. 2015.

Ball, Sarah. "What You Should Know About Shonda Rhimes: A Panoply of Eccentric Biographical Data Re: TV's First Lady Of Network Drama." *Vanity Fair*. Condé Nast, 7 Aug. 2013. Web. 2 Feb. 2015.

Collier, Aldore. "Shonda Rhimes: The Force Behind Grey's Anatomy." *Ebony* Oct. 2005: 204–8. Print.

Ogunnaike, Lola. "Shonda Rhimes." *Essence* Mar. 2012: 98–102. Print.

Rhimes, Shonda. "Shonda Rhimes." Interview by Colleen Leahey. *Fortune*. Time, 10 Oct. 2013. Web. 2 Feb. 2015.

Rose, Lacey, and Mary Rozzi. "Hollywood's Most Powerful Black, Female Showrunner." *Hollywood Reporter*. Hollywood Reporter, 2014. Web. 2 Feb. 2015.

## SELECTED WORKS

*Introducing Dorothy Dandridge*, 1999; *Princess Diaries 2*, 2004; *Grey's Anatomy*, 2005–; *Private Practice*, 2007; *Scandal*, 2012–; *How to Get Away with Murder*, 2014

—Judy Johnson

---

# Laurel Richie

**Born:** 1959

**Occupation:** President of the Women's National Basketball Association

Laurel Richie replaced Donna Orender as the president of the Women's National Basketball Association (WNBA) in May 2011, becoming the first African American woman to head a national professional sports league in the United States. Before accepting the position, Richie worked as a marketing executive at the advertising agency Ogilvy & Mather for twenty-four years. She also served as senior vice president and chief marketing officer for the Girl Scouts of the USA from 2008 to 2011.

Although Richie is not a lifelong basketball aficionado, she is a longtime advocate for women, and she has the marketing savvy to make the WNBA a much more visible—and viable—organization. "Laurel combines extraordinary marketing and brand-management skills with a tremendous enthusiasm to help evolve young women into leaders," former NBA commissioner David Stern said about the appointment, according to Jodie Valade for the Cleveland *Plain Dealer* (19 June 2011). "She joins the WNBA at such an exciting time in its history, and we know her expertise will be key to continuing the growth and success of the league."

Founded in 1996, the WNBA was not the first professional women's basketball league in the United States, but nearly twenty seasons later, it is by far the most successful; its predecessor, the Women's Professional Basketball League (WBL), lasted only three seasons before collapsing in debt. Still, that success is difficult to quantify. Superstar players such as Brittney Griner of the Phoenix Mercury, who recently signed an endorsement deal with Nike, are bringing more attention to women's basketball, but the sport has a long way to go to compete with its male counterpart. As Neil deMause wrote for the Al Jazeera America website (29 Aug. 2014), "For most sports fans, these are the two competing images of the WNBA: the arenas are either half empty or half full."

## EARLY LIFE AND EDUCATION

Laurel Janet Richie was born and raised in Shaker Heights, just outside of Cleveland, Ohio. Her father, Winston Richie, worked as a dentist and community leader. Her mother, Beatrice, was a librarian; she passed away in 2009. Richie has three siblings, sisters Beth and Anne and brother Winston Jr. In the 1950s, her father was the only black player on the Case Western Reserve basketball team, and he held season tickets for the National Basketball Association's (NBA) Cleveland Cavaliers for thirty years.

Growing up, Richie was a synchronized swimmer and a cheerleader; she did not consider herself a basketball fan, much less a player. "I have never one day played the game of basketball, not one day in my entire life," she told students at Shaker Heights High School, according to the school's newspaper, the *Shakerite* (18 Oct. 2012). As she has said in multiple interviews, however, she would characterize herself as a "trailblazer" in the mold of her parents. When she was a student at Mercer Elementary School, hers was the only African

Mike Coppola/Getty Images North America

American family in her class. To be able to buy her childhood house, her parents had to ask a white friend to act as an intermediary because the owners refused to sell the house to a black family. This kind of discrimination prepared her for many of her jobs since, Richie told Shaker Heights High students, in which she has found herself to be the only woman or the only African American in the room.

In 1977, Richie graduated from Shaker Heights High School and enrolled at Dartmouth College. During her time there, she was a dancer and a member of the Black Underground Theater of the Arts (BUTA). She was also a member of Cobra, Dartmouth's oldest all-female senior society. As a junior, she received the Randy B. Cardozo Memorial Award. Though she began her college career as a foreign-languages major, she graduated with a degree in policy studies—or, as she preferred to think of it, the psychology of decision making—in 1981.

## MARKETING CAREER

After graduation, Richie took a job with the advertising agency Leo Burnett Worldwide in Chicago. "I decided to go into advertising because I was interviewed for Burnett by [fellow Dartmouth alum] John Kovas," she told Ralph Wimbish for the *Dartmouth Alumni Magazine* (Sept.–Oct. 2011). "At forty he was the type of person I wanted to be: well read, up on current events, knowledgeable about music and the arts . . . just a really interesting sort of a man."

With the Burnett management training program completed, Richie moved to New York City in 1983. She thought about becoming an actor and went to an open-call audition. When she arrived, she told Wimbish, there were already 350 beautiful women lined up in front of her. Realizing she did not have a thick enough skin for rejection, she "happily" returned to advertising, beginning a long tenure at the firm Ogilvy & Mather in January 1984. Her twenty-four years there offered her the variety she craved, with projects that included the AT&T merger and a marketing campaign for Huggies diapers. She also worked on brand development for companies such as American Express, Pepperidge Farm, and Unilever and was involved with pro bono work for the Museum for African Art, the Hospital for Special Surgery, and the New York City Commission on Human Rights.

Richie told Adam Bryant for the *New York Times* (4 Aug. 2012) that she learned an important leadership lesson after she was made vice president at Ogilvy & Mather. She and her team were working on a successful account when she decided to take a week's vacation. When she returned from her trip, she found out that her team had approached Human Resources while she was gone. They said that they enjoyed working on the account but that they did not like working for Richie. "I remember feeling shocked, and defensive at first. But then I really stepped back and listened to what they were saying," Richie recalled. The team members were upset because they felt that ownership of the account was not being equitably shared and that Richie was taking all of the credit for their work. So, Richie said, she took steps to redefine her job as a leader. She bought Silly Putty and stretched it out while allowing people to hash out their ideas and grievances. "And we all came together," Richie said. "One of the greatest things is that at the end of the year, somebody on the team came to me and said, 'I'd walk through fire for you.'"

## WNBA

In 2008, Richie left Ogilvy & Mather to become the senior vice president of the Girl Scouts of the USA, where empowering women and girls became her primary focus. In early 2011, she traveled to Seattle to deliver the keynote address at a Girl Scouts fundraiser. Karen Bryant, the president and CEO of the WNBA's Seattle Storm, was in the audience. Though Richie did not know it at the time, her fate was sealed about three-quarters of the way through her speech, when Bryant locked eyes with two of the Seattle Storm's owners. The women all knew that the WNBA was looking for a new president. "She was just the kind of person we were looking for," Bryant recalled to Wimbish. Two weeks later, Richie got a call for an interview. She officially started her job in May 2011.

Richie is the first WNBA president who is not a former player. (Val Ackerman was a college All-Star who played professional ball in France; Orender was a point guard in the WBL in the late 1970s and early 1980s.) But given the league's growth, her marketing savvy is a much more valuable asset than any athletic skills. And although she had never attended a WNBA game before assuming the post, Richie quickly formed plans to introduce the WNBA to a new generation of fans and eradicate the pervasive perception that women's basketball is a "niche" sport—or, worse, an NBA sideshow. The players, she argues, are better than ever. "We have a generation of players who've grown up with the benefits of Title IX," Richie told deMause, referring to the 1972 law that required colleges to allot equal funding to men's and women's sports. "They are stronger. They are faster. They are basketball-savvy."

In 2014, one of the WNBA's biggest stars, Becky Hammon, was hired as an assistant coach with the NBA's championship-winning San Antonio Spurs one year after her retirement. Hammon is the first woman to hold a paid coaching position in the NBA. It was a significant milestone in the relationship between the two leagues, proving that, in terms of basketball intelligence, the girls could hold their own with the guys.

## MARKETING THE WNBA

Richie hopes to do away with comparisons between the two leagues altogether. "I'd like to create an environment similar to that in pro tennis," she told Wimbish. "Men's and women's tennis are different, but one is not better than the other." Not surprisingly, Richie approaches the problem from a marketing perspective. "They know Serena [Williams]. They know Venus [Williams]. They know Maria [Sharapova]," she said to Michel Martin on the National Public Radio (NPR) program *Tell Me More* (4 Apr. 2012). "So one of the things that I'm very focused on is having more and more sports fans get to know the women of the WNBA, their style of play, their strengths, their weaknesses, because . . . at the end of the day you're really following your favorite player."

In 2013, the top pick of the WNBA draft was Baylor University All-Star Brittney Griner, one of the league's most famous players and its first to dunk twice in one game. She is also a lesbian, and the intersection of her talent and her openness about her sexual orientation has afforded the WNBA further opportunity to reach out to the LGBT community. The league launched the WNBA Pride campaign in May 2014 in support of LGBT (Lesbian, gay, bisexual, transgender) rights, a move indicative of a new and refreshing marketing strategy. Early attempts by the WNBA to win fans marginalized players in an attempt to appeal to heterosexual white male fans; at one point, the league briefly considered adopting more form-fitting uniforms, and it continues to hold tutorials for rookies about how to apply makeup. Alex Chambers, author of the book *13 Teams: One Man's Journey with the WNBA* (2011), told deMause, "For the haters, when it comes to that, no shorts will be short enough, no dunks will be enough, no plays will be enough." Richie prefers to focus on growing the diverse group of fans that the WNBA can already claim. "I was reading one of the tweets from a father who had taken a photograph of his daughter, a little tyke with a huge basketball, saying, 'This could be the next Becky Hammon,'" she told deMause. "That's the ripple effect of what we do."

## PERSONAL LIFE

Richie lives in New York City. During her career, she has been the recipient of the YMCA Black Achievers Award and was named one of *Ebony* magazine's outstanding women in marketing and communications. Her father has remained proud, expressing his faith in her ability to lead the WNBA. "I recognize that the job she has now is not a basketball player's job," he told Valade, "and you don't have to have played the game to be able to do it right."

## SUGGESTED READING

deMause, Neil. "WNBA: Hoop Skills Not Enough for Women's Teams." *Al Jazeera America*. Al Jazeera America, 29 Aug. 2014. Web. 20 Oct. 2014.
Richie, Laurel. "Tell Me Your Idea (and Don't Mind the Silly Putty)." Interview by Adam Bryant. *New York Times*. New York Times, 4 Aug. 2012. Web. 20 Oct. 2014.
Richie, Laurel. "WNBA President Bringing Lessons from Girl Scouts." Interview by Michel Martin. *Tell Me More*. Natl. Public Radio. 4 Apr. 2012. *NPR*. Web. 20 Oct. 2014.
"2012 High School Hall of Fame Inductees." *Shakerite*. Shaker Heights High School, 18 Oct. 2012. Web. 20 Oct. 2014.
Valade, Jodie. "WNBA's New Commissioner, Former Shaker Heights Resident Laurel Richie, Maintains Her Father's Pioneering Spirit." *Cleveland.com*. Plain Dealer/Northeast Ohio Media Group, 19 June 2011. Web. 20 Oct. 2014.
Wimbish, Ralph. "Game On." *Dartmouth Alumni Magazine* Sept.–Oct. 2011: 40–43. Print.

—Molly Hagan

# Gina Rinehart

**Born:** February 9, 1954
**Occupation:** Chair and director of Hancock Prospecting

Gina Rinehart is the executive chair of Hancock Prospecting and one of the richest people in Australia.

## BACKGROUND

Gina Rinehart was born Georgina Hope Hancock on February 9, 1954, in Perth. She is the only child of Australian iron-ore magnate Langley "Lang" Hancock and his second wife, Hope Margaret Nicholas. Rinehart lived in the remote West Australian town of Nunyerry for the first four years of her life before her family moved to Perth. She attended St Hilda's Anglican School for Girls in Perth for fifteen years, where she was a top student. In 1973, she attended the University of Sydney to study economics, but she dropped out after the first year, choosing instead to work for her father in the family iron-ore business.

Rinehart inherited Hancock Prospecting from her father upon his death in 1992 and has since increased her wealth through joint ventures in the mining industry and through the purchase of stakes in various media organizations. Rinehart has appeared on Australia's list of richest people since 1992, being named the richest woman in the country in 2010 and the richest person in the country the subsequent year. She is Australia's first female billionaire.

Rinehart is also politically active, having spoken out against several proposed environmental regulations and promoting the development of land in some of Australia's more remote areas. Additionally, Rinehart has worked toward charitable causes, donating time and money to organizations in Cambodia that seek to help women and girls through educational scholarships and other initiatives.

## IRON-ORE MAGNATE

After the death of her father in 1992, Rinehart inherited his business, Hancock Prospecting, and its royalty agreement with the London-based multinational mining corporation Rio Tinto Group. She is often labeled as an heiress, although she has consistently stated that the term is inaccurate, as Hancock Prospecting was in a state of debt when it passed to her. One of Rinehart's first actions as head of the company was to propose the development of the Hope Downs iron-ore mine (named after her mother), located in Western Australia's remote Pilbara region, in a joint venture with Rio Tinto that, despite initial troubles with infrastructure, played a key role in moving the company out of debt. As of 2012, this venture was netting Rinehart an annual profit of approximately $1.9 billion. In 2014, Hancock Prospecting saw its portfolio expand to include oil and gas holdings. The company has also been active in developing the Roy Hill iron-ore mine in the Pilbara region, securing a $7.2 billion debt-funding package in March 2014.

In addition to her work in the mining industry, Rinehart has recently expanded her holdings by acquiring stakes in media companies. In 2010, she bought a stake in Ten Network Holdings, worth 10 percent, and she has subsequently taken an almost 15 percent stake in Fairfax Media. She is the largest shareholder of Fairfax Media, though she does not sit on the board of the company.

With regard to personal wealth, Rinehart has been a billionaire since 2006. Between her mining and media holdings, she was estimated by *Forbes* magazine to be worth $17.6 billion in June 2014. The Australian magazine *BRW* listed her as Australia's richest woman in 2010 and as Australia's richest person in 2011. In 2014, she ranked forty-sixth on *Forbes* magazine's list of the five hundred richest people in the world.

Rinehart and her company have often been involved in legal proceedings, and Rinehart herself is known for being a fairly litigious individual. The death of her father prompted a lengthy court battle with her stepmother, Rose Porteous, concerning the circumstances of her father's death (which was later determined to be from natural causes) and ownership of his assets. In 2011, three of Rinehart's four children commenced legal action against her in an effort to remove her as the sole trustee of the Hope Margaret Hancock Trust, which was established by Lang Hancock for his grandchildren. In 2014, her third child, Hope Welker, formally withdrew from the case.

In 2010, Rinehart helped to fund a campaign protesting the Mineral Resource Rent Tax, which passed in 2012 and levies a tax on profits generated from the exploitation of nonrenewable resources in Australia. She is generally conservative in her political views, supporting antitax groups and vocally denying the existence of anthropogenic climate change. Rinehart has made repeated statements supporting the restriction of wages for working Australians and the relaxing of regulations to encourage foreign investment.

In addition to her business and political actions, Rinehart has donated time and money to organizations that seek to work against human trafficking.

## IMPACT

As Australia's first female billionaire and one of the world's wealthiest individuals, Rinehart has been influential both in the business sector and in Australian politics. Her family has been involved in controversy both publicly and personally, and Rinehart has been known to speak out on the future of Australian business interests and politics.

## PERSONAL LIFE

Rinehart was married to Frank Rinehart from 1983 until his death in 1990. Her first marriage, to Greg Milton Hayward, ended in divorce in 1981. She has four children from her two marriages, John, Bianca, Hope, and Ginia.

## SUGGESTED READING

Bryant, Nick. "Gina Rinehart's Quest for Respect and Gratitude." *Monthly*. Monthly, May 2012. Web. 30 June 2014.

Ferguson, Adele. *Gina Rinehart: The Untold Story of the Richest Person in Australian History*. Sydney: Pan Macmillan, 2012. Print.

Finnegan, William. "The Miner's Daughter." *New Yorker*. Condé Nast, 25 Mar. 2013. Web. 30 June 2014.

Kerr, Peter. "First Lady." *BRW*. Fairfax Media, 25 May 2011. Web. 30 June 2014.

Newton, Gloria. "Lang Hancock's Daughter Comes of Age." *Australian Women's Weekly* 19 Feb. 1975: 10–11. Print.

Treadgold, Tim. "Miner's Daughter." *Forbes*. Forbes.com, 2 Feb. 2011. Web. 30 June 2014.

—Anna Phillips

# Michele A. Roberts

**Born:** September 14, 1956
**Occupation:** Executive director of the National Basketball Players Association

Bloomberg/Getty Images

When Michele Roberts was selected as the next executive director of the National Basketball Players Association (NBPA) in the summer of 2014, she became the first woman to head a major professional sports union in North America. She succeeded Billy Hunter, who had left the union almost eighteen months earlier amid turmoil. Prior to joining the NBPA, Roberts enjoyed a three-decade-plus career practicing law in Washington, DC. She began her legal career as a defense attorney before specializing in civil and white-collar litigation for such firms as Shea & Gardner; Akin Gump; and Skadden, Arps, Slate, Meagher & Flom.

Formerly hailed as one of the top trial lawyers in the United States, Roberts has already begun using her no-nonsense negotiating skills and aggressive style to help restore stability and respectability back to the NBPA. The Cleveland Cavaliers forward and union treasurer James Jones described Roberts as "calculating," "intelligent," and "authentic," as quoted by Michael Lee for the *Washington Post* (9 Nov. 2014). "Of all the candidates we saw," he added, "she was by far the best."

## EARLY LIFE AND EDUCATION

Michele A. Roberts was born on September 14, 1956, in the Bronx borough of New York City. Along with her four siblings, she was raised by her mother, Elsie, in the Melrose Houses, a low-income development in the southwestern section of the Bronx. Her father deserted the family when she was a toddler.

Roberts grew up poor in a family that relied on government assistance to survive. To supplement the family's meager welfare checks, her mother worked as a housecleaner and sold home-cooked meals. Wanting her children to make a better life for themselves, Elsie Roberts, who died in 1980, ran a strict household that emphasized the importance of education. As a re-

sult, Roberts and her siblings spent much of their free time out of school reading and studying.

Roberts's interest in law took shape when she was a child. As a form of entertainment, her mother would watch trials and arraignments at the nearby Bronx Supreme Court, and during the summer, she often accompanied her. "It was free, and we didn't have any money," Roberts recalled to Kate Fagan for website espnW (17 Dec. 2014). "And I thought it was the greatest thing in the world." After witnessing one of her older brother's friends get sent to jail at the hands of a lowly court-appointed lawyer, Roberts resolved to become a lawyer for the underprivileged.

Precocious and conscientious, Roberts attended Bronx public schools before winning a scholarship to the Masters School, a prestigious, all-girls boarding school in Dobbs Ferry, New York. She enrolled there before her sophomore year of high school. During her time at the Masters School, Roberts, one of only a handful of African Americans at the predominantly white institution, was frequently subjected to racial discrimination. To cope, she threw herself into her studies. "It was actually some of the best training for my professional life," she told Andrew Keh for the *New York Times* (16 Aug. 2014). "Once I realized that being different does not mean being inferior—I scoff at that nonsense if I see it."

Despite her trying high school experience, Roberts did well enough academically to win acceptance to Wesleyan University, graduating with a bachelor's degree in government in 1977. She then attended the Boalt Hall School of Law at the University of California at Berkeley and did volunteer work at California's notorious San Quentin State Prison, where she represented inmates on death row. In 1980 she earned her juris doctor degree.

## LAW CAREER

After passing her bar exam, Roberts was hired to work at the prestigious Public Defender Service (PDS) in Washington, DC, where she was mentored by the prominent legal theorist Charles Ogletree Jr. During her eight-year tenure with PDS, Roberts represented dozens of clients accused of violent criminal offenses. She tried more than forty jury trials and rose to chief of her office's trial division.

At PDS, Roberts established a reputation as a formidable trial lawyer with a knack for connecting to jurors. "She became so good, so quickly," Keh wrote, "that some other lawyers filled the benches just to watch her work." A steadfast champion of her clients, Roberts became known for her deft handling of underdog cases. One of her most notable involved the 1984 rape and murder of Catherine Fuller, a forty-eight-year-old mother of six. Her client was one of ten defendants to stand trial for the murder and one of only two who were acquitted.

In 1988 Roberts left PDS to enter into private practice. "At some point, you become a little jaded, and my energy level was going down," she explained to Sarah Kogod for the website SB Nation (23 Oct. 2014). "As a public defender, all I did was criminal cases, and I wanted to do something else." Roberts worked at a series of Washington, DC, law firms over the next decade, during which she began specializing in civil and white-collar criminal litigation. For a time in the 1990s, she also ran her own private firm.

In 2001 Roberts joined Shea & Gardner, a law firm based in Washington, DC. She remained with the firm until 2004, when she joined Akin Gump as a partner in the prominent firm's white-collar criminal defense practice. From 2011 to 2014, she served as a litigation partner at Skadden, Arps, Slate, Meagher, and Flom. Commonly known as Skadden, the global firm is one of the most prestigious in the world.

During a legal career that spanned more than three decades, Roberts became known as one of the best trial lawyers in the country. Among her many honors, she was named "the finest pure trial lawyer in Washington" by *Washingtonian* magazine in 2002 and business trial lawyer of the year at the Chambers USA Awards of Excellence in 2011.

## CAMPAIGNING FOR THE NBPA

Roberts's interest in leading the NBPA first took root in February 2013, when Billy Hunter, the union's longtime executive director, was fired amid conflict-of-interest and nepotism allegations. Hunter, the union head since 1996, had long fallen out of favor with players for his questionable business and negotiating tactics. His handling of the 2011 National Basketball Association (NBA) lockout was regarded as a major failure.

In the wake of Hunter's firing, Roberts, a lifelong basketball fan and longtime Washington Wizards season-ticket holder who watched a lot of televised games with her brothers growing up, began studying the history of the NBPA and the intricacies of the collective bargaining agreement (CBA). Roberts soon came up with a plan that she believed would galvanize the union and entered the fray as a candidate. "After a while, I not only convinced myself I could do this, I actually convinced myself no one could do it better," she explained to Lee.

For Roberts, her biggest challenge was convincing the union's players. Despite her impressive legal credentials, she had no prior experience in labor relations or professional sports. As a result, she was considered a long shot in the race to succeed Hunter. Nevertheless, following an arduous seventeen-month-long search led by the NBPA's executive committee, in which more than three hundred candidates were considered, she emerged as one of three finalists.

In July 2014 Roberts was elected as executive director of the NBPA, after receiving thirty-two of thirty-six votes from the executive board. With her election, she became the first female leader of a players' union for one of the top four professional sports (baseball, basketball, football, and hockey) in North America. Players were ultimately won over by Roberts's legal expertise, her rise from humble beginnings, and her grit in the face of racial and gender discrimination. During her forty-five minute pitch to players, Roberts shattered any doubts about her ability to exist in the male-dominated environs of the NBA by issuing the memorable line, "My past is littered with the bones of men who were foolish enough to think I was someone they could sleep on," as quoted by Lee.

## EXECUTIVE DIRECTOR OF THE NBPA

During the first months of her tenure as executive director of the NBPA, Roberts traveled extensively around the country meeting with representatives and players from each of the league's thirty teams in an effort to gain trust and feedback. She assembled an executive management staff and began devising a strategy that would prepare and unite players for the league's next potential CBA after the 2016–17 season. Players are widely expected to opt out of their current CBA, which lowered their share of basketball-related income from 57 to around 50 percent, shortened maximum guaranteed contracts, and enacted more severe salary cap penalties. Still, Roberts explained to Lee, "I don't want a lockout. I don't want a strike. What I want is anything any reasonable person would want—and that is labor peace."

Roberts has shared her blunt views on a number of important issues that will take center stage during the next round of labor negotiations in 2017. Among them are the salary cap system, rookie wage scales, mandatory age limits, regular-season schedules, postseason formats, and players' media availability. In an interview with Pablo S. Torre for *ESPN The Magazine* (13 Nov. 2014), Roberts called the notion of a salary cap system "un-American," staunchly opposed the NBA's proposal to raise the league age limit from nineteen to twenty, and referred to the league as a "monopoly." Meanwhile, in another conversation with Kate Fagan for espnW (25 Feb. 2015), she called the league's eighty-two game regular-season schedule "ridiculous" and criticized its media policies.

During the 2015 NBA All-Star Weekend in New York, Roberts conducted her first annual meeting as NBPA head. In March of that year she announced that she would be scheduling her first substantive meetings with NBA commissioner Adam Silver, who succeeded longtime league head David Stern in 2014. Beyond that, Roberts expressed to Kogod her ultimate goal in the position, declaring that she hopes to be remembered for making the NBPA "the strongest union on the planet."

## PERSONAL LIFE

Although Roberts may have enjoyed a comfortable home in the nation's capital as well as occasional nights out with friends after work, she has voluntarily traded that in to move back to New York and assume her new role. "This job leaves no room for a life," she admitted to Fagan. She lives in an apartment in Harlem conveniently located four blocks from the NBPA headquarters.

## SUGGESTED READING

Fagan, Kate. "Fluffy Answers Not Allowed—An Afternoon with Michele Roberts." *espnW*. ESPN Internet Ventures, 25 Feb. 2015. Web. 19 Mar. 2015.

Fagan, Kate. "Impact 25: NBA Union Chief Michele Roberts Knows Exactly What She's Doing." *espnW*. ESPN Internet Ventures, 17 Dec. 2014. Web. 19 Mar. 2015.

Keh, Andrew. "Smashing a Ceiling and a Lot of Egos." *New York Times*. New York Times, 16 Aug. 2014. Web. 19 Mar. 2015.

Kogod, Sarah. "The New Sheriff in Town." *SB Nation*. Vox Media, 23 Oct. 2014. Web. 19 Mar. 2015.

Lee, Michael. "Union Head Michele Roberts Shows She'll Be Strong Advocate for NBA Players." *Washington Post*. Washington Post, 9 Nov. 2014. Web. 19 Mar. 2015.

Torre, Pablo S. "NBPA Director: 'Let's Stop Pretending.'" *ESPN*. ESPN Internet Ventures, 13 Nov. 2014. Web. 19 Mar. 2015.

—Chris Cullen

# Favianna Rodriguez

**Born:** September 26, 1978
**Occupation:** Artist

Favianna Rodriguez is a Latina artist, activist, and entrepreneur. She grew up in Oakland, California, and is the daughter of Peruvian immigrants. Rodriguez's artwork is largely political, focusing on immigration and women's rights, but she told Tina Vasquez for *Bitch* magazine (spring 2013) that she does not like to be called a political artist. "My work has always been based on my environment, my community, my experiences—it's always just been about the life I'm living and all the forces that affect me and my community, and those who look like me," she said. "Part of being an artist is understanding what unites all of us. I've become known as a Latina artist whose work focuses on migration, but it's a human issue that impacts all of us."

After dropping out of the University of California, Berkeley, in 1999, Rodriguez launched a number of successful design organizations focused on social change. In 2009, she helped found the website Presente.org in response to vitriolic anti-immigration rhetoric, stoked in part by public figures such as CNN commentator Lou Dobbs, and a corresponding spike in hate crimes against Latinos. One of Presente's first initiatives was to force Dobbs off the air; the site joined with other immigrant groups in a successful nationwide campaign that combined art and social media to accomplish its singular goal.

The Presente campaign represented a shift in the way Rodriguez viewed interactions with the public. After attending the 2008 Democratic National Convention, she felt as if protests had become an ineffective kind of theater, and no one seemed to be listening. When it came to Dobbs, Rodriguez and her supporters shrewdly directed their ire at CNN's brand. ("CNN: Clearly Not News," read one poster.) "When you mess with their brand," Rodriguez told Peter Maiden for the San Francisco website *Indybay* (13 Mar. 2010), "you're ultimately messing with their bottom line."

Rodriguez has also founded a group and magazine called *CultureStrike*, which seeks to provide a counternarrative about immigration in the United States. For example, Rodriguez spearheaded a campaign that used the image of a monarch butterfly, she told Samantha Leal for *Latina* magazine (18 Jan. 2013), "to reimagine migration as something beautiful and natural." She explained, "Like the monarch butterfly, human beings cross borders in order to survive. The butterfly is ultimately about our right to move."

## EARLY LIFE AND EDUCATION

Rodriguez was born on September 26, 1978, and grew up in the Fruitvale neighborhood of Oakland, California. Her parents had emigrated separately from Peru in the late 1960s and met in California in the early 1970s. Rodriguez's mother worked in a dental office; her father worked in restaurants. While she was growing up, Rodriguez's parents often worked two or three jobs at a time to make ends meet. They supported their daughter's artistic pursuits but considered her love of art more of a hobby than a viable career path. "They definitely wanted me to be a doctor, or an engineer, or something meaningful that would make them very proud immigrant parents, because they didn't get the opportunity to go to college," Rodriguez told Maiden.

Rodriguez went to Centro Infantil de la Raza, a nonprofit preschool, and began to learn about art at children's programs taught through Oakland's Spanish Speaking Citizens' Foundation. She attended Catholic school until seventh grade, when her parents sent her to live with an aunt in Mexico City, Mexico, for junior high. Quality of education was a factor in the decision—Oakland schools were not up to par—but Rodriguez also told Oakland's *East Bay Express* (1 July 2009) that the city was "a little dangerous for a teenager," particularly one who was "going down the wrong path and hanging out with the wrong people."

Though initially happy to get away, Rodriguez found Mexico's traditionalist culture stifling. She was "too Americanized," she told the *Express*: "I would hang out with a lot of boys . . . [and] a lot of the queer girls. . . . I would hang out with all the outsider kids." Her behavior, she told the *Express*, was seen as fairly risqué given the time and place. "It was culture shock for me, but for everyone who interacted with me, they were probably like, '*Wow,*'" she said. Living with her aunt did not work out, so Rodriguez began renting her own room elsewhere. The independence was liberating; in several interviews, Rodriguez has described her parents as well meaning but somewhat overbearing. She was inspired by the murals she saw in the street and began to feel a strong connection to Mexican painter Frida Kahlo, who would become one of her artistic heroes.

Rodriguez returned to Oakland during her junior year of high school. Still concerned about the quality of Oakland public schools, she began attending San Leandro High School in nearby San Leandro, California, in defiance of school districting laws, but was caught and ended up graduating from Skyline High School in Oakland in 1996. After years of Saturday classes and summer math camps to augment the dismal instruction she received at school, Rodriguez was admitted to the University of California, Berkeley, where she majored in architecture and Chicano studies. She won a number of community scholarships, which helped alleviate some of the cost. In 1999, during her junior year, she took a printmaking class from a Chicana painter named Yreina Cervantez. The encounter inspired her to drop out of school and pursue her own path. "Art became a way for me to have a voice, to break tradition, and to redefine myself," Rodriguez told Leal.

## TUMIS DESIGN AND NONPROFITS

Rodriguez decided to become an entrepreneur. She wanted to create socially conscious art, and after a residency at the Center for the Study of Political Graphics in Los Angeles when she was nineteen and a stint doing paid illustration for political events, she knew that she could feasibly support herself as such an artist. But Rodriguez, who had excelled in math and science, had other tools at her disposal as well. The Internet was just beginning to take off, and Rodriguez and a handful of her friends could code and design websites. The opportunity to make art and disseminate it through the Internet, she told Vasquez, was simply "more appealing to [her] than staying in school." Still, leaving the education she had worked so hard for—just shy of a degree, no less—was a difficult decision for Rodriguez and a bitter pill for her parents. "I was told that education was the only way you could ever do things for yourself," she explained to Vasquez. The gravity of her decision made her all the more determined to succeed in her new business.

In 2001, Rodriguez cofounded TUMIS, a bilingual graphic design company that seeks out clients who are working for social change. At the time, many organizations were launching their first website and needed a designer's expertise. "From the moment we opened TUMIS, we were busy," Rodriguez told Maiden. The company is still going strong; according to TUMIS's website, it has worked with over three hundred organizations—including Power Up the Vote, INCITE!, and the social-entrepreneurship network Changemakers—on around five hundred projects. In 2009, the company moved from its small shop in the San Antonio neighborhood of Oakland to Berkeley's David Brower Center, a state-of-the-art green building named for the late environmental activist and influential Sierra Club executive director.

Other art organizations grew out of the success of TUMIS, including a printmaking studio called Taller Tupac Amaru. The collective, which Rodriguez founded with fellow graphic artist Jesus Barraza in 2003, focuses on screen prints of political posters and artwork. Around the same time, Rodriguez helped found the East-Side Arts Alliance, which fosters creativity in Oakland neighborhoods. In 2004, the Alliance bought a building on International Boulevard in Oakland and opened the Eastside Cultural Center. Rodriguez also launched a muralist program called Visual Element with Estria Miyashiro. In 2008, she and Brooklyn artist Josh MacPhee collected the work of dozens of political artists in a book titled *Reproduce and Revolt*. "I never feel stuck for ideas," Rodriguez told Maiden of her numerous projects. "I feel like I'm in the middle of a huge social justice ecosystem, where

I'm constantly seeing subjects I can approach in my work."

## PRESENTE AND CULTURESTRIKE

In 2009, Rodriguez co-founded Presente.org. According to the group's website, Presente is "a national organization that exists to amplify the political voice of Latino communities." After the successful ouster of Lou Dobbs from CNN, the group took on a slew of other issues. Some of them might seem to tackle only a small part of a larger problem—one successful campaign lobbied the Associated Press to drop the phrase "illegal immigrant" from its lexicon—but these victories have had a profound effect on the way non-Latinos interact with the migrant population and Latino culture. With the support of its vast network, Presente was also able to stop the Walt Disney Company from trademarking the Day of the Dead, a Latino cultural holiday.

In 2011, Rodriguez co-founded CultureStrike, a national grassroots organization and magazine that, according to its website, seeks to foster an arts movement around immigration. "Immigrants have become a scapegoat for things that are wrong with this country," Rodriguez said in her documentary series *Migration Is Beautiful* (2013), coproduced with recording artist Pharrell Williams and disseminated via his YouTube channel I Am Other. CultureStrike hopes to provide a counternarrative. In the documentary, Rodriguez said that people who are unhappy with the high levels of unemployment in the United States tend to blame their fellow workers rather than the people in charge—business executives and politicians—who are making money off the status quo. "Immigrants aren't to blame," she said, "greed is to blame."

## OTHER WORK

The *East Bay Express* compared Rodriguez's artwork to that of graphic artist Emory Douglas, a former minister of culture for the Black Panthers who used bold outlines and rich colors to create works in an agitprop style. Rodriguez's work often features abstracted figures; warm colors, especially oranges, reds, and pinks; and eye-catching text, such as the memorable slogan "Politicians off my poontang!" Her views on feminism, patriarchy, and sexuality are influenced by the writer and activist Cherrie Moraga. In her art and in life, Rodriguez is very open about her sexuality. She is non-monogamous and sleeps with both women and men, an attitude that she says is at odds with her upbringing and cultural heritage. "I'm a . . . woman who isn't married and doesn't have children," she told Vasquez. "This is weird enough in my family, but I'm also a sexually open person and because of it, the women in my family have been brutal. They disapprove of my 'lifestyle.'"

As an artist in residence at the Kala Art Institute in Berkeley, Rodriguez worked on a series titled *Transmutation*. The show, which was exhibited in 2013, featured more abstract work from Rodriguez. The series is self-reflective rather than overtly political; Rodriguez told Eric K. Arnold for *Oakland Local* (10 Dec. 2013) that through the work, which explores ideas such as polyamory and sex positivity, she hoped to transmit a love of sexual experiences rather than fear of or shame about sex. Like her other work, the series pushes boundaries and challenges viewers to see things differently, albeit in a much more personal realm.

Rodriguez travels around the world speaking about her artwork, women's rights, and immigration. She still lives in Oakland, though her neighborhood continues to struggle. Neighborhoods surrounding Fruitvale are experiencing gentrification, which has the effect of displacing longtime residents. Rodriguez encourages artists, who are often at the forefront of gentrification, to address the problem head-on. She hopes that residents and artists alike can tell their stories through art.

**PERSONAL LIFE**

In 2014, Rodriguez announced on Facebook that she was holding a half-off sale on her posters and prints to help raise enough money to make a down payment on her parents' Fruitvale house, which they needed to sell in order to pay off debts. The art sale, which lasted forty-eight hours, raised $20,000—much more than Rodriguez needed to make the down payment. Subsequently, her loan was approved and she signed the lease to the house. As she said to Liza Veale for *Oakland Local* (3 Apr. 2014) the response of her fans stunned her. "It was like everything I've been giving, the effort and the love, was just returning to me all at once."

**SUGGESTED READING**

Arnold, Eric K. "Oakulture: A Conversation with Oakland's Iconic Visual Artist, Favianna Rodriguez." *Oakland Local*. Center for Media Change, 10 Dec. 2013. Web. 10 Mar. 2014.

"Favianna and the New Print Revolution." *East Bay Express*. East Bay Express, 1 July 2009. Web. 10 Mar. 2014.

Maiden, Peter. "Hidden in Plain Sight: Media Workers for Social Change, Chapter 4." *Indybay*. SF Bay Area IMC, 13 Mar. 2010. Web. 10 Mar. 2014.

Rodriguez, Favianna. "Artist & Activist Favianna Rodriguez Talks Immigration, Rosario Dawson and Her New Web Series Episode." Interview by Samantha Leal. *Latina*. Latina Media Ventures, 18 Jan. 2013. Web. 10 Mar. 2014.

Rodriguez, Favianna. "Artist Statement: Don't Call Favianna Rodriguez a Political Artist." Interview by Tina Vasquez. *Bitch*. Bitch Media, 2013. Web. 10 Mar. 2014.

Rodriguez, Favianna. "Unscripted: Art and Activism." Interview by Daniel Alarcón. *Radio Ambulante*. Radio Ambulante, 22 May 2014. Web. 17 July 2014.

—Molly Hagan

# Ronda Rousey

**Born:** February 1, 1987
**Occupation:** Mixed martial artist

Ronda Rousey, the first Ultimate Fighting Championship (UFC) women's bantamweight champion, is the "world's greatest female fighter," Marlow Stern declared for the *Daily Beast* (11 Mar. 2015), expressing a sentiment felt by most observers of mixed martial arts (MMA). Since making her professional MMA debut in 2011, Rousey has amassed a perfect record of 11–0, with ten first-round finishes. She competed under the now-defunct Strikeforce banner before becoming the first woman to join the UFC, the world's leading MMA promoter, in 2012. She has led five successful defenses of her UFC women's bantamweight title, with the most recent coming in 2015.

Prior to becoming an MMA fighter, Rousey had a decorated judo career. At seventeen she became the youngest judo competitor at the 2004 Olympic Games in Athens, Greece. Although failing to medal, Rousey returned to compete at the 2008 Olympics in Beijing, China, where she earned a bronze medal; she became the first American to win an Olympic medal in women's judo since the sport debuted on the Olympic stage in 1992. Rousey is best known for ending her fights with armbars, a judo-derived submission technique.

Rousey's combination of fighting skills, good looks, and charisma has made her one of the most recognizable faces of the UFC and has helped her enjoy crossover success as a model and actress. "She's changing the way we look at women," UFC president Dana White told Rick Maese for the *Washington Post* (26 Feb. 2015).

## EARLY LIFE

Ronda Jean Rousey was born on February 1, 1987, in Riverside, California. She is the youngest daughter of Ronald Rousey, a US Army veteran, and Dr. AnnMaria De Mars, a former world-champion judoka. She has two older sisters, Maria and Jennifer, and a younger half-sister, Julia.

Rousey's path to becoming a fighter began at birth. She was born with her umbilical cord around her neck, which cut off the air supply to her brain. Diagnosed with slight brain damage, she was unable to speak coherent sentences until the age of six. Rousey's speech began to improve after her family moved from California to Minot, North Dakota. Her mother, who had earned a PhD in educational psychology after her judo career ended, accepted a teaching position at Minot State University, which had one of the top speech-therapy departments in the country. As part of the arrangement, Rousey received free treatment.

Coming out of a brief retirement, Rousey's father became a research-and-development director at Sioux Manufacturing in Devil's Lake, located 120 miles east of Minot. To avoid a daily two-hour commute, he took up residence in nearby Jamestown. Rousey eventually went to live with her father at the suggestion of her therapists. The arrangement distanced Rousey from her sisters, whose willingness to translate for her was impeding her speech development.

Rousey developed a close bond with her father, who became her biggest champion and enrolled her in competitive swimming. Ron Rousey would drive his daughter to swim practice each morning and predicted that she would become an Olympic gold medalist. "He always told her that she was going to be the best in the world," Rousey's mother told Jonathan Snowden for *Bleacher Report* (22 Feb. 2013). "He always believed in her."

Jon Kopaloff/FilmMagic/Getty Images

## SHAPED BY TRAGEDY

Empowered by her father's unflinching belief in her, Rousey developed into a champion swimmer. Her steady progress in swimming, however, came to a screeching halt in 1995, when her father committed suicide. Ron Rousey had broken his back in a freak sledding accident and had been given no hope of recovery after being diagnosed with the rare blood disorder Bernard-Soulier syndrome. "He said that he didn't want me and my sisters' last memories of him to be in a bed with tubes running in and out of him," Rousey explained to Pete Thamel for the *New York Times* (11 Aug. 2008) about her father, whose health had deteriorated so much that he was given only two years to live.

After her father's death, Rousey's interest in swimming waned. She quit the sport for good at age eleven, when she persuaded her mother to let her take up judo. By then, Rousey's family had moved back to Southern California, where she had continued to struggle with speech problems and making friends; her struggles were such that her mother homeschooled her in the fifth grade. Judo, a sport in which techniques are practiced with a partner, forced Rousey to interact with other children and gave her an outlet to overcome her lingering grief. "I really do believe judo saved me from following a much darker path," she acknowledged to Maese.

Rousey's entry into the judo world came with high expectations. Her mother was arguably the most decorated US judoka in history; in 1984 she became the first American to win a world judo championship. With the guidance of her mother, Rousey began training under world-class coaches and quickly rose through the ranks.

## TWO-TIME OLYMPIAN

By age sixteen Rousey had become the top-ranked judoka in the country, prompting her to drop out of Santa Monica High School to focus solely on her judo career; she later earned a general equivalency diploma. At seventeen she was the youngest judo competitor at the 2004 Olympic Games in Athens, Greece, where she finished ninth in the women's 63-kilogram (138.6-pound) division. Later that year she captured the gold medal in the under-twenty division at the World Junior Judo Championships in Budapest, Hungary.

For Rousey, success came with a personal price. After undergoing a dramatic growth spurt in her mid-teens, she struggled to make her weight class. Already self-conscious and insecure about her appearance, Rousey, who had earned the nickname Miss Man from high school classmates for her muscular body, became bulimic. "I started thinking if I wasn't exactly on-weight, then I wasn't pretty," she told Maese.

Six months after the 2004 Olympics, Rousey, burnt out from constant pressure, cut ties from her coach, Jimmy Pedro, and her mother. Over roughly the next two years, she moved from city to city, living in such places as Albany, Chicago, and Montreal, as she tried to find herself. During that time she continued her judo training but did so on her own terms.

In early 2007, armed with a newfound sense of independence and confidence, Rousey moved back home, returned to training with Pedro, and launched a confessional blog that won popularity in judo circles. She moved up to the more accommodating 70-kilogram (154-pound) weight class and saw immediate dividends, winning the silver medal at the 2007 World Judo Championships. Rousey's judo career culminated at the 2008 Olympic Games in Beijing, China, where she won the bronze medal in the 70-kilogram division. She became the first American judoka to win an Olympic medal.

## FROM JUDOKA TO MMA FIGHTER

After the Beijing Olympics, Rousey reached a crossroads. "I was left with no goals and no direction," she explained to Melissa Segura for *Sports Illustrated* (5 Nov. 2012). Unfulfilled by judo and unenthusiastic about having to train another four years until the next Olympics, Rousey opted to walk away from the sport to pursue other endeavors. She considered attending college and becoming a helicopter rescue swimmer for the Coast Guard before settling on professional MMA, a plan her strong-minded mother did not encourage.

Drawn by the prospect of being able to earn a living with her judo skills, Rousey began training with a group of Armenian American MMA fighters at the Glendale Fighting Club. Among them was Edmond Tarverdyan, who became one of her coaches. Tarverdyan helped Rousey round out her judo prowess with skills from other fighting disciplines, such as boxing and muay thai. "I try to treat all the fighters the same and get the most out of them. But Ronda is special," Tarverdyan affirmed to Snowden. "She listens. And she's a fast learner."

As Rousey was getting her MMA career off the ground, she bartended and worked other jobs to make ends meet. For a period, she lived without hot water and ate nothing but instant ramen noodles. Her fortunes changed in June 2010, when Darin Harvey, a successful developer-turned-MMA manager, signed her to his company Fight Tribe Management. Impressed with Rousey's fighting ability and star potential, Harvey started funding her training and organizing fights for her.

Rousey made her MMA debut as an amateur on August 6, 2010, defeating Hayden Munoz in only twenty-three seconds with an armbar submission. She breezed through two more amateur MMA fights before turning professional.

## UFC's FIRST FEMALE FIGHTER

Because of her Olympic pedigree, Rousey initially found it difficult to find willing opponents. Nevertheless, she eventually made her professional MMA debut on March 27, 2011, at a King of the Cage event in Tarzana, California. There, she dismantled Ediane Gomes, a veteran fighter from Brazil, in twenty-five seconds with her signature armbar.

Rousey recorded another victory in under a minute over her next opponent, the Canadian kickboxing world champion Charmaine Tweet. Afterward, she signed a contract with Strikeforce, then the leading MMA promoter for female fighters. As a fighter on the Strikeforce tour, which ran until 2013, Rousey amassed a 4–0 record, winning all of her fights in the first round with armbars. Her toughest challenge came in March 2012, when she needed four minutes and twenty-seven seconds to defeat wrestling specialist Miesha Tate, who submitted after suffering a gruesome dislocated elbow. With that victory, Rousey became the Strikeforce women's bantamweight (135-pound) champion. She notched a successful title defense against Canadian veteran Sarah Kaufman in August 2012.

It was after the Kaufman fight that UFC president Dana White became convinced that he should add a women's division to the sport's premier circuit. In November 2012 Rousey became the first female fighter to sign with UFC and was announced as the organization's first female bantamweight champion. "She turned me around," White, who had long been against the idea of women competing in the UFC, said of Rousey to Segura. "She's a real fighter down to the core."

## UFC DOMINANCE

On February 23, 2013, Rousey made her much-awaited UFC debut as part of the co-main event of UFC 157. She successfully defended her bantamweight title against former US marine Liz Carmouche, winning via armbar four minutes and forty-nine seconds into the first round.

Rousey's next title defense came at UFC 168 in December 2013. She faced former Strikeforce rival Miesha Tate, who lasted fifty-eight seconds into the third round before submitting to another brutal armbar. It was Rousey's first and only professional fight to date to progress beyond the first round.

In her next three title defenses, Rousey fared much better. She defeated Sara McMann, an Olympic silver medalist and then undefeated fighter, in sixty-six seconds at UFC 170 in February 2014, winning via technical knockout after landing a devastating knee to the body. Then, in July of that year, she knocked out Alexis Davis, a jiu-jitsu black belt, in sixteen seconds at UFC 175, doing so with a flurry of punches to the head.

Breaking her own record in February 2015, Rousey dispatched previously unbeaten opponent Cat Zingano with an armbar in fourteen seconds at UFC 184. The fourteen-second victory was the fastest ever in a UFC title fight. "There's no one out there that's better than me at fighting," Rousey asserted to Stern. "But there's still a lot more work to do."

## CROSSOVER SUCCESS AND PERSONAL LIFE

With her long blonde hair and athletic build, Rousey has been able to parlay her MMA success into a modeling and acting career. She appeared on the cover of *ESPN The Magazine's Body Issue* in 2012 and became the first MMA fighter to be featured in *Sports Illustrated*'s annual swimsuit edition in 2015. Rousey made her acting debut in *The Expendables 3*, a 2014 action sequel starring Sylvester Stallone and a bevy of other high-profile action stars. She has also landed film roles in *Furious 7*, the seventh installment of the *Fast & Furious* franchise, and *Entourage*, a comedy based on the popular HBO series, both of which are due out in 2015. In addition, she has served as a head coach on Fox Sports 1's reality competition series *The Ultimate Fighter*.

Rousey shares a home in Venice, California, with female MMA fighters Marina Shafir, Shayna Baszler, and Jessamyn Duke. The foursome is known in fighting circles as the Four Horsewomen, a reference to a wrestling team headed by Ric Flair in the 1980s.

## SUGGESTED READING

Maese, Rick. "UFC's Ronda Rousey Is Okay with Being Called Pretty. She Can Still Kick Any Guy's Butt." *Washington Post*. Washington Post, 26 Feb. 2015. Web. 18 Mar. 2015.

Sanneh, Kelefa. "Mean Girl." *New Yorker*. Condé Nast, 28 July 2014. Web. 18 Mar. 2015.

Segura, Melissa. "Ronda Rousey Lays the Smack Down." *Sports Illustrated*. Time, 5 Nov. 2012. Web. 18 Mar. 2015.

Stern, Marlow. "The Rise of 'Rowdy' Ronda Rousey: The 14-Second Assassin." *Daily Beast*. Daily Beast, 11 Mar. 2015. Web. 18 Mar. 2015.

Thamel, Pete. "Rousey's Journey Out of Pain, Through Judo." *New York Times*. New York Times, 11 Aug. 2008. Web. 18 Mar. 2015.

—Chris Cullen

# Darius Rucker

**Born:** May 13, 1966
**Occupation:** Musician

For more than two decades, Darius Rucker has built a career out of transcending music genres. The African American singer first came into prominence as the frontman of the pop-rock band Hootie and the Blowfish. At the height of the grunge era, their 1994 debut CD was one of the music industry's unlikeliest success stories, dominating the album charts and the airwaves for over a year. Propelled by the hit single "Hold My Hand," *Cracked Rear View* became the top-selling record of 1995 and, eventually, the sixteenth-best-selling album of all time. Although this early popularity was regarded as a fluke by the critics, the band released two more platinum albums, *Fairweather Johnson* (1996) and *Musical Chairs* (1998).

During the band's hiatus in 2008, Rucker decided to tackle the largely white country music industry. Despite some initial skepticism, Rucker's platinum debut album and lead single topped Billboard's country charts, making him the first African American singer since Charley Pride to have a number-one country single. He has since added four Billboard number ones, a gold album, a 2009 Country Music Association (CMA) Award, and a 2014 Grammy Award to

Gary Miller/FilmMagic/Getty Images

his collection. The ultimate stamp of approval was his 2012 invitation to join the Grand Ole Opry, Nashville's famous weekly country concert. "This is the completion of the conversion from Hootie into Darius the country singer," he told Chris Talbott for the Associated Press (3 Nov. 2012). "With the induction into the Opry, it's definitely complete now."

## INHERITING A LOVE OF MUSIC

Darius Carlos Rucker traces his roots back to Charleston, South Carolina, where he was born on May 13, 1966, the second youngest of six children. Despite growing up in a cramped three-bedroom West Ashley home that he shared with his single mother, his five siblings, his maternal grandmother, two of his aunts, and several cousins, Rucker recalled his childhood with absolute fondness. "We didn't have a lot, but we had everything we needed," he told Matt Hendrickson for *Parade Magazine* (15 June 2013).

From an early age, Rucker's mother, a nurse, exposed him to the sounds of Al Green, Betty Wright, and Otis Redding. Music also connected Rucker to his absent father, a traveling musician. Rucker was often glued to the radio, listening to Sunday performances by his father's gospel group, as well as to a steady diet of rhythm and blues, rock, and country. "That was where it all started for me, being able to flip through the channels and never really hearing about what label something was," he told John Wenzel for the *Denver Post* (4 Sept. 2009).

## HONING HIS PERFORMING CHOPS

Rucker, whose influences included crossover pop-country artist Kenny Rogers as well as traditional country singers Buck Owens and Charley Pride, fell in love with performing at Middleton High School, where he sang with the school's choir, the Middleton Singers. "Middleton Singers was everything for me. It was why I got up in the mornin', why I went to school," he told Dan Rather for AXS TV's *Big Interview* (21 Apr. 2014). In 1984 Rucker enrolled in the University of South Carolina (USC), and during his first year, the broadcast journalism major successfully auditioned for USC's vocal jazz ensemble, Carolina Alive. His life-changing moment came in 1985, when fellow freshman Mark Bryan overheard Rucker singing in the dorm showers and invited him to form an acoustic cover band, the Wolf Brothers.

They made their debut at Pappy's, a local college bar, performing classic-rock songs by the

Eagles, Simon and Garfunkel, and Dire Straits. They eventually recruited USC classmates Dean Felber, a former bassist in Bryan's high school cover band, and Brantley Smith, a drummer. Rucker, who had taught himself to play rhythm guitar, renamed the group. Contrary to popular belief, the name refers not to Rucker or the other band members, but to two members of Carolina Alive. "There was one guy who had big eyes and wore glasses and looked like an owl. And I started callin' him Hootie, and his best friend had these huge cheeks on him. And one night I called him the Blowfish," Rucker told Rather. The revamped Hootie and the Blowfish performed covers of the Police, U2, R.E.M., and Squeeze at fraternity parties and mixers.

## MAJOR RECORD DEAL

The group experienced another lineup change in 1989, when Smith left to focus on a music ministry career; he was replaced by Jim "Soni" Sonefeld, another USC classmate and member of fellow cover band Tootie and the Jones. Rucker eventually dropped out of college to pursue his musical career full-time. With the help of manager Rusty Harmon, they toured the Atlantic seaboard in a van, performing at various clubs in South Carolina, North Carolina, Georgia, Florida, Delaware, and Virginia. By the early 1990s Hootie and the Blowfish had recorded two cassette demos under their Fishco management company: a self-titled album in 1991 and the follow-up, *Time*, in 1992.

In 1992 the California-based independent label J. R. S. Records signed the band, but following delays with their album release, the label allowed them to terminate the contract. Hootie and the Blowfish pressed about 60,000 copies of their self-produced album *Kootchypop* (1992), which they sold at live shows and at various mom-and-pop stores across South Carolina.

*Kootchypop* quickly flew off local retailers' shelves, outselling albums from superstar acts like U2 and Pearl Jam and garnering the attention of Atlantic Records. Talent scout Tim Sommer signed Hootie and the Blowfish in 1993 after taking in two of their live performances. *Cracked Rear View*, the band's first full-length studio album, debuted in July 1994. Rucker drew from personal experience for several tracks, including "Let Her Cry," which chronicled the end of a long-term relationship, as well as "I'm Going Home" and "Not Even the Trees," both inspired by his mother's 1992 death.

Although the more upbeat "Hold My Hand" was the first single released from *Cracked Rear View*, it was not the group's first choice. "It's not even in the top four or five," Rucker told Greg Kot for the *Chicago Tribune* (12 Apr. 1996). "But it was the one song everybody liked and we thought we might get only one shot, so let's lead with it." Their big break came just a few months later, when talk show host David Letterman heard their single on the radio and invited the band to perform on the show's September 2, 1994, episode. A month later, the "Hold My Hand" video began receiving heavy rotation on the rebranded VH1 music channel.

## BREAKTHROUGH SUCCESS

Hootie and the Blowfish continued their steady climb in 1995. February was a pivotal month for the band: not only did it mark their first top-ten hit ("Hold My Hand") on Billboard's Hot 100 chart, it also marked their second *Letterman* appearance, during which the host remarked: "If you don't buy this album, there's something wrong with you"—a career-changing event. "We left that day, and by the next Monday, you could tell instantly that things were about to take off," Rucker told Chuck Dauphin for *Billboard* (3 July 2014). Album sales increased dramatically, from about 5,000 a week to around 16,000 or 17,000 a week.

By March *Cracked Rear View* was certified double platinum. In late May, not only was the album number one on the Billboard 200 but its second single, "Let Her Cry," also reached the top ten. "Only Wanna Be with You" and "Time" became the group's third and fourth consecutive top-ten hits, respectively.

After winning best new artist at the MTV Video Music Awards in September, the band capped off the year by winning four Billboard awards, including Top Billboard 200 Album for the $10 million–selling *Cracked Rear View*, which has since sold $16 million. The accolades continued for Rucker and his bandmates, who were named favorite pop/rock new artist at the 1996 American Music Awards and received Grammy Awards for best new artist and for best pop performance by a duo or group with vocals.

## BACKLASH

Although *Fairweather Johnson* debuted at the Billboard 200's top spot in April 1996, many critics were quick to dismiss the group's sophomore effort. Jim Farber, in his review for the *New York Daily News* (22 Apr. 1996), lambasted the band's "staggering blandness," calling the lyrics "generic" and the emotion "forced." Writing for *SF Weekly* (12 June 1996), notable rock critic Jim DeRogatis said, "It is certainly its predecessor's artistic equal . . . an album full of what Hootie themselves call 'silly little pop songs'—no more, no less."

Although *Fairweather Johnson* failed to duplicate its predecessor's acclaim, it achieved double platinum status and its leading single, "The Old Man and Me," reached number thirteen on the Billboard charts. After the release of their next album, the platinum-selling *Musical Chairs* (1998), Hootie and the Blowfish took a break, during which the group released a compilation of cover songs (2000's *Scattered, Smothered and Covered*) and Rucker recorded a neo-soul album, *The Return of Mongo Slade*.

After opting not to release Rucker's solo effort, Atlantic Records sold the masters to independent label Hidden Beach Recordings. However, *Back to Then* (2002), a renamed version of *The Return of Mongo Slade* that featured collaborations with Jill Scott and rapper Snoop Dogg, failed to connect with audiences. "It's just that I came from Hootie and the Blowfish, and nobody wanted to hear that from me," he told Farai Chideya for *NPR* (19 Nov. 2008).

## GOING COUNTRY

In March 2003 Hootie and the Blowfish reunited to record a self-titled CD, followed by a 2004 greatest-hits collection, *The Best of Hootie & the Blowfish: 1993 Thru 2003*. After parting ways with Atlantic, Rucker and his bandmates founded Sneaky Long Records, a joint venture with Vanguard Records. They recorded two more albums—*Looking for Lucky* (2005) and *Live in Charleston* (2006)—before taking another extended hiatus so Rucker could pursue a country music career. The band still performs at charity events.

In 2007 Rucker realized his long-awaited dream, signing with Capitol Records Nashville. "I didn't think anybody would give me a record deal," he told J. Freedom du Lac for the *Washington Post* (10 Dec. 2008). "There's a stigma about being in Hootie. I thought that would be a liability." His fears proved unfounded. In September 2008 Rucker's album, *Learn to Live*, debuted at the top of the country album charts. A month later, when his first single, "Don't Think I Don't Think About It," topped the country-singles chart, Rucker became only the second African American singer in twenty-five years to

accomplish this feat. Rucker's next two singles ("It Won't Be Like This for Long" and "Alright") also reached the top spot, the first time since 1992 that an artist's first three singles all hit number one.

After walking away with new artist of the year honors at the 2009 Country Music Association Awards, Rucker avoided the sophomore jinx with *Charleston, SC 1966* (2010), his second number-one album, which also produced two more number-one singles: "Come Back Song" and "This." The title of the gold-certified disc is a nod to his birthplace and birth year and homage to *Del Rio, TX 1959*, Radney Foster's influential 1992 debut, which was one of Rucker's inspirations.

For his follow-up, *True Believers* (2013), Rucker, a 2012 Grand Ole Opry inductee, was determined to show that his earlier success was not a fluke. "I feel like part of the family but I also still feel like I have so much to prove," he told Gary Graff for *Billboard* (20 May 2013). "There's still the naysayers . . . out there, so I've still got to make great records." It became his third consecutive number-one album, propelled by his sixth number-one hit, a cover of Bob Dylan's "Wagon Wheel," which earned him a 2014 Grammy for best country solo performance.

In 2014 Rucker released *Home for the Holidays*, a collection of Christmas songs, and "Homegrown Honey," the lead single from album *Southern Style*, scheduled for release on March 31, 2015.

## PERSONAL LIFE

Rucker lives in Charleston, South Carolina, with his wife, Beth Leonard Rucker, a former VH1 producer, their two children, Daniella Rose and Jack, and Rucker's daughter, Carolyn Pearl Phillips.

## SUGGESTED READING

Chideya, Farai. "Country Music Finds New Star in Darius Rucker." *NPR.* NPR, 19 Nov. 2008. Web. 10 Mar. 2015.

Graff, Gary. "Darius Rucker Looks to Silence the Naysayers with *True Believers*." *Billboard*. Billboard, 20 May 2013. Web. 13 Mar. 2015.

Kot, Greg. "Will Hootie Blow It." *Chicago Tribune. Tribune Publishing, 28 Apr. 1996. Web.* 10 Mar. 2015.

Rucker, Darius. Interview by Dan Rather. *The Big Interview*. AXS TV. 21 Apr. 2014. Television.

Talbott, Chris. "Darius Rucker Invited to Join the Grand Ole Opry." *Huffington Post*. TheHuffingtonPost.com, 3 Nov. 2012. Web. 12 Mar. 2015.

Wenzel, John. "After Hootie's Hits, A Rare Country Crossover." *Denver Post*. Denver Post, 4 Sept. 2009. Web. 13 Mar. 2015.

—Bertha Muteba

# Mary Doria Russell
**Born:** August 19, 1950
**Occupation:** Novelist

Author Mary Doria Russell slides among various fiction genres. Her first two novels were science fiction best sellers and propelled her to international attention. She then moved to historical novels, examining such topics as World War II, the 1921 Cairo Conference, and the Old West while maintaining her trademark consideration of religious themes. She told Ron Charles for the *Washington Post* (6 May 2009), "Part of my job as a historical novelist is to get readers to feel an intense connection with the past." Her writing has won numerous awards, including the British Science Fiction Association Award for best novel in 1997 and two nominations for the Pulitzer Prize. She considers her writing as an outgrowth of her attempts to understand her own life and her surroundings. As she told Brian McLendon for Random House, "I don't seem to be interested in writing what I know. I write what I don't know and what I want to learn about."

## EARLY LIFE AND EDUCATION
Russell was born to a US Marine Corps drill sergeant and a US Navy nurse in 1950, and she grew up in a Chicago suburb. She attended Sacred Heart Catholic School and Glenbard East High School before enrolling at the University of Illinois to study anthropology. She earned a master's degree in cultural anthropology at Northeastern University before receiving her PhD in biological anthropology from the University of Michigan in 1983.

Russell trained as a four-field anthropologist, with specializations in archaeology, linguistics, biological anthropology, and social-cultural an-

Jeffrey Beall/Wikimedia Commons

thropology. She credits her education for her outlook on humanity and feels that anthropology and religion essentially ask the same questions, except that whereas questions in science are assumed to have definite answers, questions in religion do not. As she told Amy Frykholm for *Christian Century* (2 Dec. 2008), "I find religions and ideologies interesting because they attempt to reconcile the big and little pictures—the way that individuals or groups behave within the context of history and culture."

After completing her doctorate in biological anthropology, Russell landed a three-year internship to study bone biology at Case Western Reserve University School of Dentistry, which brought her to Cleveland, Ohio. When she lost the position as a result of cost-cutting during the recession, she became a technical writer, producing manuals for scanning equipment maker Picker International and other projects.

## *THE SPARROW* AND *CHILDREN OF GOD*
For five years, Russell worked as a freelance technical writer, but the work dried up in the 1990s. In 1992 she decided to try to write a short story, expecting to give up about ten pages into it; instead she eventually produced an entire novel, *The Sparrow* (1996). Although she had always been an avid reader, Russell did not expect to become a writer. She began writing only because she failed to find any fiction that she felt

was worth reading, but she soon found herself on the task full time. As she told Joanna Connors for *Plain Dealer* (19 Aug. 2011), "I just got sucked in by the characters. I worked in total concentration, something I had never experienced before. It was difficult to tear myself away."

Yet at the same time Russell suffered a crisis of confidence, quitting the project on a weekly interval, certain that her writing was not good enough. However, each time the ideas stuck with her and soon after she was compelled to resume the story. Her characters became friends; as she told Roger C. Thompson in an interview for Random House, "My characters always teach me things, and they remain a part of my life even when I move on." Russell also developed a meticulous system of research and organization to aid her writing, including the use of carefully labeled files and an obsessively neat workspace.

The plot of *The Sparrow* was inspired by the five-hundredth anniversary of Christopher Columbus's landing in the Americas and the search for extraterrestrial life. Russell imagined that the discovery of intelligent alien life would lead to religious missions to new worlds, as did Western contact with other cultures in the past, and she chose the Jesuit order as the missionaries for her novel set in 2019. She also created new languages for the story, relying on her anthropological training in linguistics. She used the Quechua and Nepali languages as frameworks due to their unfamiliarity to Western audiences.

After completing the manuscript Russell searched for an agent but was rejected time after time. After several months she found a taker for *The Sparrow*, and the novel was quickly sold to the Random House publishing company, which released the book to almost immediate critical and popular acclaim. The book received the Arthur C. Clarke Prize for best novel in 1998, among other awards, and has been called one of the landmark works of 1990s science fiction. A sequel, *Children of God*, followed in 1998 and was similarly well reviewed.

### A THREAD OF GRACE

Rather than continuing with science fiction, Russell set her third novel, *A Thread of Grace* (2005), in 1940s Italy. She had recently converted to Judaism when she discovered the book *Benevolence and Betrayal: Five Jewish Italian Families under Fascism* (1991) by Alexander Stille. Fascinated by the real-life stories in the book, Russell found the inspiration for her next work.

Writing historical fiction rather than science fiction presented new challenges, and the foreign setting added further difficulty to the project. "None of the characters are American, and the story is set in World War II Italy, so I'm not drawing on my own language, culture, or personal experiences," Russell told McLendon. Her desire to achieve total historical accuracy was driven by her sense of responsibility to the living memory of the time period and the stories that inspired her. Meanwhile, Russell's writing was slowed by the need to care for her aging parents and deal with health issues of her own. These factors led to the seven-year gap before the work was published.

Russell determined whether characters in *A Thread of Grace* would live or die based on a coin toss, a method that her adolescent son suggested, reinforcing the arbitrary nature of who lives and dies in war. It was her responsibility as the writer to come up with the how, when, and where of the death. She was interested in the fact that although Italy was under Nazi rule for twenty months, Jews in Italy had the highest survival rate in Nazi-occupied Europe, and she wanted to investigate how that happened. Russell told McLendon about her process: "I thought of it as constructing a fictional building with historical bricks. I'd combine memories, events, incidents to compress the action or see it from the point of view of a character." *A Thread of Grace* brought Russell further positive critical attention and was nominated for the 2005 Pulitzer Prize.

### DREAMERS OF THE DAY AND DOC

Russell continued writing historical fiction for her fourth and fifth novels. She heard the September 11, 2001, terrorist attacks on the United States referred to as retaliation for the 1921 Cairo Conference, at which Western nations created the modern political boundaries of the Middle East, and realized that she knew next to nothing about that important event. Russell began research that led to her fourth novel, *Dreamers of the Day* (2008).

The novel's narrator, an American named Agnes who was in Egypt as a forty-year-old during the time of the conference, tells her story after her death, nudging this work into magical realism. Russell sees *Dreamers of the Day* as not only linking the past to the present but as reflective of her own personal connections to historical events and their legacies. Calling the book her "most autobiographical" work, she told Frykholm, "In that novel, I was attempting to understand my mother better." Her family's military connections also loomed large in her exploration of the war-torn region; her nephew, a Marine, was stationed in Iraq the day the novel was published.

Asked how she begins the research for such a complex work, Russell told Thompson, "I start with biographies. Well, actually—dialogue comes first. A character's sense of humor or lack of it, the cleverness or stolidity of expression . . . I hear characters long before I see or understand them." To get a feel for the historical period and the influences on it, Russell reads biographies and other historical works covering the four decades before the novels' opening.

For her fifth novel, *Doc* (2011), Russell shifted genres within historical fiction, creating a Western with mystery elements inspired by facts about the real life of the mythologized gunfighter Doc Holliday. She chose to base her story on real events in his life from 1878, with fictional additions. Russell explained to Connors the way that the characters came alive as she wrote: "Doc would wake me up. I'd hear, 'Write this down, darlin',' and I'd get up and write it. They really come to inhabit your head." *Doc* won the American Library Association's award for best historical fiction novel in 2011.

*Doc* also earned Russell a second Pulitzer Prize nomination, continuing her run of critical acclaim along with relatively strong commercial success. However, just as the book was released, she received notice that she was being dropped by her publisher, Random House. While Russell admitted she was hurt and surprised at the move, she acknowledged the changing trends of the industry. In 2012 her proposed sequel to *Doc* was purchased by the HarperCollins imprint Ecco.

## PERSONAL LIFE

Russell married her husband, Don, a software engineer, in 1970; the two met in high school. They live near Cleveland, Ohio, and their son Daniel was born in 1985. Russell and her husband have helped support a local school, St. Adelbert's, by paying tuition for a child and assisting with the school library, among other charity work. Russell claims she converted from atheism to Judaism in order to raise her son with moral values. She finds the Jewish faith appealing in other ways, too, as she explained to Frykholm. "One of the many reasons that I feel at home in Judaism is that it doesn't require or even expect faith per se. There is a large space

in Judaism for doubt, for questioning, for skepticism, for agnosticism, and outright atheism." After researching the role of music in the life of Doc Holliday, Russell bought a piano and began taking piano lessons. An asteroid was named "Rakhat" after a place in her novel *The Sparrow*.

## SUGGESTED READING

Connors, Joanna. "Acclaimed Author Mary Doria Russell Settles into Successful Routine in Her Lyndhurst Home Office." *Cleveland.com*. Plain Dealer, 19 Aug. 2011. Web. 30 Jan. 2015.

Rosen, Judith. "Something About Mary." *Publishers Weekly*. PWxyx, 3 Jan. 2005. Web. 30 Jan. 2015.

Russell, Mary Doria. "A Historical Novelist's Perspective on Our New Swine Flu." Interview by Ron Charles. *Washington Post*. Washington Post, 6 May 2009. Web. 30 Jan. 2015.

Russell, Mary Doria. "Tackling the Big Questions." Interview by Amy Frykholm. *Christian Century* 2 Dec. 2008: 12–13. Print.

## SELECTED WORKS

*The Sparrow*, 1996; *Children of God*, 1998; *A Thread of Grace*, 2005; *Dreamers of the Day*, 2008; *Doc*, 2011

—Judy Johnson

# Haim Saban

**Born:** October 15, 1944
**Occupation:** Entrepreneur

Haim Saban is the chair and chief executive officer of the Saban Capital Group, a privately owned investment company with numerous holdings in the media and entertainment sectors. He is responsible for introducing the wildly popular and lucrative Mighty Morphin Power Rangers franchise to the United States, selling the Fox Family Worldwide conglomerate to the Walt Disney Company for $5.2 billion (a deal that marked the largest cash transaction conducted by a single person in Hollywood history), and helping build Univision into a Spanish-language media juggernaut, among other high-profile accomplishments.

Many who have done business with Saban describe him as relentless, tenacious, and aggressive. "He's constantly focusing on 'Where am I

Michael Kovac/WireImage/Getty Images

going with this? What's the next move?'" Peter Chernin, a media executive who has negotiated with Saban, told Amy Wallace for *Upstart Business Journal* (13 Aug. 2008). Children's programming executive Andy Heyward explained to Connie Bruck for the *New Yorker* (10 May 2010) that he "has known Haim from the most ruthless and anything-goes guy in business to the biggest heart imaginable, and all points in between. . . . If you took all Haim's money away and took him to a Casbah, gave him some rugs, and said, 'Stay here'—a year later he'd have a billion dollars."

Even his detractors have admitted that Saban's journey from impoverished youth to media titan is the stuff of legend. In 2014 he was again included in the Forbes 400 as one of the wealthiest people in the United States, and he was also given the Forbes 400 Self-Made Score of 9. In 2014 *Forbes* began ranking each individual on the 400 list on a scale from 1 to 10, with a score of 1 indicating that the fortune was completely inherited. A 10, on the other hand, indicates that the individual had amassed their fortune independently of anyone and had done so from a place of poverty and while overcoming obstacles. "He could be the subject of a movie or a TV series," former President Bill Clinton told Stephanie N. Mehta for *Fortune* (1 May 2007). "He's a fascinating character."

## EARLY LIFE

Saban was born to Jewish parents on October 15, 1944, in Alexandria, Egypt, where his father's job as a clerk in a toy shop allowed the family to live modestly but comfortably. During the Suez Crisis in 1956, however, Egypt became an unwelcoming place for Jews. One day, early in the conflict, Saban was doing his homework near the open window of his apartment when an Egyptian soldier pointed a gun at him and mimed pulling the trigger. Subsequently, the family fled to safety in Israel.

Once in Tel Aviv, Saban, his grandmother, parents, and younger brother found lodging in a seedy apartment house, sharing a three-bedroom unit with two other families and using a communal bathroom often monopolized by prostitutes. His father sold office supplies door to door, desperately trying to earn a living; Saban helped out by peddling fruit on the street and other odd jobs. So hard were times that his mother could not bake a cake to serve when Saban had his Bar Mitzvah, a Jewish ceremony that marks entry into adulthood. As Mehta pointed out, however, "Saban's ability to seamlessly glide from East Coast bankers to Israeli pols to Hollywood media moguls can be traced to his peripatetic youth." Ultimately, his parents made the difficult decision to send Saban to a boarding school for the children of poor immigrants. He often dreamed of becoming rich. "Before I went to sleep, I'd close my eyes and think about it," he recalled to Wallace.

At school he set out to earn money by going door to door offering to shovel manure from barns for a fee. He soon had so many clients that he recruited fellow students as subcontractors. Saban was later expelled from school for being a troublemaker, so he enrolled in night school before the principal there told him that rather than focus on academics, he should put his business savvy to use instead.

Although Saban never completed a formal education beyond high school, his savvy, as the principal predicted, stood him in good stead. Hearing a mediocre band in 1966 at a local venue, he approached the owner and claimed to be in a much better band that would draw in greater crowds. He then approached the members of a band he knew with a proposition: if they allowed him to play bass (a skill he possessed only slightly), he would arrange lucrative engagements for them. Despite his limited musical ability, Saban was able to parlay this experience into a major concert-promotion and band-management business. In the wake of the 1973 Yom Kippur War, however, Israel experienced a significant economic downturn. With his concert-promotion business deeply in debt, Saban decided to move to Paris in 1975.

## BUSINESS CAREER

Saban remained in the entertainment industry in Paris, managing artists and producing records. Among his major clients was a young Israeli boy, Noam Kaniel, who in 1978 recorded the theme song for Goldorak, a Japanese cartoon that aired in France. "It was just one of the worst songs I ever heard in my life," Saban recalled to Andrew Ross Sorkin for the *New York Times* (5 Sept. 2004). He soon discovered, however, how lucrative music aired on televised cartoons could be. "It's really simple to understand," he told Wallace. "If you watch a half-hour sitcom, you hear a little music at the beginning, a little at the end. But cartoons open with music, have music all along and music at the end. I'm still making money on those cartoons." Saban began hiring songwriters desperate to make money, paying them an hourly wage, listing himself on the credits as co-writer, and retaining the publishing rights to the work.

In 1983 Saban relocated to Los Angeles, where he expanded his interest to include the cartoons themselves. In 1985 on a business trip to Japan, he watched a children's show that featured a quintet of spandex-wearing teen superheroes. He paid $500,000 for the rights to broadcast the program outside Asia, and while it took him almost a decade to get a network to agree to remake the campy show, the Fox network began airing *Mighty Morphin' Power Rangers* in 1993. The show became a blockbuster hit, reaching top ratings and spawning myriad toys, apparel, lunchboxes, and other merchandise. Later, Saban showed similar foreknowledge when he bought the television rights to what would become another massive hit, *Teenage Mutant Ninja Turtles*.

In 1995, Saban merged Saban Entertainment with Fox Kids Network, which in a few years was restructured as Fox Family Worldwide. The new corporation reached over 250 million homes worldwide. In 2001, Saban spearheaded a deal in which Michael Eisner, head of the Walt Disney Company, acquired Fox Family Worldwide for $5.2 billion. Saban earned $1.5 billion from the deal, and in 2007 the Saban Capital Group, which he had formed after the Disney transaction, sold its stake to a group of private equity firms. That year Saban teamed with a group of outside investors to purchase Univision, the premier Spanish-language media company in the United States. Saban now keeps 10 percent of his investment portfolio in low-interest but highly secure assets. He has joked to journalists that he calls these NPA investments, which stands for "Never Poor Again."

## POLITICAL INFLUENCE

Saban, who has dual citizenship in the United States and Israel, has asserted that he has a three-pronged plan for influencing America's policy on the Jewish state: controlling as many media outlets as he can, launching think tanks, and making political donations.

He is currently one of the largest donors in Democratic Party history. One oft-repeated story holds that in 2000 he learned that his $250,000 gift to the Democratic Congressional Campaign Committee had been surpassed by someone who had given $500,000. He immediately sent a check for another $250,000 but attached a dollar bill to assert his dominance. In 2002, he gave the Democratic National Committee $7 million to help build a new headquarters in Washington.

Saban is a particularly staunch friend and supporter of Bill and Hillary Clinton, and while he has used a significant portion of his wealth to bolster the Democratic Party, his aim in seeking to influence US politics is to ensure that the country maintains close ties to Israel. In a line often cited by other journalists, he asserted to Sorkin, "I'm a one-issue guy and my issue is Israel."

Not surprisingly, Saban has been an ardent supporter of Hillary Clinton's 2008 and 2016 presidential bids and serves as a major "bundler," persuading other wealthy people to give to her campaign. Explaining Saban's inclusion on the *Jerusalem Post*'s 2015 list of the fifty most influential Jews in the world (21 May 2015), Greer Cashman wrote, "It is his financial support of Hillary Clinton's American presidential bid that differentiates him from being a mere well-intentioned philanthropist to a kingmaker."

Fulfilling the think-tank portion of his three-part strategy, Saban founded the Saban Center for Middle East Policy at the Brookings Institution in 2002. The Center hosts an annual conference on US–Israeli relations that draws major political figures from both Jerusalem and Washington.

## PERSONAL LIFE AND PHILANTHROPY

In addition to his political contributions to US Democrats, Saban is a major donor to the Israeli Defense Forces (the nation's military). He is also engaged in a campaign to counter the Boycott, Divest, and Sanction (BDS) movement that has been mounted against Israel on many college campuses. In 1999 he and his wife, Cheryl Saban, launched the Saban Family Foundation, which supports a variety of causes, many of which are related to children's health and education.

The Sabans live in Beverly Hills, California. They have been married since 1987 and have four children—daughters Tifanie and Heidi by Cheryl's first marriage, and son Ness and daughter Tanya together. Ness (whose name means "miracle" in Hebrew) and Tanya were born in 1989 and 1991, respectively. Cheryl, who holds a doctorate in psychology, has written several self-help books and since 2009 has headed the nonprofit organization, the Cheryl Saban Self-Worth Foundation for Women and Girls.

## SUGGESTED READING

Bruck, Connie. "The Influencer." *New Yorker*. Condé Nast, 10 May, 2010. Web. 30 June 2015.

Cashman, Greer Fay, and Noa Amouyal. "50 Most Influential Jews: Most Influential Media Titans." *Jerusalem Post*. JPost, 23 May 2015. Web. 30 June 2015.

Hoffman, Allison. "Morphed: Cheryl Saban's Journey from Beach Bunny to Philanthropist." *Tablet*. Nextbook, 17 June 2009. Web. 30 June 2015.

Lowry, Brian. "Haim Saban's Mighty Transformation." *Variety*. Variety Media, 25 Feb. 2013. Web. 30 June 2015.

Mehta, Stephanie N. "The Man with the Golden Gut." *Fortune*. Time, 1 May 2007. Web. 30 June 2015.

Sorkin, Andrew Ross. "Schlepping to Moguldom." *New York Times*. New York Times, 5 Sept. 2004. Web. 30 June 2015.

Wallace, Amy. "Haim Saban, Power Ranger." *Upstart Business Journal*. American City Business Journals, 13 Aug. 2008. Web. 30 June 2015.

—Mari Rich

# Güler Sabancı

**Born:** 1955
**Occupation:** Chair and managing director of Sabancı Holding

Güler Sabancı is a member of Turkey's wealthy Sabancı family and the chair and managing director of Sabancı Holding. The first woman to head the company, Sabancı is also a noted philanthropist and patron of the arts.

## BACKGROUND

Güler Sabancı was born in 1955 in Adana, Turkey, the first child of İhsan and Yüksel Sabancı. Her grandfather Haci Omer Sabancı had begun building the family business, Sabancı Holding, in the 1920s, initially investing in the cotton industry. The company later came to encompass numerous businesses in the manufacturing, energy, banking, insurance, and retail sectors, among others.

Sabancı attended high school at TED Ankara College, a private school in Ankara, Turkey. She continued her education at Boğaziçi University in Istanbul, Turkey, where she studied business administration, and completed the advanced management program at Harvard University in Cambridge, Massachusetts.

## SABANCI HOLDING

Sabancı joined Sabancı Holding in 1978 as head of the company's tire-manufacturing division, Lassa (later renamed Brisa). She held this post for fourteen years, during which time she became known as the Rubber Queen.

In 1985, while still serving at Lassa, Sabancı became the general manager of Kordsa, Sabancı Holding's tire-cord manufacturing and trading company. There, she extended the division's reach by establishing relationships with the American plastic manufacturer DuPont as well as other international partners. During the 1990s, Sabancı championed the company's joint-venture strategy and expanded its overseas operations into Latin America and Europe. She also helped establish Sabancı University in Istanbul, a self-supporting university that opened to students in 1999. Sabancı is a member of the university's board of trustees.

After serving on Sabancı Holding's board of directors, Sabancı was appointed chair and managing director of the company in 2004. By that time, Sabancı Holding Group had become Turkey's largest financial and industrial conglomerate, comprising more than sixty companies and operating in more than ten other countries.

Sabancı's management style, which combines delegation and teamwork, is unusual in Turkey's corporate culture. One of her first acts as chair and managing director was to call a meeting to examine forthcoming trends and help the company look a decade into the future. The meeting helped Sabancı conclude that in order to increase revenues, the company needed to focus on differentiation and investing in the energy sector. As Sabancı Holding's first female head, she has worked to improve the experience of women in the workplace and often has lunch with randomly selected female employees.

## CHARITABLE WORK

Aside from her work with Sabancı Holding, Sabancı is also an active philanthropist. She serves as the head of the Haci Olmer Sabancı Foundation, which has made charitable donations totaling more than $1.5 billion since 1974. The foundation has built and restored more than 120 educational, health, and cultural facilities. It also helped establish Sabancı University and provides more than 35,000 scholarships. In 2006, the Sabancı Foundation partnered with the United Nations and the Turkish Ministry of the Interior to back a joint program focused on issues of education, employment, reproductive health, and violence against women.

On September 22, 2011, Sabancı was honored by former US president Bill Clinton with the Clinton Global Citizen Award in recognition of her women's rights initiatives and contributions to Turkish society. She has worked with numerous charitable and professional organizations, including the International Crisis Group, a nonprofit organization committed to preventing and resolving deadly conflict, for which she serves as a trustee. She was the first female board member of the Turkish Industry and Business Association and the first woman to join the European Round Table of Industrialists. In January 2013 Sabancı became a member of the supervisory board at Siemens AG, a German engineering and electronics conglomerate.

Sabancı is a noted patron of the arts in Turkey and has worked with partners such as the Ministry of Culture and Tourism to organize theater festivals and other artistic events. In 2005 she arranged for the country's first exhibition of paintings by renowned artist Pablo Picasso, which was held at the Sakip Sabancı Museum

in Istanbul, the former summer home of one of her late uncles. More than 250,000 people visited the exhibit. Sabancı serves as chair of the museum's board of trustees.

## IMPACT

Sabancı has distinguished herself in Turkey's male-dominated corporate world, becoming one of the country's most prominent businesswoman. As chair of Sabancı Holding, she expanded the business and encouraged diversification. Sabancı has also established herself as a crucial player in Turkey's political, social, and cultural spheres. She was ranked second in the *Financial Times'* 2011 Top 50 Women in World Business list and was number 60 on *Forbes* magazine's list of the world's most powerful women.

## PERSONAL LIFE

Sabancı enjoys collecting art, particularly ceramics from the medieval Seljuk period. She is also an avid winemaker.

## SUGGESTED READING

Anderson, Becky. "How Turkey's Business Superwoman Steers Empire in Man's World." *CNN.* Cable News Network, 6 Feb. 2013. Web. 26 June 2014.

"Güler Sabancı." *Sabancı Vakfi.* Sabancı Vakfi, n.d. Web. 26 June 2014.

"Güler Sabancı Recognized for Philanthropic Achievements with David Rockefeller Bridging Leadership Award." *Synergos.* Synergos Inst., 8 Oct. 2013. Web. 26 June 2014.

Sabancı, Güler. "Güler Sabancı Interview." Interview by Filiz Bikmen. *Alliance* Mar. 2013: 37–38. Print.

Smith, Helena. "First Lady of Turkish Finance." *Guardian.* Guardian News and Media, 16 Sept. 2006. Web. 26 June 2014.

—Patrick G. Cooper

---

# Pablo Sandoval

**Born:** August 11, 1986
**Occupation:** Baseball player

Pablo Sandoval is a Venezuelan-born third baseman for the Boston Red Sox. The heavy hitter joined the team in 2014, after seven seasons with the San Francisco Giants in which he established himself as a premier player and a fan favorite.

## EARLY LIFE IN VENEZUELA

Sandoval was born on August 11, 1986, in Puerto Cabello, Venezuela. He grew up as the youngest in his family—his little sister, Diana, died in a car accident before her first birthday. His parents—father, Pablo Sr., and mother, Amelia—owned a mechanical engineering firm. His father was a third baseman, as was his older brother, Michael, who pursued his own baseball career and played several seasons of minor league and independent league ball before later becoming one of Sandoval's agents. Growing up, Sandoval and his brother used to play in their two-car garage, using wadded up tape as a baseball. He would later credit this haphazard style of play for shaping his ability to command a large hitting zone, as Michael threw hard and the ball flew inconsistently.

By the time Sandoval was five, he moved out of the garage and on to a real league—though he initially refused to do anything but hit. "I just went to hit and I sat down next to my mom," Sandoval recalled to Schulman. "That was it. The coach told me to play defense and I said, 'No.'" Eventually, Sandoval played right field, throwing with his left hand. When he was nine, however, he wanted to play shortstop like his favorite player, Omar Vizquel, another native Venezuelan. Because left-handed shortstops are at a disadvantage and therefore rare, Sandoval learned to throw right-handed. Michael, who was drafted by the Minnesota Twins when Sandoval was a youngster, encouraged Sandoval's ambidexterity, and sent his younger brother right-handed gloves. Eventually Sandoval came to throw predominantly right-handed, though he retained the ability to throw with his left. He also developed his skills as a switch-hitter.

## MINOR LEAGUE CAREER

Sandoval was fourteen when baseball scouts began to take notice of him. At sixteen, he met a scout for the Texas Rangers at a two-week scouting tournament in the Dominican Republic. The scout promised to sign him, but Sandoval never heard from him again. Two weeks later, back in Venezuela, the San Francisco Giants offered him a minor league contract. Sandoval signed with the club in 2003, and made his minor league debut with the AZL Giants in Scottsdale, Arizona, in 2004. (His mother insisted that he finish high school before moving to the United States.) Sandoval played for five different minor league teams in four and a half seasons. He was playing for the Salem-Keizer

Michael Ivins/Boston Red Sox/Getty Images

As one of the league's top postseason performers, Sandoval helped lead the Giants to World Series titles in 2010, 2012, and 2014. In 2012, he became the first Venezuelan player to win World Series most valuable player (MVP), and one of only four players in Major League Baseball (MLB) history to hit three home runs during a single World Series game.

Sandoval earned the nickname Kung Fu Panda, after the plump but agile title character of a DreamWorks cartoon. (Sandoval has consistently made headlines for his weight.) "He's not a small individual by any means, yet he plays with athleticism," former Giants teammate Sergio Romo said of Sandoval to Henry Schulman for the *San Francisco Chronicle* (18 Mar. 2010). "His agility, his ability to go left and right and pick up speed, is pretty impressive." Many Giants fans adopted panda-themed apparel as Sandoval's career blossomed and his popularity grew. As a beloved face of the Giants franchise, Sandoval surprised many by rejecting all contract negotiations from the team. In November 2014 Sandoval signed a $95 million, five-year contract with the Boston Red Sox, a team looking to rebuild after finishing last in its division the previous season. Sandoval's first season with his new team got off to a rocky start. Of his and the team's struggles, Sandoval told Wayne Epps Jr. for the *Boston Globe* (24 June 2015): "It's part of the game, you have to keep fighting, you have to keep fighting."

Volcanoes (a rookie league affiliate of the Giants) in Keizer, Oregon, in 2005, when his skills began to make an impression on his fellow players. Pitcher Alex Hinshaw recalled one dazzling play in particular from Sandoval at third base. "I threw a fastball inside to a right-handed hitter," Hinshaw recalled to Schulman. "He pulled it down the line, pretty hard. Pablo tries to back-hand it. The ball was hit so hard it knocked the glove off Pablo. . . . Without even thinking about it, he picks the ball up left-handed and throws it straight to first base and gets the guy out." Hinshaw was shocked. "At that point I didn't even know Pablo could throw the ball left-handed," he said. "I stood there for a good 30 seconds and I had to look around to see if anyone else saw it. Everyone else's reaction was the same as mine: dumbfounded."

Sandoval was beginning to garner some attention during games, but off the field, the teenager was missing his family in Venezuela. In 2006 and 2007, when he was playing for the Class A San Jose Giants, Sandoval grew close to Donna and Ed Musgrave, a local couple who hosted international players for the Giants. The Musgraves helped draw the young, shy Sandoval out of his shell. "They were very special to me," Sandoval recalled in 2009, as quoted by Mark Emmons for the *San Jose Mercury News* (25 Oct. 2012). "They always seem to have fun, so I wanted to be part of it. They would act like real parents. Sometimes they would scold me if I wasn't doing something right."

## SAN FRANCISCO GIANTS

After sustained minor league success, Sandoval was called up to the major leagues on August 13, 2008. He joined his childhood idol Vizquel on the San Francisco Giants, and made his debut the next day against the Houston Astros. Giants pitcher Barry Zito began to call him Kung Fu Panda after a game on September 19, when Sandoval jumped over opposing catcher Danny Ardoin to avoid a tag and score a run. By the beginning of the Giants' 2009 season, Sandoval was the team's starting third baseman (he also served as a backup catcher until he developed bone spurs in his elbow, ending his role at that position).

Yet despite his considerable defensive prowess, Sandoval's true talent, fans quickly realized, was as a hitter. On May 12, 2009, Sandoval hit his first walk-off home run in the major leagues in a game against the Washington Nationals. "I was so excited," he told a reporter for the *San Francisco Chronicle* after the game, as quoted by Rachel G. Bowers for the *Boston Globe*, "I could not sleep thinking about it." He hit his first career grand slam nearly two months later on July 6. However, the 2010 season was a more difficult one for Sandoval. His weight—around 278 pounds—became an issue and his batting average dropped from .330 (second-best in the National League in 2009) to .268. As a result he was benched for much of the playoffs—Juan Uribe took over on third base—and had only three at-bats in the 2010 World Series. The Giants won the series 4–1 against the Texas Rangers, bringing Sandoval his first championship ring, but individually the year was a disappointment. "Those are the things that happen in your career, things that God puts in your path to see how you take them," Sandoval would later tell Monte Poole for the *Bay Area News Group* (26 Oct. 2012). "I learned from them."

Sandoval slimmed down before the 2011 season at the Giants' behest, and the team, aware of the slugger's popularity, publicly referred to his attempt to get in better shape as "Operation Panda." He made some progress, reaching 240 pounds in order to save his starting job. Indeed, Sandoval rebounded, even playing in his first All-Star Game that year, but his season was plagued by injury. He missed over forty games because of a broken hamate bone in his right hand. Still, he batted .315, hit 23 home runs, and hit for the cycle on September 15, 2011. It was a similar story for 2012, as Sandoval made his second appearance at the All-Star game though the regular season was marred by a broken hamate bone in his *left* hand. Sandoval's post-season performance that year, however, was another story entirely.

## WORLD SERIES MVP

Sandoval hit .333 in the 2012 playoff division series against Cincinnati and .310 in the National League Championship Series against St. Louis, helping to lead the Giants to the World Series against the Detroit Tigers. In game one he hit three home runs, making him at the time one of only four people in MLB history to have accomplished such a feat in the World Series. He would go on to hit an incredible .500 throughout the rest of the series and set a franchise record for the Giants with twenty-four postseason hits. He was named World Series MVP after the Giants swept the Tigers in four games. He was also presented with the Babe Ruth Award for his performance.

In 2013 Sandoval regressed somewhat, ending the season with a .278 average and fourteen home runs, while the Giants failed to make the playoffs. During the 2014 regular season he again failed to perform to his past standards, but the team made the postseason on a wild-card berth. In the wildcard game against Pittsburgh, Sandoval had two hits and scored two runs, helping the Giants advance. San Francisco then defeated Washington and St. Louis to reach the World Series once again. Sandoval hit .429 through the series, which stretched the full seven games and saw the Giants beat the Kansas City Royals to win their third championship in five seasons. Sandoval also set the MLB record for postseason hits, with twenty-six, while hitting .366 overall throughout the playoffs.

## BOSTON RED SOX

Sandoval's contract extension talks with the Giants had stalled during the 2014 season, and after the World Series he became a free agent poised for a major contract. In November he signed a five-year contract with the Boston Red Sox worth $95 million. The Giants offered him a similar deal, even suggesting that they were prepared to pay him more, but Sandoval turned them down, stunning some of his fans. At the time, Giants assistant general manager Bobby Evans told Alex Pavlovic for the *San Jose Mercury News* (24 Nov. 2014) that Sandoval characterized the move as a "difficult decision," but Sandoval later claimed he and his agent had been mistreated by the Giants' management, making his mind up to leave. He joined the Red Sox team looking to add hitting to help it rebound from a last-place finish in 2014, one year after a World Series title of their own. Sandoval's Red Sox tenure began with difficulty, as he entered the 2015 All-Star break hitting only .267 with seven home runs.

## SUGGESTED READING

Bowers, Rachel G. "Meet Pablo Sandoval, New Red Sox Third Baseman." *Boston Globe.* Boston Globe Media Partners, 24 Nov. 2014. Web. 16 July 2015.

Emmons, Mark. "Home Runs by San Francisco Giants' Pablo Sandoval Thrill Former Host Family." *San Jose Mercury News.* San Jose Mercury News, 25 Oct. 2012. Web. 16 July 2015.

Epps, Wayne, Jr. "As Weather Heats Up, So Does Pablo Sandoval." *Boston Globe.* Boston Globe Media Partners, 24 June 2015. Web. 16 July 2015.

Keri, Jonah. "Hanley Ramirez, Pablo Sandoval, and Boston's High-Risk, High-Reward Plan." *Grantland.* ESPN Internet Ventures, 24 Nov. 2014. Web. 16 July 2015.

Pavlovic, Alex. "Why Pablo Sandoval Chose Boston Red Sox over Giants." *San Jose Mercury News.* San Jose Mercury News, 24 Nov. 2014. Web. 16 July 2015.

Schulman, Henry. "All the Comforts of Far-Away Home." *San Francisco Chronicle.* Hearst Communications, 8 Mar. 2009. Web. 16 July 2015.

Schulman, Henry. "In Small-Town Oregon, the Panda Legend Was Born." *San Francisco Chronicle.* Hearst Communications, 18 Mar. 2010. Web. 16 July 2015.

—Molly Hagan

# Nadia Santini

**Born:** May 23, 1970
**Occupation:** Chef

When chef Nadia Santini took charge of the kitchen at the restaurant Dal Pescatore, she faced the difficult challenge of making her mark with her cuisine while remaining true to the history and traditions of the northern Italian restaurant, which had been in the Santini family for generations. Founded in 1925 by her husband's grandparents, Dal Pescatore (From the Fisherman) evolved over the years from a simple tavern to a more formal yet warm and welcoming rural sanctuary, becoming an internationally renowned establishment during Santini's tenure as chef. As the restaurant's popularity among both diners and critics suggests, Santini's careful balance between culinary innovation and family legacy has been an overwhelming success.

Despite the fact that she had never really had professional culinary experience or training before first stepping through the doors of Dal Pescatore, Santini managed to earn three stars from the prestigious Michelin restaurant guide for her restaurant. She eschews much of the experimentation that pervades the menus of other top-rated dining establishments, instead presenting diners with her own take on a wide array of traditional Italian dishes. "Well, today a word like 'tradition' almost seems to be a swearword," she told Jesper Storgaard Jensen for *Italy Magazine* (3 Feb. 2014). "However, we must remember that there can't be innovation without tradition. Tradition means roots. Tradition means respect for what previous generations have created."

## EARLY LIFE AND EDUCATION

Nadia Santini was born Nadia Cavaliere in the northern Italian town of San Pietro Mussolino. A largely self-taught cook, she began her culinary education at an early age, watching as her mother prepared meals using old-fashioned techniques. Her childhood experiences taught her the power of food, particularly its ability to evoke emotions in those who eat it. "When we were sitting at the table, I remember how happy I felt eating a well-prepared and delicious meal," she told Jensen. "Now and again that same feeling of happiness wells up inside me when I sit down at the table to eat."

During the early 1970s, Santini attended the University of Milan, where she studied political science and sociology. While enrolled in university she married her husband, fellow student Antonio Santini. The grandson of Antonio and Teresa Santini, the original proprietors of the restaurant Dal Pescatore, the younger Antonio belonged to a generation of the Santini family that would soon be charged with carrying on the family's legacy at the restaurant.

After the wedding, Santini was quickly ushered into her husband's food-focused family. Seeking to learn more about different types of cuisine, the newlyweds traveled to France for an extended honeymoon and spent much of their time there learning about French food and how French restaurants were run, with the intent of putting some of that knowledge to use upon their return to Italy.

## ENTERING THE FAMILY BUSINESS

The restaurant now known as Dal Pescatore, located on the edge of a regional park in the village of Runate, Italy, opened in 1925 under the direction of Antonio Santini, a fisherman, and his wife, Teresa. Then a simple country tavern, the restaurant bordered a pond and specialized in fish dishes, which Teresa prepared in a variety of traditional northern Italian styles. Teresa and Antonio's son, Giovanni, joined the family business and brought his wife, Bruna, into the fold following their marriage. During Giovanni and Bruna's tenure as heads of the restaurant, the establishment took on a more formal atmosphere and became known as Vino e Pesce (Wine and Fish). The name was changed to Dal Pescatore in 1960, several years after the birth of their son, Antonio, Santini's future husband.

© Maurice Rougemont/Corbis

After returning to Italy, Santini and her husband went to work at Dal Pescatore, where she took on some of the responsibilities in the kitchen and he joined the front-of-house staff. Cooking alongside Teresa and Bruna, Santini learned the family's signature recipes and gained hands-on experience in running a restaurant. She eventually took over the position of chef, although Bruna continued to make many of the restaurant's fresh pastas into her ninth decade.

## DAL PESCATORE: ACHIEVING MICHELIN STATUS

Under Santini's direction, Dal Pescatore has evolved to reflect her own culinary sensibilities while preserving the legacy of the previous generations of chefs. Although Dal Pescatore had long been a respected restaurant in its region and throughout Italy, it received significant international attention beginning in 1982, when it earned its first Michelin star. The Michelin restaurant guidebooks, first published early in the twentieth century as an attempt by the Michelin tire-manufacturing company to promote automobile travel in Europe, publish reviews of the best-regarded restaurants throughout the world. The rating of one Michelin star is a prestigious honor in the culinary industry, indicating that a restaurant is considered a very good one within its category of cuisine.

For Dal Pescatore, however, this one star was merely the beginning. The restaurant soon earned a second star and in 1996 received a third, becoming one of the few restaurants in Italy to hold that ranking. Santini and her staff worked hard over the following decade to maintain that prestigious designation, succeeding in that impressive accomplishment. In an interview for *Fine Dining Lovers* (3 Apr. 2013), she described the value of cooking—particularly Italian: "Its language is universal, its ethics transparent, if you cook you want to bring joy and health. Italian food is like music: a few notes can create a symphony."

The restaurant primarily serves traditional regional dishes, including a variety of housemade pastas as well as meat and fish dishes. The menus change depending on the season, but as of 2015 Dal Pescatore typically offers guests tasting menus as well as à la carte options. The restaurant also boasts a substantially stocked wine cellar; one of Santini and Antonio's sons, Alberto, serves as sommelier.

In addition to her focus on traditional foods and techniques, Santini places a significant emphasis on seasonal and local ingredients. "I grew up in the country and have spent many years living here," she explained to Jensen. "This gives you the chance to know, understand, and watch how the animals are bred and the crops cultivated. This is really the knowledge at the core of a chef's work. It's important to have a wide knowledge of the entire food chain—from the farm to the fork. We really must have more appreciation for what the earth gives us."

Among the many local ingredients regularly featured in Dal Pescatore's menu is pumpkin, a staple of cooking in the northern province of Mantua, where the restaurant is located. Dal Pescatore is particularly known for its tortelli di zucca, fresh pasta stuffed with pumpkin, and for good reason. "What's indisputable is that Nadia Santini's tortelli di zucca, literally made as the order is called at the pass, are out-of-this-world ambrosial," Sudi Pigott wrote for the *Independent* (25 Apr. 2013), "ethereally light with mesmerising agrodulce bite from the pumpkin, amaretti, parmesan and homemade mostarda." The tortelli feature prominently in many reviews of the restaurant and are often cited as a reason to make the trip to its rural location, despite the dish's relative prevalence in the region. In addition to her prominent use of pumpkin, Santini serves a variety of other local items, including Italian cheeses and traditional Mantuan desserts.

## FURTHER RECOGNITION

As a critically acclaimed chef, Santini has become known among chefs and gourmets worldwide, and interest in her cooking has spread far beyond Italy. She and her family have been featured in several books published in Italian, French, and other languages, including 2008's *Dal Pescatore: La storia e le ricette della famiglia Santini* (Dal Pescatore: the history and recipes of the Santini family). Santini has also appeared in various documentaries, including the 2010 documentary *Three Stars*, about Michelin-starred restaurants, and 2011's *Inventing Cuisine: Nadia Santini*. Although she has noted that she knows many chefs who have competed in reality television programs such as *MasterChef Italia*, she is personally averse to participating in such programs because "the show's format is very aggressive," as she explained to Jensen. "And that's not my style."

In describing fifty of the world's best restaurants of 2011, a journalist for the *Guardian* (18 Apr. 2011) wrote of Dal Pescatore that "it's easy to see what attracted the little red book [the Michelin guide] to this out-of-the-way corner of Mantua—the setting is luxurious and while the cuisine is still rigorously authentic Italian, the kitchen remains ever-receptive to new ideas or ingredients." Indeed, Dal Pescatore's status as a three-star restaurant has prompted foodies from all over the world to make the pilgrimage to Runate. However, the Michelin reviewers were not the only culinary experts to praise Santini's cooking and her restaurant's warm and welcoming atmosphere. The restaurant has been recognized as exceptional by numerous other bodies, both in Italy and elsewhere, and it has frequently been included on such lists of the world's best restaurants.

In 2013, Santini was awarded the Veuve Clicquot World's Best Female Chef award, one of several awards given in association with the annual World's 50 Best Restaurants list. Although Santini herself was widely praised following the announcement that she had won the award, she became the center of some controversy when members of the culinary community began to call attention to the award's potentially sexist nature. Many influential figures in the culinary industry questioned the purpose of an award for best female chef, arguing that the existence of such an accolade perpetuated the outdated and offensive perception that female chefs cannot compete on the level of their male counterparts. Despite this controversy, Santini remained pleased about the award, telling interviewers that it reflected not only her hard work at Dal Pescatore but also that of her entire family and explaining that she hoped to inspire other women to pursue culinary careers. Although Santini has noted on multiple occasions that she does view her approach to cooking as inherently somewhat feminine, she elaborated to interviewers that she and other female chefs have the same basic goal as their male colleagues. "Ultimately, we are all cooks and have the same objective: to create a unique and unforgettable dining experience for our guests," she told Pigott.

### PERSONAL LIFE

Santini and her husband, Antonio, married in 1974. They have two sons, Giovanni and Alberto. Both men have joined their parents in the family business: Giovanni collaborates with Santini in the kitchen, while Alberto works in the dining room alongside his father and sister-in-law. Santini enjoys working with her family and credits them for much of Dal Pescatore's success. "Dal Pescatore is always more than Nadia Santini," she explained to Pigott.

### SUGGESTED READING

Forbes, Paula. "Nadia Santini Is World's 50 Best's 2013 Best Female Chef." *Eater*. Vox Media, 3 Apr. 2013. 11 Aug. 2015.

Jensen, Jesper Storgaard. "Talking to: Nadia Santini, the World's Best Female Chef." *Italy Magazine*. Italy Magazine, 3 Feb. 2014. Web. 11 Aug. 2015.

Pigott, Sudi. "Is There a Place for Sex in the Kitchen?" *Independent*. Independent.co.uk, 25 Apr. 2013. Web. 11 Aug. 2015.

Santini, Alberto. "Alberto Santini (Dal Pescatore): The Culture of Italian Wine at Expo." Interview by Matteo Bernardelli. *Vino*. Verona Exhibition Authority, 4 Mar. 2015. Web. 11 Aug. 2015.

"World's 50 Best Restaurants 2011." *Guardian*. Guardian News and Media, 18 Apr. 2011. Web. 11 Aug. 2015.

—Joy Crelin

# Anita Sarkeesian

**Born:** 1984
**Occupation:** Media critic and blogger

Anita Sarkeesian is a pop culture critic and host of the video blog *Feminist Frequency*, which deconstructs representations of women in the media. In 2012 Sarkeesian became the target of a massive online hate campaign when she created a Kickstarter initiative to raise financial support for, or crowdfund, a set of five videos examining female characters in video games. These videos were an extension of her 2011 web series, produced in conjunction with Bitch Media, called *Tropes vs. Women*. That original series, which has garnered hundreds of thousands of views on YouTube, comprises six videos that are each between five and ten minutes long. They discuss classic female character tropes in movies, television shows, and comic books—tropes such as the "manic pixie dream girl" or the "evil demon seductress." For the second series, *Tropes vs. Women in Video Games*, the Kickstarter asked for $6,000 to film five short videos. The project raised almost $160,000—more than twenty-five times its goal—but not before Sarkeesian herself fell prey to hostile forces within the gaming community, raising a debate about the epidemic of sexual harassment on the Internet at large.

### EARLY LIFE AND EDUCATION

Anita Sarkeesian was born in 1984 in Toronto, Canada, to Armenian parents. Her father worked as a network engineer, which meant, she told Stephen Beirne for the gaming website Destructoid (2 July 2012), she "basically grew up surrounded by computers and started playing PC games at a pretty young age." She remembers playing old-school gaming systems such as NES (Nintendo Entertainment System) and SNES (Super Nintendo Entertainment System), but when she was ten years old, she begged her parents to buy her a Game Boy. It took some "serious persuasion" she told Beirne. Her mother was worried that video games would affect her child's brain—a popular notion—but she was also confused by the request, assuming Game Boys were, after all, for boys. Still, on Christmas morning, Sarkeesian got her Game Boy, and after that, she and the device, she told Beirne, "were inseparable." Her love of games has continued into adulthood and is, in part, what inspired her to discuss them in her *Tropes vs. Women* series.

Sarkeesian was raised in a liberal family; she started taking a serious interest in social issues, such as LGBT (Lesbian, Gay, Bisexual, and Transgender) rights and the anti–Iraq War movement, in high school. She earned her bachelor's degree in communication studies from California State University, Northridge, in 2007 and enrolled in York University in Toronto to complete a master's degree in social and political thought. She graduated in 2010, with a thesis titled "I'll Make a Man Out of You: Strong Women in Science Fiction and Fantasy Television."

### FEMINIST FREQUENCY

"I wasn't always a strong feminist or a self-identifying feminist at all," Sarkeesian told Sophie Perrault for the blog *Text Appeal* (17 Jan. 2011) of her college self. "Like many women, I would say things like 'I believe in equal rights but I'm not a feminist.'" Sarkeesian acknowledges that this posturing was out of step with her otherwise liberal views, but her aversion to the term *feminism* is far from unusual. It was not until Sarkeesian enrolled in Z Media Institute—a weeklong institute devoted to fostering radical social change, which was held annually in Woods Hole, Massachusetts, from 1994 to 2013—that she began to reconsider her position regarding feminism. She took a few courses with the playwright and activist Lydia Sargent, who was part of the feminist movement of the 1970s. After learning of Sargent's experiences, Sarkeesian was inspired to think about feminism in terms of privilege, class, and race. She read the work of influential authors and thinkers such as Bell Hooks, Allan G. Johnson, and Tim Wise and was encouraged to take a second look at the power structures of her own world.

In 2009, a year before she left graduate school, Sarkeesian launched a video blog, or vlog, called *Feminist Frequency* in conjunction with Bitch Media. She wanted to make videos because she hoped that they would "make feminism more accessible," as she told Nina Liss-Schultz for *Mother Jones* (30 May 2014). In one video, "Toy Ads and Learning Gender," uploaded in November 2010, Sarkeesian examines the highly gendered marketing of children's toys and how that marketing reinforces patriarchal norms. Commercials selling toys such as G.I. Joe for boys emphasize power, aggression, competition, and control. Other boy-oriented commercials, such as those for Legos or Battleship, encourage making, building, and constructing. Commercials selling toys for girls, on the other hand, are more likely to emphasize skills such as child-rearing or the importance of popularity and self-image. Creativity, if treated at all, is limited to such activities as baking a cake in a toy oven. In another video, "What Liquor Ads Teach Us about Guys," posted in June 2010, Sarkeesian—citing Hooks—discusses how sexism affects men as well as women. In many ads for alcohol, male characters are applauded for manipulating, deceiving, or objectifying women, thus reinforcing the harmful stereotype that men cannot express honest emotion.

### TROPES VS. WOMEN

In 2011 Sarkeesian created a six-segment web video series, *Tropes vs. Women*, posted on YouTube. The videos were made with the guiding principle that by observing patterns in how women are portrayed in movies, comic books, and magazines, people can better understand the more complicated gender dynamics at play in everyday life. The first video addresses a common trope known as the "manic pixie dream girl." From Meg Ryan's knocked-unconscious character, Patricia, in the movie *Joe Versus the Volcano* (1990) to Natalie Portman's eccentric Sam in *Garden State* (2004), the manic pixie dream girl embodies the ideal female muse: a woman who exists primarily as inspiration for a man. The second video discusses a less talked-about trope known as "women in refrigerators," which refers to a plot point in the story of the Green Lantern. This comic-book trope, first described by comics writer Gail Simone, involves the random and often brutal killing, rape, or disabling of a female character for the ultimate purpose of furthering a male hero's story—for example, providing him with an emotionally complex backstory or revenge narrative. Viewers of this six-segment series number in the hundreds of thousands.

### ONLINE HARASSMENT

In May 2012 Sarkeesian created a campaign page on the crowdfunding website Kickstarter. She asked for $6,000 to create a new series of videos, *Tropes vs. Women in Video Games*. This new series would be specifically focused on gaming, since, in her research for her previous video series, she had discovered that tropes permeated many video games. A deluge of hate began during the third week of funding. Sarkeesian was relentlessly harassed on her blog, Twitter, and YouTube; she received numerous threats of sexual assault, rape, and murder. In unregulated and largely anonymous chat forums, abusive gamers continued to one-up each other in their harassment. They flagged her videos as terrorism, changed her Wikipedia page, and sent her doctored images of her likeness being raped by video game characters. Some tried to hack into her e-mail account and publish her private phone number and address. "There was even a game made," she told Emily Greenhouse for the *New Yorker*'s *Elements* blog (1 Aug. 2013), "where players were invited to 'beat the bitch up' in which upon clicking on the screen, an image of me would become increasingly battered and bruised," until the screen would eventually turn red. The backlash was unusually intense, so much so that common expressions—such as cyber-bullying or trolling—did not adequately convey the scale of harassment.

In a TEDxWomen talk, given on December 1, 2012, in Washington, DC, Sarkeesian suggested that a better way of describing this behavior would be "cyber mob" and that what these gamers were engaging in was a coordinated "social activity." Her perpetrators did not see their behavior as criminal; instead they "referred to their abuse as a game." The notion that sexual harassment is merely a part of gaming culture is an old one. Underlying it, Sarkeesian pointed out in her talk, is the goal of "creating an environment that is too toxic and hostile [for women] to endure." Jasmine Silver, reporting on Sarkeesian and gamers for *Bitch* magazine (1 Nov. 2012), cited sociologist Michael Kimmel, who addressed gaming culture in his 2009 book *Guyland: The Perilous World Where Boys Become Men*. Kimmel writes (as quoted by Silver) that for young heterosexual males, the interactive yet anonymous world of online gaming "is both an escape from reality and an escape to reality." Interviewing young men about their behavior online, Kimmel found responses similar to this one: "We all know the PC drill . . . but c'mon, man. It's only a g—— game . . . it's just entertainment."

But young men—particularly young men who believe that society assigns dignity to women just to be politically correct—are only a part of the problem. As Sarkeesian noted in her TED talk, the average age of a male gamer in the United States is thirty years old. "It's not just 'boys being boys,'" she said. "It's not just 'how the Internet works,' and it's not just going to go away if we ignore it." As the number of female gamers grows, many male gamers are becoming territorial about the space that they once dominated. The same year Sarkeesian was harassed, Helen Lewis for the *New York Times* (25 Dec. 2012) reported, citing the Entertainment Software Association, that the female/male split among gamers was 47 percent to 53 percent and that the split had narrowed during the past three years. Silver pointed out that this presents an interesting duality: it's all "just a game," but at the same time male gamers "know that the space is a real, tangible thing, in need of protection."

## NEW OPPORTUNITY FOR EDUCATION

In the summer of 2012, despite the harassment she faced, Sarkeesian was able to raise close to $160,000 for the *Tropes vs. Women in Video Games* series. With the extra funds, she expanded the project to include thirteen twenty-five-minute videos and a free classroom curriculum. "I love gaming (and there are a small handful of amazing female characters out there), but the seriousness of the gender problem really cannot be overstated," Sarkeesian told the gaming website IGN (6 June 2013).

The series begins with a three-part "miniseries," as Sarkeesian termed it on *Feminist Frequency* (1 Aug. 2013), focusing on a very familiar trope: the damsel in distress. Part 1 (posted in March 2013) begins with a story about a game called *Dinosaur Planet*. The game was originally developed for *Super Mario 64* in 1999, but it was never released. One of its heroes was a female fox named Krystal, who was imbued with magical, dinosaur-fighting powers. Krystal's character ultimately became part of Nintendo's *Star Fox Adventures*; the narrative was largely rewritten so that Fox McCloud, *Star Fox*'s male protagonist, has those magical powers. Krystal herself spends most of the game trapped inside of a crystal prison—effectively becoming a damsel in distress waiting to be rescued by Fox McCloud. This particularly literal illustration of the trope, Sarkeesian says in the video, lets us understand how the "damsel in distress" robs female characters of their autonomy. In another widely viewed *Tropes vs. Women in Video Games* video, "Ms. Male Character," which was released in November 2013, Sarkeesian examines characters that are feminized versions of their male counterparts, such as Ms. Pac-Man, the original Ms. Male Character.

The overwhelming support for Sarkeesian's project represents a burgeoning cultural shift. While there remain many abusive gamers, there is also a growing number of people speaking out about online harassment—not only as it occurs in the gaming community but also as it has permeated the larger Internet. Harmful online behaviors are being scrutinized and exposed. "For the longest time, people have seen games as a children's pastime, and we as an industry have stood behind this idea," game designer James Portnow told Amy O'Leary for the *New York Times* (1 Aug. 2012). "But that's not true any longer. We are a real mass medium, and we have a real effect on the culture. We have to take a step beyond this idea that nothing we could possibly do could be negative, or hurt people."

In 2013 Sarkeesian received an honorary award from the National Academy of Video Game Trade Reviewers. The following year she was awarded the Game Developers Choice Ambassador Award and nominated for Microsoft's Women in Gaming Award. She is currently an advisor to Silverstring Media.

Sarkeesian lives in California and identifies herself as a Canadian American.

## SUGGESTED READING

Greenhouse, Emily. "Twitter's Free-Speech Problem." *Elements*. New Yorker, 1 Aug. 2013. Web. 12 June 2014.

Lewis, Helen. "Game Theory: Making Room for the Women." *New York Times*. New York Times, 25 Dec. 2012. Web. 12 June 2014.

Liss-Schultz, Nina. "This Woman Was Threatened with Rape after Calling Out Sexist Video Games—and Then Something Inspiring Happened." *Mother Jones*. Mother Jones, 30 May 2014. Web. 12 June 2014.

O'Leary, Amy. "In Virtual Play, Sex Harassment Is All Too Real." *New York Times*. New York Times, 1 Aug. 2012. Web. 12 June 2014.

Sarkeesian, Anita. "TEDxWomen Talk about Online Harassment and Cyber Mobs." *Feminist Frequency*. Feminist Frequency, 5 Dec. 2012. Web. 12 June 2014.

Silver, Jasmine. "Game Changer." *Bitch*. Bitch Media, 1 Nov. 2012. Web. 12 June 2014.

## SELECTED WORKS

*Feminist Frequency*, 2009–; *Tropes vs. Women*, 2011; *Tropes vs. Women in Video Games*, 2013–

—Molly Hagan

# Kshama Sawant

**Born:** 1973
**Occupation:** City Council member

Indian American Kshama Sawant is a Seattle City Council member in Seattle, Washington, the first socialist to be elected to the council in more than a century.

## BACKGROUND

Kshama Vivek Sawant was born in Pune, India, in 1973. Her mother, Vasundhara Ramanujam, was a teacher and later a school principal before her retirement; her father, civil engineer H. T. Ramanujam, was killed by a drunk driver when Sawant was thirteen years old. She has an older sister.

Most of Sawant's youth was spent in Mumbai, where she attended St. John's High School. She studied computer science and engineering at Sathaye College (then called Parle College) at the University of Mumbai, earning her bachelor's degree in 1994.

Sawant worked as a software engineer in Mumbai before immigrating to the United States in 1996 with her husband, Vivek Sawant. She enrolled in North Carolina State University in 2000 and earned a master's degree in economics in 2003. She then entered the university's doctorate program, working on a two-year research project on retirement-planning behavior under economics professor Robert Clark. From 2005 to 2006, Sawant was a visiting professor of economics at Washington and Lee University in Lexington, Virginia. She finished her doctoral degree in 2009 with a dissertation on elderly labor supply in rural communities. Sawant became a United States citizen in 2010.

## POLITICAL INVOLVEMENT

In 2008, Sawant, who had moved to Seattle two years earlier, became involved with the Socialist Alternative Party, an independent political party founded in the 1980s. After earning her PhD, she began teaching economics at Seattle Central Community College and Seattle University.

During the national Occupy Wall Street movement of 2011, Sawant became a leader in the movement's Seattle branch. On October 31, 2011, she participated in an all-night teach-in organized by the American Federation of Teachers, Seattle Community Colleges, Local 1789 to support the Occupy movement. From three to four o'clock in the morning, she lectured the assembled crowd on issues concerning economics and politics.

In 2012, Sawant made her first bid for public election, running for a seat in the Forty-Third District of the Washington House of Representatives. She originally ran for the position 1 seat against incumbent Jamie Pedersen but instead made it through the primary as a write-in candidate for the position 2 seat, held by the less-popular Frank Chopp. Sawant's campaign began to gain public support after an article endorsing her candidacy and socialist affiliations appeared in the *Stranger*, a Seattle alternative newspaper.

Though Sawant wanted to highlight her socialist beliefs to differentiate herself from Democratic candidates, state bylaws prohibited write-in candidates from stating a party preference. She challenged this law in August 2012, and the Washington courts ruled that the state had to allow her to list her party preference on the ballot.

## SEATTLE CITY COUNCIL

Sawant lost the general election but captured nearly 29 percent of the vote, an unexpected level of support for an openly socialist candidate. Shortly after losing the election, she announced her intention to run for city council, basing her campaign on a movement to increase Seattle's minimum wage from $9.32 to $15 per hour. The proposed figure, which was significantly higher than the $10.10 wage being debated on the federal level at the time, was based on independent economic estimates of the compensation required for working-class Seattle residents to live healthy lives unencumbered by poverty.

Sawant ran against four-term incumbent Richard Conlin, who was supported by the Democratic Party. In the November 2013 elections, Conlin gained an early lead, holding 54 percent of the vote; when the vote-by-mail ballots were counted, however, Sawant unexpectedly became the front-runner. Conlin conceded the election, making Sawant the winner by a 1,640-vote margin.

Media reactions to Sawant's victory were mixed. Some hailed it as a sign of shifting values regarding economic and social justice, while others highlighted the past and present political failures of socialism around the world as reason to doubt Sawant's qualifications and economic beliefs. Some news agencies also questioned her legitimacy as a socialist; prior to the election, political blog PubliCola had taken issue with

the fact that Sawant, who claimed to represent the "99 percent," had reported her husband's income as over $100,000. She responded on her campaign website by saying that she and her husband were separated but not legally divorced, for "emotional and private reasons," and that she did not share his income. After winning the election, Sawant released a statement announcing that she would take home only $40,000 of her $117,000 city council salary; the rest would go to what she called a "Solidarity Fund" to support social-justice causes.

## MINIMUM WAGE VICTORY

Sawant continued campaigning to raise the minimum wage to $15 per hour, delivering speeches throughout Seattle and building up a grassroots political movement. Though opposition from the business community was substantial, the proposal became so popular that the city's leadership had little choice but to support the initiative. Mayor Mike McGinn met with business leaders and the legislature to debate potential implementation compromises.

In June 2014, the city officially approved the $15 minimum wage, to be phased in over a period of three to seven years, making Seattle's minimum wage the highest in the United States. Sawant did not support the final version of the bill, believing that it had been altered by too many concessions to protect business interests. Despite her objections, news media credited Sawant as the driving force behind the historic legislation.

## IMPACT

As one of the most visible socialist politicians in the United States, Kshama Sawant has helped bring the issue of third-party viability to the forefront of the American political debate. Her role in raising Seattle's minimum wage to $15 was a crowning achievement in American political and economic history, despite her misgivings about the final result.

## PERSONAL LIFE

Sawant married Microsoft software engineer Vivek Sawant in Mumbai prior to immigrating to the United States. They have since separated but remain legally married.

## SUGGESTED READING

La Ganga, Maria L. "Socialist to Occupy Seattle City Council." *Los Angeles Times*. Los Angeles Times, 20 Nov. 2013. Web. 10 June 2014.

Rajghatta, Chidanand. "Pune-Born Socialist Kshama Sawant Scores for Seattle: Record $15 an Hour Minimum Wage for Workers." *Times of India*. Bennett, Coleman, 3 June 2014. Web. 10 June 2014.

Roose, Kevin. "Meet the Seattle Socialist Leading the Fight for a $15 Minimum Wage." *New York Magazine*. New York Media, 26 May 2014. Web. 10 June 2014.

Rosenthal, Brian M. "Richard Conlin Making Issue of Kshama Sawant's Voter Registration." *Seattle Times*. Seattle Times, 8 Oct. 2013. Web. 10 June 2014.

Sawant, Kshama. "Capitalism Is a 'Dirty Word': America's New Socialist Council Member Talks to Salon." Interview by Josh Eidelson. *Salon*. Salon Media Group, 18 Nov. 2013. Web. 10 June 2014.

Valdes, Manuel. "Socialist Kshama Sawant Elected to Seattle City Council." *Huffington Post*. TheHuffingtonPost.com, 15 Nov. 2013. Web. 10 June 2014.

—Micah Issitt

# Jeremy Scahill

**Born:** 1974

**Occupation:** Journalist

Investigative journalist Jeremy Scahill has reported from war zones and various devastated regions, in countries such as Iraq, Yemen, Somalia, Afghanistan, and Nigeria. He is the author, in addition to numerous articles, of two books, *Blackwater: The Rise of the World's Most Powerful Mercenary Army* (2007), for which he won the 2007 George Polk Book Award, and *Dirty Wars: The World Is a Battlefield* (2013). The documentary film *Dirty Wars*, in which he investigates US government's use of special military units and drone warfare as part of the ongoing "war on terror," also came out in 2013 and was nominated for the Academy Award for best documentary feature. Scahill, investigative journalist Glenn Greenwald, and documentary film director Laura Poitras are the founding editors of the online publication the *Intercept*.

Chatham House/Wikimedia Commons

## YOUTH IN REVOLT

Jeremy Scahill was born in 1974 in Milwaukee, Wisconsin. His parents, Mike and Lisa, were very mindful of and active in issues of social justice. "My dad in particular really made part of our education growing up understanding issues involving the politics of racism and war issues," Scahill told Rob Thomas for Madison. com (10 Aug. 2013). "It was part of the regular discussion in our household growing up." Scahill was the oldest of three children. According to Patrick O'Neill in an article for *Indy Week* (10 Oct. 2007), Scahill's father lived in New York City during the late 1960s and early 1970s at the headquarters of the *Catholic Worker*, an independent monthly newspaper published by the Catholic Worker Movement, which is dedicated to bringing awareness to the socially progressive teachings of the New Testament. Speaking to O'Neill about his oldest child, Mike Scahill remembered how his son, in sixth grade, volunteered to call bingo at a local Catholic church: "He just had this tremendous gift for impromptu, spontaneous speaking. It was truly a remarkable gift."

Scahill attended Wauwatosa East High School, a public high school in Wauwatosa, Wisconsin, where he was not a particularly good student. He graduated in 1992 and went on to study at the University of Wisconsin–Madison, where he became a student organizer, working primarily to advocate for the rights of homeless people.

## DROP OUT, HELP OUT

In the summer of 1995, Scahill decided to leave college to further pursue his activism and moved to Washington, DC, where he joined the Community for Creative Non-Violence, a DC–based homeless shelter and nonprofit that, according to its website, seeks to "ensure that the rights of the homeless and poor are not infringed upon and that every person has access to life's basic essentials—food, shelter, clothing, and medical care." He would, for example, take homeless people (many of whom were war veterans) to doctor's appointments, helping them deal with transportation and the paperwork.

While in DC, he met peace activist Philip Berrigan at a rally. Berrigan invited him to visit Jonah House, a commune he ran with his wife, which billed itself as a faith-based resistance community that promoted nonviolent activism. Scahill took Berrigan up on the invitation and visited Jonah House in the inner city of Baltimore, Maryland. His initial plan was to stay for a weekend, but he ended up staying for a year. Along with other Jonah House members, Scahill took part in various forms of nonviolent activism, which led to his arrest on several occasions. According to Bruce Bawer for *City Journal* (Summer 2013), in 1996 Scahill and ten other activists were arrested in Chicago for occupying a federal building as a result of their protest against the imprisonment of Leonard Peltier, a leader of the American Indian Movement who was incarcerated for killing two agents of the Federal Bureau of Investigation. In January 1997, Scahill was arrested near the Supreme Court building in the nation's capital during a protest against the death penalty.

## *DEMOCRACY NOW*

When Scahill first moved to Washington, DC, he had never heard of journalist Amy Goodman or her independent daily news program *Democracy Now*. "I heard Amy Goodman on the radio and my mind was just completely blown," he told Micah Rodman of the *Yale Herald* (12 Sept. 2013). "I started stalking her, and offering to do anything—you know, if you have a dog, I'll walk it. I'll feed your cat. I'll wash your windows. I just want to be a part of this. . . . And eventually she let me come in and volunteer, and I was there ever since. I list *Democracy Now* as my university, because that's what it was like."

Scahill started out at *Democracy Now* as an unpaid volunteer, getting coffee. By the late 1990s, he began to do reporting pieces, going out into the field with a voice recorder and getting commentary from people "on the ground" in such devastated or war-torn places as Yugoslavia and Iraq. By 1998, Scahill had the official title of producer, and that year his reporting made a significant contribution to a story about the oil company Chevron's role in the murder of two Nigerian activists. In the story, titled "Drilling and Killing: Chevron and Nigeria's Oil Dictatorship," Scahill and Goodman offered the findings of a report they produced, which argued that in May 1998 in Nigeria, where the company was drilling for oil, Chevron had transported Nigerian soldiers via helicopter to an oil platform and barge, which had been occupied by dozens of activists, who were demanding that "Chevron contribute more to the development of the impoverished oil region where they live." The Nigerian military subsequently shot and killed two of the protesters and imprisoned another eleven activists for several weeks. Goodman and Scahill received the 1998 George Polk Award for radio reporting for this documentary.

## REPORTING ON HURRICANE KATRINA

Scahill's next big story, which ultimately led to the publication of his first book, was about the private security consulting firm Blackwater (later renamed Academi). While reporting for the left-leaning magazine the *Nation* on the aftermath of Hurricane Katrina in New Orleans in 2005, Scahill wrote a story titled "Blackwater Down" (21 Sept. 2005). The article's opening paragraph paints a vivid scene right off the bat: "The men from Blackwater USA arrived in New Orleans right after Katrina hit. The company known for its private security work guarding senior US diplomats in Iraq beat the federal government and most aid organizations to the scene in another devastated Gulf. About 150 heavily armed Blackwater troops dressed in full battle gear spread out into the chaos of New Orleans. Officially, the company boasted of its forces 'join[ing] the hurricane relief effort.' But its men on the ground told a different story."

Scahill goes on to describe a kind of postapocalyptic scene in which heavily armed Blackwater employees ride around in big cars with tinted windows and no license plates. Scahill spent time with them, and they told him about their experience of working on the security detail of top US officials in Iraq, such as L. Paul Bremer and John Negroponte. The four men working for Blackwater whom Scahill spoke to in New Orleans told him their job in the city was "securing neighborhoods" and "confronting criminals." They were operating under the authority of the Department of Homeland Security, they told him, and they had even been deputized by the governor of Louisiana.

In that article, Scahill also introduced to his readers Erik Prince, Blackwater's chief executive officer and cofounder—a billionaire and a "staunch right-wing Christian." Prince, wrote Scahill, has serious financial and personal ties to various members of the Republican Party. Scahill expressed grave concern over allowing private security forces to conduct police action: for one, there is the issue of accountability, and also there is the issue of tactics. Primarily, at least at the time, Blackwater was being used (in a fairly significant way) in the war in Iraq, which also brought out various accountability issues, since as a private company Blackwater was not subject to the US military justice system and was subject to a financial incentive to prolong the war effort there.

### BLACKWATER

Scahill's first book, *Blackwater: The Rise of the World's Most Powerful Mercenary Army*, came out in February 2007. The following month, Scahill appeared on the National Public Radio program *Fresh Air*, which led to more exposure. The book, which went on to become a best seller, received mixed reviews, in part depending on which side of the political divide the reviewer was on.

The most penetrating reviews, however, offered subtle analyses: acknowledging Scahill's staggering findings—for example, that the US government had spent $5.6 billion on private security in Iraq—but criticizing him for mischaracterizing or simplifying the nature of organizations and politicians he opposes ideologically. In the *London Review of Books* (2 Aug. 2007) James Meek wrote, "As much as Scahill's book is a sincere attempt to investigate an organization with a vested financial interest in America's being at war for as long and as widely as possible, it has the unintentional side effect of hyping Blackwater in a way not so different from the way Blackwater hypes itself. We don't know how Prince feels about being described on the jacket of Scahill's book as head of 'the world's most powerful mercenary army', but I suspect the answer is: very pleased."

### DIRTY WARS

After a few years of writing and talking about Blackwater, Scahill wanted to move on. He wanted to explore other aspects of the war on terror. He and Richard Rowley, a friend and filmmaker, went to Afghanistan in early 2010. Scahill traveled around the country, interviewing locals about a series of deadly night raids. Rowley followed him around with the camera. And this is where the documentary film *Dirty Wars* (2013) starts off. In the documentary, which is shot and narrated like a thriller or noir film, Scahill serves as both the narrator and main character: Viewers see him talking to locals in Afghanistan (and later other countries), asking questions, trying to piece together the puzzle, and talking to sources inside the US military—some out in the open, some anonymous.

During his investigation, Scahill learns that a night raid in Afghanistan, which resulted in the deaths of innocent civilians, was conducted by the Joint Special Operations Command (JSOC). At the time, the name JSOC was little known, but the acronym was entered into the public lexicon after the revelation of the successful operation to assassinate Osama bin Laden, which was carried out by a JSOC unit. Scahill acknowledges that the unit is not all bad, but it seems to have gotten out of control. "Certainly, major terrorist figures have been killed," Scahill explained to Rodman. "Osama bin Laden no longer joins us on Earth. But, a tremendous number of innocent people are being killed, and I think that we've reached a point where we are creating more new enemies than we are killing actual terrorists in these operations."

In true noir fashion, at one point in the documentary, Scahill's computer is anonymously hacked with a note left on it indicating that his encryption code—which he uses to put in the names of his sources—has been broken. As the momentum in the film picks up, Scahill travels to Somalia and Yemen. In Somalia, he discovers warlords being paid by the US government to keep order and in Yemen he discovers how the US government has been using drone strikes to take out "targets," including an American-born alleged terrorist and his sixteen-year-old son. Scahill leaves the viewer with the impression that the drone program and the JSOC units, though occasionally useful, are, more often than not, dangerous to both local civilian populations and the future security of the United States. Reviews, like before, widely varied. Steven Boone, writing for RogerEbert.com (13 June 2013), complimented the film's fact-finding mission but criticized its thriller style: "Scahill is so respected and convincing that he doesn't need such propping up, so the flashy directing and editing makes it feel as though 'Dirty Wars' is trying too hard." The film nevertheless won the Cinematography Award for US documentary at the Sundance Film Festival. Scahill's book *Dirty Wars: The World Is a Battlefield* was published in April 2013 and covers similar issues, though it was not based on the film.

Scahill lives in the New York City borough of Brooklyn. He is the national security correspondent for the *Nation* and a fellow at the Nation Institute.

## SUGGESTED READING

Moss, Stephen. "Jeremy Scahill: The Man Exposing the US Dirty War." *Guardian*. Guardian News and Media, 24 Nov. 2013. Web. 18 Dec. 2014.

O'Neill, Patrick. "Author Jeremy Scahill Discusses How Blackwater Is Changing How War Is Waged." *Indy Week*. Indy Week, 10 Oct. 2007. Web. 18 Dec. 2014.

Rodman, Micah. "Sitting Down with Jeremy Scahill." *Yale Herald*. Yale Herald, 12 Sept. 2013. Web. 18 Dec. 2014.

Scahill, Jeremy. "Interview with Jeremy Scahill on 'Dirty Wars' Production, War on the Press & Bradley Manning's Trial." Interview by Kevin Gosztola. *Dissenter*. FireDogLake. com, 2 June 2013. Web. 18 Dec. 2014.

—Dmitry Kiper

# Max Scherzer

**Born:** July 27, 1984
**Occupation:** Baseball player

Max Scherzer of the Detroit Tigers is widely considered to be among the best pitchers in Major League Baseball (MLB). Described by Jeff Seidel for the *Detroit Free Press* (14 July 2013) as "a complex, cerebral pitcher, blessed with a great right arm, an inquisitive mind and a fierce, competitive spirit," Scherzer has dominated opposing hitters with a pitching repertoire that includes a blistering fastball, a devastating slider, and a curveball. After battling inconsistency in his first four major-league seasons, the first two of which were spent in the National League (NL) with the Arizona Diamondbacks,

Skoch3/Wikimedia Commons

Scherzer enjoyed a breakout year in 2012, when he helped the Tigers reach the World Series. The following year he earned his first All-Star selection and was awarded the American League (AL) Cy Young Award for his remarkable 2013 season, in which he finished among the AL leaders in a number of pitching categories. In 2014 Scherzer earned his second career All-Star selection and led the AL in wins for the second consecutive year.

## EARLY LIFE

The older of the two sons of Brad and Jan Scherzer, Maxwell M. Scherzer was born on July 27, 1984, in St. Louis, Missouri. Scherzer developed a love for baseball at an early age. "I came out of the womb throwing and hitting baseballs," he quipped to Bill Dow for *Baseball Digest* (Jan./ Feb. 2014). As a youngster, Scherzer rooted for his hometown St. Louis Cardinals and dreamed of playing in the major leagues.

Growing up, Scherzer was practically inseparable from his brother, Alex, who was three years younger. The two forged a close bond through sports and challenged each other in everything from Wiffle ball to table tennis. For Scherzer, sports not only gave him motivation to compete against his brother but also to prove himself to his peers. He was diagnosed with heterochromia, a rare condition in which the eyes are different colors, and was often teased by classmates. The teasing stopped, however, once Scherzer began to display his athletic prowess.

Scherzer attended Parkway Central High School in Chesterfield, Missouri, where he was a standout athlete. As a freshman he played varsity basketball and was the starting quarterback on the varsity football squad, but his focus was baseball. During his senior season Scherzer recorded seventy-two strikeouts in fifty innings. By then he already had a low-nineties fastball and a work-in-progress slider that was already well-regarded by scouts. He also performed well academically, and graduated with a 3.9 grade point average.

Despite being drafted by the hometown Cardinals in the forty-third round of the 2003 MLB draft, Scherzer turned down their offer in order to play college baseball, which offered him a chance to further his education. He chose to attend the University of Missouri, where he majored in finance. Under Missouri's coach Tim Jamieson, Scherzer quickly developed into one of the best collegiate starting pitchers in the country. Scherzer's brother Alex showed him how to use sabermetrics, the statistical analysis of baseball data, to understand and improve his game. Jamieson helped Scherzer change his approach and refine his mechanics, particularly his delivery, which was "so raw and violent that often his hat fell off as he unleashed a pitch," as Albert Chen wrote for *Sports Illustrated* (28 Apr. 2014). He adopted Jamieson's philosophy of "attacking in three pitches," which focuses on the importance of throwing strikes in one-and-one counts. He also tightened his throwing motion, which added more velocity to his fastball. "A lot of guys overthink and overcomplicate things," Jamieson told Chen. "Max always had the ability to take all the information, consume it, but simplify things when he's out there."

Scherzer's adjustments paid immediate dividends. During his sophomore season he went 9–4 with a remarkable 1.86 earned-run average (ERA) and a school-record 131 strikeouts over sixteen starts. He was named the Big Twelve Conference Pitcher of the Year and an All-American second team member by *Baseball America*. Following an equally impressive junior season, Scherzer, whose fastball was now clocking as high as ninety-nine miles per hour, was drafted by the Arizona Diamondbacks as the eleventh overall pick in the first round of the 2006 draft.

## EARLY MLB CAREER

Scherzer joined the Diamondbacks' organization in 2007. After brief stints with the Fort Worth Cats in the independent American Association and the Visalia Oaks in the advanced single-A California League, he was promoted to the Diamondbacks' double-A affiliate in Mobile, Alabama, the Mobile BayBears. In fourteen starts with the club, Scherzer went 4–4 with a 3.91 ERA. Prior to the 2008 season, he was promoted to the Tucson Sidewinders, in the triple-A Pacific Coast League.

After four impressive starts with the Sidewinders, Scherzer earned his first call-up to the majors on April 29, 2008, as a relief pitcher against the Houston Astros. He struck out seven batters and allowed no hits or runs in four and one-third innings, setting an MLB record for most consecutive batters retired (thirteen) in a reliever's debut. "It was a vindication that I had the talent and belonged in the major leagues," Scherzer told Dow. "To have an outing like that convinced me that I could pitch in the majors and have success."

Following his brilliant debut, Scherzer was inserted into the Diamondbacks' starting rotation. He made three starts and six relief appearances with the club before being relegated back to the Sidewinders, where he continued to appear as both a starter and reliever. He earned a second call-up to the majors on August 29, and remained with the Diamondbacks through the end of the 2008 season. Despite going winless with a 0–4 record during his rookie campaign, Scherzer posted a solid 3.05 ERA in sixteen games, seven of which were starts.

Scherzer pitched well enough as a rookie to earn a spot in the Diamondbacks' starting rotation in 2009. As the team's fifth starter, he went 9–11 with a 4.12 ERA in thirty starts and recorded 174 strikeouts in 170.1 innings. During that offseason, the Diamondbacks, who had finished last in the NL West Division with a 70–92 record, traded Scherzer to the Detroit Tigers in a three-team deal that also included the New York Yankees.

## DETROIT TIGERS AND TRANSFORMATION INTO AN ELITE PITCHER

When Scherzer joined the Tigers, many within the organization expected him to develop into "an adequate middle-of-the-rotation pitcher," as Chen noted, though some believed he had greater potential. His development, however, came slowly. After posting a 1–4 record in his first eight starts for the Tigers, Scherzer was demoted to the team's triple-A affiliate, the Toledo Mud Hens, to adjust his pitching mechanics. Tweaking his throwing motion, he recorded seventeen strikeouts over fifteen innings in two starts with the Mud Hens before being recalled to the Tigers for the remainder of the 2010 season. He finished with a 12–11 record and a respectable 3.50 ERA over thirty-one starts, while striking out 184 in 195.2 innings. His strikeout-per-nine-inning ratio (8.5) ranked sixth in the AL.

Scherzer opened the 2011 season in dominant fashion, earning wins in his first six decisions, the longest streak by a Tigers pitcher since 2006. He went on to win fifteen games and finished tied for ninth in the AL with a .625 winning percentage. Bolstered by a formidable pitching staff led by Justin Verlander, the Tigers finished with a 95–67 record and won their first AL Central title since joining the division in 1998. The Tigers advanced to the AL Championship Series, which they lost to the Texas Rangers in six games. Scherzer went 1–1 in his first two career postseason starts, striking out fourteen batters and allowing nine runs in fifteen and two-thirds innings.

Scherzer enjoyed a breakout season in 2012, despite playing most of the year with a heavy heart after a family tragedy. In June his brother, Alex, committed suicide after struggling with depression for years. The tragic news was devastating to Scherzer, who had remained very close to Alex as his pitching career developed. Baseball offered Scherzer and his family some respite from their grief. Only two days after his brother's death, he made his next scheduled start against the Pittsburgh Pirates. In a press conference held the following day, Scherzer called the start the "most difficult" of his life but said that it "was best for my family," as quoted by Jason Beck for *MLB.com* (26 June 2012). "It gave us. . . . a chance to have something we'd love and laugh about, and that's baseball." Scherzer credits his brother as an influence on his mathematical approach to the game and dedicates every start to Alex.

## CY YOUNG AWARD WINNER

Despite reaching the 2012 season's midpoint with a mediocre 8–5 record and 4.72 ERA, Scherzer had a remarkable second half, going 8–2 with a 2.69 ERA over his final fifteen starts. He placed first in the AL in strikeouts-per-nine-inning ratio (11.1) and finished second behind

Verlander with 231 strikeouts. Scherzer's stellar pitching down the stretch helped the Tigers win their second consecutive AL Central title and advance to the World Series for the first time since 2006. The Tigers were swept by the San Francisco Giants in the World Series in four games, but Scherzer continued to dominate opposing hitters, going 1–0 with a 2.08 ERA and 26 strikeouts in three postseason starts. Following his brother's death, he told Robert Sanchez for *ESPN* (6 Apr. 2013), "I couldn't be destroyed when I took the mound. . . . Instead of looking at the past, I was looking forward to what was in my future."

Scherzer carried his momentum into the 2013 season, which saw him emerge as one of the best pitchers in baseball and supplant Verlander as the Tigers' ace. Armed with the addition of a curveball, better control, refined mechanics, and a stronger mental approach, Scherzer opened the year 13–0, the first pitcher to do so since 1986. He finished the regular season with an MLB-best 21–3 record and led the AL with a 0.97 ratio of walks plus hits per inning pitched (WHIP). He ranked second in the league in both strikeouts (240) and strikeout-per-nine-inning ratio (10.1), and placed fifth in both ERA (2.90) and innings pitched (214.1).

The performance earned Scherzer his first career All-Star selection, as the starting pitcher for the AL squad, and he was a near-unanimous winner of the AL Cy Young Award. Commenting on Scherzer's remarkable year, Tigers catcher Alex Avila affirmed to Bill Dow, "Max always had great stuff, that was never in question from when he started in the big leagues, but it was just a matter of honing his skills and learning how to pitch. . . . If he remains consistent, he will put up numbers like this for years to come."

The Tigers, meanwhile, earned their third consecutive AL Central title in 2013 and advanced to the American League Championship Series (ALCS) for the third straight season. The Tigers lost the ALCS to the eventual World Series champion Boston Red Sox in six games, but in his four postseason appearances Scherzer established a new Tigers record with thirty-four strikeouts.

During the offseason Scherzer rejected a six-year, $144 million contract extension offer from the Tigers. The media questioned his decision, noting that he was gambling on continued success in hope of securing an even bigger payday in free agency. If he failed to perform to the same level he risked getting lower offers on the open market. But Scherzer put together another dominant campaign in 2014; he finished in a three-way tie for the AL lead in wins, with eighteen, and achieved career-bests in both strikeouts (252) and innings pitched (220.1). He was named to his second straight All-Star team and led the Tigers to their fourth consecutive AL Central title. Following the season, Scherzer became one of the top free agent pitchers available, and as of December 2014 he was reportedly seeking a contract in excess of $200 million.

During the offseason, Scherzer lives in Scottsdale, Arizona, with his wife, the former Erica May. They were married in November 2013.

## SUGGESTED READING

Chen, Albert. "Mad Max." *Sports Illustrated* 28 Apr. 2014: 28–33. Print.

Dow, Bill. "The Thinking Man's Pitcher." *Baseball Digest* Jan./Feb. 2014: 34–37. Print.

Sanchez, Robert. "Max Scherzer: A Brother's Passage." *ESPN*. ESPN Internet Ventures, 6 Apr. 2013. Web. 22 Dec. 2014.

Seidel, Jeff. "Detroit Tigers First-Time All-Star Max Scherzer Takes Modesty, Intellect to Mound." *Detroit Free Press*. Gannett, 14 July 2013. Web. 22 Dec. 2014.

—Chris Cullen

---

# Stacy Schiff

**Born:** October 26, 1961
**Occupation:** Writer

Stacy Schiff is an American writer specializing in biography. Her book *Saint-Exupéry: A Biography* (1994) was a finalist for the Pulitzer Prize, and her 1999 biography of Véra Nabokov, wife of the Russian writer Vladimir Nabokov, won the 2000 Pulitzer Prize in biography.

## BACKGROUND

Stacy Madeline Schiff was born in the town of Adams in the Berkshire Mountains region of western Massachusetts in 1961. Her father, Morton, managed a clothing store, while her mother, Ellen, was a professor of French literature at North Adams State College.

Schiff's passion for literature began as a young child, when she would spend several hours a week at the town library. She read the biographies of historical women such as Helen Keller, Joan of Arc, and Isadora Duncan and would later complain that the women most written about by biographers seemed to be those who were famous for being disabled or dying tragically.

She attended high school at Phillips Academy Andover in Andover, Massachusetts, before enrolling at Williams College in 1978. She graduated from Williams in 1982 with a bachelor of arts degree.

After graduating, Schiff entered the world of publishing, working as an editor for Basic Books, Viking, and finally Simon & Schuster. She also served for a time as a consulting editor for the *Paris Review*. While on lunch breaks, Schiff developed a habit of visiting libraries, where she remained drawn to biographical works.

## WRITING CAREER

Schiff came up with the idea for her first book, on the life and work of the French aristocrat, writer, and aviation pioneer Antoine de Saint-Exupéry, while she was working at Simon & Schuster. She thought at first of proposing the idea to an agent so that a writer could be found for it, but she soon decided she would rather write the book herself. In 1990 she left Simon & Schuster to work on the biography full-time.

*Saint-Exupéry: A Biography*, published in 1994, received high critical praise from luminaries in nonfiction. Esteemed American historian David McCullough lauded it as a "book not to be missed." The book was a finalist for the 1995 Pulitzer Prize in biography.

Schiff's second work was equally ambitious. *Véra (Mrs. Vladimir Nabokov): Portrait of a Marriage*, published by Random House in 1999, gives an exhaustively researched account of the life of the notoriously private Véra Nabokov, Russian novelist Vladimir Nabokov's wife of more than twenty years. *Véra* expounds on the massive influence Véra Nabokov had on her husband's work and legacy, both as his main influential voice and as a business associate, negotiating contracts with major publishing houses. The book established Schiff as one of the preeminent biographers in the United States and won the 2000 Pulitzer Prize in biography.

Schiff's next work, *A Great Improvisation* (2005), centers on venerable statesman Benjamin Franklin's time in France during the Revolutionary War. The book was praised by critics as one of the seminal texts on Franklin's widespread diplomatic influence and fostering of the Franco-American alliance that was a major factor in America's Revolutionary War victory.

Her 2010 book, *Cleopatra: A Life*, a biography of the famed Egyptian ruler, was voted one of the year's best books by notable publications such as the *New York Times* and *Kirkus*. Schiff drew on research about not only the queen herself but also the social and political climate of ancient Egypt, dispelling several myths that have surrounded Cleopatra for centuries while providing numerous new insights into her personal and political life.

## IMPACT

Schiff has emerged as one of the most celebrated and respected biographers working in the United States. Her endless dedication to researching her subjects and the epochs in which they lived and worked has led numerous critics to assert that Schiff has the ability to transform historically significant individuals into subjects more engaging that those of modern fiction writers. She has also made an effort in her writing to address a perceived lack of compelling biographies about female historical figures who are famous for their accomplishments and lasting influence rather than the tragedies of their lives or deaths.

In addition to her Pulitzer Prize win and nomination, her writing honors include fellowships from both the Guggenheim Foundation and the National Endowment for the Humanities as well as the 2006 Academy Award in literature from the American Academy of Arts and Letters.

## PERSONAL LIFE

Schiff married real estate developer Marc de la Bruyère in Lenox, Massachusetts, in May 1989. The couple has three children and divide their time between New York and Edmonton, Canada.

## SUGGESTED READING

"About Stacy." *Stacy Schiff Official Website*. Schiff, n.d. Web. 16 Mar. 2014.

Hertzel, Sarah. "Stacy Schiff's Remarkable Obsession." *StarTribune* [Minneapolis]. StarTribune, 6 Nov. 2011. Web. 16 Mar. 2014.

Schiff, Stacy. "Questions for Stacy Schiff: The Queen." Interview by Deborah Solomon. *New York Times*. New York Times, 15 Oct. 2010. Web. 16 Mar. 2014.

Schiff, Stacy. "An Interview with Stacy Schiff." Interview by Suellen Stringer-Hye. *Penn State University Library*. Penn State University, n.d. Web. 16 Mar. 2014.

"Stacy M. Schiff, an Editor, Weds." *New York Times*. New York Times, 14 May 1989. Web. 16 Mar. 2014.

## SELECTED WORKS

*Saint-Exupéry: A Biography*, 1994; *Véra (Mrs. Vladimir Nabokov): Portrait of a Marriage*, 1999; *A Great Improvisation: Franklin, France, and the Birth of America*, 2005; *Cleopatra: A Life*, 2010

—John Pritchard

---

# Amy Schumer

**Born:** 1981
**Occupation:** Comedian

Stand-up comedian and actor Amy Schumer quickly became a top talent in the world of comedy with her raunchy yet honest and uncompromising approach to humor. She first made waves for her blunt comedy about sex and relationships during the 2007 season of the reality television show *Last Comic Standing* and then for memorably roasting celebrities Charlie Sheen and Roseanne Barr. After a number of guest appearances on various comedy series, she gained even greater popularity with her own standup television special *Mostly Sex Stuff* (2012) and her sketch comedy show *Inside Amy Schumer* on the Comedy Central network, which premiered in 2013.

Schumer continued her march to mainstream fame as the writer and star of the film *Trainwreck*, produced and directed by famed comedy director Judd Apatow and scheduled for release in July 2015. In an interview with Charlotte Alter for *Time* (29 Apr. 2014), Schumer explained her approach to the trademark sexual element of her comedy: "I do want women to feel comfortable with themselves as sexual beings, and I don't think anyone should have to apologize for that or act like 'oh no, I'm a girl, I only want to have sex if its [sic] to make a baby.' But I'm just being myself. This is the stuff I think is so funny and I want to talk about."

## EARLY LIFE AND EDUCATION

Amy Schumer was born in 1981 on the Upper East Side of New York City. Like many of the families in the neighborhood, the Schumers were wealthy, and for a number of years the family prospered. Then her father was diagnosed

C Flanigan/FilmMagic/Getty Images

with multiple sclerosis (MS) when Schumer was nine, and before long his baby furniture business had collapsed and the family faced bankruptcy. The Schumers moved several times before settling on Long Island, where Amy and her siblings were raised in a small house. Schumer explained to Alter how her upbringing shaped her comedic sense: "It's a combination of a naturally good sense of humor and also a good amount of pain at a young age. We had a really dark couple of years in our house and we would just laugh about it. . . . I have such a dark sense of humor and the most awful stuff makes me laugh, and I think it's probably because of that."

Schumer's dark humor was aided by the fact that her childhood and teen years were somewhat unstable, as her parents divorced and each remarried several times, so she grew up with a revolving door of stepparents and stepsiblings. In 1999 Schumer graduated from South Side High School in Rockville Centre, New York, where she played volleyball and was voted both class clown and teacher's worst nightmare. She recalled in an interview with Terry Gross for the NPR program *Fresh Air* (25 June 2013) that although she was attentive in classes that interested her, she would often act out in those that she struggled in by "making dumb jokes" and trying to be as funny as possible to disrupt the class.

After high school graduation, Schumer studied theater at Towson University in Maryland, where she developed an interest in both dramatic

and comedic acting roles. Upon her graduation in 2003 with a degree in theater, she moved back to New York City to study at the William Esper Studio. There she worked for two years to develop her understanding of the Meisner technique, a naturalistic approach to acting, while at the same time waiting tables and tending bar between auditions. She received some acclaim for her role as a woman with breast cancer in an Off-Broadway black comedy titled *Keeping Abreast*.

### LAST COMIC STANDING

Schumer turned to stand-up comedy on a lark. One day as she passed the Gotham Comedy Club, she decided to go in and ask how she might get a chance to perform at the venue. The club happened to have an opening that night—which she could have, provided she brought at least four people along with her. She rounded up a group that included her mother, who, according to Schumer, was skeptical that her daughter was prepared to become a comedian on the spot. "She said, 'Do you have any jokes?' and I said, 'I'll figure it out,'" Schumer told Tiffany Razzano for the *Queens Chronicle* (15 May 2008). "It was pretty horrible, but I got a good response, and people couldn't believe it was my first time. Ever since that night I've just been pounding the pavement and doing it every night." She continued to perform and develop her jokes alongside her acting career.

In 2007 Schumer collaborated with several William Esper Studio alums to found the Collective, a theater company aimed at providing a network for actors to pursue and develop new work. Her first real breakthrough came that same year, when she recorded a stand-up performance for Comedy Central's *Live at Gotham* program and then was featured on the fifth season of the talent show *Last Comic Standing*. Schumer had previously auditioned and been rejected by *Last Comic Standing*, which features stand-up comedians facing off against one another, but on her second try she placed fourth in the contest despite her relative lack of experience. She explained to Razzano how her appearance on the show shaped her career but not her outlook: "I went from being completely unknown to having a fan base," she said. "But I feel the same. I still love comedy. I just don't have to sort mail to make a living anymore." She followed up with another comedy reality show appearance on *Reality Bites Back* in 2008.

Before long Schumer found herself in demand for everything from writing for *Cosmo-*

*politan* magazine to cohosting the talk show *Hoppus on Music* with musician Mark Hoppus. She received her own *Comedy Central Presents* special in 2010 and had much-acclaimed performances in *The Comedy Central Roast of Charlie Sheen* in 2011 and *The Comedy Central Roast of Roseanne Barr* in 2012. The year 2011 saw the release of her debut album featuring her comedy, titled *Cutting*. Schumer also had notable guest parts on a number of television comedies, including episodes of *30 Rock* (2009), *Curb Your Enthusiasm* (2011), and *Louie* (2012). Her feature film career began in 2012, with roles in the independent comedies *Sleepwalk with Me*, *Price Check*, and *Seeking a Friend for the End of the World*.

## MOSTLY SEX STUFF AND INSIDE AMY SCHUMER

Schumer's memorable performances across a variety of formats helped to secure her a one-hour stand-up comedy special, which premiered on Comedy Central in 2012. The title of the program was something of an in-joke, as the network executives had suggested that she add other material to her stand-up routine to move it beyond sexual humor, but Schumer suggested they simply name the special *Mostly Sex Stuff*. Throughout her stand-up career, Schumer has testified that many people—club owners and television producers and even comedy fans—are surprised to hear a young woman speak so bluntly about sex. Schumer expressed her thoughts on what she sees as a double standard to Gross, saying "There's such a stigma with being a woman who talks about sex, and there's just sort of no repercussions, I think, if you're a male comic that talks about sex. They wouldn't label you that way, I don't think." Whatever concerns Comedy Central may have had prior to the special's airing, they evaporated the day after the premiere, when *Mostly Sex Stuff* became the network's second-highest-rated special of 2012. The program was such a success that Comedy Central offered Schumer her own show.

*Inside Amy Schumer* debuted on Comedy Central in April 2013 and became the network's highest rated premiere of the year. The show, which stars Schumer and is written and executive produced by her as well, delves into many topics but never strays too far from her provocative takes on sex and relationships. Unlike a traditional sitcom or sketch comedy show, *Inside* features not only clips of Schumer doing stand-up, but also scripted skits and recorded

interviews in which Schumer asks questions of professionals in fields related to sex. Reviewing the series for the *New York Times* (31 Mar. 2014), Mike Hale remarked: "With her laserlike focus on sex and sexual politics, her willingness to get dirty (sometimes so much of a sketch or conversation is bleeped that it's impossible to follow) and her readiness to make fun of her own body and looks, Ms. Schumer brings to mind a more deadpan, twenty first-century Joan Rivers." In 2014 Schumer's work on the show brought her nominations for a Critics' Choice Television Award for best actress in a comedy series, a Primetime Emmy Award for outstanding writing for a variety series, and an American Comedy Award for best comedy actress. A third season of the series was scheduled to begin airing in April 2015.

## TRAINWRECK

In 2014 Schumer began working on her first major feature film, *Trainwreck*, in which she would costar alongside Bill Hader, Tilda Swinton, and Brie Larson. The idea for the movie, which Schumer wrote, began after director Judd Apatow, who is best known for such male-centered comedies as *The 40-Year-Old Virgin* (2005) and *Knocked Up* (2007), heard Schumer on Howard Stern's radio program and thought she would be a terrific person to work with on a film. "Most people aren't that funny—there's only a few that take it to a higher place," Apatow said of Schumer to Cara Buckley for the *New York Times* (18 July 2014). "She's insanely funny, and she has stories to tell."

Apatow contacted Schumer and asked her to write a script for him to direct. After scrapping her original idea, they developed what would become *Trainwreck*, a film about a woman in her early thirties who has an inability to commit to any relationship until she comes into contact with Hader's good-guy sports-doctor character. Schumer's character, also named Amy, is a fictionalized version of herself. She felt little stress making the film despite the pressures of mainstream attention, telling Buckley, "Making this feels like vacation. I'm the most relaxed I've been in ten years." *Trainwreck* is slated to be released in July 2015.

## PERSONAL LIFE

Schumer dated Dolph Ziggler, a professional wrestler, as well as comedian Anthony Jeselnik. She has admitted that her sex jokes sometimes make men hesitant to date her. She has also stated that she at times questions her own attractiveness and promiscuity but has committed to not getting plastic surgery.

## SUGGESTED READING

Alter, Charlotte. "Here's What Amy Schumer Thinks about Everything." *Time*. Time, 29 Apr. 2014. Web. 17 Mar. 2015.

Buckley, Cara. "From Stand-Up to Standout." *New York Times*. New York Times, 18 July 2014. Web. 17 Mar. 2015.

Hale, Mike. "Fast on Her Feet, and More Than Willing to Get Dirty." *New York Times*. New York Times, 31 Mar. 2014. Web. 17 Mar. 2015.

Razzano, Tiffany. "'Last Comic' Comedienne Settles in Astoria." *Queens Chronicle*. Queens Chronicle, 15 May 2008. Web. 17 Mar. 2015.

Schumer, Amy. "'Inside Amy Schumer': It's Not Just Sex Stuff." Interview by Terry Gross. *NPR*. NPR, 25 June 2013. Web. 17 Mar. 2015.

—Christopher Mari

© CHEMA MOYA/epa/Corbis

# Tom Sellers

**Born:** 1987
**Occupation:** Chef

Though only in his late twenties, British chef Tom Sellers has already accomplished as much as some chefs twice his age, opening his own critically acclaimed restaurant in London and earning a prestigious Michelin star after less than six months of operation. But for Sellers, such prestige and praise are secondary to the pure joys of cooking itself. "There is such freedom in cooking," he told the *Good Food Guide*. "There are no rules to be governed by, no structure by which it has to be done. It's a creative process where you never stop learning."

As a chef who entered the workforce as a teenager without having attended culinary school, Sellers might initially be perceived by some as disadvantaged when compared to his classically trained peers. That assessment, however, could not be farther from the truth. Sellers learned his craft not in the classroom but in working kitchens, first at a local pub and later in world-renowned restaurants such as Thomas Keller's Per Se and René Redzepi's Noma. After spending nearly a decade filling vital roles in British, American, and Danish kitchens, he entered the next stage of his career in 2013, when he opened Restaurant Story in London's Bermondsey district. The restaurant was met with significant critical acclaim, and Sellers has gone from a little-known cook to one of the United Kingdom's newest chefs to watch. Still, Sellers is not content to coast on his initial success; rather, he continues to tout the importance of continued effort. "I believe you only get what you want if you work hard for it," he explained to Nicky Evans for *Square Meal* (Feb. 2013). "Talent alone won't get you there."

## EARLY LIFE AND CAREER

Thomas Sellers was born in 1987 and grew up in East Leake, a village in Nottinghamshire, England. He attended the Harry Carlton Comprehensive School (now known as East Leake Academy) in Leicestershire, but did not enjoy his time there. Eventually his lack of interest in school led to his expulsion. Rather than complete his schooling elsewhere, Sellers instead entered the workforce, taking a position as a dishwasher in a local pub. He soon began taking on some of the cooking as well, a change that would shape his career from that point on. "When I started cooking, I fell in love. It's as simple as that," he told Susie Mesure for the *Independent* (8 Dec. 2013). "It was like a girlfriend, and then nothing else mattered."

Having decided to pursue a career in cooking seriously, Sellers took a position working for English chef Tom Aikens, owner of the now-closed Tom Aikens Restaurant in Chelsea,

London. Under Aikens, Sellers held a variety of positions and at times worked as many as 110 hours per week. Although the work was often strenuous, Sellers credits Aikens as one of his greatest teachers. "He taught me all the basics; now I look back and realize he was such an amazing person to have teaching me. It was very hard," he told Harry Hughes for *Q Insider* (18 Mar. 2013).

## A CHEF's TRAINING

After leaving Aikens's restaurant, Sellers, then still in his late teens, traveled to New York City to work at the restaurant Per Se, owned by acclaimed chef Thomas Keller. At that restaurant, the recipient of three Michelin stars, Sellers served as *chef de partie*—that is, a cook in charge of a particular section of the kitchen. He was greatly influenced by his time at Per Se, particularly in terms of the restaurant's management and procedures. Of those lessons, he told Evans, "The way Thomas runs his kitchen, the systems he has in place and his ethos are second-to-none—it's just a different level to what anyone else is doing."

Returning to the United Kingdom, Sellers worked for a time as a sous chef for chef Adam Byatt at the restaurant Trinity. He and Byatt remained on good terms, and Byatt would later serve as Sellers's financial backer. He also spent a year in Copenhagen, Denmark, where he worked at the restaurant Noma under chef René Redzepi. While Sellers was working for Noma, the restaurant was named the best restaurant in the world by the Diners Club World's Fifty Best Restaurants Academy. Those experiences were productive ones for Sellers, who in 2012 began to make his first forays into the restaurant business himself, opening the pop-up restaurants Foreword in London and Preface in New York. Each pop-up operated for only two nights, but Sellers succeeded in attracting both diners and critical acclaim, a crucial step in his plan to open his own dining establishment.

## RESTAURANT STORY

In April 2013 Sellers took the next step in his career, opening Restaurant Story in the Bermondsey neighborhood of London. Financially backed by Byatt, the restaurant found a home in a substantially renovated building that had once housed public restrooms. The renovations gained the restaurant significant attention long before it opened its doors, as Restaurant Story's owners reportedly spent £2 million (about $3.1 million) on the building and renovation process.

The name of the restaurant, much like those of Sellers's earlier pop-ups, suggests an association with storytelling, and Sellers, who first thought of the name as a teenager, has confirmed that this is very much intentional. "We try really hard at Story to work with the narrative side of food," he told Erin DeJesus for *Eater* (17 Apr. 2014). Each dish served at the restaurant is said to have a story associated with it, and Sellers encourages his guests to leave meaningful books in the restaurant's library, which later diners can then peruse.

## CRITICAL RECEPTION

Restaurant Story's menu has evolved since the establishment's first opening in the spring of 2013, but by mid-2015 Sellers and his team offered both lunch and dinner, with the former a choice between a lunch tasting menu and a smaller prix-fixe meal. For dinner, patrons may choose between the "Half Story" tasting menu and the more extensive "Full Story" menu. All of the tasting menus feature an iconic dish known as bread and dripping, which consists of housemade bread served with a lit candle made of beef drippings, accompanied by a garnish consisting in part of small pieces of veal tongue. As the candle melts, the liquid pools near the base of the candleholder, allowing diners to dip chunks of the bread in the freshly melted drippings. Sellers debuted the dish during the Young British Foodies (YBF) Awards in 2012, and it has since become his signature creation. In her review of Restaurant Story for the *Guardian* (4 May 2013), critic Marina O'Loughlin described the bread and dripping as "bloody lovely: earthy, piquant, meaty flavours and wobbly, crunchy, fatty textures, all in one mouthful." In many ways, the dish sums up Sellers's approach to food: creative yet simultaneously full of traditional, homey, nostalgia-inducing flavors. In addition to the bread and dripping, Restaurant Story's menu features numerous innovative dishes featuring locally sourced ingredients. The restaurant's local emphasis also extends to beverages, and its drink menu highlights many artisanal British beers.

Following its opening, Restaurant Story was met with many positive reviews from critics, and the restaurant was often fully booked. Despite this, Sellers sought to maintain his focus and avoid being distracted by the restaurant's increasing acclaim. "A restaurant is a business.

It's very easy, in this day and age, to forget that and for people to think that it's a vanity," he explained to Mesure. "However self-rewarding it can be as a chef, the end goal is to have a restaurant that's successful, not only in notoriety and accolades but in terms of a functioning business that's profitable."

## MICHELIN STAR

Although the critical response to Restaurant Story strongly suggested that Sellers had a success on his hands, this was confirmed without a doubt less than six months after the restaurant's opening, when it was awarded a Michelin star. The Michelin restaurant guides are some of the oldest extant guides of their kind, having been published by the French tire manufacturer since early in the twentieth century, and earning a Michelin star is widely considered one of the most prestigious honors in the culinary industry. Unlike other review publications, in which a one-star rating might indicate that a restaurant has poor food or service, the Michelin restaurant guides award stars only to restaurants its reviewers deem exceptional; receiving one Michelin star, then, is a significant achievement.

At the time of the publication of the 2014 Britain and Ireland Michelin dining guide, Sellers was the youngest British chef to have earned a Michelin star. He attributed much of his success to the accomplishments of Restaurant Story's entire team. "It was a credit to the team unity and spirit of the restaurant and how hard people worked," he told DeJesus. "At the end of the day, I cook to make people happy, but you can never overlook things like Michelin stars. To be awarded something so prestigious, it was an amazing feeling."

## OTHER PROJECTS

In 2014 Sellers took over the Lickfold Inn, a pub in the small town of Petworth, in southern England. The building had housed a pub for more than one hundred years, despite various changes in ownership. At the time Sellers and his backers acquired the space, however, it had been closed for about four years, much to the dismay of many in the Petworth community. Working with chef Graham Squire, Sellers transformed the space into a new restaurant that pays tribute to its century-old roots. By mid-2015, the Lickfold Inn featured a casual pub serving traditional bar snacks such as scotch eggs and an upstairs restaurant serving new takes on beloved British dishes. As with Restaurant Story, the Lickfold Inn places an emphasis on local produce and beverages. Squire serves as the establishment's head chef, but Sellers himself is a frequent visitor.

Although focusing primarily on his restaurant ventures, Sellers has occasionally appeared in cooking-focused media. He competed in the reality-television contest *Great British Menu* in 2014 and also appeared in a 2015 episode of the reality show *Burger Bar to Gourmet Star*, in which he mentored a young cook with dreams of one day opening a restaurant. He told interviewers on multiple occasions that he was in the process of writing a cookbook, and in 2014, the Orion Publishing Group announced that it would publish a collection featuring some of Sellers's best-known recipes in 2015.

## SUGGESTED READING

Mesure, Susie. "'The Haters Spur Me On': Michelin-Starred Tom Sellers on Being This Year's Hottest Property." *Independent*. Independent, 8 Dec. 2013. Web. 30 June 2015.

O'Loughlin, Marina. "Restaurant: Story, London SE1." *Guardian*. Guardian News and Media, 4 May 2013. Web. 30 June 2015.

Sellers, Tom. Interview. *Good Food Guide*. Good Food Guide, n.d. Web. 30 June 2015.

Sellers, Tom. "Restaurant Story's Tom Sellers on Media Pressure and Feeling Michelin Relief." Interview by Erin DeJesus. *Eater*. Vox Media, 17 Apr. 2014. Web. 30 June 2015.

Sellers, Tom. "Starter for 10: Interview with Tom Sellers." Interview by Nicky Evans. *Square Meal*. Monomax, Feb. 2013. Web. 30 June 2015.

Sellers, Tom. "A Very Sharp Story." Interview by Harry Hughes. *Q Insider*. Quintessentially Group, 18 Mar. 2013. Web. 30 June 2015.

—Joy Crelin

# Chris Sharma

**Born:** April 23, 1981
**Occupation:** Rock climber

American rock climber Chris Sharma is arguably the most famous and revered figure in his sport. Dubbed the "Michael Jordan of sport climbing" by Leong Siok Hui for the Malaysia Star (21 Oct. 2013), Sharma is widely credited with popularizing the climbing disciplines of bouldering, sport climbing, and deep-water soloing. After bursting onto the climbing scene as a teenager in the mid-1990s, he enjoyed a meteoric rise to the top, winning dozens of competitions and making numerous first ascents. He gained his legendary reputation, however, by developing and scaling routes, or "king lines," that continually pushed the boundaries of sport climbing. In 2001, at the age of twenty, he became the first climber to break the 5.15 barrier with his ascent of Realization (also known as Biographie Extension) in Céüse, France. Then, in 2008, he became the first to climb a route rated 5.15b, with his ascent of Jumbo Love in Clark Mountain, California. That same year he moved to the climbing-rich region of Catalonia, Spain, where he has since established many other 5.14 and 5.15-rated routes. In 2013, he made the second ever ascent of La Dura Dura in Oliana, Spain, which is one of only two 5.15c-rated climbs in the world. Personal accomplishments notwithstanding, Sharma, who is known for his unparalleled physical and mental strength, said to Hui, "I really never set out to be the best. . . . Being the best has never been a goal, climbing is more of a personal journey."

## EARLY LIFE AND EDUCATION

Chris Omprakash Sharma was born on April 23, 1981, in Santa Cruz, California. He is the only child of Bob Sharma and Gita Jahn, who were both students of the world-renowned Indian yoga mas-

Chris Sharma & Skimble/Wikimedia Commons

ter Baba Hari Dass. His parents adopted the last name of Sharma, which means "good fortune," after marrying at Dass's picturesque mountain retreat, the Mount Madonna Center, in the Santa Cruz Mountains.

Sharma's parents divorced when he was still a child. As a result he spent much of his childhood and adolescence being shuttled back and forth between parents. Sharma, who has led a mostly peripatetic lifestyle as an adult, has credited his father, who worked as a maintenance supervisor at the University of California, Santa Cruz, with giving him an early love of the outdoors. Meanwhile, he inherited his natural athleticism from his mother, a masseuse, who committed suicide in 2005 after a long battle with depression.

Like his parents, Sharma studied at the Mount Madonna Center, which helped give him a strong spiritual grounding. Growing up, he participated in a wide variety of sports, including baseball, soccer, surfing, and skateboarding. He did not start to distinguish himself as an athlete, however, until the age of twelve, when he first discovered climbing. Sharma was taken to the Pacific Edge climbing gym by his mother, who thought it was something he would like. Climbing was "a huge breakthrough in my life," he told Jack Geldard for *UK Climbing* (Aug. 2012). "Until then I was pretty mediocre at everything I tried."

## CLIMBING PRODIGY

Drawn to climbing's personal, individualistic nature, Sharma quickly fell in love with the sport. He used money earned from a paper route to purchase climbing gear and a membership at Pacific Edge, then one of the largest indoor climbing facilities in the world, and began practicing there on a daily basis. Tom Davis, the cofounder and co-owner of Pacific Edge, quickly recognized Sharma's preternatural climbing ability, noting to Christa Fraser for *Metroactive* (27 Sept.–4 Oct. 2000) that "by the end of the first year, we knew that he was something special."

Blessed with large hands and rare physical abilities, Sharma, who reportedly could lift his entire body weight with a finger at age thirteen, immediately stood out from his peers. He initially specialized in the rock-climbing subcategory of bouldering, which features short but extremely difficult unroped ascents. As Fraser put it, "The sport combines the athleticism of a gymnast, the flexibility of a yogi, the intellectual cunning of a chess player, and the metaphysics of a mystic."

Sharma won the Bouldering Nationals in Phoenix, Arizona, at age fourteen, and by fifteen, he was routinely completing 5.14-rated climbing routes. Among them included Hasta La Vista (5.14b/c) at the Hood in Mt. Charleston, Nevada; Just Do It (5.14c) at Smith Rock, Oregon; and Lung Fish (5.14a/b) in Rifle Canyon, Colorado. (While there are many different rating systems in climbing, the most commonly used Yosemite Decimal System rates climbs on a scale according to difficulty, starting at 5.0 and ending at 5.15c. Beginning at 5.10, climbs are further broken down into sublevels ranging from "a" to "d." Climbing routes, meanwhile, are traditionally named by the first person to ascend them.)

## TOP SPORT CLIMBER IN THE WORLD

Sharma attended Soquel High School in Soquel, California, for one year, before transferring to an alternative high school in Santa Cruz. Upon earning his General Educational Development (GED) from the school at fifteen, he began to focus on his climbing career full time. He landed sponsorships from the climbing retailers Prana and Five Ten and turned professional.

In 1997, under the mentorship of Boone Speed, then one of America's top sport climbers, Sharma became the first person ever to ascend Necessary Evil, a 5.14c climb in the Virgin River Gorge, located at the Utah-Arizona border, which was then regarded as the hardest route in North America. Also that year he became, at sixteen, the first male American to win an adult World Cup event. Sharma would go on to win "dozens of competitions," most by large margins, and achieve "hundreds of first ascents" at locations around the world over the next several years, as Kelli Anderson noted for *Sports Illustrated* (28 May 2001).

Sharma gained attention from mainstream media in 1999, when he won the gold medal for bouldering at the fifth annual X Games, held in San Francisco, California. Then, in February of the following year, he effectively established himself as one of the most gifted climbers ever when he became the first person to ascend the Mandala, a large granite boulder in the Buttermilks region of Bishop, California, which had long been considered impossible to climb. "One of the hardest things is having that vision—seeing something that has never been done," Sharma explained to Andrew Bisharat for *Rock and Ice* (27 Nov. 2013). "Once you see it and you do it, you're like, 'OK, maybe there's room for something harder.'"

## SPIRITUAL SOJOURN AND "REALIZATION"

Extraordinary feats notwithstanding, Sharma decided to take a sabbatical from climbing in October 2000, after growing disillusioned with the sport. He traveled extensively through Asia, focusing on Eastern philosophy and meditation and going on a 1,000-mile pilgrimage around the Japanese island of Shikoku. Sharma, who was unjustly criticized early in his career by climbing's elder statesmen for his nontechnical style and for eschewing traditional training methods, said to Tim Struby for *ESPN The Magazine* (31 Dec. 2002), "Climbing's always come very easy for me . . . Then I got to this place where I needed to learn about myself. I wanted to develop myself in ways other than climbing."

After a seven-month hiatus, Sharma returned to climbing with a newfound appreciation for the sport and a stronger sense of purpose. In July 2001, he made a first ascent of Biographie Extension, an arduous two-route, 130-foot limestone face at Céüse in the southern French Alps. With that feat, Sharma, who had previously made more than two dozen unsuccessful attempts on the route, which he renamed Realization, helped establish the first 5.15a in the world. The historic ascent marked "a huge milestone in my climbing," as Sharma told Geldard. "So much of my climbing had always been so playful and that route really tested me to see how much I wanted it."

Several days after successfully climbing Realization, Sharma won the Bouldering World Cup in Munich, Germany. He had his title rescinded, however, after testing positive for marijuana. Nevertheless, he continued to dominate on the competitive circuit, and in 2002, he won the men's rock-climbing competition at the high-profile Gorge Games in Hood River, Oregon. By early 2003 he was rated number one in the Professional Climbers Association national rankings. It was around this time that Sharma began to focus more on route projects and less on competitions. In his conversation with Bisharat, he said, "A lot of people have this desire to do something, but they often don't know what it is that they want to do. I wanted to push myself to the next level."

## IN SEARCH OF "KING LINES"

For Sharma, the next level meant scouring the globe for beautiful and inspiring routes that pushed human limits, routes or problems he would coin "king lines." In March 2005, he achieved a first ascent of a forty-foot-long roof, or upside-down climb, called Witness the Fitness, located in the Ozark Mountains of Arkansas. With a grade of V15, it is regarded as one of the most difficult roof problems ever climbed. (In bouldering, the most commonly used grade system is the V-scale, which starts at V0 and ends at V16.)

Later in 2005, he made the first ascent of Dreamcatcher, a new 5.14d route in Squamish, British Columbia. Then, in 2007, he popularized deep-water soloing, or "psicobloc," a climbing discipline that involves climbing over water without ropes or gear. That year he put up and completed a deep-water soloing line in Majorca, Spain, called Es Pontas (5.15a), which runs underneath an arresting natural sea arch. The climb, which took Sharma more than fifty attempts to complete, was featured in *King Lines* (2007), an acclaimed documentary that chronicles Sharma's life and globetrotting climbing exploits. *King Lines* is the best-known of Sharma's many climbing films.

Sharma made history again in 2008, when he became the first to ascend Jumbo Love, a 250-foot-long climb at Clark Mountain, California. The climb was the first in the world to be rated 5.15b. Shortly after ascending Jumbo Love, Sharma, who is fluent in Spanish, decided to move to the Catalonia region of Spain, which he felt was the best location to further develop his climbing. "Up until that point, in a lot of ways, I'd been just riding on my talent," he told Bisharat. "I thought . . . 'Let's see what happens if I really dedicate myself to sport climbing.'"

## ROUTING PROJECTS IN SPAIN AND OTHER ENDEAVORS

After moving to Spain, Sharma developed and climbed a number of routes in the 5.15-plus range. He completed first ascents of the second and third 5.15b routes in the world, Golpe de Estado and Neanderthal, in 2008 and 2009, respectively. Between 2008 and 2011, he added three more 5.15a routes to his credit, Papichulo, Pachamama, and Catxasa. The search for the world's hardest climb eventually brought Sharma to Oliana, a limestone crag in Catalonia containing the biggest concentration of 5.14 and 5.15 routes in the world. According to Bisharat, "Oliana has become to sport climbing what Mavericks is to surfing: a place for the biggest names in the sport to come and prove themselves."

Oliana served as the setting for Sharma's greatest career achievement. In March 2013, he made the second ascent of Oliana's La Dura Dura, a 165-foot mega-pitch route and the world's second 5.15c. The route, widely considered to be the world's hardest climb, was completed over a two-year period in collaboration with the Czech climbing prodigy Adam Ondra, who had made the first ascent one month earlier and established the first 5.15c, Change, in Flatanger, Norway, in 2012.

Sharma has continued to tackle new climbing projects in Spain and beyond. He has also pursued a number of other endeavors. In 2013, he opened his first indoor rock-climbing gym, Sender One, in Santa Ana, California, in partnership with his sponsor Walltopia. The 25,000-square-foot space, which Sharma designed himself, is one of the largest climbing gyms in California. He has also become deeply involved in shoe design through one of his other sponsors, Evolv, for whom he serves as lead shoe designer. In addition, he is the founder of the Psicobloc Masters, the first deep-water soloing contest in the United States, and the Sharmafund, a nonprofit organization dedicated to bringing rock climbing to underprivileged youths.

## SUGGESTED READING

Bisharat, Andrew. "Perfect Play: What It Took to Climb La Dura Dura (5.15c)—The World's Hardest Route." *Rock and Ice*. Big Stone, 27 Nov. 2013. Web. 22 Dec. 2014.

Fraser, Christa. "Rock Star." *MetroActive* [Santa Cruz]. Metro Publishing, 27 Sept.–4 Oct. 2000. Web. 22 Dec. 2014.

Hui, Leong Siok. "Chris Sharma Continually Rises to the Challenge." *Malaysia Star Online*. Star Publications, 21 Oct. 2013. Web. 22 Dec. 2014.

Reitman, Janet. "Karma Climber." *Los Angeles Times*. Los Angeles Times, 19 Jan. 2003. Web. 22 Dec. 2014.

Sharma, Chris. Interview by Jack Geldard. "Chris Sharma Talks 9b+." *UK Climbing*. UKClimbing Limited, Aug. 2012. Web. 22 Dec. 2014.

—Chris Cullen

# Ed Sheeran

**Born:** February 17, 1991
**Occupation:** Singer-songwriter

The British pop star Ed Sheeran, with his fiery red hair, does not seem like the stereotypical teen idol or celebrity. In addition to his "average guy" appearance, he is a singer-songwriter with an acoustic guitar who is influenced by the quick rhyming patterns of hip hop and who uses a guitar pedal to loop his voice and instrument.

In 2009 Sheeran played more than three hundred live shows after dropping out of high school to pursue a music career full time, and he first gained major international fame for his hit single "The A Team" in 2011. His second album, *x*, featured the hit song "Sing," which was influenced by the music of Justin Timberlake. Grammy Award–winning singer-songwriter Pharrell Williams appeared on (and helped produce) that track. Influential music producer Rick Rubin produced other songs on the album. Sheeran has also collaborated with musicians such as Taylor Swift and has written songs for singers Jessie Ware and Usher and the musical groups Rixton and One Direction. Sheeran's song "I See Fire" was included on *The Hobbit: The Desolation of Smaug* soundtrack (2013), and in December 2014 he received three Grammy Award nominations, for album of the year, best pop vocal album, and best song written for visual media.

## EARLY LIFE

Edward Christopher Sheeran was born on February 17, 1991, in Halifax, West Yorkshire, England. His parents, Imogen and John, are from Wexford. His father was an art historian and lecturer, and his mother was a jewelry maker. When Sheeran was still quite young, the family moved from Halifax to Framlingham, in Suffolk County. From the age of four, Sheeran sang in a church choir with his mother, and music was a big part of his life from a very early age. His parents introduced him to such musical greats as the Beatles, Bob Dylan, Van Morrison, Joni Mitchell, and Elton John, and when Sheeran was about eleven years old, his uncle gave him an acoustic guitar as a gift.

After receiving the guitar from his uncle, Sheeran taught himself to play and had no formal training. One day, his father took him to Dublin, Ireland, to see the Irish singer-songwriter Damien Rice. Sheeran enjoyed the

Ed Sheeran/Wikimedia Commons

concert and afterward he and his father ran into Rice. Although he and Sheeran only spoke for a brief time, Sheeran came away inspired and considered the encounter a life-changing moment and the beginning of his journey as a singer-songwriter. After that concert, Sheeran began writing songs, accompanied by acoustic guitar. A few years later, at the age of fourteen, Sheeran recorded his first album.

## HIGH SCHOOL AND EARLY MUSIC CAREER

In 2005, at the age of fourteen, Sheeran recorded and self-published *The Orange Room*, which was his first extended play (EP) album. It featured five songs and was a sure indicator of Sheeran's ambition, even at such a young age. After this, Sheeran went to London for the summer in order to play some live performances, but he eventually returned home to attend Thomas Mills High School. In 2006 he put out a self-titled album, and the following year he released *Want Some?* as a digital download. In 2007 Sheeran continued to perform live as much as possible and he also began working as the guitar tech for the group Nizlopi, for whom he served as the opening act in 2008. He was also opening for acts such as the Noisettes and Jay Sean.

Not surprisingly, Sheeran's burgeoning music career was having a negative impact on his studies and his ability to attend high school with any kind of regularity. Taking extended time off from school in order to record and produce an album or play live performances also did not sit well with his school's administrators. When Sheeran was sixteen, he dropped out of school and moved to London. In 2009 and at the age of eighteen, he released his second EP album, *You Need Me*. Also in 2009 Sheeran played more than three hundred live shows—playing music nearly every night and sleeping on friends' couches, all with the goal of making it in the music industry.

### EARLY FAME AND RECOGNITION

Sheeran's hard work and dedication to his music were early motivators, but it was online media that first gave him a taste of fame and recognition. John Walsh for the *Independent* (5 Dec. 2014) described Sheeran as looking like "nobody's idea of a rock hero . . . too ordinary, too inconsequential, too much of your bouncy kid brother." It was his everyday and conventional appearance, however, that made him stand out as a pop star, and his style of combining pop, folk, and hip-hop music genres proved irresistible to his future fans. When he began collaborating with British grime rappers Devlin, Sway, Wiley, and Wretch 32, his fan base grew even wider and more varied. Through it all, Sheeran continued to play live performances, and his song "You Need Me, I Don't Need You" went viral on YouTube.

In 2010, Sheeran released two albums: *Songs I Wrote with Amy* and the critically acclaimed *Loose Change*. Shortly after, Sheeran went to Los Angeles, California, to play at open-mic nights and wound up impressing actor Jamie Foxx, who in turn invited him to stay at his mansion and use the recording studio there. Sheeran also appeared on Foxx's Sirius radio show. Sheeran was then signed by Atlantic Records in January 2011 and began being managed by the Rocket Record Company, which was founded by singer-songwriter Elton John.

### +

Sheeran's first major studio album with Atlantic Records was released in 2011 and titled + (pronounced "plus"). In its first six months, the album sold one million copies in the United Kingdom, and the following year it became internationally acclaimed with the single "The A Team," which reached number 16 on the Billboard Hot 100 chart. In an interview with Andy Welch for the *Independent* (10 June 2011), Sheeran told the story of the song's inspiration: One Christmas a friend asked him to volunteer

at a homeless shelter and play some songs for the residents. It was there that Sheeran met Angel, "who was this amazing girl who really stood out—mainly because she was the only girl in the shelter." Angel told him she worked as a prostitute in order to have money for drugs. It was "a very bleak story" Sheeran told Welch. Most of the songs on +, including "The A Team," are about his experiences with other people.

While the album pleased many fans, it did not move most critics to great praise. Jon O'Brien, writing for the AllMusic website, called the album's ballads "disappointingly back-to-basics affairs" though he did say Sheeran was a "much more interesting prospect" on some of the up-tempo songs. O'Brien concluded that "with his casual jeans and hoodie and relatable tales of relationship woes, university, and getting drunk, it's easy to see why Sheeran has struck such a chord with the late-teens/early-twenties crowd. But his debut's failure to capitalize on his unique selling point means it's likely to leave everyone else nonplussed." In a combined profile of Sheeran and review of the album for the *Guardian* (8 Sept. 2011), Alexis Petridis described the song "Wake Me Up" as "halting" and suggested that listeners of the song might not be able to "keep their last meal down." Petridis offered a more positive assessment of Sheeran's ability as a whole, however, albeit with an open-ended conclusion. "Apart from his teen appeal," Petridis said, "Sheeran's strength is his melodic ability [and] a way with a really strong, radio-friendly tune as on 'The City' or 'Grade 8.' You can't help wishing he'd put said ability to slightly more edgy use, but then again, he still might."

### X

Despite receiving predominantly lukewarm reviews, Sheeran's first major album did very well on the charts. It peaked at number 5 on the Billboard 200 in 2012, and the following year it again peaked at number 5. Although Sheeran was becoming more famous and in-demand musically than ever before, his personal life was suffering. In an interview with Jon Caramanica for the *New York Times* (19 June 2014), Sheeran admitted to having had troubles with "his waistline, his romantic life, his state of mind, and more." In 2013 he played three sold-out concerts at New York City's famed Madison Square Garden, toured as the opening act for Taylor Swift's Red tour, and occasionally succumbed to the pressures and temptations of life on the road.

His next album, *x* (pronounced "multiply"), came out in 2014 and reached the number-one position on the Billboard 200 chart. It also received better reviews than +, at least in part because Sheeran was trying out new things such as sounds, genres, and production. The fact that production was overseen by Pharrell Williams and famed producer Rick Rubin also helped. Caramanica called the new album "impressive." The single "Sing" reached number 13 on the Billboard Hot 100 chart, and Caramanica called it an "obvious radio hit." Many other reviewers agreed. Sheeran told Caramanica he wanted to create a song inspired by the popular singer Justin Timberlake, and by most measures he succeeded. The record "shines more brightly," however, on the mellower songs, according to Caramanica, who specifically named "Tenerife Sea" and "Thinking Out Loud" as standout singles. In his review for the *Guardian* (19 June 2014), Petridis observed that "not all of it works," in reference to the album's new direction, but acknowledged that the ballads "evince a certain new-found maturity." Neil McCormick concurred in his review of the album for the *Telegraph* (24 June 2014), stating that "Sheeran stays true to the essential artistic notions of the classic singer-songwriter genre by treating his music as a vehicle for emotional veracity, personal revelation, and universal inclusion."

## SUGGESTED READING

Caramanica, Jon. "Ed Sheeran, Lighter and Wiser, Releases 'x'." *New York Times*. New York Times, 19 June 2014. Web. 27 Jan. 2015.

McCormick, Neil. "Ed Sheeran, *X* Review: 'Genuinely Great.'" *Telegraph*. Telegraph Media Group, 24 June 2014. Web. 27 Jan. 2015.

O'Brien, Jon. Rev. of +, by Ed Sheeran. *AllMusic*. All Music, n.d. Web. 27 Jan. 2015.

Walsh, John. "Ed Sheeran: Boy Next Door Who Made It Very Big." *Independent*. Independent.co.uk, 5 Dec. 2014. Web. 27 Jan. 2015.

Welch, Andy. "Ed Sheeran: Irish Blood, English Heart." *Independent*. Independent.co.uk, 10 June 2011. Web. 27 Jan. 2015.

—Dmitry Kiper

# Sheikh Hasina

**Born:** September 28, 1947

**Occupation:** Prime Minister of Bangladesh

Sheikh Hasina is the prime minister of Bangladesh and the daughter of Bangabandhu Sheikh Mujibur Rahman, known to Bangladeshis as the Father of the Nation. Hasina's life has been as turbulent as the history of her country, which gained independence from Britain the year she was born and then from Pakistan in 1971. As the late journalist David Frost said of Hasina when he spoke with her during an episode of the *Frost Interview* for Al Jazeera English (23 Sept. 2013), Hasina's life and the history of Bangladesh are very much "intertwined." As a young woman, Hasina survived a coup in which almost her entire family was murdered, and spent six years in exile in India. When she returned to Bangladesh she was elected the party leader of her father's Awami League in 1981 and served as prime minister of Bangladesh from 1996 to 2001. After facing corruption and extortion charges, she was reelected in 2009. Critics argue that contemporary Bangladeshi politics consist of little more than two party leaders—Hasina and her sworn rival, Khaleda Zia of the Bangladesh Nationalist Party (BNP)—bandying power back and forth at the expense of the Bangladeshi people. Others argue that, for a country that only reestab-

Carsten Koall/Getty Images Europe/Getty Images

lished its democratic process in 1991, growth takes time.

Bangladesh is one of the most populous countries in the world, but also one of the poorest and one of the most corrupt. Hasina has worked her entire life to achieve her father's vision for a "Golden Bengal," a state in which no citizen would be hungry or live in poverty. But as Bangladeshis struggle to compete in a global economy—and middle-class Bangladeshis enjoy the fruits of the unregulated labor of poor farmers and garment workers—that goal remains just out of reach.

## EARLY LIFE AND EDUCATION

Sheikh Hasina Wazed was born in Tungipara, a village in the Gopalganj district in southern Bangladesh (then East Pakistan), on September 28, 1947. That year the British Raj was divided into two independent states: the predominantly Hindu India and the predominantly Muslim Pakistan, though East and West Pakistan lay on either side of India. As Hasina was growing up, West Pakistan thrived off of the labor of East Pakistanis, and though Pakistan received significant sums of foreign aid, West Pakistan shared little of it with the eastern region. Hasina's father, Sheikh Mujibur Rahman, who became a leader of the Awami League in 1949, was instrumental in preserving Bangla, the Bengali language, when West Pakistan tried to impose its native tongue, Urdu, on the east, and later became the most significant figure in the country's fight for independence. Hasina—or "Hasu," as she was known in her family—was the eldest of five children: she had three brothers and one sister. They lived with her protective grandparents and her mother, Fazilatunnesa, was a homemaker, though she served as a member of the Awami League in Hasina's father's lengthy absences; Sheikh Mujib was frequently imprisoned between 1930s (for agitating for Indian independence) and his death in 1975. "I learned from my father, I learned from my mother how to organize a political party, how to organize a movement, [and] how to support the movement," Hasina told Frost.

Hasina attended local school until 1954, when Sheikh Mujib became a minister in the nationalist Jukta Front government. Hasina enrolled at a girl's school called Nari Shikkha Mandir (now the Sher-e Bangla Girls School and College) in Tikatuli, a historical district in the capital, Dhaka. She then attended Dhaka's Azimpur Government Girls' School and College, passing her exams in 1965. At the Intermediate Girls' College (now the Badrunnesa Government Girls' College), Hasina was a campus leader and was elected vice president of the student union. After passing her higher secondary examinations in 1967, Hasina studied honors-level Bangla language and literature at Dhaka University and earned her BA degree in 1973.

## INDEPENDENCE AND WAR

In 1966 Hasina was a student activist in her father's burgeoning independence movement. The following year he was arrested for "waging war" against Pakistan. The popular unrest seeded by Sheikh Mujib's subsequent year-long trial (and inconclusive release) made him a lightning rod for Bengali nationalism. When in 1970 the Awami League swept the national parliamentary elections, Pakistani president Ayub Khan rejected the results. The following March, Sheikh Mujib made a historic broadcast claiming independence for East Pakistan, calling the new state Bangladesh ("Bengali Nation"). West Pakistan, refusing to recognize Bangladeshi independence, launched a brutal offensive known as Operation Searchlight, during which the military systematically murdered between 300,000 and 3 million people. "Everywhere there were dead bodies," Hasina recalled to Frost. "I have seen it [with] my own eyes." The military razed major cities to the ground before India intervened militarily on behalf of the Bangladeshis in December 1971. After thirteen days of war West Pakistan surrendered, and Sheikh Mujib was sworn in as Bangladesh's first prime minister in 1972.

## HARDSHIP, COUP, AND EXILE

Euphoria over independence was quickly overtaken by distress at the country's multiple woes—a poor economy, starvation, famine, the war's devastation. In 1974 Sheikh Mujib declared a state of emergency after flooding destroyed most of Bangladesh's grain crop and 28,000 Bangladeshis died. Seeking to bring order, he became increasingly autocratic, nationalizing key industries. In November 1975 he dissolved the parliament in favor of a one-party system. The emergence of the one-party state, an emotional Hasina explained to Frost, was "because my father loved his people and he wanted to ensure people a better life." Her father's close confidante at the time, Hasina insisted in her interview that he intended to reinstate parliamentary democracy within a few years, after repairing the economy.

Unsurprisingly, Sheikh Mujib's decision did not sit well with Bangladeshis, who had supported him through years of hardship, war, and massacre. On the morning of August 15, 1975, Hasina and her younger sister, Rehana, were staying in West Germany at the house of the Bangladeshi ambassador, when he received a phone call. When he hung up without a word, he insisted that Hasina wake her husband, refusing to share any information with her directly. The ambassador told Hasina's husband—and then later, Hasina—that there had been a coup and that a group of rebel army officers had assassinated her parents, three brothers and sisters-in-law, an uncle, and several other relatives in the middle of the night.

In an interview with Frost, Hasina's son, Sajeeb Wazed, recalled that she did not tell him or his younger sister, then aged four and two, about the murders. "But what she would do instead," he recalled, "is she would cry all day." Hasina and her sister were not allowed to return to Bangladesh for the funerals. (The rebels had hoped to kill off the entire Mujib bloodline, and Hasina and Rehana were targets.) Hasina vowed to return to Bangladesh and complete her father's vision of a Golden Bengal.

## RETURN TO BANGLADESH

While Hasina was exiled in India, Bangladesh suffered a fitful period of coups and assassinations. Hasina and her family returned to their country in 1981. "I decided to come back and work for democracy," she told Frost. Hers was a fight much like her father's a decade before. She was arrested, shot at, and targeted by assassins. (In 2004 she was badly hurt when someone threw grenades into the crowd at her political rally, killing twenty-two of her supporters and injuring five hundred.) Named the head of her father's Awami League in 1981, she worked tirelessly throughout the 1980s to sow the seeds of a new democracy in Bangladesh.

Hasina even worked with Khaleda Zia of the BNP, the widow of BNP founder Ziaur Rahman, who took power after the coup that killed Hasina's father. Frost characterized the relationship between the two families, not as a mere political rivalry, but a "blood feud." The two powerful leaders were able to come together in 1991 to bring democracy back to Bangladesh, but the success of their joint endeavor did nothing to diminish the "deep hatred" and "deep mistrust" between them, Dhaka University law professor Asif Nasrul told Frost. To Hasina's consterna-

tion, Zia was named prime minister in 1991. The feud between Zia and Hasina continues to define Bangladeshi politics decades later. Asif Nasrul criticized both for equating ideology and family issues. When Frost asked if they could ever work together again, Hasina replied, "We have ideological differences."

## ELECTION AND WAR CRIMES TRIBUNALS

Hasina was elected prime minister of Bangladesh on June 23, 1996. During her five-year term, Hasina sought justice for the murder of her family and for war crimes committed against Bangladeshis in 1971. In 2001 Hasina was defeated by the BNP. Zia served as prime minister until 2006, when political unrest—fueled, many say, by the rivalry between the Awami League and the BNP—led the military to step in and establish an interim government in 2007. Both Hasina and Zia were arrested and charged with corruption. They were later released, and most of the charges were dropped. Corruption nonetheless remains endemic in Bangladesh, which in 2001 was named the world's most corrupt nation by Transparency International and in 2015 remained in the top twenty-five. In 2009 Hasina was elected prime minister for a second time. She was reelected in 2014, amid violent protests led by Zia and the BNP.

In 2010 Hasina set up war tribunals to try key Bangladeshi collaborators involved in the 1971 massacres for war crimes. Three years later the tribunals returned its first guilty verdicts—a "major triumph" for Hasina, Sabir Mustafa noted for the BBC News (21 Jan. 2013), who "made prosecution of 1971 war crimes a key goal of her government." The tribunals were not as popular in Bangladesh as one might assume. "From the beginning the tribunals have faced internal skepticism, as well as international concerns expressed by such groups as Human Rights Watch," Mustafa wrote. Some saw the tribunals as an attempt by Hasina to rid Bangladesh of people who might oppose her or her party. The first tribunals condemned former leaders of Jamaat-e-Islami, an Islamist political party that has enjoyed an alliance with the BNP since 2001.

## CHALLENGES

As Hasina's third term continues, she must contend with the violent opposition of the BNP party; in early 2015 Zia "declared an indefinite campaign of strikes and transport blockades, hoping to pressure her rival, Prime Minister Sheikh Hasina, into holding new national elections," Ellen Barry reported for the *New York Times* (12 Apr. 2015). Protesters wielding firebombs to enforce blockades have killed and maimed Bangladeshis traveling to work or school.

Hasina must also contend with the natural disasters that continue to beset the country. Climate change and rising sea levels threaten to displace millions of Bangladeshis over the next century. "A lot of places in the world [are] at risk from rising sea levels," Rafael Reuveny, an international political economist at the Indiana University at Bloomington told Gardiner Harris for the *New York Times* (28 Mar. 2014). "But Bangladesh is at the top of everybody's list."

Last but not least, Hasina must contend with Bangladesh's booming, and largely unregulated, garment industry. On April 24, 2013, the Rana Plaza garment factory in Dhaka—where underpaid, exploited workers toiled making clothes for Western companies—collapsed. It was the deadliest accident in the history of the industry, having killed 1,134 people and injuring hundreds more. Companies and the Bangladeshi government promised reform, but while they began addressing some building safety concerns, in 2015 the independent Human Rights Watch reported that many garment workers still faced physical and verbal abuse, forced overtime, and withheld wages, as well as intimidation of union organizers.

## PERSONAL LIFE

Sheikh Hasina married a nuclear scientist named M. A. Wazed Miah in 1968. She gave birth to a son named Sajeeb Wazed "Joy" on July 27, 1971, and a daughter, Saima Wazed "Putul" on December 9, 1972. Wazed Miah died in 2009.

## SUGGESTED READING

Barry, Ellen. "Turmoil between Political Leaders Has Harmed Bangladesh's People." *New York Times*. New York Times, 12 Apr. 2015. Web. 17 May 2015.

Harris, Gardiner. "Borrowed Time on Disappearing Land." *New York Times*. New York Times, 28 Mar. 2014. Web. 17 May 2015.

Mustafa, Sabir. "Bangladesh's Watershed War Crimes Moment." *BBC News*. BBC, 21 Jan. 2013. Web. 17 May 2015.

Sheikh Hasina. Interview by David Frost. *Frost Interview*. Al Jazeera English, 20 Sept. 2013. Web. 17 May 2015.

—Molly Hagan

# Sheikha al-Mayassa al-Thani

**Born:** 1983
**Occupation:** Chair, Qatar Museums

Sheikha al-Mayassa al-Thani, the younger sister of the emir of Qatar, Sheik Tamim bin Hamad al-Thani, is the chair of the Qatar Museums and one of the most influential art collectors in the world. In 2013 she was ranked the single most powerful person in the art world by the journal *ArtReview*. The following year she was listed as ninety-first on the *Forbes* list of the world's hundred most powerful women and was included on *Time* magazine's list of the hundred most influential people in the world.

Qatar, an absolute monarchy, is a small desert country jutting out into the Persian Gulf, neighboring Bahrain and Saudi Arabia, and opposite the United Arab Emirates (UAE). As a journalist for the *Economist* (31 May 2012) reported, for much of history, Qatar was "little more than a sandy backwater," known for its struggling, centuries-old pearl industry. With a population of only 2.1 million people, Qatar had the highest per-capita gross domestic product (GDP) in the world in 2013, largely thanks to its enormous oil and gas reserves. Qatar's growing international influence was demonstrated in 2010, when it won its bid to host the 2022 Fédération Inter-

Mohammed Al Kuwari/Wikimedia Commons

nationale de Football Association (FIFA) World Cup, but the emir (and his father before him) appears to be acutely aware of the fleeting nature of oil riches. His blueprint for the country's future, *Qatar National Vision 2030*, places a national emphasis on culture and education, hoping to prepare citizens for its post-oil days.

Sheikha al-Mayassa has been a crucial part of the Qatari renaissance. Her family has been collecting art for decades—some of that collection is on view at the Museum of Islamic Art, designed by architect I. M. Pei, in Doha. The museum is said to be among the best in the world—but Sheikha al-Mayassa has larger aims for the Qatar Museums, which was originally the brainchild of her father, Sheik Hamad bin Khalifa al-Thani, who abdicated in June 2013. "Above all, we want the [Qatar Museums Authority] QMA to be a 'cultural instigator,' a catalyst of arts projects worldwide," said one trustee, as reported by the *Economist*.

## FAMILY BACKGROUND

Sheikha al-Mayassa bint Hamad bin Khalifa al-Thani was born into a Qatari royal dynasty in 1983 in Doha, Qatar's capital city. The al-Thani royal family can trace its roots back to the ancient Banu Tamim tribe of Arabia and has been in power in Qatar since the mid-nineteenth century. Her father is former emir Sheikh Hamad bin Khalifa al-Thani, who deposed his father, Sheikh Khalifa bin Hamad al-Thani, in a bloodless coup in 1995. Despite his political maneuverings, Sheikh Hamad was considered a progressive ruler who, until his abdication, oversaw the enrichment of Qatar through the exploitation of its natural gas reserves and through overseas investments. He even developed the internationally respected pan-Arab news network Al Jazeera—though, as some critics have noted, there is no real freedom of press in Qatar itself—and openly funded rebel uprisings in Libya and Syria during the Arab Spring. Domestically, the emir supported social programs, charities, education, and, of course, art.

The sheikha's mother, Sheikha Mozah bint Nasser al-Missned, is the chair of Qatar Foundation for Education, Science and Community Development and founder of the Qatar Philharmonic Orchestra and the Sidra Medical Centre in Doha. She also oversaw the expansion of the country's university education program in Doha's Education City sector and was appointed a special envoy for education in 2003 by the United Nations Educational, Scientific and Cultural Organization (UNESCO). She remains, as Andrew Anthony wrote for the *Observer* (13 Dec. 2014), an embodiment of the "charming side of a family that runs a sharia state, where homosexuality is punishable by death, women are severely restricted in their liberties and foreign workers are treated like indentured labourers, stripped of their rights and forced to work in highly dangerous conditions."

## EARLY LIFE AND EDUCATION

Sheikha al-Mayassa, Sheikh Hamad's fourteenth daughter and the youngest of his three children with Sheikha Mozah, has been interested in art since she was a small child. "I always loved to paint," she explained to John Arlidge for the *London Evening Standard* (4 Oct. 2013). "My father would encourage me. He took me to art fairs, auctions, operas and concerts, in Paris and London." She went on to study literature and political science at Duke University in Durham, North Carolina, from which she graduated in 2005. For her junior year she studied abroad at the Sorbonne and the Institut d'Études Politiques de Paris.

After graduation she went on to further studies at Columbia University in New York City. During her time there, she worked for actor Robert De Niro's Tribeca Film Festival. In 2009 she organized a partnership between Tribeca Enterprises and the Doha Film Institute, which she launched and which provides financial support and training to the budding Qatari film industry; the Doha-Tribeca collaboration ended in 2013 after four successful film festivals.

Sheikh Hamad named her chair of the Qatar Museums Authority (QMA) in 2006. The QMA renamed itself the Qatar Museums in mid-2014 in an effort to appear more approachable to the public.

## QATAR MUSEUMS

As chair of the Qatar Museums, Sheikha al-Mayassa is in charge of all of the museums and galleries in Doha, including the Museum of Islamic Art (MIA); Mathaf, dedicated to modern Arab art; Fire Station, a space for artists-in-residence; the Orientalist Museum, devoted entirely to the Orientalist art movement; the 3-2-1 Qatar Olympic and Sports Museum; and two Doha galleries, QM Gallery Al Riwaq and QM Gallery Katara.

In 2016 the Qatar Museums will open the National Museum of Qatar, which will likely be the crown jewel of Qatar's museums. The building, designed by the award-winning French architect Jean Nouvel to conjure the image of the petals of a desert rose, will house galleries, an auditorium, retail stores, and a research center. It will also likely house a good portion of the artwork—much of it Western masterpieces—that Sheikha al-Mayassa and her family have collected during her tenure.

As for the Qatar Museums themselves, the sheikha has recruited a number of foreign executives and employees, including Edward Dolman, the former chair of Christie's auction house, who served as the Qatar Museums' executive director from 2011 to 2014. Jean Paul Engelen, another Christie's alum, is the director of public art.

## A VISION OF CROSS–CULTURAL EXCHANGE

Sheikha al-Mayassa views her position at the Qatar Museums as an artistic mediator between Islam and the West. "Thanks to recent history," she explained to Arlidge, "people see Islam as a violent religion. They come with bin Laden in their heads. We want to showcase, with evidence, that Islam is a peaceful religion at the heart of the most intellectually and culturally sophisticated societies throughout history. That is our message." The MIA, opened in 2008, displays rare artifacts that were once part of the royal family's private collection and speak to the "richness of Islamic art," Nicolai Ouroussoff wrote for the *New York Times* (26 Nov. 2010). The Orientalist Museum, meanwhile, focuses on the Western European movement of the same name that attempted to depict Middle Eastern life during an era that is otherwise largely undocumented. The works "are not simply relics of cultural imperialism," Ouroussoff argued, but an important part of Qatari history. "By shining a light into the darker corners of Arab history, as well as at its ancient glories, the Orientalist museum suggests an understanding—rare anywhere—that the foundations of any healthy culture must be built on an unflinching appraisal of the past."

The sheikha also hopes to introduce Western art to Qatar—even if some of that art offends the senses of the deeply conservative country. "Controversial art can unlock communication between diverse nations, peoples and histories," she told Arlidge. Of course, such an exchange of ideas is easier in theory than in practice. She has exhibited the work of controversial artist Damien Hirst—including *The Miraculous Journey*, a bronze sculpture that features a nude

boy—but the Qatari authorities recently barred her from displaying a collection of Greek statues that were nude. The sheikha has said that she hopes that the new collections will inspire a new generation of Qatari artists, but those artists will have to watch their step. In 2012 the Qatari government prosecuted a student-poet, Muhammad ibn al-Dheeb al-Ajami, for criticizing the royal family in his work. The writer was sentenced to life in prison, though that sentence was later reduced to fifteen years on appeal.

## QATAR MUSEUMS' PURCHASES AND FUNDING

The sheikha's family spends an estimated $1 billion a year on art. (By contrast, the Metropolitan Museum of Art in New York purchased $39 million worth of art in 2012.) Among the works Sheikha al-Mayassa has acquired are famous pieces by Mark Rothko, Richard Serra, Jeff Koons, Andy Warhol, Francis Bacon, Roy Lichtenstein, and Damien Hirst. When the sheikha purchased Pablo Picasso's 1901 painting *Child with a Dove* for about $79 million in 2012, the British government issued an export ban on the painting, instated to incite British galleries and museums to raise the funds needed to purchase it back. (The early Picasso piece had been in Britain since 1924 and lived in various public institutions until 2012.) In early 2011 Sheikha al-Mayassa quietly purchased Paul Cézanne's late-nineteenth-century painting *The Card Players*, for which she paid a record $250 million. It was then the most money ever spent for one work of art. That record was broken in February 2015, when the Qatar Museums was rumored to have paid a staggering $300 million for the Paul Gauguin 1892 painting *Nafea Faa Ipoipa (When Will You Marry?)*.

As Arlidge reported, Sheikha al-Mayassa and her family spend so much money on art that it affects the entire art world. Veteran New York art dealer and former Sotheby's auction-house executive David Nash told Robin Pogrebin for the *New York Times* (22 July 2013), "When they finish their buying program and withdraw from the market, they will leave a big hole which I don't see anyone else ready to fill at their level." In 2007 Sheikha al-Mayassa paid upward of $70 million for the Rothko painting *White Center*. The amount was three times as much as anyone had ever paid for one of the artist's works. One London art dealer bitterly told Arlidge, "Qatar pays over the odds, often vastly, for everything. It has skewed large sectors of the art market, which is bad for everyone—except, of course, the Qataris." The Qatar Museums does not publish its budget, which has led to speculation about where exactly the money for the artworks is coming from. Suspicions have been fueled, the *Economist* wrote, by "the family's blank refusal to confirm or deny any of the rumours and its reluctance to clarify whether its acquisitions are private or on behalf of the state." Qatar Museums operations that are public, however, include funding for exhibitions abroad. The Qatar Museums funded a show by Japanese artist Takashi Murakami in Versailles in 2010 and a Damien Hirst retrospective at the Tate in London in 2012. In 2007 Sheikha al-Mayassa bought Hirst's pill-cabinet piece for more than $20 million. It was, at the time, the most money ever paid to a living artist for a single artwork.

## COMMITTED TO EDUCATING CHILDREN

In keeping with her mother's focus on education, Sheikha al-Mayassa is committed to not only making the Qatar Museums open to schoolchildren but to improving the arts education in schools. The sheikha has plans for a children's museum to open in 2017. In an interview for the Qatar Museums website (14 May 2014), she stated her belief that "children think creatively and by exposing them to arts education and cultural institutions from a young age, it nurtures innate talent."

Sheikha al-Mayassa has also served as the chair of the nonprofit Reach Out to Asia (ROTA) since its establishment. ROTA was founded by her brother, Sheikh Tamim, in 2005 in the wake of 2004's devastating Indian Ocean earthquake and tsunami and the October 2005 earthquake in Pakistan. The organization functions under the umbrella of the Qatar Foundation, itself the brainchild of their parents, Sheikh Hamad and Sheikha Mozah. ROTA seeks to expand primary education and promote community and professional development, particularly in areas hard hit by disasters or displacement.

## PERSONAL LIFE

Sheikha al-Mayassa speaks French, English, and Arabic. She is married to her cousin Sheikh Jassim bin Abdul Aziz al-Thani. They have three children.

Though sometimes seen in trendy Western dress or business attire, Sheikha al-Mayassa frequently appears at public gatherings wearing the traditional black abaya. This choice, she noted in a 2010 TEDx Doha talk, she views not as a

religious or political statement, but rather as a cultural one. She believes that in a rapidly globalizing world, individuals are seeking out that which differentiates them and re-embracing cultural traditions such as this.

## SUGGESTED READING

Adam, Georgina. "Energy—and Ambition to Match." *Financial Times*. Financial Times, 9 Mar. 2012. Web. 9 Apr. 2015.

Arlidge, John. "Forget about the Price Tag: Qatar's Sheikha Mayassa Is Outbidding the Art World." *London Evening Standard*. 4 Oct. 2013. Web. 9 Apr. 2015.

Ouroussoff, Nicolai. "Building Museums, and a Fresh Arab Identity." *New York Times*. New York Times, 26 Nov. 2010. Web. 11 Apr. 2015.

Pogrebin, Robin. "Qatari Riches Are Buying Art World Influence." *New York Times*. New York Times, 22 July 2013. Web. 9 Apr. 2015.

"Qatar's Culture Queen." *Economist*. Economist, 31 May 2012. Web. 9 Apr. 2015.

Vogel, Carol. "Sheikha al-Mayassa Hamad bin Khalifa al-Thani of Qatar Museums." *International New York Times*. New York Times, 26 Dec. 2013. Web. 21 Apr. 2015.

—Molly Hagan

---

# Richard Sherman

**Born:** March 30, 1988
**Occupation:** Football player

"I'm the best corner in the game!" Those brash words were spoken by Seattle Seahawks cornerback Richard Sherman in a postgame interview with Fox Sports reporter Erin Andrews after he made a game-saving deflection against the San Francisco 49ers in the 2014 National Football Conference (NFC) Championship Game. The play sent the Seahawks to Super Bowl XLVIII, where they defeated the Denver Broncos to win their first Super Bowl title. Sherman's now-infamous interview instantly catapulted him to national celebrity and burnished his reputation as one of the most outspoken and polarizing players in the National Football League (NFL). For Sherman, however, it only added to a long list of attention-grabbing moments since he first entered the league in 2011, moments that have often overshadowed his stellar play on the field and remarkable journey from a little-known fifth-round draft pick to an NFL star.

From 2011 to January 2014 Sherman had more interceptions (twenty-four) and pass breakups (sixty-eight) than any other player in the league, and he established himself as one of the linchpins of a dominant Seahawks' secondary known as the "Legion of Boom." His ability to lock down opposing teams' top receivers earned him first-team All-Pro selections in 2012, 2013, and 2014 and Pro Bowl selections in 2013 and 2014. Sherman, who is equally known for his intelligence and articulate nature, said to Michael Silver for *Yahoo! Sports* (11 Dec. 2012), "I want to be the best, period. A lot of people don't think it's possible. . . . But that's what I want to be."

## EARLY LIFE

Richard Kevin Sherman was born on March 30, 1988 in Compton, California. With his older brother, Branton, and younger sister, Kristyna, Sherman was raised in a strict household. His father, Kevin, worked for the Los Angeles sanitation department, and his mother, Beverly, was a clerk for California Children's Services. Sherman has said that he inherited his drive and work ethic directly from his parents.

To keep him insulated from the dangerous streets of Compton, Sherman's parents pushed him into sports. Sherman developed an interest

Michael Buckner/WireImage/Getty Images

in football after his brother became involved in the sport, and he played on a Pop Warner team coached by his father. Lean and thin, Sherman initially shied away from physical contact, threatening to end his football career before it started, but with constant pressure from his father he persevered.

At an early age, Sherman learned how confidence and trash talk could be used as a weapon to gain a mental edge over opponents. A documentary about boxing legend Muhammad Ali left a lasting impression on him around the age of twelve. Sherman told Lee Jenkins for *Sports Illustrated* (29 July 2013) how he realized Ali "created a persona. He was a leader, an entertainer, and he knew how to break people down in the ring. I didn't really care about boxing, but I wanted to be like Ali." Sherman developed what would become his signature razor-sharp tongue by studying Ali and other athletes such as Michael Irvin and Deion Sanders who used their intelligence and psychological tactics along with their physical skills.

Sherman followed his brother to Dominguez High School in Compton, where he played football and competed in track and field. Underweight and not exceptionally tall as a freshman, Sherman overcame his physical limitations with a fearless style of play. However, after undergoing a growth spurt and filling out his frame through a weight training regimen, he became a two-way standout on the gridiron for Dominguez High. He also emerged as a track star, winning the California state championship in the triple jump as a senior. "Richard never wanted to be average or good," Keith Donerson, his highschool football coach, stated to Ben Shpigel for the *New York Times* (25 Jan. 2014). "He wanted to be great, in everything that he did."

Sherman's athletic achievements were rivaled only by his accomplishments in the classroom. He earned straight As throughout high school and graduated as the salutatorian of his class with a 4.2 grade point average (GPA). Despite being recruited as a cornerback and receiver by numerous Division I schools, Sherman ultimately chose Stanford University because of its academic reputation. He explained to Jenkins, "I wanted to make a statement. . . . I had to prove it was possible: Compton to Stanford."

## STANFORD TO SEATTLE SEAHAWKS

When Sherman arrived at Stanford on an athletic scholarship, the school was not known as a football power. He played as a receiver for the

Stanford Cardinals and led the team in catches his freshman year, though they finished with a 1–11 record. The next season the Cardinals hired coach Jim Harbaugh, who frequently clashed with Sherman and used him less and less on the field. After being limited to four games during the 2008 season due to a left knee injury, Sherman was granted redshirt status.

When he returned to team workouts in the spring of 2009, however, he found himself at the bottom of the Cardinals' receiver depth chart. After considering transferring schools, Sherman instead requested a switch to cornerback. "At receiver, you're limited," he explained to John Wilner for the *San Jose Mercury News* (10 Sept. 2013). "If the quarterback has a bad game, you're having a bad game. But at cornerback, no matter what's going on, if your man doesn't catch the ball, you're having a pretty good day. You control your own destiny." Sherman earned a starting cornerback spot and flourished at the position in his final two years at Stanford, helping the team to a 40–12 win over Virginia Tech in the 2011 Orange Bowl. He graduated with a degree in communications and a 3.9 GPA.

After performing well in a number of predraft evaluations, Sherman entered the 2011 NFL Draft expecting to be selected in the first round. However, 153 players, including thirty-one other defensive backs, were selected before he was taken by the Seattle Seahawks in the draft's fifth round. Despite realizing his dream of making it to the NFL, Sherman was "livid" over his draft placement and resolved to "destroy the league, as soon as they give me the chance," as he told Silver. The Seahawks' head coach, Pete Carroll, was meanwhile enamored with Sherman's rangy six-foot-three, 195-pound frame and believed he would fit perfectly in the team's defense, which featured physical, man-to-man coverage. Carroll described Sherman to Silver as "one of those guys who has a really classic [cornerback's] mindset. Nothing's gonna deter him from what he believes he can do."

Sherman's opportunity to prove his doubters wrong came seven games into the 2011 season, when he was inserted into the lineup as a replacement for an injured teammate. In his first NFL start, a week-eight matchup against the Cincinnati Bengals, he recorded his first career interception despite a 34–12 Seahawks loss. Sherman started the Seahawks' remaining nine games as left cornerback and finished with four interceptions and seventeen passes defended, leading all

rookies in both categories. He was subsequently named to the Pro Football Writers of America (PFWA) All-Rookie Team. The Seahawks duplicated their 7–9 record from the previous year but missed the playoffs.

## EMERGENCE AS A STAR PLAYER

In only his second NFL season, Sherman firmly established himself as one of the best cornerbacks in the league. In 2012 he started all sixteen games for the Seahawks and led the team in both interceptions (eight) and pass breakups (twenty-four), which ranked second and first in the NFL, respectively. For his performance, he was selected to his first All-Pro team.

During the season Sherman paired with Brandon Browner, a similarly imposing, six-foot-four, 220-pound cornerback, to form what Silver described as "likely the most physically imposing cornerback pairing in NFL history." As Sherman put it to Jenkins, "Seahawks corners don't back up. We don't give you room. We stay in your face all day long." Together they made up one half, along with All-Pro safeties Earl Thomas and Kam Chancellor, of a Seahawks' secondary that earned the nickname the "Legion of Boom" for their relentless, high-octane style of play. Anchored by their defense, the Seahawks finished second in the NFC West, at 11–5, and returned to the postseason. They overcame the Washington Redskins in the first round of the playoffs before advancing to the NFC divisional playoffs, where they narrowly lost to the Atlanta Falcons, 30–28.

Sherman not only gained league-wide attention for his play but also for his voluble antics. He taunted quarterback Tom Brady after the Seahawks upset the New England Patriots in week six, called Harbaugh, then the head coach of the San Francisco 49ers, a "bully" following a week-seven loss to the 49ers, and aggravated Redskins offensive lineman Trent Williams so much that Williams pushed him in the face after the Seahawks beat the Redskins in the playoffs, among other trash-talking incidents. Meanwhile, Sherman found himself at the center of a more serious controversy in November 2012, when he tested positive for the performance-enhancing drug Adderall. He later won his appeal of a four-game suspension from the league after successfully arguing that his urine sample had been tampered with.

## SUPER BOWL CHAMPION

Prior to the 2013 season, Sherman made even more headlines. First, he called the Atlanta Falcons' Pro Bowl receiver Roddy White "an easy matchup" on ESPN's *NFL Live*, and then he became embroiled in a Twitter feud with All-Pro cornerback Darrelle Revis, then a member of the New York Jets, over who was the better player of the two. Headline-grabbing incidents notwithstanding, Sherman continued to back up his words on the field. In 2013 he led the NFL with eight interceptions and led the Seahawks with sixteen pass breakups, and he made his second All-Pro team and earned his first career Pro Bowl selection. Thanks to Sherman's lockdown defense, the Seahawks allowed the fewest passing yards in the league as well as the fewest points and yards. The team finished with a 13–3 record to win the NFC West and clinch the NFC's number-one seed.

After defeating the New Orleans Saints, 23–15, in the NFC divisional playoffs, the Seahawks faced the 49ers in the NFC Championship Game. The game was decided in the final seconds after Sherman deflected a pass in the end zone intended for 49ers receiver Michael Crabtree that would have given the 49ers the lead. The Seahawks won 23–17 and advanced to the Super Bowl for the second time in the franchise's history. The team's win, however, was largely overshadowed by Sherman's postgame rant in which he proclaimed himself the game's best cornerback and disparaged Crabtree, drawing national press coverage and widespread criticism. Sherman responded to commentators who labeled him a "thug" by opening a debate about race and sports. His overnight rise to national fame did not, however, distract Sherman from Super Bowl XLVIII. On February 2, 2014, the Seahawks stifled the Broncos' record-breaking offense as they completed a 43–8 victory to earn the franchise's first Super Bowl title.

In May 2014 Sherman signed a four-year contract extension with the Seahawks worth approximately $57.4 million. The contract included $40 million in guaranteed money and made him the highest-paid cornerback in the league. Sherman lived up to his lofty contract with another All-Pro season in 2014. That year he led the Seahawks in interceptions and finished second on the team in pass breakups, with four and eight, respectively. He was named to his third straight All-Pro team and second consecutive Pro Bowl. The Seahawks again allowed the few-est yards and points in the league, en route to a 12–4 record and second straight NFC West title. In the NFC divisional playoffs, the Seahawks defeated the Carolina Panthers, 31–17. In the game, Sherman recorded his first career playoff interception. The Seahawks advanced to play in Super Bowl XLIX, where they lost to the Patriots, 28–24.

Sherman, who is known for his long, flowing dreadlocks, was named one of the one hundred most influential people in the world by *Time* magazine in 2014. That year he was also chosen to appear on the cover of EA Sports' *Madden NFL 15* video game. He has done extensive charity work and established a foundation in 2013 to help inner-city youth called Blanket Coverage, the Richard Sherman Family Foundation. Sherman and his longtime girlfriend Ashley Moss are expecting the birth of their first child in February 2015.

## SUGGESTED READING

Jenkins, Lee. "Warning: Don't Take the Bait." *Sports Illustrated* 29 July 2013: 46. Print.

Shpigel, Ben. "Seahawks' Richard Sherman Is Much More than Just Talk." *New York Times*. New York Times, 25 Jan. 2014. Web. 27 Jan. 2014.

Silver, Michael. "Seahawks' Richard Sherman Wants to 'Destroy' the NFL and Become the Best CB of All Time." *Yahoo! Sports*. Yahoo Sports–NBC Sports Network, 11 Dec. 2012. Web. 27 Jan. 2014.

—Chris Cullen

# Gwynne Shotwell

**Born:** November 23, 1963

**Occupation:** President and COO of SpaceX

Gwynne Shotwell is the president and chief operating officer (COO) of SpaceX, a commercial space exploration company based in California. As the head of day-to-day operations at the company, Shotwell oversees $5 billion in government contracts and SpaceX's nearly three thousand employees. SpaceX, which is short for the Space Exploration Technologies Corporation, was founded in 2002 by PayPal founder Elon Musk, an eccentric but visionary tech magnate who is also the chief executive officer and product architect of the electric car manufacturer Tesla Motors. Musk has publicly announced SpaceX's goals of reducing space transportation costs for governments and private customers and of colonizing the planet Mars. Both he and Shotwell have presided over SpaceX during the company's first rocket launches. Despite experiencing initial failures and frustrations in design and execution, in December 2010 SpaceX became the first private company to successfully launch, orbit, and recover a spacecraft. About two years later they sent a vehicle named *Dragon* to the International Space Station (ISS), once again making history as the first nongovernmental organization to deliver cargo to ISS and then return intact to Earth.

Regarding plans for Grasshopper, the company's newest project which involves creating a reusable, orbital spaceship and rocket launch system, Shotwell told Kiona Smith-Strickland for *Popular Mechanics* (20 June 2013), "The tests are going beautifully, which fundamentally means we're not pushing the envelope hard enough. We should have some failures with Grasshopper. We need to push harder." If it succeeds, Grasshopper would be the world's first reusable launch system.

## EARLY LIFE AND EDUCATION

Shotwell was born on November 23, 1963, in Evanston, Illinois, though she was raised in Libertyville, a suburb located about forty miles outside of Chicago. Her father, Wilbur Rowley, is a brain surgeon. Her mother is an artist. By all accounts, Shotwell, the second of three daughters, was a born engineer. She loved helping her father with odd jobs around the house—putting together a basketball net or cutting railroad ties to construct a barrier for the family's backyard garden. When she was in the third grade, she asked her mother how a car engine worked. "So my mom bought me a book on engines," Shotwell told W. J. Hennigan for the *Los Angeles Times* (7 June 2013). "I read it and became really interested in car engines, and gears and differentials." In high school, Shotwell was a straight-A student. She was also a cheerleader and played varsity basketball. Her mother suggested that she should pursue engineering as a career and took her to a Society of Women Engineers panel at the Illinois Institute of Technology. There, she met a glamorous mechanical engineer who owned her own business. Crucially, Shotwell noted to Emily Ayshford for Northwestern Engineering

NASA/Kim Shiflett/Wikimedia Commons

School's *McCormick Magazine* (Spring 2011), "she wasn't all that nerdy." Shotwell was sold.

Shotwell enrolled at Northwestern University's McCormick School of Engineering where she was one of three women in her class of thirty-six. She graduated in 1986 with a bachelor's degree in mechanical engineering. After graduation, she enrolled in Chrysler Motor's management training program in Detroit, but she was unhappy there. Shotwell decided to return to McCormick to complete her master's degree and doctorate in applied mathematics.

## EARLY CAREER

Shotwell earned her master's degree in 1988 but then put aside her plans to pursue a PhD in part thanks to a chat with her friend, a former McCormick teaching assistant named Tom Hopp. Hopp was working for Aerospace Corporation, a federally-funded research center in El Segundo, California, that oversees military space contracts. Shotwell was intrigued by the company, interviewed there, and got a job working with thermal analysis. She spent the next ten years at the company and wrote, according to Hennigan, papers on subjects dealing with conceptual small spacecraft design, infrared signature target modeling, space shuttle integration, and reentry vehicle operational risks. She enjoyed the work but she told Hennigan, "I wanted to go build, and put spacecraft together." In 1998, Shotwell became the director of the space systems division at Microcosm, Inc. in El Segundo.

Microcosm built rockets for the Air Force, but it remained a small-scale operation, and it was just what Shotwell was looking for. However, fate stepped in again and in 2002, she had lunch with a friend who was working for a new commercial space exploration company called SpaceX. Shotwell visited the company's Hawthorne, California, offices that same day, and as she walked past Elon Musk's cubicle, she told Jenny Hontz for *Northwestern* magazine (Spring 2012) that she said, "'Oh, Elon, nice to meet you. You really need a new business developer.' It just popped out. I was bad. It was very rude." Despite how Shotwell feels she handled the initial encounter, Musk called her later that day and offered her a job.

## EARLY WORK WITH SPACEX

Shotwell joined SpaceX as the vice president of business development in 2002. She was the company's seventh employee. Of her decision to join the company, Shotwell told Smith-Strickland, "I was at a point in my career where I felt like the business of space needed to be fixed, and if it wasn't, I didn't want any part of this industry. It was slow and stodgy. I told myself when I started at SpaceX that this would be my last job in this industry. If we couldn't make it work, I was out."

The company attempted its first test launch of the rocket *Falcon 1* in March 2006, but a fuel leak cut the flight short at half a minute. Still, the same year SpaceX was awarded a $278 million contract with the US government agency NASA (National Aeronautics and Space Administration) to begin developing a program to shuttle cargo and crew to the ISS. Thanks to this contract SpaceX began to turn a profit in 2007. A second attempt to launch *Falcon 1* failed in March 2007, but in 2008—the same year Shotwell was named president of the company—SpaceX received another contract from NASA for *Falcon 1* and *Falcon 9*. In August the third attempt to launch *Falcon 1* failed, but after identifying the problem, SpaceX launched a fourth attempt on September 28, 2008. This time, the launch was a success, and *Falcon 1* became the first privately funded liquid rocket to reach orbit. "[The test launch was] a remarkable testament to her ability to organize and motivate," Tim Hughes, senior vice president and general counsel at SpaceX, told Hontz of Shotwell. "Fundamentally, if you're at a startup rocket company,

you're an optimist. Gwynne's attitude, and the attitude of this company, is can-do."

## SPACEX SUCCESSES

Following the 2008 successful launch of *Falcon 1*, SpaceX began experiencing a series of achievements starting in July 2009 when the company used *Falcon 1* to successfully launch a Malaysian satellite into orbit. In June 2010 the company launched the first *Falcon 9*, a rocket capable of carrying a cargo vehicle, into low-Earth orbit. That same month, SpaceX won a $492 million contract with the satellite communications company Iridium. In December 2010 the *Falcon 9* rocket successfully launched carrying the *Dragon* spacecraft, and SpaceX became the first commercial company to launch, orbit, and recover a spacecraft.

By early 2012, the company was reportedly worth over $1 billion. In May, SpaceX launched *Falcon 9* at the Cape Canaveral Air Force Base. The rocket carried a cargo capsule intended for the International Space Station, and a few days later, *Dragon* became the first commercial spacecraft to dock at the space station. Shotwell told Smith-Strickland that watching the craft berth with the ISS was the most exciting moment of her time at SpaceX thus far. "It's a little fuzzy because it was at four in the morning, but it was an incredibly intense, nerve-racking, but really satisfying time," she said. "It's so great to be with the teams for those events, like launches or berthings. Employees are crying and screaming and laughing and jumping up and down." In December 2013 SpaceX hit another milestone—*Falcon 9* launched a communications satellite, owned by the Luxembourg-based company SES, into geostationary transfer orbit (GTO). GTO involves a satellite being placed so as to orbit with the Earth in order to maintain the same position in perpetuity. The feat was significant because it required *Falcon 9* to travel far outside of low-Earth orbit where the ISS is stationed.

## THE FUTURE OF SPACEX

SpaceX came into being at a time when the American space program found itself at a crossroads. NASA officially ended its space shuttle program in 2011, reportedly to focus on its widely publicized missions to Mars, but the organization suffered from a lack of funding (alongside accusations of wasteful spending) and a lack of sustained popular support. Space exploration is more important to civilization than it has ever been, yet it is consistently the last item on the US political docket. It has long been suggested that private companies might be able to remedy this situation, and when SpaceX started to succeed and with spacecraft built for a fraction of the cost of NASA's government-funded spacecraft, many touted a new day for space exploration. On this point, however, popular astrophysicist Neil deGrasse Tyson is not so sure. Anthony Ha for TechCrunch (8 Mar. 2014) reported on a speech Tyson gave at the Austin, Texas, South by Southwest festival in 2014. Space travel, Tyson said, is "a long-term investment" and is one "that private enterprise cannot lead." Exploration in itself, Tyson argued, has no endgame: There is no profit to be made from seeing what's out there—which is exactly what NASA exists to do.

But while, as Tyson says, it is unlikely that a private company could ever amass the resources to replace a government-run program such as NASA, there is no question that companies like SpaceX could play a significant role in facilitating long-term projects in the future. In September 2014, NASA awarded contracts to SpaceX and Boeing to develop spacecrafts that would deliver astronauts to the ISS by 2017. The partnership is a major step forward for the American space program, which previously relied on Russia to ferry astronauts back and forth at the cost of $71 million per seat. "Once NASA approves that Boeing's and SpaceX's systems meet its requirements, the systems will be certified for two to six human missions to deliver cargo and a crew of up to four to the ISS," Dan Kedmey and Jack Linshi reported for Time magazine (16 Sept. 2014). "The missions will enable NASA to nearly double today's scientific research potential, [Program Manager, Kathryn] Lueders said." Meanwhile, SpaceX continues to develop new and imagination-grabbing projects. Most recently, Musk hinted that SpaceX is planning to launch a number of advanced microsatellites to provide low-cost Internet access.

## PERSONAL LIFE

Shotwell has received several awards and honors over the years. In 2011 she was presented with the World Technology Award for her individual achievements in space. The following year she was inducted into the Women in Technology International Hall of Fame and also won the Women in Aerospace Outstanding Achievement Award for her contributions to a breakthrough aerospace project. In 2014 she was named by Forbes magazine as one of the one hundred most powerful women for that year.

Shotwell's husband Robert is an engineer at NASA's Jet Propulsion Laboratory at the California Institute of Technology. They have a son and a daughter, and the family lives in Los Angeles.

## SUGGESTED READING

Ayshford, Emily. "Alumni Profile: Gwynne Shotwell." *McCormick Magazine.* Northwestern University, Spring 2011. Web. 17 Nov. 2014.

Hennigan, W. J. "How I Made It: SpaceX Exec Gwynne Shotwell." *Los Angeles Times*. Los Angeles Times, 7 June 2013. Web. 17 Nov. 2014.

Hontz, Jenny. "Rocket Ma'am." *Northwestern.* Northwestern University, Spring 2012. Web. 17 Nov. 2014.

Kedmey, Dan, and Jack Linshi. "Boeing and SpaceX Win Major NASA Space Taxi Contract." *Time.* Time, 16 Sept. 2014. Web. 17 Nov. 2014.

Smith-Strickland, Kiona. "SpaceX President Gwynne Shotwell: The Case for Commercial Rockets." *Popular Mechanics.* Hearst Communication, 20 June 2013. Web. 17 Nov. 2014.

—Molly Hagan

# Adam Silver

**Born:** April 25, 1962
**Occupation:** NBA commissioner

When David Stern announced his intention to step down as commissioner of the National Basketball Association (NBA) in February 2014, it came as no surprise that he endorsed Adam Silver as his successor. Stern had essentially groomed Silver, a former litigation associate, to take over the multibillion-dollar league since hiring him as his special assistant in 1992. Over a two-decade-plus career with the NBA, Silver has held a series of increasingly responsible positions, including NBA chief of staff, president and chief operating officer (COO) of NBA Entertainment (NBAE), and deputy commissioner and COO of the NBA. During that time he worked closely with Stern on the league's biggest and most significant deals, including the 2011 NBA lockout.

Silver officially succeeded Stern in February 2014, becoming the NBA's fifth commissioner. He has already made an impact on the NBA in his brief tenure at the helm, most notably banning Los Angeles Clippers owner Donald Sterling from the league for life in April 2014 for making racist comments about African Americans. In contrast to the brash and outspoken Stern, Silver is known for his unassuming and accessible nature and for adopting a business-first, team-building approach. Jerry Colangelo, the director of USA Basketball, said to John Lombardo and Terry Lefton for the *SportsBusiness Journal* (21 Oct. 2013), "[Silver] has the experience, intelligence, and work ethic to do it all, but he will do it with a different style."

## EARLY LIFE AND EDUCATION

Adam Silver was born on April 25, 1962, in Rye, an affluent New York City suburb located in Westchester County. The youngest of four children, he grew up in a liberal, upper-class Jewish household. Silver's father, Edward, was a prominent labor attorney and onetime chairman of the elite New York–based white-shoe law firm Proskauer Rose who also served as special labor counsel under four New York City mayors. His mother, Melba, was a teacher, environmentalist, and fervent community activist.

Silver's parents, who both died of cancer in 2004, divorced when he was ten. Afterward, he continued to live with his mother in Rye while

Keith Allison (CC-BY-SA 2.0)

his father moved to an apartment in New York. Silver remained close with his father through regular trips to the city. He and his father bonded over watching the New York Knicks and the New York Rangers, at Madison Square Garden, as well as occasional New York Yankees games and Muhammad Ali boxing bouts that were broadcast at a theater in New Rochelle, New York. For Silver, these experiences sparked a lifelong love of sports.

While Silver, who stands six feet three inches tall, never played competitive basketball, he played Little League baseball as a child and later ran cross-country for the Rye High School track team. In high school, he was also class president and the editor-in-chief of the student newspaper. A precocious straight-A student, Silver went on to attend Duke University in Durham, North Carolina, where he earned a degree in political science in 1984.

Silver's tenure at Duke coincided with the arrival of the university's legendary head basketball coach Mike Krzyzewski, who helped transform the Blue Devils into a perennial national title contender. Though admittedly "never a paint your face kind of guy," as he told Sam Amick for *USA Today* (14 Feb. 2014), Silver went to all of the Blue Devils' home games and further immersed himself in the school's fanatical hoops culture by playing intramural basketball.

After graduating from Duke, Silver spent a year working in Washington, DC, as a legislative aid for Les AuCoin, a now-retired US congressman from Oregon. He then attended the University of Chicago Law School and did volunteer work at the school's legal assistance clinic. During his time there, he regularly attended Chicago Bulls games for the chance to see the then-burgeoning superstar Michael Jordan. Silver earned his juris doctor degree in 1988.

## PATH TO THE NBA

Silver initially followed in his father's footsteps by pursuing a law career. After passing his bar exam, he was hired as a law clerk for newly appointed federal judge Kimba Wood in the US District Court for the Southern District of New York. During his one-year stint as clerk, he "settled dozens of cases" for Wood, according to Lee Jenkins for *Sports Illustrated* (20 May 2014), impressing her with his uncanny negotiating skills. "He was proficient way beyond his years," Wood told Scott Soshnick and Mason Levinson for *Bloomberg Business* (26 Oct. 2012). "He would find ways to help me close negotiations, close settlements, that no other clerk has been able to do since."

In 1989 Silver moved into private practice as a litigation associate with Cravath, Swaine & Moore, another New York–based white-shoe law firm. He spent three years with the firm, routinely working 110-hour weeks. During this time, Silver tried a number of antitrust cases for Time Warner, which piqued his interest in the media and cable business.

Dissatisfied with his work as a lawyer and looking for career advice, Silver decided to write a letter to David Stern, who had worked with and been mentored by his father at Proskauer Rose in the 1970s. He was soon granted a meeting with the NBA commissioner. "At that point I didn't even understand what it would have meant to be working at the NBA back then," Silver admitted to Amick. "I was a fan, but had no sense of league operations." Stern gave him advice about the sports industry and suggested he pursue a job outside of New York. The prospect of leaving the city, however, did not appeal to Silver, who went back to working at his law firm.

Silver met with Stern several more times before being offered a job to serve as his special assistant. He took on the role in 1992, replacing future Women's National Basketball Association (WNBA) president and Big East Conference commissioner Val Ackerman when she went on maternity leave. "I feel as though I kidnapped Adam for the NBA on his way to a legal career," Stern later said to Marek Fuchs for the *New York Times* (10 June 2001).

## APPRENTICING WITH STERN

Silver rapidly rose through the ranks of the NBA hierarchy. After spending one year as Stern's assistant, he was promoted to chief of staff in 1993 and then to senior vice president and COO of NBA Entertainment (NBAE) in 1995. In the latter role, Silver helped oversee the development of the NBA's official website and, in 1996, its fiftieth anniversary celebrations. Bill Daugherty, former NBA senior vice president of business development, told Lombardo and Lefton, "From the beginning, it was apparent Adam was going to be a commissioner. And from the beginning, his instincts have been dead on. He could always make things happen and make them happen smoothly."

In 1997 Silver was named president and COO of NBAE. He held that role for the next nine years, during which time he was involved in every aspect of the NBA's business opera-

tions, including those of its newly launched sister league, the WNBA. In 1999 Silver helped orchestrate the launch of NBA TV, the first cable network exclusively owned and operated by a sports league. The following year Silver's role broadened to include overseeing the league's properties division. He eventually grew NBAE into one of the largest providers of sports television and Internet programming in the world.

Silver became known as a workaholic with a business-centric ethos, a global vision, and a keen foresight for melding media and technology. Throughout his rise up the NBA ranks, he worked side by side with Stern, who schooled him in the intricacies of labor relations, marketing, branding, and negotiations between media programmers and distributors. Unlike Stern, who often rubbed colleagues the wrong way with his combustible temper, outspoken nature, and autocratic management style, Silver established himself as an approachable and straightforward team builder. "Adam had the right combination of talent and intellect to be successful. . . . [He] became a real trusted alter ego for Stern," Rick Welts, the president and COO of Oakland's Golden State Warriors, said to Lombardo and Lefton.

Silver became Stern's official second-in-command in 2006, when he was named deputy commissioner and COO of the NBA. In his new role, he was an instrumental force in the NBA's biggest and most delicate dealings. In 2007 he helped negotiate the league's eight-year, $7.4 billion television deal with Turner Broadcasting, ABC, and ESPN, set to expire after the 2015–16 season. Later that year he played a central role in resolving one of the league's worst crises, a betting scandal involving veteran NBA referee Tim Donaghy. In 2008 he oversaw the launch of NBA China, a venture aimed at growing the game in the world's biggest market.

## NBA COMMISSIONER

Silver cemented his standing as Stern's successor in 2011, when he served as chief negotiator during the 2011 NBA lockout, which lasted 161 days and shortened the 2011–12 season to sixty-six games. When the lockout was finalized, Stern announced that he would no longer be commissioner when team owners and players negotiated their next collective bargaining agreement in 2017.

In October 2012 Stern endorsed Silver to succeed him when he stepped down as NBA commissioner. Stern officially retired on February

1, 2014, after thirty years in the role. That same day, Silver was unanimously elected the NBA's fifth commissioner by the NBA Board of Governors. Commenting on Stern's legacy in professional sports, Silver told Soshnick and Levinson, "David has transformed the industry, and not just the NBA. David is the one who turned sports leagues into brands."

Silver inherited a league whose annual revenues exceed $5 billion and whose games have been broadcast in 215 countries and forty-seven languages. Though admitting he has large shoes to fill, he has stated that the league still has plenty of room for growth. In April 2014 Silver held his first meeting with the NBA Board of Governors, where he addressed his stances on a number of topics, including the NBA age minimum, the draft lottery system, team schedules, and the playoff format. Among his proposed reforms is increasing the minimum age for draft eligibility from nineteen to twenty years old.

### THE STERLING SCANDAL

One week after his first Board of Governors meeting, Silver faced the first major crisis of his tenure as NBA commissioner. On April 25, 2014, the celebrity gossip website TMZ released an audio recording of Los Angeles Clippers owner Donald Sterling making racist comments about African Americans to his girlfriend. The comments caused a national uproar and caused NBA players to threaten boycotts if proper punishment were not meted out. On April 29, Silver announced his decision to ban Sterling from the NBA for life and fine him $2.5 million, the maximum amount allowable under NBA rules. He also stated the NBA's intention to terminate Sterling's ownership and force him to sell the Clippers, but Sterling's wife and Clippers co-owner Shelly Sterling negotiated a league-approved sale before official action could be taken.

Though Silver's sanctions against Sterling were the harshest ever taken against a professional sports team owner, they were met with widespread praise from NBA players and coaches. Explaining his decision, Silver told Jenkins, "This wasn't an outsider taking shots. To have these references come from within an institution that is—while far from perfect—as egalitarian as there is in society made a particular impact."

In November 2014 Silver made waves again when he published an op-ed article in the *New York Times* that declared his support for the legalization and regulation of sports gambling. He became the first major US sports league commissioner to publicly support legalized gambling outside of Nevada.

### PERSONAL LIFE

Silver is said to have a legendary wit and a penchant for practical jokes. An avid runner, he has run the New York City Marathon twice, both times completing the race in less than four hours. In 2015 he was named to the Time 100, *Time* magazine's list of the world's one hundred most influential people. Silver married his longtime girlfriend, interior designer Maggie Grise, in May 2015.

### SUGGESTED READING

Beck, Howard. "Adam Silver's Lifelong Love of Basketball Will Help Shape Focus in New Role." *Bleacher Report*. Bleacher Rept., 14 Feb. 2014. Web. 10 Sept. 2015.

Fuchs, Marek. "Native Son: Leaving the Law for a Hoop Dream." *New York Times*. New York Times, 10 June 2001. Web. 10 Sept. 2015.

Jenkins, Lee. "New Commissioner Adam Silver Is His Own Man." *Sports Illustrated*. Time, 20 May 2014. Web. 10 Sept. 2015.

Lombardo, John, and Terry Lefton. "Silver Mettle." *SportsBusiness Journal*. Amer. City Business Jour., 21 Oct. 2013. Web. 10 Sept. 2015.

Silver, Adam. "Adam Silver Q&A: New Boss Wants NBA Age Limit Raised." Interview by Sam Amick. *USA Today*. Gannett, 14 Feb. 2014. Web. 10 Sept. 2015.

Soshnick, Scott, and Mason Levinson. "Silver Taking Over NBA with Stern Completing Turnaround." *Bloomberg Business*. Bloomberg, 26 Oct. 2012. Web. 10 Sept. 2015.

—Chris Cullen

# Nancy Silverton
**Born:** June 20, 1954
**Occupation:** Chef and baker

The James Beard Foundation is named for the legendary late cookbook author, teacher, and champion of American cuisine, and the organization's mission is to celebrate, nurture, and honor the United States' diverse culinary heritage. The foundation bestows highly coveted annual awards, and in 2014, Nancy Silverton became one of the few women ever to win the award for outstanding chef. While

Astrid Stawiarz/Getty Images for Macy's

those outside the culinary world might assume that winning the title means that Silverton creates haute cuisine or inaccessibly expensive fare, she is in fact most noted for her bread and pizza.

Silverton is the founder of Los Angeles's La Brea Bakery, where she is credited with introducing to America the crusty European baguettes and boules now easily found in most supermarkets and bakeries. "I wasn't thinking of artisan bread as the next big trend," she explained to Bev Bennett for *New Products* magazine (Aug. 2007). "I looked at the market and saw an absence of crusty breads in neighborhood bakeries. That's what I wanted and it turned out other people did as well." She is currently the chef and co-owner of the restaurants Pizzeria Mozza and Osteria Mozza, located next door to each other in Los Angeles. Celebrities flock to her establishments, and there is often a several-week wait for a reservation to try Silverton's beautifully composed salads, pastas, and world-renowned pizza pies, which feature crusts that are appealingly textured and complexly flavored. She includes rye flour and malt in her dough and lets it sit for thirty-six hours before baking it at seven hundred degrees in a wood-burning oven. "At Mozza most of the comment cards say something about it being as good as sex or wanting it for their last meal," she told Alex Witchel for the *New York Times* (25 Oct. 2011). "But some say, 'Go to Italy and learn the Neapolitan way. What

pie are you making? Is it New York? Chicago? Italian?' And I say no. It's mine."

## EARLY YEARS AND EDUCATION

Nancy Silverton was born on June 20, 1954, in Los Angeles County and was raised in California's San Fernando Valley. Her father, Larry, is a retired lawyer; her mother, Doris, who died in 2001, was a writer who penned scripts for the popular soap opera *General Hospital*. Doris liked to experiment with French and Middle Eastern dishes and was strict about avoiding fast food. She rarely served kid-friendly meals such as macaroni and cheese or peanut-butter-and-jelly sandwiches, but Silverton recalls with fondness a particular lunch-box favorite: her mother's homemade egg-salad sandwiches.

Silverton herself had little interest in cooking and few career ambitions. She casually considered becoming a lawyer, like her father, and when she entered Sonoma State University, she majored in liberal arts. When she began preparing vegetarian meals in the kitchen of her dormitory, she found that she not only enjoyed cooking but had a knack for it. She dropped out before her senior year and sought an apprenticeship in a restaurant kitchen, promising to work for free in exchange for learning everything she could. She had found her calling, and she says that it is now impossible for her to envision any other career path. "I can really only think of things I would never want to do, like the person who called last night to sell me a new phone plan. What if I had to do that?" she joked to Rick Nelson for the Minneapolis *Star Tribune* (1 Feb. 2001). "If I'm not passionate about something, it's difficult for me to do it. Maybe some people can do their job and leave it behind, but not me."

Realizing that she would benefit from more formal training, she traveled to London in 1977 to study at a branch of the famed Le Cordon Bleu culinary institution in London. (Later in her career she took courses at Ecole Lenôtre, a baking school near Paris, but Silverton has said that her lack of French language skills hampered her there.)

After completing her program in London she returned to the United States. In 1979 she found work at Michael's, a high-end restaurant in Santa Monica, California, whose pastry chef, Jimmy Brinkley, opened her eyes to more creative possibilities. "Unlike when I studied at Cordon Bleu and they said don't be creative, Jimmy was a wild man, tasting, changing, and I saw how much flexibility there was in desserts," she recalled to Witchel.

In 1982, the chef Wolfgang Puck hired her as head pastry chef at his newly opened Hollywood hotspot Spago. So beloved were her desserts there that one restaurant reviewer advised his readers to buy stock in cocoa beans because of her popular chocolate torte. Silverton remained with Puck, save for a short tenure at Maxwell's Plum restaurant in New York City, until she started a new venture with fellow Spago chef Mark Peel, also her husband at the time.

## LA BREA BAKERY AND CAMPANILE

Silverton and Peel had gained a solid reputation in the California culinary world during their time at Spago, and they envisioned opening an unfussy trattoria-inspired establishment. With the help of Silverton's mother, they found a sprawling 1920s Spanish-style building said to have once been owned by the actor Charlie Chaplin. Serendipitously, the building had room for commercial ovens, and in January 1989 Silverton began presiding over La Brea Bakery, whose breads stood in stark contrast to the spongy, flavorless loaves that were then standard in most markets. The recipes centered on an original sourdough starter that she developed after much experimentation. While she has been called responsible for changing the tastes of the entire country, that change was far from immediate. "The first thing, we were a bakery, and so people were very surprised to see no cakes there and that made some people mad," Silverton explained to Russ Parsons for the *Los Angeles Times* (29 Jan. 2014). "There was another lady who kept coming in and telling us the bread was dirty, because it had flour on it. There were complaints about too many holes—the peanut butter kept falling through."

Just a few months later, Silverton and Peel opened a restaurant adjoining the bakery. That restaurant, which they named Campanile, became an indelible, even iconic, part of the area's culinary landscape. Among the most treasured of its traditions was Thursday Sandwich Night, which found Silverton at the panini grill, piling such ingredients as salty prosciutto, roasted meats, braised artichokes and leeks, and unusual cheeses onto La Brea bread.

## MOZZA AND OTHER WORK

While at Campanile, Silverton won the 1991 James Beard Foundation Award for best pastry chef, but it was at her next venture that she would earn the foundation's title of outstanding

chef. She had been approached by chef and television personality Mario Batali to join his New York City restaurant Del Posto as a pastry chef but had turned him down, not wanting to uproot her life. Instead, she casually brought up the possibility of collaborating on a California-based venture. Batali seemed uninterested at first. "He had bought into that whole stereotype of LA where there are not serious eaters and they go to bed at 9 o'clock," she recalled to Gary Baum for the *Hollywood Reporter* (14 Feb. 2013).

When Silverton approached Batali with the idea of opening a restaurant based entirely around the concept of mozzarella, inspired by the Italian mozzarella bar Obikà , he relented. "My plan was to do a little place, and it'd be just me behind the counter," she told Baum. "But, this being Mario, the scale grew." Pizzeria Mozza and Osteria Mozza opened in 2007 and 2008, respectively, and Silverton found a ready audience for her squash-blossom-and-burrata pizza, wild-boar-sauced pasta, butterscotch budino, and other creations.

Batali, according to Baum, has referred to Silverton as having "the confidence of an Italian grandmother and the touch of [cello master] Yo-Yo Ma," and the two are said to share a distinct sensibility. Batali himself told Carolynn Carreño for *Food & Wine* (July 2005), "She and I are kindred spirits in the world of simplicity and big flavor."

There are now outposts of the Mozza empire in Singapore and San Diego, among other locations. Writing for *Los Angeles* magazine (Nov. 2007), Patric Kuh opined that "to offer a gamut of Italian dining—one that runs from pizza to waiters in cuff links—is a monumental undertaking" but that Batali and Silverton were succeeding. "Silverton is a minimalist who has found in Italian fresh cheeses and pizza dough a fascination to plumb. Batali's approach is generous and all-embracing, his relationship to Italian food respectful but not reverential," Kuh wrote. He concluded, "There's one basic question that Mozza has to answer: Is it worth all the fuss? The answer is yes."

Silverton also opened the salumi-themed restaurant Chi Spacca in 2013 and has cooked as a guest chef at such Los Angeles spots as Jar and La Terza. She is the author of numerous cookbooks, including *A Twist of the Wrist* (2007) and *The Mozza Cookbook* (2011). In addition to her Beard awards, for decades she has been a fixture on various lists of the best and most influential chefs in the country.

## PERSONAL LIFE

Silverton and Peel, who divorced in 2007, have three children. Silverton maintains a home in Umbria, Italy, where she spends several weeks each year. She sold her interest in La Brea in 2001 for several million dollars but lost her entire fortune when she ignored her father's advice to diversify and invested in a fund run by Bernie Madoff, who was later convicted of financial fraud.

Witchel described the chef as "a small woman, sporting a knot of wiry hair on top of her head, and her body has a tensile quality, like a human rubber band." The description continued, "The physical work of a baker requires agility and stamina and a bent toward stubbornness, or perfectionism, and even behind [sunglasses] that attitude slammed through."

When she is not developing recipes or cooking, Silverton volunteers with Meals-On-Wheels and the Garden School Project of Los Angeles.

## SUGGESTED READING

Baum, Gary. "LA A-List Chef Nancy Silverton Gets Serious about Pork." *Hollywood Reporter*. Hollywood Reporter, 14 Feb. 2013. Web. 24 Nov. 2014.

Bennett, Bev. "Culinary Persuasion." *New Products* Aug. 2007: 32–36. Print.

Bruni, Frank. "In Los Angeles, the Accidental Pizza Maker." *New York Times*. New York Times, 9 May 2007. Web. 24 Nov. 2014.

Carreño, Carolynn. "Nancy Silverton Does the Twist." *Food & Wine*. Time, July 2005. Web. 20 Oct. 2014.

Green, Emily. "An Elegy for Campanile." *LA Weekly*. LA Weekly, 24 Oct. 2012. Web. 24 Nov. 2014.

Kuh, Patric. "Double Vision." *Los Angeles* Nov. 2007: 207–12. Print.

Winer, Laurie. "Building the Perfect Pizza." *Los Angeles* Sept. 2006: 128+. Print.

Witchel, Alex. "Mozzarella as Medium and Muse." *New York Times*. New York Times, 25 Oct. 2011. Web. 24 Nov. 2014.

## SELECTED WORKS

*Mark Peel & Nancy Silverton at Home*, 1994; *Nancy Silverton's Breads from the La Brea Bakery*, 1996; *The Food of Campanile*, 1997; *Nancy Silverton's Pastries from the La Brea Bakery*, 2000; *Nancy Silverton's Sandwich Book*, 2002; *A Twist of the Wrist*, 2007; *The Mozza Cookbook*, 2011

—Mari Rich

# Bill Simmons

**Born:** 1969
**Occupation:** Sports columnist

Bill Simmons is arguably the most influential American sportswriter of the Internet age. After a failed attempt at traditional journalism, he started the sports column The Boston Sports Guy for AOL's *Digital City Boston* website. In 2001, after building a highly dedicated readership, he was hired by the sports media conglomerate ESPN, where he became a prominent voice in the sports world. As a lead columnist for ESPN. com and *ESPN The Magazine*, Simmons became known for pioneering a style of sports writing that connected to the average sports fan. Mixing an encyclopedic sports knowledge and analysis with pop-culture references, irreverent humor, and personal asides, his columns quickly gained widespread popularity.

By the mid-2000s Simmons had become one of ESPN's most popular writers. He eventually segued his online column into other ventures, including a popular podcast, *The B.S. Report*, the award-winning documentary series *30 for 30*, the sports and culture website Grantland, and two best-selling books, *Now I Can Die in Peace: How ESPN's Sports Guy Found Salvation with a Little Help from Nomar, Pedro, Shawshank, and the 2004 Red Sox* (2005) and *The Book of Basketball: The NBA According to the Sports Guy* (2009).

Despite achieving enormous popularity and power at ESPN, Simmons was long a magnet for controversy at the network for his outspoken views. He was suspended by ESPN from the social-networking site Twitter for brief periods in both 2009 and 2013 for outspoken outbursts and was then suspended by the network for three weeks in 2014 when he harshly criticized NFL commissioner Roger Goodell. Simmons and ESPN's acrimonious relationship came to a head in May 2015, when the network unexpectedly announced it would not renew Simmons's contract.

## EARLY LIFE AND EDUCATION

An only child, William "Bill" J. Simmons III was born in 1969, to William Simmons, Jr. and Jan Corbo. He spent his early childhood grow-

Leon Bennett/Getty Images North America/Getty Images

ing up in Marlborough and Brookline, Massachusetts. Simmons's parents divorced when he was thirteen years old, after which he moved to Stamford, Connecticut, to live with his mother, who managed a jewelry store. He remained extremely close to his father and visited him often.

Simmons developed his obsession with sports, particularly basketball, as a child. He grew up rooting for Boston-area sports teams and idolized the Boston Celtics' Larry Bird. His father was a longtime Celtics season ticket holder, and Simmons regularly attended games with him at the Boston Garden. "Of the fifty happiest moments of my life, Bird and the Garden were involved in at least a dozen of them," he revealed in an article titled "An Apostle of Basketball Jesus," for ESPN.com's Page 2 (25 Apr. 2003).

Though Simmons dreamed of following in Bird's footsteps as a professional basketball player, he also fostered an early passion for writing and envisioned writing a sports column as his backup plan. As a boy, Simmons "read every conceivable type of writer" and "had hundreds and hundreds of books," as he told Jason Pinter for the *Huffington Post* (18 Mar. 2010). One of those books included David Halberstam's seminal *The Breaks of the Game* (1981), which he has cited as a major influence in his approach to sports writing.

After attending private schools in Connecticut, Simmons enrolled at the College of the Holy Cross in Worcester, Massachusetts, where he honed his craft as a writer. From his freshman through senior years, he wrote a sports column, called Ramblings, for the school newspaper, the *Crusader*; he also served as the paper's sports editor for two semesters. After earning a bachelor's degree in political science from Holy Cross in 1992, Simmons studied at Boston University. He received a master's degree in print journalism there in 1994.

## "BOSTON SPORTS GUY"

Upon completing his graduate studies, Simmons landed a job at the sports desk of the *Boston Herald*. In that role, he covered high school sports, wrote feature stories, and performed other entry-level tasks, such as "organizing Chinese-food orders," as he recalled bitterly to Rob Tannenbaum for *Rolling Stone* (29 Apr. 2014). Feeling unfulfilled and longing to write his own column, Simmons quit the paper after three years to work as a freelance writer. In an interview with Jonathan Mahler for *New York Times Magazine* (31 May 2011), he explained, "The only way to get a column back then was to go through this whole ridiculous minor-league-newspaper system and then kind of hope that other people died."

After leaving the *Herald*, Simmons started freelancing for the *Boston Phoenix*, a now-defunct alternative weekly. He struggled to make ends meet, however, and quit after three months to work as a bartender and waiter. Not long afterward, Simmons came across a new website hosted by AOL called *Digital City Boston*, which featured a columnist known as the Boston Movie Guy. After much persistence, he eventually persuaded the website's editor to give him a spinoff site. Simmons's sports and pop-culture column, The Boston Sports Guy, debuted in 1997. Originally available only through an e-mail mailing list, the column went live in 1998.

Because Simmons earned only fifty dollars a week for his column, he continued to work as a bartender and waiter at night. Nevertheless, The Boston Sports Guy, which was written from a fan's perspective and showcased the unique style for which Simmons would eventually become known, gradually started to build a strong following, thanks to a loyal network of friends who forwarded it around the then-burgeoning Internet. Simmons explained to Pinter, "I needed to bring readers to my site every day . . . and the only way that was happening was if I pushed the envelope and wrote angles that I wasn't seeing anywhere else."

## RISE TO PROMINENCE AT ESPN

Simmons's big break came in 2001, when John Walsh, ESPN's longtime executive editor, read an irreverent column he had written about that year's ESPYs, the network's annual sports awards show. Walsh subsequently invited Simmons, whose column was then attracting around twelve thousand readers a day, to write three guest columns for ESPN.com's Page 2, a sports and culture site that the network had launched in 2000. Simmons was offered a full-time position after his first article, "Is Clemens the Antichrist?" (about former Boston Red Sox pitcher Roger Clemens), generated significant buzz around the site.

As a featured columnist for ESPN.com's Page 2 and, eventually, *ESPN The Magazine*, Simmons, who simply became known as the Sports Guy, quickly developed a rabid readership for his one-of-a-kind columns, which included everything from profiles and features to confessionals, lists, running diaries, and movie reviews. He distinguished himself with his unparalleled knowledge of sports, partiality toward Boston sports teams, penchant for pop-culture minutiae, and proclivity for high word counts, with many of his columns exceeding five thousand words. "At the center of Simmons's columns is not the increasingly unknowable athlete but the experience of the fan," Mahler wrote. "His frame of reference is himself."

During his early years at ESPN, Simmons briefly scaled back his columns to foray into television writing. In 2002 he moved from Boston to Los Angeles, and in April of the following year, he began working as a comedy writer for the late-night talk show, *Jimmy Kimmel Live!* He ultimately left the show after a year and a half to focus full time on his column but remained in California. Kimmel, one of Simmons's close friends, told Warren St. John for the *New York Times* (20 Nov. 2005), "Sports is a part of Bill's life, and it's woven throughout."

By 2005 Simmons had become one of the most popular sportswriters in the country, with his columns attracting an average of five hundred thousand visitors a month. Later that year he took advantage of that popularity by releasing his first book, *Now I Can Die in Peace* (2005), a collection of his columns from the years leading up to the Boston Red Sox's historic 2004 championship season. The book spent five weeks on the *New York Times*' extended best-seller list.

## BUILDING A MEDIA EMPIRE

At ESPN, Simmons transformed himself from an online columnist to multifaceted media personality with a wide-ranging presence. Among his projects was a podcast for ESPN.com called *The B.S. Report*, launched in 2007. On *The B.S. Report*, which aired two- to three-hour-long episodes a week, Simmons discussed sports and pop culture with a wide range of guests, from athletes and celebrities to family and friends. Though initially launched as a trial ground for Simmons's radio and television voice, *The B.S. Report* later became the most downloaded podcast on ESPN.com and one of the most popular on the web. In 2013 the podcast generated thirty-two million downloads.

Also in 2007 Simmons conceived the idea for an ESPN documentary series, called *30 for 30*, that would be pegged to the network's thirtieth anniversary. Premiering in October 2009 the series featured thirty documentaries that chronicled important moments in sports during ESPN's three decades of operation. As an executive producer, Simmons lured a slew of high-profile directors to create the documentaries, including Peter Berg, Barry Levinson, Albert Maysles, and Billy Corben. The series received widespread critical acclaim, earning a Peabody Award in 2010; a second season debuted in 2012.

Simmons's second book, *The Book of Basketball*, was released in October 2009. Offering a comprehensive and humorous look at professional basketball, the 700-page, heavily footnoted book debuted at number one on the *New York Times* nonfiction best-seller list. "It's the type of book you can pick up, put down, skim ahead, consume however you want," Simmons told David Davis for *Los Angeles Magazine* (1 Nov. 2009). "By the time you're done you'll feel like you understand the NBA."

In 2010 Simmons agreed to terms with ESPN on a new five-year contract. The contract paid him an estimated five million dollars annually, making him the highest-paid sportswriter in the country. As part of the new deal, Simmons was given his own website, Grantland, which launched in 2011 in partnership with ESPN. The site was centered around provocative, long-form articles on sports and culture and featured contributions from some of the most renowned writers in the country, including Wesley Morris, Chuck Klosterman, Jonah Keri, and Colson Whitehead. Simmons served as a regular contributor to the site while serving as its editor-in-chief.

From 2012 to 2014 Simmons served as an on-air personality for ESPN's pregame show, *NBA Countdown*. Prior to the 2014–15 season, he left the show to launch his own NBA show, *The Grantland Basketball Hour*, which debuted in October 2014.

## SPLIT WITH ESPN

During his tenure at ESPN, Simmons often courted controversy for his outspokenness against network colleagues, policies, and properties. He was suspended by ESPN from the social-networking site Twitter for two weeks in 2009, when he made derisive tweets about the hosts of an ESPN-affiliate radio show. He was briefly suspended from Twitter again in 2013, when he posted critical tweets about ESPN's controversial debate show, *First Take*. In September 2014 he was suspended by the network for three weeks after lambasting NFL commissioner Roger Goodell over his handling of the Ray Rice domestic violence scandal and daring ESPN to punish him for the remarks.

On May 7, 2015, Simmons again criticized Goodell while appearing as a guest on former ESPN anchor Dan Patrick's eponymous radio show. The next day John Skipper, president of ESPN, announced that the network would not be renewing his contract. This promptly ended Simmons's fourteen-year run at the network. Simmons was to be paid through the end of his contract, set to expire in September 2015. However, he would no longer run or take part in any of the ESPN platforms he helped create. According to many media observers, his departure from ESPN instantly made him the most coveted sports media free agent.

## PERSONAL LIFE

Simmons has a daughter, Zoe, and son, Benjamin, with his wife, Kari. Kari has been referenced and made guest posts in Simmons's columns as the Sports Gal, and Simmons's father has likewise appeared as the Sports Dad.

## SUGGESTED READING

Davis, David. "He Shoots, He Scores." *Los Angeles Magazine*. Los Angeles Magazine, 1 Nov. 2009. Web. 20 May 2015.

Mahler, Jonathan. "Can Bill Simmons Win the Big One?" *New York Times Magazine*. New York Times, 31 May 2011. Web. 20 May 2015.

Miller, James Andrew, and Tom Shales. *Those Guys Have All the Fun: Inside the World of ESPN*. New York: Little, 2011. Print.

Simmons, Bill. "Interview with Bill Simmons, Author of *The Book of Basketball*." Interview by Jason Pinter. *Huffington Post*. TheHuffingtonPost.com, 18 Mar. 2010. Web. 20 May 2015.

St. John, Warren. "That Sports Guy Thrives Online." *New York Times*. New York Times, 20 Nov. 2005. Web. 20 May 2015.

Tannenbaum, Rob. "Bill Simmons' Big Score." *Rolling Stone*. Rolling Stone, 29 Apr. 2014. Web. 20 May 2015.

—Chris Cullen

# Abdel Fattah el-Sisi

**Born:** November 19, 1954
**Occupation:** President of Egypt

On June 8, 2014, Abdel Fattah el-Sisi was sworn in as the sixth president of Egypt, marking a new chapter in the country's turbulent political landscape of the 2010s. After years of military service, during which he rose to the rank of general, Sisi first came to national prominence when he was named Egypt's director of military intelligence and a member of the Supreme Council of Armed Forces (SCAF) following the Egyptian Revolution of 2011. His rise to power continued when Egypt's then president Mohammed Morsi appointed Sisi commander-in-chief of all Egypt's armed forces as well as minister of defense in August 2012. Then in July 2013 the Egyptian military, led by Sisi, and thousands of civilian protestors called for Morsi's resignation before removing him from power. This period of mass protests and violent civil unrest, including what Negar Azimi for the *New Yorker* (8 Jan. 2014) called "the bloodiest massacre in modern Egyptian history," put the country's future in jeopardy. The Egyptian people wanted a new, strong leader.

After his lead role in overthrowing Morsi, Sisi's popularity ran sky high; his picture adorned posters across the Egyptian capital city of Cairo and shops sold all manner of Sisi-branded merchandise. A Cairo resident told Waleed Abdul Rahman for the London-based Arabic newspaper *Asharq al-Awsat* (24 May 2014), "It is as if the entire city is celebrating Sisi, day and night." After resigning from the military in order to sub-

Russian Presidential Press and Information Office/Wikimedia Commons

mit his candidacy in the Egyptian presidential race, Sisi swept to victory by a large margin and was officially named the winner of the election on June 3, 2014. Sisi took power with an unprecedented level of control over the various institutions of the Egyptian state, exceeding even that of former president Gamal Abdel Nasser.

## CHILDHOOD AND EARLY MILITARY CAREER

Abdel Fattah Said Hussein Khalil el-Sisi was born on November 19, 1954, the second of eight children of Said "Hassan" el-Sisi and Malika Titani. He was raised in the Gamaleya district of Cairo, and his family was wealthy but humble, conservative but not radical, and devoutly religious. They owned a shop in the Khan el-Khalili, a bazaar that attracts tourists visiting the pyramids of Giza, where they produced decorative pieces in the arabesque style. As a youngster, Sisi worked in his family's shop after school and studied at the library at al-Azhar University. According to Patrick Kingsley for the *Guardian* (22 May 2014), Sisi was an obedient child, if a bit reclusive. "I don't think he had any interesting stories from when he was a child," Sisi's cousin Ali Hamama told Kingsley. "He was just so serious."

Sisi's involvement in the military began early, as he attended a secondary school run by the army. He then entered Egypt's military academy for training as an officer, and graduated from the

program in 1977. He served in an infantry corps and worked his way up the ranks, eventually commanding a mechanized infantry division. Although he entered service too late for combat experience in any of Egypt's wars with Israel, he quickly began rising through the ranks. Sisi gained further leadership skills upon graduating from the Egyptian Command and Staff College in 1987. In 1992 he trained at the United Kingdom's Joint Command and Staff College, and served as Egypt's military attaché in Saudi Arabia.

From 2005 to 2006 Sisi spent a year at the US Army War College in Pennsylvania studying for his master's degree. It was a tense time for American-Arab relations, with the United States involved in the Iraq War, leading to frequent arguments. Yet Sisi's American colleagues recall him as friendly, polite, and controlled, and his political personality began to develop. Sherifa Zuhur, one of Sisi's professors, told Mike Giglio for *Newsweek* (16 Aug. 2013) that Sisi "was ready for debate, but not aggressive," adding that he "can be angered, but possesses a lot of self-control and would choose not to respond when others might do so. He was not quiet because he was passive, but more contemplative, waiting, watching, and following along." During his time at the War College, Sisi also wrote a paper called "Democracy in the Middle East." In it, Giglio reported, he championed democracy based on Islamic beliefs, noting the parallel influence of Christianity on the American government.

## REVOLUTION AND RISE TO POWER

In early 2011 the revolutionary spirit of the Arab Spring uprisings swept through Cairo's Tahrir Square and the rest of Egypt. Thousands protested the alleged corruption and dictatorship of the Egyptian government. On February 11, President Hosni Mubarak stepped down after thirty years in office, ceding control of the government to the SCAF. Sisi, a relative unknown, was appointed head of military intelligence and reconnaissance and a member of the SCAF.

Within days the military announced a plan to restore the constitution (which was suspended) and the parliament (which was disbanded), and hold a presidential election, all within six months. The announcement divided Egyptian citizens, previously united against Mubarak's regime, along religious and political lines. Islamist groups, like the Muslim Brotherhood, wanted to hold elections first in hopes of influencing the contents of the new constitution. Egyptian liberals and secularists wanted to write the constitution first. The military stood as a separate group supposedly loyal to the will of the people, but many questioned the affiliations of the powerful generals, including the possibility that Sisi would support the Islamists contrary to the army's traditionally secular stance.

After Mubarak's ouster, the military government started beating and arresting protesters. In March Sisi came to widespread international attention for the first time, as he defended the so-called virginity tests administered to a group of female protestors. The "tests" were humiliating vaginal exams meant to distinguish whether or not the women were virgins because, according to Sisi, only virgins could be raped. Although Sisi's official argument was that the tests were meant "to protect the girls from rape as well as to protect the soldiers and officers from rape accusations," as quoted by G. Willow Wilson in the *Guardian* (3 Sept. 2012), critics condemned the policy as an act of intimidation. Sisi later promised Amnesty International that the practice would be ended.

The Muslim Brotherhood won a majority when parliamentary elections were finally held in November 2011. Just before the presidential run-off election in June 2012, the military shut down the parliament and gave itself the power to control the national budget and issue laws—significantly diminishing the authority of the office of the president. The Muslim Brotherhood's candidate Mohamed Morsi was elected to the presidency by popular vote, a first in the history of Egypt. Thanks to negotiations behind the scenes, Morsi appointed Sisi to replace Field Marshal Mohamed Hussein Tantawi, who had led the SCAF, as defense minister and commander-in-chief of the armed forces.

## GOVERNMENT TAKEOVER

Within a year of Morsi's election, civil unrest again flared up, as opponents of the Muslim Brotherhood voiced their dissatisfaction with the government. Sisi began to distance himself from the president, though he repeatedly stated that the military would not attempt a coup. Protests against Morsi turned violent and tensions grew while Sisi bided his time. Then on July 1, 2013, Sisi announced the military's ultimatum that Morsi resign within forty-eight hours to satisfy the people or face intervention by the army.

Morsi refused to step down and was allegedly kidnapped and detained by the army. Sisi, the de facto leader of state despite the installation of Adly Mansour as an interim president, publicly announced the military takeover on July 3, 2013. In nearly every respect, Sisi appeared to represent Egypt's old guard—not only was he a member of the military, he had been a powerful general in the Mubarak regime—but Egyptians embraced him as a revolutionary and a leader. Many considered him a national hero, and he became wildly popular. Sisi even won the tentative support of ideologically disparate groups ranging from the ultraconservative Islamist al-Nour party to the more liberal Free Egyptians Party and New Wafd Party.

Meanwhile, Sisi and the military continued to paint the Muslim Brotherhood as extremists. In an interview with Lally Weymouth for the *Washington Post* (5 Aug. 2013) a month after the coup, Sisi suggested that Morsi was merely a puppet of his organization. "The Egyptian people felt that he wasn't the man making the decisions and that he wasn't their president," he said. "The leadership was in the hands of the Brotherhood." On July 16, 2013, Sisi took the position of deputy prime minister in addition to his military role, and ten days later called for public support of "antiterrorism" measures against Morsi supporters. This led to a violent crackdown on the Muslim Brotherhood throughout the summer of 2013—killing, according to some estimates, some two thousand protestors. The military arrested the Brotherhood's top leaders, and the group was named an illegal terrorist organization in late 2013, shortly after the government passed a law making any protest impossible without an official permit.

## PRESIDENCY

Sisi resigned his military post on March 26, 2014, and announced his intention to run for president. He adopted the campaign slogan, "Long Live Egypt," and forwarded a platform to combat poverty and continue his crackdown on the Brotherhood. "There will be nothing called the Muslim Brotherhood during my tenure," he said on the campaign trail, as quoted by Kingsley. On June 3, 2014, Sisi won the presidential election with over 96 percent of the vote. He was officially sworn in on June 8, 2014.

Although Western governments expressed concern over the suppression of peaceful protest and the consolidation of power, most eventually recognized Sisi's government as legitimate. The United States did suspend its military aid package to Egypt, but began restoring it by late 2014. Nearly a year into his tenure, Sisi remained firmly in control and largely popular, though the mention of his name did not inspire the euphoria that it once did. A May 2014 poll by the Pew Research Center even found his approval rating had declined to 54 percent as citizens realized Sisi's election was not an instant cure to the country's problems. However, the former general's firm grip on power, extending throughout all elements of the state, kept him insulated from any real opposition. The BBC News (16 May 2014) summarized Egyptian sentiment regarding Sisi best: "Many Egyptians see in him the strong leader needed to overcome the instability that has beset Egypt. . . . But his ascendancy has left some worrying that it heralds a return to [an] authoritarian security state."

## PERSONAL LIFE

Sisi married Entissar Amer in 1977, and the couple has four children: Mustafa, Mahmoud, Hassan, and Aya. He is known for protecting the privacy of his family and close friends.

## SUGGESTED READING

Azimi, Negar. "The Egyptian Army's Unlikely Allies." *New Yorker*. Condé Nast, 8 Jan. 2014. Web. 18 Mar. 2015.

"Egypt: Abdul Fattah al-Sisi profile." *BBC News*. BBC, 16 May 2014. Web. 18 Mar. 2015.

Giglio, Mike. "General Al-Sisi: The Man Who Now Runs Egypt." *Newsweek*. Newsweek, 16 Aug. 2013. Web. 18 Mar. 2015.

Kingsley, Patrick. "Abdel Fatah al-Sisi: Behind the Public Face of Egypt's Soon-to-be President." *Guardian*. Guardian News and Media, 22 May 2014. Web. 18 Mar. 2015.

Weymouth, Lally. "Excerpts from *Washington Post* interview with Egyptian Gen. Abdel Fatah al-Sissi." *Washington Post*. Washington Post, 5 Aug. 2013. Web. 18 Mar. 2015.

Wilson, G. Willow. "From Virginity Test to Power." *Guardian*. Guardian News and Media, 3 Sept. 2012. Web. 18 Mar. 2015.

—Molly Hagan

# Jenny Slate

**Born:** March 25, 1982
**Occupation:** Actor, comedian

After being known for several years as the young comic who accidently swore on *Saturday Night Live* (*SNL*) in 2009, Jenny Slate has come

Mingle Media TV/Wikimedia Commons

fully into her own in recent years. Her collaboration with her husband, Dean Fleischer-Camp, on the stop-motion animated character Marcel the Shell has charmed millions through videos and best-selling books. More recently, she took on the captivating lead role in the indie film *Obvious Child* (2014), in which she portrays a young stand-up comic facing the prospect of an abortion. Slate has received widespread acclaim for both of these creative efforts, leading many entertainment reporters and film critics to conclude that she may finally be poised to make great strides as an actor.

Slate is currently involved with no fewer than four television shows, appearing as the voice of the character of Tammy in *Bob's Burgers* since 2012; as Mona-Lisa in *Parks and Recreation* from 2013 until the show's final season in 2015; as a variety of characters on *Kroll Show* since 2013; and as Jess in *Married*, which began in 2014. "It's nice to feel like I'm on the road to being an American movie actress," Slate said of her current career trajectory to Kevin Fallon for the *Daily Beast* (17 Oct. 2014). "But whatever the road is it does feel new, and it does feel good, and it feels like I made it for myself with people I know and love."

## CHILDHOOD AND EDUCATION

Jenny Sarah Slate was born on March 25, 1982, in Milton, Massachusetts. The middle of three sisters, she was raised in a Jewish and artistic household; her paternal grandmother was a survivor of the Holocaust. Together since high school, her parents still live in Milton. Ron, her father, is a published poet whose collections include *The Incentive of the Maggot* (2005) and *The Great Wave* (2009), while her mother, Nancy, is a raku potter.

One of Slate's favorite childhood memories consists of repeatedly listening to *Classic Crystal*, a greatest-hits LP by the country singer Crystal Gayle that her father had given to her. "I played it on my Fisher-Price record player over and over again," Slate told David Kamp for *Vanity Fair* (Nov. 2014). "I remember thinking that she was the most beautiful woman I had ever seen, and singing along to all the songs and just really, really yearning for an adult female experience." She also has a distinct memory of meeting former Massachusetts governor Mike Dukakis at a Boston Pops Orchestra concert.

Slate studied at the Milton Academy, a prep school for grades kindergarten through twelve. Named the valedictorian of her class, she claims that she only received the accolade because she had pressured her classmates to vote for her. Upon her graduation, she moved to New York City to study at Columbia University, where she earned her degree in English and comparative literature education while performing in sketch comedy and improv groups. She told Stacey Anderson in an interview for the *New York Times* (8 Nov. 2013) that she often uses her education in her comedy: "The things that I was interested in ranged from 20th-century poetry to plagues in Dickensian London. I use my education a lot, because I tend to make fun of the things that I love."

## EARLY CAREER AND *SNL*

Upon graduating from Columbia in 2004, she began to explore the alternative-comedy scene in New York City's East Village neighborhood, where other noted comics got their start. She had become interested in comedy in college, prompted in part through her discovery of Amy Sedaris's Comedy Central series *Strangers with Candy* on DVD but also through her fast friendship with fellow student Gabe Liedman, who would go on to become her comedic partner. In an interview for *Boston* magazine's *Boston Daily* newsletter (27 Feb. 2009), she described her comedic relationship with Liedman: "We hit it off right away. We call our relationship a nonsexual romance because I swear I locked eyes with Gabe and we made each other laugh all the

time. We have the same sense of humor. . . . He was really my first friend where I had that connection with."

Slate initially received attention as a regular commentator on pop culture topics on VH1, but soon began making appearances in 2009 on television shows like *Late Night with Jimmy Fallon* (on which she portrayed an NBC page named Jenny). She then made guest appearances on *Brothers* (2009) and *Bored to Death* (2009–10), among others. Her big break also came in 2009 when she was tapped to be one of the new cast members on NBC's long-running sketch comedy show, *Saturday Night Live*, for the 2009–10 season. Unfortunately for Slate, she accidently cursed on camera during her very first sketch. While the producers of the show were not fined for the profanity and cast members offered support, she felt that she would not likely be asked back for another season.

Despite this dark cloud, Slate reveled in the opportunity to live out part of her dream. In addition to mastering celebrity interpretations typical of the show, which included Lady Gaga and Hoda Kotb, she also played the part of an original recurring character. As Tina Tina Cheneuse, she attempted to sell custom doorbells, alarm clocks, and car horns. "I could describe it as a series of dates with someone whom you've always wanted to go out with," she told Mike Agresta for *Columbia College Today* (Fall 2011) of her time on the iconic show. "Every single second you're thinking 'Oh my God, I can't believe this is happening.'"

However, though she waited anxiously by the phone at the end of the season, her contract was not renewed. While Slate can look back with some understanding—but she has never watched the infamous clip—she remembers how the loss of her *SNL* gig had devastated her.

## COMING BACK WITH MARCEL THE SHELL

Slate faced a couple of nervous months of unemployment after departing *SNL*. Returning to her first love, stand-up comedy, was a struggle because she feared that her audience simply perceived her as the girl who had sworn on live television. Each time she did her routine, she felt like she was bombing. As a result, she developed crippling stage fright. In an interview with Terry Gross for National Public Radio (26 June 2014), she recalled how she finally cured herself: "I had some friends that went to this hypnotist to stop smoking, and I kind of love things that seem magical. And I liked that it was in Santa Monica, and I had to go near the ocean to get my brain washed out or whatever. . . . And whether or not it was real, Saturday I had a show and it was the best show I'd had in two years—and my stage fright went away."

Something that helped boost her confidence was a collaboration she began with her future husband, Fleischer-Camp. It had all started with a voice she was doing around the time her *SNL* gig was coming to an end. She told Anderson, "I wasn't fired yet. I knew I was going to be. I felt myself starting to become a bit watered down and sluggish and hard on myself in a way that is not helpful. And I started to talk in a little voice, and my husband noticed it. He was like: 'You need to remember that you're a creative person no matter what your job is. You've been a creative person forever, so continue to do that. You don't need to wait for permission from a television show that doesn't understand you.'"

That voice, however, inspired the creation of a stop-motion character—Marcel the Shell, a one-eyed tiny mollusk with pink sneakers and an oversized sense of confidence and an appealingly gentle wisdom. The film shorts are recorded in Slate and Fleischer-Camp's home, with Slate, as Marcel, improvising answers to an off-screen interviewer voiced by Fleischer-Camp. The first video, *Marcel the Shell with Shoes On*, debuted at a local comedy show before it was released on YouTube in 2010 and became an immediate cult sensation, drawing in millions of viewers. The second installment was posted in 2011. Slate is proud of the positive message that Marcel's small but self-assured character conveys. "You don't have to be in the brightest, shiniest state of being an individual to feel like you're exceptional," she explained to Fallon. Always admirers of children's literature, the couple agreed that the next step for Marcel should be a children's picture book, which was published that same year as *Marcel the Shell with Shoes On: Things about Me*. While they wrote the book together, they hired a talented oil painter to supply the unique illustrations that landed the book on the *New York Times* bestseller list.

At the behest of her agent, Slate agreed, with reluctance, to take a role in *Alvin and the Chipmunks: Chipwrecked*, which was also released in theaters in 2011. She subsequently did some more television work and voiced a character in the 2012 animated feature film adaptation of the Dr. Seuss book *The Lorax*. After an almost three-year hiatus, a third short featuring Marcel

became available on YouTube in 2014. Marcel's husband-and-wife creators followed up their first successful children's book adaptation with a second, *Marcel the Shell: The Most Surprised I've Ever Been*, later that year. They have reportedly been in talks with studios about making a full-length Marcel film.

When asked about Marcel's ever-increasing popularity, Slate suggested that much of it has to do with his inspiring personality. She explained the origins of that personality to Rachel Lubitz for the *Washington Post* (31 Oct. 2014): "I think it comes from an assertion of self-love that I felt like I needed at that time and that calm wisdom and bright intelligence of Marcel is something that is with him all the time. I think it comes from a wish that I could be always be comfortable with myself."

## OBVIOUS CHILD

In 2009 Slate starred in *Obvious Child*, a short film about a young woman who has an abortion, which was directed and co-written by Gillian Robespierre. In 2014 Robespierre asked Slate to reprise her role in a new, feature-length version of *Obvious Child*. The film takes a realistic approach to the abortion issue but never loses sight of the main character's humanity or sense of humor. "Our film is not an agenda movie in any way," Slate said to Carrie Battan for *Rolling Stone* (2 June 2014). "The whole point is that women have this procedure, and they should have it safely, and it's a part of life. It doesn't have to be this giant *obelisk* sticking out."

In the film, Slate plays a twenty-seven-year-old stand-up comic who discovers she is pregnant after a one-night stand. Realizing she does not have the emotional maturity to care for a child, she opts to have an abortion. For Slate, the role was appealing because it allowed her to use both her comedic and dramatic skills as an actor. "The character is at once really gentle and very bold and sweet, but [she] also can be rather bawdy at times," she remarked in her interview with Gross. "I do a lot of comedy work but have yet to do real vulnerable stuff." *Obvious Child* received generally favorable reviews from film critics. For her role in the film, Slate won several honors, including the 2015 Critics' Choice Movie Award for best actress in a comedy.

## PERSONAL LIFE

Having lived in New York, specifically Brooklyn, for several years during the beginning of her career, Slate eventually relocated to Los

Angeles. After seven years together, she married Fleischer-Camp, a filmmaker, in 2012. The couple has two small dogs, Reggie and Arthur.

## SUGGESTED READING

Anderson, Stacey. "Equal Parts Teeny and Terrifying." *New York Times*. New York Times, 8 Nov. 2013. Web. 17 Apr. 2015.

Battan, Carrie. "Laugh Track: Jenny Slate's Winding Road from 'SNL' to 'Obvious Child.'" *Rolling Stone*. Rolling Stone, 2 June 2014. Web. 17 Apr. 2015.

Fallon, Kevin. "The Casual Genius of Jenny Slate: 'Marcel the Shell,' 'Obvious Child,' and the Ghost of 'SNL.'" *Daily Beast*. Daily Beast, 17 Oct. 2014. Web. 17 Apr. 2015.

Lubitz, Rachel. "Jenny Slate and Dean Fleischer-Camp Talk Their Most Beloved Creation, Marcel the Shell." *Washington Post*. Washington Post, 31 Oct. 2014. Web. 17 Apr. 2015.

Slate, Jenny, and Gillian Robespierre. "The Women behind 'Obvious Child' Talk Farts, Abortion and Stage Fright." Interview by Terry Gross. *NPR*. NPR, 26 June 2014. Web. 17 Apr. 2015.

## SELECTED WORKS

*Saturday Night Live*, 2009–10; *Marcel the Shell with Shoes On*, 2010; *Alvin and the Chipmunks: Chipwrecked*, 2011; *Marcel the Shell with Shoes On, 2*, 2011; *The Lorax*, 2012; *Parks and Recreation*, 2013–15; *Kroll Show*, 2013–2015; *Obvious Child*, 2014; *Marcel the Shell with Shoes On, 3*, 2014; *Married*, 2014–15

—Christopher Mari

# Sam Smith

**Born:** May 9, 1992
**Occupation:** Singer

"You may not yet be familiar with his face but chances are that if you turned on the radio in 2013, you'll have heard Sam Smith's voice," read the official announcement that the British singer had been named the Sound of 2014 by the BBC. While Smith has released just one full-length album, *In the Lonely Hour*, industry insiders have predicted a long and successful career for him. *In the Lonely Hour* sold more than a million copies in the United Kingdom and in the United States, garnered four Grammy

Awards, and led to a show at New York City's massive Madison Square Garden that sold out in less than thirty minutes.

"Key to Mr. Smith's success has been his sweet tenor voice, which climbs to intense, androgynous peaks," Ben Sisario wrote for the *New York Times* (4 Feb. 2015). Because of the ethereal quality of his voice and his choice of romantically heartfelt material, he is often likened to fellow British singer Adele—a comparison he has found flattering but tiresome. "If we went back 30 or 40 years, there'd be many more people like that: Etta James, Ella Fitzgerald," he told Sisario. "It wasn't about the celebrity; it was about the music and the lyrics." He elaborated on that theme during an interview with Amy Wallace for *GQ* (Feb. 2015). "I love pop culture. But I feel like class and romance have gotten lost," he asserted. "We've become a bit lazy, not just in terms of music. I miss the days when girls would wear full long dresses and just stand onstage and sing. That's what I'm trying to bring back: that timeless element. I want to create music that people will be listening to in fifty years."

## EARLY YEARS

Samuel "Sam" Frederick Smith, who has two younger sisters, was born on May 9, 1992, in London, England. He was raised in the village of Great Chishill, not far from Cambridge. His father, Frederick Smith, stayed at home to raise the children, and his mother, Kate Cassidy, had a lucrative job as a bonds and currency broker. The family lived in a large home with a pool that they called the "pink house."

Cassidy hailed from a line of feminist role models—Smith's great-aunts were among the first female bankers in Great Britain—and the singer considers himself a staunch feminist as well. "When I was young, my mum and dad used to have me and my sisters come downstairs to dinner parties, and we used to sit at the table with groups of my mum's work friends," he recalled to Jessica Robertson for *Fader* magazine (June–July 2014). "I'd watch my mum hold her own until the very end with these men, who were hard businessmen." Sometimes at those parties, Smith was called upon to sing for the guests, mounting a small elevated area in the conservatory of the house and plugging in an amplifier he had purchased for himself.

When Smith was a teen, Cassidy was fired from her job in the wake of accusations that she was neglecting her duties in order to manage his fledgling career. She sued for lost salary, bonuses, and stock options, and while the court's decision was not made public, British tabloids reported that she had won £800,000.

## MUSIC EDUCATION

During the long drives to St Thomas More Catholic Primary in the town of Saffron Walden, his parents had heard him belting out tunes from the backseat—his first musical memory was of his mother playing a Whitney Houston album in the car and singing along—and they had become determined to nurture his obvious natural talent. When he was eight years old, they hired a local jazz performer, Joanna Eden, to give him formal voice lessons, and so impressed was she, that by the time he was a teen, she was hiring him on occasion to sing back-up vocals when she performed in local clubs. He also began singing with Youth Music Theatre UK (YMT), a company for performers under twenty-one, and he landed a role in their 2007 production of *Oh! Carol*, which featured the songs of Neil Sedaka. He recalled one year in which he was in six different productions, racing to rehearsals after school and foregoing social events.

Smith, who was also a member of the Bishop's Stortford Junior Operatics group and the Cantate Youth Choir, recalls that he was content "80 percent of the time," as he told Patrick Doyle for *Rolling Stone* (28 Jan. 2015).

## HUSTLING FOR FAME

While talent managers began expressing interest in him early on, little came of those discussions. "When I was 14 or 15, I was promised stardom," he told Robertson. "It was sad, actually. [My managers] would literally say, 'You're going to be this famous by next year.' I was thinking, 'Great, I can leave school at 16.' . . . It never materialized, and I looked like a complete idiot. I remember when Lady Gaga was coming out, watching her and hearing her story of how she hustled in New York for everything. I remember thinking 'Right, that's what I need to do.'"

Abandoning a series of ineffectual managers and in the wake of his parents' separation, Smith moved to London after earning his A-levels at St Mary's Catholic School to try becoming a serious songwriter and performer on his own. It was a frightening time, he has told interviewers; most of his friends were enrolling in college, and at age eighteen he was taking a series of low-level jobs, including cleaning the bathroom at a bar, to support himself. He recalled to Mark Savage for BBC News (10 Jan. 2014), "I just had to clean up everything that happened at night—which was horrendous. Then the bar I worked in last, which I kind of helped to manage, was in the City so there was a lot of chucking drunk people out."

## RECORDING CAREER TAKES OFF

It was during this period that a friend of Smith's introduced him to songwriter Jimmy Napes (James Napier), with whom he wrote "Lay Me Down." Napes sent the haunting ballad to the club-music duo Disclosure (brothers Guy and Howard Lawrence) in 2012. Impressed by his evocative falsetto, they featured Smith on their next single, "Latch," which reached the top twenty on the British charts. Guy Lawrence was shocked upon meeting Smith in person for the first time and realizing that he was a white man. "I actually thought he was going to be a black woman, like Samantha Smith or something," Lawrence told Sisario.

"Latch" caught the attention of Capitol Records president Nick Raphael, who quickly signed Smith. "It was a breakthrough made possible by something Smith hadn't yet explored musically: contrast," Robertson opined. "His voice is inherently traditional and lends itself to old standards; he has covered Judy Garland, Frank Sinatra and Chaka Khan to great effect. But pairing up with Disclosure . . . added a contemporary edge to Sam Smith that made him sound, for once, as young as his age." A similar contrast was apparent when Smith collaborated with British producer Naughty Boy on the dance track "La," which reached the top of the charts and became one of the best-selling singles of 2013.

It was his own single, "Lay Me Down," however, that Smith credits for really launching his career. It was released in March 2013, later reaching number eight on the Billboard Hot 100 chart and, even before his full-length debut album had hit the shelves, accolades began accumulating. He took home a 2014 BRIT Award in the critics' choice category, was named BBC Sound of 2014, and was tapped to perform as a musical guest on the iconic American program *Saturday Night Live*.

### IN THE LONELY HOUR

In January 2014 Smith released the seven-track EP *Nirvana*, and he followed that with *In the Lonely Hour*, which went multiplatinum in the United States. Critics, however, did not offer it universal praise; in a review for *Pitchfork* (19 June 2014), for example, Andrew Ryce complained, "Sam Smith possesses one hell of a set of pipes, able to go from a commanding lower register to an inhumanly high squawk in record time. . . . But the main problem with *In the Lonely Hour* . . . [is] it feels like the record company has groomed him within an inch of his life." Still, most critiques were complimentary. Writing for the All Music website, Andy Kellman echoed the sentiments of other reviewers when he wrote, "The dominance of stripped-down backdrops—some with merely piano, acoustic guitar, and conservative strings—is somewhat surprising. That puts all the more focus on Smith's voice and words." Kellman concluded, "This is an understated and promising first step from an unpredictable and distinctive talent."

The album—which featured the blockbuster singles "Stay with Me" and "I'm Not the Only One"—garnered Smith four statuettes at the Fifty-Seventh Annual Grammy Awards: best new artist, record of the year and song of the year for "Stay with Me," and best pop vocal album for *In the Lonely Hour*. At the 2015 BRIT Awards, Smith took home honors in the categories of British breakthrough act and global success.

Smith's triumph was tainted somewhat when "Stay with Me," which reached the number-two spot on Billboard's Hot 100 and became ubiquitous on soft-rock and top-40 radio, became the target of plagiarism charges because of its simi-larity to the 1989 Tom Petty hit "I Won't Back Down." The matter culminated in Smith awarding Petty and his cowriter, Jeff Lynne, 12.5 percent of the royalties from the song and listing them in the credits.

In May 2015 Smith underwent surgery at Massachusetts General Hospital for hemorrhaged vocal cords but was able to speak again by early June. The Australia tour that had been canceled due to his injury was rescheduled for the end of the year.

### SEXUALITY IN THE SPOTLIGHT

Smith has long been aware that he is gay and sometimes suffered harassment because of it. Once, as he was walking through Great Chishill with his father, a passing motorist had yelled a homophobic slur at him. "I was just embarrassed that my dad had to see that, because I could only imagine how you feel as a parent," he told Doyle. "I was always embarrassed for the people around me." In London, as in Great Chishill, he was sometimes subject to homophobic taunts and he was once physically attacked while walking down the street.

Tabloid journalists, initially unaware that he was gay, linked Smith to model Daisy Lowe until the two confirmed that they were simply platonic friends. (He did have a short-lived relationship with another model, Jonathan Zeizel.) Even those who did not realize Smith was gay, learned of the fact at the Grammy Awards, when he said during his acceptance speech, "I want to thank the man who this record is about, who I fell in love with last year. Thank you so much for breaking my heart, because you got me four Grammys!"

Discussing *In the Lonely Hour* with Savage, he lamented, "I've spent my whole life listening to songs about breaking up and falling in love—but I've never had a partner. I've never been in love with someone who has loved me back. So I wanted to write an album about unrequited love. An album for people who are lonely."

Smith has told journalists that he does not want his sexual orientation to define him. He explained to Sisario, "I wanted my voice to be Story No. 1 when you Googled my name. I didn't want it to be 'Sam Smith, the gay singer.' I wanted it to be 'Sam Smith, the singer who happens to be gay.'"

## SUGGESTED READING

Doyle, Patrick. "Sam Smith: The Lonely Boy inside the Big Voice." *Rolling Stone*. Rolling Stone, Feb. 2015. Web. 6 Aug. 2015.

Guiducci, Mark. "Sam Smith Pours—and Sings—His Heart Out." *Vogue*. Vogue, Mar. 2015. Web. 6 Aug. 2015.

Robertson, Jessica. "Cover Story: Sam Smith." *Fader*. Fader, June–July 2014. Web. 6 Aug. 2015.

Ryce, Andrew. Rev. of *In the Lonely Hour*, by Sam Smith. *Pitchfork*. Pitchfork Media, 19 June 2014. Web. 6 Aug. 2015.

Sisario, Ben. "Sam Smith, Up for Six Grammys, Is Getting Used to Arenas." *International New York Times*. New York Times, 4 Feb. 2015. Web. 6 Aug. 2015.

Smith, Sam. "BBC Sound of 2014: Sam Smith." Interview by Mark Savage. *BBC News*. BBC, 10 Jan. 2014. Web. 6 Aug. 2015.

Smith, Sam. "Sam Smith: The New Face of Soul." Interview by Amy Wallace. *GQ*. Condé Nast, Feb. 2015. Web. 6 Aug. 2015.

—Mari Rich

# Tracy K. Smith

**Born:** April 16, 1972
**Occupation:** Poet

## BACKGROUND

Tracy K. Smith was born on April 16, 1972, in Falmouth, Massachusetts. She was raised in Fairfield, California, the youngest of five children. Her father, originally from a small town north of Mobile, Alabama, was an optical engineer who worked on the Hubble Space Telescope.

Smith studied at Harvard University in Cambridge, Massachusetts, graduating in 1994 with a BA in English and American literature and Afro-American studies. She started writing poetry seriously during her sophomore year. While in college, she also became involved with the Dark Room Collective, a group whose dual mission was to form a supportive community of African American writers and to host a community-based reading series for writers of color. Upon graduation, Smith spent a year in her childhood home in Fairfield, where her mother was suffering from terminal cancer. After her mother's death, Smith decided to pursue a career as a poet because it was the only thing that seemed real or reliable to her.

She continued her education in the writing division at Columbia University in New York City, earning an MFA in creative writing in 1997. During her time at Harvard and Columbia, Smith studied under a number of highly respected contemporary poets, including Seamus Heaney, Linda Gregg, Mark Doty, and Henri Cole. She has stated that while she was a student, her biggest influence as a writer was the director of Columbia's poetry concentration, Lucie Brock-Broido.

## TEACHING AND WRITING POETRY

From 1997 to 1999, Smith held the Wallace Stegner Fellowship in poetry at Stanford University in Stanford, California. Her first collection of poetry, *The Body's Question* (2003), won the 2002 Cave Canem Poetry Prize, an award given to African American writers for a first book. Many of the poems are revisions of her early work from college. The first section of the book reflects her experiences with Mexican culture, gathered while she lived in Mexico during a long stretch of writer's block.

Smith moved on to teaching poetry and creative writing at several institutions, including Marymount Manhattan College; Medgar Evers College of the City University of New York; the University of Pittsburgh; and Columbia University.

In 2004 Smith received the Rona Jaffe Foundation Writers' Award, which is given to women writers early in their careers. The following year she won the Whiting Writers' Award, awarded annually to ten emerging writers. After teaching as a visiting faculty member at Princeton University for a year, Smith officially joined the faculty in 2006 as assistant professor of creative writing at the Lewis Center for the Arts. At Princeton, Smith leads intensive writing workshops that aim to inspire students in their development as writers. She encourages her undergraduates to take risks and works with them to gain confidence and to become comfortable with the peer critique process. She has also helped create the Lewis Center's Althea Ward Clark Reading Series, which invites distinguished writers to speak to students.

## *DUENDE*

During a writer's residency in Andalusia, Spain, many of the poems for Smith's second collection of poetry, *Duende* (2007), emerged. For this collection, Smith drew inspiration from different Spanish folk traditions, including flamenco dancing, as well as from the oral traditions that had captivated her during her previous visit to Mexico.

*Duende* received a great deal of critical acclaim. A year before it was published, it earned the James Laughlin Award of the Academy of American Poets, given for a writer's second book. In 2008, Smith was presented with the first Essence Literary Award for poetry, which recognizes the literary achievements of African American writers. *Duende* was also a finalist for the thirty-ninth National Association for the Advancement of Colored People (NAACP) Image Award.

### LIFE ON MARS AND OTHER WORKS

Smith's father, who died in 2008, inspired her next collection of poetry, *Life on Mars* (2011). The poems within this collection are set in an imagined world and use the solar system as a metaphor for the place to which her father has traveled upon his death. The collection won Smith the 2012 Pulitzer Prize for Poetry.

Following *Life on Mars*, Smith began writing a memoir, in which she explores the ramifications of loss after her mother's death from cancer. She is working on the book under the tutelage of German poet Hans Magnus Enzensberger as part of the Rolex Mentor and Protégé Arts Initiative, which recognizes rising artists internationally.

### IMPACT

With only three published poetry collections, Smith established herself as a distinguished voice in poetry and African American literature. She received numerous accolades and awards, including the first Essence Literary Award for poetry and the 2012 Pulitzer Prize in Poetry. As a professor of creative writing and poetry, Smith inspires and nurtures young writers.

### PERSONAL LIFE

Smith lives in Brooklyn, New York with her husband, Raphael (Raf) Allison, a visual artist and assistant professor of literature at Bard College. They have a daughter, Naomi.

### SUGGESTED READING

Brouwer, Joel. "Poems of Childhood, Grief, and Deep Space." *New York Times*. New York Times, 26 Aug. 2011. Web. 13 May 2014.

Brown, Jericho. "The Body's Boundaries, The Body's Questions." *Gulf Coast* 17.1 (2004): 123–137. Print.

Dienst, Karin. "Seeking the Magic of Poetry." *Princeton University*. Trustees of Princeton University, 7 Apr. 2008. Web. 13 May 2014.

Saxon, Jamie. "Princeton's Tracy K. Smith Wins Pulitzer Prize for Poetry." *Princeton University*. Trustees of Princeton University, 16 Apr. 2012. Web. 13 May 2014.

Smith, Tracy K. "Interview with Tracy K. Smith—'Poets Are Lucky.'" Interview by Michael Klein. *Ploughshares Literary Magazine*. Ploughshares, 30 May 2012. Web. 23 May 2014.

### SELECTED WORKS

*The Body's Question*, 2003; *Duende*, 2007; *Life on Mars*, 2011

—Patrick G. Cooper

# Timothy Snyder

**Born:** 1969
**Occupation:** Historian and professor

Fluent in several languages, including French, German, and Polish, the American historian Timothy Snyder has gained a reputation in recent decades as being a preeminent authority on the history of Central and Eastern Europe. Currently the Bird White Housum Professor of History at Yale University, he is perhaps best known for his ability to provide keen insights into major historical events through the personalities of the men and women who experienced them. His books have been translated into numerous languages and have earned multiple prestigious awards, while his scholarly articles have appeared in many of the chief historical journals. In addition to these works, he also frequently writes commentary for key news journals and newspapers and provides on-air political analysis of current events in interviews at major news organizations, including National Public Radio. His most significant works to date are *Bloodlands: Europe between Hitler and Stalin* (2010) and *Thinking the Twentieth Century* (2012), which he helped the late historian Tony Judt write.

### EARLY LIFE AND EDUCATION

Timothy David Snyder was born in southwestern Ohio in 1969. An avid reader of history from

Aleksandr Andreiko/Wikimedia Commons

a young age, he graduated from Centerville High School and began studying for his undergraduate degree at Brown University in Providence, Rhode Island. In 1991 he earned his bachelor of arts degree in European history and political science from Brown. On a Marshall Scholarship, he traveled to the United Kingdom to pursue his graduate degree at Balliol College at the University of Oxford. Initially interested in becoming a diplomat, he explained in an interview for the Connecticut *Jewish Ledger* (22 Sept. 2011) that by the time an adviser had suggested that a career as a historian might be a better fit, he had already "come to love the archival work, the travel, and the sense of discovery." He earned his doctorate in philosophy in modern history from Oxford in 1997.

Snyder has held fellowships at a number of prestigious institutions around the world, including the National Center for Scientific Research in Paris, France (1994–95), the Institute for Human Sciences in Vienna, Austria (1996), and the Olin Institute for Strategic Studies at Harvard University in Cambridge, Massachusetts (1997). From 1998 to 2001 he served as an academy scholar at the Center for International Affairs at Harvard. He has been the Housum Professor of History at Yale University in New Haven, Connecticut, since 2001. There he teaches both graduate and undergraduate courses in modern East European political history.

## FIRST BOOKS

Snyder's first work of history was *Nationalism, Marxism, and Modern Central Europe: A Biography of Kazimierz Kelles-Krauz, 1872–1905* (1997), which was translated into Polish and earned the Oskar Halecki Polish and East Central European History Award from the Polish Institute of Arts and Sciences of America in 1998. He then coedited, with Peter Andreas, *The Wall around the West: State Borders and Immigration Controls in North America and Europe*, which was published in 2000.

His first widely reviewed work of history was *The Reconstruction of Nations: Poland, Ukraine, Lithuania, Belarus, 1569–1999* (2003), which examines how, over four hundred years, Poland, Ukraine, Lithuania, and Belarus emerged as nation-states from the conflicts of Eastern Europe despite the pressures of the region's overlapping religious and ethnic groups. Snyder brings the history into the close of the twentieth century, covering the ethnic cleansings of the 1940s through the rise of Poland as an independent country following the collapse of the Soviet Union and the Eastern Bloc. Writing for the *American Historical Review* (Feb. 2004), John-Paul Himka called *The Reconstruction of Nations* "one of the most interesting works of East European history to have appeared in the last decade." Translated into five languages, the book earned several prizes, including the 2003 George Louis Beer Prize presented by the American Historical Association and the award for best book from the American Association for Ukrainian Studies in 2004.

## A MICRO LENS ON HISTORY

For his next book, *Sketches from a Secret War: A Polish Artist's Mission to Liberate Soviet Ukraine*, (2005), Snyder returned to the world of biography to document the life of Henryk Józewski, a Polish intellectual and artist who, during the first half of the twentieth century, served as both the governor of Polish Volhynia and later as an anti-Nazi and anti-Soviet resistance fighter before being jailed by the Soviets in 1953. Throughout the book, Snyder uses Józewski's personal story—which is fascinating in its own right—as a means to tell the larger tale of modern Polish history, as well as the history of much of Eastern Europe. Writing about *Sketches from a Secret War* for the *American Historical Review* (Dec. 2006), Kate Brown proclaimed, "This micro view, placed always within its larger historical and philosophical context, makes for an enticing read. . . . Like the spies he writes about, Snyder frequently crosses the borders of Polish and Soviet Ukrainian history, but he does so more fruitfully than his hapless Soviet and Polish agents." *Sketches from a Secret War* was translated into Polish and Ukrainian and won the Pro Historia Polonorum, an award for the best book on Polish history penned by a foreign scholar over the previous five years.

In 2008 Snyder also published *The Red Prince: The Secret Lives of a Habsburg Archduke*, which details the life of Wilhelm von Habsburg, a member of the famed Habsburg family that ruled a large section of Europe beginning in the thirteenth century. Wilhelm was born toward the end of his family's long reign and came of age in the first half of the twentieth-century, during which he became a passionate supporter of Ukrainian nationalism. After World War II, he sought to bring the Ukraine closer to the West but was imprisoned by Soviet authorities for his activities and died in prison. "There are few historians who possess Timothy Snyder's winning combination of languages, stylish story-telling and analytic insight; in *The Red Prince*, he has produced a gem," Mark Mazower wrote in his review of the book for the *Guardian* (20 June 2008). Translated into at least a dozen languages, the book earned a prize from the American Association for Ukrainian Studies in 2008. Its critical reception was not universally positive, however. One critic for *Publishers Weekly* (14 Apr. 2008) found that Snyder's narrow biographical focus leads to "the complexities of twentieth-century Ukrainian history sometimes [getting] short shift," noting as an example that Snyder devotes "only two sentences to the 1933 'terror famine' that killed three million peasants."

## CEMENTING HIS REPUTATION

Perhaps Snyder's best-known work is *Bloodlands: Europe between Hitler and Stalin*, which was published in 2010. In it, he depicts the brutal extermination tactics employed in Eastern Europe by Adolf Hitler of Nazi Germany and Joseph Stalin of the Soviet Union between 1933 and 1945. He discussed his commitment to provide new insight into the complex topic of this period of mass murder during his interview for the *Jewish Ledger*: "The Holocaust happened entirely behind the line that became the Iron Curtain. And the opening of the Iron Curtain, the possibility of living and researching in

Eastern Europe, was a special opportunity for my generation."

Between the two dictators, more than fourteen million people were deliberately starved, shot, or gassed to death. For Stalin, the killings were done to collectivize farming, organize the Soviet state, eliminate enemies, and consolidate power in his hands alone. For Hitler, he imagined Eastern Europe as an area to be cleared of all "undesirables"—Slavs, Poles, Jews, and Russians, among others—so that the farmlands could be taken for Germany and protected by German overlords to help feed the expanding German Reich. In a review for the *Washington Post* (16 Dec. 2010), Richard Rhodes remarked of *Bloodlands*, "By including Soviet with German mass atrocities in his purview, Timothy Snyder begins the necessary but as yet still taboo examination of the full depravity of total war as it was practiced in the twentieth century, before the advent of nuclear weapons foreclosed it." Translated into more than twenty languages, the book went on to become a best seller in the United States, Germany, Poland, and Colombia. It made around a dozen book-of-the-year lists and earned ten major awards, including the Moczarski Prize in History, the Leipzig Book Prize for European Understanding, the Ralph Waldo Emerson Award from Phi Beta Kappa, and a literature award from the American Academy of Arts and Letters. "This book absorbed me completely for a very long time, but more than anything else I've done it gave the sense, each day, that my work was worthwhile," Snyder said of writing *Bloodlands* in his interview for the *Jewish Ledger*.

## CREATIVE COLLABORATIONS AND OTHER WORK

Snyder's 2012 publication *Thinking the Twentieth Century* was written in collaboration with Tony Judt, the respected British historian best known for his studies of European history, particularly *Postwar: A History of Europe Since 1945* (2005). After Judt was diagnosed with amyotrophic lateral sclerosis (ALS), also known as Lou Gehrig's disease, Snyder sat down with Judt at his home weekly to help him write the intellectual history of the twentieth century that Judt had always wanted to compose. The resulting collaboration, formatted as an extended dialogue, is part memoir, in which Judt recalls events of the century and provides historical analysis of the trends among intellectuals and politicians over the same period. David Keymer, in a review of the book for *Library Journal* (1 Nov. 2011), proclaimed, "We may never have the full history Judt intended to write, but this marvelous précis, vibrantly alive, rich, and piquant, is one last gift from an exceptional public intellectual." The book was also translated into many languages and was notably praised by a number of periodicals, including the *Financial Times* and the *New York Times*. In 2014 he also published *Stalin and Europe: Imitation and Domination, 1928–1953* (2014), which he coedited with Ray Brandon.

Additionally Snyder has published scholarly articles in numerous journals, as well as written articles for such notable publications as the *New York Review of Books*, the *New York Times*, and the *New Republic*, among others. Through these and other media outlets, he offers analysis and historical insights into current events; for example, he has commented on the tensions between the European Union and Russia over Ukraine.

In addition to his writing, Snyder sits on the advisory boards of the Yivo Institute for Jewish Research and the Association for Slavic, East European, and Eurasian Studies. He is also a member of the Committee on Conscience of the United States Holocaust Memorial Museum. He is at work on several new books, including a biography of Karl Marx, a history of the Holocaust, a history of Eastern Europe, and a family history of nationalism.

## SUGGESTED READING

Brown, Kate. Rev. of *Sketches from a Secret War*, by Timothy Snyder. *American Historical Review* Dec. 2006: 1629–30. Print.

Himka, John-Paul. Rev. of *The Reconstruction of Nations*, by Timothy Snyder. *American Historical Review* Feb. 2004: 280. Print.

Keymer, David. Rev. of *Thinking the Twentieth Century*, by Timothy Snyder. *Library Journal* 1 Nov. 2011: 87. Print.

Mazower, Mark. "Empire State Building." Rev. of *The Red Prince*, by Timothy Snyder. *Guardian.* Guardian News and Media, 20 June 2008. Web. 17 Mar. 2015.

Rhodes, Richard. Rev. of *Bloodlands*, by Timothy Snyder. *Washington Post.* Washington Post, 16 Dec. 2010. Web. 17 Mar. 2015.

Snyder, Timothy. "Q &A with . . . Prof. Timothy Snyder: Best-Selling Author of 'Bloodlands: Europe between Hitler and Stalin.'" Interview. *Connecticut Jewish Ledger*. Jewish Ledger, 22 Sept. 2011. Web. 17 Mar. 2015.

## SELECTED WORKS

*Nationalism, Marxism, and Modern Central Europe*, 1997; *The Wall around the West* (coedited with Peter Andreas), 2000; *The Reconstruction of Nations*, 2003; *Sketches from a Secret War*, 2005; *The Red Prince*, 2008; *Bloodlands*, 2010; *Thinking the Twentieth Century* (coauthored with Tony Judt), 2012; *Stalin and Europe* (coedited with Ray Brandon), 2014

—Christopher Mari

# Gayatri Chakravorty Spivak

**Born:** February 24, 1942
**Occupation:** Philosopher

Gayatri Chakravorty Spivak is a writer, philosopher, cultural critic, and University Professor in the Department of English and Comparative Literature at Columbia University in New York City. She is best known for her 1985 essay "Can the Subaltern Speak?," a seminal text in postcolonial studies, and her 1976 translation of French philosopher Jacques Derrida's treatise *Of Grammatology*, which introduced Derrida's theory of deconstruction to the United States. She has also translated the work of Mahasweta Devi, a Bengali novelist and short story writer. Spivak studied comparative literature at Cornell University, but after penning the introduction to Derrida's work, she became a prominent deconstructionist. In her scholarly work, Spivak supplies deconstructionist readings of Marxism, globalization, postcolonialism, and feminism. In his seminar "Tracing Derrida, Post-Structuralism, and Deconstruction," Professor Martin Irvine of Georgetown University explains Derrida's theory of deconstruction this way: "Deconstruction is the procedure of thinking against the obvious, exposing that what seems natural and given in our meaning systems is in fact constructed (structured), that is, not natural, and embedded in and sustained by cultural systems of belief and ideology."

Most readers, or at least those unfamiliar with critical theory, require an intermediary to understand Derrida's work. The same can be said of Spivak, who, throughout her career, has been criticized for her dense writing yet praised for the originality of her thought. "When academics say I'm difficult to understand, I don't pay attention because I think they are saying, 'This does not deserve to be understood,'" she told Dinitia Smith for the *New York Times* (9 Feb. 2002). "No student ever complained at the end of a course." Spivak acknowledges a need for clarity, but the challenging language of theory, and the problems inherent in language itself, mean that philosophical texts have been challenging to nonspecialists for years. "I think the demand that one be comprehensible is a good demand," Spivak told Leon de Kock for *Ariel: A Review of International English Literature* (1 July 1992). "On the other hand, I also know that plain prose cheats, and I also know that clear thought hides."

In 2012, Spivak won the $630,000 Kyoto Prize in Arts and Philosophy. She donated the money to the Pares Chandra Chakravorty Memorial Literacy Project, a rural education foundation in West Bengal that she helped found in 1997. Spivak is also a founding member of the Institute for Comparative Literature and Society at Columbia University, where she began teaching in 1991.

## EARLY LIFE AND EDUCATION

Gayatri Chakravorty Spivak was born on February 24, 1942, in Calcutta (now Kolkata), in British India. Some of her earliest memories are of India's independence, achieved in 1947. "My generation was on the cusp of decolonialization," she told Alfred Artega in an interview published in Donna Landry and Gerald Maclean's book *The Spivak Reader: Selected Works of Gayatri Chakravorty Spivak* (1996). "In a way, it's more interesting to have been in my generation than to have been a midnight's child, to have been born at independence, to be born free by chronological accident."

Her father, Pares Chandra Chakravorty, was a Cambridge-educated doctor who died when Spivak was thirteen. Spivak's mother, Sivani, had a master's degree in Bengali literature. After Spivak's father died, her mother ran a working women's boarding house in Calcutta called Sarada Sangha Mohila Nivas. Later, in the United States, she helped returning Vietnam War veterans cope with post-traumatic stress disorder. Spivak has a sister named Maitreyi Chandra, who is also a professor, as well as a brother.

By her own account, Spivak was a precocious child, and she began her undergraduate education at Presidency College, Calcutta, when she was thirteen. She received her bachelor's degree in English in 1959 and began her graduate studies in India but soon decided to study in the United States. At nineteen, Spivak enrolled at Cornell University in New York. When Bulan Lahiri for India's Hindu newspaper (5 Feb. 2011) asked her if she felt isolated as a young Indian immigrant in the United States, she said, "I just came

and started going to class and never thought about the fact that wearing a sari was an odd thing. And that was also the way my Indian citizenship has remained intact. I never thought that I was supposed to change." She completed her master's degree in 1962 and taught at the University of Iowa while completing her doctorate in comparative literature at Cornell. (She chose comparative literature, she has said, because it was the only subject that offered her scholarship money.) She completed her dissertation, on Irish writer and poet William Butler Yeats, under the deconstructionist Paul de Man. The book that resulted from her thesis, *Myself Must I Remake: The Life and Poetry of W. B. Yeats*, was published in 1974.

## INTRODUCTION TO DERRIDA

While finishing her PhD, Spivak began working in 1965 as an assistant professor of British literature at the University of Iowa. Feeling cut off from the more stimulating academic world at Cornell, she would order new books to try to stay abreast of the intellectual currents of the day. It was at this time that she stumbled across Derrida. "It was by chance that I ordered [*De la*] *Grammatologie*," she told Lahiri of her encounter with the groundbreaking 1967 French text. "I didn't know Derrida's name at all. I was far, far away. There was no email, no fax, no nothing. How would I know? If I hadn't ordered that book my life would have been so totally different." Derrida was hitting his stride as a philosopher in the late 1960s and early 1970s. Spivak was not fluent in French, nor had she any formal training in philosophy. (Her thesis advisor, de Man, is remembered as another leading deconstructionist, but she worked with him before his association with Derrida.) Still, she was drawn to Derrida's book. She heard that the University of Massachusetts Press was publishing translations, and she sent the press a query touting her skills as a translator—"I had never translated anything before!" she admitted to Lahiri—but stipulating she would only translate Derrida's book if she were allowed to write the introduction as well. The publisher agreed, and Spivak was given a year's sabbatical from the University of Iowa to work on the book.

Spivak's translation, *Of Grammatology*, was published in 1976. She famously employed concepts of deconstruction in her introduction, unpacking the meaning of a preface as piece of writing in itself.

## "CAN THE SUBALTERN SPEAK?"

In 1981, the journal *Yale French Studies* asked Spivak to write an essay about French feminism. Her essay, "French Feminism in an International Frame," was published the same year. In the journal *Critical Inquiry*, she published a translation of "Draupadi," a short story by Mahasweta Devi. In her research for these writings, she came across an interview between the French philosopher and poststructuralist Michel Foucault and the postmodern French philosopher Gilles Deleuze. She was struck by the way they spoke to one another, using "presuppositions," she told Lahiri, that would never appear in their published theory. To illustrate her point, she talked about her mother, who was an American citizen. Quite simply, she said, many people, "even politically correct people," presuppose that being an American means being white. "So this is the kind of thing I was looking at," she told Lahiri, "unacknowledged presuppositions which came out in conversation but would not be acknowledged in their theoretical productions."

With such presuppositions in mind, Spivak embarked on what would become her most famous work, the essay "Can the Subaltern Speak?" The essay itself was published in 1985, but it was based on a lecture Spivak gave in 1983. The word *subaltern* was originally used to describe a junior military officer but was used by the Italian communist philosopher Antonio Gramsci to describe a marginalized or powerless person under capitalism. For Spivak, it is a person entirely outside the colonial power structure, to which her own country of India was subject for hundreds of years under British rule. In her essay, Spivak tells the story of Bhubaneswari Bhaduri, a teenage Indian woman who hanged herself in 1926. After her suicide, some suggested that Bhaduri had perhaps killed herself because of an illicit pregnancy. Spivak—who later revealed that Bhaduri was her grandmother's sister—argues that Bhaduri was not, in fact, pregnant. Bhaduri even waited for her menstrual period to begin before she killed herself, in order to head off just such rumors, but this piece of evidence, Spivak says, was forgotten or intentionally overlooked. Bhaduri's death was actually a political protest; she was ordered to commit a political assassination, and she did not want to do it. For Spivak, a subaltern identity meant that "when a young, single girl attempted to write resistance in her very body, she could not be read," as she said in a speech published in *Scholar and Feminist Online* (2006).

Spivak asks her readers to question their own history and privileges, their own relationship to a society that has been defined by white males. How might such a society, which is inherently racist and sexist, affect a reader's worldview? It is a task, Spivak said, as quoted in the introduction to *The Spivak Reader*, that concerns everyone: "'I am only a bourgeois white male, I can't speak.' Why not develop a certain degree of rage against the history that has written such an abject script for you that you are silenced? Then you begin to investigate what it is that silences you, rather than take this very deterministic position—since my skin color is this, since my sex is this, I cannot speak." Spivak also warns of the dangers of the well intentioned who claim to speak *for* the subaltern. To speak for the subaltern, Spivak asserts in her writing, is effectively to silence the subaltern—a point she negotiates in her own work.

In the 1980s, a group of South Asian scholars emerged called the Subaltern Studies Group (SSG). Many members of the SSG are considered the founders of postcolonial studies. In 1988, Spivak and historian Ranajit Guha edited a collection of essays from the SSG titled *Selected Subaltern Studies*. The late Edward Said, a Palestinian scholar and leading postcolonial theorist, wrote the anthology's introduction.

## TEACHING CAREER AND OTHER WORKS

In addition to the University of Iowa, Spivak has taught at Brown University; the University of Texas at Austin; the University of California at Santa Barbara; Université Paul Valéry in Montpellier, France; Jawaharlal Nehru University in New Delhi; Stanford University; the University of British Columbia; Goethe University in Frankfurt, Germany; Riyadh University in Saudi Arabia; and Emory University in Atlanta. She was the Andrew W. Mellon Professor of English at the University of Pittsburgh before she took a position at Columbia University in 1991. In 2007, Spivak was named a University Professor at Columbia, its highest academic rank, becoming the first woman of color to be afforded this honor.

Spivak has translated many of Devi's stories. She published *Imaginary Maps: Three Stories by Mahasweta Devi* in 1995. Other notable works include her book *Outside in the Teaching Machine* (1993), a volume of essays about the globalization of higher education; *In Other Worlds: Essays in Cultural Politics* (1998); *A Critique* of *Postcolonial Reason: Toward a History of the Vanishing Present* (1999); and *An Aesthetic Education in the Era of Globalization* (2012). In 2008, Spivak published a book called *Who Sings the Nation-State? Language, Politics, Belonging* with Judith Butler, another prominent theorist best known for her work on feminism and gender. In the book, the authors question the meaning of the word *state* in a globalized world.

In 1986, Spivak began funding primary school education in West Bengal, her home state. With a $10,000 inheritance from a friend, she founded a rural education project in 1997. The project funds six schools for about three hundred young girls and boys, ages three through thirteen, in the poor and rural district of Birbhum. The children start coming "as soon as they can toddle along," Spivak told Georgette Jasen for the Columbia University website (18 Dec. 2012). "I want them to feel that school is a comfortable place." Spivak visits the schools three or four times a year and spends two days at each school in turn. She hopes the children will learn to spell and add numbers, but more importantly, she hopes that they will understand how those operations work. She disdains learning simply by rote. "Literacy and numeracy without a good education are worth nothing," she told Jasen.

## PERSONAL LIFE

Spivak married a Cornell classmate named Talbot Spivak in 1964. His novel, *The Bride Wore the Traditional Gold* (1972), contains autobiographical tidbits from their early marriage. They divorced in 1977. In the early 1990s, Spivak separated from her second husband, Basudev Chatterji, a history professor at Delhi University.

## SUGGESTED READING

De Kock, Leon. "Interview with Gayatri Chakravorty Spivak: New Nation Writers Conference in South Africa." *Ariel: A Review of International English Literature* 23.3 (1992): 29–47. Web. 13 May 2014.

Irvine, Martin. "Derrida/Deconstruction: Seminar Notes: Tracing Derrida, Post-Structuralism, and Deconstruction." *Georgetown University*. Georgetown U, 2011. Web. 13 May 2014.

Jasen, Georgette. "Winner of Kyoto Prize Donates Award Money to Rural Indian Schools." *Columbia News*. Columbia University, 18 Dec. 2012. Web. 13 May 2014.

Lahiri, Bulan. "In Conversation: Speaking to Spivak." *Hindu*. Hindu, 5 Feb. 2011. Web. 13 May 2014.

Smith, Dinitia. "Creating a Stir Wherever She Goes." *New York Times*. New York Times, 9 Feb. 2002. Web. 13 May 2014.

Spivak, Gayatri Chakravorty. "If Only." *Scholar and Feminist Online* 4.2 (2006): n. pag. Web. 13 May 2014.

## SELECTED WORKS

Introduction, *Of Grammatology* by Jacques Derrida, 1976; *In Other Worlds: Essays in Cultural Politics*, 1987; *Selected Subaltern Studies* (with Ranajit Guha), 1988; *Outside in the Teaching Machine*, 1993; *A Critique of Postcolonial Reason: Toward a History of the Vanishing Present*, 1999; *Who Sings the Nation-State? Language, Politics, Belonging* (with Judith Butler) 2008; *An Aesthetic Education in the Era of Globalization*, 2012

—Molly Hagan

# Kathryn Sullivan

**Born:** October 3, 1951
**Occupation:** NOAA administrator

On March 6, 2014, Dr. Kathryn D. Sullivan, an oceanographer and former astronaut, was confirmed by the US Senate as the under secretary of commerce for oceans and atmosphere and administrator of the National Oceanic and Atmospheric Administration (NOAA). The administration's fleet of weather satellites and its National Weather Service supply the country with necessary data for weather forecasts. NOAA manages marine fisheries and operates the country's National Marine Sanctuaries, such as Monterey Bay in Santa Cruz and the Hawaiian Islands Humpback Whale National Marine Sanctuary on the island of Maui.

Also a longtime advocate for policies that address climate change and global warming, the organization released a report in July 2014 confirming that the earth's climatic temperature has been increasing at a steady rate. "These findings reinforce what scientists for decades have observed: that our planet is becoming a warmer place," Sullivan said in a statement, as quoted by Laura Barron-Lopez in the Congressional weekly, the *Hill* (17 July 2014). The report was compiled by 425 scientists in fifty-seven countries.

NOAA/Wikimedia Commons

Among other findings, the report explained that NOAA scientists at the Mauna Loa Observatory in Hawaii had measured the daily concentration of carbon dioxide in the atmosphere at more than 400 parts per million (ppm) for the first time since measurements began at the facility in 1958. Scientists agree that the surpassing of the 400 ppm milestone is an alarming occurrence that demands a swift response. "This report provides the foundational information we need to develop tools and services for communities, business, and nations to prepare for, and build resilience to, the impacts of climate change," Sullivan said.

Sullivan was a part of the National Aeronautics and Space Administration (NASA)'s first class to include female astronauts in 1978, and she became the first American woman to walk in space in 1984. In 1990, she served with the crew that launched the Hubble Space Telescope. After fifteen years with NASA, Sullivan was determined to put her extraterrestrial experience to use on Earth. She joined NOAA as chief scientist in 1993, and served as NOAA's acting administrator beginning in February 2013. She has been awarded honorary degrees from several universities, including Dalhousie University (1985), the Stevens Institute of Technology (1992), and Kent State University (2002). In 2014 *Time* magazine included Sullivan on its list of the one hundred most influential people in the world.

## EARLY LIFE AND EDUCATION

Kathryn Dwyer Sullivan was born on October 3, 1951, in Paterson, New Jersey, to parents Donald, an aerospace engineer, and Barbara. She recalls running out onto her front lawn to try to glimpse the first artificial satellite, the Soviet *Sputnik I*, when she was six years old. Sullivan and her family moved to the Woodland Hills neighborhood of Los Angeles, California, that same year.

Growing up, Sullivan was inspired by the country's first astronauts as well as the ocean explorations of television star and scientist, Jacques Cousteau. She devoured the regular coverage of astronauts and aquanauts alike in the pages of *National Geographic* and *Life*. "It never bothered me that everyone I was watching was male," she wrote in a blog post for the US Department of Commerce website (29 Mar. 2013). "My brother and I were raised with the view that every person has unique talents and interests and should pursue them as they see fit, regardless of what someone else thinks is 'right' for girls or boys." Glued to the television during the first lunar landing in 1969, Sullivan felt as if she were not just an observer, but a part of the event, trying to understand the mechanics of the feat as well.

Sullivan graduated from Taft High School in Woodland Hills that year and enrolled at the University of California, Santa Cruz (UCSC), where she intended to study Russian (already being fluent in French and German) and embark on "a career of global exploration," she wrote on the Department of Commerce website. Required to take three classes outside of her major, Sullivan found herself in an introductory course on marine biology during her freshman year. The required textbook was Sir Alister Hardy's memoir and travelogue *Great Waters* (1967), a book she would later say changed her life. "I realized that oceanographers led exactly the kind of life I had dreamt of as a child, lives full of inquiry, exploration, and adventure," she wrote. She had found her calling.

In 1971, Sullivan spent a year as an exchange student at the University of Bergen in Norway. When she returned, she knew that she wanted to specialize in oceanography. She graduated from UCSC with a bachelor's degree in earth sciences in 1973, and began applying for graduate programs in marine geology. She had accepted a fellowship at Oregon State when she heard back from Dalhousie University in Halifax, Nova Scotia. The university offered her a chance to join a marine expedition that summer and she accepted.

## OCEAN OR SPACE?

During her time at Dalhousie, Sullivan participated in oceanographic expeditions with the US Geological Survey, Woods Hole Oceanographic Institute, and the Bedford Institute. Research projects involved the Mid-Atlantic Ridge, the Newfoundland Basin, and fault zones off the California coast. Her greatest ambition at the time was to get a chance to explore the deep seafloor in a submersible.

Meanwhile, on a holiday visit home in 1976, Sullivan's brother, a pilot, told her that NASA was recruiting a new class of astronauts and encouraging women and minorities to apply. He was already applying and he urged his sister to do the same. She initially dismissed him—outer space was a different beast, and going that route could not possibly help her unravel the mysteries of the ocean floor.

Then she saw an ad herself. She realized that the mission specialist position sounded an awful lot like the role she had been filling on oceanographic expeditions. Despite knowing very little about the program, she decided to apply in 1977. From there, her life took a rather unexpected turn when she graduated with her doctorate in geology the following year.

## WALKING IN SPACE

Sullivan considered completing her postdoctorate at Columbia University. However, in January 1978, after a lengthy interview process, she was chosen as a member of NASA's Astronaut Group 8, the program's first class of astronauts that listed women on its roster. Among her classmates was Sally Ride, who became the first American woman in space in 1983.

Although Sullivan officially became an astronaut in August 1979, she did not embark on her first space shuttle mission, on the space shuttle *Challenger*, until October 1984. On the eleventh of that month, Sullivan became the first American woman to walk in space—she might have been the first woman of any nationality to complete a spacewalk had it not been for Soviet astronaut Svetlana Savitskaya, who beat her by a few months, completing her own spacewalk in July 1984. Still, Sullivan's feat was well documented; William J. Broad for the *New York Times* (12 Oct. 1984) reported that the thirty-three-year-old Sullivan "floated her way to history at 11:46" in the morning while making a

satellite repair. He continued, detailing her first reaction: "'That is really great,' she said as she stood up straight in the payload bay, taking in the view of the Earth and stars."

Later, Sullivan was able to better articulate the historic moment. She described the experience to Lynn Sherr, the author of *Sally Ride: America's First Woman in Space* (2014), in an interview at an event hosted by the Pew Charitable Trusts on October 8, 2014. As quoted by Hannah Waters in *Scientific American* (16 Oct. 2014), Sullivan explained to Sherr that she was struck less by the sight of the stars, than by the sight of Earth from up above. Orbiting the entire globe in an hour and a half, she saw "a sunrise or sunset every forty-five minutes"; she watched the continents sweep by in "extraordinary panoramas"; and she witnessed a dust storm off the coast of North Africa in "remarkably fine detail."

## TWO MORE MISSIONS

Almost two years after that flight, Sullivan had been working on a new project when she heard the news: the very same shuttle that had brought her on her first mission, *Challenger*, had exploded only seconds after launch, killing all seven crewmembers. Though she went to the space center as soon as possible and helped to console family members, struggling with a sense of numbness, she also knew that this tragedy would not prevent her from going into space again. "I had to fly again," she said, as quoted by James M. Clash in the *Huffington Post* (6 July 2011). "We were all there because we believed this was important work for the country."

In April 1990, Sullivan served aboard the space shuttle *Discovery* to deploy the Hubble Space Telescope. It was another historic moment for the space agency and for Sullivan; Hubble is one of NASA's most important projects and has provided the world with some of the most captivating photographs of outer space available. Hubble is still in operation. Sullivan also served as payload commander aboard the space shuttle *Atlantis* in March 1992. During the mission, Sullivan led experiments pertaining to climate and atmosphere. It was her last mission.

When it was over, she had logged a total of more than 532 hours in space. More seasoned than her first mission, she had also gained a new perspective on her role and the significance of her journeys: "But what accumulated by my third flight was an underlying dissatisfaction if all that it was for was that I got the cool view. . . . Somehow it fired in me a drive to figure out, How do you make this matter?" she stated, as quoted by Waters.

## CAREER WITH NOAA

In 1993 Sullivan left NASA and was appointed chief scientist at NOAA, a position she served until 1996. She was then named president and chief executive officer of the Center of Science and Industry in Columbus, Ohio, where, in addition to being inducted into the US Astronaut Hall of Fame in 2004, she remained until 2006. That same year, she became the first director of the Battelle Center for Mathematics and Science Education Policy at the John Glenn School of Public Affairs at Ohio State University.

In 2011 she returned to NOAA as deputy administrator. In that role, she oversaw the agency's satellite program, which, in 2012, was instrumental in predicting the destructive course of super storm Sandy. "Had we thought the brunt of the storm was going to stay out in the Atlantic, or if residents had only a day to prepare or evacuate, the results would have been even more devastating," Sullivan said in 2012, as quoted by Jason Samenow for the *Washington Post* (12 Nov. 2014).

Sullivan replaced Jane Lubchenco as acting administrator on February 28, 2013. In August, President Barack Obama nominated her to fill the post permanently. Sullivan was officially confirmed on March 6, 2014. In September 2014, NOAA's Satellite Data and Information Service network was hacked. The data feed was out of commission for two days while NOAA fixed the problem, and Samenow wrote that it was a troubling glimpse at life without the information provided by NOAA satellites. Sullivan and her team are working to address a potential data gap that could affect NOAA's polar-orbiting satellites in 2016, between when those satellites are expected to die and the launch of their replacements in 2017. In 2013, Samenow wrote, the Government Accountability Office listed the gap among the top thirty challenges facing the federal government.

## SUGGESTED READING

Barron-Lopez, Laura. "NOAA: Climate Change Is Getting Worse." *Hill*. Capitol Hill, 17 July 2014. Web. 17 Dec. 2014.

Broad, William J. "'Really Great,' Says the First Woman from US to Take a Walk in Space." *New York Times*. New York Times, 12 Oct. 1984. Web. 17 Dec. 2014.

Samenow, Jason. "Weather Satellite Data Hack and Outage: Why This Matters for Forecasting." *Washington Post*. Washington Post, 12 Nov. 2014. Web. 17 Dec. 2014.

Sullivan, Kathryn. "America's First Woman Space-Walker Remembers Shuttle Rides." Interview by James M. Clash. *Huffington Post*. HuffingtonPost.com, 6 July 2011. Web. 17 Dec. 2014.

Sullivan, Kathryn. "Spotlight on Commerce: Dr. Kathryn D. Sullivan, Acting Under Secretary of Commerce for Oceans and Atmosphere and Acting NOAA Administrator." *Commerce.gov*. US Dept. of Commerce, 29 Mar. 2013. Web. 17 Dec. 2014.

Waters, Hannah. "The Global Perspective of Space and Deep-Sea Explorer Kathryn Sullivan." *Scientific American*. Scientific Amer., 16 Oct. 2014. Web. 17 Dec. 2014.

—Molly Hagan

# George Takei

**Born:** April 20, 1937
**Occupation:** Actor, author

In an era when Asian American actors usually found work playing stereotypical roles such as servants, enemy soldiers, or ninjas, George Takei's role on the original television series *Star Trek* (1966–69) was considered groundbreaking. Takei played Hikaru Sulu, a calm and competent senior officer on the starship *Enterprise.*

Although *Star Trek* retains an enormous and fervid fan base and has spawned feature-length films, spin-off series, cartoons, conventions, toys, and more, a new generation of fans now knows Takei as a presence on social media. As of mid-2014, he had almost 1.5 million followers on Twitter and almost 8 million "likes" on his Facebook page. Takei, who came out publicly as a gay man in 2005, uses social media to post items he finds humorous or appealing and for more serious purposes as well. "Like [actress] Betty White, Mr. Takei has used naughty-oldster humor to fuel a late-career surge," Michael Schulman wrote for the *New York Times* (13 June 2014). "But his ribaldry is often in the service of social causes, whether gay rights or Japanese-American visibility."

## EARLY YEARS AND EDUCATION

George Takei (pronounced tuh-KAY) was born on April 20, 1937, in Los Angeles, California. His parents, Takekuma Norman Takei and Fumiko Emily Takei, were Anglophiles and named their son after the British monarch George VI, whose coronation took place that year. Takei has one younger brother and one younger sister.

During World War II, Takei and his family members, along with more than 100,000 other American citizens of Japanese ancestry, were forced into US internment camps. Takei was a preschooler when he was sent with his parents and siblings to California's Santa Anita Park racetrack, where they lived in the stables for several months until being moved to Camp Rohwer in Arkansas. His parents had spared him the horror of knowing they were being forcibly incarcerated by telling him they were going on a camping vacation, so he did not find Arkansas wholly unpleasant. Although he disliked how muddy the camp became during the region's frequent rains, he did not mind lining up for meals, and he believed that the searchlights following him when he went to the latrine at night were there to help guide him in the dark.

The Takei family was then transferred to Camp Tule Lake in northern California, and once the war was over they were allowed to return home. Takei was almost nine. Because of lingering prejudice, Takei's father had difficulty

finding work and was forced to take a job washing dishes in a restaurant. The family, middle class before the war but now penniless, settled in a dirty, crime-ridden area of Los Angeles. Takei's sister, who was an infant when the family entered the camps, once begged to "go home," back to the barbed wire enclosures of Rohwer.

Takei's father eventually saved enough money to buy a small dry-cleaning business and then a grocery store. He ultimately entered the real estate field, correctly reasoning that many Japanese-Americans were buying homes and businesses and would appreciate guidance from a compatriot. Gradually, the family regained its financial footing.

Takei initially studied architecture at the University of California, Berkeley. One summer, to make extra money, he answered an ad for voice artists to dub English dialogue for the Japanese monster movie *Rodan* (1956). He found he enjoyed providing the voices for his eight assigned characters, and he soon took on small roles in such shows as *Perry Mason* and *Playhouse 90* and decided to study acting. Transferring to the University of California, Los Angeles, he earned a bachelor's degree in theater in 1960 and a master's degree in 1964.

## EARLY ACTING CAREER

Early in his career Takei appeared in a pair of forgettable Jerry Lewis movies, *The Big Mouth* (1967) and *Which Way to the Front?* (1970). "When I decided to become an actor—and I had those discussions with my father—I promised him that I would not do anything that would make him ashamed," he recalled to Terry Gross for the National Public Radio show *Fresh Air* (28 July 2014). "And so I'd been avoiding stereotype roles. Until, one day, my agent came up with this . . . 'opportunity' in a Jerry Lewis movie . . . and [explained that] it's very important for a young actor to be associated with a moneymaking project." Despite the popular appeal of those pictures, Takei now deeply regrets his participation. Bright spots for him in those early days were being cast in John Wayne's well-regarded war drama *The Green Berets* (1968) and, of course, winning a role in the series that would change his life.

### STAR TREK

*Star Trek* premiered in 1966 and followed the adventures of the crew of the USS *Enterprise* as they explored the galaxy on behalf of the United Federation of Planets. "*Star Trek*," Schulman wrote, "offered something different: a chance to work with a multiethnic ensemble on a show that obliquely tackled hot-button issues like the Vietnam War and civil rights." Takei gained a reputation for fighting vehemently with the show's creator, Gene Roddenberry, on his character's behalf. Once, for example, he refused to use the samurai sword called for in the script, insisting that the prop be changed to a fencing foil instead. "I knew this character was a breakthrough role, certainly for me as an individual actor but also for the image of an Asian character: no accent, a member of the elite leadership team," he recalled to Nicole Pasulka for *Mother Jones* (Sept./Oct. 2012). "I was supposed to be the best helmsman in the Starfleet, No. 1 graduate in the Starfleet Academy. At that time there was the horrible stereotype about Asians being bad drivers. I was the best driver in the galaxy!" While *Star Trek* did not receive a great deal of attention during its original run, it proved to be a blockbuster hit in syndication. Takei appeared in many of the spin-off projects that resulted from the syndicated series such as the animated series and many of the books and video games based on the series. He also appeared in the first six *Star Trek* movies and one episode of the spin-off series, *Star Trek: Voyager*.

## CAREER AFTER *STAR TREK*

Although he was cemented in the public's mind as Sulu for decades and remains a popular draw on the science fiction convention circuit, Takei took on many other roles in the years following *Star Trek*. He has had, for example, guest roles on such shows as *Murder, She Wrote* (1987), *Miami Vice* (1987), *Malcolm in the Middle* (2006), *Will & Grace* (2006), and *Heroes* (2007–8, 2010)—and hearkening back to the voice work he did as a college student, he can often be heard portraying characters in animated programs and films, including Disney's *Mulan* (1998), *Kim Possible* (2003, 2005, 2007), and *Adventure Time* (2010, 2012).

Takei also works with shock-jock Howard Stern on occasion. Beginning in the mid-1990s, he took part in Stern's radio show from time to time to promote a project, such as his autobiography *To the Stars* (1994). Stern's producers began manipulating the tapes of his interviews to make it seem as though the supposedly strait-laced actor was using obscenity or isolating catchphrases ("Oh Myyy!" is still a favorite). Fans so enjoyed these short comic bits that in 2006 Takei was invited to serve as the announcer

when Stern debuted his irreverent show on satellite radio. He continues to be heard regularly on the show, and while he says that he dislikes some of Stern's crude language, he admires the radio host's show business acumen and his courage in expressing sometimes unpopular views.

A veteran of live theater, Takei has appeared in several productions at such esteemed venues as the Mark Taper Forum in Los Angeles and the Manhattan Theater Club. As of early fall 2014, he was preparing to star in a Broadway run of the musical *Allegiance*, which is based on his family's experiences with being interned during World War II.

## PERSONAL LIFE AND ACTIVISM

Takei realized that he was gay in about fifth grade but remained for most of his life firmly in the closet, with only his closest friends, coworkers, and family members aware of his sexual preference. As a young actor, he feared being ostracized if news of his sexuality became public. "In the early part of my career . . . there was a very popular box-office movie star—blond good looking, good actor—named Tab Hunter. He was in almost every other movie that came out," Takei recalled to Gross. "And then one of the scandals sheets of that time . . . exposed him as gay. And suddenly and abruptly, his career came to a stop. That was, to me, chilling and stunning."

Takei has admitted that leading a double life was exhausting, but for the most part he lived quietly and happily with his partner, Brad Altman, whom he had met in the 1980s when both were members of a running club. (Takei has run several marathons.)

Takei participated in the civil rights movement of the 1960s and protested the war in Vietnam, but he did not address gay rights until 2005 when California governor Arnold Schwarzenegger vetoed the state's Marriage Equality Bill. An infuriated Takei was suddenly inspired to use his fame to change public opinion. "I'd spent a lifetime being silent on the issue," he explained to an interviewer for *Winq* magazine (29 Aug. 2014), "now I had to speak up."

The Supreme Court of California legalized same-sex marriage in a ruling that took effect on June 16, 2008, and Takei and Altman were married in a Buddhist ceremony held at the Japanese American National Museum, in Los Angeles, on September 14 of that year. (They later appeared on an episode of *The Newlywed Game*, becoming the first gay couple ever to compete in the long-running program. The two are featured in the 2014 documentary film *To Be Takei*, and audiences and critics alike have remarked on their palpable love and the gruff but doting manner in which they interact.

## SOCIAL MEDIA FAME

Takei has found that using social media is among the most effective ways to spread a message. He has been on Twitter since January 2011 and on Facebook since March of that same year. "I have had a lifelong engagement with *Star Trek* fans as well as a more recent engagement with fans who know me from my guest announcer gig on Howard Stern on Sirius XM," he told Alex Knapp for *Forbes* (23 Mar. 2012). "So I naturally began with that, which produced a curious combination of geek/nerd humor and somewhat raunchy and irreverent banter. It was rather like the Sci-Fi Channel meets Comedy Central. I also had a vibrant following among LGBT [lesbian, gay, bisexual, transgender] fans who have come to embrace my message of combating idiocy with humor. It's really hard to hate someone for being different when you're too busy laughing together." Takei has published two books about his experience as a social media phenomenon, *Oh Myyy: There Goes the Internet* (2012) and *Lions and Tigers and Bears: The Internet Strikes Back* (2013).

## SUGGESTED READING

Knapp, Alex. "How George Takei Conquered Facebook." *Forbes.* Forbes, 23 Mar. 2012. Web. 18 Sept. 2014.

Pasulka, Nicole. "George Takei, the Best Driver in the Galaxy." *Mother Jones.* Mother Jones and the Foundation for National Progress, Sept./Oct. 2012. Web. 18 Sept. 2014.

Rudolph, Christopher. "George Takei Discusses Gay Rights, *Star Trek*, and Being a Comic Book Hero." *Huffington Post.* TheHuffingtonPost.com, 29 June 2013. Web. 18 Sept. 2014.

Schulman, Michael. "George Takei Is Still Guiding the Ship." *New York Times.* New York Times, 13 June 2014. Web. 18 Sept. 2014.

Takei, George. Interview by Terry Gross. "From 'Star Trek' to LGBT Spokesman, What It Takes 'To Be Takei.'" *NPR.* National Public Radio, 28 July 2014. Web. 18 Sept. 2014.

## SELECTED WORKS

*Rodan*, 1956; *Star Trek*, 1966–69; *The Green Berets*, 1968; *Kissinger and Nixon*, 1995; *Mulan*, 1998; *Heroes*, 2007–10; *The Neighbors*, 2013–14; *Allegiance: A New American Musical*, 2012–; *To Be Takei*, 2014

—Mari Rich

---

# Barbara Brown Taylor

**Born:** September 21, 1951
**Occupation:** Theologian, author

Rev. Barbara Brown Taylor is an Episcopal priest named by Baylor University as one of twelve most effective preachers in the English-speaking world, chosen from 1,500 nominees in 1996. In 1998 she astounded many by leaving her pulpit ministry to become a college professor at Piedmont College in northern Georgia, although she remains an ordained priest. Brown believes her work in the classroom is a ministry as well, as she explained to Jana Riess for *Publishers Weekly* (13 Mar. 2006), "My ordination vows are lifelong. I ended up spending a lot of time parsing them in terms of my present situation as a professor. . . . I teach undergraduate religion to a broad range of students to whom I am passionately devoted."

She is the most often requested Sunday speaker at New York's Chautauqua Institute, and speaks at the National Cathedral in Washington, DC, as well as guest lecturing at universities such as Duke and Princeton. In 2014 she appeared with Oprah Winfrey on Super Soul Sunday (Nov. 9, 2014) and was named to Time's 100 Most Influential People list.

## EARLY LIFE AND EDUCATION

Barbara Brown Taylor was born September 21, 1951, in Lafayette, Indiana, and is the eldest of three girls. Her father was a psychologist and her mother cared for the children and home. During the years after Taylor's birth her family moved multiple times, first to Kansas, then to Ohio and Alabama, and finally settling in Atlanta, Georgia, in 1965.

Taylor was baptized Catholic as an infant; however, she became serious about Christianity only while attending college at Emory University. There, religion professors joined in protests against the Vietnam War. As Taylor told

Elizabeth Dias for *Time* (28 Apr. 2014), "To be a Christian in those days was to be adventurous. It was to be countercultural. It was to be really out there. I wanted to know more, what gave them that kind of independence, what gave them that moral sense."

After Taylor graduated from Emory with a bachelor of arts degree in English in 1973, she entered Yale Divinity School and planned to pursue a career in writing, not in ministry. During her second year, she attended a Christ Episcopal Church service on the school grounds, and found the kind of worship that made sense to her. While in her third year of seminary school the Episcopal Church began to ordain women, opening a new path for Taylor, who graduated from Yale Divinity School in 1976, shortly after being confirmed in the Christ Episcopal Church. She was ordained as a deacon in the Christ Episcopal Church, in the diocese of Atlanta, in 1983. The following year, she was ordained as a priest in the same diocese.

## PARISH MINISTRY

While working her way toward ordination, Taylor spent a full year in pastoral clinical education as a hospital chaplain. She spent nearly ten years as an assistant priest at the large All Saints Episcopal Church in Atlanta. During that time she also married her husband Ed, as Episcopal priests are allowed to marry.

Taylor and her husband began looking for a way out of the bustle of Atlanta. Driving in the mountains of northeast Georgia, they saw a small Episcopal church. Taylor fell in love with the building itself and in 1990 accepted a call to the same church, Grace-Calvary Episcopal, in Clarkesville, Georgia. Not only was it her first time in charge of a congregation, but she also was moving from urban to rural ministry. During the time Taylor was working at Grace-Calvary she wrote her first two books, *The Preaching Life* (1993), and *Gospel Medicine* (1995).

The church held only eighty-two people; however, after Taylor's recognition as one of the top preachers of the day by Baylor University, busloads of people began arriving, and the church had to expand to four services. Soon tensions developed between Taylor and her congregation as a result of her overnight fame. She realized she could not continue in parish ministry, but was unsure how to leave. Her answer came when nearby Piedmont College asked her to head its newly formed religion department in 1997.

## FROM PARISH PRIEST TO COLLEGE PROFESSOR

Taylor started teaching at Piedmont in 1998. Her title at the college is the Harry R. Butman Chair in Religion and Philosophy. Taylor, writing for the *Journal of Pastoral Psychology* (Nov. 2003), explained her departure from parish ministry with these words, "I had resigned from my country church . . . with a mortgaged heart and a sense of defeat so great that I had no ready answer for people who asked me why I left. The easiest thing was to tell them that I had always wanted to teach college, which was true, but behind that answer lay truths harder to confess. I left because I could no longer lead. I left because I made no difference. I left because I ran out of love."

Leaving the ministry and becoming a professor gave Taylor more time for prayer, reading, and writing. That time allowed Taylor to explore her faith more deeply than she was able to do, previously. In addition to her teaching responsibilities, she also provides oversight for Piedmont's annual Conference on Religion and the Liberal Arts.

## LEAVING CHURCH: A MEMOIR OF FAITH

Religious publishing houses, such as the Episcopal publishing firm Cowley Publications (later acquired by Rowman & Littlefield), published Taylor's early books. When her editor left Cowley, she sought literary agent Tom Grady, who helped her land at HarperSanFrancisco, a trade publisher.

Grady selected Taylor's book idea about leaving the parish ministry in order to help her to reach a broader audience, including those she calls "edge dwellers." As she told Riess, "They have one foot in the church and one foot out. I've flourished in the institutional side of religion, but I've also felt boxed in by it and short of air. So I feel I can be a bridge to the people who call themselves 'spiritual but not religious' as well as those who are religious."

She began to write her memoir, *Leaving Church* (2006) about the events leading to the break, wanting to examine the private truths that had made her ministry a sometimes difficult task. As she wrote for *Christian Century* (25 July 2006), "As gladly as I served the public truth for years, I had a lot of private truth left over. Some of it was petty, some of it was shameful and some of it led me to question the public truth I proclaimed on a regular basis, so I boxed it up and put it in my spiritual basement.

Then one day when I was looking for a place to set a new box, I realized that some of my best stuff was down there, and that going up and down the steps was wearing me out. Soon after that I started writing a memoir, without the least idea how complicated that might turn out to be."

The book earned for Taylor an author of the year award from the Georgia Writers Association in 2006 as well as a wider readership. However, many people were confused and upset by Taylor's leaving parish ministry and then writing what some saw as a tell-all book.

Explaining the negative reception the book received, Taylor told Marcia Z. Nelson for *Publishers Weekly* (12 Jan. 2009), "As I aged both in my faith and in my life, I become interested in things beyond that center, questioned some of the central doctrines of Christianity and looked into scriptures that didn't make it into the canon. I wanted to explore what felt to me like family secrets that parish ministers aren't supposed to talk about. I broke a silence that struck some people as indiscreet."

### *LEARNING TO WALK IN THE DARK*

Taylor next turned to a study of Christian disciplines that could be practiced without the formal structure of a church. *An Altar in the World: A Geography of Faith* (2009) suggests habits such as physical labor, enduring pain, and taking off one day a week. Some of her suggestions have long been a part of Christian tradition, but she gave them a new look. For example, Sabbath, the day off, is discussed in a chapter entitled "The Practice of Saying No."

A five-year gap followed before Taylor's next book, *Learning to Walk in the Dark*, appeared in 2014. As she explained to David Crumm for *Read the Spirit* (5 May 2014), "I envy the writers who can turn out a book every year, but I teach full-time, my husband and I live on a working farm, I travel a lot to speak. And, honestly, I think it's worth taking time to actually live the kind of life that will produce something worth writing about."

Before writing *Learning to Walk in the Dark*, Taylor spent four years exploring various ways to enter darkness, seeking to challenge the too-prevalent notion in Christianity that light is good and darkness is evil. She explored caves, took an air mattress out into the yard to watch night fall and learned to walk using only the light of the stars. She also reexamined the Bible, finding that even though the concept of darkness is used negatively, good things do happen at night. She cites Abraham being told to look at the stars and Jacob wrestling with an angel.

Taylor concluded, as Dias wrote, "contemporary spirituality is too feel-good, that darkness holds more lessons than light and that contrary to what many of us have long believed, it is sometimes in the bleakest void that God is nearest." Taylor returns to an earlier Christian spirituality, which focused on the mystery that darkness held, rather than darkness as equated with sin and evil.

### PERSONAL LIFE

Taylor and her husband, Ed, live on a farm in northern Georgia. She writes in a twelve by twelve foot cabin, without plumbing or electricity, in the woods.

Taylor regards aging as a clarifying force, as she told Nelson, "I do think that 50 is a milestone. I'm grateful to have reached 50 and with limited time left, there's not time to waste on things that don't matter and don't engage the pain in the world. There's no time left to pretend."

### SUGGESTED READING

Dias, Elizabeth. "Let There Be Night. (Cover Story)." *Time* 28 Apr. 2014: 183.16 (2014): 36–41. Print. Web. 24 Feb. 2015.

Nelson, Marcia Z. "PW Talks with Barbara Brown Taylor: A Priest without a Pulpit." *Publishers Weekly* 12 Jan. 2009: 43. Print.

Riess, Jana. "PW Talks with Barbara Brown Taylor: Bridging the Holy and the Human." *Publishers Weekly* 13 Mar. 2006: 62. Print.

Taylor, Barbara Brown. "Barbara Brown Taylor." Interview by Bob Abernethy. *PBS WGBH*. Public Broadcasting Service, 9 Mar. 2007. Web. 28 Apr. 2015.

### SELECTED WORKS

*Bread of Angels*, 1997; *Home by Another Way*, 1999; *Leaving Church: A Memoir of Faith*, 2006; *An Altar in the World: A Geography of Faith*, 2009; *Learning to Walk in the Dark*, 2014

—Judy Johnson

# Jill Thompson

**Born:** November 20, 1966

**Occupation:** Comic book writer and illustrator

In a field largely dominated by men, Jill Thompson has proved herself to be one of the most inventive and respected comic book artists of the modern era. Since the early 1990s, she has worked for nearly every major comic book publisher, including Marvel Comics and DC Comics, and has received numerous awards for her work, including several Eisner Awards, the industry's equivalent of a Pulitzer Prize. She is perhaps best known for her work on such popular titles as DC's *Wonder Woman*, *Sandman*, and *Swamp Thing*. More recently, she has also published two celebrated children's book series, *Scary Godmother* and *Magic Trixie*, which she both writes and illustrates. *Scary Godmother* has proved so popular that it was adapted as a stage play in 2001 and again as two computer-animated Halloween television specials, *Scary Godmother: Halloween Spooktacular* and *Scary Godmother: The Revenge of Jimmy*, in 2003 and 2005, respectively.

In addition to being highly esteemed by her fellow creators, Thompson is also a favorite among longtime comic book fans. "It's nice that there are nice people in my industry," she said to Christopher Irving for *Graphic NYC* (30 Jan. 2012). "I

© Luigi Novi/Wikimedia Commons

like to think I'm one of them, and treat anyone who comes up to me as a friend. If you're nice enough to come up and like my work, how could I ever possibly be anything but gracious?"

## EARLY LIFE

Jill Thompson was born on November 20, 1966, and grew up in Forest Park, Illinois. An avid reader from an early age, she read everything she could get her hands on and claims she wore out her library card from overuse. She even set up her own "office" in a closet off the kitchen in her childhood home, complete with a typewriter set up on a TV tray, to try to write a novel of her own.

Thompson's entry into the world of comic books came at a similarly early age. In an interview published on the HarperCollins Canada website, Thompson recalled, "I got hooked on comic books fairly early when I bought a box of old Archie comics at a garage sale down the alley. . . . I got an orphanage crate filled with comics for a couple of bucks. But that's really what started me down this path . . . the comics in that box. I fell in love with the sequential storytelling. From there I moved on to any other comic book I could find: *Spider-Man*, *X-Men*, old monster comics." As an adolescent, she was particularly inspired by the art of John Byrne on titles such as *The Uncanny X-Men* and of George Perez on *The New Teen Titans*. She has also named Steve Rude, Craig Russell, and Paul Smith among her greatest influences.

## EARLY CAREER AND *SANDMAN*

After graduating from the American Academy of Art in Chicago in 1987, Thompson almost immediately found work in the comic book industry, illustrating titles for publishers such as Comico and First Comics; for the latter, she did the artwork for the Classics Illustrated version of Nathaniel Hawthorne's *The Scarlet Letter* (1850), published in 1989. She caught her first big break in the industry in 1990, when she took over the artistic duties on DC Comics' *Wonder Woman* series from her idol George Perez.

Thompson spent about a year working on *Wonder Woman* before her editor helped her secure a spot working on Neil Gaiman's Sandman series, which centers on the Endless, a group of godlike characters with very human attributes. As a longtime fan of the series, Thompson jumped at the chance. "Neil is one of the most excellent writers that an artist can work with," she told Irving. "One of the first things he does when he starts on a book is ask you what you like to draw, and what you don't like to draw." Their story arc, "Brief Lives," had originally been intended to run for just three issues, but the duo enjoyed working together so much that it stretched out from issues 41 to 49 of the *Sandman* series, published from September 1992 to May 1993. Thompson later wrote and illustrated several one-shot issues and miniseries featuring various characters from the series, including *The Little Endless Storybook* (2001) and *Death: At Death's Door* (2002–3), the latter of which was drawn in Japanese manga style, a first for the franchise.

Thompson returned to the world of *Sandman* in 2005 to write and illustrate the original graphic novel spinoff *The Dead Boy Detectives*. The titular characters are the ghosts of two teenage boys who died at an English boarding school decades apart; they first appeared in the *Sandman* story arc "Season of Mists," which related both their backstories and their first meeting. In *The Dead Boy Detectives*, which was also drawn in manga style and makes use of several tropes common to the genre, the boys must go undercover at an all-girls school in Chicago to find a missing student.

## OTHER COMICS

Thompson has provided the artwork for a number of DC's other comic series, including *Black Orchid* (1993), *The Invisibles* (1993, 1995, 1997), *Swamp Thing* (1994), *Books of Magic* (1996), and *Seekers into the Mystery* (1996). She also illustrated the DC miniseries *Finals* (1999), which she cocreated along with writer Will Pfeifer. Other publishers she has worked for include Marvel Comics, for which she illustrated "The Date," a Spider-Man story for issue 2 of the anthology series *Shadows and Light* (1998), and "Dazzler: Beyond the Music," also written by Pfeifer, which appeared in issue 32 of *X-Men Unlimited* (2001); the short-lived Topps Comics, for which she illustrated *The X-Files: AfterFlight* (1997); and Dark Horse Comics, for which she drew the miniseries *Badger: Shattered Mirror* (1994).

In addition, Thompson collaborated with writer Evan Dorkin on stories for each of the four *Dark Horse Book of . . .* anthologies: *Hauntings* (2003), *Witchcraft* (2004), *The Dead* (2005), and *Monsters* (2006). She won two Eisner Awards for best painter/multimedia artist of interior art for her work on these stories, in 2004 for "Stray" in *The Dark Horse Book of Haunt-*

*ings* and in 2007 for "A Dog and His Boy" in *The Dark Horse Book of Monsters* (among other work), and shared the 2005 Eisner Award for best short story with Dorkin for "Unfamiliar," in *The Dark Horse Book of Witchcraft*.

The characters in Thompson and Dorkin's *Dark Horse Book of . . .* stories later appeared in their own miniseries, *Beasts of Burden*, also written by Dorkin and illustrated by Thompson. The four-issue miniseries, which follows a pack of dogs (and a cat) as they fight supernatural threats to their hometown was published in 2009 to both critical and popular acclaim.

## SCARY GODMOTHER

Thompson had been riding the success of the comic book industry throughout the 1990s, picking her own projects, knowing that steady work was always available. Then came the bust that followed the collapse of the speculator market. Suddenly she found herself unable to find steady work as comic book stores and publishers began going out of business.

Thompson worked in comics whenever she could, but she also took on advertising work and other freelance assignments to make ends meet. With spare time on her hands, she began drawing for fun and soon developed the character of Scary Godmother, inspired primarily by the fact that her sister-in-law was pregnant and she was about to become an aunt for the first time. "I didn't realize that godmother was a religious thing and thought it was just a guardian. . . . I was lobbying very hard to become the godmother of what would become my first niece, Hannah, but at the time I was still dressing all in black," she told Irving. She continued, "I was thinking to myself, standing in the back of the Catholic Church, with my giant big shoes, and my black motorcycle jacket and big hair, that I was a scary godmother. Literally, when I said those two words together, the proverbial light bulb went off." Before long she began sketching out the character: a witch with tiny bat wings, black eyes, red hair, and a black tutu.

Though Thompson initially planned the story as a gift to her goddaughter, *Scary Godmother* soon took on a life of its own. Eventually the painted book found a home with Sirius Entertainment, which published it as a hardcover graphic novel. "The way I presented it is the only way that I've wanted to tell it—a story that I would enjoy, but just for kids," Thompson said to Irving. "In fact, there are very few comics for kids nowadays, but there should be more comics for kids. . . . I wanted to be one of the people who spends the time to make sure that we have another generation of comic book readers."

The first four *Scary Godmother* books—*Scary Godmother* (1997), *Scary Godmother: The Revenge of Jimmy* (1998), *Scary Godmother: The Mystery Date* (1999), and *Scary Godmother: The Boo Flu* (2000)—were published in a single collected volume in 2010. Thompson's various single-issue comics and miniseries were collected the following year as *Scary Godmother Comic Book Stories*.

### MAGIC TRIXIE

Thompson's other popular children's book series began with *Magic Trixie* (2008), a story about the misadventures of an elfish, gap-toothed magical little girl who cannot understand why no one will take her seriously. Like the Scary Godmother books, the series is completely written and painted by Thompson, who describes the character as a sassy combination of all of her nieces, with elements of her own childhood thrown in.

Recalling Trixie's creation in the HarperCollins Canada interview, Thompson said, "I never set out to create her or sat down at a blank page and said, 'Now I will create a new project!' I was working on a project for Vertigo/DC Comics. . . . At about the fifty-page mark, Magic Trixie popped into my head. She kept pushing aside the characters I was supposed to be drawing by dancing around and making faces. So I had to take out some paper at the end of each day and sketch and paint her. . . . And then once I had her drawn, her school friends started popping up. Next came her house. It all kind of crept in a little bit at a time."

The success of the first volume in the series has spawned two sequels: *Magic Trixie Sleeps Over* (2008), in which the title character tries sleeping at different friends' houses because she is tired of her bossy parents, and *Magic Trixie and the Dragon* (2009), in which she accidentally transforms her baby sister into a dragon.

### PERSONAL LIFE

Thompson is married to fellow comic book writer Brian Azzarello, best known for his series *100 Bullets*. The couple live in Chicago. Though they have said that they will never work together, they have, in a sense, appeared together in print: two characters in the DC miniseries *Kingdom Come* (1996), 666 and Joker's Daughter, were visually modeled on Azzarello and Thompson, respectively.

### SUGGESTED READING

Azzarello, Brian, and Jill Thompson. "Comic Book Writer Brian Azzarello and Artist Jill Thompson." Interview by Anne Elizabeth Moore. *AV Club*. Onion, 27 July 2006. Web. 13 Nov. 2014.

Behrens, Web. "Chicago Artist Jill Thompson Talks *Scary Godmother* Comics." *Time Out Chicago*. Time Out America, 30 Oct. 2012. Web. 13 Nov. 2014.

Dorkin, Evan, and Jill Thompson. Interview by Jon Jordan. *Crimespree* Sept.–Oct. 2009: n. pag. *Crimespree Magazine*. Web. 13 Nov. 2014.

Irving, Christopher. "Getting Scary, Cheery and Chatty with Jill Thompson." *Graphic NYC*. Christopher Irving and Seth Kushner, 30 Jan. 2012. Web. 13 Nov. 2014.

Thompson, Jill. "Jill Thompson on Magic Trixie." *HarperCollins Canada*. HarperCollins, n.d. Web. 13 Nov. 2014.

### SELECTED WORKS

*Sandman*, 1991–93; *Scary Godmother*, 1997; *Scary Godmother: The Revenge of Jimmy*, 1998; *Death: At Death's Door*, 2002–3; *The Dead Boy Detectives*, 2005; *Magic Trixie*, 2008; *Magic Trixie Sleeps Over*, 2008; *Beasts of Burden*, 2009; *Magic Trixie and the Dragon*, 2009

—Christopher Mari

# Chuck Todd

**Born:** 1972
**Occupation:** Journalist

In 2014, executives at NBC News chose Chuck Todd, the news division's longtime political director and White House correspondent, to become the twelfth moderator of *Meet the Press*, the network's flagship Sunday morning political talk show that first aired on television in 1947. Once a ratings powerhouse and the primary place where national leaders went to discuss issues of the day, the show had fallen on tough times since the sudden death of Tim Russert, its beloved and highly respected moderator, in 2008. NBC sought to return the program to its former glory and believes that Todd is the man to accomplish the show's revival.

Todd has amassed considerable professional experience since he began covering Washington politics in 1992. In an interview with Scott Porch for *Salon* (29 Nov. 2014), Todd explained what he sought to do with *Meet the Press* when he became the show's host: "I didn't think the format was necessarily broken, but I thought it couldn't be just a better-produced cable show. I think people are worn out of the daily news cycle. Monthly magazines are having a bit of a revival, and I'd like to think the Sunday news shows could be that for politics."

## EARLY LIFE AND JOURNALISM CAREER

Chuck Todd was born in Miami, Florida, in 1972. From 1990 to 1994, he attended George Washington University on a music scholarship. However, Todd did not graduate because he began working in 1992 at the *National Journal*'s newsletter the *Hotline*, long considered to be the best daily briefing for national politics. He worked at the *Hotline* for fifteen years, serving his last six years at the newsletter as its editor in chief. With the *Hotline*, Todd covered major news stories of the era, including the impeachment trial of President Bill Clinton in 1998 and 1999, the disputed presidential election of 2000, and the terrorist attacks of September 11, 2001. During this period he developed a reputation as an expert on political campaigns, and his expertise was frequently sought on political debate shows such as *Inside Politics* with Judy Woodruff on CNN and *Hardball with Chris Matthews* on MSNBC.

## NBC NEWS

With the help and support of Russert, who began moderating *Meet the Press* in 1991, Todd made the move to NBC News, where he became the news division's political director in March 2007. In this position—which he still holds—he provides on-air political analysis for NBC's major news programs including *Today*, *NBC Nightly News*, and *Meet the Press*. He is also the editor in chief of "First Read," NBC's online guide to political news, and he serves as the host for online political discussions at MSNBC.com. His insights into the political process are particularly apt during campaign seasons. Since moving to NBC News, he has covered both the 2008 and 2012 presidential elections. He also covered the midterm elections of 2010 and 2014 for NBC.

When Tim Russert died suddenly of a heart attack in June 2008, Todd was among the short list of candidates to replace him on *Meet the Press*. Of Russert's passing, Todd remarked in an interview for *Politics* (21 Apr. 2010):

fpc.state.gov/Wikimedia Commons

"There's no doubt things have changed. I think everyone is trying to contribute to the ballast that Tim was for the news organization, from anchors to correspondents to producers." Initially, retired NBC anchor Tom Brokaw filled in as interim moderator of *Meet the Press* before executives settled on David Gregory, a longtime White House correspondent for NBC News. Todd in turn replaced Gregory as White House correspondent in December 2008, covering the end of the George W. Bush presidency and the start of Barack Obama's term in office in January 2009. He also provided in-the-field reports from twenty-five countries on five continents. In January 2010, prior to the midterm elections in November, Todd launched MSNBC's *The Daily Rundown*, a weekday political news program, which he hosted until 2014 before being replaced by anchor José Diaz-Balart.

## MEET THE PRESS

In the years after Russert's passing, the once-dominate *Meet the Press* began falling behind in the ratings. Under Russert, the show pulled in more than $50 million a year in sponsorships and averaged about 4.5 million viewers a week, numbers that dwarfed the competition on CBS, ABC, and FOX. Throughout Gregory's tenure, however, the show's numbers continued to decline, dropping to 2.85 million viewers per week in the last quarter of 2013 and to 2.37 million in the second quarter of 2014. After executives at NBC initially expressed public support for Gregory, insiders began to leak rumors that NBC News had hired a psychology consultant and a brand consultant to study why Gregory was not connecting with viewers. Executives were also concerned when Gregory began to do radical things on the show, including brandishing an illegal high-capacity clip at Wayne LaPierre, the head of the National Rifle Association. He also accused the journalist Glenn Greenwald of aiding and abetting the fugitive Edward Snowden, who had revealed the extent of the National Security Agency's intelligence surveillance programs. After initially protesting that Gregory's job was secure, Deborah Turness, the president of NBC News, announced in August 2014 that Gregory was being removed in favor of Todd, whom she called "massively respected as one of the best, if not the best, political analysts in the business," as quoted by Bill Carter for the *New York Times* (14 Aug. 2014).

In order to take on the moderator's post on *Meet the Press*, Todd gave up both his morning program for MSNBC and his position as White House correspondent. When he began moderating *Meet the Press* in September 2014, he described it as something of a work in progress, with changes coming in bits and pieces as he and the producers experimented with different formats and varied guests, hoping to reattract viewers who preferred watching other Sunday morning political talk shows, particularly the number-one *Face the Nation* with Bob Schieffer on CBS.

"No one who watched *Meet the Press* on Sunday will be able to question Todd's preparedness or his clout. Delivering an interview with President Obama for his first show was a major coup," Manuel Roig-Franzia wrote in a review of Todd's debut as moderator for the *Washington Post* (7 Sept. 2014). "And as he questioned the president on the big issues of the moment . . . it was clear that Todd was not reading from some script written by the crew back in the studio. . . . Todd also knows how to keep his balance in an interview and not get knocked off his line of questioning." Todd has begun to move the ratings for *Meet the Press* in the right direction, often coming in second to Schieffer's highly regarded program.

## OTHER WORK AND ACHIEVEMENTS

In addition to his work with NBC News, Chuck Todd has served as an adjunct professor of political communications at Johns Hopkins University's graduate school. He also frequently writes op-ed pieces and political essays for such respected publications as the *Atlantic*, the *New York Times*, and the *Washington Post*. He is also the author of two books, *How Barack Obama Won: A State-by-State Guide to the Historic 2008 Presidential Election* (2009), which he co-authored with Sheldon Gawiser, and *The Stranger: Barack Obama in the White House* (2014). While the former was hailed as a definitive guide to the 2008 election, the latter met with more mixed reviews. Writing for the *Miami Herald* (14 Nov. 2014), Ariel Gonzalez complained that "nothing much is new in Todd's book. Expect no startling insights and revelations. The administration's highs and lows are recalled in dry, uninspiring prose that is beholden to a preconceived, one-size-fits-all thesis." When asked by Porch for *Salon* if his book was too focused on individual decisions Obama made (a criticism made by the *Washington Post*), Todd responded: "I wrote a book about Obama in Washington—his battle to change Washington. It's going to be insular. That's the nature of it."

Todd has won a number of Emmy Awards for his work as a journalist. In 2005, the *Washingtonian* named Todd to its list of the fifty best journalists. In 2012, he was named the most powerful journalist in Washington as part of *GQ*'s list of the "50 Most Powerful People in Washington." That same year, Todd won the Power Players match on the game show *Jeopardy*. Todd lives in Arlington, Virginia, with his wife Kristian and their two children.

## SUGGESTED READING

Carter, Bill. "NBC Chooses Chuck Todd to Replace David Gregory on 'Meet the Press.'" *New York Times*. New York Times, 14 Aug. 2014. Web. 5 Feb. 2015.

Gonzalez, Ariel. "Review: Chuck Todd's 'The Stranger: Barack Obama in the White House." *Miami Herald*. Miami Herald, 14 Nov. 2014. Web. 5 Feb. 2015.

Roig-Franzia, Manuel. "Chuck Todd's 'Meet the Press' Debut: A Straight-Talking Work in Progress." *Washington Post*. Washington Post, 7 Sept. 2014. Web. 27 Feb. 2015.

Todd, Chuck. Interview by Scott Porch. "Chuck Todd: 'I Wish We Didn't Focus on the Individual Personalities of Journalists.'" *Salon*. Salon Media Group, 29 Nov. 2014. Web. 27 Feb. 2015.

—Christopher Mari

# Toro y Moi

**Born:** November 7, 1986
**Occupation:** Musician

Chaz Bundick, much like his multilingual stage name Toro y Moi—"bull and" in Spanish and "me" in French, respectively—mixes a great variety of musical styles and approaches. Even before the release of his first album, *Causers of This* (2010), Toro y Moi was already the talk of the indie music world because of his single "Blessa." On his second album, *Underneath the Pine* (2011), Bundick tried to—and did—get away from the "chillwave" genre—a mix of pop and R&B, with influences from the 1960s, as well as the 1980s synthesizer sound, all made with lo-fi production. The second album was at times mellow but more focused and self-assured. On his albums *Anything in Return* (2013) and *What For?* (2015), Bundick has since continued to combine multiple influences, including 1970s rock and funk, 1990s neo-soul, and more contemporary indie sounds as well as house music. He has also made dance music under the name Les Sins and experimental works as Sides of Chaz.

## EARLY LIFE AND EDUCATION

Chazwick Bradley Bundick was born to a Filipina mother and an African American father in Columbia, South Carolina, on November 7, 1986. He began taking piano lessons around age eight, but did not enjoy them and so quit when he was ten. In seventh grade, however, he discovered the guitar, and with it a love of music. He began making his own music early on in high school, and even then he had multiple projects going at the same time. He and some fellow schoolmates played in an indie rock band called the Heist and the Accomplice, and Bundick also made his own recordings in his bedroom, influenced by the likes of Blink-182 and At the Drive-In—very different from the styles he would later draw on. He went on to attend the University of South Carolina, during which time he discovered a new appreciation for R&B, hip-hop, and funk and continued to record music. While at college he also befriended fellow musician Ernest Greene, who performs under the stage name Washed Out and is also often placed in the chillwave genre.

Bundick graduated from the University of South Carolina in the spring of 2009 with a bachelor's degree in graphic design, a profession

Michael Bezjian/Getty Images for Soho House

he was fully intending to pursue. He had held a graphic design job while at college, but they let him go shortly before graduation. He suddenly found himself working at a bagel shop without any future prospects for a career in his field. Meanwhile, however, he continued to make music. Yet Bundick had no idea how much traction his online song posts would get him.

## FIRST STEPS TO STARDOM

What he decided to do was to finish a few songs and put them up on his MySpace page, which he cleaned up, by removing everything from his page but the music. He then went on to e-mail a few music blogs without any serious expectations that his music would be heard or even appreciated. But he was pleasantly surprised. He told Andrew Stout for *Interview* (19 Jan. 2011), "When I got on my first blog I was freaking out." He even received an endorsement on the blog of hip-hop giant and tastemaker Kanye West. Under the name Toro y Moi, Bundick released two stylistically different songs on an EP: "Blessa" has a hazy summer mellow dance feel with an echoing beat that is both sharp and foggy, while "109" is a blend of the 1960s Motown R&B sound with a more contemporary lo-fi feel, similar to cult-classic indie pop artist Ariel Pink. These songs, like those on his upcoming debut album, were recorded and produced in his bedroom. In the middle of 2009 he was signed to

Carpark Records, on which he would release his first album.

Initially Bundick considered releasing two albums, one stylistically closer to "109" and the other to "Blessa," but he ultimately put out one, closer to the latter, called *Causers of This*. The album was released in February 2010—somewhat ironic timing, a number of critics noted, given that the genre of chillwave is generally associated with summer. With "Blessa" as the opening track, the full album, at only thirty-three minutes, introduced the new kid in town. The album's beat, synthesizers, and reverb took potential pop songs and turned them into an impressionistic and futuristic sound that looked forward as much as it looked back. The songs were by turn moody and atmospheric, fun and funky, and at times challenging: Bundick would put so much reverb and echo on some tracks that the beats seemed to trip over one another. The labels "chillwave," "glo-fi," and "hypnagogic pop" were applied, and other attempts to categorize the music were numerous, but the album remained difficult to pigeonhole. It was, however, generally well received by critics, both of the mainstream and blog variety, as well as by various fans.

In a review of *Causers of This* for the influential indie music site *Pitchfork* (17 Feb. 2010), Joe Colly wrote that Bundick's combination of his various influences and his own creativity resulted in "warm, wobbly pop songs that, while not always as catchy as his contemporaries', are distinctive and appealing in their own right." Colly observed that what separates Bundick from some of his musical peers is his production abilities and his use of sound to create texture. However, because the last few tracks failed to make an impression, Colly concluded, "If *Causers of This* stayed consistent through the end, it might be up there with the assured debuts of his peers; instead, it's just a few notches below." However, Mike Diver, writing for the *BBC Music* website (2010), offered a harsher criticism, calling the album "wholly generic," though admitting it to be "engrossing and entertaining." Diver concluded that it still might be worth following this artist to see where he goes next.

## CHANGING IT UP

In his sophomore effort, Bundick set out to make something different. The album, *Underneath the Pine* (2011), which was released almost exactly a year after Toro y Moi's debut album, was notably less lo-fi and hazy, though still often quite mellow and warm, and certainly more sure of itself. Bundick's voice and instruments, such as piano and guitar, came out more clearly on some tracks, and the live drums and bass in more uptempo numbers sound clearer as well, popping out rather than being over-soaked in reverb and effects. The cover of the album, like that of the first album, was made by Bundick. Whereas the debut album cover was more somber and dark, the cover of *Underneath the Pine* was more playful and perhaps even sexually suggestive: the cover image is a close-up photo, taken by Bundick himself, of pieces of the citrus fruit pomelo sticking out of his mouth and dripping juices. The album went on to reach number 50 on Billboard's Top Rock Albums chart and number 186 on the Billboard 200 chart.

Writing for *Pitchfork* (25 Feb. 2011), Ian Cohen saw the second album as a step up, calling it "a far richer and more accomplished whole." Furthermore, Cohen wrote, "Bundick's skill as an arranger is especially evident in *Pine*'s midsection," which, he said, makes "retro chic somehow still sound futuristic." Jenny Eliscu, writing for *Rolling Stone* (22 Feb. 2011), compared Bundick to another genre-bending indie musician with a diverse track record: "As Bundick reveals more of his esoteric pop sensibility, comparisons to Beck feel increasingly apt. Whatever wave Bundick is riding, he's likely to be at the front of it."

On his third album, *Anything in Return* (2013), Bundick again went for something different, something new. Being in a different place helped too. In the summer of 2011 he followed his girlfriend to Berkeley, California, where she was pursuing a doctorate in environmental engineering. Bundick had never lived outside of South Carolina before, and his new environment and new friends inspired him to reinvent himself yet again. *Anything in Return* was also the first of his albums to be recorded in a music studio, San Francisco's Different Fur. The album again featured synthesizers, but they were more assured and the beat was focused and strong, at times made for dance. Bundick's voice is also quite prominent and has a certain 90s R&B and neo-soul swagger with a contemporary flavor and influences from funk and house. Talking to Chris Martins for *Spin* (21 Jan. 2013), Bundick admitted that relocating to California "influenced my confidence in trying new things." He cited some modern sources of inspiration, such as Caribou, Four Tet, Motor City Drum Ensemble, and Floating Points.

The album is much more unambiguously dance-like than any of his previous records. "I was tired of making melancholy songs, because I'm not a sad guy," Bundick told Martins. "I tried to write a couple positive-sounding love songs, things that are saying how much I love you instead of how sad I am. The majority of the songs are more optimistic. There's definitely a brighter air to it. It's just me trying to change it up." The new approach certainly did not elude music critics, who almost as a rule pointed out that Toro y Moi cannot or will not be pinned down and reinvents himself on every album. Reviewing the album for the *Guardian* (17 Jan. 2013), Maddy Costa called Bundick "one of music's shape-shifters." Costa called the album's music "inventive and complex." In a review for *Paste* magazine (22 Jan. 2013), Jeff Gonick wrote that the album's musical complexity "keeps it from simply being a well-crafted collection of mildly catatonic funk." The record reached number one on Billboard's Top Electronic Albums chart and number sixty on the Billboard 200 chart.

### WHAT FOR?

Toro y Moi's fourth album, *What For?* (2015), signaled another change of musical direction. This time Bundick brought back the electric guitar, but the style borrowed heavily from 1970s rock of various sorts, from big and poppy to soft and mellow to psychedelic and spacey. Todd Rundgren and Electric Light Orchestra particularly influenced the sound of the album. Funk elements were still present on some tracks, however. The instrumentation was based primarily on the combination of drums, bass, guitar, and keyboards, and of course Bundick's vocals. In a review for *Pitchfork* (7 Apr. 2015), Ian Cohen observed that "Toro Y Moi's malleability is the project's most endearing quality," but concluded, rather harshly, that the album is "so passive it leaves your system the moment you're done with it." Not all critics were as lukewarm, however. Writing for *Spin* (7 May 2015), Harley Brown offered a positive review, admitting that although the album is a bit surprising at first, "it doesn't take much time to lean into this (somewhat) new iteration of Toro Y Moi's endlessly adaptable grooves like a head massage." The record reached number 123 on the Billboard 200 chart.

### PERSONAL LIFE

Bundick lives in Berkeley, California, where he has a studio in his home. When not work-ing on his music, he enjoys a variety of hobbies, including skateboarding, drawing, and making furniture.

### SUGGESTED READING

Bundick, Chaz. "Toro y Moi Is 'Not Just a Kid behind a Laptop': Chaz Bundick Sets the Record Straight." Interview by Chris Martins. *Spin*. SpinMedia, 21 Jan. 2013. Web. 17 July 2015.

Bundick, Chaz. "Toro y Moi's Chaz Bundick Doesn't Want to Go Shopping." Interview by Andrew Stout. *Interview*. Brant Publications, 19 Jan. 2011. Web. 17 July 2015.

Bundick, Chaz. "Q&A: Toro y Moi's Chaz Bundick on Being 'Straight-Up Tired of Music'." Interview by Chris Kornelis. *Rolling Stone*. Rolling Stone, 29 May 2013. Web. 17 July 2015.

Eliscu, Jenny. Rev. of *Underneath the Pine*, by Toro y Moi. *Rolling Stone*. Rolling Stone, 22 Feb. 2011. Web. 17 July 2015.

### SELECTED WORKS

*Causers of This*, 2010; *Underneath the Pine*, 2011; *Anything in Return*, 2013; *What For?* 2015

—Dmitry Kiper

---

# Lila Tretikov

**Born:** January 25, 1978

**Occupation:** Executive director of Wikimedia Foundation

In 2014 software engineer Lila Tretikov was named the executive director of the Wikimedia Foundation, which manages Wikipedia, the free online encyclopedia. Formerly the chief product officer at a software company called SugarCRM, the Russian-born Tretikov began working in the technology industry in 1999, with a company called Sun Microsystems. But it was only thanks to the twilight policies of the former Soviet Union that she made her way to Silicon Valley at all. She moved to the United States from Moscow to finish high school in the 1990s. "The only real way to improve conditions of civilizations is to provide open access to information for education and culture, and to be honest about the past," she observed in an interview with Jemima Kiss and Samuel Gibbs for the *Guardian* (6 Aug.

Lane Hartwell/Wikimedia

2014). "Otherwise we spend our lives siloed from each other and we repeat the mistakes of our grandparents." Tretikov's personal history, the reporters noted, fits neatly into the corporate ethos of Wikipedia, the world's sixth largest website, and according to the *Guardian*, the largest single source of free information in the world. It draws nearly 500 million unique visitors each month, and maintains over 32 million articles in 287 languages. Tretikov replaced former executive director, Sue Gardner, a journalist who joined Wikimedia in 2007. At the time, Wikipedia had only seven employees. As of the end of the 2013 fiscal year, the website counted more than two hundred employees with an operating budget of $35.7 million and net assets of more than $45.2 million, up from just $57,000 in 2004.

The site, which collects donations in lieu of selling advertisements, is an unusually complex organism. In addition to Wikipedia's paid employees, Tretikov oversees the site's core group of nearly three thousand dedicated Wikipedians—not all of whom were thrilled about her appointment. All told, Wikipedia counts about eighty thousand regular editors around the globe. Many of the core volunteers complained after Tretikov admitted that she had never edited an article on the site. Wikipedia is an open source wiki, which means that anyone anywhere can write for and edit the site. The democratic nature of Wikipedia is both its biggest draw and its

biggest weakness, though as Caitlin Dewey for the *Washington Post* (4 Aug. 2014) pointed out, there is "a side of the site casual readers never see: It's complex and esoteric and highly bureaucratic, with layers of editors, lengthy discussion boards called 'talk pages,' and many, many rules." If a user makes an edit, that edit is subject to the discretion of registered Wikipedia "admins" who have the power to enforce the site's editorial rules and ban users. Admins are subject to their own scrutiny through a myriad of other pages, tools, and panels. "It's a sprawling, self-moderating system," Dewey wrote. "And generally, it works." Still, as Dewey wrote, a case involving activists from A Voice for Men—a men's rights group—caused a stir around the same time Wikipedia announced some major changes in its editorial policies. The group claimed that Wikipedia was intentionally censoring its views as part of a feminist conspiracy. Among other changes, Wikipedia instated a new rule that editors must disclose if they are being paid to edit an article. Though Tretikov also hopes to employ new technologies to crack down on underhanded editing practices, as the site grows, it will be up to her to foster Wikipedia's relationship with its users without alienating them.

## EARLY LIFE AND EDUCATION

Tretikov was born in Moscow on January 25, 1978. Her father was a mathematician and her mother was a filmmaker. Tretikov was a child when Mikhail Gorbachev, the last general secretary of the Communist Party of the Soviet Union, launched two programs that would change the course of Russia's history: perestroika (restructuring) and glasnost (openness). "Glasnost was a phenomenal, renaissance period in the history of Russia and taught me much about importance of freedom of information," Tretikov told Kiss and Gibbs. Thanks to the country's new policies (and the collapse of the Soviet regime), Tretikov, who was an excellent student, was able to leave Moscow and finish high school in the United States. She moved to the Queens borough of New York City and worked as a waitress to pay for her senior year. When she came to the United States, she didn't speak any English, but she was a quick study. By graduation, she was the top student in her Shakespeare class. After high school, she enrolled at the University of California, Berkeley to study art and computer science. There, she became interested in artificial intelligence (AI) and machine learning systems, like those that can distinguish regular e-mail from spam, according to Katherine Seligman for Berkeley's *California Magazine* (9 May 2014). So enthusiastic was Tretikov to work in technology that she left Berkeley in 1999 to work as an engineer at Sun Microsystems before earning her degree. Tretikov holds more than six patents in intelligent data mapping and dynamic language applications through her work with Sun. She joined SugarCRM, a software company, as chief product officer in 2006.

## SUGARCRM AND OPEN SOURCE SOFTWARE

SugarCRM was founded by Jacob Tyler, Clint Orem, and John Roberts in 2004. The company offers customer management software based on the open source model. Companies like IBM, Microsoft, and Apple use what is known as proprietary code, which means that they develop software source code in-house. The open source software movement came about as a reaction to proprietary coding, and advocates for a "collaborative process for creating computer programs," Noam Cohen wrote for the *New York Times* (1 May 2014), "including the one that runs Wikipedia." Open source codes, like Linux and Unix, aren't associated with any particular hardware manufacturer, and allow knowledgeable users to tailor operating systems to their own individual needs. Open source technology was born out of the same idealistic impulse as Wikipedia—free information for all—but also, like Wikipedia, it is a poor money-making model. "Open [source] is not a business model, it is a production model," Mårten Mickos, the former chief executive MySQL, an open source database management system company that was sold to Sun Microsystems for $1 billion in 2008, told Quentin Hardy for the *New York Times* (23 July 2014). What that model is good for, he added, is providing "a way to experiment with a lot of possibilities, make a lot of mistakes quickly, figure out what works faster."

## WIKIPEDIA

Tretikov's experience with open source made her a perfect candidate for Wikipedia's top management position. "When I first met with her, she talked compellingly about her childhood growing up in the Soviet Union, and she was genuinely and deeply motivated by Wikimedia's mission to spread free knowledge to people everywhere in the world," Jimmy Wales, the co-founder of Wikipedia, told Liz Gannes for the tech news website *Re/code* (1 May 2014) of the foundation's decision to hire Tretikov. "I also appreciated her experience with open-source technologies, and I am really happy we found someone with a strong background in product and engineering." After beating out 1,300 candidates for the job, Tretikov officially assumed her post on June 1, 2014. Given her background, Kiss and Gibbs wrote, it is not surprising that Tretikov hopes to see Wikipedia "assert itself as a technology company, rather than a media firm." She hopes to utilize automated software to address some of the site's editorial issues; Wikipedia already uses bots to correct spelling, update standard census statistics and, according to the *Guardian*, reverse vandalism. A number of independent Twitter accounts also exist to tweet out alerts whenever an article related to a public body like Congress is updated by an IP address connected to the body. But Tretikov, with her experience in AI technologies, hopes to do even more. "In the future, an editor without coding skills will have access to tools that could allow him or her to automatically scan, identify, and fill gaps in the knowledge with a few clicks of a button," she told Kiss and Gibbs. "[Programmers] are thinking about how we can augment and improve what humans do by handing off the grunt work to the machines—enabling us to focus on the creative, ingenious tasks. Our biggest challenge is to understand how things are changing in the way humans experience technology and be there for those that aren't even online yet."

What the Wikipedia bots cannot address, however, is Wikipedia's diversity problem. Ninety percent of Wikipedia's contributors are men, most of them living in the West. Of the site's eighty thousand or so editors, women account for only 15 percent. Many pointed to the lack of female editors in 2013, when editors inexplicably began transferring the names of women from the "American Novelists" category on the site, to a subcategory called "American Women Novelists." An editor posted a notice saying that the general list was too long, but the lack of an "American Men Novelists" subcategory was seen by critics as implicitly suggesting that women writers exist in a lesser category than male writers. Such slights can have serious consequences given Wikipedia's ubiquity, a problem of which the site is well aware and with Tretikov, is working to remedy. As executive director, Tretikov has been adamant about not selling advertising space on the site, even though it has been estimated that the site could make as much as $3 billion a year if it did. "Knowledge is all about trust," Tretikov told Kiss and Gibbs. "Not being beholden to demands of the market gives us freedom to do the right thing for the user first and foremost. It allows us to be much more focused on the users and what their needs are."

Tretikov's partner, Wil Sinclair, is a software developer who has been an outspoken critic of Wikipedia. Tretikov lives in Los Gatos, in Santa Clara County, California.

## SUGGESTED READING

Cohen, Noam. "Open-Source Software Specialist Selected as Executive Director of Wikipedia." *New York Times*. New York Times, 1 May 2014. Web. 21 Oct. 2014.

Dewey, Caitlin. "Men's Rights Activists Think a 'Hateful' Feminist Conspiracy Is Ruining Wikipedia." *Washington Post*. Washington Post, 4 Aug. 2014. Web. 21 Oct. 2014.

Filipacchi, Amanda. "Wikipedia's Sexism toward Female Novelists." *New York Times*. New York Times, 24 Apr. 2013. Web. 21 Oct. 2014.

Gannes, Liz. "Wikipedia Has a New Boss: Lila Tretikov Named Executive Director of Wikimedia Foundation." *Re/code*. Revere Digital, 1 May 2014. Web. 21 Oct. 2014.

Hardy, Quentin. "Open Source and the Challenge of Making Money." *New York Times*. New York Times, 23 July 2014. Web. 21 Oct. 2014.

Kiss, Jemima, and Samuel Gibbs. "Wikipedia Boss Lila Tretikov: 'Glasnost taught me much about freedom of information.'" *Guardian*. Guardian News and Media, 6 Aug. 2014. Web. 21 Oct. 2014.

Seligman, Katherine. "The Woman to Run Wikipedia: Russian-born Former Cal Student Seen as 'White Unicorn.'" (Berkeley) *California Magazine*. Cal Alumni Assoc., 9 May 2014. Web. 21 Oct. 2014.

—Molly Hagan

# Monica G. Turner
**Occupation:** Ecologist

Monica G. Turner is a landscape ecologist and the Eugene P. Odum Professor of Ecology at the University of Wisconsin–Madison. People often think of landscape ecology as a subdivision of biology, but this is not the case, Turner insists. Landscape ecology combines many different sciences to describe ecosystems over time. Turner helped to organize the first American meeting of landscape ecologists in 1986, and in describing the meeting she offered a good definition of the field itself. "For the first time," she told Nick Zagorski for the *Proceedings of the National Academy of Sciences of the United States of America* (2 Mar. 2007), "ecologists from different places came together to meaningfully consider what it means to have spatial variation in the environment and what implications this has for the functioning of ecosystems, the movement patterns and survival of organisms, and community-level interactions."

Turner is best known for her research following the summer of 1988, when major wildfires raged in Yellowstone National Park and affected more than 35 percent of the park's total acreage. Her work led to a number of major discoveries regarding forest processes and regrowth. As she wrote in an article for *Yellowstone Science* (June 2009) about her work, "The 1988 fires presented an unprecedented opportunity to study the landscape-scale ecological effects of an infrequent natural disturbance—a large, severe fire in this case—in an ecological system minimally affected by humans." She hopes that her continuing research at Yellowstone might lay the groundwork for developing responses to human-induced climate change. Turner has published more than two hundred academic papers, edited six books, and is the coeditor in chief of the journal *Ecosystems*. She was elected to the National Academy of Sciences in 2004, and in 2008, she received the ECI Prize in terrestrial ecology from the Ecology Institute and the Robert H. MacArthur Award from the Ecological Society of America.

## EARLY LIFE AND EDUCATION

Turner was born and raised in the suburbs of Long Island outside of New York City. Despite her urban upbringing, annual camping trips in the summer sparked her love of nature. She enrolled at Fordham University in the Bronx borough of New York City in 1976 with aspirations of a career as a veterinarian or a forest ranger. The summer after her sophomore year, she got a job working for the Student Conservation Association as an interpretive ranger at Yellowstone National Park. "I had never been out of the northeast before that," Turner told Zagorski, "but the experience was just phenomenal. I was stationed at Old Faithful and had to give the evening campfire talks and the Twilight on Geyser Hill walk and also work in the visitor's center. By the end, I had learned so much and loved it that I decided against the veterinary path and to pursue something in ecology."

Though her department chair was less than enthusiastic about her plan—he encouraged her to attend medical school—Turner was determined. She completed her undergraduate honors thesis on phytoplankton growth in Long Island Sound and graduated summa cum laude, with a BS degree in biology in 1980. Turner initially wanted to attend Boston University for graduate school, but after a visit to Athens, Georgia, she decided to pursue her degree at the University of Georgia where pioneering ecologist Eugene Odum was a professor. Odum died in 2002, and in his obituary for the *New York Times* (14 Aug. 2002), Ari L. Goldman touted him as the "father of modern ecology." According to Goldman, Odum, who worked closely with Turner, "argued that ecology was not a branch of anything but an integrated discipline that brought all of the sciences together. He saw the earth as a series of interlocking environmental communities, or ecosystems, each of which embraced 'a unique strategy of development.'"

## LANDSCAPE ECOLOGY

Initially, Turner was more interested in working as a ranger than in research, but her academic journey happened to coincide with the birth of a new field in ecology. "Landscape ecology was emerging in Europe, and my doctoral advisor, Frank Golley, was one of the few US scientists who attended some of their meetings," she told Zagorski. "Whenever he came back, he would tell all of us about the goings on." Turner wrote her dissertation on the relationship between wildfires and the grazing of feral horses on Cumberland Island National Seashore in St. Marys, Georgia, and after finishing her PhD in ecology in 1985, Turner stayed in Athens to complete postdoctoral research with Odum. Their examination of the changes in land use in Georgia is considered one of the earliest US landscape ecology studies.

In 1986 Turner and Golley organized the first American meeting for landscape ecology. Turner felt invigorated by the support of the international ecologists, but not all of her colleagues were so excited. "People called it pseudoscience because of the absence of replicability [the ability to reproduce experiments], and reviewers would say it's impossible to do ecology at

these scales," she explained to Zagorski. One of Turner's papers was rejected three times before it was published. Over time, however, other scientists warmed to the new discipline. In 1994, Turner joined the faculty at the University of Wisconsin–Madison. In 2005, she was named the Eugene P. Odum Professor of Ecology in the Department of Zoology.

## SUMMER OF FIRE

After completing postdoctoral research with Odum in 1987, Turner moved to Tennessee to accept a fellowship at Oak Ridge National Laboratory, where she became a research staff scientist in 1989. It was a major moment for landscape ecology and also a turning point in Turner's career. During her seven years at Oak Ridge, Turner and her colleagues developed key models and concepts that are now standard in the field—"things like the fact that you can have thresholds in the connectivity of habitats across landscapes, or a series of predictions we made for species movement patterns and the spread of disturbances," she explained to Zagorski. Early on, Turner met with a forest ecologist named Bill Romme. Romme, who had extensively studied the fire history of Yellowstone National Park, had attended Turner's first landscape ecology meeting in 1986. Turner wanted to apply the models she had developed at Oak Ridge to a real landscape, so the two agreed to collaborate. She made plans to visit the park in 1988 and use Romme's data in her research, but in June she was forced to rethink everything.

According to *National Geographic*, more than one hundred thousand wildfires clear four to five million acres of land in the United States on average each year. Four out of five of those fires are started by humans, but naturally occurring wildfires can be good for forests, hastening regeneration and eliminating disease from an ecosystem. In June 1988 a combination of lightning and human carelessness sparked wildfires in Yellowstone National Park. Though wildfires can be very dangerous—moving at speeds of up to fourteen miles an hour—there was little cause for concern until July, when the unusually hot, dry weather fanned the flames. The US National Park Service employs what is colloquially known as a "let it burn" policy. In other words, fires that begin naturally are allowed to run their course, but by August, drought conditions and sixty-mile-per-hour winds had produced a fire the magnitude of which shocked even scientists. On August 20 alone, the flames consumed more than 55,000 acres, doubling the acreage that had already burned. A horrified public watched the saga unfold on television. "Yellowstone is a beloved icon," Scott McMillion, a reporter for the *Bozeman Daily Chronicle* in Montana, told Liane Hansen and Laura Krantz for NPR's *Weekend Edition* (29 Aug. 2008). "It was a celebrity fire in a celebrity place. Everyone knows about Yellowstone and there was an impression that it was being allowed to burn to the ground."

## "RISING FROM THE ASHES"

The flames did not fully subside until November; Turner arrived at the park in October. Instead of studying Yellowstone's forest history, she observed and researched its recovery. Turner and Romme began their studies in the summer of 1989. Lacking funds, they recruited volunteers—including Turner's mother—to help them measure acres of burnt trees. It was strenuous, hot work. Turner told Jill Sakai in an article for *On Wisconsin* (Summer 2008), the University of Wisconsin's alumni magazine, that it "was like being in an oven." One of Turner's first projects involved the regrowth of lodgepole pine, the most populous tree species in the park. Turner reasoned that the regrowth of the lodgepole pines would look similar in different regions of the park—this did not prove to be the case. In one region, almost no trees grew back, but in another, there was a dense forest of them. In ecology, Turner explained to Sakai, "that's an ecologically huge range. Turner and her team discovered that the variation could be attributed to a trait called cone serotiny. "Lodgepole pine trees produce one of two different cone types," Sakai wrote, "one that opens to scatter seeds as soon as it matures and another—called serotinous—that is coated with a thick resin that seals seeds inside until melted open by the heat of a fire." Trees with serotinous cones were unevenly distributed throughout the forest, it seemed, so regions that appeared homogenous before the fire grew back in very different ways.

Turner continues to be impressed by Yellowstone's incredible resiliency. Among the other surprises Turner and her team uncovered after the fire included a profusion of wildflowers in 1990 (scientists expected most plant regrowth to be slow); a decline, rather than an increase, in invasive species; and the appearance of seedling aspen—a plant that was previously thought to only reproduce from existing roots. To accommodate all of the new data, Turner assembled an interdisciplinary team including scientists from across the country and experts in a variety of fields, including soil chemistry, botany, and entomology. "She excels at getting the right team of people together to address complex questions about landscapes," Phil Townsend, Turner's colleague at Madison, told Sakai. "She's really the glue that holds them together."

Turner continues to study ecological systems at Yellowstone. Some of her recent work involves the complex relationship between wildfires and bark beetles, considered a pest and huge threat to trees, and the ecological effects of climate change and their impact on future disturbance regimes.

## SUGGESTED READING

Goldman, Ari L. "Eugene P. Odum Dies at 88; Founded Modern Ecology." *New York Times*. New York Times, 14 Aug. 2002. Web. 20 Jan. 2015.

Hansen, Liane, and Laura Krantz. "Remembering the 1988 Yellowstone Fires." *Weekend Edition Sunday*. NPR, 29 Aug. 2008. Web. 20 Jan. 2015.

Sakai, Jill. "Rising from the Ashes." *On Wisconsin*. University of Wisconsin–Madison, Summer 2008. Web. 20 Jan. 2015.

Turner, Monica. "Ecological Effects of the '88 Yellowstone Fires: A Story of Surprise, Constancy, and Change." *Yellowstone Science* 17.2 (2009): 24–49. Print.

"Wildfires: Cold, Dry, Windy." *National Geographic*. National Geographic Society, n.d. Web. 20 Jan. 2015.

Zagorski, Nick. "Profile of Monica G. Turner." *Proceedings of the National Academy of Sciences of the United States of America*. Natl. Acad. of Sciences, 2 Mar. 2007. Web. 20 Jan. 2015.

—Molly Hagan

# Deborah Turness

**Born:** 1967

**Occupation:** Television news executive

Deborah Turness became the president of NBC News in 2013. She spent twenty-five years at Britain's ITV News and was one of the few British journalists invited to a banquet at Buckingham Palace when US president Barack Obama visited Britain in 2011. She told Tara Conlan for the *Guardian* (5 July 2010), "News is the best drama on television because it's real." She was an early proponent of offering digital content along with print news. She began to shake up things at NBC News almost as soon as she arrived. As she explained to Bill Carter for the *New York Times* (25 Aug. 2014), "Some change isn't easy. It's painful, but an organization has to go through it. And a lot of that is still ahead."

## EDUCATION AND EARLY CAREER

Turness was born and raised in Hertfordshire, England. She graduated from the University of France with degrees in French and English. She remained in Paris, working for the British Channel 4 News. Her great coup was to gain an interview with French president Jacques Chirac, even persuading him to speak in English for the interview.

Beginning in 1988, Turness worked at the British station ITN, the major competitor of the British Broadcasting Corporation (BBC), as a producer, working in bureaus in Paris and Washington, DC.

In 2002 Turness took a position with public service broadcaster Channel 4 as a series producer on the new morning show *RI:SE* after the former producer, Mark Killick, left the show a mere four days after it premiered. As Killick's replacement, Channel 4 promptly hired Turness from ITN, where she was deputy editor of 5 News. Given her thirteen years at ITN, her arrival generated hope. However, it was not a good

Eamonn McCabe/Redferns/GettyImages

fit; she left the job after only six months, having failed to gain an audience. The show itself was cancelled the following year.

## FROM ITV TO NBC

After her stint at Channel 4, Turness returned to ITN, working as editor of ITV News in 2004. One of her innovations was to replace reporters sitting behind a desk with reporters standing or perching on stools.

Coworkers appreciated her work ethic when, in addition to her regular duties, she agreed to chair the 2010 Edinburgh International Television Festival, a key festival for British television. As Steve Anderson, a BBC producer who would later join Turness at NBC, told Conlan, "No one could ever pay Deborah enough. She does the work of ten people and always has the appetite for more. And she manages it all with charm and without petty politics."

ITN has a partnership with NBC to provide content for special events, such as the 2011 wedding of Prince William and Kate Middleton; Turness oversaw coverage of that wedding. The ITV News at Ten team won a 2010 British Academy of Television and Arts (BAFTA) Award for their coverage of the earthquake in Haiti. Turness received kudos for maintaining the network's integrity while competitors such as the BBC and News Corps were scandal-ridden.

Turness accepted an offer to become president of NBC News in 2013. Andrea Mitchell, an NBC correspondent, told Bryan Burrough for *Vanity Fair* (May 2015), "Deborah is very creative, very competitive, and very ambitious in the best sense of the word. I think it's been an impressive retooling."

## MOVING ON

Turness's role at NBC has been somewhat less than that of Steve Capus, whom she succeeded after his eight-year tenure. Capus resigned, frustrated with a new administrative structure that became NBC Universal, a combination of NBC News plus two cable news programs, MSNBC and CNBC, all headed by Patricia Fili-Krushel. The new division employed more than two thousand people. Unlike Capus, Turness is not in charge of the cable networks CNBC or MSNBC; instead, she reported to Fili-Krushel. Turness holds daily nine a.m. meetings, known as the Exchange, with the editorial staff, including those who attend by video conference call.

One of her first priorities was to reinvigorate the *Today* show, which lagged behind the other major networks' morning shows. ABC's *Good Morning America* had taken over the number-one slot, causing NBC a significant loss of advertising revenue. With rumors of host Matt Lauer departing, the *Today* show was floundering. Turness's arrival made the difference for Lauer, who told Carter, "We have all been impressed by how she is able to focus on every aspect of the organization. For the first time in a very long time everybody wants to be on the team."

With the *Today* show—NBC News's most profitable broadcast—stabilized, the second program to attract Turness's attention was the Sunday morning *Meet the Press*, which had been losing market share since the death of Tim Russert in 2008. In December 2013 Turness asked those working on the show for a mission statement, as well as their ideas on what did and did not work on the show. That show was also losing the ratings war in broadcast television, prompting suspicion that the host, David Gregory, might be replaced. The show's producer, Adam Verdugo, left for CBS News. By August 2014 Gregory was out and Chuck Todd was in.

## ADJUSTMENTS

Turness was unused to dealing with news personalities who made more than a million dollars annually and had a steep learning curve on dealing with the talent. Once she realized that these people had agents through whom she needed to communicate, things improved.

At the same time, however, news staff in Washington, DC, was cut, and Antoine Sanfuentes, the former Washington bureau chief, announced his retirement, effective January 2014.

Despite all the upheaval and a greater degree of scrutiny than she was used to in British television news, Turness remained positive. She told Carter, "It has been an incredibly productive year. I have achieved more in the first year than I ever thought I could." One of those achievements was to centralize booking guests for all the shows, so that shows were no longer competing for interviewees.

Turness was also eager to bring NBC into the digital age. She offended some at the network by her statement in a *New York Times* interview that the network had been "asleep" for the preceding fifteen years. She brought the digital news service into the overall organization; before her arrival it had been a separate unit.

## EBOLA

In 2014 Ashoka Mukpo, an American cameraman working for NBC in Liberia, was diagnosed with Ebola. A writer and freelancer who had been working in the African country for three years, he was hired by NBC to work with their chief medical correspondent, Dr. Nancy Snyderman. The following day he tested positive for Ebola, the fifth United States citizen to be affected.

The station pledged care for Mukpo and arranged a flight back to the United States for treatment. Turness informed the station's employees, "We are doing everything we can to get him the best care possible. He will be flown back to the United States for treatment at a medical center that is equipped to handle Ebola patients."

In addition, NBC chartered a plane for the remainder of their staff in Liberia to return to the United States, where they remained in quarantine for twenty-one days. None contracted the virus, and Mukpo recovered.

## BRIAN WILLIAMS CONTROVERSY

NBC news commentator Brian Williams was an embedded journalist in Iraq during 2003; he later claimed that a helicopter in which he was a passenger had been shot down. Iraq veterans disputed the account on social media. According to them, the helicopter had not even been fired on. Williams apologized on air and to military personnel for his exaggeration, but stronger action seemed necessary. Turness—along with Fili-Krushel and Steve Burke, CEO of NBC Universal—was part of the 2015 NBC decision to suspend Williams, in light of his embellishing his experiences in Iraq. Lester Holt replaced Williams on NBC's *Nightly News*.

When the news of Williams's suspension broke in February, Turness sent an e-mail to the news staff, which was published by the military newspaper *Stars and Stripes* (7 Feb. 2015). She included a positive message: "Since joining NBC News, I've seen great strength and resilience. We are a close-knit family, and your response this week has made that even clearer. As a relentless news agenda marches on, thank you again for continuing to do what we do best— bring the most important stories of the day to our audience."

Although Williams had signed a lucrative five-year contract the previous December, he was subsequently given a six-month leave without pay, but not fired from the network for this falsifying of his experience. "We felt it would have been wrong to disregard the good work Brian has done and the special relationship he has forged with our viewers over twenty-two years," Roger Yu and Melanie Eversley quoted Turness as saying in *USA Today* (12 Feb. 2015).

In the wake of the scandal, NBC turned to the head of its investigative reporters, Richard Esposito, to work with a lawyer, looking further into Williams's public statements for lack of veracity. His statements about Hurricane Katrina and his reporting from Tahrir Square in Cairo during the Arab Spring are among additional accounts that may have been inflated.

NBC also turned to Andrew Lack to become chair of NBC News and MSNBC, replacing Fili-Krushel. Lack had once been president and chief operating officer of NBC. He had groomed Williams for the job of news anchor, a fact that some saw as offering hope for Williams's tenure at NBC.

Media watchers place the Williams debacle in the context of five difficult years that followed Comcast's acquisition of the network and a series of missteps. Turness, with her lack of experience in US journalism, is sometimes listed among those missteps.

## PERSONAL LIFE

Turness was formerly married to television journalist Damien Steward, who was also a roadie for the rock band the Clash. She is married to John Toker, former communications director for Britain's intelligence and security, now a stay-at-home father. The couple live in Bronxville, New York, with their two daughters.

Turness loves a challenge, as is evident from her also once having competed in a Beijing-to-Paris off-road car rally that lasted thirty-three days. As she told Yael Kohen and Karen Schwartz for *Marie Claire* (Sept. 2014), "It was a really big job, and the thing is, it's about transformation, which I love. Look, if I'd been told, 'NBC is exactly the way we want it, it works, it purrs, it hums, come in, keep driving it,' I wouldn't have been interested."

## SUGGESTED READING

Burrough, Bryan. "The Inside Story of the Civil War for the Soul of NBC News." *Vanity Fair*. Condé Nast, May 2015. Web. 21 Apr. 2015.

Carter, Bill. "NBC News President Rouses the Network." *New York Times*. New York Times, 24 Aug. 2014. Web. 20 Apr. 2015.

Conlan, Tara. "Deborah Turness: 'News Is the Best Drama on Television.'" *Guardian*. Guardian News and Media, 5 July 2010. Web. 11 May 2015.

Fernandez, Bob. "Brian Williams' Troubles Are Just the Latest Plaguing NBC's News Division." *Philadelphia Inquirer*. Philadelphia Inquirer, 13 Feb. 2015. Web. 20 Apr. 2015.

Kohen, Yael, and Karen Schwartz. "Change Agents." *Marie Claire* 21.9 (2014): 222–26. Print.

"Text of Email on Brian Williams from NBC News President to Editorial Staff." *Stars and Stripes*. Stars and Stripes, 7 Feb. 2015. Web. 20 Apr. 2015.

Yu, Roger, and Melanie Eversley. "NBC Suspends Brian Williams 6 Months." *USA Today*. USA Today, 12 Feb. 2015. Web. 8 Apr. 2015.

—Judy Johnson, MLS

# Anya Ulinich

**Born:** 1973
**Occupation:** Author and illustrator

The Russian-born Anya Ulinich started out as an artist, then became a writer, and then combined her two talents to become a highly regarded graphic novelist. Ulinich published her debut novel, *Petropolis*, in 2007. Like Ulinich, the main character of that novel comes to Phoenix, Arizona, from Russia as a teenager and tries to adjust to her new homeland. For her second novel, *Lena Finkle's Magic Barrel* (2014), Ulinich returned to her roots as an artist and made a clever, funny graphic novel that also leaned heavily on autobiography for much of its material. The main character, Lena Finkle, is a twice-divorced Russian Jew living in New York City, looking for romantic relationships on the Internet while also trying to take care of her children. The combination of words and images works well: "Through moody, diary-like sketches, the book traces her harrowing and exhilarating romantic adventures, along with vivid, funny evocations of her Russian childhood and her life with her daughters," wrote Katie Roiphe for the *Financial Times* (5 Sept. 2014).

## EARLY LIFE

Anya Ulinich was born in 1973 in Moscow, Russia (then part of the Soviet Union). She grew up on the outskirts of Moscow in a typical Soviet-

Jonathan Fickies/Getty Images for Jumpstart for Children

The technique she learned in art school was the official art of the Soviet Union, known as Socialist realism. Not to be confused with social realism, Socialist realism paintings were essentially idealized pictures of Soviet leaders and common workers. Ulinich was accepted to the Stroganov Moscow State University of Arts and Industry, but she did not get a chance to pursue an education there because she moved to the United States with her mother, father, and brother.

**COMING TO THE UNITED STATES**

The Ulinich family arrived in Phoenix, Arizona, in 1991, with basically no money and an uncertain future regarding their immigration status (they came on tourist visas). Seventeen years old at the time, Ulinich continued to paint and draw, which, she told Kinsella, "became the only things that I did well" after arriving in the United States. The situation at home became more volatile and sad: her parents, normally even-tempered people, became stressed and depressed given the uncertainty of their employment, living situation, and immigration status. They had to wait for the US Immigration and Naturalization Service to accept their asylum application. (Starting in the 1980s it became easier for Jews living in the Soviet Union to immigrate to countries such as the United States. But there was still a lot of red tape.) In the "Modern Love" column for the *New York Times* (11 Mar. 2007), Ulinich wrote in detail about that time in her life. She described her parents as "nervous wrecks" and recalled how her mother would cry and her father would scream. All Ulinich knew was that she had to get out of their tiny apartment.

**EDUCATION**

Soon after arriving in Phoenix, Ulinich began attending a graphic-design trade school, which did not ask for her immigration documents or status. For work, she cleaned houses for cash. At the trade school she met a young man, and soon, as Ulinich wrote for the *New York Times* column, "I hit upon a solution to all of our problems." She decided to marry him, whom she likened to Bart Simpson (of the television series *The Simpsons*) because the first time she saw him he was eating a Butterfinger chocolate bar. Marrying him would, so to speak, kill two birds with one stone: she could move out of her parents' apartment and her immigration status would no longer be unstable (she could become a perma-

style high-rise building. Her father worked as a bureaucrat in the mining industry and her mother was a museum administrator. At school she did not fit in, and once her peers figured out she was Jewish (at first she was taken for Georgian or Armenian) she had an even harder time. In an interview with Paul Berger for *Forward* (25 July 2014), she referred to her school days as "brutal." In an interview with Kevin Kinsella for the website MaudNewton.com (18 Sept. 2007), Ulinich referred to her time in school as consisting of "ten years of boredom layered with trauma."

Though the school offered a good education in math and science, there was no real arts curriculum. However, Ulinich found a safe haven of sorts in the central part of Moscow, where she took art classes three times a week—something she would have mixed feelings about later in life, but it was an experience that nonetheless shaped her technical skills as an artist. (Unlike the heroine of her debut novel, Ulinich began taking art classes not in her mid-teens but at the age of four.) "My teachers' methods would make any American educator cringe," she told Kinsella. "One guy used to approach his students from behind with a butter knife and, without a word, scrape parts of their paintings that he didn't like. However, I loved even the meanest and the craziest of my art teachers. They were the only people, besides my parents, who cared to teach me."

nent resident of the United States as the wife of a US citizen).

Before the wedding at the courthouse, Ulinich wrote, "I sensed I was making a mistake." But the other option—losing her boyfriend and returning to live with her family—was unthinkable. The marriage did not last long. Her husband drank a lot and went out late, she "nagged and cried," and the fights they had "got so loud that our downstairs neighbors threatened to call the police." They divorced, and a few years later Ulinich remarried.

Ulinich studied art at Arizona State University, and after receiving encouragement from a teacher she transferred to the Art Institute of Chicago during her junior year. She graduated in 1996. After graduation, she worked for a tech company in Chicago but found no "spiritual fulfillment," she told Berger. She painted at home but found no satisfaction from it: on dark canvases she painted allegorical images and texts, but she found the images to be obvious and boring. She could not express her feelings and frustrations adequately with paint, but she was still too afraid to try writing because of her self-consciousness about her fluency in English.

At the age of twenty-three she became pregnant; she also applied to graduate school and got in. On a full scholarship, she attended the University of California, Davis, where she studied for two years. During her first year, she took a break from painting to make installations and sculptures; she resumed painting during her second year, and felt the first drop of originality. Her paintings had more expressive qualities, and she began to write on her own. Ulinich received her MFA in 2000, after which she, her husband, and their daughter moved to New York City.

## DEBUT NOVEL

Ulinich stayed home at her Brooklyn apartment taking care of her firstborn child, Sofia. A few years later she gave birth to her second daughter, Rebecca. While taking care of her kids, Ulinich could not paint. It was a matter of time, space, and safety (oil paints and thinners are hazardous), so she eventually took to writing. In what became an origin story of sorts, Ulinich cared for her children during the day, and after her husband came home from work, she went to cafés in the evening to write. In interviews Ulinich explained that writing was the only real creative option available to her in a café. But her immersion in writing was not simply a matter of practicality: Ulinich had stories inside her that were

waiting to get out, and she ultimately accepted that those stories had to be told with words and not paints. Her new medium was not only more portable but also the best method for her to unleash her creativity.

Published in 2007, her novel *Petropolis*, like many first novels, was semiautobiographical, at least in its foundation. The heroine, Sasha Goldberg, is a Russian Jew who emigrates from the former Soviet Union, though she grows up not in Moscow but in a town in Siberia called Asbestos 2. Although she cannot play music and is too heavy to dance ballet (a disappointment to her mother, Lubov), Sasha loves to draw and clearly has a talent for it. Her mother encourages her to attend art school in Moscow, after which Sasha tries to figure out a way to come to the United States to find her absent father. At the age of sixteen, she comes to Phoenix, Arizona, as a mail-order bride. She then escapes to Chicago to work as a maid for a rich family. Later, she makes her way to the New York City borough of Brooklyn. A reviewer for *Kirkus* (20 May 2010) called the book "admirably ambitious, if clunky, coming-of-age fare." On a slightly more generous note, a reviewer for *Publishers Weekly* concluded: "Though Sasha's mental letters home and some timeline hiccups work against the momentum, cultural assimilation humor is the order of the day, and Ulinich provides it by the bucketful."

## *LENA FINKLE'S MAGIC BARREL*

For her second novel, *Lena Finkle's Magic Barrel* (2014), Ulinich combined her new love of writing with her artistic training to create a graphic novel. However, the book went beyond combining Ulinich's literary influences Anton Chekhov and Bernard Malamud with the influence of graphic novelists such as Harvey Pekar and Marjane Satrapi. That is the case David L. Ulin made in his review for the *Los Angeles Times* (18 July 2014). The book, Ulin wrote, "has no antecedents . . . it transcends its influences so thoroughly it creates a form, a language, all its own."

Whereas the heroine of *Petropolis* was a teenager, the heroine of *Lena Finkle's Magic Barrel* (the book's name is a reference to Malamud's short story "The Magic Barrel") is a woman in her late thirties. "The drawings are dramatic, stormy, intense, witty—it's somehow always dark, or overcast, or night-time—and Ulinich often breaks out of comic-book panels into full-page sketches, crammed with bubbles of her spirited, brainy commentary," wrote Roiphe.

Like her debut novel, *Lena Finkle's Magic Barrel* is semiautobiographical (even the drawings of Lena Finkle, the main character, strongly resemble photographs of Ulinich). In Arizona, Lena avoids marrying a significantly older Hasidic Jew and instead marries a young American named Chance. Lena leaves Chance, marries another man, and moves to New York City; but she and her second husband eventually divorce too. A substantial part of the book is in fact about Lena's adventures (or rather, misadventures) in the dating world. With much help from the Internet, Lena goes on dates with all sorts of men. The story takes a turn when Lena meets a man on a bus, in the real world, who gives her a collection of short stories by Malamud.

## PERSONAL LIFE

Ulinich lives in Brooklyn with her daughters, Sofia and Rebecca. Her first and second marriages ended in divorce. Her stories and essays have appeared in the *New York Times*, *N+1*, and *PEN America Journal*.

## SUGGESTED READING

Berger, Paul. "Anya Ulinich Makes Her Graphic Debut." *Forward*. Forward Assn., 25 July 2014. Web. 8 Sept. 2015.

La Rocco, Claudia. "Could Be 'Girls,' Only She's Divorced and a Parent." Rev. of *Lena Finkle's Magic Barrel*, by Anya Ulinich. *New York Times*. New York Times, 4 Aug. 2014. Web. 8 Sept. 2015.

Roiphe, Katie. "Graphic Novelist Anya Ulinich." *Financial Times*. Financial Times, 5 Sept. 2014. Web. 8 Sept. 2015.

Ulin, David L. "'Lena Finkle's Magic Barrel' Conjures a New Literary Form." Rev. of *Lena Finkle's Magic Barrel*, by Anya Ulinich. *Los Angeles Times*. Los Angeles Times, 18 July 2014. Web. 8 Sept. 2015.

Ulinich, Anya. "Dreaming of a Life of Privilege, But First . . . ." *New York Times*. New York Times, 11 Mar. 2007. Web. 8 Sept. 2015.

Ulinich, Anya. Interview by Kevin Kinsella. *Maud Newton*. Maud Newton, 18 Sept. 2007. Web. 8 Sept. 2015.

—Dmitry Kiper

# Don Valentine

**Born:** June 1932
**Occupation:** Venture capitalist

Don Valentine is a pioneer of venture capitalism who founded the extraordinarily successful firm Sequoia Capital in 1972. According to George Anders and Alex Konrad for *Forbes* magazine (26 Mar. 2014), Sequoia "has backed startups that now command a staggering $1.4 trillion of combined stock market value, equivalent to 22 percent of NASDAQ" since its founding.

Valentine himself was an original investor in some of Silicon Valley's most iconic companies, including Atari, Oracle, Cisco Systems, and Apple. He is also a bona fide eccentric in the already-eccentric Silicon Valley; for one thing, he is incredibly wealthy yet famously frugal. Rich Karlgaard reported for *Forbes* (9 Dec. 2005) that when Valentine attended board meetings for his start-ups, he would remove the handed-out documents from their generic binders. "Then he would shove the binder back to the CEO," Karlgaard wrote. "'These binders cost money,' Valentine would say, loud enough for the room to hear. 'Spend it on something more useful.'" He has been painted as both a market guru responsible for intuiting some of the greatest tech booms of the twentieth century and a cold-blooded titan focused only on the bottom line. In an older interview for *Inc.* magazine (1 May 1985), he was described as "prickly" and "gruff sometimes to the point of rudeness." While in an early managerial position, the interviewer reported, Valentine was even said "to have scolded a subordinate so severely on one occasion that the poor fellow fainted dead away."

Valentine got his start as a salesman in the semiconductor business in the early 1960s. Semiconductors, most of which are created with silicon, are found in transistors and the microprocessor chips in computers. Their value function lies between a conductor and an insulator; simply put, semiconductors have the capability to both conduct electricity and not conduct electricity. Without semiconductors, computer technology as it exists today would not be possible. After finding success in the semiconductor industry, Valentine began investing in fledgling companies. By the early 1970s, he had quit his sales job and founded Sequoia Capital, one of Silicon Valley's earliest and, today, most successful venture-capital firms. Valentine ceded

managerial control of Sequoia in the mid-1990s, though it continues to build on its reputation.

The year 2014 was one of the firm's best ever, as Sequoia reaped the benefits of its investments in companies such as Instagram, Airbnb, Dropbox, and WhatsApp. Unlike other venture capitalists, or VCs, Valentine is not the nurturing type; his particular genius, according to some, is less for people than for markets. "He bets on markets that are ready to explode," Karlgaard wrote. "Deep in his salesman's bones, Valentine knew the market for microcomputers (Apple), databases (Oracle), and routers (Cisco) would go nuclear before other investors did."

## EARLY LIFE AND EDUCATION

Donald T. Valentine was born in June 1932 and grew up in the New York City suburb of Yonkers. His father was a delivery-truck driver and minor official in the Teamsters. Valentine graduated from Mount Saint Michael Academy, an all-boys Roman Catholic school in the Bronx, in 1950 and went on to attend Fordham University.

Valentine traveled to the West Coast for the first time in the early 1950s as a member of the US military. "I discovered that there were places where it didn't snow in your driveway," he told Rob Walker in an interview for Stanford University's *Silicon Genesis* oral history project (21 Apr. 2004). "And I decided that I was not going to live in New York State any longer. I was eventually going to live in California." Still, Valentine had to put his California dreams on hold,

at least for a few years. After the service, he returned to New York, where he did factory work for Sylvania Electric Products, a company that made various electronic components, including cathode-ray tubes, semiconductors, and vacuum tubes. Valentine moved around within the company and eventually landed a job in sales engineering. In 1957, he arranged to be transferred to California.

## SEMICONDUCTOR BUSINESS

In California, Valentine made his first shrewd business observation. He was convinced, he told Walker, that the future of components was in semiconductors. He also saw that Sylvania Electric had little technical respect for the product. In 1959, he took a job as a salesperson for Fairchild Semiconductor, then a two-year-old company that had developed a way to mass-produce silicon transistors and semiconductors. "It was my first taste of being in a start-up company instead of a giant corporation like Sylvania," Valentine told Walker. He soon found that he thrived in such an environment.

Fairchild grew incredibly fast; during his second year, Valentine's personal sales figures exceeded the company's revenues for the previous year. He eventually became the company's sales manager, a position he held "for a period that I think I measure more in dollars than in years," he said to Walker. "We went during my tenure from about twenty million or twenty-five million [dollars] to a hundred and fifty million."

In 1967, Valentine and several other Fairchild employees left to take over National Semiconductor, a public company that, he told Walker, "had very little product, very little profitability, and not very much momentum." During his three years there, Valentine significantly increased National's revenue and became more acquainted with the investment interests of the company. He had begun to make personal investments in small businesses when he was at Fairchild, some of which were clients with Fairchild and, later, National. "The interesting thing is not a lot has changed," Valentine said to Walker, referring to his strategy for making investment decisions. "At Fairchild and National my interest was investing in companies that were addressing very large markets and solving a specific kind of problem. . . . Out of that period of four or five years [at National] I hammered out this more intuitive investment selection process based on huge markets and solutions that made a significant short-term commercial sense." More than thirty years later, Sequoia was still following the same basic strategy, focusing on companies with a significant target market: "It turns out it's much easier to build a new start-up company in an environment where the markets are large than it is to try to develop a market based on some technology for which there's not an obvious solution."

## SEQUOIA CAPITAL

In the late 1960s, "venture capital" was not yet a term in common use. Companies that funded start-ups were known as small business investment companies, or SBICs, and the investments they offered were called "private placements." Valentine recalled to Udayan Gupta for his book *Done Deals: Venture Capitalists Tell Their Stories* (2000). In 1970, Valentine was approached by the Capital Group, a large investment company in Los Angeles that he had previously worked with while at National. The Capital Group asked him if he would be interested in investing in start-up companies full time, and Valentine decided that he would.

The Capital Group was launching a venture-capital firm for clients who wanted to invest in small businesses. In 1972, Valentine founded Capital Management Services, which later became Sequoia Capital. The firm's first big coup came a few years later, in 1977, when Valentine decided to invest in Apple Computer. The company was run by a twenty-year-old Steve Jobs, whom Valentine described to Walker as "un-degreed, some people said unwashed, and he looked like [North Vietnamese president] Ho Chi Minh." Jobs had been referred to Valentine by Nolan Bushnell, founder of the video-game company Atari, one of Sequoia's early investment and Jobs's employer at the time. As Valentine explained to Gupta, the advent of microprocessors and his familiarity with the technology "made the evolution of the PC obvious." Despite this, Sequoia unloaded its Apple stock a short eighteen months later, a decision that remains one of the company's biggest regrets.

In 1987, Valentine oversaw a deal that Michael S. Malone and Shelley Pannill, writing for *Forbes* magazine (29 May 2000), called "his masterpiece." Husband and wife Leonard Bosack and Sandra Lerner had founded Cisco Systems in 1984 to market their multiprotocol router, a computer-networking device and software that had been developed by a research team at Stanford University. Though the company was profitable from the beginning, most VCs were not able to recognize the long-term potential of the router. Valentine foresaw Cisco's profitable future and invested $2.3 million. The partnership was a profitable one for Valentine; as of January 2015, Cisco was worth more than $139 billion.

By 1990, Sequoia's initial $5 million fund had become $150 million. In 1995, Sequoia partner Michael Moritz was approached by two young Stanford students named David Filo and Jerry Yang. The two men had founded a website called Yahoo!, which had begun as a directory of Filo and Yang's favorite links and websites. Sequoia invested close to $2 million in the company, and under its guidance, Yahoo! grew quickly and went public almost exactly one year later.

## LATER CAREER

Valentine ceded managerial control of the company to Moritz and Douglas Leone in the mid-1990s. Since then, he has served more as a business adviser than a businessman, forwarding his own intriguing worldview through panels and lectures. He appeared in the 2011 documentary *Something Ventured*, about the birth and early growth of venture capitalism. At the technology conference TechCrunch Disrupt SF in 2013, he expressed his love of risk-takers and his disdain for MBA graduates. "The key to making great investments is to assume that the past is wrong and to do something that's not part of the past, to do something entirely differently," he told the group, as reported by Romain Dillet and Darrell Etherington for *TechCrunch* (11 Sept. 2013).

Under Valentine's watch, the culture at Sequoia remains that of a band of outsiders, populated by people much like Valentine himself. "We want people who come from humble backgrounds and have a need to win," Leone said to Anders and Konrad. At Disrupt SF, Valentine echoed that sentiment in his characteristically gruff way; when one panelist admitted that he did not invest in people who graduated from Harvard Business School, Valentine agreed: "I'm very discriminate. I'm against all business schools."

## SUGGESTED READING

Anders, George, and Alex Konrad. "Inside Sequoia Capital: Silicon Valley's Innovation Factory." *Forbes*. Forbes.com, 26 Mar. 2014. Web. 17 Dec. 2014.

Dillet, Romain, and Darrell Etherington. "VC Titans Tom Perkins and Don Valentine Articulate What Makes a Good VC." *TechCrunch*. AOL, 11 Sept. 2013. Web. 17 Dec. 2014.

Karlgaard, Rich. "Don Valentine, Venture Capitalist." *Forbes*. Forbes.com, 9 Dec. 2005. Web. 17 Dec. 2014.

Malone, Michael S., and Shelley Pannill. "The Best VCs." *Forbes* 29 May 2000: 98–105. Print.

Valentine, Don. "Peaks and Valleys." *Inc.* Mansueto Ventures, 1 May 1985. Web. 17 Dec. 2014.

Valentine, Don. "Sequoia Capital." *Done Deals: Venture Capitalists Tell Their Stories*. Ed. Udayan Gupta. Boston: Harvard Business School P, 2000. 165–77. Print.

Valentine, Don. Interview by Rob Walker. *Silicon Genesis: An Oral History of Semiconductor Technology*. Stanford U, 21 Apr. 2004. Web. 17 Dec. 2014. Transcript.

—Molly Hagan

# Lynn Vincent

**Born:** 1962
**Occupation:** Author

Lynn Vincent may not be known by most to be a *New York Times* best-selling author, but many of the books she has written, such as *Same Kind of Different as Me* (2006), *Going Rogue* (2009), *Heaven Is for Real* (2010), and *Unsinkable* (2011) are. The reason for that is that Vincent is a collaborator, or ghostwriter, who specializes in writing compelling narrative nonfiction for people who have done or experienced remarkable things. Unlike many authors who hope for complete creative control, Vincent willingly shares the credit on a book cover with the subject of her work. Sometimes, as in the case of *Going Rogue*, in which she served as Sarah Palin's ghostwriter, not at all. What matters most to Vincent is that she has been fortunate enough to craft compelling, page-turning books that get people talking. As she explained to Peter Rowe for the *San Diego Union-Tribune* (2 Apr. 2011), "My real passion is writing about ordinary people living extraordinary lives and having extraordinary experiences."

Stewart F. House/Getty Images for Sony Pictures Entertainment

## EARLY LIFE

Lynn Vincent was born in 1962 in Springfield, Massachusetts, but moved frequently during her childhood. Her parents were unmarried when she was born; her father later became a computer programmer and her mother a lab technologist. Her mother, however, was an alcoholic by the time Lynn was born, and Lynn recalls that as a young child she was often left alone while her mother drank at a local bar near where the family lived in Cocoa Beach, Florida. Her parents divorced when she was three, after which time Lynn lost contact with her father. It would be decades before she spoke with him again.

Vincent's mother soon married a man who was later drafted into the US Army, and they had a daughter when Vincent was five. During his stint in the Army, Vincent's stepfather was stationed in Germany and Hawaii, and although he tried to bring some balance to the family dynamic, he ultimately divorced Vincent's mother, leaving the two young girls alone in a very unstable environment. "The living room would be full of guys—bikers, drug dealers," Vincent said to Ariel Levy for the *New Yorker* (15 Oct. 2012). "I remember eating a lot of Chunky Sirloin Burger soup and Minute rice. I'd fix that for my sister and me, because there was no cooking going on, no domesticity."

Vincent and her sister were sexually molested when Vincent was thirteen and her sister was eight. Their mother was aware of what was happening but did nothing to stop it. After her mother lost her job, they were evicted from the house they had been renting. At first they squatted in an abandoned house and later in a tent on the beach. Vincent ran away at fourteen after her mother choked her because of something her mother's boyfriend had said. She hopped on a bus and never went back. "All I had on was a sundress over a bathing suit, and no shoes," she recalled for Rowe.

## EDUCATION AND THE US NAVY

In 1977, when she was about fifteen, Vincent went to live with her maternal grandmother in Scottsboro, Alabama. Although a difficult adjustment, her time with her grandmother brought some needed stability to her life after years of anarchy. She attended Scottsboro High School and went to church on Sundays. She graduated from high school and entered Jacksonville State University in Alabama, but she quit before completing her undergraduate degree. Part of the reason, she believes, was her experimentation with sex and drugs. Another part is that she believes that many children of alcoholics never finish what they start. "When I was in college and we were supposed to be reading 'Beowulf,' I was reading Stephen King," Vincent said to Levy. "I would really dig the more modern writers like Twain, but I feel like an intellectual failure because I could not appreciate these things like 'Beowulf.' I don't feel like I can wear the tweed jacket with the leather elbow patches and smoke a pipe."

Vincent joined the US Navy at twenty-one and became a Navy air traffic controller, a job she thoroughly enjoyed, once she began applying herself to the tasks at hand. Recalling her service for Levy, she remarked: "For the first year, I was really kind of laissez-faire. A senior chief . . . really inspired me: I began to straighten out my uniform, my punctuality." She remained in the Navy for eight years, until 1992, serving through Operations Desert Shield and Desert Storm. She also worked as a control tower supervisor at the Navy Fighter Weapons School, popularly known as "Top Gun," in San Diego.

## WORKING WRITER

In 1991 Vincent experienced a Christian conversion after attending Horizon Christian Fellowship and Maranatha Chapel in San Diego.

Afterward she felt that her growing belief in the Scripture was true. Her newfound Christianity also gave her the strength to leave the Navy in favor of a career in writing and she soon sold her first article to *San Diego Woman* magazine. She also wrote for America Online, *Big Hollywood*, *Bank Marketing*, *Advisor Today* and specialty publications printed by the *Wall Street Journal*. But her big break came in 1998 when *World*, a biweekly Christian magazine based in North Carolina, began buying her stories. From 1998 to 2009 she served as a writer and features editor for that magazine. "The first time I heard 'Hi, Lynn, this is *World* magazine,' on my answering machine, I literally injured myself on the way to the phone," she told Levy.

At *World* she covered current events, politics, and cultural issues from a Christian perspective. She would go on to pen over one thousand articles for the magazine. Some of the more notable articles she wrote were investigative pieces.

## BEST-SELLING COLLABORATOR

Vincent has written ten books, primarily as a collaborator or ghostwriter. Nine of them have been published since 2005. In most cases, she has been hired by the author to help him or her commit their thoughts to paper. Typically she has several face-to-face meetings with her potential coauthor and uses that time to ask questions about the coauthor's life and beliefs. After the meetings, she follows up with a phone interview in order to delve deeper into the book's subject matter. One of Vincent's coauthors was William G. Boykin, former US general and deputy undersecretary of defense for intelligence under President George W. Bush from 2002–7. Recalling to Rowe his experience writing his autobiography *Never Surrender* (2008), he said, "She abused me for a year. . . . Working with her is like having two wives, two mothers, two sergeant majors. She's bossy, she's a step ahead of you at every turn—and I'd work with her tomorrow in a heartbeat."

In addition to coauthoring General Boykin's biography, Vincent worked with conservative journalist Robert Stacy McCain to write *Donkey Cons* (2006), which takes the Democratic Party to task for what the authors argued were its associations with corruption and shady dealings. Despite these two politically themed books, Vincent's works tend to be more in the vein of *Same Kind of Different as Me*, in which she describes the unusual friendship between her coauthors— Ron Hall, a white wealthy art dealer, and Denver

Moore, a homeless black man who later volunteered at the Fort Worth Union Gospel Mission. The book sold slowly at first, but then took off after *Sky*, the in-flight magazine on Delta, ran an excerpt. Before long it was being recommended at reading groups and church organizations and at independent bookstores throughout the country. It first hit the *New York Times* Best Sellers list in March 2008 and has sold upwards of a million copies. Hall, Moore, and Vincent went on to coauthor a sequel, *What Difference Do It Make?* (2009).

Two of Vincent's other titles are *Prodigal Comes Home* (2007), a memoir coauthored with Michael English, the American Christian singer who was rocked by scandal, and *The Blood of Lambs* (2009), a book coauthored by Kamal Saleem, a former terrorist. Yet Vincent is probably best known for a book in which her name does not appear on the title page: *Going Rogue*, Sarah Palin's 2009 autobiography, written shortly after she was picked by Senator John McCain to run as the vice presidential candidate on the 2008 Republican ticket. Although often mocked in the media, Palin has found success as a television commentator and as an author. *Going Rogue* is one of only four political biographies to sell over a million copies. Due to a nondisclosure agreement, Vincent is unable to say why her name did not make the cover, but she was glad to have had the opportunity. "You can starve to death as a collaborator," Vincent remarked to Samuel P. Jacobs for *Newsweek* (17 Apr. 2011). "If the Sarah Palin project didn't come through when it did, I would have been eating a lot of ramen."

### HEAVEN IS FOR REAL

Vincent's greatest commercial success to date has been *Heaven Is For Real*, the 2010 book she coauthored with Todd Burpo, a pastor in a small town in Nebraska. In the book, they describe how Burpo's three-year-old son had a near-death experience, after which the boy described meeting people in the afterlife that he could not possibly have known, including a sister who died in a miscarriage and a great-grandfather he never knew, as well as meeting Biblical figures like Samson, John the Baptist, and Jesus. "We all are perhaps desperate to know what is on the other side of the veil after we die," Matt Baugher, vice president and publisher of the publishing house for *Heaven Is for Real*, said, to Julie Bosman for the *New York Times* (11 Mar. 2011). "This was a very down-to-earth, conservative, quote-

unquote normal Midwestern family. We became fully convinced that this story was valid. And also that it was a great story that would just take off."

The book, which had an initial print run of 40,000, captivated readers around the world and has been translated into thirty-five languages. It went back to print almost two-dozen times and has become a runaway *New York Times* Best Seller, selling millions of copies. As of June 2014 there are more than 10 million copies of *Heaven Is for Real* in print. It was made into a major motion picture in 2014 that grossed over $100 million.

### PERSONAL LIFE

Lynn Vincent completed her liberal arts degree at New York's Excelsior College. She is married to Danny Vincent, whom she met while they were both serving in the Navy. They have two sons and live in San Diego County. On her website Vincent describes herself as an "unabashed evangelical" and a registered Republican with a Libertarian streak. Her most recent book is *Unsinkable* (2011), which she coauthored with Abby Sunderland. It describes Sunderland's attempt to sail solo around the world as a teenager.

### SUGGESTED READING

Bosman, Julie. "Celestial Sales for Boy's Tale of Heaven." *New York Times*. New York Times, 11 Mar. 2011. Web. 21 June 2015.

Jacobs, Samuel P. "Palin's Ghost Writer, Lynn Vincent." *Newsweek*. Newsweek, 17 Apr. 2011. Web. 21 June 2015.

Levy, Ariel. "Lives of the Saints." *New Yorker*. Condé Nast, 15 Oct. 2012. Web. 18 June 2015.

"Lynn Vincent." *Lynn Vincent*. Lynn Vincent, 2011. Web. 18 June 2015.

Rowe, Peter. "Lynn Vincent: The Most Successful Writer You've Never Heard Of." *San Diego Union-Tribune*. San Diego Union-Tribune, 2 Apr. 2011. Web. 21 June 2015.

### SELECTED WORKS

*Same Kind of Different as Me* (with Ron Hall and Denver Moore), 2006; *Donkey Cons* (with Robert Stacy McCain), 2006; *Prodigal Comes Home* (with Michael English), 2007; *Never Surrender* (with William G. Boykin), 2008; *The Blood of Lambs* (with Kamal Saleem), 2009; *What Difference Do It Make?* (with Ron Hall and Denver Moore), 2009; *Going Rogue* (with Sarah Palin),

2009; *Heaven Is for Real* (with Todd Burpo), 2010; *Unsinkable* (with Abby Sunderland), 2011

—Christopher Mari

# Binyavanga Wainaina

**Born:** January 18, 1971
**Occupation:** Author

Binyavanga Wainaina is a Kenyan memoirist and public intellectual. In 2014 he published a "lost chapter" from his 2011 memoir, *One Day I Will Write about This Place*, in which he revealed that he is gay. The timing was significant. In Nigeria, gay men were being rounded up and beaten by mobs, and in January 2014 President Goodluck Jonathan signed into law a bill that banned same-sex relationships, outlawed gay-rights activism, and mandated prison terms of up to fourteen years for offenders. Uganda followed suit, criminalizing gay sex in February 2014. The laws, along with the death from AIDS of a gay friend unable to tell even his friends about his illness, inspired Wainaina to go public. In Nairobi, Kenya, where he lives, the response was largely supportive. Still, some 98 percent of Nigerians opposed gay rights, as did 90 percent of Kenyans. Wainaina attributes the resurgence of homophobia in African countries to much the

Nightscream/Wikimedia Commons

same root causes that have helped it thrive elsewhere: fear and politics. It is a religious issue, one that, in Nigeria, unites Islamists and Pentecostals, Wainaina notes. Additionally, many conservative Africans view homosexuality as a Western import (although Western influence, in the form of missionaries and evangelism, has been a significant contributor to homophobia in African countries). Speaking of President Jonathan to Tim Adams for the *Observer* (16 Feb. 2014), Wainaina said, "Your economic miracle is stalling, your popularity is tanking, and so in your desperation you create not just an anti-gay law but you blink your eyes to a wave of thuggery, beatings, whippings and everything else."

Wainaina won the 2002 Caine Prize for African Writing and in 2005 wrote a satirical essay, "How to Write about Africa," for the British literary magazine *Granta* that effectively launched his international writing career. He founded the journal *Kwani?* (a Swahili expression that means "so what?") in 2003 and served as director of the Chinua Achebe Center for African Literature and Languages at Bard College. In 2013 *Foreign Policy* magazine named Wainaina one of its Twitterati 100. The Internet has been an important part of Wainaina's career, and he has expressed hope that sites like Facebook and Twitter will help foster a community of writers among Africa's fifty-four diverse nations. "You have all these young writers in Nigeria who know writers in Kenya because they met on Facebook and so-and-so's workshop," he told Rob Spillman for *BOMB* magazine (Summer 2011). "You start to get the sense of this piling up of power and production, which is now larger than the sum of any parts you can see. That certainly has meant more to writing out of the continent than any other thing."

## EARLY LIFE

Kenneth Binyavanga Wainaina was born on January 18, 1971. (His family calls him Ken, but Wainaina prefers to use his middle name.) His mother, a Ugandan, ran a hair salon in Nakuru, Kenya, and his father was a Kenyan business executive, the CEO of the marketing company Pyrethrum Board of Kenya. He died in 2011. In Wainaina's "lost chapter" essay, "I Am a Homosexual, Mum," he imagines telling his mother (who died in 2000) that he is gay. Wainaina writes that he knew he was gay when he was five years old, though he might not have had the words to express it. When he was seven years old, he recalls shaking a man's hand at the

Nakuru Golf Club. "Then I am crying alone in the toilet because the repeat of this feeling has made me suddenly ripped apart and lonely," he writes. "The feeling is not sexual. It is certain. It is overwhelming. It wants to make a home. It comes every few months like a bout of malaria and leaves me shaken for days, and confused for months. I do nothing about it." Even aside from his sexual confusion, Wainaina felt himself to be the oddest of his siblings—an older brother, Jimmy, and two younger sisters, Ciru and Chiqy. He was a daydreamer and had trouble conforming to the strictures of school life. To Adams, he recalled as a kindergartener being asked to put his crayons in a box: "I remember thinking, 'Why is everyone finding this so easy? Why should the crayons be in the box?'"

## EDUCATION

As a youth Wainaina found solace in imported cultural icons like ABBA, the Bee Gees, and Michael Jackson. He read voraciously; his mother revoked his library privileges when she discovered that he avoided doing math homework for an entire year and was reading novels in class. At boarding school Wainaina chafed against his parents' desire for him to become a doctor, lawyer, or engineer. He became depressed and began peeling his fingernails with razor blades. In 1991, after graduation, he left Kenya to study commerce at the University of Transkei in South Africa, where apartheid, the country's repressive system of racial segregation, was in its death throes. (The policy officially ended in 1994.) Wainaina did not take well to his studies; he stopped going to class and moved into an outbuilding with only a mattress and a pile of books. In 1996 Wainaina moved to Cape Town, where he began writing food and travel articles and worked as a professional cook. He later tweeted, as quoted by South Africa's *Books Live* (20 Apr. 2015), "I became an African in South Africa. [Black South Africans] taught me to understand the possibilities of engaged political action." He returned to Kenya in 2001, where he rented a room in a hostel on the periphery of a Nairobi slum. Later, he earned his master's degree in creative writing from the University of East Anglia in Norwich.

## EARLY WRITING CAREER

In 2002 Wainaina's autobiographical novella, *Discovering Home*, won the prestigious Caine Prize for African Writing. The work began as a long e-mail to a friend. Buoyed by his success, Wainaina and a group of artists, writers, and intellectuals in Nairobi used the prize money to found a literary journal called *Kwani?* in 2003. Wainaina served as the journal's first editor. In the mid-2000s, while living in London, Wainaina wrote a scathing e-mail to the editor of the literary magazine *Granta*, criticizing the naïveté of an old issue that centered on the African continent. To his surprise, Wainaina heard back from *Granta*'s new editor, Ian Jack, right away, and in 2005 another editor asked him to contribute a piece to *Granta*'s new "Africa" issue. Wainaina considered writing a short story and eventually turned in a piece about the Irish musician and activist Bob Geldof. It was, by Wainaina's own admission, not very good, and was rejected. Sometime later, the editor e-mailed Wainaina with the idea of simply publishing Wainaina's original e-mail. Wainaina tweaked the piece and sent it in. The result, "How to Write about Africa," became the most-forwarded essay in *Granta*'s history and contained biting directives satirizing European writing about Africa. "In your text, treat Africa as if it were one country," he advises. "Never have a picture of a well-adjusted African on the cover of your book, or in it, unless that African has won the Nobel Prize. An AK-47, prominent ribs, naked breasts: use these. If you must include an African, make sure you get one in Masai or Zulu or Dogon dress." The essay garnered Wainaina international attention. People (all of them white, Wainaina noted) began writing to him, asking him to "approve" their writing about Africa or seeking his permission to write about the continent at all. "I have considered investing in a rubber stamp," he jokes in a July 2010 essay called "How to Write about Africa II: The Revenge" in *Bidoun*, a New York–based magazine focusing on Middle Eastern art. "Now I am 'that guy,' the conscience of Africa: I will admonish you and give you absolution."

## ONE DAY I WILL WRITE ABOUT THIS PLACE

After nearly seven years of writing, Wainaina published a memoir called *One Day I Will Write about This Place* in 2011. The "place" in the title refers to Wainaina's changing sense of home during his turbulent coming-of-age in several African countries. "He does not present one mythical continent, but rather a fractured, complex, and ever-shifting collection of experiences," Jena Salon wrote in her review of the book for *Bookforum* (22 July 2011). "Sentence to sentence he jams ideas together, mimicking the way Michael

Jackson, soccer, and school qualifying exams have influenced his world as much as corrupt politicians, ethnic killings, and famine." The memoir was well received by critics and was given a boost with US readers when Oprah Winfrey's magazine included it on its summer reading list for 2011. It was, however, missing a very important part of Wainaina's identity. He rectified that omission when he published his "lost chapter" in January 2014. In the essay, Wainaina imagines telling his mother, on her deathbed, that he is gay. In real life, neither of Wainaina's parents ever found out that he was gay; when his mother died, he was still in Cape Town and unable to leave due to visa issues, and his father's fatal stroke came the day after Wainaina had resolved to come out to him. Wainaina contends that he waited to come out publicly partly because his private coming out was so difficult. He did not have sex with a man until he was thirty-three years old and did not classify himself as a gay man until he was thirty-nine. In addition to his essay, Wainaina also released a six-part video series called *We Must Free Our Imaginations*, or as he referred to it on Twitter, *What I Have to Say about Being Gay*. In the first video, he talks about his high hopes for the children of Africa's collective new generation. "I want to see a continent where every kind of person's imagination . . . does not have to look for 'being allowed.'"

## PERSONAL LIFE

Wainaina lives in Karen, a suburb of Nairobi.

## SUGGESTED READING

Adams, Tim. "Binyavanga Wainaina Interview: Coming Out in Kenya." *Guardian*. Guardian News and Media, 16 Feb. 2014. Web. 15 May 2015.

"'I Became an African in South Africa'—Read Binyavanga Wainaina's Heartfelt Response to the Xenophobic Violence." *Books Live*. Times Media, 20 Apr. 2015. Web. 16 May 2015.

Salon, Jena. Rev. of *One Day I Will Write about This Place*, by Binyavanga Wainaina. *Bookforum*. Bookforum, 22 July 2011. Web. 16 May 2015.

Wainaina, Binyavanga. Interview by Rob Spillman. *BOMB*. BOMB, Summer 2011. Web. 16 May 2015.

Wainaina, Binyavanga. "How to Write about Africa II: The Revenge." *Bidoun*. Bidoun Projects, July 2010. Web. 16 May 2015.

Wainaina, Binyavanga. "I Am a Homosexual, Mum." *Observer*. Guardian News and Media, 21 Jan. 2014. Web. 15 May 2015.

"Will Binyavanga Wainaina Change Attitudes to Gay Africans?" *BBC News*. BBC, 24 Jan. 2014. Web. 16 May 2015.

—Molly Hagan

---

# Cher Wang

**Born:** September 14, 1958
**Occupation:** Cofounder and chair of HTC

Cher Wang is a Taiwanese entrepreneur and the cofounder of the HTC Corporation.

## BACKGROUND

Cher Wang was born Wang Hsiueh-Hong in Taipei, Taiwan, on September 14, 1958, one of seven children born to her father and his second wife. Wang also has two half-siblings. Her father, Wang Yung-Ching, was the second richest man in Taiwan and the founder of the plastics and petrochemicals conglomerate Formosa Plastics Group. Wang's parents were very strict and encouraged Wang to focus on athletics when not busy with schoolwork; Wang played both tennis and basketball. Her father also took her on monthly visits to a hospital he financed.

For their secondary education, the Wang children were sent abroad to private schools. Some of her siblings went to study in London, England, but the United States attracted Cher Wang, and she enrolled at the College Preparatory School in Oakland, California in 1974. She lived with a local pediatrician and his family while her older sister Charlene Wang lived nearby in the Bay Area. After finishing high school, she entered the University of California, Berkeley, as a music major with ambitions to play the piano professionally. After three weeks, however, she switched her major to economics. She earned her bachelor's degree in economics in 1981 and later received her master's degree from the university.

Wang got a job in 1982 with First International Computer, a Taiwanese computer and components manufacturer founded by her sister Charlene in 1980. With First International Computer, Wang sold motherboards and went on to oversee the personal computer division.

## ENTREPRENEUR AND EXECUTIVE

In 1987, Wang cofounded VIA Technologies, Inc., a manufacturer of integrated circuits. Ten years later, she founded the High-Tech Computer Corporation (HTC) with Peter Chou. One of her inspirations for the company came about when she was still working for First International Computer. The job required her to carry large, heavy cases of computer parts. Wang wondered if it was possible to make these devices smaller and more portable.

During the early years of the company, Wang's job was to develop relationships with customers and vendors whose products were required by HTC. The company originally manufactured notebook computers, but after a few years, Wang and her partners had to decide whether to continue focusing on notebooks or transition to handheld devices, which had been showing potential growth as a market.

Wang believed that because of the sheer amount of competition in the notebook industry, HTC should focus its efforts on developing handheld devices. Once they switched over, the company saw a 29-percent increase in revenue.

In 1998, HTC began designing and manufacturing some of the first touch-screen and wireless handheld devices. Through her work building relationships with clients, Wang had become close partners with executives at T-Mobile, a mobile telecommunications company. This allowed HTC to secure the rights to develop the first smartphone with the Android operating system. After unveiling the phone, HTC was sued by Apple Computers over twenty alleged infringed patents. HTC countersued and the two companies eventually came to a licensing agreement in 2012.

On April 30, 1999, Wang became a director at HTC, and on June 20, 2007, she was appointed the company's chair of the board. She has taken on a more active role in the company's daily operations to increase their sales following a drop in its Taiwan shares. During the first quarter of 2014, HTC saw a 23-percent drop in sales. Following this, Wang has shifted the company's focus to the mid-tier market, which she believes the company missed out on in 2013. In March 2014, HTC released a much-promoted new model of phone, the HTC One M8, which received very positive reviews.

Aside from her work in technology, Wang has also engaged in several philanthropic efforts. She has funded the prestigious American Physical Society's Oliver E. Buckley Condensed Matter Prize, given by her alma mater, the University of California, Berkeley. The award is given to researchers who make notable contributions in the field of condensed matter physics. Wang's funding doubled the amount of award money.

She also funded the Berkeley-Tsinghua Program for Advanced Study in Psychology, a collaborative program between the university's psychology department and that of Tsinghua University in Beijing, China. In 2011 she helped found Guizhou Forerunner College in southwest China, where students from low-income families can receive three years of low-cost education.

Wang is also chair of three Taiwan-listed companies and is on the board of directors of numerous other technology-related companies, including Everex Systems, Inc.

## IMPACT

Wang is one of the most powerful female executives in the technology industry. Her company, HTC, was at one point producing one out of every six smartphones sold in the United States. Wang's extraordinary insight into technology trends has led her to make HTC a billion-dollar business while also establishing a number of other technology-related businesses. In 2005, the periodical *Business Week* honored her as an innovator in its "25 Leaders on the Forefront of Change" list. The American business magazine *Forbes* listed her as number fifty-four on their list of "The World's 100 Most Powerful Women" in 2014.

## PERSONAL LIFE

Wang is married to Chen Wen-Chi, the chief executive officer of VIA Technologies. Together they have two sons. They are both nondenominational Christians, and spirituality plays a large part in her life. They split their time between houses in Mountain View, California, and Taipei, along with an apartment in Beijing.

## SUGGESTED READING

"Cher Wang: Founder of Taiwan Smartphone Maker HTC." *CNBC*. CNBC, n.d. Web. 17 June 2014.

Culpan, Tim, and Bruce Einhorn. "HTC's Wang Parachutes Back to Reverse Falling Phones Sales." *Bloomberg*. Bloomberg, 17 Apr. 2014. Web. 17 June 2014.

Holson, Laura M. "With Smartphones, Cher Wang Made Her Own Fortune." *New York Times*. New York Times, 26 Oct. 2008. Web. 17 June 2014.

Linfei, Wu, ed. "HTC's Billionaire Chair Cher Wang Leads the Battle vs. Apple." *Women of China*. Women's Foreign Lang. Pub. of China, 27 Oct. 2011. Web. 17 June 2014.

Paczkowski, John. "From Motherboards to Mobile: HTC's Cher Wang at AsiaD." *All Things Digital*. Dow Jones, 20 Oct. 2011. Web. 17 June 2014.

—Patrick G. Cooper

# Pendleton Ward

**Born:** 1982
**Occupation:** Creator of *Adventure Time*

Pendleton Ward is the creator of *Adventure Time*, an animated program that reviewers seem to relish describing almost as much as they enjoy watching. Emily Nussbaum, for the *New Yorker* (21 Apr. 2014), called it "a post-apocalyptic allegory full of helpful dating tips for teenagers, or like World of Warcraft as recapped by Carl Jung. It can be enjoyed, at varying levels, by third graders, art historians, and cosplay fans. . . . *Adventure Time* is one of the most philosophically risky and, often, emotionally affecting shows on TV. It's beautiful and funny and stupid and smart, in about equal parts." Eric Kohn for *Indiewire* (17 Oct. 2013), expressed similar sentiments, writing, "*Adventure Time* is teeming with thoughtful nuances, bold innuendo and bona fide genre-based storytelling. The blend of advanced subtext, bafflingly surreal tangents and nonsensical asides makes it hard to pin down the show's precise appeal—but you can't dispute the outlandish comic timing, lovable characters and insanely catchy songs."

By its seventh season on Cartoon Network, *Adventure Time* had spawned an enormous variety of merchandise, including a best-selling video game, and garnered two Emmy Awards and a British Academy of Film and Television Arts (BAFTA) Award. Ward, who quietly stepped down from running the show during its fifth season, although he continued to serve as writer and storyboard artist, says that winning the admiration of his fellow cartoonists is more important than any ostensibly prestigious statuette. "The best feeling is meeting people that I

Ilya S. Savenok/Getty Images North America/ Getty Images

admire and respect and finding out that they even watch the show," he explained to Noel Murray for the *A.V. Club* (21 Mar. 2012). "Just meeting Matt Groening [the creator of *The Simpsons*] and knowing that he likes the show is like the coolest award that you can even win. The 'Matt Groening Has Seen It and Likes It Award.'"

## EARLY LIFE AND EDUCATION

Pendleton Ward, the youngest of three brothers, was born in 1982 and raised in San Antonio, Texas. While he never met his father, his mother, artist Bettie Ward, was a strong force in his life. Bettie was exceptionally supportive of Ward's artistic tendencies, although she has told interviewers that at one point she resorted to hiding her Post-it notes because he was constantly using them to make flip books—small volumes with a series of pictures that appear to animate when the pages are rapidly turned.

Ward was aware from a young age that he was different from most of his peers. "As a kid I was very conscious of trying to be functional and not be too odd," he told Neil Strauss for *Rolling Stone* (2 Oct. 2014). "I liked figuring out how people worked. I had a notebook, and I'd take notes about people." Somewhat overweight and with an unfashionable bowl haircut, he found a few kindred spirits at his local comic book shop, where he purchased supplies for the role-playing game Dungeons and Dragons, to which he remains devoted and which, in later years, deeply influenced his work.

Ward was an avid watcher of animated shows, particularly *The Simpsons*, *Ren and Stimpy*, and *Beavis and Butthead*, and as early as second grade he would draw characters from those programs and sell them to his classmates for a nickel. Bettie sent him to as many art classes as she could, and in high school he attended a summer program at the California Institute of the Arts, generally known as CalArts. When it came time for Ward to apply for college, the Character Animation Program at CalArts was the natural choice for him; the college boasted big names such as John Lasseter, chief creative officer of Walt Disney and Pixar Animation Studios, as well as Tim Burton, known for producing the film *The Nightmare before Christmas* (1993) and directing *Charlie and the Chocolate Factory* (2005).

Ward, widely recognized as one of the most distinctive and talented animators in the CalArts class of 2005, participated in a year-end showcase prior to earning his bachelor of fine arts degree. Sitting in the audience during the showcase was a producer from the Channel Frederator Network, an independent animation studio, who encouraged him to pitch an idea.

## CAREER BEGINNINGS

In 2006, after his CalArts graduation, Ward pitched *Adventure Time*, about a kindly human boy named Finn and his gruff dog, Jake, traveling together through a postapocalyptic world filled with unusual characters, to the Frederator Network. Ward had heard the network was looking for seven-minute animated shorts to air on a Nickelodeon channel called *Random! Cartoons*; however, his pitch was rejected.

Fred Siebert the owner of Frederator, recalls seeing an early version of *Adventure Time*: "At the time I was in my mid-50s, and I'd been making cartoons for 15 years," he said, as quoted by Jason Krell, in his article for *Animation* (18 Apr. 2014). "And like every other idiot executive, I thought I knew what made a good cartoon, and this did not fit it, on the surface . . . his drawings looked funny—like funny weird—compared to all the other cartoons. We had already introduced, you know, 15 years before, a new style of cartoons with *Dexter's Laboratory*, *Cow and Chicken*, and *The Powerpuff Girls*. In my mind, those were cartoons."

After Nickelodeon's rejection, Ward released *Adventure Time* on YouTube in 2007, and it amassed more than three million views within a year.

Ward spent from 2008 to 2009 storyboarding and writing for a Cartoon Network show called *The Marvelous Misadventures of Flapjack*, about a young boy, a talking whale, and a pirate named Captain K'nuckles, created by a CalArts colleague. The Cartoon Network was, thankfully, more amenable to Ward's quirky vision than Nickelodeon had been, and that same year he received approval to turn *Adventure Time* into a full-fledged series, which officially premiered on April 5, 2010. "If the show hadn't been picked up, I would have moved to the Midwest and gotten a cheap apartment," Ward told Strauss. "I would have been that guy with a telescope watching my neighbors, getting pizza and putting a sign on the door that says 'Leave the pizza outside.' But I was forced into a situation where I had to maintain my social dignity."

## ADVENTURE TIME

Instead of decamping to the Midwest, Ward found himself at the helm of an undisputed hit, which garnered an increasingly appreciative audience as the story developed. "Online summaries make it sound like a wacky romp," Nussbaum wrote. "But, as the series progresses, an eerie backstory emerges. The candy-tinted world we're seeing has a terrible history: while Finn is surrounded by magical beings, virtually every other human appears to have been killed or transformed, during something called the Mushroom War." That blend of darkness and whimsy "comes from a really genuine place," as Ward told Kevin Ohannessian for *Fast Company* (12 Nov. 2012). "All of those elements feel really natural to me. [It doesn't] feel bizarre to me, to write about magic, to write about strange creatures. It all feels right out of my childhood."

Although he enjoyed the camaraderie of the writers' room, Ward found running the show unexpectedly taxing. "In the beginning, Fred Seibert kept telling me that the workload is more than you can ever imagine. Like, there's no possible way that you can prepare yourself for the amount of stress and work that you're going to have," he recalled to Murray. "And I didn't. I had no idea it would be so intense, especially in the beginning. . . . I wanted to cry and vomit every day and there were a lot of sleepless nights."

*Adventure Time* won its first Emmy Award, for outstanding individual achievement in animation, in 2013 and a second Emmy, for an outstanding short-format animated program, in

2014. Then, in the middle of *Adventure Time's* fifth season, in 2014, Ward stepped down as showrunner, handing the reins to storyboard artist and CalArts classmate Adam Muto. "Dealing with people every day wears on you," he told Strauss. "To spend that extra energy and time you don't have, to make something that's worth making, to make it awesome, wears you out. . . . And the more popular it gets, the more the ancillary things—like the merchandise and games and everything—keep getting bigger." Those ancillary things now include a staggering array of apparel, bedding, books, gadgets, toys, games, and more.

## PERSONAL LIFE

A generously proportioned, lavishly bearded figure, Ward remains somewhat shy. He much prefers, he has told numerous interviewers, to simply remain at home when not working, eating pizza and playing video games.

## SUGGESTED READING

Kohn, Eric. "Does the Obsessive *Adventure Time* Fandom Overlook the Depths of Pendleton Ward's Cartoon Network Hit?" *Indiewire*. Indiewire.com, 17 Oct. 2013. Web. 15 Mar. 2015.

Krell, Jason. "How Pendleton Ward and His Friends Created a New Era of Cartoons." *Animation*. Gawker Media, 18 Apr. 2014. Web. 12 May 2015.

Nussbaum, Emily. "Castles in the Air: The Gorgeous Existential Funk of *Adventure Time*." *New Yorker*. Condé Nast, 21 Apr. 2014. Web. 15 Mar. 2015

Strauss, Neil. "*Adventure Time*: The Trippiest Show on TV." *Rolling Stone*. Rolling Stone, 2 Oct. 2014. Web. 15 Mar. 2015.

Ward, Pendleton. "*Adventure Time* Creator Pendleton Ward." Interview by Noel Murray. *A.V. Club*. Onion, 21 Mar. 2012. Web. 15 Mar. 2015.

Ward, Pendleton. "It's *Adventure Time*! Pendleton Ward Talks about His Hit Cartoon." Interview by David M. Ewalt. *Forbes*. Forbes.com, 15 Nov. 2011. Web. 15 Mar. 2015.

Ward, Pendleton. "Pendleton Ward on Keeping *Adventure Time* Weird." Interview by Kevin Ohannessian. *Fast Company*. Fast Company, 12 Nov. 2012. Web. 15 Mar. 2015.

## SELECTED WORKS

*The Marvelous Misadventures of Flapjack*, 2008–9; *Adventure Time*, 2010–; *Bravest Warriors*, 2012–13

—Mari Rich

# Kerry Washington

**Born:** January 31, 1977
**Occupation:** Actor

## BACKGROUND

Kerry Marisa Washington was born on January 31, 1977, in the Bronx, New York. She grew up in the Bronx with her mother, Valerie, a professor and educational consultant, and her father, Earl, a real estate broker. Her mother is of Jamaican American descent and her father is an African American from South Carolina. As a child, Washington dreamed of working at a SeaWorld theme park, where she could work with killer whales, but in her teenage years she was drawn to the theater.

Washington took dance lessons at a Boys and Girls Club in the Bronx and participated in the TADA! Youth Theater in New York City. At age thirteen she worked with NiteStar, a health education theater program in New York. With NiteStar, Washington put on productions that addressed social issues such as sexuality, domestic violence, substance abuse, and discrimination. She attended the Spence School, a prestigious, all-girls private school on Manhattan's Upper East Side. There she appeared in school theater productions and sang in an a cappella group. She also took acting lessons at Michael Howard Studios in Manhattan.

After graduating from the Spence School in 1994, Washington was awarded a theater scholarship to George Washington University in Washington, DC. There she designed an interdisciplinary major, concentrating on anthropology, psychology, and sociology while also taking performance study courses and serving as a resident assistant in Thurston Hall. She graduated in 1998.

## FILM AND TELEVISION WORK

Although Washington had some minor acting roles in college, including an appearance in the educational television series *Standard Deviants* (1996), she made her film debut costarring in the drama *Our Song* (2000). The following year, she gained even more attention in the popular dance film *Save the Last Dance* (2001). Critics gave the film mixed reviews, but it was a success at the box office and helped raise Washington's profile in Hollywood. Also in 2001, she made guest appearances in shows such as *NYPD Blue*, *Deadline*, and *Law & Order*. From there, Washington began working consistently in a diverse range of both films and television series.

Washington appeared alongside renowned actor Anthony Hopkins and comedian Chris Rock in the action comedy *Bad Company* in 2002. After appearing in films *The Human Stain* (2003) and *Sin* (2003), she starred in the independent comedy *She Hate Me* (2004), directed by Spike Lee. Washington then took on her biggest role yet as Della Bea Robinson, the wife of acclaimed singer Ray Charles, in the biopic *Ray* (2004). The film received numerous award nominations and wins, and Washington won the National Association for the Advancement of Colored People (NAACP) Image Award for outstanding actress in a motion picture. Next, she appeared in the superhero film *Fantastic Four* (2005) and landed a recurring role on the show *Boston Legal* (2005–06).

She garnered widespread acclaim for her performance as Kay Amin, the wife of feared Ugandan dictator Idi Amin, in the drama *The Last King of Scotland* (2006). Her performance earned her three award nominations, including one from the Black Reel Awards, which recognizes achievements of African Americans in film. She reunited with Rock for the romantic comedy *I Think I Love My Wife* (2007) and reprised her *Fantastic Four* role in the film's sequel, *Fantastic 4: Rise of the Silver Surfer* (2007).

After appearing in films such as *Lakeview Terrace* (2008), *Night Catches Us* (2010), and *The Details* (2011), Washington won a second NAACP Image Award for her portrayal of Broomhilda von Shaft in the Western *Django Unchained* (2012). Her performance in this role also earned her the BET Award for best actress.

Beginning in 2012, Washington took on her biggest role yet as the lead in the ABC political thriller *Scandal*, in which she plays Olivia Pope, the owner of a crisis management firm that protects the images of high-profile clients. The series received mainly favorable reviews when it premiered on April 5, 2012, and went on to earn several awards and nominations, including a third NAACP Image Award for Washington. At the 2013 Primetime Emmy Awards, she became the first African American woman since 1995 to be nominated for the award for outstanding lead actress in a drama series. She was also nominated for a 2014 Golden Globe Award for best performance by an actress in a television drama series. *Scandal* was renewed for a third season in 2013.

## IMPACT

In a short amount of time, Washington became a popular and widely acclaimed actor in both film and television. She has garnered numerous awards and nominations, including three NAACP Image Awards. Washington has used her fame to help draw attention to various social and political causes, including V-Day, an organization that raises awareness of violence against women.

## PERSONAL LIFE

On June 24, 2013, Washington married professional football player Nnamdi Asomugha in Hailey, Idaho. On October 30, 2013, the couple announced that Washington was pregnant with their first child.

## SUGGESTED READING

Davis, Allison P. "Washington Heights." *Elle*. Hearst Communications, 14 Nov. 2012. Web. 14 Mar. 2014.

Kamp, David. "Ms. Kerry Goes to Washington: The First Lady of *Scandal* Speaks." *Vanity Fair*. Condé Nast, Aug. 2013. Web. 14 Mar. 2014.

Powell, Kevin. "Kerry Washington: Woman on Top." *Ebony*. Ebony Magazine, 9 May 2013. Web. 14 Mar. 2014.

Vega, Tanzina. "*Scandal* on ABC Is Breaking Barriers." *New York Times*. New York Times, 16 Jan. 2013. Web. 14 Mar. 2014.

Voss, Brandon. "The A-List Interview: Kerry Washington." *Advocate*. Here Media, 31 Oct. 2013. Web. 14 Mar. 2014.

## SELECTED WORKS

*Our Song*, 2000; *Save the Last Dance*, 2001; *Bad Company*, 2002; *She Hate Me*, 2004; *Ray*, 2004; *Fantastic Four*, 2005; *The Last King of Scotland*, 2006; *I Think I Love My Wife*, 2007; *Django Unchained*, 2012; *Boston Legal*, 2005–06; *Scandal*, 2012–

—Patrick G. Cooper

# Reggie Watts

**Born:** 1972

**Occupation:** Comedian and musician

Reggie Watts is a musician and comedian often labeled "alternative" for his unusual blend of improvisation, physicality, nonsensical use of language, accents, impressions, and beatboxing. "He embodies the paradox of the cult star: a charismatic, powerfully original performer who probably deserves to be super-famous but whose originality disqualifies him from all the usual channels of super-fame," Sam Anderson wrote for *New York* magazine (30 May 2010). Watts does not fit neatly with other comedy-music acts such as Flight of the Conchords, a New Zealand duo who once had a show on HBO, or longtime parody songwriter "Weird Al" Yankovic. He prefers to think of his particular brand of performance art as "ambient comedy," he told Nicole Tourtelot for *Esquire* magazine (2 Dec. 2008). His riffs are surreal and absurd but funny enough to have won him a large and devoted fan base.

Watts was a full-time musician in Seattle and then part of the underground performance scene in New York before becoming a frequent guest on late-night talk shows. In 2010 late-night host Conan O'Brien invited him to go on tour, and in 2012 Watts began hosting a parody talk show with comedian Scott Aukerman called *Com-*

Erika Goldring/WireImage/Getty Images

*edy Bang! Bang!* on the IFC network. He left the show in 2015 to become the bandleader on James Corden's *The Late Late Show* on CBS.

## EARLY LIFE AND EDUCATION

Reginald "Reggie" Lucien Frank Roger Watts was born on a military base in Stuttgart, Germany, in 1972. His mother is an ethnic Frenchwoman who speaks little English (Watts himself is fluent in French). His father, who died in 2007, was African American and worked for the US Air Force. By the time Watts was four years old, he had lived in Spain and Italy, though he spent most of his childhood in Great Falls, Montana. He began studying classical piano when he was five. He loved music—he grew up listening to James Brown and Miles Davis—but he was genuinely fascinated by the mechanics of the world: how it worked and the stories that make things the way they are. In his interview with Anderson, he recalls marveling at the deep oddity of orchestra practice. "All these people with horsehaired wooden sticks and strings, looking at a bunch of symbols on a piece of paper. And the bass players are tall and look like their instruments, and the cellists have long hair and look like cellists. I'm sitting there like, *What is this?*" Watts, who also played violin, was kicked out the orchestra for disobedience when he was sixteen. At Great Falls High School, he had a rock band called Autumn Asylum and dabbled in drama, student council, and football—"not because I loved football," he explained to Emma Allen for the *New Yorker* (16 Mar. 2015), "but because I wanted to experience football as a construct."

## EARLY CAREER AS A MUSICIAN

Watts moved to Seattle, Washington, when he was eighteen years old. He attended the Art Institute of Seattle and studied jazz at the Cornish College of the Arts. He played in a handful of rock and jazz bands with names like Action Buddy, Ironing Pants Definitely, and Micron 7. In 1996 he joined a band called Maktub that performed rock, jazz, and R & B. (Watts came across the word—which means "it is written" in Arabic—while reading Paulo Coelho book *The Alchemist*.) The band toured with G-Love in 1998 and released their first album, *Subtle Ways*, in 1999. Maktub released four more albums between 2002 and 2009. Watts remained with the band until the end, though he pursued other projects throughout. In 2004 he released a solo EP called *Simplified*, but he also started getting into comedy. He performed with a few sketch-comedy groups in Seattle before moving to New York City in 2004. Watts honed his eclectic style, drawing inspiration from other unusual acts like Stella, a trio that included Michael Showalter, Michael Ian Black, and David Wain, all from the early 1990s sketch television show *The State*.

## BREAKTHROUGH AS A COMEDIAN

Watts began performing alt-comedy showcases, quickly winning the praise of those whom he had admired. "He's like a magician," Showalter told Dave Itzkoff of the *New York Times* (28 May 2010). Watts even caught the attention of the musical artist and producer Brian Eno, who asked him to play at his daughters' birthday parties. Writers for Conan O'Brien introduced the late-night talk-show host to Watts's work, and in 2010 O'Brien invited Watts to open for him on his Legally Prohibited from Being Funny on Television Tour. "I wanted the opening act to make a statement about the tour," O'Brien told Itzkoff. "I wanted it to be someone who would surprise people creatively, blend music and comedy, and have a very different voice from my own." Watts certainly fit those requirements, though he feared his tastes were too offbeat even for O'Brien's fans. He was wrong. Audiences loved him and welcomed him into the comedy mainstream. The same year Watts released his first hour-long stand-up special for Comedy Central, recorded in 2009, called *Why S——— So Crazy*.

As a solo performer, Watts never writes any of his acts in advance—"That would suck," he told Anderson when the interviewer suggested it. He finds each moment of his act in the environment itself, like playing a jazz solo, following a muse that he refers to mystically as "the Source." "The environment is giving you stuff constantly: a woman yelling something, an animal making a weird sound in the forest, a window being rolled up, static on a radio. Someone turns to you and says something in the same key as the radio," he said. "If you pay attention to the world, it's an amazing place. If you don't, it's whatever you think it is."

## TED TALK AND TELEVISION

The year 2012 was big for Watts. In February he gave a memorable TED talk called "Beats That Defy Boxes." He began by pacing the stage with a serious expression but speaking in a nonsensical blend of languages. Landing in an upper-crust British accent, Watts intoned, "That's one of things I enjoy most about this convention. It's not so much, as so little has to do with what everything is." Watts has called such riffing working from a template—in this case, the template is a TED talk. He uses templates and cultural signifiers (like jargon or accents) and remixes them to showcase their inherent absurdity. Like his own experience sitting in the orchestra as a school kid, Watts invites people to laugh and to ask—looking around at a quiet room full of people respectfully listening to a man with a microphone—"what is this"? The same year Watts released his second comedy special, called *Reggie Watts: A Live in Central Park* (2012), and director Steven Soderbergh asked him to make a cameo in his thriller *Bitter Pill* (2012).

Also in 2012 Watts began hosting a parody talk show called *Comedy Bang! Bang!* with comedian Scott Aukerman on the IFC network. The show grew out of Aukerman's eponymous podcast—for which Watts wrote the theme song. For a year Watts also had his own improvisational "sister" show called *Reggie Makes Music* (2012–13) online. The podcast, which runs separately from the television series, is a surreal and strange brew that does not lend itself to a visual medium. As Erik Adams wrote for the *AV Club* (8 June 2012), it is a send-up of radio shows, while the television show is a parody of talk shows, television, and film. Comparing it to another "anti-talk show," *Between Two Ferns with Zach Galifianakis*, Adams wrote that *Comedy Bang! Bang!* eschews the "public-access" aesthetic in favor of "an accessible sleekness while remaining proudly peculiar and lo-fi." Watts was the show's bandleader but also, when the show devolved from celebrity interview to sketch, one of its performers. Watts left the show when he was asked to join *The Late Late Show with James Corden* in 2015.

## THE LATE LATE SHOW WITH JAMES CORDEN

According to Watts, in an interview with Lucas Kavner for *Vulture* (23 Mar. 2015), he was wrapping up his gig with *Comedy Bang! Bang!* when he got a phone call from English comedian James Corden in 2014. He admits that he was initially annoyed by Corden's offer to join the show—he had been looking forward to taking some time off. "But then I met with James and he seemed like a cool cat. He had a lot of good energy, he was down with crazy ideas. The producer was really cool, too," he told Kavner. "But it took me a while to decide whether to do it." Eventually of course, Watts did sign on. His addition to the cast was announced in December 2014. The talk show premiered in March 2015. Unlike other talk-show hosts (David Letterman, for example), Corden is first and foremost a performer; he won a Tony Award for the Broadway comedy *One Man, Two Guvnors* in 2012. Corden's hosting style and his affinity for musical sketches appear to give Watts the perfect home for his talents. James Poniewozik for *Time* magazine (24 Mar. 2015) wrote that Watts "was an inspired choice" for the show. "Let's hope the show gives him an active role; it'll be interesting to see if his experimental comedy style can mesh with Corden's¦" he added.

In 2014 Watts teamed comedian Sarah Silverman, Tim Heidecker and Eric Wareheim of the comedy duo Tim and Eric, and actor Michael Cera to create a comedy collective and YouTube channel called Jash. He lives in Los Angeles, where *The Late Late Show* is filmed.

## SUGGESTED READING

Adams, Erik. "Comedy Bang! Bang!: Comedy Bang! Bang!" *AV Club*. The Onion, 8 June 2012. Web. 19 May 2015.

Allen, Emma. "Sidekick." *New Yorker*. Condé Nast, 16 Mar. 2015. Web. 19 May 2015.

Anderson, Sam. "The Mad Liberationist." *New York*. New York Media, 30 May 2010. Web. 19 May 2015.

Itzkoff, Dave. "Always the Quick-Change Artist, from Skits to Songs to Stand-Ups." *New York Times*. New York Times, 29 May 2010. Web. 19 May 2015.

Kavner, Lucas. "Reggie Watts on His New Gig as Bandleader of *The Late Late Show* and Why He Was Initially Annoyed by the Offer." *Vulture*. New York Media, 23 Mar. 2015. Web. 19 May 2015.

Poniewozik, James. "On James Corden's Late Night Debut, It's One More Mr. Nice Guy." *Time*. Time, 24 Mar. 2015. Web. 19 May 2015.

Tourtelot, Nicole. "The YouTube Star Who's Crazy in a Funny Way." *Esquire*. Hearst Communications, 2 Dec. 2008. Web. 19 May 2015.

## SELECTED WORKS

*Why S—— So Crazy*, 2010; *Reggie Watts: A Live at Central Park*, 2012; *Comedy Bang! Bang!*, 2012–15; *The Late Late Show with James Corden*, 2015

—Molly Hagan

# Russell Westbrook

**Born:** November 12, 1988
**Occupation:** Basketball player

Known as one of the most athletic players in the National Basketball Association (NBA), Russell Westbrook of the Oklahoma City Thunder has helped transform the point guard position with his speed, explosiveness, and aggressive style of play. An unheralded prospect coming out of high school, Westbrook had a fairly undistinguished two-year career at the University of California, Los Angeles (UCLA), before being selected in the first round of the 2008 NBA Draft. Since then, he has emerged as one of the NBA's marquee players. Westbrook has paired with forward Kevin Durant, the 2014 NBA Most Valuable Player, to form one of the top tandems in the league and has helped turn the Thunder into a perennial playoff contender. From 2011 to 2013, he earned three consecutive All-Star selections and was named to three All-NBA second teams. Thunder coach Scott Brooks said of Westbrook to Chris Mannix for *Sports Illustrated* (18 June 2012), "Some people have this old-school picture of what a point guard should be. He is not it. But he is so important to us that he can't be."

## EARLY LIFE

The older of the two sons of Russell Westbrook Sr. and Shannon Westbrook, Russell Westbrook was born on November 12, 1988, in Long Beach, California. He grew up in the suburbs of southern Los Angeles County, including Hawthorne and Torrance. He has a brother, Raynard, who is two years younger.

Westbrook was drawn to basketball through his father, who had been an athlete at Los Angeles' Thomas Jefferson High School. As a boy Westbrook often accompanied his father to parks and gyms in south central Los Angeles, where he spent countless hours watching him play pickup basketball games. He started joining his father on the courts at the age of seven. Russell Westbrook Sr., who had served time in prison on a drug conviction, resolved to keep his son off the streets and tirelessly pushed him to develop his basketball skills.

When Westbrook was eight, he began practicing at the Jesse Owens Park gym, where he met Reggie Hamilton, the coach of the LA Elite traveling team. Hamilton granted Westbrook a roster spot on the team and assisted in his development. "Russell was always focused," Hamilton recalled to Darnell Mayberry for *NewsOK* (19 Feb. 2011). "He wasn't distracted by anything. He had a vision at a young age of what he wanted to do and where he wanted to get."

To achieve his basketball goals, Westbrook worked diligently on his shooting, which was marginal at best when he first started out. Under the guidance of his father, he shot upwards of five hundred shots at various ranges and angles every day after school. He supplemented his shooting work with arduous calisthenics-based workouts. "We would shoot for hours and it was that extra effort that got him to where he's at," Westbrook's father told Arash Markazi for ESPN Los Angeles (30 Apr. 2010), adding, "That's all he wanted to do."

## HIGH SCHOOL AND COLLEGE CAREER

Westbrook attended Leuzinger High School in Lawndale, California, where he enjoyed a late-blooming basketball career. As a freshman he stood five feet eight inches and weighed only

Keith Allison/Wikimedia Commons

140 pounds. Hampered by his small size, Westbrook did not become a starter on the varsity basketball team until his junior year. Still, he impressed coach Reggie Morris and his teammates with his maturity and work ethic. "Russell is an overachiever," Morris told Mannix. "He never takes days off; he's never short on effort. He's always trying to prove himself, and he feeds off the fact that people don't believe in him."

Westbrook's basketball fortunes improved dramatically during the summer before his senior year, when he had a four-inch growth spurt, which transformed him into a highly coveted prospect. Now six feet one (he would grow two more inches in college), with a nearly eighty-inch wingspan, 180-pound frame, and size-fourteen feet, Westbrook was able to dunk for the first time and take advantage of his athleticism. As a senior he helped lead Leuzinger to the state regional quarterfinals, and colleges began to take notice. He was recruited by several of the nation's top basketball programs but chose to remain close to home, accepting a scholarship to UCLA.

Westbrook spent just two seasons at UCLA, during which he was used mostly as a backup guard and defensive specialist by coach Ben Howland. During his sophomore year, he saw his role increase after Bruins starting point guard Darren Collison was injured. He averaged 12.7 points in thirty-nine games and earned Pac 10 Defensive Player of the Year honors. He helped lead the Bruins to the 2008 NCAA Final Four, where they lost to the University of Memphis, 78–63. After the loss, Westbrook chose to forgo his final two seasons of college eligibility and enter the 2008 NBA Draft.

## OKLAHOMA CITY THUNDER

Westbrook, who averaged an unremarkable 8.3 points per game over the course of his two seasons at UCLA, drew only moderate interest from teams entering the 2008 draft. Many teams were unsure how to use him because of his status as a "tweener" combo guard—one who is able to play at both point guard and shooting guard. Despite such uncertainty, the Oklahoma City Thunder, then still known as the Seattle SuperSonics, were impressed enough with Westbrook's athleticism, toughness, and makeup to select him with the fourth overall pick in the draft, surprising many analysts. Westbrook told Markazi, "I've always had to prove myself to people. . . . I had to show them that I could do this and I could do that and paying no mind to what the critics said."

Westbrook wasted little time living up to his lofty draft position. During his rookie season in 2008–9, he played in all eighty-two games for the Thunder and averaged 15.3 points, 5.3 assists, and 4.9 rebounds. He became only the fifth rookie age twenty-one or under to average at least 15 points, 5 assists, and 4 rebounds in a season (the others are Magic Johnson, Allen Iverson, LeBron James, and Chris Paul). He was named to the NBA All-Rookie First Team and finished fourth overall in the NBA Rookie of the Year voting.

Westbrook built on his solid rookie campaign in his sophomore season, averaging 16.1 points, 8 assists, and 4.9 rebounds in eighty-two games. He teamed up with superstar forward and NBA scoring champion Kevin Durant to lead the Thunder to a 50–32 record and their first postseason berth. Towards the end of the regular season, Durant spoke of Westbrook's role to Ric Bucher for *ESPN The Magazine* (5 Apr. 2010): "He's the leader. If you watch us play in games or practices, he's the one who keeps us together." Though the Thunder lost to the eventual NBA champion Los Angeles Lakers in the first round of the playoffs, the team's fifty wins marked a twenty-seven game improvement from the previous season.

During the 2010–11 season Westbrook "transformed into a transcendent talent," as Mayberry wrote. He played in all eighty-two games for the third straight year and bettered his per-game averages in points (21.9) and assists (8.2). He also finished with a career-high three triple-doubles, which tied him for second in the league. He was named to his first All-Star team, as a reserve for the Western Conference, and received All-NBA Second Team honors for the first time in his career. By the end of the regular season, Westbrook had amassed more than 4,000 points, 1,500 assists, and 1,000 rebounds, making him only the fifth player in NBA history to accomplish such a feat in his first three seasons.

## REACHING THE NBA FINALS

Anchored by the one-two punch of Westbrook and Durant, the Thunder improved their record to 55–27 and won their first Northwest Division title in 2010–11. The Thunder advanced to the Western Conference Finals, where they were defeated by the eventual NBA champion Dallas Mavericks in five games. In seventeen playoff games, Westbrook averaged 23.8 points, 6.4 assists, and 5.4 rebounds. However, he led all playoff participants in turnovers (78), a statistic

he also ranked first in during the regular season. Westbrook's propensity for turnovers, a byproduct of his hyperaggressive playing style, led coach Scott Brooks to bench him in the fourth quarter of game two of the Western Conference finals. According to Brooks, all of Westbrook's mistakes are "pure," as he told Tom Spousta for the *New York Times* (15 May 2012). "It's not like it's selfish. It's competitive. He's passionate, and he displays it every game."

Midway through the 2011–12 season, which was shortened due to a lockout, Westbrook signed a five-year contract extension with the Thunder worth about $80 million. He rewarded their faith in him by finishing fifth in the league with a career-high 23.6 points per game. He also scored a career-high 45 points during a March contest against the Minnesota Timberwolves. He earned All-Star and All-NBA second team selections for the second straight year. Westbrook and Durant together averaged 51.6 points per game, more than any tandem in the league. The Thunder, meanwhile, continued to build on their success by winning their second consecutive Northwest Division title and advancing to the NBA finals for the first time, where they were eliminated by the Miami Heat in five games.

## INJURY AND RETURN

In 2012–13 Westbrook led the Thunder in games played (82) for the fifth straight season. He averaged 23.2 points and was named to his third straight All-Star and second-team All-NBA teams. The Thunder finished with a franchise-best 60–22 record, which helped them clinch their third straight division title and the number-one seed in the Western Conference playoffs. The Thunder defeated the Houston Rockets in the first round before being upset by the Memphis Grizzlies in the Western Conference semifinals.

In the second game of the Thunder's series against the Rockets, Westbrook suffered a lateral meniscus tear in his right knee after colliding with Rockets guard Patrick Beverley. The injury forced him to undergo season-ending surgery and was considered one of the main reasons why the Thunder lost to the Grizzlies in the conference semifinals.

Prior to the 2013–14 season, Westbrook underwent a second surgery on his right knee that forced him to miss the first two games of the regular season. It ended his streak of consecutive regular season games played at 394, which was then the longest active streak in the league. Westbrook appeared in twenty-five games before undergoing a third surgery on his right knee, which caused him to miss more time. He returned to the lineup in February 2014, but received limited minutes the rest of the season, averaging 21.8 points. The Thunder won their fourth straight division title and earned the number-two seed in Western Conference. They advanced to the Western Conference Finals, where they lost to the eventual NBA champion San Antonio Spurs in six games.

Westbrook regained his All-Star form in the playoffs, where he averaged 26.7 points, 8.1 assists, and 7.3 rebounds in nineteen games. He became the first player in the playoffs to average at least 26 points, 8 assists, and 7 rebounds since Oscar Robertson in 1964.

During the 2014–15 season, Westbrook missed fourteen games after suffering a small fracture in his right hand. In addition to the Thunder, he has played for the US men's national basketball team in international competitions. He won a gold medal at the 2010 FIBA World Championship in Turkey, and another at the 2012 Olympic Games in London.

## PERSONAL LIFE

Westbrook has won attention around the league for his sense of style. He has often showed up to postgame interviews wearing rimless glasses, skinny jeans, and colorful, one-of-a-kind shirts, choices that have turned him into a fashion icon. In 2014 Westbrook released a fashion line in conjunction with the department store Barneys New York and launched his own line of sunglasses. "I love basketball and I love fashion," he told Bee Shapiro for the *New York Times* (11 Sept. 2013). "But if it weren't for basketball, a lot of the opportunities I have now wouldn't have come about."

## SUGGESTED READING

Mannix, Chris. "Leading Man." *Sports Illustrated* 18 June 2012: 44–50. Print.

Markazi, Arash. "Westbrook: The Honor Guard." *ESPN LA*. ESPN Internet Ventures, 30 Apr. 2010. Web. 5 Jan. 2015.

Mayberry, Darnell. "Russell Westbrook's Journey from Community Center Gyms to the NBA All-Star Game." *NewsOK*. NewsOK. com, 19 Feb. 2011. Web. 5 Jan. 2015.

—Chris Cullen

# Mary Jo White

**Born:** December 27, 1947
**Occupation:** Chair of the US Securities and Exchange Commission

Mary Jo White was born in Kansas City, Missouri. After earning a bachelor's degree from the College of William and Mary in 1970, she intended to become a therapist. She earned a master's degree in psychology from the New School for Social Research in New York. While sitting in on one of her husband's law classes, White decided to become a lawyer. She earned a law degree from Columbia Law School in 1974. In 1976, she joined the New York law firm Debevoise & Plimpton as an associate. Between 1983 and 1990, she served as a litigating partner for the firm.

Having earned a law degree, White became a successful practicing attorney. From 1978 to 1981, she was assistant US attorney for the Southern District of New York. Between 1990 and 1993, she served as assistant and then acting US attorney for the Eastern District of New York. She remained in this role until President Bill Clinton appointed her US attorney for the Southern District of New York in 1993. White was the first woman in the district's history to be appointed to this position. In this capacity, she oversaw numerous high-profile cases, including the prosecution of mobster John Gotti and terrorist Ramzi Yousef, one of the perpetrators of the 1993 World Trade Center bombing.

Prior to her appointment to the United States Securities and Exchange Commission, White served as litigation department chair at Debevoise & Plimpton.

## SEC CHAIRWOMAN

President Barack Obama nominated White as chairwoman of the US Securities and Exchange Commission (SEC) on February 7, 2013. In praise of her career achievements and reputation as a tough prosecutor, President Obama remarked, "You don't want to mess with Mary Jo." White's nomination received some criticism in the press regarding her work as private lawyer for Wall Street executives—in particular, her work in defense of former Bank of America chief executive Ken Lewis, who faced a civil fraud lawsuit. Nevertheless, departing SEC Chairwoman Mary Schapiro cited White's private sector experience as a crucial asset. White's nomination was confirmed by the United States Senate on April 8, 2013. As chairwoman of the SEC, White oversees the enforcement of federal securities laws and financial sector regulations—including laws pertaining to the stock market. However, the SEC does not have the authority to sentence fraudulent businesspeople to prison terms or undertake traditional criminal investigations involving surveillance. The organization combats criminal financial activity through civil lawsuits and the application of federal fines.

Prior to White's appointment as its chief executive, the SEC garnered headlines for its failure to detect a massive, decades-spanning Ponzi scheme perpetrated by investment manager Bernie Madoff. Moreover, upon White's arrival as chairwoman, the SEC continued to face widespread political pressure to apportion blame and punishment for nefarious corporate activity that helped catalyze the global financial crisis of 2007–8. Upon taking office, White worked to reorganize the SEC's implementation of new regulations contained within the Dodd-Frank Act—legislation aimed at reforming various business practices on Wall Street and providing increased legal protections to the American consumer. White rejected a previously approved settlement agreement with hedge fund manager Phillip Falcone—who stood accused of securities fraud—on the grounds that it was too lenient. White required an admission of guilt in addition to the payment of a fine from Falcone in the subsequent agreement reached in August 2013. In her first year as chairwoman, White made an effort to improve morale at the SEC, meeting more frequently with commissioners Luis Aguilar, Daniel Gallagher, Kara Stein, and Michael Piwowar and meeting less frequently with representatives of the largest Wall Street firms.

White caused controversy in late 2013 when she dropped consideration of corporate political spending from the SEC's regulatory agenda. White's predecessor, Chairwoman Schapiro, had previously agreed to put under consideration a new SEC rule requiring corporate disclosure of political donations. In testimony before the House Financial Services Committee, White responded to questioning regarding the SEC's long-term formulation of the rule by saying, "No one is working on a proposed rule." Supporters have countered critics of White's decision by stating that regulations regarding political fundraising are out of the SEC's wheelhouse

and should be taken up by the Federal Election Commission.

In March 2014, author Michael Lewis published *Flash Boys: A Wall Street Revolt.* The book alleges that the cooptation of electronic trading by ultra-wealthy investment organizations has resulted in a rigged national stock market. Lewis argues that digital technology has created a stock trading infrastructure that provides an unfair advantage to those with access to firms with computer systems possessing the ability to learn and react to public trades in microseconds. Although *Flash Boys* caused the Federal Bureau of Investigation, the US Attorney General, and New York State prosecutors to begin investigating illegal trading schemes among electronic trading outfits, White denied Lewis's allegations in testimony to a congressional committee in April 2014. "The markets are not rigged," stated White, describing them as "the strongest and most reliable in the world."

Among the other issues considered by White as SEC chairwoman are conflict minerals reporting regulations and laws surrounding investor protections for crowdfunding.

**IMPACT**

In addition to her legal career, White has served as a member of the Council on Foreign Relations and an executive committee member of the NASDAQ Stock Market. In 2012, White was named Regulatory Lawyer of the Year by the Chambers USA Women in Law Awards. Her other career accolades include the George W. Bush Award for Excellence in Counterterrorism, the Women of Power and Influence Award from the National Organization for Women, and the Sandra Day O'Connor Award for Distinction in Public Service.

**PERSONAL LIFE**

White and her husband, John, were married in 1970. John White, a former head of the SEC's corporate finance division, is a lawyer with the New York law firm Cravath, Swaine, and Moore. The couple has one son.

**SUGGESTED READING**

Cassidy, John. "Two Reasons Why Mary Jo White Is a Bad Choice for the S.E.C." *New Yorker.* Condé Nast, 25 Jan. 2013. Web. 14 May 2014.

Chasan, Emily. "SEC Nominee Has History as Corporate Friend and Foe." *Wall Street Journal.* Wall Street Journal, 24 Jan. 2013. Web. 14 May 2014.

"Cop or Suspect?" *Economist. Economist Media Group,* 24 Jan. 2013. Web. 14 May 2014.

Eaglesham, Jean, and Liz Rappaport. "The Six Degrees of Mary Jo White." *Wall Street Journal.* Wall Street Journal, 25 Jan. 2013. Web. 9 May 2014.

Lemann, Nicholas. "Street Cop." *New Yorker.* Condé Nast, 11 Nov. 2013. Web. 14 May 2014.

Reaves, Jessica. "Time.com Profile: Mary Jo White." *Time.* Time, 13 Mar. 2001. Web. 14 May 2014.

"SEC Biography: Chair Mary Jo White." sec. gov. *United States Securities and Exchange Commission,* n.d. Web. 14 May 2014.

—Joshua Pritchard

Jessica L. Tozer/Wikimedia Commons

# Heather Willauer

**Occupation:** Analytical chemist and inventor

Dr. Heather Willauer is a research chemist at the Naval Research Laboratory (NRL) in Washington, DC. In September 2013, Willauer and her team within the NRL's Materials Science and Technology Division successfully flew a model airplane using jet fuel that had been synthesized from seawater. The feat, which was officially announced by the NRL in April 2014, captured the imaginations of news outlets across the world. In an article for the *International Business Times* (8 Apr. 2014) on the program's revolutionary potential Christopher Harress wrote, "The development of a liquid hydrocarbon fuel could one day relieve the military's dependence on oil-based fuels and is being heralded as a 'game changer' because it could allow military ships to develop their own fuel and stay operational 100 percent of the time, rather than having to refuel at sea."

Still, Willauer, who has led the project for the past decade, cautions against celebrating seawater as an alternate source of fuel too soon. With more funds and more time to refine the technology, she estimates that seawater-sourced jet fuel could be a viable commercial product in about ten to fifteen years. According to projections the new fuel will cost between three and six dollars per gallon when first introduced, and could eventually compete with traditional fuels. As Willauer perfects the conversion process she has been thrust to prominence in the global conversation on alternative energy.

## EARLY LIFE AND EDUCATION

Heather Dawn Willauer graduated from Berry High School in Birmingham, Alabama. She earned her BS degree in chemistry from Berry College, located in Rome, Georgia, in 1996. She received her PhD in analytical chemistry from the University of Alabama in 2002, and completed her postdoctoral research at the NRL as a National Research Council postdoctoral associate. She officially joined the NRL as a full-time research chemist in 2004.

The NRL is a scientific research and development hub founded in 1923 that serves both the US Navy and the US Marine Corps. In the early 2000s, Willauer and the NRL began researching alternative energies for naval vessels. The department was increasingly concerned about the world's diminishing fossil fuel supply and the country's reliance on oil from foreign suppliers, though it was motivated by economic and operational challenges more than environmentalism. In particular, refueling ships at sea can be expensive and dangerous, while returning to port is expensive and time consuming. "If [the Navy] made fuel at sea," Willauer told Marina Koren for the *National Journal* (13 Dec. 2013), "they wouldn't be buying it." This ideal scenario became the goal of Willauer's chief research project, which she began in 2007.

In 2009 the Department of the Navy established ambitious energy goals, including the intention to cut its commercial fleet oil usage by an unprecedented 50 percent by 2015. Significantly, the announcement signaled that the Navy would attempt to obtain half of its total amount of jet fuel from alternative sources by 2020. By then Willauer's project, which was already well underway, was seen as an important candidate system for eventually improving past those goals.

## FUEL FROM SEAWATER

The basis of Willauer's program was the deceptively simple-sounding effort to transform ordinary seawater into a fuel source. The ultimate goal was to find a way to synthesize jet fuel from a source other than oil. She and her team were first interested in the potential of seawater because the abundant resource contains about 140 times the amount of carbon dioxide ($CO_2$) that can be found in the air. Water also contains hydrogen, which, like carbon, is an essential part of hydrocarbon—the organic compound found in crude oil—so Willauer looked to the sea as a source. The next step was to find a way to extract both elements directly from seawater at the same time to improve efficiency and the feasibility of implementing the strategy in a field setting. That relatively straightforward task would take years to perfect.

In 2013 Willauer's team reached "a big breakthrough," as she told Harress. "For the first time we've been able to develop a technology to get $CO_2$ and hydrogen from seawater simultaneously," she said. The equipment that Willauer and her team developed to perform the extraction works in two parts. First, the NRL's proprietary E-CEM (electrolytic cation exchange module) Carbon Capture Skid extracts both dissolved and bound carbon dioxide from the seawater at 92 percent efficiency by re-equilibrating carbonate and bicarbonate to carbon dioxide and producing hydrogen at the same time. Next, "using a metal catalyst in a separate reactor system," Ben Coxworth reported for *Gizmag* (9 Apr. 2014), "the $CO_2$ and hydrogen gases [are] then converted into a liquid hydrocarbon fuel."

The details of the process are highly complex, but Kurt Kleiner described the means of extraction for *New Scientist* magazine (18 Aug. 2009) as a variation of the chemical reaction known as the Fischer-Tropsch process. The Fischer-Tropsch process, which produces hydrocarbons out of raw material "feedstocks" of carbon monoxide and hydrogen, is commonly utilized in the creation of synthetic fuel. The process that Willauer is developing however, uses $CO_2$ as a feedstock—a small but significant difference.

Once the conversion process was developed, the technology's potential became apparent. "Depending on the transition metal for the catalyst—for example iron, cobalt, nickel, copper—you can make methanol, you can make olefins that could be converted to jet fuel, you can make natural gas, all kinds of neat things," Willauer told Jessica Tozer for *Armed with Science*, the official US Department of Defense science blog (11 Apr. 2014). "It's amazing."

## TESTING AND IMPACT

In September 2013 Willauer's team successfully flew a model airplane running on the seawater-sourced fuel, but they did not officially announce the results of the test until April 2014. Once the accomplishment was confirmed, the possible implications of the technology quickly generated media attention. Vice Admiral Philip Cullom told Harress the successful experiment was "a huge milestone" for the military. "In the Navy, we have some pretty unusual and different kinds of challenges," Cullom said. "We don't necessarily go to a gas station to get our fuel. . . . Developing a game-changing technology like this, seawater to fuel, really is something that reinvents a lot of the way we can do business when you think about logistics, readiness." Cullom further emphasized the potential impact of the fuel on naval operations to Tozer, stressing how it removes the soft targets such as fuel tankers, other supply vehicles, and infrastructure that are major vulnerabilities when using fossil fuels.

The environmental aspects of the technique did not go unnoticed. Koren wrote that, according to Willauer, the E-CEM cells essentially capture carbon dioxide for free, making the process cleaner than hydrogen production through electrolysis. However, a large amount of energy is still required, and burning the resulting fuel does release pollutants like traditional hydrocarbon fuels. But Willauer stressed to Tozer that "It's a net-zero carbon footprint. . . . I'm not getting fossil fuel out of the ground and putting more $CO_2$ in the air, I'm actually using the $CO_2$ from the environment." Yet some skeptics have criticized this claim, arguing that while it may work for large Navy vessels powering the process with nuclear generators, in other applications the necessary power input may cancel out any environmental benefits.

## NEXT STEPS

After the successful flight of the model plane, Willauer and her team turned their focus to the next steps for the designer fuel, most critically towards finding a way to produce it in larger quantities. Willauer discussed the progress and future of the program for *Sea Technology* magazine (1 Apr. 2014), including ongoing tests at the NRL's Center for Corrosion Science and Engineering facility in the Gulf of Mexico that simulate "conditions that will be encountered in an open-ocean process." She noted that it took three E-CEM modules a day to produce a gallon of fuel, but that the tests have provided valuable information on how to increase production and decrease energy consumption. Successfully moving forward on this next step, Willauer stressed, heavily rests on future funding. Meanwhile, at the main NRL lab in Washington, DC, where Willauer is based, her team is scaling up production from a plug flow reactor to a commercial reactor in an effort to produce more hydrocarbons and ultimately, more fuel.

In addition to her team at NRL, Willauer collaborates with colleagues in various groups including the Office of Naval Research P38 Naval Reserve Program and Newport News Shipbuilding (NNS). As far as future private sector partnerships, Willauer is open and encouraging. "We do basic research, but the idea really is . . . for the technologies we develop, we want to get that out there in the public for commercial use," she told Francis Rose for the *In Depth with Francis Rose* radio program. Given the budget constraints of the federal government, Rose pointed out, private partnerships—won after demonstrating the commercial possibilities of a technology—may be the wisest course of action for scientists like Willauer. With financial support from the private sector, Willauer estimates that seawater-sourced fuel could become an industrial reality in about ten years, though she acknowledges that that estimate is optimistic. "We do have a long way to go," she told Rose. She cited scalability and efficiency as the project's biggest challenges going forward. Her ultimate goal, she told Rose, would be for seawater-sourced fuel to serve as what is known as a "drop-in replacement," meaning that the Navy could use the fuel with its existing equipment and technology.

Willauer married Jeffrey William Baldwin, a fellow research chemist, on July 1, 2000. They live in Washington, DC.

## SUGGESTED READING

Coxworth, Ben. "Navy Powers Model Plane Using Fuel Made from Seawater." *Gizmag*. Gizmag, 9 Apr. 2014. Web. 11 Dec. 2014.

Harress, Christopher. "Goodbye, Oil: US Navy Cracks New Renewable Technology to Turn Seawater into Fuel, Allowing Ships to Stay at Sea Longer." *International Business Times*. IBT Media, 8 Apr. 2014. Web. 11 Dec. 2014.

Koren, Marina. "Guess What Could Fuel the Battleships of the Future?" *National Journal*. National Journal Group, 13 Dec. 2013. Web. 10 Dec. 2014.

Parry, Daniel. "Scale Model WWII Craft Takes Flight With Fuel From the Sea Concept." *U.S. Naval Research Laboratory*. Dept. of the Navy, 7 Apr. 2014. Web. 10 Dec. 2014.

Rose, Francis. "Dr. Heather Willauer, Research Chemist, U.S. Naval Research Laboratory." *In Depth with Francis Rose*. Federal News Radio, 22 Apr. 2014. Web. 10 Dec. 2014.

Tozer, Jessica L. "Energy Independence: Creating Fuel from Seawater." *Armed with Science*. US Dept. of Defense, 11 Apr. 2014. Web. 11 Dec. 2014.

Willauer, Heather. "Transforming Seawater into Designer Fuel." *Sea Technology*. Compass, Apr. 2014. Web. 14 Dec. 2014.

—Molly Hagan

# Willem-Alexander Claus George Ferdinand

**Born:** April 27, 1967
**Occupation:** King of the Netherlands

Willem-Alexander is the king of the Netherlands. He is the seventh head of the Dutch monarchy since 1815, having assumed the throne after the abdication of his mother, Queen Beatrix.

## BACKGROUND

Willem-Alexander Claus George Ferdinand was born in the city of Utrecht in the central Netherlands on April 27, 1967, to Princess Beatrix of the Netherlands and Claus van Amsberg, also known as Prince Claus of the Netherlands. He was later joined by two brothers, Prince Johan Friso and Prince Constantijn. As the queen's eldest son, Willem-Alexander was in line for the Dutch throne from birth.

Willem-Alexander spent his childhood at the royal home at Drakensteyn Castle. He attended a Protestant primary school in The Hague, where his classmates came from a variety of social backgrounds. His mother ascended to the throne of the Netherlands when he was thirteen, making him the heir apparent.

In his teenage years, Willem-Alexander became increasingly rebellious, and at the age of sixteen he was sent to Atlantic College in Cardiff, Wales, for two years. He earned his International Baccalaureate from the school in 1985 and then returned to the Netherlands for compulsory military service. At the conclusion of his service he enrolled in undergraduate studies at Leiden University in western Holland, from which he graduated with a degree in history in 1993.

Throughout his studies and military service, Willem-Alexander maintained an interest in flying, gaining a private pilot's license in 1985, followed by a commercial pilot's license in 1987 and a military pilot's license in 1994. In the late 1980s he flew as a volunteer for the African Medical Research and Education Foundation and for the Kenya Wildlife Service.

## POLITICS AND KINGSHIP

In 1997, at the age of thirty, Willem-Alexander became an outspoken critic of the state of the Netherlands' water resources, advocating for increased flood protection for the nation's multitude of low-lying cities and the conservation of clean drinking water. He became the patron of the Global Water Partnership in 1998.

The prince's avid interest in sports contributed to his being named a member of the International Olympic Committee (IOC). He was appointed in 1998 and sat on various commissions, often related to marketing, over the course of his fifteen years on the committee. The prince became a prominent voice in the planning and promotion of the Olympic Games that occurred during his tenure with the IOC.

In 2000, he was named chair of the Dutch Integrated Water Management Commission, an organization tasked with monitoring water-related legislation and financial policy within the Netherlands. One of the body's major successes under his leadership was the establishment of flood safety standards throughout the country. The same year, he chaired the Second World Water Forum in The Hague.

United Nations Secretary-General Kofi Annan named Willem-Alexander chair of the United Nations Advisory Board on Water and Sanitation in 2006. As chair, the prince oversaw the UN's international political and financial strategies for wastewater management and pollution prevention.

The prince held the post until 2013, when his mother, Queen Beatrix of the Netherlands, announced her decision to abdicate the throne after a thirty-three-year reign. Willem-Alexander was the first man to succeed to the throne of the Netherlands since 1890; the three monarchs who preceded him were Beatrix, his grandmother Juliana, and his great-grandmother Wilhelmina.

Willem-Alexander assumed the throne on April 30, 2013, before a joint session of the Dutch parliament. Then forty-six years old, he was the youngest monarch in Europe at the time.

Upon taking the throne, Willem-Alexander resigned from both the IOC and the UN and was granted an honorable discharge from the Dutch armed forces, but he retained an interest in the areas of sports, water management, and defense. In September 2013, he was presented with the Olympic Order in Gold by the president of the IOC.

## IMPACT

King Willem-Alexander has gone to considerable lengths to distance the Dutch royal family from the stuffy reputation of many monarchies, keeping a daily blog, making numerous appearances worldwide, and remaining a publicly active supporter of the nation's teams at international sporting competitions. He has also worked to ease tension between the royal family and the throngs of Dutch media who remain interested in their political and personal lives, establishing legislation that sets clear guidelines regarding media availability and photo opportunities.

## PERSONAL LIFE

Willem-Alexander married Argentinean banking executive Máxima Zorreguieta in 2002. The couple has three daughters. The oldest, Catharina-Amalia, born in 2003, is heir apparent.

## SUGGESTED READING

Brooks, James. "Willem-Alexander: Profile of Europe's Youngest King." *Telegraph*. Telegraph Media Group, 30 Apr. 2013. Web. 19 Mar. 2014.

"Dutch Crown Prince Quits IOC in Preparation to Become King." *Sports Illustrated*. Time, 29 Jan. 2014. Web. 19 Mar. 2014.

"His Majesty King Willem-Alexander." *Het Koninklijk Huis*. Netherlands Government Information Service, n.d. Web. 20 Mar. 2013.

"King Willem-Alexander of the Netherlands: Biography." *Hello*. Hello, 2013. Web. 19 Mar. 2014.

Teffer, Peter. "Dutch Welcome Willem-Alexander's Ascension to Dutch Throne." *Christian Science Monitor*. Christian Science Monitor, 30 Apr. 2013. Web. 19 Mar. 2014.

"Willem-Alexander: Guardian of Global Water Management." *Hollandtrade.com*. Netherlands Enterprise Agency, n.d. Web. 19 Mar. 2014.

—John Pritchard

# Pharrell Williams

**Born:** April 5, 1973

**Occupation:** Rapper, record producer, and fashion designer

Pharrell Williams is a Grammy Award–winning producer, rapper, and singer-songwriter. Williams and his producing partner Chad Hugo—together they formed a duo called the Neptunes—have been behind some of the biggest hip-hop and pop hits of the past twenty years, including Snoop Dogg's "Drop It Like It's Hot," Nelly's "Hot in Herre," Jay-Z's "I Just Wanna Love You," and Britney Spears's "I'm a Slave 4 U." "At one point in 2003," Justin Jones wrote for the *Daily Beast* (6 Aug. 2014), "the duo were responsible for one-third of the Billboard 100, and 43 percent of songs on the airwaves in the United States." After a seven-year dry spell, Williams dominated the airwaves again as the face of the two biggest hits of the summer in 2013. He appeared with Robin Thicke in the song "Blurred Lines," and also on the track "Get Lucky," with the French electronic duo, Daft Punk. That year, he became the twelfth artist in history to claim both the number one and number two slots on the Billboard 100, simultaneously. "By 2013, I had accepted my role as the . . . camouflage,"

Pharrell told Lynn Hirschberg for W Magazine (7 May 2014) of his long career as a producer. "I was the guy next to the guy, rather than the guy himself. All my formative years, I spent standing next to Jay [Z] or Justin [Timberlake] or all those kings. I've always learned from the masters, whether it's in music or art or fashion. But in 2013, it was different: Suddenly, it was not about being the camo anymore."

In addition to his musical career, which includes work with his alt-rap trio N*E*R*D, Williams is a prolific fashion designer, artist, and business mogul. He has partnered with clothing companies including Bionic Yarn—a company that makes textiles out of recycled plastic bottles—Timberland, and Rizzoli, and he makes leather-clad bicycles with a company called Brooklyn Machine Works. With the trendy menswear designer Mark McNairy, he designed a high-end clothing label for Bloomingdale's called Bee Line, and with the Japanese streetwear designer, Nigo, founded the clothing labels Billionaire Boys Club and Ice Cream in 2003. The collaboration, at its peak, counted sales of about $15 million. In 2011, Williams signed a licensing deal with Jay-Z's Roc Apparel Group. Under the agreement, Ice Cream became a youth apparel collection. Williams unveiled a new line, the Billionaire Girls Club, in 2013. In 2012, he published a coffee table book called *Pharrell: Places and Spaces I've Been*, featuring conversations with other artists and photographs of products he has designed. When asked why he chooses to take on such an astonishing array of projects, Williams told Eric Wilson for the *New York Times* (1 Aug. 2012), "I am overly ambitious, because I realize it can be done. I don't want to end up being a circus act, doing my most famous tricks when I'm seventy."

## EARLY LIFE AND EDUCATION

Williams was born in Virginia Beach, Virginia, on April 5, 1973. His mother, Carolyn, is a retired schoolteacher and his father, Pharoah, was a handyman. The oldest of three brothers, Williams spent his early childhood living in the projects, but his family moved to the suburbs when he was seven years old. When he was twelve, Williams met Chad Hugo at a school for high achieving students. The two boys began playing together and experimenting with beats and samples. Later, they both attended Princess Anne High School in Virginia Beach. Williams told Joe La Puma for *Complex* magazine (2 Dec. 2013) that he didn't belong to one particular social group as a teenager. He had black friends, he said, but kids called him "Oreo" because he also hung out with the white skater kids and listened to the Dead Kennedys, a punk band, and the thrash band, Suicidal Tendencies. But Williams idolized Nirvana's Kurt Cobain, the godfather of the Seattle grunge scene, and P. Diddy, one of hip-hop's first major moguls. "It was two different times, those were moments where two different groups of people from different cultures liberated themselves and did not give a f—— what anyone else had to say," Williams told La Puma. "So as a teenager, that's what I was." Williams got his big break in the early 1990s while he was still in high school. He was drummer in an R & B group with Hugo and two others called the Neptunes, and the band played the school talent show. Fortuitously, the Grammy Award–winning New Jack Swing producer, Teddy Riley, had recently set up a studio a few blocks away from the school. At the time, Riley was working with artists like Whitney Houston and Michael Jackson. He attended the talent show and signed the band shortly after they graduated. Williams marvels at the serendipity now. "Who the f—— goes to Virginia?" Williams asked La Puma. "I know who goes to Virginia. *He* went to Virginia, and he went for a specific reason. . . . But I know I was meant to be affected by his decision."

## THE NEPTUNES AS PRODUCERS

The four-man band never took off, but Williams wrote Riley's verse on the 1992 Wreckx-n-Effects song "Rump Shaker." In 1993, the Neptunes (then just Williams and Hugo) worked on the remix of SWV's "Right Here." The song, which hit number two on the Billboard charts, samples Michael Jackson's 1983 single "Human Nature," and features a brief cameo from Williams near the end of the track. In 1995, they earned a production credit on Blackstreet's "Tonight's the Night" featuring SWV and Craig Mack. By the late 1990s, the Neptunes began to really distinguish themselves from Riley's smooth R & B sound. Indicative of their new sound—which Ryan Bassil for *Vice* (26 Sept. 2013) described as a "fashionable melange of psychedelic pop, classic rock, and new wave"—were Ma$e's "Lookin' at Me" featuring Puff Daddy, which reached number eight on the charts, and Noreaga's "Superthug" featuring Kelis. In 1999, the Neptunes produced debut albums for the hip-hop duo Clipse, and the singer-songwriter Kelis. The Neptunes also wrote and produced Kelis's 2003 smash hit "Milkshake." The Clipse debut didn't fare as well as expected, and the group was dropped from their label, but in 2013, *Complex* magazine dubbed the 2002 Clipse song "Grindin" the best Neptunes beat of all time. As Bassil points out, the beat inspired other artists to copy it, including one-hit wonder J-Kwon in his 2004 song "Tipsy."

The turn of the millennium marked the beginning of the Neptunes' transition from pure hip-hop producers to "maestros of the modern day pop song," Bassil wrote. In 2000, the Neptunes produced Jay-Z's first number one hit on the hip-hop/R & B Billboard chart, "I Just Wanna Love You." Williams makes a cameo on this track as well, crooning the song's title. The song caught the attention of pop superstar Britney Spears, who was at the height of her popularity and working on her third studio album. She enlisted the Neptunes to produce her next single. The result was the sexy and hypnotic—and decidedly off-brand—"I'm a Slave 4 U." The song was a smash for Spears, and effectively shattered her teenybopper image. Her performance of the song at the 2001 MTV Video Music Awards, during which she draped a live python around her neck, is one of the most iconic in the award show's history.

Hot off the success of collaborations with Spears and Jay-Z, the Neptunes wrote or produced songs for No Doubt ("Hella Good" in 2002), Busta Rhymes ("Pass the Courvoisier, Part II," featuring

P. Diddy and Pharrell in 2002) and a remix of Garbage's 2001 single "Androgyny." They also produced Beyonce's first solo single, "Work It Out" in 2002. But it was during the next few years that the Neptunes really hit their stride with Nelly's "Hot in Herre" (2002); Gwen Stefani's "Hollaback Girl" (2005); and Snoop Dogg's "Drop It Like It's Hot," (2004). The song was a major breakthrough for Snoop, Bassil wrote. "The track, which featured a synth lifted from Danish electro group Laid Back's 1983 single 'White Horse' manipulated to sound like it's saying Snoop's name, awarded the rapper with his first number one on the Billboard Chart after twelve years in the game."

In 2003, Williams and Hugo won a Grammy Award for best pop vocal album of the year for Justin Timberlake's debut solo album *Justified*. That same year, they won a Grammy for producer of the year, a title that they had previously been awarded in 2002 by both the hip-hop magazine the *Source*, and *Billboard*. Williams's production philosophy is simple, he told La Puma: just let each artist shine. "I don't paint the Mona Lisa," he said, "I just build the backdrops for the painting."

### N*E*R*D AND SOLO CAREER

In 2001, Williams, Hugo, and Shay Hayley began making their own alt-rap music under the name N*E*R*D. Their debut album *In Search Of . . .* (2002) won the Shortlist Prize for Artistic Achievement in Music. Their subsequent albums include *Fly or Die* (2004), *Seeing Sounds* (2008), and *Nothing* (2010) have garnered the group a cult following. As other collaborations began to dry up, Williams found time to record a solo album, *In My Mind*, which was released in 2006. The music website Pitchfork panned the record and lambasted Williams for making an album without his partner, Hugo. Its first single, "Can I Have It Like That," featuring Gwen Stefani, peaked at a lackluster forty-nine on the Billboard charts, but the record enjoyed decent sales and was even nominated for a Grammy for best rap album in 2007. Meanwhile, mainstream pop appeared to have moved passed the Neptunes' sound. The duo did not have a single top forty hit between 2006 and 2013. But Williams kept himself busy with other musical projects. He composed the soundtrack for the popular 2010 animated children's movie *Despicable Me*, and in 2012, worked with Hans Zimmer to score the eighty-fourth annual Academy Awards.

In 2013, Williams found himself back on top with two infectious summer anthems: "Blurred Lines" and "Get Lucky," and followed up on his success a few months later with another pop gem called "Happy," a song he wrote for the *Despicable Me 2* (2013) soundtrack. In March 2014, he released his second solo album, *G I R L*—which featured guest spots from Justin Timberlake, Miley Cyrus, and Alicia Keyes—to positive critical reception. Williams appeared as a judge on the seventh season of the Emmy Award–winning reality competition show, *The Voice* in 2014.

### PERSONAL LIFE

Williams reportedly married longtime girlfriend, Helen Lasichanh, a model and fashion designer in a small ceremony in France in August 2013. They celebrated the marriage more publicly aboard a yacht in Miami in October of the same year. The couple wore plaid. Williams and Lasichanh have a son, Rocket Ayer Williams, who was born in 2008. Williams wrote a song called "Rocket's Theme," in honor of his son, for the *Despicable Me* soundtrack.

### SUGGESTED READING

Bassil, Ryan. "The Evolution of the Neptunes." Noisey. Vice Media, 26 Sept. 2013. Web. 21 Oct. 2014.

Hirschberg, Lynn. "The Art of Being Pharrell." W Magazine. Condé Nast, 7 May 2014. Web. 21 Oct. 2014.

Jones, Justin. "How Pharrell Williams Finally Made It to the Top." Daily Beast. Daily Beast, 6 Aug. 2014. Web. 21 Oct. 2014.

La Puma, Joe. "Gravitational Pull." Complex. Complex Media, 2 Dec. 2013. Web. 21 Oct. 2014.

Wilson, Eric. "Pharrell Williams Has an Idea." New York Times. New York Times, 1 Aug. 2012. Web. 21 Oct. 2014.

### SELECTED WORKS

*In Search Of . . .* , 2002 (with N*E*R*D); *In My Mind*, 2006; *Nothing*, 2010 (with N*E*R*D); *Despicable Me 2* soundtrack, 2013; *G I R L*, 2014

—Molly Hagan

# Walter Ray Williams Jr.

**Born:** October 6, 1959
**Occupation:** Professional bowler

In 2009, an exclusive panel of professional bowlers and media representatives convened to rank the fifty greatest bowlers of the Professional Bowlers Association's (PBA) first fifty years, in celebration of the PBA Tour's fiftieth anniversary. Walter Ray Williams Jr., a longtime veteran of the sport and world champion horseshoe pitcher, was ranked second behind the late Earl Anthony, who had won a record forty-one PBA Tour titles during his fourteen-year career in the 1970s and early 1980s. Williams surpassed Anthony's career titles record in 2006. To date, Williams has garnered forty-seven PBA Tour titles and has been named the PBA Player of the Year a record-setting seven times, most recently in 2010. In August 2014 bowling journalist Chuck Pezzano reported that Williams had bowled 22,926 games in 775 PBA Tour events to compile a lifetime average of 218-plus. "To put that simply," Pezzano wrote in his column for the *North Jersey Record* (11 Aug. 2014), "an average league bowler rolling 100 games a season would be required to average 219 for 229 years to match the feat."

The decision to rank Anthony ahead of Williams was a controversial one among fans and professional bowlers. "He's the very best, I think, ever," Norm Duke, a PBA Hall of Fame bowler, said of Williams in an interview with John Branch for the *New York Times* (23 Feb. 2011). "And he certainly doesn't look like anything special. That's one thing about Walter—there's nothing physical or otherwise that sets him apart. It's his sheer determination."

Williams began his career as a professional bowler while completing his degree in physics and is known for his slow and unaffected style of play. His revolution-per-minute rate, or the rate at which he rolls the bowling ball, is a relatively sluggish three hundred, while his competitors routinely break five hundred. Such power players have come to dominate the sport after PBA Hall of Famer Mark Roth pioneered the style in the late 1970s. "When I first came out, my rev rate was probably in the middle-high average," Williams explained to Branch. "Now I'm at the low end of the spectrum." Williams, however, prizes accuracy above force. "If you don't hit the pocket, it doesn't matter," he told Branch.

## EARLY LIFE AND HORSESHOE PITCHING

Williams was born in San Jose, California, to Walter Ray and Esther Williams on October 6, 1959. He was the middle of seven children. He began pitching horseshoes in 1969. He soon earned the nickname "Dead-Eye," and won his first junior world championship in horseshoe pitching in Middlesex, New Jersey, in 1971, becoming the youngest junior world champion ever. He was featured in an issue of *Sports Illustrated* and was asked to appear as a guest on *The Dick Cavett Show*. He went on to win the junior world champ title again in 1972 and 1975. His younger brother Jeff won the junior world champ title twice, and his youngest brother, Nathan, won six Arizona state titles. Even Williams's parents took up the sport and eventually received achievement awards from the National Horseshoe Pitching Association (NHPA). "When it was time to do the dishes every evening, we would have a little round-robin competition, and the loser would have to wash them," Williams's father recalled to Brad Herzog for *Sports Illustrated* (27 Nov. 1995). "Walter Ray didn't have to wash many dishes."

"My dream when I was really young was to be a professional horseshoe player and make money that way," Williams told Herzog. "But it didn't take too long to realize that probably wasn't going to work." Though there are hundreds of tournaments held across the country each year, many of them paid less than the cost of a set of horseshoes. Williams decided he needed to pursue a different career, but he never stopped pitching shoes. He entered his first NHPA men's competition in 1977 and earned the Men's World Champion title in 1978. He won five more NHPA world championships, in 1980, 1981, 1985, 1991, and 1994. For a time, he even served as the national league's official statistician. He was inducted into the NHPA Hall

SGranitz/WireImage

of Fame in 1988 and still considers the sport his first love.

## EARLY BOWLING CAREER

Williams began bowling when he was a youth, and started to take the sport seriously in his late teens. He entered local professional tournaments and was even able to pay for part of his college tuition with his winnings. Williams graduated from California State Polytechnic University in Pomona with a bachelor's degree in physics in 1984 even though he had already embarked on his professional bowling career, having joined the PBA Tour full time in 1983. He completed his undergraduate thesis on the physics of a bowling ball rolling down a lane. "I think it gave me a different viewpoint," he said of his education to Herzog. "I don't think I necessarily looked at bowling or the bowling lane like a lot of other people did."

Though bowling itself is an age-old sport, professional bowling enjoyed a heyday during the 1960s and 1970s when professional bowlers received hefty endorsement deals and tournament prizes to rival the salaries of National Football League players of the day. Bowling was having its cultural moment as a professional sport, and pro bowlers presided over that culture. They appeared in commercials for beer and Wonder Bread, and bowling was broadcast into living rooms across the country through televised tournaments on ABC Sports every Saturday afternoon. By the 1980s, the sport had begun to lose a bit of its luster. It was clear that bowling was no longer considered elite, but it was popular, and its biggest stars were still making good money.

## PBA PLAYER OF THE YEAR

Williams earned his first PBA Player of the Year title in 1986, and he won five championships between 1986 and 1987. By the early 1990s, he hit his stride, winning his sixth tour title in 1991, the Japan Cup. In 1993, Williams won a whopping seven tour titles and snagged the PBA Player of the Year title for the second time. He was inducted into the PBA Hall of Fame in 1995 and went on to win three consecutive Player of the Year titles in 1996, 1997, and 1998. Despite Williams's success in the 1990s, the PBA was losing money in its partnership with ABC. The network chose not to renew its contract with the PBA in 1997. Williams won the last televised match on ABC against Pete Weber, who was ranked second only to Williams and who tailed Williams on

the all-time earnings list by less than five thousand dollars.

By 2000 the PBA was deeply in debt and on the verge of collapse when a trio of Microsoft veterans offered to buy the league for five million dollars. Their journey to revitalize the PBA, which included hiring marketing executives from Nike, was the subject of the 2004 documentary, *A League of Ordinary Gentlemen*, in which Williams stars alongside bowling legends Pete Weber, Chris Barnes, and Wayne Webb. Despite the setbacks for the league, Williams's career continued to thrive. He won another Player of the Year title in 2003 and a second Japan Cup in 2006. Williams tied Anthony's record forty-one PBA Tour titles on March 26, 2006, at the Denny's World Championship in Indianapolis. Williams was named Player of the Year again in 2010. Williams told Branch that he thought he would be retired when he was forty years old. "When I got to thirty-five, I kept saying, 'Two more years, two more years, two more years, two more years.' Here I am, fifty-one, still doing it. I'd like to think I can do it two more years," he said. Williams is still burning up the lanes, despite persistent arthritis in his fingers. He closed the 2012–13 season as the first player to knock down five million pins in PBA Tour competitions.

## PERSONAL LIFE

On tour, Williams is known to travel in a trailer and often spends the night in the bowling alley parking lot. Unlike most professional bowlers playing today, Williams has never had to take a second job to supplement his income. Over the course of his career, he has earned about $4.4 million, averaging about $147,000 per year. The sport's decline—evident in its declining salaries—could be attributed to a shift in how Americans view the sport. Statistics show that Americans are visiting bowling alleys in droves, but most consider bowling a recreational activity rather than a sport, Williams told Zachary Crockett for *Priceonomics* (21 Mar. 2014). Still, Williams takes heart in the millions of children who are picking up bowling each year. "Most of us in the sport side of bowling are hoping that the sport side is revitalized and all of the young talented bowlers have a great future ahead of them," he told Crockett.

Williams met his wife, Paige Pennington, at a horseshoe tournament in San Jose, California, in 1985. Pennington was there to support her mother, who was competing. Soon after that, her mother called her to tell her, as she recalled to Susan Smiley-Height for the *Ocala Star Banner* (2 May 2006), that "the horseshoe guy is bowling on TV." The couple began dating and married ten years later. They adopted a daughter named Rebecca in 2007. Williams has said that he chose to build his home in Ocala, Florida, so that he could spend more time on his golf game. He also enjoys playing chess.

## SUGGESTED READING

Branch, John. "Still Throwing Strikes, Ball After Ball." *New York Times*. New York Times, 23 Feb. 2011. Web. 16 Nov. 2014.

Herzog, Brad. "A Dead Ringer for a Bowler: That Man Pumping Iron Winners Sure Looks Like the PBA's Walter Ray Williams Jr." *Sports Illustrated*. Time, 27 Nov. 1995. Web. 16 Nov. 2014.

Pezzano, Chuck. "Bowling: Walter Ray Williams Jr. Is the Greatest." *Record* [North Jersey]. North Jersey Media Group, 11 Aug. 2014. Web. 16 Nov. 2014.

Putz, Andrew. "Fear and Bowling." *Cleveland Scene*. Cleveland Scene, 10 Aug. 2000. Web. 16 Nov. 2014.

Smiley-Height, Susan. "Three Sports, Two Halls of Fame, One Guy." *Ocala Star Banner*. Ocala.com, 2 May 2006. Web. 16 Nov. 2014.

—Molly Hagan

# Anne Wojcicki

**Born:** July 28, 1973
**Occupation:** Founder of 23andMe

Anne Wojcicki is the cofounder and acting CEO of the personal genomics and biotech company 23andMe, which is responsible for providing testing and interpreted results to individual customers.

## BACKGROUND

Anne Wojcicki was born on July 28, 1973, in San Mateo County, California. Wojcicki and her two older sisters, Susan and Janet, grew up in Palo Alto, California, near Stanford University, where her father, Stanley, worked as a professor of particle physics. Her mother, Esther, is a high school journalism teacher. Wojcicki has said that both her parents were very frugal and passionate about doing good in society, values that Wojcicki herself continues to hold.

Upon graduating from Yale University in 1996 with a degree in biology, Wojcicki worked for a decade with health-care investments in the biotech industry. Several of those years were spent living and working in New York, where Wojcicki found the culture of Wall Street to be vastly different from that of her native California. In 2000, tired of the fast-paced, money-oriented environment of Wall Street, Wojcicki quit her job and returned to California. She planned to attend medical school, but doctors she knew discouraged her from following that career path due to the debt involved. Although she ultimately did not pursue a career in medicine, she maintained an interest in the relationship between health and genetics.

## BIOTECH ENTREPRENEURSHIP

Wojcicki cofounded 23andMe in 2006, along with Linda Avey and Paul Cusenza. Avey and Cusenza have since left the company, and Wojcicki serves as its CEO. 23andMe is a company that offers rapid genetic testing and interpretation of the results for individuals. For $99 and a DNA sample, the company provides a report on genetic risk factors for diseases such as Alzheimer's and Parkinson's, without requiring the person being tested to go through a medical professional for the information.

Wojcicki has spoken frequently about her goals in founding 23andMe, stating that her interest lies in giving individuals access to their own medical and genetic information, as well as in gathering large amounts of data for the purposes of research and further medical study. She is passionate about health care on a personal level, rather than simply on a business level, unlike the companies she worked for in New York, which she found to be interested only in profits.

In her role as CEO, Wojcicki has had to deal with backlash from governmental organizations such as the Food and Drug Administration (FDA), as well as criticism from members of the medical community. The FDA and various medical professionals have expressed misgivings about allowing individuals to have access to their own genetic data without a doctor serving as a middleman in the process. Wojcicki disagrees that this is a cause for concern, as she generally believes that being aware of one's own medical and genetic risks is better than being kept in the dark. She argues that having information about a health risk allows an individual to take preventive action on the matter and that everyone is entitled to the opportunity to do so.

In addition, Wojcicki has spoken in interviews about her frustration that modern, Western medicine focuses less on prevention than on treating disease after the fact and that the decisions made in the health-care system are focused largely on finances and revenue, rather than the best interests of the patients.

## CHARITABLE DONATIONS

Wojcicki has used her personal connections in Silicon Valley, as well as those established through her marriage to Google cofounder Sergey Brin, to raise funds for and awareness of her company. She has also, along with Brin, contributed significant amounts of money to charitable causes, largely through the Brin Wojcicki Foundation, which supports human rights and antipoverty initiatives. In addition, Wojcicki and Brin have donated money to the Michael J. Fox Foundation for Parkinson's research—largely motivated by Brin's own high risk factor for developing the disease, which he discovered through 23andMe's testing.

Wojcicki, along with Brin, Facebook founder Mark Zuckerberg and his wife, and entrepreneur Yuri Milner, is responsible for funding the Breakthrough Prize in Life Sciences, an award of $3 million for research and discoveries that aim to extend the human lifespan.

## IMPACT

Wojcicki has worked successfully in STEM (science, technology, engineering, and mathematics) fields and serves as CEO of the company she helped found. Her work with 23andMe has advanced the field of personal genomics and made it possible for individuals to have access to at least a base level of knowledge about their own genetic structure.

## PERSONAL LIFE

Wojcicki has two sisters, one of whom, Susan Wojcicki, serves as senior vice president of advertising and commerce for Google. Both of Wojcicki's sisters, as well as her parents, still live near Wojcicki in California. Wojcicki married Google cofounder Sergey Brin in 2007; the couple, who have two children, announced their separation in 2013.

## SUGGESTED READING

Bilton, Nick. "Brin and Wojcicki Give $500,000 to Charity Behind Wikipedia." *New York Times*. New York Times, 18 Nov. 2011. Web. 18 June 2014.

Davies, Kevin. *The $1,000 Genome: The Revolution in DNA Sequencing and the New Era of Personalized Medicine*. New York: Free, 2010. Print.

"Leadership Team." *23andMe Media*. 23andMe, n.d. Web. 18 June 2014.

Lee, Timothy. "The FDA Should Leave 23andMe Alone." *Washington Post*. Washington Post, 25 Nov. 2013. Web. 18 June 2014.

Murphy, Elizabeth. "Inside 23andMe Founder Anne Wojcicki's $99 DNA Revolution." *BioHealth Innovation*. BioHealth Innovation, 14 Oct. 2013. Web. 16 June 2014.

Teeman, Tim. "Married to Mr Google." *Times* [London]. Times Newspapers, 4 Feb. 2012. Web. 18 June 2014.

—Anna Phillips

# Shailene Woodley

**Born:** November 15, 1991
**Occupation:** Actor

Shailene Woodley has been appearing on-screen since the age of five. In 2014 she starred in the movie *Divergent*, based on the first book in Veronica Roth's best-selling dystopian trilogy, and then starred in the movie version of John Green's young adult novel, *The Fault in Our Stars*, where she played Hazel, a teen battling cancer. "To exaggerate the extent to which films are 'hotly anticipated' is standard in Hollywood, but in the case of Woodley's next two roles, that sense is genuine and palpable," Gaby Wood wrote for *Marie Claire* (17 Mar. 2014), referring to those films. "The slick mega-explosion of the *Divergent* franchise, for which Woodley trained in martial arts, hand-to-hand combat, and knife-throwing, is one thing. The implacable, eloquent heartbreak of *The Fault in Our Stars* is another. That Woodley can do both is, somehow, incrementally incredible." Acknowledging that teens are now at the forefront of popular culture and that her current fame is emblematic of that phenomenon, Woodley told the interviewer "I think there's this big rise right now in giving teenagers the worth that they have. For so long they were—and still are—depicted in movies and TV

Georges Biard/Wikimedia Commons

shows as codependent whiners or rich, beautiful, diamond-clad daughters or dumb cheerleader types. But teenagers are so smart. . . .There is a zest for life that you have at that age that is so beautiful."

Critics agree that Woodley possesses a rare talent and that since coming to widespread attention playing George Clooney's angst-ridden daughter in *The Descendants* (2011), she has steadily honed her stage presence. "What continues to shine through is an inner strength, as Woodley never lets her teen girls fall into caricature or victimization," Drew Fortune wrote for the *AV Club* (23 Oct. 2014). "Credit the material, but Woodley makes each character relatable—the atypical girl next door with layers of depth beneath natural beauty."

## EARLY LIFE AND CAREER

Shailene Woodley was born on November 15, 1991, in Simi Valley, California. She has one younger brother, Tanner. Their mother, Lori, is a school counselor, and their father, Lonnie, was a school principal who later became a family therapist. Woodley has said that having parents in the helping professions greatly influenced her. "Empathy and compassion were ingrained into me in a very young age," she told Rob Lowman for the *Los Angeles Daily News* (14 Mar. 2014). "I feel like a lot of people don't learn about those values until later in life, but I was very fortunate to have two parents who made sure that they

were two very important things in my brother's and my lives."

Woodley began modeling at age four. A year later, Lori and Lonnie were approached by an agent who believed their young daughter might find some success acting. Woodley has said that they were so removed from Hollywood and its ethos that they had no idea what duties an agent actually performed. Still, they agreed, with the stipulations that she remain true to herself and try to have a good time, and Woodley began taking acting lessons and going to auditions.

## EARLY ACTING CAREER

Although Woodley recalled to Lowman, "I would literally be told 'no' 500, 600 times at auditions, finally get one 'yes' for a small commercial and then get told 'no' 600 more times," she relished the challenge even as a child. She eventually began appearing regularly in television ads, and in 1999 she got her first role in the made-for-TV movie *Replacing Dad*, a drama about a family coming to terms with the husband's infidelity. Then in 2001, Woodley played the recurring character Kristin Debreno on *The District* (2000–), until 2003. In 2004 Woodley had a small role in the *Everybody Loves Raymond* episode "Party Dress" (16 Feb. 2004) and also played the young Kaitlin Cooper for six episodes on the television series *The O.C.* (2003–7). She also had small parts in the television series *Crossing Jordan* (2001–7). When she was thirteen, she starred as Felicity, a Colonial youngster, in *An American Girl Adventure*, a 2005 video based on the popular line of historically garbed dolls.

Although Woodley had avoided committing working on a long television series for fear that it would not allow her the time to attend public high school, in 2008, with the end of her secondary studies looming, Woodley began starring in *The Secret Life of the American Teenager* (2008–13). The series, which was shown on the ABC Family channel, followed the life of a high school student who struggles through an unplanned pregnancy and teen motherhood. The show was among the highest rated ever to air on the channel, and Woodley—although she has since expressed reservations about the credibility of the plotline and overall message—abandoned her tentative plans to study interior design at New York University in order to remain in the cast.

## BREAKTHROUGH TO FAME

In 2011 Woodley took on what critics consider her breakthrough role appearing opposite George Clooney in *The Descendants* a movie about a wealthy landowner in Hawaii who must deal with grasping relatives, a rebellious daughter, and an unfaithful wife who has been seriously injured in a boating accident. Many critics singled out a particularly powerful scene in which Woodley's character brutally informs her father of her mother's infidelity, and another in which she cries while underwater. "Dynamite is the word for Woodley, who deserves to join Clooney and the movie on the march to awards glory," Peter Travers wrote for *Rolling Stone* (15 Nov. 2011). Those sentiments were prescient; Woodley was nominated in 2012 for a Golden Globe Award for best performance by an actress in a supporting role in a motion picture, but did not win. However, that same year she won both an Independent Spirit Award for best supporting actress, and an MTV Movie Award for breakthrough performance.

Her next high-profile big-screen role came in the 2013 film *The Spectacular Now*, about two high school students falling gradually in love. Some reviewers found fault with the film's somewhat formulaic plot—he is a hard-partying bad boy who believes in living in the moment, while she is the sensitive and studious girl who changes him—even those who quibbled found the performances noteworthy. Woodley and Miles Teller, the male lead, shared the US Dramatic Special Jury Award for acting at the Sundance Film Festival as "two young actors who showed rare honesty, naturalism and transparency and whose performances brought up the best in each other."

After appearing in the critically unsung independent film *White Bird in a Blizzard* (2014), in which she portrays a girl whose mother has disappeared, Woodley starred in the two films that have attracted buzz, thanks in some part to the popularity of their source material. Veronica Roth's *Divergent* books, and John Green's *The Fault in Our Stars*, had already sold millions of copies each and had perched on the major best-seller lists for lengthy periods before being adapted for the screen. Reviews for both pictures were almost uniformly good, with Woodley's naturalistic acting and appealing presence winning much of the attention. Headlines began touting her as the next Jennifer Lawrence (the star of the blockbuster *Hunger Games* franchise, to which the *Divergent* series is often com-

pared), and while Woodley admitted to journalists that she had reached out to Lawrence for advice before accepting the role, she quipped that the main similarities between the two were that they both had short hair and female body parts. In early 2015, *Insurgent*, the second film in the *Divergent* trilogy, was released, and the third, *Allegiant*, is expected to be filmed in two parts and released in 2016 and 2017, respectively.

Despite the runaway success of films like *The Fault in Our Stars* and *Divergent*, Woodley hopes to be offered more adult roles in the future. Her upcoming projects include *Snowden*, where she will play Lindsay Mills, the girlfriend of Edward Snowden, in the Oliver Stone–helmed biopic about the Central Intelligence Agency (CIA) computer contractor who leaked thousands of classified documents to journalists.

## PERSONAL LIFE

Woodley's interests include travel, environmentalism, sustainable living, and herbalism. She lives in Los Angeles, but has admitted in interviews that she has no fixed residence, having given her California home to her grandmother. Instead, she says that she stays with friends and lives out of a suitcase.

## SUGGESTED READING

Friedman, Devin. "Crush of the Year: Shailene Woodley." *GQ*. Condé Nast, Dec. 2014. Web. 6 Mar. 2015.

Lowman, Rob. "*Divergent*'s Shailene Woodley Talks Blockbuster and Maintaining Compassion, Empathy." *Los Angeles Daily News*. LA Daily News, 14 Mar. 2014. Web. 6 Mar. 2015.

Wood, Gaby. "Shailene Woodley: This Is What Badass Looks Like." *Marie Claire*. Hearst Communications, 17 Mar. 2014. Web. 6 Mar. 2015.

Woodley, Shailene. "Shailene Woodley." Interview by Emma Stone. *Interview Magazine*. Brant Publications, 16 July 2013. Web. 6 Mar. 2015.

Woodley, Shailene. "Shailene Woodley's Natural Life." Interview by Sarah Bruning. *Natural Health*. American Media, n.d. Web. 6 Mar. 2015.

Woodley, Shailene. "Shailene Woodley on Nudity, Gregg Araki, and Being a Foodie." Interview by Drew Fortune. *A.V. Club*. Onion, 23 Oct. 2014. Web. 6 Mar. 2015.

## SELECTED WORKS

*The Secret Life of the American Teenager*, 2008–13; *The Descendants*, 2011; *The Spectacular Now*, 2013; *Divergent*, 2014; *The Fault in Our Stars*, 2014

—Mari Rich

---

# Nick Woodman

**Born:** June 24, 1975
**Occupation:** Entrepreneur

Nick Woodman, the founder and chief executive officer of the camera company GoPro, has earned the nickname "the mad billionaire" for his highly caffeinated surfer-dude persona and penchant for thrill-seeking adventures. A born entrepreneur, Woodman founded his first startup, an online gaming company called FunBug, in 1999, two years after he graduated from the University of California, San Diego (UCSD). After that company failed amid the dot-com bust, he launched GoPro in 2002. The company originally developed straps to fasten other makers' cameras to surfers' wrists, but GoPro eventually evolved into a maker of durable palm-sized cameras and accessories. Thanks to the concurrent proliferation of social media platforms, particularly video-sharing sites such as YouTube, GoPro soon became the fastest-growing camera company in the world and virtually synonymous with first-person action videos.

Woodman, who was described by Oliver Jones for the *Daily Beast* (30 Jan. 2015) as "a kind of Bill Gates of the selfie generation," led GoPro's growth, privately bootstrapping the company before taking on a sizable investment from five venture capital firms in 2011. Upon taking GoPro public in June 2014, Woodman became an instant billionaire. He has since transformed the camera-maker into a full-fledged media company.

## EARLY LIFE AND EDUCATION

The youngest of three children, Nicholas D. "Nick" Woodman was born on June 24, 1975, in Santa Clara County, California. His father, Dean, was a successful businessman and investment banker; in the 1970s, he brokered Pepsi's acquisition of Taco Bell. Woodman's mother stayed at home to raise him and his two sisters. After his parents divorced, the prominent venture capitalist Irwin Federman became his stepfather.

John Chiala/CNBC/NBCU Photo Bank
via Getty Images

Woodman grew up in the affluent Silicon Valley enclave of Atherton. At an early age, he was exposed to the entrepreneurial ethos by his father and his father's network of friends, many of whom were founders of successful startups. Before entering the startup world, however, Woodman developed an intense passion for surfing. He became enamored with the sport at the age of eight, when he came across idyllic photos of Oahu's North Shore from *Surfer* magazine in a friend's bedroom. "I didn't even know that world existed," Woodman admitted to Serena Renner for *Triton* (Sept. 2013), UCSD's alumni magazine. "But from then on, I knew I wanted to live in that world."

Woodman attended the Menlo School, an independent college preparatory school in Atherton. A natural athlete, he played on the school's football and baseball teams. By the time he entered his senior year, however, Woodman had dropped team sports to focus solely on surfing. He established Menlo's first surf club and raised money for the club by selling T-shirts at high school football games. Throughout his senior year, he routinely woke up at five o'clock in the morning and drove forty-five minutes from Atherton to the coast to surf. His obsession with surfing was such that, after graduating in 1993, he enrolled at UCSD largely because of its close proximity to the beach.

At UCSD, Woodman immediately fell in with a group of surfers. The group woke up each morning to surf at Black's Beach, a nearby world-famous surf break, and surfed again after classes were over for the day. "Going to UCSD was like going to heaven," as Woodman put it to Renner. Woodman graduated from UCSD with a bachelor's degree in visual arts and a minor in creative writing in 1997.

## BEGINNINGS OF A BILLION-DOLLAR IDEA

Upon graduating from college, Woodman resolved to launch a successful company by the age of thirty. In 1999 he raised $3.9 million in venture capital to start an online gaming and marketing company called FunBug. The company enjoyed popularity on the web but ultimately failed to generate sufficient revenue, and by early 2002 it dissolved amid the dot-com bust. For Woodman, the experience proved humbling. "I feel like I went through the Great Depression," he told Tom Foster for *Inc.* (26 Jan. 2012). "All these companies are being successful around you, you're on that track, and then the market collapses, and you're out of a job."

Following FunBug's failure, Woodman embarked on a five-month surfing expedition through Australia and Indonesia with his girlfriend and future wife, Jill Scully. It was during this time that the seed for GoPro began to germinate. Woodman had long been frustrated by his inability to capture high-quality images of him and his friends riding waves. Unlike world-class surfers, amateurs like Woodman did not have the luxury of bringing along professional cameramen to chronicle their wave-riding exploits; at the time, disposable waterproof cameras with unsteady rubber-band wrist straps were their only option.

Taking matters into his own hands, Woodman created a makeshift wrist strap using the ankle end of a broken surfboard leash. A disposable waterproof camera was then firmly affixed to the strap with rubber bands. After experimenting with different prototypes of the strap during his surfing sojourn, Woodman returned to California rejuvenated, and in the fall of 2002, he founded Woodman Labs, which would ultimately become known as GoPro Inc. To raise capital for the company, he and Jill sold bead-and-shell belts that they had imported from Indonesia. For three months, the couple lived out of a 1974 Volkswagen bus and traveled up and down the California coast selling the belts.

## ENTERING THE CAMERA BUSINESS

After earning $10,000 in profits from belt sales, Woodman, who also received a combined $235,000 investment from his parents, moved back into his father's home in Sausalito, California, where he continued to develop and test prototype straps. It was not long, however, before Woodman realized that he had to change his business model. "Every camera I used would flood or break after a big wipeout," he noted to Robert Moritz for *Popular Mechanics* (June 2012). "I realized I shouldn't be a strap company, but a camera company."

For Woodman, the move into the camera industry was "akin to going from intramural hoops to an NBA tryout," Moritz wrote. And the initial estimate of two months to build a marketable and durable enough product ended up taking two years. After an exhaustive search, Woodman eventually found a Chinese company online that made a low-cost and reusable 35-millimeter camera for snorkelers. The company, called Hotax, agreed to modify their camera with his strap mounts and plastic waterproof cases, which he mailed to them along with $5,000. During this two-year development phase, Woodman routinely worked eighteen-hour days, stopped surfing, and largely kept himself isolated from friends and family. "I was so scared that I would fail again that I was totally committed to succeed," he said in an interview with Ryan Mac for *Forbes* (4 Mar. 2013).

Woodman's dream became a reality in September 2004, when he introduced GoPro's first product, a wrist-mounted 35-millimeter camera called the GoPro Hero, at the Action Sports Retailer convention in San Diego. There, a Japanese distributor bought $2,000 worth of the cameras. Shortly afterward, Woodman hired his friend and onetime college roommate, Neil Dana, as GoPro's first employee, tagging him to help out with sales. The twosome began peddling the GoPro Hero to surf shops and specialty sports retailers around the country, and in 2005, the company made $350,000 in sales. That money allowed Woodman to hire more staff and transition into digital and video production.

## DIGITAL, VIDEO, AND BEYOND

In 2006 GoPro released its first Digital Hero wrist camera, which featured ten-second video capabilities without audio. A breakthrough occurred later that year when Woodman strapped a camera onto the roll bar of a race car. Impressed by the footage, Woodman redesigned the camera to be even more durable and immediately launched plans to add specialty camera mounts and accessories to GoPro's product line.

The first GoPro camera with sound, the Digital Hero 3, was launched in 2007. It was around this time that GoPro's popularity began to surge, thanks largely in part to the rise of YouTube. Bolstered by thousands of consumers uploading original GoPro-tagged content to the site, GoPro's sales tripled. GoPro sales jumped even further in 2008, when the company generated more than $8 million in revenue. That year GoPro introduced the Digital Hero 5, the first of its cameras to feature wide-angle lenses, and released its first camera mounts for helmets, vehicles, ski poles, and surfboards.

In late 2009 Woodman oversaw the launch of GoPro's first high-definition camera, the Hero HD, which ushered in a period of phenomenal growth for the company. Featuring high-resolution video and selling for $200 to $400, the Hero HD line propelled GoPro to the forefront of palm-sized point-of-view camera brands and helped the company bring in revenues of $64 million in 2010. That same year the electronics giant Best Buy and outdoor retailer REI began carrying GoPro cameras and accessories in their stores.

In 2011 Woodman led GoPro's acquisition of the digital-video software company, Cineform, and raised $88 million for the company from five venture capital firms, in efforts to grow its global presence. That year GoPro released an enhanced version of its Hero HD camera, the HD Hero2, and introduced its 3D Hero System, which allowed consumers to combine two 2D cameras in a single housing to shoot 3D video and photos. "You have to strive to be a top player or you shouldn't bother doing this in the first place," Woodman explained in his interview with Moritz. "If you're just muddling along, you're going to get smoked."

## GOPRO IPO AND EXPANSION

After totaling $234 million in revenue in 2011, GoPro pulled in $526 million in 2012, thanks to the introduction of its more compact HD Hero3 product line. The company then amassed $985 million in revenue in 2013. To further raise GoPro's profile, Woodman took the company public in June 2014. GoPro sold its stock at $24 per share for its initial public offering (IPO) and was valued at nearly $3 billion. After GoPro's IPO, Woodman, the company's largest shareholder with a 48 percent stake, instantly became a billionaire. GoPro closed out 2014 with $1.4 billion in revenue, a 41 percent increase from the previous year propelled by strong sales of the company's latest Hero line, the GoPro Hero4.

After GoPro's IPO, Woodman positioned the company not only as a market-leading camera maker but also as an all-encompassing media brand. In addition to having a number of wildly popular YouTube channels, GoPro entered into the realm of sports broadcasting through partnerships with the National Hockey League and ESPN's Winter X Games. The company also sponsored a number of extreme-sports athletes from around the world, including the surfer Kelly Slater, snowboarder Shaun White, and the Austrian skydiver Felix Baumgartner, who wore five Hero2 cameras during his historic jump from the edge of space in October 2012. In 2014 GoPro sponsored the Association of Surfing Professionals World Championship Tour and Big Wave World Tour. In 2015 the company formed partnerships with the communication services provider Vislink and the Marriott hotel chain and added its GoPro Channel app to LG Smart TVs, Microsoft's Xbox gaming console, and to the Roku media streaming platform. Commenting on GoPro's expansion efforts, Woodman told Gavin Brett for the *Telegraph* (28 Feb. 2015), "You could think about GoPro as an iPod-like phenomenon that has yet to launch its iTunes."

Though GoPro has continued to remain firmly rooted in the action-sports world, the company's cameras have been used for all kinds of purposes. Besides being used on countless reality-television shows, news programs, and feature films, such as the Lucasfilm-produced World War II movie *Red Tails* (2012), GoPros have also been used by scientists for various research projects, surgeons during operations, and members of the US military on training exercises, among others. As of 2015, at least one new GoPro video was uploaded to YouTube every minute "The short video synonymous with GoPro is a kind of post-literate diary," Nick Paumgarten wrote for the *New Yorker* (22 Sept. 2014), "a stop on the way to a future in which everything will be filmed from every point of view."

## PERSONAL LIFE

Woodman and his wife, Jill, have three sons, and Woodman captured each of their births with a GoPro camera. In 2014 Woodman was listed as the highest-paid CEO in America, with an estimated $284.5 million in earnings. According to

*Forbes* magazine, he had an estimated net worth of over $2.5 billion as of 2015.

## SUGGESTED READING

Brett, Gavin. "How GoPro Cameras Have Made Nothing Unfilmable, By the Man Who Invented Them." *Telegraph*. Telegraph Media Group, 28 Feb. 2015. Web. 14 July 2015.

Foster, Tom. "The GoPro Army." *Inc.* Inc., 26 Jan. 2012. Web. 14 July 2015.

Jones, Oliver. "GoPro Founder Nick Woodman Was Just a Surfer Dude with a Billion Dollar Idea." *Daily Beast*. Daily Beast, 30 Jan. 2015. Web. 14 July 2015.

Mac, Ryan. "The Mad Billionaire behind GoPro: The World's Hottest Camera Company." *Forbes*. Forbes.com, 4 Mar. 2013. Web. 14 July 2015.

Moritz, Robert. "Guts, Glory, and Megapixels: The Story of GoPro." *Popular Mechanics* June 2012: 74–151. Print.

Paumgarten, Nick. "We Are a Camera." *New Yorker*. Condé Nast, 22 Sept. 2014. Web. 14 July 2015.

Renner, Serena. "The Best Ride of Our Lives." *Triton*. Regents of the University of California, Sept. 2013. Web. 14 July 2015.

—Chris Cullen

---

# Lawrence Wright

**Born:** August 2, 1947
**Occupation:** Journalist

Journalist Lawrence Wright is a staff writer at the *New Yorker*. Much of his work focuses on American foreign policy and global politics. His book on global terrorism and the terrorist attacks of September 11, 2001, *The Looming Tower: Al-Qaeda and the Road to 9/11*, was awarded the Pulitzer Prize in 2007. Outside of journalism, Wright is also a screenwriter and playwright.

## BACKGROUND

Lawrence Wright was born in Oklahoma City, Oklahoma, on August 2, 1947, but was raised in Texas. After graduating from Woodrow Wilson High School in Dallas in 1965, he enrolled at Tulane University. After completing his undergraduate work at Tulane, Wright attended the American University in Cairo, Egypt. He taught English at the university while earning a master's degree in applied linguistics. Wright received his graduate degree in 1969. He returned to the United States in 1971, taking a position as a writer at the *Race Relations Reporter* in Nashville, Tennessee. In 1973, he began writing for the Southern Regional Council publication *Southern Voices* in Atlanta, Georgia. Wright published his first book, *City Children, Country Summer: A Story of Ghetto Children among the Amish*, in 1979.

Wright took a position at *Texas Monthly* in 1980. That same year, he was hired as a contributing editor at *Rolling Stone*. In 1984, he published his second book, *In the New World: Growing Up in America, 1964–1984*, in 1987. Wright joined the *New Yorker* in 1992. In addition to writing about current events in politics and international affairs, he has produced hundreds of articles for the *New Yorker* covering Middle East politics—including the Israeli-Palestinian conflict and American-Pakistani foreign relations. Wright has also produced long-form nonfiction pieces for the magazine, covering such topics as Mexican businessman Carlos Slim and the US Central Intelligence Agency. In 1993, Wright published his third book, *Saints and Sinners*. The book explores the duplicitous lifestyles of various religious leaders, including preacher Jimmy Swaggart. In 1999, Wright published *Twins: And What They Tell Us about Who We Are*. He published his first work of fiction, *God's Favorite: A Novel*, in 2000.

## *THE LOOMING TOWER*

In 2006, Wright published *The Looming Tower: Al-Qaeda and the Road to 9/11*. The book traces how influential religious leaders in Egypt and throughout the Middle East helped to inspire the founding of the al-Qaeda terrorist network by Osama bin Laden. Wright traces the evolution of al-Qaeda, providing detailed descriptions of the personalities and motivations of those involved. In addition to exploring the development of al-Qaeda, *The Looming Tower* investigates the response of American officials to the growing threat of international terrorism. The book was one of the first to explore in depth the communications problems between the Federal Bureau of Investigation and the Central Intelligence Agency in working to counteract incidents of terrorism. According to Wright, a climate of departmental competitiveness between the two agencies played a significant role in al-Qaeda and Bin Laden's successful implementation of the terrorist attacks on New York, Washington, DC, and Pennsylvania on September 11, 2001.

The *Looming Tower* was a commercial success and received widespread critical acclaim. In 2006, it was awarded a *Los Angeles Times* Book Prize in history and named a *New York Times* editors' choice. *Time* magazine named the book among the best books of the year. In 2007, Wright was awarded the Pulitzer Prize for General Nonfiction. The book continued to earn accolades from journalistic and publishing institutions throughout 2007, including the Lionel Gelber Prize and the J. Anthony Lukas Book Prize.

## IMPACT

Wright's experience living and working in the Middle East and his years reporting on foreign affairs and international politics made *The Looming Tower* a great success. The book helped to inform academics, policy makers, and the general public on how and why the September 11 attacks occurred. Wright has developed a reputation for tackling difficult topics and creating informative, well-researched nonfiction. In 2013, he published *Going Clear: Scientology, Hollywood, and the Prison of Belief*, an exploration of the Church of Scientology, its leaders, and its adherents in the entertainment industry.

## PERSONAL LIFE

Wright lives in Austin, Texas. In his spare time, he plays keyboards in the blues band Who Do.

## SUGGESTED READING

"About." *lawrencewright.com.* Lawrence Wright, n.d. Web. 11 Apr. 2014.

Ankrum, Nora. "The Decoder." *Austin Chronicle.* Austin Chronicle Group, 27 Aug. 2010. Web. 17 Apr. 2014.

Guarino, Mark. "Lawrence Wright on 'Going Clear.'" *Chicago Tribune.* Tribune Company, 18 Jan. 2013. Web. 17 Apr. 2014.

"Lawrence Wright's Biography." *Redroom*.com. Red Room Omnimedia Corp., n.d. Web. 17 Apr. 2014.

"Lawrence Wright." *newnewjournalism.com.* Robert S. Boynton, n.d. Web. 17 Apr. 2014.

"*The Looming Tower*." *Kirkus Reviews.* Kirkus Media, n.d. Web. 17 Apr. 2014.

Maslin, Janet. "An Effort to Untangle Scientology's Mysteries." *New York Times.* New York Times, 13 Jan. 2013. Web. 17 Apr. 2014.

McGrath, Charles. "A Careful Writer Stalks the Truth about Scientology." *New York Times.* New York Times, 2 Jan. 2013. Web. 17 Apr. 2014.

## SELECTED WORKS

*City Children, Country Summer: A Story of Ghetto Children among the Amish,* 1979; *God's Favorite: A Novel,* 2000; *In the New World: Growing Up in America, 1964–1984,* 1987; *Saints and Sinners,* 1993; *Twins: And What They Tell Us about Who We Are,* 1999; *The Looming Tower: Al-Qaeda and the Road to 9/11,* 2006; *Going Clear: Scientology, Hollywood, and the Prison of Belief,* 2013

—Joshua Pritchard

# Wu Yajun

**Born:** 1964
**Occupation:** Chair of Longfor Properties

Wu Yajun, the billionaire founder of real estate company Longfor Properties, is one of the wealthiest businesswomen in China. In 2012 she was the richest woman and the fifth-richest person in the country, with a net worth of $6.2 billion; then she divorced her husband, ceding 30 percent of the company to him. In 2014, she was the fifth-richest woman and thirty-sixth-wealthiest Chinese overall, with a net worth of $3.2 billion. Most journalists describe Wu as "self-made" thanks to her middle-class upbringing and career as an engineer and journalist before starting Longfor in 1995 with her then husband Cai Kui; but Wu is also one of China's most elusive figures. As Hu Yuanyuan wrote for *China Daily* (4 Jan. 2010), "She has adopted the 'Three Nos' principle from the very start—no appearances on television, no interviews and no autographs." In 2003, Hu reported, Wu was listed as one of the fifty most influential people in China's real estate industry by a luxury magazine called the *Hurun Report*, but a misspelling of her name and lack of corroborating information led most readers to believe she was a man.

Despite the mystery that surrounds her personal story, Wu's rise is a good illustration of China's fraught, though enormously lucrative, real estate market. In 2011, four of the five wealthiest women in China were real estate moguls. "As one of the only tangible investment vehicles" for China's emerging middle class, "property—housing in particular—has attracted Chinese citizens who see it as a smart place to park their cash," Laurie Burkitt wrote for the *Wall Street Journal* (29 Sept. 2011). The government changed its policy regarding individual home ownership nearly twenty years ago. Today, buying property is considered less risky than investing in the stock market, and the Chinese are not allowed to invest abroad. Indeed, according to a report by Lesley Stahl for the television news magazine *60 Minutes* (3 Mar. 2013), property values have skyrocketed, leading some Chinese to sink their money into as many as five or ten apartments. The boom, Stahl reported, has created what is possibly "the largest housing bubble in human history. . . . No nation has ever built so much so fast."

## EDUCATION AND EARLY CAREER

Wu was born in Chongqing, China, in 1964. A former colleague told Andrew Vanburen for *Next Insight* (5 Aug. 2013) that Wu was the daughter of a dressmaker. Wu herself does not discuss her personal history; much of what is known about her early life comes from secondhand sources. Though one of the richest women in the world, Wu came from relatively humble beginnings. "Yajun's family was very ordinary, and of average means," a neighbor told Vanburen. "I used to take some of my clothes to her mother, a seamstress, for mending."

Wu was a good student, and made friends with one of her teacher's daughters, a girl named Zhang Wei. Today, Zhang is one of Wu's most

© Imaginechina/Corbis

trusted business partners. Wu attended the state-run Northwestern Polytechnic University in Xi'an, China, and graduated from the Department of Navigation Engineering in 1984. (She later earned her MBA degree in the executive program at the Cheung Kong Graduate School of Business in Beijing in 2007.) For four years, Wu worked as a mechanical engineer before taking a job with the China Shirong News Agency in 1988. Her transition to journalism foretold her future career, as the China Shirong News Agency is a mouthpiece for the Chongqing Construction Bureau. Wrote Vanburen, "Her tenure in the media profession was instrumental in exposing her to the movers and shakers among the region's real estate players and policy makers." Wu left the newspaper in 1993, and in 1995, with start-up capital of 10 million yuan (about $1.6 million at 2015 exchange rates), she and her husband, Cai Kui, founded a realty company called Chongqing Zhongjianke Real Estate. Within a year, they renamed it Longfor Properties.

## LONGFOR PROPERTIES

According to a former senior manager at Longfor (as reported by Hu), shortly after founding Longfor, Wu took a trip to Shenzhen to visit the headquarters of Vanke, one of the largest residential property developers in China. From the executives at Vanke, Wu learned to practice financial transparency. When she returned to Longfor, she hired New York City–based Pricewaterhouse-Coopers as the company's auditor. Longfor's first project, a townhouse community called Longfor Garden Nanyuan, broke ground in Chongqing in 1995. "Although [Wu] had no development experience at the time, [Longfor Garden Nanyuan] was regarded as a great success in Chongqing because of its fine construction, scenery, fittings and property management," Hu wrote. The project served as a template for Longfor's subsequent properties, and the duplication, according to an article in the *Want China Times* (23 Oct. 2012), has allowed Longfor to maintain a high rate of turnover. "At Longfor, it may take only five months for a project to break ground after securing the land, while the average time for the process is eight months," according to the article. Managers determine what kind of project they want to build—townhouse, high-rise, villa, or, more recently, business complex or shopping mall—and tweak the Longfor stock design to fit that plot of land. *Want China Times* described the formula as "90 percent duplication and 10 percent innovation."

## ECONOMIC AND POLITICAL POWER

Longfor began expanding rapidly in 2000, and its sales exceeded 2 billion yuan ($322 million) in 2008. The company went public, with a strong initial public offering on the Hong Kong Stock Exchange on November 19, 2009. Longfor set up a commercial property department in 2010; that year, the company owned nearly 20 million square miles of land in ten cities. As of 2013, Wu was a member of China's National People's Congress (NPC), in theory the country's highest legislative body. Among its nearly three thousand members are some of the wealthiest businesspeople in China. In 2012, Michael Forsythe reported for *Bloomberg* (27 Feb. 2012) that the seventy richest members of the NPC added more to their wealth in a single year, 2011, "than the combined net worth of all 535 members of the US Congress, the president and his Cabinet, and the nine Supreme Court justices." A professor at Northwestern University in Evanston, Illinois, told Forsythe, "The rich in China have strong incentive to become 'within system' due to the relative weakness in the rule of law and of property rights." Being an NPC member "means that one's commercial or political rival cannot easily throw one in jail or confiscate one's property."

## CHINESE REAL ESTATE BUBBLE

In 2011 the Chinese government began placing restrictions on housing purchases and loans in an effort to address the rising cost of housing. Stahl described it as a "one apartment policy" that makes it "very hard to buy more than one apartment in major cities." Still, 2011 was a banner year for the real estate market, with many buyers exploiting loopholes—even going so far as to divorce their partners—to acquire more property. That year Wu was named, briefly, the wealthiest woman in the world with the equivalent of $6.6 billion in assets. Since then, the economy has slowed, stoking fears of a downturn on the scale of the 2008 financial crisis (when the US housing bubble burst). The real estate market appears "unstoppable," Kenneth Rapoza wrote for *Forbes* (4 May 2015), despite a brief dip in 2014, when housing sales fell 7.8 percent and housing prices dropped 4.5 percent. As of early 2015, real estate accounted for 25 to 30 percent of China's gross domestic product (GDP), but the sector is "overbuilt," Minxin Pei wrote for *Fortune* (21 Jan. 2015), and the writing is on the wall. "More than 60 million empty apartments await buyers," Pei wrote. In 2013, Stahl travelled to a district in Zhengzhou, where miles upon miles of apart-

ments—all owned—stood empty. Such places, of which there are many in China, are known as "ghost cities," though Wade Shepard for *Reuters* (22 Apr. 2015) objects to the term. A ghost town is a place that has experienced economic prosperity and "died," Shepard wrote. "What China has is the opposite of ghost towns: It has new cities that have yet to come to life."

The development of land—as evidenced by the high turnover rate at Longfor—is quick; populating the land is another matter. China is in the midst of mass urbanization, and such a shift requires trust in an uncertain path. In 2015, Longfor (along with other developers) is trying to avoid financial disaster by diversifying their investments. Underneath its booming exterior, China's economic growth is at a twenty-four-year low. Longfor is projecting slower growth in contracted sales in 2015, while trying to rid itself of inventory—that is, empty apartments and land reserves. Survival has become a key word in the real estate industry. "Due to the country's high debt [to GDP] ratio, the room for supporting the property market through a monetary policy relaxation is now limited," Shao Mingxiao, Longfor's chief executive, told Langi Chiang and Sandy Li for the *South China Morning Post* (18 Apr. 2015). Risks have grown "as local governments quickened the pace of land sales to help repay trillions of yuan of debt, adding to the housing glut," Chiang and Li explained. Wu, as quoted by Chiang and Li put the company's strategy more bluntly: "If you make a turn after seeing an iceberg, you will hit it. You have to turn around the moment you feel [there is an iceberg ahead]."

## SUGGESTED READING

Burkitt, Laurie. "Landed Ladies Top List of China's Richest Women." *Wall Street Journal*. Dow Jones, 29 Sept. 2011. Web. 26 June 2015.

Chiang, Langi, and Sandy Li. "Developers Cut Sales Targets as Profit Dips." *South China Morning Post*. South China Morning Post, 18 Apr. 2015. Web. 1 July 2015.

Hu Yuanyuan. "The Property Billionaire Who Shuns Publicity." *China Daily*. China Daily, 4 Jan. 2010. Web. 26 June 2015.

Rapoza, Kenneth. "China Real Estate Is Unstoppable." *Forbes*. Forbes, 4 May 2015. Web. 28 June 2015.

Shepard, Wade. "The Myth of China's Ghost Cities." *Reuters*. Thomson Reuters, 22 Apr. 2015. Web. 28 June 2015.

Vanburen, Andrew. "Wu Yajun: Ex-Journalist Now PRC Property Billionaire." *Next Insight*. Next Insight, 5 Aug. 2013. Web. 24 June 2015.

"What Other Companies Longfor: Wu Yajun's Secrets of Success." *Want China Times*. Want China Times, 23 Oct. 2012.Web. 26 June 2015.

—Molly Hagan

# Yao Chen

**Born:** October 5, 1979
**Occupation:** Actor

Yao Chen is a well-known Chinese actor and outspoken microblogger. The US–based microblogging site Twitter is banned in China, but Yao has amassed more than seventy-one million followers—"more . . . than the population of Britain," according to Sarah Keenlyside for the *Sunday Telegraph*'s *Stella* magazine (24 Aug. 2014)—on its Chinese equivalent, Sina Weibo (or Weibo for short), earning her the nickname "Queen of Weibo."

While many actors are politically active in the United States, the character of Yao Chen's role in China is a bit different. As the Chinese chafe against a decades-old culture of self-censorship, citizens are increasingly voicing their discontent with government propaganda, political labor camps, and "liberal" Chinese president Xi Jinping online, and Yao's subtly political musings on Weibo have captured the zeitgeist of the modern nation. When the Guangzhou-based newspaper *Southern Weekend* ran afoul of Chinese censors in January 2013, Yao posted a quote from Russian writer and former Soviet gulag prisoner Alexander Solzhenitsyn—"One word of truth shall outweigh the whole world"—alongside a photo of the newspaper's logo.

Yao is in a unique position to affect the political discourse in China, in part because she is so beloved by China's middle class. "Her online advocacy is shifting the goalposts for what is permissible in Chinese cyberspace and has helped make it safe for the masses to join her on the frontlines," Dan Levin wrote for *Prospect* magazine (Apr. 2012). "As the government ramps up its efforts at internet censorship, Yao is a test case for how online expression in China will evolve." While Yao is all but unknown in Hollywood, as she speaks very little English and

ChinaFotoPress/ChinaFotoPress via Getty Images

has never appeared in an American film, she has received some international recognition for her activism; in 2014, *Time* magazine named her among the one hundred most influential people in the world, and *Forbes* ranked her eighty-third on its list of the world's most influential women.

## EARLY LIFE

Yao Chen was born on October 5, 1979, in Fujian Province in southeast China. She is an only child. Her father was a train driver and her mother was a postal worker. She described her father as very humble and giving, telling Keenlyside, "I would always overhear him and my mum discussing how they could help others." Because his friends erroneously assumed that his job allowed him to purchase train tickets for Chinese New Year before the general public, Yao recalled, he used to wake up at dawn to stand in line and buy tickets for them rather than disappoint them with the truth.

In 1993, when Yao was fourteen years old, she won a full scholarship to study folk dance at the Beijing Dance Academy. She later enrolled at the prestigious Beijing Film Academy. The tuition, she told Levin, was far more than her parents could reasonably afford, yet her father brought her the money in a bag full of notes and coins. "It was the first time she noticed he had grey hair," Levin reported. She attended the academy from 1999 to 2003.

Yao made her television acting debut in 2002 in the drama *City Man and Woman*. Her breakout role came four years later, in the martial-arts sitcom *My Own Swordsman* (2006), set in an inn during a fantastical version of China's Ming dynasty; Yao played a martial-artist-turned-waiter. She reprised her role in the successful film adaptation of *My Own Swordsman* in 2011.

## FILM CAREER AND OTHER ROLES

As an actor, Yao is best known for appearing in a number of romantic comedies, including the 2009 movie *Sophie's Revenge*, coproduced with a South Korean film company. One of her most popular films is *Color Me Love* (2010), in which she plays a young rural woman who moves to Beijing to work at a magazine run by tough, demanding editor-in-chief Zoe, played by *Twin Peaks'* Joan Chen. Her other credits include *If You Are the One 2* (2010), *Love in Cosmo* (2010), and the action film *Firestorm* (2013).

Yao made her stage debut in 2009 as the title character in *Du Lala's Promotion*, adapted from the 2007 Chinese novel, *A Story of Lala's Promotion*; the novel, about a young woman's rise through the high-powered corporate world, also inspired a movie and a television series. The same year, she starred as a guerilla fighter in the tremendously popular espionage television series *Lurk*.

In 2012 Yao appeared in the critically acclaimed film *Caught in the Web*, from renowned director Chen Kaige. The movie, which was adapted from a popular novel, is about a woman who is persecuted on the Internet after a reporter films her denying her bus seat to an old man; Yao plays the reporter's editor. *Caught in the Web* screened at the Toronto International Film Festival in 2012 and was China's official entry in the foreign-language film category of the Eighty-Fifth Academy Awards, although it did not make the final list of nominees.

## QUEEN OF WEIBO

Sina Weibo was launched in 2009, shortly after the Chinese government permanently banned Twitter, and quickly became one of the most popular websites in China. Weibo functions much like Twitter, but, as Levin notes, one can get a lot more mileage out of 140 characters in Mandarin than in English. Yao joined the site in 2010; by July 2011, she had amassed more than ten million followers.

The summer of 2011 defined Yao's role as a figure for social justice on Weibo. In June, she reported that one of her relatives in China's Hunan Province had attempted suicide by drinking rat poison because, as Levin explained, "the government had appropriated her land for the construction of a reservoir and when the woman attempted to petition local officials for fair compensation, she was detained." Such a story is all too common in China, but Yao's decision to share it was highly unusual, even radical. She deleted the post soon after she wrote it, but not before it had been saved, shared, and forwarded by thousands of her fans.

Next, in late July, two high-speed trains collided in the Zhejiang Province, killing forty people and injuring nearly two hundred more. Weibo users accused the government of disposing of wreckage from the crash and attempting to tamper with media reports of the crash. Rumors began to circulate that the crash had been caused by one of the train operators, who was among the dead and who had been a friend of Yao's father. In response, Yao wrote a passionate defense of the operator, who, according to Levin, had "sacrificed himself to save others by pulling the emergency brake rather than fleeing the train." His name was subsequently cleared by the Chinese government, though no investigation was ever undertaken to find out what did cause the crash.

## QUIET RIOT

In March 2012, the Chinese government began taking steps to censor Weibo's three hundred million users. All microbloggers were required to register using their real names and identity numbers, allegedly to prevent rumors from spreading. The government also went out of its way to censor celebrities such as Yao; under the new regulations, posts by any Weibo user with more than one hundred thousand followers must be subjected to "item-by-item examination" before they can be published.

Under constant surveillance, Yao is careful to sugarcoat her critical barbs; in one post about the country's toxic pollution, she joked that the only way her young son would ever see a blue sky was in a book. She also offers her followers ways to help others in a manner that highlight societal ills without explicitly naming them. "I don't think what I've earned comes free," she explained to an interviewer for the Chinese magazine *Southern People Weekly* in 2011, as quoted by Levin. "I'm required to do something more with my life." On one occasion, she posted news about a four-year-old boy who was kidnapped by human traffickers, accompanied by the boy's father's phone number; on another, she solicited donations for surgery for a young girl who had been brutally raped. One of her fans, university student Wang Peijia, told Levin, "Yao has become the channel for ordinary people to tell their miserable stories and inflict the pressure of public opinion on government decisions."

On the topic of her Internet musings, Yao is modest, perhaps wisely so. "I'm not interested in politics," she said to Keenlyside. "I just focus on the people in the society I live in. I only comment on things that touch me directly." Yao has largely avoided any repercussions for her activism, though she is not immune to censorship; according to Levin, her posts are occasionally deleted or suddenly, without explanation, made visible to only her. But such incidents are merely inconvenient when compared to the plight of dissidents who take a harder line. In February 2012, Levin reported, the Chinese dissident Zhu Yufu was sentenced to seven years in prison for posting a poem online that called for street protests.

## PERSONAL LIFE

Yao married her film-academy classmate and fellow actor Ling Xiaosu in 2004; the couple divorced in 2011. She married a second time in November 2012, to cinematographer Cao Yu in Queenstown, New Zealand, and gave birth to a baby boy in July 2013. Yao will not reveal her son's name, referring to him simply as Xiao Tudou, or "little potato."

Yao attributes her concern for others partly to her upbringing and partly to her conversion to Christianity in 2003. When she was twenty-five, she spent a summer reading the Bible, and she often quotes verses to her Weibo followers. She even admits to attending a non-government-sanctioned—and therefore illegal—church. (Faith is another controversial topic in China, where religion is heavily regulated and was once outright banned.)

In 2010, the United Nations High Commissioner for Refugees (UNHCR) named Yao a goodwill ambassador in China. In this role, she has visited refugee camps in Ethiopia, Lebanon, and Thailand, and she shares her impressions and even her diary entries with her fans and followers on Weibo. The communication has been a tremendous boon for the organization; Keenlyside reported that Chinese donations to the UNHCR tripled between 2012 and 2013.

## SUGGESTED READING

Keenlyside, Sarah. "Yao Chen Interview: Meet China's Answer to Angelina Jolie." *Telegraph*. Telegraph Media Group, 24 Aug. 2014. Web. 15 Dec. 2014.

Levin, Dan. "Provocateur in Heels." *Prospect* Apr. 2012: 52–55. Print.

McKinsey, Kitty. "Chinese Actress Yao Chen Shares Refugees' Stories with Millions of Fans." *UNHCR: UN Refugee Agency UK*. UNHCR, 1 Apr. 2011. Web. 16 Dec. 2014.

Osnos, Evan. "Solzhenitsyn, Yao Chen, and Chinese Reform." *New Yorker*. Condé Nast, 8 Jan. 2013. Web. 16 Dec. 2014.

Solomon, Erika. "Chinese Star Yao Chen Turns Cameras onto Syrian Refugees in Lebanon." *UNHCR: UN Refugee Agency UK*. UNHCR, 21 May 2014. Web. 16 Dec. 2014.

## SELECTED WORKS

*My Own Swordsman* (television), 2006; *Lurk*, 2009; *Sophie's Revenge*, 2009; *Color Me Love*, 2010; *My Own Swordsman* (film), 2011; *Caught in the Web*, 2012; *Firestorm*, 2013

—Molly Hagan

# Yitang Zhang
**Born:** 1955
**Occupation:** Mathematician

In 2013, a virtually unknown mathematician named Yitang Zhang, who goes by the name Tom, unlocked a problem that had plagued mathematicians for over one hundred years. Zhang is a professor at the University of New Hampshire, though for a majority of his life he toiled in obscurity, working odd jobs, including as a bookkeeper at a Kentucky Subway sandwich franchise, while pondering number theory in his spare time. In 2010, nearly ten years after acquiring his teaching position and writing his first paper, Zhang decided to tackle a problem called twin prime conjecture. A prime number is a number that can only be divided by itself and the number 1, such as 3 and 7, and twin primes are prime numbers that are separated by only one number, such as 3 and 5 or 29 and 31. Twin prime conjecture is the opinion that there are an infinite number of twin primes. Zhang attacked the conjecture from an unusual angle by proving the bounded gaps conjecture. He asserted that prime numbers, no matter how large,

Courtesy of the John D. and Catherine T. MacArthur Foundation

will always be separated by a gap no larger than 70 million. The number itself, Kenneth Chang wrote for the *New York Times* (20 May 2013), is "an arbitrary large number." What it proves is far more important.

The discovery is significant because there has been historically very little that mathematicians could be certain about prime numbers, other than that there are an infinite number of them. Their positions on a number line, however, appear to be random. Zhang's proof is a decisive step toward solving the twin prime conjecture; in fact, since the publication of his paper, other mathematicians have reduced that gap to 246. The conjecture will be solved when the gap can be proven at 2. "You have to imagine this coming from nothing," Eric Grinberg, a former colleague of Zhang's, told Alec Wilkinson for the *New Yorker* (2 Feb. 2015). "We simply didn't know. It is like thinking that the universe is infinite, unbounded, and finding it has an end somewhere." Zhang offered his stunning proof to the mathematics community in a 2013 paper called "Bounded Gaps between Primes." The fact that it was Zhang who made the discovery was remarkable for several reasons, the first being his age. "No mathematician should ever allow himself to forget that mathematics, more than any other art or science, is a young man's game," Wilkinson quoted British mathematician G. H. Hardy as saying. Zhang was fifty-five when he came to the problem and nearly sixty when he

published his proof. The second remarkable aspect of Zhang's story was his nonstanding within the mathematics community itself. Nobody had ever heard of him.

## EARLY LIFE

Zhang was born in Shanghai in 1955. His father was a college professor who taught electrical engineering, and his mother was a secretary in a government office. Zhang was fascinated by numbers from a young age, becoming, as he explained to Wilkinson, "very thirsty for math." When his parents moved to Beijing for work, Zhang stayed in Shanghai where he was raised by his grandmother, who was illiterate. When the Cultural Revolution closed schools in the 1960s, Zhang read math books that he ordered from a local bookstore. At the age of thirteen, he moved to Beijing to be with his parents, but at fifteen, he was sent to work on a rural farm with his mother, and his father was sent to a different farm in another part of China. According to Kathrin Hille for the London *Financial Times* (20 Sept. 2013), about 17 million urban Chinese youth were sent to work in the countryside to perform hard labor in the 1960s and 1970s. Hille quoted former Chairman Mao Zedong who oversaw the massive relocation program, "It is very necessary for the educated youth to go to the countryside and undergo re-education by the poor peasants." On the farm, Zhang was forbidden to read. "People did not think that math was important to the class struggle," he told Wilkinson.

## EDUCATION AND AN INTEREST IN NUMBER THEORY

Zhang moved back to Beijing a few years later and got a job in a lock factory. Meanwhile, he caught up on high school subjects, learning four year's worth of physics, chemistry, and history in a few months in order to pass the entrance examination for China's Peking University. He enrolled as a freshman at the age of twenty-three. During his senior year he decided that number theory would be his specialty, but his professor, who was also the university president, forced him to major in algebraic geometry, believing that it was more important. Zhang received his bachelor's of science degree in 1982 and his master's degree in 1984.

Number theory, which has existed since ancient times, is the study of the relationships between natural numbers, or positive whole numbers, including prime numbers. It is part of a field known as pure mathematics, a field that

Wilkinson quoted Hardy as describing as "the most austere and the most remote" of the arts and sciences. Pure mathematics is distinct from applied mathematics because it has no immediate practical purpose. "My result is useless for industry," Zhang told Wilkinson. There is, however, a particular aesthetic to pure math, Wilkinson wrote. Proofs like Zhang's are considered beautiful in the same way that a piece of art or a piece of music is considered beautiful.

## PURDUE UNIVERSITY AND SUBWAY SANDWICHES

When Zhang received his master's degree in 1984, visiting professor T. T. Moh of Indiana's Purdue University invited Zhang and several other students to complete their graduate studies in the United States. Moh specialized in an extremely complicated yet unsolved problem within algebraic geometry called the Jacobian conjecture, which was beyond the grasp of even the brightest graduate student. Zhang was interested in the conjecture, but he knew he couldn't prove it outright. Instead, he attempted to prove one of its implications. His work must have been impressive, because when Zhang announced that he was giving up algebraic geometry to study number theory, Moh was deeply disappointed. "When I looked into his eyes, I found a disturbing soul, a burning bush, an explorer who wanted to reach the North Pole," Moh recently wrote of Zhang, as quoted by Wilkinson. The two parted on poor terms, though the particulars of the split are unclear.

Zhang earned his doctorate in algebraic geometry from Purdue University in 1991. He had not published any papers and thus had difficulty finding a job in academia after graduation. He then lived with friends in New York City and Lexington, Kentucky, where he joined a group supporting Chinese democracy. A chemist in the group had recently opened a Subway sandwich franchise, and he invited the perpetually unemployed Zhang to keep the store's books. "Sometimes, if it was busy at the store, I helped with the cash register," Zhang told Wilkinson. "Even I knew how to make the sandwiches, but I didn't do it so much." In his spare time, he studied number theory at the University of Kentucky library. In 1999, a former classmate helped him get a temporary position as a lecturer teaching calculus at the University of New Hampshire. Zhang was only promoted to a full professorship in 2014 after the publication of his famous proof.

## FINDING AN OPEN DOOR

Zhang was fifty-five in 2010 when he began working on the bound gap problem, but it wasn't until July 3, 2012, that he found what he referred to as an "open door," or an entry point. He was visiting his friend Jacob Chi, a music professor at Colorado State University–Pueblo. Zhang had agreed to teach Chi's son calculus, so he lived with the family for a month, working with Chi's son, for an hour each morning. He saw the time in Colorado as a retreat from working, and he didn't bring any of his notes on the trip. On the afternoon of July 3, Zhang recalls, he was walking in Chi's backyard, hoping to spot a deer. Inexplicably, looking off into the mountains, he instead found the open door he had been looking for.

## "BOUNDED GAPS BETWEEN PRIMES"

The twin prime conjecture, which asserts that there are an infinite number of twin primes, remains unsolved. Wilkinson explained it this way: "Euclid's proof [in 300 BCE] established that there will always be primes, but it says nothing about how far apart any two might be. Zhang established that there is a distance within which, on an infinite number of occasions, there will always be two primes."

Zhang finished writing his paper in late 2012 and sent it off to mathematics' most prestigious journal, *Annals of Mathematics* on April 17, 2013. Publication in *Annals* is extremely competitive, and it did not help Zhang's case that no one working there had ever heard of him. Still, the paper made it past its first reading and then was reviewed by Rutgers professor Henryk Iwaniec and University of Toronto professor John Friedlander. The men were shocked by what they found and enthusiastically recommended Zhang's paper for publication, writing to editor Nicholas Katz of Princeton (as quoted by Wilkinson) that the results were "of the first rank," and as far as its accuracy, they wrote, "Although we studied the arguments very thoroughly, we found it very difficult to spot even the smallest slip." Zhang heard from *Annals* within three weeks—an unheard-of turnaround for the publication—and called his wife to tell her that his name might soon appear in the national news.

## RECOGNITIONS AND HONORS

When word got out about Zhang's paper, he began receiving invitations from prestigious universities like Harvard to present his findings. By the end of May—little more than a month after he submitted his paper and before it was even published—other mathematicians were already hard at work tweaking Zhang's proof to lower the separation bound that he had proven at 70 million. By July, a team of mathematicians had successfully lowered the bound to 4,680. The current bound stands at 246.

In 2013, Zhang won the Ostrowski Prize for outstanding achievement in pure mathematics, and in 2014 he won a coveted MacArthur Fellowship, as well as the Frank Nelson Cole Prize in Number Theory. He also spent six months in 2014 studying at the Institute for Advanced Study at Princeton University. His time there is the subject of a 2015 documentary by filmmaker George Csicsery called *Counting from Infinity: Yitang Zhang and the Twin Prime Conjecture*.

## PERSONAL LIFE

Zhang met his wife Yaling, who goes by Helen, at a Chinese restaurant on Long Island, New York. They have been married for twelve years. Helen dislikes New Hampshire winters and lives in San Jose, California, in the home that she and Zhang own. She works at a beauty salon, and Zhang lives with her during school vacations.

## SUGGESTED READING

Chang, Kenneth. "Solving a Riddle of Primes." *New York Times.* New York Times, 20 May 2013. Web. 15 Mar. 2015.

Hille, Kathrin. "China's 'Sent-Down' Youth." *Financial Times.* Financial Times, 20 Sept. 2013. Web. 14 Mar. 2015.

Kiersz, Andy. "A Math Genius Who Made Major Breakthrough About Prime Numbers Just Won a \$625,000 Prize." *Business Insider.* Business Insider, 17 Sept. 2014. Web. 26 Mar. 2015.

Wilkinson, Alec. "The Pursuit of Beauty." *New Yorker.* Condé Nast, 2 Feb. 2015. Web. 13 Mar. 2015.

—Molly Hagan

# Malala Yousafzai

**Born:** July 12, 1997
**Occupation:** Activist

Malala Yousafzai had been a thorn in the side of the Pakistani Taliban since at least the age of eleven when she began publicly blogging for the BBC about life in her town under the Taliban's oppressive rule. A bright and inquisitive student, she was especially distressed that their rigid interpretation of Islamic law called for banning education for girls. With schools being shuttered and often destroyed, Yousafzai also appeared in a series of documentaries made by the *New York Times* to bring attention to the issue. Taliban leaders found the attention unwelcome, and on October 9, 2012, a gunman boarded the school bus on which Yousafzai was riding and shot her in the head.

Although gravely injured, Yousafzai survived and subsequently continued her activism on an even wider stage. "In trying, and failing, to kill Malala, the Taliban appear to have made a crucial mistake," Aryn Baker wrote for *Time* (19 Dec. 2012). "They wanted to silence her. Instead, they amplified her voice. Since October her message has been heard around the world, from cramped classrooms where girls scratch out lessons in the dirt to the halls of the UN and national governments and NGOs, where legions of activists argue ever more vehemently that the key to raising living standards throughout the developing world is the empowerment of women and girls. Malala was already a spokesperson; the Taliban made her a symbol."

So powerful a symbol did Yousafzai become, in fact, that in 2014 she garnered a Nobel Peace Prize—the first Pakistani person ever to do so, and at seventeen, she also became the youngest-ever recipient of the prize. "I tell my story, not because it is unique, but because it is not," she said at the Nobel ceremony in Oslo. "I am Malala. But I am also Shazia. I am Kainat . . . I am those 66 million girls who are deprived of education. And today I am not raising my voice, it is the voice of those 66 million girls."

## CHILDHOOD

Malala Yousafzai was born on July 12, 1997, in the Swat District of Pakistan, an area known for its abundant natural beauty and as a tourist destination. Yousafzai was named for Malalai of Maiwand, a famous female Pashtun poet; the name means "grief-stricken." Yousafzai was raised in the town of Mingora, and her father, Ziauddin, is a poet and former student activist who sat on Mingora's Qaumi Jirga (community council). Believing strongly in education for all, he ran the private Khushal School, named for Khushal Khan Khattak, a seventeenth-century Pashtun warrior and poet celebrated for standing up to the Mongols. There the classes included English, physics, biology, and math, among other topics.

Yousafzai's mother, Tor Pekai, never attended school and is rarely seen in public. (The family is Sunni, and Tor Pekai adheres to the traditional practice of Purdah—or separation from unrelated men. Still, she is widely described as a source of quiet strength and support for her daughter and husband.) Yousafzai has two brothers, Khushal and Atal, and during her Nobel acceptance speech she quipped, "I am pretty certain that I am . . . the first recipient of the Nobel Peace Prize who still fights with her younger brothers. I want there to be peace everywhere, but my brothers and I are still working on that."

When Yousafzai was very young, the family lived in a two-room apartment connected to the school. They later moved to a larger home with a garden. Even as a toddler, Yousafzai regularly accompanied her father to work at the school and often sat with the older children and absorbed all she could. "Right from the beginning, Malala was my pet," Ziauddin told Marie Brenner for *Vanity Fair* (Apr. 2013). "She was

always in the school and always very curious." Yousafzai was soon writing long essays, reciting Urdu poetry, and winning debate contests. Among her favorite books was Paulo Coelho's *The Alchemist*, and when other young girls were decorating their hands with henna drawings of flowers and swirls, she adorned hers with mathematical equations. In other ways, Yousafzai was a typical preadolescent girl, watching a reality show called *My Dream Boy Will Come to Marry Me* and rooting for her favorite cricket players.

## EARLY ACTIVISM

In mid-2008, the Pakistani Taliban—formally known as Tehrik-i-Taliban Pakistan (TTP) and closely linked to the Afghan Taliban and al Qaeda—began gaining control in the Swat Valley and imposing strict Sharia law. They banned the sale of DVDs, ordered beauty shops to shut down, and announced their intention to close girls' schools. At the age of eleven, Yousafzai accompanied her father to the press club in Peshawar and gave a speech titled "How Dare the Taliban Take Away My Basic Right to Education?" While many in attendance criticized Ziauddin for allowing her to give a speech that was sure to anger members of the militant Islamist group, he asserted that his daughter knew her own mind and wanted to speak out.

Foreign journalists were drawn to the events taking place in the Swat Valley, and the BBC approached Ziauddin to help them find a schoolgirl to blog for them. After the first candidate declined because of her fear of the TTP, Yousafzai stepped in and corresponded with the British media outlet under a pseudonym. In early January 2009 she wrote, "I was afraid going to school because the Taliban had issued an edict banning all girls from attending schools. Only 11 students attended the class out of 27. On my way from school to home I heard a man saying 'I will kill you.' I hastened my pace [but] to my utter relief he was talking on his mobile and must have been threatening someone else over the phone." In all, she wrote almost forty entries using the pen name Gul Makai. She rarely hesitated to make her opinions known in person, and proclaimed on a televised show hosted by anti-Taliban broadcaster Hamid Mir, "All I want is an education, and I am afraid of no one."

When the *New York Times* sent a documentary team to film the final days of school for girls in the Swat Valley, Ziauddin somewhat reluctantly allowed his family to be the focus of the project. "A close friend said, 'This documentary will do

Russell Watkins, Dept for Int'l Development/
Wikimedia Commons

more for Swat than you could do in 100 years.' I could not imagine the bad consequences," he told Brenner, explaining that no one believed that the Taliban would attempt to assassinate a schoolgirl.

By the time the Taliban were driven from Swat, some four hundred schools had been destroyed, the vast majority of them girls' schools. Yousafzai used her increased profile to campaign to raise government spending on education and encourage parents to allow their daughters to attend classes. Several rebuilt schools were named in her honor.

## ASSASSINATION ATTEMPT AND ITS AFTERMATH

Yousafzai's high profile and willingness to speak out continued to enrage Taliban leaders, and on October 9, 2012, two men stopped her school bus, which held about a dozen girls and a handful of teachers. They boarded the bus, and while one began conversing with the driver, the other approached the girls and asked, "Which one of you is Malala?" Uneasy, some glanced quickly at her, and the gunman fired, shooting her in the head. Her friend, Shazia, screamed, and the man reacted by shooting her and a third girl.

The bullet that had been aimed at Yousafzai grazed the exterior of her skull, hit her jawbone, traveled through her neck and lodged in the muscle above her left shoulder blade. Pakistani doctors worked feverishly to remove the bullet, and within days she was flown to Queen Elizabeth Hospital in Birmingham, England, for further treatment. In a series of lengthy surgeries, British doctors inserted a titanium plate in her skull and provided her with a cochlear implant. Photos of Yousafzai in her hospital bed—looking weak but gazing unflinchingly at the photographer—galvanized public outrage. Cards and gifts flooded into the facility, and Yousafzai had several well-known visitors, including the president of Pakistan, Asif Ali Zardari.

Maulana Fazlullah, the leader of the Taliban in Swat during that time, publicly admitted to ordering the assassination attempt. "We did not want to kill her, as we knew it would cause us a bad name in the media," Sirajuddin Ahmad, a spokesman for the group, told Baker a few months after the failed attempt. "But there was no other option."

## NOBEL PRIZE AND OTHER AWARDS

Yousafzai garnered several notable international prizes before and after being shot. In 2011 she won Pakistan's National Youth Peace Prize, which has since been renamed the National Malala Peace Prize. She was in the running as *Time*'s Person of the Year in 2012, and the following year she was named by the editors of the magazine as one of the one hundred most influential people in the world. She won a Mother Teresa Memorial Award for Social Justice in 2012, and in 2013 she was awarded the Simone de Beauvoir Prize for Women's Freedom for her international human rights work.

In 2014, Yousafzai received one of the most prestigious awards in the world: the Nobel Peace Prize. She shared the prize with Indian Kailash Satyarthi, a fellow children's rights activist. In a press release, the Nobel Committee announced that it "regards it as an important point for a Hindu and a Muslim, an Indian and a Pakistani, to join in a common struggle for education and against extremism."

Later in the year, Yousafzai won the $50,000 World Children's Prize, which she ultimately donated to the United Nations Relief and Works Agency for Palestine Refugees for the purpose of rebuilding schools in the Gaza Strip that were damaged in the Israel-Hamas conflict.

## PERSONAL LIFE

The Yousafzai family remained in England after Malala recuperated. Ziauddin was appointed the United Nations Special Advisor on Global Education and the educational attaché to the Pakistani Consulate in Birmingham. He also chairs the board of the Malala Fund, a nonprofit group dedicated to promoting education for all girls worldwide and helping them to stand up for their right to education.

In 2013, Yousafzai's memoir, *I Am Malala*, co-written by journalist Christina Lamb, was published to near-universal acclaim. She now attends Birmingham's Edgbaston High School for Girls, and she told a reporter for *BBC News* (19 Mar. 2013), "I think it is the happiest moment that I'm going back to school, this is what I dreamed, that all children should be able to go to school because it is their basic right." She continues to speak out on issues of importance to her, including the kidnapping of Nigerian schoolgirls by Boko Haram and the plight of Syrian refugees.

## SUGGESTED READING

Baker, Aryn. "Runner Up: Malala Yousafzai, The Fighter." *Time.* Time, 19 Dec. 2012. Web. 17 Feb. 2015.

Brenner, Marie. "The Target." *Vanity Fair.* Condé Nast, Apr. 2013. Web. 17 Feb. 2015.

Husain, Mishal. "Malala: The Girl Who Was Shot for Going to School." *BBC.* BBC, 7 Oct. 2013. Web. 27 Apr. 2015.

Lamb, Christina. "My Year with Malala." *Sunday Times.* Times Newspapers, 9 Nov. 2013. Web. 17 Feb. 2015.

Shamsie, Kamila. "It's Hard to Kill. Maybe That's Why His Hand Was Shaking." *Guardian.* Guardian News and Media, 7 Oct. 2013. Web. 17 Feb. 2015.

Taseer, Shehrbano. "The Girl Who Changed Pakistan: Malala Yousafzai." *Newsweek.* Newsweek, 22 Oct. 2012. Web. 17 Feb. 2015.

Tohid, Owais. "My Conversations with Malala Yousafzai, the Girl Who Stood Up to the Taliban." *Christian Science Monitor.* Christian Science Monitor, 11 Oct. 2012. Web. 17 Feb. 2015.

—Mari Rich

# Riccardo Zacconi

**Born:** 1967
**Occupation:** Entrepreneur

Riccardo Zacconi is the cofounder and CEO of King Digital Entertainment, the online gaming company that created the popular puzzle game *Candy Crush Saga.* Zacconi cut his teeth as a management consultant in Germany before entering the tech world in the late 1990s. In 1999 he became the managing director of the Internet portal Spray, which flopped in 2001. He cofounded King.com (as it was then called) in 2003. The gaming company first turned a profit in 2005 and began developing games for the social network giant Facebook in 2011. King launched *Candy Crush Saga* for mobile, far and away its most popular game, in November 2012. In 2015 Nic Fildes for the London *Times* (11 Apr. 2015) reported that *Candy Crush* games are played 957 million times a day, mostly by 91 million dedicated users. The game itself is childishly easy, yet highly addictive. Players arrange different colored candies, matching like colors or highlighting certain patterns, on a grid to win points. *Candy Crush*, as Ben Machell wrote in an article for the London *Times* (13 May 2013), is "distracting, disposable, and easy to learn, enjoyed by people who wouldn't dream of spending a weekend playing *World of Warcraft* or

*Call of Duty* but want something to keep them occupied on their commute or during the TV ad breaks."

Players see *Candy Crush* as a casual way to while away a few minutes, but Zacconi sees a turning of the tide. "There is something really dramatic happening in the way users consume content," he told Katherine Rushton for the *Telegraph* (19 Jan. 2013). He called games like *Candy Crush* "snackable" entertainment because gamers can stop and start play whenever they want. To facilitate this flexible gameplay, King Digital made it possible for users to start playing a game on one device and pick it up on a different device at the same point in the game—King was one of the first companies to offer such capabilities. King Digital makes money off the game, which is free to download, by selling bonuses (such as extra lives) for one dollar or slightly more depending on the advantage. Rushton speculated that, thanks to those extras, King Digital's revenues quadrupled in 2012 alone. Despite exponential growth after debuting *Candy Crush* for mobile, King Digital's 2014 initial public offering (IPO) fared poorly; some investors were concerned that the company relied too heavily on the popularity of one game while others were spooked after King's competitor, Zynga, the company that makes the games *FarmVille* and *Words with Friends*, debuted a disappointing IPO in 2011. Nevertheless, Zacconi is enthusiastic about the company's future. "We have cracked mobile reach and mobile monetization," he told Rushton for the *Telegraph* (26 Mar. 2014), emphasizing King Digital's independence from Facebook. "This puts us in the driving seat."

## EDUCATION AND EARLY CAREER

Zacconi was born in Rome, Italy, in 1967. He earned his bachelor's degree in economics from LUISS University (Libera Università Internazionale degli Studi Sociali Guido Carli), a private university in Rome, in 1991. After graduation he took a position at the London and Munich offices of L.E.K. Consulting, a global business consulting firm. In 1993 he became a management consultant at the Munich office of the Boston Consulting Group. He remained with the company until 1999, after which he headed the German unit for a Swedish news, search, and e-mail portal (in the mold of Google or Yahoo!) called Spray Network. Zacconi and his partners planned to take the company public in March 2000, the same month that the value of dot-com companies peaked before falling into sharp decline. They sold Spray to rival Lycos Europe in 2000.

After the sale, Zacconi served as an entrepreneur-in-residence at the Silicon Valley–based venture capital firm Benchmark Capital Partners from 2001 to 2002 and worked as the vice president of European sales and marketing for the online dating company uDate.com, where he met Melvyn Morris, the CEO of uDate and the future chair of King Digital. (Morris, King's largest shareholder, resigned as the chair of King in November 2014.) When uDate sold for $150 million and merged with Match.com in 2002, Zacconi persuaded Morris and Toby Rowland, the son of the late British mining tycoon Roland "Tiny" Rowland, to back a new venture.

## FOUNDING KING.COM

Zacconi and his colleagues from Spray reunited to found King.com in 2003. Zacconi told Rushton that the team was wiser thanks to its first failed project. "The dot-com crash was a wake-up call," he said (19 Jan. 2013). "It was not a very pleasant experience but it was very rich. We learnt that you have got to think long-term and stick to healthy economic principles." The founders of King.com—including chief creative officer Sebastian Knutsson, chief technical officer Thomas Hartwig, studio chief Lars Markgren, and developer Patrik Stymne—wanted to specialize in low-stakes gambling games that

could be played on Yahoo!, one of the few Internet companies to survive the dot-com crash, and Microsoft's MSN. They poured all of their money into the company. Zacconi lived for free in a friend's spare room—to say a lot was riding on the success of King is an understatement. "It was not an easy time. I cut all my costs to zero. The room was small but I had all my properties [possessions] in there," he recalled to Rushton (28 June 2014).

A particularly significant moment for the company occurred on December 24, 2003. Zacconi and his then partner Rowland spent the night tensed over a fax machine, waiting for a letter of financial support from Morris that would make or break their fledgling company. Morris had promised to back the company, but no official paperwork had been signed. When the coveted investment contract began to come in, the fax machine broke down. Still, King received the promised financing, and as Juliette Garside remarked in an article for the *Guardian* (7 June 2014), the company "lived to fight another day."

In 2005 the private equity firm Apax Partners became an investor, offering about $36 million to King, and the technology venture capital firm Index Ventures invested $7 million in 2005. It was the first year the company turned a profit. By 2009 Zacconi saw the shift in the market: people wanted to play games with their friends and were gravitating toward social-networking sites such as Facebook to do it. Developers at King Digital began making games that could be adapted for the social-networking site, such as *Bubble Witch Saga*, in which fairy-tale witches shoot bubbles, and a digital version of the traditional Chinese game mah-jongg.

## KING'S PARTNERSHIP WITH FACEBOOK

In 2011 King Digital formed an official partnership with Facebook, though Zacconi was careful to maintain King Digital's image as an independent company. (The perception that King's competitor Zynga was dependent on the social network is widely believed to have sunk its trading debut in 2011.) A Facebook version of the game *Bubble Witch* launched, to great success, in September 2011. Other games include *Pet Rescue Saga* and *Papa Bear Saga*, but Zacconi and King Digital struck gold when they launched a mobile application of *Candy Crush Saga*, another game they had initially created for Facebook, in November 2012. Players can play the game on their phones but can also post their progress to their

Facebook page. (The levels—each of which is designed to take about three minutes—get progressively more difficult.) Machell remarked that, with this strategy, "a solitary pursuit is suddenly made social, like a book group for a game." The connection to social media also makes a single-player game into a competitive one. As Zacconi told Machell, one night he and his wife were playing *Candy Crush* on their respective devices. She quickly surpassed him, working her way up the levels, and he began buying extra lives—"which I never normally do," he said, just to beat her. The popularity of the game propelled King Digital to overtake Zynga as the most popular game developer on Facebook, but its appeal extends beyond Facebook users. "I thought we had a problem with our data," Zacconi recalled to Machell, when he saw just how many people were playing the game. "But then I realized it was a mass phenomenon, bigger than I ever thought." The same year King Digital hired executives from Zynga and Electronic Arts and opened offices in Bucharest, Romania, and Barcelona, Spain.

### KING'S UPS AND DOWNS

The company experienced a period of rapid growth in 2013, nearly doubling its workforce to more than seven hundred employees. At King Digital, approximately three developers are assigned to one project at a time—as opposed to Zynga, where hundreds of employees work on any given game. A new game debuts on the King Digital website each month. "If a game doesn't work, it fails fast and cheap," Zacconi told Rushton (19 Jan. 2013). Games that do well are singled out for further investment. Like *Candy Crush*, Zacconi aims to make games that "are easy to learn, but . . . difficult to master," he told Oscar Williams-Grut for the *Independent* (10 Aug. 2013).

After the success of *Candy Crush*, rumors about a possible King Digital IPO abounded in 2013. Despite high hopes and widespread media hype, the company's stock-market debut in March 2014 was one of the worst of the year. The company lost over $1 billion of value, fueling fears of another tech bubble. But Zacconi appeared hopeful; King Digital's IPO was still one of the best showings for a British tech company on the New York Stock Exchange. King Digital's success has been a rollercoaster ride. Profits slumped in 2014 as profits from *Candy Crush* fell, but things were looking up for the company as of early 2015, when King Digital

introduced a sequel to the game called *Candy Crush Soda Saga*. However, as Zacconi explained to Garside, "Our strategy is not based on building another hit game like *Candy Crush*. Our strategy is to build a portfolio of games." King's former chair, Morris, in an interview with Garside, expressed his confidence in Zacconi's ability to lead the company to further success: "His charisma, integrity, sense of fair play, and abundant humility allow him to gently lead from the front. Many entrepreneurs fail because they are so single-minded they struggle to scale their business beyond their own limitations. Riccardo succeeds because he allows his management to share the challenges and rewards."

### PERSONAL LIFE

Zacconi is married, and his wife is of Chinese and Swedish descent. Together they have one son. The family lives in London, where King Digital's main office is located.

### SUGGESTED READING

Fildes, Nic. "You Have to Think Ahead to Solve the Puzzle, Says King Digital Chief." *Times* [London]. Times Newspapers, 11 Apr. 2015. Web. 5 Aug. 2015.

Garside, Juliette. "How King Digital Entertainment's CEO Conquered the Gaming World." *Guardian*. Guardian News and Media, 6 June 2014. Web. 5 Aug. 2015.

Machell, Ben. "The Man behind Candy Crush." *Times*. Times Newspapers, 13 May 2013. Web. 5 Aug. 2015.

Rushton, Katherine. "Riccardo Zacconi: King.com Looking for Growth Rather than Floatation." *Telegraph*. Telegraph Media Group, 19 Jan. 2013. Web. 5 Aug. 2015.

Rushton, Katherine. "Candy Crush Maker's Shares Tumble on Debut." *Telegraph*. Telegraph Media Group, 26 Mar. 2014. Web. 5 Aug. 2015.

Rushton, Katherine. "Sunday Interview: King's Riccardo Zacconi." *Telegraph*. Telegraph Media Group, 28 June 2014. Web. 5 Aug. 2015.

Williams-Grut, Oscar. "Candy Crush Saga: Studio behind Game with Over 44m Monthly Users Promises More Hits." *Independent*. Independent.co.uk, 10 Aug. 2013. Web. 5 Aug. 2015.

—Molly Hagan

# Zhou Long

**Born:** July 8, 1953
**Occupation:** Composer

Zhou Long is a Chinese American composer. In 2003, he received a lifetime achievement award from the American Academy of Arts and Letters. His music for the 2011 opera *Madam White Snake*, won the Pulitzer Prize for music.

## BACKGROUND

Zhou Long was born in Beijing, China, on July 8, 1953. He is one of two children; the other being his younger sister. Both of Zhou's parents had a profound appreciation for the arts, notably music, and encouraged their son to pursue piano lessons as a young child. Zhou's father was a painter and professor of fine arts, while his mother was a Western-style vocal instructor.

A musical prodigy, Zhou's childhood study of the piano was deterred in 1966 during China's Cultural Revolution, which led to his relocation to a government-run farm where he raised and harvested wheat, beans, and corn. The composer would later credit this arduous time as being hugely influential on his work. While on the farm, Zhou taught himself revolutionary songs on the accordion to pass the time. The then teen-aged Zhou was assigned to be musical director for a local dance troupe after injuring his back during work.

Zhou ultimately returned to music, studying under Wu Zuqiang at the Central Conservatory of Music in Beijing from 1978–83. By his early twenties, he had become knowledgeable in the traditional music of his home country as well as music theory, conducting, and classical composition.

Upon his graduation from the Beijing conservatory in 1983, Zhou took a position as composer in residence with the National Broadcasting Symphony Orchestra, also in Beijing. There, he penned pieces of music to accompany Chinese state radio and television productions.

After establishing himself as one of China's emerging young composers, Zhou accepted a fellowship to pursue advanced music studies at New York University in 1985. During his time in New York, Zhou studied under renowned composers Chou Wen-chung (Zhou Wenzhong) and George Edwards. He received a doctor of musical arts degree from the school in 1993.

## COMPOSER

Early in his career, Zhou began to establish his signature style, melding traditional Chinese musical thinking with Western instrumentation in "Song of the Ch'in" (1982), a piece for string quartet that emulates the sounds of an ancient, seven-stringed Chinese instrument. The piece won Zhou first prize in the 1985 Chinese National Composition Competition.

In the United States, his piece for solo cello entitled "Rites of Chimes" debuted in 2000 at the Smithsonian Institute's Freer Gallery of Art in Washington, DC, in a performance by famed cellist Yo-Yo Ma.

Zhou's collaboration with Yo-Yo Ma continued in 2003, when he served as composer in residence at the Seattle Symphony's Silk Road Project Festival, with Ma serving as his fellow collaborator and cellist.

In addition to penning several chamber, orchestral, and choral works throughout the 2000s, Zhou became a United States citizen in 1999, en route to establishing himself as one of the foremost professors of classical music in the United States.

He received a lifetime achievement award for his contributions to music from the American Academy of Arts and Letters in 2003, before embarking on a career as a lecturer of master-level music courses at a variety of prominent universities, notably Columbia University and the University of California, Berkeley.

Zhou's late-2000s collaboration with fellow Chinese American artist Cerise Lim Jacobs would solidify his place as a prominent figure in contemporary orchestral music. He composed original music to accompany Jacob's libretto for *Madam White Snake*, an opera based on a narrative from Chinese folklore. The opera revolves around a demon that transforms itself into a beautiful woman in order to experience love.

Both critics and audiences lauded the opera for its atmospheric spectacle and rich musical accompaniment drawing on ancient Chinese themes. The work, produced in coordination with Opera Boston and the Beijing Music Festival, marked a rare lengthy visit by a visiting Chinese arts organization to the United States.

The work was praised for its deft combination of Eastern and Western musical traditions. Zhou was awarded the 2011 Pulitzer Prize for music for his contribution to the work. It was the first full-length operatic work to be awarded a Pulitzer since 1962.

## IMPACT

Zhou Long's contributions to classical music have been lauded for their seamless combination of traditional Chinese musical themes and Western musical traditions in composition. The composer has also drawn praise for his inclusion of Chinese philosophical and spiritual ideals in his works.

Zhou Long has established himself as one of the foremost professors of classical music presently working in the United States, and has given lectures and master classes at several prestigious institutions, notably Duke University, Cornell University, the San Francisco Conservatory, and the Manhattan School of Music.

## PERSONAL LIFE

Zhou Long is married to the composer and violinist Chen Yi.

## SUGGESTED READING

Eichler, Jeremy. "Curtain Rises on Ancient Chinese Myth." *Boston Globe* Boston Globe Media Partners, 1 Mar. 2010. Web. 10 June 2014.

Green, Edward. "The Impact of Buddhist Thought on the Music of Zhou Long: A Consideration of *Dhyana*." *Contemporary Music Review* 26.5/6 (2007): 547–67. Print.

Huizenga, Tom. "Zhou Long Wins Music Pulitzer for Fairy Tale Opera." *NPR*. NPR, 18 Apr. 2011. Web. 25 May 2014.

Kors, Stacy. "An Operatic Blend of Cultures." *Columbia Magazine*. Columbia Alumni Association, 2011. Web. 10 June 2014.

Ng, David. "Composer Zhou Long Wins Pulitzer Prize for 'Madame White Snake.'" *Los Angeles Times*. Los Angeles Times, 19 Apr. 2011. Web. 10 June 2014.

"Zhou Long Biography." *Twentieth Century and New Music*. Oxford UP, 2014. Web. 10 June 2014.

## SELECTED WORKS

*Chinese Folk Songs; Poems from Tang; Soul,* 1998; *The Ineffable,* 1998; *Out of Tang Court,* 2002; *Tales from the Cave,* 2004; *Wild Grass,* 2009; *Madam White Snake,* 2011; "Song of the Ch'in," 1982; "Rites of Chimes," 2000; "Two Poems from T'ang," 2004

—John Pritchard

# Anita Zucker
**Occupation:** Business executive

Anita Zucker is the chair and CEO of the InterTech Group, a conglomerate that was founded by her late husband, Jerry Zucker, in 1983. The daughter of Holocaust survivors, Zucker is a philanthropist and billionaire who adheres to her personal philosophy that she characterizes with the Hebrew phrase "Tikkun Olam." "It literally means 'Repair the World,'" she told Jo Hunter for *Wealth Magazine*, sponsored by BB&T (Branch Banking and Trust) Wealth (Summer 2012). "We all have an obligation to take care of each other and the planet." Zucker has focused most of her philanthropic endeavors in Charleston, South Carolina, the city that has been her home since 1978. She has served as the president of the Charleston Metro Chamber of Commerce as well as the Education Foundation of the Charleston Metro Chamber of Commerce, which she helped found. She has also served as chair of the Advisory Board of the Charleston Area HUB for Math, Science, and Technology at the College of Charleston. Zucker even owns a handful of Charleston businesses, including the Carolina Ice Palace, the Original Ms. Rose's Fine Food and Cocktails, Tristan Restaurant, and fifty percent of the South Carolina Stingrays, a minor league hockey team. But Zucker, a former schoolteacher, has directed most of her energy—and a sizeable chunk of her $2.1 billion fortune—to education. She is interested in nurturing Charleston children early with the aim of preparing them to find living wage jobs as an adult.

Zucker's goals are rooted in the region's shameful history of slavery—South Carolina counted the highest slave population in the United States in 1860—and racism. A 2012 report from the Civil Rights Project, as quoted by Paul Thomas of the Charleston *Post and Courier* (4 Nov. 2013), confirms that disparities between the state's black (and Latino) and white citizens are only getting worse. "Black and Latino students in the South attend schools defined by double isolation by both race and poverty," the report explained. "The South reports high overall shares of students living in poverty, but students of different racial backgrounds are not exposed equally to existing poverty. The typical black and Latino student in the region goes to a school with far higher concentrations of low-income students than the typical white or Asian student." Another study, this one from the Southern Education Foundation in October 2013, reported that high-poverty students were the "new majority" in the United States. Given the numbers, Thomas estimated that 54.7 percent of South Carolina public school students were living in poverty. Such numbers, Thomas wrote, make it imperative to address poverty and education reform as one and the same issue. One of Zucker's most recent projects, The Tri-County Cradle to Career Collaboration (TCCC) through the College of Charleston, attempts to do just that. The collective initiative is based on a successful program in Cincinnati, Ohio, called STRIVE. TCCC, which includes a strong health component, encompasses a child's life both in and out of school. "Children can't be expected to learn," Andy Owens of the *Charleston Regional Business Journal* (13 June 2013) paraphrased Medical University of South Carolina president and TCCC board member Ray Greenberg as saying, if they "are worried about getting enough to eat."

## EARLY LIFE AND EDUCATION

Anita Goldberg was born in Jacksonville, Florida, to Rose (née Mibab) and Carl Goldberg. Her parents were Holocaust survivors from Volodymyr-Volynskyi, Poland (now Ukraine). Both Rose and Carl suffered horribly during the war. Most of their family members were killed, including Carl's first wife and young daughter. "They were conscripted to work crews in Poland," Zucker told W. Thomas McQueeney for his book *The Rise of Charleston: Conversations with Visionaries, Luminaries & Emissaries of the Holy City* (2011) of her parents. "They were among the very few of the lucky ones because they had specific jobs." Zucker's sister, Eva, was born in a displaced persons camp in Germany in 1946, and the family came to the United States, sponsored by the Hebrew Immigration Aid Society, in 1949. Zucker was born shortly thereafter, followed by her younger sister, Susie. Zucker told Jennifer Berry Hawes for the Charleston *Post and Courier* (11 Nov. 2014) that education played an important role in her and her sister's lives because her parents—particularly her mother, who was just a teenager when she was shuttling refugees from safe house to safe house and living in a hole in the ground beneath a farmer's barn—were deprived of a formal education themselves. "Education played a tremendous role in our lives," she said. "We want to bring those opportunities and access to all of our children."

Zucker met her future husband, Jerry Zucker, when his parents, who were also Holocaust survivors and taught at her religious school, introduced the two. The couple were married on June 21, 1970, before enrolling as undergraduates at the University of Florida. "My life was not the typical life of a person who walks in and joins a sorority," she told Elizabeth Hillaker Downs for the University of Florida's *Florida Magazine* (5 Aug. 2011). The couple even owned two businesses at the time: ROC Records (where Zucker kept inventory) and the New Deli delicatessen (where she made sandwiches). She graduated with a BA degree in education in 1972, and Jerry graduated with a triple major in chemistry, mathematics, and physics the same year. She earned a master's of education degree in educational administration and supervision from the University of North Florida and the couple moved to Charleston in 1978.

## INTERTECH GROUP AND HUDSON BAY COMPANY

Jerry Zucker, a lifelong inventor, founded the InterTech Group, a chemical company, in 1983. The company makes everything from plastic tarps to cryogenic insulation. InterTech Group has expanded exponentially over the years, becoming a conglomerate and acquiring the Hudson's Bay Company (HBC) in 2006. Founded in Canada in 1670 as a fur-trading venture, HBC is North America's longest-running company. The acquisition made the Zuckers extraordinarily rich, but unfortunately, Jerry was diagnosed with brain cancer the same year. Zucker had been working as InterTech's director of community relations since the births of the couple's children, and Jerry was adamant that she take over the company when he died. The couple spent long hours discussing the company's next steps. "Our marriage was a partnership in the best sense of the word," Zucker told Hunter. Jerry died at the age of fifty-eight in 2008, and Zucker became the company's chair and CEO. It was a rough year for the company with the shift in management and the tanking economy, Zucker recalled to Hunter. Her son, Jonathan, quit his IT job to become InterTech's president. The two made the risky decision to sell HBC. "Our goal was to simplify and find ways to gain efficiencies," Zucker told Hunter. "It paid off."

## TEACHING AND EDUCATION PHILANTHROPY

Zucker taught English and social studies in elementary schools in Florida and South Carolina for eleven years before joining her husband at InterTech. Though she hasn't taught in years, she has been a lifelong supporter of education with a long resume of philanthropic gifts to educational institutions. A few of her more recent initiatives and accomplishments include her appointment as a member of the Education and Economic Development Coordinating Council of the State (EEDACC) by South Carolina governor Mark Sanford in October 2005. The council was charged with implementing 2005 legislation that affected K–16 education in all South Carolina schools. In 2012, she was appointed to the South Carolina Aerospace Task Force—which focused on strategic plans for workplace development—by the secretary of commerce, Bobby Hitt.

In 2011 Zucker established a professorship within the University of Florida's School of Education dedicated to early childhood studies, and in October 2014, she gave $5 million to the school to help train teachers in early childhood education. The money will go toward the Anita Zucker Center for Excellence in Early Childhood Studies, which will focus on children from birth to age five and their families. Crucially, the center will also collaborate with local, state, and national partners to provide health and family support. Zucker has also sponsored the Anita Zucker Alumni Challenge, matching gifts to the UF School of Education dollar-for-dollar. "Education really is the key to unlocking doors for later learning and success in life," she told Larry Lansford for the UF school website (11 Oct. 2014), adding that the "early childhood years are the most critical time for learning."

In November 2014, Zucker announced a $4 million donation to the School of Education at the Citadel, or the Military College of South Carolina, in Charleston. (Zucker took classes in education there when she moved to Charleston in 1978.) The college renamed the school the Zucker Family School of Education. The new school will include the Anita Zucker Institute for Entrepreneurial Educational Leadership. Zucker also serves as the vice-chair of the Charleston Promise Neighborhood Board, an organization that works with four specific high-poverty schools in Charleston. She holds honorary doctoral degrees from the College of Charleston and the Medical University of South Carolina, and in 2013, she received the Wilkins Award for Excellence

in civic leadership. "We just can't drop kids," Zucker told a reporter for *Charleston Magazine* (1 Jan. 2014). "If I'm a manufacturer, and I'm producing a product for Boeing, I can't produce it at 80 percent and say it's okay. God forbid I should make a plane crash. So why should we allow a child to crash? We can't complete a child's education and say it's good enough, you're 80 percent there."

Zucker has three adult children, Jonathan, Andrea, and Jeffrey, as well as five grandchildren.

## SUGGESTED READING

Berry Hawes, Jennifer. "Anita Zucker Donates $4 Million to the Citadel's Education School." *Post and Courier* [Charleston]. Post and Courier, 11 Nov. 2014. Web. 15 Dec. 2014.

"Fast Forward." *Charleston Magazine*. Gulfstream Communications, 1 Jan. 2014. Web. 15 Dec. 2014.

Hunter, Jo. "Legacy for Life." *Wealth Magazine*. BB&T Wealth, Summer 2012. Web. 15 Dec. 2014.

Lansford, Larry. "Zucker Provides Lead Gift for $10 Million Early Childhood Studies Initiative." *University of Florida News*. U of Florida, 11 Oct. 2014. Web. 15 Dec. 2014.

McQueeney, W. Thomas. *The Rise of Charleston: Conversations with Visionaries, Luminaries & Emissaries of the Holy City*. Charleston: History, 2011. Print.

Owens, Andy. "Tri-County Cradle to Career Collaborative Finds Home at College." *Charleston Regional Business Journal*. SC Biz News, 13 June 2013. Web. 15 Dec. 2014.

Thomas, Paul. "Fight Poverty to Fix S.C. Schools." *Post and Courier* [Charleston]. Post and Courier, 4 Nov. 2013. Web. 15 Dec. 2014.

—Molly Hagan

# Andrey Zvyagintsev

**Born:** February 6, 1964
**Occupation:** Director

Andrey Zvyagintsev is widely regarded as the most prominent contemporary Russian film director. He has often drawn comparisons to the late Russian auteur Andrei Tarkovsky, "whose allegorical and enigmatic epics his work echoes," as Shaun Walker wrote of Zvyagintsev's films for the *Guardian* (6 Nov. 2014). A former ac-

© Ian Gavan/epa/Corbis

tor, Zvyagintsev was virtually unknown in 2003 when he cowrote and directed his first feature, *The Return*, a dark family drama set in Siberia, Russia. The film won the Golden Lion at that year's Venice Film Festival and became an international success, catapulting Zvyagintsev to the forefront of world cinema. Zvyagintsev has since directed three other highly acclaimed full-length features: *The Banishment* (2007), *Elena* (2011), and *Leviathan* (2014), the latter of which earned a Golden Globe Award and an Academy Award nomination for best foreign language film.

## EARLY LIFE AND EDUCATION

Andrey Zvyagintsev was born on February 6, 1964, in Novosibirsk, the largest city in the Siberian region of what was then the Soviet Union. (Zvyagintsev's first name is also commonly spelled Andrei.) Zvyagintsev was raised by his mother, who was a high school literature teacher. His father abandoned the family when he was six years old. As a result, Zvyagintsev had a peripatetic childhood, moving from place to place, as his mother struggled to make ends meet.

Zvyagintsev grew up "well outside the Moscow-St. Petersburg axis that dominates Russian culture," Larry Rohter wrote for the *New York Times* (18 Dec. 2014). Nevertheless, he developed an early passion for the theater, which offered an escape from his isolated surroundings. As Zvyagintsev recalled to Walker, he spent many of his boyhood schooldays "dreaming of theater, obsessed with it."

After completing his secondary education, Zvyagintsev attended the theatrical school in Novosibirsk, where he studied acting. Upon graduating in 1984, he was conscripted into the Red Army's theater troupe. He remained with the troupe until 1986, when he moved to Moscow to continue his acting studies at the Russian Academy of Theatre Arts (GITIS). Zvyagintsev has cited the films *Bobby Deerfield* (1977) and *. . . And Justice for All* (1979), directed by Sydney Pollack and Norman Jewison, respectively, as the inspiration for him to further his training as an actor.

## EARLY CAREER

After graduating from GITIS in 1990, Zvyagintsev began acting in experimental theater productions. He supported himself by working a series of menial jobs, including as a janitor and street cleaner. "I was a zero with no prospects," he told a Russian interviewer in 2011, as quoted by Courtney Weaver for the *Financial Times* (23 Jan. 2015). "The feeling that I lived with in those days, it's not even depression. . . . It's being a loser, a zero, nothing."

Throughout the 1990s, Zvyagintsev continued to act on stage while landing small parts in Russian television serials and feature films. Those acting roles, however, provided him with insufficient income, leading him to shift his focus to directing. In 1993, at the suggestion of a friend, Zvyagintsev accepted a job filming a commercial for a furniture store, which helped him understand the "shooting process," as he told Erica Abeel for *Indiewire* (2 Feb. 2004). He further taught himself the craft of filmmaking by becoming a habitué of Moscow's Muzei Kino cinema museum. He also immersed himself in the works of such European directors as Ingmar Bergman, Michelangelo Antonioni, and Éric Rohmer.

Zvyagintsev's big break came after he was discovered by Russian producer Dmitry Lesnevsky, one of the cofounders of the Russian television network REN TV. In 2000, Lesnevsky hired Zvyagintsev to direct three episodes of the Russian detective series *The Black Room*. Lesnevsky, whom Zvyagintsev described to Abeel as his "godfather," then persuaded him to develop and direct his first film. "It wasn't a conscious decision; I guess I just felt more comfortable there," Zvyagintsev said of his move behind the camera in an interview with Helen Barlow for the Australian Special Broadcasting Service's website (22 June 2012).

## RISE TO PROMINENCE WITH *THE RETURN*

Zvyagintsev's feature directorial debut, *The Return*, was produced by Lesnevsky and released in 2003. Shot on 35-millimeter film and made on a shoestring budget of $500,000, the film tells the story of two Russian teenage brothers, Andrei and Ivan (played by Vladimir Garin and Ivan Dobronravov, respectively), who arrive home one day to discover that their hardened and mysterious father (Konstantin Lavronenko) has returned after a twelve-year absence. In an effort to get to know his sons again, the father takes them on a fateful fishing trip, during which he tries to teach them life lessons through tough love. While Andrei attempts to win his father's approval, Ivan defiantly objects to his demands.

*The Return* was screened at the 2003 Venice Film Festival, where it took home the coveted Golden Lion, the festival's top prize. Critics unanimously praised the film, which was likened to the work of Tarkovsky because of its allegorical and ambiguous nature. Abeel wrote that *The Return*, which was filmed around Lake Ladoga and the Gulf of Finland, was an "esthetic marvel" and that it evoked "a pre-Revolutionary religious and mystical strain in Russian thought, from Dostoyevsky to the philosopher Berdyaev."

Following its Venice triumph, *The Return* was sold for distribution all over the world. It earned a Golden Globe nomination for best foreign-language film and propelled Zvyagintsev to the forefront of world cinema. "For the first time I realized what I was doing was needed, that there were people who wanted to see my movie," Zvyagintsev told Barlow. "It was the big moment in my life." The success of the film was partly overshadowed by the tragic death of Garin, who drowned in a lake two months before its showing in Venice. Zvyagintsev dedicated the Golden Lion to Garin, who was only sixteen at the time of his death.

### THE BANISHMENT AND ELENA

Zvyagintsev spent three years working on his next feature film, *The Banishment*, which is loosely based on Armenian author William Saroyan's 1953 novel *The Laughing Matter*. It centers on a small-time criminal, Alex (Konstantin Lavronenko), and his wife, Vera (Maria Bonnevie), who embark on a trip to the countryside with their two children. Though initially well intentioned, the trip becomes rife with tension when Vera reveals to Alex that she is pregnant, setting in motion a calamitous series of events.

*The Banishment*, which was also produced by Lesnevsky, premiered at the 2007 Cannes Film Festival, where it was nominated for the Palme d'Or. Though the highly anticipated film failed to win that coveted award, its star, Lavronenko, took home the award for best leading actor at the festival. Like *The Return*, *The Banishment* drew critical comparisons to Tarkovsky, but it failed to generate the same kind of clamorous praise. It received generally mixed reviews, with critics praising its powerful visuals but disliking its laborious pace, long running time, contrived plot, and rampant ambiguity. *The Banishment* "looks as if it really ought to be a masterpiece, but somehow there is something missing, or something hidden," Peter Bradshaw wrote in a review of the film for the *Guardian* (14 Aug. 2008). "There is an outstanding film somewhere inside this sprawling mass of ideas, which might have been shaped more exactly in the edit."

Zvyagintsev's third feature-length film, *Elena* (2011), examines the widening gap between the rich and poor in Russia. Produced by Alexander Rodnyansky and featuring music by renowned American composer Philip Glass, the film follows an eponymous middle-aged housekeeper (Nadezhda Markina) and her husband, an elderly business tycoon named Vladimir (Andrey Smirnov), as they clash over their different socioeconomic backgrounds following a string of unexpected events. *Elena* premiered in the Un Certain Regard section of the 2011 Cannes Film Festival, where it won the Special Jury Prize. Barlow, expressing the sentiment of many critics, declared the film "a minor masterpiece."

### LEVIATHAN

The idea for Zvyagintsev's fourth feature film, *Leviathan*, first came to him while he was directing a short segment for the 2008 anthology film *New York, I Love You*. (The segment was ultimately cut from the film's theatrical release.) It was during this time that Zvyagintsev heard the story of Marvin John Heemeyer, a muffler-repair shop owner from Colorado who, in 2004, demolished thirteen buildings with a fortified bulldozer after becoming outraged over a failed zoning dispute. After the rampage, Heemeyer took his own life. "It was like a finished script," Zvyagintsev told Mark Olsen for the *Los Angeles Times* (30 Dec. 2014). "I already had a vision of what to do."

Zvyagintsev's vision for *Leviathan* meant adapting the Heemeyer story to fit the Russian temperament. It also included drawing from a number of literary influences, including the biblical book of Job, Heinrich von Kleist's 1808 novella *Michael Kohlhaas*, and Thomas Hobbes's 1651 treatise on the theory of social contract, also titled *Leviathan*. The resultant story centers on a hard-drinking, middle-aged auto-repair shop owner, Kolya (Aleksey Serebryakov), who becomes embroiled in an acrimonious dispute with a corrupt local mayor, Vadim (Roman Madyanov), over the generations-long ownership of his land, which is located in a remote fishing village near the Barents Sea. Kolya, who lives on the land with his second wife, Lilya (Elena Lyadova), and his teenage son, Roma (Sergey Pokhodaev), calls upon a lawyer friend, Dmitri (Vladimir Vdovichenkov), for help, but his efforts prove futile as his life quickly unravels.

*Leviathan* was produced by Rodnyansky and partly financed by Russia's Ministry of Culture. It premiered at the 2014 Cannes Film Festival, where Zvyagintsev and his fellow screenwriter, Oleg Negin, won the award for best screenplay. Also featuring original music by Glass, *Leviathan* received rapturous reviews from critics, many of whom hailed the ambitiously complex film a masterpiece. Rohter described the film as "a quintessentially Russian tragedy suffused with political and religious overtones," while Olsen observed that it had "the deep, expansive feel of a classic Russian novel."

In addition to its critical acclaim, *Leviathan* received a number of awards and honors. It took home the award for best film at the London Film Festival and won the Golden Globe award for best foreign-language film. It was also Russia's official submission for the Academy Award for best foreign-language film, a selection that surprised many due to its harsh criticism of Russian president Vladimir Putin and his government. In response to a question regarding the controversial political undertones of the film, Zvyagintsev

told Walker, "My position is that of a cinema director. I'm not politically active. But I can't not react to what is happening around me." *Leviathan* subsequently became one of the five Academy Award nominees in that category.

## PERSONAL LIFE

Following the success of *Leviathan*, Zvyagintsev began looking for investors for his next project. He typically prefers to keep details of his personal life private.

## SUGGESTED READING

Barlow, Helen. "*Elena*: Andrei Zvyagintsev Interview." *SBS*. Special Broadcasting Service, 22 June 2012. Web. 10 Aug. 2015.

Olsen, Mark. "Filmmakers See a Bigger Message in Russia's *Leviathan*." *Los Angeles Times*. Los Angeles Times, 30 Dec. 2014. Web. 10 Aug. 2015.

Rohter, Larry. "Champion of the Lone Russian Everyman." *New York Times*. New York Times, 18 Dec. 2014. Web. 10 Aug. 2015.

Walker, Shaun. "*Leviathan* Director Andrei Zvyagintsev: 'Living in Russia Is Like Being in a Minefield.'" *Guardian*. Guardian News and Media, 6 Nov. 2014. Web. 10 Aug. 2015.

Weaver, Courtney. "Russian Director Andrei Zvyagintsev." *Financial Times*. Financial Times, 23 Jan. 2015. Web. 10 Aug. 2015.

Zvyagintsev, Andrey. "Return of the Prodigal Father; Andrey Zvyagintsev Talks about *The Return*." Interview by Erica Abeel. *Indiewire*. Indiewire.com, 2 Feb. 2004. Web. 10 Aug. 2015.

## SELECTED WORKS

*The Return*, 2003; *The Banishment*, 2007; *Elena*, 2011; *Leviathan*, 2014

—Chris Cullen

## Tariq Aziz
## (Mikhail Yuhanna)
**Born:** Mozul, Iraq; April 28, 1936
**Died:** Nasiriyah, Iraq; June 5, 2015
**Occupation:** Deputy prime minister of Iraq

Iraq's minister of foreign affairs from 1983 to 1991, Tariq Aziz was the voice of the Iraqi dictator, Saddam Hussein, charged with the impossible task of justifying Hussein's brutal policies to the Western world. As Iraq's deputy foreign minister, he was a ubiquitous personality in world news during the first Gulf War that followed Iraq's invasion of Kuwait.

Aziz was born to a relatively poor family of Chaldean Catholics in a country that is ninety-five percent Muslim. He studied English literature at Baghdad's College of Fine Arts and began his career in journalism at the *Baghdad al-Jumhuriyah* ("The Republic"). As he became politically active, he gravitated toward the militaristic faction of the Ba'ath party. He became editor in chief of the Ba'athist newspaper *al-Thawra* (the "Revolution") in 1968, and changed his Christian name to Tariq Aziz ("noble path"). In 1974, he became the party's minister of information, later joining the ruling Revolutionary Command Council. Upon Saddam Hussein's rise to the top, Hussein appointed Aziz the deputy prime minister (sometimes referred to as the "chief propagandist" by the Western press.). Being a Christian "outsider" worked to Aziz's advantage in that Saddam Hussein would never see Aziz as a threat to his power. Aziz narrowly escaped an assassination attempt in 1980—an event that helped precipitate Iraq's debilitating eight-year war with Iran.

In 1990, Iraq invaded its southern neighbor, Kuwait, precipitating a swift and devastating military reaction by the United States—a short war commonly known as "Desert Storm." Following that war, Aziz resigned as deputy prime minister, but remained Hussein's foreign policy advisor. Following US President George Bush's "regime change" attack in 2002, Aziz turned himself in to US authorities. (He had been designated number forty-three in the United States' "playing card" list of its top fifty-five most wanted enemies.) Aziz remained imprisoned until his death on June 5, 2015. His wife, Violet, and their four children survive him.

*See Current Biography 1991.*

## Herman Badillo
**Born:** Caguas, Puerto Rico; August 21, 1929
**Died:** New York, NY; December 3, 2014
**Occupation:** Politician, United States Congressman, lawyer, accountant

Arriving in America at the very cusp of a Puerto Rican immigration tsunami, Herman Badillo became the first Puerto Rican representative in the U. S. Congress, and a fixture in New York politics. A four-term Congressman, Badillo advocated for urban renewal, antipoverty programs, voting rights and bilingual education. Badillo began his political career in 1960 as the Chairman of the East Harlem "Kennedy for President Committee." He served as the Bronx borough President for three years and claimed to have brought in some $1 billion in improvements and new construction for the Bronx. He served as Mayor Robert F. Wagner's Commissioner of Relocation—a position that earned Badillo some enemies in the Puerto Rican community, some of whom felt he betrayed them and dubbed him the man for "minority removal." He was Deputy Mayor under Ed Koch in the late 70s. Badillo himself made four unsuccessful bids for New York City Mayor.

Most remarkably, Herman Badillo arrived in the United States when he was eleven, without a home (he was orphaned at age five), nor did he speak English. Raised by relatives scattered across the country, Badillo settled with an aunt in New York City. Improving education was paramount both personally, and as a life-long political mission. (Badillo graduated magna cum laude from City College, and was class Valedictorian at Brooklyn Law School.) He was admitted to the New York Bar in 1955, and, a year later, earned his accreditation as a C.P.A. When not holding a position in public office, Badillo practiced law, and in 1999, he was the Chairman of City University of New York (CUNY) where he raised admission standards. He published one book *One Nation, One Standard: An Ex-Liberal on How Hispanics Can Succeed Just Like*

*Other Immigrant Groups.* (Sentinel; December 28, 2006.) As the title suggests, Badillo moved, politically, to the right by the end of his career, running for Comptroller on a fusion ticket with Rudolph Giuliani.

Herman Badillo died of complications from congestive heart failure in New York City on December 3, 2014.

*See Current Biography 1971.*

# Ernie Banks

**Born:** Dallas, Texas; January 31, 1931
**Died:** Chicago, Illinois; January 23, 2015
**Occupation:** Baseball player, Chicago Cubs ambassador

With a nickname like "Mr. Sunshine," it's easy to imagine Ernie Banks as a friendly, enthusiastic man, someone for whom the glass was always half full. He was also one of the most talented baseball players in the history of the sport, setting numerous performance records. He was named the National League's Most Valuable Player (MVP) for two years straight, in 1958 and 1959. In the 1958 season, he led both the American and National leagues in home runs with 47, and in runs batted in with 129. His batting average was 313. The first African American to wear the Cubs' uniform when he joined the team in 1953, Banks set a major league record by playing in 424 consecutive major league games. (He was stopped by an infected finger.) In 1955, Banks set another record by hitting five grand slams (home runs with bases loaded). That same year he was named shortstop for the Sporting News All-Star Major League Team. He won the National League Golden Glove award in 1960. In his *New York Times* article (August 24, 1955), Arthur Delaney wrote "informed baseball men are agreed that Banks is unquestionably the best shortstop in the business right now. He's a graceful, flowing fielder with wide range, a strong arm and good speed."

Ernie Banks was born in 1931, in Dallas, Texas, one of eleven children. Though he showed no real interest in sports, Banks' father insisted that he at least give it a try. (Banks' father had been a semi-professional baseball player.) The boy tried football, basketball, and track and field, but baseball became his passion. While in high school Banks met Mollye Louise Ector whom he married in 1953, following a two-year

stint in the Army. The marriage was short-lived, and Banks married Eloyce Johnson, who gave birth to twin sons within a year of their marriage. A daughter was born several years later. In all, Banks was married four times.

Following his playing years, Banks served as a team ambassador. He was inducted into the Baseball Hall of Fame in 1977, and in 1999, he was named to the major league baseball "All-Century Team." The Cubs retired his number (14) in 1982, the first Cubs player to be so honored. In 2008, a statue of Banks—"Mr. Cub"—was installed at Wrigley Field. He received the designation "Living Legend" by the Library of Congress in 2009, and in 2013, Banks received the Presidential Medal of Freedom. Ernie Banks suffered a heart attack and died in Chicago on January 23, 2015. His survivors include his fourth wife, Liz Ellzey, and his four children.

*See Current Biography 1959.*

# Marion S. Barry, Jr.

**Born:** Itta Bena, Mississippi; March 6, 1936
**Died:** Washington, DC; November 23, 2014
**Occupation:** American politician

Marion S. Barry served for four terms as the mayor of Washington, DC (1979–1991; 1995–1999). The first black activist to be elected mayor of a major American city, Barry remained popular and politically influential despite a long series of scandals and controversies.

At LeMoyne College, a historically black college in Memphis, Tennessee, Barry became active in the National Association for the Advancement of Colored People (NAACP). He graduated in 1958 and earned a master's degree in organic chemistry from Fisk University in 1960. Barry became the first chairman of the Student Nonviolent Coordinating Committee (SNCC), serving for less than a year (1960–1961). He left to become a doctoral student in chemistry, but in 1964 he went to work for SNCC full-time without having taken his degree.

Barry's work for SNCC brought him to Washington, DC, in June 1965. As SNCC became more militant, Barry struck out on his own, organizing protests and boycotts. He was elected to the school board in 1971. In 1974, when the District of Columbia gained home rule, he was elected as an at-large member to the District's first council. He was reelected in 1976 and in 1978 successfully ran for mayor.

At the outset of Barry's tenure, Washington boomed, but conditions for the majority of the city's black poor continued to deteriorate. Allegations of corruption among his associates grew ever louder. Barry made no effort to curb his flamboyant personal style, and rumors circulated about his womanizing and drug use. Arrested in 1990 on drug charges following an Federal Bureau of Investigation (FBI) sting operation, he was convicted on one count of drug possession and acquitted on a second misdemeanor count. The jury deadlocked on 12 additional charges. Barry lost the 1990 mayoral election—his only electoral defeat.

Barry completed a drug and alcohol rehabilitation program and served six months in a minimum security federal prison. He then turned the experience to political advantage in an improbable political comeback. Barry blamed racism for his arrest, claiming that the federal government was out to get him—charges that resonated in his divided city. In 1992 he was returned to the council as the member for Ward 8, and two years later he defeated sitting mayor Sharon Pratt Kelly in the Democratic mayoral primary. He easily won the general election.

In his fourth term, Barry grappled unsuccessfully with the same problems he had faced previously. In 1995 Congress created the District of Columbia Financial Control Board to rein in city spending, and in mid-1997 nine city departments were put under the board's control, effectively stripping Barry of power. The following year he announced that he would not run for reelection.

In succeeding years Barry was dogged by various scandals, including a misdemeanor assault, drug charges, tax evasion charges, and numerous parking and traffic violations. Nevertheless, in 2004 he was again elected to the city council for Ward 8, and he served until 2014, the year his memoir, *Mayor for Life: The Incredible Story of Marion Barry Jr.* (written with Omar Tyree) was published. Barry's record of creating jobs for the District of Columbia's poor young black residents remains his foremost achievement.

He died of cardiac arrest in Washington, DC, on November 23, 2014. He is survived by his fourth wife, Cora Masters Barry, and his son, Marion Christopher Barry.

*See Current Biography 1987, 1996.*

# William Baum

**Born:** Dallas, Texas; November 21, 1926
**Died:** Washington, DC; July 23, 2015
**Occupation:** Roman Catholic prelate, cardinal

Cardinal William Baum had the longest tenure of any American priest, marking thirty-nine years as an American Catholic prelate and cardinal. He was the archbishop of Washington, DC from 1973 to 1980, and he welcomed Pope John Paul II to Washington, DC in 1979.

William Wakefield Baum was born in Dallas, Texas, and was drawn to the priesthood from a very early age. His father, Harold E. White, was Presbyterian, and his mother was Catholic. It is unclear whether or not his parents divorced before his father's death, but Baum and his mother moved to Kansas City, Missouri. She married a Jewish businessman, Jerome Charles Baum, and her young son, William, assumed Baum's name. He was drawn to the Catholic Church from a very young age, serving as an altar boy at St. Peter's Church in Kansas City. He attended the parish school, then entered the Kansas City Saint Joseph diocesan junior seminary, before moving on to the Kendrick Seminary in St. Louis. Baum was ordained in 1951, becoming an associate pastor in Kansas City, and teaching at Avila College. He also studied in Rome for two years, earning a doctorate in theology at the Angelicum Athenaeum.

Baum's particular area of expertise was ecumenism—relations with the "separated brethren" of other Christian denominations and Judaism—and he was brought to Rome to give advice, do research, and prepare position papers for the Vatican Council II (1962 to 1965). He spoke fluent Italian. When he became the bishop of Springfield, Missouri in 1970, his episcopal motto, borrowed from Saint Paul, was "ministry of reconciliation." He was committed to racial equality and to fighting the armaments race among powerful nations.

A furor erupted over the Washington archdiocese's purchase of a $525,000 Chase Mansion as a residence for Archbishop Baum. In protest, a dissident priest named Edward Guinan went on a twenty-five day hunger strike, saying such a large sum of money should be spent on helping the needy. Baum rescinded the purchase.

Baum was archbishop when the Supreme Court made abortion legal, and he remained a staunch abortion opponent. Baum also established a "Black Secretariat," formed to implement the full participation of DC's African American population in archdiocesan life. They succeeded in giving the African American Catholics a voice in the selection or rejection of priests and nuns who would serve in the predominantly African American parishes.

Cardinal William Baum died on July 23, 2015 at a Catholic care facility in Washington, DC. He was eighty-eight.

*See Current Biography 1976.*

# Lawrence Peter "Yogi" Berra

**Born:** St. Louis, Missouri; May 12, 1925
**Died:** West Caldwell, New Jersey; September 22, 2015
**Occupations:** American professional baseball player, coach and manager

Yogi Berra was an award-winning baseball catcher who was equally known for his colorful personality, and witticisms deemed "Yogi-isms," such as "When you come to a fork in the road, take it," and "It's deja vu all over again." The cartoon character, Yogi Bear, was inspired by Berra. As a manager, he brought both the Yankees and the Mets to the World Series.

Berra grew up in the Italian neighborhood of St. Louis, Missouri, and enjoyed playing sports with his friends. Although he always wanted to be a professional baseball player, he took a job in a coal yard after graduating eighth grade to earn money for his family. In 1941, he was asked to be a part of the Stockham Post American Legion junior team, where he earned his nickname Yogi after his resemblance to a yogi in a film. He joined the minor leagues after spending a year with the Navy during World War II.

He was a catcher who was also an especially successful hitter; although he didn't have the highest batting average, he hit an unusual 358 home runs during his career. According to the *New York Times*, Berra was "praised by pitchers for his astute pitch-calling, Berra led the American League in assists five times, and from 1957 through 1959 went 148 consecutive games behind the plate without making an error, a major league record at the time." He is at the center of many of baseball's most fabled stories. In 1947,

he hit the first-ever pinch-hit home run during a World Series game. This culminates in a record-breaking career: "All told, his Yankees teams won the American League pennant 14 out of 17 years. He still holds Series records for games played, plate appearances, hits and doubles" (*New York Times*).

Starting in the 1960s, he began his career as a coach and manager. He was the manager of the Yankees, and then the Mets, and then the Yankees again. He is known for a feud with George Steinbrenner, the eccentric Yankees manager, and Steinbrenner eventually apologized for his treatment of Berra.

His affable personality and clever remarks led to his popularity with baseball fans of all ages. He was also featured in many commercials as the endorsing celebrity, broadening his fame.

Berra died at the age of ninety in West Caldwell, New Jersey. His three sons, each of whom had professional athletic careers, and eleven grandchildren survive him. His wife, Carmen Berra (née Short) passed away in 2014.

*See Current Biography 1952.*

# Mario Biaggi

**Born:** New York, New York; October 26, 1917
**Died:** New York, New York; June 24, 2015
**Occupation:** US Congressman, lawyer, and decorated police officer

As a nineteen-year veteran congressman, Mario Biaggi had a reputation for his commitment to community service, social conservatism, and ethnic politics. He was outspoken on such issues as Soviet-Jewish emigration, and the conflict in Northern Ireland, winning the unflagging loyalty of the large Irish, Italian, and Jewish voting blocs in his congressional district.

Born to poor Italian immigrants from Lombardy, Biaggi was raised in a Harlem tenement. He joined the New York City Police Department in 1942, and remained an officer for twenty-three years, earning twenty-eight commendations for heroism—a department record. He was seriously injured in an attempt to stop a runaway horse, and walked with a limp the remainder of his life. In 1961, he became the first New York state police officer to be inducted into the National Police Officer's Hall of Fame. After a Bronx shootout he was awarded the Police Medal of Honor for Valor, the department's highest distinction.

Upon hearing Biaggi speak, the dean of the New York Law School, Daniel Gutman, offered him a full scholarship to study law. He earned his LL.B. degree in 1963, and worked for the Republican administration of Governor Nelson Rockefeller, and from 1963 to 1965, he was the assistant to the New York secretary of state. In 1968, with his stellar law enforcement reputation, Biaggi won the congressional race for the New York 24th District, ending sixteen years of Republican incumbency. In 1973, he launched a campaign to become the mayor of New York City, but sustained heavy political blows when the *New York Times* reported he had invoked his Fifth Amendment protection against self-incrimination during a grand jury testimony, thus tarnishing his reputation.

His political career took a fatal hit in 1988 when he was convicted of extortion in a $3.5 million Wedtech Corporation no-bid defense contract, and a year later, of accepting illegal gratuities for a vacation in Florida. Biaggi was sentenced to eight years in prison, serving a little over two. His wife, Marie, predeceased him in 1997. His four children, eleven grandchildren, and four great-grandchildren survive him.

*See Current Biography 1986.*

# Theodore Bikel

**Born:** Vienna, Austria; May 2, 1924
**Died:** Los Angeles, California; July 21, 2015
**Occupation:** Actor, folk singer

Theodore Bikel was an actor and singer known for his versatility. In his 1994 biography he claimed that, when asked which of his talents he enjoyed most, he responded with "Versatility in itself." He originated the role of Captain von Trapp in *The Sound of Music* on Broadway, and in fact, Rogers and Hammerstein wrote the song "Edelweiss" to exploit Bikel's folk singing skills. For decades, he starred as Tevye in *Fiddler on the Roof*, performing the role more than two thousand times. He played Zoltan Karpathy in the 1964 film version of *My Fair Lady*, and received an Oscar nomination for his performance in the 1958 movie *The Defiant Ones*, which also starred Sidney Poitier and Tony Curtis. He played opposite Vivien Leigh in *A Streetcar Named Desire.* He applied his skills to the small screen in a wide variety of shows, from *The Twilight Zone* to *Charlie's Angels.*

Theodore Bikel was born in Vienna but rejected calling himself "Viennese" because of the city's treatment of its Jewish population during World War II. He considered himself "an Austrian-born Jew." Two years before the Nazi's invaded Poland, Bikel's family immigrated to Palestine. His original family name was Cohen, but according to Richard Severo of *The New York Times* (21 July 2015) "his great-grandfather. . . arrived at the name Bikel by pointing his finger at random in an old prayer book and combining the first letters of the Hebrew words in the sentence where his finger landed."

At times, Bikel was better known for his singing than his acting. He sang in over twenty languages, and recorded twenty-four albums with titles like *Folk Songs of Israel, Songs of a Russian Gypsy,* and *Songs of the Earth.* He founded the Newport Folk Festival.

Bikel was also politically active, attending the 1968 Democratic National Convention as a delegate, and was an officer in the American Jewish Congress. He was arrested after protesting the plight of Soviet Jewry in front of the Soviet Embassy in Washington.

Theodore Bikel was married four times. His first two marriages ended in divorce. His third wife, the conductor and pianist Tamara Brooks, predeceased him in 2012. Bikel leaves behind his wife, journalist Aimee Ginsburg, his four sons, and three grandchildren.

*See Current Biography 1960.*

# Julian Bond

**Born:** Nashville, Tennessee; January 14, 1940
**Died:** Fort Walton Beach, Florida; August 15, 2015
**Occupation:** NAACP chairman, Georgia assemblyman, professor, writer

A pioneer in the civil rights movement, Julian Bond was one of the co-founders of the Student Nonviolent Coordinating Committee that led the student sit-ins at Greensboro, North Carolina, lunch counters. At the 1968 Democratic National Convention, he was nominated for vice president (the first African American to be so honored) on Eugene McCarthy's bid for the White House, though Bond was disqualified due to his age. (He was twenty-eight years old.) Bond was a member of the Georgia General Assembly for twenty years. In 1998 he was the chairman of the national board of directors for the National Association for the Advancement of Colored People (NAACP).

Julian Bond's father, Horace Mann Bond, was the president of Lincoln University, the nation's oldest private African American college, during his son's childhood. As such, Julian Bond had the opportunity to meet many luminaries such as Albert Einstein, Paul Robeson, and W.E.B. DuBois. Bond attended a private Quaker preparatory school. His first experience of racism occurred when the school asked that he not wear his school jacket while he was dating a white girl. In 1957 the family moved to Atlanta where Bond's father became the dean of the School of Education at Atlanta University. Julian Bond attended Morehouse College as an English major. He took a philosophy course taught by Martin Luther King, Jr. He co-founded the Committee on Appeal for Human Rights (COAHR), the organization that staged a series of sit-ins in whites-only establishments that served as a catalyst for the desegregation of lunch counters throughout Atlanta. COAHR merged with the Student Nonviolent Coordinating Committee (SNCC). Bond became the organization's communications director.

Bond married Alice Louise Clapton, with whom he had five children, in 1961. Bond became the managing editor at the *Atlanta Inquirer*. He was elected to the Georgia House of Representatives in 1965, but fellow legislators prevented him from being seated due to his antiwar stance, until the US Supreme Court ruled his exclusion was unconstitutional. In 1971, Bond became the first president of the Southern Poverty Law Center.

In 1987, after Bond lost the race for the fifth Congressional district to his former friend, John Lewis, his marriage began to disintegrate. His wife accused him of drug use and adultery, an accusation she later rescinded. He married Washington lawyer Pamela Horowitz in 1990.

Bond received twenty-five honorary degrees, and was a professor of history at George Washington University, and at the University of Virginia. He published the book, *A Time To Speak, A Time To Act*. His poetry and articles have appeared in numerous publications, including Langston Hughes' anthology *New Negro Poetry U.S.A.*

Julian Bond died on August 15, 2015. His wife, his five children from his first marriage, two siblings, and eight grandchildren survive him.

*See Current Biography 2001.*

---

# Malcolm Boyd

**Born:** Buffalo, New York; June 8, 1923
**Died:** Los Angeles, California; February 27, 2015
**Occupation:** Episcopal priest, social activist, and author

Malcolm Boyd was an Episcopal priest who believed that the place for the gospels was in the streets. Sometimes referred to as "secular clergy," or as a "pop evangelist," Boyd was among the first white ministers to work toward a desegregated south. Although *Mademoiselle* magazine once referred to him as a "disturber of the peace," Boyd called himself a "Christian existentialist." But the greatest controversy of his life was his 1976 admission that he was homosexual.

Boyd had not originally planned to live the life of a clergyman. He graduated from the University of Arizona with a degree in journalism. He worked for an advertising agency in Hollywood, California. In 1949, he formed a radio and television agency with Mary Pickford and Buddy Rogers, acquiring such a favorable reputation that he was elected the first president of the Television Producers' Association of Hollywood.

To the astonishment of all who knew him, in 1951 Boyd decided to abandon his career to study for the Episcopal ministry. His first assignment as a priest was an all-white parish in a largely African-American section of Indianapolis, where he was shocked to learn the depth of prejudice in middle-class America. He became a popular college chaplain at Colorado State University, where he began holding informal talks and hearing confessions in coffee houses. Re-assigned to Wayne State University, he joined twenty-seven other Episcopal priests on a "prayer pilgrimage"—a form of "freedom ride" for civil rights. While at Wayne State, he began writing plays and poetry about racial injustice. He began to read his "prayers" with guitar accompaniment in taverns and coffeehouses. Boyd published more than two dozen books of "prayers," which read like stories. His most famous was a book of prayers called *Are You Running with Me Jesus?*

In 1976, at a Chicago Episcopal convention, Boyd came out as a gay man. The admission marked, once again, a new direction for Boyd's life, as he became an activist for gay rights. In 1985, he led the first "AIDS mass." He formed consciousness-raising groups for homosexuals, and wrote books about gay spirituality.

In his 1969 memoir, *As I Live and Breathe,* Boyd explained the extraordinary twists and turns in his life, writing "the single great war of my life has been against fragmentation and for wholeness, against labels and for identity." Malcolm Boyd died due to complications of pneumonia on February 27, 2015. His life-partner and spouse, Mark Thompson, survives him.

*See Current Biography 1968.*

# Benjamin Crowninshield "Ben" Bradlee

**Born:** Boston, Massachusetts; August 26, 1921

**Died:** Washington, DC; October 21, 2014

**Occupation:** Journalist, executive editor, and author

When asked about his extraordinary success as a "newsman" at the *Washington Post,* Ben Bradlee summed up his entire leadership strategy in six short words: "Hire people smarter than you are"—a tall order for someone with Bradlee's background. Ben Bradlee graduated from Harvard University in 1942, following in the footsteps of 10 generations of Bradlee men. He managed to graduate early by doubling his workload, in order to join the U. S. Navy and fight in the war. His wartime experiences had a far greater impact on his work than any educational institution, even Harvard.

His early career began at the *Washington Post,* but after failing to advance quickly enough, he became the press attaché for the U. S. Embassy in Paris. Not long after, *Newsweek* hired him as its chief European correspondent, then promptly reassigned him to its Washington bureau, where he reported on the 1960 presidential election, and Richard Nixon's 1962 gubernatorial campaign.

Ben Bradlee had a close friendship with President John F. Kennedy—the two had been neighbors in Georgetown—a relationship that had no small effect on Bradlee's career as a journalist. He regularly scooped *Time* magazine on important issues. Eventually, Bradlee would write a book—*Conversations with Kennedy*—that described his informal encounters with the Kennedys.

When Bradlee learned from a friend, Osborn Elliott, the managing editor at *Newsweek,* that the magazine was looking for a buyer, Bradlee immediately called Philip Graham, owner of the *Washington Post,* who promptly bought the news magazine—an event that changed the course of Ben Bradlee's life. Graham hired him to be the magazine's Washington bureau chief. By 1968, Bradlee was named vice-president and executive editor of the *Post.* Under his leadership the *Post* garnered seventeen Pulitzer Prizes, and a Public Service Award for its work on the Watergate scandal. In June of 1971, the *Post* attained a generous portion of the Pentagon Papers. Upon publication of its initial article, the paper was under a court injunction to stop. The case would be taken up by the Supreme Court, setting important precedent on First Amendment presumption against prior restraint. His congratulatory memo to his staff reveals a great deal about Bradlee's managerial style. He wrote, "The guts and energy and responsibility of everyone involved in this fight...has impressed me more than anything in my life. You are beautiful." To insure fair and accurate reporting, Bradlee hired an in-house ombudsman to criticize the *Post*'s performance in print.

In 2013, President Barack Obama bestowed the Presidential Medal of Freedom on Bradlee, who came to epitomize the quintessential newsman. Ben Bradlee died of natural causes on October 21, 2014, at his home in Washington, DC. He was ninety-three years old. He is survived by his third wife, Sally Quinn, and his four children.

*See Current Biography 1975.*

# Sarah Brady

**Born:** Kirksville, Missouri; February 6, 1942

**Died:** Alexandria, Virginia; April 3, 2015

**Occupation:** American gun-control activist and wife of James S. Brady

Sarah Brady's occupation as a gun-control advocate began on March 30, 1981, when her husband, James Brady—press secretary to President Ronald Reagan—was critically injured in an assassination attempt on the president. James Brady took a bullet to the head, leaving him permanently paralyzed. Subsequent to Brady's injuries, Sarah Brady found her young son handling a loaded handgun, which he had pointed directly at his mother thinking it was a toy. Around the same time, Mrs. Brady learned that the US Congress was considering a bill to repeal key provisions of the Gun Control Act of 1968. She considered it her personal call to action.

Born Sarah Jane Kemp on February 6, 1942 in Missouri, Brady was raised around guns due to her father's profession as a Federal Bureau of Investigation (FBI) agent. Brady's first job upon graduating from the College of William and Mary, was as a schoolteacher. However, four years later, she signed on as an assistant to the campaign director of the National Republican Congressional Committee in Washington, DC where, in the late 1960s, she met James Brady. The two married in 1973. While she held several positions in Republican administration offices, her husband delved into national politics. In 1980, he served as the director of public affairs and research in Ronald Reagan's presidential campaign. Upon winning the election, Reagan appointed Brady White House press secretary.

After the events of 1981, Sarah Brady began speaking out about handguns being too easily available. In 1985, Brady helped forge an alliance between the gun-control organization, Handgun Control, and numerous law enforcement agencies. The National Rifle Association (NRA), an anti-gun-control organization, was not happy. Brady would spend the next twenty years fighting to institute safer gun control measures. In 1987, Brady and Handgun Control were instrumental in getting a number of congressmen to sponsor a bill that mandated a seven-day waiting period prior to a handgun purchase. The bill became known as the Brady Bill. It took years of political wrangling, but in 1993, Congress passed an amended version of the bill.

Later, Mrs. Brady lobbied for a ban on assault-weapons. She also helped found, and served as the chairwoman of, the Brady Campaign to Prevent Gun Violence, and the Brady Center to Prevent Gun Violence, from 2000 until she died on April 3, 2015 due to pneumonia. Her husband, James Brady, predeceased her. Her son, Scott Brady, a stepdaughter, and a brother survive her.

*See Current Biography 1996.*

# Leon Brittan

**Born:** London, England; September 25, 1939

**Died:** London, England; January 21, 2015

**Occupation:** British politician

Leon Brittan was a British barrister and Conservative politician who helped orchestrate and administer the General Agreement on Tariffs and Trade (GATT). GATT's chief aim was to reduce tariffs, and other barriers to trade, between member nations. As the European Commission (EC) competition commissioner, Brittan was charged with leveling the European playing field in preparation for market unification—a task that left him in the difficult position of opposing his own conservative prime minister, Margaret Thatcher, who was shocked by some of his stances.

In 1974, Brittan was elected to Parliament, as a "backbencher" (noncabinet member). In 1979, Prime Minister Thatcher appointed Brittan minister of state for the Home Office (another noncabinet post). In 1981, however, Thatcher promoted him to serve as chief secretary to the treasury. He was credited with keeping government spending to a minimum. In 1985, Thatcher's government suffered a scandal, commonly referred to as the "Westland helicopter scandal." Documentation was leaked, regarding Thatcher's alleged unfair and clandestine support for an American consortium, and of discouraging the European group. (It became a juggernaut over Thatcher's entire industrial policy and style of leadership.) Brittan was accused of leaking the information, and giving misleading testimony to Parliament. Brittan, who never confirmed his culpability for the leak, resigned in an effort to protect Thatcher. (He had assumed she would reappoint him to parliament. She did not. She had him knighted and sent him to the EC.) Brittan served in numerous roles at the EC, including vice-president in 1999.

For the last year of his life Brittan faced allegations that, in the 1980s, he improperly handled evidence in a child sex abuse case involving prominent political figures. (Files related to the claims, and for which he was responsible, disappeared when he was minister of the Home Office.) His home was searched and he, himself, was accused of rape and child molestation, though he would never be tried. On January 21, 2015, Leon Brittan died before the case could go any further, leaving many disappointed that they would never know what happened to the child sex abuse dossier, and what it contained. Leon Brittan died in his home after a lengthy battle with cancer. He is survived by his wife, Diana Peterson, and two stepdaughters.

*See Current Biography 1994.*

# Edward William Brooke, III

**Born:** Washington DC, October 26, 1919

**Died:** Coral Gables, Florida, January 3, 2015

**Occupation:** Politician and US Senator

In November 1966, Edward Brooke became the first African American elected, by popular vote, to the US Senate. Defying stereotypes, Edward Brooke was an African American, yet he avoided being categorized as a civil rights icon; he was a Republican with a Democratic constituency; he was Episcopalian in a largely Catholic city; he was a politician who avoided publicity. Fiercely independent, Brooke refused to support his party's candidate, Barry Goldwater, in the 1964 Republican National Convention. Yet, he remained wildly popular in Massachusetts.

Edward Brooke was born in Washington DC, to Helen and Edward Brooke, a lawyer with the Veteran's Administration. Although he knew he was "negro," he never felt underprivileged because of race. He was told he was a descendant of Thomas Jefferson and of a British admiral, Sir Philip Boes Broke. After graduating from Howard University in 1941, Brooke served with the all-Negro 366th Combat Infantry Regiment, in World War II, winning a Bronze Star and the Combat Infantry Badge. Following the war, Brooke remarked that the German prisoners received better treatment than African American soldiers. (*New York Times,* January 3, 2015)

(Years later, he would serve as the national judge advocate and state commander of Amvets, a veterans of war organization.)

Brooke attended law school at Boston University, graduating with an LL.B. and an LL.M. in 1948. He worked to build his private law practice, while dabbling briefly in state politics. In 1960, the state's Republicans selected Brooke as their candidate for the Massachusetts secretary of state. Although he lost that bid, he gained statewide recognition. The newly elected Republican governor, John A. Volpe, appointed Brooke chairman of the Boston Finance Commission and he immediately made headlines by uncovering corruption in city agencies. In 1962, he was elected Massachusetts's attorney general, where he gained a reputation as a serious crime buster, bringing in scores of indictments, some for high-ranking politicians. In 1966, Massachusetts elected Brooke as their representative to the US Senate, where he championed anti-poverty and fair housing initiatives.

President George W. Bush awarded Senator Brooke the Presidential Medal of Freedom in 2004. By the time of his death, Brooke had served as chancellor of the Old North Church in Boston, was president of the Boston Opera Company, a fellow of the American Academy of Arts and Sciences, and was a trustee of Boston University. Brooke died at home in Coral Gables, Florida, on January 3, 2015. He is survived by his second wife of thirty-five years, Anne Fleming Brooke, his four children, and four grandchildren.

*See Current Biography 1967.*

# Rene Burri

**Born:** Zurich, Switzerland; April 9, 1933

**Died:** Zurich, Switzerland; October 20, 2014

**Occupation:** Swiss photographer

For Rene Burri, the ability to capture the pulse of life in a photograph depended a great deal on persistence and luck—something one can't cultivate. While he captured great events and large personalities, it was his sense of composition, of geometry and architecture, (an early fascination that lasted his lifetime) that made Burri one of the most important figures in the history of photography. He is known for his iconic pictures of larger-than-life characters—Che Guevarra smoking his cigar—but many of his images are of common people just to the side of great events, as though seen through the corner of the eye. Burri explained that his main interest was in the links shared between human beings, between man and society.

Rene Burri's curiosity about the larger world grew from watching his chef father bring home lobsters, clams, and oysters, provoking Burri to fantasize about their exotic places of origin, instilling his desire for exploration. Initially, to follow his passion for adventure, Burri wanted to make documentary films, but with no film schools in Zurich, he chose to study photography. In 1954, Burri undertook compulsory military service, where he spent much of his time documenting events through film. Burri would later credit these years as fundamental to his development as a photojournalist. Afterward, while waiting to catch a glimpse of Pablo Picasso (and perhaps photograph the artist), in Paris, Burri found the offices of the photographic cooperative, Magnum Photos, and joined as an associate correspondent. (He would eventually be elected European president of the cooperative.) Henri Cartier-Bresson became his mentor. While his initial goals were journalistic in nature, he became skeptical about how world events were depicted in new media, namely television. He wanted to capture something more fundamental, something that lasted beyond the news story. He documented the Six-Day War, Vietnam, and Cambodia in the late 60s, U. S. President Ronald Reagan meeting Mikhail Gorbachev, the student protests at Tiananmen Square, and the collapse of the Berlin Wall. His photos were published in periodicals such as *Time, Life, Vogue,* and *National Geographic.*

Rene Burri died in Zurich, Switzerland on October 20, 2014. He is survived by his second wife, Clotilde Blanc, and his three children.

*See Current Biography 2007.*

# Jane Byrne

**Born:** Chicago, Illinois; May 24, 1934
**Died:** Chicago, Illinois; November 14, 2014
**Occupation:** Former Chicago mayor

Despite having never run for office, and with very little political experience, Jane Byrne stirred up the long-entrenched Democratic machine that had dominated Chicago's political landscape for decades. And she made it seem ef-

fortless. Her foray into politics began when she volunteered in the 1960 presidential campaign of John F. Kennedy—an attempt to recover from the loss of her young husband, a marine pilot who was killed in a crash in 1959. Soon after joining the campaign, Byrne was offered the post of secretary-treasurer of the Chicago organization. Her first foray into politics gave her access to Kennedy's prominent supporters, and she made such an impression on Kennedy that he offered her a position in Washington following his election. She declined, though she did accept social engagements from the Kennedys. She also garnered the attention of Mayor Richard J. Daley, who quickly took her on as his protégé. In 1964, Daly appointed Mrs. Byrne to a minor post on the federal antipoverty program, where she learned the ropes, from ward level to the mayor's office. Four years later, he named her commissioner of consumer sales, weights, and measures, making her the first woman in his cabinet. She transformed the office, advocating for consumer justice, thus earning the trust and respect of citizens and politicians alike.

Byrne was fiercely devoted to her mentor, Mayor Daley. After he suffered a stroke, she castigated those who eagerly planned his succession, calling them "little men of greed," and "political vultures." After Daly's death two years later, these same men exacted revenge, stripping her of her position with the Cook County Democratic organization. She remained in the administration of Daly's predecessor, Michael Bilandic, but the relationship was not a good one, and Byrne eventually accused him of "fraudulent and conspiratorial action." He fired her. Her response was to run against him in the next Democratic primary. Byrne won an extraordinary 82 percent of the vote, beating an incumbent Mayor from her own party, even though she had little political experience. She became Chicago's first and only female mayor. Determined to increase efficiency while cutting the budget, she carried out shakeups of the city's sanitation operations and police department, replacing several high-profile commissioners and top government officials. She faced a series of strikes by public employees' unions. Her mercurial temperment, with a penchant for high-profile hirings and firings, unsettled City Hall, but she still managed to strengthen the city's finances, and revitalize the downtown. Her term and her political career ended on April 29, 1983. Though she attempted a comeback, she would not win another election.

Byrne married journalist Jay McMullen in 1978, and published her memoir, *My Chicago*, in 1992. On November 14, 2014, Jane Byrne died in Chicago due to complications from a stroke. She is survived by her daughter Kathrine, and her grandson, Willie.

*See Current Biography 1980.*

# Billy Casper

**Born:** San Diego, California; June 24, 1931
**Died:** Springville, Utah; February 7, 2015
**Occupation:** American professional golfer

At the height of his career, from 1956 to 1975, Billy Casper won fifty-one Professional Golfers' Association (PGA) tour titles, and in 1966 to 1968, Billy Casper was the top income earner on the PGA tour. He placed seventh on the tour's all-time victory list, winning titles for sixteen consecutive years. Casper won three major championships. He was acknowledged as one of the finest putters in the history of the game.

Billy Casper began golf instruction when he was five, on his grandfather's three-hole course on his ranch in New Mexico. He attended the University of Notre Dame on a golf scholarship, but he couldn't abide the cold Indiana winters, and left to join the US Navy, where he spent most of his time teaching and playing golf. From 1959 through 1962, Casper consistently ranked fourth among money winners, and he was the top income earner from 1966 to 1968. In 1964, Casper was named putter of the year by the Golf Writers Association of America, and *Golf* magazine included Casper in its All-America Pro Team as a putter. He was named the PGA player of the year in 1966.

In 1964, Billy Casper started experiencing health problems that affected him mentally. He became "grumpy and fidgety," Casper told Erwin Shrake of *Sports Illustrated* (7 Feb. 1966). He said, "Everything on the course bothered me . . . I was always sick." Eventually, his extreme weight gain and moodiness was traced to severe food allergies that also plagued his wife and son. After his diagnosis, and a special diet, Casper improved. Known to be deeply devoted to his family, Billy Casper was drawn to the Mormon faith in the mid-1960s, and he and his wife joined the Church of Jesus Christ of Latter-day Saints in 1966.

In 1978, Billy Casper was inducted into the Golf Hall of Fame. From 1981 to 1989, he played on the Senior Tour. Billy Casper died on February 7, 2015. He is survived by his wife of sixty-two years, Shirley, eleven children (six of whom are adopted), seventy-one grandchildren, and numerous great-grandchildren.

*See Current Biography, 1966.*

# Yves Chauvin

**Born:** Menen, Belgium; October 10, 1930
**Died:** Tours, France; January 27, 2015
**Occupation:** French chemist and Nobel laureate

In 2005, the French chemist, Yves Chauvin, received a Nobel Prize in chemistry, for his research into the chemical reaction called "metathesis", which literally means "changing places." Chauvin's discovery provided a powerful new means of synthesizing certain molecules, under mild conditions, and with little waste. (Prior to his revelations, the process created tremendous waste in energy and hazardous byproducts.) He described metathesis as a process where chemicals perform something of a dance. Two dancing pairs bond into a single dancing unit, then swap partners and break apart into new pairs. The bond of the secondary "dancers" (atoms) is a stronger, double bond. The bonding agent is a metal-carbon catalyst (an organometallic compound).

Chauvin's results benefit a number of industries, from herbicide and fuel producers to pharmaceuticals manufacturers. His discovery provided new methods for environmentally friendly chemical production. Upon his acceptance of the Nobel Prize, Chauvin felt that most of the credit belonged with his fellow recipients, Robert R. Schrock and Robert H. Grubbs, both of whom took Chauvin's findings and applied them to a variety of organic compounds. (They were co-recipients with Chauvin.)

Chauvin earned his degree from the Lyon School of Chemistry, Physics, and Electronics in 1954, though he never earned a Ph.D. After graduating, he took an industrial job, but his creative, inventive mind was not a good fit. Chauvin recalled how managers adhered to a status quo, with no room for invention or creativity. So, in 1960, Chauvin joined the Institut Français du Pétrole in Rueil-Malmaison, France, where he spent the majority of his career as the director of research.

Yves Chauvin died in Tours, France, on January 27, 2015. His survivors include his two sons, and grandchildren.

*See Current Biography 2007.*

# Eugenie Clark

**Born:** New York, New York; May 4, 1922
**Died:** Sarasota, Florida; February 25, 2015
**Occupation:** American ichthyologist

Often referred to as the "shark lady," Eugenie Clark was a scientist who specialized in researching sharks and poisonous fish in tropical waters. She was also a pioneer in marine conservation and the use of scuba gear for research purposes—one of the first scientists to research marine life in its natural environment.

Born and raised in New York City, Clark spent a great deal of her childhood at the New York Aquarium (then known as the Battery Park Aquarium) while her mother worked in lower Manhattan. Her father died when she was just two years old. She studied zoology at Hunter College, and also at the University of Michigan's biological station during the summers. She continued her graduate studies at New York University.

Clark's first job in the field, was as research assistant to Dr. Carl Hubbs of the Scripps Institute of Oceanography in LaJolla, California. At Scripps, she learned to scuba dive. Over the course of her lifetime, she would conduct research at many of the world's premier oceanography research institutions. Clark also conducted research for the US Navy at the Loma Linda School of Tropical Medicine. In 1950, she won a Fulbright Scholarship to work at the Ghardaqa Biological Station of Fuad University in Egypt. She worked for the American Museum of Natural History, the Wildlife Conservation Society, and in 1955, Clark established her own aquatic research center, Sarasota Florida's Mote Marine Laboratory and Aquarium. The "Mote" offers twenty-four research and conservation programs, with labs on six campuses, and more than 200 staff. Mote's scientists conduct research in oceans surrounding the seven continents.

Clark wrote numerous articles for *National Geographic,* including the classic "Sharks: Magnificent and Misunderstood." In 1953, she published her autobiography about her underwater experience, called *Lady with a Spear.* The National Geographic Society, awarded her over a dozen grants, and she appeared in several TV specials. Clark wrote three books, and published dozens of articles. At the time of her death, she had an article out for review.

In addition to her research, Clark taught marine biology at the University of Maryland from 1968 to 1992. She also, famously, taught then Crown Prince Akihito of Japan how to snorkel.

Eugenie Clark's last dive was in 2014, in the Red Sea, on her 92nd birthday. She married five times, and had four children, all of whom survive her, along with a grandson.

*See Current Biography 1953.*

# Lucien Clergue

**Born:** Arles, Bouches-du-Rhone, France; August 14, 1934
**Died:** Nimes, France; November 15, 2014
**Occupation:** Fine art photographer, educator

Lucien Georges Clergue was a small boy when his home was destroyed during World War II. A few years later, his mother died. The death, destruction, and loss experienced in those early years haunted Clergue for the rest of his life. His style might be characterized as dark. His black and white images are as haunting as they are beautiful, and his still images, full of motion, as if they are performance art. Clergue explained, "Three subjects are my main interest: death, life, and a kind of no-man's land in between. The death of the bulls at the bullfight, the nude female in true nature, landscape … is the essentials of my permanent research to find the beginnings of our world and ourselves" (from the California Museum of Photography website). Clergue's early work reflected his interests, with images of mannequins and animal carcasses. He was fascinated with Gypsy culture, which drew him in through music, another of Clergue's passions. (He took violin lessons when he was quite young, and his mother envisioned him attending a conservatory, but had to discontinue the lessons due to the expense.) While photographing the Romani community, Clergue met the flamenco guitarist Manitas de Plata, whom he eventually took to the United States for a tour. Clergue managed de Plata's recording career.

Besides being gifted with a lense, Lucien Clergue was also extremely lucky. In 1953, he met Pablo Picasso at a bullfight, a passion they both shared, and showed him his photographs. Picasso asked to see more, and Clergue responded with *Saltimbanques* ("acrobats"), a collection of children in circus garb, standing in the ruins of his city, Arle. According to Clergue's daughter, Anne, Picasso remarked "Clergue's photographs are from God's own sketchbooks." The two became lifelong friends, and Picasso introduced Clergue to other artists and poets. In 1957, *Corps Memorable*, a series of nudes illustrating the poems of Paul Eluard, was published. The cover featured a Picasso drawing. Clergue would later publish a memoir, *Picasso mon ami* ("Picasso, My Friend") in 1993. By the time of his death, Clergue had published more than 75 books.

In addition to his career as a photographer, Clergue directed more than 20 short films and documentaries, one of which (*Delta de sel*) was selected for screening at the Canne Film Festival. Lucien Clergue's list of honors and awards is extensive. In 2003, Clergue was named a chevalier of the Legion d'honneur; in 2006 he became the first photographer elected to the Academie des Beaux-Arts. He received the Lucie Award (from an international photography organization) in 2007, and in 2008 he was made a commandeur of the Ordre des Arts et des Lettres. He chaired the Academie des Beaux-Arts (a French learned society).

Clergue died in Nimes, France, on November 15, 2015. He is survived by his wife of 42 years, Yolanda, and their daughters, Anne and Olivia.

*See Current Biography 2000.*

cal language called "harmolodics" that allowed musicians of all genres to collaborate. With harmolodics whole ensembles could improvise in unison, combining harmonies, melodies, speed, and rhythm. Most critics agree that Coleman was a musical genius.

Ornette Coleman was born and raised in Fort Worth, Texas, a segregated southern town, with a small African American population. His father was a cook and a mechanic who died when his son was just seven years old, leaving Coleman's mother, Rosa, to raise her four children. Coleman's extended family was highly musical. His sister, Truvenza (Trudy) Coleman was a vocalist and trombonist. His uncle was the guitarist and singer T-Bone Walker. Coleman bought his first saxophone when he was fourteen, but his family couldn't afford lessons. Through serendipity he mistook the low 'C' on his saxophone for the 'A' in the instruction book. He didn't realize his mistake for several years, but it had a profound effect on his music.

Coleman weathered harsh criticism for his eccentricities. Thelonious Monk and Miles Davis dismissed his work. Most fellow musicians and critics either considered him a genius or a fraud. There was little middle ground. His vision included a style that bridged the worlds of jazz and classical music. He collaborated with the music world's elite, including Don Cherry, Charlie Haden, Scott LaFaro, Billy Higgins, Lou Reed, and Ed Blackwell. His work had a profound effect on John Coltrane and Eric Dolphhy. In 1967, Coleman was awarded a Guggenheim grant, the first ever for jazz composition, and was one of only twenty winners of the 1994 MacArthur Foundation "genius" awards. In 2007, he won both a Grammy Lifetime Achievement Award and a Pulitzer Prize in Music. He released over fifty albums in his lifetime.

Coleman's son, the legendary jazz drummer, Denardo Coleman, survives him.

*See Current Biography 1961.*

# Ornette Coleman

**Born:** Fort Worth, Texas.; March 9, 1930
**Died:** New York, New York; June 11, 2015
**Occupation:** Jazz saxophonist, composer

As a jazz musician, Ornette Coleman defied the conventions of harmony and tone, creating a new style of jazz composition that was harsh, inchoate, and atonal. Sometimes referred to as the "father of free jazz," he developed a new musi-

# Jackie Collins

**Born:** London, England; October 4, 1937
**Died:** Beverly Hills, California; September 19, 2015
**Occupation:** Author

Jackie Collins was a prolific novelist known for her creation of the "bonkbuster" novel, famous among women and teens for erotic content and disreputable gossip. Although her novels were often considered to be lowbrow, they were immensely popular. She sold more than 500 million books, and they were translated into forty different languages, which is unusual for a contemporary novelist.

Collins was born in London and had a difficult childhood. After her expulsion from high school, she moved to Hollywood, where an older sister, Joan Collins (later made famous on the hit television show, *Dynasty*) was living. She quickly adapted to a glamorous Hollywood lifestyle, and claimed to have had a "brief but fabulous affair" with the older Marlon Brando when she was 15 years old. She was married twice and divorced once.

Collins' plotted her thirty-two novels around scandalous content about sex, Hollywood affairs, organized crime, and feisty female protagonists. According to *The Guardian*, "Jackie Collins more or less invented the form of storytelling now recorded in the Oxford English Dictionary as 'bonkbuster,'" a British slang term meaning "a type of popular novel characterized by frequent explicit sexual encounters." Because of her proximity to Hollywood, her books were exceptionally successful as it was assumed that the plots were based in part on real gossip. Many of her books became films or television shows (such as *The Stud* and *The Bitch*) that featured her sister as the leading actress.

Collins passed away from breast cancer on September 19, 2015. She kept her illness secret up until a week before her passing, writing a final letter to readers urging them to get mammograms in order to detect their own symptoms of breast cancer early. As her website states: "How fitting that the woman who held Hollywood's deepest secrets, kept her own stage four breast cancer diagnosis quiet for the past six and a half years." Her brother, sister, three daughters, and six grandchildren survive her.

*See Current Biography 2000.*

# Marva Collins

**Born:** Monroeville, Alabama; August 31, 1936
**Died:** Beaufort County, South Carolina; June 24, 2015
**Occupation:** Educator

Marva Collins was a dynamic schoolteacher who came to national attention when she was featured on a segment of the television news show *60 Minutes*. She founded the Westside Preparatory School in Chicago in 1975, transforming supposedly "unteachable" ghetto children into accomplished readers who quoted Shakespeare and Socrates.

Collins herself attended a one-room schoolhouse, and the personal attention she received there influenced her teaching methodology. Growing up in the segregated South, Collins witnessed, first-hand, the disparities between white students and African American. She graduated from Clark College in Atlanta, eventually moving to Chicago where she became a substitute teacher. Appalled by the low quality of Chicago's inner-city schools, she took her $5,000 retirement funds and built her own school where she developed the curriculum now known as the "Collins Method." She came under some criticism because of her outspoken candor regarding Chicago's public school system, but Collins had no tolerance for ineffective teachers. The second floor of Collins' home became her schoolhouse. She salvaged books from school dumpsters and hand copied other books. Collins' approach focused on phonics, math, and reading, eschewing traditional "Dick and Jane" readers. Her students read classical literature.

Collins came to national attention when the *Chicago Sun-Times* ran a story about her. In 1979, Morley Safer interviewed her for *60 Minutes*, and in 1981, CBS produced a movie about her. At that time the waiting list for getting into her school grew to one thousand.

In 1985, the entertainer Prince, provided $500,000 for Collins to found Westside Prep's National Teacher Training Institute, where she trained over one hundred thousand teachers, principals, and administrators. Marva Collins has received numerous awards and accolades including honorary doctorate degrees from Howard University, Amherst College, and Dartmouth College. President George W. Bush awarded her the National Humanities Medal.

Marva Collins' sons, Patrick and Eric, a sister, Cynthia, and her mother, Bessie Mae Johnson, survive her.

*See Current Biography 1986.*

# Charles Correa

**Born:** Secunderabad, India; September 1, 1930

**Died:** Mumbai, India; June 16, 2015

**Occupation:** Architect

One of the most celebrated architects of India, Charles Correa's structures were designed to save India's environment with open, self-ventilated, and affordable buildings. Correa saw architecture as "an agent of change."

Charles Correa studied under architect Buckminster Fuller at the University of Michigan in Ann Arbor, and earned his graduate degree in architecture from the Massachusetts Institute of Technology (MIT), returning to India in 1958 to establish a private practice. Correa designed the Gandhi Memorial at Sabarmati when he was just twenty-eight. Some of his early structures were known as "tube" housing—energy-efficient buildings that minimized surface area exposed to the sun, and utilized natural air convection. He was the chief architect of "New Bombay," a working community across the harbor from the city of Bombay. (One of his deepest concerns was Mumbai's unrelenting growth and urban sprawl.) In 1984, Correa co-founded Mumbai's Urban Research Institute, and in 1985, Prime Minister Rajiv Gandhi named him chairman of the National Commission on Urbanization. Correa's numerous international creations include the Brain Science Centre at the Massachusetts Institute of Technology, Toronto's Ismaili Centre, Champalimaud Centre in Lisbon, and the permanent Mission of India at the United Nations in New York.

His major awards include the Royal Gold Medal from the Royal Institute of British Architects, and the Gold Medal from the Indian Institute of Architects. He taught at Harvard University, MIT, and the University of London.

Charles Correa is survived by his wife, Monika, his two children, and five grandchildren.

*See Current Biography 2000.*

# Philip Miller Crane

**Born:** Chicago, Illinois; November 3, 1930

**Died:** Jefferson, Maryland; November 8, 2014

**Occupation:** United States representative from Illinois, former presidential candidate

Prior to his participation in the 1964 Goldwater for President campaign, Philip Crane had little use for politics or politicians. So it is ironic that a scant five years later, he would be running for elective office in a bid to gain the Illinois Thirteenth Congressional District's seat vacated by Donald Rumsfeld (who left to work in Nixon's cabinet). Crane became a pillar of Republican neo-conservatism. In 1973, he founded the Republican Study Committee to ensure Republican leadership did not stray too far from the conservative line, and he helped found the conservative Heritage Foundation. Crane's stance on most issues reads like a bible of American conservative philosophy. He called for the suspension of the Paris peace talks on Vietnam, and he favored cuts in foreign aid. He proposed drastic cuts in financial support of the United Nations. However, Crane hit hardest on domestic issues, blasting high taxes, inflation, and federal support for education. He argued that the social security system should be left to private insurers and that college education should be reserved for those with IQs of at least 115. He opposed federal funds for abortions and the ratification of the Equal Rights Amendment. Crane stated his goal was to "maximize free choice and minimize trespass," a philosophy he promoted in his three books: *The Democrat's Dilemma* (1964); *The Sum of Good Government* (1976); and, *Surrender in Panama: The Case Against the Treaty* (1978).

One of Crane's greatest disappointments was when Ronald Reagan overlooked him as a running mate in 1976. By the middle of 1978, Crane decided to make his own bid for the White House. While he had early success, in 1979 Crane's campaign ran into financial woes, and his reputation was tarnished when William Loeb, an archconservative publisher of the *Manchester Union Leader*, ran a full-page editorial accusing Crane of womanizing and drinking too heavily. Crane pulled out of the race by April of 1980. Philip Crane was the longest-serving Republican member of the House of Representatives at the time of his defeat in the 2004 election.

Crane's conservatism was part of his family heritage. His father, a psychiatrist, was a speechwriter for Senator Robert Taft, Sr., and he wrote a syndicated advice column dubbed "The Worry Clinic." Philip Crane spent two years in the Army, and returned to earn a doctorate in history from Indiana University. Prior to his political career, he taught at Bradley University in Peoria, and at Westminster Academy. After marrying Arlene Catherine Johnson in 1959, the two had eight children.

Crane died of lung cancer on November 8, 2014, at age eighty-four. His wife, Arlene and a daughter, Rachel, predeceased him. He is survived by seven children and numerous grandchildren.

*See Current Biography 1980.*

# Mario Cuomo

**Born:** New York, New York; June 15, 1932
**Died:** New York, New York; January 1, 2015
**Occupation:** Politician and former governor of New York State

Larger than life, and as popular nationally as he was in New York State, Mario Cuomo was an icon of American liberalism. He served as the governor of New York State for twelve years, from 1983 through 1994. While many considered Cuomo a strong contender for national office, he always claimed that he owed his complete attention to the state of New York. President Bill Clinton came close to nominating him to the US Supreme Court, but Cuomo pulled out of contention at the last minute.

Mario Cuomo was born and raised in Queens, New York, the third child of Andrea and Immaculata Cuomo who had emigrated from Salerno, Italy. He attended St. John's University on a scholarship grant that he supplemented by playing semiprofessional basketball. He received his LL.B. degree in 1956 at the top of his class. By 1963, Cuomo was a partner in a law firm and an adjunct professor at St. John's University. Cuomo quickly earned a reputation as an advocate for the working-class poor and as a master negotiator. He was appointed New York's secretary of state in 1975, the same year that he was appointed a special prosecutor for nursing home violations. In 1977, with his unsuccessful bid for New York City mayor, Cuomo earned the recognition of Governor Carey, who selected

him as New York's lieutenant governor. Cuomo won national acclaim when he gave an inspired keynote address at the 1984 Democratic National Convention.

While Cuomo was a popular governor, he was dogged by gridlock in the divided state legislature. He was criticized for not instituting innovative programs to deal with such problems as the AIDS epidemic and the growth in crack cocaine addiction. When New York's economy started to falter in the late 1980s, Cuomo instituted budget cuts, but was reluctant to slash social welfare programs too severely. State reserve funds began to dwindle and deficits mounted. He lost his fourth bid to the governorship to George Pataki.

By the end of his life, Mario Cuomo's son, Andrew, was elected governor of New York, the first father and son pair to hold the office. Mario Cuomo died from heart failure, at his home in Manhattan, New York, on January 1, 2015—the day his son, Andrew, was sworn in for his second term as governor of New York. Survivors include his wife, Matilda, his five children—Chris, Madeline, Margaret, Maria, and Andrew—and fourteen grandchildren.

*See Current Biography 1983.*

# Alvin Ralph "Al" Dark

**Born:** Comanche, Oklahoma; January 7, 1922
**Died:** Easley, South Carolina; November 13, 2014
**Occupation:** American professional baseball player and manager

An extraordinary athlete who excelled in any sport he tried, Alvin Dark attended Louisiana State University in 1941, on an athletic scholarship. Dark played varsity basketball, hit .350 in baseball, and led the football team in rushing, passing, and punting from the halfback position. Upon graduation, he was actually drafted by the NFL's Philadelphia Eagles, but chose to sign with baseball's Boston Braves. As a pro baseball player, he was a three-time National League All-Star shortstop with three solid .300 seasons. He played professional ball for fourteen years, with impressive complete tallies, (incorporating his minor league figures), of 2,089 hits, a .289 batting average, 126 home runs, 727 runs-batted-in, and a fielding average of .959. By the end of his playing career, Dark had played with the Boston

Braves (and named rookie of the year), the New York Giants (where he was a three-time All Star shortstop and team captain), the St. Louis Cardinals, the Chicago Cubs, Philadelphia Phillies, and, finally, the Milwaukee Braves. He played in three World Series contests.

Dark began his new career as a team manager in 1960. The following year the Giants won the National League pennant. Dark went on to manage the Chicago Cubs, the Kansas City Athletics, and the Cleveland Indians, and the San Diego Padres. As manager he led his teams to two world series contests.

Despite such an impressive record, Dark will probably be remembered most for the off-hand (and he claimed, misquoted) remark that "so many Negro and Spanish-speaking players on the team … are just not able to perform up to the white player when it comes to mental alertness." At the time, Dark was the team manager for the New York Giants. Though Willie Mays and Jackie Robinson strongly defended him, even saw him as a mentor whom they greatly respected, Dark was branded a bigot. His reputation was further damaged when it was revealed that Dark had an ongoing affair with a stewardess (who became his second wife). Though he was reluctant to break up his first family (on religious grounds, he opposed divorce), he followed through, finally marrying Jacolyn Troy following her attempted suicide.

Dark died of Alzheimer's disease on November 13, 2014, at his home in Easley, South Carolina. He is survived by his second wife, Jacolyn Troy Dark; four children from his first marriage; two adopted children from his second marriage; and numerous grandchildren and great-grandchildren.

*See Current Biography 1975.*

# Oscar de la Renta

**Born:** Santo Domingo, Dominican Republic; July 22, 1932

**Died:** Kent, Connecticut; October 20, 2014

**Occupation:** Fashion designer

From common sidewalks to the red carpet, and from entertainers to heads of state, Oscar de la Renta was a superstar in the world of high fashion. Not only did this fashion icon dress celebrities, he became a celebrity himself. When Oscar de la Renta, (whose birth name was Oscar Aristides Renta Fiallo) left his native Dominican Republic at the age of 19, it was to attend art school in Madrid, where he hoped to become an abstract painter. As a means of income, he drew clothing for newspapers and fashion magazines. Mrs. John Lodge, the wife of America's Ambassador to Spain, noticed his drawings, and was so impressed that she commissioned him to design the dress for her daughter's debut. Both the dress and its wearer graced the cover of *Life* Magazine. With that encouragement, de la Renta abandoned painting to join Cristobal Balenciaga, the world-famous Madrid house of couture, though he had little fashion experience. He moved to America in the early 1960s to work as a designer for Elizabeth Arden, but a few scant years later, he bought into the Seventh Avenue firm of Jane Derby Inc., which catered to women who bought simple aristocratic clothing with a custom-order look.

While de la Renta has received numerous awards and accolades, one of his greatest rewards was his invitation to dress America's first ladies. Beginning with Jacqueline Kennedy, de la Renta earned entry into White House dressing rooms, becoming good friends with Nancy Reagan and Hillary Clinton. Mr. de la Renta received two Coty awards honoring his influence in the fashion industry, and was named to the Coty Hall of Fame. He also received a lifetime achievement award from the Council of Fashion Designers of America, the Neiman Marcus Award, and Italy's Tiberio d' Oro. De la Renta was also a philanthropist and patron of the arts. He founded an orphanage in his native country, where he found and adopted his son, Moises. He was a board member of the Metropolitan Opera, Carnegie Hall and WNET. In 1980, de la Renta donated his services to redesign the Boy Scouts' uniforms.

De la Renta died from cancer at his home in Kent, Connecticut on October 20, 2014. He is survived by his second wife, Annette Engelhard, and his four children.

*See Current Biography 1970.*

# Suleyman Demirel

**Born:** Islamkoy, Isparta, Turkey; November 1, 1924

**Died:** Ankara, Turkey; June 17, 2015

**Occupation:** Former Turkish prime minister

With seven terms as Turkey's prime minister, and one term as president, Suleyman Demirel was a political survivor who was known for his ability to mediate between rivals and to build coalitions. He survived two military coups and two attempts on his life.

Demirel considered himself a "peasant boy," born to an Anatolian farmer. He was a brilliant student who became a civil engineer following his graduation from the University of Istanbul with a specialty in hydraulics. He continued his training in the United States, and would return in 1954 as an Eisenhower Exchange Fellow. He was appointed director-general of the state water works until he joined the army in 1960. He had little interest in politics until 1961 when he was elected to the National Assembly (the lower house of the national parliament). He was elected prime minister in 1965. At forty-one, he was the youngest man to hold the office.

Turkey is a country where the East meets the West, both literally and figuratively, so many of the challenges Demirel faced as prime minister concerned Turkey's identity as a Muslim country that was also a member among the powerhouse nations of the United Nations. Conflict arose between the ideals of progress and tradition. There was religious unrest and tension with Turkey's neighbors. Demirel's career withstood two coup attempts. He was ousted from power in 1971, only to launch an incredible comeback. Following another coup in 1980, Demirel was banned from politics, but a referendum in 1987 plowed the way for his 1991 comeback. He served as Turkey's president from 1993 to 2000. He is remembered as a taciturn leader who upheld traditional values while, at the same time, generating economic growth through his belief in private enterprise.

*See Current Biography 1980.*

# Assia Djebar (Fatima-Zohra Imalayan)

**Born:** Cherchell, Algeria; June 30, 1936

**Died:** Paris, France; February 7, 2015

**Occupation:** Algerian novelist, film maker, translator

A French-language novelist who chronicled Muslim women's struggles for emancipation, Assia Djebar was often considered a strong contender for the Nobel Prize for literature. Her candor was shocking to some, and uncharacteristic for a woman so devoted to her faith, as she explored the role of women in Algeria's struggle for independence from France.

Raised in a small, seaport town on the Algerian coast, Djebar was one of only two girls to attend a Quranic private school where she acquired a deep sense of faith. She was the first Algerian woman to attend the prestigious École Normale Supérieure (Higher Teacher Training School) in France, and she earned a history degree from Le Sorbonne. At twenty, Djebar joined a student strike to support Algeria's struggle for independence from France. (Her brother was imprisoned in France.) In 1958, Djebar married a fellow resistance fighter, Ahmed Ould-Rouïs. (They later divorced and Djebar eventually married fellow writer, Malek Alloula.) She chose to write under a pseudonym to save her family from embarrassment. However, a spelling error from "Djebbar" to "Djebar" changed the meaning of her name from "one who praises Allah," to "one who heals." Djebar taught history at the University of Algiers, and was the head of the university's French section. In 1995, Djebar moved to the United States and taught French literature at Louisiana State University, and later, at New York University.

Djebar's awards are many, and include the International Prize of Palmi, the Peace Prize of the Frankfurt Book Fair, the International Critics' Prize at Venice Biennale, the International Literary Neustadt Prize, and the Marguerite Yourcenar Prize for Literature. In 1978, Djebar directed the film *La nouba des femmes du Mont Chenoua* ("The Mount Chenoua Band of Women"), for which she won the prestigious Grand Prize at the Venice Film Festival. In 2005, she was elected to the French Academie Francaise,

France's top literary institution, the fifth woman to be so honored, and the first Algerian.

Assia Djebar died on February 7, 2015. Her daughter, Djalila, survives her.

*Note: There is no current EBSCO biography.*

# Carl Djerassi

**Born:** Vienna, Austria; October 29, 1923
**Died:** San Francisco, California; January 30, 2015
**Occupation:** American chemist, professor, and author

Often referred to as the "father of the pill," Carl Djerassi's work spawned a worldwide cultural revolution in human sexuality. Under the enormity of that accomplishment, his many additional scientific discoveries are often overlooked. At the tender age of nineteen, Djerassi synthesized one of the first antihistamines. He pioneered research in mass spectrometry, and developed environmentally friendly methods for pest control. He was also a novelist, poet, and playwright, coining the term "science-in-fiction" to describe his writing genre, that tackled the personal and social dilemmas, the moral and ethical implications, brought about by achievements in science.

Carl Djerassi was born in Vienna, Austria to Jewish parents, both physicians, who fled as the Nazis gained power. He and his mother traveled to England, then the United States; his father returned to his native Bulgaria. (His parents were divorced, something Djerassi only learned about many years later.) Arriving in America with no money, Djerassi wrote to Eleanor Roosevelt, explaining his situation and requesting financial assistance with his education. He was offered a scholarship to Presbyterian college in Missouri. He completed his chemistry degrees from Kenyon College, and later, the University of Wisconsin.

Carl Djerassi had not set out to research birth control when, at twenty-six, he went to Mexico City as the associate director of research for the pharmaceutical company, Syntex. He was actually looking to produce a wonder drug for treating arthritis, and he needed to find an inexpensive way to synthesize cortisone. At that time, a key element—diosgenin, necessary for developing cortisone—could only be extracted from slaughterhouse animals, a costly endeavor. In an effort to reduce costs, his research involved isolating diosgenin from native yams. As it turned out, diosgenin is also used in preparing progestogen, a female sex hormone. Djerassi learned that synthetic progestogen was much more potent than the natural occurring hormone. He sent his synthetic progestrogen to three colleagues— Min Chuch Chang, Gregory Pincus, and John Rock—who conducted research on the drug's efficacy in birth control. Their work resulted in the world's first oral contraceptive.

Djerassi received the National Medal of Science in 1973, and was conferred eighteen honorary doctorates. He won the first Wolf Prize in Chemistry, the Priestly Medal (the American Chemical Society's highest award), and he was one of the first scientists to receive both the National Medal of Science and the National Medal of Technology. He was the author of more than 1,200 scientific publications and seven monographs. He taught at Wayne State University early in his career, moving to Stanford University in 1959, where he remained an emeritus professor of chemistry.

Carl Djerassi died from liver and bone cancer on January 30, 2015. His son, Dale Djerassi; his stepdaughter, Leah Middlebrook; and a grandson, Alexander M. Djerassi, survive him.

*See Current Biography 2001.*

# E. L. Doctorow (Edgar Lawrence Doctorow)

**Born:** New York, New York; January 6, 1931
**Died:** New York, New York; July 21, 2015
**Occupation:** Writer, author

According to the Modern Library editorial board, author E. L. Doctorow was considered one of the best American novelists of the twentieth century. His historical fiction often included real-life characters like Harry Houdini, J. P. Morgan, Sigmund Freud, and Booker T. Washington, who interacted with his fictional characters. His most widely acclaimed novels include *The Book of Daniel*, *Ragtime*, *Billy Bathgate*, and *The March*.

From the time Edgar Lawrence Doctorow was in the third grade, he wanted to become a writer. He attended the selective Bronx High School of Science (where he worked on the literary magazine *Dynamo*), then Kenyon College in Ohio for his bachelor's degree. He served two years in the US Army before he found work as a reader for Columbia Pictures. (His work at Columbia inspired him to write his first novel, *Welcome to Hard Times*, a parody of the numerous western scripts he had to read.) He eventually worked as an editor with the new American Library, and rose to the level of editor-in-chief, then vice president at Dial Press where he worked with such notable writers as Norman Mailer, James Baldwin, and Richard Condon.

He left Dial Press in 1969 so he could finish his third novel, *The Book of Daniel*, which would become his first best seller. (Based roughly on the Rosenberg spy case, the novel would be made into the movie *Daniel*, starring Timothy Hutton, in 1983.) In 1975, Doctorow published another blended fictional historical hit, *Ragtime*, for which he won the National Book Critics Circle Award. The film version would pick up an Oscar nomination in 1981, and a stage adaptation would earn a Tony nomination for a Broadway musical in 1998. Doctorow received a PEN/Faulkner Award for fiction for his subsequent novel, *Billy Bathgate*, also adapted for a movie starring Dustin Hoffman. In all, Doctorow won three National Book Critics Circle Awards, a National Book Award, two PEN/Faulkner Awards, a gold medal for fiction from the American Academy of Arts and Letters, and a Library of Congress Prize for American Fiction, among others. He was also inducted into the New York State Writers Hall of Fame.

E. L. Doctorow died from lung cancer on July 21, 2015. His wife of sixty years, Helen Esther Setzer, and their three children, Caroline, Richard, and Jenny, survive him.

*See Current Biography 1976.*

# Ivan Doig

**Born:** White Sulpher Springs, Montana; June 27, 1939

**Died:** Seattle, Washington; April 9, 2015

**Occupation:** American author

Often characterized as a "western" writer, Ivan Doig's stories, whether fiction, non-fiction, or autobiographical, chronicle a hard life in a bygone era on the plains of western Montana. Ivan Doig wrote thirteen novels, and four works of non-fiction, including his highly acclaimed autobiography, *This House of Sky: Landscapes of a Western Mind.*

Ivan Doig was an only child, born to a sheep ranch hand, Charlie Doig, and a ranch cook, Berneta Ringer Doig. His mother died from an asthma attack on his sixth birthday, and his father tried raising him alone for several years, before giving in and asking for help from Doig's maternal grandmother, Elizabeth "Bessie" Ringer. With the help of his high-school English teachers, Doig received a scholarship to Northwestern University in Evanston, Illinois, where he earned a B.S. and an M.A. degree in journalism. He spent one year in Texas, on active duty with the US Air Force Reserve, before finding work composing editorials for a newspaper chain, and eventually, as assistant-editor at *Rotarian* magazine. In 1965, he married Carol Dean Muller. The two moved to Seattle, and Doig enrolled at the University of Washington, receiving a Ph.D. in US history in 1969.

His father and grandmother died in the early 1970s, prompting Doig to write a memoir documenting his father's generation. The memoir, *This House of Sky: Landscapes of a Western Mind*, was nominated for a National Book Award. His first three novels—a trilogy—chronicle the first century of Montana's statehood, following the McCaskill family. All of Doig's writing has garnered praise for his powerful descriptions and musicality. In 2007, Doig received the Wallace Stegner Award. Often compared to Wallace Stegner, Doig resisted his characterization as a "western" author, stating that he never thought of himself as a western writer, claiming on his website "to me, language—the substance on the page, that poetry under the prose—is the ultimate 'region,' the true home, for a writer."

Ivan Doig died from multiple myeloma on April 9, 2015. His wife, Carol Muller Doig survives him.

*See Current Biography 2011.*

# Nelson Doubleday

**Born:** Oyster Bay, New York; July 20, 1933

**Died:** Locust Valley, New York; June 17, 2015

**Occupation:** Publisher, baseball executive

Nelson Doubleday was the grandson of Frank Nelson Doubleday, founder of one of the major American publishing dynasties. Working his way up the executive ladder Nelson Doubleday became the company president in 1978. Two years later, he purchased the floundering, last place New York Mets baseball franchise, which he would transform into world champions within a few short years.

Nelson Doubleday was born into privilege, attending the most elite private schools in the Northeast. In 1955, he graduated from Princeton University with a degree in economics. After serving in the US Air Force for several years, he started at the "bottom" with an entry-level job at his father's publishing house—at that time, the largest hardcover book publisher in the country. Having been groomed for leadership, he was named executive vice-president in charge of sales in 1967. By May of 1978, Doubleday was elected chief executive officer of Doubleday and Company, publishing more that seven hundred titles a year.

In 1980, Doubleday became the majority owner of the New York Mets baseball team, putting up eighty-percent of the then record $21.1 million. (The other owners were Fred Wilpon and the City Investing Corporation.) By 1984, the Mets became a profit-making pennant contender, winning the pennant in 1986. By that time, receipts at Shea Stadium exceeded $6 million.

Doubleday's publishing company did not fair so well, as revenue began a downward spiral with book sales nearly half that in 1978. Some observers blamed the decline on Doubleday for paying too much attention to the Mets. Doubleday stepped aside, becoming chairman of the board.

When it came time to sell his fifty-percent share of the Mets franchise, he argued bitterly with his partner, Fred Wilpon, thinking that the franchise was undervalued.

Nelson Doubleday died at home from a short bout of pneumonia. He was eighty-one. Doubleday's wife, Sandra, four daughters, two stepchildren and two sisters survive him.

*See Current Biography 1987.*

# William Donlan (Don) Edwards

**Born:** San Jose, California; January 6, 1915
**Died:** Carmel, California; October 1, 2015
**Occupation:** US Congressman

One of the most effective liberal members of Congress, Don Edwards spent thirty-two years protecting the civil and constitutional rights of women and minorities for equal access to housing, voting, and jobs. As chairman of the Judiciary Committee's subcommittee on civil and constitutional rights for twenty years, he shepherded some of the country's most important civil rights bills through the legislative process.

Founder of a successful California land title firm, Edwards was voted President of the Young Republicans in Santa Clara County in 1950. By the time he ran for Congress in 1962, however, he'd become a Democrat, disillusioned with the Grand Old Pary (GOP) and the House Committee on Un-American Activities (HUAC); after his election, he fought to abolish it, finally succeeding in 1975.

One of his first votes as a freshman congressman was for the landmark Civil Rights Act of 1964. He vigorously backed the Voting Rights Act of 1965, and traveled to Mississippi with the Freedom Riders during the height of the civil rights turmoil. In 1982, he helped draft an extension of the Voting Rights Act that committed the federal government to preventing abuses in states with a history of turning black voters away from the ballot box.

An early environmentalist, in 1968 he introduced legislation that created the 21,000-acre South San Francisco Bay National Wildlife Refuge, which would bear his name upon his retirement from Congress in 1995.

Among other bills he helped pass were the Fair Housing Act, the Americans With Disabilities Act, and the Civil Rights Act of 1991. He fought against domestic overreach in intelligence gathering. In 1971, Edwards assumed the role of House floor manager for the Equal Rights Amendment (ERA). In 1978, when it became clear that three quarters of states would not vote for the amendment within the seven years allotted, he pushed through a 39-month extension, though the ERA failed to win approval by the new cutoff date of June 30, 1983. Still, he was considered the "father of the ERA."

As the congressional representative for part of Silicon Valley, Edwards was honored in 1982 by the Semiconductor Industry Association for his 'interest in and support of high technology industries." He received the Hubert H. Humphrey Civil Rights Award that year for his "devoted service in the cause of equality."

A 1936 graduate of Stanford University, Edwards attended Stanford University Law School.

From 1940 to 1941, he was a special agent with the Federal Bureau of Investigation (FBI). In World War II, he fought in the South Pacific. An early opponent of the Vietnam War, he also opposed apartheid in South Africa, and the 1991 war in the Persian Gulf. He became known as "the conscience of Congress." In 2003, he was awarded the Congressional Distinguished Service Award.

Edwards died on October 1, 2015, and is survived by four sons.

*See Current Biography 1983.*

# Edward M. Egan

**Born:** Oak Park, Illinois; April 2, 1932
**Died:** New York, New York; March 5, 2015
**Occupation:** American cardinal of the Roman Catholic Church

The ninth Catholic archbishop of the Archdiocese of New York, Cardinal Edward Egan will be remembered for his restoration of financial stability to the archdiocese of New York. However, he will also be remembered for closing well-loved Catholic schools, and the consolidation of parishes in order to meet his financial goals. He was also accused of mishandling a string of accusations of sexual abuse at the hands of Catholic priests. A staunch conservative, Egan was outspoken on the issues of sex education, abortion, and birth control, scolding New York City Mayor, Rudolph Giuliani, for taking communion during the pope's visit, because Giuliani supported abortion rights. He criticized Father Robert Nugent and Sister Jeannine Gramick for ministering to lesbian women and gay men, and their families.

Cardinal Egan was ordained as a priest in 1957, after graduating from a seven-year program that combined traditional college courses with four years of theological study. Some years later, he graduated summa cum laude with a degree in canonical law from Gregorian University in Rome. He was a canonical lawyer and judge, spending nearly half of his career in Rome, following an executive trajectory. He returned to the United States to serve as secretary to Chicago's John Cardinal Cody, who supported civil rights and school desegregation. Egan was active in interfaith organizations. From 1973 until 1985, Egan was a judge for the Sacred Roman Rota, a court in the Vatican's judiciary. In 1985,

he was appointed as vicar for education under New York's Archbishop John O'Connor, and in 1988, he became bishop of the Bridgeport, Connecticut diocese of Fairfield County.

The late 1990s saw a series of lawsuits brought against the Church, for alleged sex abuse by priests. Egan was sharply criticized, as he appeared to minimize the suffering of the victims. In 2002, he offered something of an apology on behalf of the church, but retracted his apology a decade later.

Egan was the cardinal of New York on September 11, 2001, when terrorists brought down the World Trade Center buildings. He spent the day distributing rosaries to the living and anointing the dead. Many felt it was Egan's finest hour, as he urged levelheaded caution to an angry and hurt population. He attended many of the funerals of those killed that day.

Cardinal Egan retired in 2009, the first archbishop in the archdiocese to do so, since his predecessors had died in office. Cardinal Egan died of cardiac arrest on March 5, 2015.

*See Current Biography 2001.*

# Suzette Haden Elgin

**Born:** Louisiana, Missouri; November 18, 1936
**Died:** January 27, 2015
**Occupation:** American linguist, science fiction writer, educator, and poet

Suzette Haden Elgin was a linguist who believed in the power of language to transform an individual's perceptions of reality. She was a specialist in applied psycholinguistics, which involves the interrelationships between language, thinking, and culture. Elgin considered language the most powerful instrument for social change. She wrote more than thirty books including eleven science fiction novels, a series of self-help books beginning with *The Gentle Art of Verbal Self-Defense,* reference works on linguistics, and a handbook for writing science fiction poetry. Elgin went so far as to create a new language, called Laadan, for her fictional worlds.

Suzette Elgin was raised in Jefferson City, Missouri. Her mother was a teacher, and her father was a lawyer, (as was her grandfather and four uncles), and Elgin credits her passion for language to the stimulating conversation she grew up with. In high school, she studied numerous languages, in an effort to shed what she called the "ignorant hillbilly myth." She attended the University of Chicago, earning an Academy of American Poets Award in her first year. In 1958, she won a Eugene Saxon Memorial Trust Fellowship in poetry from *Harper's* magazine. Elgin married young, and found work as a secretary and translator to help with her husband's education. After the birth of two daughters and a son, her husband (Peter Haden) died at the age of 29. About a year later, she married George Elgin, a sales manager.

Suzette Elgin wrote her science fiction novels to help pay for school as she pursued her Ph.D. in linguists from the University of California (UC) at San Diego, where she eventually became a faculty member. In 1978, Elgin founded the Science Fiction Poetry Association, and in 1981, she founded the Ozark Center for Language Studies, an institution dedicated to reducing violence and educating the public about linguistics. In 2013, the Science Fiction Poetry Association created the Elgin Award in her honor.

Suzette Elgin died on January 27, 2015 from the effects of fronto-temporal dementia.

*See Current Biography 2006.*

# Helen Eustis

**Born:** Cincinnati, Ohio; December 31, 1916
**Died:** New York, New York; January 11, 2015
**Occupation:** American author and translator

Helen Eustis is remembered as a versatile writer whose first novel, *The Horizontal Man*, won her an Edgar Award for best first mystery novel of 1946. Her second novel, *The Fool Killer*, was adapted for a film by the same title, starring Anthony Perkins and Edward Albert.

Helen Eustis was an only child when her mother died in the 1918 flu epidemic. Her stockbroker father remarried providing her with two stepsisters and a stepbrother. Challenged with adjusting to a ready-made family, Eustis found refuge in books, and claimed that she started writing as a means of reestablishing her own sense of importance for herself. Eustis attended Smith College as an art major, and was encouraged to continue writing when she was awarded a medal for a novel she wrote (a novel that remained unpublished). She studied psychology at Columbia University, and wrote advertising copy for several companies, but her professional ambitions were put on hold when she married her former English professor, Alfred Young Fisher, and had a son. She began writing short stories that appeared in *New Yorker, Mademoiselle, Harper's Bazaar,* and *Saturday Evening Post,* among others. Eustis won wide acclaim with her two novels, *The Horizontal Man,* and *The Fool Killer.* In addition, she published a collection of short stories, *The Captains and the Kings Depart,* and a children's story called *The Rider on a Pale Horse,* parts of which were first published in *The Saturday Evening Post.* Another novel, *Mr. Death and the Redheaded Woman,* was published in 1983.

In her later years, Eustis translated books from French into English. She was twice divorced, and had one son. Helen Eustis died on January 11, 2015 in New York City. Her son, Adam Fisher, survives her, along with three grandchildren.

*See Current Biography 1955.*

# Kenan Evren

**Born:** Alasenhir, Ottoman Empire;   July 17, 1917
**Died:** Ankara, Turkey; May 9, 2015
**Occupation:** President of the Republic of Turkey, military officer

Kenan Evren is remembered as the leader of the 1980 Turkish coup d'état that dissolved the Turkish Parliament, and left the country under military rule through the National Security Council. At the time, Evren was the chief of the general staff, and led the country until he was elected president in 1982 for a seven-year term.

Evren was born in western Turkey after his parents emigrated from the Balkans. His father was a Muslim imam, though Evren was educated in military schools, graduating from the School of Artillery and the Army Staff College. He advanced rapidly, becoming chief of staff of the Turkish Brigade of the North Atlantic Treaty Organization (NATO) Forces during the Korean War. He was later promoted to chief of army operations, and attained the rank of general in 1964.

The 1980 coup is considered one of the bloodiest in Turkey's modern history, though it did not start out that way. In fact, it was a bloodless coup until the military began imprisoning political agitators. Over half a million people were imprisoned. Three hundred died under torture and bad prison conditions. Fifty were executed. As president, Evren suspended numerous human rights for the sake of political stability, and changed the constitution that he claimed was "too luxurious" for the current climate.

However, his leadership helped restore order at a time of great upheaval when leftist Marxist and ultra-nationalist parliamentarians were coming to blows in the streets. Following the coup, Turkey's economy grew and Turkey became an important market for the West. Evren promoted women's rights, including the legalization of abortion.

Evren remained a controversial figure, hated by liberals but also lauded for keeping Turkey from utter anarchy and civil war. In 2010, his immunity from prosecution was reneged and Evren was charged and convicted of "crimes against the state." Stripped of his rank, he was sentenced to life imprisonment, a largely symbolic gesture since Evren was permanently hospitalized after his large intestine was removed.

Kenan Evren died of multiple organ failure on May 9, 2015. His three daughters survive him.

*See Current Biography 1984.*

## John B. Fairchild

**Born:** Newark, New Jersey; March 6, 1927
**Died:** New York, New York; February 27, 2015
**Occupation:** American publisher and fashion critic

John Fairchild was the president of Fairchild Publications, which published several trade journals, including the popular *Women's Wear Daily* (*WWD*). The brash Fairchild was anything but politic, pulling no punches, in both assessing and influencing fashion trends. Under his aegis, the gossipy, irreverent trade journal became the most influential publication on American fashion, proving that fashion editors, as well as designers and retailers, could dictate fashion to substantial numbers of women.

Fairchild Publications, founded by John Fairchild's grandfather, Edmund Fairchild, did not initially attract young John, who had aspirations of becoming a scientist. He attended

Princeton University, but found he had no aptitude for math, and, after a stint as an Army speechwriter at the Pentagon, he graduated from Princeton, with a degree in humanities. In 1951, he began working as a reporter for *WWD*, covering the New York retail scene. He earned fame—or notoriety—by panning top designers' collections, printing sketches before release dates, and reporting unsubstantiated gossip. He became publisher in 1960 and, while maintaining factual, useful trade stories, he added photographs of high society, with sketches, notes on fashion trends, and gossip. He even introduced reviews of plays, books, films, and restaurants in the market news column known as "Eye."

He was ruthless (and some would say rude) about the wives of politicians, in particular, assigning them catty monikers. Mrs. Nixon became "Her Goodiness," and Mrs. Johnson was called "Her Efficiency." Once, when asked by reporters if she read *WWD*, Jacqueline Kennedy Onassis replied with a sigh, "I try not to."

John Fairchild made stars of fashion designers, such as Oscar de la Renta, and Yves St. Laurent. Those whom he panned have remained more obscure. He remained chairman of the board for thirty years, "retiring" in 1972, though he continued to write under the pseudonym Louise J. Esterhazy. He also founded the well-respected fashion magazine W.

John Fairchild died on February 27, 2015. His wife, three sons, and a daughter survive him.

*See Current Biography 1971.*

## Malcolm Fraser

**Born:** Toorak, Victoria, Australia; May 21, 1930
**Died:** March 20, 2015
**Occupation:** Former Australian Prime Minister

Malcolm Fraser rose to the office of prime minister following Australia's gravest constitutional crisis to date. He was elected on December 13, 1975, by a record margin, following the dissolution of Parliament due to a stalemate between the Labor and Liberal political parties, after the Labor Prime Minister, Gough Whitlam, was embroiled in a scandal of Watergate proportions. Fraser, the leader of the Liberal party, ordered the liberal senate to withhold funding, effectively denying vital funds to the opposition Labor party, and the Labor prime minister, effectively bringing the government to a standstill. In a stunning move, the governor general, Sir John Kerr, dissolved parliament, and appointed Fraser interim prime minister, to organize a caretaker government. The ensuing election campaign was hostile. Workers walked off their jobs. Fraser and Kerr were intended victims of letter bombs. However, Fraser's liberal party won by a landslide.

Malcolm Fraser was born to a barrister and gentleman farmer, descended from aristocratic Jacobites who fled Scotland in 1745. His grandfather, Sir Simon Fraser, was one of the first men to represent Victoria State in the senate. Fraser earned an M.A. degree in philosophy, economics, and political science from Magdalen College, Oxford University, in 1952. In 1955, he won a seat in parliament—the youngest member at that time. For ten years, he sat on the backbench until, in 1966, he was appointed minister for the army. He supported conscription and was a hawk on Vietnam. He ordered the controversial build-up of Australian defense capabilities in the Indian Ocean, in response to a growing Soviet naval presence in the area.

During his tenure as prime minister, Malcolm Fraser was a champion of the rights of indigenous people. He supported multiculturalism, and set up a national broadcasting station, SBS, to provide multilingual services. He formed close ties with African leaders, especially in opposition to apartheid. After his eight-years as Australia's prime minister, Fraser continued pro-humanitarian international efforts. He was the chairman of a UN group of advisors on issues of African commodity markets. He created the international aid network, "Care Australia," and was an international observer in elections in Tanzania, Pakistan, and Bangladesh. Fraser broke from his party in his later years, opposing its stance against refugees and asylum-seekers.

Malcolm Fraser died on March 20, 2015. Tamie, Fraser's wife of fifty-nine years, and his four children survive him.

*See Current Biography 1976.*

# John Freeman

**Born:** London, England; February 19, 1915
**Died:** London, England; December 20, 2014

**Occupation:** Diplomat, politician, journalist, television personality

John Freeman was a man of many trades, and he mastered them all. He was a politician, a diplomat, a writer and editor, a chairman, a television personality, and a university professor. Though he was an intensely private man, he spent much of his life in the limelight. Success seemed to come easily to Freeman who did not pursue fame, prestige or high office as much as they seemed to pursue him. He claimed that he only stood for Parliament because he was sure he would lose. He was wrong. As a decorated war hero, addressing Parliament, Freeman's eloquence reportedly moved Winston Churchill to tears. As a politician, Freeman became a champion of the working class and a proponent of Socialism, serving in a number of sub-cabinet positions. He was such a prominent figure that his peers considered him a potential Prime Minister.

Freeman, the politician, became disenchanted when the government chose to trim National Health Service benefits. He resigned from politics to become, first, Deputy Editor and then Editor at the *New Statesman,* a left wing, Labour Party weekly. Freeman moved the paper slightly to the right, to appeal to a broader readership. He worked with the BBC on numerous radio and television productions, becoming a household name when he hosted "Face to Face" where he conducted his interviews facing his subjects, and away from the camera. Freeman earned a reputation as "a merciless inquisitor," interviewing such greats as Bertrand Russell, Martin Luther King, Carl Jung, and Evelyn Waugh. The inquisitor revealed little about himself, however. Freeman was so intensely private that the *New Statesman* has since characterized him as "pathologically private." (March 7, 2013) Freeman's radio and television connections led to his appointment as Chair of the Independent Television News, Governor of the British Film Institute, and Vice-President of the Royal Television Society.

Though he did not seek the position, Freeman was appointed High Commissioner to India in 1965, and then, in 1968, he was transferred to the United States as the U. K. Ambassador.

A popular fixture in Washington, Freeman befriended Henry Kissinger and President Richard Nixon (whom he had vilified scant years earlier in the *New Standard*). In his later years, he became a visiting professor of International Relations at U.C. Davis in California.

An attractive man with an erect bearing, Freeman was the epitome of "suave" and "debonair," listed as one of Britain's Ten Best Dressed Men. He was married four times. His third wife, Catherine Dove, a gregarious woman, seventeen years his junior, is often credited with much of her husband's success as a diplomat.

John Freeman died at a nursing facility in London on December 20, 2014.

*See Current Biography 1969.*

# Jane Freilicher

**Born:** New York, NY; November 29, 1924
**Died:** New York, NY; December 9, 2014
**Occupation:** Artist

Though Jane Freilicher denied being a landscape artist, (once quipping "if I were a landscape painter, I'd probably go to the Alps"), she was a still life artist. Art critic Amei Wallach observed in *Newsday* (September 14, 1986) "Jane Freilicher [was] a still life painter who compose[d] landscapes as if they were still lifes." Subjects that might have come off as quaint or facile in another artist's hands, (most of her paintings invariably included a vase of flowers and a landscape), evoked a certain wistfulness and anxiety about time and change. Behind the easy visual appeal of her light-drenched paintings of Long Island meadows and marshes, tranquil and unpeopled cityscapes, lurks a serious debate on the nature of reality. The influence of the great painters Henri Matisse, Pierre Bonnard, and Edouard Vuillard are undeniable. Freilicher managed to blend abstract expressionism and realism, invention, and observed fact into a fluid, lyrical style all her own.

Jane Freilicher was a painter among poets—a member of the so-called second generation of New York School, a community of painters, writers, choreographers, and musicians—that included such greats as the poets John Ashberry, Kenneth Koch, Frank O'Hara, and Ted Berrigan. She had a life-long friendship with the painter and musician, Larry Rivers, whom she met through her first husband, Jack Freilicher

(whom she married right out of high school at age 17). Though her marriage was annulled a few years later, her friendship with Larry Rivers lasted throughout her life. And it was Rivers who persuaded Freilicher to join the Hans Hofmann school of fine arts. Her work as Hofmann's protégé was pivotal to her craft. Art was not easy for Freilicher who explained that she really struggled with her painting. For her, "every inch of a painting is a decision," but she was driven to "do beautiful things." She painted not to express herself, but to discover her own feelings.

Jane Freilicher married her second husband, Joseph Hazan, in 1957, and was with him for over fifty years. He died in 2012. Freilicher died on December 9, 2014, in New York City, and is survived by her daughter Elizabeth Hazan. She was ninety years old.

*See Current Biography 1989.*

# Brian Friel

**Born:** Killyclogher, Tyrone, Northern Ireland; January 9, 1929
**Died:** Green Castle, County Donegal, Ireland; October 2, 2015
**Occupation:** Irish playwright, director, author

Brian Friel was one of the greatest playwrights of his time, often characterized as an Irish Chekov. His plays have been performed by some of the greatest actors in contemporary theater, such as Liam Neeson and Meryl Streep. His play, *Dancing at Lughnasa* won three Tony Awards in 1992, including best play, and would be made into a film starring Meryl Streep.

It has never been determined whether he was born on the 9th or 10th of January. He was raised in Londonderry, Ireland, the grandson of illiterate, rural peasants. He followed in his father's footsteps, becoming a teacher after attending St. Columb's College (an alma mater he shared with the great poet, Seamus Heaney, and Nobel Peace Prize recipient, John Hume). Another graduate and fellow writer, Seamus Deane, would help Friel and Heaney, found the Field Day Theater Company in 1980, in a response to the political turbulence and violence in a divided Northern Ireland. Friel was working as a teacher in Derry, when he began writing—short stories first, then drama. In 1954, his first play, *A Sort of Freedom,* was broadcast on the BBC. That same year he married Anne Morrison. His big break came some ten years later, when his play *Philadelphia, Here I Come,* was produced on Broadway. His plays were performed worldwide. At one time, three of his plays were in production, simultaneously. Friel also became known for his adaptations of Anton Chekov's work. In August, 2015, just before his death, Friel was acknowledged with a festival of the arts in his honor, in Belfast.

Brian Friel died peacefully at his home in Green Castle. He and his wife, Anne, had five children. Their eldest daughter, Paddy, predeceased him. Friel's wife and their four other children survive him.

*See Current Biography 1974.*

# Edgar Froese

**Born:** Tilsit, East Prussia, Germany; June 6, 1944
**Died:** Vienna, Austria; January 20, 2015
**Occupation:** German electronic musician and composer

Edgar Froese was an electronic music pioneer, who founded the musical group Tangerine Dream in 1967. Froese explained that he had originally set out to emulate western Rock and Roll legends such as Jimi Hendrix and Eric Clapton, before realizing that his group needed to find a way to express their own background and experience, claiming that "Germans have no roots in rock music" (*Guardian,* 25 Jan. 2015). Froese began exploring synthesizers and sequencer rhythms, challenging himself to add what he called a "human touch," to produce moving electronic scores.

Born in East Prussia, Froese and his family were forced to move to Germany following World War II, and Froese grew up in West Berlin. From an early age, he was fascinated with Dadaist and surrealist art. One of his earliest jobs was to organize multimedia events in the home of the surrealist painter, Salvador Dali. Froese joined a rock band called The Ones, but soon struck out on his own, forming Tangerine Dream, which focused on psychedelic-rock style with jazz-inflected guitar lines. In an effort to create their own original sound, Tangerine Dream began creating music produced with found objects, filtered through various electronic effects processors, to engender near trance-inducing sound. In 1973,

the popular deejay, John Peel began promoting their sound, and within ten years, the group was composing movie scores for box-office hits like *Thief* (1981), *Risky Business* (1984), and *Three O'clock High* (1987).

Though Froese declared that his style of music was strongly related to his state of consciousness—the daily working, thinking, behaving processes—he resisted being characterized as "New Age." In all, Tangerine Dream received seven Grammy Award nominations, holding the record for the artists with the most consecutive nominations—five from 1992 to 1996.

Edgar Froese died suddenly, and unexpectedly, from a pulmonary embolism on January 20, 2015. He was seventy years old. His survivors include his second wife, Bianca Acquaye, and his son, Jerome, who performed with Tangerine Dream from 1990 to 2006.

*See Current Biography 2005.*

# Peter Gay
# (Peter Joachim Froelich)

**Born:** Berlin, Germany; June 20, 1923
**Died:** New York, New York; May 12, 2015
**Occupation:** Historian, author, professor

Dr. Peter Gay was a world-renowned scholar on the enlightenment, and on the works of Sigmund Freud, winning the National Book Award for his work four times, in 1967, 1969, 1975, and 1988. The 1967 and 1969 awards were for his two volumes of *The Enlightenment: An Interpretation,* subtitled *The Rise of Modern Paganism,* which reframed how the world thinks about the enlightenment. From seeing great philosophers, such as Voltaire, as irresponsible or superficial rationalists, Gay classified their thought as a transformation of classical paganism, rejecting Christian authority to develop a humanitarian or deist philosophy. Gay saw the historian's task as part science—discovering and objectively analyzing the facts—and part art—the style with which one communicates the facts.

He was also interested in psychoanalysis, and a great proponent of Sigmund Freud. In the mid-1970s, he was a nonmedical research candidate at the Western New England Institute for Psychoanalysis. In *Freud for Historians* he attempted to dispel the mutual ignorance between historians and psychoanalysts.

Gay was born in Berlin, a German-Jew whose family narrowly escaped the Nazi scourge by emigrating to Cuba in 1939 on one of the last ships not turned away at the border. Born Peter Joachim Froelich, he anglicized his surname to Gay—a literal translation of his German name. The family eventually settled in Colorado where Gay earned a B.A. degree. He earned his Ph.D. in political science from Columbia University, where his dissertation combined historiography with political science. In 1955–1956, Gay was a Hodder Fellow at Princeton University. In 1962, he became a professor of history at Columbia, holding Guggenheim fellowships in 1967 and 1968. His book *Weimar Culture* received the Ralph Waldo Emerson Award, as well as the American Book Award. In 1969, Gay moved to Yale University where he was named the Sterling Professor of History. He retired from Yale in 1993.

Gay's numerous accolades included the Netherlands Academy of Arts and Sciences Heineken prize, University of Munich's Geschwister School prize in 1999, and a lifetime distinction award from the American Historical Association in 2004. The *New York Times* named him America's preeminent cultural historian.

Peter Gay died on May 12, 2015 at the age of ninety-one. His wife, sociologist Ruth Slotkin, predeceased him in 2006. His three stepdaughters survive him.

*See Current Biography 1986.*

# Frank Gifford

**Born:** Santa Monica, California; August 16, 1930

**Died:** Greenwich, Connecticut; August 9, 2015

**Occupation:** Professional football player, sportscaster

Frank Gifford was the number-one football draft choice in 1952, when he signed on with the New York Giants. He would remain with the Giants for twelve seasons, racking up 5,434 yards rushing, catching 367 passes, making six interceptions, and forty-three touchdowns. He also threw for fourteen touchdowns—the most for any non-quarterback in National Football League (NFL) history. Gifford was selected for the pro-bowl

eight times, in three different positions, and was inducted into the Football Hall of Fame in 1977.

Frank Gifford's father, Weldon Gifford, was an iterant oil driller during the Depression, which meant Frank and his two older siblings never attended one full year in any school during his elementary school years. The family moved forty-seven times before Gifford made it to high school in Bakersfield, California, where he joined the football team. His coach, Home Beatty, persuaded Gifford to concentrate on his studies, in part, so he could qualify for a football scholarship at the University of Southern California (USC). In his 1993 memoir, *The Whole Ten Yards*, Gifford claimed that his coach at USC, Jeff Cravath, ". . . simply didn't know what to do with a quarterback turned halfback who was also a good defensive back, punter, and placekicker." It meant Gifford spent a great deal of time learning patience on the bench. However, during his final USC season, Gifford scored seven touchdowns, rushed for 841 yards, completed thirty-two of sixty-one passes, snared three interceptions and kicked for twenty-six extra points. He played in two All-Star bowl games. As the number-one draft pick with the NFL, Gifford was picked up by the New York Giants. He suffered a horrific injury in 1960 that sent him to the hospital with a deep brain concussion and a fractured vertebra. He thought he was finished. (He wasn't; he returned in 1962.)

With his movie-star good looks, Gifford took acting classes and supplemented his income by working on films, doubling for Jerry Lewis in one comedy, and coaching Tony Curtis on football moves in another. The president of ABC Sports, Roon Arledge, asked Gifford to join a new weekly live broadcast of football games on Monday nights. The program would become a staple in homes across the country. In 1977, Gifford received an Emmy Award as TV's outstanding sports personality. He covered numerous Olympic games and hosted ABC's Wide World of Sports. He received the Christopher Award for his coverage of the 1983 Special Olympics.

In 1982 Gifford met TV personality Kathy Lee Johnson, and the two were married in 1986. Together they created The Association to Benefit Children, with its Cody Gifford House and Cassidy's Place, charities named after their two children, among others, to serve children living in poverty.

Frank Gifford died at home from a heart attack on August 9, 2015. His wife, Kathy Lee Gifford, their two children, three children from a previous marriage, and three grandchildren survive him.

See Current Biography 1995.

# Martin Gilbert

**Born:** London, England; October 25, 1936
**Died:** London, England; February 3, 2015
**Occupation:** English historian and biographer

Penning more than ninety books over his lifetime, Sir Martin Gilbert also had the distinction of writing the longest biography in publishing history. His tomes on the life of Winston Churchill was more than 7,285 pages for six narrative volumes, not accounting for the eleven companion volumes of source materials (such as letters and memoranda) totaling over 6,500 pages. It took Martin Gilbert twenty-six years to complete Winston Churchill's official biography while, at the same time, establishing himself as a foremost scholar of modern Jewish history.

After graduate school at St. Anthony's College at Oxford, Martin Gilbert was made a fellow at Merton, Oxford, where he joined the research staff of Randolph Churchill, who was his father's official biographer. Upon the younger Churchill's death (only three years after his father's death), Gilbert was chosen to complete the vast project, which was supposed to last ten years. It took him more than twenty. Gilbert was a meticulous detective, insisting on primary sources for his research. All told, Gilbert had at his disposal, fifteen tons of material on Churchill. Later, in 1991, he wrote a condensed Churchill biography of 1,000 pages.

Martin Gilbert was well traveled. From 1957 to 1962, he visited a number of Middle Eastern and Eastern European nations. Fluent in several languages, he was able to read Russian newspapers, and was disturbed by the anti-Semitic attacks he found there. He became a vociferous champion of the "refuseniks"—Soviet Jews denied permission to emigrate from the Soviet Union. Though not raised as a religious Jew, Gilbert became an ardent Zionist after several visits to Israel—one at the outbreak of the Yom Kippur War. It was Gilbert's many publications on Jewish affairs that established his reputation in the United States, well before his recognition as a Churchill scholar.

His first book on Jewish history, *A Jewish History Atlas,* was published in 1969. In 1978, he published *Exile and Return: The Struggle for Jewish Statehood.* Gilbert's magnum opus on the holocaust, *The Holocaust: The Jewish Tragedy,* was published in 1986. He also wrote volumes on the history of World War II. In his book, *The Appeasers,* written in collaboration with Richard Gott, Gilbert made a devastating case against the men who effectively encouraged German aggression, seeking a Nazi alliance.

Gilbert was a gregarious, amiable man, a characteristic that gave him access to numerous world leaders, including American presidents and British prime ministers. He became a close friend of England's Gordon Brown who, in 2009, selected Gilbert to sit on the Chilcot inquiry panel, charged with investigating the war in Iraq. Martin Gilbert was appointed Commander of the Most Excellent Order of the British Empire (CBE) in 1990, and was knighted in 1995.

Martin Gilbert died on February 3, 2015 in London. He is survived by his wife, Esther Goldberg, and three adult children.

See Current Biography 1991.

# Frank Daniel Gilroy

**Born:** New York, New York; October 13, 1925
**Died:** Monroe, New York; September 12, 2015
**Occupation:** Playwright, screenwriter, director, producer

Frank D. Gilroy realized his passion for writing at a young age, growing up as an only child in the Bronx. He began to write short stories in his teens, and, after doing quite poorly in high school, was drafted into the US Army from 1943 to 1946, where he wrote stories for the army newsletter.

Upon returning home, he was accepted to only two colleges of the forty he applied to. One of these two schools was Dartmouth College where he learned that his ideal genre of writing was playwriting. Seemingly directionless, Gilroy dropped out of Yale graduate school, worked odd jobs to support himself, and wrote scripts for television (mostly for Westerns). He wrote plays in his spare time. Eventually, he developed a steady career in television, which allowed him more time to focus on his plays.

Gilroy's first play, *Who'll Save the Plowboy?*, was performed off-Broadway in 1962, winning the Obie Award for best American play of that season. He is primarily known, however, as the writer of *The Subject Was Roses*, which garnered enormous critical acclaim after it premiered on Broadway in 1965. The play is about a young veteran returning from World War II, with his two parents vying for his affection and attention. The original production starred Martin Sheen as the son and Irene Dailey and Jack Albertson as the parents. *The Subject Was Roses* won both the Tony Award and the Pulitzer Prize in 1965. The play was later adapted to a feature film by Gilroy himself. Although he wrote many plays after "Roses," it was by far his biggest success and most enduring legacy.

His plays were known for their simplicity and sparseness; they often contained only two or three characters, in ordinary settings, and took place in the course of a day or two. He wrote both one- and two-act shows ("Roses" was in two acts) but he was best known for his one-act shows. In the introduction of *A Way With Words: Five One Act Plays*, upon being asked whether or not he always knows beforehand that a play will be in one act, he responded, "There is no 'always' when it comes to writing except that the most proven and skilled practitioner knows that he or she is *always* one play away from being an amateur."

Frank Gilroy passed away at the age of eighty-nine in his home in Monroe, New York, near the Catskill Mountains. His wife, Ruth Gaydos, a sculptor and writer, and their three sons, all of whom followed him into the film profession, survive him.

*See Current Biography 1965.*

# Leon Gorman

**Born:** Nashua, New Hampshire; December 20, 1934

**Died:** Yarmouth, Maine; September 3, 2015

**Occupation:** Former president of L. L. Bean; outdoorsman

Leon Gorman was the grandson of Leon Lenwood Bean, more famously known as L. L. Bean, the outdoor and sportswear company that originated in Maine. Gorman is known for his innovation in L. L. Bean operations that led to its massive success as a leading outdoor sportswear retailer.

Gorman was born in 1934 and attended Bowdoin College in Maine. His grandfather died in 1967, and Gorman was the only one interested in taking over the company, becoming president at the age of thirty-two. He had previously worked as a treasurer for the business and shared his grandfather's passion as an outdoorsman. He was known for his conservation work in Maine, a state that takes great pride in its association with L. L. Bean. According to *The New York Times*, "With 5,000 workers, Bean is one of Maine's top private employers."

L. L. Bean is known for valuing its employees and for customer satisfaction, allowing customers to return any item regardless of when it was purchased. Gorman kept this philosophy, but added many others when he was president. He increased catalog mailings, brought the number of stores from one to twenty-four, and adapted quickly to online shopping in the 1990s. He also added home furnishings and sporting supplies to their product line. L. L. Bean is best known for its rubber-soled hunting boots.

After his retirement, Gorman served as chairman of the board for the company from 2001 to 2013. He was also an acclaimed philanthropist. According to the real estate blog Movoto, he was named the richest person in Maine in 2012 and 2014.

Gorman passed away from cancer in his Maine home on September 3, 2015. He is survived by his wife, Lisa, three children, two stepchildren, several grandchildren, and his brother, James.

*See Current Biography 1997.*

# Gunter Grass

**Born:** Danzig-Langfuhr, Germany; October 16, 1927

**Died:** Lubeck, Germany; April 13, 2015

**Occupation:** German novelist

Novelist Gunter Grass is most well known for his 1959 novel *The Tin Drum,* which literary critics consider to be one of the greatest works of modern European literature, and with its publication, Grass was recognized as an important literary figure. A film version of the novel received numerous honors, including the Golden Palm award at the Cannes film festival, and an

Oscar for best foreign language film. Grass was equally well-known for what became his role as Germany's moral compass, urging his compatriots to come to terms with their recent Nazi past. Grass was also an accomplished sculptor, artist, poet, playwright, and musician who, according to German chancellor Angela Merkel, "accompanied and shaped Germany's post war history."

Grass was just coming of age during the height of Nazi power. At age ten, he was a Pimpf (or Hitler "cub"), and at fourteen, he joined the Hitler Youth. In his 2006 autobiography, *Peeling the Onion,* Grass revealed that he had also been a tank gunner in the Waffen SS. The admission created a firestorm as many Germans felt betrayed by their so-called moral compass, who waited too long in admitting his own role in the Nazi machine. As a prisoner of war, Grass was forced to view the newly liberated Dachau death camp as part of his de-Nazification process.

Something of a renaissance man, Grass apprenticed as a stonemason and tombstone engraver, studied painting with Otto Pantock, and sculpture with Sepp Mages. He played drums in a jazz band and wrote poetry. He was invited to join a group of avant-garde writers, Gruppe 47, in the mid-1950s, and his work began to appear in literary journals. He gained recognition as a playwright. Moving to Paris in 1956, Grass began working on his novel *The Tin Drum*. Upon bestowing Grass's Nobel prize, the Royal Swedish Academy praised Grass's gift for "reviewing contemporary history by recalling the disavowed and the forgotten: the victims, losers, and lies that people wanted to forget because they had once believed in them."

The author campaigned against German reunification because he felt, after so many years under communism, East Germany had a character all its own, and because a unified Germany could once again, pose a threat to neighboring nations.

Grass held honorary doctorate degrees from Harvard University and Kenyon College. He was eighty-seven at the time of his death on April 13, 2015.

*See Current Biography 1999.*

# Michael Graves

**Born:** Indianapolis, Indiana; July 9, 1934
**Died:** Princeton, New Jersey; March 12, 2015
**Occupation:** American architect, designer, and professor

Michael Graves was a pioneer of post-modern architecture, who considered a building as a means of communication. He intended his buildings to register a "mythic and ritual structure of society." In all, he designed over three hundred and fifty buildings, and designed thousands of products, from teapots to wheelchairs.

Graves earned a B.S. degree from the University of Cincinnati in 1958, and an M.A. in architecture from Harvard University. He won the Prix de Rome and the Arnold W. Brunner Fellowship, and began his two-year residency at the American Academy in Rome. In 1962, he became a lecturer in architecture at Princeton University, where he would remain for the rest of his career.

Graves was associated with the group of architects and teachers called the Conference of Architects for the Study of the Environment (CASE), where he met Peter Eisenman. They discussed education in architecture and the difficulties of urban planning. Later the two joined with three other architects, (Richard Meier, John Hejduk, and Charles Gwathemy) to make up the "New York Five" who, in 1972, published a book by the same name. Their discussion focused on the nature and function of architecture. Graves wanted his building structures to register a "mythic and ritual structure of society." Graves mixed the classic architecture of Egypt, Greece, Italy, and France with modern idioms such as constructivism, futurism, and cubism, bringing a human touch to design. In 2002, Graves famously designed scaffolding for restoration work on the Washington Monument that became a work of art in itself.

Graves' career took an interesting twist when he began designing household products. His conical stainless teakettle, with a red bird whistle, which he designed for Alessi, is a classic. He created designs for Target and J.C. Penney stores, with the idea that good design should be available to everyone.

In 2003, Graves suffered a debilitating infection that affected his spine, leaving him confined to a wheelchair. His experiences in hospital rooms led him to develop interiors and product design tailor-made for the medical field.

Mr. Graves received the National Medal of Arts from President Bill Clinton in 1999, and the Gold Medal of the American Institute of Architects in 2001. Michael Graves died on March 12, 2015, leaving behind his companion, Minxia Linn, two sons, a daughter, and three grandsons.

*See Current Biography 1989.*

# Robert P. Griffin

**Born:** Detroit, Michigan; November 6, 1923
**Died:** Traverse City, Michigan; April 16, 2015
**Occupation:** American politician

Robert Griffin was a Republican politician from Michigan, who served in both Houses of Congress and included eight years as the minority whip. In 1968, he filibustered to block President Lyndon Johnson's nomination of Judge Abe Fortas to the US Supreme Court. He co-authored the Landrum-Griffin bill, (now known as the Landrum-Griffin Act) in an effort to curb labor racketeering. He is most remembered for his call to his friend, Richard Nixon, to resign the presidency in 1974, following the Watergate scandal.

Born to a blue-collar factory worker in Detroit, Michigan, Robert Griffin was the first person in his family to graduate from college. He attended Central Michigan University, and received his law degree from Michigan State University.

In 1969, Griffin was elected Minority Whip, his party's number two position, (behind House Minority leader, Gerald Ford) which he held for eight years. He was on the short list of potential running mates for Richard Nixon, whom he would later vote to impeach, against his party line—an act that led directly to Nixon's resignation. Griffin was considered a rising star, helping to orchestrate the rise of Gerald Ford, who became vice president in 1973. After Ford lost the 1976 presidential election, Griffin's career started to wane. After losing his senate seat, Griffin was elected to the Michigan Supreme Court in 1987. The Traverse City courthouse was renamed the Robert P. Griffin Hall of Justice in 2006.

Robert Griffin died on April 16, 2015. His wife of sixty-seven years, Marjorie, and a son, Judge Richard Griffin, survive him.

*See Current Biography 1960.*

# Denis Healey

**Born:** Mottingham, London, England; August 30, 1917
**Died:** Afriston, England; October 3, 2015
**Occupation:** British politician, Member of Parliament

Denis Healey was one of the most powerful men in Parliament's Labour party. He was the Defence Secretary from 1964 to 1970, and Chancellor of the Exchequer under Harold Wilson, from 1974 to 1979.

Denis Healey first got involved in politics by becoming a pacifist. However, in 1936 while he attended Balliol College, Oxford, he became alarmed by the emergence of Adolf Hitler. Healey joined the communist party, feeling it was the only party that took a firm stance against Nazism. He left in protest a few short years later, due to the 1939 Nazi-Soviet pact. Healey fought with the British Army, serving with the Royal Engineers in North Africa, Sicily, and Italy, during World War II. Following the war, Healey switched loyalties to the Labour Party, and caught the attention of those in power when he spoke at the 1945 Labour Party Conference, declaring, "The upper classes in every country are selfish, depraved, dissolute and decadent."

As Defence Secretary he made controversial cuts to British bases in Singapore, Malaysia, and elsewhere in the Far East, and cancelled expensive weapons development, putting more emphasis on maintaining alliances with Western allies such as the North Atlantic Treaty Organization (NATO). He drew criticism from the Right for his defense strategy, and from the Left for his support of the US policy in Vietnam, though he did keep Britain out of the war. Later, as Chancellor of the Exchequer, he inherited a badly sagging economy. The Organization of the Petroleum Exporting Countries (OPEC) was raising oil prices, and miner strikes meant the country was on a three-day week. Healey was forced to seek help from the International Monetary Fun (IMF), once more drawing heavy criticism. (His own party booed as he explained the necessity of spending cuts to secure the IMF deal.) Some have argued that it was Healey's tough measures that paved the way for Margaret Thatcher's longevity as prime minister, and the Tory Party's eighteen-year reign. Thatcher inherited a rebounding economy after Healey took the political hard knocks.

Denis Healey was blessed with a remarkably happy marriage to Edna Edmunds, whom he married in 1945. He once quipped that he didn't need the love of his colleagues. He had the love of his wife. Denis Healey passed away on October 3, 2015. His wife predeceased him in 2010. Their son and two daughters survive him.

*See Current Biography 1971.*

# Theodore M. Hesburgh

**Born:** Syracuse, New York; May 25, 1917
**Died:** Notre Dame, Indiana; February 26, 2015
**Occupation:** American priest and college president

Father Theodore Hesburgh was the transformative leader and president of the University of Notre Dame for thirty-five years, from 1952 to 1987. During his tenure, the university went from a glorified Catholic liberal arts college to a respected and highly selective university. When asked to sum up the priest's achievements at Notre Dame, his assistant, George Schuster, said "He has taken this university into the mainstream of American Life." Hesburgh sat on the United States Commission on Civil Rights for fifteen years, chairing the Commission from 1969 to 1972. In 1962 he graced the cover of *Time Magazine*, and in 1964 Hesburgh walked hand-in-hand with Dr. Martin Luther King, Jr., at a rally at Soldier Field in Chicago.

Born in Syracuse, New York, Hesburgh reportedly wanted to become a priest from the age of four. He attended Notre Dame and the Gregorian University in Rome, receiving his bachelor of arts degree in 1940. In 1943, he was ordained at the Holy Cross major seminary in Washington, DC, and in 1945 he earned his doctorate in theology at Catholic University. While he had hoped to serve as a missionary abroad, the Congregation of Holy Cross assigned him to Notre Dame University as a teacher of religion, and as chaplain to the World War II veterans on campus.

After his promotion to president of the university, he relieved a number of restrictions on students (such as curfews, lights out, and Mass checks), fostering an "open" campus. Within the first twenty-five years of his presidency, $150,000,000 was raised for new professorships, higher salaries, the expansion of engineering and science programs, the Center for the Study of Man in Contemporary Society, and the Center for the Study of Civil Rights, among many others. The university passed from exclusively clerical hands to a predominantly lay board of trustees.

In 1954, Hesburgh joined the board of the National Science Foundation and, later, became chairman of the board of trustees for the Rockefeller Foundation. He sat on numerous charitable foundations boards. The most important of his extracurricular posts was with the federal government as an Eisenhower appointee to the US Commission on Civil Rights. Under the Carter administration, Hesburgh became chairman of the Overseas Development Council, concerned with helping developing countries, and headed the American delegation to the United Nations Conference on Science and Technology. He also chaired the Select Commission on Immigration and Refugee Policy. Among Hesburgh's myriad honors, he was awarded the US Medal of Freedom, and has received over ninety honorary degrees. The University of Notre Dame campus library was renamed the Theodore Hesburgh Library following his retirement in 1987.

Theodore Hesburgh, CSC was ninety-seven years old at the time of his death.

*See Current Biography 1982.*

# Dean Elmer Hess

**Born:** Marietta, Ohio, December 6, 1917
**Died:** Huber Heights, Ohio; March 2, 2015
**Occupation:** Christian minister and air force colonel

Dean Hess is most remembered for his role in "Operation Kiddy Car," an effort to relocate orphaned Korean children from the approaching Communist troops. His actions resulted in the founding of the US Air Force Orphanage on Cheju Island, Korea. He flew more than 313 combat missions over Germany and Korea.

Dean Hess had dreamed of becoming a minister studying at Marietta College in preparation for the ministry as a full-time profession. He graduated in 1941, and soon thereafter, became an ordained minister. However, following the Japanese attack on Pearl Harbor, Hess enlisted in the US Army Air Corps. Having learned to fly through Marietta's government subsidized civilian-pilot training program, Hess became a flight instructor in Dothan, Alabama, where he also served as a temporary chaplain. Upon his request, he was eventually assigned to the Ninth Air Force in Europe, joining the 511th Fighter Squadron in France. On a mission, in December of 1944, an errant bomb he had released accidently hit a school for the children of war workers, an action that some claimed led to his interest in caring for the children of war.

Though he returned home to earn his M.A. in history, and was only a few months shy of earning his Ph.D., Hess was called to active duty in the Air Force in 1950. He was sent to Japan and, at the outbreak of the Korean War, began training South Korean pilots to fly the F-51 plane. He was eventually promoted to lieutenant colonel.

In 1951, Hess had begun gathering homeless Korean orphans, helping them find food and shelter. When Seoul was threatened by Communist troops, Hess appealed to the Fifth Air Force to help him evacuate the children. The Air Force sent fifteen C-54 planes to fly hundreds of children to safety, an operation dubbed Operation Kiddy Car." Hess helped establish an orphanage and, upon returning home, raised money through his speaking engagements and public appearances. In 1956, a movie starring Rock Hudson was produced, chronicling his work. He donated all proceeds to the orphanage.

After retiring from the Air Force in 1969, Hess taught high school history, economics, and psychology. Dean Hess died on March 2, 2015. His four children, seven grandchildren, and ten great-grandchildren survive him. Hess's wife, Mary Lorentz Hess, predeceased him in 1996.

*See Current Biography 1957.*

# James M. Hester

**Born:** Chester (Delaware) Pennsylvania; April 19, 1924

**Died:** Princeton, New Jersey; December 31, 2014

**Occupation:** American educator and college administrator

James Hester began his service as the eleventh president of New York University (NYU) on January 1, 1962. At the time, NYU was still considered a "commuter" school, but Hester envisioned its growth potential with improved laboratories, library services, and athletic facilities. His biggest challenges were financial. He raised tuition to nearly triple that of 1952; however, he also increased teaching salaries, built the twelve-story Elmer Holmes Bobst Library, and worked to improve recruitment outside of the New York metropolitan area. In 1972, the university sold its Bronx campus in an effort to consolidate resources, closed the engineering school, and required some of the other departments to pay their own way. Hester is credited with transforming NYU from a regional college into a world-renowned research institution.

The son of a Navy chaplain, Hester was well traveled as a child. In 1942, Hester moved to Princeton University where he attended on scholarship, graduating with dual degrees in humanities and history (magna cum laude). He entered the US Navy's accelerated pre-officer training program, and was also in the US Marine Corps Reserve, where he learned Japanese. He attended Pembroke College of Oxford University in England as a Rhodes Scholar.

Hester worked for the advertising research firm Gallup and Robinson while he finished his doctorate in international affairs at Oxford. His first foray into education was in post-war Japan where he worked as an education supervisor. In 1957 he was hired as provost of Long Island University's Brooklyn Center, and eventually became the institution's vice president. He was a member of the Princeton University chapel advisory council, and a trustee of the Brooklyn Institute of Arts and Science. In 1960, Hester became the dean of the Graduate School of Arts and Sciences.

Following his tenure at NYU, Hester became rector at the United Nations University in Tokyo. He also served on the President's Task Force on Higher Education where he recommended the expansion of Federal student scholarships, grants for graduate schools, and tax incentives to encourage private donations to education. He was the president of the New York Botanical Garden, and sat on the Board of the American Council on Education. Finally, he was president of the Guggenheim Foundation from 1989 to 2004.

James Hester died on December 31, 2014 in Princeton, New Jersey. He is survived by his brother, Raymond; his sister, Virginia; his wife, Janet; his three children, Janet Gerrish, Margaret Giroux, and Martha Stafford; and, seven grandchildren.

*See Current Biography 1962.*

# James Horner

**Born:** Los Angeles, California; August 14, 1953

**Died:** Ventucopa, California; June 22, 2015

**Occupation:** Composer

James Horner composed music for over one hundred movies, manipulating the hearts and minds of his audiences under the direction of some of the biggest names in the movie industry. His screen credits include two of the highest grossing films in history: *Titanic* and *Avatar.* The music for *Titanic* remains the highest selling film score of all time. In all, Horner was nominated for eleven Academy Awards, winning two Oscars; he won two Golden Globe awards; and he netted four Grammy Awards after eleven nominations. A number of these awards were for his song "My Heart Will Go On," and for "Somewhere out There" (for the movie *An American Tale*), which he co-wrote with Barry Mann and Cynthia Weil.

Though he was born in California, James Horner spent most of his childhood in London where he studied piano at London's Royal College of Music. He returned to the United States to study music composition at the University of Southern California, and continued his graduate studies in music theory and composition at the University of California at Los Angeles (UCLA). He had made up his mind to resist the movie industry, hoping to build his career in music academia, becoming a "serious" composer, but he found himself exhilarated while helping students at the American Film Institute in Los Angeles. His first commercial film was Oliver Stone's *The Hand*, but his "big break" came when Horner snatched the opportunity to do the score for *Star Trek II: The Wrath of Khan.*

Some critics accused Horner of "borrowing" from other composers, even borrowing from his own previous work when writing a new score. He responded by explaining that some directors would insist that he write something that sounded like the music of a particular composer. He also maintained that it is impossible to be completely original, moreover originality is not the goal in composing for a film.

James Horner was tragically killed on June 22, 2015 after his S312 Tucano turboprop plane crashed in the Los Padres National Forest. He leaves behind his wife, Sarah, and their two daughters.

*See Current Biography 1997.*

# Satoru Iwata

**Born:** Sapporo, Japan; December 6, 1959

**Died:** July 11, 2015

**Occupation:** Japanese businessman, gamer

At the time of his death, Satoru Iwata was the president and CEO of the high-tech game maker, Nintendo.

Satoru Iwata created his first electronic games on his Hewlett Packard Pocket calculator, which was cutting edge technology at that time. His baseball game had no graphics or user interface and all game play was represented by numbers. Still, the game was a success, and Iwata was inspired by the enthusiasm he saw as he watched his friends play. After graduating from high school in 1978, Satoru Iwata attended the Tokyo Institute of Technology to study engineering and early computer science. (At that time, there were no classes in videogame programming.) He spent a lot of time in the only retail store he could find that specialized in computers. Finding an apartment near that store, he and a small group of friends formed the club that eventually became known as the HAL Laboratory. (The club was named after the malevolent computer in the film *2001: A Space Odyssey.*) The small group began creating game software for Nintendo with titles like Balloon Fight and Nintendo Entertainment System (NES) Open Golf. Iwata is credited with helping to create the best-selling games featuring a small, spherical creature named Kirby. (Nintendo has since released numerous games in the Kirby franchise.) Iwata played key roles in developing some of Nintendo's most popular games including those featuring Mario and his brother, Luigi, which have become Nintendo's flagship characters.

By 1999, Iwata had rescued the HAL company, which had grown to ninety employees, from the brink of insolvency, gaining the attention of the longtime president of Nintendo, Hiroshi Yamauchi who hired Iwata as company president—the first in Nintendo's history who was not a family member. As president, Iwata was committed to producing simple games that would appeal to all levels of players. Though there were rough patches, under Iwata's reign the company developed the extremely success-ful DS (dual-screen) and Wii brands, which tar-geted a demographic of families and less hard-core gamers. Iwata brought a genial face to the gaming giant with his "Iwata asks," a series of interviews with gaming developers.

In June of 2014, Iwata underwent surgery to remove a cancerous growth from his bile duct. He succumbed to the cancer on July 11, 2015. His wife, Kayoko, survives him.

*See Current Biography 2007.*

# Louis Jourdan
# (Louis Henri Gendre)
**Born:** Marseille, France; June 19, 1921
**Died:** Beverly Hills, California; February 13, 2015
**Occupation:** French actor

Louis Jordan was a French actor who spent a great deal of his career trying to avoid the ste-reotypical roles of a Continental charmer. For Jordan, his natural elegance, his accent, and his dark good looks hindered his desire for more complex, less insipid characters.

Jourdan was born in Marseille, France, to a hotel owner who also promoted the Canne Film Festival. In 1938, he began studying drama with Rene Simon, at Ecole d'art Dramatique, with hopes of directing films. However, he could not escape his handsome features, which begged to be in front of the camera lense. His first movie was *Le Corsaire* with Charles Boyer, in 1939.

Jourdan's movie career was interrupted by World War II. Too young to fight, he was asked to report to a movie set to make "nonpolitical" films.  Instead, he escaped to join the French resistance, helping to print anti-German leaflets and carrying messages. After France was freed by allied forces, the talent scout, David Selznick, came across Jourdan's work and brought him to Hollywood. Though he starred in a number of films, he was slow to take off. He left Holly-wood for Broadway in 1954, and also returned for a number of projects in France. In 1956, he was selected by Alan Jay Lerner and Frederick Loewe to play the part of Gaston, his most fa-mous role, in the move *Gigi*, to the delight of moviegoers and critics alike. He was nominated for a Golden Globe Award for the role, in 1959.

Off the screen, in 1987, Jourdan served as a nongovernmental representative to the United Nations Commission on Human Rights (UN-CHR) in Geneva.

Louis Jourdan died on February 13, 2015. Jourdan's wife of sixty years, Berthe Frederique Takar, and his son, predeceased him.

*See Current Biography 1967.*

# Robert W. Kastenmeier
**Born:** Beaver Dam (Dodge), Wisconsin; January 24, 1924
**Died:** Arlington, Virginia; March 20, 2015
**Occupation:** U. S. Congressman

Robert Kastenmeier was a member of the U.S. House of Representatives for thirty-six years of continuous service. He spent twelve of those years as a member of the House Judiciary Com-mittee. Kastenmeier was the voice of liberal conscience, supporting civil rights, and cam-paigning against poverty and unemployment. After Kastenmeier and fifteen other Democratic Congressmen failed in their attempt to persuade the House Foreign Affairs Committee to hold a full public hearing on U.S. involvement in Vietnam, Kastenmeier decided to hold "grass-roots" hearings. The hearings were held in July of 1965, with more than fifty witnesses testify-ing, including foreign policy experts and private citizens. The transcript of the hearings, including an introduction by Kastenmeier, was published under the title *Vietnam Hearings: Voices from the Grass Roots* in 1966.

Kastenmeier was a champion of human rights, both at home and abroad. In 1960, the *New York Times* published his letter calling for a pledge by the United States not to resort to biological war-fare unless it was used by an enemy first. The *Times* letter would become the first of many. In 1962, in another *Times* letter, Kastenmeier de-plored Congressional proposals to legalize wire-tapping. He wrote to President John F. Kennedy calling for an end to American complicity in the use of torture. In 1965, he wrote to President Johnson, criticizing the use of gas by American forces in the Vietnam War.

On the issues at home, Kastenmeier sat on a special Committee that charged the Army and the Commerce Department for neglecting small businesses in assigning government contracts. He was a staunch supporter of equal rights, and fought against those who sought to disenfranchise African American voters. He oversaw the first major overhaul of US copyright law in 1976, and he played a key role in the Watergate hearings.

Upon Kastenmeier's retirement in 1991, Chief Justice William Rehnquist offered a resolution that commended him for his service in the administration of justice–an unprecedented honorific. He received a Warren Burger Award for Excellence for his dedication and contributions.

Robert Kastenmeier died peacefully at his home in Arlington, Virginia, on March 20, 2015. His wife of sixty-two years, Dorothy, survives him.

*See Current Biography 1966.*

# Frances O. Kelsey

**Born:** Cobble Hill, British Columbia, Canada; July 24, 1914

**Died:** London, Ontario, Canada; August 7, 2014

**Occupation:** Physician, United States government employee

Dr. Frances Kelsey, a medical doctor with the US government's Food and Drug Administration (FDA), was responsible for preventing countless birth defects by withholding the certification of the drug thalidomide for marketing in the United States. She withstood pressure from the drug manufacturer, which characterized her as a hairsplitting, stubborn, and unreasonable bureaucrat. She had been on the job for one month. In 1962, Dr. Kelsey received the President's Award for Distinguished Federal Civilian Service, the highest honor accorded to a US government employee.

Born in British Columbia, Canada, Frances Oldham received her BS and MSc degrees from McGill University in Montreal. She moved to Chicago and earned her PhD degree in pharmacology in 1938 from the University of Chicago, where she met and married her colleague, Fremont Ellis Kelsey. Frances earned her medical degree from the University of Chicago in 1950. Dr. Kelsey had become a naturalized US citizen in 1956. Upon her husband's appointment to the division of general medical sciences at the National Institutes of Health (NIH), Kelsey accepted a position with the FDA evaluating applications from pharmaceutical firms for licenses to market new drugs. On September 8, 1960, she received an application for the clearance of the drug thalidomide, a sleeping medication that was being prescribed to pregnant women to help with morning sickness. Kelsey noticed that the drug behaved differently in animals and withheld approval, pending further investigation. She informed the manufacturer, Richardson-Merrell, that she worried it might contribute to birth defects. Soon thereafter, she received reports that there was evidence of an epidemic of newborns with deformed limbs.

Democratic senator Estes Kefauver lauded Kelsey's actions on the floor of the US Senate and proposed that she be given the Award for Distinguished Federal Civilian Service. On August 7, 1962, President John F. Kennedy presented her with the gold medal with a citation recognizing that her refusal to approve the drug prevented a major tragedy. Kelsey herself testified before a Senate subcommittee on the need for greater regulation of experimental use of drugs not cleared for the US market. In December of 1962, the Kefauver-Harris Amendment was added to the Food, Drug and Cosmetic Act (FDCA) of 1938, based largely on the thalidomide case. Dr. Kelsey was pegged to head the new investigational drug branch of the FDA.

The day before her death on August 7, 2015, Dr. Kelsey was presented with the insignia of Member of the Order of Canada. Her two daughters, a sister, and two grandchildren survive her.

*See Current Biography 1965.*

# Kirk Kerkorian

**Born:** Fresno, California; June 6, 1917

**Died:** Los Angeles, California; June 15, 2015

**Occupation:** Financier, entrepreneur, consultant

Kirk Kerkorian was a self-made billionaire who played a key role in the rise of Las Vegas as a gambling destination. He made his fortune by buying and selling stakes in casinos, automobile manufacturers, movie studios, and airlines, with an uncanny intuition about when to buy and when to sell his investments. Automobile executive, Lee Iacocca told Reuters, "He [was] a born gambler with a sixth sense for sniffing out value" (16 June 2015).

Kerkorian was born in abject poverty, the grandson of Armenian immigrants in California's great Central Valley. His father grew fruit for a living, and the young Kirk started earning money for the family when he was just nine. The family became itinerant following the recession of 1921, moving over twenty times during Kerkorian's childhood, eventually ending up in Los Angeles. He dropped out of school, never achieving more than an eighth-grade education. He lied about his age and joined the Civilian Conservation Corps. With what little money he made, he began buying broken down cars and fixing them up for resale—a pattern of buying and selling he would follow for the rest of his life.

In World War II he served as a pilot, transporting airplanes from Canada to Britain. The pay was high ($1,000 per transport) because these missions were extremely dangerous. He made enough money by the end of the war to purchase surplus airplanes and open a flight school to help veteran pilots attain commercial licenses. Eventually he created a charter airplane shuttle between Los Angeles and Las Vegas, taking the wealthy on gambling sprees. In 1962, he bought eighty acres of land in Las Vegas for $900,000—the site for the future Caesar's Palace—generating $2 million each year in rent. Six years later, he sold it for $5 million. According to *Bloomberg Business*, by the time Kerkorian was eighty, he controlled over half of the hotel rooms on the Las Vegas strip. (16 June 2015) In the course of his lifetime, he bought and sold MGM studios three times. He made several attempts at buying automobile manufacturers, acquiring stakes but never full control.

Kerkorian had been an amateur boxer and an avid tennis fan, playing in the Men's National Championships well into his nineties, in the over-85 bracket. He was also a philanthropist who distributed about $1 billion in aid to Armenia following a devastating earthquake. He donated $14 million to the University of Las Vegas, and $100 million to the University of California, Los Angeles (UCLA).

At the time of his death, Kirk Kerkorian was worth $3.6 billion. Married and divorced three times, Kerkorian is survived by his two daughters, Tracy and Linda.

*See Current Biography 1996.*

# B. B. King
# (Riley B. King)

**Born:** Itta Bena, Mississippi; September 16, 1925

**Died:** Las Vegas, Nevada; May 14, 2015

**Occupation:** Legendary blues performer

Born and raised on a Mississippi Delta cotton plantation, Riley B. King would become an iconic blues musician, a pioneer who brought the blues to the mainstream music world, playing with, and mentoring, some of the world's foremost rock stars at venues like the Apollo Theater and Carnegie Hall.

B. B. King began his music career as a DJ for Memphis-area radio stations where he earned the moniker "Beale Street Blues Boy," later shortened to "Blues Boy," and finally, just "B. B." In 1949, King began recording songs with Sam Phillips, who later founded Sun Records. One defining moment in King's career happened at a Twist, Arkansas "juke joint" when a fire broke out. King exited the building only to realize he had forgotten his guitar, and ran back into the burning building to retrieve it. He later heard the fire was started when two men were fighting over a woman named Lucille. He henceforth named his guitar Lucille as a reminder not to fight over women. Though King would acquire and use numerous guitars, each was named Lucille.

King used his guitar responsively rather than as a mere accompaniment to his voice. His guitar had an active role in the story he was telling. In a 2006 Associated Press (AP) interview, King claimed he didn't want his audience to "just hear the melody." He wanted his audience to "relive the story, because most of the songs have pretty good storytelling." It wasn't until the middle to late 1960s that King's career took off after the young guitarist, Mike Bloomfield, unabashedly worshipped and copied King's playing, introducing King to white audiences. He began making TV appearances in 1969, and toured with the Rolling Stones. As his popularity grew, it was painful to him that, despite increased African American pride and awareness, most of his race still spurned the blues. By early 1970, *Guitar Player* magazine named King the world's top blues guitarist.

King was nominated for thirty Grammy Awards, winning fifteen, and in 1987, he received a Grammy lifetime achievement award.

He was inducted into the Blues Hall of Fame in 1980, and the Rock and Roll Hall of Fame in 1987. His 1965 album, *Live at the Regal,* has been preserved by the Library of Congress' National Recording Registry. In 2012, the story of King's life was chronicled in the documentary, *The Life of Riley.* The production featured appearances by Bono (of U2 fame), Aaron Neville, Ringo Star, and Carlos Santana, among many others. That same year, he performed at the White House.

King was married and divorced twice, and fathered fifteen children. He died in his sleep, on May 14, 2015, from complications of Diabetes and Alzheimer's disease.

*See Current Biography 1970.*

# Galway Mills Kinnell

**Born:** Providence, Rhode Island; February 1, 1927
**Died:** Sheffield, Vermont; October 28, 2014
**Occupation:** American poet and translator

Galway Kinnell was a modern transcendentalist whose work sprang from his intimacy with the writings of Emily Dickinson, Edgar Allen Poe, Percy Bysshe Shelley, and William Butler Yeats. His writing demonstrated his reverence for the tiny empty space where the sacred and profane meet, sometimes using savage images to elicit the most sublime understanding. He has been celebrated as one of America's most prominent poets. In 1983, his *Selected Poems* won a Pulitzer Prize for Poetry and an American Book Award. From 1989–1993, he was a celebrated poet laureate of Vermont.

Born to a working class family, Kinnell grew up in the mill town of Pawtucket, Rhode Island. From a very young age, Kinnell recognized the musical rhythm in his mother's Irish lilt, claiming he had learned "how language could sing." He attended Princeton University where the poet, Charles G. Bell, recognized his talent—a stark contrast to the New Critical dicta of the program instructors, John Berryman and R. P. Blackmur. (Kinnell's roommate was the equally celebrated poet, W. S. Merwin.) There was something old-fashioned in Kinnell's writing, something unpretentious. Bell invited him to attend the summer poetry workshop at Black Mountain College in North Carolina, where he was introduced to the writing of François Villon, which he would one

day translate into English. In 1960, he published his first book of poetry, *What a Kingdom It Was;* he would go on to write nineteen books of poetry, and five books of poetry translations of the poetry of Yves Bonnefoy, François Villon, Yvan Goll, and Rainer Maria Rilke.

Kinnell taught at the University of Iran in Tehran, as a Fulbright lecturer. He lectured at the University of Grenoble and at the University of Nice. Though he claimed academic life made him "restive," Kinnell taught in a number of U.S. universities, eventually finding his home as director of New York University's creative writing program.

Kinnell died of leukemia on October 28, 2014 at his home in Sheffield, Vermont. He was eighty-seven. He is survived by his wife, Barbara Bristol; his son, Fergus; his daughter, Maud Kozodoy; and two grandchildren.

*See Current Biography 1986.*

# Christopher Lee

**Born:** London, England; May 27, 1922
**Died:** London, England; June 7, 2015
**Occupation:** British actor

The British cinema's undisputed master of the macabre, Christopher Lee could transform his normally charming, aristocratic self into a villain or vampire as soon as the cameras were rolling. Knighted in 2009, he was awarded the British Academy of Film and Television Arts (BAFTA) fellowship in 2011.

Like his American counterpart, Vincent Price, Christopher Lee tried to avoid being typecast as a villain, but his film credits are heavy laden with such roles. He came to public attention after playing Frankenstein's creature in the Hammer Productions film, *The Curse of Frankenstein* in 1957, and that identification became indelible when he made his first Dracula movie. Lee considered *The Wicker Man,* to be his best work. He was Roger Moore's nemesis, Scaramanga, in the 1974 James Bond film, *The Man with the Golden Gun.* He collaborated on several films with Tim Burton, including *Corpse Bride, Charlie and the Chocolate Factory,* and *Alice in Wonderland.* Most recently, Lee played Saruman the White in Peter Jackson's *Lord of the Rings series.* (He had long hoped to play Tolkien's character Gandalf, but was too old for the part by the time production began.) At the time of his death, Lee was working on a movie called *The 11th,* co-starring Uma Thurman, about the September 11 attacks on the World Trade Center. He appeared in more than two hundred and fifty movies—a world record.

Never a man to fear taking risks, Lee started a new heavy metal recording career, with the 2010 release of his "Let Legend Mark Me as the King" on his ninetieth birthday. Three years later he recorded *Charlemagne: The Omens of Death,* a metal album about his great ancestor, Charlemagne. In 2013, his song "Jingle Hell," featured on his album, *A Heavy Metal Christmas,* shot to number twenty-two on Billboard's Hot 100. While Lee considered it his job to "make the unbelievable believable," in actuality, he made the unbelievable quite real.

Christopher Lee died on June 7, 2015. He was ninety-three years old. He was married to the former Danish Model, Birgit Kroencke, for over fifty years. Lee's survivors include his wife and their daughter, Christina.

*See Current Biography 1975*

# Albert Leonard (Al) Rosen

**Born:** Spartanburg, South Carolina; February 29, 1924
**Died:** Rancho Mirage, California; March 13, 2015
**Occupation:** American baseball player and executive

Third baseman, Al Rosen, spent his entire major league career playing for baseball's Cleveland Indians. In 1953, he was unanimously voted the most valuable player in the American League. That same season, he finished just shy of earning baseballs "triple crown" which is based on a player's batting average, home runs, and runs batted in (RBI). Rosen hit 43 home runs, 145 RBI, and maintained a .336 batting average, losing that season's highest batting average, by a tiny fraction, to Mickey Vernon's .337 batting average. Rosen drove in one hundred runs for five straight seasons. In 1955, he appeared on the cover of *Sports Illustrated.* He played in the all-star game for four consecutive seasons, from 1952 to 1955.

Following his baseball career, Rosen worked as a stockbroker for twenty years, until he joined the New York Yankee's executive management team, (he was already a minority owner of the team) at the request of the owner, George Steinbrenner, in 1978. Rosen stayed for one season. In 1980, he became the president and general manager of the Houston Astros, and from 1985 to 1992, he worked for the San Francisco Giants.

Al Rosen died on March 13, 2015. He is survived by his wife, Rita, his three sons, two stepchildren, four grandchildren, and one great-grandchild. Rosen's first wife, Terry, predeceased him in 1971.

*See Current Biography 1954.*

# Philip Levine

**Born:** Detroit, Michigan; January 10, 1928
**Died:** Fresno, California; February 14, 2015
**Occupation:** American poet

Pulitzer Prize-winning poet, Philip Levine wrote about his childhood in Detroit during the Great Depression, his Russian Jewish roots, his time in Spain in the mid-1960s, racial and social injustices, and his four years working difficult industrial jobs in Detroit following World War II. He penned twenty books of poetry, and three non-fiction books, including an autobiography, and translated two volumes of Spanish texts into English. He was named US Poet Laureate for 2012 to 2013.

Philip Levine was born to working-class, Jewish parents in Detroit, Michigan. He was just five years old when his father died, leaving his mother to support three boys on her salary as an office manager. He had two brothers—one, his identical twin. Levine began working for Chevrolet and Cadillac at the tender age of fourteen, where he learned more than just the assembly line. As a young man, he encountered the violence, unemployment, and poverty that would provide the stories and images he recounted in his poetry, winning the moniker "poet of the working class," and "poet of industrial America." As a narrative poet, (poems built around a story and characters), Levine was accessible, using common language and images. He was "down to earth," and he revealed a deep sensitivity to the dignity of hard work.

Philip Levine attended Wayne State University, and earned an M.F.A. from the highly respected writing program at the University of Iowa, where his mentors were John Berryman and Robert Lowell. Levine taught creative writing and literature at California State University at Fresno from 1958 to 1992, as well as serving as a writer-in-residence at numerous other universities, including Vanderbilt, Princeton, Tufts, Columbia, and New York University (NYU). He was named Outstanding Professor at Fresno in 1977 and in 1978, Outstanding Professor for the entire California State University system.

Among his many honors are the Pulitzer Prize, two National Book Awards, and two National Book Critic Circle Awards. He earned two Guggenheim Foundation fellowships and three fellowships from the National Endowment for the Arts (for which he served as chair of the Literature Panel). He was also Chancellor of the Academy of American Poets from 2000–2006.

Philip Levine died from pancreatic cancer on February 14, 2015. His wife of 60 years, Frances Levine, his three sons, two brothers, five grandchildren, and a great-granddaughter survive him.

*See Current Biography 2012.*

# Peg Lynch

**Born:** Lincoln, Nebraska; November 24, 1916
**Died:** Becket, Massachusetts; July 24, 2015
**Occupation:** Radio and television writer, actress

Peg Lynch is credited with writing and acting in the first "sitcom" on radio and television. Lynch's 1938 *Ethel and Albert* series was originally written for the radio station KATE in Albert Lea, Minnesota, as three-minute "fillers," but the series became so popular that by 1944, the program had expanded to a fifteen-minute, five-days-a-week series for the National Broadcasting Company (NBC). *Ethel and Albert* moved to commercial television in 1950, with ten-minute guest shots on the Kate Smith hour. *Ethel and Albert* was arguably about nothing but the everyday light-hearted minutiae of married life, and has been deemed a precursor to *Seinfeld*, with topics like whether or not the garage door was locked, and how to care for a toothache. The characters of Ethel and Albert Arbuckle were portrayed so realistically that they took on real-life personalities of their own.

Margaret Frances Lynch (Peg) was born in Lincoln, Nebraska to sales executive, Hugh Lynch. Upon his death when Peg was just two,

the family moved to Rochester, Minnesota. Lynch's greatest ambition was to be a writer. She graduated from the University of Minnesota in 1937, with a degree in English. In 1948 Lynch married Odd Knut Ronning, a consulting engineer with a machine manufacturing company. They had one daughter, Astrid King. Survivors include King, her husband, Denis King, and their son, Alexander.

*See Current Biography 1956.*

# Brian Macdonald

**Born:** Montreal, Québec, Canada; May 14, 1928
**Died:** Stratford, Ontario, Canada; November 29, 2014
**Occupation:** Choreographer, dance director, teacher

Though he harbored a deep respect for classical ballet, Brian Macdonald's inventive spirit could hardly be contained by tradition. Macdonald's career started with his love of music. (He taught himself to play piano after a few lessons.) From 1949 to 1951 he was a music critic for the *Montreal Herald*, after which he joined the national ballet as a dancer. He did not begin studying dance until he was 20, but he had developed the necessary strength and flexibility through his proficiency as a figure skater. As fortune would have it, an arm injury limited his potential as a dancer, and he turned his attention to choreography, joining the newly created Canadian National Ballet Company. He moved to Winnipeg in 1958 where the Royal Winnipeg ballet performed his first work, *The Darkling*. In 1962, he was one of six choreographers invited to Watch Hill, Rhode Island, by Mrs. Rebekah Harkness (who sponsored the workshop for the Joffrey Ballet). There, Macdonald created *Time Out of Mind*, a work of dizzying pace and myriad movement suggesting tension and violence. It remains one of his most powerful works. Ken Winters of the *Winnipeg Free Press* (February 1, 1964) commented, "Here is a work which is modish, deft, cheeky, handsome and utterly beguiling."

Brian Macdonald's career was peripatetic, as he crossed the globe with performances in New York, Chicago, London, Leningrad, Stockholm, and Oslo. He was brave, creatively planning a ballet on race relations and a surrealistic mixed-media piece in collaboration with Salvador Dali. In 2002, he created a production to commemorate the terror attacks of September 11, 2001.

Macdonald received many awards and accolades. In 1967, he received the Order of Canada, his country's highest honor, and in 2008, Macdonald received the Governor General's Performing Arts Award for lifetime artistic achievement. He ventured into Broadway, reviving numerous Gilbert and Sullivan musicals, and was nominated for a Tony award in 1987, for Best Choreography and Best Direction of a Musical.

Macdonald married twice. His first wife, Olivia Wyatt, was killed in an automobile accident in 1959. Brian Macdonald died from cancer in Stratford Ontario, on November 29, 2014. He is survived by his second wife, ballerina Annette av Paul of the Royal Swedish Ballet. Macdonald was eighty-six

*See Current Biography 1968.*

# Tom Magliozzi

**Born:** Cambridge, Massachusetts; June 28, 1937

**Died:** Belmont, Massachusetts; November 3, 2014

**Occupation:** Radio personality and talk show host

By all accounts, the most memorable things about Tom Magliozzi was his infectious laugh. Magliozzi was one half of "Click and Clack, the Tappet Brothers," hosts of a weekly radio show—called Car Talk—that became a mainstay of National Public Radio (NPR) programming. In the hour-long show, listeners called the brothers with questions about car troubles, ostensibly to get advice on how to handle their car woes. But the show was much more about the irreverent banter between the two, about themselves, their audience, and the automobile culture, including many anecdotes about humorous past experiences. While the brothers laughed at themselves, and each other, there was always a sense of warmth in their humor.

Raised in a "gritty" Italian neighborhood in east Cambridge, Massachusetts, Magliozzi boasted of an ideal childhood where he had anything a kid could ever want. He was the oldest of three children, born to Louis and Elizabeth Magliozzi. Most of his listeners would be

surprised to learn that in 1958, Tom Magliozzi graduated from the Massachusetts Institute of Technology (MIT) with a dual degree in chemical engineering and economics. While at MIT, he participated in the ROTC, and spent six months in the Army Reserve. Some years later, he earned a masters degree in business administration, and a Ph.D. in marketing. For eight years, he taught at Boston and Suffolk Universities. During this time, Tom and his brother, Ray, had the idea to create a "do-it-yourself" auto garage. While that venture failed, they eventually opened a traditional auto repair shop known as Ray's Garage. In 1977, Magliozzi was invited (along with other mechanics), to field listener questions for the Boston University public radio station, WBUR. He was the only one who showed, and Car Talk was born out of the experience. He has been honored with a Peabody Award and was inducted into the National Radio Hall of Fame.

Tom Magliozzi died on November 3, 2014 in Belmont, Massachusetts from complications of Alzheimer's disease. He is survived by his three children, two former wives, his brother, a sister, and five grandchildren.

*See Current Biography 2006.*

# Judith Malina

**Born:** Kiel, Schleswig-Holstein, Germany; June 4, 1926

**Died:** Ingelwood, New Jersey; April 10, 2015

**Occupation:** American actress and theatrical director

Not only did Judith Malina and her husband, Julian Beck, co-found the Living Theatre, (the oldest experimental theater in the United States) they co-founded a movement that placed them in the upper echelon of New York's bohemian avant-garde arts scene. Influenced by similar theater movements in Europe, Malina and Beck began to address contemporary political issues through provocative performances. In particular, they were proponents of an anarchist-pacifist vision of world peace, which they named the "Beautiful Non-violent Anarchist Revolution."

Though born in Kiel, Germany, Malina and her parents immigrated to the United States when she was four. Her father was a rabbi, and her mother had dreams of becoming an actress. In 1932, the Malina family traveled to Germany for a visit, and, upon returning, worked to spread the word about the anti-Semitism and cruelty they witnessed. At a very young age, Judith Malina called herself a pacifist, to her father's chagrin. She dropped out of high school after her father's death, and began studying drama at the New School for Social Research's Dramatic Workshop. Her classmates included Marlon Brando and the playwright, Tennessee Williams. There she met Julian Beck, an abstract-expressionist painter who had recently dropped out of Yale. They married, though they characterized their marriage as an "open" one.

Beck and Malina founded the Living Theatre in 1947, the longest producing theater company in New York and the United States, with the express intention of building a "citadel of emotionally direct expression." They produced plays, in an unconventional staging of poetic drama, by Picasso, Brecht, Gertrude Stein, Paul Goodman, Lorca, and Auden. In the 1960s, they took the theater to Europe, evolving into a collective. In the 1970s, they produced dramas in unconventional venues from prison cells in Brazil to steel mills in Pittsburgh. The theater found a permanent home in 1993 in New York City.

Judith Malina died on April 10, 2015 in Inglewood, New Jersey. Two children survive her.

*See Current Biography 2011.*

# Moses Malone

**Born:** Petersburg, Virginia; March 23, 1955
**Died:** Norfolk, Virginia; September 13, 2015
**Occupation:** Professional basketball player

Moses Malone, known by fans as the "Chairman of the Boards," was an award-winning, record-breaking professional basketball player. He was the first high school student in contemporary basketball to bypass college and play professionally upon his high school graduation. According to ESPN, "His 16,212 rebounds still rank fifth on the National Basketball Association's (NBA) all-time list." He was also named most valuable player three times, and all-star nine times during his career. He often played center. During the prime of his career, he was six feet, ten inches, and weighed two hundred and fifteen pounds.

Malone grew up in a low-income family with a single mother and a passion for basketball. Although his father was only five foot six, Moses

was six foot three by adolescence, and quickly outgrew his basketball friends. His prowess, intensity, and determination were made clear on his Petersburg High team, where he wrote on a slip of paper that it was his goal to go straight to the pros. After almost signing with the University of Maryland, he was instead recruited to the American Basketball Association's (ABA) Utah Stars, where he led in offensive rebounds for the whole team. After the ABA disbanded and its players joined the NBA, he was briefly on the Portland Trailblazers and Buffalo Braves before being drafted to the Houston Rockets.

His career with the Houston Rockets was incredibly successful as the coach established the team's collective strategy based on Malone's skill. The team, which had been mediocre, skyrocketed under Malone's leadership and offensive rebounding skills, which were the highest in the league three times during his time on the team.

Malone is most associated with the next team he joined, the Philadelphia 76ers. On this team, he reportedly served as a mentor to many younger players who would grow to become famous, such as Charles Barkley, who gave a eulogy at Malone's funeral, calling him "dad."

Malone's quiet and down-to-earth nature stood as a contrast to other flashy players of the time, such as Magic Johnson and Larry Bird. He was soft-spoken, hardworking, and honest in both his playing and his manner of speech.

Malone passed away as a result of cardiovascular disease in a hotel room in Norfolk, Virginia at the age of sixty. He is survived by his two adult sons with ex-wife Alfreda Malone, and his six-year-old son, Micah Francois, with girlfriend Leah Nash.

*See Current Biography 1986.*

# Mary Ellen Mark

**Born:** Philadelphia, Pennsylvania; March 20, 1940
**Died:** New York City, New York; February 26, 2015
**Occupation:** Documentary photo–journalist

Sometimes referred to as "a snake charmer of the soul," Mary Ellen Mark captured a haunting vulnerability in her subjects, and is considered to be one of the greatest documentary photographers of her time, with exhibits in museums around the world. Her photography has appeared in *Look*, *Life*, the *New Yorker*, the *New York Times Magazine*, *Rolling Stone*, and *Vanity Fair*. In all, she published eighteen books of photography.

Mark chose to enter the social fabric of some of the most vulnerable populations in the world: runaway children on the streets of Seattle; prostitutes on the streets of Bombay, India; and, Mother Teresa's Missions of Charity in Calcutta. For one of her earliest projects—titled *Ward 81*—Mark spent six weeks in a women's maximum–security mental ward at Oregon State Hospital. Though observation was at the center of her work, Mark entered and became part of the world of her subjects. Mark explained that eventually she developed a "sense of being almost psychic about things," anticipating what her subjects might do while analyzing who they are. Her images of society's marginalized populations are chilling.

Mark has received an extraordinary number of awards and accolades, including the 2014 Lifetime Achievement in Photography Award from the George Eastman House. Her numerous grants and fellowships include many of the most prestigious awards in photography and journalism, including a Walter Annenberg Grant, the John Simon Guggenheim Fellowship, and three fellowships from the National Endowment for the Arts. She won the 1980 Page One Award for Excellence in Journalism from the *New York Times Magazine*; the Robert F. Kennedy Journalism Award for photojournalism in 1981, 1983, and 1985. In a recent poll of readers of the magazine *American Photography*, she was voted the favorite female photographer of all time.

Mary Ellen Mark died from a bone marrow, blood disease. Her husband, Martin Bell, with whom she made an Academy Award nominated film *Streetwise*, survives her.

*See Current Biography 1999.*

---

# Colleen McCullough

**Born:** Wellington, New South Wales, Australia; June 1, 1937

**Died:** Norfolk Island, Australia; January 29, 2015

**Occupation:** Australian novelist

Colleen McCullough was a prolific writer who penned twenty-five books before her death on January 29, 2015. She is most widely recognized as the author of *The Thorn Birds,* a sweeping family saga set on a sheep farm in the Australian Outback. The novel was famously portrayed in the 1977, ten-hour ABC television miniseries by the same name. The book has sold more than thirty million copies worldwide, has been translated into twenty languages, has never been out of print, and was on the *New York Times'* bestseller list for over a year.

McCullough was raised in Sydney, Australia, by cold, disinterested parents who were verbally abusive, calling her ugly, fat, and dumb. She had dreams of becoming a physician, but was stayed by a physical allergy to disinfectant used in medicine at the time. She earned a bachelor's degree in medical technology, with a specialty in neurophysiology. In 1967, McCullough moved to the United States at the invitation of the chairman of the neurology department at the Yale University School of Medicine. She remained there for over ten years, managing the school's neurological research laboratory, going so far as designing special equipment for the doctors, and working as a medical illustrator.

Colleen McCullough was known for her bold, indomitable personality. She claimed to have penned *The Thorn Birds* as a means of overcoming the painful breakup of a love affair, writing two long drafts over a nine-week period. (She would write eight more in as many months. The book is nearly 700 pages long.) Negative critical reviews didn't seem to faze her. A 1996 profile in the *Philadelphia Inquirer* characterized McCullough as "supremely unafflicted by self-doubt" (*New York Times*, 29 Jan., 2015). When rumor spread that she had plagiarized part of her novel, *The Ladies of Missalonghi*, she responded that she had too many of her own good ideas to work with, so why would she steal from another writer?

Colleen McCullough married late in life. She had avoided marriage because of the model her parents provided, and because she felt men's egos were too fragile. However, in 1984, she married Ric Robinson, the only man who could, in her words, control her. She claimed that his gentle spirit was intimidating for her.

Colleen McCullough died on January 29, 2015. She was seventy-seven years old. Her survivors include her husband, Ric, two stepchildren, and two step-grandchildren.

*See Current Biography 1982.*

# Rod McKuen

**Born:** Oakland, California; April 29, 1933
**Died:** Beverly Hills California; January 29, 2015
**Occupation:** American poet, composer, lyricist, performer

A prolific poet, songwriter, and composer, Rod McKuen was one of the best-selling writers of verse in American history. Although critics did not universally praise his work, considering him too sentimental and simplistic, McKuen became an immensely popular writer, entertainer, and cultural icon in the 1960s and 1970s.

Rod McKuen is said to have composed over 1,500 songs, many becoming classics that defined an era. He recorded over 200 albums, with 63 going golden and platinum worldwide. His most popular songs include "Seasons in the Sun," "Jean," and "A Boy Named Charlie Brown." Johnny Cash, Barbara Streisand, Madonna, and Dolly Parton have all covered McKuen's songs. Frank Sinatra liked him so much he commissioned McKuen to write an entire album for him, (*A Man Alone*) which included the hit "Loves Been Good to Me." McKuen's "The City: Suite for Narrator and Orchestra" was nominated for a Pulitzer Prize in 1973, and his work was nominated for two Academy Awards—one for "Jean" (written for the movie *The Prime of Miss Jean Brodie*) and one for "A Boy Named Charlie Brown" (written for an animated film by the same name.) He penned dozens of poetry collections.

With just four years of education, McKuen ran away from home when he was eleven years old, to escape his step-father's abuse. At just sixteen, with the help of his friend, Phyllis Diller, McKuen became a popular deejay in the San Francisco Bay area. In 1953, he was drafted to fight in the Korean War where he served as a public information specialist, writing psychological warfare scripts. In 1959, he traveled to New York City, where he wrote and performed his first hit—"Mister Oliver Twist." He sang the song so much that he strained his vocal chords, which would never recover, leaving him with a raspy, gravelly voice that became his unique sound. In 1963, McKuen traveled to France where he became a lifelong friend and protégé of the French singer/songwriter, Jacques Brel. The two collaborated, and in 1966, McKuen's English album *Seasons in the Sun*, won the French

Grand Pri du Disque as the best album of the year. The song by the same title was, in part, a translation of Brel's work. McKuen's song "If You Go Away" was voted song of the millennium by the French performing society.

Upon his return to the United States, McKuen began writing musical scores for Twentieth Century Fox films. In 1976, he published a memoir *Finding My Father: One Man's Search for Identity,* which followed his search for the father who had abandoned him, calling attention to the rights of adopted children.

McKuen died on January 29, 2015, leaving behind his half-brother, Edward McKuen Habib.

*See Current Biography 1970.*

# Jayne Meadows (Jayne Meadows Allen; Jayne Cotter)

**Born:** Wuchang, China; September 27, 1919
**Died:** Encino, California; April 26, 2015
**Occupation:** American actress

Actress Jayne Meadows received multiple Emmy nominations for her work in several television series, but she is most remembered for her long-standing role as a panelist on the game show "I've Got a Secret," which is where she met her second husband, celebrity comedian Steve Allen.

Meadows was born to Episcopal missionaries in China, where she spent her early childhood. The family moved to the United States when Meadows was eight, making their home in the North East. Her first acting roles were for the stage, where she appeared in the Broadway comedies "Another Love Story," (1946) and "Kiss Them for Me" (1945). Her role as a shrewish foster sister in "Enchantment" (1949) won her the *Cosmopolitan* Movie Citation of the month. In 1952, Meadows became a regular panelist on the game show "I've Got a Secret"—one of the most popular shows in the 1950s—where she met and married Steve Allen, who hosted the game show from 1964 to 1973. The two became one of the most recognizable couples in Hollywood. Meadows was nominated for an Emmy in 1977 for her role in a PBS show "Meeting of Minds." She received two more Emmy nominations for her work on "St. Elsewhere" (1987), and for the comedy show, "High Society" (1996). In the early 1980s, Meadows received the Susan B. Anthony Award for her positive portrayal of women in her acting roles.

Jayne Meadows' husband, Steve Allen, predeceased her in 2000. She is survived by her son, Bill Allen, her three stepsons, Stephen, Jr., Brian, and David, as well as by grandchildren.

*See Current Biography 1958.*

# Mike Nichols

**Born:** Berlin, Germany; November 6, 1931
**Died:** New York, New York; November 19, 2014
**Occupation:** Film and stage director, producer, actor

The protean director and producer Mike Nichols worked in theater, film, and television, and was among the elite few to win an Emmy, Grammy, Oscar, and Tony award. Nichols began his career in improvisational theater in Chicago with the Compass Players (later called Second City), and gained early fame for his comedy act with fellow Compass Players member, Elaine May. His experience as an actor made him "an actors director" according to many who worked with him. After Nichols and May broke up, Nichols ventured into theater, directing Neil Simon's *Barefoot in the Park,* a Broadway sensation that made him a star, virtually overnight. By 1966 he had four simultaneous hits on Broadway: Simon's *Barefoot in the Park* and *The Odd Couple,* Murray Schisgal's *Luv,* and *The Apple Tree,* a three-act musical starring Barbara Harris. That year he made his directorial film debut in Edward Albee's *Who's Afraid of Virginia Woolf?,* which garnered five Academy Awards out of thirteen nominations. His second film, *The Graduate* (1967), was immediately viewed as iconic, and with *Catch-22* (1970) he became the first film director to command $1 million per film. Nichols was a great collaborator with playwrights, screenwriters, and performers. The playwright Neil Simon has been quoted as saying, "People who work with Mike are spoiled for all time, because he is the best, the brightest, the strongest, and it's never as much fun with anyone else."

Michael Igor Peschkowsky, later known as Mike Nichols, was born on November 6, 1931, in Berlin, Germany, to Brigitte (Landauer) Peschkowsky and Pavel Nikolaevich Peschkowsky, a Russian-Jewish physician who anglicized his surname to Nichols in 1938, after escaping from Nazi Germany to the United States. In 1939 Mike Nichols and his three-year-old brother joined their father in New York City; their mother followed in 1941. Nichols attended private schools in Connecticut and New York City.

Nichols won an Academy Award, a Grammy Award, four Emmy Awards and nine Tony Awards. He was also a three-time British Academy of Film and Television Arts (BAFTA) Award winner. His other honors included the Lincoln Center Gala Tribute in 1999, the National Medal of Arts in 2001, the Kennedy Center Honors in 2003, and the AFI Life Achievement Award in 2010. His films garnered a total of 42 Oscar nominations and seven awards. He won a Tony Award for his revival of *Death of a Salesman,* just two years before his death.

Nichols, married four times, claimed that he found the love of his life in broadcast journalist, Diane Sawyer, whom he married in 1984. Nichols died of a heart attack on November 19, 2014, at his apartment in Manhattan. He was eighty-three years old. His survivors include his wife, Diane, his three children, Max, Daisy, and Jenny, and four grandchildren.

*See Current Biography 1992.*

# Jean Nidetch

**Born:** New York, New York; October 12, 1923
**Died:** Parkland, Florida; April 29, 2015
**Occupation:** World-wide Organization Founder and business executive

Jean Nidetch was the founder of Weight Watchers International, "the world's best weight-loss program" according to *US News and World Report,* for five years running. Millions who suffer from obesity have found a simple solution that includes a sensible, medically approved, food plan, education, and a social support network.

Jean Nidetch had a humble beginning as the daughter of a cab driver and a manicurist. She explained that food was both a reward and a salve in the home where she grew up. She, her sister, Helen, and her mother were all obese. In 1947, she married Marty Nidetch. While their first child died in infancy, they later had two boys, David and Richard.

When, as a Brooklyn housewife, Nidetch had had enough of dieting, she enrolled in a weight loss program at the New York City Department of Health Obesity Clinic. However, she still found it too easy to "cheat." In a moment of inspiration, or desperation, Nidetch invited six overweight friends to her house to discuss their weight-loss difficulties. The group agreed to follow the healthy meal plan and to meet weekly. Nidetch realized that her real battle was mental, and that required a mental or psychological solution. Nidetch had discovered the power of social networking, and as the circle of supportive friends grew, Weight Watchers was born.

Two friends from the program, Al and Felice Lippert, helped Nidetch turn Weight Watchers into a business that would eventually sell to H. J. Heinze, in 1978, for $7.2 million.

After Weight Watchers, Nidetch continued to promote her healthy plan of eating, and she worked to help disadvantaged teens and women get an education. (She was denied a college education due to her father's unexpected death during her freshman year.) Nidetch won recognition from the Horatio Alger Association for her success, having grown from disadvantaged circumstances. In 1993, the University of Nevada, Las Vegas awarded her an honorary doctorate, and in 1994, established the Jean Nidetch Women's Center to help nontraditional students earn a degree. In 2013, Weight Watchers celebrated its 50th anniversary.

Two sons predeceased Jean Nidetch. Her second son, David, and three grandchildren survive her.

*See Current Biography 1973.*

# Leonard Nimoy

**Born:** Boston, Massachusetts; March 26, 1931
**Died:** Bel Air, California; February 27, 2015
**Occupation:** American actor and director

Leonard Nimoy is most remembered for his role as the Vulcan character, "Spock"—an alien, unemotional, highly logical being—in the television series *Star Trek*. The series has garnered such a cult following, and has aired in so many syndicated re-runs over the past fifty years, that most television viewers would be surprised to know the series lasted just three seasons.

Born and raised in Boston, Massachusetts, to Jewish immigrant parents, Nimoy became interested in acting at a very young age, and left for California when he was seventeen. Though he had been studying theater at Boston College, he found the lure of Hollywood too powerful. In his autobiography, *I Am Not Spock,* Nimoy claimed he was always drawn to the "outsider" personae, and to exploring the connections between human and alien (or outsider). He saw his love for Quasimodo in *The Hunchback of Notre Dame,* and for Boris Karloff's interpretation of Dr. Frankenstein's monster, as preparation for the Spock role. Even in his childhood, as a Jewish boy in a largely Italian neighborhood, Nimoy felt "alien." (He later explained that his iconic hand gesture accompanied by the greeting "live long and prosper" was actually derived from an old Jewish blessing.)

Though he loved and admired the character he played in the series, Nimoy was never able to fully shed the role. Though he went on to play other roles in film and television, including characters in the series *Mission Impossible, Dragnet,* and *Twilight Zone,* viewers always identified him as "Spock." In fact, Nimoy himself claimed to "sense Vulcan speech patterns, Vulcan social attitudes, and even Vulcan patterns of logic and emotional suppression in [his] behavior." Nimoy once quipped that Spock was his best friend. In addition to his television roles, Nimoy acted on stage and directed movies, including the box office hit *Three Men and a Baby* in 1987. He received an Emmy award for his performance in the television movie, "A Woman Called Golda."

Leonard Nimoy died of chronic obstructive pulmonary disease on March 27, 2015. His wife, Susan Bay, and his two children survive him.

*See Current Biography 1977.*

# Elena Obraztsova

**Born:** Saint Petersburg, Russia; July 7, 1939
**Died:** Leipzig, Germany; January 12, 2015
**Occupation:** Russian opera diva, stage director, and professor

Over the course of her career, opera diva Elena Obraztsova was one of the first Russian singers to become internationally famous. She was granted unprecedented access to western audiences, as an exemplary Russian artist, from the very beginning of her career in 1964, when she first joined the Bolshoi Opera troupe. She was considered one of the Bolshoi's greatest stars, performing in all of the world's great theaters, including La Scala in Milan, Covent Garden in London, the Metropolitan Opera in New York, and the Vienna State Opera.

By the time she was five years old, Obraztsova knew she wanted to sing. Her father, an engineer by trade, sang and played the violin, and Obraztsova credits her love of music to the many nights he and his friends played and sang at home. However, he did not encourage Elena to sing professionally. He felt her voice was too "tinny," and encouraged her to attend technical college. Still, Obraztsova felt it was her destiny to sing, so in 1958, she enrolled at the Leningrad Conservatory. Soon after her graduation, in 1964, she traveled to Japan and Italy with the Bolshoi Opera, performing at La Scala in Milan, and then at the Montreal World Expo in 1967. Obraztsova performed over thirty classic operatic roles of the Russian and European theater. In her later years, she taught at the Moscow Conservatory, and in Tokyo and St. Petersburg. She was the artistic director of the Mikhailovsk Theater opera troupe, and in 2011, she created a charitable foundation to promote music education.

Obraztsova's life was not without controversy. She had a long-standing, public rivalry with another celebrated Russian soprano, Galina Vishnevskaya, presumably because of Vishnevskaya's support of the author, Alexander Solzhenitsyn. Obraztsova won criticism because of her alleged close relationship with Russian authorities. She left her first husband, the physicist Vyacheslav Makarov, for Algis Zhuraitis, a conductor at the Bolshoi, who would become her second husband.

Elena Obraztsova died in Germany on January 12, 2015. She is survived by a daughter from her first marriage, Elena Vjacheslavovna Makarova, (also a singer), and a grandson.

*See Current Biography 1983.*

---

# Frei Otto

**Born:** Siegmar, Saxony, Germany; May 31, 1925
**Died:** Leonburg, Germany; March 9, 2015
**Occupation:** German architect and professor

Frei Otto was a groundbreaking German architect who spent his life designing structures using minimal materials. Sometimes referred to as the "titan of tent architecture" or the "architect of air," Otto's structures comprised lightweight materials gently stretched over angular support beams. His forms mimicked what he observed in nature, from spider webs to tortoise shells, to the extent that he considered himself more of a natural scientist than architect. He attributed his passion for soft, pliable, floating canopies as a reaction to the rigid architecture of the Third Reich. Otto's goal was to design lightweight, cheap structures, with minimal impact on the environment, and for the betterment of all humanity, including the poor.

Born on May 31, 1925, to a family of sculptors, Otto spent his boyhood in Berlin. By the time he was fifteen, he was building and flying gliders to familiarize himself with the principles of thermodynamics. In 1942, Otto designed a two-engine swept-wing plane, and in 1943 he was drafted into the German air force. He was a prisoner in a camp near Chartres, France, from 1945 to 1947, where he used the time studying structural engineering theory and working on civil engineering projects. The dearth of building materials during wartime challenged Otto, who later attributed his interest in minimal construction to his wartime experiences.

Upon his release from prison, Otto studied architecture and developed new buildings from the rubble of war. Later, he studied urban planning and the history of American cities at the University of Virginia and as a consultant with New York City's Fred Severud. He graduated from Berlin's Technische Universitat where his doctoral dissertation was called "Das hangende Dach" ("The Suspended Roof").

In 1957, Otto founded the Development Center for Lightweight Construction in Berlin where he researched pneumatic membrane structures. In 1964, he founded the Institute for Lightweight Structures at the University of Stuttgart. He eventually returned to the United States as a teacher and lecturer at a number of universities, including Yale University, the University of California at Berkeley, the Massachusetts Institute of Technology, and Harvard University.

Otto's most widely recognized and highly acclaimed structures include the German Pavilion at the 1967 Montreal Expo, the aviary at the Munich zoo, and the stadium roof for the 1972 Olympics in Munich.

Ironically, Otto was awarded the prestigious Pritzger Prize the day following his death. Fortunately, Otto was aware of the coming award prior to his death. Frei Otto died on March 9, 2015 two months shy of his ninetieth birthday.

*See Current Biography 1971.*

# Jacques Parizeau

**Born:** Montreal, Québec Province, Canada; August 9, 1930
**Died:** Montreal, Québec Province, Canada; June 1, 2015
**Occupation:** French-Canadian politician, economist

Jacques Parizeau was considered the architect of the "quiet revolution" that nearly won independence for the province of Québec from the Canadian federation.

Jacques Parizeau was born to a "very bourgeois" (as he described it) family in the Outremont section of Montreal—an enclave of the city's French-speaking upper class. His mother, Germaine Parizeau, worked alongside leaders of the Québec women's rights movement, and her volunteer activities during World War II won her the Order of the British Empire award. His father was a civil servant who founded an insurance brokerage that became the most powerful in Québec, amassing the largest family fortune in the entire province. Parizeau attended the Institute d'Études Politiques, in Paris, and the London School of Economics under the guidance of the world-renowned economist, James Edward Meade.

In the late 1950s, he became a researcher for the Bank of Canada, the country's central government-owned bank, and eventually returned to Québec as an economics advisor for the provincial government, where he became involved in the watershed "quiet revolution" movement, contributing to the growth of the provincial government. Parizeau helped establish a provincial pension plan and the nationalization of Québec's electricity utilities. By the late 1960s, Parizeau believed the only way to maintain Québec's cultural uniqueness was to separate from Canada as a sovereign nation. In 1969, he joined the newly formed Parti Québécois (PQ) under the leadership of René Lévesque. By 1976, the PQ won the provincial election, and Parizeau was named the finance minister and president of the Treasury Board. After unemployment reached 15.9 percent and the deficit climbed to more than $3 billion, Lévesque asked Parizeau to resign. He refused. However, in late 1988, Parizeau assumed leadership of the PQ, and support for Québec's independence rose to 60 percent. However, the recession was of greater concern with the electorate. When the 1995 election failed, by a very small margin, to pass a referendum on separation, Parizeau uttered a career-ending statement. He blamed the loss on "money and the ethnic vote." Under intense criticism, Parizeau resigned. It became the perception in immigrant communities that the PQ was a collection of "old-school francophones" and the party never regained traction. While he continued to work behind the scenes, Parizeau would never assume leadership again.

Jacques Parizeau died on June 1, 2015 following a long illness. His first wife, Alice, predeceased him. His wife, Lisette Lapointe, and his two children survive him.

*See Current Biography 1993.*

# Ian Player

**Born:** Johannesburg, Gauteng, South Africa; March 27, 1927
**Died:** KwaZulu-Natal, South Africa; November 30, 2014
**Occupation:** Conservationist

Ian Player is credited with saving the white rhinoceros from extinction. Years of poaching had decimated the white rhino population, which had declined to just 300 animals. (One outbreak of disease could have completely destroyed the white rhino population.) Player arranged to capture and transfer male-female pairs to zoos and wildlife sanctuaries around the world to reproduce in safety; they were later released back into the wild. The population at the time of his death was well over 13,000. His techniques have since become the standard for rescuing endangered species.

Ian Player became a conservationist at a time when wilderness preservation and animal protection were not popular concepts. Local South African populations blamed wild animals for destroying crops and spreading diseases. Though Player had been a substitute game ranger in Lake St. Lucia on the Kwazulu-Natal coast, it wasn't until he befriended the seasoned Zulu bushman,

Magqubu Ntombela, that he gained a passion for preservation. Player claims to have been steeped in the racial prejudice of his country (South Africa), and his strict Anglican upbringing, which taught that anything remotely pagan was evil. Player once shared in astonishment, "Here [I am] now living and working in the wilderness… guided by a man who communicates with the animals—talks to them, thinks like them, imitates them, loves them." His relationship with Ntombela would inform his beliefs and his commitment to wildlife for the rest of his life. (He and Ntombela were so close, they referred to each other as teacher, brother, and even father.)

Player was not only concerned about wildlife, however. He considered himself a humanist and dreamed of imparting wilderness values, as embodied by Magqubu's teachings, to a world increasingly removed from nature. In 1974, he helped create the Wilderness Leadership Foundation (WLF) with a mission of education and conversation, as a way of fulfilling that dream. Since then, the WLF has become a clearinghouse of sorts, supporting Save the Elephants, Noah's Ark relocation program, and the Cheetah Conservation Fund. In 1977, Player established the World Wilderness Congress (WWC), the world's longest-running international public environmental forum.

He believed in the healing power of dreams, and was fascinated with the theories of Carl Jung. Player authored three books. On November 30, 2014, Ian Player died from complications following a stroke, in his home in KwaZulu-Natal province of South Africa. Survivors include his wife, Anne Farrer Player, their three grown children, his brother, golf pro Gary Player, and a sister.

*See Current Biography 2002.*

*York Harold Tribune* (September 21, 1962) she could "assume the characteristics of a magical creature . . . The audience applauded and wept . . . Indeed the length of the applause . . . exceeded the length of the solo itself."

The dancer did not have an easy life. In 1937 her father, Mikhail, a Jewish Russian diplomat, was arrested and executed as an "enemy of the people" for his Trotskyite sympathies. Her mother, silent film star Rachel Messerer, was arrested a year later, spending three years in a labor camp. Plisetskaya's aunt, ballerina Sulamith Messerer, cared for the young girl. Born into a musically gifted family, two of Plisetskaya's mother's siblings were accomplished dancers; her aunt danced with the Bolshoi Ballet, and her uncle was a choreographer.

Because of her family's political background, Russian authorities kept Plisetskaya on a tight leash as a "severe defection risk." When the Bolshoi made its Western debut in 1956, Plisetskaya was not with them. However, after her marriage to composer Rodion Shchedrin, Khrushchev had a change of heart, and in 1959 Plisetskaya became an international sensation following her US debut.

Though she plagued the Soviet government with her outspoken candor, she was awarded the Lenin Prize and three Orders of Lenin. The French honored her with a Chevalier of the Legion of Honour. From the Paris Academy of Dance, Plisetskaya won the Anna Pavlova Prize. In 2006, Vladimir Putin awarded Plisetskaya the top state honor for her "services to the fatherland."

Maya Plisetskaya died from heart failure on May 2, 2015. Her husband, Rodion Shchedrin, and her brother, Azari Plisetsky, survive her.

*See Current Biography 1963.*

## Maya Plisetskaya

**Born:** Moscow, USSR; November 20, 1925
**Died:** Munich, Germany; May 2, 2015
**Occupation:** Russian prima ballerina

Maya Plisetskaya, prima ballerina of the Bolshoi Ballet, was one of the most remarkable ballerina's of the Soviet era. Her style combined great technical precision with extraordinary fluidity. What's more she learned new parts with remarkable rapidity. She is best known for her portrayal of *The Dying Swan* where, according to the *New*

## Yevgeny Primakov

**Born:** Kiev, Ukrainian, Union Soviet Socialist Republics; October 29, 1929
**Died:** Moscow, Russia; June 26, 2015
**Occupation:** Russian prime minister, foreign minister, Soviet spymaster

Yevgeny Primakov was a top Russian official during a period of great transition for the Union of Soviet Socialist Republics (USSR). He was a lead architect of perestroika, a policy that ushered in a new era of economic, political, and social restructuring. He was integral in shaping the USSR's Middle East policy, and served as Russia's prime minister from October 1998 to May 1999, one of the most popular in Russian history, though his tenure was short-lived.

Primakov was born to a Jewish mother and a Russian father who vanished during a Stalinist purge. Though born in the Ukrainian capital of Kiev, he was raised in Tbilisi, the capital of Georgia. He graduated from the Institute of Oriental Studies in 1953, and received a degree in economics from the M. V. Lomonosov Moscow State University in 1956. Following graduation, he worked as the Middle East correspondent for *Pravda,* the official newspaper of the Communist Party, until 1970. He was fluent in Arabic and cultivated close relationships with a number of influential Arab leaders. In 1970, Primakov was named deputy director of the Institute of World Economy and International Relations (MEMO)—the country's top foreign policy think tank. He was closely associated with Mikhail Gorbachev and was a member of the Politburo (the governing body of the Communist Party), serving as Gorbachev's special envoy to Iraq where he worked to avert a war between Saddam Hussein and the United States. In 1991, Primakov became the director of the Committee for State Security (KGB), and would continue as head of the Russian Foreign Intelligence Service once the KGB was dissolved. In 1996, President Boris Yeltsin named him foreign minister. Yeltsin fired him eight months later because he had failed to establish a solid economic plan.

Primakov's first wife, Laura, and his son, Alexander, both died young due to heart disease. His second wife, Irina, and his daughter, Nana, survive him.

*See Current Biography 1999.*

# Paul Prudhomme

**Born:** Opelousas, Louisiana; July 13, 1940
**Died:** New Orleans, Louisiana; October 8, 2015
**Occupation:** Cajun chef, author

Chef Paul Prudhomme is said to have invented the spicy "blackening" process so common in Cajun cooking. Shortly after word got out about his Cajun-style fare, Cajun mania swept the country, putting America on the culinary map. His enthusiasm for the food he was raised on, and his pleasure in observing its effect on his patrons, translated into tremendous success for Prudhomme.

Chef Paul Prudhomme was raised in a large family, the youngest of thirteen children. He was seven years old when he began working with his mother, cooking for a large crowd in a kitchen that had no electricity. He learned how to garden and how to slaughter farm animals. His first attempt at a restaurant, a hamburger stand, failed. Prudhomme was seventeen years old. He embarked on his self-created apprenticeship program by traveling around the country to learn from other cooks, from truck stops to posh resorts. None would match his mother's skill at combining spices. He began working for Ella and Dick Brennan, owners of the popular Commander's Palace, in 1975. Eventually, he talked them into trying some of his Cajun cuisine, which was virtually unheard of at that time, even in Louisiana. The fare became wildly popular. Blackened redfish became so popular, according to John Pope of the *Times Picayune*, "… in 1987, Louisiana had to halt the slaughter by banning the sale of redfish caught off its coast until 1992." (8 Oct. 2015)

In 1979, Prudhomme and his wife, Kay Hinrichs Prudhomme, opened K-Paul's Louisiana Kitchen, a restaurant specializing in Cajun and Creole fare. The place was so popular, and seating so tight, that patrons sat at large tables with perfect strangers. The restaurant had such a reputation that patrons would wait in long lines for hours to get in. Prudhomme appeared on television shows. He published more than a dozen cookbooks, and even created his own line of Cajun style spice blends known as Magic Seasoning Blends.

Paul Prudhomme died on October 8, 2015. His first wife, Kay Hinrichs Prudhomme, predeceased him in 1992. His second wife, Lori Prudhomme, survives him.

*See Current Biography 1997.*

# Richard Rainwater

**Born:** Fort Worth, Texas; June 15, 1944
**Died:** Fort Worth, Texas; September 27, 2015
**Occupation:** Investor, philanthropist

At the time of his death, Richard Rainwater had an estimated net worth of $3 billion, the world's 663rd wealthiest person, ranked 236th in the United States. He had started out for graduate school at Stanford University's school of business, with four hundred dollars and a car.

Richard Rainwater was born in Fort Worth, Texas, to second-generation, Lebanese immigrants. (The name, Rainwater, is courtesy of a Cherokee Indian ancestor.) His mother was a saleswoman at J.C. Penney, and his father owned a modest wholesale grocery business. Rainwater attended school at the University of Texas at Austin, majoring in math and physics. While attending Stanford's school of business, he met fellow Fort Worth native, Sid Richardson Bass, the nephew of the oil millionaire, Sid Richardson. The two became good friends. Following graduate school, Rainwater was a trader for Goldman, Sachs & Company, but at Sid's request, Rainwater joined his friend in working for the Basses. He successfully invested their money in Texaco and Disney. (It was Rainwater who brought in Michael Eisner for the struggling Disney.) Starting with a $50 million Bass fortune, by the time Rainwater left, sixteen years later, Bass was worth $5 billion. Rainwater decided to strike out on his own, having set his sights on building his own fortune. Rainwater invested in oil, buying when oil was just nine dollars a barrel. By the mid-1980s, he had created an oil empire, with influence around the world. In 1989, he partnered with the future president, George W. Bush, in purchasing the Texas Rangers baseball team.

In 1991, Rainwater married the South Carolina investment banker, Darla Moore, who quickly became his chief financial deputy. That same year, Rainwater set up a charitable organization to help children living in poverty. In 2009, Rainwater learned that he had the rare neurological brain disease, progressive supranuclear palsy (PSP). Within the short time he had left, Rainwater donated over $50 million for research into the condition. He had not appeared in public since 2010. He died, peacefully, at home on September 27, 2015. He leaves behind his wife, two sons and a daughter.

*See Current Biography 1999.*

# Ruth Rendell

**Born:** London, England; February 17, 1930
**Died:** London, England; May 2, 2015
**Occupation:** Novelist

Novelist Ruth Rendell considered herself a "compulsive writer," spending a minimum of five hours a day writing and rewriting. Her compulsion resulted in over sixty novels and seven short story collections. Many of her stories have been serialized on television, or made into feature films. While she was a writer of "crime fiction," critics have suggested that Rendell "transcended the genre," a compliment she paid little heed to. Rendell felt she was not a great writer, but that her goal was to entertain. One of her most enduring, "entertaining," characters was Chief Inspector Reginald Wexford, a relatively erudite investigator who defies the officer stereotype. He is happily married, and at peace with himself and the world. On the other side of the law, Rendell likes plumbing the dark pathologies that haunt contemporary life. She had an artistic preoccupation with psychopaths, and she tried to occupy the criminal mind.

Rendell was an only child whose mother suffered from multiple sclerosis. Her parents' marriage was not happy, and Rendell was raised primarily by a housekeeper, though she describes her father as patient and kind, not unlike inspector Wexford. For a short time, she was a reporter for the *Chigwell Times*, but quit before being fired for reporting on a speech during which the speaker had died. She had not attended the meeting and wrote her story based on his pre-released speech. While there, she did meet fellow journalist, Don Rendell, whom she married in 1953. The couple divorced in 1975, but remarried two years later.

Rendell received numerous accolades for her work, winning three Edgar Awards, four Gold Daggers, and one Diamond Dagger award from the Crime Writers' Association. Her writing made her a wealthy woman who donated a great deal to charity. She was made a Labour life peer in 1997, a member of the House of Lords.

Rendell's husband predeceased her in 1999. Her son, Simon, survives her.

*See Current Biography 1994.*

Dr. Ronan's wife of 57 years, the former Elena Vinade, predeceased him in 1996.

*See Current Biography 1969.*

## William J. Ronan

**Born:** Buffalo, New York; November 8, 1912
**Died:** West Palm Beach, Florida; October 15, 2014
**Occupation:** New York State public official, transportation chairman, and university professor

Following his appointment as chairman of the Metropolitan Transportation Authority (MTA) in 1967, William Ronan was one of the most powerful public officials in the country. The appointment, effective in March 1968, placed virtually all mass transportation in the New York metropolitan area under Ronan's control. At the time, the MTA had over 52,000 employees and an estimated gross annual income of $6 billion.

Ronan brought a great deal of experience to the job. He had been a professor of government at New York University (NYU), and Dean of the school of public service. During World War II, Ronan enlisted in the Navy where he was the Assistant Director of Personnel of the Office of Foreign Relief in Washington, DC. In 1958, he was appointed secretary to New York Governor, Nelson A. Rockefeller, where he and the governor hashed out plans to rescue faltering railroads in the New York metropolitan area. Ronan's plan was to put all commuter transportation from bridges to airports, subways to trains, under one umbrella agency. This consolidation allowed Ronan to steer income from toll bridges and tunnels, into the failing New Haven and Long Island railroad lines. The six years of Ronan's tenure as MTA chair were not easy. There were chronic problems of vandalism and declining ridership. He received death threats and his image was burned in effigy in Long Island after he increased fares, and he had to hire police protection. However, his legacy has been far reaching. Even after he left the MTA, Ronan's work led to the expansion and completion of the Metro-North Railroad in 1983.

On October 15, 2014, Dr. Ronan died at his home in West Palm Beach, Florida. He was one hundred and one years old. He is survived by two daughters, his partner, Bette Machon, three grandchildren, and three great-grandchildren.

## Jean Ritchie

**Born:** Viper, Kentucky; December 8, 1922
**Died:** Berea, Kentucky; June 1, 2015
**Occupation:** Folk singer, folklorist, author

Referred to as the "mother of folk," Jean Ritchie brought America's heritage of folk music to the mainstream, inspiring vocal artists like Bob Dylan, Emmylou Harris, and Linda Ronstadt. She introduced, performed, and preserved a rich body of homespun, traditional songs from her Appalachian childhood.

Jean Ritchie was born into a musical family, the youngest of fourteen children reared in mountain poverty, in a three-room house where she and her nine sisters shared a single bedroom. She and a number of her siblings attended the Hindman Settlement School, part of the movement known as "progressivism" conceived around the idea that students from all social classes should know and educate each other, and honor and preserve a student's background. The Ritchie family was one of two great "ballad-singing" families from Kentucky. (The other family was the Combs from an adjacent county.) Ritchie received her degree in social work from the University of Kentucky, graduating Phi Beta Kappa. She taught elementary school during World War II, then worked at New York's Henry Street Settlement where she taught music, and gained exposure to the New York folk music scene, meeting Pete Seeger, Lead Belly, Woody Guthrie, and The Weavers. She appeared regularly on Oscar Brand's Folksong Festival on WNYC radio. She met her future husband, photographer George Pickow, at a square dance.

In 1952, Ritchie won a Fulbright Scholarship to trace the origins of Appalachian folk songs in the British Isles. While there, she appeared at the Royal Albert Hall, and on the BBC radio. That same year she recorded her first solo album, and Oxford University Press published her first book, *The Swapping Song Book*. Another book, *Singing Family of the Cumberlands*, documented her family's story. *Rolling Stone Magazine* awarded Ritchie with a Critics Award in 1977. In 2002, Ritchie received a National Endowment for the Arts heritage fellowship, and was inducted into the Kentucky Hall of Fame. Ritchie was largely responsible for creating the Newport folk festival. In all, she published over thirty books, and thirty-three record albums. In 2014, a number of artists, including Judy Collins, Kathy Mattea, Robin and Linda Williams, among many others, recorded the tribute album *Dear Jean: Artists Celebrate Jean Ritchie.*

Though she lived in Port Washington, New York, following her husband's death in 2010, she retired to Berea Kentucky where she died at home on June 1, 2015. Her sons, Peter and Jonathan, survive her.

*See Current Biography 1959.*

# Ann Rule
# (Ann Rae Stackhouse,
# Andy Stack)

**Born:** Lowell, Michigan; October 22, 1931
**Died:** Seattle, Washington; July 26, 2015
**Occupation:** True-crime author

When Ann Rule struck up a friendship with the caring and sensitive colleague who volunteered with her at the Seattle crisis center, she could hardly have suspected him of brutal murder, especially given Rule's experience as a criminal psychologist. However, to her horror, the man—Ted Bundy—was a twenty-four year old serial murderer who easily won her trust and friendship. Rule went on to write the best-selling novel *The Stranger Beside Me* about her friendship with Bundy. At the time she met Bundy, she was already a writer of true crime novels. Because she had been a good writer, she majored in writing at the University of Washington, though her ambition was to work in law enforcement. She also studied psychology, criminology, and penology, and joined Seattle's police force after graduating. Her career in law enforcement was short lived, however. Her extreme near-sightedness prevented her from passing the eye exam.

Throughout her childhood, Rule spent her summers with her grandfather who was a sheriff. Her passion for law enforcement grew out of the question of why innocent children grow up to become criminals. She married her husband, Bill Rule, and became a writer in the late 1960s, writing true-crime stories for newspapers and national magazines. Rule divorced in 1972 and raised her four children alone. She took night courses in crime-scene investigation and other law enforcement topics, earning an MA in criminal psychology. She began writing under the pseudonym "Andy Stack" because crime stories sold better if readers thought a man had written them. Two of her books were adapted for television. *Small Sacrifices* became a miniseries that won a George Foster Peabody Award.

The Federal Bureau of Investigation (FBI) and the justice department have consulted with Rule for her expertise in serial murder. She had also been featured on the crime show *48 Hours*.

Her books often detailed the near-heroic efforts of law enforcement to solve a case. In the early 1980s, Rule helped develop the FBI's Violent Crime Apprehension Program (VI-CAP). She received the Washington State Governor's Award and two Anthony Awards at the annual World Mystery Convention. The Mystery Writers of America nominated two of her books for Edgar Awards.

In a sad turn of events in early 2015, two of Rule's sons were accused of theft and forgery on her accounts. At the time, she was confined to a wheelchair and in poor health. Ann Rule died of congestive heart failure on July 26, 2015. Her four children, numerous grandchildren, and great-grandchildren survive her.

*See Current Biography 2000.*

# Oliver Sacks

**Born:** London, England; July 9, 1933
**Died:** New York, New York; August 30, 2015
**Occupation:** Neurologist, author

Oliver Sacks was a neurologist and writer who shared his fascination with the mystery of human consciousness. Most of his books were written for laymen and attempted to overcome the rigid categorizations of contemporary medical science. His was a quest for a holistic and humanistic practice that transcended the confines of standard scientific empiricism.

Sacks was most interested in exploring the interaction between physiological, biological, and psychological factors, and their manifestation as disease. Early in his career, Sacks worked with patients who were victims of a global pandemic of encephalitis lethargica ("sleeping sickness"). Most of these patients lived in suspended animation, thrown into states of coma or, as Sacks would write in *Awakenings*, "states of sleeplessness so intense as to preclude sedation." Thinking that a personal, humane atmosphere was more conducive to therapy, Sacks brought one group of such patients together and began treating them with L-Dopa, a medication for treating Parkinsons patients. The results were as astonishing as they were tragic. Patients began to "come to," only to discover that decades had passed without their knowledge. Then they began to relapse into states of catatonia or unconsciousness. After documenting and publishing his observations, Sacks was puzzled by the tepid response from the medical community. Convinced that no "scientific presentation" could capture the depth and complexities of what his encephalitic patients experienced, Sacks wrote his book, *Awakenings,* for a lay audience. His experience would be the subject of a BBC documentary, and a full-length feature film starring Robin Williams and Robert de Niro.

Since Sacks was a polymath, equally at home in science and the arts, and with intriguing titles like *The Man Who Mistook His Wife for a Hat*, and *An Anthropologist on Mars*, Sacks cultivated a personal appeal, sharing his natural curiosity to which most of his readers could relate.

Both of Sacks' parents were physicians who inspired a love of medicine in each of their four sons. Born in London, Oliver Sacks studied medicine at Queens College, Oxford, with his internship at Mount Zion Hospital in San Francisco, and his residency at the University of California, Los Angeles (UCLA). He was a consulting neurologist at Beth Abraham hospital in New York, and held academic positions at New York University and Columbia University. He received a Guggenheim fellowship in 1989.

In February of 2015, Sacks learned he had liver cancer. He succumbed to the disease on August 30, 2015. His partner, writer Bill Hayes survives him.

*See Current Biography 1985.*

# Donald Saddler

**Born:** Van Nuys, California; January 24, 1918

**Died:** Englewood, New Jersey; November 1, 2014

**Occupation:** American choreographer, dancer, and theater director

Donald Saddler was a man of extraordinary energy, creating dance for every conceivable venue, from television to opera, Broadway to ballet, animated feature films to United Service Organizations (USO) performances in World War II. Through his career that spanned more than six decades, Saddler directed and/or choreographed for any number of big city opera houses, including the Metropolitan Opera, New York City Opera, and the Washington opera. He created ballets for the Ballet Theater (now known as the American Ballet Theater), Cincinnati Ballet, the Harkness Ballet, and the Joffrey Ballet. Saddler's movie credits include *April in Paris, By the Light of the Slivery Moon,* and *The Happy Hooker.* He choreographed multiple Tony Award broadcasts. For Saddler, dancing was as essential as air.

Originally, Donald Saddler began dancing to recover from a childhood bout of scarlet fever. Born and raised in Van Nuys, California, Saddler lived just a stone's throw from Culver City and the MGM studios, where he spent his school breaks. Fred Astaire was Saddler's dance idol, and Saddler's first dance instructor, Nico Cherisse (Cyd Cherisse's husband) told him he needed to learn ballet in order to dance like Fred Astaire. Eventually, he became a chorus dancer in MGM musicals, using any earnings to pay for dance lessons.

Saddler's 1953 debut on Broadway, Leonard Bernstein's *Wonderful Town*, brought him a Tony award for choreography. His creativity went beyond dance numbers as he choreographed actors' movements on stage, where every gesture was planned, each step meticulously taken to evoke a mood or quality of character. He often used popular or social dance forms. Between 1954 and 1960, Saddler choreographed a number of productions for the Italian musical stage, producing almost one show each year, and winning the Maschera d'Argento award (the Italian equivalent of the Tony Award).

Saddler claimed that he was a bit like the character Billy Elliot, explaining "I only knew who I was when I was dancing." His last public performance (at the age of eighty-one) was in 2001—a revival of Sondheim's *Follies*, in which he also performed with life-long friend, and fellow octogenarian, Marge Champion. Saddler died at the age of ninety-six on November 1, 2014. He had no immediate survivors.

*See Current Biography 1975.*

# Tomaž Šalamun

**Born:** Zagreb, Croatia; July 4 1941
**Died:** Ljubljana, Slovenia; December 27, 2014
**Occupation:** Poet

By all accounts, Tomaž Šalamun was a force of nature, a man who never outgrew the vivacity of his youth. And his poetry reflected that sometime frenetic pace with images, sprinkled, almost haphazardly, throughout his poetry—that coalesced into a whole, much more than the sum of its parts. Born in Zagreb, Yugoslavia in 1941, Šalamun lived through an extraordinary time of change for his country. Inheriting the Stalinist noose on artistic expression and then, in the early 1990s, living through a civil war that transformed one single Yugoslavia into six distinct ethnic nations—a process of integration and dissolution—Šalamun developed a poetic style that mirrored his experience.

Two events set the direction for Šalamun's life. Though he was born something of a prodigy with piano, Šalamun had refused to do anything "artistic" after an argument with his father. It wasn't until he was a grown man that he heard a "tremendously charismatic" poetry reading by the Slovenian poet, Dane Zajc, that Šalamun felt poetry capture his spirit. In the second event, Salamun published his poem "Duma 1964," a blasphemous re-write of a canonized patriotic poem, (as recalled by Aleš Debeljak in the *Afterwards: Slovenian Writing 1945–1995.*) Šalamun was arrested and jailed. However, by 1964, Yugoslavia had opened trade with the west, and the young poet's arrest drew international attention. He left prison, after five days, with a reputation as a revolutionary.

For Šalamun, the compulsion to write was a fierce taskmaster, bred in response to the intellectual dishonesty of the period. His poems explored the striking dichotomy between the physical ugliness of the Eastern Europe of his day and its cultural riches. He traversed the globe, learning, writing, and teaching. He participated in an "Information Show" at the Museum of Modern Art (MoMA) in 1970, and attended the prestigious International Writing Program at the University of Iowa where he studied numerous American poets. The most important discovery for his work, was the poetry of kindred spirit, John Ashberry. Šalamun served as a writer-in-residence at Yaddo (a writer's retreat in Saratoga Springs, New York), and he was a Fulbright Fellow at Columbia University.

In all, Šalamun wrote more than 40 collections of poetry. (His first book, *Poker*, was published when he was just 25). His work has been translated into more than 20 languages. His awards include Prešeren Prize, the Jenko Prize, and the prestigious Pushcart Prize. Tomaž Šalamun died on December 27, 2014. He was seventy-three years old.

*See Current Biography 2007.*

# Carl E. Sanders

**Born:** Augusta, Georgia; May 15, 1925
**Died:** Atlanta, Georgia; November 16, 2014
**Occupation:** Former Governor of Georgia, a politician, and a lawyer

Upon taking office as the governor of Georgia, Carl Sanders had reform on his mind, with the specific goal of improving Georgia's image as a backward and racist state. As the youngest governor in the country at the age of thirty-seven, Sanders worked to improve education by raising minimum standards, building new schools, and raising pay for teachers. He increased state funding for higher education, and implemented the Governor's Honors Program, "a six-week supplemental enrichment program" held each summer for high achievers in the state's high schools. Though he considered himself a segregationist, he led the transition toward racial desegregation, cooperating with U.S. Presidents Kennedy and Johnson in complying with civil rights laws. As Governor, Sanders sought international trade and investment, bringing in over one billion dollars worth of new industry to Georgia.

Carl Sanders began his political career in 1954 when he was elected to be a representative of Richmond County in the lower chamber of Georgia's General Assembly. Sanders established himself so solidly with his constituents that he served for six years (quite a rarity) in the state Senate. (Under Federal mandate, Governor Sanders would implement the reapportionment of state districts, eliminating the county "rotation system" that had allowed Sanders such a lengthy tenure.) He served as floor leader in 1959, and as president pro tempore from 1960–1962. Many of his peers felt Sanders was destined for national leadership. Although President

Johnson offered him several federal positions, he was through with politics. Following his term as governor, Sanders established his own law practice that became one of Atlanta's largest law firms.

Carl Sanders was born and raised in Augusta, Georgia, the eldest of two sons for Carl Thomas Sanders and Roberta J. (Alley) Sanders. At the onset of World War II, Carl (the younger) enlisted in the Army Air Forces. Two years later, as a lieutenant, he became one of the first to pilot a B-17, (Flying Fortress) heavy bomber, in combat.

Governor Sanders died in Atlanta on November 16, 2014 at the age of eighty-nine. He is survived by Betty, his wife of sixty-seven years, his son and daughter, their spouses, and five grandchildren.

*See Current Biography 1964.*

# Marlene Sanders

**Born:** Cleveland, Ohio; January 10, 1931
**Died:** New York, New York; July 14, 2015
**Occupation:** Broadcast journalist

Marlene Sanders was a news broadcaster at a time when network news was a man's purview. She was the first woman to anchor a network evening news broadcast, the first to cover the Vietnam War, on location in Vietnam, and the first to rise to the position of vice president of news at a television network. Her work included writing, producing, and appearing on camera.

Marlene Sanders originally set out to major in speech at Ohio State University, but left after a year to travel and, later, she studied acting at the Sorbonne. In 1955, while working as an assistant to the producer at a summer theatre in Rhode Island, Sanders met the broadcast journalist Mike Wallace, who found a position for her as a production assistant on his newscast. She began work as an associate producer and writer on the news program *Night Beat.* She gradually began to assume broadcast responsibilities. In 1964 she won a Writer's Guild of America Award for her documentary *The Battle of the Warsaw Ghetto.* Shortly thereafter, she was hired as a correspondent for *News with a Woman's Touch* newscast. (Topics covered such womanly fare as food, decorating, raising children, and fashion.) Her big break in front of the camera occurred when anchorman Ron Cochran lost his voice and Sand-

ers was pegged to replace him. In 1966 Sanders was sent to Vietnam for three weeks. The resulting footage was shown on Peter Jennings' evening news report. In 1971, Sanders replaced Sam Donaldson while he was on assignment in Vietnam. In 1972, she was named a full-time documentary producer at ABC. Documentary topics included the right to die, questions regarding gender roles for men and women, and life-threatening problems such as breast cancer. In 1977, Sanders moved to CBS News.

Sanders won three Emmy Awards for her documentaries; two were for her work as a writer and correspondent at CBS on *What Shall We Do About Mother?* about the rising elder care crisis, and another for her work on *Nurse, Where Are You?* about a rising nurse shortage. She was the Broadcast Woman of the Year in 1975, and won a Silver Satellite Award for overall contributions to the industry. She retired from CBS in 1987, and taught journalism part-time at Columbia University.

Marlene Sanders died of cancer on July 14, 2015. Her husband, Jerome Toobin, died in 1984. Their son, Jeffrey Toobin, and three grandchildren survive her.

*See Current Biography 1981.*

# Carl E. (Emil) Schorske

**Born:** New York, New York; March 15, 1915
**Died:** New Jersey; September 13, 2015
**Occupation:** American cultural historian, author, and professor

An internationally acclaimed cultural historian, professor, and scholar, Carl E. Schorske was an authority on nineteenth- and early twentieth-century Europe. The Dayton-Stockton Professor of History, Emeritus, at Princeton University in Princeton, New Jersey, he was the author of several groundbreaking books, including *Fin-de-Siècle Vienna: Politics and Culture* (1979), a Pulitzer prize-winning collection of essays that describe late-imperial Vienna's burgeoning artistic, political, and intellectual life amidst a background of social and political tumult.

A brilliant lecturer, Professor Schorske began his academic career in 1946, when he joined the history department at Wesleyan University in Middletown, Connecticut. From 1960 to 1969, he was a professor of history at the University of California, Berkeley–where, in 1966, he was recognized by *Time* magazine as one of the country's ten "great teachers."

Born in New York City, he grew up in the suburb of Scarsdale, New York, and attended Columbia University. He earned his MA at Harvard University in Cambridge, Massachusetts, before joining the German Research Section of the Office of Strategic Services (OSS), the forerunner of the Central Intelligence Agency (CIA), during World War II.

In 1946 he joined the Council of Foreign Relations' German studies group, whose purpose was to report on postwar Germans' cultural and economic situation. His first book, which he co-authored, was *The Problem of Germany* (1947), which summarized the group's suggestions for the country's successful reintegration.

In 1955, after returning to Harvard for his PhD, he published his second book, *German Social Democracy, 1905–1917: The Development of the Great Schism* (1955), which analyzed the consequences of the Social Democratic Party's replacement by reformist and radical factions.

*Fin-de-Siècle Vienna: Politics and Culture*, for which he won the 1981 Pulitzer Prize for general nonfiction, features seven essays that focus on the era's cultural creativity and describe how a revolt against a previous generation's rationalism and liberalism provoked counter-politics of the irrational, including ethnic nationalism and anti-Semitism. Professor Schorske was also the author of *Thinking with History: Explorations in the Passages to Modernism* (1998).

In addition to the Pulitzer Prize, he was the recipient of numerous other honors, including Guggenheim and MacArthur fellowships and honorary degrees from Wesleyan, Princeton, and the University of Salzburg, in Austria.

Four children, three grandchildren and two great-grandchildren survive him.

*See Current Biography 1999.*

---

# Gunther Schuller

**Born:** New York, New York; November 22, 1925

**Died:** Boston, Massachusetts; June 21, 2015

**Occupation:** Composer, conductor, French horn player, educator, writer

Gunther Schuller was a self-taught, Pulitzer Prize winning musician and composer who coined the term "third stream," which refers to the fusion of jazz and classical music. He played the French horn for the Metropolitan Opera Orchestra, the New York Philharmonic Symphony Orchestra, and was co-conductor (with David Baker) of the Smithsonian Jazz Masterworks orchestra. From 1967 to 1977, Schuller served as the president of the New England Conservatory of Music, and was the artistic director of the Berkshire Music Center at Tanglewood. He published several books considered classics of jazz scholarship: *Horn Technique* (1962), *Jazz: Its Roots and Musical Development* (1968), and *The Swing Era* (1989). In his title *The Compleat Conductor* (1997), Schuller examines, from the conductor's viewpoint, eight works from the standard orchestral repertory.

Gunther Schuller was born into a musical family. His grandfather was a conductor and music teacher in Germany, while Schuller's father, Arthur Schuller, joined the New York Philharmonic Symphony Orchestra as a violinist, playing there from 1923 to 1964. By the age of fifteen, Gunther Schuller began playing professionally with the New York Philharmonic as a substitute hornist, while studying music at the Manhattan School of Music. However, he quit his schooling altogether when he began touring with the American Ballet Theater in 1943. The same year, he became the principle hornist of the Cincinnati Symphony Orchestra. Schuller took great pride in the fact that he never earned a degree, including a high school diploma.

He became enamored with jazz after listening to Duke Ellington, and soon his chamber music took on characteristics of jazz. He named this jazz-infused classic music, "third stream." By 1959, Schuller gave up performance, devoting himself full-time to composition. His early composition, *Spectra*, was quite avant-garde. Commissioned by the New York Philharmonic and performed at Carnegie Hall, Schuller arranged the orchestra in seven distinct instrumental groups across the stage, achieving a stereophonic projection.

Schuller had a significant impact on music education in the United States, serving on the faculties of New York's Manhattan School of Music and Yale University's School of Music while he was also appointed president of the New England Conservatory.

Schuller received numerous awards and accolades. In 1974, he won a Grammy Award. He was an elected member in the National Institute of Arts and Letters and the American Academy and Institute of Arts and Letters. Schuller won a MacArthur Foundation grant in 1991, and a Pulitzer Prize in 1994. He won two Guggenheim Fellowships and *DownBeat's* Lifetime Achievement Award for Jazz. In 2011, he published his autobiography, *Gunther Schuller: A Life in Pursuit of Music and Beauty."*

Gunter Schuller died from complications with leukemia on June 21, 2015. His two sons, Edwin and George, and his brother, Edgar, survive him.

*See Current Biography 1964.*

# Robert H. Schuller

**Born:** Alton (Sioux), Iowa; September 16 1926

**Died:** Artesia, California; April 2, 2015

**Occupation:** American clergyman and televangelist

The Reverend Robert Schuller was a unique minister whose teachings emphasized positive thinking—his term was "possibility thinking"—over the shame-based theology of his televangelist peers. Heavily influenced by the social psychologist, Norman Vincent Peale, author of *The Power of Positive Thinking,* Schuller initiated the mega-church phenomena that swept across the country in the 1970s through the 1990s. At the pinnacle of his success, Schuller's church brought in between $30 million and $50 million per year, and he reached an audience of millions with his *Hour of Power* syndicated television and radio broadcasts.

Beginning in the mid-1950s, the Reformed Church of America, asked Schuller to establish a congregation in Orange County, California. With just a $500 stake, Schuller had to be creative in finding a venue for his new church. He rented the Orange Drive-In Theatre near the Santa Ana Freeway, and stood on the roof of the concessions building, preaching to congregants in their cars. His slogan became "Worship as you are/In the family car." He continued his radio/car broadcasts throughout his career, calling his unique congregation a walk-in/drive-in church. Though he would come to build an astonishing glass cathedral (dubbed the "Crystal Cathedral"), his ministry would always include a "drive-in" component.

Schuller's sermons covered topics like hope in the face of adversity, the family as therapeutic fellowship, and self-love as a "dynamic force for success." Unlike most televangelists, Schuller felt controversial social, political, or theological issues were not topics for the pulpit, but rather, they should be broached in a setting where dialogue was possible.

After Schuller's retirement in 2003, his Crystal Cathedral Ministries went into a rapid financial decline, finally declaring bankruptcy in 2010, and leaving a schism between his children. Robert Schuller was diagnosed with esophageal cancer in 2013, and on April 2, 2015, he succumbed to the disease. His wife, Arvella, predeceased him in 2011. His son and four daughters survive him.

*See Current Biography 1979.*

# Richard Schweiker

**Born:** Norristown, Pennsylvania; June 1, 1926

**Died:** Pomona, New Jersey; July 31, 2015

**Occupation:** US Senator from Pennsylvania

Richard Schweiker had the distinction of being the first vice presidential nominee before the Republican convention to nominate its presidential candidate for the 1976 election. Surprising his party, and Schweiker himself, Republican contender, Ronald Reagan, named Schweiker his running mate in his first bid for the White House. Schweiker was one of the more liberal Republicans, supporting civil rights legislation, Medicare, and Social Security increases, and Reagan, one of the most conservative Republicans, thought Schweiker's record would pull his ticket to the center against Gerald Ford's nomination. They failed to win their party's nomination, and Schweiker's subsequent move to the right had some of his fellows labeling him a blatant opportunist.

Richard Schweiker had no political ambitions as he quickly rose to vice-president of sales in the family business—the American Olean Tile Company. But Schweiker was drawn to community service following the death of his brother in World War II. (Schweiker himself served in the US Navy on the combat aircraft carrier Tarawa.) He had been a prize-winning debater at Pennsylvania State University. In 1960, he ran against the conservative incumbent, John LaFore, in Pennsylvania's Thirteenth Congressional District, and won with a 61.8 percent share of the votes. In 1968, he won a senate seat against the liberal Democrat, Joseph Clark. Schweiker's voting record ran afoul of the Nixon administration by rejecting two of Nixon's Supreme Court nominees, earning him a place on the list of the Chief Executive's "enemies." In early May of 1974, Schweiker became the third Republican Senator to call for Nixon's resignation. He came to national attention when he was selected for the Senate Select Committee on Intelligence Operations, investigating Central Intelligence Agency (CIA) and Federal Bureau of Investigation (FBI) abuses of power.

In 1976 the former California Governor, Ronald Reagan stunned political observers by selecting a running mate, Richard Schweiker, before the Republican convention, in his attempt to derail Gerald Ford's campaign. They failed to win the nomination. Schweiker did not seek re-election following two terms. After Reagan's rise to the presidency in 1980, he pegged Schweiker to head the U.S. Department of Health and Human Services. Schweiker left after two years to run the Washington-based trade group, the American Council of Life Insurance.

Richard Schweiker married Clair Joan Coleman, the original "Miss Claire" on the children's television series *Romper Room*, in 1955. The two had two sons and three daughters. Schweiker died from an infection on July 31, 2015. His wife, Claire, predeceased him in 2013. A sister, five children, twenty-three grandchildren, and one great-grandchild survive him.

*See Current Biography 1977.*

# Stuart Scott

**Born:** Chicago, Illinois; July 19, 1965
**Died:** Avon, Connecticut; January 4, 2015
**Occupation:** Sports news broadcaster

Sports news anchorman, Stuart Scott, was just forty-nine years old when he died on January 4, 2015. Widely celebrated for his flair and creativity in the broadcast booth, Scott managed to transform the lexicon of sports commentary. Some of his trademark catchphrases—known as "Stu-isms" among his colleagues and sports fans—have even spread into non-sports-related popular culture. Many of the popular "Stu-isms" were derived from the West Coast hip-hop culture, and Scott was sharply criticized by some for what they considered to be faux hip-ness. Scott's response was always that his speech in the broadcast booth mirrored his speech on the street. His easy, laid back style brought a younger, more diverse crowd to the sports network. Popular "Stu-isms" include "boo-yah," "can I get a witness to the congregation," and "cool as the other side of the pillow." Fans also enjoyed the banter between Stuart Scott and Rich Eisen—an unlikely duo. Scott was an African-American hipster, and Eisen, an East Coast Jew.

While he was born in Chicago, Illinois, Scott grew up in Winston-Salem, North Carolina, with his two sisters and a brother. Scott was an athlete himself, with big dreams of playing professional football. In high school, he played basketball, baseball, and tennis, and acted in the school's theater productions. Four colleges vied to recruit him, but he chose to attend the University of North Carolina (UNC), in Chapel Hill, as a walk-on athlete. (His brother also attended UNC.) Scott's college sports career was short-lived however. A series of eye surgeries kept him from the field and the court, so he channeled his passion for sports into broadcasting. In his early career, he worked for a series of radio and television programs, but his big break came in 1993, when he sent a demo tape to the newly formed ESPN2.

Scott conducted one-on-one interviews with such sports icons as Michael Jordan, Lebron James, and Tiger Woods. He interviewed two presidents, Bill Clinton and Barack Obama. In 2007, an emergency appendectomy revealed malignant tumors throughout Scott's abdomen. With brief bouts of remission, he fought the cancer for the rest of his life. He was awarded the Jimmy V Award for Perseverance in July of 2014. Scott leaves behind his two daughters, Sydni and Taelor, his parents, and three siblings.

*See Current Biography 2012.*

# Miriam Shapiro

**Born:** Toronto, Ontario, Canada; November 15, 1923
**Died:** Hampton Bays, New York; June 20, 2015
**Occupation:** Feminist artist, educator

Miriam Shapiro was one of the originators of the feminist-art movement in the early 1970s. She was a leader of the pattern-and-decoration (P&D) genre that incorporated painting, sketching, and collage to create an altogether new art form that Shapiro dubbed "femmage." She derived her art from distinctly female experience, such as child-rearing, household chores, and "crafts" that she felt were undervalued by feminists and the broader patriarchal society. Shapiro was drawn to Abstract Expressionists and began incorporating "women's work" such as quilting, embroidery, applique, and crochet into her art. She was also one of the first artists to use a computer for creating art. The result was hard-edged, geometrically structured, intensely colored canvases.

Miriam Shapiro was born in Toronto, Canada, but spent most of her childhood in New York, the only child of Jewish immigrants. Her father was an artist and Socialist intellectual who studied at the Beaux-Arts Institute. Both parents encouraged their daughter to study art. She earned a bachelor of art degree, a master's degree in printmaking, and a master of fine arts degree—all from the State University of Iowa where she met her husband, Paul Brach.

In 1971, Shapiro joined the staff at the California Institute of the Arts in Valencia, California, where she teamed up with Judy Chicago to create a feminist art program that sought to address women's self-esteem. They received national attention for their collaborative work "Womanhouse"—a whole-house installation in which individual students and artists sought to "echo the feelings of a woman's place," that reminds [one] of the magic of childhood, fantasy control over the tremors of the heart" (Artnews.com, 23 June, 2015). Shapiro wrote three books: *Women and the Creative Process* (1974), *Rondo, An Artist's Book* (1988), and *Miriam Shapiro: A Retrospective, 1953–1980* (1980). She earned numerous awards, among them a National Endowment for the Arts Fellowship, a Ford Foundation Fellowship, a Guggenheim Fellowship, a Sowhegan Medal, a Rockefeller Fellowship, and the Women's caucus for Art Award. She was also awarded six honorary doctoral degrees.

Miriam Shapiro died on June 20, 2015. Her son, Peter von Brandenburg survives her.

*See Current Biography 2000.*

# Omar Sharif (Michel Demitri Shalhoub)

**Born:** Alexandria, Egypt; April 10, 1932
**Died:** Cairo, Egypt; July 10, 2015
**Occupation:** Egyptian actor

The Egyptian actor, Omar Sharif, is best known for two of his movie roles, both winning him prestigious acting accolades. He won an Oscar nomination in 1963 for his performance as a tribal chief, Sherif Ali, in *Lawrence of Arabia.* He won a Golden Globe from the Hollywood Foreign Press Association in 1966 as Best Actor in a dramatic role for his performance in *Doctor Zhivago*, a movie based on Boris Pasternak's novel of the same name. Sharif was a versatile actor, playing a Russian poet/physician caught in a love triangle; a Spanish priest; a German policeman; crown prince Rudolf of Austria; and an Arabian tribal chieftain.

Of Syrian-Lebanese descent, Sharif was born into an affluent Catholic family. His father was a timber merchant. Sharif attended western-style boarding schools, and never learned to speak Arabic as a child. (The family spoke French.) His parents were friends with King Farouk, with whom Sharif's mother played bridge. Before his debut with western audiences, Sharif was a well-known actor to Arabic-speaking audiences. He created a stir by kissing the young starlet, Faten Hamama, on screen. The two would marry a few years later after Sharif converted to her Islamic faith.

Sharif was known to be something of a philanderer, having affairs with a number of his co-stars. Off-screen, he was known to have a bad temper, brawling with a Beverly Hills parking attendant, and head butting a French policeman in a casino. Sharif was also a world-class bridge player, ranking in the top fifty players, worldwide.

According to Sharif's son, Tarek Sharif, the movie star was diagnosed with Alzheimer's disease, though he died of a heart attack on July 10, 2015. His son survives him.

*See Current Biography 1970.*

# Dean Smith

**Born:** Emporia, Kansas; February 28, 1931
**Died:** Chapel Hill, North Carolina; February 7, 2015
**Occupation:** American basketball coach

Dean Smith was the legendary basketball coach of the University of North Carolina (UNC) Tar heels who, at the time of his retirement in 1997, had the most wins (879) of any coach in the National Collegiate Athletic Association (NCAA) Division I, men's basketball tournament. Many considered him one of the greatest coaches of all time.

Though he had been the assistant basketball coach at the University of Kansas, the game's birthplace, and again, for the U.S. Air Force in Germany, Dean Smith's big break came when he signed on with the coaching staff at UNC, in Chapel Hill, North Carolina. Originally hired as an assistant coach, Smith moved to head coach in 1961 following a recruiting scandal involving head coach Frank McGuire.

By the time of his retirement in 1997, Smith was one of the winningest coaches of all time, with 879 wins in 36 years. In 1976, Smith coached the US Olympic basketball team that won a gold medal. One measure of his success is the success of the players he coached. A full fifty percent of his players continued to play professional basketball after graduating. He coached twenty-five National Basketball Association (NBA) first round draft picks. Five of his players were voted NBA Rookie of the Year. A significant number of legendary players have called Smith "coach," including Michael Jordan, James Worthy, and Sam Perkins.

On the court, he emphasized teamwork over individual success, and praised the athlete with an assist over the athlete making the shot. (It is common for a UNC scorer to point to the man who assisted him.) Smith was responsible for creating a number of innovations in college basketball, including the four-corners offence, commonly known as stalling, which motivated the NCAA to institute the "shot clock," limiting the amount of time an offensive team can take to make a shot. The "tired signal" allowed a player to take himself out of the game if he was over-tired.

Dean Smith was inducted into the Basketball Hall of Fame in 1983. ESPN named him among the top five greatest coaches in any sport,

not just basketball. Upon his retirement, *Sports Illustrated* named him coach of the year. UNC named its new basketball arena the Dean Smith Center (commonly referred to as the "Dean Dome") after him. In 2013, President Barack Obama awarded Smith the Presidential Medal of Freedom.

While Smith's statistics are remarkable, he is also remembered for his kindness and integrity. Dean Smith died on February 7, 2015. He is survived by his wife of 39 years, Linnea, his five children, seven grandchildren, and one great granddaughter.

*See Current Biography 1994.*

# William Jay Smith

**Born:** Winnfield, Louisiana; April 22, 1918
**Died:** Pittsfield, Massachusetts; August 18, 2015
**Occupation:** Poet, translator, literary critic, professor

William Jay Smith was a celebrated poet, translator, scholar, and the US Poet Laureate. Several of his poetry collections were contenders for the National Book Award. He won the Henry Bellamann Award for creative achievement in poetry in 1970, from the National Institute of Arts and Letters, and received a grant from the National Endowment for the Arts in 1972. His first collection of children's poetry, *Laughing Time*, is considered a classic among historians of children's literature. He also served in the Vermont House of Representatives from 1960 to 1962.

William Smith has often been thought of as a New England poet, perhaps because of his ties to Vermont, but he was actually born in Winnfield, Louisiana, a town his grandfather, a soldier in the Confederate Army, helped found. Smith's father was a soldier and clarinetist in the US Army band. William Smith earned his BA and MA from Washington University, majoring in French. He continued his studies in French at the Institut de Touraine, Université de Poitiers. His knowledge of French also won him a commendation from the French Admiralty for his work as a liaison officer aboard the French sloop La Grandiére.

Smith taught French and English at Columbia University. In 1947 to 1948, he studied English literature at Oxford University as a Rhodes Scholar. From 1948 to 1950, Smith studied Italian literature and language at the University of Florence in Italy. In the early 1950s he moved to Pownal, Vermont, to focus on his writing. While working as a consultant, Smith urged the Library of Congress to record poets reading their poetry to capture the identifiable music in their poetic language. Tapes of Smith reading his poetry were used in the television program *Mr. Smith and Other Nonsense*, broadcast on WETA-TV in Washington, DC, on Christmas day in 1969.

From 1959 to 1967, Smith was the poet-in-residence and a lecturer at Williams College, where he was also in charge of the creative writing program. He taught courses in children's literature and European literature at Hollins College in 1965 and 1966. He was a visiting professor of writing and acting chairman of the writing division of the School of the Arts at Columbia University. From 1968 to 1970, William Smith was the US poet laureate.

William Smith died from pneumonia on August 18, 2015. Survivors include his wife of forty-eight years, Sonja Haussmann Smith, a son and stepson, two grandchildren, and two great-grandchildren.

*See Current Biography 1974.*

# Ken Stabler

**Born:** Foley, Alabama; December 25, 1945
**Died:** Gulfport, Mississippi; July 8, 2015
**Occupation:** Professional football player

The left-handed football player, Ken Stabler, earned his nickname, "the Snake," because of his uncanny ability to slice through opposing defense with precise, last minute touchdown spirals. In 1973 he led the Oakland Raiders to the title in the American Football Conference (AFC)-West with the best all-around quarterbacking performance, completing 163 of 260 throws for 1,997 yards, fourteen touchdowns, and only ten interceptions, breaking Sammy Baugh's three-decade-old record for single-game passing efficiency. He threw an astounding 86.21 percent pass completion. Stabler's performance was so dramatic that some of his memorable plays have earned nicknames—"ghost to the post," and "Holy Roller."

Ken Stabler was born on Christmas day in 1945. He was born with natural athletic talent, receiving attractive offers from major league baseball upon his high school graduation. He chose to play football with the University of Alabama. According to coach Paul ("Bear") Bryant, in his junior year Stabler was the best college quarterback he ever saw, taking the Crimson Tide through an undefeated season. He was selected in the second round draft in 1968, by the Oakland Raiders, but was sidelined by a knee operation that kept him benched through much of the 1971 and 1972 seasons. (A bad knee plagued him throughout his career.) However, in 1974 Sporting News named him Player of the Year, and the Associated Press cited him as the National Football League's (NFL) Most Valuable Player (MVP). In 1976 Stabler led the Raiders to their best recorder ever (13-1), compiling a completion percentage of 66.7, at that time, the highest in football history since 1945. He played for the Houston Oilers from 1980 to 1981, and the New Orleans Saints from 1982 to 1984.

Stabler had a reputation for hard living, drinking, and womanizing. Discouraged by media reports, Stabler stopped talking to reporters altogether. In 1979, Stabler was involved in a strange incident where a Sacramento Bee reporter, Bob Padecky, was detained by police after they found a key case full of cocaine hidden in the fender of his car. The police determined that Padecky had been "framed." (The implication was that Stabler had something to do with the incident.)

Ken Stabler was married and divorced twice, and had three daughters. In February of 2015, Stabler revealed he had colon cancer. He succumbed to the disease on July 8, 2015. His sister, three daughters, Kendra, Alexa, and Marissa, and two grandsons survive him.

*See Current Biography 1979.*

# Phil Stern

**Born:** Philadelphia, Pennsylvania; September 3, 1919
**Died:** Los Angeles, California; December 13, 2014
**Occupation:** Photographer

From Darby's Rangers to the Rat Pack, Phil Stern documented an era remembered mostly in black and white. A combat photographer in Italy during World War II, and one of Hollywood's most renowned still photographers, Stern had nearly unlimited access to Hollywood film sets, recording sessions, and parties that allowed him to capture on film such movie celebrities as James

Dean, Marilyn Monroe, and Joan Crawford in a variety of candid poses—images of celebrities from the inside out. Few of the era's big stars escaped his lens. Yet, Stern was so unobtrusive, so invisible, his photographs capture these icons in very human moments—James Dean pulling on a sweater, Humphrey Bogart on a swing with his daughter.

Phil Stern was born in Philadelphia, but he grew up in the Bronx, New York, one of three boys, to a family of Jewish immigrants from Russia. He began his career as a photograph engraver during the day, and a photographer for the *New York City Police Gazette* in the evening. Stern moved to Los Angeles, California, in 1941, working freelance for a number of publications, including *Life, Collier's, Look,* and the *New York Times Magazine*. He joined the Army to serve as a combat photographer for Darby's Rangers, an elite American fighting squad, stationed overseas, and sustained significant injuries. Upon returning home, Stern was hired by movie studios to shoot publicity stills. He took advantage of his access to the stars, capturing candid moments behind the glamour. He also shot numerous album covers featuring artists such as Louis Armstrong, Ella Fitzgerald, Art Tatum, and Billie Holiday.

Although Stern often mingled with the stars, he was never one of them, and one gets the sense that he never fell prey to the wealth and glamour that surrounded them. He developed a close relationship with John Wayne, however. In an interview with Judy Raphael, he explained, "We got drunk together. He'd call me a bomb-throwing Bolshevik and I called him a raving right-wing Neanderthal! We were an odd couple." When Frank Sinatra was put in charge of entertainment for President-elect John F. Kennedy's inaugural celebration, Stern left a note in Sinatra's dressing room asking Sinatra to select him as the photographer. Stern made it easy. He left three blank boxes on the note—options for his reply: "Yes," "I'll think about it," and "[expletive] off." One of Stern's most iconic images is of Sinatra lighting Kennedy's cigarette at that event.

In December 1993, the Govinda Gallery in Washington DC exhibited a retrospective of Stern's work, and Knopf published *Phil Stern's Hollywood*, a compilation of some of his best work.

Phil Stern was married to the model, Rose Mae Lindou. They had four children: one daughter and three sons. Stern died of emphysema in Los Angeles on December 13, 2014. His survivors include his two sons, eight grandchildren, and a legacy of images from a bygone era.

*See Current Biography 2001.*

# Brandon Stoddard

**Born:** Bridgeport, Connecticut; March 31, 1937

**Died:** Los Angeles, California; December 22, 2014

**Occupation:** American television executive, producer

ABC entertainment executive Brandon Stoddard first came to public attention in the late 1970s when, as the network's senior vice-president in charge of dramatic programs, motion pictures, and novels for television, he was largely responsible for the telecast of the highly rated and critically acclaimed miniseries *Roots*. Though he was not the first to produce a miniseries, he demonstrated mastery over the form with productions like *Masada, The Winds of War,* and *The Thorn Birds*. He took risks tackling such thorny issues as nuclear war, incest, and homosexuality. *Roots* was, in fact, the first television program to present a story about slavery from a black point of view. The series was unprecedented in that ABC televised the 12-hour saga over eight consecutive nights. By the end of the series, *Roots* had become the highest-rated entertainment program in the history of the medium. (The concluding installment won a staggering 71 percent share of the viewing audience.)

Some speculate Stoddard was so successful because he knew his audience, perhaps due to his experience with demographic studies in advertising. He had earned a bachelor's degree in American Studies from Yale, and a law degree from Columbia University. Finding law to be "unbelievably boring," he decided to try his hand at advertising, in an era when advertising agencies played a major role in television programming. Stoddard first came to ABC in 1970 as the director of daytime programming. After two years, he was promoted to vice-president of daytime programming, where he developed the ABC Afterschool Special, a series of one-hour dramatic specials and documentaries aimed at young people. *Schoolhouse Rock* was another concept developed under his direction—short, musical, educational film clips about history, government, science, and basic grammar. Within another two years, Stoddard was named network vice-president of motion pictures for television.

Stoddard had been promoted to president of American Broadcasting Company (ABC) Entertainment when, in March of 1989, he resigned to become the head of ABC's new in-house production unit. Upon retiring from ABC, Stoddard taught graduate students at the University of Southern California's (USC) school for Cinema and Television. He was inducted into the Television Academy Hall of Fame in March, 2014. Brandon Stoddard died at his home in Los Angeles after a battle with cancer. He is survived by his wife, Mary Anne Dolan, a sister, two daughters, and four grandchildren. He was seventy-seven years old.

*See Current Biography 1989.*

# Robert Stone

**Born:** New York, New York; August 21, 1937
**Died:** Key West, Florida; January 10, 2015
**Occupation:** American novelist

Robert Stone was a renowned author whose novels addressed the brutality and despair of an America that lost its innocence in Vietnam and in Central America. Each of his novels creates an appalling, drug-ridden world of brutality, violence, and despair, where he examines victimization, godlessness, and nihilism. Though he wrote just eight books, Stone won numerous writing prizes, including the William Faulkner Foundation Award (for "notable first novel"), the National Book Award for Fiction, a Guggenheim Fellowship for Creative Arts, a Dos Passos Prize, and the Ambassador Book Award for Fiction. Two of his novels were adapted for film— *A Hall of Mirrors* (released as *WUSA*) and *Dog Soldiers* (released as *Who'll Stop the Rain*).

Robert Stone was born and raised in New York City. His father was not involved in his upbringing, (his parents were never married) and his mother suffered from schizophrenia. For four years, between the ages six and nine, Stone lived in a Marist Brothers orphanage, and he credits the Marist Brothers education with his ability to write. (He attended Archbishop Malloy High School in Manhattan.) He did not graduate from high school, (though he eventually earned his GED). In 1955, he enlisted with the US Navy where he served as a journalist for the United Force Press Service. Upon leaving the Navy,

Stone returned to New York to work as an editorial assistant for the *New York Daily News*. He moved to New Orleans in the late 1950s, which factored heavily in creating the settings for his novels. He received a Stegner fellowship in the creative writing program at Stanford University where he met Ken Kesey, and fell in with the group of "Merry Pranksters" that included Jack Kerouac and Allen Ginsberg. Though he didn't stay with the group long, he was aboard the Merry Praksters bus on the 1964 cross-country trip recounted by Tom Wolfe in *The Electric Kool-Aid Acid Test* (1968). Through his experimentation with the drug culture of the sixties, Stone began exploring his deep-rooted religious sensibility, viewing everything as a mystical process. His experiences would feature heavily in his first novel, *A Hall of Mirrors.* Stone worked as a writer-in-residence at numerous universities, including Princeton, Amherst College, Stanford University, the University of Hawaii, Harvard University, University of California at Irvine, and New York University.

Robert Stone had a peaceful, stable home life in a small New England town. He met his wife, Janice G. Burr, in 1958, and they had two children, a daughter and son. He died on January 10, 2015 from chronic obstructive pulmonary disease. He is survived by his wife, Janice, their two grown children, Deidre and Ian, and a daughter from another relationship, Emily Burton, and six grandchildren.

*See Current Biography 1987.*

# Louise Suggs

**Born:** Atlanta, Georgia; September 7, 1923
**Died:** Sarasota, Florida; August 7, 2015
**Occupation:** Professional golfer

Louise Suggs was one of the finest female golfers in the history of the sport, winning more than sixty-one amateur and professional tournaments. (Her professional victories totaled a record-breaking forty-nine.) Having won virtually every major event in women's golf, she was inducted into golf's Hall of Fame in 1951. Her lowest round was a 66. In 1961, she won the Palm Beach par-three invitational tourney, beating five other women, and twelve male professionals, including such illustrious players as Sam Snead, Lew Worsham, and Dow Finsterwald.

Louise Suggs was born in Lithia Springs, Georgia, a health resort outside of Atlanta that her grandfather founded years earlier. (Her grandfather was born on the property in a clay-floored cabin.) Her father was a left-handed pitcher for the Crackers baseball team, which her grandfather owned. Beginning when she was twelve, Suggs learned to play golf on the Lithia Springs nine-hole course. By the time she was fifteen, she reached the finals in the Georgia State amateur tournament. By 1940, she won the Georgia title, and in 1941 she took the Southern women's championship. In 1945, she won seven out of ten tournaments. By 1946 she was regarded as one of the top three female golfers.

In addition to playing the game, Suggs designed her own line of women's golf attire. She served as the president of the Ladies' Professional Golfer's Association, and she co-authored the book *Gold for Women*. In the introductory chapter, Suggs wrote, "Golf is very much like a love affair. If you don't take it seriously, it's no fun; if you do, it breaks your heart. Don't break your heart, but flirt with possibility."

Louise Suggs died in Sarasota, Florida on August 7, 2015.

*See Current Biography 1962.*

# A. Alfred Taubman

**Born:** Pontiac, Michigan; January 31, 1924

**Died:** Bloomfield Hills, Michigan; April 17, 2015

**Occupation:** American real estate executive and philanthropist

Alfred Taubman's flair for moving merchandise and his architect's eye made him a major developer of immensely profitable, meticulously managed shopping malls. He is credited with changing the way Americans shop by moving retail shops indoors, away from urban downtown areas. Taubman attempted to make his malls sources of "fantasy fun, and entertainment," renting space to restaurants, movie theaters, and ice-skating rinks. He created the idea of "overcoming threshold resistance," referring to the value of wide-open entranceways for store-fronts, open to public spaces. With his innate understanding of consumer behavior, he developed a multi-billion dollar industry that made him one of *Forbes* 400 richest individuals.

Taubman was born to working-class, German Jewish immigrants. During the Great Depression, he began working at the age of nine. He served as an aerial photographer during World War II, and was one of the first to observe the damage following the bombing of Hiroshima, Japan. Taubman studied architecture at the University of Michigan and at the Lawrence Institute of Technology, working as a shoe salesman and construction worker to help pay for college, though he never graduated. He would later donate over $200 million to the University of Michigan (the largest donation in the school's history), where the university's college of Architecture and Urban Planning bears his name. He established and funded the Taubman Center for State and Local Government at Harvard University, the Program in American Institutions at the University of Michigan, and Brown University's Public Policy and American Institutions program.

In addition to his vast development empire, Taubman sat on the boards of Chase Manhattan Bank of New York, R.H. Macy Co., and Getty Oil. In 1983, he rescued the ailing Sotheby's auction house, but the billionaire served nine months of a two-year jail sentence in 2002, for anti-trust violations between Sotheby's and its rival, Christie's.

Alfred Taubman died from a heart attack at the age of ninety-one, on April 17, 2015. His daughter, two sons, two stepchildren, nine grandchildren, and one great-grandson survive him.

*See Current Biography 1993.*

# Clark Terry

**Born:** St. Louis, Missouri; December 14, 1920

**Died:** Pine Bluff, Arkansas; February 21, 2015

**Occupation:** American jazz musician

Known by fans and fellow musicians alike as "Mumbles," Clark Terry was a world-class trumpeter and flugelhornist, who mentored jazz legends like Miles Davis and Quincy Jones. They credit Terry as an extraordinary influence on their early careers. With more than 900 recordings, Terry was one of the most recorded musicians in the history of jazz, recording with Ella Fitzgerald, Charles Mingus, Thelonious Monk, Dizzy Gillespie, and other leading jazz artists.

Clark Terry was born to a poor family with eleven young mouths to feed, so when he expressed interest in learning to play the trumpet, his parents couldn't afford the trumpet or the lessons. The resourceful Terry devised a trumpet out of a length of garden hose, a funnel, and a piece of lead pipe as a mouthpiece. His neighbors, tired of hearing his homemade horn, pooled their money to buy the boy a trumpet. He tricked a trumpet-playing friend into showing him everything he had learned in his lessons, thereby giving Terry lessons, second-hand.

Terry gained a national reputation while playing for Charlie Barnet. Over the course of his career, he had the rare distinction of playing with both Count Basie and Duke Ellington. He played with Ellington for nine years, from 1951 to 1959, and left to become the first African American to play in the National Broadcasting Corporation (NBC) studios. Terry performed for such shows as "The Arthur Murray Dance Party," and "Music on Ice." He played alongside Doc Severinsen, Joe Newman, and Jimmy Maxwell in the "Tonight Show" band. He also played freelance gigs, once claiming he had enough W-2 forms to fill a suitcase. He enjoyed playing advertising jingles and backing up rock groups where he could remain anonymous.

Terry was an enthusiastic teacher and role model as well, becoming something of an itinerant teacher and mentor upon leaving NBC. He was especially drawn to teaching because he never had a teacher when he was young, and he wanted to give children every opportunity possible. In his autobiography, Miles Davis claimed that one of the most important events in high school, was meeting Clark Terry when he visited Carbondale, Illinois. He became Davis's idol. In the 1970s, the US State Department sent Terry on something of a public relations mission to the Middle East, Pakistan, India, and Africa.

Clark Terry died in hospice care on February 21, 2015. His wife, two stepsons, numerous grandchildren, and great-grandchildren survive him.

*See Current Biography 2000.*

# Jeremy Thorpe

**Born:** Surrey, England; April 29, 1929
**Died:** London, UK; December 4, 2014
**Occupation:** British politician and parliamentarian

Jeremy Thorpe was born to privilege with a staunchly conservative family whose record of public service dates back centuries, (all the way to Robert de Thorpe, Chief Justice of the Common Pleas in 1356). He was one of three children, and the only son of John Henry Thorpe, a barrister and King's Counsel who was a Member of Parliament from 1919–1923. Jeremy Thorpe was stricken with tuberculosis at the age of six, and had to stay isolated in a separate cottage, on his own with two servants to care for him. He spent seven months in a spinal carriage. With war imminent in 1940, he and his sisters were sent to the United States to stay with an aunt in Massachusetts, and Thorpe became an ardent admirer of President Franklin D. Roosevelt. These years would have a lasting impact on Thorpe's life. When he returned home, his father, with whom he was very close, died from a massive stroke in 1944. The stuffy British class system was another shock, a stark contrast to his experience in America. He would spend the rest of his life as a member of the Liberal party, breaking his family's centuries-old tradition.

Thorpe began his political career early, at Trinity College, Oxford. He won the presidency of the Liberal Club, the Law Society, and the Russell and Palmerstone Club. In 1951, he became president of the Oxford Union—the debating society recognized as an important stepping-stone to a career in British politics. Some of his contemporaries found his elegant dinner parties and extravagant clothes at odds with the zeal of the Liberal party. Though he lost his first bid for the House of Commons, he used the loss as a lesson and worked to become familiar—on a first-name basis—with his constituents in North Devon. He won the next round in 1959, in a historically conservative district. The charismatic Thorpe was a champion of Western European unity, in favor of giving genuine power to the European Parliament, strengthening the Common Market. He was also a staunch supporter of the Anti-Apartheid Movement.

In 1970, Thorpe's wife, Caroline Allpass, was killed in a car accident, leaving him with an infant son. He married Marion Stein, Countess of Harewood, in 1973. More trouble was soon to follow, however. Within two years, Thorpe's career was irretrievably in shambles. In one of the most spectacular scandals of the twentieth century, Thorpe was prosecuted for plotting the murder of a homosexual lover who had been blackmailing him since the early 1960s. Though he was acquitted, the incidents and revelations destroyed his career, and he retired to private life. In the early 1980s, he was diagnosed with Parkinson's disease, which eventually took his life on December 4, 2014. He is survived by his son, Rupert.

*See Current Biography 1974.*

# Reies Lopez Tijerina

**Born:** Fall City, Texas; September 21, 1926
**Died:** El Paso, Texas; January 19, 2015
**Occupation:** American Chicano activist

Reies Lopez Tijerina was a civil rights crusader who championed the property rights of Spanish-Americans (a distinct group from other Hispano-American populations) in the American Southwest. In 1963, after something of a "messianic vision," Tijerina—an itinerant preacher—founded the Alianza Federa de los Puelos Lires (Federal Alliance of Free City States), an organization committed to the repatriation of the 594,500-acre Tierra Amarilla land grant (in New Mexico) that had belonged to his Spanish ancestors, through an agreement between Spanish viceroys and Mexico. (The land was ceded to the United States following the 1848 Treaty of Guadalupe Hidalgo.) Tijerina also established close ties with such Chicano activists as Cesar Chavez and Corky Gonzales.

Reies Tijerina was born to an itinerant farm worker who claimed he was heir to a Spanish land grant near Laredo, Texas. His mother, who died when Tijerina was just a boy, was a devout Catholic whose prayers and Bible recitations would one day feed Tijerina's mystical visions. He became a wandering fundamentalist minister. In the 1950s, he conceived a utopian "community of Justice and harmony" called Valle de la Paz (Valley of Peace) on sixteen acres of Arizona land. While seventeen Spanish-American families joined him, the surrounding community resented their presence and harassed the group, finally burning down a number of buildings. The community folded, though Tijerina continued to live on the property.

In 1967, Tijerina's organizing efforts culminated in an armed raid on a county court house in Tiera Amarilla, New Mexico, after men from his group were jailed for "arresting" two forest rangers, as trespassers on their land. Following the courthouse raid, Tijerina's group took a newspaper reporter and a deputy sheriff as hostages, and Tijerina became something of a folk hero of the New Left. Later, in 1969, Tijerina tried to make citizen's arrests of Supreme Court appointee Warren Burger; the Los Alamos Laboratory director, Norris Bradbury; and, New Mexico Governor, David Cargo. He saw jail time in both federal and state prisons. Tijerina's fiery demeanor earned him some enemies within his Alianz, and in 1978 he was ousted as head of the movement, and fell into obscurity.

In his last years, Tijerina turned his efforts to getting his third wife into the United States from Mexico. She survives him, along with eight of his children, and numerous grandchildren.

*See Current Biography 1971.*

# Leo Tindemans

**Born:** Zwijndrecht, Antwerp, Belgium; April 16, 1922
**Died:** Edegem, Belgium; December 26, 2014
**Occupation:** Prime Minister of Belgium and the European Parliament, politician

Belgium's political history has been complex and fractious, with divisions among religious, cultural and linguistic parties, so it is ironic that a man from such a strife-torn government, who failed to get his own party's full support for a regionalization program designed to ease ethnic tensions, would be widely recognized as a man who brought unity to Europe, and a founding father of the European Union (EU). But, such a man was Leo Tindemans.

Tindemans was born to a Flemish Roman Catholic family, on April 16, 1922 in Zwijndrecht, Belgium, near Antwerp. He earned degrees in commercial, economic, and consular sciences. Though he started his career as a journalist in Antwerp, Tindemans soon became a civil servant in the economic department of Belgium's Ministry of Agriculture. He served as mayor of Edegem, a residential suburb of Antwerp, concurrently while serving in Belgium's national government. Tindemans was a member of the Social Christian party, and was the party's national secretary general from 1958 to 1966. Long interested in the movement for European unity, he eventually became vice-chairman of the European Union of Christian Democrats. In March of 1974, Tindemans was elected Prime Minister of Belgium after Belgian Parliament was dissolved due to the failure of plans to construct a Belgian-Iranian oil refinery.

In 1974, Tindemans proposed that the Common European Market establish a top-level committee to study the feasibility of the creation of a Western European political union by 1980. And, in 1976, he published a forty-one page report calling on member states (of Western European) to accept an obligation to work toward common objectives on major issues involving economic, defense, and foreign policies, as well as the development of energy sources, scientific research, and aid to underdeveloped countries. Tindemans expressed the hope that his report would generate major discussions about a unified European body. Tindemans likewise, co-founded and chaired the first multi-national political party—the European Peoples Party (EPP). In a landslide vote, Tindemans was elected Prime Minister of the European Parliament. The preference vote totaled nearly 1 million in favor of his leadership, and earned Tindemans the monikers "man of a million votes," and "Mr. Europe."

In 1981, Tindemans returned to Belgian politics as the Belgian Foreign Minister. He took special interest in a growing trend toward democracy in Africa, and, in 1989, was a key player in Belgium's policy to forgive Zaire's national debt to Belgium, and one-third of it's commercial debt. In his retirement from politics, Tindemans taught international relations and European policy at the Catholic University of Leuven. In 1995 he co-created Crisis Group, an international organization committed to "acting as the world's eyes and ears for impending conflicts, and with a highly influential board that could mobilise effective action from the world's policymakers." (*CrisisGroup.org;* "About Us")

Leo Tindemans died on December 26, 2014 in Edegem, Belgium. He is survived by his wife, Rosa Naesens, four of his children, and twelve grandchildren.

*See Current Biography 1978.*

# Charles Hard Townes

**Born:** Greenville, South Carolina; July 28, 1915

**Died:** Oakland, California; January 27, 2015

**Occupation:** American physicist, professor, and Nobel laureate

Dr. Charles Townes was one of the greatest physicists of the twentieth century, receiving the Nobel Prize for his invention, the "maser," (an acronym for microwave amplification by stimulated emission of radiation), an instrument to measure time more absolutely, irrespective of the motions of the sun and stars. Scientists had long known that disturbances in the motions of celestial bodies caused unpredictable variation in the Earth's rotation around the sun, causing a loss or gain of one second or more every year. The maser, a precursor to the laser, proved remarkably important in a number of scientific areas. In communications, the maser amplified radio signals. In astronomical research on the nature of planets and galaxies, the maser made a more accurate measurement of the Earth's rotation. And, in testing cosmological theories, it was used to conduct laboratory tests that proved the validity of Einstein's theory of relativity. Products that use Towne's technology include everything from CD and DVD players, to laser scalpels and code scanners at the market.

Townes studied physics and modern languages at Furman University in Greenville, South Carolina. He finished his master's degree at Duke University, and his PhD at the California Institute of Technology. While working at Bell Telephone Laboratories, his initial research was in weapons systems, with important contributions to navigation and radar bombing. Beginning in 1948, Townes taught at Columbia University, where he became executive director of the radiation laboratory, then, later, head of the physics department. In 1959, the US Institute for Defense Analyses (IDA) offered him the position of vice-president and research director. (The IDA is a nonprofit organization designed to bring together scientists and government defense planners.) In 1961, he left the IDA to become provost of the Massachusetts Institute of Technology.

Townes received numerous awards for his scientific research. In addition to his Nobel Prize, he was honored by the Franklin Institute, the Academy of Sciences, and the American Academy of Arts and Sciences. He received a

Guggenheim Fellowship in 1955, and two Fulbright Fellowships to teach in France and Japan. In 2005, he received the prestigious Templeton Prize, awarded for Progress toward research or discoveries about spiritual realities.

Townes died on January 27, 2015 in Oakland, California. He is survived by his wife of seventy-four years, Frances Brown, four daughters, six grandchildren, and two great-grandchildren.

*See Current Biography 1963.*

poetry. In October of 2011, Tranströmer won the Nobel Prize for Literature, the first Swedish poet to do so since 1974. His other honors included the Lifetime Recognition Award from the Griffin Trust for Excellence in Poetry, and the Petrarch Prize in Germany.

Tomas Tranströmer died at home following a short illness. His wife, Monica Bladh, and their two daughters survive him.

*See Current Biography 2012.*

# Tomas Tranströmer

**Born:** Stockholm, Sweden; April 15, 1931
**Died:** Stockholm, Sweden; March 26, 2015
**Occupation:** Swedish poet and psychologist

The Nobel Prize-winning, Swedish poet, Tomas Transtömer, published his first collection of poetry at twenty-three, while he was still a student of psychology and the history of literature, poetics and religion at Stockholm University. He continued to publish more than twelve collections of poetry, which have been translated into more than fifty languages, including English. His American translators have included, most notably, the poets Robert Bly and Robin Fulton.

Transtömer's writing was informed by his passion for music and nature. His poems were philosophical, introspective, and musical, as well as simple and straightforward. After graduating from Stockholm University, he worked as a psychologist, providing rehabilitation and therapy at the Roxtuna Prison for Boys, counseling convicts, drug addicts, and juvenile delinquents. He considered his work as a psychologist and his work as a poet to be equally important and mutually influential.

In the 1970s, he was still almost unknown to the English-speaking world, but in the early 1980s, American poets, Robert Bly and Robin Fulton began translating Transtömer's work, garnering enthusiastic high praise. (His close friendship with Robert Bly lasted until Transtömer's death in March of 2015.) In 1981, Robert Fulton translated Transtömer's *Selected Poems,* the first comprehensive English collection of Transtömer's poetry.

In November of 1990, when he was fifty-nine, Transtömer suffered a massive stroke that left him partially paralyzed, and nearly unable to speak. Yet, he went on to write some of his best

# Jon Vickers

**Born:** Prince Albert, Saskatchewan, Canada; October 29, 1926
**Died:** Ontario, Canada; July 10, 2015
**Occupation:** Canadian opera singer

Sometimes referred to as "God's Tenor" due to his refusal to perform certain roles he considered blasphemous, Jon Vickers was an intense opera icon. Considered one of the world's top tenors, Vickers won two Grammy Awards and numerous honorary degrees, performing on the world's greatest stages.

Originally, Jon Vickers had no aspirations to sing professionally. He was born into a large (with seven children) and poor farming family. However, the family loved to sing. Vickers once characterized his family as a poor version of the von Trapp singers. In addition to being a school principal, Vickers' father was a minister who gave his children a strong religious identity. Originally, Vickers wanted to go to medical school, but he found his way blocked by the influx of war veterans hoping to do the same. Vickers worked odd jobs such as managing a Woolworth's department store, but in his spare time, he participated in community theater productions. One female lead, Mary Morrison, recognized his talent, and played a recording of his voice for authorities at the Toronto Royal Conservatory of Music, which subsequently offered Vickers a scholarship. He studied with the former operatic britone, George Lambert and landed lead roles on the world's greatest stages, including the Metropolitan Opera in New York, and Covent Garden in London.

Having been raised on a farm, Vickers had a strong physical presence and a sublime singing voice. According to the *Los Angeles Times* (12 July 2015), Herbert Breslin (Luciano Pavarotti's manager), "likened Vickers' voice to an iron column that weeps tears." Apparently Vickers was not easy to work with. When preparing for rehearsals he not only memorized his own parts, but those of the other performers as well, and he was impatient with those he considered ill prepared. In 1976, Vickers actually pulled out of a role—Wagner's *Tannhäuser*—just one month before its opening because the role contradicted his religious convictions. (Some critics argued he pulled out due to the strain on his voice.)

Jon Vickers was a devoted husband and father. He avoided travel as much as possible to be with his family. His first wife, Henrietta Outerbridge, whom he married in 1953, predeceased him in 1991. He married Judith Panek Stewart in 1993. He is survived by his five children from his first marriage, eleven grandchildren, and two great-grandchildren.

*See Current Biography 1961.*

# Dan Walker

**Born:** Washington, DC; August 6, 1922
**Died:** Chula Vista, California; April 29, 2015
**Occupation:** Former governor of Illinois, politician

Governor Dan Walker was a controversial figure with a meteoric rise to fame and power, and an equally precipitous decline that ended with eighteen months behind bars. He eschewed the political machine that dominated Illinois politics, including the powerful Chicago mayor (and fellow Democrat) Richard J. Daley.

Following in his father's footsteps, Dan Walker enlisted as a Navy seaman in 1939, serving on minesweepers and destroyers in the Pacific before his entry into the US Naval Academy. Following his graduation from Northwestern University Law School in 1950, Walker served successively as a clerk to the US Supreme Court Chief Justice Fred Vinson, deputy chief commander of the US Court of Military Appeals, and as assistant to Illinois Governor Adlai Stevenson. Governor Otto Kerner appointed him to the Illinois Public Aid Commission, and he was twice elected president of the Chicago Crime Commission.

Walker first came to national attention as head of the blue-chip National Commission on the Causes and Prevention of Violence that compiled the controversial report—later named the "Walker Report"—on the student-police

confrontations at the 1968 Democratic National Convention. His study found that some policemen demonstrated "unrestrained and indiscriminate . . . violence." Walker castigated Mayor Richard Daly and the police for dropping a "blue curtain" of secrecy, and Daly's order to "shoot to kill arsonists and shoot to maim looters."

Walker helped cultivate his populist image by walking 1,197 miles across the state of Illinois with a promise to renew the "hardworking, law-abiding, God-fearing people's" faith in government. His strategy got him elected. However, Walker's confrontational politics did not win him friends, and he suffered from a general inability to get his major proposals passed into law (though he was successful in helping to create a mass transit system for Chicago). He was not re-elected, and Democrats would need twenty-six years to regain the governor's mansion.

Following his political career, Walker acquired First American Savings and Loan of Oak Brook, and his life began to unravel. In 1986, Walker was convicted of bank fraud, using loans from his own savings and loan to finance his other businesses and lavish lifestyle.

Dan Walker died on April 29, 2015. His wife, Lily Stewart, and seven children survive him.

*See Current Biography 1976.*

# Ben Wattenberg

**Born:** New York, New York; August 26, 1933
**Died:** Washington, DC; June 28, 2015
**Occupation:** Demographer, political author

Ben Wattenberg has been characterized as "Panglosian"—over-optimistic about the state of the nation. In the mid-1960s, while many political commentators felt the country was falling to pieces, Wattenberg claimed the quality of life was actually improving in virtually all segments of society, backing up his assertions with census data and public-opinion polls. He was a senior fellow at the American Enterprise Institute (a conservative think tank), and hosted a number of public broadcasting programs such as *Think Tank with Benn Wattenberg, Ben Wattenberg at Large,* and *In Search of Real America.* He published eleven books, and hosted a documentary for PBS called *Heaven on Earth: The Rise and Fall of Socialism.*

Joseph Ben Zion Wattenberg was born in New York City to lawyer, Judah Wattenberg, and Rachel (Gutman) Wattenberg, immigrants from eastern Russia. He attended Hobart College in Geneva, New York. Upon graduation from Hobart, he spent two years in the Air Force. He was a prolific writer. Though he wrote for numerous publications like *Ladies' Home Journal* and *The Reporter*, he came to national prominence with his fourth book, *The U.S.A.: An Unexpected Family Portrait of 194,067,296 Americans Drawn from the Census*, which he co-wrote with Richard Scammon (former head of the US Census Bureau), with whom he eventually authored numerous books. In 1970, just shy of the election, they published *The Real Majority*, an authoritative analysis that revealed the key to electoral success were the "middle-aged, middle-class, middle-minded" voters. They speculated that the hope for Democrats to recapture the White House was to take a firm "law-and-order" stance on social issues and to avoid measure that exacerbated racial tensions. They concluded that the nation's leader should "trust the people and listen to the people before leading the people."

Wattenberg helped found the Coalition for a Democratic Majority, in an effort to move the Democratic Party toward the center. He was a researcher and speechwriter for President Lyndon B. Johnson's administration, and helped Hubert Humphrey return to the Senate after his 1968 defeat in the presidential election.

Wattenberg had a way with words, coining unique terms like "neo-manifest destinarian" and "redistributionist capitalist." He considered himself "pro-natal" on abortion.

Ben Wattenberg died from complications from surgery on June 28, 2015. His survivors include his one son, Daniel; his three other children, Ruth, Sarah, and Rachel; his sister, actress Rebecca Schull; his wife, Diane Abelman; and four grandchildren.

*See Current Biography 1985.*

# Alan Weinstein

**Born:** New York, New York; September 1, 1937

**Died:** Gaithersburg, Maryland; June 18, 2015

**Occupation:** Archivist, historian, educator, writer

Alan Weinstein was the ninth archivist of the US National Archives and Records Administration (NARA), and was a professor of history at several major universities, including Smith College, Georgetown University, and Boston University. He co-authored the book *Perjury: The Hiss-Chambers Case,* a National Book Award winner that was controversial, not so much due to its content, as to the fact that Weinstein remained tight-lipped about his primary sources in violation of the American Historical Associations' Standards of Professional Conduct. In all, he wrote six books and his writing was included in numerous edited collections.

In 1985 Weinstein founded and became president of the Center for Democracy, a nonprofit organization for promoting democracy throughout the world. The center held conferences and worked with teams monitoring elections, among them the Philippines' 1986 election, and Nicaragua's 1989 election. The center drew attention in the 1990s when it formed a working relationship with Boris Yeltsin who used it to fax messages during the 1991 right-wing attempted coup in Moscow. Weinstein became the source of information about events in Moscow for the White House, the State Department, and the press.

In 2004, President George W. Bush nominated Weinstein for the post of national archivist, which raised concerns among archivists and historians who worried that the White House had chosen Weinstein because of his perceived penchant for secrecy. They feared that Weinstein's assignment was Bush's attempt to keep his father's (George H. W. Bush) presidential papers, due to be made public, out of the hands of critics. The Senate nevertheless, confirmed Weinstein who devoted much of his time to the presidential library system.

Weinstein's academic awards include two Senior Fulbright Lectureships, the American Council of Learned Societies' Fellowship, and the Commonwealth Fund Lectureship at the University of London. For his promotion of democracy work, he was awarded the UN Peace Medal, and two Silver Medals from the Council of Europe.

Alan Weinstein was the son of Russian-Jewish immigrants who owned a deli in the Bronx, New York. He earned a degree in history from the City University of New York, and a master's degree and a doctorate from Yale University. Weinstein died from complications from pneumonia on June 18, 2015. His wife, Adrienne Dominguez, his two sons from a previous marriage, a stepson, and three grandchildren survive him.

*See Current Biography 2006.*

# Richard von Weizsäcker

**Born:** Stuttgart, Baden-Wurttemberg, Germany
**Died:** January 31, 2015
**Occupation:** Former president of the Federal Republic of Germany

Sometimes referred to as Germany's liberator, former President Richard von Weizsäcker was the first president to govern a united Germany after the collapse of the Berlin Wall. For Weizsäcker, the only way for Germany to be free from the wreckage of the Holocaust, was to take responsibility, and dismiss the notion that German citizens didn't know what was happening in their country. Weizsäcker was hailed as the conscience of the nation after his moving speech to commemorate the fortieth anniversary of Germany's surrender, and the end of World War II. Weizsäcker said, "Anyone who closes his eyes to the past, is blind to the present." He travelled to Israel in 1985, and accompanied the Israeli ambassador to see the German premier of the highly acclaimed film *Schindler's List*. In 1986, Weizsäcker addressed a joint session of the British Parliament, the first German to do so.

Born in a castle on the family estate, to a long line of patrician theologians, educators, statesmen, and scientists, Richard von Weizsäcker was a lawyer and businessman before entering politics as a member of the Christian Democratic Union. Weizsäcker's father had been a career diplomat and former naval officer, who served as a state secretary of the German foreign office, and as an ambassador to the Vatican during the Nazi regime. He was tried for war crimes, though there was some evidence he had resisted Hitler. The senior Weizsäcker was imprisoned for two years of a seven-year term. (Even Winston Churchill had considered his sentence a mistake.)

The elder Weizsäcker's work as a diplomat meant his son grew to be a cosmopolitan individual. Richard von Weizsäcker attended schools in Basel, Bern, Copenhagen, and Oslo. He studied law and history for a year, in Grenoble, France, and at Oxford University. In 1938, he joined the German Wehrmacht, and in 1939 he took part in the invasion of Poland, though he developed a marked distaste for Nazism. After the war, he would take time away from his law studies, to help in his father's defense at the Nuremberg trials. After resuming his studies, he obtained his doctor of jurisprudence degree in 1954.

He spent his early career in private corporate management until 1967, when he left industry to devote himself full-time to church affairs. He had been heavily involved in the Evangelical Church, serving in various posts on its executive committees. He had joined the dominant Christian Democratic Union (CDU) in 1954, and by 1972, he was chairman of the party's commission on basic principles, playing a key role in drafting the party's manifesto. He was elected to the Dundestag in 1969, serving as its vice president from 1979 to 1981, after which, he became the mayor of West Berlin. He was elected to the presidency in 1984, and retired ten years later.

Richard von Weizsäcker is survived by his wife, and three of his four children.

*See Current Biography 1985.*

# P. D. James (Phyllis Dorothy James White)

**Born:** Oxford, England; August 3, 1920
**Died:** Oxford, England; November 27, 2014
**Occupation:** Novelist

Many P. D. James fans would be shocked to learn that her formal education ended when she was just 16. (Her father "was not disposed to" educating girls.) She was an avid reader however, a trait that would provide both education and solace over the course of her lifetime. By some standards, she was not a prolific writer. (She wrote 21 novels, one memoir, and another book about her writing process, by the time of her death). She stole a few early morning hours to hone her craft as she had to work full time as a civil servant to support herself and her two children. Her husband, Ernest Conner Bantry White, a young physician, returned from World War II a broken man. He suffered from mental illness (probably schizophrenia), spending much of their marriage in mental hospitals, until his death in 1964. James raised her two daughters on her own. One daughter, Clare, was born during the devastating Nazi rocket bombing of London.

Most of James' novels are about crime, and much of her knowledge of crime came from her various positions in the civil service. She worked for years in the criminal policy department, and eventually became a specialist in juvenile delinquency. Prior to her qualification for civil service, James worked for the National Health Service where she gained much of her medical knowledge about murder. Unlike her mystery-writing predecessors (e.g., Agatha Christy and Dorothy Sayers), James' treated murder victims much the same as she would any other character. She made them real. They had personalities and history. Her depictions of murdered corpses were brutal and realistic. She believed that anything less would trivialize human life. James also wrote about crime because, early on, she believed that detective stories, would be more readily published for an unseasoned, unknown writer. She cherished crime stories' webs of intrigue that demanded painstaking construction—a quality she prized. Her careful analysis of human behavior, her eye for details of sociocultural implication, and faculty for tense, absorbing storytelling distinguished her from other "mystery writers." Common themes in her stories explored life in a closed, cloistered community; the plight of the chronically ill; the suffering of prolonged dying; and, the quest for identity—a quest that involves learning to love and forgive.

Her most beloved character has been master detective, Commander Adam Dalgliesh of Scotland Yard, a "ruthless, unorthodox" detective who is also intelligent and sensitive. (He writes and publishes poetry.) The Commander appears in the majority of her novels.

P. D. James is among the very few writers who never received a rejection letter. Her accolades include the Silver Dagger from the British Crime Writers Association; an Edgar from the Mystery Writers of America; and the Edgar Allen Poe Scroll Award. James was decorated with the Order of the British Empire in 1983 and was named a peer of the House of Lords in 1991; her honorary title is Baroness James. Phyllis Dorothy James died on November 27, 2014. She is survived by her two daughters, Clare and Jane; a sister, Monica; five grandchildren; and eight great-grandchildren.

*See Current Biography 1980.*

# Robert E. White

**Born:** Melrose, Massachusetts; September 21, 1926
**Died:** Arlington, Virginia; January 13, 2015
**Occupation:** American diplomat

Robert E. White was a US ambassador to Central and South America who advocated for social reform and who, ultimately, sacrificed his own career in order to stand up for his convictions against the brutal rightists that governed his host country, El Salvador. He is most widely remembered for his denunciation of the Salvadoran "anachronistic power structure" that supported the "death squads" that terrorized the country's lower class population. At times, he criticized the US policies he was there to uphold.

White's career began in 1963, when he was sent to the Consulate General in Guayaquil, Ecuador, to serve as deputy principal officer. In the late 1960s, White was director, at the US embassy in Managua, Nicaragua, and then later, in Bogotá, Colombia. In 1975, as Washington's deputy representative to the Organization of American States (OAS), White began stirring the diplomatic waters by appealing to member nations to strengthen their respect for human rights. He explicitly criticized the host government for its violations of those rights. He was officially reprimanded, but Washington withdrew the reprimand after White threatened to resign.

In 1977, President Jimmy Carter sent White to Paraguay as the US ambassador, and with the support of a group of US Congressmen, White urged the Asuncion government to extradite Josef Mengele, the physician known to have participated in torturing and killing thousands during the holocaust. In 1979, White was sent to El Salvador as the US ambassador where he tried to keep the government on the path to reform. Following the overthrow of the Humberto government, ultraconservatives resorted to terrorism to regain power. Right-wing gunmen murdered Archbishop Oscar Arnulfo Romero as the social-activist priest celebrated mass. White's life was also threatened, and he was barricaded in the embassy for several days. Not long after, four American Catholic churchwomen, considered leftist because of their social work among the poor, were found murdered.

When Ronald Reagan won the 1980 presidential election, Robert White's days in the Foreign Service were numbered. Reagan and his administration were convinced that the unrest in Central America was instigated by Cuba and the Soviet Union. They criticized envoys like White whom they felt were working, improperly, as social reformers. Just weeks into Reagan's presidency, White received notice that he was being "automatically retired." He sharply criticized Reagan's handling of South American policy, and charged that the Reagan administration covered up important documents he had supplied, that named Archbishop Oscar Romero's assassin, along with the names of six wealthy Salvadorans living in Miami who helped finance the "death squads."

Upon his "retirement," White became the president of the Center for International Policy, a liberal think tank in Washington. Robert White died on January 13, 2015, from prostate and bladder cancer. He is survived by his wife of fifty-nine years, Maryanne Cahill White, three children, a brother, and three grandchildren.

*See Current Biography 1984.*

# Edward Gough Whitlam

**Born:** Kew, Melbourne, Australia; July 11,1916
**Died:** Elizabeth Bay, Sydney, Australia; October 21, 2014
**Occupation:** Former Australian prime minister, politician, and UNESCO ambassador

Edward Gough Whitlam's three-year tenure as the prime minister of Australia was as transformative as it was divisive. Gough Whitlam almost single-handedly brought sweeping reforms in international relations and in social services, following twenty years of opposition, conservative rule. Yet, in just three short years, he was dismissed as Prime Minister in 1975, in response to a stubborn deadlock in the Senate over the passage of a budget . The event became known as "The Dismissal" in Australian lore.

Whitlam's list of accomplishments in those three short years, reads like an extraordinary laundry list of reform, that included the withdrawal of Australian troops from Vietnam; equal pay for women; a new ministry of aboriginal affairs (the first of it's kind); withdrawal of support of South Africa due to its apartheid policies; normalization of diplomatic ties with China, (he was the first Australian prime minister to

visit China); the establishment of a universal health care insurance known as Medibank; the establishment of no-fault divorce; laws to ban discrimination based on race or sex; and, education reforms. His government established the first national parks in Australia and was committed to environmental protection. Yet, economic conditions dogged his every move. Many of his reforms were expensive, the world was in a recession, unemployment rose, and government deficits ballooned.

Following his ouster in 1975, Whitlam became a visiting fellow at the Australian University, and in 1979, he became a visiting professor at Harvard. In 1983, he was appointed Australian ambassador to the United Nations Educational, Scientific, and Cultural Organization (UNESCO). He and his wife, Margaret, were part of the team responsible for bringing the summer Olympics to Sydney in 2000. Whitlam wrote several books reviewing his time in office, and he remained quite active in Labor Party politics.

Edward Gough Whitlam died on October 21, 2014. Whitlam's wife of seventy years predeceased him in 2012. He is survived by his four children, five grandchildren, and nine great-grandchildren.

*See Current Biography 1974.*

# Miller Williams

**Born:** Hoxie, Arkansas; April 8, 1930
**Died:** Fayetteville, Arkansas; January 1, 2015
**Occupation:** Poet and professor

Few people knew of the poet Miller Williams, until President Bill Clinton selected him to write and read a poem at his 1997 inauguration. Williams is also the country singer, Lucinda Williams's, father. The two have appeared on stage together, and the title for one of Lucinda's Williams's albums, *Down There Where the Spirit Meets the Bone,* is a line from one of her father's poems.

Miller Williams and former President Clinton had become acquainted when they each taught at the University of Arkansas in the 1970s. Williams was the co-director of the graduate program in creative writing, as well as the director of the university's program in translation. He later founded and directed the University of

Arkansas Press. Other notables acquainted with Williams include former president, Jimmy Carter, and a young protégé, Billy Collins, who was the US Poet Laureate from 2001 through 2003.

Williams's original career interest was in science. He received a B.S. degree in biology from Arkansas State College in 1951, and his M.S. in zoology from the University of Arkansas. From 1952 until 1960, he was a biology professor at several southern colleges. His career took a different turn, however, when he won a Breadloaf Fellowship in poetry in 1961. In 1963, he won an Amy Lowell traveling scholarship in poetry, and he served as a visiting professor at the University of Santiago, Chile (where he also served as the first US delegate to the Pan American Conference of University Artists and Writers). Though he was relatively obscure to non-writers, he was well known to some of the best writers of the era. Upon the recommendations of several well-known writers—Flannery O'Connor, Howard Nemerox, and Richard Yates—and with no college degrees in English, Louisiana State University hired him as an English instructor. (That same year, Williams was a Fulbright professor at the National University of Mexico City.)

Williams's first volume of poetry, *A Circle of Stone,* was published in 1964. In all, Miller wrote or translated twenty-eight books, most of which are volumes of poetry. He also translated poetry by German, French, Italian, and Spanish poets, and penned the well-known poetry textbook, *How Does a Poem Mean?*.

Miller Williams died on New Year's Day, 2015. His three children and wife, Rebecca Jordan Hall, survive him.

*See Current Biography 1997.*

## Julie Wilson

**Born:** Omaha, Nebraska; October 21, 1924
**Died:** New York City, New York; April 5, 2015
**Occupation:** American actress and cabaret singer

Julie Wilson is most remembered for her signature song, "I'm Still Here" by Stephen Sondheim. The cabaret singer broke into show business through racy burlesque shows, fighting her way to center stage despite a weak voice. She appeared in such musicals as *Kiss Me Kate, Gypsy, South Pacific, The Pajama Game, Company,* and *A little Night Music.* Wilson retired in 1976

to care for her two sons and ailing parents, only to revive her career in the early 1980s. In 1988, Wilson was nominated for a Tony Award for her performance as the speakeasy owner "Flo" in the Peter Allen show *Legs Diamond.* She continued to perform well into her mid-eighties.

Wilson gained a passion for performing at a young age, singing with local bands at the age of fourteen. She studied drama and music at Omaha University. Her life in cabaret had her constantly moving throughout the Midwest and northeast where she performed in gambling clubs and nightclubs, including such famous venues as New York's Latin Quarter, Mocambo, and the legendary Copacabana. Following a United Service Organization (USO) tour of Europe, she performed on Broadway's stages.

Wilson was married three times, though none of her marriages were long lived. She had two sons with her second husband, Michael McAloney. Julie Wilson died following a series of strokes, on April 5, 2015. Her son, Michael McAloney Jr., predeceased her. She is survived by her second son, a writer, actor, and producer Holt McCallany, and a granddaughter.

*See Current Biography 2000.*

## Jim Wright (James Claude Wright, Jr.)

**Born:** Fort Worth, Texas; December 22, 1922
**Died:** Fort Worth, Texas; May 6, 2015
**Occupation:** Congressman and former speaker of the US House of Representatives

Jim Wright was a surprise nominee in 1976 when Democrats in the House of Representatives elected him as their new majority leader. Wright was a moderate in a party increasingly dominated by liberals, who had a reputation as a skilled mediator and conciliator in bringing consensus on national issues. His career would weather heavy political artillery, and would usher in a new era in the relationship between the president and the speaker, as well as changing the tone of the discourse between house Republicans and Democrats. He would be the first speaker of the house to resign amidst an ethics investigation, though charges against him were baseless.

Born and raised in northeast Texas to a working class family, Wright attended public schools, and graduated from the University of Texas. He served as a pilot and flight instructor in the US Army Air Force in World War II. Afterward, he joined the local chapter of the Young Democrats, and in 1946, won election to the Texas state legislature. In 1954 Wright challenged incumbent representative Wingate Lucas in the Democratic primary, winning his seat in the US House of Representatives.

Wright earned a reputation as a formidable foe, considered matchless in his determination. Within weeks of taking office as speaker, Wright went to battle with President Ronald Reagan over spending and handling the national debt. In 1987, he took advantage of the stock market collapse to force the White House into accepting tax increases, but his tactics won him no friends, and his maneuvers and manipulations of parliamentary procedure shook even his supporters. Later, his solitary nature would be his undoing as he failed to garner support following a concerted smear campaign by Newt Gingrich, who accused Wright of accepting royalties from lobbyists who bought large quantities of his book—something allowed by House rules. When he asked the ethics committee for an immediate trial to address the allegations, he was denied, leaving time for his political reputation to further erode. He resigned on June 6, 1989—something he would later regret—as his way of protesting the "mindless cannibalism" that the charges against him represented.

After leaving office, Wright taught political science at Texas Christian University. For his legacy, Wright was most proud of the critical role he played in brokering peace (in spite of Republican President Ronald Reagan's best efforts) in the Nicaraguan civil war. On November 22, 1963, Wright was in the motorcade when President John F. Kennedy was assassinated.

Jim Wright died May 6, 2015. His wife of forty-three years, Betty Hay, predeceased him. Four of his five children with his first wife, Mary Ethelyn, survive.

*See Current Biography 1979.*

# Hermann Zapf
**Born:** Nurnberg, Bavaria, Germany; November 8, 1918
**Died:** Darmstadt, Germany; June 4, 2015
**Occupation:** Calligrapher, typographer, book designer

Hermann Zapf was one of the world's foremost calligraphers and type designers who reimagined the alphabet from hand drawn calligraphy to fonts for the computer age. Fonts named "Palatino," "Optima," and "Zapf Dingbats"—so familiar to computer-users—were Hermann Zapf designs. He created well over fifty typefaces.

Hermann Zapf was born at the end of World War I in Nurnberg, Bavaria. As a boy, he loved science, and had hoped to become an electrical engineer. However, World War II diverted his professional trajectory. His father, a union organizer, was dismissed from his job as a metal worker, and spent a short time as a prisoner in Dachau. His father's reputation made it difficult for Zapf to find work. He first worked at a printing plant, retouching photography. A calligraphy and typography exhibition of Rudolf Koch's work inspired Zapf's interest, and he began teaching himself calligraphy by studying manuscripts in the Nurnberg city library. After designing his own typeface, he began compiling material for his book *Alphabete und Schriftblätter.* (The English translation is *Pen and Graver: Alphabets and Pages of Calligraphy.*) In 1941, he was conscripted into the German army, but his ineptitude as a soldier led to his assignment to the army's geographic department, designing maps for a cartographic unit in France.

After the war, Zapf moved to Frankfurt to become the artistic director at the Stempel type foundry. He traveled to the United States in the early 50s to attend exhibitions of his work. In 1960 Zapf was invited to conduct a six-week seminar in book design at the Carnegie Institute of Technology, as the Andrew Mellon Distinguished Visiting Professor at the College of Fine Arts. Zapf was among the earliest type designers to acknowledge the need for multiple, computer-generated typefaces. His designs have become ubiquitous.

Herman Zapf died on June 4, 2015. His wife, Gudrun von Hesse, survives him.

*See Current Biography 1965.*

# CLASSIFICATION BY PROFESSION

## ACTIVISM

Hawa Abdi
Noorjahan Akbar
Nina Davuluri
Donald Glover
David Graeber
Neil Harbisson
Sam Kass
Lawrence Lessig
Rick Lowe
Thuli Madonsela
Alexis Ohanian
Ai-jen Poo
Malala Yousafzai

## ARCHITECTURE

Hafeez Contractor

## ART

Duncan Campbell
Neil Harbisson
Rick Lowe
Catherine Martin
Favianna Rodriguez
Sheikha al-Mayassa al-Thani
Jill Thompson
Anya Ulinich

## BUSINESS

Anat Admati
Folorunsho Alakija
Gavin Andresen
Brandee Barker
Arundhati Bhattacharya
Rosalind Brewer
Nolan Bushnell
Safra A. Catz
Solina Chau
Roy Choi
Vijay Govindarajan
Marillyn Hewson
Elizabeth Holmes
Renée James
Abigail Johnson
Travis Kalanick
Jørgen Vig Knudstorp
Chanda Kochhar
Susan Gregg Koger
Donna Langley

Alicia Munnell
Elvira Nabiullina
Phebe Novakovic
Kevyn Orr
Ruth Porat
Laurene Powell Jobs
Laurel Richie
Gina Rinehart
Michele A. Roberts
Güler Sabancı
Gwynne Shotwell
Lila Tretikov
Don Valentine
Cher Wang
Pharrell Williams
Wu Yajun
Anita Zucker

## COMEDY

Key & Peele
Kumail Nanjiani
John Oliver
Chelsea Peretti
Reggie Watts

## DESIGN

Yves Béhar

## EDUCATION

Vijay Govindarajan
David Graeber
Amy Gutmann
Victor Davis Hanson
Lawrence Lessig
Claudia Rankine
Timothy Snyder

## ENGINEERING

Mylswamy Annadurai

## ENTREPRENEUR

Garrett Camp
Tony Fadell
Hu Shuli
Travis Kalanick
Susan Gregg Koger
Alexis Ohanian

Peng Lei
Jonah Peretti
Haim Saban
Anne Wojcicki
Nick Woodman
Riccardo Zacconi

## FASHION

Mel Ottenberg
Phoebe Philo
Pharrell Williams

## FILM

Anthony Anderson
Matthew Bomer
John Boyega
Carrie Brownstein
Lizzy Caplan
Yao Chen
Emilia Clarke
Ellar Coltrane
Megan Ellison
Gal Gadot
Bobby Holland Hanton
Kevin Hart
Sally Hawkins
Tom Hiddleston
Liya Kebede
Jennifer Lee
Kate Mara
Idina Menzel
Ezra Miller
Chris O'Dowd
Joshua Oppenheimer
Chris Pratt
Lynne Ramsay
Amy Schumer
George Takei
Kerry Washington
Shailene Woodley
Andrey Zvagintsev

## FOOD

Roy Choi
Dominique Crenn
Sam Kass
Christopher Kostow
Sarah Kramer
Virgilio Martínez Véliz
Nadia Santini
Tom Sellers
Nancy Silverton

## GOVERNMENT & POLITICS

Lloyd Austin
Ashton Carter
Tammy Duckworth
Josh Earnest
Abdel Fattah el-Sisi
Willem-Alexander Claus George Ferdinand
Maura Healey
Margaret Hamburg
Sheikh Hasina
Michelle Howard
Atifete Jahjaga
Kevin Johnson
Sergey Lavrov
Mia Love
Loretta Lynch
Mari Pangestu
Petro Poroshenko
Kshama Sawant
Mary Jo White

## HEALTH

Martin Makary

## HISTORY

Victor Davis Hanson
Timothy Snyder

## INVENTOR

William Kamkwamba

## JOURNALISM

Emily Bazelon
Charles M. Blow
Ta-Nahisi Coates
Tavi Gevinson
Anand Gopal
Hu Shuli
Julia Ioffe
Sarah Koenig
Elizabeth Kolbert
Rich Lowry
Jeremy Scahill
Bill Simmons
Chuck Todd
Lawrence Wright

## LAW
Preet Bharara

## LITERATURE
Malorie Blackman
John Darnielle
Anand Gopal
N.K. Jemisin
Phil Klay
Elizabeth Kolbert
Jhumpa Lahiri
Patricia Lockwood
Lois Lowry
Elizabeth McCracken
Dinaw Mengestu
Evan Osnos
Claudia Rankine
Tom Reiss
Mary Doria Russell
Stacy Schiff
Tracy K. Smith
Barbara Brown Taylor
Jill Thompson
Anya Ulinich
Lynn Vincent
Binyavanga Wainaina

## MATHEMATICS
Maryam Mirzakhani
Yitang Zhang

## MUSIC
Sheila Kay Adams
Aloe Blacc
Carrie Brownstein
Charli XCX
John Darnielle
Davido
Lana Del Rey
Donald Glover
Ariana Grande
Susie Ibarra
Kim Kashkashian
La Roux
Zhou Long
Jenny Lewis
Idina Menzel
Ingrid Michaelson
Andris Nelsons
Anna Netrebko
Pitbull
Darius Rucker

Ed Sheeran
Sam Smith
Toro y moi
Reggie Watts
Pharrel Williams

## NONFICTION
Vijay Govindarajan
N.K. Jemisin
Sarah Kramer
Clifford Pickover
Anita Sarkeesian
George Takei

## PHILOSOPHY
Gayatri Chakravorty Spivak

## RADIO
Diane Rehm

## RELIGION
Barbara Brown Taylor

## SCIENCE
Hawa Abdi
Myles Allen
Richard Alley
Gavin Andresen
Danielle Bassett
Raphael Bousso
Jennifer Eberhardt
François Englert
Jules A. Hoffman
Elizabeth Holmes
Maxim Kontsevich
John Kovac
Robert Lanza
Saul Perlmutter
Clifford Pickover
Kathryn Sullivan
Monica G. Turner
Heather Willauer

## SPORTS
Jamie Anderson
Simone Biles
Dustin Brown
Madison Bumgarner
Mo'ne Davis

Mahendra Singh Dhoni
Anna Fenninger
Ryan Hunter-Reay
Nyjah Huston
Kevin Johnson
Duncan Keith
Dennis Kimetto
Jürgen Klinsmann
Eddie Lacy
Kawhi Leonard
Andrew Luck
Marc Márquez
Maya Moore
Neymar
Laurel Richie
Ronda Rousey
Pablo Sandoval
Max Scherzer
Chris Sharma
Richard Sherman
Hakuhō Shō
Adam Silver
Russell Westbrook
Walter Ray Williams Jr.

## TECHNOLOGY

Nolan Bushnell
Mark Cerny
Tony Fadell

## TELEVISION

Anthony Anderson
Matthew Bomer
John Boyega
Lizzy Caplan
Emilia Clarke
Laverne Cox
Donald Glover
Ariana Grande
Kevin Hart
Key & Peele
Sarah Koenig
Kate Mara
Ronald D. Moore
Chris O' Dowd
Chris Pratt
Shonda Rhimes
Amy Schumer
Jenny Slate
Deborah Turness
Ward Pendleton Ward
Kerry Washington
Shailene Woodley